PEARSON

ALWAYS LEARNING

Matt Davis

Meaningful Statistics

Fifth Custom Edition

Pearson Learning Solutions, 330 Hudson Street, New York, New York, 10013
A Pearson Education Company
www.pearsoned.com

Printed in the United States of America

1 2 3 4 5 6 7 8 9 10 V092 18 17 16 15

000200010271972589
000200010271971140

CB/CC

ISBN 10: 1-323-23039-4
ISBN 13: 978-1-323-23039-8

Additional Resources for Students and Instructors

In addition to the material found in the pages of this textbook, you can find many other useful items on the Online Resources Page for the textbook. The resources page contains:

Lecture Notes Packets: These packets can be used as templates by instructors teaching from the Meaningful Statistics text. These packets are also useful for students to take notes while watching the lecture videos below.

Lecture Videos: These videos can be used by instructors as part of a distance education course, a hybrid course, or a flipped classroom. These videos are also useful for students who would like to hear a different perspective on the material. Students watching these videos should download and print the corresponding notes packets above so that they can take notes while watching.

StatCrunch Lab Projects: The textbook already has technology projects at the end of the chapter, but they are not technology specific. These projects are similar, but they have specific directions for completing the tasks using StatCrunch.

StatSims Applications: These apps are required for the Technology projects assigned in the text and for the StatCrunch projects above. These apps will run on Window XP or later. They do NOT run on Mac OS.

Data Collection Projects: These projects can be assigned to give students some experience working with statistics in the world around them.

Printable Formula Sheet: The book has a formula sheet as a removable card inside the back cover. Some students prefer to download and print a paper copy rather than removing the one from the book. A PDF version of the card is available here.

Casio Calculator Directions: The textbook includes instructions for the TI-83/84 calculators. Similar instructions for Casio graphing calculators are posted online.

Location of Additional Resources:

I have posted a Meaningful Statistics Resource Page on my school webpage. The easiest way to find this page is to perform a Google search for "Matt Davis Chabot". One of the top links will take you to my Chabot Directory. One click from there and you will be on my school page. You will find a link there for Meaningful Statistics.

Having trouble finding the page online? Feel free to email me at mdavis@chabotcollege.edu and I can send you a direct line to the resources page.

Table of Contents

Chapter 1 - An Introduction to Statistics

Chapter Problem: *Are multi-vitamins a waste of money?*

According to an article published in the December 2011 issue of the International Journal of Epidemiology, "Long-term antioxidant supplementation has no effect on health-related quality of life." These conclusions were the results of a 6-year study of 8112 total participants carried out by Nancy University in France. Half of the participants were given a multi-vitamin containing vitamin C, vitamin E, beta-carotene, selenium, and zinc. The other participants were given a placebo. The researchers assessed their health at the beginning of the trial. When researchers analyzed how many in each group had gone on to develop serious illnesses during the trial, they found very little differences.

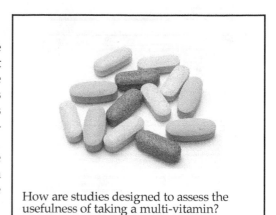

How are studies designed to assess the usefulness of taking a multi-vitamin?

By the end of this text, we will want to understand all of the math and statistics that are used to draw the conclusions in such a study. In this chapter, our goal will be to understand how the participants were chosen, how the study was designed, and to understand how this should affect the way we consider the conclusions from such studies. We will examine this study in more detail in the chapter problem at the end of this chapter.

Introduction:

Welcome to your introduction to the subject of Statistics. Before we begin learning any of the specific ideas, let's begin with a brief discussion of what the course will be all about. Students often come into this course with many questions. Is it just like the Algebra I have been taking? Are there going to be word problems? Is this a number crunching course? Does any of this really apply to my major? These are a few of the common questions students ask about Statistics. Just in case you are wondering about these questions, the answers are: It's different from algebra, but you will use some of the skills you learned in that class. There are words in most of the problems, but the words usually just describe the situation. It is rare that you will actually need to translate the words you read into a mathematical equation. We will do some of the number crunching you're expecting in the first few chapters. However, we will take advantage of technology to make this more manageable. You may or may not end up doing your own statistical studies in your area of interest. However, we all are faced with information that comes from statistical studies and it is important that we know how to evaluate the information that is presented.

People often ask these questions because they think of Statistics as an unknown topic, but the truth is, you have had a lot of contact with statistics in your everyday life. Simple forms include your instructor giving you the class average for a midterm, the scoreboard at a ballpark giving you the batting average of your favorite player, or the news reporting the median cost of buying a home in your city. Other types of Statistics tell you how many grams of fat are in the food you eat, the amount of chocolate eaten by the average person, or the percentage of the vote a politician is likely to get in an upcoming election.

Figure 1: Estimated Median New Home Price in 2007 in 1,000 Dollars

By the end of this course, you will understand how all of the above calculations are made. Statistics is different from the Algebra you took preparing for this course, and that means that before we can do statistics, we need to become familiar with the words, notations, and tools used in statistics. Because of this, most chapters will begin with an introduction to new vocabulary before you start making any statistical calculations. In this vein, most of chapter one will be devoted to learning the vocabulary of statistics so we can speak the language as we move on to make calculations in the later chapters. We will accomplish this goal in the following sections:

Section 1.1	Descriptive and Inferential Statistics
Section 1.2	Observational Studies and Designed Experiments
Section 1.3	Acceptable Methods of Data Collection
Section 1.4	Problematic Methods of Data Collection
Section 1.5	Variables and Data

Let's get started.

Section 1.1 – Descriptive and Inferential Statistics

As we learn statistics, we will see that we can separate the work we do into two types. One type is known as **descriptive statistics** and the other is called **inferential statistics**.

Definition: *Descriptive Statistics*

Descriptive statistics consists of methods of organizing and summarizing data so that it is easier to read and understand. Here are a few examples of the use of descriptive statistics.

- Computing an average of many data values
- Grouping data into separate classes using a table
- Creating a graph so that people can interpret our data visually

---

Before we can define the other type of statistical work, it is important to define a couple more statistical terms:

> **Definitions**: *Populations and Samples*
>
> **Population**: the group of people or things you will state conclusions about in your study.
>
> **Sample**: the part of the population from which you actually collect your data.

> **Definition**: *Inferential Statistics*
>
> **Inferential statistics** involves using data collected from a sample to make decisions about the population of interest. That is, we try to infer information about the whole based on data from just a part.
>
> *Examples*: Familiar examples of this are opinion and election polls. It is common for surveys to be taken of part of the public, yet the results are often stated for the whole state or country.

The main goal of this class will be to use samples to make inferences about populations. However, we will begin by studying descriptive statistics so that we can organize and summarize the data we will later use to make our inferences.

Example 1.1: *Approval ratings*

Polls are often taken to determine the level of support the President of the U.S. has from Americans. In September 2009, a Rasmussen poll of 1500 likely voters showed that 695 of those polled approved of the job President Obama was doing. As a result of this poll, it is then reported that 46.3% of Americans feel that the president is doing a good job. Answer each of the following:

a) Identify the population.

b) Identify the sample.

c) Is this study descriptive or inferential?

Do Americans approve of the job the President is doing?

Solution:

a) The population is all Americans. The study is interested in how all Americans feel about their President.

b) The sample is the 1500 likely voters that were surveyed and actually provided data by answering the question.

c) The study is inferential because it was eventually reported that 46.3% of Americans think the President is doing a good job, despite the fact that the data was collected from 1500, not all Americans.

> **Caution**: *Descriptive work is part of an inferential study*
>
> The study above does involve descriptive statistics as well, because the person doing the study had to go through the 1500 responses to the questions and summarize it by saying that 695 people supported the President. But, due to the fact that conclusions were drawn about a larger group than the 1500, we must state that the study is inferential.

Example 1.2: *Classifying Statistical Studies*

Consider each of the following situations and state whether the situation is a descriptive or inferential study. If the study is inferential, then state the sample and the population.

a) A statistics class took an exam and the average score on the exam was found to be 78.5.

b) A college is interested in the success rates of students taking their statistics course. They follow up on 70 students who took Intermediate Algebra last semester and are taking Statistics this semester. They find that 49 of those students pass the Statistics course. They conclude that 70% of students who take Intermediate Algebra will pass their Statistics course if they take it the next semester.

c) A survey was taken of the Temperature in 100 major world cities. The average temperature in those cities is found to be 67.2 °F.

d) The temperature from part (c) is 1.3 °F higher than found in a study 20 years earlier. The researcher concludes that this provides evidence of global warming.

Solution:

a) We are only summarizing this data for the purpose of describing those we collected the data from. This is descriptive statistics.
b) Conclusions are being drawn about more students than those we collected data from. This is inferential statistics. The sample is the 70 students who were tracked in the study. The population would appear to be all students who will take Statistics the semester after taking Intermediate Algebra.

c) We are only summarizing data and the result is only applied to the cities from which the data was collected. This is descriptive statistics.

d) This time, an attempt is made to extend our results to the entire Earth. This is inferential statistics. The sample is the 100 cities chosen. The population is the entire Earth.

Key Concept: *There is always a descriptive part to a study*

It would be very hard to make inferences from your data if you did not organize or summarize it first. That means that an inferential statistical study will always start out with descriptive statistical techniques and will become inferential at the point that conclusions are drawn about a larger group than those from which the data was collected.

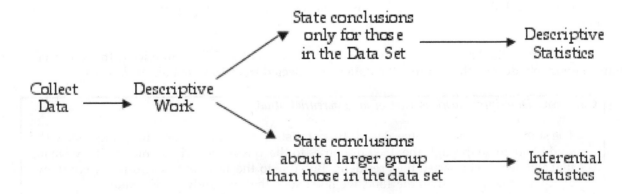

WRAP SESSION: *Thinking about the target of the conclusions*

Example 1.3: *Average Income Level*

Whether or not a person is satisfied with the money they make often depends on how it compares to the amount of income earned by those around them. One way of making such comparisons is to determine the average income for a group of people. Suppose that we obtained the income of 2000 randomly chosen Americans and computed the average income level. Suppose that the average income level was found to be $37,721 per year.

a) Would the 2000 people chosen be the population of interest or just a sample?

b) State a conclusion that would make this a descriptive study.

c) State a conclusion that would make this inferential statistics.

How much do we need to be satisfied?

Solution:

a) We really don't have enough information to answer this question. It depends on the group of people for which the conclusion is ultimately stated.

b) The average income level for the 2000 randomly chosen Americans is $37,721 per year.

c) Based on a sample of 2000 Americans, it is estimated that the average income level for Americans is $37,721 per year.

Let's practice what we have learned with some exercises.

Exercise Set 1.1

Concept Review: Review the definitions and concepts from this section by filling in the blanks for each of the following.

1) When you are only seeking to organize or summarize your data, this is referred to as _____ statistics.

2) When you attempt to draw conclusions about the population, based on information you obtained from a sample, that is known as _____ statistics.

3) The group of people or things you wish to state your conclusions about is known as the_____.

4) The _____is the part of the population that your data is collected from.

Applications: Practice the ideas learned in this section within the context of real world applications.

5) To estimate the average depth of the snow at a Lake Tahoe resort, 41 different locations on the mountain are chosen and the depth of the snow is measured at each location.
a) Identify the population.
b) Identify the sample.

6) A snowboarder wants to determine if the average price of snowboard bindings falls below $100 by the end of the season. During the month of April, she randomly chooses 25 pairs of bindings from local stores and notes the current price. Based on those 25 pairs, she estimates that the average price of bindings at the end of the season is about $93.77.
a) Identify the population.
b) Identify the sample.

7) A teacher is interested in what percentage of students would admit to texting while driving. The teacher surveys 85 students and finds out that 47 of them admitted to texting while driving in the past week.
a) Identify the population.
b) Identify the sample.

8) In 2009, a survey of 1280 Americans found that 602 of them have high speed internet at home. Based on this, it was estimated that 47% of Americans had high speed internet at home at that time.
a) Identify the population.
b) Identify the sample.

9) A manufacturer has built a new hybrid SUV and needs to estimate the average gas consumption for city driving conditions. They tested 12 of the vehicles in city driving conditions.
a) Identify the population.
b) Identify the sample.

10) In June 2011, a poll was conducted by the Gallup organization investigating whether or not Americans were confident in the public school system. Of the 1,020 adults surveyed, 348 expressed confidence in the U.S. public school system.
a)   Identify the population.
b)   Identify the sample.

11) A math teacher gives a test to a group of 38 students. He calculates the average score for these students for the sole purpose of reporting the information to the students when he returns the test.
a)   Would the 38 students be the population or just a sample?
b)   What type of statistics is the teacher doing?

12) A researcher is interested in the milk production of dairy cows. She measures the volume per day from 40 cows chosen from various farms around the country. She will use her data to estimate the average milk production per day for dairy cows.
a)   Are the 40 cows the population or just a sample?
b)   What type of statistics is the researcher doing?

13) In an effort to predict the winner in the January 2010 Massachusetts senate race, a Suffolk University poll asked 500 likely voters who they were planning to vote for.
a)   Are these 500 likely voters the population or just a sample?
b)   What type of statistics is the pollster doing?

14) A car salesman that works on commission is asked to state his monthly income during the last year for a credit card application. Because his income varies greatly from month to month, he decides to use the average of all 12 months during that year.
a)   Are the 12 months the population or just a sample?
b)   What type of statistics is the car salesman doing?

15) A snowboarding magazine conducts a survey of all the winter resorts in the Lake Tahoe area. The average adult lift ticket price for the Lake Tahoe area is calculated and published in the magazine.
a)   Are the adult lift ticket prices obtained the population or just a sample?
b)   What type of statistics is the magazine doing?

16) The editors of an electronics magazine would like to publish an estimate of the average cost of different brands of HDTV's. They randomly select 19 different 42" HDTV's and find the average of their prices. They publish the results in their magazine and label the result as the average cost of 42" HDTV's.
a)   Are the 19 prices obtained the population or just a sample?
b)   What type of statistics is the magazine doing?

17) A survey conducted in 2011 sampled 2,077 video game players and found that 41.49% of them were female.
a)   State a conclusion that would make this a descriptive study.
b)   State a conclusion that would make this inferential statistics.

18) In March 2008, the list price of 39 homes with 5 or more bedrooms for sale in Malibu, CA was obtained. The average price for these 39 homes was found to be $6,282,692.
a)   State a conclusion that would make this a descriptive study.
b)   State a conclusion that would make this inferential statistics.

19) A sports writer decides to keep track of the points scored by the star on the local basketball team. He keeps track of the points scored by this player for the first 10 games of the season. The average is computed and found to be 26.3 points per game.
a)   State a conclusion that would make this a descriptive study.
b)   State a conclusion that would make this inferential statistics.

20) A gambler observes 100 plays of the game of roulette. He notices that the ball landed on a red number 48% of the time.
a)   State a conclusion that would make this a descriptive study.
b)   State a conclusion that would make this inferential statistics.

Section 1.2 – Observational Studies and Designed Experiments.

In addition to identifying statistical work as descriptive or inferential, it is also important to differentiate between **observational studies** and **designed experiments**. The type of conclusions we can draw from our work is determined by this distinction. Therefore, let's figure how to tell the two types of studies apart.

Definitions: *Observational Studies and Designed Experiments*

Observational Studies: In this type of study, the researchers simply gather or record data that already exists in the world. This is often referred to as "natural" data. They do not have any influence on the data values. They merely record the data. Examples include the following.

- Opinion polls where you are asking someone to share an opinion that they already have
- Quality control studies where you check existing products for defects

Designed Experiments: In this type of study, the researcher has some control over the subjects being studied. This control includes the ability to make choices on behalf of the subject. The researchers will often intentionally change the value of a variable of interest. Examples include the following.

- When testing medicines, the researchers typically randomly split subjects into two groups and give the real medicine to one of the two groups and a placebo to the other.

In a purely statistical sense, designed experiments are more desirable than observational studies because by randomly deciding which people receive a treatment and which people do not you can avoid biases in your results that can occur when self selection is allowed. For example, suppose we want to study the effects of cigarette smoking on life expectancy. If we simply compute the lifespan of people who smoke to those who don't, we will not be sure what is causing the differences in life expectancy. Suppose the smokers have a shorter lifespan. Is that the result of the smoking or is it because of the lack of education and health care coverage that is more common in smokers than nonsmokers? We can note the difference in life expectancy, but we cannot be sure what is causing it. This is the problem with results found in observational studies. We can see the link, but we are unsure of the underlying cause.

However, suppose we did this as a designed experiment. In this case, we would obtain a random sample and then the researcher would randomly split this sample into two groups. One group would not be allowed to smoke and the other group would be forced to smoke. Now, unless we are unlucky, we will have roughly split up the factors such as education and healthcare evenly among the two groups, so the only clear distinction between the groups would be smoking versus nonsmoking. If we find that the smokers have a shorter lifespan, we can now be more certain that the smoking is the cause. This is because smoking is the only variable that is clearly different between the two groups in this case. It must be noted that we would not do such a study with people, because it would be a clear violation of peoples' rights if we forced them to smoke. Such studies are done, but they are done with mice rather than people. In this case, we can try to make sure that both groups are as similar as possible except for the smoking so that we can be more sure of a possible cause and effect relationship between smoking and lifespan. That is to say, we can make sure that both groups of mice have access to the same foods, toys, daylight etc.

> **Point to Remember**: *The ability to show cause and effect*
>
> In a designed experiment, you can show a cause and effect relationship between the variables studied. However, in an observational study, you can only show that there is a relationship between two variables. You will not be sure whether the relationship is casual or one of cause and effect. Because of this, we need to be careful that we do not overstate the results of an observational study.

One of the main reasons we are studying this topic is so that we can recognize the type of study that is being done. This will then tell us how strong of a conclusion we can reach from the information gained in the study. We will now look at these ideas in the context of some examples.

Example 1.4: *Cell Phones vs. Binge Drinking*

Recent research has revealed that adults who live in cell phone only households (no land-line phone) are twice as likely to binge drink (five or more alcoholic drinks during one day during the past year).

a) Do you think that this is an observational study or a designed experiment? Explain.

b) Based on the results of the research, can we conclude that living in a cell phone only household causes people to binge drink? Explain.

Does the lack of a land-line cause people to binge drink?

Solution:

a) I suspect that this was an observational study. Most likely, they performed a survey among many households and asked if they had a cell phone only, or also a land-line. In order for this to be a designed experiment, they would have to randomly assign adults to live in a cell phone only home and others to have a land-line. It's hard to imagine people volunteering to have this choice made for them.

b) Because this is observational only, we cannot prove cause and effect. Perhaps an alternate explanation is that younger adults are more likely to live in a cell phone only home and are also more likely to binge drink.

Example 1.5: *Laptop Batteries vs. Room Temperature*

A researcher is interested in the effects of temperature on the lifetime of laptop batteries. She takes 90 new laptops and randomly splits them into three groups. The first group is placed in a room that is kept at 110 °F, the second group is placed in a room that is kept at 70 °F, and the final group in placed in a room that is kept at 30 °F. All three groups are given the same program to run and the lasting times of the batteries are measured. The results showed that those kept at 30 °F lasted the longest and those kept at 110 °F had their batteries run out the fastest.

Does the air temperature affect the battery life of your laptop?

a) Do you think that this is an observational study or a designed experiment? Explain.

b) Based on the results of the research, can we conclude that higher temperatures cause laptop batteries to run out faster? Explain.

Solution:

a) This sounds like a designed experiment. With the nice round numbers for the temperatures, I assume that the researcher controlled the temperature. Also, the computers were randomly split and assigned to rooms. They were not already in those rooms being used regardless of the study.

b) Yes, because this is a designed experiment with random assignment. The only variable left to explain the difference in lasting time for the batteries would be the temperature. Perhaps, at higher temperatures, the computers fan must run more to keep the processor cool.

MORE ABOUT DESIGNED EXPERIMENTS: *The language of Designed Experiments*

The proper design and implementation of a statistical experiment is incredibly complex and difficult to achieve perfectly. It is a topic worthy of an entire course or text. However, in this book, we will simply introduce some of the key ideas involved in designing an experiment. There are four key elements that must exist in a well-designed experiment. The researchers must decide what **treatment** options will be applied to the subjects. They must **control** which subject is given each **treatment**, but they also must use **randomization** in this process. Finally, they must make sure they **repeat** the experiment enough times to ensure that the results are meaningful. These ideas are summarized by the definitions below.

Definitions: *Treatments, Control, Randomization, and Replication*

Treatments: These are the different values for a variable that will be assigned to the subjects by the experimenter. Examples include:
- Real medicine vs. placebo
- Plants grown in 60 degree room vs. 85 degree room

Control: Two or more treatment options should be possible for the subjects in the experiment. A **control group** where no treatment is given is often one of the options.

Randomization: It must be randomly decided which treatment a subject is to receive in the experiment. The subject cannot have been the one to make this choice.

Replication: This refers to the idea that we will conduct the experiment using many subjects. The result from any one subject is hard to use to draw conclusions. However, if a large sample is used, then the patterns that emerge can lead us to meaningful conclusions.

In addition to the factors listed above, researchers often use **blinding** when conducting a designed experiment. If the subject knows which treatment they are receiving this may alter the way they answer questions or perform tasks. Also, if the researcher knows which treatment a subject is receiving, they may subconsciously act in different ways towards subjects receiving different treatments. These actions could then end up affecting the outcome of the experiment. If experiments are not carefully controlled and if blinding is not used, then we may end up with some **confounding variables**. Let's define these new terms and then examine all of this with an example. All of this is usually done so that we can see the effect of the treatments on a particular variable of interest, called the **response variable**.

Definitions: *Single and Double Blind Experiments, Response Variable, Confounding Variables*

Single Blind Experiments: This means that the subject is not aware of which treatment they are receiving.

Double Blind Experiments: This means that in addition to the subject not being aware of which treatment they are receiving, the researchers that interact with these subjects are also not aware of which treatment group they are in. The treatment group of the subjects is assigned, but kept secret until the experiment is finished. After the experiment, the treatment group is available to the researchers.

Response Variable: When different treatments are applied in a designed experiment, we wish to see how these affect a particular variable. This variable is called the response variable.

Confounding Variables: If the variations in experimental outcomes can realistically be caused by more than one variable, then we say that we have confounding variables. This is troubling because it means that we are unable to determine the cause and effect relationship that we are seeking.

One final thing to consider when setting up a designed experiment is the ethics involved. When testing is done using human subjects, there are two basic principles of data ethics that need to be followed. They are listed in the following point to remember.

Definitions: *Basic Principle of Data Ethics*

Informed Consent: The participants need to be informed of any risks that may be involved in participating in the study. You should obtain participants consent in writing before they participate in your study.

Confidentiality: The identity of your participants should be kept confidential.

Example 1.6: *Weight Watchers vs. Doctor's Advice*

A 2011 study by the UK Medical Research Council compared the effectiveness of the commercial weight loss program 'Weight Watchers' to following a weight loss program given by the person's doctor. 772 overweight and obese adults in Australia, Germany, and Britain were randomly assigned to either a 1-year free membership for Weight Watchers or to 'Standard Care' by their doctor. Those assigned to the Weight Watchers program, on average, lost about twice as much weight as those in the other group.

What is the best way to lose weight?

a) What elements of experimental design were used in this study?

b) What confounding variables might exist in this weight loss scenario? Do you think they were adequately addressed in this study? Explain.

c) A 2011 Yahoo News story about this study had the headline "Weight Watchers Works." Based on the details of the study provided, does it seem like this headline is justified? Explain.

d) Discuss how data ethics should be addressed in this study.

Solution:

a) The study had two treatments, Weight Watchers and standard doctor care. The researchers did control which group each participant was in and the participants were randomized into the groups. There were 772 participants, so replication was also part of this study. Blinding probably did not make sense and was not used. Though not mentioned, it would be assumed that the participants gave informed written consent and that their identities were kept confidential.

b) Genetics is always a possible confounder in medical studies, though it is hard to imagine how genetics would direct people to one form of care over another. Motivation could also be a confounder here. People who choose to pay for a weight loss program might be more motivated to lose weight than directed to try to lose weight by their doctors. However, in this study, the participants did not make this choice, the researchers did. In addition, the program was free to them.

Both of the above confounders as well as others have been addressed by having the researchers control the choice of treatment by randomly assigning a treatment group to each subject.

c) Yes, this seems to be a well designed experiment with enough replication for the results of the study to be meaningful.

d) The risks involved in the study should have been clearly explained to the participants and the researchers should have obtained written consent from the participants. The identity of the participants should remain confidential.

> **Key Concept**: *Randomization and Confounding Variables*
>
> The biggest problem with confounding variables is that they can affect the subjects' choice of treatment. This makes it confusing to know whether it was the treatment or the reason for the subjects' choice of treatment that caused the change in the response variable. The best way to deal with this problem is to randomize the choice of treatment for each subject.

WRAP SESSION: *An Example involving Blinding*

Example 1.7: *Experimental Design in a Taste Test*

A supermarket has its own brand of cola that it sells to compete against Coke and Pepsi. The store brand is less expensive and the store would like to conduct a study to show that people like it as much as the major brands. They randomly choose customers out front of the store to take a taste test involving all three types of cola. The researchers randomly assign the colas to three cups labeled A, B, and C. They then pass these cups to those running the tasting booth without telling them which cup contains which brand. The participants then taste from each cup and choose their favorite. The process is repeated 150 times.

How should we design a soda taste test?

a) What are the treatments used in this experiment?

b) What is the response variable of interest?

c) Does the study include replication? Explain.

d) Would you consider this study to involve blinding? If so, is it single or double blinded? Explain.

e) Were efforts taken to avoid confounding variables? Explain.

Solution:

a) The treatments are the different types of soda used. There are 3 treatments: store brand cola, Coke, and Pepsi.

b) The participants' choice of favorite soda.

c) Yes. They conducted the process 150 times with different randomly chosen customers.

d) I would say that this is a double-blind study. The customers were not told which brands of soda were in the cups and those conducting the test also did not know which type of soda each cup contained. If the customers could recognize the taste of the Coke and Pepsi, then this would remove the blinding from some customers.

e) Yes. By double-blinding the study at least two possible confounding variables are removed. If the customers knew which cup contained which brand, then they might vote based on product loyalty rather than on taste. Also, if those conducting the study knew which cups contained which brands, then they might have subconsciously tried to encourage participants to choose the store brand.

Let's practice what we have learned with some exercises.

Exercise Set 1.2

Concept Review: Review the definitions and concepts from this section by filling in the blanks for each of the following.

21) In an Observational study, the researchers simply collect _____ data. This type of study _____ show cause and effect.

22) A designed experiment is one where the researchers design and _____ the experiment. This type _____ show cause and effect.

23) In a designed experiment, the different values for a variable that will be assigned to the subjects by the experimenter are known as the _____ .

24) In a designed experiment, if neither the participants nor those interacting with the participants are aware of what treatments are given to each participant, then this is known as a _____ _____ experiment.

25) In order to avoid the effects of confounding variables, it is important that we use _____ to assign subjects to either a control or treatment group.

26) In order to make sure that differences between the treatment groups and the control group is not just due to random variation, we need to conduct our experiments using many subjects. This is known as _____ .

Applications: Practice the ideas learned in this section within the context of real world applications.

27) A recent study showed that people who sleep more than 8 hours a day tend to live significantly longer than those who sleep 8 hours a day.
a) Do you suspect that this was an observational study or a designed experiment? Explain.
b) Can we conclude that extended sleep causes people to live longer? Explain.
c) Identify a possible confounding variable.

28) A study conducted on an allergy medication involved 100 patients who were split randomly into two groups. One group received the allergy medication and one group received a placebo. No participant was told which group they were in. The study showed that those taking the medication were significantly more likely to report drowsiness than those taking a placebo, rather than the medication.
a) Would you classify this as an observational study or a designed experiment? Explain.
b) Can we conclude that the allergy medication causes drowsiness? Explain.
c) Identify a possible confounding variable.
d) Discuss how data ethics should be addressed in this study.

29) A farmer was interested in the effects of a certain fertilizer on his tomato crops. He used the fertilizer on half of his plants, but not on the other. He noticed a significantly higher quantity and quality of tomatoes from the plants that received the fertilizer.
a) Would you classify this as an observational study or a designed experiment? Explain.
b) Can the farmer conclude that the fertilizer is the cause of the better results? Explain.
c) Identify a possible confounding variable.

30) A study revealed that students who take math classes during the evening tend to have significantly higher success rates than those who take similar classes during the day.
   a) Would you classify this as an observational study or a designed experiment? Explain.
   b) Does this show that a student who has had trouble with math during the day would be well advised to switch to evening classes for math? Explain.
   c) Identify a possible confounding variable.

31) A math teacher is interested in the connection between completing homework and test results. The teacher randomly splits the members of the class into two groups. One group is required to complete homework before taking the test. The other group is not. It was found that those required to do homework performed better on the test.
   a) Would you classify this as an observational study or a designed experiment? Explain.
   b) Does this show that a student who is struggling on exams, but is not doing the homework, would be well advised to start doing it? Explain.
   c) Identify a possible confounding variable.

32) A study has shown that the more fast food restaurants a city has, the more tire stores it tends to have.
   a) Would you classify this as an observational study or a designed experiment? Explain.
   b) Should this be considered evidence that eating fast food causes people to drive in a way that wears their tires out faster? Explain.
   c) Identify a possible confounding variable.

33) A study of 514 families with children revealed that the first-born child tends to have the highest IQ and the youngest child in the family tends to have the lowest. In addition, the study showed that children in larger families, on average, had lower IQs than those in smaller families.
   a) Do you suspect that this was an observational study or a designed experiment? Explain.
   b) Based on your answer to part (a), would you feel that the researchers would be justified to say that large families cause lower IQs? Explain.
   c) Identify a possible confounding variable.

34) A 2011 study, published in the Annals of Internal Medicine compared a weight loss procedure known as duodenal switch to the more common and less risky gastric bypass surgery. The study involved 60 severely obese patients who were randomly assigned to one of the two procedures. The duodenal switch patients, on average, lost about 50 pounds more in the two years following the procedures.
   a) Would you classify this as an observational study or a designed experiment? Explain.
   b) Based on your answer to part (a), would you feel that the researchers would be justified to say that duodenal switch patients will experience greater weight loss than gastric bypass patients? Explain.
   c) Identify a possible confounding variable.
   d) Discuss how data ethics should be addressed in this study.

35) This problem is a continuation of problem (29) about the farmer testing out a new fertilizer on his tomato crops.
   a) What are the treatments used in the experiment?
   b) What is the response variable of interest?
   c) Does the study include replication? Explain.
   d) Would you consider this study to involve blinding? Explain.
   e) Were efforts taken to avoid confounding variables? Explain.

36) This exercise is a continuation of exercise (28) about the link between an allergy medication and drowsiness.
   a) What are the treatments used in the experiment?
   b) What is the response variable of interest?
   c) Does the study include replication? Explain.
   d) Would you consider this study to involve blinding? Explain.
   e) Were efforts taken to avoid confounding variables? Explain.

37) This problem is a continuation of problem (31) about the teacher investigating the relationship between students being required to do homework and the resulting test scores.
   a) What are the treatments used in the experiment?
   b) What is the response variable of interest?
   c) Does the study include replication? Explain.
   d) Would you consider this study to involve blinding? Explain.
   e) Were efforts taken to avoid confounding variables? Explain.

38) This problem is a continuation of problem (34) about the study comparing the duodenal switch with gastric bypass surgery.
   a) What are the treatments used in the experiment?
   b) What is the response variable of interest?
   c) Does the study include replication? Explain.
   d) Would you consider this study to involve blinding? Explain.
   e) Were efforts taken to avoid confounding variables? Explain.

39) In 2011, McGill University in Montreal conducted a study to see if a parent holding a baby while blood was drawn reduced the amount of pain experienced by the baby. The study involved 62 preemies that needed multiple heel stick procedures for blood tests. The investigators had mom and dad alternate who was holding the baby. In the study, the babies were observed to experience about 17.5% less pain when held by the mothers.
   a) What elements of experimental design were used in this study?
   b) What confounding variables might exist in this pain test study? Do you think they were adequately addressed in this study? Explain.
   c) A Reuters news article reporting on this study had the headline "Mom better than dad at soothing baby's pain." Based on the details on the study provided, does it seem like this headline is justified? Explain.
   d) Discuss how data ethics should be addressed in this study.

40) The author of this text gave two forms of an exam to 60 of his Statistics students. One form was printed on yellow paper and the other form was printed using green paper. The different forms were randomly assigned to the students taking the exam. Suppose that the average score was 10 points higher on the yellow form of the exam. The students in the class concluded that the green test must have been harder.

a) What elements of experimental design were used in this study?

b) What confounding variables might exist in this pain test study? Do you think they were adequately addressed in this study? Explain.

c) Based on the details on the study provided, does it seem like the students feeling that the green test was harder were justified? Explain.

Section 1.3 – Acceptable Methods of Data Collection

We have now seen some of the types of statistical studies that can be conducted. In all types of statistical studies, we are going to be working with data. But where does it come from? Do we just take any data that is handy or do we somehow carefully pick the values we need or will our method be something else entirely? In this section, we will discuss the standard method of data collection, upon which, all of our mathematics is based. We will also discuss some of the acceptable variations of this method commonly used by those doing statistical studies. Let's start with a definition.

Definition: *Census*

> A **census** is the act of taking data from the entire population of interest rather than just using a sample from the population. You could also say that, if you are taking a census, then your sample consists of the entire population.

People don't usually take a census when doing a study. There are several reasons for this. One reason is that the data collection process can be very time consuming and also very expensive. Another problem is that, in some studies, the process of data collection can damage or destroy the item from which data is collected. For example, we would not want to take a census when crash testing a new car or testing the lifetime of a non-rechargeable battery. Because of the problems with a census, we generally take a sample when conducting a study, but that introduces a different problem.

When you collect a sample and use the data you collected to make estimates about the population, you invariably end up with some error in your estimates. This is not to say that we will make a mistake in our sampling methods or calculations. It is just acknowledging that a sample is unlikely to produce the exact answer we would have gotten had we taken a census. Therefore, when we take a sample we want to use a procedure that will minimize the **sampling error** that we get.

Definition: *Sampling Error*

> **Sampling Error** is the error that results from using a sample to estimate a quantity rather than taking a census to find its true value. The sampling error is the difference between the estimate and the true value of the quantity.

Let's take a look at an example where a poor job is done of selecting the sample.

Example 1.8: *IQ of college students*

A speech student at UC Berkeley is planning on giving a speech about IQs among college students in California. They go to the school library and obtain 50 volunteers to take a standard IQ test. They use the average IQ score for these 50 students as an estimate for the average IQ of all college students in California.

Will a student's survey on IQ be accurate?

a) Do you think that this estimate is likely to be exactly correct for the average IQ of all California college students? Explain.

b) Do you think the estimate will be too high or too low? Explain.

Solution:

a) No. Anytime you use a sample to estimate a population quantity, the estimate will most likely contain sampling error.

b) If this were a well-chosen sample, then we would not really have a good answer for this question. It would be a 50-50 chance as to whether it was too high or too low. However, this was not a well-chosen sample. Not only did the student choose only students from UC Berkeley (a university with high entrance requirements), but the student also only chose students from the library. Students in the library might tend to have higher IQs than the ones found in the pub or campus bowling alley.

Key Concept: *Avoid biased Samples*

This was not a good sampling technique because it was **biased** (see definition below) towards students with above average IQs.

This example leads us to a couple of definitions. The key concept above mentioned that the sample in the last example was **biased** towards above average IQs. We do not want biased samples, we would prefer to have **representative** samples. Here are the relevant definitions.

Definition: *Representative and Biased Samples*

Representative Sample: A representative sample is one where all relevant characteristics of the population are present in the same proportion in the sample as they exist in the population. If 37% of the population has trait 'A', then 37% of the sample should have trait 'A'.

Biased Sample: A biased sample is one where important characteristics are either over or under represented in the sample. This pulls or skews our estimate away from the correct answer.

Example 1.9: *Representing gender in a workplace survey*

A large company wants to survey their employees to see if they feel that satisfied with their opportunities to move up in the company. If 29.2% of the employees at this company are women, then how many women should be in a sample of size 200 if gender is to be properly represented?

Solution:

How do we decide how many women and men to include in our sample?

This is a fairly straightforward process. We want to make sure that the sample has the same proportion (or percentage) of women in it as the company does. So we want our sample to be 29.2% women. Because the sample size is 200, we simply multiply as follows.

$$29.2\% \text{ of } 200 = (0.292)(200) = 58.4$$

Sample size must always be a whole number. We round our answer to the nearest integer, 58. So we should have 58 women in our sample so that they are properly represented.

The example above shows that it is fairly easy to properly represent an important characteristic if you know what percentage of the population it makes up. However, there are many important characteristics for which we do not have this information. After all, you could not know this percentage unless you had taken a census of the population and we mentioned previously that, for many good reasons, this rarely happens. Another thing to consider is that we often do not even know what all the important characteristics are in a given population.

Suppose that we are conducting a study to estimate the average income of workers in a given city. Is it important to properly represent the different heights for the workers? It would seem like the answer to this would be no, but what if it is learned that taller people tend to have higher income levels? Then this would be an important characteristic. You never know what variables might be important, so you would like them all to be properly represented, but as was stated earlier, we don't have a census to tell us the percentages needed for each characteristic. So what do we do? The answer may surprise you. We choose our sample using the method of **simple random sampling**.

Definition: *Simple Random Sample*

   A **simple random sample** is one in which every sample of a given size is equally likely to be the one chosen.

A random sample does not ensure that all characteristics will be properly represented, however, it does give every characteristic a fair chance at being represented. It may seem like we are leaving it up to luck and hoping to get a representative sample by random chance, but the truth is, we have to get unlucky to get a biased sample. So, with just normal luck, a simple random sample will provide us with a fairly representative sample.

The following graph shows the ratio of a randomly selected trait over a large number of trials. Notice that as the number of trials increases the ratio of the trait in the sample approaches the true percentage (in decimal form) of the trait in the population of interest. This shows us that for a large sample size, random sampling is likely to produce a reasonably representative sample.

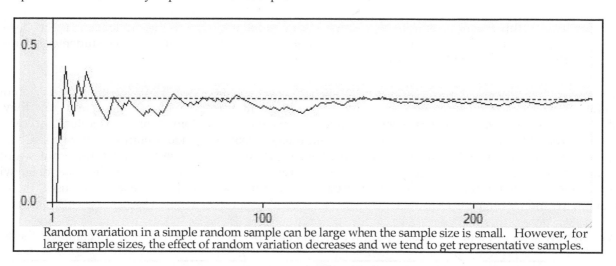

Random variation in a simple random sample can be large when the sample size is small. However, for larger sample sizes, the effect of random variation decreases and we tend to get representative samples.

METHODS: *Ways to obtain a simple random sample*

OK, so we have decided to randomly choose our sample, but this doesn't just mean to close your eyes and choose. If it is really going to be a simple random sample, then every sample of a given size must be *equally likely* to be the one chosen. The easiest way to visualize this method being carried out is the method of drawing names from a hat. Imagine that you wrote the names of all the people in your population on separate pieces of paper and then mixed them up in a (large) hat. If you want a sample of size 50, then simply draw out 50 names from the hat. This will absolutely get the job done, but writing down all those names is similar to taking a census, so it is unlikely we would do it this way. So now what?

The most common solution to this problem is the use of random number generators. We assign each item in the population a number. For example, if our population is the workers in America, then we could use their social security number as this number. We then use a computer or calculator to choose random numbers for us and then we pick the items that correspond to those numbers selected. Before we get to an example, we need a to define a couple of new terms.

Definition: *Sampling with or without replacement*

Sampling with Replacement is a method where after an item is selected, it is returned to the sampling pool. This means that the same item could possibly be chosen multiple times in a single sample.

Sampling without Replacement is a method where, after an item is selected, it is not returned to the sampling pool. This means that the same item cannot be selected more than once in a single sample.

Let's look at an example that demonstrates the use of a random number generator.

Example 1.10: *Using Random Number Generators*

Suppose that a small college has 1583 students. A campus researcher wants to randomly choose 150 students, without replacement, from the college to complete a survey. Explain how the 150 students could be randomly chosen using a random number generator.

Solution:

The first step in this process would be to assign a natural number to each of the students at the college. One simple way to do this would be to obtain an alphabetically arranged list of the students and then just number them from 1 to 1583 starting with the first name on the list.

The next step is to use a random number generator to choose numbers from 1 to 1583 giving every student an equal chance at being chosen. We will explore a few specific number generators and explain how they work at the end of this section. For now let's assume that we have a random number generator that can easily choose a random integer from 1 to 1583. Obtain an integer from the random number generator. Choose the student that corresponds to that number on your list of students. Continue to repeat the process until 150 unique students have been selected. Because it was requested that the sampling be done without replacement, if the random number generator ever selects a number that has already been used, then ignore that choice and obtain a new number.

We can now send out a notice to the 150 students that have been chosen and have them complete the survey.

Caution: *Ignore repeats for sampling without replacement*

Most random number generators choose their numbers with replacement. If you are using the method of sampling without replacement, then you simply ignore repeated numbers and continue selecting until you have obtained the required number of distinct values.

ALTERNATIVE SAMPLING METHODS: *Acceptable variations on simple random sampling*

While simple random sampling is the method we base the mathematics of statistics on, there are times when people apply variations to this method of selection. We shall quickly look at a few of the most common variations as well as the reasons they are used and the consequences of making these adjustments. We will begin with the method of **systematic sampling**.

Definition: *Systematic Sampling*

Systematic sampling is a form of sampling where we equally space our sample items throughout the population of interest. Because like items are often near each other, this can help avoid getting a biased sample. Examples include:
- Choosing every 9th student in a class
- Choosing an item every 10 minutes from an assembly line

Let's look at the procedure and then illustrate it with an example.

Point to Remember: *Procedure for obtaining a systematic random sample*

1. Divide the population size, N, by the desired sample size n. Round the answer down to the nearest integer and call that k. (This represents the space between picks.)
2. Now use a random number generator to choose a random integer from 1 to k. Call the randomly chosen integer m. (This represents the starting point for our first pick.)
3. Now pick the items from the population numbered m, m + k, m + 2k, . . .

Example 1.11: *Choosing students from a class*

A teacher in a large lecture hall wishes to choose 20 students at random. He would prefer not to have friends together in this group so he decides to use systematic random sampling to obtain the 20 students needed. He numbers the students beginning with the student in the front left and then going across the rows from the front row to the back row. This way, students who normally sit together will not be in the same group. Suppose the class contains 196 students:

How can we get a systematic random sample from a large group of students?

a) Use the procedure in the preceding box to obtain a systematic random sample of size 20 from the integers 1 to 196.

b) Explain why this method is not the same as simple random sampling.

c) Do you think that using this method increases or decreases the teacher's chance of getting a representative sample? Explain.

Solution:

a) First, we need to divide the population size, 196, by the desired sample size, 20, and round down to get k.

$$\frac{196}{20} = 9.8 \Rightarrow k = 9$$

Secondly, use a random number generator to choose a random integer between 1 and 9.

Let's suppose it produces the number 3.

Finally, plug into the formula m, m + k, m + 2k, . . . until 20 numbers are obtained.

3, 12, 21, 30, 39, 48, 57, 66, 75, 84, 93, 102, 111, 120, 129, 138, 147, 156, 165, 174

b) In a simple random sample, all samples of size 20 would be equally likely to be chosen as each other. With a simple random sample, we could end up with all students from the first two rows of the room. With systematic sampling, this would not be possible.

c) This method should increase our chance of getting a representative sample because it spreads the students picked throughout the room. People sitting next to each other often have things in common. Avoiding putting them in the sample together helps decrease the chance of getting a biased sample.

Key Concept: *Always Round Down*

Even though 9.8 is closer to 10 than 9, we always round down when choosing the value for k. If we round up, it is possible we would reach the end of the list, but not have enough students.

One drawback of rounding down is that you might never get an item at the very end of the list in your sample. Notice 174 is rather far away from the last number 196.

Another commonly used variation on simple random sampling is the method of **cluster sampling**. Cluster sampling is often employed to speed up the sampling process to save time and money. It is also used at times where getting individuals to participate may be difficult, but getting a whole group is easier. Let's look at the definition and then see how it works through an example.

Definition: *Cluster Sampling*

Cluster sampling is a form of sampling where we identify groups of items that exist in our population and then we choose several of these groups rather than selecting one individual item at a time.

Consider the following, suppose we wanted to obtain a sample of 300 bananas. We could choose bunches of bananas rather than single bananas and we might only need to choose 15 bunches rather than 300 individual bananas. This would make our work faster, but if one banana in a bunch is rotten, it is likely the other ones are also. Bananas on the same bunch will tend to have much in common and this increases our chance of getting a biased sample. Let's look at the procedure and a quick example.

Point to Remember: *Procedure for obtaining a cluster sample*

1. Decide on some natural form of grouping that exists in your data to use as the cluster.
2. Divide the desired sample size, n, by the average size of one of the clusters. Round this number up to the nearest integer.
3. Now use simple random sampling to choose the number of clusters you arrived at in step 2.

Example 1.12: *Cluster sampling the student body*

The office of instructional research at a community college with 12,000 students wants to conduct a student satisfaction survey. They would like to have about 600 students participate in the survey, but they are worried that if they randomly select 600 students and ask them to stop by for 30 minutes to fill out the survey, then many students may decline the offer. However, if they randomly choose whole classes, they feel they are more likely to get compliance from the instructor of that class. Suppose that the average class size at this college is 28.3 students.

a) What would be considered the clusters in their sampling procedure?

b) How many clusters should they choose?

c) What biases might be introduced due to the cluster sampling?

d) What biases might have been introduced if they just asked individual students to participate?

Solution:

a) The classes at the community college.

b) First we divide the sample size of 600 by the average cluster size, 28.3. $\dfrac{600}{28.3} \approx 21.2$

   We then round this up to 22. So, we should sample 22 classes.

c) Because we are choosing whole classes at a time, we will get many students with common characteristics. This can cause a bias towards those characteristics. If we happen to choose a class taught by the most popular teacher on campus, that might make the survey biased towards satisfied students.

d) If we only surveyed students who were willing to volunteer to spend 30 minutes of their time filling out the survey, then our sample would be biased against busy students who have no time to spare.

We will now turn our attention to one final variation on the method of simple random sampling. Sometimes, researchers may feel that certain characteristics are so important to the outcome of the study that they are unwilling to trust chance to represent them properly. In such cases, they turn to the method of **stratified sampling**.

> **Definition**: *Stratified Sampling*
>
> A **stratified sample** is one where certain important characteristics are purposely and carefully chosen in the sample in the same proportion (or percentage) that they exist in the population.

You should recognize some of this terminology from the definition of a representative sample. Because of this, we will see that procedure and example below are very similar to the work we did with representative samples earlier in the text.

> **Point to Remember**: *Procedure for obtaining a stratified sample*
>
> 1. Decide which characteristic you wish to use to stratify your sample. These characteristics separate your population into subpopulations.
> 2. For each characteristic, multiply the percentage of that characteristic in the population with the desired sample size.
> 3. Now choose a sample of the size determined in step 2 from each subpopulation.
> 4. Combine the samples from each subpopulation into one larger sample.

Example 1.13: *Stratifying by grade level*

A university is going to conduct a study on study habits among its students. The university has 16,909 students. 4509 are freshmen. 3812 are sophomores. 4593 are juniors. 3995 are seniors.

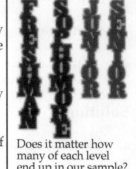

a) If they wish to obtain a stratified sample of size 800 based on class level, how many students should they choose from each class level?

b) Do you think that stratifying in this way will increase or decrease the chance of obtaining a representative sample? Explain.

Does it matter how many of each level end up in our sample?

Solution:

a) Let's start with the freshmen. Basically, what we need to do is calculate the percentage of students at the university that are freshmen and then determine how many students out of 800 would create the same percentage.

$$\text{Percentage of freshmen: } \frac{4509}{16909} \approx 26.667\%$$

26.667% of $800 = 0.26667 \cdot 800 = 213.336 \approx 213$, so we would want 213 freshmen.

As we continue on with the other class levels we can combine the two steps and just multiply the sample size of 800 directly by the fraction used to calculate the percentage.

$$\text{Sophomores: } \frac{3812}{16909} \cdot 800 \approx 180.354 \approx 180$$

$$\text{Juniors: } \frac{4593}{16909} \cdot 800 \approx 217.304 \approx 217$$

$$\text{Seniors: } \frac{3995}{16909} \cdot 800 \approx 189.012 \approx 189$$

The numbers above would be our answers except for one problem. If we add them up, the total is 799. This happened because every number was rounded down. So we need to add in one more student, but from which category? This is a little tricky, but I would add one more sophomore because that number was rounded down more than any of the others, so rounding that one up to 181 brings in less error than if we rounded up one of the others. So the final answer would be:

Sample 213 freshmen, 181 sophomores, 217 juniors, and 189 seniors.

b) Study habits probably vary greatly among the different class levels of the students. Representing any important characteristic properly should increase your chance of having a representative sample overall. There are probably many other important factors that we are leaving to chance, but stratifying at least one should still improve our sample.

TECHNOLOGY SECTION: *Random Number Generators*

This section demonstrates how to use the random number generators on two popular graphing calculators and on two popular statistics software packages. For each type of technology, we will learn how to obtain a sample without replacement of 12 integers chosen from 1 to 100.

TI-83/84:

The TI calculator has a random integer function. The user specifies a lower boundary and an upper boundary and the function chooses an integer in that range. This function picks one integer at a time and it does so WITH replacement. To obtain twelve integers from 1 to 100 without replacement, we would do the following steps.

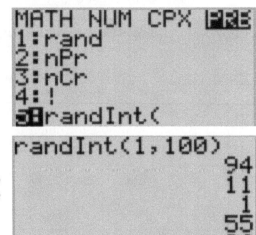

The randInt function is found under the MATH and then PRB menu. So, we choose MATH>PRB>randInt(, and then enter as follows.

randInt(1,100) and then press ENTER.

If we then press ENTER again, it will provide another integer from 1 to 100. We will repeat the process until we have 12 distinct numbers. The results are as follows.

94, 11, 1, 55, 86, 98, 62, 84, 21, 95

Point to Remember: *Procedure for obtaining random integers on the TI-83/84*

The structure we will use is randInt(A , B)

This command is found by selecting MATH and then PRB. You put the lowest number you want as a possibility in place of A and the largest possible number in place of B. The sampling is done with replacement, so if a number is repeated ignore it and choose another.

Note: It will sometimes happen that a number in the list is repeated. If you need a sample chosen without replacement and this happens, simply ignore that number and continue selecting until you have the required number of *distinct* values.

EXCEL:

1. Click in any of the cells in the worksheet.
2. Click in the f_x box.
3. Type in "=RANDBETWEEN(1,100)" and then press ENTER. (Notes: Don't type the quotes, but you must type the equal sign. Change the 1 to whatever you want to be the smallest possible integer. Change the 100 to whatever you want to be the largest possible integer.)
4. Repeat the process for additional random picks.

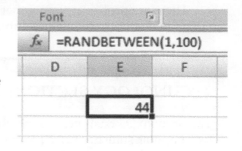

STATCRUNCH:

The following steps illustrate how to use StatCrunch to obtain a simple random sample of size 12, without replacement, from the integers 1 to 100.

1. From the STATCRUNCH window, click Data > Sequence Data. Fill in the pop up window as shown to the right. 2. Click on the Create sequence button.	**From:** 1 **To:** 100 **By:** 1 **Repeat each value:** 1 time(s) **Repeat the sequence:** 1 time(s) (Snapshot) (Cancel) (Create sequence!)
3. From the Data menu, choose Sample columns. 4. Fill in the pop up window as shown to the right. If you want to sample with replacement, make sure you click that option. 5. Select Stacked with a sample id so that your sample is stored in a new column. 6. Click the Sample Column(s) button to obtain your sample.	**Select Columns:** Sequence / Sequence **Sample size:** 100 **Number of samples:** 1 ☐ Sample with replacement ☐ Sample all columns at one time ☐ Save row ids for samples **Store samples:** ◯ Split across columns ◉ Stacked with a sample id (?) (Snapshot) (Cancel) (Sample Column(s))

MINITAB:

The following steps illustrate how to use Minitab to obtain a simple random sample of size 12, without replacement, from the integers 1 to 100.

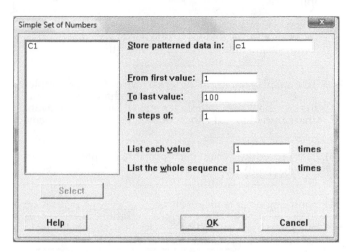

1. Enter the integers from 1 to 100 in C1 by doing the following: From the menus, choose CALC > Make Patterned data > Simple Set of Numbers

2. Fill in blanks in the pop up form as shown in the screen shot on the right.

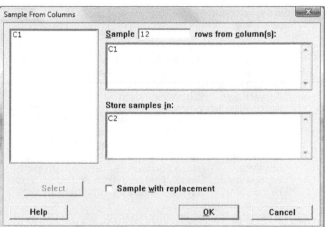

3. Now choose the random sample by going to the menus and selecting CALC > Random Data > Sample from Columns

4. Fill in the blanks in the pop up form as shown in the screen shot to the right.

5. Leave the box at the bottom unchecked unless you really want sampling with replacement.

6. The sample can be seen in the worksheet in column C2 or it can be displayed in the session window.

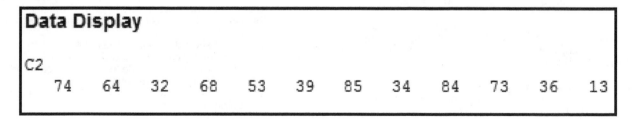

Exercise Set 1.3

Concept Review: Review the definitions and concepts from this section by filling in the blanks for each of the following.

41) When you collect data from the entire population of interest, that is known as taking a _____ . Two disadvantages of this are that it can be _____ or _____ .

42) To minimize our sampling error, we want our samples to be _____ rather than biased. This means that the sample contains all the relevant characteristics of the population in the same _____ as they exist in the population.

43) The procedure where each possible sample of a given size is equally likely to be the one chosen is referred to as _____ _____ _____ .

44) Sampling error is the result of _____ variation in our samples. However, the variation decreases as our sample size gets _____ . This helps us to get roughly representative samples.

45) Sampling without _____ is a method where after an item is selected, it is _____ returned to the sampling pool.

46) Each of the following is an advantage and/or disadvantage of an alternative sampling method. Identify the sampling method for each.
   a) Advantage: Choosing data that is already naturally in a group speeds up the sampling process. Disadvantage: Items naturally grouped together usually have common characteristics and this increases the chance of a biased sample.
   b) Advantage: This method guarantees that certain important characteristics are properly represented. Disadvantage: this requires some census knowledge and is more work than a simple random sample.
   c) Advantage: By equally spacing the members of your sample throughout the sample you decrease your chance of getting a biased sample.

Mechanics: Practice using random number generators on the technology of your choice before moving to the real world applications.

47) Use a random number generator to select a random sample of size 10 (with replacement) from the integers from 1 to 20.

48) Use a random number generator to select a random sample of size 10 (without replacement) from the integers from 1 to 20.

49) Use a random number generator to select a random sample of size 15 (without replacement) from the integers from 20 to 60.

50) Use a random number generator to select a random sample of size 15 (with replacement) from the integers from 20 to 60.

51) Choose a systematic random sample of size 12 from the integers from 1 to 100. Use a random number generator as needed.

52) Choose a systematic random sample of size 15 from the integers from 1 to 200. Use a random number generator as needed.

Applications: Practice the ideas learned in this section within the context of real world applications.

53) Suppose that Disneyland wants to estimate the average wait time for riders of Space Mountain. They want to time the wait time for 32 riders during the course of the day. They would like to use a systematic method of obtaining the sample. Suppose that they expect about 5400 riders during the day.
   a) Describe the procedure they should use to obtain this sample.
   b) What is the advantage of choosing the riders in a systematic way?

54) A candy company wants to get an estimate of the average number of pieces of candy in its bags. They would like to use a systematic random sample to select 35 of the next 500 bags that come down the conveyor belt.
   a) Describe the procedure they should use to obtain this sample.
   b) What is the advantage of choosing the bags in a systematic way?

55) A large poker room has 50 poker tables. Each table has 10 players seated at it. The manager wishes to obtain a sample of 60 players to fill out a survey. Suppose that they want to choose 60 players using cluster sampling.
   a) What should they use as their clusters? Why?
   b) How many clusters should they choose?
   c) How should they decide which particular clusters to include in the survey?
   d) Discuss the advantages and disadvantages of using cluster sampling.

56) A wine maker wants to study the grapes in one of his vineyards to test them for sugar content. He would like to have a sample of about 1000 grapes and he knows that there are about 40 grapes in each bunch of this variety. He plans to use cluster sampling to obtain the sample.
   a) What should he use as the clusters? Why?
   b) How many clusters should he choose?
   c) How should he decide which particular clusters to include in the survey?
   d) Discuss the advantages and disadvantages of using cluster sampling.

57) 6 months after the election of a new governor in a certain state, a newspaper wishes to estimate the approval rating of this new governor among the state's voters. When the governor was elected, the party breakdown of the voters in that election was: Democrat 51.7%, Republican 43.1%, other 5.2%.
   a) If we want to stratify based on political party, what should be the party breakdown in the current sample of 980 voters?
   b) Discuss the advantages and disadvantages of using stratified sampling for this application.

58) At Chabot college 3,332 students are 19 or younger, 4,393 are 20-24, 1,859 are 25-29, 2,269 are in their thirties, and 3,222 are forty or over.
   a) How many students should be chosen from each age group to obtain a sample of size 250 that is stratified based on age?
   b) Discuss the advantages and disadvantages of using stratified sampling for this application.

59) A 2011 Rasmussen Reports study reported that 86% of American Adults believe that it's a good idea for police cars to use surveillance cameras to monitor what happens when officers approach and apprehend suspects. The article states that these results are based on a national survey of 1,000 adults.
   a) What type of sampling procedure do you suspect they used?
   b) What might have been the motivation for using this sampling procedure?
   c) Do you think that this procedure will result in a representative sample and an accurate estimate of the true percentage of Americans that believe this about surveillance cameras? Explain.

60) A mountain biker wants to estimate his average speed on a ride with a lot of climbing and descents. He notes his speed after one minute and then every two minutes after that during a 60-minute ride.
   a) What type of sampling procedure is the mountain biker using?
   b) What might have been the motivation for using this sampling procedure?
   c) Do you think that this procedure will result in a representative sample and an accurate estimate of the true average speed? Explain.

61) A California newspaper wants to conduct a survey on the prevalence of racism in California. They decided to take their sample in such a way as to include the same percentage mixture of races in their sample as make up the adult population of California.
   a) What type of sampling procedure is the newspaper using?
   b) What might have been the motivation for using this sampling procedure?
   c) Do you think that this procedure will result in a representative sample and an accurate estimate of the population? Explain.

62) A city soccer league is hosting a large youth soccer tournament featuring teams from all over the state. They want to get feedback from some of the parents of the children who played in the tournament. Rather than asking all of the parents to fill out the survey, they randomly selected eight of the teams and asked all the parents for the kids on those teams to fill out the survey.
   a) What type of sampling procedure is the league using?
   b) What might have been the motivation for using this sampling procedure?
   c) Do you think that this procedure will result in a representative sample and an accurate estimate of the feelings of the parents of all kids involved in the tournament? Explain.

63) A student is doing a project to estimate the average number of study hours per week for math students. The student obtains the study times for 50 students in the school's math tutoring lab and uses that as the sample.
   a) Explain why this is not a representative sample for all the math students at the college.
   b) What biases might be introduced into the results due to the sample used?

64) When evaluating the effectiveness of teachers, most colleges have the teacher's students fill out a survey during the last week or two of school. This survey asks several questions about the quality of instruction.
   a) Explain why taking the sample at the end of the semester might not get all of the instructors students.
   b) What biases might be introduced into the results due to the sample used?

65) A student is trying to gather data for a project where they plan to estimate the percentage of people in her community that drink coffee beverages that include shots of espresso, such as a café mocha. She collects data by interviewing people as they exit the local Starbucks.
   a) Explain why this will probably not produce a representative sample for the people in the student's community.
   b) What biases might be introduced into the results due to the sample used?
   c) This sample might be considered acceptable if the student changed the target population from people in her community to what other group?

66) A student turned in a report on a study about children with progressive myopia. The article stated that all of the children in the study were Chinese-Canadians.
   a) The student stated that this was a representative sample. Do you agree with him? Explain.
   b) What biases might be introduced into the results due to the sample used?
   c) This sample might be considered representative if the population was changed from all children with progressive myopia to what other group?

Section 1.4 – Problematic Methods of Data Collection

In the previous section, we discussed acceptable variations to the method of simple random sampling. However, there are many sampling techniques that are commonly used that should never be considered acceptable variations. In fact, one of the worst abuses of Statistics occurs when someone uses an inappropriate sampling method, but then follows it up with correct statistical procedures. There is a feeling that, if the math is done correctly, then that will make up for the poor sampling procedure that was used. The truth is, all the math we apply is based on simple random samples. If we don't properly include the random element in our samples, then we can't expect reliable results regardless of how flawlessly we execute the statistical procedures that follow.

In this section, we will describe some sampling methods that should never be used when conducting a statistical study. If you ever read a study that used one of these sampling methods, then you should disregard the results (even if you like them). Sometimes the use of these sampling methods is the result of innocent mistakes by well-intentioned, but not statistically savvy people. Other times, such results have been purposely created to mislead you to support the cause of those conducting the survey.

We will begin by looking at one of the most commonly made sampling mistakes. This mistake is often made when non-statisticians attempt to collect data. It is most commonly seen when a television show or web site conducts a poll among its viewers. Rather than randomly choosing their participants, they allow people to volunteer to participate. This is collect **volunteer sampling**.

Definition: *Volunteer Sampling*

Volunteer Sampling: In this form of sampling, you allow the participants to volunteer to participate in the study. You don't randomly choose the participants, rather you invite members of the population to participate and you take whoever comes. These are very common and are usually referred to as **Non Scientific Studies**.

Examples: Call in / Text in / Web voting or polling. Many television programs, radio programs, and web sites ask questions of their audiences and invite them to respond with their choices. Businesses and organizations will often invite all of their customers or clients to participate in a survey and then take whatever responses are returned as their sample.

The Major Problem: Such data sets are usually not representative. Just because those running the poll / survey did not choose the participants, does not mean the results will be random. Some subgroups in your population are more inclined to participate than others and the results will be biased towards their viewpoint.

Note: In designed experiments, data collection ethics would demand that human subjects volunteer to participate. However, the volunteers are then randomly assigned to different treatment groups to reduce the effects of confounding variables on the response variable. Volunteer studies are most troublesome in opinion polls, which are observational rather than designed.

Another common mistake made by non-statisticians is the use of **convenience samples**. They are not asking for volunteers, but they do not randomly select their participants either. They just get data from the easiest available targets.

Definition: *Convenience Sampling*

Convenience Sampling: This means that we just collect the data that is easiest for us to obtain. Perhaps we only survey people we know, or that go to our school. We make no attempt to give every member of the population an equal chance at participating, we simply collect data from whatever sources are most convenient to us.

Examples: A student is giving a speech in a class and wants to collect data to support his point. He conducts a poll among his classmates, coworkers, friends, and family. A farm worker is asked to get a sample of 100 tomatoes from his 2000-acre farm for testing. He goes out and picks 100 tomatoes from plants near the building where he is working.

The Major Problem: Such data sets are not representative. Those whom you normally associate with are probably more likely to have opinions similar to your own. This would bias the study towards your point of view. Tomatoes that have all been grown in the same small area share similar soil quality, temperature, etc. The result will be biased toward the condition of the crop in that one small area.

In the next sampling method, it could be fair to say that those doing the statistical work did not seek a sample at all. They had no initial interest in studying a topic, but data has come to their attention that seems surprising or strange in some way. Because this data seemed so unusual, they decided to do some statistical analysis of it. It may seem harmless enough, but this can cause serious bias in the results. This is called **using attention getting data** and is defined as follows.

Definition: *Using Attention Getting Data:*

Attention Getting Data: This occurs when something that regularly produces data, suddenly produces data that stands out as unusual. You don't normally do statistical studies on this, but because this data seemed so strange to you, you decide to conduct a study based on this data set.

Examples: A regular gambler notices that a roulette wheel has produced a red number on ten consecutive plays of the game. She uses this result to show that the wheel is biased towards the red numbers. A sports radio talk show host notices that a baseball player is leading the majors with 11 homeruns in the first 14 games of the season. He uses this data to say he thinks the player will likely hit about 127 homeruns during the course of the season.

The Major Problem: It is normal for random experiments to occasionally produce what appear to be unusual results if we observe this experiment over a long time period. While this data is random to some extent, we have decided to only use the portion of the data that stood out as unusual. This will severely bias our study towards providing "evidence" supporting our position. The roulette wheel and the baseball player will most likely fall back into more normal patterns if we continue to observe them.

A variation on the problem of using attention-getting data, is the process of using **pre-existing data**. In this case you may have been planning to investigate a certain item all along. However, you do not state the theory that you are trying to prove until after you have collected the data. Worse yet, you may decide what theory you will seek to prove only after seeing the trends in the data.

Definition: *Using Pre-Existing Data:*

Pre-Existing Data: This occurs any time you collect and examine a data set before you decide what you are going to try to prove from that data.

Examples: A person tosses a coin 100 times. It lands showing the heads side 63 times. The person decides to use this data to show that the coin is biased towards heads. A consumer buys 36 cans of soda and carefully measures the amount in each of the cans. The average amount per can is 11.8 ounces. The consumer decides to use this data set to try to show that the soda company is, on average, under filling the cans.

The Major Problem: If the data gives us our opinion, then the data will automatically be biased towards supporting that opinion. It is fine to get an idea of what you want to prove by using data that has been randomly selected. However, once you come up with what you want to show, you must take a new random sample to try to prove your point.

We will end the discussion of problematic sampling techniques with one final type of sample to avoid. This type is called **handpicking your data**. This happens anytime someone makes sure that they only use data that supports their case. They may randomly select a sample and then discard data that doesn't fit their theory or they purposely only collect data that fits their theory. Someone doing this is either very naïve about how statistics works or they are purposely seeking to distort the facts.

Definition: *Hand Picking Your Data:*

Hand Picked Data: This is a method where you purposely seek out data that meets a certain criteria or possibly throw out any data that doesn't.

Examples: Choosing data from a top 10 or top 40 lists. Examining only the results from the best performer or the worst performer on a test, game, sport etc. Throwing out data that doesn't fit your theory.

The Major Problem: It is actually fine to look at such a list or leaders, but you should never consider this to be a representative sample of your population. Such data sets should be seen as populations themselves. Study them if you want, but do not try to make inferences about the larger group they were selected from. In the case of throwing out data that doesn't fit your theory, you are purposely distorting your data set in a way that helps you prove your point.

Let's take a look at a couple of examples that illustrate the use of a problematic sampling method and the biases that can result.

Example 1.14: *Olympics too Dangerous?*

While practicing for the men's luge competition at the 2010 Vancouver Olympics, Georgian competitor Nodar Kumaritashvili crashed and died. A few days later, CNN conducted a poll on its web page asking readers the question: "Have the Olympics become too dangerous?" After almost 100,000 votes had been cast, 72% of the respondents had answered "No". The site stated that this was not a scientific poll. Suppose that we wanted to use this as an estimate of the views of Olympic viewers in general.

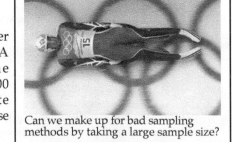

Can we make up for bad sampling methods by taking a large sample size?

a) Identify the type of problematic sampling that caused them to state that this was not a scientific poll.

b) What potential biases could this introduce in the results of the study?

c) Does the large sample size make up for the sampling method?

Solution:

a) This study was conducted using a volunteer sample. Participants were not randomly selected.

b) CNN viewers and readers might not be representative of the general viewers of the Olympics. Also, because they are not randomly chosen, one choice or the other may feel a stronger compulsion to participate and respond. This would bias the outcome towards their viewpoint.

c) 100,000 participants is considered a huge sample size. However, large sample sizes do not make up for poor sampling techniques.

Example 1.15: *A biased coin?*

A Statistics teacher gives each of his 50 students a quarter and asks each of them to flip their coins 100 times. The teacher then polls the students to see who got the most lopsided results. One of the students reports that they obtained 61 tails and only 39 heads. This student's data is chosen and analyzed. It is determined that the chance of 61 tails or more in a random sample from a fair coin is only about 1.8%. Based on this evidence, it is concluded that this student's quarter is biased towards tails.

a) What problematic sampling method was used?

b) Do you feel that they are justified in deciding that the coin is biased towards tails? Explain.

c) If they wish to properly investigate this coin, what would you recommend that they do?

Solution:

a) I would say that they have handpicked their data set. They had 50 data sets to choose from and they purposely chose the most lopsided one. Also, they did not decide to check for biased towards tails until after they had seen the data set. This means that they are using pre-existing data.

b) It could be, but I doubt that it is. If there is a 1.8% chance of seeing this many tails or more in 100 tosses, then it should not be considered surprising that it happened once in a group of 50 students. 1 student out of 50 is 2%, which is pretty close to the calculated probability of this event occurring with a fair coin.

c) If the results so far have them suspicious that this coin is biased towards tails, then they should toss it 100 more times and use the new data set to test this theory.

OTHER PROBLEMS WITH DATA: *Loaded Questions and Suspicious Sources*

All the examples above concern faulty sampling techniques. However, even if a study is using a true simple random sample, there are still other problems that can lead to bias in the results. If a survey contains **loaded questions**, then even a random sample can be biased towards a certain answer.

> **Definition**: *Loaded Questions*
>
> **Loaded Question**: A survey question that has been worded in such a way that it encourages one answer over others.

Example 1.16: *Support for Healthcare reform*

During the healthcare reform debates in 2010, a pollster asked the following question: "Do you support a government takeover of healthcare?" Out of 560 people surveyed, approximately 62.6% answered "No". It was then reported that a recent polled showed that 62.6% of Americans were opposed to healthcare reform.

How important is the wording of the poll questions that are asked?

a) Explain why this is considered a loaded question.

b) What would be better language for a poll question on this matter?

Solution:

a) The question characterizes the health care reform plan as a government takeover of healthcare. This strong language probably encouraged a "No" answer from the participants.

b) Better question: "Do you support the currently proposed healthcare reform plans?"

One final caution is to always be wary when the sponsor of a study has a vested interest in reaching a certain conclusion. It is not uncommon for companies to fund the research that ultimately will support the product they sell. However, because we know they have a vested interest in a positive result, we may wish to examine their methods more carefully.

> **Definition**: *Suspicious Sources*
>
> **Suspicious Sources:** When those conducting or funding the study have a vested interest in a certain result, this is considered a suspicious source. This study may in fact be completely valid, but it is a good idea to try to verify that random sampling was used and that loaded questions were not asked on the surveys.

Example 1.17: *Cure for baldness?*

In February 2010, the Rogaine website contained the following claim: "In clinical testing, ROGAINE® Foam regrew hair in 85% of men after 4 months when used twice daily."

a) If this clinical testing was funded by the Rogaine company, does this make the result suspicious? Explain.

b) Can this claim be automatically dismissed as false? Explain.

How does the source of the study affect the reliability of the conclusions?

Solution:

a) Because they are interested in selling this product, a study they fund that shows it is effective is suspicious. Before believing such results, further details about who conducted the study and the methods used should be examined.

b) No! Almost all studies conducted to prove that products are effective are funded by those wishing to sell the product. If those conducting the study do not have a clear incentive to find a favorable result for the company and if they use valid sampling techniques and statistical methods, then the results can still be believed.

Let's practice with some exercises.

Exercise Set 1.4

Concept Review: Review the definitions and concepts from this section by filling in the blanks for each of the following.

67) If you are presented with a study that used problematic sampling methods then you should _____ the results.

68) A survey question that has been worded in such a way that it encourages one answer over others is called a _____ _____ .

69) When those conducting or funding the study have a vested _____ in a certain result, this is considered a _____ source.

70) When a poll is conducted using the method of volunteer sampling, they usually refer to it as a _____ _____ study.

Applications: Practice the ideas learned in this section within the context of real world applications.

71) To determine who Americans think is the best singer on American Idol, the show creates toll free telephone numbers for the viewers to use to call in and vote for their favorite performer. The one receiving the least votes each week is then out of the competition.
a) What problematic sampling method was used?
b) What biases might be introduced into the results due to the problematic sampling method?

72) In June 2011, a former student of the author e-mailed him a Yahoo news article that stated that a British cake decorator cracked a record 29 eggs with double yolks in a row. The article stated that the odds of getting 29 in a row are 1 in "10 raised to the power of 87".
a) What is the problem with using the decorators egg experience data to do statistical calculations?
b) What biases might be introduced into the results due to the problematic sampling method?

73) A poker player regularly plays 10 player tournaments online. At one point he wins three of these in a row. He knows that if he is an average player, his chance of winning 3 in a row would be about 1 in 1000. Because this is so unlikely for an average player, he decides he must be an above average player.
a) What problematic sampling method was used?
b) What biases might be introduced into the results due to the problematic sampling method?

74) A gambler wants to check a die to see whether or not it is fair. After rolling the die 257 times, he notices that the roll of the die produced the number "5" 59 times. He then uses this data to show that the die is biased towards the number "5".
a) What problematic sampling method was used?
b) What biases might be introduced into the results due to the problematic sampling method?

75) In the 1970's a naturalist at Glacier Bay National Park was talking with a researcher who was collecting data on the historical rate of advance for one of the glaciers in the park. The naturalist noticed that the researcher had crossed many of the data points on the map out. When asked why these data points were crossed off, the researcher stated that they were removed as errors because they did not fit the model for the rate at which the glacier had advanced.
a) What problematic sampling method was used?
b) What biases might be introduced into the results due to the problematic sampling method?

76) In September 2011, a Reuters article stated that a recent poll had shown that "The world still thinks Americans are the "coolest nationality". The data was collected from 30,000 people across 15 countries from members of the social networking site Badoo.com who chose to respond to a posted survey.
a) What problematic sampling method was used?
b) What biases might be introduced into the results due to the problematic sampling method?
c) Is this remedied by the extremely large sample size? Explain.

77) When the author of this text was taking a speech class as a freshman at Sacramento State, he collected data for a speech on the unreasonableness of a 55 mph highway speed limit by asking his classmates, friends, and coworkers how fast they typically drove on the freeway. He then used this data to support his argument that the speed limit should be raised.
   a) What problematic sampling method was used?
   b) What biases might be introduced into the results due to the problematic sampling method?

78) After 18 games were played in the 2007 baseball season, New York Yankee Alex Rodriguez led the majors in homeruns with 14. Using these 18 games as the sample, it is estimated that he will hit 126 homeruns by the end of the 162 game season.
   a) What problematic sampling method was used?
   b) What biases might be introduced into the results due to the problematic sampling method?

79) A statistics student decides to check the fairness of a coin. She flips the coin 100 times and it lands showing heads 61 times. She then went on to use this data to show that the coin was biased towards heads.
   a) What problematic sampling method was used?
   b) What biases might be introduced into the results due to the problematic sampling method?

80) A student at Chabot College believed that the college should change to a plus/minus grading system. He collected data to support his case by surveying his classmates and instructors. When he tried to survey his instructor, he was told that his data collection method was flawed.
   a) What problematic sampling method was used?
   b) What biases might be introduced into the results due to the problematic sampling method?

81) A poll question about the death penalty asked the following: "Do you support government sanctioned murder of those convicted of acts of terrorism?"
   a) Explain why this would be considered a loaded question.
   b) What would be better language for a poll question on this matter?

82) A poll question about the issue of abortion asked the following question: "Do you believe that a mother should be able to kill her unborn child if the pregnancy is in any way an inconvenience to her?"
   a) Explain why this would be considered a loaded question.
   b) What would be better language for a poll question on this matter?

83) In August 2011, designer Kenneth Cole came under fire for his social media campaign that was said to trivialize serious issues. One of their survey questions asked the following: "If gun owners are 4.5 times more likely to be shot in an assault, are guns an effective form of self-defense?"
   a) Explain why this would be considered a loaded question.
   b) What would be better language for a poll question on this matter?

84) One of the demands of the "Occupy Movement" in 2011 was for higher taxes on the wealthiest Americans. One poll question at most time asked the following: "Do you agree with most Americans that the super rich should have their taxes raised so that they can start paying their fair share?"
   a) Explain why this would be considered a loaded question.
   b) What would be better language for a poll question on this matter?

85) Between songs, a radio disc jockey stated that a recent study had shown that people who listen to the radio tend to be happier. The radio host was referring to the conclusion in an article written by the planning director of the United Kingdom's Radio Advertising Bureau.
   a) Why should this be considered a suspicious source for this information?
   b) Does the fact that this is a suspicious source mean that this is not a true claim? Explain.

86) A 2011 article on massage.com stated that a new study showed that a 12-minute exercise can help reduce pain in office workers. The details of the study stated that the study utilized elastic tubing to perform the exercises. A disclosure in the article stated that the Thera-Band Company provided the elastic tubing to the researchers.
   a) Why should this be considered a suspicious source for this study?
   b) Does the fact that this is a suspicious source mean that this is not a true claim? Explain.

87) A commercial for a medical office that performs laser surgery to improve the condition of the gums of people with periodontal disease stated the following. "Studies have shown that those suffering from periodontal disease have an increased risk of heart attack and stroke."
   a) Why should this be considered a suspicious source for this information?
   b) Does the fact that this is a suspicious source mean that this is not a true claim? Explain.

88) In 2010, the Jenny Craig weight loss system ran an add comparing their program to Weight Watchers. The commercial claimed that a study had shown that "Jenny Craig clients lost, on average, over twice as much weight as those on the largest weight-loss program."
   a) Why should this be considered a suspicious source for this information?
   b) Does the fact that this is a suspicious source mean that this is not a true claim? Explain.

Section 1.5 – Variables and Data

Now that we have talked about the ways we can obtain our sample, it is time to take a look at the types of questions we will be interested in as well as the answers to those questions. Statistically, that means it's time to take a look at **variables** and **data**.

Definitions: *Variables and Data*

Variables: A variable is a characteristic that can vary from one person or item selected to another. It might be the question we ask in a poll or a measurement we take on an assembly line product.

Data: Data is the specific answer we get to our question or the specific measurement for an item selected. Data is the value the variable takes on for a specific person or item.

When we select data we want to classify it as **categorical** or **quantitative**. We generally treat these two types of data in quite different manners, so it is important to know right away which situation you are in.

Definition: *Categorical Data*

Categorical Data: The root word here is category. It is called categorical because it is often used to separate data into groups or categories. This type of data is generally in word form rather than number form.

Caution: While categorical data is generally non-numeric, if a piece of data is a number which merely represents a category, but does not actually count or measure anything, then it is still considered categorical.

Examples of categorical data include the following. We might ask someone their favorite flavor of ice cream or whom they will be voting for in an upcoming election. Their answer will come in words, not numbers. We might group people by eye color or gender, which are nonnumeric categories. This type of data is also referred to as **qualitative** data because we are describing qualities of the data using words rather than numbers.

Definition: *Quantitative Data*

Quantitative Data: This time the root word is quantity and we will be looking at variables that take on numeric values. We might measure the time it takes a person to eat a bowl of their favorite flavor of ice cream or we might ask them how many elections they have voted in during the past ten years. The answer will be a number this time rather than a word description. This type of data is also referred to as numerical data.

Caution: While quantitative data is generally given as a number, if a piece of data is a word or letter that has a numeric value, then it is still considered quantitative. For example: A 'B' grade in a course has a value of 3.0 grade points.

In addition to classifying data as categorical and quantitative, quantitative data can be broken down into two subtypes. The subtypes are **discrete** and **continuous** and they are defined below.

> **Definitions**: *Discrete and Continuous Quantitative Variables*
>
> **Quantitative-Discrete**: If two possible values of the variable have numbers that exist between them, but those numbers in between are not possible values of the variable, then we are working with a discrete variable. We can also say that, with discrete variables, gaps exist between the possibilities. Mathematically speaking, we say that a discrete variable has a finite or countable number of values. Discrete variables often, but not always, are the result of counting.
>
> **Quantitative-Continuous**: A variable is continuous if all the numbers between any two given possibilities are themselves possibilities. With continuous variables, there are no gaps between the possibilities. Mathematically speaking, we say that a continuous variable has possible values that form an interval and there will be an infinite and uncountable number of possibilities.

All of the definitions above tell us how to classify a variable. There are times when we are also asked to classify data. To do this you simply determine the classification of the variable and apply the same answer to the data. For example, because eye color is a categorical variable, a person with blue eyes is a piece of categorical data. Let's take a look at several examples to help clarify the definitions given.

Example 1.18: *Shoe Sizes*

A simple random sample of 79 people is taken. They are asked to specify their shoe size (by U.S. measurements).

a) What is the variable?

b) Give an example of a possible data value.

c) Classify the variable.

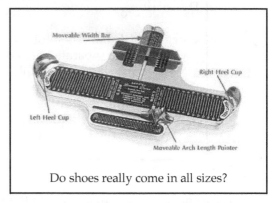

Do shoes really come in all sizes?

Solution:

a) The variable is the shoe size.

b) A possible data value would be size 10.

c) Because the data values are numeric, it is a quantitative variable. The answer could be 10 or 11, but could it be in between? Yes, it could be a size $10\frac{1}{2}$. Does this mean it is continuous? No, it can't be a size 10.783088, so there are gaps between the possibilities. This means that we have another quantitative-discrete variable.

Example 1.19: *Filling Soda Cans*

A simple random sample of 120 soda cans is taken from a bottling plant assembly line. Each is measured for the number of fluid ounces it contains.

a) What is the variable?

b) Give an example of a possible data value.

c) Classify the variable.

Sampling can be used to estimate the accuracy of a soda can filling machine.

Solution:

a) The variable is the amount of soda in a selected can.

b) A possible data value would be 12.043 fluid ounces.

c) Because the data value is numeric, this is a quantitative variable. Because it is quantitative, we must classify it further as either discrete or continuous. 12.1 and 12.2 ounces are both possible values for the variable, and so are the infinitely many numbers in between, so this is a quantitative-continuous variable.

> **Key Concept**: *Consider what is possible*
>
> The measurements for the 120 cans will be a finite and thus discrete set of numbers. However, when making this classification, we always look at the set of *possibilities* for the data values, and the set of possibilities forms an interval.

Example 1.20: *Nathan's Hot Dog Eating Contest*

Every July 4th in Coney Island, Nathan's hosts a hot dog eating contest. In 2011, contestant Joey Chestnut took first place by eating 62 hot dogs in 10 minutes. Contestants are not given credit for partially eaten hot dogs. Suppose we want to collect the data for the number of hot dogs eaten by the contestants in the upcoming year's competition.

a) What is the variable?

b) Give an example of a possible data value.

c) Classify the variable.

How many hot dogs could you eat in 10 minutes?

Solution:

a) The variable is the number of hot dogs eaten by a given contestant.

b) A possible data value would be 17 hot dogs.

c) Because the answer to the question is numeric, this is a quantitative variable. The problem states that partial hot dogs do not count. So only whole numbers are possible making this quantitative – discrete.

Example 1.21: *Fake Medicines in Africa*

A 2011 Gallup poll found that counterfeit drugs are widespread in sub-Saharan Africa. They surveyed a random sample of 1,000 African adults and asked them the following: "Are you aware of the presence of fake medicine in this country?" In Cameroon, 91% of the respondents were aware of such fake drugs.

a) What is the population of interest in this study?

b) What is the variable in this study?

c) What are some possible data values?

d) Classify the variable.

How common are fake medicines is Africa?

Solution:

a) The article ended up stating a conclusion about how common these fake drugs are in sub-Saharan Africa, so the population in this study would be all of the adults living in sub-Saharan African countries. Notice that we do need not mention the variable when stating the population of interest.

> **Caution:** *Population vs. Variable*
>
> It is common for students to state the variable when asked about the population in a study. Be careful to avoid this mistake.

b) The variable is the response given by individual participants to the question "Are you aware of the presence of fake medicine in this country?"

c) Possible answers to the question might be "Yes", "No", or "Not Sure".

d) Because the answers are all non-numeric word based answers, this should be considered a categorical variable.

> **Caution:** *Variables apply to individual subjects.*
>
> You might be tempted to list this variable as quantitative because of the 91% number reported for Cameroon. However, the variable applies only to the individuals being asked the question. The 91% is a summary number for many of these individuals.

It's time to practice by doing some exercises.

Exercise Set 1.5

Concept Review: Review the definitions and concepts from this section by filling in the blanks for each of the following.

89) A variable that takes on non-numeric values is known as a _____ variable.

90) If the variable takes on numeric values, then it is known as a _____ variable.

91) Quantitative variables whose possible values have _____ between them are known as discrete.

92) Quantitative variables whose possible values do not have gaps between them, but rather form an _____ are known as continuous.

Applications: Practice the ideas learned in this section within the context of real world applications.

93) A random sample of 85 students are asked to name their favorite beverage.
   a) What is the variable?
   b) Give an example of a possible data value.
   c) Classify the variable.

94) A random sample of 845 registered voters are asked whom they will vote for in the 2012 presidential election.
   a) What is the variable?
   b) Give an example of a possible data value.
   c) Classify the variable.

95) A random sample of 212 Californians are asked to state the number of speeding tickets they have received in the last 3 years.
   a) What is the variable?
   b) Give an example of a possible data value.
   c) Classify the variable.

96) A random sample of 19 koala bears are observed and the amount of time they spent sleeping during a 24-hr period is recorded.
   a) What is the variable?
   b) Give an example of a possible data value.
   c) Classify the variable.

97) A random sample of 12 giraffes are measured and the height of each is recorded.
   a) What is the variable?
   b) Give an example of a possible data value.
   c) Classify the variable.

98) 46 math classes are randomly selected and the number of students taking the final exam is counted in each class.
   a) What is the variable?
   b) Give an example of a possible data value.
   c) Classify the variable.

99) A random sample of 24 community college students is taken and the students are asked what their favorite type of food is.
   a) What is the variable?
   b) Give an example of a possible data value.
   c) Classify the variable.

100) A sports statistician looks over the records for the 2011 football season and records the number of sacks for each of the defensive players on the New York Giants.
   a) What is the variable?
   b) Give an example of a possible data value.
   c) Classify the variable.

101) A random sample of 24 types of SUVs is obtained and each one is tested to find the braking distance required to come to a stop from 65 mph.
   a) What is the variable?
   b) Give an example of a possible data value.
   c) Classify the variable.

102) A census is conducted in a small town for the purpose of determining the blood type of all the people who live there.
a) What is the variable?
b) Give an example of a possible data value.
c) Classify the variable.

103) A 2011 Rasmussen Reports poll asked 1,014 Americans the question: "Do you think it's a good idea to get rid of the existing income tax code and replace it with something simpler?" The study concluded that 61% of likely U.S. voters prefer a simpler tax code.
a) What is the population of interest in this study?
b) What is the variable?
c) Classify the variable.

104) In an effort to help users know if other purchasers have been happy with a product, Amazon.com allows purchasers to rate the products they buy on Amazon. Users can rate a product from a low of 1 star to a high of 5 stars. Partial stars are not allowed. They then display the average rating. One type of Sony headphones had received an average rating of 4.29 stars after 979 reviews.
a) What is the population of interest in this study?
b) What is the variable?
c) Classify the variable.

105) According to a 2011 Gallop poll, "More Americans are Now Normal Weight than Overweight." These results are based on a random sample of 90,070 adults who were asked many questions including "What is your current weight, in pounds?"
a) What is the population of interest in this study?
b) What is the variable?
c) Classify the variable.

106) According to a 2011 Gallop poll, "Majority of Britons Distrust the Media." These results are based on a random sample of 1,000 adults who were asked "In this country, do you have confidence in the quality and integrity of the media?"
a) What is the population of interest in this study?
b) What is the variable?
c) Classify the variable.

107) A 2011 Time/CNN article had the headline "Cheers, Ladies! A Drink a Day May Mean Good Health in Older Age." The article stated that research had found that those who reported having one or two drinks a day in middle age were significantly more likely to maintain good health as they aged, compared to women who did not drink at all. Harvard researchers collected the data from 13,894 women who filled out surveys about their drinking habits around age 58 and then had their health assessed again at age 70.
a) What is the population of interest in this study?
b) What is the treatment variable?
c) Classify the treatment variable.
d) What is the response variable?
e) Classify the response variable.

108) A math instructor conducted a study among her students to examine the link between TV viewing habits and student test scores. The students were asked to report the average number of hours per week that they watch TV and these numbers were then compared to the students test scores on the next exam. After examining the data, the instructor concluded that students who watch more TV will tend to have lower test scores.
a) What is the population of interest in this study?
b) What is the treatment variable?
c) Classify the treatment variable.
d) What is the response variable?
e) Classify the response variable.

Chapter Problem – A Study on the Effects of Multi-Vitamins

Are multi-vitamins a waste of money?

According to an article published in the December 2011 issue of the International Journal of Epidemiology, "Long-term antioxidant supplementation has no effect on health-related quality of life." These conclusions were the results of a 6-year study of 8112 total participants carried out by Nancy University in France. Half of the participants were given a multi-vitamin containing vitamin C, vitamin E, beta-carotene, selenium, and zinc. The other participants were given a placebo. The researchers assessed their health at the beginning of the trial. When researchers analyzed how many in each group had gone on to develop serious illnesses during the trial, they found very little differences. For example, 30.5% of the participants taking the supplement suffered a major health 'event', such as cancer or heart disease. However, in the placebo group, this happened to 30.4% of the participants. The article claimed that it was a randomized, double blind, placebo-controlled trial. The researchers concluded "Long-term supplementation with antioxidant vitamins and minerals had no beneficial effect in this trial."

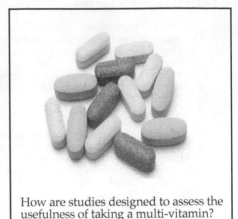

How are studies designed to assess the usefulness of taking a multi-vitamin?

a) What is the population of interest in this study?

b) Is this an observational study or a designed experiment? Explain.

c) What were the treatments used in the study?

d) What is the response variable of interest?

e) What steps were taken to control possible confounding variables such as genetics?

f) The article claims that this was a double blind study. Specifically for this study, what do you think that meant?

g) What ethical steps should have been taken in this study?

h) Do you feel that the researchers are justified in claiming that supplementation with vitamins has no beneficial effect?

Chapter 1: Technology Project

Use the technology of your choice to complete problem 1 below.

1)   The goal of this problem is to simulate 2 keno draws where 20 numbered balls are chosen from a bin containing balls numbered from 1 to 80.

  a) Enter the pool of numbers 1 through 80 into the data area of the statistics application. (Most application have a method to quickly fill a column with sequential or patterned data.)

  b) Use the application to choose 20 of the 80 numbers, without replacement, and store them in a new column.

  c) Repeat the process to again choose 20 numbers 1 to 80 and store them in a new column.

  d) Name the appropriate columns 'Draw 1', 'Draw 2'

  e) Display the <u>results</u> of your 2 draws. (Do NOT display the pool of numbers 1 to 80.)

  F) Make a list of any numbers from your first Keno draw that were repeated in the second Keno draw? Does the fact that you have repeated numbers violate the sampling without replacement requirement that was specified? Explain.

2)   This problem uses the application "SuperLottoPlus" which is located in the StatSims folder. The California Super Lotto Plus game consists of 5 numbers chosen from balls numbers 1 to 47 followed by 1 number, known as the mega number, chosen from different balls numbered 1 to 27.

  A) When playing this lottery, do you suspect that there are any allowed sets of numbers to be avoided? Or is any pick just as good as any other? Explain.

  b) Enter your name in the textbox provided. Click the QUICK PICK button to choose 5 regular numbers and a mega number randomly. Change the number of plays to 1000000. (No commas!)

  c) Click the ONE PLAY button a few times to try your luck and see how you do. Now click the Automatic button to finish up the 1,000,000 plays.

  d) Copy the window to memory by holding down the ALT key and pressing the "Print Screen" key on the keyboard. This is typically the key to the right of the F12 key and it is often labeled "PRINT SCRN / SYSREQ". You can now paste an image of the window into your report by choosing PASTE.

  E) The "Summary of All Plays" output shows the frequency for each type of win for these numbers. Add up the number of wins to find the total number of wins and then divide that total by the number of plays to calculate the percentage of winning plays for these numbers. Show the work for the percentage.

  F) Locate and **interpret** the average profit or loss per play. Negative values (losses) are in parentheses.

  g) Click the clear button to get set up for a new simulation. In the text boxes provided, enter regular numbers of 1, 2, 3, 4, 5 with a mega number of 6.

  h) Click the ONE PLAY button a few times to try your luck and see how you do. Now click the Automatic button to finish up the 1,000,000 plays.

  i) Copy the window to memory by holding down the ALT key and pressing the "Print Screen" key on the keyboard. This is typically the key to the right of the F12 key and it is often labeled "PRINT SCRN / SYSREQ". You can now paste an image of the window in your report by choosing PASTE.

  J) Use the "Summary of All Plays" output again to determine the total number of wins for these numbers and then use that to calculate the percentage of winning plays for these sequential numbers.

  K) Locate and **interpret** the average profit or loss per play. Negative values (losses) are in parentheses.

  L) Calculate the difference between the winning percentages from parts (E) and (J). Would you say that the difference in the winning percentages between the million quick picks and the million plays of 1, 2, 3, 4, 5, 6 is large enough to be convincing evidence that one of those choices was better than the other one OR would you say that the difference is small enough that it is plausible that the difference is just due to random variation? Pick the option that makes the most sense and write it in your report.

Chapter 1: Chapter Review

Section 1.1

- Descriptive statistics consists of method of organizing and summarizing data so that it is easier to read and understand.
- The population is the group of people or things that conclusions are stated about.
- The sample is the part of the population from which data is actually collected.
- Inferential statistics involves using data collected from a sample to make decisions involving the population of interest.
- All statistics tends to contain descriptive work, but if we go on to make estimates about a larger population than we collected data from, then we still consider it to be inferential statistics.

Section 1.2

- In an observational study, the researchers simply gather or record data that already exists in the world. They do not have any influence on the data values.
- In designed experiments, the researchers have some control over the subjects being studied. This often includes the ability to make choices on behalf of the subject.
- Designed experiments can show cause and effect relationships, but observational studies can merely establish associations or links between the variables studied.
- Treatments are the different values for a variable that will be assigned to the subjects by the experimenter.
- A control group where no treatment is given is often one of the options.
- Randomization means that it must be randomly decided which treatment a subject is to receive in the experiment.
- Replication refers to the idea that we will repeat the experiment on many subjects. This helps to reduce the effects of random variation and allows the true patterns to emerge in the data.
- Single blinded experiments are ones where the subject is not aware of which treatment they are receiving.
- In a double-blinded experiment, the researcher is also not aware of which treatment has been given to subjects that they interact with.
- Data ethics require you to get informed written consent from your participants. You should also keep the identity of the participants confidential.
- Confounding variables exist when the variation in the experimental outcomes can realistically be caused by more than one variable.

Section 1.3

- A census is the act of taking data from the entire population of interest rather than just using a sample from the population.
- Sampling error is the error that results from using a sample to estimate a quantity rather than taking a census to find its true value.
- A representative sample is one where all relevant characteristics of the population are present in the same proportion in the sample as they exist in the population.
- A biased sample is one where important characteristics are either over or under represented in the sample.
- A simple random sample is one in which every sample of a given size is equally likely to be the one chosen.
- Sampling with replacement is a method where after an item is selected, it is returned to the sampling pool and could be chosen again.

Section 1.3 (Continued)

- Sampling without replacement is a method where after an item is selected, it is not returned to the sampling pool. This means the same item cannot be selected twice.
- Systematic sampling is a form of sampling where we equally space our sample items throughout the population of interest.
- Cluster sampling is a form of sampling where we identify groups of items that exist in our population and then we choose several of these groups rather than selecting one individual item at a time.
- A stratified sample is one where certain important characteristics are purposely and carefully chosen in the sample in the same proportion (or percentage) that they exist in the population.

Section 1.4

- If problematic sampling methods are used to obtain data, then the results of the study should be disregarded.
- Volunteer sampling is a method that allows the participants to volunteer to participate in the study. Many web and television polls are like this. They tend to call them non-scientific studies.
- The major problem with volunteer sampling is that not all segments of the population are equally motivated to participate and this usually creates a bias in the data obtained.
- In convenience sampling, we just collect the data that is easiest for us to obtain.
- The problem with convenience sampling is that it tends to get large clumps of the same characteristics and this biases the study towards those characteristics.
- Studies based on attention getting data are biased towards determining that we have just experienced an "unusual" result.
- If pre-existing data has formed an opinion that we wish to conduct a study on, then we must generate new random data to test this opinion.
- Hand picking data biases the results towards whatever the researcher is seeking to prove. This can be done intentionally or unintentionally.
- Large sample sizes do not make up for the problems caused by problematic sampling methods.
- A loaded question is one that has been worded in such a way that it encourages one answer over others.
- Suspicious sources are ones that fund or conduct a study and have a vested interest in the results turning out a certain way.
- Just because the source is suspicious doesn't mean that the information is bad. It just means that you should be a little more skeptical and investigate the details further.

Section 1.5

- A variable is a characteristic that can vary from one person or item selected to another.
- Data is the specific answer we get to our question or the specific measurement for an item selected.
- Data is the value the variable takes on for a specific person or item.
- Categorical data is generally in word form rather than number form.
- Quantitative data takes on numerical values that measure or count something.
- Quantitative discrete variables have gaps that exist between the possible values of the variable.
- Quantitative continuous variables have possibilities that form an interval. No gaps exist between the possibilities.

Review Diagrams:

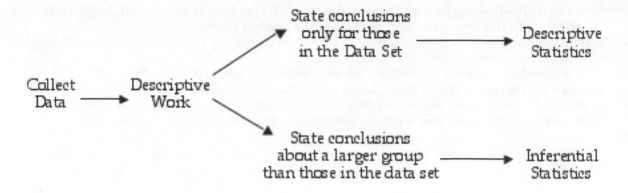

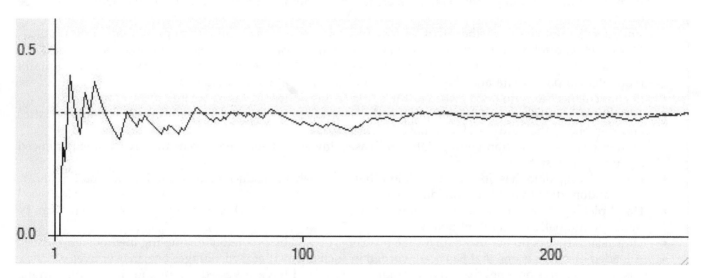

Large random samples tend to represent all characteristics in roughly the same proportion in which they exist in the population. Random variation can cause bias in small sample, but this effect is reduced as the sample size is increased.

Chapter 1: Review Exercises

1) A sports writer wants to write a story on players moving directly from high school to play in the NBA. As part of his research, the writer finds the ages of all the current NBA players. He then computes the average age. In his column, he states that the average age of current NBA players is 27.13 years old.
   a) Are the NBA players the population of interest or just a sample?
   b) Which type of statistics was done by the writer?

2) A statistics teacher wants to summarize the results of her students on the first test they take in her class. She grades the test and then computes the average score for all the tests. She then reports this average to her class when she returns the exam.
   a) Are the students in her class the population of interest or just a sample?
   b) Which type of statistics was done by the teacher?

3) A 2012 Reuters Health article stated that "Kids who were breastfed as babies may have a lower risk of asthma than those who were formula fed." The conclusion was based on a UK study that followed 1,500 kids from their birth in the mid 1990's.
   a) Identify the population of interest.
   b) Identify the sample being used.
   c) Which type of statistics is was this?

4) A researcher from the U.S. Mint is given the task of estimating the average age of pennies in circulation in America. To accomplish this goal the researcher randomly samples 100 pennies in circulation and computes the average age.
   a) Identify the population of interest.
   b) Identify the sample being used.
   c) Which type of statistics is the researcher doing?

5) A 2014 study by the American Academy of Neurology investigated whether or not your blood type can affect your memory in later years of life. The study compared 495 subjects who developed memory problems with 587 subjects that developed no such problems. State whether the following conclusions are descriptive or inferential.
   a) People that develop memory problems in their later years are 1.5 times more likely to have type AB blood than their counterparts that do not develop such memory problems.
   b) Among the 1,082 subjects in the study, people with AB blood type made up 6% of the group who developed memory problems. In comparison, only 4% of those without such memory problems had type AB blood.

6) A national restaurant chain is considering introducing a new menu with higher prices. They are hoping that such a change will increase revenue. They decide to test out the new menus in one of their locations. During the first 40 days of using the new menus, the revenue for the restaurant falls by 9.12%. State whether the following conclusions are descriptive or inferential.
   a) For the 40-day test period, the revenue at the test restaurant fell by 9.12%.
   b) Based on the test of the new menus, it is estimated that if these new menus are introduced throughout the national chain, then the restaurants will see a drop in revenue of about 9.12%.

7) In 1973 Lillian Belmont and Francis Marolla published family size, birth order and intelligence test. The study showed that on a standardized intelligence tests, the lower the birth order of the child, the lower their test scores tended to be. That is, the first-born child tends to score better than the second born and so on.
   a) Would you classify this as an observational study or a designed experiment?
   b) Can you conclude that being born later causes the child to have lower intelligence?
   c) Give a possible confounding variable.

8) In 2012, a WebMD article had the title "Walking in High Heels Changes How Women Walk." It refers to a study where nine young women who wore heels for 40 hour per week or more were compared to 10 young women who rarely wore high heels. The researchers discovered that the women who regularly wore high heels walked differently than those who didn't, even when they were in their bare feet.
   a) Would you classify this as an observational study or a designed experiment?
   b) Can you conclude that wearing high heels causes young women to walk differently?
   c) Give a possible confounding variable.

9) A 2014 study by researchers at the University of Queensland investigated the effects of texting while walking. The study used 26 healthy adults as subjects. The subjects were monitored as they walked repeatedly along a 28-foot stretch of hallway. Sometimes they walked without a phone. Sometimes they walked while reading a long text. Other times they were asked to walk while composing a text. The researchers noticed that texting activity significantly distorted the subjects gait and walking form. Texters were also noticed to take shorter steps, walk slower, and deviate more from a straight line.
   a) Is this an observational study or a designed experiment? Explain.
   b) What are the treatments used?
   c) What is the response variable of interest?
   d) Does the study include replication? Explain.
   e) Would you consider this study to involve blinding? Explain.

10) A spark plug manufacturer claims that using their spark plugs in your car will increase your gas mileage by about 10%. To test this theory a mechanic randomly chooses ten different vehicles and tests their gas mileage in both city and highway conditions. The mechanic then replaces the spark plugs in these cars with the new spark plugs. The cars are then tested again using the same driving conditions.
   a) Is this an observational study or a designed experiment? Explain.
   b) What are the treatments used in the experiment?
   c) What is the response variable of interest?
   d) Does the study include replication? Explain.
   e) Would you consider this study to involve blinding? Explain.

11) A soup company wants to check the accuracy of its filling machines. To make sure that the sample they use is spread out over an hour's time, they want to use the method of systematic sampling. They know that the machine fills about 5000 cans per hour. They would like to systematically choose 35 cans from the conveyor as they move by during the next hour.
   a) Explain the details of how this systematic sampling process should be executed.
   b) Execute this plan using a random number generator to state which cans out of the 5000 should be selected.
   c) What advantages or disadvantages will this have over a simple random sample of size 35 from the hour's production?

12) A banana farmer wants to obtain a sample of about 1000 bananas from the farm to check for ripeness, quality, pests, etc. A typical bunch of bananas contains about 200 bananas. To save time and effort, the worker asked to obtain the sample of bananas decides to choose whole bunches rather than individual bananas.
   a) What type of sampling variation is the worker considering?
   b) Explain the details of how this plan could be executed.
   c) What are the advantages or disadvantages of using this method to obtain the sample?

13) In May 2007, a Rasmussen poll estimated that 36.3% of Americans reported themselves to be Democrats, 30.8% claimed to be Republicans, and then remaining 32.9% claimed other political affiliations. Suppose that a national poll on the issue of the U.S. becoming energy independent is to be conducted at this time. The pollsters wish to conduct a survey of 600 Americans using a sample that is stratified by political affiliation.
   a) What should be the breakdown of the number of Democrats, Republicans, and Other affiliations used in the sample?
   b) What are the advantages or disadvantages of stratifying the sample in this way?

14) The coordinators of a college math and science tutoring center want to get feedback from the students that use the center. They know from the login computer that 59.7% of the students that use the center are seeking help with math, 19.1% need help with chemistry, 14.9% need physics help, and 6.3% need help with Biology. The coordinators would like to survey 240 students stratified by the subject the students are seeking help with.
   a) What should be the breakdown of the number of math, chemistry, physics, and biology students used in the sample?
   b) What are the advantages or disadvantages of stratifying the sample in this way?

15) A coin toss is used to decide who will receive the opening kick-off in the Super Bowl. In February 2010, the Saints won the coin toss. This made it 14 consecutive years that the coin toss was won by the NFC team. After calculating that there is only a 1 in 16,384 chance that the NFC would have won 14 coin tosses in a row, an AFC fan becomes convinced that the coin toss must somehow be rigged in favor of the NFC.
   a) What is the problem with the way this data and "study" was decided on and carried out?
   b) Should we agree with this fan that the coin toss is "rigged" in favor of the NFC? Explain.

16) A Facebook user wishes to conduct a study to see what percentage of all Facebook users update their status at least once per week. She monitors the activity of her Facebook friends over a one-week period and notices that 37.2% of them updated their status during that time period. From this she estimates that about 37.2% of all Facebook users update their status during any given 1-week period.
   a) What problematic sampling method was used?
   b) What, if any, biases might this cause in the results of the study?

17) In the weeks following the 2012 shootings at the Sandy Hook Elementary School in Connecticut, surveys were conducted about changing gun laws. Some of the surveys asked "Do you support an increase in gun control laws?" while others asked "Do you support strengthening current gun laws?".
   a) Do you feel that the first wording favors a certain answer? Explain.
   b) Do you feel that the second wording favors a certain answer? Explain.

18) A survey about Climate Change asked the following question: "Do you agree with the vast majority of scientists that global warming is happening or are you a global warming denier?"
   a) Explain why this would be considered a loaded question.
   b) What would be better language for a poll question on this matter?

19) In 2012, Republicans in some states were trying to pass laws requiring picture ID to be presented by voters at the polls when they vote in elections. Studies published by the Brennan Center stated that such laws have a racist effect on voter participation. Supporters of voter ID laws pointed out that the Brennan Center receives much of its funding from George Soros. Soros is well known for supporting Democrat causes.
   a) Should the Brennan Center be considered a suspicious source for results on this topic? Explain.
   b) What might be a considered a less suspicious source for such studies?

20) In the 2006 movie, "Thank You for Smoking", tobacco companies funded research by the Academy of Tobacco Studies. The research by this group was unable to find a link between smoking and lung cancer.
   a) Should this be considered a suspicious source for results on this topic? Explain.
   b) What might be a considered a less suspicious source for such studies?

21) A sportswriter wishes to conduct a study on the average pitch count for starting pitchers in major league baseball. He wants to estimate the percentage of the time a starting pitcher throws at least 100 pitches in the game. He randomly chooses 500 games and notes the pitch counts for the starting pitchers involved.
   a) Identify the population of interest.
   b) What is the variable?
   c) Give an example of a possible data value.
   d) Classify the variable.

22) During the tough economic times in 2010, a pollster wanted to survey people about changes in their spending habits. They asked participants the following question: "As compared with 2 years ago, would you say that you are currently spending more, spending less, or spending about the same?"
a) What is the population of interest?
b) What is the variable?
c) Give an example of a possible data value.
d) Classify the variable.

23) A student turned in a report about a study they had read on the relationship between the number of concussions football players had suffered and how that related to problems retaining new information later in life. The student stated that this was a designed study. Explain why this almost certainly could not be the case.

24) A student turned in a report about a study they had read on "Breadwinning" moms. The student stated that the sample could not have been representative because the study only involved 5,000 working moms when there are actually millions of working moms. Is the student making a valid criticism? Explain.

25) A 2012 article published by Health.com had the headline "Coffee drinking linked to longer life." Researchers from the National Institutes of Health followed more than 400,000 healthy men and women between the ages of 50 and 71 for up to 13 years. During that time period, 13% of the participants died. The study found that men and women who drank six or more cups of coffee per day were 10% to 15% less likely, respectively, to die during the study.

a) Identify the population of interest in this problem.
b) Identify the sample used.
c) What were the variables in the study?
d) Classify the variables from part (c).
e) Is this an observational study or a designed experiment? Explain.
f) Based on this study, can we conclude that drinking coffee causes people to live longer? Explain.
g) What are some possible confounding variables in the study?

26) A February 2012 article on WebMD had the title "Purple potatoes lower blood pressure in overweight people". The study tracked 18 middle-aged adults. Half of them were asked to eat the skin and flesh of six to eight small purple potatoes at lunch and dinner for a period of four weeks, while the others did not eat them. The purple potato eaters had a 4% drop in diastolic pressure and a 3% drop in systolic pressure compared to the non purple potato eaters.

a) What were the treatments used in the experiment?
b) Did the experiment include randomization? Explain.
c) Did the experiment involve replication? Explain.
d) What was the primary response variable of interest?
e) The headline of "Purple potatoes lower blood pressure in overweight people" seems to indicate cause and effect. Do you think this is justified? Explain.
f) Discuss how data ethics should have been addressed in this study.

27) According to a January 2012, Yahoo! News article, blogging can help calm anxious teens. The study included 161 Israeli high school students who were experiencing some level of social anxiety. The students were randomly divided into six groups. Four of the groups were assigned to blog, one group wrote in a private diary, and one group did nothing. Two of the blogging groups focused their posts on their social problems. Two were free to write about any topic. One group from each of those two options allowed comments on their posts. The researchers assessed all of the teen's social anxiety levels before and after the 10-week experiment. The greatest improvements in anxiety levels occurred in the group that blogged about their social problems and were open to comments.
a) What were the treatments used in the experiment?
b) Did the experiment include randomization? Explain.
c) Did the experiment involve replication? Explain.
d) What was the primary response variable of interest?
e) The headline of "Blogging can help calm anxious teens" seems to indicate cause and effect. Do you think this is justified? Explain.
f) Discuss how data ethics should have been addressed in this study.

28) A study is going to be conducted to investigate the charitable donations given by the people in a small town. The main goal is to obtain an estimate of the *percentage of gross household income that is donated to charity*. It is known that, of the 1,973 households in this town, 387 households have a gross income below $25,000/year, 562 households have gross income of at least $25,000 but less than $50,000/year, 893 households have gross income of at least $50,000 but less than $100,000/year, and 131 households have income of at least $100,000/year.

They feel that people's income level is probably a very important characteristic to properly represent in the sample. So they chose a random sample of 50 households stratified by income level and obtained the gross annual income and amount of charitable contributions for each of the households selected. They then computed the desired *percentage of annual income given to charity* for each household. They next computed the average of these 50 different percentages to obtain their estimate for the percentage of gross household income that is given to charity in this town.

a) It is stated above that they stratified the sample by income level. How many households should have been chosen from each income group?
b) Identify the population of interest in this problem.
c) Identify the sample used.
d) What is the *variable* of interest in this problem?
e) Give an example of a possible data value.
f) Classify the variable.
g) Is this an observational study or a designed experiment? Explain.
h) If at the end of the study the researchers state "The average percentage of gross annual income given to charities by the 50 households selected is 7.9%", then would you consider this to be an example of descriptive or inferential statistics? Explain.
i) If at the end of the study the researchers state "We estimate that the average percentage of gross annual income given to charities by the households in this city to be 7.9%", then would you consider this to be an example of descriptive or inferential statistics? Explain.

Chapter 2 – Organizing and Displaying Data

Chapter Problem: *Top 40 Grossing Movies in the U.S. (Since 1977)*

Every year billions of dollars are spent by people going to the movies. Award shows such as the Academy Awards and the Golden Globes attempt to judge which movies were the best each year. Among movie fans, there will sometimes be discussions of which movies were the best of all time. Because different people appreciate different aspects of movies, it is hard to ever reach much agreement as to which movies are the best, but what if we let the money do the talking? At the end of this chapter, we will examine the list of the top 40 grossing movies in the United States since 1977. In addition to seeing the list, we will also try to examine the data set to see what these great movies have in common. Are they geared towards families or college students? What time of year do these top movies tend to be released? When

What is the best movie of all time?

faced with a large list of movies and trying to see the patterns that exist in the data, it can be very helpful to group and graph the data. In this chapter, we will see how this is done and then we will apply these skills to these top-grossing movies in the chapter problem.

Introduction:

In chapter 1, we mainly focused on the process of collecting data. But, once you have it, what should you do next? In many cases, you will have collected a very large amount of data and looking at the raw data you have collected is often overwhelming and unenlightening. If we want to start seeing important patterns that may exist in our data, then we must organize it. The most common way to organize a large set of data is to group it in a table. This will be the task of Section 2.1.

In addition, once our data sets have been organized or grouped, we will then often want to give the users of our data and ourselves a visual representation of the data. This can be done using a wide variety of charts and graphs and we will take a look at some of those in Sections 2.2 and 2.3.

Finally, once our data has been organized and graphed, we will often be concerned with determining the likely shape of the distribution of the population from which the data was drawn. The work we do with our sample can give us much insight into this question. We will examine this idea further in Section 2.4. So the chapter is laid out before us as follows.

Section 2.1   Grouping Data
Section 2.2   Graphing Data
Section 2.3   Stem-and-Leaf Diagrams
Section 2.4   Common Distribution Shapes

Let's get started.

Section 2.1 – Grouping Data

As mentioned above, once we have collected our data, we then want to start organizing it in order to see patterns. We also want to organize our data in a way that condenses it into a smaller more manageable size. The most common way this is done is through the use of a **grouped data table**. We will explore one of these in the situation that follows and then we will summarize all the pertinent definitions.

Final Exam Scores *(A discussion of grouping discrete data sets)*

The final exam scores (out of 100 points possible) for a group of 43 statistics students are shown below.

91	53	75	64	72	88	90	94	86
70	99	75	53	98	71	81	79	43
94	54	42	69	94	93	79	92	83
90	71	51	98	75	98	92	82	81
81	66	94	52	69	26	96		

Our goal is to organize this data set by constructing a **grouped data table**.

What patterns exist in final exam scores?

A grouped data table generally consists of 4 columns. The first column consists of the classes. The classes are the different groups our data will be separated into. We will begin with the class 20 – 29 (read "20 thru 29") and use equal widths after that. Because the first class ends at 29 it makes sense to begin the next class at 30. The ending point of the first class, 29, was 9 more than its beginning point 20. If we follow that pattern, then the second class should end at 39. So, the second class is 30 – 39 and we will continue in this fashion until we have a class that will hold the largest value in the table, in this case 99. (See below.)

The next step in the process is to add a **frequency** column. The **frequency** for any class is just the count of the number of data values that fall into that class description. To find these frequencies, we simply scan through the data set looking for all numbers in the range 20 – 29, and then list that in the frequency column for the row including the class 20 – 29. We then repeat the process for all the remaining classes until we come up with the table below. We also, want to obtain a total for this column. Because it is not possible to total the classes, we will shade that cell of the table.

Score	Frequency		
20 – 29	1		
30 – 39	0		
40 – 49	2		
50 – 59	5		
60 – 69	4		
70 – 79	9		
80 – 89	7		
90 – 99	15		
	43		

Caution: *It is easy to miss a value*

Scanning through to count the frequency for a class is not always exciting and it's easy to pass by a number without counting it. As you go through the list, cross off data values as you count them. That way, if you miss something, you will know which value you missed and thus which class it belongs in.

Key Concept: *Empty Classes*

If a class is empty as in 30 – 39, we should still show this class in the table. It helps us to see that the score in the 20's is separated from the other scores.

At this point, the table should be making it easier for us to see some patterns in the data. For example, I can now see that scores in the 90's (A's) were the most common group and that the person who scored only 26 on the final was a bit of an unusual score as no other scores are close to that one.

While the frequency information does reveal some patterns in the data, it is often the case that people like to think about the percentage of items in a group rather than the count. To help us see this information we add a **relative frequency** column to our table. **Relative frequencies** are obtained by dividing the frequency of a class by the total frequency and writing the answer in decimal form. For example, for the first class we get: $\frac{1}{43} \approx 0.0233$

Continuing in this manner for the remaining classes produces the following.

Score	Frequency	Relative Freq	
20 – 29	1	0.0233	
30 – 39	0	0.0000	
40 – 49	2	0.0465	
50 – 59	5	0.1163	
60 – 69	4	0.0930	
70 – 79	9	0.2093	
80 – 89	7	0.1628	
90 – 99	15	0.3488	
	43	1.0000	

Key Concept: *Rounding Issues*

Division by 43 produced infinitely many decimal places. When rounding a relative frequency, it is recommended that you use at least 4 decimal places. Show these decimal places on all your relative frequencies, even if some or all of them are zeros.

The total of this column should always be 1.0000 or 100%. However, sometimes, due to rounding error, you might get something slightly different like 0.9999 or 1.0001.

By adding this extra column of information, we can now see that scores in the 90's made up about 34.88% of the data set. Many people prefer this information to just a raw count.

The final step in creating a grouped data table is to add in a **midpoint** column. When we group data, we lose touch with the original data values. Instead of knowing someone scored a 26, we merely know that someone had a score in the 20's. Often, people who collect data only present the data in grouped form. If we wanted to make a calculation, such as average final exam score, then we don't have the data anymore to make that calculation. So the **midpoint** of a class serves as a representative for all of the values in that class (we will see this put to use in Chapter 3.) To calculate the **midpoint** we simply take the average of the two boundaries of our class. For example, for the first class we get the following midpoint.

$$\frac{20+29}{2} = 24.5$$

We continue in the same manner for the remaining classes.

Score	Frequency	Relative Freq	Midpoint
20 – 29	1	0.0233	24.5
30 – 39	0	0.0000	34.5
40 – 49	2	0.0465	44.5
50 – 59	5	0.1163	54.5
60 – 69	4	0.0930	64.5
70 – 79	9	0.2093	74.5
80 – 89	7	0.1628	84.5
90 – 99	15	0.3488	94.5
	43	1.0000	

Key Concept: *Using Patterns*

There is usually a clear pattern to the midpoints. If you wish to use this pattern to fill in the numbers rather than continuing to compute averages, that is fine. However, when doing so, it is important to always check the last midpoint and make sure that it is appropriate for the class it represents.

While a total for midpoints is possible to compute, it has no use. Therefore, the total cell for that column has been shaded. When making these tables in the future, we will only show the completed table, rather than showing it in stages.

One of the main reasons we group data is to be able to reveal patterns in the data set. Now that the data has been grouped, many things are easier to see than with the raw data. The highest counts are in the classes with scores of 70 and above. So, most people "passed" this test. There is only 1 score in the 20's and none in the 30's, so the score in the 20's is probably a bit of an unusual occurrence. I can now easily see that 34.88% of the scores were in the 90's. This fact was hidden in the raw data set.

Now that we have completed our table, let's carefully define all of the terms that are used to describe the parts of the table we filled in.

Definitions: *Group Data Table and Related Items*

Grouped Data Table: A group data table consists of classes, frequencies (with a total), relative frequencies (with a total), and midpoints (if appropriate). We will see examples in this section where there is no need for a midpoint.

Classes: The classes are the groups that we divide our data set into.

Lower Cutpoint: This is the name we give to the left hand boundary of our classes. For example, for the class 20 – 29, the lower cutpoint is the 20. This is the smallest number that can be contained in this class.

Upper Cutpoint: This is the name we give to the right hand boundary of our classes. For example, for the class 20 – 29, the upper cutpoint is the 29. For discrete data, this is the largest number that can be contained in this class (this will not be true for continuous data).

Width: The width of a class is the difference between the lower cutpoint for that class and the lower cutpoint for the next higher class. For example, for the class 20 – 29, the width is 30 – 20 = 10.

Frequency: The frequency of a class is the number of items that fall in that class.

Relative Frequency: The relative frequency of a class is the ratio (or fraction) of the number of items in that class to the total number of items in the data set. The relative frequency for a class should be written in decimal form. It is usually interpreted as a percent.

    Rounding Rule: When rounding a relative frequency, you should use at least 4 decimal places and use a consistent number of decimal places for all of your entries, including the total.

Midpoints: The midpoint for a class is the average of the lower and upper cutpoints of the class. The midpoint can serve as a representative for hidden data values when calculations need to be made.

GROUPING CONTINUOUS DATA: *What changes need to be made?*

When we group continuous data, we will make a small adjustment in the way we do things. In our last example, we had consecutive classes of 20 – 29 and 30 – 39, but if we had continuous data, we could have a value like 29.3. It doesn't fit in either of those classes, so what do we do? Can we change the classes to 20 – 30 and 30 – 40? No, this would fix the problem for 29.3, but now what about a data value of 30? It would now fit in two different classes and we don't want that to happen. Another possible fix would be to change the classes to 20 – 29.9 and 30 – 39.9. While this works for 29.3, what would we do with the data value 29.93?

The way we handle this is to change from 20 – 29 (read "20 thru 29") to 20 – < 30 (read "20 thru less than 30"). The values 29.3 or 29.93 would now fit in this class because they are less than 30, but the value 30 would not, i t would still go in the next class which would be 30 – < 40 (read "30 thru less than 40"). Let's see how this works by looking at an example where we group continuous data.

Example 2.1: *Calories in Potato Chips (A continuous example)*

To test the calorie content of a brand of potato chips, a random sample of 50 1-serving size bags is obtained. Each serving is tested to determine the number of calories. The test yielded the following calorie data for the 50 different servings.

140.08	140.80	131.35	140.85	143.31	143.60	140.68	136.26	142.83	143.11
131.47	140.56	135.73	138.50	140.11	137.61	143.25	145.54	139.56	143.44
141.84	140.64	143.49	136.29	140.49	142.00	140.10	139.23	138.41	132.92
135.70	144.49	140.09	139.31	144.91	140.57	149.31	137.12	144.28	138.98
134.50	136.55	141.17	138.29	143.33	138.92	130.68	136.29	148.85	144.96

How many calories are you getting when you eat a serving of potato chips?

a) Construct a grouped data table for the calorie data. Use equal class widths beginning with 130 – < 132 as the first class in the table.

b) How many of the servings contained less than 140 calories?

c) What percentage of the servings contained at least 144 calories?

Solution:

a) If our first class is 130 – < 132, then the next should be 132 – < 134. The largest value in the data set is 149.31, so we must continue until we reach the class 148 – < 150. We will then count the frequency for each class. For example, there are 3 numbers in the range 130 – < 132. So the frequency for this class is 3. After the frequencies are completed we divide each by 50 to get the relative frequencies, and finally, we compute a midpoint for each of the classes. The result is as follows.

Calories	Frequency	Rel Freq	Midpoint
130 – < 132	3	0.06	131
132 – < 134	1	0.02	133
134 – < 136	3	(0.06)	135
136 – < 138	6	0.12	(137)
138 – < 140	8	0.16	139
140 – < 142	13	0.26	141
142 – < 144	9	0.18	143
144 – < 146	5	0.10	145
146 – < 148	0	0.00	147
148 – < 150	2	0.04	149
	50	1.00	

$$\frac{3}{50} = 0.06$$

$$\frac{136+138}{2} = 137$$

Caution: *Rounding rule violated?*

While it may appear that the rounding rule for relative frequencies has been violated, it has not. All of the relative frequencies in the table are exact and thus we have not rounded them at all. Even when they are exact, it is important to keep a consistent number of decimal places in all the values, including the total.

b) We can just add up all of the frequencies for the classes with less than 140 calories.

   $3 + 1 + 3 + 6 + 8 = 21$ servings contained less than 140 calories.

c) For this one, we just add the relative frequencies for classes with at least 144 calories and then convert the answer to percentage form.

   $0.10 + 0.00 + 0.04 = 0.14 = 14\%$ of the servings contained at least 144 calories.

Key Concepts: *Naming Columns, Empty Classes, and Computing Midpoints*

Naming Columns: It is better to give a description of the type of data values you are working with, i.e. "Calories", rather than just writing classes at the top of the class column.

Empty Classes: We have included a class that was empty because it is surrounded by classes that do contain data. It is always important to allow your reader to see such gaps in the data.

Computing Midpoints: Even though the upper cutpoint of a class is not included in that class, we still use that number when computing the midpoints. Thus, the first midpoint came from the calculation: $\dfrac{130 + 132}{2} = 131$. You should also note that for this problem the midpoints could easily been done in your head by just thinking of the number half way between 130 and 132 rather than averaging.

GROUPING GUIDELINES: *Things to keep in mind when choosing classes*

Now that we have successfully completed a couple of grouping examples, it would be good to mention the guidelines for determining the classes to use. This has not been an issue up to this point because we have always been told what class to start with. However, this certainly would not be the case with data you collect in real life. There is no reason to expect that data collected in the field would come with a suggestion as to which class to begin with. People who collect and group data must make these decisions on their own. When doing so, they often use the following guidelines.

Point to Remember: *Grouping Guidelines*

- When writing the class descriptions, use the '– ' symbol for discrete data, but use '– <' for continuous data. Examples: Write 10 – 19 for the number of people in line, but write 10 – < 20 for the number of minutes a student spends on a quiz.
- The number of classes should be between 5 & 20. If you have too many classes, then you still have an overwhelming amount of information to absorb. If you have too few classes, then it will be hard to see patterns that exist in the data. For smaller data sets, it is best to try to go with between 5 & 10 classes.
- Each piece of data should fit into *exactly* one class. Every data value must fit somewhere and no data value should fit in more than one class.
- When possible, classes should all be the same width. Occasionally data sets have extreme values in them that make this impractical.
- The lower cutpoints should be nice numbers if possible. Choose lower cutpoints of 10, 20, 30 etc. rather than 8, 15, .22, . . .

Let's use these guidelines to help us make a decision on how to group the data in the following example.

Example 2.2: *Matching birthdays in a group of 30 people (Single Value Grouping)*

A student was interested in the frequency with which a day of the year would be a shared birthday for two or more students in a class of 30 students. To investigate this question, she chose a random sample of 67 classes that each contained 30 students. She then surveyed these classes to obtain the birthdays of the students and then looked for days of the year that were shared birthdays for 2 or more classmates. So a data value of 0 represents a class where no people shared the same birthday. A data value of 1 represents a class where exactly one day of the year was a common birthday for at least 2 people out of the 30 in the class. A data value of 2 would mean that two different dates during the year would be a shared birthday for 2 or more classmates. The data is as follows.

Do most groups of 30 people include a birthday match?

1	1	3	1	1	2	2	1	1	0	1	1	1	0
1	0	0	2	1	2	1	1	2	1	3	2	3	0
1	0	0	1	0	2	1	1	0	1	2	2	1	0
0	1	0	0	0	3	1	2	1	2	1	1	0	0
0	4	0	2	2	2	1	1	0	2	1			

a) Construct a group data table making classes that follow the guidelines.

b) What percentage of the time did a class of size 30 contain at least one shared birthday?

Solution:

a) The tricky part of this problem is deciding what the classes should be. The first thing we should note is that this is quantitative discrete data, so we would expect to use the thru symbol. Our smallest data value is 0, so we should start there, perhaps 0 – 2? If we did this, then the next class would be 3 – 5 and we would not need any more classes. This would only be two classes and the guidelines say that we should use at least 5, so we need smaller classes. What if we used 0 – 1? Then the next classes would be 2 – 3 and 4 – 5 and we would only get 3 classes. So we need even smaller classes. The only option left is 0 – 0 and that is basically what we will do, though it would seem strange to write 0 – 0 when the only number that fits in that class is zero. When only one number can fit in a class, we just write that single number when describing the class. We would then find the frequencies and compute the relative frequencies in the normal manner. Because we're once again rounding the relative frequencies, we used 4 decimal places all the way down that column. The results are shown in the table below.

$$\frac{28}{67} \approx 0.4179$$

Shared Dates	Frequency	Relative Freq
0	19	0.2836
1	28	0.4179
2	15	0.2239
3	4	0.0597
4	1	0.0149
	67	1.0000

Key Concept: *No Midpoint*

The purpose of a midpoint is to serve as a representative value for hidden data. However, when we use single value grouping, none of our data is hidden. So we do not need a midpoint in our table this time.

A table where each class consists of a single possible value is known as **single value grouping**.

b) This happened in all but 19 of the classes, so it happened $\dfrac{67-19}{67} = \dfrac{48}{67} \approx 0.7164 = 71.64\%$ of the time.

We could also have answered this question by using the relative frequencies, but because they are rounded numbers, it is best to use the frequencies.

Definition: *Single Value Grouping*

Single Value Grouping: When each class consists of only a single possible value, we say we are using single value grouping in our table. No midpoint is needed for single value grouping.

GROUPING CATEGORICAL DATA: *How we handle non-numerical data*

Grouping categorical data is a lot like single value grouping. It usually doesn't make any sense to combine several different word descriptions into one class, so every possible value of our categorical variables ends up being its own class. Because grouping categorical data is like single value grouping, it should not come as a surprise to learn that we will not use a midpoint when grouping this type of data. It's hard to imagine how we would average words, so not having a midpoint is good news. Let's work out the details in an example.

Example 2.3: *m&m colors (Grouping Categorical Data)*

I recently bought a large bag of milk chocolate m&m's. I shook the bag to mix them well and then scooped out a sample of 84 pieces of candy. The colors were as listed in the table below.

Are m&m colors evenly distributed in a typical bag?

Green	Green	Blue	Yellow	Green	Red	Yellow	Blue
Blue	Green	Red	Yellow	Green	Blue	Yellow	Yellow
Green	Orange	Yellow	Blue	Brown	Orange	Yellow	Blue
Orange	Orange	Brown	Red	Red	Yellow	Yellow	Green
Red	Yellow	Orange	Green	Brown	Blue	Blue	Green
Blue	Yellow	Green	Blue	Yellow	Brown	Red	Orange
Orange	Blue	Red	Orange	Blue	Red	Red	Blue
Red	Red	Blue	Orange	Red	Orange	Yellow	Blue
Blue	Orange	Red	Blue	Orange	Brown	Green	Orange
Blue	Orange	Orange	Green	Brown	Blue	Green	Blue
Brown	Brown	Orange	Brown				

a) Make a grouped data table using the colors as the classes.

b) Was it easier to see which colors were most and least common before or after grouping the data? Explain.

Solution:

a) No real surprises here. We let the colors be the classes. We count the frequencies and we calculate the relative frequencies. No midpoint is used for categorical data. See the table that follows.

Color	Frequency	Relative Freq
Brown	9	0.1071
Yellow	13	0.1548
Red	13	0.1548
Blue	20	0.2381
Orange	16	0.1905
Green	13	0.1548
	84	1.0001

Key Concept: *Technology Tip*

Graphing calculators make it possible to calculate all of the relative frequencies at once. This can speed up the process and is especially helpful for larger tables. See directions for doing this in appendix A and B.

This time our rounded relative frequencies did not add up exactly to 1. This is just due to normal rounding error and it should not be adjusted or changed in any way.

b) Before the data was grouped, the list of text was overwhelming. After the data is grouped, we can quickly and easily see that the most common color was Blue and the least common color was Brown. It's much easier for a consumer of this information to simply look at the frequencies rather than carefully examining the entire set of raw data.

So we have now covered all the different types of grouping that we will encounter. What we have learned is summarized in the following point to remember.

Point to Remember: *Key Points for Grouping Data*

The following is a brief list of the key things to consider when grouping data.
- You must consider whether you have categorical or quantitative data.
- If the data is quantitative, then you need to consider whether it is discrete (use the – symbol) or continuous (use the – < symbol).
- The role of a midpoint is to be a representative value for all possibilities in the class.
- If you are dealing with single value grouping or categorical data, then no midpoint is needed.
- Totals should be given only for the frequency and relative frequency columns.
- Be consistent with the number of decimal places used for relative frequencies, including the total.

Let's practice with some exercises.

Exercise Set 2.1

Concept Review: Review the definitions and concepts from this section by filling in the blanks for each of the following.

1) The left hand boundary of the class description is called the lower_____and the right hand boundary is called the_____.

2) The number of items in each class is known as the _____of the class.

3) The ratio of the number of items in each class to the total number of items in the data set is known as the _____ _____.

4) The midpoint of a class is the _____ of the lower and upper cutpoints. This value is often used as a representative for the data values in that class when making computations.

5) The difference between consecutive lower cutpoints is known as the class_____ .

6) We use the - < symbols when grouping _____ data, but we just use the – symbol alone when grouping_____ data.

Applications: Practice the ideas learned in this section within the context of real world applications.

7)   The points scored by LeBron James of the Miami Heat in each of the 79 regular season games he played in during the 2010-11 season are shown below.

31	16	15	20	20	20	23	20	35	23
20	32	29	25	25	20	23	30	18	38
22	17	33	25	25	20	21	32	32	19
36	27	18	20	25	38	25	26	44	27
34	38	24	39	23	24	51	19	12	41
16	22	27	23	31	29	25	27	29	26
26	31	19	27	21	19	43	33	19	32
33	27	35	27	31	29	23	27	34	

Points	Frequency	Rel Freq	Midpoints
10 – 14	1	0.0127	12
15 – 19	11	0.1392	
	20	0.2532	
	7	0.0886	
	3	0.0380	
	79		

a)   Complete the grouped data table above.
b)   What is a good representative for the score from the most commonly occurring class?

8)   The heights of 34 randomly selected adult male giraffes are shown below. The heights are in feet.

17.08	17.14	16.15	15.64	17.65	17.55
15.76	16.80	17.94	17.54	15.97	17.92
17.27	16.03	18.14	16.37	17.06	17.46
16.90	18.84	17.70	16.91	16.93	17.01
17.22	17.33	17.55	17.20	18.27	17.97
16.63	17.05	14.61	16.95		

Height	Frequency	Rel Freq	Midpoints
14.5 - < 15.0	1	0.0294	14.75
15.0 - < 15.5			
	3	0.0882	
	3	0.0882	
	10	0.2941	
	8	0.2353	
	1	0.0294	
	34		

a)   Complete the grouped data table above.
b)   What is a good representative for the height from the most commonly occurring class?

9)   Super Bowl winners as of Feb. 2011 are below.

Super Bowl	City	Nickname
I	Green Bay	Packers
II	Green Bay	Packers
III	New York	Jets
IV	Kansas City	Chiefs
V	Baltimore	Colts
VI	Dallas	Cowboys
VII	Miami	Dolphins
VIII	Miami	Dolphins
IX	Pittsburgh	Steelers
X	Pittsburgh	Steelers
XI	Oakland	Raiders
XII	Dallas	Cowboys
XIII	Pittsburgh	Steelers
XIV	Pittsburgh	Steelers
XV	Oakland	Raiders
XVI	San Francisco	49ers
XVII	Washington	Redskins
XVIII	Los Angeles	Raiders
XIX	San Francisco	49ers
XX	Chicago	Bears
XXI	New York	Giants
XXII	Washington	Redskins
XXIII	San Francisco	49ers
XXIV	San Francisco	49ers
XXV	New York	Giants
XXVI	Washington	Redskins
XXVII	Dallas	Cowboys
XXVIII	Dallas	Cowboys
XXIX	San Francisco	49ers
XXX	Dallas	Cowboys
XXXI	Green Bay	Packers
XXXII	Denver	Broncos
XXXIII	Denver	Broncos
XXXIV	St. Louis	Rams
XXXV	Baltimore	Ravens
XXXVI	New England	Patriots
XXXVII	Tampa Bay	Buccaneers
XXXVIII	New England	Patriots
XXXIX	New England	Patriots
XL	Pittsburgh	Steelers
XLI	Indianapolis	Colts
XLII	New York	Giants
XLIII	Pittsburgh	Steelers
XLIV	New Orleans	Saints
XLV	Green Bay	Packers

Nickname	Frequency	Rel Freq
Steelers		
49ers		
Cowboys		
Packers		
Raiders		
Redskins		
Patriots		
Giants		
Colts		
Dolphins		
Broncos		
Jets		
Chiefs		
Bears		
Rams		
Ravens		
Buccaneers		
Saints		
	45	

a)   Complete the grouped data table above.
b)   Why is no midpoint needed?
c)   Which team(s) has the most Super Bowl wins?

10) The number of games required to determine a winner in each of the best of 7 play-off series in the NBA in 2011.

5	6	4	5	6	5	6	6
6	5	7	4	5	5	6	

# Games	Frequency	Rel Freq
4	2	0.1333
7	1	0.0667
	15	

a) Complete the grouped data table above.
b) Why was a midpoint not needed?
c) What appears to be the most common number of games played in a best of 7 series?

11) At the beginning of the Spring semester, I asked a random sample of 31 Statistics students how many movies they saw in the theater over the Winter break. Their responses are shown in the table below.

5	1	1	0	1	0	2	0
1	0	1	1	0	3	10	1
1	3	1	0	1	3	1	0
1	0	3	1	1	0	1	

# Movies	Frequency	Rel Freq
0	9	0.2903
1		
2		
3	4	0.1290
5		
10		
	31	

a) Complete the grouped data table above.
b) What percentage of the students saw at least 3 movies during the break?

12) In January 2012, a random sample of 32 Americans were asked what level of confidence they had in the stability of the U.S. banking industry. Their responses are shown below. Data is based on a Rasmussen Reports poll.

Weak	Moderate	Weak	None
Weak	Weak	Weak	Weak
Weak	Neutral	Weak	Weak
Strong	Weak	Weak	Weak
Moderate	None	Weak	Strong
Weak	Weak	Weak	Moderate
None	Moderate	Moderate	Moderate
Moderate	Moderate	Weak	Moderate
Moderate	Strong	Moderate	

Confidence	Frequency	Rel Freq
Strong	3	0.0857
Moderate		
Neutral		
Weak		
None	3	0.0857
	35	

a) Complete the grouped data table above.
b) What percentage of those sampled were at least moderately confident in the stability of the U.S. banks?

13) The duration of labor, in hours, for a random sample of 28 pregnant women during natural childbirth was recorded and is shown in the table below.

9.3	20.2	24.7	21.2	10.6	15.0	27.6
13.9	17.9	17.5	3.3	11.1	15.9	8.0
8.9	30.2	8.8	19.8	16.5	19.3	21.8
7.2	6.5	19.7	14.6	18.2	7.9	21.9

Labor Time	Frequency	Rel Freq	Midpoints
0 – < 5	1	0.0357	2.5
5 – < 10			
10 – < 15			
15 – < 20			
20 – < 25	5	0.1786	22.5
	28		

a) Complete the grouped data table above.
b) What percentage of the women had labor that lasted less than 20 hours?

14) In January 2012, according to Realtor.com, there were 18 new listings for homes for sale in Pocatello, Idaho with 5 or more bedrooms. The year those homes were built are shown in the table below.

2010	1959	2001	1965	2006	2007
2005	2007	2001	2006	2005	2001
1975	2005	1984	1960	1980	1959

Year	Frequency	Rel Freq	Midpoints
1951 – 1960	3		
1961 – 1970	1	0.0556	
1971 – 1980	2	0.1111	
1981 – 1990	1		
	18		

a) Complete the grouped data table above.
b) What percentage of the homes were built after 1980?

15) A new long lasting DVD player is tested for the lasting time of its battery under normal use conditions. A random sample of 45 units, produced the following battery durations, in hours.

4.42	4.22	4.92	4.81	5.79	7.46	4.58	4.16
6.93	7.92	4.45	5.97	6.10	7.23	4.25	6.68
5.54	6.33	5.90	3.75	6.35	4.98	5.05	5.14
4.21	6.13	6.39	5.35	6.11	6.16	6.64	7.13
6.85	6.03	6.57	6.28	5.48	4.56	5.33	5.03
5.18	4.30	4.93	4.82	4.62			

a) Construct a grouped data table using classes of equal width beginning with 3.5 - < 4
b) Is it common for these batteries to last longer than 7 hours? Explain.

16) The braking distances, in feet, required to reach a complete stop from a speed of 60 mph are given below for a random sample of 37 SUVs. The distances have been rounded to the nearest 10th of a foot.

145.9	141.1	134.7	139.6	149.7	138.7
144.6	143.9	147.5	145.0	149.7	151.0
142.6	149.0	156.5	141.1	138.1	156.4
151.1	149.9	145.6	148.6	149.2	141.1
137.8	143.9	146.3	153.9	145.0	145.7
146.3	152.4	147.9	155.4	137.9	145.0
149.8					

a) Construct a grouped data table using classes of equal width beginning with $134 - < 137$.
b) What percentage of the vehicles were able to stop in less than 140 ft?

17) The owner of "Everything Grows", a plant business in Danville, CA wishes to increase traffic to the company's website. To accomplish this goal, he paid for a search engine optimization. A random sample of 18 days after the optimization was completed had the following number of hits:

27	37	33	11	32	5
31	6	11	23	22	29
13	9	33	21	35	37

a) Construct a grouped data table using classes of equal width beginning with $5 - 9$.
b) Prior to the optimization, the site was typically getting about 17 hits per day. What percentage of the time did the site get more hits than that after the optimization?
c) Does this seem like solid evidence that the site is getting more hits after the optimization? Explain.

18) The following is a random sample of the blood type for 51 Americans.

O+	O+	A+	B+	B+	O-	A+	O+	A+
B+	O+	O+	B+	A-	O+	O-	A+	B+
A+	A-	B+	A+	O+	A+	A+	O+	O+
O+	O+	O-	A+	O+	O+	A+	O+	A+
A+	B+	O+	A+	O+	B+	A+	A-	B+
O-	A+	A+	O+	A+	A+			

a) Construct a grouped data table based on the blood type. Positive and negative blood types should each be in their own class.
b) What was the most and least common blood types in the sample?
c) Do you think that the relative frequencies from your table are the same as for all Americans? Explain.

19) The chapter 2 homework score, out of 5 points possible, for a stat class with 43 students are shown below.

0	4	4	4	4	3	4	4	0
5	4	5	5	4	3	5	4	2
4	2	4	4	5	5	5	4	4
5	4	4	2	4	5	4	3	3
3	4	3	4	4	5	4		

a) Construct a grouped data table for the scores. Decide on the most appropriate classes to use.
b) If the teacher is hoping that most of the students score at least a 3, do you expect that the teacher will be satisfied? Explain.

20) The prices from a random sample of 30 digital cameras are listed below. The sample was taken in April 2007 and the prices have been rounded to the nearest dollar.

90	130	150	200	180	200
220	250	250	230	300	250
250	300	300	300	300	350
330	350	350	400	400	600
650	800	900	1100	1500	3800

a) Group using equal width classes beginning with $0 - 249$. You need only create a frequency distribution. That is, include classes and frequencies, but leave off relative frequency and midpoints.
b) Repeat part (a), but this time group using $1 - 200$ as the first class, and use equal width classes except for the last class which will be '1001 and over'.
c) Which do you feel was the better grouping?

21) In December 2011, a random sample of 47 Americans were asked "How serious a problem is global warming?" There responses are shown below. Data is based on a study by the Pew Research Center.

Very	Very	Not	Somewhat
Not	Very	Very	Very
Very	Not Too	Not Too	Very
Not Too	Not	Somewhat	Very
Somewhat	Unsure	Very	Somewhat
Not Too	Somewhat	Somewhat	Not
Not	Very	Somewhat	Very
Very	Not Too	Somewhat	Somewhat
Not Too	Very	Not	Somewhat
Very	Somewhat	Not Too	Not Too
Very	Somewhat	Very	Very
Not	Very	Not	

a) Construct a grouped data table based on the responses.
b) What percentage of these Americans think that global warming is at least a somewhat serious problem?
c) Do you think this is the same as for the percentage of all Americans at that time? Explain.

22) An algebra class was assigned a practice final to take online before the actual final. The students were allowed to take the practice final as many times as they wished. The number of attempts for each of the students is shown in the table below.

8	2	0	3	1	3
0	3	4	1	3	1
2	3	1	0	2	1
2	0	2			

a) Construct a grouped data table based on the number of attempts. Use Single Value grouping.
b) Do any of the data values stand out now that they have been grouped? Explain.
c) Do you think it is better to show or not show the empty classes in this table? Explain.

Section 2.2 – Graphing Data

Grouping data is an excellent way to condense and organize a large data set, however, it can still be difficult for some people to process the information that is being presented to them in table form. It is very common for people to be better at processing information that is in a graphical form rather than a numerical one. In this section, we will explore various ways of taking both raw and grouped data and making a graphical representation of the data. The most commonly used graphical representation for data sets is a **histogram**. Let's define the term and then look at some examples.

Definitions: *Frequency and Relative Frequency Histograms*

Frequency Histogram: A frequency histogram is a bar chart for quantitative data that uses the heights of the bars to illustrate the frequencies of the classes. It can be used for discrete or continuous data.

Relative Frequency Histogram: A relative frequency histogram is a bar chart for quantitative data that uses the heights of the bars to illustrate the relative frequencies of the classes.

Example 2.4: *Final Exam Scores*

The final exam scores (out of 100 points possible) for a group of 43 statistics students are shown grouped in the table below.

Can a histogram help reveal the patterns in final exam scores?

Classes	Frequency	Relative Freq	Midpoint
20 – 29	1	0.0233	24.5
30 – 39	0	0.0000	34.5
40 – 49	2	0.0465	44.5
50 – 59	5	0.1163	54.5
60 – 69	4	0.0930	64.5
70 – 79	9	0.2093	74.5
80 – 89	7	0.1628	84.5
90 – 99	15	0.3488	94.5
	43	1.0000	

a) Construct a frequency histogram for the scores.

b) Construct a relative frequency histogram for the scores.

c) Compare the visual impact of the two different histograms.

Solution:

a) The finished product is shown below. Because you will make this graph in several steps, please read all the comments that follow the graph.

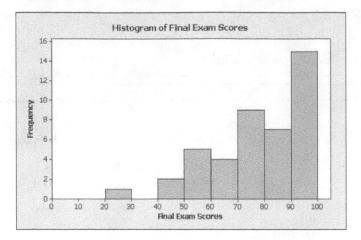

We always put our variable on the horizontal axis and our frequency on the vertical axis. Axes should be labeled. Notice, in the histogram above, we labeled the horizontal axis as 'Final Exam Scores' and labeled the vertical axis as 'Frequency'.

The bars extend from lower cutpoint to lower cutpoint. This means there will not be gaps between the bars unless there is an empty class. Therefore, we did have a gap in the 30's because there were no test scores in that range. However, we do not show a gap between the end of the class 40 – 49 and the beginning of the class 50 – 59 because no scores could have fallen between those classes. We drew the bar for 40 – 49 from 40 to the next lower class limit of 50.

Because you will draw your axes and bars by hand, graph paper and a straight edge are highly recommended. This will help ensure bars of equal width and proper ratios among the heights of the bars.

b) This is done just like the previous histogram except the vertical axis now represents the relative frequency of the class rather than the frequency.

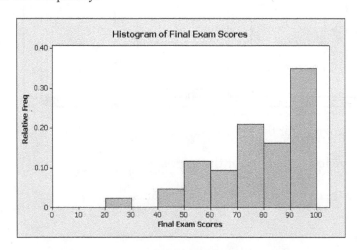

Always try to scale the vertical axis in such a way so as to make the top of the tallest bar appears at or just below the top of your graph grid. It is also important to attempt to use a nice scale. Above, the numbering is 0, 0.10, 0.20, etc.

c) There is no apparent difference between the visual impact of the two graphs. In fact, when you first glance at them, they appear to be exactly the same graph. The only difference is the labeling on the vertical axis.

> **Key Concept**: *Similarity of Frequency and Relative Frequency Histograms*
>
> Because these two versions of a histogram look so much alike, it really doesn't make sense to create both of them (unless asked). Just decide what is more important to your reader, the count or the percent, and go with the appropriate graph.

VARIATIONS: *Continuous data, Single value grouping, and Categorical data*

Now that we have seen the histograms for a quantitative discrete data set, it is time to look at how variations in our data set and grouping style affect the graphs we make. Let's take a look at a quantitative continuous data set next.

Example 2.5: *Calories in Potato Chips*

To test the calorie content of a brand of potato chips, a random sample of 50 serving size containers is obtained. Each serving is tested to determine the total number of calories. The calorie data for the 50 servings are shown grouped in the table below.

Can graphing the potato chip calories better reveal the pattern in them?

Calories	Frequency	Relative Freq	Midpoint
$130 - <132$	3	0.06	131
$132 - <134$	1	0.02	133
$134 - <136$	3	0.06	135
$136 - <138$	6	0.12	137
$138 - <140$	8	0.16	139
$140 - <142$	13	0.26	141
$142 - <144$	9	0.18	143
$144 - <146$	5	0.10	145
$146 - <148$	0	0.00	147
$148 - <150$	2	0.04	149
	50	1.00	

a) Construct a frequency histogram for the calorie data.

b) What information about the data set is evident upon viewing the graph?

Solution:

a) The complete histogram is shown below. See the comments that follow below.

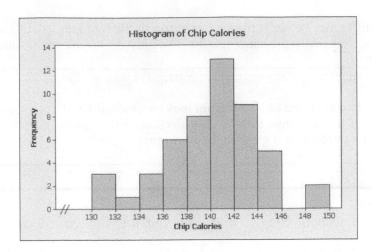

Just like for the discrete data set, we also draw the bars from lower cutpoint to lower cutpoint when making histograms for continuous data.

If the horizontal scale had started at zero and gone all the way to 150, then the histogram would have been seen as spikes on the far right hand side of the graph. To spread the data across the full space, we broke scale and began numbering at 130. The two slash marks on the horizontal axis are there to alert the reader that there has been a break in scale.

b) The most common amount of calories per serving is between 140 and 142 calories. However, some contain as few as 130 calories and some as much as 150. Most of the servings had calories amounts near the center of 140.

Key Concept: *Breaking the horizontal scale*

For graphical displays, it often doesn't look good to have the intersection of the vertical and horizontal axes represent the number zero. We may wish to cut out a portion of the horizontal scale to bring the graph closer or we may sometimes push zero to the right to keep the bars from overlapping our vertical scale. In such cases, we need to draw in the double slash shown on the number line to indicate this break in the normal scale.

Caution: Making a break in scale for a histogram makes the graph misleading. This should be avoided. We will discuss this further at the end of this section.

The above example illustrates that there is really not much of a difference between constructing a histogram for discrete data versus continuous data. However, for the case of single value grouping we will see a significant change occur. Let's take a look.

Example 2.6: *Matching birthdays in a group of 30 people (Single Value Grouping)*

A student was interested in the frequency with which a day of the year would be a shared birthday for two or more students in a class of 30 students. To investigate this question, she chose a random sample of 67 classes that each contained 30 students. She then surveyed these classes to obtain the birthdays of the students and then looked for days of the year that were shared birthdays for 2 or more classmates. A data value of 0 represents a class where no people shared the same birthday. A data value of 1 represents a class where exactly one day of the year was a common birthday for at least 2 people out of the 30 in the class. A data value of 2 would mean that two different dates during the year would be a shared birthday for 2 or more classmates. The grouped data is as follows.

Is 4 birthday matches in a group of 30 unusual?

Shared Dates	Frequency	Relative Freq
0	19	0.2836
1	28	0.4179
2	15	0.2239
3	4	0.0597
4	1	0.0149
	67	1.0000

a) Construct a relative frequency histogram for the number of shared birth dates.

b) What information stands out in the graphical representation of the data?

Solution:

a) The completed histogram is shown. See the comments that follow below.

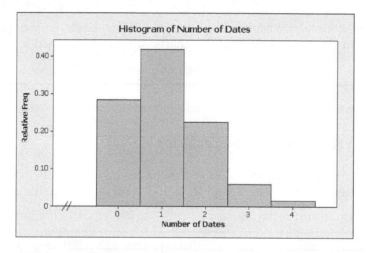

You should notice a big difference between the way the bars were drawn in the previous two examples and this one. Instead of the bars being drawn from lower cutpoint to lower cutpoint, when we do single value grouping, we center the bars over the single value they represent. Also, because this is quantitative data, we do not want gaps to exist between the bars. To meet both of these goals, the bars must go from 1/2 mark to 1/2 mark. So, for example, the bar for 2 shared dates starts at 1.5 and ends at 2.5. If we had followed the old model and started the bar at 2 and ended it at 3, some readers may have been confused about whether that was the bar for 2 shared dates or 3 shared dates.

We once again broke the horizontal scale. This time, we did not break scale to move the bars closer to the vertical axis; rather we broke scale to move the bars off of the vertical axis. Notice that if we did not break the scale, then the zero bar would have obscured the vertical number line. Whenever we break scale, we also show the double slash mark on the horizontal axis between the vertical axis and the start of our numbering.

b) From this graph it stands out that it is very common for there to be at least 1 matching birthday among a group of 30 people. 1 match is the most common and no matches happened less than 30% of the time. We might also notice that it was rare for there to be 4 shared birthdays and more than that never happened.

> **Point to Remember**: *Cutpoints for Single Value Grouping*
>
> For single value grouping, the histogram bars are always centered over the single value. The bars start and end halfway between the numbers being represented by the histogram bars.

GRAPHING CATEGORICAL DATA: *Bar Charts and Pie Charts*

The final variation is for categorical data. We actually have to make a change in terminology for this one. A histogram is a bar graph for quantitative data, but graphing categorical data, we simply refer to the graph as a **bar graph**. When working with categorical data, it is also common to make **pie charts** as well as bar graphs.

> **Definitions**: *Bar Charts and Pie Charts*
>
> **Bar Graphs** are very similar to histograms in the way they present the data visually. However, histogram is a name used for quantitative data. When the similar graph is made for categorical data, it is called a bar chart.
>
> **Pie Charts** are a circular graph where sections of the circle or pie are divided up to represent the various classes. Pie charts are commonly used to present categorical data.

Let's take a look at an example.

Example 2.7: *m&m colors (Graphing Categorical Data)*

I recently bought a large bag of milk chocolate m&m's. I shook the bag to mix them well and then scooped out a sample of 84 pieces of candy. The colors were as listed in the table below.

Are m&m colors evenly distributed in a typical bag?

Color	Frequency	Relative Freq
Brown	9	0.1071
Yellow	13	0.1548
Red	13	0.1548
Blue	20	0.2381
Orange	16	0.1905
Green	13	0.1548
	84	1.0001

a) Construct a bar graph to illustrate the frequencies for the colors.

b) Construct a pie chart to illustrate the relative frequencies for the colors.

c) Do you suspect that the differences in the heights of the bars are convincing evidence that the colors in the bag are not uniform or could the differences just be due to random variation? Explain.

Solution:

a) The completed graph is shown below. See the comments that follow for explanations of the difference between this bar graph and the preceding histograms.

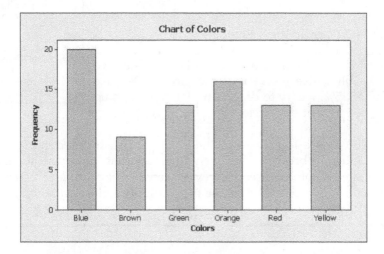

For quantitative data, we number the horizontal number line and then placed the bars. For categorical data, we draw the bars and then label the bars.

Because we do not have a horizontal number line, there is no natural flow from one bar into another. Because of this, we now put gaps between the bars. Also, because there is no number line, we never need to show a break in scale.

b) The completed pie chart is shown below. See the comments that follow.

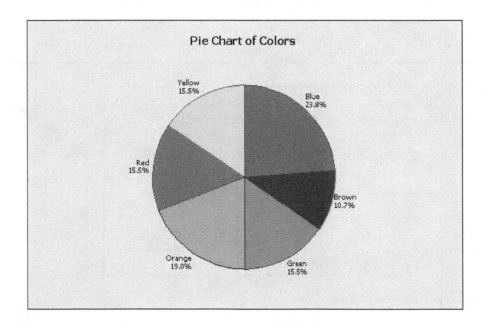

There are two ways that we can construct a graph like the one shown above. One of them is technical and very mathematical. The other is more casual. Let's talk about the wedge for blue using both approaches.

Technical: First, we take a compass and draw a circle. Then we consider the fact that there are 360° in a circle and that blue is supposed to make up 23.8% of that. So, we calculate 23.8% of 360°. We get $(0.238)(360°) = 85.68°$. We would then take out our protractor and measure an $85.68°$ angle and draw in the wedge.

Casual: We do the best we can to draw a circle by hand. Then we notice that the blue slice is 23.8% of the circle. Because this is just under 25%, we try to draw a wedge that uses up slightly less than 1/4 of the circle.

> **Key Concepts**: *Pie Chart Tips*
>
> If we really want the nice picture obtained through the technical method, we should use a computer (as I did for this graph.) For work completed by hand, the casual method makes the most sense.
>
> Look for nice sums when using the casual method. Red, Orange, and Green add up to 50%. So cut the circle in half and then split that half among these 3 colors.

c) From the two graphs, we can see that most of the colors are distributed fairly evenly. However, blue appeared about twice as much as brown.. Intuitively, the fact that there are about twice as many blues as browns seems like more than a coincidence. However, we will learn in later chapters that for samples of this size, such a difference could reasonable just be the result of random variation.

DOTPLOTS: *A visual representation of raw quantitative data sets*

The final graph that we will look at in this section is known as a **dotplot**. **Dotplots** can be useful for seeing gaps and clusters that exist in a data set. They also help us see values that stand apart from the rest of the data set. Such values are important and we will look at them in much more detail in Chapter 3.

> **Definition**: *Dotplots*
>
> **Dotplot**: A dotplot is a simple graph used to show the location of every individual piece of data. It consists of a horizontal number line with dots plotted above the line in the location of the data values. If two or more data values are the same or very close together, then they are stacked.

Let's get acquainted with a dotplot through an example.

Example 2.8: *Final Exam Scores (Seen through a dotplot)*

The final exam scores (out of 100 points possible) for a group of 43 statistics students are shown below.

91	53	75	64	72	88	90	94	86
70	99	75	53	98	71	81	79	43
94	54	42	69	94	93	79	92	83
90	71	51	98	75	98	92	82	81
81	66	94	52	69	26	96		

What can a dotplot show us that was hidden in a histogram?

a) Construct a dotplot for the data set.

b) Do any data value stand apart by themselves? Discuss.

c) Normally, the instructor for this class uses 70 as a lower boundary for C grades and 80 as a lower boundary for B grades. Do these seem like the best boundaries for these grades based on the dotplot? Explain.

Solution:

a) To construct a dotplot, we simply draw a horizontal number line that spans all the scores in our data set. We then plot a dot just above the number line for each piece of data. If two people have the same score or very close scores, then we stack the dots so that they can each be clearly seen. The results are as shown below.

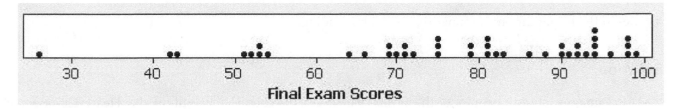

b) The score of 26 really seems to be off by itself. This score is low enough, that it probably should be checked for a possible error in data entry. However, the two scores in the forties suggest that low scores do occur on this test. So, the 26 might just be a really poor performance by a student.

c) No, the gaps in the data occur just below 70 and 80. Perhaps better boundaries would be 69 for the C grades and 79 for the B grades. The 69s and 79s seem to be clustered with the scores above them rather than the ones below them.

MISLEADING GRAPHS: *Don't make them. Don't be fooled by them.*

All of the graphs that have been shown in the examples above are carefully constructed to make sure that they were not misleading. However, sometimes people get a little careless when they construct their graphs and make a mistake that causes the graph to become misleading. Even when we are only a consumer of statistical work, we still need to be aware of this problem. Sometimes, people will purposely make this "mistake" with the intention of misleading you with their graphs. For both of the reasons mentioned above, it is very important that we learn how to avoid and recognize misleading graphs. Let's take a look at such a graph in an example.

Example 2.9: *Leading Causes of Death in America*

According to the CDC, the number of deaths for the top three causes in America for the year 2007 are as shown in the bar chart below. The graph has been constructed in such a way so as to make it misleading.

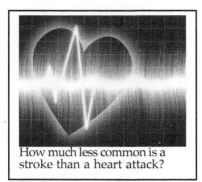

How much less common is a stroke than a heart attack?

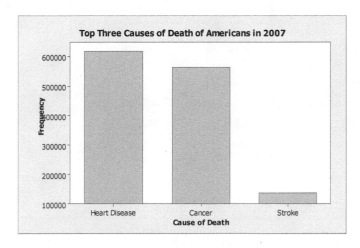

a) Just looking at the visual in the graph (but not the frequency scale), how many times more common is heart disease than stroke as the cause of death among Americans?

b) Now use the vertical scale to estimate the frequency for heart disease and stroke. How many times more common is heart disease than stroke as the cause of death among Americans?

c) What is wrong with the graph that makes it misleading?

d) Re-do the histogram in a manner that is not misleading.

Solution:

a) If I imagine stacking copies of the Stroke bar until it reaches the height of the Heart Disease bar, it appears that Heart Disease is about 15 times more common than Strokes as a cause of death.

b) Estimating the frequencies by using the height on the vertical scale. It appears that Heart Disease has a frequency of approximately 610,000 while for Stroke it appears to be about 140,000. Now, we can do the math as follows:

$$\frac{610,000}{140,000} \approx 4.36,$$ So Heart Disease is actually only 4.36 times more common than Stroke.

c) The problem with this graph that the frequency scale does not start at zero, rather it starts with 100,000. This means that the bottom part of all the bars is missing. This is called a truncated graph.

The error has had the effect of exaggerating the differences in the bars by not showing them in proper proportion. We saw this exaggeration as we worked through parts (a) and (b) above. We make bar graphs to allow the reader to interpret visually, but in this case the visual will mislead them.

d) Here is the graph with a proper vertical scale. Notice that the bar for Heart Disease actually does look a little more than 4 times as tall as the bar for Stroke.

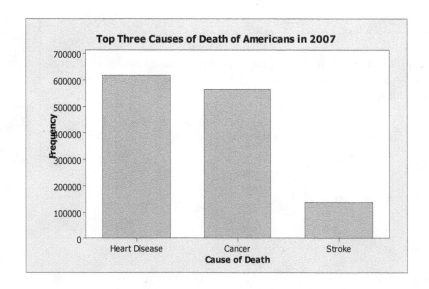

Point to Remember: *Keeping a consistent scale is vital*

When creating histograms and bar graphs, it is important to remember to keep your scale consistent and start the vertical scale at zero. To do otherwise distorts the heights making your graph misleading.

If using a double slash to indicate a break a scale, imagine that it extends a cut all the way through the graph. A break in the vertical scale extends horizontally and can't be used for bar graphs or histograms. A break in the horizontal scale extends up vertically and should not pass through key parts of the graph.

Let's practice with some exercises.

Exercise Set 2.2

Concept Review: Review the definitions and concepts from this section by filling in the blanks for each of the following.

23) For a standard histogram, the bars are drawn from _____ _____ to _____ _____ . So, unless there is an empty class, there will be no _____ between the bars.

24) When doing a histogram for single value grouping, the bars start and end at _____ marks.

25) For categorical data, there is no natural flow from one bar to the next, so we do put _____ between the bars.

26) For histograms, we label the _____ line, but for bar charts, we label the _____ .

27) For dotplots, if data values are repeated or if they are very close to each other, then we _____ the dots.

28) If an inconsistent scale chops off the bottom of all our bars, this throws off the proportions between the bars. Such graphs can be _____ .

Applications: Practice the ideas learned in this section within the context of real world applications.

29) A student tossed 8 coins 1000 times and counted the number of heads for each toss of the 8 coins. A frequency histogram for the number of heads that resulted each time is shown below.

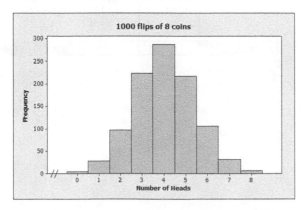

a) Based on the histogram, do you think that it is possible that all possibilities from 0 to 8 heads are equally likely and that the difference in this graph is just random variation? Explain.
b) If you were going to toss 8 coins and had to guess how many heads there would be, what number would you guess? Explain.
c) Use the graph to approximate the number of times the 8 coins showed at least 6 heads.

30) In 2006, the Pew Research Center asked a random sample of 3,014 American adults how happy they were. The results are summarized in the chart below.

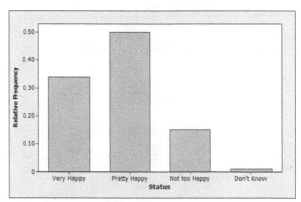

a) Use the graph to estimate the percentage of those sampled that were 'Not too Happy' at that time.
b) Use your answer to part (a) to estimate the number of those sampled that were 'Not too Happy' at that time.
c) Use the graph to approximate the number of people in the sample that were at least 'Pretty Happy'.

31) In the 2011 main event of the World Series of Poker there were 6,865 entrants. When only 366 players remained, the ages of the players were as shown in the graph below.

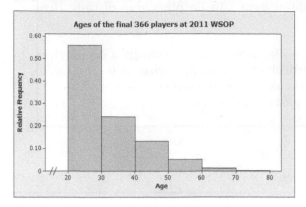

a) Use the graph to estimate the percentage of the remaining players that were younger than 30.
b) Use your answer from part (a) to approximate the number of players that are younger than 30.
c) Do you think we should consider this to be a representative sample of the ages of the original 6,865 entrants? Explain.
d) What does this graph tell you about age and success in poker tournaments? Explain.

32) A student rolled a die 600 times and counted the number of times each number ended up on the top. A frequency histogram for the number of times each number ended up on top is shown below.

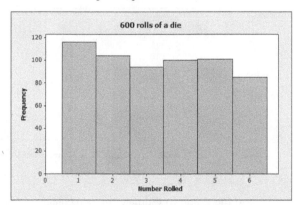

a) Based on the histogram, do you think that it is possible that all possibilities from 1 to 6 are equally likely and that the difference in this graph is just random variation? Explain.
b) If you were going to roll this die and guess which number would show up on top, what number would you guess? Explain.
c) Use the graph to approximate the number of times the die showed at a 2 or lower.

33) The grouped data table below is for the lasting time in hours for the battery of a new long lasting DVD player.

Time	Freq	Rel Freq	Midpoints
3.5 - < 4.0	1	0.0222	3.75
4.0 - < 4.5	7	0.1556	4.25
4.5 - < 5.0	8	0.1778	4.75
5.0 - < 5.5	7	0.1556	5.25
5.5 - < 6.0	4	0.0889	5.75
6.0 - < 6.5	9	0.2000	6.25
6.5 - < 7.0	5	0.1111	6.75
7.0 - < 7.5	3	0.0667	7.25
7.5 - < 8.0	1	0.0222	7.75
	45	1.0001	

a) Construct a frequency histogram for lasting time of the batteries.
b) Construct a relative frequency histogram for the lasting time of the batteries.
c) What do you notice about the two graphs?

34) The grouped data table below is for the braking distances, in feet, required to reach a complete stop from a speed of 60 mph for a random sample of 37 SUVs.

Distance	Freq	Rel Freq	Midpoints
134 – < 137	1	0.0270	135.5
137 – < 140	5	0.1351	138.5
140 – < 143	4	0.1081	141.5
143 – < 146	9	0.2432	144.5
146 – < 149	5	0.1351	147.5
149 – < 152	8	0.2162	150.5
152 – < 155	2	0.0541	153.5
155 – < 158	3	0.0811	156.5
	37	0.9999	

a) Construct a frequency histogram for braking distances for the SUVs.
b) Construct a relative frequency histogram for the lasting time of the batteries.
c) What do you notice about the two graphs?

35) The owner of "Everything Grows", a plant business in Danville, CA wishes to increase traffic to the company's website. To accomplish this goal, he paid for a search engine optimization. The grouped data table for a random sample of 18 days after the optimization was completed is shown below.

Web Hits	Freq	Rel Freq	Midpoints
5 – 9	3	0.1667	7
10 – 14	3	0.1667	12
15 – 19	0	0.0000	17
20 – 24	3	0.1667	22
25 – 29	2	0.1111	27
30 – 34	4	0.2222	32
35 – 39	3	0.1667	37
	18	1.0001	

a) Construct a frequency histogram for number of hits per day after the optimization.
b) Prior to the optimization, the website was getting about 17 hits per day. Based on the graph does it look like things have improved after the optimization? Explain.

36) The table below shows the number of sacks for the 32 NFL teams during the 2007 football season.

# of sacks	Freq	Rel Freq
20 – 23	2	0.06250
24 – 27	3	0.09375
28 – 31	7	0.21875
32 – 35	5	0.15625
36 – 39	8	0.25000
40 – 43	3	0.09375
44 – 47	3	0.09375
48 – 51	0	0.00000
52 – 55	1	0.03125
	32	1.00000

a) Construct a frequency histogram for the sacks.
b) What stands out about the sack data now that you have seen it graphically?

37) The table below is for the chapter 2 homework score, out of 5 points possible, for a stat class with 43 students.

Score	Frequency	Rel Freq
0	2	0.0465
1	0	0.0000
2	3	0.0698
3	6	0.1395
4	22	0.5116
5	10	0.2326
	43	1.0000

a) Construct a relative frequency histogram for their scores.
b) If one of these homework assignments were randomly selected, what would you guess for the score of that assignment? Use your graph to justify your choice.

38) The table below shows the number of goals scored by the losing team in a random sample of 47 NHL games.

Goals	Frequency	Rel Freq
0	8	0.1702
1	19	0.4043
2	15	0.3191
3	4	0.0851
4	1	0.0213
	47	1.0000

a) Construct a relative frequency histogram for the number of goals.
b) If you were given two guesses at the score for the losing team in a randomly selected NHL game, what would you guess for the score of the losing team? Use your graph to justify your choices.

39) The chart below shows the colors obtained in a random sample of 99 peanut butter m&m's.

Color	Frequency	Rel Freq
Blue	25	0.2525
Brown	15	0.1515
Green	16	0.1616
Orange	17	0.1717
Red	11	0.1111
Yellow	15	0.1515
	99	0.9999

a) Construct a frequency bar chart for the colors.
b) Create a pie chart for the relative frequencies.
c) Does it seem reasonable to believe that these m&m's have been taken from a population where the colors are actually distributed evenly? Explain.
d) Which of the two graphs do you feel was more useful in answering this question? Explain.

40) The chart below shows the blood types for a random sample of 51 Americans.

Blood Type	Frequency	Rel Freq
O+	17	0.3333
A+	18	0.3529
B+	9	0.1765
AB+	0	0.0000
O-	4	0.0784
A-	3	0.0588
B-	0	0.0000
AB-	0	0.0000
	51	0.9999

a) Construct a frequency bar chart for the blood types.
b) Create a pie chart for the relative frequencies.
c) Are you convinced by this data that 'positive' blood types are more common than 'negative' ones for all Americans? Explain.
d) Which of the two graphs do you feel was more useful in answering this question? Explain.

41) In December 2011, a random sample of 47 Americans were asked "How serious a problem is global warming?" There responses are summarized below. Data is based on a study by the Pew Research Center.

How Serious?	Frequency	Rel Freq
Very	18	0.3830
Somewhat	12	0.2553
Unsure	1	0.0213
Not Too	8	0.1702
Not	8	0.1702
	47	1.0000

a) Construct a relative frequency bar chart for the responses.
b) Create a pie chart for the relative frequencies.
c) In the sample, a majority of people feel that global warming is at least a somewhat serious problem. Do you think this could just be the result of random variation or does it reflect what is happening in the population? Explain.

42) In January 2012, a random sample of 32 Americans were asked what level of confidence they had in the stability of the U.S. banking industry. Their responses are summarized below. Data is based on a Rasmussen Reports poll.

Confidence	Frequency	Rel Freq
Strong	3	0.0857
Moderate	11	0.3143
Neutral	1	0.0286
Weak	17	0.4857
None	3	0.0857
	35	1.0000

a) Construct a relative frequency bar chart for the responses.
b) Create a pie chart for the relative frequencies.
c) In the sample, a majority of people have weak if any confidence in the stability of the U.S. banking system. Do you think this could just be the result of random variation or does it reflect what is happening in the population? Explain.

43) The points scored by LeBron James of the Miami Heat in each of the 79 regular season games he played in during the 2010-11 season are shown below.

31	16	15	20	20	20	23	20	35	23
20	32	29	25	25	20	23	30	18	38
22	17	33	25	25	20	21	32	32	19
36	27	18	20	25	38	25	26	44	27
34	38	24	39	23	24	51	19	12	41
16	22	27	23	31	29	25	27	29	26
26	31	19	27	21	19	43	33	19	32
33	27	35	27	31	29	23	27	34	

a) Create a dotplot for the data set.
b) Point out a few things about LeBron's scores that were easier to notice in the dotplot than in the set of raw data.

44) An algebra class was assigned a practice final to take online before the actual final. The students were allowed to take the practice final as many times as they wished. The number of attempts for each of the students is shown in the table below.

8	2	0	3	1	3
0	3	4	1	3	1
2	3	1	0	2	1
2	0	2			

a) Create a dotplot for the data.
b) Do any of the data values stand apart from the rest? Explain why this is important to notice.

45) The duration of labor, in hours, for a random sample of 28 pregnant women during natural childbirth was recorded and is shown in the table below.

9.3	20.2	24.7	21.2	10.6	15.0	27.6
13.9	17.9	17.5	3.3	11.1	15.9	8.0
8.9	30.2	8.8	19.8	16.5	19.3	21.8
7.2	6.5	19.7	14.6	18.2	7.9	21.9

a) Create a dotplot for the data.
b) Do you notice any patterns or anything unusual about the data now that it has been plotted?

46) A random sample of 38 Statistics students were asked how many minutes they had exercised in the last 24 hours. Their responses are shown below.

30	4	0	15	0	40	0	30
1	7	160	120	30	0	5	189
3	120	60	0	60	80	30	30
0	180	60	60	0	45	45	80
0	0	120	0	30	0	4	

a) Create a dotplot for the data.
b) Do you notice any patterns or anything unusual about the data now that it has been plotted?

47) Consider the graph below for the letter grade distribution of a college history course.

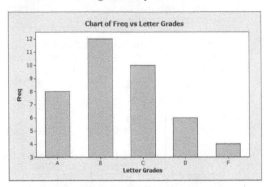

a) Just looking at the bars (but not the scale), how does the number of D's compare to the number of F's?
b) Looking at the scale, what is the actual ratio of D's to F's?
c) What mistake was made in creating this graph that makes it misleading?
d) Draw a new sketch of the histogram that is not misleading.
e) Now how does the number of D's visually compare to the number of F's?

48) Consider the graph below for the medal counts for the top 10 countries at the 2010 winter Olympics in Vancouver.

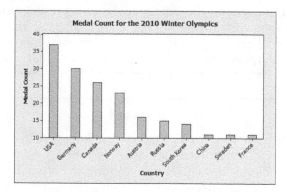

a) Just looking at the bars (but not the scale), how does the number of Medals for South Korea seem to compare to the number for China?
b) Looking at the scale, what was the actual ratio for those countries?
c) What mistake was made in creating this graph that makes it misleading?
d) Draw a new sketch of the histogram that is not misleading.
e) Now how does the number of medals for South Korea visually compare to China?

49) During the 2011 NFL season, the Green Bay Packers extended their streak of consecutive wins to 18 games. At that time ESPN showed a graphic like the one below to show the number of minutes that the Packers had trailed during the streak by quarter.

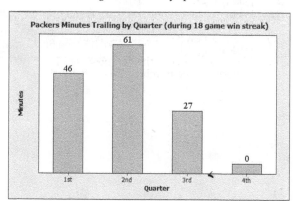

a) What mistake was made in creating this graph that makes it misleading?
b) Draw a new sketch of the histogram that is not misleading.
c) Now that you have seen both versions of the graph, why do you think they chose to draw the graph the way they did?
d) Recommend a better way that ESPN could have handled the presentation of this data.

50) The histogram below is showing the results of randomly selecting 1000 integers from 1 to10, with replacement.

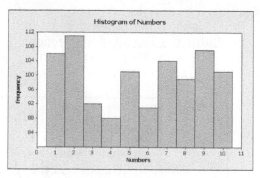

a) Just looking at the bars (but not the scale), does it seem like the difference in the heights could just be due to random variation in the sample? Explain.
b) What mistake was made in creating this graph that makes it misleading?
c) Draw a new sketch of the histogram that is not misleading.
e) Now does it seem like the difference in the heights could just be due to random variation in the sample? Explain.

Section 2.3 – Stem-and-Leaf Diagrams

The graphs introduced in the previous section are all useful for giving the reader a visual representation of a data set. However, with the exception of the dotplot, once we switch to the visual, the original (or raw) data becomes hidden. The goal of this section is to show a method of graphing your data in a type of histogram that maintains contact with the original data set. We will accomplish this goal using a **stem-and-leaf** diagram. Because the graph shows you every original number in the data set, it is best used for smaller data sets.

Definition: *Stem-and-Leaf Diagram*

Stem-and-Leaf Diagram: A stem and leaf diagram is a visual display made out of the numbers themselves. The beginning digit of the number, the stem, is used to make the classes and the next digit of the number, the leaf, is used to form the visual. The leaves corresponding to each stem can be spread out over multiple lines if needed to improve the visual.

Let's take a look at an example to see how this works.

Example 2.10: *Student Perseverance*

During a recent semester, the number of students taking the final in each of the 59 math classes offered at a college was recorded. Typically, these classes start with around 45 students each. The data is shown below.

25	18	24	21	28	36	28	27	12	29	26	9
34	27	36	19	32	36	10	26	24	38	33	12
21	46	34	29	24	35	31	33	36	20	18	31
15	35	28	33	28	35	30	41	31	19	17	21
18	23	18	17	21	39	23	16	22	14	18	

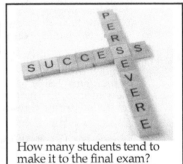

How many students tend to make it to the final exam?

a) Construct a stem-and-leaf diagram for the data set.

b) Order the stem-and-leaf diagram for the data set.

c) Construct an ordered stem-and-leaf diagram using 2 lines per stem.

Solution:

a) To construct a stem-and-leaf diagram, we split each number into two parts. The stem is the first digit of the number; we use this to make the classes. The leaf is the second digit of the number; we use this to form the visual. To make the diagram, we place the different possible stems, in order, on the left side of a vertical line. On the right side of this line, we place the leaves. The leaves will then stack up horizontally and form a visual similar to a histogram. Let's take a look at the results of entering the first row of data into the diagram.

```
0 | 9
1 | 8 2
2 | 5 4 1 8 8 7 9 6
3 | 6
4 |
```

The first number was 25, the 2 is on the left side of the vertical line and the 5 is in the first box on the right hand side. The next number was 18, so we entered a 8 on the right side of the vertical line in the row starting with the 1. The number in the row starting with 0 represents 09 or 9. Now let's fill in the rest of the rows of data.

0	9																				
1	8	2	8	9	0	2	4	8	8	8	5	9	7	7	6						
2	5	4	1	8	8	7	9	6	1	2	7	6	4	3	1	9	4	0	3	8	8	1
3	6	4	6	2	6	8	3	9	4	5	1	3	6	1	5	3	5	0	1			
4	6	1																			

You should now be able to see the visual we are going for in this picture. It's like a histogram lying on its side with the leaves forming the bars. So we have grouped the data and graphed it all at the same time and we can still see the individual data values as well. For example, the two numbers in the forties can be seen to be 46 (40 + 6) and 41 (40 + 1).

b) It is rare that someone would make a stem-and-leaf diagram and not order it. Notice that the leaves in the diagram above are currently not in order. For example the last row reads 46 and 41 rather than 41 and 46. We can fix this rather quickly by ordering the leaves on each row. The result is shown below.

> **Caution:** *Spacing is Critical*
>
> It is critical that the spacing of the leaves be consistent when making a stem and leaf diagram. The leaves form the bars, so if we are inconsistent with the spacing, then we distort the visual. For this reason, graph paper is recommended.

0	9																				
1	0	2	2	4	5	6	7	7	8	8	8	8	8	9	9						
2	0	1	1	1	1	2	3	3	4	4	4	5	6	6	7	7	8	8	8	8	9	9
3	0	1	1	1	2	3	3	3	4	4	5	5	5	6	6	6	6	8	9			
4	1	6																			

c) The stem-and-leaf diagrams shown above are considered to have one line per stem because each stem is only used on one row. However, this gave us a diagram with only 5 classes or bars. This is acceptable, but perhaps we could better visualize the patterns in this data set if we had more classes. One way to do that would be to split each line into two groups. For example the class for 20 – 29 could be split into two classes, 20 – 24, and 25 – 29. To do this we just list the 2 as a stem twice, once for the lower 20's and once for the upper 20's. The other stems would similarly be listed twice each. The results are as follows.

0	9										
1	0	2	2	4							
1	5	6	7	7	8	8	8	8	9	9	
2	0	1	1	1	1	2	3	3	4	4	4
2	5	6	6	7	7	8	8	8	8	9	9
3	0	1	1	1	2	3	3	3	4	4	
3	5	5	5	6	6	6	6	8	9		
4	1										
4	6										

> **Key Concept:** *Never start with an empty class*
>
> The reason we only list the stem 0 a single time is because, if we had listed it twice, the first 0 would represent the class 0 – 4 and the second 0 would be for the class 5 – 9. However, you should never begin or end with an empty class.

> **Key Concept**: *Ordered Stem-and-Leaf is the standard*
>
> Because people are generally only interested in ordered stem-and-leaf diagrams, in the future, you will only see directions asking you for the ordered stem-and-leaf diagram. However, if the data set you are working with is not in order, then it might be a good idea to make a non-ordered stem-and-leaf diagram first as scratch work.

> **Point to Remember**: *Procedure for creating an ordered stem-and-leaf diagram*
>
> - Decide what your stems will be and whether you want one line per stem or two. The goal is to have between 5 and 20 classes. Stems are typically the first digit or two of your numbers.
> - Draw a vertical line and place the stems in order on the left side of the line. Remember: We should never begin or end with an empty line.
> - The leaves will be the digit in the next place to the right of your stem. If the leaf unit is not the ones place, then you should specify the leaf unit on your diagram. Place the leaves to the right of the vertical line. Do not worry about order this time.
> - Redo the diagram placing the leaves in order. Remember, consistent spacing is vital on a stem-and-leaf diagram. Use graph paper if necessary.

VARIATIONS: *Using Non-Standard Stems and Leaves*

The previous example is the most common form of stem-and-leaf diagram. However, there are times when you want to make a stem and leaf, but it doesn't make sense to use a class width of 10 or 5. The following example shows a case where it makes sense to deviate from the standard stem-and-leaf. Let's take a look at why this happens and how we deal with it.

Example 2.11: *SAT scores*

A random sample of 50 high school students produced the following combined SAT scores.

1510	1720	1590	1440	1030	1870	1530	1580	1300	910
1540	1630	1830	1610	1150	1060	1680	1330	1720	1520
890	1360	1510	1790	1640	1370	1490	1790	1510	1230
1490	1610	1640	1650	1630	1490	1250	1690	1430	1320
1520	1160	1270	1470	1610	2040	1520	1640	1380	1530

What should we expect for the typical combined score on the SAT test?

a) Create an ordered stem and leaf diagram using the hundreds place as the stem and the tens place as the leaf.

b) What patterns do you see looking at the grouped / graphed data?

Solution:

a) Notice that on this first run through, I did not put the leaves in order. It is generally faster to just do a quick version that is in the order the data was listed.

Note: leaf unit is the tens place.

08	9
09	1
10	3 6
11	6 5
12	7 5 3
13	6 7 3 0 8 2
14	9 4 7 9 9 3
15	1 4 2 9 1 3 2 8 1 2 3
16	3 1 4 1 5 4 3 1 8 9 4
17	2 9 9 2
18	3 7
19	
20	4

Key Concepts: *Variation of units*

You can use multiple digits for the stem, but the leaf is always written as a single digit. If that means dropping off digits from the number, then do not round.

The standard stem-and-leaf diagram has the tens digits as the stem and the ones digit as the leaf. If you do something different from that standard, then you need to label your units at the top of the diagram as was done on the left.

I entered the data by going through the columns. It could also been done using the rows, it doesn't matter. I chose to put a zero in front of the 8 and 9 stems for a consistent look, but that is optional.

You always show only a single digit for the leaf. If there are digits after that, zero or otherwise, you do not put them in the diagram. When the leaf unit is not the ones place, that needs to be mentioned as we did above.

Finally, we finish the job by putting the leaves in order. This one is going to be our final answer, so the spacing is now critical. Of course, the spacing above is perfect, but when doing these by hand the spacing is not important on the non-ordered version.

Note: leaf unit is the tens place.

08	9
09	1
10	3 6
11	5 6
12	3 5 7
13	0 2 3 6 7 8
14	3 4 7 9 9 9
15	1 1 1 2 2 2 3 3 4 8 9
16	1 1 1 3 3 4 4 4 5 8 9
17	2 2 9 9
18	3 7
19	
20	4

Caution: *Reading adjusted units*

Because the leaf is in the tens place, if we read numbers off of the diagram, we need to remember to add the zero. For example, we have a 4 in the 20 row. So the number is 20 hundreds + 4 tens or $2000 + 40 = 2040$.

b) Most of the scores are in the middle of the data set. The most common occurrence is for the score to be in the 1500s or 1600s. Combined scores below 1000 or above 1800 seem to be very rare.

WRAP SESSION: *Reading a Stem-and-Leaf Diagram*

Example 2.12: *Sleeping the night before the big test?*

The amount of sleep, in hours, was recorded for a random sample of 35 statistics students the night before they took a midterm exam. A stem-and-leaf diagram for the data collected is shown below.

Are statistics students getting enough sleep the night before they take exams?

Note: leaf unit is the tenths place.

```
1 | 3
2 | 6
3 | 0 3 5 6 8 9
4 | 1 1 3 6 8
5 | 0 1 2 5 6 7 7 9
6 | 1 1 4 5 7 8 8 8 9
7 | 4 8
8 | 1 2 5
```

a) Write out the sleep amounts represented by the row with a stem of 4.

b) What percentage of the students slept at least 6 hours the night before the exam?

c) Suppose we were to construct a grouped data table where each row of the stem-and-leaf diagram represented the classes. Write out what the class description would be fore such a table.

Solution:

a) The note at the top of the table indicates that the leaf unit is the tenths place. That means that the stems would represent the ones place. Therefore the numbers in the fourth row of the stem-and-leaf diagram are 4.1, 4.1, 4.3, 4.6, and 4.8.

b) We would count all the students on the rows with stems 6 or higher. There are 9 students on the row with a stem of 6, 2 on the row with a stem of 7, and 3 on the row with a stem of 8. So we get:

$$\frac{9+2+3}{35} = \frac{14}{35} = 0.40 = 40\%$$

c) Sleep time is a continuous variable, so we should use the '– <' symbol to write out the class descriptions. The classes appear to be: $1.0 - < 2.0$, $2.0 - < 3.0$, $3.0 - < 4.0$, $4.0 - < 5.0$, $5.0 - < 6.0$, $6.0 - < 7.0$, $7.0 - < 8.0$, and $8.0 - < 9.0$,

Let's practice with some exercises.

Exercise Set 2.3

Concept Review: Review the definitions and concepts from this section by filling in the blanks for each of the following.

51) Because a stem-and-leaf diagram is interpreted like a histogram, it is extremely important that we have consistent _____ between the numbers.

52) For a standard stem-and-leaf diagram, the width of the classes is ____ . If we use two lines per stem, then the width is ___ .

Applications: Practice the ideas learned in this section within the context of real world applications.

53) A random cluster sample of 69 NBA players from games played on Jan 14, 2012 produced the following minutes played per player. The players were chosen by using all players from both teams from 3 randomly selected games. A stem-and-leaf diagram for the minutes is shown below.

```
0 | 0000000011
0 | 5566899
1 | 0144
1 | 5556667789999
2 | 02233444
2 | 5666689
3 | 122333
3 | 5588999
4 | 002244
4 | 5
```

a) Write out the actual data values for the second to last line of the graph (the first use of the 4 stem).
b) If you considered each row of this graph to represent a class from a grouped data table, then what are the class descriptions?
c) What percentage of the players played at least 35 minutes?

54) In January 2012, a random sample of 30 statistics students with cars were asked to give the gas mileage, in mpg, for their vehicles. A stem-and-leaf diagram for the mileages is shown below.

```
1 | 4
1 | 7788
2 | 00011244
2 | 55567888
3 | 0000024
3 | 5
```

a) Write out the actual data values for the second line of the graph (the second use of the 1 stem).
b) If you considered each row of this graph to represent a class from a grouped data table, then what are the class descriptions?
c) What percentage of the vehicles get less than 20 mpg?

55) In January 2012, a random sample of 43 statistics students were asked to state their current GPA. A stem-and-leaf diagram for the GPA's is shown below.

Leaf Unit is 0.1

```
1 | 99
2 | 234
2 | 55568
3 | 0000000223344444
3 | 555556777788888
4 | 00
```

a) Write out the approximate data values for the third line of the graph (the second use of the 2 stem).
b) If you considered each row of this graph to represent a class from a grouped data table, then what are the class descriptions?
c) What percentage of the students have at least a 3.0?
d) Why isn't there a second line for the stem of 4?

56) In January 2012, the author of this book collected data on all 109 of his Facebook friends. The number of wall posts for each of his friends is displayed in the stem-and-leaf diagram below.

Leaf Unit is the tens place

```
 0 | 00001111111111222233444444
 0 | 5555566677778889999
 1 | 00001112222233333334
 1 | 566677889
 2 | 000001222344
 2 | 6667788
 3 | 234
 3 | 55889
 4 | 04
 4 | 56
 5 |
 5 | 9
 6 | 2
 6 | 89
 7 |
 7 |
 8 |
 8 |
 9 | 4
 9 |
10 | 0
```

a) Write out the approximate data values for the second use of the 3 stem.
b) If you considered each row of this graph to represent a class from a grouped data table, then what are the class descriptions for the first 6 classes?
c) What percentage of the friends have at least 500 wall posts?
d) Why isn't there a second line for the stem of 10?

57) A random sample of 41 community college statistics students were asked how many hours per week they expected to work at a job during the Spring 2012 semester. Their responses are shown in the table below.

9	12	0	8	20	40	40	0	25
20	20	16	12	20	0	0	10	20
0	20	25	10	0	0	25	8	20
30	0	0	0	5	14	20	14	8
0	7	30	20	20				

a) Create an ordered stem-and-leaf diagram for the data set.
b) Create an ordered stem-and-leaf diagram using two lines per stem.
c) Which one better shows the patterns in the data set?

58) The points scored by the winning teams in a sample of 48 games played during the 2011 NFL season are shown below.

20	22	51	10	21	22	31	37	33	8
29	13	26	20	20	31	23	32	28	10
27	30	21	49	38	25	19	35	38	38
20	41	16	22	48	27	13	30	34	20
33	31	27	17	42	44	38	38		

a) Create an ordered stem-and-leaf diagram for the data set.
b) Create an ordered stem-and-leaf diagram using two lines per stem.
c) Which one better shows the patterns in the data set?

59) The test scores of 38 stat students on their first exam are shown in the table below.

61	80	37	74	80	46	75	79
50	96	29	45	76	61	54	81
68	94	73	108	89	49	79	93
62	83	62	72	91	86	41	47
66	76	22	90	99	86		

a) Create an ordered stem-and-leaf diagram for the data set.
b) What patterns do you see in the graphed version of the data set?

60) An intermediate algebra class was assigned an online practice midterm. The midterm was timed with a maximum allowed time of 150 minutes. The times for the 28 students in the class are shown below.

141.2	141.0	118.8	109.7	146.9	93.0
90.7	129.0	123.5	150.0	128.4	99.0
124.3	150.0	146.7	104.8	87.5	91.8
77.3	97.3	144.8	85.3	136.3	107.2
100.8	56.5	71.9	129.6		

a) Create an ordered stem-and-leaf diagram for the data set.
b) What patterns do you see in the graphed version of the data set?

61) A random sample of 41 Big Macs were purchased and analyzed for calorie content. The number of calories in each of the sandwiches is shown in the table below.

563.0	578.7	554.6	556.5	559.5	588.4
556.0	553.1	552.2	573.3	563.9	574.1
570.3	564.7	568.3	563.7	549.1	558.6
557.3	568.6	574.1	556.0	570.7	558.6
557.4	547.8	555.4	573.0	558.5	564.4
553.7	555.3	566.6	572.5	558.0	566.5
557.6	565.9	574.6	555.2	580.4	

a) Create an ordered stem-and-leaf diagram for the data set. Use two lines per stem. Make the leaf unit the ones place (standard).
b) Does it appear that it is rare for a Big Mac to have 580 or more calories? Explain.

62) The sale price for a random sample of 35 pairs of snowboard bindings from April 2011 are listed in the table below.

103	48	74	162	130	54
61	65	118	56	57	51
123	85	54	97	65	122
70	76	125	145	70	105
51	83	67	72	65	68
94	72	90	139	193	

a) Create an ordered stem-and-leaf diagram for the data set. Use two lines per stem. Make the leaf unit the ones place (standard).
b) Does it appear that it is rare for a pair of binding to cost more than $150 in April? Explain.

63) During the 2008-2009 academic year, a random sample of 30 public 4-year colleges was obtained and the cost of tuition and fees were recorded. The costs, in dollars, were as follows.

9,354	14,399	5,600	7,061	2,711	14,694
5,910	8,534	8,232	8,746	6,146	6,567
7,926	4,516	7,777	6,608	10,416	4,529
2,922	5,340	2,740	6,900	4,011	3,207
7,719	1,356	5,834	3,346	8,084	6,530

a) Create an ordered stem-and-leaf diagram for the data set using the hundreds digit for the leaves.
b) Based on your graph, which if any of the costs seems unusual for the data set? Explain.

64) The eggs sold in grocery stores come in a variety of sizes. Three common sizes that are sold are large, extra large, and jumbo. A random sample of 48 eggs labeled as extra large was taken. The weights of the eggs, in ounces, were as shown below.

2.20	2.29	2.21	2.20	2.31	2.14	2.21	2.33
2.27	2.30	2.24	2.34	2.26	2.08	2.20	2.11
2.12	2.27	2.34	2.34	2.47	2.28	2.24	2.01
2.24	2.29	2.35	2.33	2.30	2.05	2.25	2.30
2.13	2.15	2.23	2.31	2.33	2.07	2.24	2.30
2.16	2.18	2.19	2.16	2.23	2.21	2.22	2.20

a) Create an ordered stem-and-leaf diagram for the data set using the hundredths digit for the leaves. Use two lines per stem.
b) Based on your graph, which if any of the weights seems unusual for the data set? Explain.

Section 2.4 – Common Distribution Shapes

In the last two sections, we have spent a lot of time coming up with graphical representations of our data sets. We mentioned that a good reason for doing this is that many people can process information much better in a visual form than in a numerical one. This is true, but it is not the only reason we made the decision to graph our data sets. The other reason for doing this is to try to determine the shape of the population from which the data set was drawn. At least roughly knowing the shape of populations will be important in later sections. This information helps us determine the appropriate statistical process to apply. In Chapter 7 we will begin to see how the shape of the population affects our ability to do certain statistical procedures. For now, we need to become acquainted with a few key distribution shapes. There are perhaps infinitely many shapes that a data set can take on, but here are a few that we should be familiar with as we progress through the course.

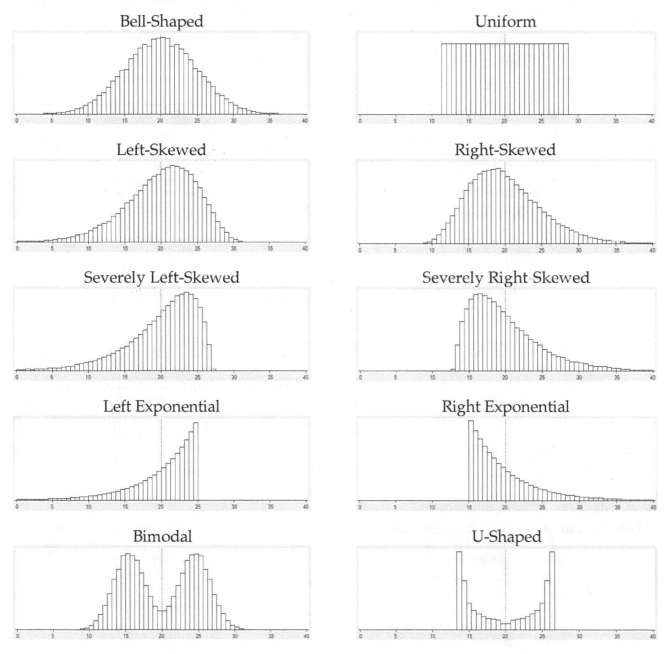

We will probably never see a histogram from a sample that we feel looks as good as any of the shapes shown above, but it will be our job to decide which of these shapes the histogram we are working with most resembles.

Soon, we will look at more detailed descriptions of the distributions shown above, but first we need a couple of general definitions.

Definitions: *Symmetric vs. Skewed Distributions*

Symmetric: A distribution is said to be symmetric if the two sides of the curve are mirror images of one another. For a symmetric curve, you should be able to fold vertically down the middle of the picture and the two sides should match up perfectly.

Skewed: A distribution is said to be skewed to one side if, compared to its high point, it extends further out in one direction than the other. The name skewed comes from the fact that the average of the data set will be pulled in the direction of the further extremes. Skewed distributions are never symmetric.

Now that we have had a glimpse at some key distribution shapes, let's take a moment to formally define each of them and give some extra description of the key characteristics for each type of graph.

Definitions/Descriptions/Examples: *The Key Distribution Shapes*

Bell-Shaped: A bell-shaped distribution has its highest bars in the center. As you move away from the center of the data set, the histogram bars will get shorter and shorter. The histogram bars eventually get so short on each side that they begin to blend in with the horizontal axis. We say that the curve has "tails" on each side. This means it is most common for data to lie in the center and the further you get away from the center the more rare the data values become. The distribution is symmetric. Examples include:

- Heights of men
- Heights of women
- Standardized Test Scores

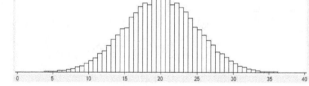

Uniform: Data that has the uniform distribution has histogram bars of equal height all the way across the data set. All data values occur an equal amount of the time. This means that if we randomly select a data value, all possible values are equally likely to occur. This distribution is symmetric. Examples of uniform data include:

- Numbers selected using simple random sampling
- Lottery balls chosen with replacement

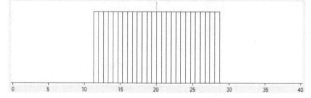

Left-Skewed: A left-skewed distribution has its highest bars on the right side. The values on the left have shorter bars that form a longer tail on the left. Most of the data is on the right side in a left-skewed distribution. The extremes are on the left side. Skewed distributions are not symmetric. Examples include:

- Scores on test where the average is around a 'B' grade.
- Batting average of minor league baseball players (because the extremes on the right get moved to the pros.

Right-Skewed: A right-skewed distribution has its highest bars on the left side. The values on the right have shorter bars that form a long tail on the right. Most of the data is on the left side in a right-skewed distribution. The extremes are on the right side. Skewed distributions are not symmetric.
- Batting averages in Major League Baseball (where the lower batting averages get sent to the minor leagues)
- Hourly pay rate at a small business (where only the managers are extremes)

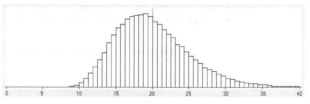

Severely Left-Skewed: This type is similar to left-skewed, but the differences between the two sides are more severe. The drop on the right will be short and fast, but there will be a much longer tail on the left side.
- The scores on an assignment that is just graded based on completion
- Scores given by judges in a figure skating competition.

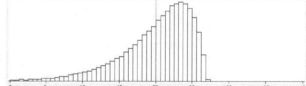

Severely Right-Skewed: This type is similar to right-skewed, but the differences between the two sides are more severe. The drop on the left will be short and fast, but there will be a much longer tail on the right side.
- The cost of homes in a city where most homes are similar, but some homes are very large.
- Income levels in the U.S. where more people are bunched together, but some people are extremely wealthy.

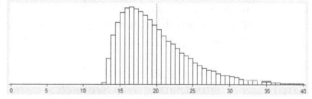

Left Exponential: This distribution is very similar to a severely left-skewed distribution. However, there is no drop on the right at all. The highest bar is on the right and the bars keep dropping off to the left forming a very long tail.
- Scores on an assignment so easy that below average students can still get a perfect score.
- Time spent on a very difficult quiz were the most common occurrence was for the student to run out of time

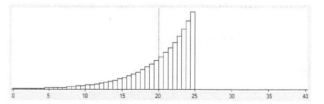

Right Exponential: This distribution is very similar to a severely right-skewed distribution. However, there is no drop on the left at all. The highest bar is on the left and the bars keep dropping off to the right forming a very long tail.
- Amount paid out by an auto insurance in claims to its customers (Most people will not make a claim at all.)
- Salaries for Major League Baseball players (Most players make the minimum salary.)

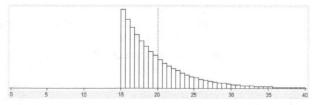

Bimodal: Bimodal distributions have two high points. Typically they are formed when two populations with different high points are joined together into one big population. The one shown here might be the result of looking at the heights of men and women. In general, these distributions could end up being either symmetric or skewed.

- The heights of the men and women at a large college
- The weights of male and female tigers

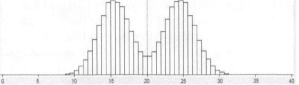

U-Shaped: The U-shaped distribution is an unusual case. It is bimodal, but both of the high points are on the extreme edges of the data set. One way this could occur would be if two exponential type populations were combined.

- The scores by students on a very easy quiz and a very hard quiz mixed together into one data set.
- The time spent solving a puzzle that is really easy with the correct insight but almost impossible without the insight. There is also a maximum amount of time allowed.

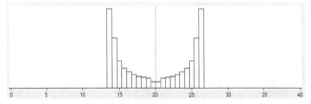

While it would be nice if we could use the graph of sample data to identify the shape of the population to the levels of detail of the ten distributions given above, it is usually enough to properly identify the distribution of the population into rough categories. The example that follows shows us the broad categories that we are most interested in.

Example 2.13: *Identifying characteristics of the distributions.*

Consider the ten shapes listed above.

a) Which distributions are roughly bell-shaped?

b) Which distributions are severely skewed?

c) Describe the remaining distributions?

Solution:

a) Even with the addition of the word roughly, we still can only put one type in this category. The only one that fits is the bell-shaped distribution.

b) Four of the distributions meet this description. Two of them are obvious by name: severely left-skewed and severely right skewed. The other two, despite not having the name skewed in their name, are left exponential and right exponential. These last two are the most severely skewed of the ten.

c) Of the five that are left, they all share an important characteristic. While they are not bell-shaped, they are also not severely skewed. Three of these are in fact symmetric: uniform, bimodal, and u-shaped. The remaining two are skewed, but not severely: left-skewed and right-skewed.

In Chapter 7 and beyond, checking the requirements of our procedures will often require us to look at a fairly small sample and choose the most likely category for the population from the three discussed in the previous example. These three categories are important enough to be memorized.

> **Point to Remember**: *bell-shaped, severely skewed, and not severely skewed*
>
> **Bell-shaped**: The bell shaped distribution is the most desirable one in statistics. When we start our work with a bell-shaped distribution, we are able to do our most powerful work, even with small samples.
>
> **Severely Skewed**: Severely skewed populations often make it harder for us to do our work in later chapters. When we discover that we are sampling from a severely skewed population, we are usually forced to use large sample sizes to overcome this shape.
>
> **Not Severely Skewed**: If our data does not come from a bell-shaped distribution, then the next best thing is one that is symmetric or not severely skewed. From such populations, we can still do powerful work with relatively small sample sizes.

IDENTIFYING THE POPULATION: *Making observations through a cloudy window*

The main reason we will look at graphs of data sets is to try to determine the shape of the distribution of the population from which the data set was taken. It could be the case that we have a graph of the population data, but that is rare. It is much more likely that we will have sample data. In this case, it is critically important to remember that we are NOT trying to determine the shape of the sample data; we are trying to determine the shape of the population from which it was taken. When completing this task, the following theorem will be very useful.

> **Point to Remember**: *Determining the shape of a population's distribution*
>
> **Theorem 2.1**: If a random sample is taken from a population, then the shape of the distribution of the sample is approximately the same as the shape of the distribution of the population. However, the shapes from a random sample will almost always be somewhat different from the population due to random variation.
>
> The bigger the sample we take, the better approximation the sample data's shape will be for population's distribution. Conversely, the smaller our sample, the more difficult it will be to determine the shape of the population by looking at graphs of the sample data. Very small samples give us only a very rough approximation of their population. Remember from Chapter 1: The amount of random variation in a sample tends to get smaller as the sample size increases.
>
> All three of the samples below are taken from the same population. Notice how it is very difficult to recognize the population from the small sample, but it is easier by the time we see the largest sample.
>
>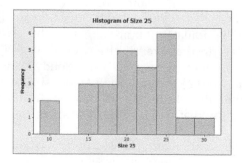

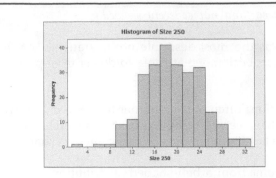
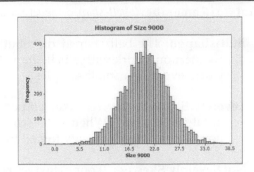

Hopefully it true shape was clear by the final histogram. The population is actually bell-shaped. Random variation made this very hard to see in the sample of size 25. Even in the sample of size 9000, the shape of the population is not perfectly revealed.

So, according to this theorem, the more data we have in a sample, the easier it will be to determine the shape of the population. However, this also means that for smaller samples, we will only get a hint of the population's shape from our graph of the sample data. So, when we have small samples, it is fairly common that we cannot decide with confidence the shape of the distribution of the population. Here's an analogy to this theorem.

The cloudy window analogy:

Suppose that a stranger introduces us to an individual and then offers us $1000 if we can simply pick the individual out of a line up one hour from now. This sounds simple and we are hopeful that we are about to make a quick and easy $1000. We study the individual carefully, noting hair color and style, skin tone, height, weight, etc. However, when we observe the lineup of individuals, we are forced to look through a cloudy window. Do we have a chance of making an informed choice or will we end up just guessing? The cloudy window makes our job tougher, but we should still be able to do better than just a random guess.

Perhaps minor features cannot be made out, but we should still be able to use height to help us. Perhaps hair or skin color can be made out. Even with a very cloudy window, we should still be able to eliminate some of the candidates.

Now, imagine this twist. Suppose that we are told that we could give up $200 of our prize for the opportunity to polish the window a little. Would it help? Would it be worth it? It is likely that if we polish the window, we will be able to distinguish some of the more minor features that we committed to memory and this might make it much easier to identify our target. Probably we should take this offer.

This lineup is from a popular movie from 1995, can you identify the movie or any of the actors?

Trying to identify a well-known population from a sample is a lot like the situation described above. If the sample size is small, then it is like looking through a very cloudy window. Perhaps the best we can do is eliminate some shapes. If we are allowed to increase the sample size, it may make the study more expensive. However, this larger sample size will also start showing us more details and we will have a better chance at figuring out the shape of the population that the sample was drawn from.

Enough theory, let's try to identify some populations based on graphs of sample data.

Example 2.14: *Identifying populations by looking at graphical representations of samples*

For each of the visual representations of sample data shown below, try to identify which of the distributions discussed in this section is the best candidate for the shape of the population from which the data set was taken.

a) The dotplot below is for a sample of final exam scores for students of a certain statistics instructor.

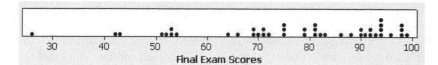

b) This histogram on the right shows the number of shared birth dates in a sample of 67 classes containing 30 students.

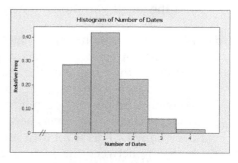

c) The histogram on the right represents a sample of 1000 randomly chosen integers from 1 to 10.

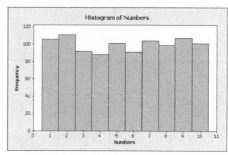

d) The stem-and-leaf diagram below illustrates the combined SAT scores for a sample of 50 students.

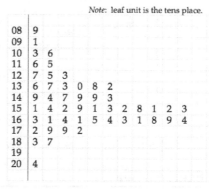

Note: leaf unit is the tens place.

```
08 | 9
09 | 1
10 | 3  6
11 | 6  5
12 | 7  5  3
13 | 6  7  3  0  8  2
14 | 9  4  7  9  9  3
15 | 1  4  2  9  1  3  2  8  1  2  3
16 | 3  1  4  1  5  4  3  1  8  9  4
17 | 2  9  9  2
18 | 3  7
19 |
20 | 4
```

e) The bar chart to the right illustrates the mixture of colors in a random sample of 84 milk chocolate m&m candy pieces.

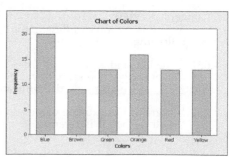

Solution:

a) The dotplot seems to indicate that the population of final exam scores for students of this instructor is left-skewed or perhaps severely left-skewed. The data gives two strong clues that this is the case. First, most of the scores are on the right side of the number line. Second, the extreme values (those that seem to stand apart from the rest of the data) are on the left. One of them is extremely far to the left.

b) The histogram leads me to believe that the population is right skewed. The tallest two bars are on the left and the bars on the right drop lower and lower forming a short tail on the right hand side.

c) It appears that this data is from a uniform population. This is based on the fact that all the bars are roughly the same height. This sample is clearly not uniform because not all of the bars are exactly the same height. However, because this is the graph for the sample it could still be from a uniform population and the small variations in height are likely just the result of the random variation in the sample.

d) We must start by noticing that a stem-and-leaf diagram is like a histogram turned on its side. Because of this, the top is like the left and the bottom is like the right. For this particular graph, it is hard to be certain of the shape of the population, but we can rule out some of the possibilities right away. The population does not appear to be uniform, right-skewed, exponential, u-shaped, or even severely left-skewed. The population might be left-skewed based on the slightly longer tail on the left (top) than on the right (bottom). However, because there is a tail on the left and the right, it could be that the population is bell-shaped. This is a fairly small sample, only 50 students. If we had a larger sample, it would be easier to decide between the two remaining choices. I can at least confidently say that the population is not severely skewed. This is actually helpful information.

e) This bar graph is for categorical data. Distribution shapes are only applied to quantitative data. Therefore, it is not appropriate to give a distribution shape for the population from which this sample was taken.

Caution: *the dangers of small samples and categorical data*

Small Sample Sizes: While just looking at the graph for part (d) above, we were not able to narrow down to a single choice from the distribution of the population. However, it is stated that these are combined SAT scores and standardized test scores are often normally distributed. In fact, SAT scores are usually bell-shaped. This shows how difficult it can be to accurately identify a population based on a small random sample.

Categorical Data: Because the bars for categorical data can be arranged in any order, it does not make sense to describe the shape of the distribution for categorical data.

Let's practice the ideas we've learned with some exercises.

Exercise Set 2.4

Concept Review: Review the definitions and concepts from this section by filling in the blanks for each of the following.

65) If the left and right hand sides of a distribution are mirror images of one another, then we refer to that as a _____ distribution.

66) If a graph has extreme values on one side, but not on the other, then it is referred to as either a left or right _____ distribution.

67) When we look at the graph of sample data, we are not actually trying to determine the shape of the sample, rather we are trying to determine the shape of the distribution of the _____ from which it was taken.

68) Due to the effects of random variation, it can be difficult to determine the distribution of the population from sample data if the sample size is too _____ .

Applications: Practice the ideas learned in this section within the context of real world applications.

69) The dotplot shown below is for the list prices of a sample of 39 homes (5+ bedrooms) from Malibu, CA in March 2008.

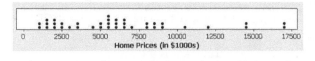

a) Based on this sample data, what is the best choice for this likely distribution of the population from which the sample was taken? Explain.
b) What would make it easier to decide the correct choice for the population?

70) A histogram is shown below for the points scored by the winning teams in a sample of 48 games played during the 2011 NFL season.

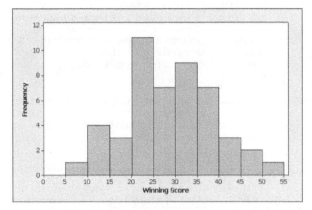

a) Based on this sample data, what is the best choice for this likely distribution of the population from which the sample was taken? Explain.
b) What would make it easier to decide the correct choice for the population?

71) A histogram is shown below for the number of goals scored by the losing team in a random sample of 47 NHL games from the 2011 season.

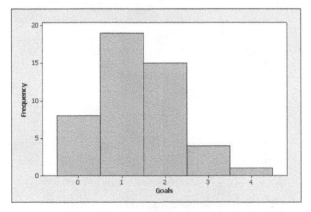

a) Based on this sample data, what is the best choice for this likely distribution of the population from which the sample was taken? Explain.
b) Explain why this shape makes sense that the data would take on this shape for the number of goals for the losing team in an NHL game.

72) The stem-and-leaf diagram for the braking distances required to reach a complete stop from a speed of 60 mph is given below for a random sample of 37 SUVs.

```
13 |4
13 |77889
14 |1112334
14 |55555566778999999
15 |1123
15 |566
```

a) Based on this sample data, what is the best choice for this likely distribution of the population from which the sample was taken? Explain.
b) What would make it easier to decide the correct choice for the population?

73) A student tossed 8 coins 1000 times and counted the number of heads for each toss of the 8 coins. A frequency histogram for the number of heads that resulted each time is shown below.

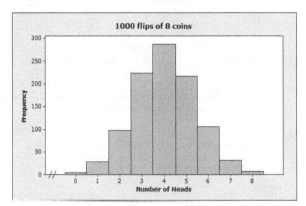

a) Based on this sample data, what is the best choice for this likely distribution of the population from which the sample was taken? Explain.
b) Explain why this shape makes sense that the data would take on this shape for the number of heads that would result from tossing 8 coins.
c) Do you think the lack of perfect symmetry in the graph is convincing evidence that the coin is not fair or do you think it just reflects the random variation in the sample? Explain.

74) A student rolled a die 600 times and counted the number of times each number ended up on the top. A frequency histogram for the number of times each number ended up on top is shown below.

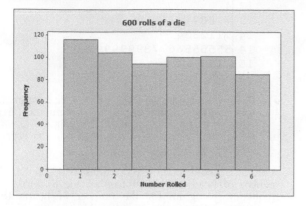

a) Based on this sample data, what is the best choice for this likely distribution of the population from which the sample was taken? Explain.
b) Explain why this shape makes sense that the data would take on this shape for the number of times each of the six sides of the die ended up on top.
c) Do you think the fact that the graph is not perfectly level is convincing evidence that the die is not fair or do you think it just reflects the random variation in the sample? Explain.

75) In the 2011 main event of the World Series of Poker there were 6,865 entrants. When only 366 players remained, the ages of the players were as shown in the graph below.

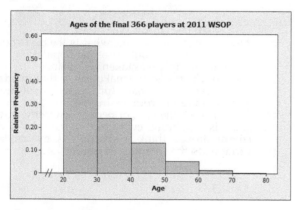

a) Based on this sample data, what is the best choice for this likely distribution of the population from which the sample was taken? Explain.
b) Suppose that the rules were changed so that the age requirement was reduced from 21 to 10 years old to enter these tournaments. What do you think the shape of the graph would be then? Explain.

76) The points scored by LeBron James of the Miami Heat in each of the 79 regular season games he played in during the 2010-11 season are graphed in the dotplot below.

a) Based on this sample data, what is the best choice for this likely distribution of the population from which the sample was taken? Explain.
b) Do you think that the multiple peaks in this graph are meaningful to the application or just random variation from the sample? Explain.

77) In January 2012, a random sample of 43 statistics students were asked to state their current GPA. A stem-and-leaf diagram for the GPA's is shown below.

Leaf Unit is 0.1

```
1 | 99
2 | 234
2 | 55568
3 | 000000223344444
3 | 555556777788888
4 | 00
```

a) Based on this sample data, what is the best choice for this likely distribution of the population from which the sample was taken? Explain.
b) Given that this was a sample of community college students that mostly take this class just before they transfer, explain why this shape makes sense for the data.

78) In January 2012, the author of this book collected data on all 109 of his Facebook friends. The number of wall posts for each of his friends is displayed in the stem-and-leaf diagram below.

Leaf Unit is the tens place

```
 0 | 000011111111111222233444444
 0 | 5555566677778889999
 1 | 000011122222333334
 1 | 566677889
 2 | 000001222344
 2 | 6667788
 3 | 234
 3 | 55889
 4 | 04
 4 | 56
 5 |
 5 | 9
 6 | 2
 6 | 89
 7 |
 7 |
 8 |
 8 |
 9 | 4
 9 |
10 | 0
```

a) Based on this sample data, what is the best choice for this likely distribution of the population from which the sample was taken? Explain.
b) Give a logical explanation for why Facebook wall post data tends to take on this shape.

79) The duration of labor, in hours, for a random sample of 28 pregnant women during natural childbirth was recorded and is shown in dotplot below.

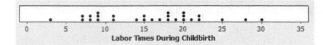

a) Based on this sample data, what is the best choice for this likely distribution of the population from which the sample was taken? Explain.
b) Can you think of a reasonable explanation for why there is a cluster of data around 8 hours and another around 19 hours? Explain.

80) A random cluster sample of 69 NBA players from games played on Jan 14, 2012 produced the following minutes played per player. The players were chosen by using all players from both teams from 3 randomly selected games. A stem-and–leaf diagram for the minutes is shown below.

```
0| 0000000011
0| 5566899
1| 0144
1| 5556667789999
2| 02233444
2| 5666689
3| 122333
3| 5588999
4| 002244
4| 5
```

a) Based on this sample data, what is the best choice for this likely distribution of the population from which the sample was taken? Explain.
b) Explain why it might make sense for the data for teams that play 5 players at a time but have 12 players on the team might have two peaks in the number of minutes played.

81) In December 2011, a random sample of 47 Americans were asked "How serious a problem is global warming?" There responses are summarized below. Data is based on a study by the Pew Research Center.

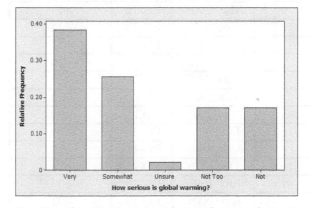

Based on this sample data, what is the best choice for the likely distribution of the population from which the sample was taken? Explain.

82) In 2006, the Pew Research Center asked a random sample of 3,014 American adults how happy they were. The results are summarized in the chart below.

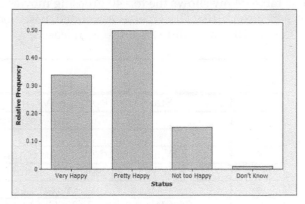

Based on this sample data, what is the best choice for the likely distribution of the population from which the sample was taken? Explain.

83) Suppose that you went to an electronics store and collected the amount of money paid for each HDTV sold on a given day. What shape do you think the distribution of the data would most resemble? Explain.

84) Suppose that a class of 40 students took an exam that a majority of students did not finish by the end of the time allowed. What shape do you think the distribution of the test times would most resemble? Explain.

85) Suppose that we randomly selected 1000 American adults and obtained their heights. What shape do you think the distribution of the data would most resemble? Explain.

86) Suppose that my mother never drives her car on Saturdays, but on Sunday she always makes the 30 mile round trip to church. On the weekdays, she drives a random distance between 0 and 30 miles running errands. Suppose that we randomly selected several days and recorded the miles driven by her and then graphed the miles data using a dotplot. What shape do you think the distribution of the miles data would most resemble? Explain.

Chapter Problem – Top 40 Grossing Movies in the U.S. since 1977

The table below shows the top 40 grossing movies since 1977 by U.S. box office receipts, adjusted for inflation, as of February 2010. The gross is estimated based on how much the movie would have made if it sold as many tickets in 2010 as it did when it was released.

Rank	Title	Release Date	Rating	Receipts (in millions)
1	Star Wars Episode IV: A New Hope	May 1977	PG	1221
2	ET: The Extra-Terrestrial	June 1982	PG	1008
3	Titanic	Dec 1997	PG-13	966
4	Star Wars Episode V: The Empire Strikes Back	May 1980	PG	724
5	Star Wars Episode VI: Return of the Jedi	May 1983	PG	697
6	Avatar	Dec 2009	PG-13	689
7	Star Wars Episode I: The Phantom Menace	May 1999	PG	636
8	Jurassic Park	June 1993	PG-13	635
9	Raiders of the Lost Ark	June 1981	PG	613
10	Forrest Gump	July 1994	PG-13	602
11	The Lion King	June 1994	G	574
12	Close Encounters of the Third Kind	Nov 1977	PG	558
13	The Dark Knight	July 2008	PG-13	557
14	Grease	June 1978	PG	536
15	Shrek 2	May 2004	PG	527
16	Spider-Man	May 2002	PG-13	521
17	Independence Day	July 1996	PG-13	519
18	Beverly Hills Cop	Dec 1984	R	496
19	Ghostbusters	June 1984	PG	493
20	Home Alone	Nov 1990	PG	492
21	Pirates of the Caribbean: Dead Man's Chest	July 2003	PG-13	485
22	Batman	June 1989	PG-13	468
23	The Lord of the Rings: The Return of the King	Dec 2003	PG-13	466
24	National Lampoon's Animal House	July 1978	R	454
25	Spider-Man 2	June 2004	PG-13	451
26	The Passion of the Christ	May 2005	R	448
27	Star Wars Episode III: Revenge of the Sith	May 2005	PG-13	445
28	The Lord of the Rings: The Two Towers	Dec 2002	PG-13	434
29	The Sixth Sense	Aug 1999	PG-13	432
30	Tootsie	Dec 1982	PG	426
31	Finding Nemo	May 2003	G	423
32	Back to the Future	July 1985	PG	422
33	Harry Potter and the Sorcerer's Stone	Nov 2001	PG	420
34	The Lord of the Rings: The Fellowship of the Ring	Dec 2001	PG-13	411
35	Twister	May 1996	PG-13	410
36	Superman	Dec 1978	PG	410
37	Men in Black	July 1997	PG-13	409
38	Transformers: Revenge of the Fallen	June 2009	PG-13	402
39	Mrs. Doubtfire	Nov 1993	PG-13	399
40	Indiana Jones and the Temple of Doom	May 1984	PG	391

Use the chart above to answer the questions that follow on the next page.

a) Create a grouped data table for the receipts (in millions). Begin with the class $300 - < $400.

b) Create a frequency histogram for the table you made in part (a).

c) What if any distribution shape does this most resemble? Explain.

d) Would you expect the box office receipts data (adjusted for inflation) for all movies made since 1977 to have a similar shape? Explain.

e) Below is a chart for the month-released data. What stands out to you about the results?

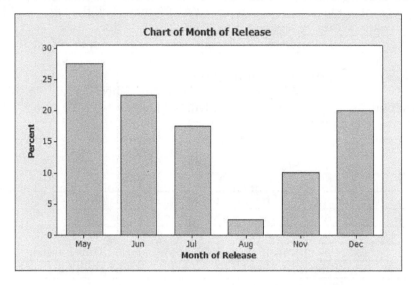

f) Below is a pie chart for the rating of the movies. Often, movie producers will edit movies a bit if necessary to change an R rating to a PG-13 rating. Does the pie chart seem to justify this? Explain.

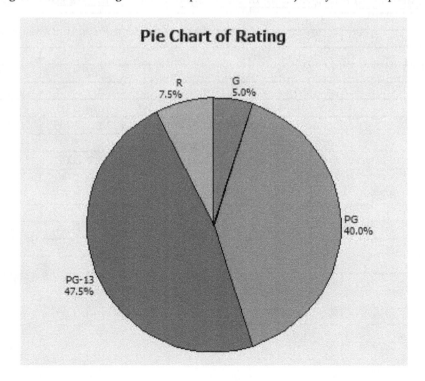

Chapter 2: Technology Project

1) The problem uses the application "Histogram Dist Quiz" located in the StatSims folder.
   a) Enter your name in the textbox provided. Change the sample size to 4000. Click the Start Quiz button.
   b) Take the quiz. If you miss a question, study the graph and the right answer in the pop-up window so that you get it right next time you see it. Take the quiz until you get at least 10 of 12 correct.
   c) Hold down the "ALT" key and press the "PRNT SCRN" button to copy the application window to memory. If the graph vanishes when you press "ALT", then click the "Refresh" button and try again. Paste the window image into your report in Word or a Google doc.
   d) Click clear and change the sample size to 100 and then click start quiz. Take the quiz until you get at least 9 of 12 correct.
   e) Use "ALT / PRNT SCRN" to copy and paste this window into your report.
   F) How much harder, if at all, would you say the quiz became when the sample size was reduced?
   g) (*Challenge*) See how many you can get correct with a sample size of 25. Use "ALT / PRNT SCRN" to copy and paste this window into your report.

Use the technology of your choice to complete problems 2 and 3 below.

2) a) Enter the data from Exercise (15) from Section 2.1 into your statistics application and name it.
   b) Create a histogram beginning with the class $3.5 - < 4$ and ending with a class that contains the max data value.
   c) Create a dotplot for the data.
   D) Based on the histogram and or dotplot of this sample, what would you guess is the distribution of the population? Explain.
   E) What change would you recommend to those collecting the sample so that the answer to (D) could be easier to determine? (See the notes that follow Theorem 2.1 in Section 2.4.)
   f) Create a stem-and-leaf diagram for the data using 1 line per stem.
   g) Create a stem-and-leaf diagram for the data using 2 lines per stem.
   H) Write out the class descriptions (lower and upper cutpoints) for each of the lines of the stem and leaf on part (g).

3) a) Enter the blood types from Exercise (40) into your statistics application and name the column.
   b) Enter the frequencies into another column.
   c) Use the technology to create a bar chart for the data.
   d) Use the technology to create a pie chart for the data.
   E) What key piece of information is clearly shown on the bar chart, but is missing on the pie chart?

Chapter 2: Chapter Review

Section 2.1

- A grouped data table contains classes, frequencies, relative frequencies, and midpoints (when appropriate).
- The lower cutpoint and upper cutpoint of a class are simply the left and right hand boundaries for the class description.
- The width of a class is the difference between consecutive lower cutpoints.
- The frequency of a class is a simple count of the number of items contained in the class.
- The relative frequency of a class is the ratio of the number of items in that class to the total number of items in the data set.
- Relative frequencies should be written in decimal form. If you must round them, use at least 4 decimal places.
- The midpoint for a class is the average of the lower and upper cutpoints of the class.
- The midpoint serves as a representative for the hidden data values when calculations need to be made.
- We use the '–' symbol for grouping discrete data and the '–<' for continuous data.
- We usually want to have between 5 and 20 classes when we group data.
- Do not begin or end your list of classes with an empty class.
- Each piece of data should fit into exactly one class.
- For single value grouping, no midpoint is needed.
- For grouping categorical data sets, no midpoint is needed.

Section 2.2

- A frequency histogram is a bar chart for quantitative data that uses the heights of the bars to illustrate the frequencies of the classes.
- A relative frequency histogram is a bar chart for quantitative data that uses the heights of the bars to illustrate the relative frequencies of the classes.
- Whether we are working with discrete or continuous data sets, the bars are drawn from lower cutpoint to lower cutpoint. This means that histograms do not have gaps between the bars.
- If you make a break in scale, remember to put the double slash mark on the number line. Breaks in scale are used to remove large unused sections of the number line or to move bars off of the vertical number line.
- For single value grouping, the bars are drawn directly on top of the numbers. The bars start and end at the midpoints of the single values that are your classes. No gaps should exist between the bars.
- A bar graph is the name used for categorical data.
- We label the bars rather than number the line for categorical data.
- There are gaps between the bars for categorical data.
- Pie charts are best done using technology. If drawing them by hand, look for nice percentages or sums of percentages to make it easier to judge the sizes of the slices.
- A dotplot consists of a horizontal axis with dots drawn above it for each data value.
- Dotplots help us see gaps and clusters in our data set and can show us values that stand apart from the rest of the data set.
- Be careful to stay consistent with the numbering on any axis to avoid making misleading graphs.

Section 2.3

- A stem and leaf diagram makes use of the raw data to form the visual.
- Part of the number makes up the class and the other part forms the graph.
- Typically the stem is the tens place digit and the leaf is the ones place, but other variations are permitted as long as the units are explained.
- A vertical line is drawn in to separate the stems from the leaves. This line acts as the axis for the graph.
- It is vital to carefully space the leaves to avoid making a misleading graph.
- Even though an ordered stem and leaf diagram is the standard, it is sometimes easier to make a non ordered stem and leaf first to help sort the raw data.
- You can make 2 or 5 lines per stem if needed to increase the number of classes.

Section 2.4

- Knowing the shape of the population's distribution is often important in later chapters to determine what procedures can be used to analyze the data.
- Even though we want to know the shape of the population, we usually only have graphs that are based on sample data.
- The graph of sample data gives us a hint as to what the shape of the population will be. Small samples only give us a rough idea of the population shape. Large samples can give us a very good idea of the shape of the population.
- The ten most important shapes for us are bell-shaped, uniform, left-skewed, right-skewed, severely left-skewed, severely right-skewed, left exponential, right-exponential, bimodal, and u-shaped.
- It is often good enough to recognize the population as bell-shaped, not severely skewed, or severely skewed.
- Symmetric distributions are one where the two sides are mirror images of one another.
- A skewed distribution is one where the data extends farther from the high point in one direction that in the other.
- Trying to determine the shape of the population by examining sample data can be like trying to identify a person through cloudy glass.

Review Diagrams:

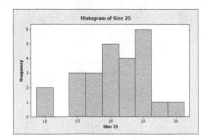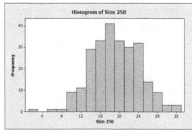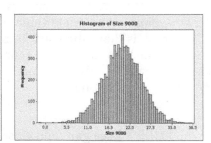

Small samples make it hard to determine the shape of the population. As the sample size becomes larger, it becomes easier to make out the true shape of the population.

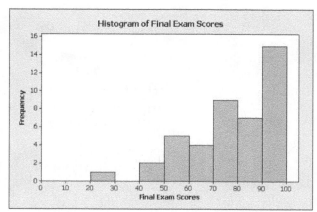

- Even for discrete classes like 70 – 79, we draw the bars from lower cutpoint to lower cutpoint.
- This means that there are no gaps between the bars, unless there is an empty class.

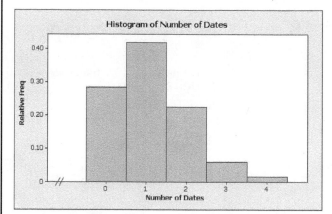

- For single value grouping, the bars go from half mark to half mark. So, the bars are centered over the value they represent.
- When zero is moved from its normal spot, we indicate this with slash marks on the number line.

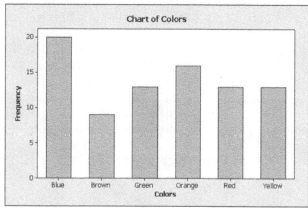

- For categorical data, we label the bars rather than numbering the line.
- Because there is no natural flow from one class to the next, there are gaps between the bars.

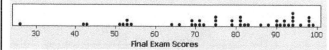

- In a dotplot, when you have repeated values or even values that are very close to each other, we stack them.
- Dotplots are used to show the location of the data values and they help us spot unusual data values.

Key Distribution Shapes

Bell-Shaped
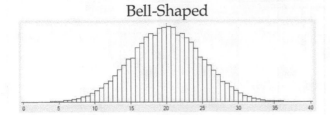

Uniform
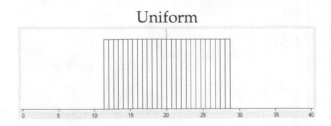

Left-Skewed
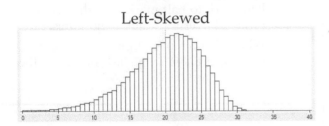

Right-Skewed
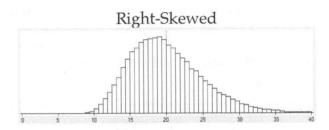

Severely Left-Skewed
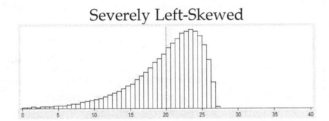

Severely Right-Skewed
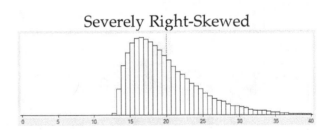

Left Exponential
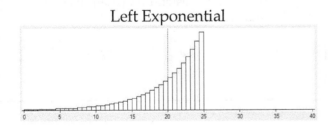

Right Exponential
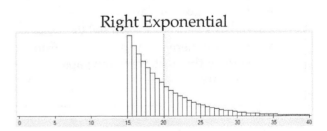

Bimodal
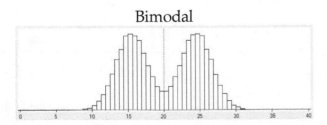

U-Shaped
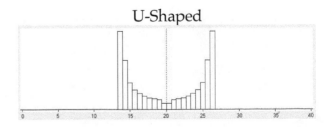

Chapter 2: Review Exercises

1) In January 2015, a nationwide survey was conducted regarding gas prices in the U.S. A random sample of 36 stations produced the following prices per gallon for regular unleaded gasoline.

1.83	2.26	2.22	2.22	1.96	2.18
2.03	2.05	1.95	1.93	1.99	1.98
1.73	2.36	1.80	3.37	2.01	1.93
2.04	1.89	2.49	2.57	2.04	2.10
1.92	2.01	2.25	2.12	2.53	2.88
1.93	2.18	2.29	1.94	1.88	1.99

a) Create a grouped data table for the data set beginning with the class $1.60 - < 1.80$.
b) Create a relative frequency histogram for the data set based on the classes from part (a) above.
c) What distribution shape do you think the population of gas prices had at that time? Explain.
d) What does this shape tell us about gas prices?

2) Starting on September 1, 2010, the author of this text attempted to lose weight by counting all calories consumed each day. The number of calories consumed for breakfast during each of the days of September is recorded in the table below.

172	290	635	350	862	240	290
586	202	333	280	289	319	280
517	446	335	483	354	290	75
290	196	614	915	291	421	400
165	232					

a) Create a grouped data table for the data set beginning with the class $0 - < 100$.
b) Create a relative frequency histogram for the data set based on the classes from part (a) above.
c) If we consider this to be a sample of breakfast calorie amounts for the author, then what distribution shape do you think the population of all breakfast calories would be? Explain.
d) What does this shape tell us about the author's breakfast habits?

3) An online poker player routinely plays in 9-player online tournaments. She kept track of the place she finished for 28 tournaments.

2	3	1	7	7	9	1
9	2	1	9	1	7	1
2	4	2	3	1	2	8
1	1	1	4	8	1	8

a) Make a grouped data table for the data using the method of single value grouping.
b) Create a frequency histogram for data using the single value classes from part (a).
c) The poker player makes a profit when she finishes in 1st, 2nd, or 3rd place. She loses money all other times. What does the table and graph tell you about her results?

4) A random sample of 27 college students was taken and the number of moving violations (speeding tickets, etc.) received in the last 3 years was obtained. The data is as follows:

0	4	1	0	1	2	0
1	0	0	0	1	4	0
2	2	0	2	0	1	0
11	0	0	0	2	6	

a) Make a grouped data table for the data using the method of single value grouping.
b) Create a frequency histogram for data using the single value classes from part (a).
c) What stood out to you once the data had been grouped and graphed?

5) In January 2015, a random sample of 28 college students was asked to name their preferred web browser. Their responses are shown below.

Safari	Explorer	Chrome	Chrome
Explorer	Safari	Safari	Chrome
Safari	Safari	Firefox	Chrome
Chrome	Chrome	Firefox	Explorer
Chrome	Safari	Safari	Chrome
Chrome	Chrome	Safari	Safari
Chrome	Explorer	Safari	Chrome

a) Create a grouped data table for their responses.
b) Create a bar chart for the frequencies.
c) Create a pie chart for the relative frequencies.
d) What info is easier to see now that the data has been grouped and graphed?

6) A random sample of 24 third graders was asked to name their favorite color. Their responses are shown below.

Pink	Blue	Red	Green
Blue	Red	Pink	Pink
Green	Pink	Orange	Pink
Pink	Blue	Blue	Red
Blue	Pink	Red	Blue
Purple	Purple	Pink	Pink

a) Create a grouped data table for their responses.
b) Create a bar chart for the frequencies.
c) Create a pie chart for the relative frequencies.
d) What info is easier to see now that the data has been grouped and graphed?

7) A random sample of Master's thesis projects for 30 randomly selected graduate students in English yielded the following number of pages.

50	74	54	77	63	71
49	55	55	47	54	42
52	50	65	52	54	120
48	102	40	66	51	51
59	83	52	48	87	60

a) Create a grouped data table for the data set beginning with the class $40 - 49$.
b) Create a dotplot for the data set.
c) What shape distribution do you suspect the population this sample was drawn from has? Explain.

8) A random sample of 35 randomly selected community college statistics students were asked how many units they were taking the semester they took Statistics. Their responses are shown below.

14	16	15	4	10	4
12	13	13	14	10	11
4	8	9	18	12	16
4	11	18	15	12	12
10	13	15	11	18	12
8	15	14	12	7	

a) Create a grouped data table for the data set beginning with the class $4 - 6$.
b) Create a dotplot for the data set.
c) What shape distribution do you suspect the population this sample was drawn from has? Explain.
d) Do you notice anything surprising in the graph? What might explain this?

9) A European roulette wheel only has 1 green slot, numbered 0. Similar to an American style wheel it also has red and black slots numbered from 1 to 36. A random sample of 49 plays of a European wheel produced the following numbers.

21	16	33	3	13	23	17
11	24	11	31	2	4	34
31	10	16	22	18	29	11
23	6	13	15	1	14	11
31	23	31	20	33	19	31
4	0	31	6	10	24	8
10	5	0	6	24	9	7

a) Create an ordered stem-and-leaf diagram for the data set using 1 line per stem.
b) Create an ordered stem-and-leaf diagram using 2 lines per stem.
c) Based on this sample data, what distribution shape do you think best describes the long-term list of numbers this wheel would produce?

10) A company produces a wall mount for large size HDTVs. The box claims that the wall mount can safely hold weights up to 200 pounds. In a recent test, they randomly chose 30 wall mounts and increased the amount of weight on them until they failed. The failure weights, in pounds, are listed below.

253	245	258	238	221	248
263	255	265	270	222	245
237	226	223	244	217	212
249	273	231	247	243	276
228	260	229	221	242	263

a) Create an ordered stem-and-leaf diagram for the data set using 1 line per stem.
b) Create an ordered stem-and-leaf diagram using 2 lines per stem.
c) Based on this sample data, what distribution shape do you think best describes the failure weights for these wall mounts?

11) A histogram for a random sample is shown below.

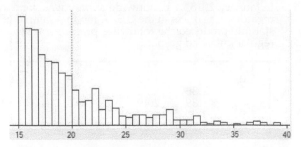

a) What shape distribution would you guess that the population has? Explain.
b) If the population really does have shape you specified in part (a), then why doesn't the graph look *exactly* like that shape?

12) A histogram for a random sample is shown below.

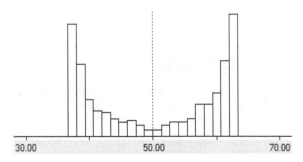

a) What shape distribution would you guess that the population has? Explain.
b) If the population really does have shape you specified in part (a), then why doesn't the graph look *exactly* like that shape?

13) A dotplot for a random sample is shown below.

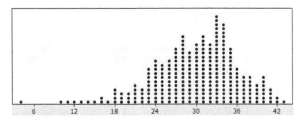

a) What shape distribution would you guess that the population has? Explain.
b) Random variation causes sample histograms to look only roughly like the true shape of the population. What can be done to reduce this effect of random variation?

14) A dotplot for a random sample is shown below.

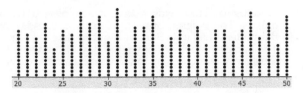

a) What shape distribution would you guess that the population has? Explain.
b) Random variation causes sample histograms to look only roughly like the true shape of the population. What can be done to reduce this effect of random variation?

15) A stem-and-leaf diagram for a random sample is shown below.

```
0 |8
1 |
1 |
2 |2
2 |5566778
3 |0011122222244444
3 |555556666677777788899999
4 |00000000001111111111222222222222222233333333333334444444444
4 |55556666666666666677777777778888888888888888999999999999
5 |00000000000000001111111111111112222222222233333333344444444
5 |555555555566666666677777777778888888888999999999
6 |00000001111112222222233333444444
6 |55555556677777999
7 |011
7 |559
8 |
8 |
9 |0
```

a) What shape distribution would you guess that the population has? Explain.
b) If the sample size was dramatically increased, what effect do you think that would have on the shape of this graph?

16) A stem-and-leaf diagram for a random sample is shown below.

```
 3 |444678
 4 |113344566666777778888889
 5 |0011222234445556666677788888999
 6 |02222333444455555556777
 7 |011112334455567777788888899999
 8 |12234444456666
 9 |011233456777778889
10 |00222235666
11 |001223344789
12 |224589
13 |022346679
14 |1267
15 |14
16 |27
17 |002
18 |779
19 |08
20 |123
21 |4
```

a) What shape distribution would you guess that the population has? Explain.
b) If the sample size was dramatically increased, what effect do you think that would have on the shape of this graph?

17) The histogram below shows the distances for 31 Hammer Throws for women competing at the 2012 Sacramento State Hornet Invitation track meet.

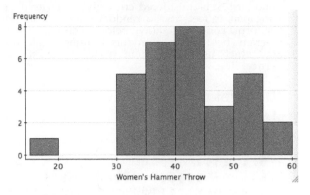

a) Create the grouped data table that corresponds to the histogram shown above.
b) Criticize the numbering used by StatCrunch on the horizontal axis.
c) What might explain the data value that stands apart from the rest?

18) The points scored by the winning teams in a sample of 48 games played during the 2007 NFL season are shown below.

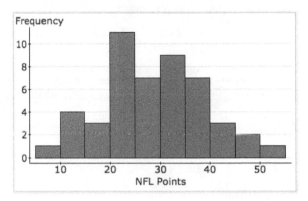

a) Create the grouped data table that corresponds to the histogram shown above.
b) If you were to randomly select 111 games from that NFL season, how many of those games would you expect to have the winning team scoring at least 20 points? Explain and show work.

19) The California condor is the largest North American Land bird. It is considered critically endangered. The wingspan, in feet, from a random sample of 65 adult California condors is shown below. The stem and leaf diagram below was produced using StatCrunch. StatCrunch uses a colon in place of the standard vertical line.

Decimal point is at the colon.
Leaf unit = 0.1

```
   7 : 8
   8 : 134444
   8 : 5556666666777888888899
   9 : 000111111222333344444444
   9 : 5556666779
  10 : 01
```

a) Write out the best estimate of the wingspans for the California condors represented by the fifth line of the graph.
b) Create the grouped data table that corresponds to the stem and leaf diagram shown above.
c) What is your best guess at the distribution for the wingspans of all adult California condors? Explain.
d) What percentage of the California condors have wingspans of at least 9.5 feet?

20) A sample of 45 community college students were asked how far they lived from the college, in miles. The Stem-and-Leaf diagram shown below summarizes their responses. Standard units are used for the stems and leaves. The graph was made using StatCrunch. StatCrunch uses a colon in place of the standard vertical line.

```
  0 : 112333344
  0 : 5555666666777888899
  1 : 0000022333
  1 : 5566
  2 : 2
  2 : 5
  3 :
  3 : 5
```

a) Write out the best estimate of the mileage for the students represented by the fourth line of the graph.
b) Create the grouped data table that corresponds to the stem and leaf diagram shown above.
c) What is your best guess at the distribution of the distances from school for the students at this college? Explain.
d) What percentage of the college students live less than ten miles from campus?

21) A statistics class was asked to complete a survey online. The assignment was given on a Tuesday and the students had until Sunday night to take the survey. The bar graph below shows the day of the week that the survey was taken by the 45 students in the class.

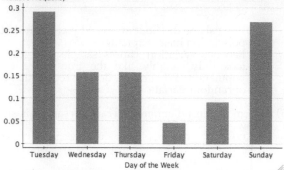

a) Why is this referred to as a bar graph rather than as a histogram?
b) Create the grouped data table that corresponds to the bar graph shown above.
c) Would you order the bars as shown or reorder them so that Sunday is first? Explain.
d) How many of the students waited until the weekend to fill out the survey?

22) According to Forbes Magazine, the top 6 valued U.S. companies on 8/11/2011 were as shown in the graph below.

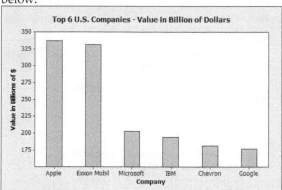

a) Ignoring the scale and only looking at the height of the bars, how many times more valuable does it appear Apple was than Google at this time? Explain.
b) Now, use the scale to estimate the value of Apple and Google at that time. How many times more valuable was Apple than Google according to the numbers?
c) What error was made to make this graph misleading?

Chapter 3 - Descriptive Measures for Populations and Samples

Chapter Problem: *2014 British Open Championship Golf Tournament*

On the final day of the 2014 British Open Championship golf tournament, 72 golfers participated in the day's play. Rory McIlroy, from Northern Ireland, shot a 71 that day and won the championship with a four-day total score of 271. In this tournament, two other golfers, Sergio Garcia of Spain and Rickie Fowler of the U.S. tied for second place. On the final day, Sergio shot a score of 66, but his four-day total was 273. Rickie shot a 67 and also finished with a four-day total score of 273. In order to tie with Rory and force a play-off, Sergio would have needed to shoot a 64 on the final day and Rickie would have needed to shoot a 65.

The questions we want to tackle regarding this are as follows: Given the scores shot by the other golfers, did Rory McIlroy have an unusually good score on the final day? Would it have taken an unusually good score for someone to catch him? What would be the expected score range for a professional golfer that day? In addition to answering these questions, we will also use the data from that day to illustrate the need for checking a data set for suspicious values before making statistical calculations. In this chapter we will explore the necessary tools for answering the questions above and many other similar ones. After all of the needed tools are introduced in the chapter we will return to explore the 2014 British Open Championship in the chapter problem.

Would it have been realistic for one of Rory McIlroy's competitors to make up the necessary strokes on the final day of the 2014 British Open golf tournament to force a play-off to decide the Championship?

Introduction:

In the last chapter we learned how to organize data into charts and graphs. In this chapter we will learn how to numerically summarize data using a few important quantities calculated from the data. Our main focus will be calculating measures of center and spread for a data set and learning how to use these to get an idea of what is expected and what is unusual in a data set. In addition, we will learn how percentiles and quartiles can help us understand where a specific person or item fits into a larger data set. We will also learn a new graph that helps us detect errors and unusual observations in a data set. This chapter meets many students' expectations of what a statistics class is about, as we will begin making some involved calculations with our data sets in this chapter. We will explore all of this and much more in the following sections:

Let's get started.

Section 3.1 - Measures of Center

In this section we will discuss a few different measures of center for a data set. Most statistical work is done with sample data. However, it is the goal of inferential statistics to use sample values to estimate population values. Because of this, our goal is to become familiar with both population and sample measures of center. We will begin by examining the **mean**, a familiar value with a new name.

Definition: *Population Mean and Sample Mean*

Mean: the mean (or arithmetic mean) of a data set is the quantity you probably already know as the average. To calculate a mean we simply add up all the data values and then divide by the number of data values we have. The population mean is denoted by μ, a Greek letter pronounced "mew". The sample mean is denoted by $\overline{x}$, pronounced "x-bar".

Formulas: Note, $\sum x$ means add up all the data values

$$\text{Population Mean} = \mu = \frac{\sum x}{N} \; ; \; N = \text{population size}$$

$$\text{Sample Mean} = \overline{x} = \frac{\sum x}{n} \; ; \; n = \text{sample size}$$

Rounding Note: If you decide to round your answer for a mean, then you should use *at least* one more decimal place than was used in the original data set.

Let's look at an example.

Example 3.1: *U.S. box office gross for the 2014 best picture nominees*

In 2014, the Academy Awards had 9 movies nominated for the best picture award. *12 Years a Slave* won best picture that year. All 9 nominees are shown in the table below together with their gross U.S. box office receipts, in millions of dollars (Source: IMDb.com).

56.7	12 Years a Slave	116.9	The Wolf of Wall St.
37.7	Philomena	107.1	Captain Phillips
150.1	American Hustle	274.0	Gravity
17.6	Nebraska	25.6	Her
27.3	Dallas Buyers Club		

Is the Oscar for best picture a reflection of a movie's box office success?

a) Find the mean U.S. box office gross for the movies. Assume that the calculation is being made solely for the purpose of describing that year's best picture nominees.

b) What percentage of the movies had below average U.S. box office grosses?

Solution:

a) Because the results are only being used to summarize the year's nominees, this will be a population mean. The total for the 9 movies is $813 million.

$$\text{Population mean} = \mu = \frac{\sum x}{N} = \frac{813}{9} \approx 90.33 \Rightarrow \$90.33 \text{ million}$$

Because the original data was given with 1 decimal place, the rounding rule for means requires that we use at least two decimal places if we round our answer.

Caution: *Which kind of mean?*

When we are asked to find the mean, we must remember that it could be a sample or a population mean. We must use the context of the problem to determine which type is needed.

Key Concept: *Rounding Error*

It is common to round answers. When you do so, you should use the approximately equal symbol, $\approx$, to make it clear that you have introduced rounding error.

b) 5 of the 9 movies had below average grosses. So, the percent is: $\dfrac{5}{9} \approx 0.5556 = 55.56\%$

Example 3.2: Average *Cell Phone Bill for College Students*

In November 2014, a random sample of 14 college students was asked to report the amount of their most recent cell phone bill. The data below shows those amounts, in dollars.

| 278 | 200 | 250 | 88 | 30 | 53 | 140 |
| 45 | 60 | 77 | 80 | 114 | 100 | 200 |

What does it really mean to have an above average cell phone bill?

a) Find the mean of the data set if the results will be used to estimate the average cell phone bill for all college students.

b) Did the student who paid $114 have an above or below average phone bill? Explain.

c) Was the $114 phone bill in the top or bottom half of the results for this data set? Explain.

d) What percentage of the phone bills were above average?

Solution:

a) Because the results are only going to be used to estimate the average phone bill for all college students, this is a sample data set. Therefore, we will be finding a sample mean this time. To find the mean we start by adding together all of the data values. The sum of the data set is 1715. There are 14 values in the set, so we get:

$$\text{Sample Mean} = \bar{x} = \frac{\sum x}{n} = \frac{1715}{14} = 122.5 \quad \Rightarrow \text{ The sample mean is } \$122.50$$

b) This student's phone bill of $114 is lower than the mean of $122.50. So, it is a below average phone bill.

c) 8 of the 14 phone bills in the data set are lower than $114. Therefore, the phone bill of $114 is in the top half of the data set.

d) Only 5 of the 14 phone bills, {278, 200, 250, 140, 200}, were above the average of $122.50.

So, the percentage is: $\dfrac{5}{14} \approx 0.3571 = 35.71\%$

In the preceding phone bill example, we saw that only 35.71% of the phone bills were above the average of $122.50. This may seem counter intuitive, but it is a fairly common occurrence. The reason this happened in that example was that a few of the students had phone bills that were much higher than the rest of the phone bills. Extremes can have a large effect on the mean of a data set by pulling the mean towards them. This is often considered to be one of the disadvantages of using a mean as a measure of center.

> **Key Concept:** *Extremes pull the mean in their direction.*
>
> One disadvantage of the mean is that it can be strongly affected by extreme values in the data set. When this happens the mean of the data set might not be near what people intuitively think of as the middle of the data set. Extremes on one side of a data set tend to pull or *skew* the mean in the direction of those extremes.

THE MEDIAN: *Another type of measure of center*

Despite the fact that extremes can pull the mean away from the middle of the data set, they are still a very important quantity in statistics. Later in the chapter, we will see that we measure the spread of a data set by examining the difference between individual data values and the mean of the data set. The mean is also commonly used to calculate an individual's "fair share" when items are pooled together and then redistributed equally. Another important quality of the mean is that it creates a center of mass or balancing point for the values in a data set. However, sometimes people really are looking for a value that splits a data set into two equal halves. Because people are often interested in knowing whether their data is in the top or bottom half of a data set, it is useful to define a measure of center that splits a data set into an upper and lower half. The **median** attempts to do exactly that.

Definition: *The Median of a data set*

Median: The median, denoted M, of an *ordered* data set is:
   a) the value in the middle of the set (if the number of data values is odd) OR
   b) the mean of the two middle values (if the number of data values is even).

Location of the Median: the following formula can be used to help determine the location of the median of a data set. This is useful when a data set becomes too large for us to recognize the middle of a data set visually.

$$\text{For population data: } L_M = \frac{1}{2}(N+1), \text{ OR for sample data } L_M = \frac{1}{2}(n+1)$$

Note: If the location is a decimal value, then we find the mean of the two values in the locations surrounding the calculated location.

$$\text{Example: } L_M = 6.5 \Rightarrow M = \frac{(6\text{th number})+(7\text{th number})}{2}$$

Example 3.3: *Cell Phone Bills (Revisited)*

The cell phone bills from a random sample of 14 college students from Example 3.2 are shown again below.

278	200	250	88	30	53	140
45	60	77	80	114	100	200

a) Find the median of the data set.

b) Use the student whose bill was $114 to explain why the median might be a better measure of center for this data set than the mean of $122.50.

Solution:

a) The median is found for ordered data sets. This data set is not in order, so we must start by putting it in order. The ordered list is shown below.

$$30, 45, 53, 60, 77, 80, 88, 100, 114, 140, 200, 200, 250, 278$$

Because there are an even number of data values, the median will be the mean of the two middle values in this ordered list. We can use the location formula to determine which values to use.

$$L_M = \frac{1}{2}(n+1) = \frac{1}{2}(14+1) = 7.5 \quad \Rightarrow \text{Median} = M = \frac{88+100}{2} = \$94$$

The median of \$94 accomplishes our goal of dividing the data set into an upper and lower half. We have 7 phone bills below \$94 and 7 above \$94.

b) If the goal is to give college students a sense of whether they have one of the more expensive plans or one of the cheaper plans, then the median is probably more appropriate than the mean. Notice that the student whose bill was \$114 had a below average phone bill, but was actually in the top half of the data set because that student's bill is above the median of \$94.

It was mentioned earlier that the mean of a data set could be pulled or skewed by extreme values in a data set. When extremes pull the mean to the left of the median this indicates that the data set is left-skewed. If extremes pull the mean to the right of the median, then this indicates that the data set is right-skewed. If a data set is roughly symmetric, then the mean and the median will be about the same. In the example above, the more expensive cell phone bills have pulled the mean, \$122.50, to the right of the median, \$94. Therefore, that data set would be considered to be right-skewed. This is summarized and illustrated in the following Point to Remember.

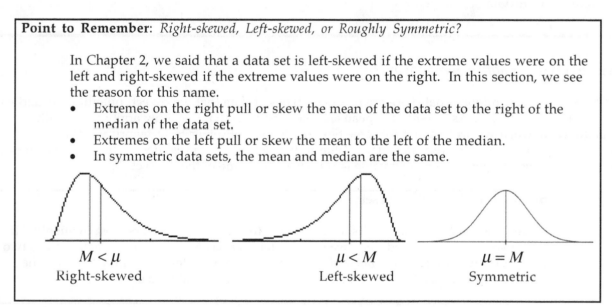

Point to Remember: *Right-skewed, Left-skewed, or Roughly Symmetric?*

In Chapter 2, we said that a data set is left-skewed if the extreme values were on the left and right-skewed if the extreme values were on the right. In this section, we see the reason for this name.
- Extremes on the right pull or skew the mean of the data set to the right of the median of the data set.
- Extremes on the left pull or skew the mean to the left of the median.
- In symmetric data sets, the mean and median are the same.

$M < \mu$ $\mu < M$ $\mu = M$

Right-skewed   Left-skewed   Symmetric

Example 3.4: *U.S. box office gross for 2014 best picture nominees (Revisited)*

All 9 best picture nominees from 2014 are shown in the table below together with their gross U.S. box office receipts, in millions of dollars (Source: IMDb.com).

56.7	12 Years a Slave	116.9	The Wolf of Wall St.
37.7	Philomena	107.1	Captain Phillips
150.1	American Hustle	274.0	Gravity
17.6	Nebraska	25.6	Her
27.3	Dallas Buyers Club		

a) Find the median of the data set.

b) In Example 3.1, we found the mean of this data set to be \$90.33 million. Comparing this with the median, would you describe this data set as left-skewed, right-skewed, or neither? Explain.

Solution:

a) The first thing we have to do is put the data in order:

$$17.6 \quad 25.6 \quad 27.3 \quad 37.7 \quad 56.7 \quad 107.1 \quad 116.9 \quad 150.1 \quad 274.0$$

Because there is an odd number of data values, the median will be the middle value in the ordered list. We can use the location formula to determine which value to use.

$$L_M = \frac{1}{2}(N+1) = \frac{1}{2}(9+1) = 5 \quad \Rightarrow \quad \text{Median} = M = 56.7$$

The median of $56.7 million accomplishes our goal of dividing the data set into an upper and lower half. We have 4 receipt totals below $56.7 million and 4 above it.

b) In Example 3.1 we found that $\mu \approx \$90.33$ million. This value is further to the right in the list than the median, because it has been pulled (skewed) by the extreme value $274.0 million. Therefore, this is a right-skewed data set.

THE MODE: *Another measure of center?*

In Chapter 1, we mentioned that there are two main types of data that we collect, quantitative and categorical data. One of the drawbacks to both the mean and the median is that they only apply to quantitative data. So what do we do when we are looking for some type of measure of center for categorical data? One answer is to look for the most frequently repeated data value in the set. This can be done with both numbers and word values. This most frequently repeated value is known as the **mode** of the data set.

> **Definition:** The Mode of a data set
>
> **Mode**: The mode of a data set is the data value (or values) that occurs most frequently. If no values are repeated, then we say the data set has *No Mode*. If the data set has two modes, we say that it is *bimodal*. If there are three modes we call it *trimodal*. The mode can be applied to both quantitative and categorical data sets.

Example 3.5: *Teacher Evaluations*

It is common for students to be asked to evaluate the performance of the instructor in the classes they take. On one such evaluation, the students were asked to rate their instructors "logic and clarity of explanations." They were asked to rate the instructor from a low of 1 to a high of 5. The ratings for one instructor from a class of 27 students are shown below.

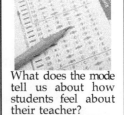

What does the mode tell us about how students feel about their teacher?

| 3 | 5 | 5 | 5 | 2 | 5 | 4 | 3 | 5 | 4 | 4 | 5 | 1 | 5 |
| 2 | 4 | 2 | 5 | 4 | 2 | 3 | 5 | 1 | 3 | 4 | 3 | 5 | |

a) Find the mode of the data set.

b) Interpret the mode of the data set.

Solution:

a) Again, the first thing we should do is put the data in order:

1	1	2	2	2	2	3	3	3	3	3	4	4	4
4	4	4	5	5	5	5	5	5	5	5	5	5	

All the values in this data set are repeated: 1 (2 times), 2 (4 times), 3 (5 times), 4 (6 times), and 5 (10 times). The mode is not all repeated numbers, but only the one that repeats the most often. In this case, the rating of 5 is the most repeated value.

$$\text{Mode} = 5$$

b) The most common rating given to the instructor in the category "logic and clarity of explanations" was a 5. Because this is the highest possible rating, it appears that the most common perception is that the instructor is doing a great job in this area.

Even though we call the mode a measure of center, it really could be anywhere in the data set. Nothing would prevent the lowest or highest (as in the previous example) number in the data set from being the mode. If it is the one with the most repeats, it is the mode, regardless of its location in the data set.

Let's look at an example where we are dealing with categorical data.

Example 3.6: *Favorite Paris Tourist Sites*

After completing a 4-day tour of Paris and the surrounding areas, the members of a tourist group were asked to choose the favorite thing that they saw. Their answers are shown in the table below.

This is clearly a Paris icon, but is it the top tourist attraction?

Sacre Coeur	Eiffel Tower	Notre Dame	Louvre
Louvre	Eiffel Tower	Louvre	Musee d'Orsay
Louvre	Eiffel Tower	Champs Elysees	Champs Elysees
Notre Dame	Louvre	Arc de Triomphe	Notre Dame
Eiffel Tower	Montmarte	Eiffel Tower	Arc de Triomphe

a) Find the mode of the data set.

b) Explain why the mode is more appropriate for this data set than the mean or the median.

Solution:

a) Two values are tied for the most repeats. The Eiffel Tower and the Louvre both show up 5 times. Therefore, this data set has two modes: Eiffel Tower and the Louvre.

b) It is not possible to find the mean for categorical data and the data must be ordered to find the median. True, we could put the data into alphabetical order, but then the middle value really doesn't mean anything in terms of most popular tourist sites. The mode does get to the heart of the question: "What was the most popular site among this group of tourists?"

CHOOSING THE APPROPRIATE MEASURE OF CENTER: *How to Decide*

We have now seen three different measures of center, but which one should we choose when working with a particular data set? We will now look at a few of the distinguishing features of the different measures and see how this helps us pick a particular measure when working with a data set.

Measure of Center	Interpretations	Best Choice for:
Mean	• Center of Mass • Balances total distance of data on the left with distances on the right. • Fair or equal share value when redistributing items among group members.	• Situations where the total of the data values is important. • Finding a balancing point for the data set. • Finding the fair share when sharing the total among group members.
Median	• Attempts to separate the lower 50% of the data set from the upper 50%.	• Situations where we want to let people know if they are in the top or bottom half of the data set. • Skewed data sets where estimating the total is not our goal, so we don't want extremes affecting the center.
Mode	• The most commonly repeated value.	• Categorical data where means and medians cannot be computed.

Example 3.7: *Choosing the most appropriate measure of center*

For each of the data sets below, decide what would be the most appropriate measure of center to use for the situation described. Explain your reasoning.

a) A newspaper has collected home price data for an area and wants to give people in that area an idea of what a typical home costs.

b) Blood type data is collected and the researchers want to know what the most common blood type is.

c) A student has taken 5 tests in a class and is interested to know how she is doing in the class.

Solution:

a) They should use the median because half of the homes will be less expensive than the median and half of the homes will be more expensive. If they used the mean, it would probably come out higher because of really expensive homes in the area skewing the mean to the right.

b) Because this is categorical data and they are looking for the most common value, they should use the mode.

c) Because all scores will ultimately count in the grade, the student should use the mean. Extreme test scores will affect the grade and therefore should be taken into account. The total is important in this case. The mean becomes more useful when the total is important.

Example 3.8: *Using the mean to estimate totals*

a) In Example 3.2, we found the mean for our random sample of 14 student cell phone bills to be $122.50. Suppose that bookstore is offering a promotion where they will randomly select 30 students who purchase textbooks from them and the bookstore will pay those students' most recent cell phone bill. How much should they expect to pay?

b) In Example 3.1, we found that the mean gross box office receipts for the 9 nominees for best picture to be $90.33 million. Explain why it would not be appropriate to use this mean to estimate the total gross box office receipts for a random sample of 25 other movies from that year.

Solution:

a) Because $122.50 was the mean from a random sample, it should be considered to be a reasonable estimate of the mean cell phone bill for all students. If the bookstore were to randomly choose 30 students, they should expect to get a similar value for the mean of that group. Therefore, we can get a reasonable estimate for what the bookstore should end up paying by multiplying the sample mean by the number of students.

$$\text{Expected Payment} = 30 \cdot \bar{x} = 30(122.50) = \$3,675$$

b) They key to making the estimate above is that the sample mean was a reasonable estimate of the population mean. This should be true with a random sample, which should be a representative sample. However, in the gross box office receipts example, we were looking at the gross for the 9 nominees for best picture. It is fine to examine this data set as a population, but it should not be considered to be a representative sample of all movies from that year. This data set was handpicked rather than randomly selected. Therefore, we should not expect the mean from this data set to be a good estimate for the mean of all movies from that year.

WRAP SESSION: *Looking at all the measures side by side*

We will now look at one final example that shows all of the different measures of center for a single data set. This will help us see the differences and benefits of the different measures. This example will also explore how changes to the extreme values affect the various measures of center.

Example 3.9: *Salaries for the 2009 World Series Champions*

In 2009, the New York Yankees won the World Series. Many baseball fans feel that the Yankees enjoy so much success because their owners are willing to spend so much money on players' salaries. The salaries for the players on the 2009 Yankee roster are shown below. Salaries are shown in millions of dollars.

Is the Yankee success partially due to high player salaries?

0.40	0.43	1.25	5.00	13.00	16.50
0.40	0.43	1.40	5.40	13.00	20.63
0.40	0.46	2.13	5.50	13.10	21.60
0.41	0.53	3.75	6.00	15.00	33.00
0.42	1.24	5.00	6.55	15.29	

a) Find the mean of the data set. Assume we are only using this to describe the 2009 Yankee Salaries.

b) Find the median of the data set.

c) Find the mode of the data set.

d) Which of these measures of center would best tell a player on that team where his salary ranks among the other players? Explain.

e) Which measure of center would be best to use when arguing that the Yankees have success due to their high payroll? Explain.

f) What effect would it have on the 3 measures of center if the highest salary were changed from 33.00 to 55.00?

Solution:

a) Because we are only seeking to describe the 2009 Yankee salaries and we have all of them, this is population data. Therefore, we will calculate the population mean.

$$\mu = \frac{\sum x}{N} = \frac{208.22}{29} = 7.18 \text{ or } \$7.18 \text{ million}$$

b) Normally, we begin this process by putting the data set in order. Fortunately, this has already been done for this data set. So, we can just calculate the location and identify the median.

$$L_M = \frac{1}{2}(29+1) = 15 \implies M = 5.00 \text{ or } \$5.00 \text{ million}$$

c) There are several values that are repeated twice in this data set. However, the most repeated was 0.40, which occurred 3 times in the data set. So the mode is 0.40 or $0.40 million.

d) The median would be the best for that because it separates the top half of the salaries from the bottom half. The mean has been skewed to the right by the extremely high salaries. This means that you can be in the top half of the salaries, but still have a below average salary. The worst measure for this would be the mode. In this case, the mode turned out to be the minimum salary for the team. So, every player on the team is at or above the mode.

e) The mean would be the best because it incorporates the total the team spent on salaries during the 2009 season. If the Yankees have a higher mean salary then other teams, then that will indicate that they are spending more on salaries. This might not be true if we used the median or the mode.

f) If the top salary on the Yankees were changed from 33.00 to 55.00, it would have no effect at all on the mode or the median. However, because it would change the grand total, it would end up affecting the mean. The mean should become even more skewed to the right by such a change. Let's verify this.

$$\mu = \frac{\sum x}{N} = \frac{230.22}{29} \approx 7.939$$

In the example above, we saw that while the mean was skewed by the extreme values in the data set, the median is not affected by these extremes. When a value is not affected by the extremes in the data set, we say that the value is **resistant**.

Definition: *resistant*

Resistant: If the value of a calculated quantity is not affected, either at all or only very little, by the extremes in the data set, then that value is said to be resistant.

Note: The median is resistant, but the mean is not.

Let's practice what we have learned with some exercises.

Exercise Set 3.1

Concept Review: Review the definitions and concepts from this section by filling in the blanks for each of the following.

1) $\bar{x}$ is the symbol for the _____ mean and μ is the symbol for the _____ mean.

2) The median of an odd data set is the value in the _____ of the ordered list. If the number of values is even, then the median is the _____ of the two middle values.

3) L_M stands for the _____ of the median.

4) The mean is the _____ point of a data set. It balances the total _____ of the data on the left with _____ on the right. The mean is considered to be the _____ share value.

5) The mode is the data value that is _____ the most. If no values are repeated, then we say that there is _____ _____ .

6) Extremes in a data set pull or _____ the mean in the direction of the extremes. The median is not affected by extremes. This tells us that the median is _____ .

7) Use the median when you want to separate the data set into a lower _____ and an upper _____ . Use the mean if the _____ is important.

8) The mode is the only appropriate measure of center to use when working with _____ data.

Mechanics: Practice using the formulas from this section on each of the following. Include the appropriate symbol with each answer.

9) Suppose this is population data.

19	21	15	16	18	19
14	22	15	22	21	19
23	24	23	9	17	18

a) Calculate the mean for the data set.
b) Calculate the median of the data set.
c) Find the mode(s) for the data set.

10) Suppose this is population data.

22	16	18	13	19	18
16	15	19	7	5	13
14	16	17	15	18	

a) Calculate the mean for the data set.
b) Calculate the median of the data set.
c) Find the mode(s) for the data set.

11) Suppose this is sample data.

63.98	33.11	61.88	62.68	58.36	69.75
50.64	76.2	26.53	65.89	72.40	23.45

a) Calculate the mean for the data set.
b) Calculate the median of the data set.
c) Find the mode(s) for the data set.

12) Suppose this is sample data.

12.8	1.0	0.8	2.8	4.2	4.1
13.4	4.4	5.5	3.9	4.2	

a) Calculate the mean for the data set.
b) Calculate the median of the data set.
c) Find the mode(s) for the data set.

Applications: Use the procedures shown in the examples of this section to calculate any requested quantities. Label all of your answers with the appropriate symbols.

13) The following data set contains the number of hits a child got in all 15 little league games played during the season. We are only interested in summarizing his hits for the season.

1	2	2	4	2
2	0	4	1	1
1	0	0	3	1

a) Calculate the mean for the data set.
b) Calculate the median of the data set.
c) Find the mode(s) for the data set.
d) Which of the three measures would you use if you were trying to decide if this player is the best hitter on the team? Explain.
e) Would you describe this data set as left-skewed, right-skewed, or neither? Explain.

14) The following data set represents the number of cars sold per month by a salesperson during the last year. We are only seeking to summarize the year's data.

6	4	4	7	9	4
2	7	5	7	5	4

a) Calculate the mean for the data set.
b) Calculate the median of the data set.
c) Find the mode(s) for the data set.
d) Which of the three measures would you use if you were trying to decide the sales person of the year at this car lot? Explain.
e) Would you describe this data set as left-skewed, right-skewed, or neither? Explain.

15) The monthly utility bills for the month of May were collected from a random sample of 12 homes in a city and were as follows. We are trying to make estimates about utility bills in May for the entire city.

274	172	104	134	214	358
236	152	117	172	198	263

a) Calculate the mean for the data set.
b) Calculate the median of the data set.
c) Find the mode(s) for the data set.
d) If you lived in this town and your May utility bill was $197, then would you expect that you were in the lower half of the utility bills for the city or in the upper half? Explain.
e) Would you describe this data set as left-skewed, right-skewed, or neither? Explain.

16) A local golf course randomly selected 23 players on a Saturday and asked them to report their scores for that day's gold game. Their sorted scores are shown below. We want to use these scores to make estimates about all the golfers that played this course that Saturday.

71	81	85	85	88	88
89	89	91	93	93	93
95	96	96	97	98	98
98	99	100	102	106	

a) Calculate the mean for the data set.
b) Calculate the median of the data set.
c) Find the mode(s) for the data set.
d) If you played a round of golf at this course on that particular Saturday and your score was 92, then would you expect that you were in the lower half of the scores for the day or the upper half? Explain.
e) Would you describe this data set as left-skewed, right-skewed, or neither? Explain.

17) The adult lift ticket prices for a random sample of 16 U.S. ski/snowboard resorts are listed in the table below. The prices are for the 2014/2015 season. (Source: OnTheSnow.com). We wish to make estimates about adult lift ticket prices in the U.S. for that year.

95	75	42	90	78	62
102	54	118	35	47	29
50	68	69	39		

a) Calculate the mean for the data set.
b) Calculate the median of the data set.
c) Would you describe this data set as left-skewed, right-skewed, or neither? Explain.
d) During that season, if you randomly chose 23 ski/snowboard resorts and bought one adult lift ticket from each one, what would you expect for the total cost of the 23 tickets?

18) A gamer is playing the drums on the hard level in the game *Rock Band*. The data set below shows the percentage of notes played correctly for 9 randomly selected songs. We wish to use this data to make estimates about the gamer's abilities for all the songs in the game.

86	77	90	91	94
89	92	92	91	

a) Calculate the mean for the data set.
b) Calculate the median of the data set.
c) Would you describe this data set as left-skewed, right-skewed, or neither? Explain.
d) If the gamer were to play all of the songs in this game, would you expect the gamer to play at least 90% of the notes correctly most of the time? Explain.

19) A group of 5th graders were allowed to buy milkshakes on a class field trip. The flavors chosen by each of the 20 kids are shown below.

Strawberry	Strawberry	Chocolate	Vanilla
Vanilla	Strawberry	Strawberry	Vanilla
Vanilla	Strawberry	Chocolate	Vanilla
Banana	Chocolate	Vanilla	Vanilla
Vanilla	Vanilla	Chocolate	Chocolate

a) What is the only appropriate measure of center for this data set? Explain.
b) Find the mode(s) for the flavors chosen by this group of 5th graders.
c) Interpret the mode.

20) A group of college students are asked the make of the car that they own. Students that do not drive a car responded with none. The results are shown below.

None	Ford	Chevy	Mazda
Honda	Toyota	Mazda	Honda
Honda	Toyota	Toyota	Audi
Hyundai	Mazda	Toyota	Toyota
None	Ford	Honda	None

a) What is the only appropriate measure of center for this data set? Explain.
b) Find the mode(s) for the make of car owned by this group of college students.
c) Interpret the mode.

21) A random sample of 11 Holstein dairy cows was taken and the annual milk production, in liters, was measured for each of the cows. The results are shown below. We wish to use this data to make estimates for the annual milk production for all Holstein dairy cows.

8007	7667	7192	6985
8023	7577	6623	7685
7122	8062	7894	

a) Calculate the mean for the data set.
b) Calculate the median of the data set.
c) What percentage of these dairy cows have an above average annual milk production?
d) A dairy farmer is planning on buying 47 Holstein dairy cows. What should he expect his total annual milk production to be from these 47 cows?

22) The top 15 grossing movies, for the opening weekend, as of January 6, 2015, are as follows (Source: BoxOfficeMojo.com). The data is in millions of dollars. We wish to summarize the receipt data for these 15 movies.

Movie	Gross
The Avengers	207.4
Iron Man 3	174.1
Harry Potter: Deathly Hallows Part 2	169.2
The Dark Knight Rises	160.9
The Dark Knight	158.4
The Hunger Games: Catching Fire	158.1
The Hunger Games	152.5
Spider-Man 3	151.1
The Twilight Saga: New Moon	142.8
The Twilight Saga: Breaking Dawn Part 2	141.1
The Twilight Saga: Breaking Dawn Part 1	138.1
Pirates of the Caribbean: Dead Man's Chest	135.6
Iron Man 2	128.1
Harry Potter: Deathly Hallows Part 1	125.0
The Hunger Games: Mockingjay Part 1	121.9

a) Calculate the mean for the data set.
b) Calculate the median of the data set.
c) What percentage of the movies have an above average gross?
d) Explain why it would not be accurate to use the mean of this data set to estimate the total opening weekend gross for the next 25 movies to be released.

23) The Beech 1900 Turboprop aircraft has a capacity of 18 passengers. On a recent full flight, the weights of the passengers, in pounds, were as shown below. We wish to summarize the weights of these passengers.

133	146	182	22	186	209
224	151	105	164	155	199
115	89	159	70	141	173

a) Calculate the mean for the data set.
b) Calculate the median of the data set.
c) What percentage of the passengers have a below average weight?
d) Which of the measures of center would be more useful to an airline worker who needed to make sure that the total weight of the cargo and passengers was below the maximum allowed level? Explain.

24) A random sample of 16 Intermediate Algebra students completed a chapter quiz using an online homework system. The time, in minutes, spent by each of the 16 students on the assignment is shown below. We wish to use this data to make estimates about all such students that will take this quiz.

35	46	13	38	47	35
25	37	36	41	42	29
41	44	12	22		

a) Calculate the mean for the data set.
b) Calculate the median of the data set.
c) What percentage of the students have a below average time?
d) Which of the measures of center should be given to a student who is asking how long the typical student spends taking this quiz? Explain.

25) The appraised value of all the homes on a short street were obtained and listed in the table below. The values listed are in thousands of dollars. We wish to summarize the appraised values for this street.

525	461	477
523	598	430
517	559	507

a) Calculate the mean for the data set.
b) Calculate the median of the data set.
c) Which of these two values would be most useful to the county property tax collector? Explain.
d) Which of the two values would be most useful to an owner on this street who wanted to know if he had one of the more expensive homes on the street? Explain.
e) Suppose that the home appraise at 598 thousand dollars was remodeled and had a large addition built and now appraised for 815 thousand dollars. What effect if any would this have on the mean and median of the data set?

26) A random sample of 14 college students were surveyed and asked how many minutes they exercise per week. The times reported are shown below. We wish to use these times to estimate the exercise time for all college students.

120	0	0	240	445	300	90
0	360	90	60	0	150	300

a) Calculate the mean for the data set.
b) Calculate the median of the data set.
c) Find the mode(s) for the data set.
d) Suppose that the student that reported 445 minutes of exercise actually only worked out 145 minutes. What effect if any would correcting this value have on the mean and median of the data set?
e) Which measure of center do you feel is most appropriate for this application? Explain.

27) For each of the following situations, explain whether the mean, median, or mode would be the most appropriate measure of center. Briefly explain your answer.

a) The eye color of all the students in a class is noted. We are looking for the most common eye color.
b) A person has all his weekly paycheck stubs for the past year. He wants to make a statement about his weekly income level.
c) The income levels for all the people who live in a certain city are collected. We want to make a statement about the typical income level for that city.

28) For each of the following situations, explain whether the mean, median, or mode would be the most appropriate measure of center. Briefly explain your answer.

a) A golfer has all his scores for the last year and he wants to know his typical score (perhaps for establishing his handicap).
b) A candy company counts the number of pieces of candy that went into each of its bags. It wants to print a number on the bags telling people how many pieces to expect, on average, per bag.
c) A researcher wants to make a statement about the most common blood type among people in a given country.

29) The hourly salaries, in dollars per hour, for each of the 15 employees at a local flower shop are shown below. We wish to summarize these salaries.

9.75	10.25	11.50	14.00	13.50
12.50	9.75	19.75	9.75	10.25
10.00	9.75	10.25	11.75	9.75

a) Calculate the mean for the data set.
b) Calculate the median of the data set.
c) Find the mode(s) for the data set.
d) Would you describe this data set as left-skewed, right-skewed, or neither? Explain.
e) Which of these measures of center would best tell an employee of this flower shop where they rank among the other employees? Explain.
f) Which of these measures of center would be best for the owner to use when thinking about payroll expenses? Explain.
g) What effect would it have on the 3 measures of center if the highest paid employee's hourly rate were changed from $19.75/hour to $29.75/hour?

30) After the field in the 2014 WSOP was reduced to 693 players remaining from the initial field of 6,683 players, a random sample of 18 players was chosen. The ages of those 18 players are shown below. We wish to make estimates about the 693 players that made the money.

23	34	24	21	22	42
22	26	23	21	34	21
50	29	21	36	22	61

a) Calculate the mean for the data set.
b) Calculate the median of the data set.
c) Find the mode(s) for the data set.
d) Would you describe this data set as left-skewed, right-skewed, or neither? Explain.
e) Which of these measures of center would best tell a player if they were one of the younger or older players remaining? Explain.
f) Which of these measures of center would be best for pointing out the most common age? Explain.
g) What effect would it have on the 3 measures of center if the oldest player was 75 rather than 61?

Section 3.2 – Percentiles, Quartiles, and Boxplots

In Section 3.1 we found the median of a data set. The job of the median was to cut a data set into two equal parts, the lower and upper half. For some data sets, we may wish to cut the data set into more parts. In this section we will explore the process of finding percentiles and quartiles. The job of the percentiles will be to cut a data set into 100 equal parts. Similarly, the job of the quartiles will be to cut a data set into 4 equal parts. We will also see that the quartiles are just a special case of the percentiles. Once we have learned to find these numbers, we will learn how to make a new graph, called a boxplot. Boxplots are a visual display of the four equal parts of a data set.

PERCENTILES AND QUARTILES:

Percentiles are very commonly used in everyday life. If you take a standardized test like the SAT, you will generally be told what **percentile** your score is. If you take your child to the doctor for an annual check-up, the doctor will tell you the child's **percentile** for height and weight. For example, as a parent, your child's doctor may tell you that the child is at the 30th **percentile** for weight. What does that mean? Should you be concerned? Let's take a look at the definition.

Definition: *Percentiles*

Percentiles: Percentiles attempt to divide an ordered data set into 100 equal parts. It takes 99 numbers to accomplish this task. They are denoted $P_1, P_2, P_3, \ldots, P_{99}$. P_k is the kth percentile and it attempts to have k% of the data set below it and (100-k)% of the data set above it. For example, P_{30} is the 30th percentile and it attempts to have 30% of the data values below it and 70% of the data values above it.

Location: Just like for the median, the key to finding a percentile is to know where it is located in the ordered list of data. The formulas for the location of P_k are as follows.

$$\text{Population: } L_{P_k} = \frac{k}{100}(N+1) \quad \text{or} \quad \text{Sample: } L_{P_k} = \frac{k}{100}(n+1)$$

Note: If L_{P_k} is a decimal value, then we find the mean of the two values in the locations surrounding L_{P_k}. Example: $L_{P_k} = 14.4 \Rightarrow P_k = \dfrac{(14\text{th number}) + (15\text{th number})}{2}$

Dividing a data set into 100 equal parts may be a common thing to do, but it doesn't make a lot of sense when you have a small data set. How do you divide a data set into 100 equal parts when the data set only contains 15 data values? In such cases it might make sense to simply divide the data set into 4 equal parts. The numbers that accomplish this job are called **quartiles**.

When people hear the name **quartile**, they generally think that they will be finding four numbers. However, it only takes 1 median to cut a data set into two parts and similarly it only takes 3 **quartiles** to cut a data set into 4 equal parts. The **quartiles** are defined as follows:

Definition: *Quartiles*

Quartiles: Quartiles attempt to divide an ordered data set into 4 equal parts. It takes 3 numbers to accomplish this task. They are denoted Q_1, Q_2, Q_3. See below.

First Quartile: The first quartile, denoted Q_1, attempts to have 1/4 of the data set below it and 3/4 of the data set above it. Because $1/4 = 25\%$, $Q_1 = P_{25}$.

Second Quartile (Median): The second quartile, denoted Q_2, attempts to have 2/4 of the data set below it and 2/4 of the data set above it. Because 2/4 is the same as 1/2, $Q_2 = M$ (the median).

Third Quartile: The third quartile denoted Q_3, attempts to have 3/4 of the data set below it and 1/4 of the data set above it. Because $3/4 = 75\%$, $Q_3 = P_{75}$.

Locations: Similar to the percentiles, the key to finding a quartile is to know where it is located in the ordered list of data. The formulas for the locations are shown below.

Population data: $\quad L_{Q_1} = \dfrac{1}{4}(N+1) \qquad L_M = \dfrac{1}{2}(N+1) \qquad L_{Q_3} = \dfrac{3}{4}(N+1)$

Sample data: $\quad L_{Q_1} = \dfrac{1}{4}(n+1) \qquad L_M = \dfrac{1}{2}(n+1) \qquad L_{Q_3} = \dfrac{3}{4}(n+1)$

Note: If the location is a decimal value, then we find the mean of the two values in the locations surrounding the calculated location.

Example: $L_{Q_1} = 6.75 \Rightarrow Q_1 = \dfrac{(6\text{th number}) + (7\text{th number})}{2}$

Let's explore these new definitions with an example.

Example 3.10: *Counting Calories*

Starting on September 1, 2014, the author of this text attempted to lose weight by counting all calories consumed each day. The number of calories consumed for dinner during each of the days of September is recorded in the table below.

357	688	483	862	569	923	828	320	700	1337
1196	365	687	614	402	702	1000	1050	1350	336
485	946	464	724	1215	806	1007	683	594	783

Can counting calories help us lose those extra pounds?

a) Find the 40th percentile.

b) Find P_{63} and *interpret* in terms of the application.

c) Find the quartiles of the data set.

Solution:

a) Before finding percentiles or quartiles, we have to put the data set in order.

320	336	357	365	402	464	483	485	569	594
614	683	687	688	700	702	724	783	806	828
862	923	946	1000	1007	1050	1196	1215	1337	1350

We want the 40th percentile, or P_{40}. Therefore, we know that k = 40. Our data set has 30 data values, so $N = 30$. Using the location formula we get:

$$L_{P_{40}} = \frac{40}{100}(30+1) = 12.4$$

If the location had been a whole number, then we would have just taken the data value in that location. Because the location number lies between two whole numbers, we will take the mean of the data values in those two locations. So, in this case, we need to find the mean of the data values in the 12th and 13th spots of the ordered list. These numbers are 683 and 687. They are circled in the table below.

320	336	357	365	402	464	483	485	569	594
614	683	687	688	700	702	724	783	806	828
862	923	946	1000	1007	1050	1196	1215	1337	1350

So, we get: $P_{40} = \dfrac{683 + 687}{2} = 685$

b) Because we are asked to find P_{63}, the value of k = 63. So, this time we get:

320	336	357	365	402	464	483	485	569	594
614	683	687	688	700	702	724	783	806	828
862	923	946	1000	1007	1050	1196	1215	1337	1350

$$L_{P_{63}} = \frac{63}{100}(30+1) = 19.53 \Rightarrow P_{63} = \frac{806 + 828}{2} = 817$$

Interpretation: About 63% of the dinners in September had less than 817 calories and about 37% of the dinners in September had more than 817 calories.

c) The data values have already been ordered, so we can jump right in with the location formulas.

$$L_{Q_1} = \frac{1}{4}(30+1) = 7.75 \qquad L_M = \frac{1}{2}(30+1) = 15.5 \qquad L_{Q_3} = \frac{3}{4}(30+1) = 23.25$$

These are the location of the quartiles, but they are not the quartiles themselves. We now return to our ordered list and circle and highlight the numbers in the set that need to be averaged to finish off the quartiles.

320	336	357	365	402	464	483	485	569	594
614	683	687	688	700	702	724	783	806	828
862	923	946	1000	1007	1050	1196	1215	1337	1350

So we get: $Q_1 = \dfrac{483+485}{2} = 484$ $M = Q_2 = \dfrac{700+702}{2} = 701$ $Q_3 = \dfrac{946+1000}{2} = 973$

Key Concepts: *A few notes about finding quartiles*

The previous example brought up a few points that we will want to remember when doing future quartile problems.

- **We refer to Q_2 as the median.** Referring to the second quartile would be like referring to the fraction $2/4$. We would usually reduce this fraction to $1/2$ and in the same way, we will usually just refer to Q_2 as the median or M.
- **Quartiles only attempt to divide the data into four equal parts.** It is not always possible to break a data set into four equal parts. In the last example, we had 30 data values and 30 is not divisible by 4. The process we use creates four equal parts when it is possible and does as good a job as we could hope for when perfection is not possible.

Interpreting percentiles and quartiles is a very important skill in everyday life, yet many people have trouble with it. Before we move on to the next topic, let's get some more practice interpreting these numbers.

Example 3.11: *Interpreting Percentiles and Quartiles*

a) You take your 7-year-old daughter to the doctor for her regular check up. After measuring her height, the doctor tells you that your daughter is at the 30th percentile for height for 7-year-old girls. What does this mean?

b) Your son takes the SAT math test during his senior year of high school. His results show that he is at the 63rd percentile. How should you interpret this result?

Solution:

a) The 30th percentile has 30% of the data set below it and 70% of the data set above it. In this case, the data set is all 7-year-old girls. *Interpretation:* Your daughter is taller than 30% of 7-year-old girls and shorter than the other 70% of 7-year-old girls. Your daughter is probably a little shorter than typical for her age.

b) The 63rd percentile has 63% of the data set below it and 37% of the data set above it. *Interpretation:* Your son scored higher on the SAT math test than 63% of other people who took it and he scored lower on the SAT math test than the other 37% of people who took it. Your son is probably a little better at math than the typical person who took the SAT math test.

> **Caution: Percentile is not your percentage**
>
> It is a common mistake for people to think that being the 63rd percentile on a test means that they scored 63% on the test. The percentile does not tell you your grade or score. Rather it tells you the percentage of others that you were higher than. In the case of a test, the 63rd percentile is a score in the top half and is probably a decent result.

FIVE NUMBER SUMMARY: *Bringing in the minimum and maximum values*

When we use quartiles to divide a data set into four equal parts, it is common for people to want to know where the first part starts and where the last part ends. Because of this fact, we often include the minimum data value and the maximum data value with the quartiles to form a **five number summary** of the data set.

> **Definition:** *Five Number Summary*
>
> **Five Number Summary**: The five number summary is simply a list consisting of the minimum, Q_1, M, Q_3, and the maximum listed in order. We often just write the answer using set braces as shown below.
>
> $$\{Min,\ Q_1,\ M,\ Q_3,\ Max\}$$

Let's practice quartiles again by finding this five number summary for a new data set.

Example 3.12: *Battery life for the Nintendo DSi*

Shortly after Nintendo introduced the DSi game system, people noticed that the charge on the battery didn't last quite as long as it had for the previous version, the DS. An article claimed that the battery would last between 8 and 12 hours using the low brightness setting. A random sample of 19 DSi's was taken and tested for battery life during use in the low brightness setting. The following lasting times were produced.

Will the DSi's battery last until you finally get your turn?

9.30	10.51	11.14	9.94	9.44	8.23	10.19	10.34	10.10	8.97
8.59	9.63	9.69	10.67	9.23	10.60	5.66	10.21	11.53	

a) Determine the five number summary for the data set.

b) Interpret Q_3 in terms of the application.

Solution:

a) Anytime we are finding quartiles, we must start by putting the data in order. This will also make it easier to spot the minimum and maximum data values in the set.

5.66	8.23	8.59	8.97	**9.23**	9.30	9.44	9.63	9.69	**9.94**
10.10	10.19	10.21	10.34	**10.51**	10.60	10.67	11.14	11.53	

Next, we will find the location of the quartiles. These will point us to the quartiles themselves.

$$L_{Q_1} = \frac{1}{4}(19+1) = 5 \Rightarrow Q_1 = 9.23$$

$$L_M = \frac{1}{2}(19+1) = 10 \Rightarrow M = 9.94$$

$$L_{Q_3} = \frac{3}{4}(19+1) = 15 \Rightarrow Q_3 = 10.51$$

> **Key Concept:** *Exact Locations*
>
> When the locations turn out to be integers, there is no need to average any values to find the quartiles. We simply go to the location specified and the data value in that spot is the quartile that we need.

We now simply include the minimum and maximum times to get the five number summary.

Five Number Summary: $\{5.66,\ 9.23,\ 9.94,\ 10.51,\ 11.53\}$

b) The third quartile separates the lower 3/4 of the data set from the upper 1/4, so we get the following.

  Interpretation: About 3/4 or 75% of the DSi's had batteries that lasted less than 10.51 hours and the remaining 1/4 or 25% of the DSi's had batteries that lasted longer than 10.51 hours.

BOXPLOTS: *A Visual Representation of the Five Number Summary*

In Chapter 2, we saw that summarizing data sets can make it easier for people to understand some of the patterns in the data, but these patterns are often more obvious if we can find a visual representation for them. The visual representation of the five number summary is a graph called a **boxplot**. Let's discuss the procedure for making this graph and then try it with an example.

Definition: *Boxplots (NOT Modified)*

  Boxplots: A boxplot is a visual representation of the five number summary for a data set. To draw a boxplot we complete the following steps.

  - Draw a horizontal axis and label it in such a way as to contain the entire range of the data set.
  - Draw vertical lines at Q_1, M, and Q_3. Draw horizontal lines to enclose these three lines into a box. Leave some space between the axis and the box.
  - Extend horizontal lines (whiskers) from each side of the box. The whiskers should connect to the middle of each side of the box and extend to the minimum and maximum of the data set (unless drawing a modified boxplot which we will look at later in the section).

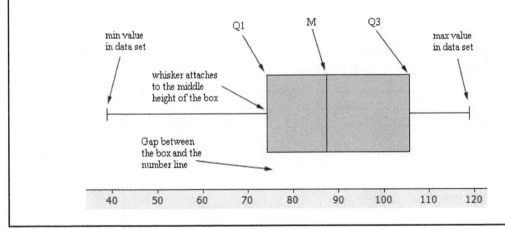

Example 3.13: *Counting Calories (The Boxplot)*

On September 1, 2014, the author of this text attempted to lose weight by counting all calories consumed each day. The number of calories consumed for dinner during each of the days of September is recorded in the table below.

Can counting calories help us lose those extra pounds?

357	688	483	862	569	923	828	320	700	1337
1196	365	687	614	402	702	1000	1050	1350	336
485	946	464	724	1215	806	1007	683	594	783

a) Find the five number summary for the data set.

b) Use the five number summary to draw a boxplot for the data.

c) Based on the boxplot, would you say that the shape of the distribution of the data set is best described as uniform, left-skewed, right-skewed, or bell-shaped? Explain.

Solution:

a) We already found the quartiles for this data set in Example 3.10. We now include the minimum and maximum data values to get the five number summary : $\{320, 484, 701, 973, 1350\}$

b) We will begin the boxplot by drawing a horizontal number line similar to the one used for a dotplot. Try to choose a nice scale that will allow for all the possibilities in your data set. Then, begin the boxplot by drawing a box that goes from Q_1 to Q_3. Make sure that you leave a gap between the number line and the box. Draw another vertical line at the median. Finally draw whiskers from the middle of each side of the box that extends to the minimum and maximum data values.

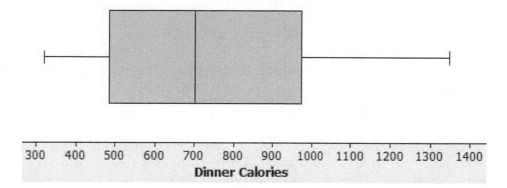

c) The boxplot has four parts: the left whisker, the left side of the box, the right side of the box, and the right whisker. Each of these parts represents 1/4 of the data set. Therefore, the more space on the number line covered by a part of the graph, the more spread out the data is in that part. The less space a part takes up, the less spread out the data is in that part.

Using this idea, we can see that the data on the right is more spread out than the data on the left. This means that histogram bars would be shorter on the right and taller on the left. This tells us that we are looking at a right-skewed distribution.

Another clue is that there are greater extremes on the right than on the left. We know that extremes are a key indication of which way data is skewed.

Using boxplots to determine the shape of the distribution of a data set can be a little tricky at first. We will discuss this topic in more detail later in this section.

MODIFIED BOXPLOTS AND OUTLIERS: *Detecting errors and unusual observations*

When working with data sets, it is often important to notice data values that lie far away from the majority of the other data values. We will call such values **outliers**. When **outliers** exist in a data set, they have a large effect on values such as the mean. They can also affect our ability to perform certain statistical procedures discussed in later chapters. The following definitions give us a technique for identifying **outliers** in a data set.

Definitions: *The range, interquartile range, fences, and outliers*

Range: The range of a data set, denoted R, is the difference between the largest and smallest values in the data set. The largest data value is called the maximum. The smallest data value is called the minimum.

$$Range = R = \text{maximum} - \text{minimum}$$

The Interquartile Range (IQR): The interquartile range is the distance between the third quartile, Q_3, and the first quartile, Q_1. In a boxplot, this is also the length of the box. The IQR is calculated as shown below.

$$IQR = Q_3 - Q_1$$

Upper and Lower Fences: The lower fence is located $1\frac{1}{2}$ box lengths to the left of the box on a boxplot and the upper fence is located $1\frac{1}{2}$ box lengths to the right of the box. The fences are calculated as shown below.

$$\text{Lower Fence} = LF = Q_1 - 1.5 \cdot IQR \qquad \text{Upper Fence} = UF = Q_3 + 1.5 \cdot IQR$$

Outliers: Outliers are values that lie far away from the majority of the other data values. Because the box in a boxplot represents the middle half of the data set, we say that a value will be considered an outlier if it lies more than $1\frac{1}{2}$ box lengths away from the box. This means that we will consider a value to be an outlier if it is below the lower fence or above the upper fence. The following is a list of key things to know about outliers.

- Any data values that lie more than $1\frac{1}{2}$ box lengths away from the box in a boxplot are considered outliers.
- Outliers are values that do not lie within the lower and upper fences.
- If any outlier visually stands far apart from other data values, then it should be investigated as a possible error in the data set.
- Outliers on a single side of a data set are indicators of severely skewed data sets. Severely skewed data sets often cause problems with statistical procedures in later chapters.

While technically, the formulas presented above are enough for us to find outliers in a data set, it would be useful to have a visual tool to help us identify these outliers. You may have noticed that many of the definitions above explained things in terms of boxplots. That is because we will use a modified version of boxplots to help us identify and display outliers.

Definition: *Modified Boxplots*

Modified Boxplots: A modified boxplot is a standard boxplot with fences added to help identify outliers in the data set. In a modified boxplot we modify the whisker of a boxplot if it contains outliers. The steps to make a modified boxplot are as follows.

- Draw a horizontal axis and label it in such a way as to contain the entire range of the data set.
- Draw vertical lines at Q_1, M, and Q_3. Draw horizontal lines to enclose these three lines into a box. Leave some space between the axis and the box.
- Calculate the IQR and use it to calculate the upper fence, UF, and the lower fence, LF. Draw these fences onto the graph as vertical dashed lines. (If a fence does not lie within the range of your axis, then that fence is not needed and it does not need to be drawn in.)
- If any of your data values are to the left of the lower fence or to the right of the upper fence, then mark them with an asterisk, *. These values are considered to be outliers.
- Draw your whiskers from the middle of the sides of the box and extend them to the largest and smallest data values that lie within the fences.

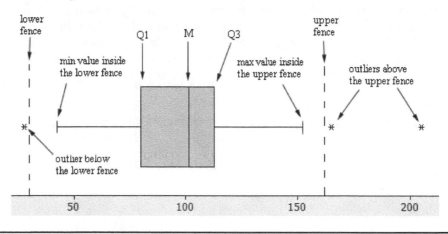

Example 3.14: *Battery life for the Nintendo DSi (Modified Boxplot)*

Shortly after Nintendo introduced the DSi game system, people noticed that the charge on the battery didn't last quite as long as it had for the previous version, the DS. An article claimed that the battery would last between 8 and 12 hours using the low brightness setting. A random sample of 19 DSi's were taken and tested for battery life during use in the low brightness setting. The following lasting times were produced.

Will the DSi's battery last until you finally get your turn?

| 5.66 | 8.23 | 8.59 | 8.97 | **9.23** | 9.30 | 9.44 | 9.63 | 9.69 | **9.94** |
| 10.10 | 10.19 | 10.21 | 10.34 | **10.51** | 10.60 | 10.67 | 11.14 | 11.53 | |

a) Calculate the Range, Inter quartile Range, IQR, for the data set.

b) Calculate the lower and upper fences for the data set.

c) Use the fences to make a modified boxplot for the data.

d) What concerns do you now have about the 5.66-hour data value? Explain.

e) If we assume that the 5.66 hours is an error and we disregard it, then what shape is the best guess for the distribution of the population that this sample was taken from? Explain.

Solution:

a) The data set is in order. Therefore, we can get the range with a quick subtraction.

$$Range = R = \text{maximum} - \text{minimum} = 11.53 - 5.66 = 5.87 \text{ hours}$$

In Example 3.12, we put the data in order and found the quartiles. They are shown in bold in the data set above. Therefore, for the interquartile range, or IQR, we get the following.

$$IQR = Q_3 - Q_1 = 10.51 - 9.23 = 1.28$$

b) The lower fence $= LF = Q_1 - 1.5 \cdot IQR = 9.23 - 1.5 * 1.28 = 7.31$

The upper fence $= UF = Q_3 + 1.5 \cdot IQR = 10.51 + 1.5 * 1.28 = 12.43$

c) A modified boxplot begins just like a regular one. We start by drawing the box and the median line. However, before we draw the whiskers, we will draw vertical dashed lines representing our lower and upper fences (if they fit within the range of the data set). If a fence does not fit within the data range, then that means that you do not have outliers on that side and you do not need to draw that fence. Our lower fence, 7.31, does fit the within the range of the data set, so we will add it onto our graph.

Any data value beyond the fence will be marked with an * denoting it as an outlier. The value 5.66 falls into this category. We still draw whiskers, but rather than extending to the minimum value, we will now go to the smallest data value that is not beyond the fence. For this example, because 5.66 will be an outlier, we will draw our whisker to the next lowest value in the data set, 8.23.

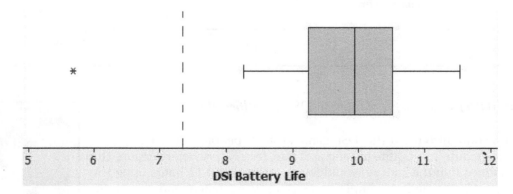

d) Not only is the 5.66 beyond the lower fence, but it is also very far away from the next lowest time of 8.23 hours. When an outlier is so far from any other data values, we should always be concerned that it might be an error in the data set. Perhaps, this was a typo and is not really 5.66 hours, but rather some higher, more normal time. Another possibility is that the data was improperly collected. All the data in this set is supposed to be from DSi's set to the low brightness setting. Perhaps this DSi was set to high brightness and that is why the time was so low. Finally, it is always possible that this data value is correct, but just an unusual observation.

e) If we disregard the outlier, then we should conclude that this data set is perhaps taken from a bell-shaped or uniform population. We should pick one of these two because of the symmetry of the box and whiskers. We would lean towards bell-shaped because the whiskers are a bit longer than the two sections of the box. This indicates tails on each side. However, they are not substantially longer than the box and thus the extra length on the whisker could just be random variation on a population that is actually uniform.

SIDE-BY-SIDE BOXPLOTS: *Using Boxplots to Make Comparisons*

In addition to using boxplots to learn about a single data set, boxplots can also be a useful tool for making comparisons between two data sets. The example below illustrates this idea.

Example 3.15: *Shower time by Gender*

A random sample of college students were surveyed and asked to estimate the length of time, in minutes, that they spent in the shower the last time they took a shower. The results are illustrated by the two modified boxplots shown below. The results are separated into two groups using gender.

Do college women spend more time in the shower than college men?

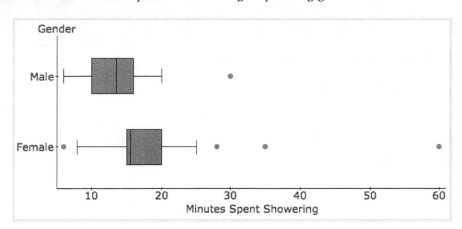

a) What do the small circles past the end of the whiskers represent?

b) Use the modified boxplots to estimate the five number summary and the range for each of the genders.

c) Do the boxplots shown support the idea that college women spend more time in the shower than college men? Use details from the graph to support your case.

Solution:

a) All of these values appear to be more than1.5 box lengths away from the box. This would indicate that the small circles represent outliers in the two data sets.

b) For the men: The left whisker ends at the minimum, the box starts at Q1, there is a line in the box at the median, the box ends at Q3. Because there is an outlier on the right, the outlier represents the max (rather than the end of the whisker). So, using the number line to estimate these values, we get the following:

$$\text{5-Number Summary} \approx \{6,\ 10,\ 13,\ 16,\ 30\},\ R = 30 - 6 = 24$$

We use the same idea for the women. Only we will use the outlier on the left as the minimum.

$$\text{5-Number Summary} \approx \{6,\ 15,\ 16,\ 20,\ 60\},\ R = 60 - 6 = 54$$

c) It is certainly not true that all college women take longer showers than the men. We see from the boxplots that the upper fourth of the men are taking long showers than the lower half of the women. However, it does appear that the college women tend to take longer showers than the men. For example, almost all of the upper 75% of the female shower times are longer than 75% of the male shower times. It is also noteworthy that the women's shower times are much more spread out than the men's. We can see this in that the range for women is 54 minutes while for men it is only 24 minutes.

WRAP SESSION: *Putting it all together*

Let's take a look at one final example to see everything we have learned in this section in a single application.

Example 3.16: *Las Vegas Cab Fares*

A random sample of 40 cab rides initiated on the Las Vegas Strip produced the following fares in dollars.

Can a modified boxplot help us spot an unusual cab fare?

12.50	18.26	22.11	6.90	17.55	20.32	17.52	18.72	21.39	17.91
11.10	13.00	28.64	16.46	15.74	24.18	36.90	19.17	15.16	14.08
21.21	19.22	17.13	31.50	16.99	23.00	22.96	14.99	17.48	9.54
20.43	42.90	19.80	17.67	16.44	17.22	13.86	16.42	20.86	26.62

a) Find the 90th percentile. Interpret this number in terms of the application.

b) Determine the Five Number Summary for the data set.

c) Create a modified Boxplot.

d) Comment on the shape of the distribution.

e) Comment on any outliers.

Solution:

Before we can find percentiles or quartiles, we must put the data in order. The sorted data is shown below.

6.90	9.54	11.10	12.5	13.00	13.86	14.08	14.99	15.16	**15.74**
16.42	16.44	16.46	16.99	17.13	17.22	17.48	17.52	17.55	**17.67**
17.91	18.26	18.72	19.17	19.22	19.80	20.32	20.43	20.86	**21.21**
21.39	22.11	22.96	23.00	24.18	26.62	28.64	31.50	36.90	42.90

a) The 90th percentile is denoted P_{90}. First we find the location and then the percentile.

$$L_{P_{90}} = \frac{90}{100}(40+1) = 36.9 \Rightarrow P_{90} = \frac{26.62+28.64}{2} = 27.63$$

Because the location number was between 36 and 37, we found the mean of the 36th and 37th values in the ordered data set.

Interpretation: 90% of the cab fares in this sample are less than $27.63 and the remaining 10% of the cab fares are greater than $27.63. So, in the population, we would also expect that about 90% of all cab rides in Las Vegas cost less than $27.63.

b) The five number summary is: $\{Min, Q_1, M, Q_3, Max\}$. The min is 6.90 and the max is 42.90, but the median and quartiles are not quite as easy to identify. For these values we need to first find the location and then use the location to determine the value in question.

$$L_{Q_1} = \frac{1}{4}(40+1) = 10.25 \Rightarrow Q_1 = \frac{15.74+16.42}{2} = 16.08$$

$$L_M = \frac{1}{2}(40+1) = 20.5 \Rightarrow M = \frac{17.67 + 17.91}{2} = 17.79$$

$$L_{Q_3} = \frac{3}{4}(40+1) = 30.75 \Rightarrow Q_3 = \frac{21.21 + 21.39}{2} = 21.30$$

> **Caution:** *Technology and Quartiles*
>
> There are at least 8 different methods used for finding quartiles and they produce slightly different answers in many cases. It is possible and even likely that the technology you use will not produce the same values as the method here.

All of the location values were decimal numbers, so in each case we found the mean of the two values in the surrounding locations. The numbers involved in the calculations are shown in bold in the table above. Putting these quartiles together with the minimum and maximum gives us the five number summary.

$$\{Min, Q_1, M, Q_3, Max\} = \{6.90, 16.08, 17.79, 21.30, 42.90\}$$

c) We will begin by drawing a horizontal axis and choosing the scale. Because the minimum value is 6.90 and the maximum is 42.90, a good scale would be to start at 5 and number in fives. Next we draw the box from Q_1 to Q_3. Remember to leave space between the box and the axis. We then finish the box by adding the vertical line at M.

After completing the box, we will calculate the IQR and the fences to see if we have any outliers.

$$IQR = Q_3 - Q_1 = 21.30 - 16.08 = 5.22$$

$$\text{Lower Fence} = LF = Q_1 - 1.5 \cdot IQR = 16.08 - 1.5 * 5.22 = 8.25$$

$$\text{Upper Fence} = UF = Q_3 + 1.5 \cdot IQR = 21.30 + 1.5 * 5.22 = 29.13$$

The minimum of 6.90 is below the lower fence, so it is considered an outlier. Also, the largest 3 fares are all above the upper fence, so they are also considered outliers. We will draw in the fence as vertical dashed lines and then mark all four of the outliers using an *. Finally, we extend the whiskers to the smallest data value inside the fences, 9.54, and to the largest data value inside the fences, 28.64. The completed graph is shown below.

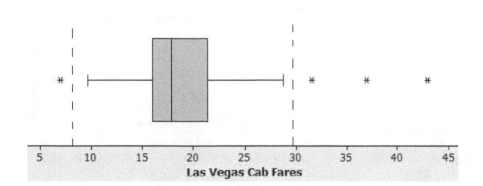

Las Vegas Cab Fares

> **Key Concepts:** *Fences and Whiskers*
>
> The fences are supposed to be located about 1.5 box lengths away from each side of the box. You should inspect them visually to see that this appears to have happened.
>
> When drawing the whiskers, a useful trick is to cross off all outliers from your data set and then draw the whiskers to the remaining minimum and maximum values.

d) If we consider the outliers to be part of the whiskers (as they would be in an unmodified boxplot) then the right whisker is much longer than the left whisker. Also, the right section of the box is wider than the left side section. Together these facts point towards the conclusion that this distribution is right-skewed.

e)　None of the outliers actually appear to be out of place in this data set. I suspect that they just represent one unusually short cab ride and 3 unusually long ones. They do not really stand apart from the rest of the data enough to raise suspicion that they represent errors in the data set.

It is important that we be able to roughly identify the distribution of our data set by looking at a boxplot. The following point to remember summarizes some of the key features of boxplots that help reveal the shape of the distribution.

Point to Remember: *Boxplots and Distribution Shapes*

Boxplots and Distribution Shapes: The following facts will help us determine the shape of a distribution based on features of a boxplot from the data. Recall: each of the four sections of a boxplot represents the same number of data values. Therefore . . .
- Narrow segments of a boxplot correspond to tall bars on a histogram.
- Wide sections of a boxplot correspond to short bars on a histogram.
- Whiskers that are longer than the box represent tails on a histogram.
- Whiskers that are shorter than the sections of the box represent the tallest bars on that side of the histogram.
- A whisker on one side that is much longer than the whisker on the other side indicates that the distribution is skewed towards the side of the longer whisker.

Examples: Here are a few boxplots for some of the most common distribution shapes. Each of these is from a random sample of size 200 from the indicated population. A dotplot of the actual data values is shown below the boxplot.

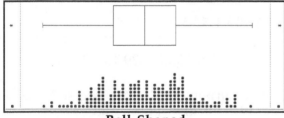

Bell-Shaped

The long whiskers on each side indicate symmetric tails on both sides with taller bars in the center. The boxplot is also roughly symmetric. Outliers may or may not exist.

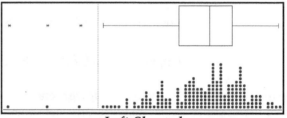

Left-Skewed

The whisker and outliers on the left extend much farther than the whisker on the right. This indicates a longer tail on the left than on the right. Outliers are only present on left.

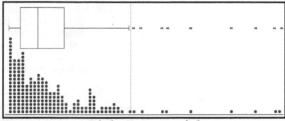

Right Exponential

The shortest segment of the graph is on the left and the segments keep getting longer as we move to the right. This indicates that the tallest bars are on the left with the tail on the right. Expect outliers on the right side.

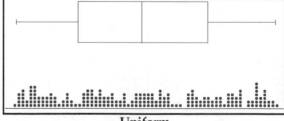

Uniform

Each of the four segments of the graph is approximately the same width. This indicates that the histogram bars would be roughly the same height all the way across the graph. There should not be any outliers.

Now it's time for some exercises.

Exercise Set 3.2

Concept Review: Review the definitions and concepts from this section by filling in the blanks for each of the following.

31) P_{12} is called the 12th _____ and it attempts to have 12% of the data set _____ it.

32) If $L_{Q_1} = 5.75$, then Q_1 is the mean of the ____ and ____ values in the ordered data set.

33) The five number summary consists of the _____ , _____ , _____ , _____ , and the _____ listed in _____ .

34) The range of a data set can be found by subtracting the _____ from the _____ .

35) The IQR is found by taking the difference between ____ and ____ . Graphically, it represents the length of the _____ in our boxplot.

36) The fences on a boxplot lie ____ box lengths away from the box. Any values that are outside the fences are considered to be _____ .

37) An outlier that stands apart visually from the rest of the data set is likely to be an _____ .

38) The whiskers on a modified boxplot extend to the largest and smallest _____ _____ that lie within the _____ .

Mechanics: Practice using the formulas from this section on each of the following.

39) Consider the data set below to be population data.

25	21	24	16	29	19
21	32	26	19	24	

a) Find all three quartiles for the data set.
b) Find the 28th percentile.
c) Find the five-number summary.
d) Calculate the range.

40) Consider the data set below to be sample data.

57	36	55	41	64	44
52	69	47	43	54	52
65	51				

a) Find all three quartiles for the data set.
b) Find the 63rd percentile.
c) Find the five-number summary.
d) Calculate the range.

41) Consider the data set below to be sample data.

5.7	6.3	4.1	8.4	5.2	5.3
5.5	8.0	5.1	4.0	3.9	2.8
3.6	2.3	5.4	4.4	4.6	

a) Find all three quartiles for the data set.
b) Find the 45th percentile.
c) Find the five-number summary.
d) Calculate the range.

42) Consider the data set below to be population data.

0.99	0.93	1.22	0.77	1.22	1.25
0.21	1.23	0.35	0.96	0.79	1.36
1.36	1.66	0.85	0.69		

a) Find all three quartiles for the data set.
b) Find the 91st percentile.
c) Find the five-number summary.
d) Calculate the range.

Applications: Use the procedures shown in the examples of this section to complete the following. Label all of your answers with the appropriate symbol. Show work.

43) A random sample of 11 college students were asked how much they pay per year for car insurance. The results, in dollars per year, are shown below.

900	1200	900	600	1400	2500
2000	480	500	1200	1200	

a) Find and interpret the 43rd percentile.
b) Find the five number summary.
c) Calculate the range of the data set.

44) A random sample of 13 college students were asked how many minutes they spent on social media last week. The results are shown below.

80	150	0	70	1260	300	420
90	1080	360	360	50	60	

a) Find and interpret the 90th percentile.
b) Find the five number summary.
c) Calculate the range of the data set.

45) The monthly utility bills for the month of May were collected from a random sample of 12 homes in a city and were as follows.

274	172	104	134	214	358
236	152	117	172	198	263

a) Find and interpret the 80th percentile.
b) Find the five number summary.
c) Calculate the range of the data set.

46) The hourly salaries, in dollars per hour, for each of the 15 employees at a local flower shop are shown below.

9.75	10.25	11.50	14.00	13.50
12.50	9.75	19.75	9.75	10.25
10.00	9.75	10.25	11.75	9.75

a) Find and interpret the 67th percentile.
b) Find the five number summary.
c) Calculate the range of the data set.

47) A local golf course randomly selected 23 players on a Saturday and asked them to report their scores for that day's golf game. Their sorted scores are shown below.

71	81	85	85	88	88
89	89	91	93	93	93
95	96	96	97	98	98
98	99	100	102	106	

a) Find and interpret the value of P_{55}.
b) Find the five number summary.
c) Create a modified (if necessary) boxplot.
d) Give a possible explanation for any outliers.

48) A random sample of 19 college students were surveyed and asked to take a guess at the number of calories in a McDonald's Big Mac Sandwich. Their guesses are shown below.

500	541	500	900	500	546
600	350	500	2500	870	140
3281	2000	1200	100	1200	460
2000					

a) Find and interpret the value of P_{42}.
b) Find the five number summary.
c) Create a modified (if necessary) boxplot.
d) According to McDonald's, there are 563 calories in a Big Mac. Use the graph to discuss what the students' knowledge on this topic.

49) The owner of a 2014 Ford Focus recorded the gas mileage for the car for a random sample of 19 tanks of gas. The sample produced the following highway gas mileages, measured in miles per gallon.

30.6	33.6	29.8	32.1	27.4
32.4	31.3	32.1	31.5	30.6
31.2	33.0	32.8	32.6	29.1
32.0	30.8	31.5	32.5	

a) Find and interpret the value of P_{88}.
b) Find the five number summary.
c) Create a modified (if necessary) boxplot.
d) Give a possible explanation for any outliers.

50) The following is a price list, rounded to the nearest dollar, for each of the pictures in an art studio.

133	13	78	517	968	295
360	253	60	193	703	929
356	944	623	683	38	608
219	1063	901	490	527	446
159	238	144	295	158	416
909	78	227	533	319	200
1535	77	70	2160	446	821

a) Find and interpret the value of P_{15}.
b) Find the five number summary.
c) Create a modified (if necessary) boxplot.
d) Give a possible explanation for any outliers.

51) A random sample of 23 people who hiked round trip from Yosemite Valley to the top of Half Dome was taken. The round trip hiking times, in hours, for those sampled are shown below.

13.4	11.7	12.9	10.8	15.5	12.5
12.4	11.4	11.0	11.5	12.0	12.8
12.1	10.9	11.8	11.1	10.7	12.4
14.1	9.8	10.4	11.9	13.0	

a) Find the five number summary.
b) Create a modified (if necessary) boxplot.
c) What is the most likely shape for the population of round trip hike times? Explain.
d) Give a possible explanation for any outliers.

52) A random sample of 22 people who hiked down and back out of the Grand Canyon was taken. The round trip hiking times, in hours, for those sampled are shown below.

9.65	9.93	11.76	8.70	9.83	11.10
12.78	5.32	10.56	9.91	11.71	11.77
13.55	11.78	11.51	12.75	12.74	12.84
11.51	12.68	11.20	9.10		

a) Find the five number summary.
b) Create a modified (if necessary) boxplot.
c) What is the most likely shape for the population of round trip hike times? Explain.
d) Give a possible explanation for any outliers.

53) An Intermediate Algebra class completed a homework assignment using an online homework system. The time, in minutes, spent by each of the 22 students on the assignment is shown below.

79	317	229	115	116	158
213	103	130	215	73	101
42	117	97	75	137	157
110	520	128	210		

a) Find the five number summary.
b) Create a modified (if necessary) boxplot.
c) What is the most likely shape for the distribution of the homework completion times? Explain.
d) Give a possible explanation for any outliers.

54) The National UFO Reporting Center collects data on UFO sightings. They collected 491 such reports in December of 2014. The duration of the sightings from a random sample of 18 reports is shown below. The durations of the sightings have been rounded to the nearest minute. So a 25 second sighting is listed as 0 minutes.

10	0	0	2	8	3
5	0	3	5	1	15
20	15	120	60	10	35

a) Find the five number summary.
b) Create a modified (if necessary) boxplot.
c) What is the most likely shape for the distribution of the quiz times? Explain.
d) What does this shape tell us about the duration of UFO sightings?

55) After about two-thirds of the players had been eliminated from a poker tournament, the number of chips possessed by each of the remaining players was noted. The counts are shown below.

7387	5160	13472	2670	12930
4905	11260	5475	7700	6480
21952	8704	8455	4626	14620
2595	5020	25015	5790	4000
11535	5455	7855	29670	15140
18605	1150	16455		

a) Find the five number summary.
b) Create a modified (if necessary) boxplot.
c) What is the most likely shape for the distribution of the chip stacks? Explain.
d) At the beginning of a poker tournament, all of the players start with an equal amount of chips. What does this shape tell us about what happens to those chips over time?

56) The ages of all 33 of the employees at a midsize architecture firm are provided in the table below.

46	33	25	62	53	43	60
39	47	50	26	40	42	70
56	58	27	41	57	35	53
36	47	64	52	39	47	43
45	38	57	31	29		

a) Find the five number summary.
b) Create a modified (if necessary) boxplot.
c) What is the most likely shape for the distribution of the ages? Explain.
d) Which of the four sections of the graph illustrates where the ages at the firm are the most spread out? Explain.

57) A random sample of 28 people who wear glasses, for reading only, was chosen. Those sampled were asked at what age they first needed to wear the glasses. The age data, in years, is given below.

48	42	51	38	49	25	41
50	48	36	49	44	41	40
51	44	22	44	50	53	47
28	45	39	51	44	42	32

a) Find and interpret the 67th percentile for the ages.
b) Find the five number summary.
c) Create a modified (if necessary) boxplot.
d) What is the most likely shape for the distribution of the ages? Explain.
e) What does this tell us about the age at which people start to need glasses when reading?

58) A statistics instructor decided to collect some data from a mountain bike ride. He noted his speed every 2.5 minutes using his cycling computer. The speed data sampled is shown below.

3.8	4.5	3.4	12.1	8.0	2.8	3.1
6.9	3.1	3.3	4.0	11.8	19.2	9.4
4.1	4.7	9.8	3.4	3.1	8.5	13.4

a) Find and interpret the 67th percentile for the mountain bike speeds.
b) Find the five number summary.
c) Create a modified (if necessary) boxplot.
d) What is the most likely shape for the distribution of the speeds? Explain.
e) What does this graph tell you about the statistics instructor's bike ride?

59) The modified boxplot of the scores on the Math portion of the SAT test for a sample of 579 high school students is shown below.

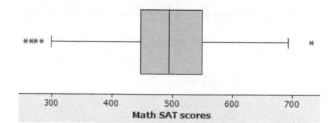

a) Use the boxplot to estimate the five number summary for the scores.
b) What shape distribution would you say these scores have? Explain.
c) What does this shape tell us about SAT math scores?
d) What do the outliers represent in terms of the application? Explain.

60) The main event of the 2010 World Series of Poker began with 7,319 players. The modified boxplot below shows the ages of the last 366 remaining players during that year's main event.

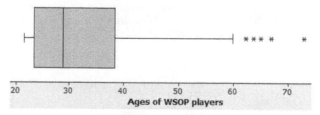

a) Use the boxplot to estimate the five number summary for the ages.
b) What shape distribution would you say these ages have? Explain.
c) What does this shape tell us about the ages of poker players near the end of the tournament?
d) What do the outliers represent in terms of the application? Explain.

61) A random sample of 35 students were given an online survey and asked to enter their GPA's. The data, as entered by the students, is shown below followed by a boxplot.

2.81	3.84	2.36	3.83	3.50	3.27	3.34
2.50	1.91	3.67	3.00	3.55	23.1	3.06
2.51	3.38	2.21	3.53	3.75	4.00	4.00
3.25	2.65	3.73	3.61	3.40	3.80	2.47
3.00	3.00	3.51	3.47	2.98	3.35	3.73

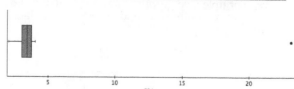

a) Which data value does the • represent in this graph?
b) What explanation would you give for this large data value?
c) If it were up to you, what would you do with this value before further analysis of this data?
d) Would you handle this outlier differently if it was 53.1 rather than 23.1? Explain.

62) A Church surveyed a random sample of 26 of its members and asked them how many miles they traveled to come to the service. Their responses, in miles, are shown below followed by a boxplot of the data.

15	10	6.5	8	16	15	12.7
12	5	3.8	35	25	16	2
12	5.9	6	9	1	10	6.3
7	8	9	8.2	13		

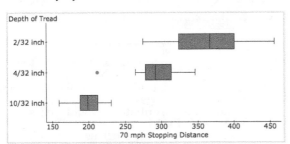

a) Which data values do the •'s represent in this graph?
b) What explanation would you give for these large data values?
c) If it were up to you, what would you do with these values before further analysis of this data?
d) Would you handle the outlier of 35 differently if it was 355? Explain.

63) The boxplots below represent the 70 mph stopping distances for a random sample of sports sedans on wet pavement. The test was conducted with new tires (10/32 in. of tread), worn tires (4/32 in. of tread), and nearly worn out tires (2/32 in. of tread). Based on a 2007 study by the Tire Rack.

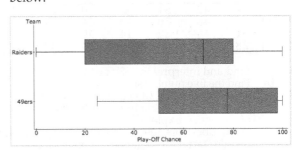

a) Use the modified boxplots to estimate the five number summary for the new tires.
b) Use the modified boxplots to estimate the five number summary for the worn tires.
c) Use the modified boxplots to estimate the five number summary for the nearly worn out tires.
d) Do these boxplots support the conclusion that the depth of tire tread affects the 70 mph stopping distance for sports sedans? Explain.
e) What other key differences stand out about the stopping distances from the three tread depths?

64) The boxplots below represent the prices obtained for regular unleaded gasoline from random samples of gas stations in California and in Nevada in January of 2015.

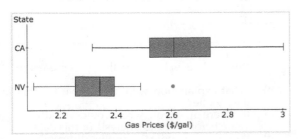

a) Use the modified boxplots to estimate the five number summary for the prices in CA.
b) Use the modified boxplots to estimate the five number summary for the prices in NV.
c) Do these boxplots support the conclusion that Californians pay more for a gallon of gas than Nevadans? Explain.
d) What other key differences stand out about the prices from the two states?

65) The boxplots below show the median percentage of income donated to charity for each of the 50 states in the U.S. The boxplots have been separated based on whether Barack Obama or Mitt Romney won that state in the 2012 Presidential election. Source: The Chronicle of Philanthropy.

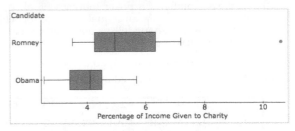

a) Use the modified boxplots to estimate the five number summary for states that Obama won.
b) Use the modified boxplots to estimate the five number summary for states that Romney won.
c) An article by the National Review stated that "Liberals are an uncharitable bunch". Do these boxplots support that conclusion? Explain.
d) What other key differences stand out about the results from the two groups of states?

66) In August 2014, a random sample of fans of the Oakland Raiders and the San Francisco 49ers were surveyed and asked what they thought the chances were that their team would make the play-offs that year. Boxplots of the percent chance are shown below.

a) Use the modified boxplots to estimate the five number summary for Raiders fans.
b) Use the modified boxplots to estimate the five number summary for 49ers fans.
c) Which group of fans was more optimistic about their team's chances of making the play-offs? Explain.
d) Do you think the differences could just be due to random variation? Explain.

Section 3.3 – Measuring Variation

In Section 3.1, we looked at measures of center, but that does not tell us the whole picture. Another important factor to look at for a data set is measures of variation. In other words, we need to know how spread out the data is as well as where it is centered. Let's examine this by comparing two population data sets.

PreCalculus Exams: *A discussion of the Range of a data set*

A small high school had a PreCalculus class containing only 7 students. The data sets below represent their test scores on the first and second exams given in the course. The teacher wishes to compare the results on the two exams to see how the class has progressed since the first exam.

Test I	63	68	72	83	91	93	97
Test II	59	78	80	83	84	85	98

Begin the comparison of the two sets of exams by finding the mean, median and mode.

Using the techniques from Section 3.1 we find the following results:

	mean	median	mode
Test I	$\mu = 81$	$M = 83$	None
Test II	$\mu = 81$	$M = 83$	None

Because there are no repeats in either set, there was no mode.

Because the means and medians are both the same, our measures of center have failed to differentiate between these two sets of tests despite the facts that they are different. This is because they are different in their variation or spread, not in their centers.

Situations like the one above point out the need to measure the variation of a set. This will give us a numerical method to differentiate between sets like the ones above. One logical way to attempt to measure the variation or spread in a data set is to use the range, R, from Section 3.2.

Find the Range for each of the two sets of test scores:

Test I	63	68	72	83	91	93	97
Test II	59	78	80	83	84	85	98

The two data sets are already in order, so it is very easy to spot the maximum and minimum values in the data set.

$$\text{For Test I: } R = 97 - 63 = 34 \qquad \text{For Test II: } R = 98 - 59 = 39$$

The good news is that the range does point out a difference between the two data sets by noting the larger difference between the maximum and minimum scores that occurs in the second set of test scores. The bad news is that, because the range only uses two of the data values, we may have incorrectly identified which data set was more spread out overall. Consider the following dotplots of the data sets.

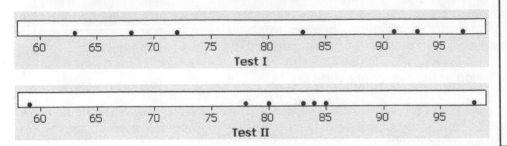

The graphs to the left show that while it is true that the range, R, is larger in data set two, this is mainly because of only 2 of the 7 students in the class. Overall, the test scores on test 1 are somewhat evenly spread out. However, for test II, 5 of the 7 scores are clumped together. We need a measure of variation that notices this by using all of the data values.

As you can see from the dotplots above, it would probably be more accurate to say that while data set II had a bigger difference between the extreme values, it appears that the data in set I is more spread out or varied as a whole. We need to find a way to detect variation that occurs within the data set as well as at the extremes so that we can get an overall sense of the spread within a data set. The **standard deviation** will give us a way to do just that. We will develop the formula for this quantity by working out the **standard deviation** for the test scores from data set I. A complete definition and formula will be provided following the discussion.

PreCalculus Exams: *A discussion of the Standard Deviation of a data set*

The following are the test scores for all of the students in a small high-school PreCalculus class.

Test I	63	68	72	83	91	93	97
Test II	59	78	80	83	84	85	98

Find the standard deviation needed to describe the variation in data set I.

We have scores for all of the students in the class, so we will be computing a population standard deviation. The standard deviation attempts to measure the typical distance away from the mean for the values in a data set. So the first step in the process will be to determine how far away from the mean each data value is. It is handy to make a table to help with this process. The first column will be the test scores and the second will be the deviations (differences) from the mean. Recall: for data set I, $\mu = 81$. The first entry in this new column will be $x - \mu = 63 - 81 = -18$. When we are finished with this column, we will look at the total to get a sense of the overall deviation from the mean for this data set.

Test Score x	Deviation $x - \mu$
63	-18
68	-13
72	-9
83	2
91	10
93	12
97	16
	0

$x - \mu = 68 - 81 = -13$

$x - \mu = 93 - 81 = 12$

A negative on a deviation indicates a value that was to the left of the mean and a positive indicates a value to the right of the mean.

Because the mean of a data set represents the balancing point between the distances to the left and the right of the mean, we will always get a zero for the total of this column. Because of this, we need to do something to make sure the negatives and positives don't cancel out. Otherwise, we will be left with the impression that there is no deviation overall.

There are two options we could choose to eliminate the negatives. One would be to take the absolute value (or just remove the negatives), the other is to square the deviations so that the negatives become positive. While just removing the negatives may seem simpler, when it comes to the calculus that underlies the statistics we will do, it is much easier to work with squaring than with an absolute value. For this reason and others, we will choose squaring as our method of dealing with the negative deviations. So, we will add a new column to the table, $(x-\mu)^2$.

Test Score x	Deviation $x-\mu$	$(x-\mu)^2$
63	-18	324
68	-13	169
72	-9	81
83	2	4
91	10	100
93	12	144
97	16	256
	0	1078

$(-13)^2 = 169$

$(12)^2 = 144$

Now that we have added these squared deviations, we should, like in an average, divide by the number of pieces of data. This gives us:

$$\frac{\sum(x-\mu)^2}{N} = \frac{1078}{7} = 154$$

If this is our measure of the typical distance a data value is from the mean, then we have failed miserably. The farthest any value was from the mean was 18 points, so 154 does not represent the typical distance. The answer seems way too big. Why did this happen?

The reason our answer is currently so big is because we have squared all of the deviations. We need to do something to undo this. The inverse operation to squaring is taking the square root, so we will finish this calculation by doing just that.

$$\sqrt{\frac{\sum(x-\mu)^2}{N}} = \sqrt{154} \approx 12.410$$

This new value seems to be a much better measure of the typical distance away from the mean for the scores on test I. 4 of the 7 tests were less than 12.410 points away from the mean and 3 of the 7 tests were more than 12.410 points away from the mean. We will now formally define the **population standard deviation** calculated above. Also, because it will be common for us to be working with sample data rather than population data, we will also define the **sample standard deviation**.

Definitions: *Population and Sample Standard Deviation*

Standard Deviation: the standard deviation gives us an overall measure of the variation, or spread, of a data set. It measures the typical distance away from the mean in a data set. If we have population data, we will calculate the population standard deviation, σ (a Greek letter pronounced "sigma"). If we have sample data, then we will calculate the sample standard deviation, s.

Formulas:

$$\text{Population Standard Deviation} = \sigma = \sqrt{\frac{\sum(x-\mu)^2}{N}} \; ; \; N = \text{population size}$$

$$\text{Sample Standard Deviation} = s = \sqrt{\frac{\sum(x-\bar{x})^2}{n-1}} \; ; \; n = \text{sample size}$$

Rounding Note: If you decide to round your answer for a standard deviation, then you should use *at least* five digits. Notice the emphasis is on digits not on decimal places. We count all digits before and after the decimal point, unless they are merely there as place holders. For those who have taken science courses, this could also be stated as using at least 5 significant figures.

You may have been surprised by the '$n-1$' in the denominator of the formula for s rather than just 'n'. The simplest explanation for this is that samples tend to have less variation in them than the population from which they were selected. Because, ultimately, we want to use 's' as an estimate for σ, we want to inflate its size a little to make it a better estimate of σ. This is accomplished by making the denominator of the formula a little smaller. The reason for the specific choice '$n-1$' is calculus based and, therefore, will not be detailed in this book.

Example 3.17: *PreCalculus Exams (Comparing the Spread or Variation)*

A small high school had a PreCalculus class containing only 7 students. The data sets below represent their test scores on the first and second exams given in the course. The teacher wishes to compare the results on the two exams to see how the class has progressed since the first exam. He calculated the measures of center for the data set and they failed to differentiate between the two sets of tests scores. He found the range to be higher in data set II, but he would like to compare a measure of the overall spread for the two sets.

Test I	63	68	72	83	91	93	97
Test II	59	78	80	83	84	85	98

a) In the preceding discussions, we calculated the standard deviation of data set I to be 12.410. Without making any new calculations, explain how you think the standard deviation of data set II will compare to data set I.

b) Calculate the standard deviation for data set II.

c) Does the standard deviation for the test II scores compare as expected to the one for the test I scores? Explain.

Solution:

a) Even though data set II has a larger range than data set I, the middle 5 scores for test II are clustered much closer together than the middle 5 scores for test I. Because the standard deviation measures the overall spread for the data set, this tight clustering of the middle 5 values in data set II should cause it to have a smaller standard deviation than test I.

b) We will make a table to help us calculate the standard deviation. Recall that, for data set II, $\mu = 81$.

Test Score x	Deviation $x - \mu$	$(x - \mu)^2$
59	-22	484
78	-3	9
80	-1	1
83	2	4
84	3	9
85	4	16
98	17	289
	0	812

$(-22)^2 = 484$

$x - \mu = 83 - 81 = 2$

Thus, $\sigma = \sqrt{\dfrac{\sum(x-\mu)^2}{N}} = \sqrt{\dfrac{812}{7}} = \sqrt{116} \approx 10.770$

c) As we expected from the discussion in part (a), the standard deviation for test II was smaller than for test I. The results of all calculations made in this section for the two tests are shown below.

	mean	median	mode	Range	St Dev
Test I	$\mu = 81$	$M = 83$	None	$R = 34$	$\sigma \approx 12.410$
Test II	$\mu = 81$	$M = 83$	None	$R = 39$	$\sigma \approx 10.770$

While the range is larger for data set II, the smaller value for the standard deviation reflects the fact that the middle portion of the data was more tightly packed in data set II compared to data set I as illustrated by the dotplots seen earlier in this section.

> **Point to Remember:** *Using standard deviation to compare the spread in data sets*
>
> The more overall variation in a data set, the larger its standard deviation. Conversely, the less overall variation in a data set, the smaller its standard deviation. Thus, one basic use of the standard deviation is determining which of two data sets is more spread out by comparing the size of their standard deviations.

In addition to standard deviation, we also use **variance** when describing the variation or spread in a data set. **Variance** is simply the square of the standard deviation. While we will focus on the standard deviation for now, **variance** will be important in later chapters and in more theoretical statistical courses that you may take after this one. Because it is so closely related to standard deviation, we present the definition of **variance** here.

Definitions: *Sample and Population Variance*

Variance: Variance is the value that we take the square root of to obtain the standard deviation. Variance can also be thought of as the average of the squared deviations from the mean for a data set. Variance can be calculated for a sample or a population.

Sample Variance: Because variance is the square of the standard deviation, we represent the sample variance using the symbol, s^2.

$$\text{In symbols: } s^2 = \frac{\sum (x - \bar{x})^2}{n-1}$$

Population Variance: We use the symbol σ^2 for population variance.

$$\text{In symbols: } \sigma^2 = \frac{\sum (x - \mu)^2}{N}$$

Let's look at an example involving sample data and variance.

Example 3.18: *Number of Facebook friends for college students*

A statistics student is interested in the number of Facebook friends that college students have. She randomly selects 12 students and asks them how many Facebook friends they have. The student is going to use the data obtained below to make estimates about all the students at her college. The number of friends data is shown below.

| 420 | 199 | 289 | 312 | 425 | 145 | 30 | 143 | 219 | 86 | 122 | 153 |

a) Find the mean of the data set.

b) Find the standard deviation.

c) Find the variance.

d) Explain why the standard deviation seems to be a better description of the overall spread in this data set than the variance.

Solution:

a) The problem states that calculations are being made for the purpose of estimating values for all the students at the college. Because we only have a sample of 12 students, this is sample data. Therefore, we will be finding the sample mean, $\bar{x}$.

$$\text{Sample mean} = \bar{x} = \frac{\sum x}{n} = \frac{2543}{12} \approx 211.9$$

The answer was rounded, so we used one decimal place more than was used in the original data set.

b) We begin the process of finding the sample standard deviation by making a table for the deviations from the mean similar to the one we made for the population standard deviation, σ. However, because this is sample data, the deviations are calculated using $\bar{x}$ rather than μ.

Friends x	Deviation $x - \bar{x}$	$(x - \bar{x})^2$
30	-181.9	33087.61
86	-125.9	15850.81
122	-89.9	8082.01
143	-68.9	4747.21
145	-66.9	4475.61
153	-58.9	3469.21
199	-12.9	166.41
219	7.1	50.41
289	77.1	5944.41
312	100.1	10020.01
420	208.1	43305.61
425	213.1	45411.61
2543	0.2	174610.92

$(86 - 211.9)$

$(-66.9)^2$

$$\text{Sample standard deviation} = s = \sqrt{\frac{\sum (x - \bar{x})^2}{n-1}} = \sqrt{\frac{174610.92}{11}} \approx 125.99$$

Recall from the previous section that the rounding rule for standard deviations is to use at least 5 digits in your answer. So we have used the minimum requirement of 5 digits in our answer.

c) Because the variation is s^2, we can just square our answer from part (b).

$$s^2 = (125.99)^2 \approx 15{,}873.48$$

d) The largest deviation in our data set was 213.1, for the value 425 friends. The smallest deviation in our data set was 7.1, for the value 219 friends. The value of $s \approx 125.99$ is about half way between these two and, therefore, seems like a reasonable measure of how spread out the data values are. However, the variation, $s^2 \approx 15{,}873.48$, is far larger than any of the distances from the mean in our data set.

WRAP SESSION: *The standard deviation tells us how much variation to expect in a data set*

In Example 3.17, we used the standard deviation to compare the variation in two data sets. The standard deviation also has a use when working with a single data set. For most data sets, the percentage of the data values that lies within 1, 2, or 3 standard deviations of the mean is fairly consistent. We will get a glimpse of this idea in the next example and we will pursue it in detail in Section 3.5.

Example 3.19: *Age of fast food restaurant employees*

A small fast food restaurant has 15 employees. The ages, rounded to the nearest tenth of a year, of all the hourly employees (excluding the manager) are given in the table below.

19.9	17.1	18.5	23.8	23.6	18.9	16.9	16
25.2	20.5	20.0	17.3	20.7	20.3	17.4	

a) Determine the mean and standard deviation of the ages for this population.

b) What percentage of the employees have an age that falls within 1 standard deviation of the mean age?

c) What percentage of the employees have an age that falls within 2 standard deviations of the mean age?

Solution:

a) We will make the standard table again to assist us with the calculations.

Age x	Deviation $x - \mu$	$(x-\mu)^2$
*19.9	0.15	0.0225
17.1	-2.65	7.0225
*18.5	-1.25	1.5625
23.8	4.05	16.4025
23.6	3.85	14.8225
*18.9	-0.85	0.7225
16.9	-2.85	8.1225
16.1	-3.65	13.3225
25.2	5.45	29.7025
*20.5	0.75	0.5625
*20.0	0.25	0.0625
*17.3	-2.45	6.0025
*20.7	0.95	0.9025
*20.3	0.55	0.3025
*17.4	-2.35	5.5225
296.2	-0.05	105.0575

> **Key Concept**: *rounding the mean*
>
> When using tables to calculate the standard deviation, it is easiest to use a mean that has been rounded using the minimum number of decimal places, 2 in this case. This does hurt the accuracy a bit, but when accuracy is our number one concern, we will use a different method (see Section 3.4).

> **Technology Tip**: *Speeding up the tables*
>
> Graphing calculators or statistical software packages can be used to speed up the process of filling in these tables. See the appendix for the technology that you use (located at the back of the text.)

$$\text{Thus, } \mu = \frac{\sum x}{N} = \frac{296.2}{15} \approx 19.75 \text{ and } \sigma = \sqrt{\frac{\sum (x-\mu)^2}{N}} = \sqrt{\frac{105.0575}{15}} \approx 2.6465$$

b) The key to answering this question is understanding the center column of the table above. $x - \mu$ is the directed distance of each data value from the mean. If we ignore the negative signs, then the numbers in this column tell us the distance each data value is away from the mean. If this distance is less than σ, then that data value lies less than 1 standard deviation away from the mean. All such ages have been marked above with a single *.

We now simply divide the number of ages that were less than 1 standard deviation away from the mean by the total size of the population. This gives us:

$$\frac{9}{15} = 0.60 = 60\%$$

> **Key Concept**: *% within 1 standard deviation*
>
> For most data sets we encounter, we will find about 50% to 80% of the data set lies within 1 standard deviation of the mean.

c) This time we want all ages that lie within 2 standard deviations of the mean. To accomplish this we calculate $2\sigma \approx 5.2930$. Any ages with deviations smaller than this should be counted. Except for the 25.2 year old employee, all the deviations are less than $2\sigma \approx 5.2930$, so for this one we get:

$$\frac{14}{15} \approx 0.9333 = 93.33\%$$

> **Key Concept**: *% within 2 standard deviations*
>
> For most data sets we encounter, we will find about 90% to 100% of the data set lies within 2 standard deviations of the mean.

The graphs below illustrate the work done in parts (b) and (c) of the preceding example.

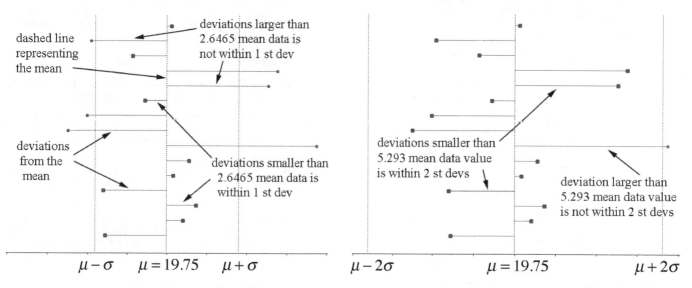

> **Key Concept**: *Finding the percentage of data within 1, 2, or 3 standard deviations of the mean*
>
> **Population Data**: Count the values of $|x - \mu|$ that are smaller than σ, 2σ, or 3σ. Divide that count by the total number of data values, N. Convert to a percentage.
>
> **Sample Data**: Count the values of $|x - \bar{x}|$ that are smaller than s, $2s$, or $3s$. Divide that count by the total number of data values, n. Convert to a percentage.

The approach for answering parts (b) and (c) in the examples above works great if you have made a table to find your standard deviation. In the next section, we will learn a different approach to this type of question if the table is not available.

Exercise Set 3.3

Concept Review: Review the definitions and concepts from this section by filling in the blanks for each of the following.

67) The standard deviation measures the amount of _____ in a data set.

68) A deviation measures the directed _____ from the data value to the _____ .

69) Before adding the deviations, we _____ them to get rid of the negatives. We balance this by taking the _____ _____ of the sum.

70) The more spread out a data set is, the _____ its standard deviation will be.

71) σ is the symbol for the _____ standard deviation and s is the symbol for the _____ standard deviation.

72) Variance is the _____ of the standard deviation.

Mechanics: Practice using the formulas from this section on each of the following. Include the appropriate symbol with each answer. Show tables.

73) Assume this is population data.

| 3 | 13 | 11 | 10 | 20 | 18 | 12 |

a)   Calculate the range for the data set.
b)   Calculate the standard deviation of the data set.

74) Assume this is sample data.

| 22 | 16 | 18 | 13 | 19 | 18 |
| 14 | 16 | 17 | 15 | 18 | |

a)   Calculate the range for the data set.
b)   Calculate the standard deviation of the data set.

75) Assume this is sample data.

| 151.7 | 143.9 | 184.4 | 172.9 |
| 141.8 | 115.4 | 186.1 | 118.7 |

a)   Calculate the range for the data set.
b)   Calculate the standard deviation of the data set.

76) Assume this is population data.

| 12.8 | 1.0 | 0.8 | 2.8 | 4.2 | 4.1 |
| 13.4 | 4.4 | 5.5 | 3.9 | 4.2 | |

a)   Calculate the range for the data set.
b)   Calculate the standard deviation of the data set.

77) Assume each data set represents sample data.

| Set I | 10 | 12 | 29 | 35 | 47 |
| Set II | 49 | 50 | 57 | 59 | 68 |

a)   Calculate the standard deviation for set I.
b)   Calculate the standard deviation for set II.
c)   Which of the two data sets has more overall variation? Explain.

78) Assume each data set represents population data.

| Set I | 9 | 19 | 14 | 20 | 23 | 24 | 19 |
| Set II | 36 | 41 | 35 | 73 | 41 | 67 | 83 |

a)   Calculate the standard deviation for set I.
b)   Calculate the standard deviation for set II.
c)   Which of the two data sets has more overall variation? Explain.

Applications: Use the procedures shown in the examples of this section (make tables and use formulas) to calculate any requested quantities. Label all of your answers with the appropriate symbol.

79) The monthly utility bills for the month of May were collected from a random sample of 12 homes in a city and were as follows. We are trying to make estimates about the variation in utility bills in May for the entire city.

| 274 | 172 | 104 | 134 | 214 | 358 |
| 236 | 152 | 117 | 172 | 198 | 263 |

a)   Calculate the range for the data set.
b)   Calculate the standard deviation of the data set.
c)   What percentage of the bills lie within 1 standard deviation of the mean?

80) A random sample of 9 light bulbs was tested and the bulbs were found to have the following lifetimes, in hours. We wish to make estimates about all the variation in lifetimes for all such light bulbs.

| 701.9 | 667.3 | 960.2 | 820.1 | 511.2 |
| 660.6 | 769.0 | 876.8 | 913.5 | |

a)   Calculate the range for the data set.
b)   Calculate the standard deviation of the data set.
c)   What percentage of the bulbs lie within 1 standard deviation of the mean?

81) The appraised value of all the homes on a short street were obtained and listed in the table below. The values listed are in thousands of dollars. We only wish to summarize the variation in appraised values for this street.

525	461	477
523	598	430
517	559	507

a)   Calculate the range for the data set.
b)   Calculate the standard deviation of the data set.
c)   What percentage of the homes lie within 1 standard deviation of the mean?

82) The top 15 grossing movies, for the opening weekend, as of January 6, 2015, are as follows (Source: BoxOfficeMojo.com). The data is in millions of dollars. We only wish to summarize the variation in the receipt data for these 15 movies.

Movie	Gross
The Avengers	207.4
Iron Man 3	174.1
Harry Potter: Deathly Hallows Part 2	169.2
The Dark Knight Rises	160.9
The Dark Knight	158.4
The Hunger Games: Catching Fire	158.1
The Hunger Games	152.5
Spider-Man 3	151.1
The Twilight Saga: New Moon	142.8
The Twilight Saga: Breaking Dawn Part 2	141.1
The Twilight Saga: Breaking Dawn Part 1	138.1
Pirates of the Caribbean: Dead Man's Chest	135.6
Iron Man 2	128.1
Harry Potter: Deathly Hallows Part 1	125.0
The Hunger Games: Mockingjay Part 1	121.9

a) Calculate the range for the data set.
b) Calculate the standard deviation of the data set.
c) What percentage of the movies lie within 1 standard deviation of the mean?

83) The two data sets below contain the ages of all the people in the sibling group of the author and his spouse. Boxplots are shown for the ages in each of the two families. We only wish to describe the variation in ages in each of these families.

Author	59	57	54	51	49	47	42
Spouse	41	38	35	35	33	31	27

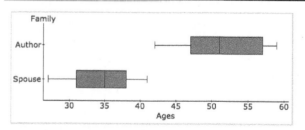

a) Which family's ages do you think will have a larger standard deviation? Explain using the boxplots above.
b) Calculate the standard deviation for the author's sibling group.
c) Calculate the standard deviation for the spouses sibling group.
d) Which of the two sibling groups has more overall variation? Explain.

84) The number of runs in each game for each team during the 2014 World Series is given below. Boxplots are shown for the number of runs for each team during the 7-game series. We only wish to describe the variation in runs for these two teams.

Giants	7	2	2	11	5	0	3
Royals	1	7	3	4	0	10	2

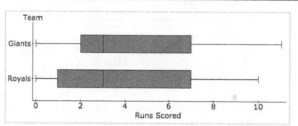

a) Which team's set of runs scored do you think will have a larger standard deviation? Explain using the boxplots.
b) Calculate the standard deviation for the Giants.
c) Calculate the standard deviation for the Royals.
d) Which of the two teams' runs had more overall variation? Explain.

85) A random sample of 11 Holstein dairy cows was taken and the annual milk production, in liters, was measured for each of the cows. The results are shown below. We wish to use this data to make estimates for the variation in annual milk production for all Holstein dairy cows.

8007	7667	7192	6985
8023	7577	6623	7685
7122	8062	7894	

a) Calculate the standard deviation.
b) What percentage of the milk productions lie within 1 standard deviation of the mean?
c) What percentage of the milk productions lie within 2 standard deviation of the mean?

86) The lap times for the first ten attempts at a new track on *Project Gotham 3* (car racing video game) are listed in the table below. Times are rounded to the nearest hundredth of a second. We only wish to describe the variation in these race times.

86.49	83.79	80.04	81.41	77.05
80.01	78.31	76.84	76.35	75.07

a) Calculate the standard deviation.
b) What percentage of the race times lie within 1 standard deviation of the mean?
c) What percentage of the race times lie within 2 standard deviation of the mean?

87) The adult lift ticket prices for a random sample of 16 U.S. ski/snowboard resorts are listed in the table below. The prices are for the 2014/2015 season. (Source: OnTheSnow.com). We wish to make estimates about the variation in adult lift ticket prices in the U.S. for that year.

95	75	42	90	78	62
102	54	118	35	47	29
50	68	69	39		

a) Calculate the standard deviation.
b) What percentage of the lift ticket prices lie within 1 standard deviation of the mean?
c) What percentage of the lift ticket prices lie within 2 standard deviation of the mean?

88) The National UFO Reporting Center collects data on UFO sightings. They collected 491 such reports in December of 2014. The duration of the sightings from a random sample of 18 reports is shown below. The durations of the sightings have been rounded to the nearest minute. So a 25 second sighting is listed as 0 minutes. We wish to make estimates about the variation in the duration of all UFO sightings.

10	0	0	2	8	3
5	0	3	5	1	15
20	15	120	60	10	35

a) Calculate the standard deviation.
b) What percentage of the durations lie within 1 standard deviation of the mean?
c) What percentage of the durations lie within 2 standard deviation of the mean?

89) The hourly salaries, in dollars per hour, for each of the 15 employees at a local flower shop are shown below. We only wish to summarize the variation for these salaries.

9.75	10.25	11.50	14.00	13.50
12.50	9.75	19.75	9.75	10.25
10.00	9.75	10.25	11.75	9.75

a) Calculate the range for the data set.
b) Calculate the standard deviation.
c) What percentage of the hourly salaries lie within 1 standard deviation of the mean?
d) What percentage of the hourly salaries lie within 2 standard deviation of the mean?

90) A random sample of 19 college students were surveyed and asked to take a guess at the number of calories in a McDonald's Big Mac Sandwich. Their guesses are shown below. We wish to make estimates about the variation in the guesses for the number of calories in a Big Mac for all college students.

500	541	500	900	500	546
600	350	500	2500	870	140
3281	2000	1200	100	1200	460
2000					

a) Calculate the range for the data set.
b) Calculate the standard deviation.
c) What percentage of the guesses lie within 1 standard deviation of the mean?
d) What percentage of the guesses lie within 2 standard deviation of the mean?

Section 3.4 - Grouped Data and Using Technology

In the previous sections, we have looked at examples where we are given raw data, but we also need to know how to handle data that has been organized and grouped into a table. It is common for people conducting statistical work to organize large sets of raw data by putting it in a grouped data table. This makes the data set much more manageable, but it can complicate the process of finding the mean and standard deviation. Also, we need to learn how to use technology to speed up many of our calculations. We will explore both of these topics in this section. We will begin by exploring grouped data in the discussion example below.

Average age of college students (*A discussion of mean and standard deviation for grouped data*)

The following is a frequency distribution for the ages of a randomly selected sample of 137 college students. While it is easier to digest this data by viewing an organized table, the fact that we have lost the raw data will change the way we approach calculations for this data set.

Ages	Frequency
15 – < 20	40
20 – < 25	44
25 – < 30	25
30 – < 35	13
35 – < 40	8
40 – < 45	5
45 – < 50	0
50 – < 55	2
	137

Suppose that we wanted to find the mean for this sample of students. How would we go about making the calculations? In theory, finding the mean should be very easy. Simply add up all the ages and divide by the number of students in the sample. However, this is not as easy as it sounds.

The first big issue we must deal with is that we actually do not know the ages of any of the students in this sample. For example, there are 40 students in the first age group, but we do not know their actual ages. We only know that they are somewhere between 15 and 20 years old. The way we will handle this will be to use the midpoint as an estimate for the ages of all the people in this and all other classes in the table. The midpoint of the first class is 17.5, the average of 15 and 20, so we will do our work under the pretense that all 40 of the people in that class are 17.5 years old. We continue in the same fashion with the other classes and produce the table shown to the right.

Now, we will try to use these midpoints to estimate the mean age of these students. Because this is sample data, we will compute the sample mean, $\bar{x}$. Because there are 137 students in the sample our denominator will be 137. This means that we will have to add up 137 ages to get the numerator. To achieve this we must count each midpoint repeatedly to account for all the students in each class. This might look as shown below.

Age (midpoint) x	Frequency f
17.5	40
22.5	44
27.5	25
32.5	13
37.5	8
42.5	5
47.5	0
52.5	2
	137

$$\bar{x} = \frac{\sum x}{n} \approx \frac{17.5+17.5+ \cdot \cdot \cdot +17.5+22.5+ \cdot \cdot \cdot +22.5+27.5+ \cdot \cdot \cdot +27.5+ \cdot \cdot \cdot +52.5+52.5}{137}$$

This would be very tedious work. Rather than adding the 17.5 to itself 40 times, it would be much faster and easier to just multiply the 17.5 by the frequency for that class. Making this multiplication adjustment gives us the following.

$$\bar{x} = \frac{\sum xf}{n} \approx \frac{17.5(40)+22.5(44)+27.5(25)+ \cdot \cdot \cdot +52.5(2)}{137} = \frac{3417.5}{137} \approx 24.945$$

When dealing with grouped data, we will always make the adjustment shown above. Therefore, all formulas for grouped data will involve multiplying by the frequency before we find sums. All the mean, standard deviation, and variance formulas for grouped data are given below.

Point to Remember: *mean, standard deviation, and variance formulas for grouped data*

Sample measures for grouped data:

$$\bar{x} = \frac{\sum x \cdot f}{n} \qquad s = \sqrt{\frac{\sum(x-\bar{x})^2 f}{n-1}} \qquad s^2 = \frac{\sum(x-\bar{x})^2 f}{n-1}$$

Population measures for grouped data:

$$\mu = \frac{\sum x \cdot f}{N} \qquad \sigma = \sqrt{\frac{\sum(x-\mu)^2 f}{N}} \qquad \sigma^2 = \frac{\sum(x-\mu)^2 f}{N}$$

Note: When the actual x-values for the data set are unknown because each class could possibly contain many different values, we will use the midpoint of each class as the x-value for all the members of that class. Using midpoints for the x-values causes all answers to be estimates rather than exact.

Let's examine the practical use of these formulas by looking at another example.

Example 3.20: *Laughter in Social Interactions*

Studies have shown that, on average, adults laugh about once per hour while they are awake. Because this is an average, it might contain many hours per day when adults are working in isolation. A psychologist believes this number will be much higher for adults interacting socially with others. A random sample of 184 adults engaged in conversations with friends or strangers was taken and the number of times each person laughed during a 1-hour period was recorded. The table below summarizes the results.

Is laughing a social activity?

Laughs per Hour	Frequency
0 – 9	1
10 – 19	10
20 – 29	41
30 – 39	81
40 – 49	37
50 – 59	12
60 – 69	2
	184

a) Find the mean and standard deviation for the number of laughs per person per hour in this sample.

b) What percentage of the data set lies within 2 standard deviations of the mean?

Solution:

a) The first thing we should notice is that this problem involves sample data. So, we will be finding $\bar{x}$ and s, rather than μ and σ. We will start by finding the midpoints for each class. We will then calculate the sample mean. Finally we will use the mean to help calculate the standard deviation. We will make a table to help organize all of the work.

Laughs (midpoint) x	Frequency f	$x \cdot f$	$(x - \bar{x})^2 f$
4.5	1	4.5	909.6256
14.5	10	145	4064.256
24.5	41	1004.5	4232.2496
34.5	81	2794.5	2.0736
44.5	37	1646.5	3582.5472
54.5	12	654	4723.5072
64.5	2	129	1780.8512
	184	6378	19295.1104

$x \cdot f = 14.5(10) = 145$

$(24.5 - 34.66)^2 * 41$

Key Concept: *the order of the calculations.*

You must calculate the value of the mean before you can compute the values in the last column.

From this table we can calculate the sample mean: $\bar{x} = \dfrac{\sum xf}{n} \approx \dfrac{6378}{184} \approx 34.66$

Now that we have the sample mean, we can find and add the remaining column needed to calculate the standard deviation.

The sample standard deviation is: $s = \sqrt{\dfrac{\sum (x - \bar{x})^2 f}{n-1}} \approx \sqrt{\dfrac{19295.1104}{183}} \approx 10.268$

b) In the past we calculated this by comparing the values of $|x - \bar{x}|$ to $2s$. However, this time, we did not list the '$x - \bar{x}$' column in our table. Because of this, we will now switch to a new method for answering this type of question. We will calculate the cutoffs that lie two standard deviations on either side of the mean and then count the data values that lie between these cutoffs. The cutoffs are calculated as follows:

Left Cutoff: $\bar{x} - 2s = 34.66 - 2*10.268 = 14.124$ **Right Cutoff:** $\bar{x} + 2s = 34.66 + 2*10.268 = 55.196$

When we count the data values that lie between these cutoffs, we have to make sure that we count *all* of the values that lie between them. To do this, we must remember to count the frequency for each class rather than just counting the number of classes. The smallest midpoint that lies between the cutoffs is 14.5. The largest midpoint that lies between the cutoffs is 54.5. Counting the frequencies for these midpoints and dividing by the sample size, we get the following:

$$\frac{10+41+81+37+12}{184} \approx 0.9837 = 98.37\%$$

Another, often better option, is to subtract away all of the frequencies that do not lie between our two cutoffs from the total. All of the midpoints lie between these cutoffs except for 4.5 and 64.5 with frequencies of 1 and 2 respectively. Using the subtraction method gives us:

$$\frac{184-1-2}{184} \approx 0.9837 = 98.37\%$$

Key Concept: *Finding the percentage of data within 1, 2, or 3 standard deviations of the mean using the cutoff method*

Population Data: Use if the values of $|x - \mu|$ are not available.
- Calculate the lower and upper cutoffs for the number of standard deviations requested. Use cutoffs of $\mu \pm \sigma$ if counting within 1 standard deviation, use $\mu \pm 2\sigma$ for two standard deviations, and use $\mu \pm 3\sigma$ for three standard deviations.
- Count all of the data values that lie between the desired cutoffs.
- Divide that count by the total number of data values, N.
- Convert to a percentage.

Sample Data: Same idea as above, but the cutoffs are $\bar{x} \pm s$, $\bar{x} \pm 2s$, or $\bar{x} \pm 3s$.

Grouped Data: Make sure that you are counting frequencies rather than just counting the number of classes.

In the examples that we have seen so far, we needed to use the midpoint as a representative for the unknown values in each class. If we are working with single value grouping, we do not need to do this. A common situation where this arises is in the computation of grade point average or GPA. The following example illustrates this point.

Example 3.21: *Computing Grade Point Average (or GPA)*

The table below shows the number of units completed with grades of A, B, C, D, and F for a community college student. The student is applying to transfer to a 4-yr university and needs to calculate his GPA (grade point average).

Grade Received	A (4.0)	B (3.0)	C (2.0)	D (1.0)	F (0.0)
Number of Units	12	27	21	3	1

a) Use the units as frequencies to compute the GPA that the student should report on his application.

b) Compute the standard deviation for the grade points received by this student.

c) What percentage of the units taken have grade points that lie within 2 standard deviations of the mean?

Solution:

a) Because we will be using all of the courses that the student has taken at the community college, this should be considered population data. Therefore, we will be computing a population mean, μ. We will use the grade points, A = 4.0, B = 3.0, etc. as our x-values. We will use the number of units at each grade as the frequency.

x (Grade Points)	freq (units)	$x \cdot f$
4.0	12	48
3.0	27	81
2.0	21	42
1.0	3	3
0.0	1	0
	64	174

$$\mu = \frac{\sum x \cdot f}{N} = \frac{174}{64} \approx 2.72$$

b) To calculate the standard deviation, we must add the column $(x - \mu)^2 \cdot f$ to the table above.

x (Grade Points)	freq (units)	$x \cdot f$	$(x - \mu)^2 \cdot f$
4.0	12	48	19.6608
3.0	27	81	2.1168
2.0	21	42	10.8864
1.0	3	3	8.8752
0.0	1	0	7.3984
	64	174	48.9376

$(3.0 - 2.72)^2 * 27$

$$\sigma = \sqrt{\frac{\sum (x - \mu)^2 f}{N}} = \sqrt{\frac{48.9376}{64}} \approx 0.87444$$

c) We will use the cutoff method to answer this question.

$$\mu - 2\sigma = 2.72 - 2*0.87444 = 0.97112 \qquad \mu + 2\sigma = 2.72 + 2*0.87444 = 4.46888$$

All of the grade point possibilities lie between these cutoffs except for 0.0 with only 1 unit at this grade point level. This gives us:

$$\frac{64 - 1}{64} \approx 0.9844 = 98.44\%$$

You may have noticed that the process of making tables to compute the mean and standard deviation for a data set can be quite tedious. This is especially true when sets of raw data become large or if grouped data sets contain many different classes. Fortunately, modern calculators and software packages can compute these values for us if we enter the data and give the correct instructions. We conclude this section with directions for finding the mean and standard deviation using various forms of technology.

TECHNOLOGY SECTION: *Finding the mean and standard deviation for raw or grouped data sets*

While computing the values of the mean and standard deviation using tables and formulas is important for our understanding of the meaning of these quantities, it is much more common for people doing statistical work to make use of technology to speed up the process and to decrease the risk of arithmetic errors. Using the calculator will also allow us to quickly move past the calculation and focus on the meaning and use of the quantities we are computing. The use of technology also makes it more reasonable to work with large data sets or messy numbers that may be common in real life examples. The following examples will show you how to quickly make the calculations on various technology platforms.

TI-83/84:

Mean and Standard Deviation for Raw Data: Use these directions if the data set is given as a list of numbers.

1. Choose STAT > EDIT > Edit . . and you will be taken to the list editor screen.
2. Enter the data set one number at a time into L1. Press ENTER after each number.
3. Choose STAT > CALC > 1-Var Stats and then use the keypad to select L1, and finally press the ENTER key.
4. If you entered sample data, then use $\bar{x}$ for the sample mean and Sx for the sample standard deviation (change the symbol to s .) If you entered population data, then use $\bar{x}$ for the population mean (but change the symbol to μ), and use σx for the population standard deviation (change the symbol to σ .)
5. See the screen shots below.

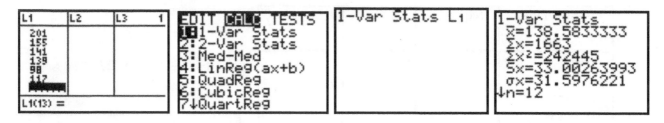

Mean and Standard Deviation for Grouped Data: Use these directions if the data set is given in a grouped data table.

1. Enter the x-values (midpoints if needed) into L1.
2. Enter the frequencies into L2.
3. Choose STAT > CALC > 1-Var Stats and then use the keypad to select L1, then press the comma key, and then use the keypad to select L2, and finally press the ENTER key.
4. Choose the appropriate mean and standard deviation as described in step 4 above.
5. See the screen shots below.

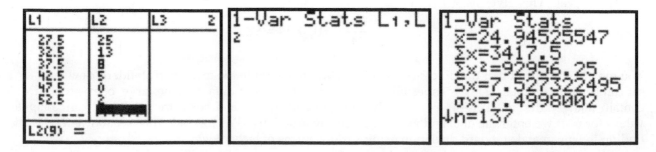

STATCRUNCH:

Mean and Standard Deviation for Raw Data: Use these directions if the data set is given as a list of numbers.

1. Enter the data set one number at a time into the var1 column. Press RETURN after each number.
2. Choose STAT > Summary Stats > Columns.
3. Click on var1 in the select columns box and then click the Calculate button.
4. If you entered sample data, then use 'Mean' for the sample mean (label it as $\bar{x}$) and 'Std. Dev.' for the sample standard deviation (label it as s .) If you entered population data, then use 'Mean' for the population mean (label it as μ). Unfortunately, StatCrunch does not calculate the population standard deviation, so we will need to use a trick to get it from their output. To get the population standard deviation we must multiply 'Std. Dev.' by $\sqrt{\dfrac{N-1}{N}}$. After completing this multiplication, we label the population standard deviation as σ .
5. See the screen shots below.

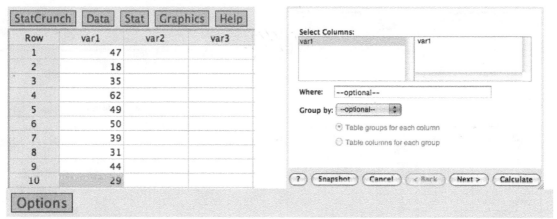

Summary statistics:

Column	n	Mean	Variance	Std. Dev.	Std. Err.	Median	Range	Min	Max	Q1	Q3
var1	10	40.4	160.04445	12.650867	4.0005555	41.5	44	18	62	31	49

$$\text{Converting from } s \text{ to } \sigma: \quad \sigma = 12.650867 \cdot \sqrt{\frac{9}{10}} \approx 12.002$$

Mean and Standard Deviation for Grouped Data: At the time of this writing, StatCrunch appears not to offer any simple way of calculating the mean and standard deviation for grouped data. When working with grouped data, you will need to continue to make tables and use the formulas from this section if StatCrunch is the only technology option available to you.

MINITAB:

<u>Mean and Standard Deviation for Raw Data</u>: Use these directions if the data set is given as a list of numbers.

1. Enter the data set one number at a time into the C1 column. Press RETURN after each number.
2. Choose Stat > Basic Statistics > Display Descriptive Statistics.
3. Click in the Variables box and then double click on C1. Click the OK button.
4. If you entered sample data, then use 'Mean' for the sample mean (label it as $\bar{x}$) and 'StDev' for the sample standard deviation (label it as s .) If you entered population data, then use 'Mean' for the population mean (label it as μ). Unfortunately, Minitab does not calculate the population standard deviation, so we will need to use a trick to get it from their output. To get the population standard deviation we must multiply 'StDev' by $\sqrt{\dfrac{N-1}{N}}$.   After completing this multiplication, we label the population standard deviation as σ .
5. See the screen shots below.

Descriptive Statistics: C1

Variable	N	N*	Mean	SE Mean	StDev	Minimum	Q1	Median	Q3	Maximum
C1	10	0	40.40	4.00	12.65	18.00	30.50	41.50	49.25	62.00

$$\text{Converting from } s \text{ to } \sigma: \ \sigma = 12.65 \cdot \sqrt{\frac{9}{10}} \approx 12.001$$

<u>Mean and Standard Deviation for Grouped Data</u>: At the time of this writing, Minitab appears not to offer any simple way of calculating the mean and standard deviation for grouped data. When working with grouped data, you will need to continue to make tables and use the formulas from this section if Minitab is the only technology option available to you.

EXCEL:

<u>Mean and Standard Deviation for Raw Data</u>: Use these directions if the data set is given as a list of numbers.

1. Enter the data set one number at a time into the cells of the desired column. Press RETURN after each number.
2. From the "Data" tab, choose Data Analysis > Descriptive Statistics and click OK.
3. Specify the cell range that contains your data in the Input Range box. (See below.)
4. In the Output Range Box, specify the cell that you would like to be the upper left corner of the output chart that Excel produces.
5. Check the Summary Statistics box and then click OK. Resize the columns as needed to improve readability of the output.
6. If you entered sample data, then use 'Mean' for the sample mean (label it as $\bar{x}$) and 'Standard Deviation' for the sample standard deviation (label it as s .) If you entered population data, then use 'Mean' for the population mean (label it as μ). If you need the population standard deviation, see the steps following the screen shots.
7. See the screen shots below.

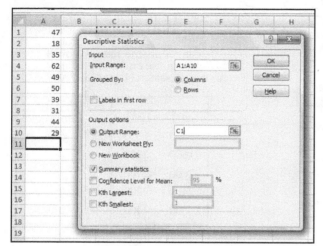

<u>Population Standard Deviation for Raw Data</u>: Use this procedure to find σ for population data.

1. Click on the cell where you would like to store the population standard deviation.
2. Type "=STDEVP(A1:A10)" and press enter. A1 and A10 represent the first and last cells containing your data and will vary from data set to data set.
3. See the screen shot below.

	C2		f_x	=STDEVP(A1:A10)	
	A	B	C	D	E
1	47				
2	18		12.0016666		
3	35				
4	62				
5	49				
6	50				
7	39				
8	31				
9	44				
10	29				

Exercise Set 3.4

Concept Review: Review the definitions and concepts from this section by filling in the blanks for each of the following.

91) When calculating the mean and standard deviation for data that has been grouped into classes, use the _____ of each class in place of the x-values.

92) When using midpoints for grouped data calculations, all of the answers will be _____ .

93) When counting the number of data values within 1, 2, or 3 standard deviations of the mean for grouped data, remember to count the _____ for each class rather than counting the _____ of classes.

94) When computing GPA, the number of _____ takes the place of the frequencies in all of your calculations.

Mechanics: Practice using the formulas from this section on each of the following. Include the appropriate symbol with each answer. Show tables.

95) Assume this is sample data

x-value	Frequency
1	22
2	17
3	10
4	7
5	2
	58

a) Calculate the mean for the data set.
b) Calculate the standard deviation for the data set.

96) Assume this is population data

x-value	Frequency
4	12
5	23
6	41
7	15
	91

a) Calculate the mean for the data set.
b) Calculate the standard deviation for the data set.

97) Assume this is population data

Classes	Frequency
0 - <10	7
10 - <20	10
20 - <30	6
30 - <40	4
40 - <50	1
	28

a) Calculate the mean for the data set.
b) Calculate the standard deviation for the data set.

98) Assume this is sample data

Classes	Frequency
400 - 599	3
600 - 799	19
800 - 999	46
1000 - 1199	33
1200 - 1399	9
	110

a) Calculate the mean for the data set.
b) Calculate the standard deviation for the data set.

Applications: Use the procedures shown in the examples of this section (make tables and use formulas) to calculate any requested quantities. Label all of your answers with the appropriate symbol. Show work.

99) In August 2014, a random sample of 52 homes for sale in Hayward, CA was taken and the size of the homes, in square feet, was recorded. The results are summarized in the table below (Source: Realty.com). We wish to use our results to make estimates about all homes for sale in Hayward, CA.

Size	Frequency
800 - <1200	14
1200 - <1600	6
1600 - <2000	8
2000 - <2400	14
2400 - <3200	8
3200 - <4400	2
	52

a) Calculate the mean for the data set.
b) Calculate the standard deviation for the data set.

100) A random sample of 43 community college students was taken and we asked them how many minutes it takes them to get to school. Assume we wish to use the data to make estimates about all students at this college.

Commute Time	Frequency
0 – < 10	7
10 – < 20	13
20 – < 30	14
30 – < 40	6
40 – < 50	2
50 – < 60	0
60 – < 70	1
	43

a) Calculate the mean for the data set.
b) Calculate the standard deviation for the data set.

101) Amazon allows customers to rate the products they buy as 1, 2, 3, 4, or 5 stars. The table below shows the results for the Coleman 4-Person Instant Tent. Suppose that we are only making calculations to describe the satisfaction level for the 360 customers that rated this product.

Number of Stars	Frequency
5	249
4	75
3	16
2	12
1	8
	360

a)   Calculate the mean for the data set.
b)   Calculate the standard deviation for the data set.

102) The scores for the Chapter 3 homework assignment of all 70 students in a statistics instructor's sections have been listed in the following table together with their frequencies. We are only making calculations to describe these students' scores.

Score	Frequency
0	3
1	2
2	6
3	12
4	28
5	19
	70

a)   Calculate the mean for the data set.
b)   Calculate the standard deviation for the data set.

103) The table below shows the number of units earned at each letter grade for a college student. Calculate the GPA for the student.

Grade	Units
A (4.0)	15
B (3.0)	37
C (2.0)	20
D (1.0)	4
F (0.0)	3
	79

104) The table below shows the number of units earned at each letter grade for a college student. Calculate the GPA for the student.

Grade	Units
A (4.0)	24
B (3.0)	16
C (2.0)	9
D (1.0)	0
F (0.0)	1
	50

Applications using technology: Use the built in procedures of your calculator or statistics package to calculate the requested means and standard deviations. If possible, use the given value of $\sum x^2$ to verify your data entry.

105) The ages of all 33 of the employees at a midsize architecture firm are provided in the table below. Calculations are being made to summarize the ages of these employees.

46	33	25	62	53	43	60
39	47	50	26	40	42	70
56	58	27	41	57	35	53
36	47	64	52	39	47	43
45	38	57	31	29		

Note: $\sum x^2 = 71,699$

a)   Calculate the mean for the ages.
b)   Calculate the standard deviation for the ages.

106) A random sample of 23 bags of salt water taffy was taken from a coastal gift store. The number of pieces of candy in each bag was counted and the results are listed in the following table.   We wish to use the results to make estimates about all such bags.

45	40	42	38	40	42
40	43	38	39	41	40
42	40	38	42	41	41
44	40	37	41	42	

Note: $\sum x^2 = 38,176$

a)   Calculate the mean for the number of pieces of taffy per bag.
b)   Calculate the standard deviation for the number of pieces of taffy per bag.
c)   Suppose that you bought 77 bags of taffy from this store. How many total pieces of candy would you expect to get?

107) In January 2015, a nationwide survey was conducted regarding gas prices in the U.S.   A random sample of 36 stations produced the following prices per gallon for regular unleaded gasoline. We will use our results to make estimates about national gas prices in the U.S.

1.83	2.26	2.22	2.22	1.96	2.18
2.03	2.05	1.95	1.93	1.99	1.98
1.73	2.36	1.80	3.37	2.01	1.93
2.04	1.89	2.49	2.57	2.04	2.10
1.92	2.01	2.25	2.12	2.53	2.88
1.93	2.18	2.29	1.94	1.88	1.99

Note: $\sum x^2 = 167.6315$

a)   Calculate the mean for the prices.
b)   Calculate the standard deviation for the prices.
c)   Suppose that while making a 3000-mile road trip across the country that you had to stop several times for gas and that you purchased 114.7 gallons of gas total. How much would you expect the total gas bill to be for the trip?

108) A company produces a wall mount for large size HDTVs. The box claims that the wall mount can safely hold weights up to 200 pounds. In a recent test, they randomly chose 30 wall mounts and increased the amount of weight on them until they failed. The failure weights, in pounds, are listed below. We wish to make estimates about the failure weights for all such wall brackets.

253	245	258	238	221	248
263	255	265	270	222	245
237	226	223	244	217	212
249	273	231	247	243	276
228	260	229	221	242	263

Note: $\sum x^2 = 1,787,482$

a) Calculate the mean for the failure weights.
b) Calculate the standard deviation for the failure weights.

109) An Intermediate Algebra class completed a homework assignment using an online homework system. The time, in minutes, spent by each of the 22 students on the assignment is shown below. We wish to summarize the times for these students.

79	317	229	115	116	158
213	103	130	215	73	101
42	117	97	75	137	157
110	520	128	210		

Note: $\sum x^2 = 762,338$

a) Calculate the mean for the data set.
b) Calculate the standard deviation for the data set.

110) An Intermediate Algebra class completed a chapter quiz using an online homework system. The time, in minutes, spent by each of the 18 students on the assignment is shown below. We wish to summarize the times for these students.

50	41	13	36	47	35
25	37	36	41	42	29
41	44	12	22	35	46

Note: $\sum x^2 = 24,242$

a) Calculate the mean for the data set.
b) Calculate the standard deviation for the data set.

111) A random sample of 27 college students was taken and the number of moving violations (speeding tickets, etc.) received in the last 3 years was obtained. The data is shown below. We will use our results to make estimates about the number of moving violations for all college students.

0	4	1	0	1	2	0
1	0	0	0	1	4	0
2	2	0	2	0	1	0
11	0	0	0	2	6	

Note: $\sum x^2 = 214$

a) Calculate the mean for the number of violations.
b) Calculate the standard deviation for the data set.
c) If you asked this question of 47 college students, how many total tickets would you expect?
d) What percentage of the data values lie within 1 standard deviation of the mean?

112) A random sample of 24 Facebook accounts was taken and number of words in their last status update was noted. We wish to make estimates about the number of words in all status updates on Facebook. The word counts are shown below.

30	4	25	18	6	9
27	45	55	2	67	26
5	1	15	24	18	30
43	8	8	8	2	13

Note: $\sum x^2 = 17,195$

a) Calculate the mean number of words.
b) Calculate the standard deviation for the number of words.
c) If you looked at a random sample of 93 Facebook posts, what would expect the total word count to be for those posts?
d) What percentage of the data values lie within 1 standard deviation of the mean?

113) After about two-thirds of the players had been eliminated from a poker tournament, the number of chips possessed by each of the remaining players was noted. The data will only be used to summarize the chip counts of the remaining players. The counts are shown below.

7387	5160	13472	2670	12930
4905	11260	5475	7700	6480
21952	8704	8455	4626	14620
2595	5020	25015	5790	4000
11535	5455	7855	29670	15140
18605	1150	16455		

Note: $\sum x^2 = 4,242,872,899$

a) Calculate the mean number of chips per player.
b) Calculate the standard deviation for the chip counts.
c) What percentage of the chips counts lie within 1 standard deviation of the mean?
d) What percentage of the chip counts lie within 2 standard deviations of the mean?

114) The following is a price list, rounded to the nearest dollar, for all of the pieces in an art studio. Calculations are only being made to summarize the prices of these pieces of art.

133	13	78	517	968	295
360	253	60	193	703	929
356	944	623	683	38	608
219	1063	901	490	527	446
159	238	144	295	158	416
909	78	227	533	319	200
1535	77	70	2160	446	821

Note: $\sum x^2 = 17,460,123$

a) Calculate the mean price for the art in the studio.
b) Calculate the standard deviation for the prices.
c) What percentage of the data values lie within 1 standard deviation of the mean?
d) What percentage of the data values lie within 2 standard deviations of the mean?

115) A concert for a popular band at a major arena is sold out. A random sample of 34 tickets for sale online produced the following ticket prices. The results will be used to make estimate about the prices of tickets available online for this concert.

165	130	110 ◡	280†	220	290†
165	130	249	135	150	419✗
179	140	259	139	179	209
160	169	309✝	129	165	130
275⑥	199	209	240	345✗	135
159	225	140	239		

Note: $\sum x^2 = 1{,}520{,}094$

a)   Calculate the mean of the ticket prices.
b)   Calculate the standard deviation for the prices.
c)   If you were to purchase 5 tickets to this sold out show online, what should you expect the total cost to be?
d)   What percentage of the data values lie within 1 standard deviation of the mean?
e)   What percentage of the data values lie within 2 standard deviations of the mean?

116) The points scored by the winning teams in a sample of 48 games played during the 2007 NFL season are shown below.   The results will be used to make estimates about the winning scores in all games that season.

20	22	51	10	21	22	31	37	33	-8
29	13	26	20	20	31	23	32	28	-10
27	30	21	49	38	25	19	35	38	38
20	41	-16	22	48	27	-13	30	34	20
33	31	27	17	42	44	38	38		

Note: $\sum x^2 = 43{,}026$

a)   Calculate the mean number of points for the winning teams.
b)   Calculate the standard deviation for the number of points scored by the winning team.
c)   What percentage of the point totals lie within 1 standard deviation of the mean?
d)   What percentage of the point totals lie within 2 standard deviations of the mean?

117) A statistics instructor decided to estimate his average speed while mountain biking. He decided to note his speed at quarter mile intervals using his cycling computer. The speed data sampled is shown below.

4.2	6.0	19.5	3.2	23.6	11.8	2.9
8.4	5.6	2.8	25.1	16.8	7.3	30.2
5.0	3.8	27.5	3.4	8.7	4.4	18.1
14.9						

Note: $\sum x^2 = 4588$

a)   Calculate the mean of the sample speeds.
b)   Calculate the standard deviation of the speeds.
c)   Given that the actual ride covered a distance of 5.48 miles and took 0.86 hours to complete, use the formula $d = r \cdot t$ to find the true average speed for this mountain bike ride.
d)   Assuming that all the speeds were recorded correctly, what was wrong with the sampling technique that caused such a bad estimate in part (a) of this problem?

118) A statistics instructor decided to estimate his average speed while mountain biking. He decided to note his speed every 2.5 minutes using his cycling computer. The speed data sampled is shown below.

3.8	4.5	3.4	12.1	8.0	2.8	3.1
6.9	3.1	3.3	4.0	11.8	19.2	9.4
4.1	4.7	9.8	3.4	3.1	8.5	13.4

Note: $\sum x^2 = 1362.38$

a)   Calculate the mean of the sample speeds.
b)   Calculate the standard deviation of the speeds.
c)   Given that the actual ride covered a distance of 5.48 miles and took 0.86 hours to complete, use the formula $d = r \cdot t$ to find the true average speed for this mountain bike ride.
d)   Comment on the importance of good sampling techniques. Hint: Compare with Exercise 117.

119) The moving violation data from problem (111) has been summarized in the following table. Recall: This was sample data.

# violations	Frequency
0	13
1	5
2	5
4	2
6	1
11	1
	27

Note: $\sum x^2 = 214$

a)   Calculate the mean of the number of violations.
b)   Calculate the standard deviation for the number of violations data.
c)   Explain why, despite being grouped, the answers are exactly the same as in exercise (111).

120) The art prices from problem (114) have been grouped into the following table. Recall: This was population data.

Price	Frequency
0 - 199	12
200 - 399	10
400 - 599	7
600 - 799	4
800 - 999	6
1000 - 1199	1
1200 - 1399	0
1400 - 1599	1
1600 - 1799	0
1800 - 1999	0
2000 - 2199	1
	42

Note: $\sum x^2 = 17{,}439{,}410.5$

a) Calculate the mean of the prices.
b) Calculate the standard deviation of the prices.
c) Explain why the answers are not exactly the same as in exercise (114).

121) A study was conducted to investigate the braking distance for SUV's. The braking distances, in feet, required to reach a complete stop from a speed of 60 mph for was collected for a random sample of 37 SUVs. The results will be used to estimate the 60 mph braking distance for all such SUV's.

Distance	Freq
134 – < 137	1
137 – < 140	7
140 – < 143	16
143 – < 146	29
146 – < 149	20
149 – < 152	14
152 – < 155	5
155 – < 158	2
	94

Note: $\sum x^2 = 1{,}997{,}543.5$

a) Calculate the mean of the braking data.
b) Calculate the standard deviation of the data.
c) What percentage of the data values lie within 1 standard deviation of the mean?
d) What percentage of the data values lie within 2 standard deviations of the mean?

122) The table below shows the number of goals scored by the losing team in a random sample of 47 NHL games.

Goals	Frequency
0	8
1	19
2	15
3	4
4	1
	47

Note: $\sum x^2 = 131$

a) Calculate the mean of the goal data.
b) Calculate the standard deviation of the data.
c) What percentage of the data values lie within 1 standard deviation of the mean?
d) What percentage of the data values lie within 2 standard deviations of the mean?

123) The ages of all 360 NBA players at the start of the 2004-2005 season have been grouped in the table below. We wish to summarize the age data for this group.

Age	Freq
18 – < 22	57
22 – < 26	119
26 – < 30	87
30 – < 34	53
34 – < 38	30
38 – < 42	14
	360

Note: $\sum x^2 = 275{,}104$

a) Calculate the mean of the age data.
b) Calculate the standard deviation of the data.
c) What percentage of the data values lie within 1 standard deviation of the mean?
d) What percentage of the data values lie within 2 standard deviations of the mean?

124) At one point during the ESPN broadcast of the 2010
World Series of Poker Main Event, the remaining ages
of the 366 remaining players were shown in grouped
form. We will use the data below to summarize the
ages of the remaining 366 players.

Age	Freq
21 – < 30	205
30 – < 40	88
40 – < 50	48
50 – < 60	19
60 – < 70	5
70 – < 80	1
	366

Note: $\sum x^2 = 422,526.25$

a) Calculate the mean of the age data.
b) Calculate the standard deviation of the data.
c) What percentage of the data values lie within 1
standard deviation of the mean?
d) What percentage of the data values lie within 2
standard deviations of the mean?
e) ESPN reported that the average age of these
players was 26 years old. Can that be correct
given the data that they presented? Explain.

125) The table below shows the number of units earned at
each letter grade for a university student. Calculate the
GPA for the student.

Grade	Units
A (4.0)	9
A- (3.7)	5
B+ (3.3)	6
B (3.0)	14
B- (2.7)	7
C+ (2.3)	4
C (2.0)	12
C- (1.7)	0
D+ (1.3)	0
D (1.0)	3
D- (0.7)	0
F (0.0)	1
	61

Note: $\sum x^2 = 526.98$

126) The table below shows the number of units earned at
each letter grade for a university student. Calculate the
GPA for the student.

Grade	Units
A (4.0)	3
A- (3.7)	7
B+ (3.3)	9
B (3.0)	24
B- (2.7)	17
C+ (2.3)	11
C (2.0)	21
C- (1.7)	0
D+ (1.3)	0
D (1.0)	15
D- (0.7)	0
F (0.0)	9
	116

Note: $\sum x^2 = 738.96$

Section 3.5 - Interpreting the Standard Deviation

There are two main interpretations of the standard deviation. The first one, discussed in Section 3.3, is that the more spread out a data set is, the larger its standard deviation tends to be. In that section, we used that idea to decide which of two sets had more overall variation. However, a far more important interpretation of the standard deviation is that it gives us a sense for what the typical distance away from the mean is for the data in a set. Our goal is to learn how to use this interpretation to help us determine when values in a data set should be considered unusual. We will examine this idea in the following discussion.

Heights of Female High School Seniors (*A Discussion of the Standard Deviation*)

The following are the heights, in inches, of all 50 girls in the senior class of a small high school.

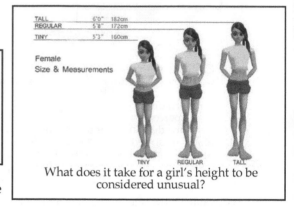

56.8	60.7	61.8	63.0	63.7	65.0	65.6	66.3
57.8	60.8	62.3	63.1	63.8	65.0	65.6	66.5
58.6	61.5	62.3	63.4	63.9	65.0	65.8	66.5
59.5	61.6	62.5	63.4	64.1	65.0	66.1	66.6
60.1	61.6	62.6	63.7	64.4	65.2	66.2	66.7
67.9	68.5	69.3	69.9	70.2	70.3	70.8	71.2
71.3	74.7						

What does it take for a girl's height to be considered unusual?

Using technology, we find the mean and standard deviation to be $\mu = 64.764$ inches and $\sigma \approx 3.6868$ inches.

Determine the percentage of the heights that lie within 1 standard deviation of the mean.

To help us visualize the situation, we will look at a dotplot of the data set and then number that dotplot in a special way to help us answer the question. We will start off by labeling the mean and then we will label on each side by adding and subtracting the standard deviation. This will give us a visual sense of how much data is within 1 standard deviation of the mean. The calculations for determining the values that lie 1 standard deviation away from the mean are shown below:

$$\mu - \sigma = 64.764 - 3.6868 = 61.0772 \quad \& \quad \mu + \sigma = 64.764 + 3.6868 = 68.4508$$

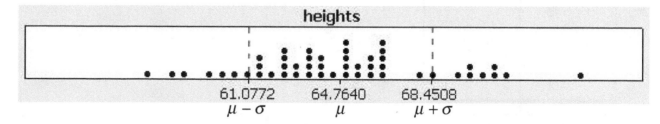

From the visual we can see that there is a large percentage of the data within these boundaries. We can look at the original data set above and count how many data values actually lie between 61.0772 and 68.4508. We find that there are 34 girls who have heights in this range (all the ones from 61.5 inches to 67.9 inches.) So the final answer to this question is:

$$\frac{34}{50} = 0.68 = 68\% \text{ of the heights lie within 1 standard deviation of the mean.}$$

Determine the percentage of the heights that lie within 2 standard deviations of the mean.

Here we just repeat the process, but now we want to go 2 standard deviations on each side of the mean. The calculations are as follows:

$$\mu - 2\sigma = 64.764 - 2(3.6868) = 57.3904 \quad \& \quad \mu + 2\sigma = 64.764 + 2(3.6868) = 72.1376$$

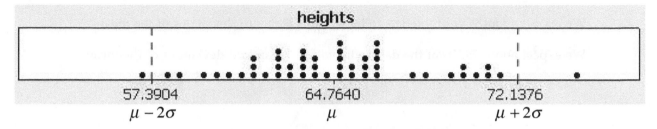

We should now notice that most of the data lies within 2 standard deviations of the mean. When we count all the heights that lie between these boundaries, we get the following result:

$$\frac{48}{50} = 0.96 = 96\%$$ of the heights lie within 2 standard deviations of the mean.

Determine the percentage of the heights that lie within 3 standard deviations of the mean.

Finally we repeat the process one more time, but this time extending out 3 standard deviations away from the mean as follows:

$$\mu - 3\sigma = 64.764 - 3(3.6868) = 53.7036 \quad \& \quad \mu + 3\sigma = 64.764 + 3(3.6868) = 75.8244$$

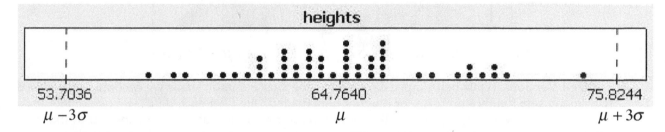

We now notice that all of the data lies within our boundaries. So our final result is that we have:

$$\frac{50}{50} = 1 = 100\%$$ of the heights lie within 3 standard deviations of the mean.

We have examined the percentage of data that lies within 1, 2, and 3 standard deviations of the mean for the heights of these female high school seniors, but if we performed the same task for other data sets, we would see that we typically obtain answers very similar to the ones above. We want to be able to apply what we learned from examining the data set above to future data sets we encounter. The ideas we have seen for these heights are generalized in the following Point to Remember.

Point to Remember: *The Empirical Rule for Bell-Shaped data (and generalized for most other sets)*

The Empirical Rule: For bell-shaped data sets, the Empirical Rule tells us the percentage of data that we should expect to lie within 1, 2, or 3 standard deviations of the mean.

We expect about 68% of the data to lie within 1 standard deviation of the mean.

We expect about 95% of the data to lie within 2 standard deviations of the mean.

We expect about 99.7% of the data to lie within 3 standard deviations of the mean.

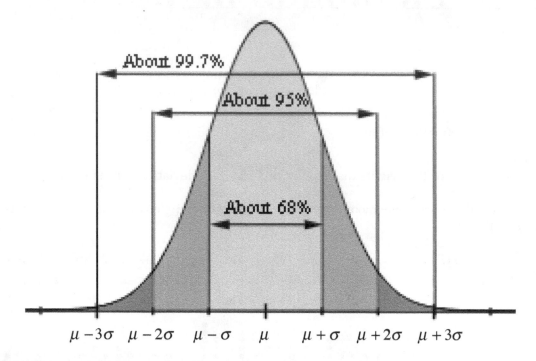

$$\mu - 3\sigma \quad \mu - 2\sigma \quad \mu - \sigma \quad \mu \quad \mu + \sigma \quad \mu + 2\sigma \quad \mu + 3\sigma$$

Generalized Version: While bell-shaped data may be the most common shape we encounter, we also deal with many sets that are uniform, or roughly bell-shaped, etc. For such data sets, we cannot provide such precise percentages, but it is still nice to have a rough idea of what is expected in those cases. Also, even if the population is bell-shaped, the sample will only be roughly bell-shaped due to random variation. If data sets contain severe outliers or have peaks near the maximum (severely left-skewed), the minimum (severely right-skewed), or both (U-shaped), then they may violate the ranges given below. However, for most other types of data sets, we expect the following:

We expect about 50% to 80% of the data to lie within 1 standard deviation of the mean.

We expect about 90% to 100% of the data to lie within 2 standard deviations of the mean.

We expect about almost 100% of the data to lie within 3 standard deviations of the mean.

In simple words: For most data sets we get a *majority* of the data within 1 standard deviation, *most* of the data within 2 standard deviations, and usually *all* or *almost all* of the data within 3 standard deviations of the mean.

Note: The Empirical Rule can also be used in conjunction with the sample mean and standard deviation.

APPLICATION OF THE EMPIRICAL RULE: *Deciding what is considered unusual or rare*

We will now turn our attention to using the empirical rule to help us decide when a data value should be considered unusual. While the word "unusual" often has a negative connotation, in statistics, we consider something to be unusual because it is "rare" or occurs a low percentage of the time. Unusual things can be unusually good, unusually bad, or just a surprise.

The majority of a data set (68% for bell-shaped and 50% to 80% for most others) lies within 1 standard deviation of the mean. So any data that lies in this interval is considered to be *normal*. However, this only accounts for 50% to 80% of the data, so it does not make sense to refer to the other 20% to 50% as unusual. On the other hand, because most of the data set (95% for bell-shaped and 90% to 100% for most others) lies within 2 standard deviations of the mean, only 0% to 10% of the data lies beyond 2 standard deviations. For bell-shaped data sets, only the top 2.5% and the bottom 2.5% are more than 2 standard deviations away from the mean. This represents a much smaller fraction of the data set. Because values like this occur a low percentage of the time, we tend to consider these values to be *unusual*. Moreover, because we usually get all or almost all of our data (99.7% for bell-shaped) within 3 standard deviations of the mean, anything beyond that would be very rare and is considered to be *very unusual*. Data that lies between 1 and 2 standard deviations away from the mean is hard to classify. Whether or not those data values are considered unusual will vary from person to person and from situation to situation. We call this the *gray area*. The following chart summarized this discussion.

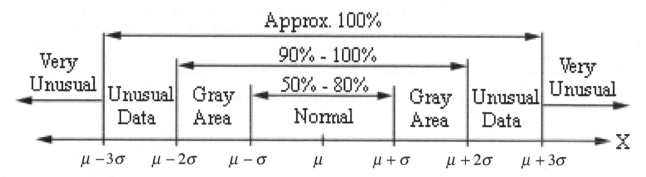

We should notice that the further a data value is located away from the mean, the more rare, and therefore, the more unusual the data value is considered to be. When we are wondering if a data value is unusual or not, it would be very burdensome to compute all of the cutoffs shown on the chart above. It would be very helpful if somehow we could just compute a single number that would tell us where our data value is located on the chart above. Such a calculation does exist and it is called the **z-score** of a data value.

Definition: *The z-score of a data value*

    z-score: The z-score for a data value tells us the number of standard deviations a data value is away from the mean. z-scores can be computed using the mean and standard deviation from either a sample or the population. The formulas are as follows:

$$\text{Population:}\quad z = \frac{x - \mu}{\sigma} \qquad\qquad \text{Sample:}\quad z = \frac{x - \bar{x}}{s}$$

    Rounding Rule: To achieve consistent answers in later chapters, z-scores should always be rounded to *exactly* 3 decimal places.

    Note: The more standard deviations away from the mean a data value is, the more unusual it is considered to be.

According to the chart above, any data value that is more than 2 standard deviations away from the mean is considered to be either unusual or very unusual. Therefore, any data values that lie within 2 standard deviations of the mean would not be considered unusual. Based on this idea, we say the usual or **expected range** for a variable is the set of all possible values that lie within 2 standard deviations of the mean.

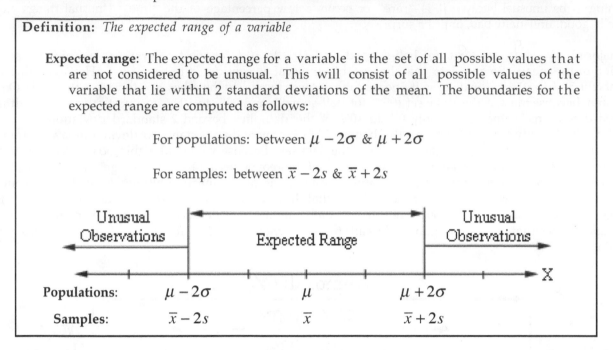

Definition: *The expected range of a variable*

    Expected range: The expected range for a variable is the set of all possible values that are not considered to be unusual. This will consist of all possible values of the variable that lie within 2 standard deviations of the mean. The boundaries for the expected range are computed as follows:

$$\text{For populations: between } \mu - 2\sigma \ \& \ \mu + 2\sigma$$

$$\text{For samples: between } \overline{x} - 2s \ \& \ \overline{x} + 2s$$

Let's take a look at an example to see how these rules and definitions help us determine what values in a given data set are considered to be unusual.

Example 3.22: *Heights of Female High School Seniors (Revisited)*

The following are the heights of all 50 girls in the senior class of a small high school.

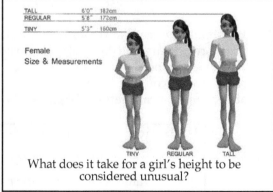

What does it take for a girl's height to be considered unusual?

56.8	60.7	61.8	63.0	63.7	65.0	65.6	66.3
57.8	60.8	62.3	63.1	63.8	65.0	65.6	66.5
58.6	61.5	62.3	63.4	63.9	65.0	65.8	66.5
59.5	61.6	62.5	63.4	64.1	65.0	66.1	66.6
60.1	61.6	62.6	63.7	64.4	65.2	66.2	66.7
67.9	68.5	69.3	69.9	70.2	70.3	70.8	71.2
71.3	74.7						

Recall: the mean and standard deviation for this data is $\mu = 64.764$ inches and $\sigma \approx 3.6868$ inches.

a) Would the girl that is 74.7 inches tall be considered unusually tall for this school? Explain.

b) Which was a more unusual height, that of the shortest girl or that of the tallest girl? Explain.

c) Find the expected range for the heights of the girls at this school. That is, what height range would a senior girl in this school have to fall in, so that her height would not be considered unusual?

d) Suppose a new senior girl moves to this school and we are told that her height has a z-score of 1.753. What does this tell us about the height of this new girl?

Solution:

a) Whenever we are asked whether or not a given data value is unusual or not, the best strategy is to find the z-score and use that to answer the question.

$$z = \frac{x - \mu}{\sigma} = \frac{74.7 - 64.764}{3.6868} \approx 2.695$$

This tells us that the height in question is 2.695 standard deviations above the mean. Because 74.7 inches is more than 2 standard deviations above the mean, it would be fair to say that this girl would be considered unusually tall among the senior girls at this school.

> **Key Concept:** *Why unusual is important*
>
> While it may not be polite to talk about whether someone is unusually short or unusually tall, this is a very important statistical topic. When analyzing data it is important to make note of unusual observations because they may point out errors in our data set or possibly a problem with the process we are analyzing.

b) We will compute the z-scores for both of these girls. Whichever girl is more standard deviations away from the mean will be considered the more unusual one.

For the shortest girl: $z = \dfrac{x - \mu}{\sigma} = \dfrac{56.8 - 64.764}{3.6868} \approx -2.160$ standard deviation from the mean

For the tallest girl: $z = \dfrac{x - \mu}{\sigma} = \dfrac{74.7 - 64.764}{3.6868} \approx 2.695$ standard deviations from the mean

Because the height of each of these girls is more than 2 standard deviations away from the mean, both of them have heights that would be considered unusual in their school. However, the tallest girl's height is more unusual because it is 2.695 standard deviations away from the mean while the other one is only 2.160 standard deviations away.

c) Any girl whose height was more than 2 standard deviations away from the mean would be considered unusual or possibly very unusual. So any girl whose height lies within 2 standard deviations would not be considered unusual. We compute the boundaries of the expected range as follows.

$$\mu - 2\sigma = 64.764 - 2(3.6868) = 57.3904 \quad \& \quad \mu + 2\sigma = 64.764 + 2(3.6868) = 72.1376$$

So the expected height range for these girls is anywhere between 57.3904 inches and 72.1376 inches.

d) Knowing that her height has a z-score of 1.753 tells us many things about her height. First of all, because the z-score is positive we know that she has an above average height. Using the units of z-scores, we can say that her height is 1.753 standard deviations above the mean height for girls at this school. Because this is less than 2 standard deviations above the mean, she is not unusually tall. However, because her standard deviation is more than 1 standard deviation, she would probably be considered somewhat tall rather than normal height. We can also use her z-score to calculate her height. If we were told that she was 2 standard deviations above the mean, the her height would be $x = \mu + 2\sigma$. For a z-score of 1.753, we simply change the 2 in that formula to 1.753 as follows.

The new girl's height = $x = \mu + 1.753 \cdot \sigma = 64.764 + 1.753(3.6868) \approx 71.22$ inches tall.

The previous example shows us that whenever we are asked if a data value is unusual or not, we will answer this question by computing the z-score for the data value. Because of this, it is useful to have a version of normal vs. unusual chart that is scaled based on z-scores rather than the original x values. The modified version of the chart is shown below. We also see that it is useful to be able to change a z-score back to an x-value. The formula for doing that is show below the new z-score chart.

Point to Remember: *Interpreting the z-score of a data value*

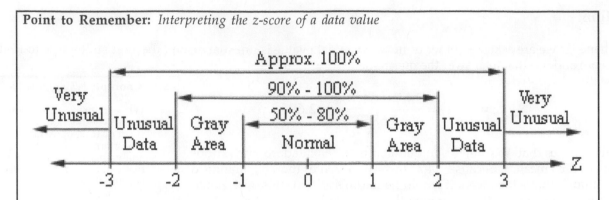

Notes: After we calculate the z-score for a data value, we locate its position on the chart above to classify it. A negative on a z-score indicates that the data value in question was below the mean rather than above it.

Point to Remember: *Converting a z-score to an x-value*

If you are given a z-score and need to convert it back to an x-value, then substitute the given z-score into one of the formulas below. Which formula you would use depends on whether you started with population data or sample data.

For Populations: $x = \mu + z\sigma$ **For Samples:** $x = \bar{x} + z \cdot s$

Notes: Even though the formulas show addition, if your data value is to the left of the mean, then the z-score will be negative. Adding the negative z-score multiplier will result in subtraction in the formulas.

Example 3.23: *Length of the line at Starbucks*

The number of people in line at a local Starbucks at 8:00 a.m. was observed on a random sample of 34 days. The sample produced a mean of 8.33 people with a standard deviation of 3.9448 people.

a) Based on the sample, would it be unusual to find 15 people in line at 8:00 a.m. at this particular Starbucks? Explain.

b) Based on the sample, would it be unusual to find no people in line at 8:00 a.m. at this particular Starbucks? Explain.

How many people do we expect to see at 8:00 a.m. in our local Starbucks? How many would it take for us to consider it to be unusual?

c) Find the expected range for the number of people in line at 8:00 a.m. at this particular Starbucks. That is, how many people could be in line, so that it would not be considered unusual?

d) Suppose that a statistics student went to this Starbucks before class this morning and reported that the length of the line had a z-score of –1.351. What does that tell us about the line the student encountered at Starbucks?

Solution:

a) Whenever we are asked if a particular value of a variable is unusual, it is best to calculate the z-score for that value. So we will calculate the z-score for 15 people. In this problem, the mean and standard deviation provided came from a sample, so we use the following.

$$z = \frac{x - \bar{x}}{s} = \frac{15 - 8.33}{3.9448} \approx 1.691$$

The z-score tells us that 15 people is 1.691 standard deviations above the mean. Because 15 people in line is less than 2 standard deviations away from the mean, we would not consider this to be an unusual observation.

b) For this one, we will calculate the z-score for zero people in line.

$$z = \frac{x - \bar{x}}{s} = \frac{0 - 8.33}{3.9448} \approx -2.112$$

The z-score tells us that zero people in line is 2.112 standard deviations below the mean. Because zero people is more than 2 standard deviations away from the mean, we would consider that to be unusual.

c) To not be considered unusual, the number of people in line must be less than 2 standard deviations away from the mean. We will start by calculating the two numbers that are exactly 2 standard deviations away from the mean.

$$\bar{x} - 2s = 8.33 - 2*3.9448 = 0.4404 \text{ and}$$

$$\bar{x} + 2s = 8.33 + 2*3.9448 = 16.2196$$

Caution: *Expected range for a discrete variable*
When calculating the expected range for a discrete variable, there are two important things to remember.   • We should adjust the numbers we calculate so that they make sense as possible values of the variable.   • When making this adjustment, we are not rounding. We consider the smallest possible value that fits in the range and the highest possible value that lies in the range.

Because the number of people in line must be a whole number, we will start with the smallest integer in this range and extend to the highest integer in the range. Therefore, we expect the number of people in line at 8:00 a.m. at this particular Starbucks to be anywhere from 1 to 16 people. Notice in the graph below that even though 0.4404 is closer to 0 than 1, we use 1 because 1 is in the expected range, but 0 is an unusual observation.

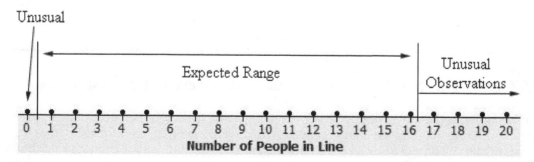

d) The z-score of –1.351 tells us that the student encountered a below average length line this morning at Starbucks. However, it was not an unusually short line. We can also calculate how long the line was.

The number of people in line = $x = \bar{x} + z \cdot s = 8.33 - 1.351(3.9448) \approx 3$ people in line.

The z-score is a very useful way to decide if a value is unusual or not, but it is also a great tool for comparing two items that many people might think cannot be compared. When we compute the z-score for a variable, we are changing the units from inches, pounds, dollars, etc. to the number of standard deviations away from the mean. This process is called **standardizing** and is very helpful in making comparisons.

Definition: *standardizing variables*

Standardizing: Computing the z-score for a value of a variable is referred to as standardizing. We say this because the units are changed from inches, pounds, dollars, etc. to the number of standard deviations away from the mean.

Recall: The more standard deviations a value is from the mean, the more unusual or rare it is considered to be.

Let's see how standardizing can help us make a comparison that many might think to be difficult if not impossible.

Example 3.24: *Comparing apples and oranges*

The mean number of seeds in apples is 10.7 with a standard deviation of 2.305 seeds. The average weight of ripe oranges is 154 grams with a standard deviation of 16.22 grams. Which would be considered more unusual, an apple that had 14 seeds or a ripe orange that only weighed 135 grams? Explain.

Is it possible to compare apples and oranges?

Solution:

To answer this question, we will compute the z-score for each of the hypothetical fruits described above.

$$\text{The apple: } z = \frac{x - \mu}{\sigma} = \frac{14 - 10.7}{2.305} \approx 1.432 \qquad \text{The orange: } z = \frac{x - \mu}{\sigma} = \frac{135 - 154}{16.22} \approx -1.171$$

Neither of these data values would be considered unusual as their z-scores reveal that both of them lie within 2 standard deviations of the mean. Despite this fact, we would still say that the apple with 14 seeds is more unusual than the 135 gram orange because the 14 seeds is more standard deviations away from its mean than the 135 gram weight.

AN IMPORTANT DISTINCTION: *Sometimes we should expect the unusual*

It is important to point out the difference between something being considered an unusually high or low value in a data set and it being unusual that such an item would exist. For example, in most cities it is safe to say that someone earning $1,000,000 or more has an unusually high income. What we mean by this is that only a small percentage, let's say 1%, of people in the city earn this much. However, if 1% of the people earn this much and there are 200,000 people living in the city in question, then 1% of these people or 2000 of them should earn $1,000,000 or more. So while this is an unusually high income, we still should not be surprised to see that it exists in this city. Let's look at another example.

Example 3.25: *Ages of people living in the United States*

In 2008, based on Census Bureau figures, the United States had a population of 301,237,703. The average age of these people was estimated to be 37.31 years old with a standard deviation of 22.550 years old.

a) If we randomly selected a person from the U.S. at this time and it turned out that they were 100 years old, would that be considered unusual? Explain.

b) Would it be unusual for there to be a 100 year old person in the U.S. at that time? Explain.

Is it considered unusual in the U.S. to be 100 years old? It depends.

Solution:

a) This is actually a pretty straightforward z-score question.

$$z = \frac{100 - 37.31}{22.550} \approx 2.780$$

Yes, the z-score shows us that a 100-year old person would be more than 2 standard deviations away from the mean. Therefore, they would be considered to be unusually old (a rare and precious commodity.)

b) No, this would not be unusual at all. This may be surprising given the z-score, but it does make sense. By the Empirical Rule we expect almost 100% of the data values in most sets to lie within 3 standard deviations of the mean. However, that means that we expect a small percent, let's say 0.01%, of the population to be above that mark. Out of a population of 301,237,703 people, that would mean that there might be about 30,000 people in that group.

The example above illustrates a concept worth remembering.

Key Concept: *what we mean by unusual*

When we refer to a data value as being unusual, we mean that such values are a rare occurrence percentage wise. However, in a large population, things that occur only a small percentage of the time can still occur many times.

COEFFICIENT OF VARIATION: *Deciding if the standard deviation is acceptable*

There are many processes where, even if we were achieving the desired mean, we still might be unhappy with the process because the variation in the data values is too large. We would like to have a way of deciding what standard deviations represent unacceptable levels of variation. The problem is, the larger the mean of a data set is, the larger the standard deviation tends to be. This indicates that when considering how much variation is acceptable, we should take the size of the mean into account. We do this by calculating the **coefficient of variation**.

Definition: *Coefficient of Variation*

Coefficient of Variation: The coefficient of variation, denoted CV, is the ratio of the standard deviation to the mean of a data set. The CV is sometimes called the **variation percentage**.

For populations: $CV = \dfrac{\sigma}{\mu} \cdot 100\%$ For samples: $CV = \dfrac{s}{\overline{x}} \cdot 100\%$

Example 3.26: *Testing the consistency of an IV pump*

A consultant is testing the consistency of a medical IV pump. Not only is it important that the pump deliver the correct mean amount of medication, but it is also very important that it deliver the medication with only a small amount of variation. A pump that has too much variation can at times be delivering levels of medication that are ineffective or unsafe for the patient. The consultant is testing a pump that is supposed to deliver 20 cc of medication per hour. It is vital that the percentage of variation for the pump be below 15%. A sample of 8 test runs of the pump produced the following data in CCs per hour.

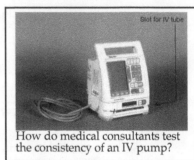

How do medical consultants test the consistency of an IV pump?

| 20.99 | 18.32 | 19.36 | 20.60 | 19.06 | 17.68 | 20.15 | 21.33 |

a) Determine the appropriate mean and standard deviation for the data set.

b) Does it appear that the level of variation for this pump is acceptable? Explain using the CV.

Solution:

a) It is stated that this is sample data, so we use technology to find $\overline{x}$ and s.

$$\overline{x} \approx 19.686 \qquad\qquad s \approx 1.3007$$

b) The percentage of variation is another name for the coefficient of variation.

$$CV = \frac{s}{\overline{x}} \cdot 100\% \approx \frac{1.3007}{19.686} \cdot 100\% \approx 6.61\%$$

Because the CV is less than 15%, this pump seems to have an acceptable level of variation.

Let's practice these new ideas with some exercises.

Exercise Set 3.5

Concept Review: Review the definitions and concepts from this section by filling in the blanks for each of the following.

127) According to the Empirical Rule for bell-shaped data sets, we expect about _____ of the data to lie within 1 standard deviation of the mean, about _____ of the data to lie within 2 standard deviations of the mean, and about _____ of the data to lie within 3 standard deviations of the mean.

128) If we generalize the Empirical Rule to try to include most data sets, then we say that we expect about _____ of the data to lie within 1 standard deviation of the mean, about _____ of the data to lie within 2 standard deviations of the mean, and almost _____ of the data to lie within 3 standard deviations of the mean.

129) A data value is considered to be unusual if it is more than ____ standard deviations away from the mean, and it is considered very unusual if it is more than ____ standard deviations away from the mean.

130) A z-score measures the number of standard _____ that a data value is away from the _____. When rounding a z-score, always use _____ ____ decimal places.

131) The expected range for data values is anything that lies within ____ standard deviations of the mean.

132) The CV stands for the coefficient of _____. It is the _____ of the standard deviation to the mean. The CV is sometimes called the _____ percentage.

Mechanics: Practice using the formulas from this section on each of the following.

133) A continuous population has a mean of 45.34 and a standard deviation of 13.315.
a) Find the z-score for a data value of 57.8.
b) Find the expected range for the data values from this population.
c) A data value has a z-score of 2.071. What does this tell us about that data value?

√ 134) A continuous population has a mean of 85.66 and a standard deviation of 22.087.
a) Find the z-score for a data value of 51.9.
b) Find the expected range for the data values from this population.
c) A data value has a z-score of 0.857. What does this tell us about that data value?

135) A discrete population has a mean of 150 and a standard deviation of 29.85. The population only consists of whole number possibilities.
a) Find the z-score for a data value of 75.
b) Find the expected range for the data values from this population.
c) A data value has a z-score of –1.209. What does this tell us about that data value?

136) A discrete population has a mean of 5.5 and a standard deviation of 1.7207. The population only consists of whole number possibilities.
a) Find the z-score for a data value of 10.
b) Find the expected range for the data values from this population.
c) A data value has a z-score of –3.027. What does this tell us about that data value?

137) A population has a mean of 187.6 and a standard deviation of 23.055. Calculate the coefficient of variation.

138) A sample has a mean of 5.088 and a standard deviation of 3.2272. Calculate the coefficient of variation.

Applications: Check to see how the data sets below match up with the percentages given in the Empirical Rule.

139) In January 2015, a nationwide survey was conducted regarding gas prices in the U.S. A random sample of 36 stations produced the following prices per gallon for regular unleaded gasoline. We will use our results to make estimates about national gas prices in the U.S.

1.83	2.26	2.22	2.22	1.96	2.18
2.03	2.05	1.95	1.93	1.99	1.98
1.73	2.36	1.80	3.37	2.01	1.93
2.04	1.89	2.49	2.57	2.04	2.10
1.92	2.01	2.25	2.12	2.53	2.88
1.93	2.18	2.29	1.94	1.88	1.99

Note: $\bar{x} \approx 2.135$, $s \approx 0.31974$

a) Determine the percentage of the data that lies within 1 standard deviation of the mean.
b) Determine the percentage of the data that lies within 2 standard deviations of the mean.
c) Determine the percentage of the data that lies within 3 standard deviations of the mean.
d) Compare your answers to parts a, b, c with the Empirical Rule.

√140) A random sample of 23 bags of salt water taffy was taken from a coastal gift store. The number of pieces of candy in each bag was counted and the results are listed in the following table. We wish to use the results to make estimates about all such bags.

45	40	42	38	40	42
40	43	38	39	41	40
42	40	38	42	41	41
44	40	37	41	42	

Note: $\bar{x} \approx 40.7$, $s \approx 1.9641$

a) Determine the percentage of the data that lies within 1 standard deviation of the mean.
b) Determine the percentage of the data that lies within 2 standard deviations of the mean.
c) Determine the percentage of the data that lies within 3 standard deviations of the mean.
d) Compare your answers to parts a, b, c with the Empirical Rule.

Applications: Practice using and interpreting z-scores in the context of real world applications.

141) The round trip times for hiking to the top of Half Dome in Yosemite National Park from the valley floor have a mean of 11.8 hours with a standard deviation of 1.05 hours.
   a) Would a hiking time of 13.5 hours to make the round trip be unusually slow? Explain.
   b) Would it be unusual for a hiker to complete the round trip in only 8 hours? Explain.
   c) Find the expected range. That is, what round trip time would a hiker need to have for it to NOT be considered unusual?
   d) A hiker's time has a z-score of 1.308. What does this tell us about the hike time for that person?

142) The round trip times for hiking to the bottom of the Grand Canyon and back have a mean of 11 hours with a standard deviation of 1.54 hours.
   a) Would a hiking time of 15 hours to make the round trip be unusually slow? Explain.
   b) Would it be unusual for a hiker to complete the round trip in only 9 hours? Explain.
   c) Find the expected range. That is, what round trip time would a hiker need to have for it to NOT be considered unusual?
   d) A hiker's time has a z-score of 2.077. What does this tell us about the hike time for that person?

143) A math test had a mean score of 77 and a standard deviation of 13.207. (Assume the test scores must be whole number values.)
   a) Would a test score of 97 on this test be considered unusually high? Explain.
   b) Would a test score of 27 on this test be considered unusually low? Explain.
   c) Find the expected range for the scores on this test. That is, what scores would NOT be considered unusual?
   d) A student's score has a z-score of –2.347. What does this tell us about the test score for that student?

144) A certain brand of soda is produced containing an average of 12 ounces of soda with a standard deviation of 0.0439 ounces.
   a) Would it be unusual for a soda can to contain only 11.93 ounces? Explain.
   b) Would it be unusual for a soda can to contain 12.1 ounces? Explain.
   c) What amounts would a make up the expected range for this data set?
   d) A can has a z-score of –0.565. What does this tell us about the amount of soda in that can?

145) The players in a baseball league had a mean batting average of 0.270 with a standard deviation of 0.053.
   a) Would a batting average of 0.300 be considered unusually high? Explain.
   b) Would a batting average of 0.400 be considered unusually high? Explain.
   c) Find the expected range. That is, what batting average would a player need to have for it to NOT be considered unusual?
   d) A player's batting average has a z-score of –3.188. What does this tell us about the batting average for that player?

146) The players in a baseball league average 16.3 homeruns per season with a standard deviation of 9.4 homeruns.
   a) Would hitting only 5 homeruns be considered unusually low? Explain.
   b) Would hitting 43 homeruns be considered unusually high? Explain.
   c) Find the expected range. That is, how many homeruns would a player need to have for it to NOT be considered unusual?
   d) A player's home run count has a z-score of –1.628. What does this tell us about that player's homerun total?

147) The wide receivers in a football league have an average of 53 receptions (passes caught) per season with a standard deviation of 19.8 receptions.
   a) Would catching only 15 passes in a season be considered unusually low? Explain.
   b) Would catching 100 passes in a season be considered unusually high? Explain.
   c) Find the expected range. That is, how many receptions would a player need to have for it to NOT be considered unusual?
   d) A player's reception total has a z-score of 0.859. What does this tell us about the number of receptions for that player?

148) The running backs in a football league rush for an average of 905.6 yards per season with a standard deviation of 351.58 yards.
   a) Would rushing for only 250 yards in a season be considered unusually low? Explain.
   b) Would rushing for 2000 yards in a season be considered unusually high? Explain.
   c) Find the expected range. That is, how many yards would a player need to have for it to NOT be considered unusual?
   d) A player's rushing total has a z-score of 3.053. What does this tell us about the rushing total for that player?

149) Which would be considered more unusual, a Half-Dome hiking time of 13.4 hours from Exercise (141) or a student scoring 100 on the math test from Exercise (143)? Explain.

150) Which would be considered more unusual, a Grand Canyon hiking time of only 8 hours from Exercise (142) or a soda can from Exercise (144) containing only 11.92 ounces of soda? Explain.

151) Which would be considered more unusual, a player with a batting average of only 0.200 from Exercise (145) or a wide receiver with 110 receptions from Exercise (147)? Explain.

152) Which would be considered more unusual, a baseball player from Exercise (146) with 25 homeruns or a running back from Exercise (148) with 1100 yards? Explain.

153) A community college student has a GPA of 3.56 under a system that does NOT include +/- grades. Assume the standard deviation for this student is 0.493.
   a) Would it be considered unusual for this student to get a 'D' (1.0)? Explain.
   b) Find the expected range. That is, what letter grades could this student get that would NOT be considered unusual?

154) A university student has a GPA of 2.84 under a system that does include +/- grades. Assume the standard deviation for this student is 1.092.
   a) Would it be considered unusual for this student to get a 'D' (1.0)? Explain.
   b) Find the expected range. That is, what letter grades could this student get that would NOT be considered unusual?

155) In a certain year, the combined SAT scores for all people taking the test had a mean of 1524.6 and a standard deviation of 235.95.
   a) Would a combined SAT score of 2100 be considered unusually high? Explain.
   b) Would it be unusual for there to be combined scores of 2100 or above in the data set from that year? Explain.

156) Suppose that adult women have an average height of 64.6 inches with a standard deviation of 2.94 inches.
   a) Would a woman who is 6'2" be considered unusually tall? Explain.
   b) Would it be unusual for there to be women who are 6'2" or above? Explain.

Applications: Calculate the coefficient of variation to answer the following questions in the context of real world application.

157) One filling machine is used to fill 12-ounce cans of soda. A sample of cans filled by this machine had a mean of 12.03 ounces with a standard deviation of 0.1035 ounces. A second machine is used to fill 1-gallon (128 ounces) milk containers. A sample of the milk containers had a mean of 128.15 ounces with a standard deviation of 0.2568 ounces.

   a) Calculate the coefficient of variation for the soda filling machine.
   b) Calculate the coefficient of variation for the milk filling machine.
   c) Which device should be considered to be the more consistent? Explain.

158) A supermarket has 10 registers open. Each register has its own line. Customers ready to check out pick the line for the register they wish to wait for. An electronics store also has 10 registers open. However, they have one single line that all customers wait in. When a register open up, the first customer in the single line goes to that register. The wait times at the supermarket have a mean of 5.7 minutes with a standard deviation of 3.207 minutes. The wait times at the electronics store have a mean of 8.75 minutes with a standard deviation of 1.574 minutes.

   a) Calculate the coefficient of variation for the supermarket wait times.
   b) Calculate the coefficient of variation for the electronics store wait times.
   c) Would it be unusual for a customer to be in line for over 12 minutes at the supermarket? Explain.
   d) Would it be unusual for a customer to be in line for more than 12 minutes at the electronics store? Explain.
   e) If having individual lines at each register and having 1 single line for all the registers is known to produce the same average wait time, then is there any advantage to having a single line? Explain.

159) A hospital needs to choose between two medical pumps. The pumps cost the same amount, so the decision will be based entirely on the accuracy and consistency of the pumps. They tested each of the pumps 6 times at a setting of 50 mg/hour and obtained the following sample flow rates, in mg/hr.

| Pump 1 | 48.3 | 48.9 | 48.4 | 53.7 | 58.0 | 43.2 |

| Pump 2 | 48.0 | 47.6 | 50.8 | 49.2 | 51.9 | 53.9 |

Note : Pump 1: $\sum x^2 = 15{,}180.59$

Pump 2: $\sum x^2 = 15{,}169.86$

   a) Calculate the mean and standard deviation for pump 1.
   b) Calculate the mean and standard deviation for pump 2.
   c) Which pump's average was closest to the target of 50 mg/hour?
   d) Calculate the coefficient of variation for each of the two pumps.
   e) Which pump is more consistent? Explain.
   f) Which pump would you recommend the hospital to buy? Explain.

160) On the Myth Busters episode, *Vector Vengeance*, 3 devices were tested with the goal of propelling a soccer ball at 60 mph with the best consistency. They tested 3 different machines: the kicking robot, the ball chucker, and the air cannon. The following speeds in mph were obtained for samples of size 5 for each device.

| Kicking Robot | 58 | 56 | 59 | 58 | 59 |

| Ball Chucker | 59 | 63 | 60 | 57 | 58 |

| Air Cannon | 58 | 59 | 59 | 58 | 57 |

Note: Robot: $\sum x^2 = 16{,}826$

Chucker: $\sum x^2 = 17{,}663$

Cannon: $\sum x^2 = 16{,}939$

   a) Calculate the mean and standard deviation for the kicking robot.
   b) Calculate the mean and standard deviation for the ball chucker.
   c) Calculate the mean and standard deviation for the air cannon.
   d) Which device's average was closest to the target of 60 mph?
   e) Calculate the coefficient of variation for each of the three devices.
   f) Given that consistency was the most import factor to the Myth Buster team, which device should they use to propel their soccer balls? Explain.

Chapter Problem: 2014 British Open Championship Golf Tournament

On the final day of the 2014 British Open Championship golf tournament, 72 golfers participated in the day's play. Rory McIlroy, from Northern Ireland, shot a 71 that day and won the championship with a four-day total score of 271. In this tournament, two other golfers, Sergio Garcia of Spain and Rickie Fowler of the U.S. tied for second place. On the final day, Sergio shot a score of 66, but his four-day total was 273. Rickie shot a 67 and also finished with a four-day total score of 273. In order to tie with Rory and force a play-off, Sergio would have needed to shoot a 64 on the final day and Rickie would have needed to shoot a 65.

The following data set provides the scores during the final round of the 2014 British Open golf tournament for all the golfers who played that day.

71	66	67	65	65	66	67	68	65	67
70	68	69	72	67	68	68	68	67	69
69	72	65	68	72	67	70	71	72	73
73	69	69	71	72	72	73	74	67	67
69	71	71	71	71	76	69	70	70	71
68	71	74	72	73	74	75	70	70	71
71	74	74	71	73	75	71	74	75	79
87	78								

a) Find the five number summary for the data set.

b) Create a modified boxplot for the data set.

c) Identify any outliers in the data set. Give two reasonable explanations for the outlier?

d) The truth is that the 87 was a typo. That golfer actually scored a 78 that day. Change the 87 back to its correct value of 78. Use the corrected value of 78 when answering the questions below. (You do not need to adjust your answers to parts a, b, and c above.)

e) Based on the boxplot (ignoring the now changed outlier), comment on the shape of the distribution.

f) The right whisker is longer than the left whisker. What does that tell us about the data located in those sections?

g) Find the appropriate mean and standard deviation of the new data set with the outlier changed to 78. Include symbols with your answers. **Note:** $\sum x^2 = 359{,}001$

h) Would you say that Rory had an unusually low score the day he won this event? Explain using z-scores.

i) Would it have taken an unusually good round for either Sergio or Rickie to have tied Rory and forced a play-off? Explain using z-scores.

j) Find the expected range for the scores. That is, what range would a score have to lie in so that it would not be considered unusual?

k) What percentage of the golfers' scores (87 changed to 78) lie within the expected range?

Chapter 3: Technology Project

1) Use the technology of your choice to complete this problem.
   a) Enter and name the data from Exercise (53) from Section 3.2 into the statistics application.
   b) Use the application to find the five number summary.
   c) Use the application to find the mean and standard deviation for the data set.
   d) Use the application to sort the data.
   E) Calculate the value of Q3 using the sorted list and methods from Section 3.2 (Do this by hand, not using the software application).
   F) Various statistics applications use different methods of finding the quartiles. Compare your answer for the third quartile from part (E) to that of the statistics application. Did you get the same exact answer or just something close?
   g) Use the statistics application to create a modified boxplot for the data set.
   H) Did the boxplot show any outliers? If so, how were they marked by the application?
   I) Show the calculations needed to find the upper fence and verify that the outlier was past the fence (Use your statistics application's values for Q1 and Q3 when making the fence calculations.)
   J) Give two possible reasons why a value in the data set would be so high.

2) For this problem, we will use the application 'Standard Deviation Demonstration' from the webpage.
   a) Enter your name into the textbox on the upper right of the window.
   b) Change the sample size to 11 and press the 'Get Data' button.
   c) You can move data values around by clicking on them once to grab them and then clicking again where you want to release them. Try to move the data values around until all but one of the values are above the mean.
   D) Fill in the blanks: The mean balances the total _____ on the left and right side.

3) This problem will use the 'Boxplot Simulation' application.
   a) Enter your name into the textbox provided. Change the sample size to 23 and the population to Uniform.
   b) Click the Get Data button and then check the box that says "Show a Dotplot".
   c) Move the data values around until your boxplot looks like the one shown below. Hint: Calculate the *locations* of the quartiles for 23 data values to know which values represent the quartiles.

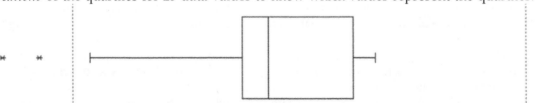

   D) The left side of the box is much narrower than the right side of the box. In general, what does that tell us about the data represented by those two parts of the graph?

4) This Problem uses the application "Boxplot Dist Quiz" from the webpage.
   a) Enter your name in the textbox provided. Change the sample size to 500. Click the Start Quiz button.
   b) Take the quiz. If you miss a question, study the graph and the right answer in the pop-up window so that you get it right next time you see it. If you score 8.5 or lower, then click clear and start quiz again.
   c) Click clear and change the sample size to 100 and then click start quiz. See if you can get at least 8 of 10 correct.
   D) How much harder, if at all, would you say the quiz became when the sample size was reduced?
   g) See how many you can get correct with a sample size of only 25.

Chapter 3: Chapter Review

Section 3.1: Measures of Center

- The mean is the statistical name for the average. To find the mean, we add all the data values and divide by the number of values. If rounding a mean, use at least one more decimal place than was used in the original data set.

- $\bar{x}$ is the symbol for the sample mean. $\bar{x} = \dfrac{\sum x}{n}$, where n is the sample size.

- μ is the symbol for the population mean. $\mu = \dfrac{\sum x}{N}$, where N is the population size.

- When rounding answers, we are introducing error. We should use the approximately equal symbol, $\approx$, to make this clear to the reader.
- The extremes in a data set skew or pull the mean in their direction. Because of this, it is common that the mean does not split the data set into a top and bottom half.
- The median is the value that attempts to split a data set into a top and bottom half.
- Data sets must be put in order before the median can be found.
- When we have an even number of data values, the median is the mean of the two middle values.

- Use a location formula, $L_M = \dfrac{1}{2}(N+1)$ or $L_M = \dfrac{1}{2}(n+1)$, to help locate the median in larger data sets.
- The mode of a data set is the value (or values) that occurs most frequently.
- The mean can be thought of as a balancing point for the data set. It balances the total distance of data on the left with the distance to the data on the right. The mean represents a fair or equal share when redistributing items among a group. The mean is affected by extremes.
- The mean is the best choice when the total of the data values is important, or when we are looking for a balancing point, or when trying to find a fair share when distributing the total to the group.
- The median separates the lower 50% of a data set from the upper 50%. The median is not affected by extreme values in the data set.
- The median is best used in situations where we want to let people know if they are in the top or bottom half of the data set. We should also use the median when we don't want the extremes to weigh heavily on the measure of center.
- The mode is best for categorical data where means and medians cannot be computed.
- Resistant quantities are not affected at all or only very little by the extremes in the data set. The median is resistant, but the mean is not.
- In a right-skewed data set, the mean has been pulled by extremes to the right of the median.
- In a left-skewed data set, the mean has been pulled by extremes to the left of the median.
- In a symmetric data set, the mean and median are equal to each other.

Section 3.2: Percentiles, Quartiles, and Boxplots

- Percentiles attempt to divide a data set into 100 equal parts.
- P_k has $k\%$ of the data below it and $(100-k)\%$ of the data set above it.
- Location of the Percentiles: For Populations: $L_{P_k} = \dfrac{k}{100}(N+1)$ or for Samples: $L_{P_k} = \dfrac{k}{100}(n+1)$
- Quartiles attempt to divide a data set into 4 equal parts.
- We usually refer to Q_2 as the median, M.
- We must always remember to put the data set in order when finding percentiles or quartiles.
- If the location of a quartile or percentile turns out to be a decimal value, then we average the two numbers in the locations surrounding that value. $L_{Q_1} = 6.75 \Rightarrow Q_1 = \dfrac{(\text{6th number}) + (\text{7th number})}{2}$
- The five number summary consists of the following: $\{Min, Q_1, M, Q_3, Max\}$
- **Warning:** Because many different procedures exist for finding quartiles, the values of Q_1 and Q_3 given by technology do not always match the ones we get by hand.
- A boxplot is a visual representation of the five number summary.
- There should be at least a small gap between the axis and the boxplot.
- The biggest clue that we get from boxplots about distribution shape is from the whiskers. Long whiskers represent tails. Long whiskers on only one side indicate that the distribution is skewed to that side.
- The range, R, is the difference between the maximum and the minimum values in the data set.
- The $IQR = Q_3 - Q_1$ and it represents the length of the box from the boxplot.
- The lower and upper fences are located $1\frac{1}{2}$ box lengths away from the box in a boxplot.
- Values located outside of the fences are considered to be outliers and are marked with an *.
- If an outlier visually stands far apart from the rest of the data, then it might be an error in the data.
- A modified boxplot is one where the upper and lower fences are found and outliers are marked.
- The whiskers on a modified boxplot extend to the largest and smallest data values that lie within the upper and lower fences.

Section 3.3: Measuring Variation

- The range gives us a quick sense of spread or variation, but it can be misleading at times because it only uses two of the data values.
- The standard deviation gives us an overall measure of the variation, or spread, in a data set. It measures the typical distance away from the mean in a data set.
- σ is the symbol for the population standard deviation.
- s is the symbol for the sample standard deviation. Remember to divide by $n-1$, rather than N, when calculating the sample standard deviation.
- It is vital that you be able to recognize whether you are working with sample data or population data and that you then apply the correct symbols to your means and standard deviations.
- The variance of a data set is the square of the standard deviation. Population: σ^2 or Sample: s^2
- When rounding standard deviations, we should use at least 5 digits, or significant figures, in our answer.
- The more overall variation in a data set, the larger its standard deviation.
- We expect to get about 50% to 80% of a data set within 1 standard deviation of the mean. We expect to get about 90% to 100% of a data set within 2 standard deviations of the mean.

Section 3.4: Grouped Data and Using Technology

- When calculating the mean and standard deviation for grouped data, we use the midpoint of the classes as our x-values. This makes the answers estimates of the true values.
- When working with grouped data, we must always multiply by the frequency before we find any sums.
- GPA calculations are the same as the mean for grouped data, but we use the number of units in place of the frequency.
- When using technology to find the mean and standard deviation, use the given value of $\sum x^2$ to verify that you have entered the data correctly.

Section 3.5: Interpreting the Standard Deviation

- The Empirical Rule says that, for bell-shaped data sets, we expect about 68% of the data to lie within 1 standard deviation of the mean, about 95% of the data to lie within 2 standard deviations of the mean, and about 99.7% of the data to lie within 3 standard deviations of the mean.
- For most other data sets, we expect about 50% to 80% of the data within 1 standard deviation, about 90% to 100% of the data to lie within 2 standard deviations of the mean, and almost 100% of the data to lie within 3 standard deviations of the mean.
- The z-score tells us how many standard deviations a data value is away from the mean.
- For populations: $z = \dfrac{x - \mu}{\sigma}$. For Samples: $z = \dfrac{x - \bar{x}}{s}$.
- z-scores should be rounded to exactly 3 decimal places.
- z-scores standardize data values by converting them from their original units to the number of standard deviations away from the mean.
- z-scores can be converted back to x-values using the following formulas:
  For populations: $x = \mu + z\sigma$; For Samples: $x = \bar{x} + zs$.
- The more standard deviations away from the mean a data value is, the more unusual it is considered to be.
- Data that lies more than 2 standard deviations away from the mean is considered to be unusual, meaning rare.
- The expected range for a data set consists of all possible values of the variable that lie within 2 standard deviations of the mean.
- When finding the expected range for a discrete variable, remember to consider the smallest and largest values that lie within 2 standard deviations rather than rounding your boundaries.
- When we state that a data value is unusual, we mean that it only occurs a low percentage of the time in the data set. This means that we would be surprised if such a value were randomly selected. However, in large data sets, it is normal for many unusual data values exist within the data set.
- The coefficient of variation or variation percentage is the ratio of the standard deviation to the mean, interpreted in percentage form. The formulas are as follows:

  For populations: $CV = \dfrac{\sigma}{\mu} \cdot 100\%$ For samples: $CV = \dfrac{s}{\bar{x}} \cdot 100\%$

- The coefficient of variation can help us compare the variation in data sets with different units or data sets that contain different sized numbers from each other.

Review Diagrams:

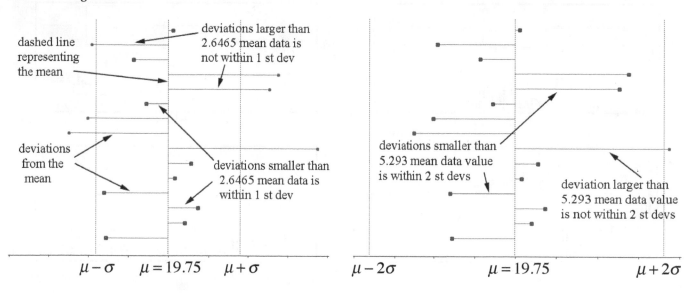

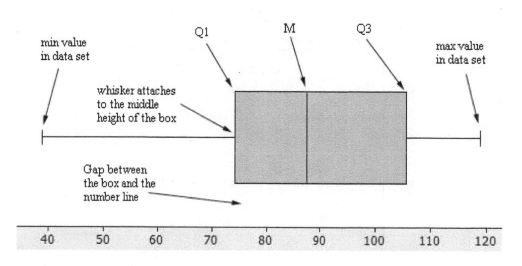

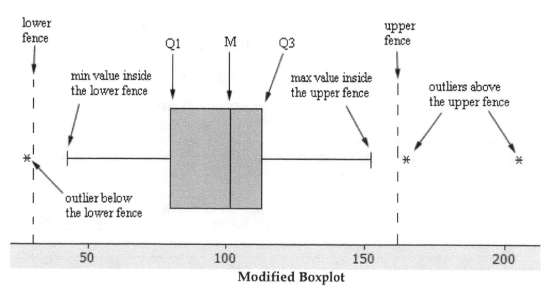

Modified Boxplot

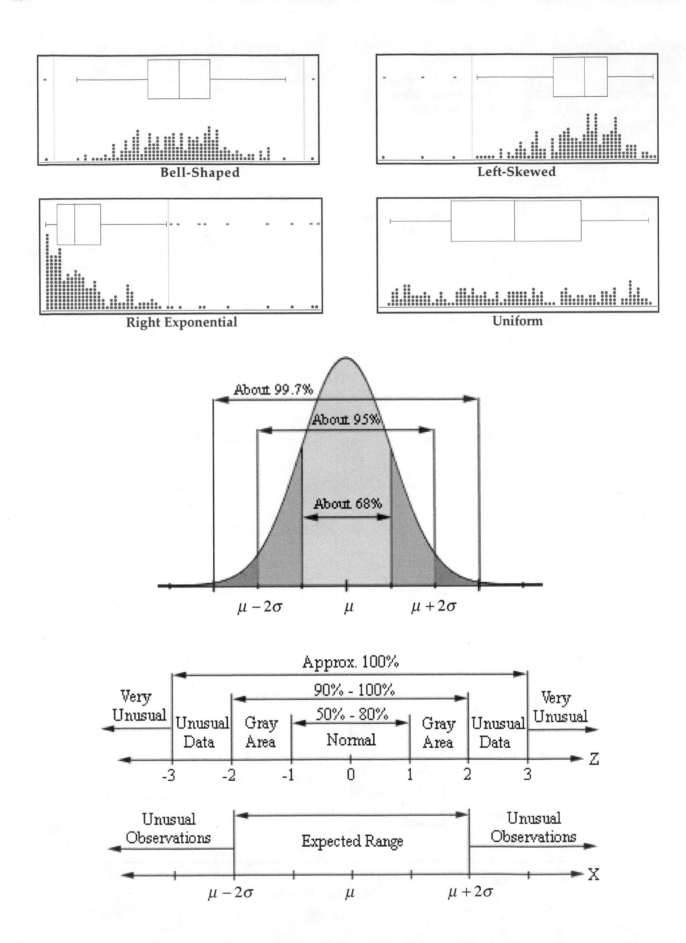

Chapter 3: Review Exercises

Mechanics: Use formulas and tables as needed to find the requested quantities. Show your work rather than using technology to get to the answers. Include symbols with your answers.

1) Assume that the data below is sample data.

10	6	4	10	1	1	3	7
6	10	2	7	5	9	8	

   a) Find the appropriate mean for the data set.
   b) Find the median for the data set.
   c) Find the mode(s) for the data set.

2) Assume that the data below is population data.

3.27	2.70	2.96	3.08	2.26	3.27	3.10
2.63	3.03	3.01	2.76	3.34	3.39	2.82

   a) Find the appropriate mean for the data set.
   b) Find the median for the data set.
   c) Find the mode(s) for the data set.

3) The data below was collected from the entire group that we wish to state conclusions about.

46.1	24.0	8.5	28.7	26.6	28.0	29.4	36.1

   a) Calculate the range for the data set.
   b) Calculate the mean for the data set.
   c) Calculate the standard deviation for the data set.

4) The data below was collected from only part of the group that we wish to state conclusions about.

343	354	372	326	282	445	510

   a) Calculate the range for the data set.
   b) Calculate the mean for the data set.
   c) Calculate the standard deviation for the data set.

5) Assume that we are making calculations to summarize the data below.

x-value	Frequency
4	12
5	23
6	41
7	27
8	18
9	7
	128

   a) Calculate the mean for the data set.
   b) Calculate the standard deviation for the data set.

6) Assume that we will use the results of our calculations to make estimates about a larger group.

Classes	Frequency
0 - <10	1
10 - <20	0
20 - <30	5
30 - <40	18
40 - <50	25
50 - <60	14
	63

   a) Calculate the mean for the data set.
   b) Calculate the standard deviation for the data set.

7) Consider the data set below to be sample data.

37.2	55.4	14.6	70.6	64.0	73.4
97.8	62.5	41.6	42.4	42.2	21.1
65.0	73.4	30.7	18.2	31.6	47.5

   a) Find all three quartiles for the data set.
   b) Find the 61st percentile.

8) Consider the data set below to be population data.

375	567	523	530	401	609
609	693	440	427	651	599
424	305	429	341	493	

   a) Find all three quartiles for the data set.
   b) Find the 15th percentile.

9) A continuous population has a mean of 4009.66 and a standard deviation of 1322.087.

   a) Would 6000 be considered an unusually high data value? Explain.
   b) Would 1000 be considered an unusually low data value? Explain.
   c) Find the expected range for the data values from this population.

10) A discrete sample has a mean of 50.7 and a standard deviation of 19.85. The population only consists of whole number possibilities.

   a) Would 100 be considered an unusually high data value? Explain.
   b) Would 35 be considered an unusually low data value? Explain.
   c) Find the expected range for the data values from this sample.

11) A sample has a mean of 501.6 and a standard deviation of 93.639. Calculate the coefficient of variation.

12) A population has a mean of 32.17 and a standard deviation of 0.098546. Calculate the coefficient of variation.

Applications: Use the techniques and formulas learned in this section to answer each of the following. Use of technology is expected if $\sum x^2$ is given to verify data entry. Write symbols with your answers where appropriate.

13) A random sample of 14 college students that owned cars were asked how many years old their cars were. The age data for these 14 cars are shown below. Assume that we will use our results to make estimates about the ages of all college students' cars.

2	18	6	3	23
5	3	12	5	4
5	1	4	9	

 a) Calculate the mean for the data set.
 b) Calculate the median of the data set.
 c) Find the mode(s) for the data set.
 d) Would you describe this data as left-skewed, right-skewed, or neither? Explain.
 e) Which of these measures of center would be best for helping students decide if their car was in the younger or older half of student cars? Explain.

14) For 15 days, I kept track of the number of diapers used per day for my 7-month old niece Sofia. The data is shown below. We wish to summarize the diaper use for these 15 days.

7	7	8	5	8
8	9	13	9	8
7	7	5	10	10

 a) Calculate the mean for the data set.
 b) Calculate the median of the data set.
 c) Find the mode(s) for the data set.
 d) Would you describe this data as left-skewed, right-skewed, or neither? Explain.
 e) Which of these measures of center would be best for planning how many diapers to buy for the next 15 days? Explain.

15) To prepare for a midterm, an Intermediate Algebra class was encouraged to take a practice test online. They were told to take it as many times as needed until they were satisfied with their score. The number of hours spent taking the practice test is shown below. We wish to summarize the times for the class.

2.4	5.3	2.4	2.0	1.9	2.5
2.5	5.5	0.9	1.5	4.5	2.1
2.5	0.9	2.1	3.5	6.6	5.0
2.5	4.9	4.1	3.3	2.8	7.1

Note: $\sum x^2 = 326.18$

 a) Calculate the range for the data set.
 b) Calculate the mean for the data set.
 c) Calculate the standard deviation of the data set.

16) Statistics students were surveyed about their Facebook accounts. They were asked how many people had commented or clicked "like" on their last status update. The totals for the most recent status updates of 17 students are shown below. Assume that we will use this data to make estimate about all statistics students who use Facebook.

9	4	1	2	4	1
2	0	3	9	7	5
4	4	3	7	13	

Note: $\sum x^2 = 546$

 a) Calculate the range for the data set.
 b) Calculate the mean for the data set.
 c) Calculate the standard deviation of the data set.
 d) Suppose that we randomly selected 100 Facebook posts made by college students. How many total comments or "likes" should we expect?

17) A gambler has been reading books about how to count cards and gain an advantage in the game of Blackjack. He decides to test his knowledge by playing for 2 hours per night over a 30-day period. The amount won or lost per session, in dollars, is shown below. Losses are shown as negative amounts. We will use our results to make estimates about the long term results should he continue to play.

120	-70	65	-160	195	-20
-20	-50	-40	-40	-315	-555
-45	485	165	-80	-240	-360
-50	185	40	-115	80	-165
40	-120	-110	-115	-150	-120

Note: $\sum x^2 = 1,122,375$

 a) Calculate the mean for the data set.
 b) Calculate the standard deviation for the data set.
 c) Suppose that we were to randomly select 200 sessions of blackjack for this gambler. What should we expect for the total profit or loss?
 d) What percentage of the data values lie within 1 standard deviation of the mean?
 e) What percentage of the data values lie within 2 standard deviations of the mean?

18) An online poker player routinely plays in 9-player online tournaments. She keeps track of the place she finishes for 28 tournaments. We will use our results to make estimates about her long-term results in the future.

2	3	1	7	7	9	1
9	2	1	9	1	7	1
2	4	2	3	1	2	8
1	1	1	4	8	1	8

Note: $\sum x^2 = 662$

 a) Calculate the mean for the data set.
 b) Calculate the standard deviation for the data set.
 c) What percentage of the data values lie within 1 standard deviation of the mean?
 d) What percentage of the data values lie within 2 standard deviations of the mean?

19) A survey asks people how many televisions they have in their household. The results are shown in the table below. Assume calculations will be used to make estimates about the number of televisions in all households.

# of TVs	Frequency
0	15
1	47
2	88
3	147
4	98
5	34
6	12
7	3
	444

Note: $\sum x^2 = 4719$

a) Calculate the mean number of TVs per household.
b) Calculate the standard deviation for the data.
c) Suppose that we were to randomly select 50 such households. How many TV's altogether would we expect among those households.
d) What percentage of the households lie within 1 standard deviation of the mean?
e) What percentage of the households lie within 2 standard deviations of the mean?

20) A Lake Tahoe Ski resort keeps track of the number of lift tickets purchased per day during the 2009/2010 season. The results are shown in grouped form in the table below. Assume the results will be used to summarize the ticket sales for the season.

# Tickets sold	Frequency
0 – 999	7
1000 – 1999	15
2000 – 2999	22
3000 – 3999	45
4000 – 4999	31
5000 – 5999	22
6000 – 6999	13
7000 – 7999	9
8000 – 8999	3
	167

Note: $\sum x^2 = 3,289,073,542$

a) Calculate the mean of the age data.
b) Calculate the standard deviation of the data.
c) Suppose that 40 days were randomly selected. How many total tickets should we expect to be sold on those 40 days?
d) What percentage of the days have ticket totals that lie within 1 standard deviation of the mean?
e) What percentage of the days have ticket totals that lie within 2 standard deviations of the mean?

21) During the 2009/2010 season, a professional basketball team scored an average of 102.5 points with a standard deviation of 7.3 points.

a) Would a score of 120 points be considered unusually high for this team? Explain.
b) Would a score of 80 points be considered unusually low for this team? Explain.
c) Find the expected range for the scores by this team during that season. That is, what scores would NOT be considered unusual?
d) For one of the games, the z-score for the number of points scored was 2.808. What does this tell us about the number of points scored by this team in that game?

22) A random sample of 115 movie theaters was taken and the price of a standard adult ticket was obtained. The sample produced a mean of $10.79 with a standard deviation of $1.57.

a) Would it be unusual for an adult ticket to cost $8? Explain.
b) Would it be unusual for an adult ticket to cost $15? Explain.
c) What amounts would make up the expected range for the adult ticket prices? That is, what prices could an adult have paid to go to the movie and it would NOT be considered unusual.
d) Suppose you found a movie theater where the adult ticket price had a z-score of –1.936. What does this tell you about the cost of an adult ticket at that theater?

23) A filling machine is used to fill bags with pretzel sticks. The machine is supposed to put an average of 550 pretzels per bag. A sample of bags filled by this machine had a mean of 548.9 pretzel sticks with a standard deviation of 8.261 sticks. The company has a strong desire to have a consistent product and demands that the variation percentage be less than 1%.

a) Calculate the coefficient of variation for the pretzel bag filling machine.
b) Is the machine working with the consistency that the company desires? Explain.

24) A professional poker player plays two different forms of poker. He plays no limit Texas Hold'em where he averages a profit of $320 per session with a standard deviation of $412. He also plays limit Omaha High-Low split where he averages a profit of $275 per session with a standard deviation of $173 per session.

a) Calculate the coefficient of variation for the Texas Hold'em profits.
b) Calculate the coefficient of variation for the Limit Omaha High-Low split profits.
c) Which would be more unusual, for the player to lose $100 playing Texas Hold'em or Playing the Omaha game? Explain.
d) Which would be more unusual, for the player to win $1000 playing Texas Hold'em or Playing the Omaha game? Explain.
e) Explain why the poker player might prefer to play the Texas Hold'em game.
f) Explain why the poker player might prefer to play the Omaha game.

25) Starting on September 1, 2010, the author of this text attempted to lose weight by counting all calories consumed each day. The number of calories consumed for breakfast during each of the days of September is recorded in the table below.

172	290	635	350	862	240	290
586	202	333	280	289	319	280
517	446	335	483	354	290	75
290	196	614	915	291	421	400
165	232					

a) Find and interpret the 90th percentile for the breakfast calories.
b) Find the five number summary.
c) Create a modified (if necessary) boxplot.
d) What is the most likely shape for the distribution of the breakfast calories? Explain.
e) Comment on any outliers.

26) A car dealership kept track of the number of cars sold per month for a two-year period. The number of cars sold in each of the 24 months is shown in the table below.

80	165	85	104	86	94
111	78	102	77	123	82
82	86	47	100	106	90
89	77	114	117	87	128

a) Find and interpret the 10th percentile for the number of cars sold per month.
b) Find the five number summary.
c) Create a modified (if necessary) boxplot.
d) What is the most likely shape for the distribution of the number of cars sold per month? Explain.
e) Comment on any outliers.

27) A statistics teacher rated the efforts of his students as either acceptable or unacceptable in three areas of test preparation: Homework, Technology Projects, and Review Assignment. The boxplots below represent the performance of the students on the exam that followed. The students' test scores were separated into 4 groups based on the number of areas in which that had acceptable preparation.

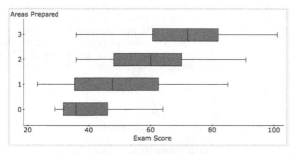

a) Use the modified boxplots to estimate the five number summary for the least prepared group of students.
b) Use the modified boxplots to estimate the five number summary for the most prepared group of students.
c) Do these boxplots support the idea that better preparation leads to better test scores? Explain.

28) The most famous movie awards show is probably the Academy Awards (or Oscars) Ceremony. However, many other organizations also vote for the best movie in a given year. One of the newer awards shows is the MTV movie awards. The tables below show the gross U.S. box office receipts for all ten of the recent nominees for best picture from the each of the two award shows (Source: IMDb.com). Boxplots for the two groups of movies are shown below the tables.

2009 Oscar Nominees

Gross	Movie
12.6	The Hurt Locker
749.5	Avatar
256.0	The Blind Side
115.5	District 9
12.6	An Education
120.5	Inglorious Basterds
47.4	Precious
9.0	A Serious Man
293.0	Up
83.8	Up in the Air

2009 & 2010 MTV Nominees

Gross	Movie
191.5	Twilight
533.3	The Dark Knight
90.6	High School Musical 3
318.3	Iron Man
141.3	Slumdog Millionaire
296.6	New Moon
334.2	Alice in Wonderland
749.5	Avatar
277.3	The Hangover
302.0	Harry Potter and the Half-Blood Prince

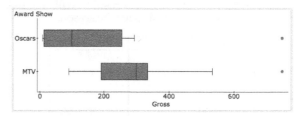

a) Which group of movies appears to have been more popular among moviegoers? Use the boxplots to support your answers.
b) Based on what you see in the two boxplots, which group of movies do you think have a larger standard deviation for their grosses? Explain.
c) Use the actual grosses from the tables to compute the mean and standard deviation for each group. Include the appropriate symbols.
d) Did the calculated standard deviations from part (c) match your prediction from part (b)? If not, what do you think you missed in the boxplots that caused the difference?
e) Use the boxplots to estimate the median gross for each of the two groups.
f) Which do you believe would be better for numerically comparing the popularity of the two groups of movies, the means or the medians? Explain.

Chapter 4 – Linear Regression

Chapter Problem: *Is a junk food diet harmful to your child's IQ?*

In February of 2011, an article published in the *Journal of Epidemiology & Community Health* stated that there is evidence that a poor diet of high fat, sugar and processed food in early childhood may be associated with small reductions in IQ in later childhood, while a healthy diet, of nutrient rich foods may be associated with small increases in IQ. The study was based on data collected from 3996 children. They recorded their eating patterns at age 3 and later checked their IQ's at age 8.5 years old. Specific results of the study stated that children whose dietary score was 1 standard deviation above average (towards healthy eating) showed an average increase in IQ of 1.20 points at age 8.5 years. On the other hand, children whose dietary score was 1 standard deviation below average (towards junk food) showed an average decrease in IQ of 1.67 points.

Does the type of food a child eats at age 3 have an effect on their intelligence at age 8.5?

In this chapter, we will want to ask the following questions about this study: How can we use a data plot to help spot this pattern in the data? If we see a linear pattern to the data, how can we find an equation to best describe the pattern? How useful is this equation for making predictions about IQ based on observed dietary patterns? Does an association between eating habits and IQ prove that junk food is harmful to a child's IQ? We will investigate this study and these questions again in the chapter problem at the end of the chapter.

Introduction:

In previous chapters, we have been performing descriptive statistics on data sets involving only a single variable. We have looked at things such as: calories in potato chips, number of shared birthdays, colors of m&m's, final exam scores, points for Baron Davis, etc. In this chapter, we will begin looking at data sets that contain two different variables. Examples will include: the size and price of homes; the ERA's for a baseball team's pitchers and the number of wins for the team; the age of a person and their peak heart rate, the mileage on a car and the price it sells for, the type of food a child eats and their IQ, etc.

When we begin dealing with two variables, the natural thing to look for is a relationship. If we find a relationship, then we will start trying to describe that relationship, use it to make predictions, and quantify the relationship between the two variables in question. When variables are related, the relationship can take many forms. In this chapter, we will only be studying linear relationships between variables. Because of that, we will begin with a review of the algebra of lines and then we will move on to apply statistics to those ideas. We will do this through the following sections.

Section 4.1   Linear Equations in Statistics
Section 4.2   Linear Regression
Section 4.3   Coefficient of Determination, r^2
Section 4.4   Linear Correlation, r

Let's get started.

Section 4.1 – Linear Equations in Statistics

This chapter will discuss linear relationships between variables. To do the work we need to do, we must be comfortable with many of the ideas from algebra concerning linear equations. However, when we work with lines in statistics, we use some different notation and we focus on different aspects of the lines. Let's begin with a quick review of one of the common forms of the equation of a line in algebra, the slope intercept form. The equation is: $y = mx + b$. In this equation, the m represents the slope and the b is the y-coordinate of the y-intercept. In the algebra setting, the x is usually referred to as the independent variable, or the input, and the y is usually called the dependent variable, or the output of the equation. In statistics, we also will use the slope intercept form of the equation, however, we will use some different variables in the equation and refer to the variables in a different manner. In statistics, the standard form of the equation will be:

$$y = b_0 + b_1 x$$

So, you can see that we have removed the m and the b and replaced them with b_1 and b_0. Also, the order of the constant term and the variable term has been switched. These changes may seem arbitrary, but they have been done to allow for the flexibility to add more parts to the equation, something that is done in more advanced statistical work. As we continue into this chapter, we will learn that the primary purpose of a linear equation will be to use the x value to make a prediction for the y value. Because of this purpose, we will now call the x value the **predictor** (also known as the **explanatory variable**) and the y value the **prediction** (also known as the **response**). Because b_1 is the coefficient of x, it is the slope and b_0 is the y-coordinate of the y-intercept. This discussion is summarized below.

Definitions: *slope, y-intercept, and variables*

The standard form of a linear equation in statistics is $y = b_0 + b_1 x$; where:

- x is the predictor or explanatory variable
- y is the prediction or response variable
- b_1 is the slope
- b_0 is the y-coordinate of the y-intercept

GRAPHING TECHNIQUES: *A quick review of one method of graphing a line*

Now that we have seen the new notation, let's begin our review with graphing linear equations. In algebra, we learn many different ways to graph a linear equation. In statistics, we will focus on the table method where we substitute in x-values to find the corresponding y-values and then we plot the points and draw our line.

Example 4.1: *Sketching the graph of linear equations*

a) Sketch the graph of $y = 5 + 3x$

b) Sketch the graph of $y = 4 - \dfrac{3}{2}x$

c) Discuss the biggest difference in the graphs that can be attributed to the slopes.

Solution:

a) Generally, the simplest way to sketch a graph is to choose any x-values you wish, substitute them into the equation and then solve for the corresponding y-values. This is how we will begin here. To try to get points in several locations on the graphs, we can choose one negative value, one positive value, and zero for our x-values.

$x = 0 \implies y = 5 + 3(0) = 5 + 0 = 5 \implies (0, 5)$ is one ordered pair on the graph. Similarly we get:

$x = -3 \implies y = 5 + 3(-3) = 5 - 9 = -4 \implies (-3, -4)$ and

$x = 2 \implies y = 5 + 3(2) = 5 + 6 = 11 \implies (2, 11)$

This information is often organized using a table as shown below.

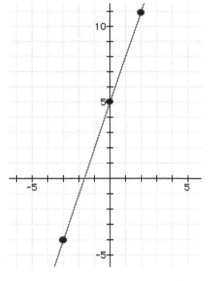

x	y
0	5
-3	-4
2	11

We now simply plot these three ordered pairs and connect them with a straight line, as shown on the right.

b) We are free to choose any x-values we want; however, because the coefficient of x is a fraction, we should choose all even numbers for x, so that we will get whole numbers for the y-values.

$x = 0 \implies y = 4 - \dfrac{3}{2}(0) = 4 - 0 = 4 \implies (0, 4)$ is one ordered pair on the graph. Similarly we get:

$x = -2 \implies y = 4 - \dfrac{3}{2}(-2) = 4 + 3 = 7 \implies (-2, 7)$ and

$x = 4 \implies y = 4 - \dfrac{3}{2}(4) = 4 - 6 = -2 \implies (4, -2)$

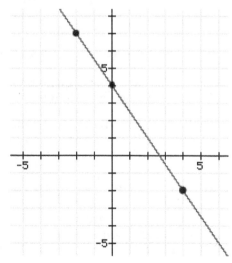

x	y
0	4
-2	7
4	-2

We now simply plot these three ordered pairs and connect them with a straight line, as shown on the right.

c) The most noticeable difference between the two graphs is that the first one has increasing y-values from left to right (because of its positive slope), whereas the second one has decreasing y-values, when read from left to right (because of its negative slope).

The effect of the slope of a line on the direction of that line is summarized in the following point to remember.

Point to Remember: *The connection between the slope and direction of a line*

The slope of a line is related to its graph as shown below.

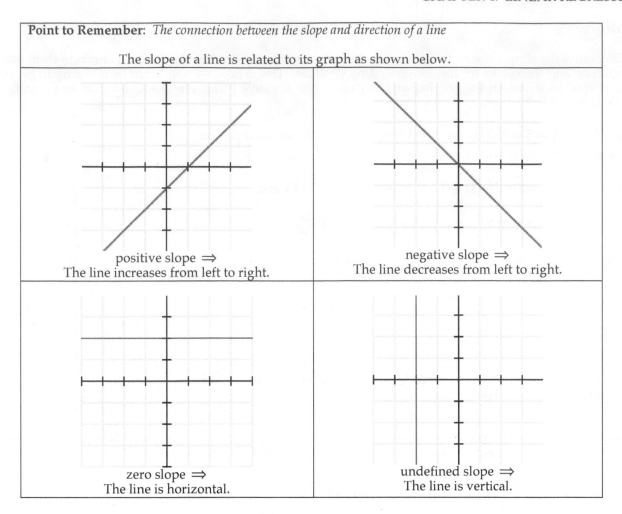

positive slope $\Rightarrow$
The line increases from left to right.

negative slope $\Rightarrow$
The line decreases from left to right.

zero slope $\Rightarrow$
The line is horizontal.

undefined slope $\Rightarrow$
The line is vertical.

APPLICATIONS: *Applying what we know about lines to real life situations*

Now that we have done a quick review of graphing lines, we want to see how lines can be applied to applications. In statistics, we are almost always looking at an application, so we don't just have an abstract equation to graph; rather we have one where the variables and graph tell us something about a real life situation. Though we will still use the same skills as in the previous examples, we will have to refine them for the application we are working with. Let's look at some examples.

Example 4.2: *Age vs. Target Heart Rate*

The target heart rate for aerobic exercise is given by the equation $r = 165 - 0.75x$, where r is the heart rate in beats per minute and x is the person's age in years.

a)   Use the equation to calculate the target heart rate for a person of age 20.

b)   Sketch the graph for the equation.

c)   Use the graph to estimate the target heart rate for a person of age 54.

d)   Interpret the slope in terms of the application.

e)   Find the value of the y-intercept and explain why it is not relevant for this problem.

How is a person's age related to target heart rate during aerobic exercise?

Solution:

a) We substitute the 20 in for x and we get: $r = 165 - 0.75(20) = 150$ beats per minute, or 150 bpm.

b) To graph, we need at least one more point. Let's use 80. $r = 165 - 0.75(80) = 105$. So we now have two ordered pairs, (20, 150) and (80, 105).

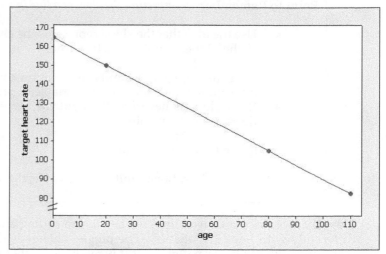

x	y
20	150
80	105

Connecting these points with a straight line produces the graph.

Notice that we only showed target heart rates from 80 to 170 on our scale. It is common when graphing a line tied to an application to only show the part of the number line that is relevant to the data we are likely to see.

c) Using the graph to estimate the target heart rate is a little different from using the equation. Rather than entering the age into the equation, we will go to age 54 on the horizontal axis and then draw a vertical line up to the line. Then, we will draw a horizontal line from there to the target heart rate. See below.

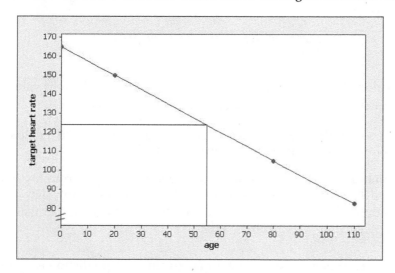

Based on the graph it appears that the target heart rate for a 54 year old is about 124 bpm.

d) The slope is the coefficient of the input variable (age or x in this case). For this equation the slope is –0.75. To interpret this number in terms of the application, we will begin by returning to its algebraic definition. In algebra we define slope as the change in output variable (r in this problem) divided by the change in input variable (x in this problem). We then put units on the changes in output and input and use them to help us make our interpretation.

$$slope = \frac{\text{change in r}}{\text{change in x}} = \frac{\Delta r}{\Delta x} = -\frac{0.75}{1} = \frac{-0.75 \text{ bpms}}{1 \text{ year}}$$

When interpreting a slope in terms of an application, it is usually best to work from the bottom up. So we say: For each additional year of age, the target heart rate decreases by 0.75 bpm.

e) The y-intercept in this problem is 165 bpms and it represents the target heart rate during aerobic activity for a newborn baby. It's hard to imagine that a newborn baby will be on a treadmill trying to lose a bit of weight.

It is very common in statistical applications that the y-intercept is not relevant. This is because a zero input in many applications does not make sense for the data we are working with. Our focus will be on interpreting the slope rather than on the y-intercept. Guidelines for interpreting the slope are given below.

Point to Remember: *Interpreting the slope of a line in terms of an application.*

- Use the idea that the slope represents the change in y divided by the change in x.
- If the slope is not a fraction, then write the slope as a fraction by putting a 1 in the denominator.
- Add the appropriate units for y (output variable or response) to the numerator and the appropriate units for x (input variable or predictor) to the denominator.
- If the slope is negative, then put the negative sign in the numerator and interpret it as a decrease in the y-value.

Template for interpretations:

For each additional unit of the x-value, the y-value is *changed* by the slope.

Now that we have reviewed lines in the algebra setting and with an application, it is time to look at what we do differently with lines in statistics. The biggest change is that, when we start dealing with real life data, it often takes on a roughly linear pattern, but it is rarely perfectly linear. This means that it will not be possible to actually draw a line that hits all of our data points. When this happens, we try to draw a line that is a good fit to the pattern. However, this line will miss some or all of the points. When a line misses a point, we call the vertical distance that it misses by the **prediction error** or the **residual**. The formal definition of this error and some related items are given below.

Definitions: *Observed y-value, scatterplot, prediction equation, predicted y-value, prediction error (residual)*

Observed y-value: If (x, y) is an ordered pair from a data set, then the value y is referred to as an observed y-value (because we "saw" it in the data set.)

Scatterplot: A scatterplot is a graph where all of the ordered pairs in a data set are graphed. This allows us to see patterns that may exist in the data set.

Prediction Equation: The equation of the line that we "fit" to a roughly linear data set is referred to as a prediction equation. To let people know that an equation is a prediction equation, we write it using $\hat{y}$ (say "y-hat") rather than y. So the equation is written as: $\hat{y} = b_0 + b_1 x$.

Predicted y-value: When we substitute for an x-value in a prediction equation, the output, $\hat{y}$, is called the predicted y-value.

Prediction Error or Residual: The prediction error (or residual) is the difference between the observed y-value and the predicted y-value. Prediction Error is denoted by e.

$$\text{Prediction Error} = e = (\text{observed } y) - (\text{predicted } y) = y - \hat{y}$$

- If the error is positive, then our line passed below the actual or observed y-value.
- If the error is negative, then our line passed above the actual or observed y-value.

(See the graph on the following page for illustrations of these definitions.)

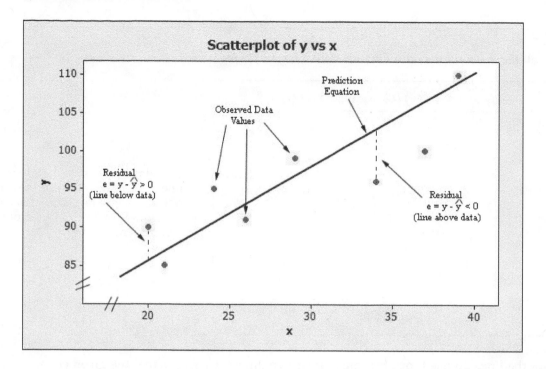

In this section, the prediction equation will be provided for us. In the next section, we will learn how to find them ourselves. Let's look at an example to get a better feel for these definitions in the context of an application.

Is there a pattern to the college enrollments of young adults in the US.?

Example 4.3: *Percent of 18 to 24 year olds enrolled in college*

The table below shows the percentage of 18 to 24 year olds in the U.S. that were enrolled in college during a sample of years from 1973 to 2008. This data is based on information from the U.S. Census Bureau (October reports).

Year (x)	1973	1977	1980	1985	1990	1995	1997	2000	2005	2006	2007	2008
% in college (y)	24.0	25.9	25.5	27.8	32.3	34.4	36.7	35.8	38.6	37.1	38.8	39.6

a) Create a scatterplot for the data set. What pattern do you see in the data?

b) Sketch the graph for the equation $\hat{y} = -855.394 + 0.44571x$ together with the ordered pairs. (This equation was found using algebra and the first and last data points. We will learn a better method for finding prediction equations in the next section.) Does it seem like a good fit to the data set? Explain.

c) Interpret the slope in terms of the application.

d) Use the equation to estimate percentage of 18 to 24 year olds in the U.S that were enrolled in college in 1980 (Round answer to the nearest hundredth of a percent). What is the prediction error or residual for the observed data point $(1980,\ 25.5)$?

e) Use the equation to estimate percentage of 18 to 24 year olds in the U.S that were enrolled in college in 1997 (Round answer to the nearest hundredth of a percent). What is the prediction error or residual for the observed data point $(1997,\ 36.7)$?

f) Find the sum of the squared prediction errors for the entire data set.

Solution:

a) Plotting all the ordered pairs produces the following scatterplot.

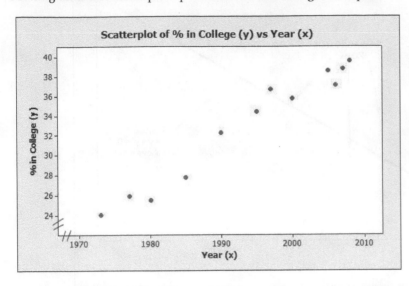

The data seems to produce a roughly linear pattern. Because the data tends to rise from left to right, it seems that the percentage of 18 to 24 year olds attending college is increasing.

b) To graph the line, we need to substitute at least two different x-values into the given equation. Because the problem states that the line was created using the first and last data values, we will use 1973 and 2008 as our x-values.

$$\hat{y} = -855.394 + 0.44571(1973) \approx 23.99 \Rightarrow (1973,\ 23.99)$$

$$\hat{y} = -855.394 + 0.44571(2008) \approx 39.59 \Rightarrow (2008,\ 39.59)$$

We now plot these two points and connect them with a straight line. Notice that these two points from the prediction equation are plotted as X's rather than dots. This keeps us from mixing up predicted points from actual observed data values.

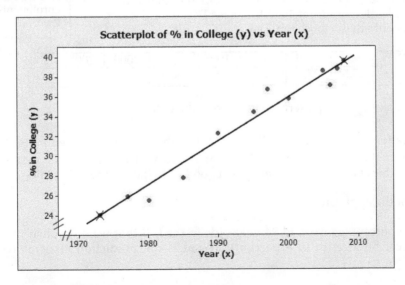

c) The slope is the coefficient of the x-variable in the prediction equation. So the slope is 0.44571. So we now write this as a fraction and add the units as follows.

$$slope = \frac{\text{change in } \hat{y}}{\text{change in x}} = \frac{\Delta \hat{y}}{\Delta x} = \frac{0.44571}{1} = \frac{0.44571\%}{1 \text{ year}}$$

Interpreting this from the bottom up, we get the following interpretation: For each additional year that goes by, the percent of 18 to 24 year olds attending college tends to increase by about 0.44571%.

d) To make estimates using the prediction equation, we simply substitute the given year in for the x-value.

$\hat{y} = -855.394 + 0.44571(1980) \approx 27.11\%$ of 18 to 24 years olds enrolled in college in 1980.

Looking at the data set, we see that the actual percentage in 1980 was 25.5%. So our prediction error (or residual) is calculated as follows:

$e = y - \hat{y} = 25.5 - 27.11 = -1.61$

(The error is negative because the line passed over the point.)

e) Once again, we simply substitute the given year in for the x-value to make the prediction.

$\hat{y} = -855.394 + 0.44571(1997) \approx 34.69\%$ of 18 to 24 years olds enrolled in college in 1997.

Looking at the data set, we see that the actual percentage in 1997 was 36.7%. So our prediction error or residual is calculated as follows:

$e = y - \hat{y} = 36.7 - 34.69 = 2.01$ (The error is positive because the line passed below the point.)

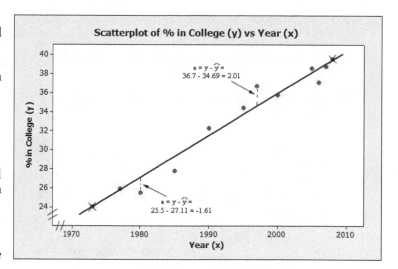

f) To find the sum of the squared prediction errors, we must find the predicted values for the other ten observed data values. We will then calculate the errors for those points and then square them. Finally we take the sum. The work is organized in the table shown below.

x	y	$\hat{y}$	$e = y - \hat{y}$	e^2
1973	24.0	23.99	0.01	0.0001
1977	25.9	25.77	0.13	0.0169
1980	25.5	27.11	-1.61	2.5921
1985	27.8	29.34	-1.54	2.3716
1990	32.3	31.57	0.73	0.5329
1995	34.4	33.80	0.60	0.3600
1997	36.7	34.69	2.01	4.0401
2000	35.8	36.03	-0.23	0.0529
2005	38.6	38.25	0.35	0.1225
2006	37.1	38.70	-1.60	2.5600
2007	38.8	39.15	-0.35	0.1225
2008	39.6	39.59	0.01	0.001
				$\sum e^2 = 12.7717$

$\hat{y} = -855.394 + 0.44571(1985) \approx 29.34\%$

$e = y - \hat{y} = 34.4 - 33.80 = 0.60$

$e^2 = (-1.60)^2 = 2.5600$

In the next section, we will see how the sum of squared errors calculated above is used to determine the best fitting line to a data set.

It's time to try some of these as exercises.

Exercise Set 4.1

Concept Review: Review the definitions and concepts from this section by filling in the blanks for each of the following.

1) The standard form of a line in statistics is $y = b_0 + b_1 x$, where b_0 is the _____ and b_1 is the _____ .

2) The x-variable is usually referred to as the predictor or the _____ variable.

3) The y-variable is usually referred to as the prediction or the _____ variable.

4) Interpretation of the slope: For each _____ unit of the x-value, the y-value is changed by the _____ .

5) If (x, y) is an ordered pair in our data set, then we refer to the y as an _____ y-value.

6) $\hat{y}$ represents a _____ y-value and it is found by substituting for an x-value in the _____ equation.

7) A _____ is a graph where all of the ordered pairs in a data set are graphed.

8) Prediction _____ is the difference between the observed y-value and the predicted y-value.

Mechanics: Practice graphing lines by finding at least 2 ordered pairs that solve the equations and then use those points to sketch the graph.

9) Graph: $y = -5.4 + 3.71x$,
   Assume $0 \le x \le 10$.

10) Graph: $y = 1.09 + 2.066x$,
    Assume $15 \le x \le 30$.

11) Graph: $y = -34.56 - 15.85x$,
    Assume $100 \le x \le 500$.

12) Graph: $y = 54.5 + 12.51x$,
    Assume $-50 \le x \le 150$.

Applications: Apply the mechanics learned above in the context of the following applications.

13) The value of a color copier owned by a small business is estimated by the equation $v = 1500 - 250y$, where v is the value in dollars and y is the age in years.
   a) Interpret the slope in terms of the application.
   b) Interpret the "y-intercept" in terms of the application.
   c) Use the equation to estimate the value of the copier after 2 years.
   d) Sketch a graph for the equation.
   e) Use the graph to estimate the value of a color copier that is 3.5 years old.
   f) What is the largest age that could be entered into this equation? Explain.

14) The height h (in thousands of feet) of an airplane t minutes after it begins its descent is given by the formula $h = 30 - 2.5t$.
   a) Interpret the slope in terms of the application.
   b) Interpret the "y-intercept" in terms of the application.
   c) Use the equation to estimate the height of the plane 10 minutes after it begins its descent.
   d) Sketch a graph for the equation.
   e) Use the graph to estimate the height of the plane 5 minutes after it begins its descent.
   f) What is the largest time that can be entered into this equation? Explain.

15) The cost c, in dollars, of shipping a package weighing 1 lb or more, but less than 20 lbs, is given by the formula $c = 2.8w + 21.05$, where w is the weight of the package, in lbs.
   a) Interpret the slope in terms of the application.
   b) Find the value of the "y-intercept" and explain why it is unimportant in this problem.
   c) Use the equation to estimate the cost of shipping a 14.7-pound package.
   d) Sketch a graph for the equation.
   e) Use the graph to estimate the cost of shipping a package weighing 7 lbs.

16) In order to have enough water pressure to hold up a barefoot water skier, the boat needs to travel at a high rate of speed. A common formula used by boat drivers to estimate the speed needed is $v = 20 + \dfrac{w}{10}$, where v is the speed of the boat (in mph) and w is the weight of the barefooter (in lbs.) This formula will work for barefooters weighing between 50 and 250 lbs.
   a) Interpret the slope in terms of the application.
   b) Find the value of the "y-intercept" and explain why it is unimportant in this problem.
   c) Use the equation to estimate the speed required for a 215 lb. barefooter.
   d) Sketch a graph for the equation.
   e) Use the graph to estimate the speed required for a 175 lb. barefooter.

17) The cost c, in dollars, of renting a moving van for a day and driving it m miles is given by the equation $c = 29.99 + 0.19m$. While the rental company does not place a limit on the number of miles that we can put on the moving van, let's assume we are only interested in 500 miles and below.
   a) Interpret the slope in terms of the application.
   b) Interpret the "y-intercept" in terms of the application.
   c) Sketch a graph for the equation.

18) The cost of throwing a birthday party at a popular kid's party center is given by the formula $c = 50 + 10k$, where c is the cost in dollars and k is the number of kids. They require a minimum of 10 kids to book a party and the maximum capacity is 40 kids.
   a) Interpret the slope in terms of the application.
   b) Find the value of the "y-intercept" and explain why it is unimportant in this problem.
   c) Sketch a graph for the equation.

19) The data below was recorded by a video game player while playing *Project Gotham Racing 3*. All the data was collected with the same car on the same track. The x-value is the number of attempts and the y-value is the lap time, in secs.

Attempt # (x)	1	2	3	4	5
Lap time (y)	86.49	83.79	80.04	81.41	77.05
Attempt # (x)	6	7	8	9	10
Lap time (y)	80.01	78.31	76.84	76.35	75.07

   a) Create a scatterplot for the 10 data values.
   b) Sketch the graph of the equation $\hat{y} = 85.443 - 1.0739x$ with the data values in the scatterplot. Does it seem like the line is a good fit to the data set?
   c) Interpret the slope of the line in terms of the application.
   d) Find the prediction error (residual) for the ordered pair (3, 80.04).

20) The data below was recorded by a video game player while playing *Rock Band*. All the data was collected for a single song played on the drums at the hard level. The x-value is the number of attempts and the y-value is the percentage of notes successfully played.

Attempt # (x)	1	2	3	4	5
% success (y)	85	88	89	90	88
Attempt # (x)	6	7	8	9	
% success (y)	91	91	90	95	

   a) Create a scatterplot for the 9 data values.
   b) Sketch the graph of the equation $\hat{y} = 85.4 + 0.850x$ with the data values in the scatterplot. Does it seem like the line is a good fit to the data set?
   c) Interpret the slope of the line in terms of the application.
   d) Find the prediction error (residual) for the ordered pair (5, 88).

21) A mountain bike rider has a computer that monitors his heart rate, mileage, and time during rides. This information is used to estimate the number of calories burned on the ride. The data for the ride time, in minutes, and the calories burned for 15 recent rides is shown in the table below. The scatterplot together with a prediction line is provided below the data set.

Ride Time (x)	45	74	58	55	83
Calories Burned (y)	499	861	659	657	984
Ride Time (x)	73	63	54	51	92
Calories Burned (y)	816	781	622	595	1067
Ride Time (x)	77	70	85	63	82
Calories Burned (y)	844	815	975	745	1007

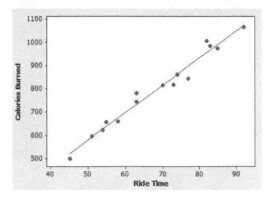

$$\hat{y} = -7.96 + 11.7526x$$

   a) Use the prediction equation provided to estimate the number of calories burned for a 67 minute ride.
   b) Interpret the slope of the line in terms of the application.
   c) Find the prediction error (residual) for the ordered pair (77, 844).
   d) Find the prediction error (residual) for the ordered pair (82, 1007).

22) Samples are taken most years to estimate the percentage of adults who smoke cigarettes in the U.S. The table below lists the year and percentage for 9 such samples. The scatterplot together with a prediction line is provided below the data set. The equation of the prediction line is also provided. *Source: Center for Disease Control.*

Year (x)	1970	1980	1990	2000	2002
% smokers (y)	37.4	33.2	25.5	23.3	22.5
Year (x)	2003	2004	2007	2010	
% smokers (y)	21.6	20.9	20.8	19.3	

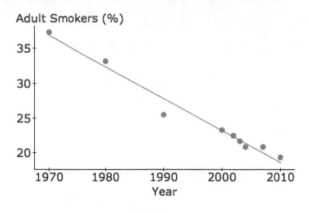

$$\hat{y} = 935.07 - 0.4559x$$

a) Use the prediction equation provided to estimate the percentage of smokers in the U.S. in 1996.
b) Interpret the slope of the line in terms of the application.
c) Find the prediction error (residual) for the ordered pair (1990, 25.5).
d) Find the prediction error (residual) for the ordered pair (2010, 19.3).

23) According to the Office of Institutional Research at Harvard University, the student tuition, in dollars, for a sample of 7 years was as shown below. A scatterplot of the data set is shown below with a prediction equation. *Source: Harvard Magazine.*

Year (x)	1981	1985	1990	1995
Tuition (y)	6000	9800	13545	18485
Year (x)	2000	2005	2010	
Tuition (y)	22765	28752	34976	

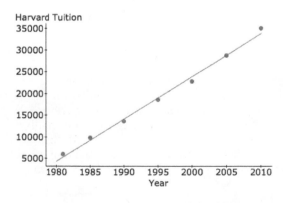

$$\hat{y} = -1{,}934{,}953.6 + 979.450x$$

a) Does the prediction line seem like a good fit to the data set? Explain.
b) Interpret the slope of the line in terms of the application.
c) Find the sum of the squared prediction errors for the entire data set. That is, find $\sum e^2$.

24) You may occasionally here reports on the news about the cost per barrel for crude oil. This is the product that is refined into the gasoline we use in our cars. It is natural to wonder about the relationship between the price of crude oil and the price of gasoline. The chart below shows a sample of 6 days where the price of oil ($/barrel) and the national average in the U.S. for regular unleaded gasoline ($/gallon) are recorded. (The data is based on info from gasbuddy.com from late 2010 / early 2011.)

Oil (x)	81	90	87	103	110	97
Gas (y)	2.86	3.01	3.10	3.47	3.82	3.42

A scatterplot of the data set is shown below with a prediction equation.

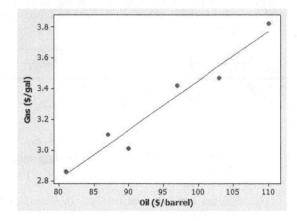

$$\hat{y} = 0.235 + 0.03217x$$

a) Does the prediction line seem like a good fit to the data set? Explain.
b) Interpret the slope of the line in terms of the application.
c) Find the sum of the squared prediction errors for the entire data set. That is, find $\sum e^2$.

Section 4.2 - Linear Regression

In the previous section, we began exploring the idea of fitting a line to a data set that has a roughly linear pattern. In that section, the line was provided for us. In this section, we want to learn a statistical process that uses all of the data values to determine the equation of the line that best describes and fits the pattern we see. The philosophy we will use to find this line is that the smaller the overall prediction error a line has, the better fit it is considered to be. This is known as the **least squares criterion**.

THE LEAST SQUARES CRITERION:

> **Definitions:** *The least squares criterion and the Sum of Squared Error*
>
> **Least Squares Criterion:** The smaller the overall prediction error for a prediction line, the better fit it is considered to be. Because some prediction errors are positive and some are negative, we square the errors when getting a total error calculation.
>
> **Sum of Squared Error:** The sum of squared error for a prediction equation is the sum of the squared prediction errors (or residuals). The formula is $\sum e^2 = \sum (y - \hat{y})^2$.
>
>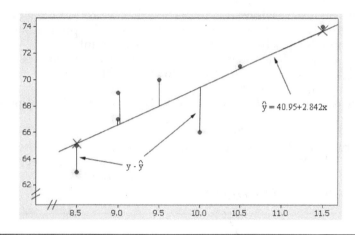

The least squares criterion gives us a method to compare two lines and determine which one is the better fit to a given data set. However, for any given data set, there are infinitely many lines that are candidates for the best fitting line. Every small adjustment to the slope or the y-intercept creates a new line for us to consider. Our task is to somehow use the least squares criterion to pick a winner from all these potential prediction equations. The process of doing this is outlined below.

THE LINEAR REGRESSION EQUATION: *A formula for the best fitting line*

So, we now see that our goal is to examine infinitely many possible fit lines and determine which one fits the best. We have decided that our criterion will be that the line that has the smallest sum of squared error is the best fitting line. When and if we find the equation for this line, we will call it the **linear regression equation**. So our task is to look at every possible slope and y-intercept and determine which pair of these creates the smallest sum of squared error. This goal may sound impossible (worse than a needle in a haystack), but it can be done. However, it does require multivariate calculus. Because this text does not assume that you have a calculus background, we will skip the calculus work and go straight to the formula that the calculus process produces.

Definition: *Linear Regression Equation*

Linear Regression Equation: The best fitting line for a data set is referred to as the linear regression line. The equation for that line is $\hat{y} = b_0 + b_1 x$ where

$$b_1 = \frac{\sum(x - \bar{x})(y - \bar{y})}{\sum(x - \bar{x})^2} \quad \text{and} \quad b_0 = \bar{y} - b_1 \bar{x}$$

Predictions: Because we use linear regression for data sets that have roughly linear patterns, we cannot expect the equation to make perfect predictions for individuals or items in the data set. We use linear regression to predict the *average* y value, for specified x-values.

This formula may look quite intimidating, but we will see that it is not nearly as bad as it looks. It is also important to remember that we are skipping a lot of calculus work and going straight to the formula. When finding the regression equation, we will typically round both the slope and the y-intercept. The rules for that are shown below, followed by an example of both finding the regression equation and using the rounding rules.

Point to Remember: *Rounding Rule for Linear Regression*

Rounding Rules for Regression: It is important that we round the slope and y-intercept in such a way that the rounding error does not affect the predictions from our equation. Consider the following when rounding the slope and y-intercept.
- Choose a y-value that you think is typical of the largest y-values in your data set.
- Use at least one more *decimal place* for the y-intercept than you would need for a predicted y-value of this size.
- Use at least one more *digit* for the slope than you would need for a predicted y-value of this size.

Note: These are probably the most complicated rounding rules in the text. However, they do use the phrase *at least*. So, when in doubt, use more decimal places and digits than you think are necessary. This will ensure that the rounding error does not adversely affect your predictions.

Example 4.4: *Practicing the mechanics of the Regression Equation formulas*

Consider the data set below to be a random sample of ordered pairs.

x	1	2	4	7	9
y	1	3	4	7	6

a) Create a scatterplot to verify that the data set has a roughly linear pattern.

b) Use the preceding formulas to determine the linear regression equation for the data set. Round in such a way that predictions made from this equation will be accurate to the nearest hundredth.

c) Verify the good fit by graphing the line with the data set.

d) Determine the sum of squared errors for the regression equation.

Solution:

a) Recall: We create a scatterplot by plotting the x and y-values from the
   table as ordered pairs. Shown to the right.

   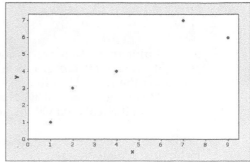

   While these points do not seem to be perfectly linear, they do appear to
   form a roughly linear pattern.

b) To use the formulas provided, we need to find a few sums: $\sum x$, $\sum y$,
   $\sum (x-\bar{x})(y-\bar{y})$, and $\sum (x-\bar{x})^2$. To calculate the last two sums,
   we must first find the values of $\bar{x}$ and $\bar{y}$. Because we have five ordered pairs, we will use n = 5.

$$\bar{x} = \frac{\sum x}{n} = \frac{23}{5} = 4.6 \quad \text{and} \quad \bar{y} = \frac{\sum y}{n} = \frac{21}{5} = 4.2$$

Next, we will make a table to find the values of $(x-\bar{x})(y-\bar{y})$ and $(x-\bar{x})^2$. Then we will find the total for
each of these columns.

x	y	$(x-\bar{x})(y-\bar{y})$	$(x-\bar{x})^2$
1	1	11.52	12.96
2	3	3.12	6.76
4	4	0.12	0.36
7	7	6.72	5.76
9	6	7.92	19.36
23	21	29.4	45.2

$(2-4.6)(3-4.2) = 3.12$

$(7-4.6)^2 = 5.76$

So, the sums are $\sum (x-\bar{x})(y-\bar{y}) = 29.4$ and $\sum (x-\bar{x})^2 = 45.2$. We now substitute these values into
the formulas and we get the following.

$$b_1 = \frac{\sum (x-\bar{x})(y-\bar{y})}{\sum (x-\bar{x})^2} = \frac{29.4}{45.2} \approx 0.6504 \quad \text{and}$$

$$b_0 = \bar{y} - b_1 \bar{x} = 4.2 - \frac{29.4}{45.2} * 4.6 \approx 1.208$$

> **Caution:** *Calculation Tip*
>
> Even though we rounded
> the answer to b_1, we should
> use the exact answer when
> calculating b_0. This helps
> prevent the rounding error
> from spreading.

So the linear regression equation is: $\hat{y} \approx 1.208 + 0.6504x$

Rounding Note: The largest y-value in this data set was 7. If we wrote this y-value to the nearest hundredth, it
would be 7.00. Because this has two decimal places, we used three decimal places when writing the intercept.
Because there are 3 digits total in 7.00, we would need at least 4 digits in our slope.

c) For this part, we need to plot the data along with a graph of the linear regression line. To graph the line, we
   need at least two ordered pairs. It is best to pick x-values that are far apart from each other, so we will use
   x = 1 and x = 9. This produces the following points.

$$x = 1: \hat{y} \approx 1.208 + 0.6504(1) \approx 1.86 \Rightarrow (1, 1.86)$$

$$x = 9: \hat{y} \approx 1.208 + 0.6504(9) \approx 7.06 \Rightarrow (9, 7.06)$$

So, we plot these two points and connect them with a straight line to get the graph below. When plotting the points on the regression line, we will use X's rather than dots. This is done so that we don't mix up our graphing marks with the real data values from the data set.

While this is not a perfect fit (because it doesn't hit all the points), it does look like a good fit to the data set because it follows the overall pattern and passes over some points and under others.

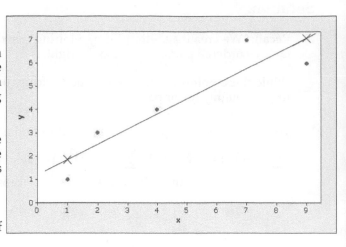

d) It is helpful to use a chart when calculating the sum of squared errors.

x	y	$\hat{y}$	$e = y - \hat{y}$	e^2
1	1	1.86	-0.86	0.7396
2	3	2.51	0.49	0.2401
4	4	3.81	0.19	0.0361
7	7	5.76	1.24	1.5376
9	6	7.06	-1.06	1.1236
				3.6770

$$y - \hat{y} = 3 - 2.51 = 0.49$$

$$\hat{y} \approx 1.208 + 0.6504(7) \approx 5.76$$

$$(y - \hat{y})^2 = (7 - 5.76)^2 = 1.5376$$

So for our regression line, we get $\sum e^2 = 3.677$. By itself, this is hard to interpret. However, the claim of linear regression is that this is smaller than the sum of squared error for any other possible prediction equation. We will examine this further in the examples that follow.

Now that we have practiced the mechanics of linear regression, let's return to the example involving the percentage of 18 to 24 year olds enrolled in college over the last few decades. We will find the linear regression equation for this data set and verify that it is a better fit than the line used in the previous section.

Example 4.5: *Percent of 18 to 24 year olds enrolled in college (Revisited)*

The table below shows the percentage of 18 to 24 year olds in the U.S. that were enrolled in college during a sample of years from 1973 to 2008. This data is based on information from the U.S. Census Bureau (October reports).

Does linear regression create a better prediction equation for estimating college enrollments?

Year (x)	1973	1977	1980	1985	1990	1995	1997	2000	2005	2006	2007	2008
% in college (y)	24.0	25.9	25.5	27.8	32.3	34.4	36.7	35.8	38.6	37.1	38.8	39.6

a) Use tables and formulas to find the linear regression equation for this data set. Round in such a way that predictions will be reliable to the nearest hundredth of a percent.

b) Graph the regression equation together with the data. Does the linear regression equation seem to be a good fit to the data set? Explain.

c) Find the sum of squared errors for the linear regression equation and verify that it is smaller than the sum of squared error found for the previous prediction equation used in Example 4.3.

Solution:

a) This is the same task as in the previous example, only this time our data set is bigger and contains "messy" data. That's real data for you. To use the formulas provided, we need to find a few sums: $\sum x$, $\sum y$, $\sum(x-\bar{x})(y-\bar{y})$, and $\sum(x-\bar{x})^2$. When finding many sums for a data set, it is best to use a table to organize the work. There are 12 ordered pairs, so we use $n=12$.

x	y
1973	24.0
1977	25.9
1980	25.5
1985	27.8
1990	32.3
1995	34.4
1997	36.7
2000	35.8
2005	38.6
2006	37.1
2007	38.8
2008	39.6
23,923	396.5

$$\bar{x} = \frac{\sum x}{n} = \frac{23{,}923}{12} \approx 1993.58$$

$$\bar{y} = \frac{\sum y}{n} = \frac{396.5}{12} \approx 33.04$$

Next, we find the values of $(x-\bar{x})(y-\bar{y})$ and then of $(x-\bar{x})^2$. We also find the total for each column.

x	y	$(x-\bar{x})(y-\bar{y})$	$(x-\bar{x})^2$
1973	24.0	186.0432	423.5364
1977	25.9	118.3812	274.8964
1980	25.5	102.3932	184.4164
1985	27.8	44.9592	73.6164
1990	32.3	2.6492	12.8164
1995	34.4	1.9312	2.0164
1997	36.7	12.5172	11.6964
2000	35.8	17.7192	41.2164
2005	38.6	63.4952	130.4164
2006	37.1	50.4252	154.2564
2007	38.8	77.2992	180.0964
2008	39.6	94.5952	207.9364
23,923	396.5	772.4084	1696.9168

$$(1980-1993.58)(25.5-33.04) = 102.3932$$

$$(2000-1993.58)^2 = 41.2164$$

So, the sums are $\sum(x-\bar{x})(y-\bar{y}) = 772.4084$ and $\sum(x-\bar{x})^2 = 1696.9168$. We now substitute these values into the formulas and we get the following.

$$b_1 = \frac{\sum(x-\bar{x})(y-\bar{y})}{\sum(x-\bar{x})^2} = \frac{772.4084}{1696.9168} \approx 0.45518 \quad \text{and}$$

$$b_0 = \bar{y} - b_1\bar{x} = 33.04 - \frac{772.4084}{1696.9168} * 1993.58 \approx -874.405$$

So the linear regression equation is: $\hat{y} \approx -874.404 + 0.45518x$

Rounding Note: I put three decimal places in the y-intercept, because we want two decimal places in our predictions. The largest y-value in our table was 39.6. If we wrote this out to the hundredths place, it would be 39.60. Because this value has 4 total digits in it, I used 5 digits when writing the slope. All this is to ensure predictions are accurate to the nearest hundredth of a percent.

b) We simply plot all the data values as ordered pairs. We can then add the graph of our linear regression equation by finding two ordered pairs using the equation. It is usually a good idea to use a small x-value and a large x-value when graphing the line. We will use 1975 and 2003.

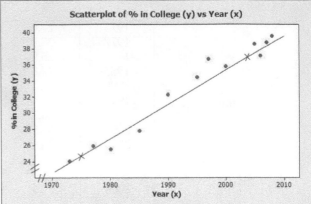

$x = 1975$: $\hat{y} \approx -874.405 + 0.45518(1975) \approx 24.58$

$$\Rightarrow (1975,\ 24.58)$$

$x = 2003$: $\hat{y} \approx -874.405 + 0.45518(2003) \approx 37.32$

$$\Rightarrow (2003,\ 37.32)$$

Plotting these two new points produces the graph shown to the right. The regression line appears to be a good fit as it seems to follow the pattern of the data with some values above the line and other below it.

c) We begin this process by using the regression equation to find the values of $\hat{y}$ for all of the x-values in our data set. The work is shown for the first point and then the results for the rest of the points are shown in the table.

x	y	$\hat{y}$	e^2
1973	24.0	23.67	0.1089
1977	25.9	25.49	0.1681
1980	25.5	26.85	1.8225
1985	27.8	29.13	1.7689
1990	32.3	31.40	0.8100
1995	34.4	33.68	0.5184
1997	36.7	34.59	4.4521
2000	35.8	35.96	0.0256
2005	38.6	38.23	0.1369
2006	37.1	38.69	2.5281
2007	38.8	39.14	0.1156
2008	39.6	39.60	0.0000
			12.4551

(1973, 24.0):

$\hat{y} \approx -874.405 + 0.45518(1973) \approx 23.67$

$\Rightarrow e^2 = (y - \hat{y})^2 = (24.0 - 23.67)^2 = 0.1089$

So, for our regression line, the sum of squared error is: $\sum e^2 \approx 12.4551$.

This is in fact a little bit smaller than the $\sum e^2 = 12.7717$ that we found for the prediction line in Example 4.3. This small difference indicates that we actually had a pretty good fit in Example 4.3. However, as promised, the regression line fits better.

USING TECHNOLOGY: *Finding Regression Equations with various technologies*

While it was still manageable, the previous example shows that finding regression equations with real data can be a messy process. The amazing thing to consider is that 12 data points is actually considered to be a small data set. Imagine the work required if our data set had 112 data values. Because of the tedious and messy nature of finding regression equations by hand, most people employ some form of technology to speed up and simplify the process. The steps below show how to use 4 common forms of technology to find regression equations. For all of these we will use the data set from Example 4.4.

x	1	2	4	7	9
y	1	3	4	7	6

MINITAB:

1. Enter the x-values into C1 and the y-values into C2. (These should be renamed to match the application.)
2. Choose STAT > Regression > Regression . . .
3. Enter the y-column for the response variable and the x-column for the predictor.
4. Click the OK button.
5. The output will show a form of the equation with a lot of rounding error. You can improve the accuracy by replacing the slope and intercept in their equation with the values given below in the output.
6. Write down the equation using the y-intercept (Constant) and the slope (x) provided in the output.

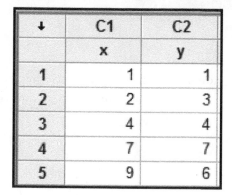

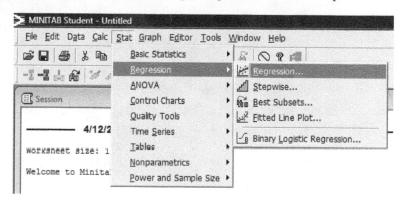

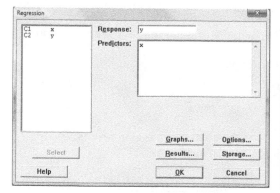

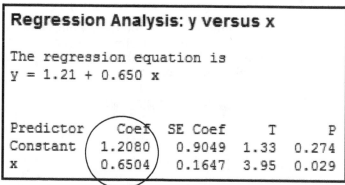

So the equation is: $\hat{y} \approx 1.208 + 0.6504x$

TI 84:

1. Choose STAT > EDIT
2. Enter the x-values into L1 and the y-values into L2.
3. Choose STAT > CALC > 8:LinReg(a+bx)
4. Specify the list L1 and L2 and press enter. "LinReg(a+bx) L1, L2"
5. Write down the equation using the y-intercept (a) and the slope (b) provided by the calculator

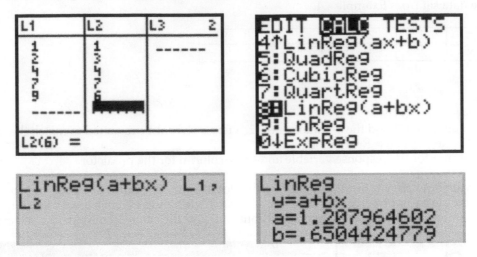

So the equation is: $\hat{y} \approx 1.208 + 0.6504x$

Checking Data Entry: Many problems in the homework provide a value for $\sum xy$. Verifying that you are getting the same value on the TI-84 is a good way to avoid data entry errors from ruining your equation. To see the value of $\sum xy$ on the TI-84, do the following.

Choose STAT > CALC > 2: 2-Var Stats L1, L2   (Press ENTER and then scroll down.)

STATCRUNCH:

1. Enter the x-values into var1 and the y-values into var2. (Rename these to match the application.)
2. Choose STAT > Regression > Simple Linear
3. Use the pull down menu's to choose the appropriate x and y variables.
4. Click the Calculate button.

StatCrunch	Edit	Data	Stat
Row	x		y
1	1		1
2	2		3
3	4		4
4	7		7
5	9		6

Options

Simple linear regression results:
Dependent Variable: y
Independent Variable: x
$y = 1.2079647 + 0.6504425\ x$
Sample size: 5
R (correlation coefficient) = 0.9158
R-sq = 0.8387285
Estimate of error standard deviation: 1.107097

So the equation is: $\hat{y} \approx 1.208 + 0.6504x$

EXCEL:

1. Enter the x-values into cells in column A and the y-values into cells in column B. Use the first cell in each column to provide names for the variables.
2. Click on the DATA tab and then click Data Analysis on the far right. Select Regression and click OK.
3. Choose the appropriate range of cells for the Y Range and the X range. In the Output Range, select the cell that you would like to be the upper left of the regression output. Click OK.
4. In the output, look for the y-intercept and slope (labeled X Variable) under Coefficients. Use these to write your equation.

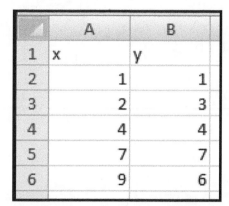

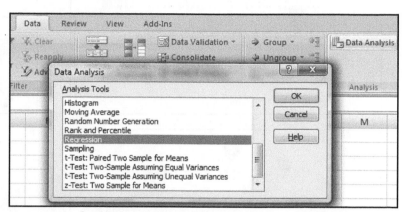

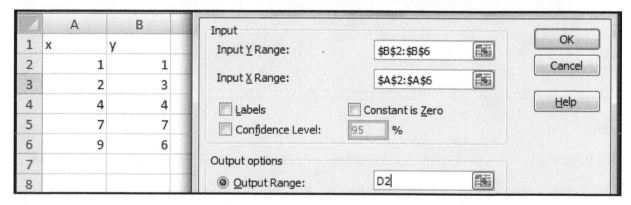

So the equation is: $\hat{y} \approx 1.208 + 0.6504x$

DECIDING WHEN REGRESSION IS APPROPRIATE: *What the scatterplot tells us*

We have now seen how to calculate the linear regression equation both by hand and with the aid of technology. The technology makes it very easy to find the regression equation, but that doesn't mean that it is always appropriate. We should only try to fit a line to a data set if the scatterplot reveals that the data has a roughly linear pattern. The following example illustrates this point.

Example 4.6: *Deciding if linear regression is appropriate*

For each of the data plots shown below, decide whether or not a linear regression would be appropriate for the data set. Justify your answers.

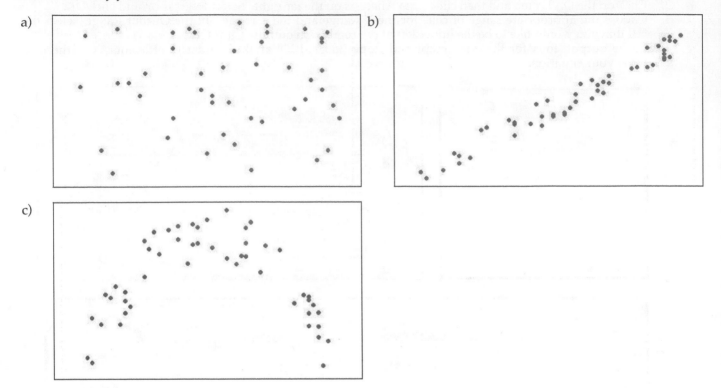

a)

b)

c)

Solution:

a)   No, there is no pattern to the plot, linear or otherwise. Therefore, linear regression is not appropriate.

b)   Yes, there is a roughly linear pattern to the data set, so a linear regression would be appropriate.

c)   No. linear regression is not appropriate, because, even though there is a pattern to the data set, it is not a roughly linear pattern. Based on the pattern of the data, it might be appropriate to try to find the equation of the best fitting parabola to the data set, but not a line. (In this text, only linear regression is covered. However, other shapes such as parabolas can be done.)

Point to Remember: *We only do linear regression for roughly linear data sets*

Linear Regression should only be done when the data set in question forms a linear pattern. If the data set in question has a strong pattern that is not linear, then other types of regression may be more appropriate. If no pattern exists at all in the data set, then no type of regression should be done. Why spend all the time and effort to find the best fitting line, if the data does not have at least a roughly linear pattern?

POTENTIAL PROBLEMS: *What problems can arise in linear regression?*

There are a two troubling types of data values that can cause problems in the process of linear regression. One of these occurs when the data set has a roughly linear pattern, but one of the data values does not fit the pattern. Such data values are referred to as **outliers**. The other issue occurs when we have a data value that does fit the linear pattern, but still stands apart from the rest of the data. Such values are referred to as **potentially influential observations**. Both outliers and potentially influential observations tend to have a larger effect on how the regression equation turns out than the rest of the data values. We need to know what to do when such data values exist in our samples. Let's look at the formal definition and a visual of the situation.

Definitions: *Outliers and Potentially Influential Observations*

Outlier: In the context of linear regression, an outlier is a data value whose y-value does not fit the linear pattern formed by the rest of the data set. As always, an outlier could represent an error or it might just be an unusual observation. In either case, an outlier should usually be examined carefully before calculations are made.

Potentially Influential Observation (PIO): This is a data value whose x-value stands apart from the other data values in the data set. Such data values might fit the linear pattern of the rest of the data set. However, because they have a larger effect on the regression equation than other data values, you may wish to consider whether or not they should remain in the data set for the regression calculations.

Note: It is possible for a data value to be considered both an outlier and a potentially influential observation. This would occur if the x-value is much larger or smaller than most data values AND it does not fit the linear pattern.

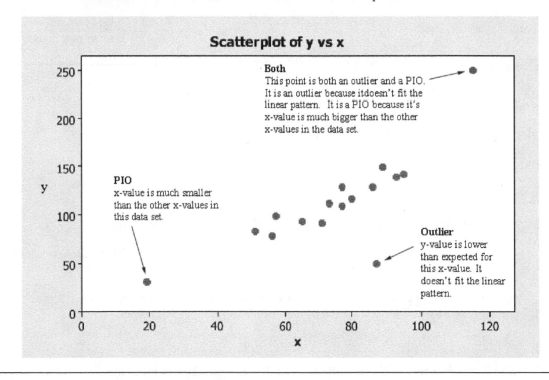

Scatterplot of y vs x

Another problem arises with linear regression when we try to make predictions using our linear regression equation for x-values that do not fit the range of our data set. When we see a linear pattern and model that pattern with a linear equation, that model should only be used to make predictions for x-values within the range of the x-values in our sample data. This type of prediction is known as an **interpolation**. If we try to expand these predictions using x-values outside of the range of those in our sample, we may get much larger prediction error than we expect. This can happen if the pattern we see does not continue outside of the x-values we have collected. This change in the pattern is referred to as **model breakdown**. Making such predictions is unwise and we call them **extrapolations**. The formal definitions are as follows.

> **Definitions**: *Interpolation, Extrapolation, and Model Breakdown*
>
> **Interpolation**: This is the process of using a regression equation to make predictions for x-values that lie within the range of the given x-values in the sample data set. Such predictions are considered to be wise/reliable.
>
> **Model Breakdown**: When a linear pattern exists for x-values in a certain range, but then begins to change outside of that range, then we refer to this as model breakdown.
>
> **Extrapolation**: This is the process of using a regression equation to make predictions for x-values that lie outside of the range of the given x-values in the sample data set. Such predictions are not wise/reliable because the linear pattern that led us to compute the regression equation may not continue beyond the range of the data we saw in our data set.

Let's examine all of these new concepts with an example.

Example 4.7: *Quarterback Passer Rating vs. Number of Team Wins*

It is commonly believed among football fans that the quarterback is the most critical player on the team. The NFL rates the performance of a quarterback using a complex formula that incorporates many elements of the quarterback's job. A perfect rating using this formula would be 158.3. The table below lists the passer rating from the 2012 regular season for a sample of 9 NFL quarterbacks together with the number of regular season wins by their teams. (*Source*: ESPN.com)

How important is the quarterback to an NFL team?

Player Name	Passer Rating (x)	Team Wins (y)
Tom Brady	98.7	12
Drew Brees	96.3	7
Matt Cassel	66.7	2
Jay Cutler	81.3	10
Peyton Manning	105.8	13
Cam Newton	86.2	6
Aaron Rodgers	108.0	11
Tony Romo	90.5	8
Matthew Stafford	79.8	4

a) Create a scatterplot for the data set. Does linear regression seem appropriate? Explain.

b) Use technology to find the linear regression equation. Round in such a way that predictions made from this equation will be reliable to the nearest tenth of a win.

c) Use the regression equation to predict the average number of wins for a team whose quarterback has a passer rating of 105. Interpret this prediction in terms of the application.

d) Graph the regression line with the data set to verify a good fit.

e) Would it be wise / reliable to use the equation to predict the number of wins for a team whose quarterback has a passer rating of 124? Explain.

f) Which data value is the best candidate to be called an outlier? Explain.

g) Give two possible explanations for why this point stands apart from the rest.

h) Which data value is the best candidate to be called a potentially influential observation? Explain.

Solution:

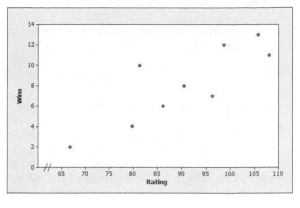

a) We create a scatterplot by plotting the ordered pairs. Shown to the right. Linear regression is appropriate for this data set, because there is a roughly linear pattern to the data set.

b) The process will vary depending on the technology you are using, but the regression equation is as shown below.

$$\hat{y} \approx -12.94 + 0.2329x$$

Rounding Note: The highest number of wins in the data set was 13 wins. If we wrote this to the nearest tenth of a win, it would be 13.0 wins. Because this has one decimal place, we used two decimal places when writing the intercept. Because there are 3 digits total in 13.0, we would need at least 4 digits in our slope.

c) To use a regression equation to make predictions, we simply substitute the predictor of interest into the equation for the x-value and calculate the y-value, or prediction. So we get:

$$x = 105: \ \hat{y} \approx -12.94 + 0.2329(105) \approx 11.5 \Rightarrow (105, \ 11.5)$$

Interpretation: We predict that the average number of wins for teams whose quarterback had a passer rating of 105 would be about 11.5 wins.

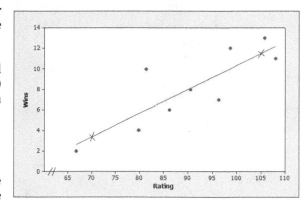

d) To graph the regression line, we need to find at least two ordered pairs on the line. We already have the ordered pair (105, 11.5) from our work above. We get another ordered pair by choosing a new x-value and substituting it into the equation.

$$x = 70: \ \hat{y} \approx -12.94 + 0.2329(70) \approx 3.4 \Rightarrow (70, \ 3.4)$$

We now plot these points (using X's rather than dots) with the actual data points and then connect the two points from the equation using a straight line.

e) Making a prediction of the average number of wins for a team whose quarterback has a passer rating of 124 is NOT wise/reliable because size 124 was not within the range of the passer ratings we were given in our sample data set (Our data set went from a minimum of 66.7 to a maximum of 108.0). Such predictions are not wise because the linear pattern we see in our data set might not continue beyond the data we have collected in our sample.

f) An outlier is a data value whose y-value stands apart from the linear pattern. The best candidate for that description in this data set is the ordered pair (81.3, 10). With Jay Cutler having a quarterback rating of only 81.3, it seems like 10 wins was an unusually high amount.

> **Key Concept:** *Extrapolations*
>
> Stating that a prediction is not wise does not mean that the prediction is necessarily a bad one. It just means we can't rely on it to be a good prediction. Maybe it is, maybe it is not.

g) Outliers are often errors, so we normally double-check this data value. If the data value is actually correct, we often look for other explanations for why this team won so many games. Perhaps this team relies more on a running game than a passing game. Or alternatively, maybe they rely on their defense to win.

h) A potentially influential observation is an ordered pair whose x-value stands apart from other data values in the data set. The best candidate for that in this data set is the ordered pair (66.7, 2). That quarterback has a much lower passer rating than the other quarterbacks in the sample. It is useful to have this quarterback in the data set, because it allows us to see that the linear pattern continues down to rating as low as 66.7.

WRAP SESSION: *An example with a negative slope*

It's now time to take a look at all the aspects of regression in one final example.

Example 4.8: *Vehicle weight vs. gas mileage*

In April 2011, a random sample of 28 new vehicles was obtained and data was collected on the curb weight of the vehicle (in lbs.) and the overall gas mileage (the average of the city and highway miles in mpg.) The following table shows the make and model of each vehicle together with its curb weight and overall mileage. A scatterplot of the data has also been provided. We wish to see if we can use this data to compute a prediction equation for gas mileage of cars based on curb weight.

Can the curb weight of a vehicle be a good predictor of its overall gas mileage?

Make / Model	Curb Weight	Overall Mileage	Make / Model	Curb Weight	Overall Mileage
Audi A3	3219	25.5	Honda Pilot	4319	20
BMW 5 Series	3814	27	Hummer H2	6614	10
BMW X5	4960	21	Jaguar XJ	4045	19.5
Cadillac CTS	3872	21	Jeep Wrangler	3760	17
Cadillac Escalade	5488	16	Mazda RX-8	3111	19.5
Chevy Camaro	3780	22.5	Mercedes-Benz M-Class	4630	18
Chevy Tahoe	5636	18	MINI Cooper Convertible	2701	31.5
Chrysler Town and Cntry	4652	21	Mitsubishi Outlander	3384	25.5
Dodge Grand Caravan	4510	21	Nissan Altima Sedan	3180	27.5
Dodge Viper	3454	17.5	Porsche Cayenne	4398	18.5
Ford Fusion	3285	27	Subaru Outback	3386	23
Ford Ranger SuperCab	4760	24.5	Toyota Land Cruiser	5765	15.5
GMC Sierra Crew Cab	5095	16.5	Toyota Prius	3042	49.5
Honda Civic	2588	30	VW Golf	2968	28

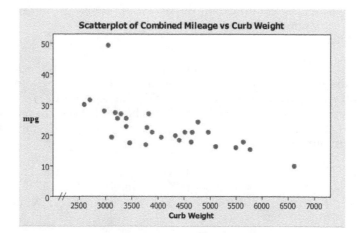

a) Does a linear regression seem appropriate? Explain.

b) Which vehicle is the best candidate to be called an outlier? Explain. Can we explain why this car did not fit the pattern? How should we handle this outlier?

c) Which vehicle is the best candidate to be called a potentially influential observation (PIO)? Explain. How should we handle this PIO?

d) Remove the outlier from the data set and then use technology to find the linear regression equation. Round your answers so that predictions made from the equation will be reliable to the nearest hundredth of a mpg.

e) Use the regression equation to predict the average gas mileage for a 2815 lb. vehicle. Is this a wise prediction?

f) Would it be wise to use this equation to predict the average mileage for a 9000 lb. vehicle? Explain.

g) Interpret the slope of the line in terms of the application.

h) Graph the regression line with the scatterplot.

Solution:

a) Yes, there is a roughly linear pattern to the scatterplot.

b) The data point in the upper left corner of the scatterplot appears to be an outlier. It does not fit the linear pattern. Its mileage seems unusually high, even for a low weight vehicle. Looking at the data set, it appears that this is the Toyota Prius. This is the only hybrid vehicle in this chart. That is most likely the reason that it gets such high gas mileage. Because this vehicle is the only hybrid in the data set, it probably should be removed. This assumes that we will only use our prediction equation for non-hybrids.

c) The vehicle in the lower right corner of the scatterplot could be considered a PIO. This vehicle is much heavier than the other vehicles in the data set. Looking at the data set, it appears that this is the Hummer H2. If we are confident that we will not be making predictions for vehicles weighing more than 5765 lbs., then we could remove this data point. However, if it is possible that we might make predictions for vehicles over 5765 lbs., then the Hummer helps us see that the linear pattern continues and keeps such predictions from being considered extrapolations.

d) We should enter all of the data, except for the Toyota Prius Hybrid, into the technology of our choice. Output from various technologies is shown below.

Minitab

```
The regression equation is
Overall Mileage = 37.8 - 0.00393 Curb Weight


Predictor         Coef    SE Coef      T      P
Constant        37.775      2.542   14.86  0.000
Curb Weight   -0.0039320   0.0005990  -6.56  0.000


S = 3.11256   R-Sq = 63.3%   R-Sq(adj) = 61.8%
```

TI-84

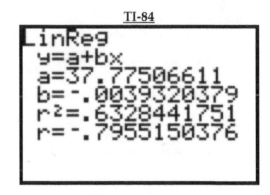

StatCrunch

Simple linear regression results:

Dependent Variable: Mileage

Independent Variable: Weight

Mileage = 37.775066 – 0.003932038 Weight

Sample size: 27

R (correlation coefficient) = -0.7955

R-sq = 0.63284415

Estimate of error standard deviation: 3.1125581

Excel

SUMMARY OUTPUT				
Regression Statistics				
Multiple R	0.795515			
R Square	0.632844			Coefficients
Adjusted R Squ	0.618158		Intercept	37.77506611
Standard Error	3.112558		Curb Weight	-0.00393204
Observations	27			

Rounding: The highest mileage in our data set is 31.5 mpg. If we wrote this to the nearest hundredth it would be 31.50. Because this value has 2 decimal places, we need to write our intercept using at least 3 decimal places. Because 31.50 has 4 digits, we will write our slope using at least 5 digits. The slope here is a very small number and we must remember that the leading zeros do not count as digits. The equation is as follows

$$\hat{y} \approx 37.775 - 0.0039320x$$

e) A prediction for a 2815 lb. vehicle should be reliable because this weight is within the range of curb weights in our data set. To make the prediction, we simply substitute this value into our regression equation.

$$x = 2815 \Rightarrow \hat{y} \approx 37.775 - 0.0039320(2815) \approx 26.71 \text{ mpg}$$

f) It would not be wise to make a prediction for a vehicle weighing 9000 lbs. It is possible that the linear model will not continue for vehicles weights above the ones in our data set. Because the linear model could break down for vehicles of this size, it would be unwise to make such an extrapolation.

> **Key Concept**: *Is it wise to predict*
>
> When asked if it would be wise or reliable to make a prediction, our answer is based on the x-value alone. We do not need to make the prediction to decide if it is wise or not.

g) The slope is the coefficient of x, -0.0039320. We will start with the scratch work of writing this as a fraction representing the change in response over the change in predictor. We will then add the units and interpret from the bottom up.

$$slope = \frac{\Delta\hat{y}}{\Delta x} = \frac{-0.0039320}{1} = \frac{-0.0039320 \text{ mpg}}{1 \text{ lb.}} = \frac{-0.0039320 \text{ mpg}}{1 \text{ lb.}} \cdot \frac{1000}{1000} = \frac{-3.9320 \text{ mpg}}{1000 \text{ lb.}}$$

The standard interpretation is: For every additional 1 lb. of curb weight, the average overall gas mileage decreases by 0.003932 mpg.

Because this is such a small change in gas mileage per pound, it might be better to interpret as follows. For every additional 1000 lbs. of curb weight, the average overall gas mileage decreases by 3.932 mpg.

h) From part (e), we have the ordered pair $(2815, 26.71)$. We need one more ordered pair to graph and it is best if we use a point from the opposite end of the weights, such as 6000 lbs.

$$x = 6000 \Rightarrow \hat{y} \approx 37.775 - 0.0039320(6000) \approx 14.18$$
$$\Rightarrow (6000, 14.18)$$

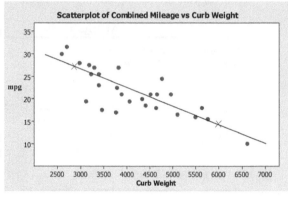

Plotting these two ordered pairs produces the line shown to the right with the scatterplot. Notice that we have removed the Toyota Prius from the data set.

This last example showed us how we might deal with outliers and potentially influential observations that show up in our data sets. This information is summarized in the following Point to Remember.

> **Point to Remember**: *How to handle outliers and PIO's in a data set: To remove or not to remove?*
>
> *Outliers*: If a data set contains an outlier, it should be inspected carefully. If you determine that the outlier was the result of an error in data entry or data collection, then you should fix or remove the outlier from the data set before making calculations. If the outlier simply represents an unusual observation, then it should stay in the data set.
>
> *PIO's*: If the data set contains a PIO, then you must consider whether or not the data point is valuable in extending the predictions we can make with the regression equation. However, you should remove the PIO from the data set if you are confident that all predictions you will be making have x-values that lie within the range of the data values that would remain.

Let's practice what we have learned with some exercises.

Exercise Set 4.2

Concept Review: Review the definitions and concepts from this section by filling in the blanks for each of the following.

25) The best fitting line for a data set is called the _____ line.

26) The regression line is the one with the smallest possible sum of squared _____. An error is the difference between the height of an actual data point and the height of the line at that same ____ -value.

27) Linear regression should only be done if a plot of the data values has a roughly _____ pattern.

28) When we use a regression equation to make a prediction, we are always predicting the _____ y-value.

29) It is not wise to make predictions using ____-values that are outside of the _____ of the given data.

30) If the x-value of a data point stands out, then we call it a _____ _____ _____ .
    If the y-value does not fit the linear pattern, then we call it an _____.

31) y stands for the _____ y-value of a piece of data.
    $\bar{y}$ stands for the _____ of all the y-values in the data set. $\hat{y}$ stands for a _____ y-value using an x-value in the regression equation.

32) When a linear pattern exists for x-values in a certain range, but then begins to change outside of that range, then we refer to this as _____ _____.

Mechanics: The following exercises will help practice the mechanics of finding the sum of squared errors and the linear regression equation.

33) Consider lines A and B to be possible fit lines for the data set shown below:

Line A: $y = 6 + 4x$ Line B: $y = 7 + 3.5x$

x	3	5	6	8	8	11
y	21	25	24	30	41	50

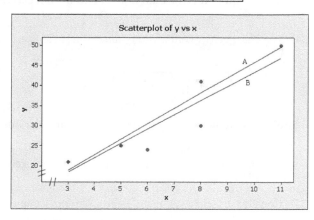

a) Based only on looking at the above graph, which line appears to be the better fit for the data set, A or B?
b) Determine the sum of squared error for each fit line.
c) Which line is the better fit according to the least squares criterion? Explain.

34) Consider lines A and B to be possible fit lines for the data set shown below:

Line A: $y = 11 - 0.8x$ Line B: $y = 10.5 - 0.7x$

x	-2	0	3	6	9
y	13	10	8	7	4

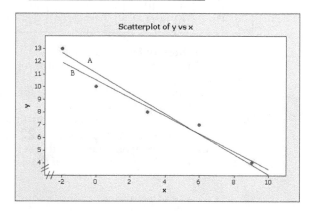

a) Based only on looking at the above graph, which line appears to be the better fit for the data set, A or B?
b) Determine the sum of squared error for each fit line.
c) Which line is the better fit according to the least squares criterion? Explain.

35) The chart below contains the same data set as exercise (33).

x	3	5	6	8	8	11
y	21	25	24	30	41	50

a) Use tables and formulas to determine the linear regression equation for the data set.
b) Verify that the regression line has a smaller sum of squared error than lines A and B from exercise (33).

36) The chart below contains the same data set as exercise (34).

x	-2	0	3	6	9
y	13	10	8	7	4

a) Use tables and formulas to determine the linear regression equation for the data set.
b) Verify that the regression line has a smaller sum of squared error than lines A and B from exercise (34).

37) Consider the data set below to be a random sample.

x	-3	0	2	5	8	9	12
y	21	15	15	12	3	4	-4

a) Create a scatterplot for the data set.
b) Does a linear regression seem appropriate? Explain.
c) Use tables and formulas to determine the linear regression equation for the data set.
d) Use the linear regression equation to find the predicted y-values for $x = -2$ and $x = 11$.
e) Use your answers from part (d) to sketch the regression line with the scatterplot of the data.

38) Consider the data set below to be a random sample.

x	7	9	10	13	16	20	21	24
y	9	13	16	22	27	35	37	44

a) Create a scatterplot for the data set.
b) Does a linear regression seem appropriate? Explain.
c) Use tables and formulas to determine the linear regression equation for the data set.
d) Use the linear regression equation to find the predicted y-values for $x = 8$ and $x = 22$.
e) Use your answers from part (d) to sketch the regression line with the scatterplot of the data.

39) For each of the data sets shown in the scatterplots below, is a linear regression appropriate? Explain.

a)

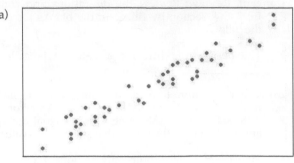

b)

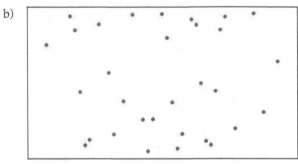

c)

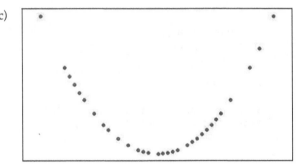

40) For each of the data sets shown in the scatterplots below, is a linear regression appropriate? Explain.

a)

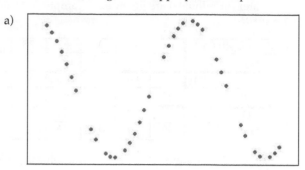

b)

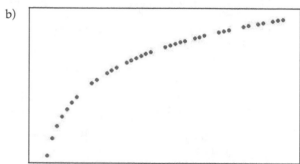

c)

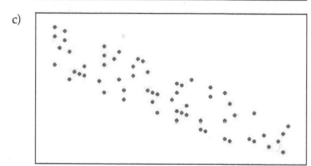

Applications: Use technology to help find the regression equations in the context of the following applications. Answer all follow-up questions. If the technology you use provides you with $\sum xy$, then use the value given to verify data entry.

41) A random sample of 16 Americans yielded the following data on age, in years, and peak heart rate, in beats per minute (bpm).

Age (x)	88	55	64	90	45	40
Peak (y)	137	167	146	135	172	170
Age (x)	67	75	81	48	89	80
Peak (y)	150	143	144	171	133	141
Age (x)	84	37	36	25		
Peak (y)	130	182	185	201		

a) Make a scatterplot for the 16 data values.
b) Does a linear regression seem appropriate? Explain.
c) Use technology to find the regression equation. Round your answer so that predictions made from the equation will be reliable to the nearest 0.1 bpm. **Note:** $\sum xy = 150{,}378$
d) Use the regression equation to predict the average peak heart rate for a 30-year-old American. Is this a wise prediction? Explain.
e) Graph the regression line on the scatterplot from part (a).
f) Interpret the slope of the line in terms of the application.

42) The size of a TV is listed by the measurement of the screen diagonal, in inches. In February 2014, a sample of 8 Vizio TV's for sale on the Costco website produced the following sizes and prices (rounded to the nearest dollar.)

TV Size (x)	32	39	40	47
Price (y)	230	350	490	650
TV Size (x)	60	65	60	70
Price (y)	760	1180	1300	1680

a) Make a scatterplot for the 8 data values.
b) Does a linear regression seem appropriate? Explain.
c) Use technology to find the regression equation. Round your answer so that predictions made from the equation will be reliable to the nearest $1. **Note:** $\sum xy = 389{,}060$
d) Use the regression equation to predict the average price for a 55-inch Vizio TV. Is this a wise prediction? Explain.
e) Graph the regression line on the scatterplot from part (a).
f) Interpret the slope of the line in terms of the application.

43) A random sample of 15 homes for sale in Hayward, CA in May of 2011 yielded the following values for the size (in square feet) and the list price (in thousands of dollars).

Size (x)	1140	1637	1600	2659	2452
Price (y)	625	710	715	870	991
Size (x)	924	1470	880	918	1412
Price (y)	479	489	540	490	490
Size (x)	1128	1031	1119	1592	1119
Price (y)	535	560	590	600	610

a) Make a scatterplot for the 15 data values.
b) Does a linear regression seem appropriate? Explain.
c) Use technology to find the regression equation. Round your answer so that predictions made from the equation will be reliable to the nearest $100. **Note:** $\sum xy = 14{,}019{,}198$
d) Use the regression equation to predict the average list price of a 2200 square foot home. Is this a wise prediction? Explain.
e) Graph the regression line on the scatterplot from part (a).
f) Explain why it would not be wise to use the equation to predict the average list price of a 3400 square foot home.
g) Interpret the slope of the line in terms of the application.
h) Explain why the two big houses could be useful to have in the data set.

44) The author of this text is a recreational scuba diver. The maximum depth (in feet) and the time under water (in minutes) are given for a sample of 18 of his dives.

Max Depth (x)	42	46	90	62	25	30
Time (y)	31	37	25	30	45	45
Max Depth (x)	56	60	35	35	60	50
Time (y)	41	48	44	40	45	45
Max Depth (x)	36	48	35	44	42	41
Time (y)	46	38	31	34	28	38

a) Make a scatterplot for the 18 data values.
b) Does a linear regression seem appropriate? Explain.
c) Use technology to find the regression equation. Round your answer so that predictions made from the equation will be reliable to the nearest tenth of a foot. **Note:** $\sum xy = 31{,}450$
d) Use the regression equation to predict the average dive time at a depth of 75 ft. Is this a wise prediction? Explain.
e) Graph the regression line on the scatterplot from part (a).
f) Explain why it would not be wise to use the equation to predict the average dive time of a 15-foot deep dive.
g) Interpret the slope of the line in terms of the application.
h) Explain why the 90-foot deep dive is useful to have in the data set.

45) The table below shows the ERAs (Earned Run Averages) for the pitching staffs and number of wins for each of the 15 American League teams during the 2013 baseball season.

Team	ERA (x)	Wins (y)
Royals	3.45	86
Athletics	3.56	96
Tigers	3.61	93
Rangers	3.62	91
Rays	3.74	92
Red Sox	3.79	97
Indians	3.82	92
Yankees	3.94	85
White Sox	3.98	63
Orioles	4.20	85
Angels	4.23	78
Blue Jays	4.25	74
Mariners	4.31	71
Twins	4.55	66
Astros	4.79	51

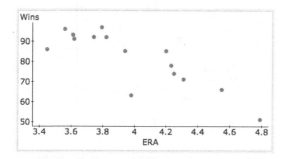

a) Does a linear regression seem appropriate? Explain.
b) Use technology to find the regression equation. Round your answer so that predictions made from the equation will be reliable to the nearest 0.1 wins. **Note:** $\sum xy = 4804.44$
c) Use your regression equation to find the value of $\hat{y}$ when $x = 4.11$. Interpret this prediction in terms of the application.
d) Interpret the slope of the line in terms of the application.
e) Which data point is the best candidate to be called an outlier? Explain.
f) Which data point is the best candidate to be called a potentially influential observation? Explain.

46) Patrick was a college statistics student that was also on his school's golf team. When Patrick was assigned to collect data for a class project, he came up with the following theory. He thought that the farther he stood away from the hole on a putting green, the less likely it would be that he would make a put. To test his theory, he took 20 puts from each of several different distances. The distance is measured in feet and he recorded the number of made puts (out of 20) for each distance. The data he collected is in the table below.

Distance (x)	3	6	9	12
Putts Made (y)	19	17	14	12
Distance (x)	15	18	21	24
Putts Made (y)	5	6	2	0

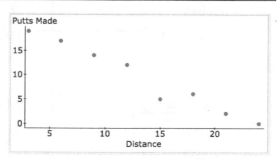

a) Does a linear regression seem appropriate? Explain.
b) Use technology to find the regression equation. Round your answer so that predictions made from the equation will be reliable to the nearest tenth of a made putt. **Note:** $\sum xy = 654$
c) Use your regression equation to find the value of $\hat{y}$ when $x = 11$. Interpret this prediction in terms of the application.
d) Interpret the slope of the line in terms of the application.
e) There is one data value that stands out a little from the rest. Which one is it? Would this data value best be described as an outlier or a potentially influential observation? Explain.

47) The table below shows the gross domestic product (GDP, in Billions of U.S. dollars) and the daily oil consumption (in barrels/day) the 30 countries with the highest GDPs. Data is from 2011 estimates.

Country	GDP (x) (in Billions)	Oil Con (x) (Thousands)
USA	16245	19150
China	8358	9400
Japan	5960	4452
Germany	3426	2495
France	2611	1861
United Kingdom	2418	1622
Brazil	2254	2029
Russia	2030	2199
Italy	2013	1528
India	1875	3182
Canada	1821	2209
Australia	1564	961
Spain	1322	1441
Mexico	1184	2073
South Korea	1130	2195
Indonesia	878	1292
Turkey	788	646
Netherlands	770	1009
Saudi Arabia	711	2643
Switzerland	631	243
Iran	552	1845
Sweden	524	221
Norway	500	351
Poland	490	565
Belgium	483	296
Argentina	477	618
Austria	394	278
Thailand	386	988
South Africa	384	553
United Arab Em	384	545

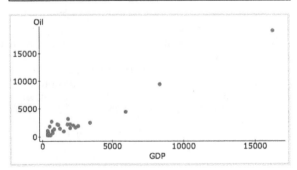

a) Use technology to find the regression equation. Round your answer so that predictions made from the equation will be reliable to the nearest 0.1 thousand barrels per day.

Note: $\sum xy = 471,354,374$

b) Interpret the slope in terms of the application.
c) There is one data value that stands out from the rest. Which one is it? Would this data value best be described as an outlier or a potentially influential observation? Explain.
d) Explain why it is probably not appropriate to use this equation to predict the oil consumption for any country regardless of GDP.

48) The table below shows the number of points that the favorite in the Super Bowl was expected to win by together with the actual point difference in the game. If the favorite won, then a positive difference is shown. If the favorite lost the game, then a negative is shown. 21 recent Super Bowls are included. The favorite is shown first in each game.

Teams	Expected Margin (x)	Actual Game Difference (y)
SF vs. CIN	7	4
SF vs. DEN	12	45
BUF vs. NYG	7	-1
WAS vs. BUF	7	13
DAL vs. BUF	6.5	35
DAL vs. BUF	10.5	17
SF vs. SD	18	21
DAL vs. PIT	13.5	10
GB vs. NE	14	14
GB vs. DEN	12	-7
DEN vs. ATL	7.5	15
STL vs. TEN	7	7
BAL vs. NYG	3	27
STL vs. NE	14	-3
OAK vs. TB	3.5	-27
NE vs. CAR	7	3
NE vs. PHI	4	3
PIT vs. SEA	4	11
IND vs. CHI	7	12
NE vs. NYG	14	-3
PIT vs. AZ	6.5	4

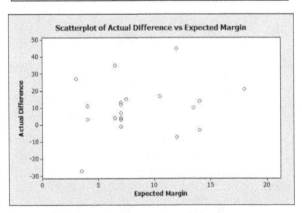

a) Use technology to find the regression equation. Round your answer so that predictions made from the equation will be reliable to the nearest 0.1 points. Note: $\sum xy = 1934$

b) Interpret the slope in terms of the application.
c) Which games are the best candidates to be called outliers? Explain.
d) Which game is the best candidate to be called a PIO? Explain.
e) Based on the scatterplot, does it appear that the expected margin is a good predictor of the actual game outcome? Explain.

49) A statistics student is an avid tea drinker. He has an *Aroma* electric water kettle. The kettle once started will bring the water to a boil and, when it senses that the water has reached boiling temperature, it shuts off. He was curious if there was a linear relationship between the amount of water in the kettle and the time it takes to reach boiling. He filled the kettle with various volumes of water (measured in liters) and then recorded the time (in seconds) that it took for the kettle to boil the water and shut off. The data is shown below followed by a scatterplot of the data.

Volume (x)	0.58	0.65	0.80	1.20
Time (y)	220	260	288	406
Volume (x)	1.04	0.90	0.85	0.73
Time (y)	345	287	305	276

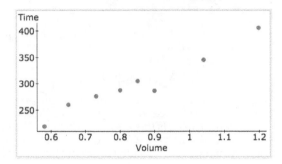

a) Does a linear regression seem appropriate? Explain.

b) Use technology to find the regression equation. Round your answer so that predictions made from the equation will be reliable to the nearest 0.1 seconds. **Note:** $\sum xy = 2092.03$

c) Use your regression equation to find the value of $\hat{y}$ when $x = 0.98$. Interpret this prediction in terms of the application.

d) Interpret the slope of the line in terms of the application.

e) Would you consider any of the data values to be outliers or potentially influential observations? Explain.

50) The data below was obtained from a random sample of 23 Algebra students during the Spring 2011 semester. A practice midterm was taken online with unlimited attempts. The maximum score possible on the practice midterm was 20 points. The actual midterm was taken with pencil and paper and students were given a single attempt. 105 points were possible on the actual midterm. A scatterplot of the data is provided below.

Practice (x)	14	14	11	14	15	18
Actual (y)	86	73	78	68	96	90
Practice (x)	15	19	15	17	19	16
Actual (y)	77	84	56	72	101	77
Practice (x)	17	18	19	18	8	14
Actual (y)	91	77	97	78	77	84
Practice (x)	15	0	12	6	16	
Actual (y)	94	17	32	51	75	

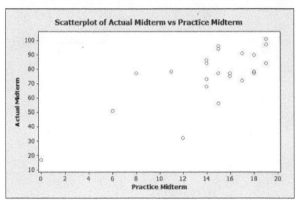

a) Does a linear regression seem appropriate? Explain.

b) Use technology to find the regression equation. Round your answer so that predictions made from the equation will be reliable to the nearest 0.1 point. **Note:** $\sum xy = 26,334$

c) Use your regression equation to find the value of $\hat{y}$ when $x = 17$. Interpret this prediction in terms of the application.

d) Interpret the slope of the line in terms of the application.

e) Would you consider any of the data values to be outliers or potentially influential observations? Explain.

(51 – 52) Use this table for the next two exercises. The information below is for a random sample of 12 Mustang GT convertibles taken in May of 2007.

Age (In years)	Price (in $100s)	Miles
1	256	26692
2	289	13759
3	228	25396
3	199	39264
4	185	55690
4	163	62482
5	119	69071
5	170	41841
5	169	25000
6	175	51600
7	115	82000
7	120	79000

51) Consider the Mustang data given above. Let the mileage be the x value and the price be the y-value. A scatterplot for the data set is shown below.

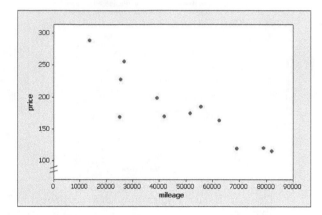

a)   Use technology to find the regression equation. Round your answer so that predictions made from the equation will be reliable to the nearest $1. **Note:** $\sum xy = 92,397,962$

b)   Use the regression equation to predict the average price of a Mustang GT convertible with 35,000 miles on it. Is this a wise prediction? Explain.

c)   Explain why it would not be wise to use the equation to predict the average price of a Mustang GT convertible with 120,000 miles on it.

d)   Interpret the slope of the line in terms of the application.

e)   Make up x and y values for an additional piece of data that, if added to the data set, would be an obvious outlier. Explain why it would be an outlier.

f)   Make up x and y values for an additional piece of data that, if added to the data set, would be an obvious PIO. Explain why it would be a PIO.

52) Consider the Mustang data given above. Let the age be the x value and the price be the y-value. A scatterplot for the data set is shown below.

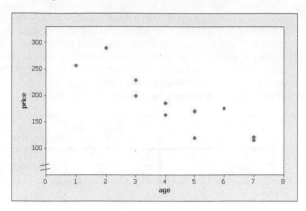

a)   Use technology to find the regression equation. Round your answer so that predictions made from the equation will be reliable to the nearest $1. **Note:** $\sum xy = 8492$

b)   Use the regression equation to predict the average price of a 6-year-old Mustang GT convertible. Is this a wise prediction? Explain.

c)   Explain why it would not be wise to use the equation to predict the average price of a 40-year-old Mustang GT convertible.

d)   Interpret the slope of the line in terms of the application.

e)   Make up x and y values for an additional piece of data that, if added to the data set, would be an obvious outlier. Explain why it would be an outlier.

f)   Make up x and y values for an additional piece of data that, if added to the data set, would be an obvious PIO. Explain why it would be a PIO.

Section 4.3 – Coefficient of Determination

In the previous section, we learned when and how to find a linear regression equation. Now we have an important question to answer. How useful is the regression for making predictions? To best answer this question, we have to consider both what we mean by using regression and what the alternative to using regression would be. When we say that we are using regression to make predictions, we are implying that we will use the x-value to help predict the y-value. In contrast to this, if we did not use regression, then we would not use the x-value to help us estimate the y-value. So what would we do instead? Typically, the answer is, we would use the average y-value from our data values as the estimate. Using the average y-value as the prediction makes sense because it produces the smallest sum of squared error when using a constant prediction for all data values.

To help us understand this comparison, let's consider the quarterback passer rating vs. number of wins from Example 4.7. We have seen that we can use the passer rating of a quarterback to help predict the number of wins for his team, but what if we didn't know the passer ratings for these quarterbacks, rather we just had the number of wins data for their teams. If someone, then told us to predict the number of wins for a randomly selected team, what would we do? It would be a common practice to use the average number of wins from our data set as the prediction. So, for this example, the question of usefulness can be translated as follows. Is using a quarterback's passer rating in the linear regression equation to predict the number of wins for his team more useful than just using the average number of wins from our sample as the estimate? We will now look at this question in detail in the discussion that follows.

Quarterback Passer Rating vs. Number of Team Wins
(A discussion of the usefulness of regression)

It is commonly believed among football fans that the quarterback is the most critical player on the team. The NFL rates the performance of a quarterback using a complex formula that incorporates many elements of the quarterback's job. A perfect rating using this formula would be 158.3. The table below lists the passer rating from the 2012 regular season for a sample of 9 NFL quarterbacks together with the number of regular season wins by their teams. (*Source*: ESPN.com)

Is quarterback passer rating a useful predictor for the number of team wins?

Player Name	Passer Rating (x)	Team Wins (y)
Tom Brady	98.7	12
Drew Brees	96.3	7
Matt Cassel	66.7	2
Jay Cutler	81.3	10
Peyton Manning	105.8	13
Cam Newton	86.2	6
Aaron Rodgers	108.0	11
Tony Romo	90.5	8
Matthew Stafford	79.8	4

We found the regression equation for this data set to be $\hat{y} \approx -12.94 + 0.2329x$ in Example 4.7. We will now investigate how useful this equation is by answering a series of questions.

Question 1: If we use the average number of wins for the teams from this sample as our prediction for each of the number of wins in the sample, then what would be the sum of squared error? That is, find

$$\sum e^2 = (y - \overline{y})^2.$$

Let's take a look at this visually. If we find the average number of wins for the teams in our sample, then we get $\overline{y} \approx 8.111$. In the graph that follows, the horizontal line represents this average number of wins for the teams in the sample and the vertical lines represent the error that would

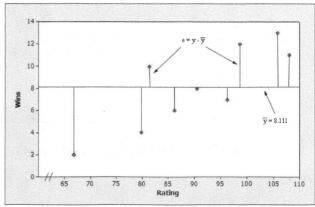

result from using this line to predict the number of wins for each of the individual teams in our sample.

Now let's compute the sum of these squared errors using a table similar to the ones used in Section 4.2.

x	y	$\bar{y}$	$e = y - \bar{y}$	$e^2 = (y - \bar{y})^2$
98.7	12	8.111	3.889	15.124
96.3	7	8.111	-1.111	1.234
66.7	2	8.111	-6.111	37.344
81.3	10	8.111	1.889	3.568
105.8	13	8.111	4.889	23.902
86.2	6	8.111	-2.111	4.456
108.0	11	8.111	2.889	8.346
90.5	8	8.111	-0.111	0.012
79.8	4	8.111	-4.111	16.900
				110.886

So, for $\bar{y}$, the sum of squared error is: $\sum e^2 = \sum (y - \bar{y})^2 \approx 110.886$

Question 2: If we use linear regression to make the predictions, what would be the sum of squared error? That is, find $\sum e^2 = (y - \hat{y})^2$.

Again, we will look at this visually first. The line shown below is the regression line and the vertical lines represent the error that results from using the regression line to make predictions.

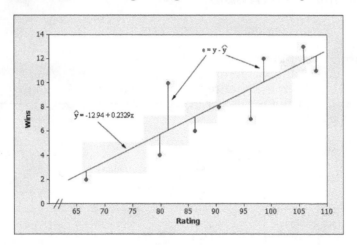

Now let's compute the sum of these squared errors using a table similar to part (a).

x	y	$\hat{y}$	$e = y - \hat{y}$	$e^2 = (y - \hat{y})^2$
98.7	12	10.047	1.953	3.814
96.3	7	9.488	-2.488	6.190
66.7	2	2.594	-0.594	0.353
81.3	10	5.995	4.005	16.040
105.8	13	11.701	1.299	1.687
86.2	6	7.136	-1.136	1.290
108.0	11	12.213	-1.213	1.471
90.5	8	8.137	-0.137	0.019
79.8	4	5.645	-1.645	2.706
				33.570

So, for $\hat{y} \approx -12.94 + 0.2329x$, the sum of squared error is: $\sum e^2 = \sum (y - \hat{y})^2 \approx 33.570$

Question 3: What is the percent reduction in squared error when we use linear regression rather than the average number of wins to make our predictions?

Let's begin by computing the amount of the reduction in squared error. This is fairly straightforward. We take the amount of error from using $\bar{y}$, $\sum e^2 = \sum (y - \bar{y})^2 \approx 110.886$, and then we subtract the error that remains when we use $\hat{y} \approx -12.94 + 0.2329x$, $\sum e^2 = \sum (y - \hat{y})^2 \approx 33.570$. This yields:

$$\text{Amount of reduction in squared error} = 110.886 - 33.570 = 77.316$$

Now to get the percent reduction in squared error we simply divide this amount by the error we originally had when using $\bar{y}$ to make the predictions. This yields:

$$\text{Percent reduction in squared error} = \frac{77.316}{110.886} \times 100\% \approx 69.73\%$$

Question 4: Would you say that regression is useful here? Explain.

I would definitely say that the regression has been useful. We have removed just under 70% of the squared error in our predictions. If the choice is between using the average number of wins to make predictions or using regression and reducing my squared error by 69.73%, then I'll choose regression any day!

THE COEFFICIENT OF DETERMINATION: *Formalizing the discussion*

Clearly, the information we obtained in the previous discussion is very useful to know about a linear regression we have performed. In fact, the percent reduction in squared error is so important, we will formally define it and give the formula for calculating it.

> **Definition**: *Coefficient of Determination*
>
> **Coefficient of Determination**: The coefficient of determination is the percent reduction in squared error when we use linear regression rather than the average of the y-values in our sample to make predictions. It is denoted by r^2 and the formula is as shown below.
>
> $$r^2 = \frac{\text{removed squared error}}{\text{original squared error}} = \frac{\sum (y - \bar{y})^2 - \sum (y - \hat{y})^2}{\sum (y - \bar{y})^2}$$
>
> *Rounding Note*: As will be the case with all numbers that can be interpreted as a percentage, we will use at least 4 decimal places when rounding r^2.

Because the process of linear regression produces the line with the smallest possible sum of squared error, we know that it cannot be worse than using the average y-value from the sample. Also, the best we can hope for is that regression will remove all of the errors. Therefore, r^2 will always be between 0 and 1 inclusive.

In the discussion about passer rating and number of wins, we learned that one interpretation of the coefficient of determination is that it represents the percent reduction in squared error when we use linear regression rather than the average y-value to make our predictions. This is a good interpretation, but there is another one that is also used. People often say that r^2 represents the percentage of variation in the y-values that can be explained by using the x-value in the regression equation. Let's take a look at the reasoning behind this explanation.

Imagine someone is looking at the data on passer rating and number of wins, but that they are only looking at the number of wins for the teams (perhaps they were not given the passer ratings). They calculate the average number of wins and they notice that some teams won more games than average and some teams won less games than average. They do not understand why there is so much variation in the number of wins.

Another person then comes along and tells them that they need to consider the passer ratings for each team's quarterback. They explain that those with better quarterbacks often win more games and they provide the person with the regression equation that can be used to make predictions for the number of wins for these teams. After using the regression equation to make predictions, we still notice that some teams win more games than we expected and some win less. However, some of the variation has been reduced or explained away by linear regression. See the graphs that follow.

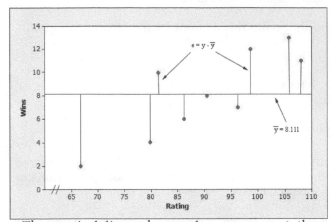

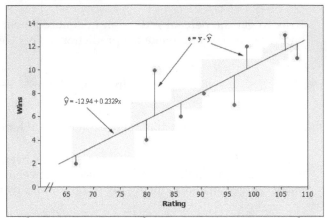

The vertical lines shown above represent the variations from the average number of wins that the person can't seem to explain for himself.

The vertical lines shown above represent the variations from the number of wins predicted by the regression equation.

Point to Remember: *Interpretation of r^2 and the Usefulness of Linear Regression*

Interpretations of r^2:

- r^2 represents the percent reduction in squared error when we make predictions by using the x-value in the linear regression equation rather than always just using the average y-value as our prediction.

- r^2 represents the percentage of variation in the y-values that can be explained by using the x-value in the regression equation.

Usefulness of regression:

- $r^2 = 1$ indicates that the data was perfectly linear and that all prediction error has been removed. The closer r^2 is to 1, the more useful the regression is.

- $r^2 = 0$ indicates that linear regression produces the horizontal line that has the same height as the average of the y-values. The closer r^2 is to 0, the more we fear that the regression was not useful at all.

LOOKING DEEPER: *It's just no use!?*

If r^2 is near zero, then people will often say that the regression is not useful at all. This may seem strange, but let's look a little deeper at this idea. Suppose that r^2=0.10. This means that we are getting a 10% reduction in squared error when we use linear regression rather than the average y-value to make our predictions. Isn't it useful to get rid of 10% of your errors? Or would you rather keep them all? Imagine I told you that I know a little study trick that will remove 10% of the errors you normally make when taking a test. This would mean that instead of missing say 30 points on the test, you only miss 27 points. Isn't it useful to gain those three points by using the study trick? Of course it is.

The problem is that the 10% reduction in error is for the sample data, but we usually apply the regression equation to the population. Values obtained from samples only provide an estimate of what is happening in the population. So, it is feared that if the error removed in the sample is 10%, then for the population it might actually be 0%. So, in conclusion, any amount of error removed is useful, however, if it appears that regression has only little use in the sample, then it may in fact have no usefulness in the population we apply it to.

USING TECHNOLOGY: *Finding the Coefficient of Determination Using Various Technologies*

The method we just developed to find r^2 is very good for understanding the interpretation. However, we can also quickly obtain this number using technology. We will now explore how to use technology to quickly find this number and we will then use the time saved to work on interpreting it. The steps below show how to use 4 common forms of technology to find the coefficient of determination. For most technologies, this does not require any extra work. The number is usually produced at the same time as the regression equation. For all of these we will use the data set from Example 4.4.

x	1	2	4	7	9
y	1	3	4	7	6

MINITAB:

1. Enter the x-values into C1 and the y-values into C2. (These should be renamed to match the application.)
2. Choose STAT > Regression > Regression
3. Enter the y-column for the response variable and the x-column for the predictor.
4. Click the OK button.
5. Look for R-Sq in the output.

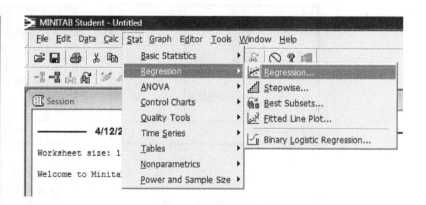

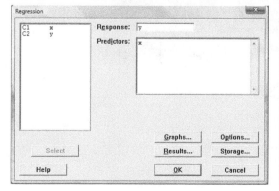

So the coefficient of determination is: $r^2 \approx 0.839$

TI-84:

The default setting on the calculator does not give r^2 to us, but we can turn on a feature that will make it provide r^2 along with the regression equation. This procedure only needs to be done once and, from then on, your calculator will automatically give you the value of r^2 when you compute your regression equation. Just follow the steps below to turn on the feature.

Choose: CATALOG > DiagnosticOn > Enter > Enter (See screen shots below.)

 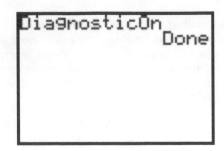

Note: Catalog is found above the zero key and you just have to scroll down to find DiagnosticOn

1.   Choose STAT > EDIT
2.   Enter the x-values into L1 and the y-values into L2.
3.   Choose STAT > CALC > 8:LinReg(a+bx)
4.   Specify the list L1 and L2 and press enter. "LinReg(a+bx) L1, L2"

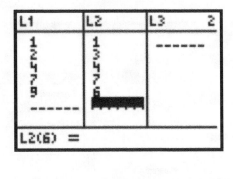 

So the coefficient of determination is: $r^2 \approx 0.8387$

STATCRUNCH:

1. Enter the x-values into var1 and the y-values into var2. (Rename these to match the application.)
2. Choose STAT > Regression > Simple Linear
3. Use the pull down menu's to choose the appropriate x and y variables.
4. Click the Calculate button.

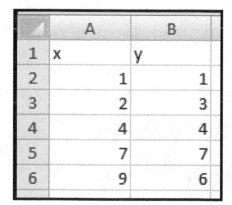

StatCrunch	Edit	Data	Stat
Row	x		y
1	1		1
2	2		3
3	4		4
4	7		7
5	9		6

Options

Simple linear regression results:
Dependent Variable: y
Independent Variable: x
y = 1.2079647 + 0.6504425 x
Sample size: 5
R (correlation coefficient) = 0.9158
R-sq = 0.8387285
Estimate of error standard deviation: 1.107097

So the coefficient of determination is: $r^2 \approx 0.8387$

EXCEL:

1. Enter the x-values into cells in column A and the y-values into cells in column B. Use the first cell in each column to provide names for the variables.
2. Click on the DATA tab and then click Data Analysis on the far right. Select Regression and click OK.
3. Choose the appropriate range of cells for the Y Range and the X range. In the Output Range, select the cell that you would like to be the upper left of the regression output. Click OK.
4. In the output, look for R Square in the Regression Statistics section.

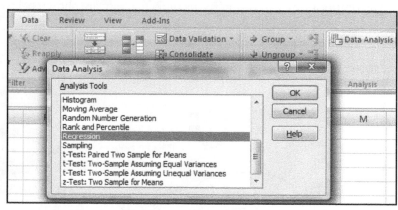

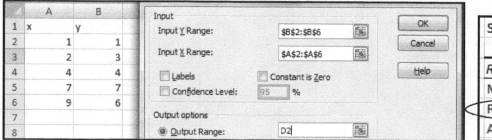

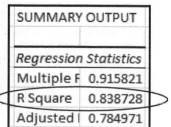

So the coefficient of determination is: $r^2 \approx 0.8387$

Let's look at a new example where we use technology to quickly find r^2 and then spend most of our effort on interpreting what it means in terms of the application.

Example 4.9: *Row number vs. Exam results*

During a recent Algebra exam given by the Author, the row number for each of the students taking the exam was recorded. The rows were numbered from 1 in the front row to 5 in the back row of the classroom. The data set that follows is a random sample of 19 of these students.

Can the row number a student sits in for an exam predict the exam score?

Row Number, x	3	4	5	4	1	5	1	2	5	3	5	2	3	1	4	2
Exam Score, y	77	78	94	56	91	90	78	51	43	84	84	72	73	75	17	97

a) What do you think (without examining the data in the table) would be the relationship between these two variables?

b) Use technology to determine the value of the coefficient of determination, r^2.

c) Interpret r^2 in terms of the application.

d) So, would you consider where someone sits to be a useful predictor of success on the exam? Explain.

Solution:

a) It is a common perception that the best students in the class sit in the front of the class and that the lesser students sit in the back. If this is true, then I would expect that larger row numbers would result in lower test scores.

b) The output from 4 common forms of technology are shown below.

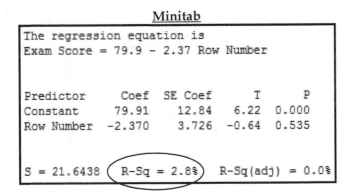

Minitab

```
The regression equation is
Exam Score = 79.9 - 2.37 Row Number


Predictor      Coef   SE Coef      T      P
Constant      79.91    12.84    6.22  0.000
Row Number    -2.370    3.726   -0.64  0.535


S = 21.6438   R-Sq = 2.8%   R-Sq(adj) = 0.0%
```

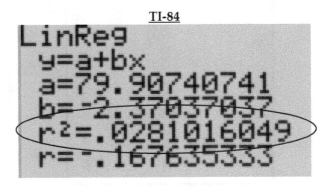

TI-84

```
LinReg
y=a+bx
a=79.90740741
b=-2.37037037
r²=.0281016049
r=-.167635333
```

StatCrunch

Simple linear regression results:
Dependent Variable: Exam Score
Independent Variable: Row Number
Exam Score = 79.90741 - 2.3703704 Row Number
Sample size: 16
R (correlation coefficient) = -0.1676
R-sq = 0.028101604
Estimate of error standard deviation: 21.643822

Excel

SUMMARY OUTPUT	
Regression Statistics	
Multiple F	0.167635
R Square	0.028102
Adjusted	-0.04132

So the coefficient of determination is: $r^2 \approx 0.0281$

c) There are two standard interpretations for r^2, both are given below.

We get a 2.81% reduction in squared error when we make predictions of Algebra students' exam scores by using their row number in the regression equation rather than just always using the overall average score as our prediction.

2.81% of the variation in exam scores can be explained by using the students' row numbers in the regression equation.

d) If this value of r^2 were from the population rather than a sample, then we might say that there was at least a small amount of usefulness to the regression equation. However, because this value of r^2 is from the sample and is so close to zero, we have to worry that this equation will not be useful at all when applied to the population. So, it appears from this sample that a student's row number is not really useful in predicting the student's exam score.

WRAP SESSION:

Let's take a look at all these ideas with one more example.

Example 4.10: *Vehicle weight vs. gas mileage*

In April 2011, a random sample of 27 new vehicles were obtained and data was collected on the curb weight of the vehicle (in lbs.) and the overall gas mileage (the average of the city and highway miles in mpg.) The following table shows the make and model of each vehicle together with its curb weight and overall mileage. In Example 4.8, we found the linear regression equation for this data set. Now we wish to see if that equation is useful. (Note: the Toyota Prius has been removed from the sample given in Example 4.8 because it was the only hybrid vehicle.)

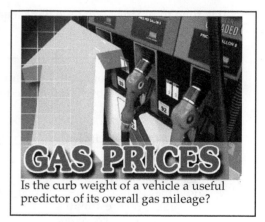

Is the curb weight of a vehicle a useful predictor of its overall gas mileage?

Make / Model	Curb Weight	Overall Mileage	Make / Model	Curb Weight	Overall Mileage
Audi A3	3219	25.5	Honda Pilot	4319	20
BMW 5 Series	3814	27	Hummer H2	6614	10
BMW X5	4960	21	Jaguar XJ	4045	19.5
Cadillac CTS	3872	21	Jeep Wrangler	3760	17
Cadillac Escalade	5488	16	Mazda RX-8	3111	19.5
Chevy Camaro	3780	22.5	Mercedes-Benz M-Class	4630	18
Chevy Tahoe	5636	18	MINI Cooper Convertible	2701	31.5
Chrysler Town and Cntry	4652	21	Mitsubishi Outlander	3384	25.5
Dodge Grand Caravan	4510	21	Nissan Altima Sedan	3180	27.5
Dodge Viper	3454	17.5	Porsche Cayenne	4398	18.5
Ford Fusion	3285	27	Subaru Outback	3386	23
Ford Ranger SuperCab	4760	24.5	Toyota Land Cruiser	5765	15.5
GMC Sierra Crew Cab	5095	16.5	VW Golf	2968	28
Honda Civic	2588	30			

a) Use technology to find the coefficient of determination, r^2.

b) Interpret r^2 in terms of the application and squared error.

c) Interpret r^2 in terms of the application and the variation in the y-values.

d) Would you consider the linear regression done previously for this problem to be useful? Explain.

Solution:

a)   Using the StatCrunch output shown on the right (or the technology of your choice), we find the coefficient of determination, $r^2 \approx 0.6328$

b)   We get a 63.28% reduction in squared error when we use the curb weight in the regression equation to predict the overall gas mileage rather than just always using the average overall mileage from the sample as our prediction.

> **StatCrunch Output**
>
> **Simple linear regression results:**
> Dependent Variable: Mileage
> Independent Variable: Weight
> Mileage = 37.775066 – 0.003932038 Weight
> Sample size: 27
> R (correlation coefficient) = –0.7955
> R-sq = 0.63284415
> Estimate of error standard deviation: 3.1125581

c)   63.28% of the variation in the overall gas mileages can be explained by using the curb weight in the regression equation.

d)   Yes! Even though this is only a sample, we see that about 63.28% of the squared prediction errors have been removed by using regression. I would much rather remove 63.28% of the squared error than keep it all.

It is time to practice what we have learned with some exercises.

Exercise Set 4.3

Concept Review: Review the definitions and concepts from this section by filling in the blanks for each of the following.

53) r^2 is called the coefficient of _____ .

54) $\sum (y - \bar{y})^2$ represents the total squared error if we used the _____ y-value from our data set to make our estimates rather than the linear _____ equation.

55) $\sum (y - \hat{y})^2$ represents the total squared error if we used the linear _____ equation to make predictions.

56) $\dfrac{\sum (y - \bar{y})^2 - \sum (y - \hat{y})^2}{\sum (y - \bar{y})^2}$ represents the

_____ reduction in squared error when we make predictions by using the x-value in the regression equation rather than just always using the overall average y-value to make our _____ .

57) If r^2 is near 0, then we fear that the regression is _____ _____ .

58) If r^2 is near 1, then the regression is _____ _____ .

Mechanics: The following exercises will help practice the mechanics of finding the coefficient of determination. These exercises are also meant to help us visualize what is being calculated.

59) The graph below shows a data set together with a horizontal line representing the average y-value for the data set. The sum of the squared errors is given below the graph.

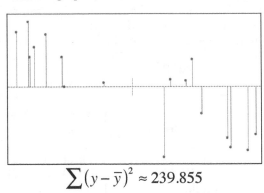

$$\sum (y - \bar{y})^2 \approx 239.855$$

This graph shows the same data set together with the linear regression line. The sum of the squared errors is given below the graph.

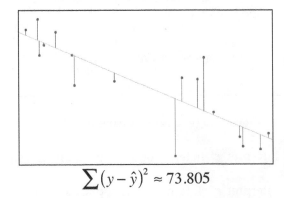

$$\sum (y - \hat{y})^2 \approx 73.805$$

Use the two sum of squared errors provided to calculate the coefficient of determination, r^2.

60) The graph below shows a data set together with a horizontal line representing the average y-value for the data set. The sum of the squared errors is given below the graph.

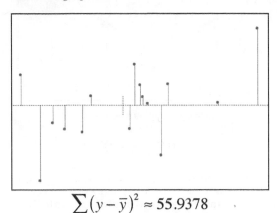

$$\sum (y - \bar{y})^2 \approx 55.9378$$

This graph shows the same data set together with the linear regression line. The sum of the squared errors is given below the graph.

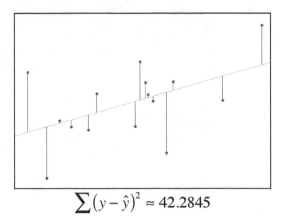

$$\sum (y - \hat{y})^2 \approx 42.2845$$

Use the two sum of squared errors provided to calculate the coefficient of determination, r^2.

61) In the graph shown below, consider the horizontal line to represent the average y-value for the data set and the slant line to represent the linear regression equation.

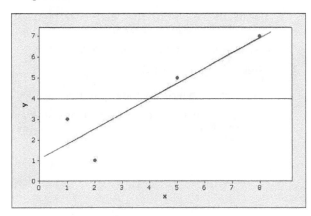

Use only the graph of the data to do the following.
a) Use the graph above to estimate the value of
$$\sum (y - \bar{y})^2$$
by first estimating the difference in height between each of the data values and the horizontal line.
b) Use the graph above to estimate the value of
$$\sum (y - \hat{y})^2$$
by first estimating the difference in height between each of the data values and the slanted regression line.
c) Use your answers from parts (a) and (b) to estimate the value of r^2.

62) In the graph shown below, consider the horizontal line to represent the average y-value for the data set and the slant line to represent the linear regression equation.

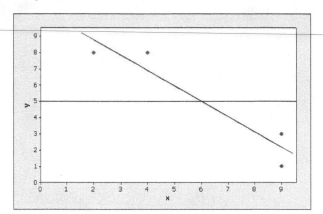

Use only the graph of the data to do the following.
a) Use the graph above to estimate the value of
$$\sum (y - \bar{y})^2$$
by first estimating the difference in height between each of the data values and the horizontal line.
b) Use the graph above to estimate the value of
$$\sum (y - \hat{y})^2$$
by first estimating the difference in height between each of the data values and the slanted regression line.
c) Use your answers from parts (a) and (b) to estimate the value of r^2.

63) Consider the data below to be a random sample.

x	3	5	6	8	8	11
y	21	25	24	30	41	50

Use tables and formulas to calculate the coefficient of determination, r^2.

64) Consider the data below to be a random sample.

x	-2	0	3	6	9
y	13	10	8	7	4

Use tables and formulas to calculate the coefficient of determination, r^2.

Applications: Apply what we have learned about the coefficient of determination in the context of real world applications. Use technology, when indicated, to help find the r^2. If the technology you use provides you with $\sum xy$, then use the value given to verify data entry.

65) According to the Office of Institutional Research at Harvard University, the student tuition, in dollars, for a sample of 7 years was as shown below. A scatterplot of the data set is shown below with the regression equation. *Source: Harvard Magazine.*

Year (x)	1981	1985	1990	1995
Tuition (y)	6000	9800	13545	18485
Year (x)	2000	2005	2010	
Tuition (y)	22765	28752	34976	

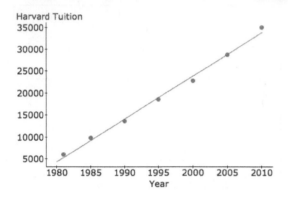

$$\hat{y} = -1{,}934{,}953.6 + 979.450x$$

a) Based on the graph, does the linear regression appear to be useful? Explain.
b) Use tables and formulas to calculate the coefficient of determination, r^2.
c) Does the value of r^2 you obtained in part (b) agree with your answer from part (a)? Explain.

66) You may occasionally here reports on the news about the cost per barrel for crude oil. This is the product that is refined into the gasoline we use in our cars. It is natural to wonder about the relationship between the price of crude oil and the price of gasoline. The chart below shows a sample of 6 days where the price of oil ($/barrel) and the national average in the U.S. for regular unleaded gasoline ($/gallon) are recorded. (The data is based off of info from gasbuddy.com from late 2010 / early 2011.)

Oil (x)	81	90	87	103	110	97
Gas (y)	2.86	3.01	3.10	3.47	3.82	3.42

A scatterplot of the data set is shown below with the regression line.

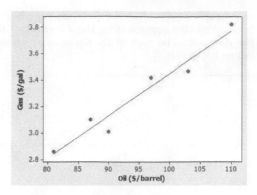

$$\hat{y} = 0.235 + 0.03217x$$

a) Based on the graph, does the linear regression appear to be useful? Explain.
b) Use tables and formulas to calculate the coefficient of determination, r^2.
c) Does the value of r^2 you obtained in part (b) agree with your answer from part (a)? Explain.

67) The data below was recorded by a video game player while playing *Project Gotham Racing 3*. All the data was collected with the same car on the same track. The x-value is the number of attempts and the y-value is the lap time, in seconds. A scatter plot and the regression equation are shown for the data.

Attempt # (x)	1	2	3	4	5
Lap time (y)	86.49	83.79	80.04	81.41	77.05
Attempt # (x)	6	7	8	9	10
Lap time (y)	80.01	78.31	76.84	76.35	75.07

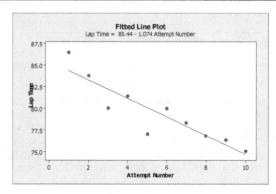

a) Based on the graph, does the linear regression appear to be useful? Explain.
b) Use technology to find r^2 for the data set.
   Note: $\sum xy = 4285.88$
c) Interpret r^2 in terms of the application.
d) Based on the value of r^2, does it appear that attempt # is a useful predictor of lap time? Explain.

68) The data below was recorded by a video game player while playing *Rock Band*. All the data was collected for a single song played on the drums at the hard level. The x-value is the number of attempts and the y-value is the percentage of notes successfully played. A scatter plot and the regression equation are shown for the data.

Attempt # (x)	1	2	3	4	5
% success (y)	85	88	89	90	88
Attempt # (x)	6	7	8	9	
% success (y)	91	91	90	95	

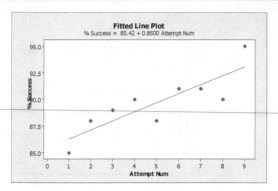

a) Based on the graph, does the linear regression appear to be useful? Explain.

b) Use technology to find r^2 for the data set. **Note:**
$$\sum xy = 4086$$

c) Interpret r^2 in terms of the application.

d) Based on the value of r^2, does it appear that attempt # is a useful predictor of % success? Explain.

69) A random sample of 15 homes for sale in Hayward, CA in May of 2011 yielded the following values for the size (in square feet) and the list price (in thousands of dollars).

Size (x)	1140	1637	1600	2659	2452
Price (y)	625	710	715	870	991
Size (x)	924	1470	880	918	1412
Price (y)	479	489	540	490	490
Size (x)	1128	1031	1119	1592	1119
Price (y)	535	560	590	600	610

a) Use technology to find r^2 for the data set.
Note: $\sum xy = 14,019,198$

b) Interpret r^2 in terms of the application and squared error.

c) Interpret r^2 in terms of the application and the variation in the y-values.

d) Based on the value of r^2, does it appear that the size of the homes in Hayward is a useful predictor of price? Explain.

70) The table below shows the ERAs (Earned Run Averages) for the pitching staffs and number of wins for each of the 15 American League teams during the 2013 baseball season.

Team	ERA (x)	Wins (y)
Royals	3.45	86
Athletics	3.56	96
Tigers	3.61	93
Rangers	3.62	91
Rays	3.74	92
Red Sox	3.79	97
Indians	3.82	92
Yankees	3.94	85
White Sox	3.98	63
Orioles	4.20	85
Angels	4.23	78
Blue Jays	4.25	74
Mariners	4.31	71
Twins	4.55	66
Astros	4.79	51

a) Use technology to find r^2 for the data set.
Note: $\sum xy = 4804.44$

b) Interpret r^2 in terms of the application and squared error.

c) Interpret r^2 in terms of the application and the variation in the y-values.

d) Based on the value of r^2, does it appear that a teams ERA is a useful predictor for the number of wins they will have during the season? Explain.

71) A mountain bike rider has a computer that monitors his heart rate, mileage, and time during rides. This information is used to estimate the number of calories burned on the ride. The data for the ride time, in minutes, and the calories burned for 15 recent rides is shown in the table below.

Ride Time (x)	45	74	58	55	83
Calories Burned (y)	499	861	659	657	984
Ride Time (x)	73	63	54	51	92
Calories Burned (y)	816	781	622	595	1067
Ride Time (x)	77	70	85	63	82
Calories Burned (y)	844	815	975	745	1007

a) Use technology to find r^2 for the data set.
Note: $\sum xy = 847,488$

b) Interpret r^2 in terms of the application and squared error.

c) Interpret r^2 in terms of the application and the variation in the y-values.

d) Based on the value of r^2, does it appear that the ride time is a useful predictor of the number of calories burned? Explain.

72) The author of this text is a recreational scuba diver. The maximum depth (in feet) and the time under water (in minutes) are given for a sample of 18 of his dives.

Max Depth (x)	42	46	90	62	25	30
Time (y)	31	37	25	30	45	45
Max Depth (x)	56	60	35	35	60	50
Time (y)	41	48	44	40	45	45
Max Depth (x)	36	48	35	44	42	41
Time (y)	46	38	31	34	28	38

a) Use technology to find r^2 for the data set.

   Note: $\sum xy = 31,450$

b) Interpret r^2 in terms of the application and squared error.

c) Interpret r^2 in terms of the application and the variation in the y-values.

d) Based on the value of r^2, does it appear that the maximum depth during the dive is a useful predictor of the dive time? Explain.

73) A random sample of 12 digital cameras in May of 2007 yielded the following data on the number of mega pixels and the suggested price of the camera (in dollars). A scatterplot for the data is shown below.

Meg-Pixs(x)	5.0	5.0	6.3	6.0	6.0	7.2
Price (y)	300	250	220	150	230	200
Meg-Pixs(x)	7.1	7.2	8.3	8.0	10.2	10.1
Price (y)	150	350	180	200	1000	350

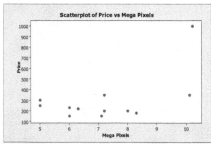

a) Use technology to find r^2 for the data set.

   Note: $\sum xy = 28,270$

b) Based on the scatterplot, which camera is the best candidate to be called an outlier? Explain.

c) Remove the ordered pair (10.2, 1000) from your data set. Now use technology to find r^2 for the modified data set. **Note:** $\sum xy = 18,070$

d) Did removing the outlier have much of an effect on the value of r^2? Explain.

e) Suppose that it turns out that this outlier camera is the only SLR camera in the sample. Choose the most appropriate version of r^2 and interpret it in terms of the application.

f) Based on the value of r^2 used in part (e), does it appear that the number of mega pixels for a digital camera is a useful predictor of the price? Explain.

74) The table below shows the number of points that the favorite in the Super Bowl was expected to win by together with the actual number of point difference in the game. If the favorite won, then a positive difference is shown. If the favorite lost the game, then a negative is shown. 21 recent Super Bowls are included. The favorite is shown first in each game.

Teams	Expected Margin (x)	Actual Game Difference (y)
SF vs. CIN	7	4
SF vs. DEN	12	45
BUF vs. NYG	7	-1
WAS vs. BUF	7	13
DAL vs. BUF	6.5	35
DAL vs. BUF	10.5	17
SF vs. SD	18	21
DAL vs. PIT	13.5	10
GB vs. NE	14	14
GB vs. DEN	12	-7
DEN vs. ATL	7.5	15
STL vs. TEN	7	7
BAL vs. NYG	3	27
STL vs. NE	14	-3
OAK vs. TB	3.5	-27
NE vs. CAR	7	3
NE vs. PHI	4	3
PIT vs. SEA	4	11
IND vs. CHI	7	12
NE vs. NYG	14	-3
PIT vs. AZ	6.5	4

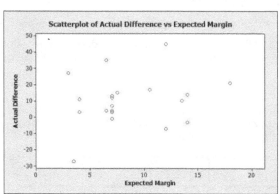

a) Use technology to find r^2 for the data set.

   Note: $\sum xy = 1934$

b) Based on the scatterplot, which game is the best candidate to be called an outlier? Explain.

c) Remove the ordered pair (3.5, -27) from your data set. Now use technology to find r^2 for the modified data set. **Note:** $\sum xy = 2028.5$

d) Did removing the outlier have much of an effect on the value of r^2? Explain.

e) If it turns out that the data value (3.5, -27) is not an error, but just an unusual result, then interpret either the value of r^2 from part (a) or (c). Choose the one that you feel is most appropriate.

f) Based on the value of r^2 used in part (e), does it appear that the expected margin is a useful predictor of the actual outcome? Explain.

75) The table below shows the population (in millions) and the total medal count for the top 24 countries during the 2012 summer Olympics.

Country	Population (x) (in Millions)	Total Number of Medals (y)
USA	318	104
China	1361	88
Russia	144	81
Great Britain	61	65
Germany	81	44
Japan	127	38
Australia	22	35
France	66	34
South Korea	50	28
Italy	60	28
Netherlands	17	20
Ukraine	45	20
Hungary	10	18
Canada	35	18
Spain	47	17
Brazil	201	17
Cuba	11	15
Kazakhstan	17	13
New Zealand	5	13
Iran	77	12
Jamaica	3	12
Belarus	9	12
Kenya	44	11
Czech Republic	11	10

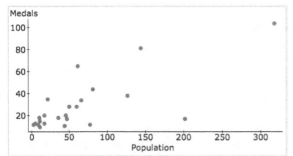

Note: To save space, China was excluded from the graph due to their large population.

a) Based on the scatterplot, does it appear that a country's population is a useful predictor of the number of medals won? Explain.

b) Use technology to find r^2 for the data set.

   Note: $\sum xy = 191,332$

c) Interpret r^2 in terms of the application.

d) If China had been included in the graph, it would have caused the data points in the lower left corner to all look clumped together. Do you think it was a wise choice to remove it from the graph? Explain.

e) Considering the method of data collection, do you think that population is really a useful predictor of the number of medals won? Explain.

76) A recreational poker player kept track of the number of hours played and the profit or loss (in dollars) for his last 15 sessions. Losses are shown as negative profits. The data is shown below.

Hours Played (x)	2	2	1	3	4
Profit (y)	60	-162	255	-113	202

Hours Played (x)	1	1	4.5	3.5	6
Profit (y)	65	43	269	227	382

Hours Played (x)	2.5	5	0.5	2.5	1.5
Profit (y)	-111	34	-100	210	243

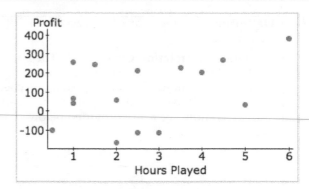

a) Based on the scatterplot, does it appear that hours played is a useful predictor of profit for this player? Explain.

b) Use technology to find r^2 for the data set.

   Note: $\sum xy = 5,657$

c) Interpret r^2 in terms of the application.

d) Based on your answer to part (a) and (b), would you say that the value of r^2 shows that hours played is a useful predictor of average profit for this player or is it a reasonable possibility that hours played is not a useful predictor and that the only reason $r^2 > 0$ is because of random variation? Explain.

e) In your opinion, and based on this data, would you say that the fact that this player won money should be attributed to luck or skillful play? Explain.

Section 4.4 – Linear Correlation

In the previous section, we learned about the coefficient of determination. Despite the fact that this number had direct visual meaning for us, it is not the number most commonly used to discuss the strength of linear regression. In this section, we will explore a new number called the **linear correlation coefficient**, or **correlation**. This number is one of the two square roots of the coefficient of determination. We will always use technology to get the **correlation**. Because of this, we will focus all of our energy in this section on learning what the **correlation** tells us about the linear pattern of the data set and the application we are working with. Let's take a look at the formal definition and formula.

Definition: *The linear correlation coefficient OR correlation, r*

   Linear Correlation Coefficient: The linear correlation, r, is one of the square roots of r^2. Because we only cover linear regression in this text, we will often refer to r simply as the correlation. The linear correlation coefficient is a numerical measure of the strength and direction of the linear pattern between our variables. Two equivalent formulas for computing r are provided below.

$$r = \frac{\sum(x-\bar{x})(y-\bar{y})}{\sqrt{\sum(x-\bar{x})^2 \sum(y-\bar{y})^2}} \qquad \textbf{OR} \qquad r = \frac{\sum z_x z_y}{n-1}$$

   Note: In the second formula, $z_x z_y$ represents the product of the z-scores for the x and y coordinates of each ordered pair in the data set.

   Rounding Note: We will round r using at least 4 decimal places.

   Technology Note: It is useful to see the two formulas above as they each reveal some important properties of the linear correlation coefficient. However, we will typically use technology to calculate r and then focus our efforts on interpreting it.

To Begin interpreting the linear correlation, it is useful to think of some synonyms for the word correlation. Here is a partial list of them: relationship, connection, link, etc. So when we examine the strength of the linear correlation between two variables, we are trying to determine how strong of a relationship or connection the variables have.

Let's begin with a visual. In the graphs that follow, we see scatterplots together with the linear correlation coefficient for the corresponding data set. We will use these to help us develop our interpretation of correlation.

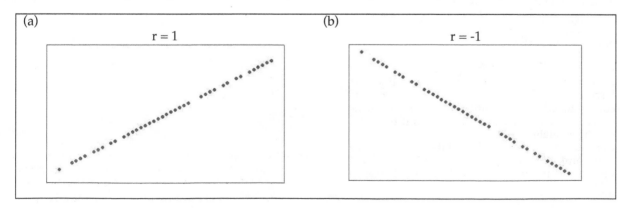

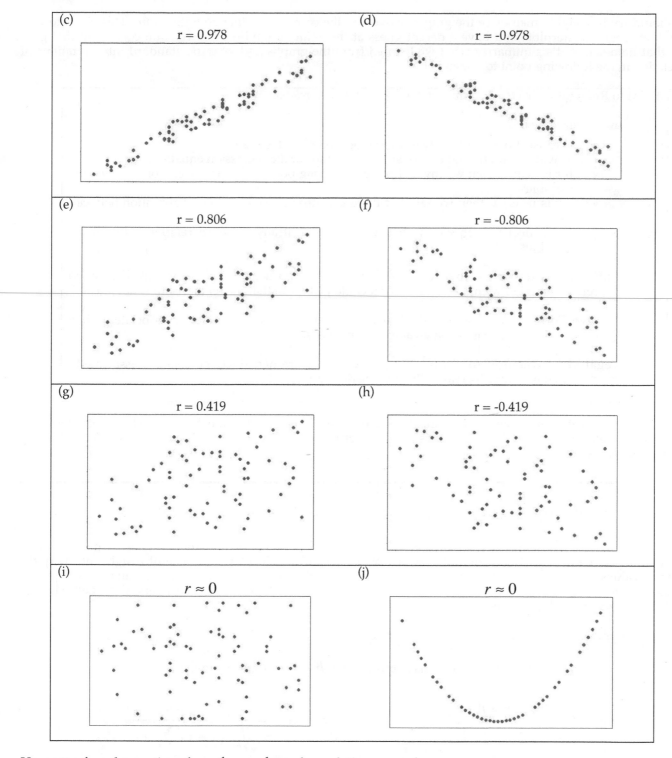

Here are a few observations from the graphs and correlations seen above.

- The stronger the linear pattern for the two variables, the closer the correlation is to either 1 or –1.
- The only difference between a positive and negative correlation is the direction of the linear pattern. If the slope is positive, then the correlation is positive. If the slope is negative, then the correlation is negative.
- Even when the linear relationship is very weak visually, the correlation can still be substantially far away from zero (see graphs (g) and (h)).
- A correlation at or near zero can mean that there is no pattern at all to the data, as in graph (i), or it could mean that there is a pattern, but that it is not a *linear* one, as in graph (j).

We should try to roughly memorize the graphs above and the correlations that go with them. This will allow us to look at future scatterplots and have a decent guess at the value of the linear correlation coefficient that goes with that data set. Let's summarize what we learned from the graphs and give the standard interpretations of correlation in the following point to remember.

Point to Remember: *Notes and interpretation for the linear correlation, r*

Interpretations of r:

- Because r is one of the two square roots of r^2, $-1 \leq r \leq 1$.
- r will always have the same sign as the slope of the regression equation.
- If r is near 1, then we say that there is a strong positive linear correlation between the variables.
- If r is near –1, then we say that there is a strong negative linear correlation between the variables.
- If r is near 0, then we say that there is weak if any *linear* correlation between the variables.

Caution: It is important to remember that a correlation near 0 can mean that there is no relationship between the variables or it could just mean that the relationship is not linear.

Positive Correlation (or association): If variables are positively correlated (associated), then as the x-value increases, the y-value also increases.

Negative Correlation (or association): If variables are negatively correlated (associated), then as the x-value increases, the y-value decreases.

All of the interpretations given above are based on the visuals that came before. However, there are mathematical reasons for these interpretations as well. For those interested in the math, please read the following looking deeper section.

LOOKING DEEPER: *What do the two formulas for correlation reveal about it?*

Even though we use technology to calculate the value of r, it is still useful to know the formulas for making these calculations by hand. The two different versions of the formula each offer some useful insight into why the different values of r are interpreted as stated in the box above. We can also use one of the formulas to see the individual contribution that each ordered pair makes towards the final value of the correlation, r. Let's use the two formulas to answer a few questions.

Why do the slope and the correlation always have the same sign?

Let's answer this by comparing the formulas for the slope, b_1, and the correlation, r.

$$\text{Slope: } b_1 = \frac{\sum(x - \bar{x})(y - \bar{y})}{\sum(x - \bar{x})^2} \qquad\qquad \text{Correlation: } r = \frac{\sum(x - \bar{x})(y - \bar{y})}{\sqrt{\sum(x - \bar{x})^2 \sum(y - \bar{y})^2}}$$

These quantities both have positive denominators because all the terms are squared. Therefore, the numerator determines the sign of each fraction. But, the numerators are exactly the same, so the answers always have the same sign.

What does it mean when the correlation is at or near zero?

Because the correlation and slope have the same sign, if the correlation is zero, then the slope also has to be zero. This tells us that a correlation of zero means that we have a horizontal regression line. Therefore, there is no overall trend of increasing or decreasing in the data set.

Why does perfectly linear data have a correlation of ± 1?

The simplest way to answer this question is to recall that r is one of the square roots of r^2 from the previous section. Therefore, if $r = \pm 1$, then $r^2 = 1$. This means that the regression equation is removing 100% of the squared prediction error when compared to making estimates of the y-values by always using the overall average y-value of the data set. The only way that 100% of this error can be eliminated is if the regression equation passes directly through every data point. This can only happen with a perfectly linear data set.

How do we know that the regression line will always pass through the point $(\overline{x}, \overline{y})$?

This is fairly easy to show, we simply substitute $\overline{x}$ into the regression equation and verify that the output is $\overline{y}$. Our regression equation is given by:

$$\hat{y} = b_o + b_1 x \text{ where } b_0 = \overline{y} - b_1\overline{x} \implies \hat{y} = (\overline{y} - b_1\overline{x}) + b_1 x. \text{ Substituting } \overline{x} \text{ in for } x \text{ yields:}$$

$$\implies \hat{y} = \overline{y} - b_1\overline{x} + b_1\overline{x} \implies \hat{y} = \overline{y} \text{ (The two } \overline{x} \text{ terms cancel out.)} \implies (\overline{x}, \overline{y}) \text{ is on the line.}$$

Can we tell if an individual data value is contributing a positive or negative amount to the linear correlation?

To answer this question, it is best to consider the formula: $r = \dfrac{\sum z_x z_y}{n-1}$

Each individual data value contributes a value of $z_x z_y$ to the numerator of this formula. This represents the product of the two z-scores for the x-value and y-value of an individual data value. If this product is positive for a given ordered pair, then that ordered pair is contributing a positive value to the correlation. If that product is negative for a given ordered pair, then that ordered pair is contributing a negative value to the correlation. Once you learn the technique, it is fairly easy to determine visually if the contribution of an ordered pair is negative to positive.

If both of the z-scores for an ordered pair are positive or if they are both negative, then the product will be positive. This occurs when both the x and y values are above average or when both the x and y values are below average. In the figures show below, a vertical line has been drawn in representing $\overline{x}$ and a horizontal line has been drawn in representing $\overline{y}$. If the ordered pair is located to the upper right of the mean lines or the lower left of the mean lines, then we will get a positive contribution to r. If the z-scores for the x and y values of an ordered pair have opposite signs, then that point makes a negative contribution to the correlation. Such ordered pairs would be located to the upper left of the mean lines or to the lower right of the mean lines.

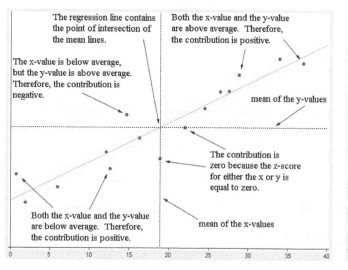

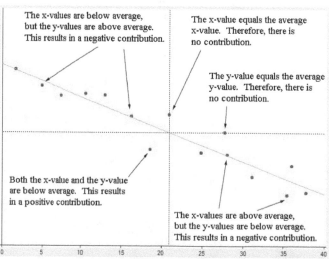

Now that we have gained some insight into how the formulas work, we will look at how to calculate the linear correlation coefficient using technology. After that, we will practice with some examples.

USING TECHNOLOGY: *Finding the Linear Correlation Coefficient Using Various Technologies*

We will now learn how to use technology to quickly find r and we will then use the time saved to work on interpreting it. The steps below show how to use 4 common forms of technology to find the linear correlation coefficient, r. For some technologies, this does not require any extra work. The number is often produced at the same time as the regression equation. For all of these examples, we will use the data set from Example 4.4.

x	1	2	4	7	9
y	1	3	4	7	6

MINITAB:

1. Enter the x-values into C1 and the y-values into C2. (These should be renamed to match the application.)
2. Choose STAT > Basic Statistics > Correlation
3. Choose both the x-column and the y-column as your variables (order does not matter).
4. Click the OK button.
5. The Pearson correlation is the number you need.

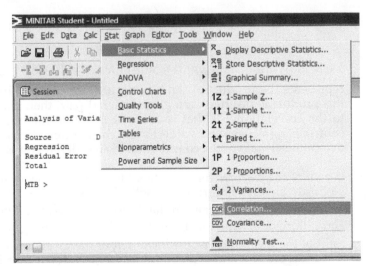

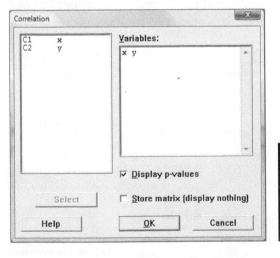

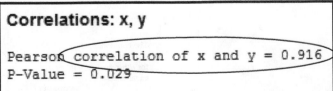

Correlations: x, y

Pearson correlation of x and y = 0.916
P-Value = 0.029

So the linear correlation coefficient is: $r \approx 0.916$

TI-84:

Provided that you have set DIAGNOSTIC ON in the previous section, the correlation will be part of your output whenever you do a linear regression. Therefore, there are no changes to our work in this section.

1. Choose STAT > EDIT
2. Enter the x-values into L1 and the y-values into L2.
3. Choose STAT > CALC > 8:LinReg(a+bx)
4. Specify the list L1 and L2 and press enter. "LinReg(a+bx) L1, L2"

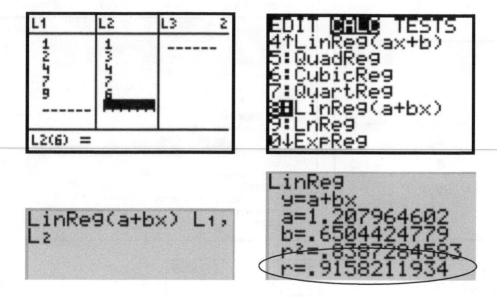

So the linear correlation coefficient is: $r \approx 0.9158$

STATCRUNCH:

StatCrunch automatically provides the linear correlation coefficient as part of the output to linear regression. So, no changes need to be made in this section.

1. Enter the x-values into var1 and the y-values into var2. (Rename these to match the application.)
2. Choose STAT > Regression > Simple Linear
3. Use the pull down menu's to choose the appropriate x and y variables.
4. Click the Calculate button.

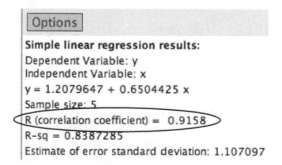

So the linear correlation coefficient is: $r \approx 0.9158$

EXCEL:

1. Enter the x-values into cells in column A and the y-values into cells in column B. Use the first cell in each column to provide names for the variables.
2. Click on the DATA tab and then click Data Analysis on the far right. Select Correlation and click OK.
3. Choose the appropriate range of cells for the Input Range. Choose both the x-column and the y-column together In the Output Range, select the cell that you would like to be the upper left of the correlation output. Click OK.
4. In the output, look for the correlation as the decimal number in the lower left of the table.

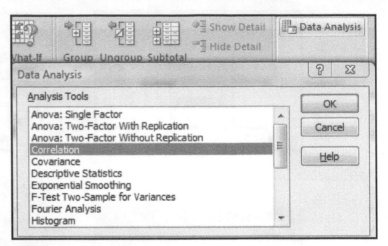

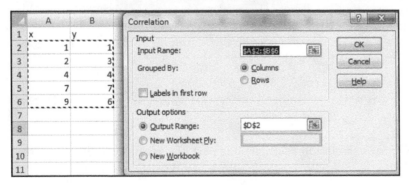

So the linear correlation coefficient is: $r \approx 0.9158$

EXAMPLES: *Finding and interpreting the correlation in the context of applications*

Example 4.11: *Quarterback Passer Rating vs. Number of Team Wins*

It is commonly believed among football fans that the quarterback is the most critical player on the team. The NFL rates the performance of a quarterback using a complex formula that incorporates many elements of the quarterback's job. A perfect rating using this formula would be 158.3. The table below lists the passer rating from the 2012 regular season for a sample of 9 NFL quarterbacks together with the number of regular season wins by their teams. A scatterplot of the data is also provided. The horizontal and vertical lines drawn through the data represent the mean lines for the x and y values. (*Source*: ESPN.com)

Is quarterback passer rating correlated with winning NFL games?

Player Name	Passer Rating (x)	Team Wins (y)
Tom Brady	98.7	12
Drew Brees	96.3	7
Matt Cassel	66.7	2
Jay Cutler	81.3	10
Peyton Manning	105.8	13
Cam Newton	86.2	6
Aaron Rodgers	108.0	11
Tony Romo	90.5	8
Matthew Stafford	79.8	4

a) By comparing the scatterplot for this data set (see figure on the right) with the ones shown earlier in this section, take a guess at the linear correlation coefficient, r.

b) Use technology to find the linear correlation coefficient, r.

c) Interpret r in terms of the application.

d) Using the mean lines shown on the scatterplot, determine which quarterbacks are not making a positive contribution to the linear correlation.

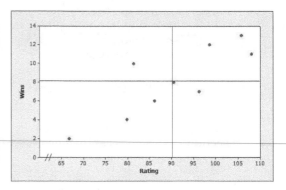

Solution:

a) The data has an upward pattern, so the correlation will be positive. The linear pattern does not seem as good as the one in graph (c) nor does it seem as bad as the pattern in graph (g). So, I will guess a number closer to the one in graph (e). My guess is that the correlation is $r \approx 0.8$.

b) Technology methods will vary. A screenshot from the TI-84 is shown to the right.

We get: $r \approx 0.8350$

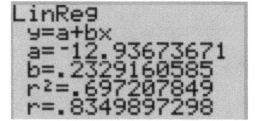

c) This value is reasonably close to 1, so I will say that there is a fairly strong positive linear correlation between the passer rating for a team's quarterback and the number of wins for the team.

Key Concept: *Specify Linear Correlation*

It is always important to state that this is a linear correlation in your interpretation. Even though we only cover linear regression in this text, there are many other types of regression.

d) Any of the quarterbacks having a data point to the upper left or to the lower right of the mean lines is making a negative contribution to the linear correlation. This appears to be the case for Jay Cutler with a rating of 81.3 and 10 wins (upper left). This also applies to Drew Brees with a rating of 96.3 and only 7 wins (lower right). Both the rating and number of wins for Tony Romo are very close to their respective average lines. This means that his data point is contributing almost nothing to the linear correlation.

Example 4.12: *Vehicle weight vs. gas mileage*

In April 2011, a random sample of 27 new vehicles were obtained and data was collected on the curb weight of the vehicle (in lbs.) and the overall gas mileage (the average of the city and highway miles in mpg.) The following table shows the make and model of each vehicle together with its curb weight and overall mileage. (Note: the Toyota Prius has been removed from the sample given in Example 4.8 because it was the only hybrid vehicle.)

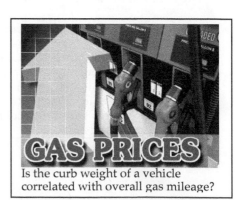

Is the curb weight of a vehicle correlated with overall gas mileage?

Make / Model	Curb Weight	Overall Mileage
Audi A3	3219	25.5
BMW 5 Series	3814	27
BMW X5	4960	21
Cadillac CTS	3872	21
Cadillac Escalade	5488	16
Chevy Camaro	3780	22.5
Chevy Tahoe	5636	18
Chrysler Town and Cntry	4652	21
Dodge Grand Caravan	4510	21
Dodge Viper	3454	17.5
Ford Fusion	3285	27
Ford Ranger SuperCab	4760	24.5
GMC Sierra Crew Cab	5095	16.5
Honda Civic	2588	30

Make / Model	Curb Weight	Overall Mileage
Honda Pilot	4319	20
Hummer H2	6614	10
Jaguar XJ	4045	19.5
Jeep Wrangler	3760	17
Mazda RX-8	3111	19.5
Mercedes-Benz M-Class	4630	18
MINI Cooper Convertible	2701	31.5
Mitsubishi Outlander	3384	25.5
Nissan Altima Sedan	3180	27.5
Porsche Cayenne	4398	18.5
Subaru Outback	3386	23
Toyota Land Cruiser	5765	15.5
VW Golf	2968	28

a) By comparing this scatterplot with the ones shown earlier in this section, take a guess at the linear correlation coefficient, r.

b) Use technology to find the linear correlation coefficient, r.

c) Interpret r in terms of the application.

d) Does this correlation show that larger curb weights cause a decrease in mileage? Explain.

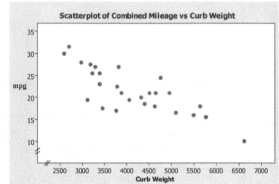

Solution:

a) This graph has a downward pattern, so I will guess a negative number. It is not as tight of a linear pattern as graph (d), but most of the points form a tighter linear pattern than graph (f), so I will guess $r \approx -0.85$.

b) Technology methods will very. A screenshot from StatCrunch is shown to the right.

We get: $r \approx -0.7995$

Simple linear regression results:
Dependent Variable: Overall Mileage
Independent Variable: Curb Weight
Overall Mileage = 37.775066 − 0.003932038 Curb Weight
Sample size: 27
R (correlation coefficient) = −0.7955
R−sq = 0.63284415
Estimate of error standard deviation: 3.1125581

c) There is a fairly strong negative linear correlation between the curb weight and the overall gas mileage.

d) Despite the fact that the correlation is strong, we cannot conclude that this is a cause and effect relationship. This is always true with observational studies. Probably in most cases, adding weight will decrease the mileage. However, it is possible that we would add a new component that improves gas mileage, but at the same time adds to the curb weight.

The result of the last part from the above example is summarized in the following point to remember.

Caution: *Correlation vs. Causality*

Linear correlation, no matter how strong, does not prove that there is a cause and effect relationship between the variables. It just shows that there is a strong relationship between the variables. It could be cause and effect, but strong correlation is not proof of that. Sometimes the true cause is some other **lurking variable** (a variable that is not included in the study, but that affects the variables being studied.)

WRAP SESSION:

Example 4.13: *Row number vs. Exam results*

During a recent Algebra exam given by the Author, the row number for each of the students taking the exam was recorded. The rows were numbered from 1 in the front row to 5 in the back row of the classroom. The data set that follows is a random sample of 19 of these students.

Is the row you sit in during a test correlated with your eventual exam score?

Row Number, x	3	4	5	4	1	5	1	2	5	3	5	2	3	1	4	2
Exam Score, y	77	78	94	56	91	90	78	51	43	84	84	72	73	75	17	97

a) What would you expect to see for the value of the linear correlation coefficient between the row number and the test scores for these students?

b) Create a scatterplot for the data set and then use it to guess at the linear correlation coefficient, r.

c) Use technology to find the linear correlation coefficient, r.

d) Interpret r in terms of the application.

e) If you were a student in this class and you sat in the back row and did poorly on the exam, would you move to the front for the next exam? Explain.

f) Which ordered pair in this data set is the best candidate to be called an outlier? Explain.

g) If this is not an error, but rather just an unusual data value, then should it be removed or left in the data set? Explain.

Solution:

a) My experience as a teacher leads me to believe that these variables will have weak if any linear correlation. So, I expect $r \approx 0$. However, it is a believed by some that the highest grades will come from the front and the lowest ones from the back row. So, some might expect a negative correlation.

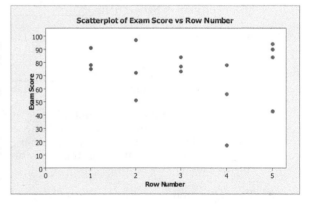

Scatterplot of Exam Score vs Row Number

b) To create a scatterplot, we simply plot all of the ordered pairs in the data set. Such a plot is shown on the right. There does not seem to be much of a linear pattern to the data set at all. However, the data does seem to decrease a little bit as we move to the right. Therefore, I guess that $r \approx -0.15$.

c) Technology methods will very. A screenshot from Excel is shown to the right.

We get: $r \approx -0.1676$

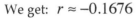

	Row Number	Exam Score
Row Number	1	
Exam Score	-0.167635333	1

d) Because this value is near zero, I would say that there is weak if any negative linear correlation between the variables. Notice that the correlation is negative which gives some support to the idea that the scores get lower as the row number gets higher. However, a correlation of –0.1676 really is pretty weak as it produces $r^2 \approx 0.0281$ which indicates that, in the sample, only 2.81% of the variation in exams scores can be explained by using the students' row number in a regression equation. In the population, row number might not explain any of the variation in test scores.

e) Moving to the front of the class for the next exam is not justified for many reasons. Here are a few. This is an observational study and correlation does not imply cause and effect. Even if it did, the correlation in this case is so small, it could just be the result of random variation in the data rather than a link between the variables. It is probably best for the student to sit where he or she feels most comfortable.

f) I would say that the ordered pair (4, 17) is an outlier. Not only does it seem like it is an unusually low score for a person sitting in row 4, but it seems like an unusually low score for the entire course. It certainly does not seem to fit the pattern of the rest of the data set.

g) Despite the fact that removing that student would support my theory stated in part (a), if it is not an error, then it needs to stay in the data set. Otherwise, I could rightly be accused of hand picking the data to support my theory.

Now that we have seen a few examples, it is time to practice with some exercises.

Exercise Set 4.4

Concept Review: Review the definitions and concepts from this section by filling in the blanks for each of the following.

77) r is known as the linear _____ coefficient.

78) The linear correlation coefficient always has the same sign as the _____ of the regression line.

79) If r is close to 1, then there is a _____ _____ linear correlation between the _____ .

80) A positive correlation (or _____) means that as the x-value gets larger, the y-value gets _____ .

81) If r is close to -1, then there is a _____ _____ linear correlation between the _____ .

82) A negative correlation (or _____) means that as the x-value gets larger, the y-value gets _____ .

83) If r is close to 0, then there is _____ if any _____ correlation between the variables.

84) A strong correlation does not always indicate a _____ and effect relationship between the two variables. It is possible that there are other _____ variables that are affecting the variables under consideration in the study.

85) The regression line always passes through the point _____ .

86) If an ordered pair is to the upper right or lower left of the mean lines, then it makes a _____ contribution to the linear correlation. If the ordered pair is on one or both of the mean lines, then the contribution to the linear correlation is _____ .

Applications: Apply what we have learned about the linear correlation coefficient in the context of real world applications. Use technology, when indicated, to help find the r. If the technology you use provides you with $\sum xy$, then use the value given to verify data entry.

87) A mountain bike rider has a computer that monitors his heart rate, mileage, and time during rides. This information is used to estimate the number of calories burned on the ride. The data for the ride time, in minutes, and the calories burned for 15 recent rides is shown in the table below.

Ride Time (x)	45	74	58	55	83
Calories Burned (y)	499	861	659	657	984
Ride Time (x)	73	63	54	51	92
Calories Burned (y)	316	781	622	595	.067
Ride Time (x)	77	70	85	63	82
Calories Burned (y)	344	815	975	745	.007

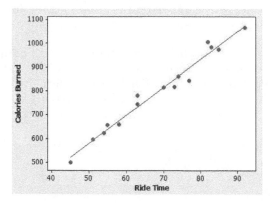

a) Take a guess at the linear correlation coefficient, r.

b) Use technology to find the linear correlation coefficient, r. **Note:** $\sum xy = 847,488$

c) Interpret r in terms of the application.

d) In your opinion, is the longer ride causing more calories to be burned, or do you suspect some other lurking variable? Explain.

88) Samples are taken most years to estimate the percentage of adults who smoke cigarettes in the U.S. The table below lists the year and percentage for 9 such samples. The scatterplot together with the regression line is provided below the data set. *Source: Center for Disease Control.*

Year (x)	1970	1980	1990	2000	2002
% smokers (y)	37.4	33.2	25.5	23.3	22.5
Year (x)	2003	2004	2007	2010	
% smokers (y)	21.6	20.9	20.8	19.3	

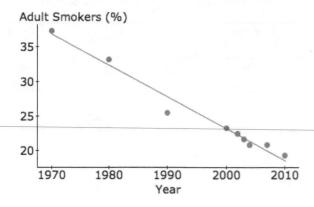

a) Take a guess at the linear correlation coefficient, r.
b) Use technology to find the linear correlation coefficient, r. **Note:** $\sum xy = 447{,}491$
c) Interpret r in terms of the application.
d) In your opinion, is the passing of time causing the percentage of smokers to decrease, or do you suspect some other lurking variable? Explain.

89) A random sample of 15 homes for sale in Hayward, CA in May of 2011 yielded the following values for the size (in square feet) and the list price (in thousands of dollars).

Size (x)	1140	1637	1600	2659	2452
Price (y)	625	710	715	870	991
Size (x)	924	1470	880	918	1412
Price (y)	479	489	540	490	490
Size (x)	1128	1031	1119	1592	1119
Price (y)	535	560	590	600	610

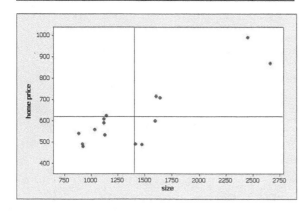

a) Take a guess at the linear correlation coefficient, r.
b) Use technology to find the linear correlation coefficient, r. **Note:** $\sum xy = 14{,}019{,}198$
c) Interpret r in terms of the application.
d) What percentage of the homes are clearly making a positive contribution to the correlation? Use the horizontal and vertical mean lines shown in the scatterplot to explain.
e) There are two ordered pairs in the data set that could be described as PIO's. Remove them from the data set and recalculate the value of r.
f) Discuss whether or not these two ordered pairs should be removed from the data set or not.

90) A random sample of 16 Americans yielded the following data on age, in years, and peak heart rate, in beats per minute (bpm).

Age (x)	88	55	64	90	45	40
Peak (y)	137	167	146	135	172	170
Age (x)	67	75	81	48	89	80
Peak (y)	150	143	144	171	133	141
Age (x)	84	37	36	25		
Peak (y)	130	182	185	201		

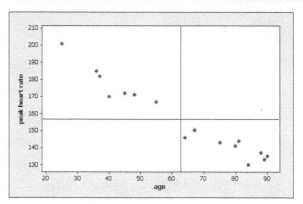

a) Take a guess at the linear correlation coefficient, r.
b) Use technology to find the linear correlation coefficient, r. **Note:** $\sum xy = 150{,}378$
c) Interpret r in terms of the application.
d) What percentage of the people sampled are clearly making a negative contribution to the linear correlation? Use the horizontal and vertical mean lines shown in the scatterplot to explain.
e) There is a single ordered pair in this data set that could possibly be considered a PIO. Remove that value from the data set and recalculate the value of r.
f) Discuss whether or not this ordered pair should be removed from the data set or not.

91) The table below shows the average price of regular unleaded gas in the U.S. (in $/gallon) together with the number of hybrid electric vehicles (HEVs) sold in the U.S. for various years. (HEV sales are from the alternative fuels data center.)

Year	Gas Price (x) ($/gal)	HEV sales (y)
2000	1.38	9,350
2002	1.36	36,035
2003	1.51	47,600
2004	1.84	84,199
2005	2.08	209,711
2006	2.87	252,636
2007	2.97	352,274
2008	3.99	312,386
2009	2.65	290,271
2010	2.70	274,210
2011	3.58	268,755
2012	3.53	382,704

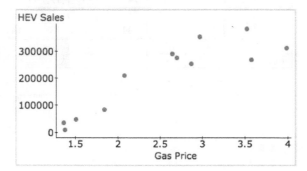

a) Take a guess at the linear correlation coefficient, r.

b) Use technology to find the linear correlation coefficient, r. **Note:** $\sum xy = 7,565,324.05$

c) Interpret r in terms of the application.

d) Based on this study, if gas prices were to fall drastically next year, would you expect sales of hybrids to decline as well? Explain.

e) Discuss possible lurking variables.

92) The data below was obtained from a random sample of 23 Algebra students during the Spring 2011 semester. The students' handwriting was rated from 1 (very messy) to 5 (very neat). The midterm was taken with pencil and paper. 105 points were possible on the midterm. A scatterplot is shown below the data table.

Handwriting, x	3	4	3	3	4	4
Midterm, y	86	73	78	68	96	90

Handwriting, x	4	3	2	3	4	3
Midterm, y	77	84	56	72	101	77

Handwriting, x	4	5	4	4	2	4
Midterm, y	91	77	97	78	77	84

Handwriting, x	2	3	4	1	4	
Midterm, y	94	17	32	51	75	

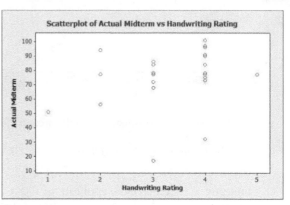

a) Take a guess at the linear correlation coefficient, r.

b) Use technology to find the linear correlation coefficient, r. **Note:** $\sum xy = 5912$

c) Interpret r in terms of the application.

d) Based on this study, if you knew someone who was struggling in algebra, would you advise them to spend time and money on a handwriting coach? Explain.

e) Discuss possible lurking variables.

(93 – 94) Use this table for each of the following problems. The information below is for a random sample of 12 Mustang GT convertibles taken in May of 2007.

Age (In years)	Price (in $100s)	Miles
1	256	26692
2	289	13759
3	228	25396
3	199	39264
4	185	55690
4	163	62482
5	119	69071
5	170	41841
5	169	25000
6	175	51600
7	115	82000
7	120	79000

93) Consider the Mustang data given above. Let the mileage be the x-value and the price be the y-value. A scatterplot for the data set is shown below. The vertical and horizontal lines represent the mean of the x and y values.

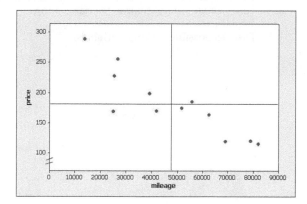

a) Take a guess at the linear correlation coefficient, r.
b) Use your calculator to find the linear correlation coefficient, r. **Note:** $\sum xy = 92{,}397{,}962$
c) Interpret r in terms of the application.
d) What percentage of the cars are clearly making a negative contribution to the linear correlation? Use the horizontal and vertical mean lines shown in the scatterplot to explain.
e) Do you suspect that putting miles causes the value of the car to decrease? Explain.
f) Discuss possible lurking variables.

94) Consider the Mustang data given above. Let the age be the x-value and the price be the y-value. A scatterplot for the data set is shown below. The vertical and horizontal lines represent the mean of the x and y values.

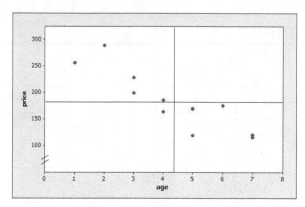

a) Take a guess at the linear correlation coefficient, r.
b) Use your calculator to find the linear correlation coefficient, r. **Note:** $\sum xy = 8492$
c) Interpret r in terms of the application.
d) What percentage of the cars are clearly making a negative contribution to the linear correlation? Use the horizontal and vertical mean lines shown in the scatterplot to explain.
e) Do you suspect that time passing causes the value of the car to decrease? Explain.
f) Discuss possible lurking variables.

(95 – 96) The table below shows the ERAs (Earned Run Averages) for the pitching staffs the number of wins, and the number of home runs for each of the 15 American League teams during the 2013 baseball season.

Team	ERA	Wins	Home Runs
Royals	3.45	86	112
Athletics	3.56	96	186
Tigers	3.61	93	176
Rangers	3.62	91	176
Rays	3.74	92	165
Red Sox	3.79	97	178
Indians	3.82	92	171
Yankees	3.94	85	144
White Sox	3.98	63	148
Orioles	4.20	85	212
Angels	4.23	78	164
Blue Jays	4.25	74	185
Mariners	4.31	71	188
Twins	4.55	66	151
Astros	4.79	51	148

95) The plot below shows the ERAs as the x-value and the number of wins as the y-value.

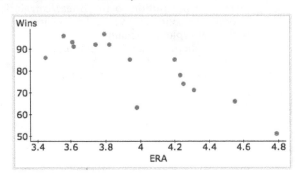

a) Take a guess at the linear correlation coefficient, r.
b) Use your calculator to find the linear correlation coefficient, r.

Note: $\sum xy = 4804.44$

c) Interpret r in terms of the application.
d) Do you suspect that pitchers with higher ERAs cause their teams to have less wins? Explain.
e) Discuss possible lurking variables.

96) The plot below shows the number of home runs as the x-value and the number of wins as the y-value.

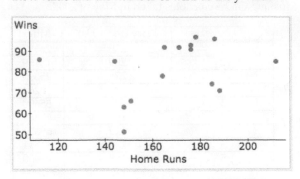

a) Take a guess at the linear correlation coefficient, r.
b) Use your calculator to find the linear correlation coefficient, r.

Note: $\sum xy = 204,978$

c) Interpret r in terms of the application.
d) Do you suspect that batters hitting more home runs cause their teams to have more wins? Explain.
e) Discuss possible lurking variables.

97) A random sample of 12 digital cameras in May of 2007 yielded the following data on the number of mega pixels and the suggested price of the camera (in dollars). A scatterplot for the data is shown below.

Meg-Pixs(x)	5.0	5.0	6.3	6.0	6.0	7.2
Price (y)	300	250	220	150	230	200
Meg-Pixs(x)	7.1	7.2	8.3	8.0	10.2	10.1
Price (y)	150	350	180	200	1000	350

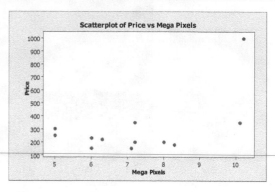

a) Use technology to find r for the data set.

Note: $\sum xy = 28{,}270$

b) Based on the scatterplot, which camera is the best candidate to be called an outlier? Explain.

c) Suppose that it turns out that this outlier camera is the only SLR camera in the sample. Should it be removed? Explain.

d) Remove the ordered pair (10.2, 1000) from your data set. Now use technology to find r for the modified data set. Note: $\sum xy = 18{,}070$

e) Did removing the outlier have much of an effect on the value of r? Explain.

f) Based on the new value of r, is it fair to say that if you want more mega pixels on your camera, then you should be prepared to pay more? Explain.

g) Discuss possible lurking variables.

98) The table below shows the number of points that the favorite in the Super Bowl was expected to win by together with the actual number of point difference in the game. If the favorite won, then a positive difference is shown. If the favorite lost the game, then a negative is shown. 21 recent Super Bowls are included. The favorite is shown first in each game.

Teams	Expected Margin (x)	Actual Game Difference (y)
SF vs. CIN	7	4
SF vs. DEN	12	45
BUF vs. NYG	7	-1
WAS vs. BUF	7	13
DAL vs. BUF	6.5	35
DAL vs. BUF	10.5	17
SF vs. SD	18	21
DAL vs. PIT	13.5	10
GB vs. NE	14	14
GB vs. DEN	12	-7
DEN vs. ATL	7.5	15
STL vs. TEN	7	7
BAL vs. NYG	3	27
STL vs. NE	14	-3
OAK vs. TB	3.5	-27
NE vs. CAR	7	3
NE vs. PHI	4	3
PIT vs. SEA	4	11
IND vs. CHI	7	12
NE vs. NYG	14	-3
PIT vs. AZ	6.5	4

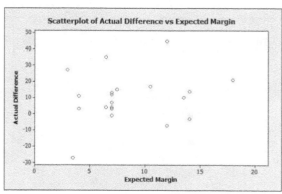

a) Use technology to find r for the data set.

Note: $\sum xy = 1934$

b) Based on the scatterplot, which game is the best candidate to be called an outlier? Explain.

c) Remove the ordered pair (3.5, -27) from your data set. Now use technology to find r for the modified data set. Note: $\sum xy = 2028.5$

d) Did removing the outlier have much of an effect on the value of r? Explain.

e) If it turns out that the data value (3.5, -27) is not an error, but just an unusual result, then should the value of r from part (a) or (c) be the one used? Explain.

f) Using the value of r from part (e), interpret the correlation in terms of the application.

Chapter Problem – Junk Food Diet and Children's IQ

Is a junk food diet harmful to your child's IQ?

In February of 2011, an article published in the *Journal of Epidemiology & Community Health* stated that there is evidence that a poor diet of high fat, sugar and processed food in early childhood may be associated with small reductions in IQ in later childhood, while a healthy diet, of nutrient rich foods may be associated with small increases in IQ. The study was based on data collected from 3996 children. They recorded their eating patterns at age 3 and later checked their IQ's at age 8.5 years old. Specific results of the study stated that children whose dietary score was 1 standard deviation above average (towards healthy eating) showed an average increase in IQ of 1.20 points at age 8.5 years. On the other hand, children whose dietary score was 1 standard deviation below average (towards junk food) showed an average decrease in IQ of 1.67 points.

Does the type of food a child eats at age 3 have an effect on their intelligence at age 8?

In the questions that follow, we will do a mini trial to see how this study might have played out. The data below represents a random sample of 40 such children in this diet vs. IQ experiment. The data displayed below is based on the results from the actual experiment. A scatterplot of the data set has also been provided.

Diet Score at 3, x	0.4	-0.8	0.0	0.9	0.3	-1.7	-1.0	1.4	-1.8	2.3	0.6	-0.5	0.2	2.7
IQ at 8.5 years, y	95	96	102	102	106	96	97	102	99	110	102	108	106	104

Diet Score at 3, x	-0.7	-0.1	2.0	2.1	0.6	1.7	-1.9	-0.2	0.0	0.5	0.3	-1.5	-1.1	-1.3
IQ at 8.5 years, y	108	92	113	103	94	99	101	92	96	109	97	98	100	95

Diet Score at 3, x	-0.4	0.7	-0.5	0.7	0.2	-1.5	0.9	-0.9	1.3	1.8	-2.8	-0.4
IQ at 8.5 years, y	108	117	100	100	94	105	109	103	109	97	95	94

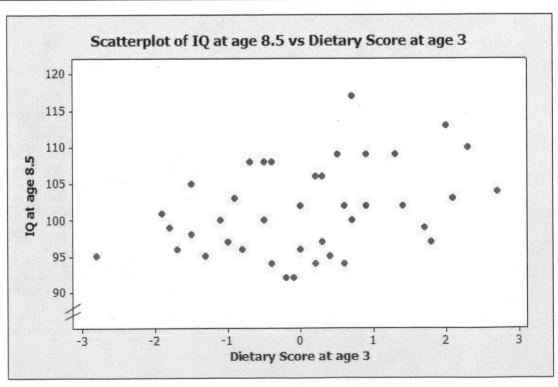

Directions: Answer each of the following using the data and scatterplot from the previous page.

a) Based on the scatterplot, does a linear regression seem appropriate? Explain.

b) What data point is the best candidate to be called an outlier? Explain. How should we deal with this data point?

c) What data point is the best candidate to be called a potentially influential observation? Explain. How should we deal with this data point?

d) Using all of the data given above and the technology of your choice, find the linear regression equation. Round in such a way that predictions made using the equation are accurate to the nearest tenth of an IQ point. **Note:** $\sum xy = 364.5$

e) Use the regression equation to predict the average IQ for an 8.5-year-old child who had a dietary score of 1 at age 3. Repeat for a child who had a dietary score of 0 at age 3.

f) Explain why it would not be wise to use this equation to predict the average IQ of an 8.5-year-old child who had a dietary score of 4.2 at age 3.

g) There was a child in the data set with a dietary score of 2.7 and an IQ of 104. What was the residual, or prediction error, for this child?

h) Interpret the slope of the regression equation in terms of the application.

i) Use technology to find the coefficient of determination, r^2, and then interpret it in terms of the application.

j) Use technology to find the linear correlation coefficient, r, and then interpret it in terms of the application.

k) Can you think of any other lurking variables, besides the dietary score, that could explain the variation in IQ?

l) If you were the parent of a 3-year-old child, should this study have any effect on the way you feed them? Explain.

Chapter 4: Technology Project

Use the technology of your choice to complete the problems below.

1) a) Enter and name the age and peak heart rate data sets from exercise (41), Section 4.2, into your statistics application.
   b) Use the application to create a scatterplot for the data set.
   C) Does a linear regression seem appropriate? Explain using the plot of the data values.
   d) Use the application to find the linear regression equation for the data set.
   E) Use the equation to predict the average peak heart rate for a 30 year old. Repeat for an 80 year old. Round your answers to the nearest tenth and include the units.
   F) Use the predictions from part (E) to draw the regression line onto your scatter plot from part (b). Do this by hand on the printout.
   G) Interpret the slope in terms of the application.
   h) If not already produced in part (d), then have the application find the coefficient of determination, r^2.
   I) Interpret r^2 in terms of the application.
   j) If not already produced in part (d), then have the application find the linear correlation coefficient, r.
   J) Interpret r in terms of the application.

2) For this problem, you need to run the application 'Regression Demonstration' from the StatSims folder.
   a) Enter your name in the textbox in the upper right of the window.
   b) Set the sample size to 15 and set the level of variation to "little" and then press "GET DATA".
   c) Move points around by clicking and dragging so that the plot contains exactly 1 outlier and 1 potentially influential observation.
   d) Click "Reg Line", "Mean Lines", "Show Errors", and "Calc R and R^2".
   e) Hold down the ALT key and then press the "PRINT SCRN" button to copy the window. Paste the image of the window to word.
   F) Circle and label the outlier and PIO in Word or on the print out.
   G) (Use the values of "Sum of Reg Errors^2", $\sum (y-\hat{y})^2$, and "Sum of Ybar Errors^2", $\sum (y-\bar{y})^2$, to calculate R^2. (Show your work!)

3) This problem will also use the application 'Regression Demonstration'. Click the "Clear" button to get ready for a new problem.
   a) Set the Sample Size to 200 and the Amount of Variation to "Random". Click on "Get Data". If the data comes up perfectly linear, then press clear and get data again.
   b) Type in a guess for the correlation in the box provided.
   c) Click on Reg Line and Calc R and R^2.
   d) Calculate the difference between your guess at the correlation and the true correlation. If you missed by more than 0.05, then return to step (a).
   e) Hold down the ALT key and then press the "PRINT SCRN" button to copy the window. Paste the image of the window to word.

Chapter 4: Chapter Review

Section 4.1: Linear Equations in Statistics

- The standard form of a linear equation in statistics is $y = b_0 + b_1 x$.
- The variable x is known as the predictor or the explanatory variable.
- The variable y is known as the prediction or the response variable.
- The slope is b_1 and the y-intercept is b_0.
- The simplest way to sketch the graph of a line is to make a table of ordered pairs. Create the ordered pairs by picking x-values and substituting them into the equation to find the y-values.
- If the slope is positive, then the line increases from left to right. If the slope is negative, then the line decreases from left to right. If the slope is zero, then the line is horizontal.
- The slope of a line represents the change in y over the change in x. So, we interpret it as follows: For each additional unit of the x-value, the y-value is *changed* by the slope.
- If (x, y) is an ordered pair from a data set, then the value y is referred to as an observed y-value (because we "saw" it in the data set.)
- A scatterplot is a graph where all of the ordered pairs in a data set are graphed. This allows us to see patterns that may exist in the data set.
- The equation of the line that we "fit" to a roughly linear data set is referred to as a prediction equation. To let people know that an equation is a prediction equation, we write it using $\hat{y}$ ("y-hat") rather than y. So the equation is written as: $\hat{y} = b_0 + b_1 x$.
- When we substitute for an x-value in a prediction equation, the output, $\hat{y}$, is called the predicted y-value.
- The prediction error (or residual) is the difference between the observed y-value and the predicted y-value (denoted e). $e = (\text{observed y}) - (\text{predicted y}) = y - \hat{y}$

Section 4.2: Linear Regression

- The least squares criterion states that the smaller the sum of squared prediction errors for a line, the better fit to the data set it is considered to be. $\sum e^2 = \sum (y - \hat{y})^2$
- The best fitting line for a data set is referred to as the linear regression line. The equation for that line is
$$\hat{y} = b_0 + b_1 x \quad \text{where} \quad b_1 = \frac{\sum (x - \bar{x})(y - \bar{y})}{\sum (x - \bar{x})^2} \quad \text{and} \quad b_0 = \bar{y} - b_1 \bar{x}.$$
- We will typically find the regression equation using technology.
- When writing your regression equation, use at least one more *decimal place* for the y-intercept than you would need for predictions and use at least one more *digit* for the slope than you would need for predictions.
- We use linear regression to predict the *average* y value, for specified x-values.
- Linear regression should only be done if a scatterplot reveals that the data set has a roughly linear pattern.
- In the context of linear regression, an outlier is a data value whose y-value does not fit the linear pattern formed by the rest of the data set. If inspection of this data value reveals that it is an error, then it should be fixed or removed before the regression equation is found.
- A potentially influential observation is a data value whose x-values stands apart from the other data values in the data set. If we will be making predictions for x-values similar to the PIO, then we should keep it in the data set, otherwise it should be removed before the regression equation is found.
- Interpolation is the process of using a regression equation to make predictions for x-values that lie within the range of the given x-values in the sample data set. Such predictions are considered to be wise/reliable.
- Extrapolation is the process of using a regression equation to make predictions for x-values that lie outside of the range of the given x-values in the sample data set. Such predictions are not wise/reliable because the linear pattern that led us to compute the regression equation may not continue beyond the range of the data we saw in our data set.
- When a linear pattern exists for x-values in a certain range, but then begins to change outside of that range, we refer to this as model breakdown.

Section 4.3: Coefficient of Determination, r^2

- The coefficient of determination is the percent reduction in squared error when we use linear regression rather than the average of the y-values in our sample to make predictions. It is denoted by r^2.

$$r^2 = \frac{\text{removed squared error}}{\text{original squared error}} = \frac{\sum(y-\bar{y})^2 - \sum(y-\hat{y})^2}{\sum(y-\bar{y})^2}$$

- r^2 represents the percent reduction in squared error when we make predictions by using the x-value in the linear regression equation rather than always just using the average y-value as our prediction.
- r^2 also represents the percentage of variation in the y-values that can be explained by using the x-value in the regression equation.
- $r^2 = 1$ indicates that the data was perfectly linear and that all prediction error has been removed. The closer r^2 is to 1, the more useful the regression is.
- $r^2 = 0$ indicates that linear regression produces the horizontal line that has the same height as the average of the y-values. The closer r^2 is to 0, the more we fear that the regression was not useful at all.

Section 4.4: Linear Correlation, r

- The linear correlation coefficient, r , is one of the square roots of r^2. We often refer to r simply as the correlation. The formulas are: $r = \dfrac{\sum(x-\bar{x})(y-\bar{y})}{\sqrt{\sum(x-\bar{x})^2\sum(y-\bar{y})^2}}$ **OR** $r = \dfrac{\sum z_x z_y}{n-1}$
- The linear correlation coefficient is a numerical measure of the strength of the linear pattern between our variables.
- Because r is one of the two square roots of r^2, $-1 \le r \le 1$.
- r will always have the same sign as the slope of the regression line.
- If r is near 1, then we say that there is a strong positive linear correlation between the variables. If variables are positively correlated, then as the x-value increases, the y-value also increases.
- If r is near –1, then we say that there is a strong negative linear correlation between the variables. If variables are negatively correlated, then as the x-value increases, the y-value decreases.
- If r is near 0, then we say that there is weak if any *linear* correlation between the variables.
- It is important to remember that a correlation near 0 can mean that there is no relationship between the variables or it could just mean that the relationship is not linear.
- Linear correlation, no matter how strong, does not prove that there is a cause and effect relationship between the variables. It just shows that there is a strong relationship between the variables. It could be cause and effect, but strong correlation is not proof of cause and effect.
- Lurking variables are variables that are not included in the study, but that affect the variables being studied.
- A regression line always passes through the ordered pair $\left(\bar{x}, \bar{y}\right)$.
- If a data point is to the upper right of the mean lines or to the lower left of the mean lines, then it makes a positive contribution to the linear correlation.
- If a data point is to the upper left of the mean lines or to the lower right of the mean lines, then it makes a negative contribution to the linear correlation.
- If a data point is on one or both of the mean lines then it does not make a contribution to the correlation. You could also say that its contribution is zero.

Review Diagrams:

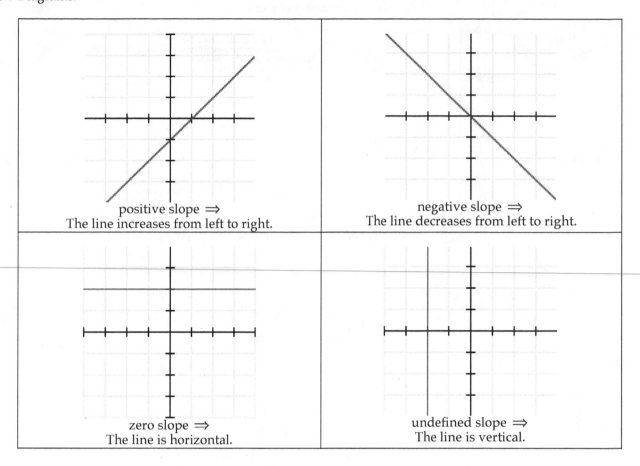

positive slope $\Rightarrow$
The line increases from left to right.

negative slope $\Rightarrow$
The line decreases from left to right.

zero slope $\Rightarrow$
The line is horizontal.

undefined slope $\Rightarrow$
The line is vertical.

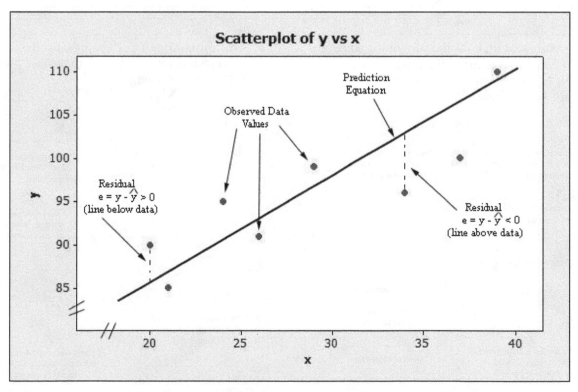

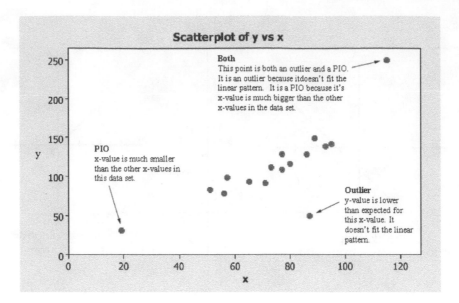

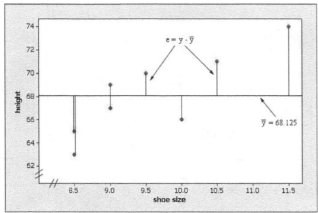

The denominator of r^2 is the sum of the squared errors if $\bar{y}$ is used to make the predictions.

$$\sum (y - \bar{y})^2$$

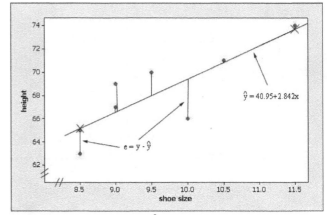

The numerator of r^2 represents the squared error that is removed if we make our predictions using the linear regression line.

$$\sum (y - \bar{y})^2 - \sum (y - \hat{y})^2$$

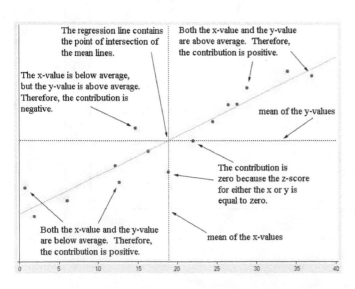

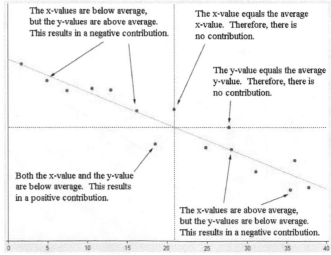

Sample values of r

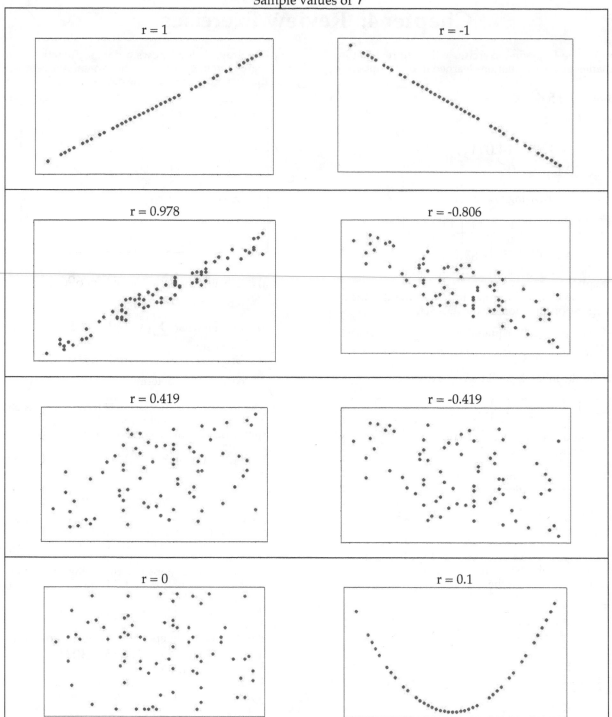

Chapter 4: Review Exercises

Mechanics: The following exercises will help review the mechanics of the calculations learned in this chapter.

1) Graph: $y = 15.4 - 2.71x$,

   Assume $1 \le x \le 5$.

2) Graph: $y = -3.05 + 14.071x$,

   Assume $20 \le x \le 50$.

3) Consider the following to be sample data.

x	5	6	8	10	13	15
y	10	9	8	5	5	0

   a) Create a scatterplot for the data set.
   b) Does linear regression seem appropriate? Explain.
   c) Use tables and formulas to determine the linear regression equation for the data set.
   d) Find the sum of squared errors, $\sum e^2$, for the regression equation.

4) Consider the following to be sample data.

x	-2	0	2	5	7	10	11
y	14	16	22	29	36	42	42

   a) Create a scatterplot for the data set.
   b) Does linear regression seem appropriate? Explain.
   c) Use tables and formulas to determine the linear regression equation for the data set.
   d) Find the sum of squared errors, $\sum e^2$, for the regression equation.

5) The graph below shows a data set together with the regression line and also a horizontal line representing the average y-value for the data set.

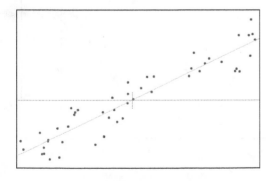

   a) Explain what $\sum (y - \bar{y})^2 = 877.331$ represents graphically.

   b) Explain what $\sum (y - \hat{y})^2 = 108.468$ represents graphically.

   c) Use the two sums provided to calculate the coefficient of determination, r^2.

6) The graph below shows a data set together with the regression line and also a horizontal line representing the average y-value for the data set.

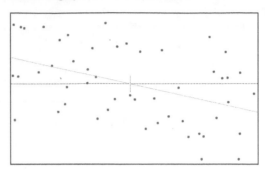

   a) Explain what $\sum (y - \bar{y})^2 = 696.122$ represents graphically.

   b) Explain what $\sum (y - \hat{y})^2 = 558.404$ represents graphically.

   c) Use the two sums provided to calculate the coefficient of determination, r^2.

Applications: Apply the concepts learned in this chapter to the following applications. Use technology where appropriate. If the technology you use provides you with $\sum xy$, then use the value given to verify data entry.

7) The cost of catering a banquet is given by the equation $C = 99 + 15.99G$, where C is the total cost in dollars for G guests to attend the banquet. The banquet hall requires a minimum of 50 guests and allows a maximum of 200 guests.
   a) Interpret the slope in terms of the application.
   b) Use the equation to find the cost of 124 guests attending the banquet.
   c) Sketch a graph for the equation.

8) The cost of a landscaper to work on a yard project is given by the equation $C = 75 + 30H$, where C is the total cost of the job, in dollars, and H is the number of hours it takes. Assume that the maximum number of hours for this landscaper's projects is 120 hours.
   a) Interpret the slope in terms of the application.
   b) Use the equation to find the cost if the job takes 25 hours.
   c) Sketch a graph for the equation.

9) A random sample of 6 homes with solar panels installed on the roof was taken in San Joaquin County, CA. The areas, in square meters, together with the energy output, in kilowatt-hours per day, are listed in the table below. The data is based on information obtained from www.solar-estimate.org. The scatterplot is also shown together with the regression line.

Area (x)	12.7	69.9	84.4	29.9	117.5	57.6
Energy (y)	88.1	452.2	474.7	194.7	742.0	301.3

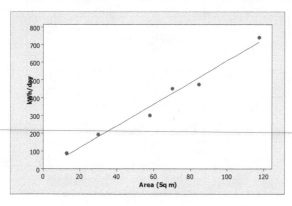

$$\hat{y} = -2.76 + 6.1010x$$

a) Use the prediction equation provided to estimate the average energy output for houses with 100 square meters of solar panels on the roof.
b) Interpret the slope of the line in terms of the application.
c) Find the sum of the squared prediction errors for the entire data set. That is, find $\sum e^2$.

10) A random sample of 6 wake boarders were asked for their weight and the speed of the boat they prefer when wakeboarding. The weights in pounds and the speed, in mph, are listed in the table below. The scatterplot is also shown together with the regression line.

Weight (x)	132	146	170	175	194	231
Speed (y)	18	20	23	22	22	28

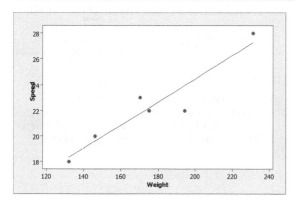

$$\hat{y} = 6.38 + 0.09037x$$

a) Use the prediction equation provided to estimate the average preferred boat speed for 165-pound wake boarders.
b) Interpret the slope of the line in terms of the application.
c) Find the sum of the squared prediction errors for the entire data set. That is, find $\sum e^2$.

11) Adding fluoride to drinking water systems is commonly credited with reducing tooth decay. The data below is based on information from the Center for Disease Control. For a sample of 8 years, the percentage of the U.S. population drinking fluoridated water is provided together with the mean number of decayed, missing, or filled permanent teeth (DMFT) for 12-year-olds in the U.S.

Year	% drinking fluoridated water, x	DMFT y
1968	42%	4.0
1972	46%	3.8
1975	50%	3.5
1978	50%	3.1
1981	51%	2.6
1985	55%	2.1
1988	56%	1.6
1991	57%	1.3

a) Make a scatterplot for the 8 data values.
b) Does a linear regression seem appropriate? Explain.
c) Use technology to find the regression equation for using the percent drinking fluoridated water to predict DMFT. Round your answer so that predictions made from the equation will be reliable to the nearest hundredth of a tooth. **Note:**

$$\sum xy = 1084.6$$

d) Use the regression equation to predict the average DMFT for 12-year-olds during the year 1968.
e) Graph the regression line with the scatterplot from part (a).
f) Interpret the slope of the line in terms of the application.
g) Does this data support the idea that fluoridating water helps reduce tooth decay? Explain.
h) Given that similar declines in tooth decay occurred in other developed nations, even though they did not fluoridate their water, what other lurking variables might explain the decline in tooth decay?

12) *Stump Cruncher Tree Service* of Rio Linda, CA offers a stump removal service to its customers. The time required to remove a stump varies based on type of tree and the size. The data below shows the time required to remove various amounts of stumps for a sample of 7 recent jobs.

Stumps (x)	3	2	3	1	5	2	10
Hours (y)	4.9	4.6	5.1	1.3	7.6	3.7	20.4

a) Make a scatterplot for the 7 data values.
b) Does a linear regression seem appropriate? Explain.
c) Use technology to find the regression equation. Round your answer so that predictions made from the equation will be reliable to the nearest tenth of an hour. **Note:** $\sum xy = 289.9$
d) Use the regression equation to predict the average number of hours required to complete the removal of 4 stumps.
e) Graph the regression line with the scatterplot from part (a).
f) Interpret the slope of the line in terms of the application.
g) How might this equation be useful to the owner of this business?
h) Identify any outlier or potentially influential observations in the data set. Explain why this value might be useful to have in the data set.

13) A sample of 15 chicken sandwiches from fast food restaurants is given below. For each sandwich the number of grams of fat is provided together with the number of calories in the sandwich. The scatterplot is shown below the data.

Restaurant	Sandwich	Fat Grams	Total Cals
Burger King	TenderCrisp	44	790
	TenderGrill	19	510
Carl's Jr.	Charbroiled BB	4.5	360
	Charbroiled Club	25	550
Chick-Fil-A	Chicken Salad S-wch	15	350
	Chargrilled Chicken	3.5	270
Hardee's	Big Fillet	37	800
	Spicy	25	470
Jack In the Box	Regular	21	400
	Sourdough Grilled	28	530
KFC	Honey BBQ Snacker	3	210
	Double Crunch	23	470
McDonald's	Crispy Chicken Club	28	660
	McChicken	16	360
Wendy's	Crispy	14	320

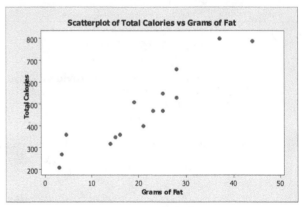

a) Does a linear regression seem appropriate? Explain.
b) Take a guess at the linear correlation coefficient, r.
c) Use technology to find the regression equation. Round your answer so that predictions made from the equation will be reliable to the nearest hundredth of a calorie. **Note:** $\sum xy = 170,765$
d) Use technology to find the values of r and r^2.
e) Interpret the slope of the line in terms of the application.
f) Interpret r in terms of the application.
g) Interpret r^2 in terms of the application.
h) Would you say that the number of grams of fat in a chicken sandwich is a good predictor of the total number of calories overall? Explain.

14) When a football team has the ball between the opponent's 20 yard line and the goal line, it is said that they are in the Red Zone. This should give the team with the ball an excellent chance to score. The data below shows the Red Zone scoring percentage for the NFC teams during the 2010 regular season together with the number of wins.

Team	Red Zone Scoring %	Number Wins
Dallas	59.57%	6
NY Giants	57.41%	10
Philadelphia	52.46%	10
Washington	51.16%	6
Detroit	45.45%	6
Green Bay	75.00%	10
Chicago	49.09%	11
Minnesota	43.48%	6
Atlanta	60.66%	13
Tampa Bay	52.27%	10
New Orleans	51.47%	11
Carolina	30.30%	2
San Francisco	47.62%	6
Seattle	54.55%	7
Arizona	33.33%	5
St Louis	33.33%	7

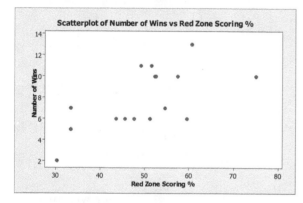

a) Does a linear regression seem appropriate? Explain.
b) Take a guess at the linear correlation coefficient, r.
c) Use technology to find the regression equation. Round your answer so that predictions made from the equation will be reliable to the nearest tenth of a win. Note: $\sum xy = 6592.23$
d) Use technology to find the values of r and r^2.
e) Interpret the slope of the line in terms of the application.
f) Interpret r in terms of the application.
g) Interpret r^2 in terms of the application.
h) Would you say that the Red Zone scoring percentage is a good predictor of the number of wins for a team? Explain.

(15 – 16) Use this table for the next two exercises. The following table provides national average for gas price, the unemployment percentage, and President Obama's approval rating for a random sample of 10 dates.

Date	Gas ($/gal)	Unemploy-ment %	Approval Rating (%)
7/2009	2.50	9.7	52
9/2009	2.51	9.5	50
11/2009	2.63	9.4	50
1/2010	2.70	10.6	47
3/2010	2.78	10.2	45
5/2010	2.87	9.3	48
7/2010	2.72	9.7	45
10/2010	2.82	9.0	43
1/2011	3.08	9.8	46
3/2011	3.52	9.2	43

15) This problem will investigate the link between unemployment and presidential approval rating.
a) What relationship, if any, do you suspect exists between the unemployment rate and approval rating? Explain.
b) Make a scatterplot for the 10 data values. Use unemployment rates for the x-value and approval rating for the y-value.
c) Take a guess at the linear correlation coefficient, r.
d) Use technology to find the values of r and r^2. Note: $\sum xy = 4522.9$
e) Interpret r in terms of the application.
f) Interpret r^2 in terms of the application.
g) What do you suspect is the true cause of the positive correlation seen in this problem? Explain.

16) This problem will investigate the link between gas prices and presidential approval rating.
a) What relationship, if any, do you suspect exists between gas prices and approval rating? Explain.
b) Make a scatterplot for the 10 data values. Use gas price for the x-value and approval rating for the y-value.
c) Take a guess at the linear correlation coefficient, r.
d) Use technology to find the values of r and r^2. Note: $\sum xy = 1313.46$
e) Interpret r in terms of the application.
f) Interpret r^2 in terms of the application.
g) Does it seem reasonable to you that these two variables would be negatively correlated as seen in this data set? Explain.

(17 – 18) Use this table for the next two exercises. The information below was obtained from a random sample of 23 stat students during the Fall 2010 semester. The homework scores are out of a possible 25 points. Exam 1 covered chapters 1 thru 4 of this text and had 100 points possible. The course grade is the students' overall ending percentage for the class.

HW Points	Exam #1 Score	Course Grade (%)
21	89	86.6
20	64	78.9
20	55	53.9
18	73	81.7
10	49	23.9
23	97	94.5
15	72	91.0
18	84	80.8
10	68	24.8
17	42	32.2
23	92	94.3
18	46	37.7
23	94	91.1
24	92	93.5
20	83	70.9
23	93	90.8
16	58	43.9
19	81	88.9
5	58	51.4
24	89	94.8
20	85	86.6
23	73	71.2
21	59	73.5

17) The scatterplot below shows the HW points as the x-value and the Exam #1 score as the y-value. The linear regression equation, r, and r^2 are provided below the scatter plot.

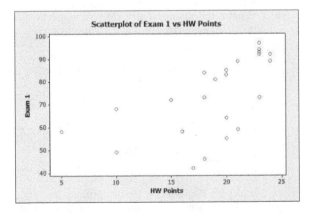

$$\hat{y} \approx 34.44 + 2.097x,$$

$$r \approx 0.6033, \ r^2 \approx 0.3639$$

a) Which data value is the best candidate to be called a potentially influential observation? Why might the instructor wish this data value could be removed? Should it stay in the data set or be removed?

b) Use the regression equation to predict the average exam 1 score for a student scoring 13 points on the homework assignments. Is this a wise prediction? Explain.
c) Would it be wise to use the equation to predict the average exam 1 score for students who scored zero points on the homework assignments? Explain.
d) Interpret the slope of the line in terms of the application.
e) Interpret r in terms of the application.
f) Interpret r^2 in terms of the application.
g) Does this data show that getting good homework scores is the cause of better exam scores? Explain.

18) The scatterplot below shows the Exam #1 score as the x-value and the Course Grade (%) as the y-value. The linear regression equation, r, and r^2 are provided below the scatter plot.

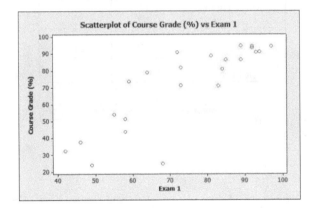

$$\hat{y} \approx -16.97 + 1.1953x,$$

$$r \approx 0.8450, \ r^2 \approx 0.7140$$

a) Which data value is the best candidate to be called an outlier? Explain what might have happened with this student.
b) Use the regression equation to predict the average course grade for student scoring a 70 on exam #1. Is this a wise prediction? Explain.
c) Interpret the slope of the line in terms of the application.
d) Interpret r in terms of the application.
e) Interpret r^2 in terms of the application.
f) Does this data show that the exam 1 score is a good predictor of overall course grade? Explain.

Chapter 5 – Probability and Random Variables

Chapter Problem: *The Art of the Chase*

For most of the history of poker, it was seen as a game of luck played by gamblers. In 1986, professional poker player, Billy Baxter sued the U.S. government for a tax refund claiming that his poker playing should be seen as a business entitled to deductions for expenses, travel costs etc. Baxter was successful in his case arguing that his profits were not the result of luck, but skill. One of the findings of the court was "The money, once bet, would have produced no income without the application of Baxter's skills." Since this time, most of those familiar with poker will concede that skill does play a roll in poker success. After that, a new debate was opened up: Is the primary skill needed to be successful the psychological ability to "read" people or is the primary skill the application of mathematics?

Does statistical and mathematical knowledge win out over luck or psychology in poker?

Until around 2003, most people would have argued the psychological people reading skills were more important than the math. However, around that time, many people began playing poker against others on online poker sites. On these sites, you had no visual or audio contact with your opponent. Because of this, many players started spending more time studying the mathematical and statistical strategies that could be used in poker. These players soon rose to the top of the professional poker player ranks. Now, virtually all professional poker players understand that mathematical and statistical analysis can greatly improve their results. The emphasis in this chapter will be on learning how we apply probability to sampling, not to learning poker. However, at the end of this chapter, we will use the skills we have learned to get a glimpse at how probability helps poker players make better decisions.

Introduction:

I have heard it said that probability is the science of uncertainty. At first, this phrase may seem a bit strange. We often think of science as a process that tries to uncover hidden truths. So how do we apply it to situations where things are uncertain or unpredictable? When we flip a coin, it is uncertain whether we will get heads or tails, this is true. And when we learn probability theory, we will find that we still cannot predict the result of a single toss of a coin with any decent reliability. However, probability will help us reveal the long-term patterns of the tossed coin.

So, suppose we learn how to use probability to understand the long-term patterns of a tossed coin or a rolled die. What does that have to do with statistics? The answer lies in our samples. Recall, we choose our samples randomly. This means there will be uncertainty in what results we get. However, we will eventually learn to apply the probability we learn to help us better understand the accuracy of an estimate that is obtained from a *random* sample.

It is true that the main reason we will study probability is to help us with inferential statistics based on random samples, but that doesn't mean we can't find some other applications of probability along the way. One of the more interesting applications of probability is to various games of chance, including gambling. In this chapter, we will learn the basics of probability along with some more advanced probability rules. We will then discuss random variables so that we can find means and standard deviations for random events. Finally, we will look at the probability of experiments that have two possible results, classified as success and failure. We will explore all of these ideas in the following sections:

Let's get started.

Section 5.1 – Classical Probability and Notation

I think that the easiest way to understand probability is to look at a few probability questions and go through the answers to those. After we discuss a few example questions, we will then carefully define classical probability and clarify the procedure for calculating classical probabilities. Let's jump in.

Calculating Probabilities: *(Discussion Examples)*

Determine the probability for each of the following:

a) A fair coin is tossed. What is the probability that it will show the heads side?

b) A balanced die is rolled. What is the probability that it will land showing the number 4 on top?

c) A balanced die is rolled. What is the probability that it will land showing an even number?

How is calculating the probability that Josh Hamilton will hit a home run different than for calculating probabilities for a coin or a die?

d) What is the probability that Josh Hamilton will hit a home run in a given plate appearance?

Solution:

a) A fair coin has two sides each of which are equally likely to occur. So, the probability of heads is given by:

$$P(heads) = \frac{1}{2} = 0.5 = 50\%$$

$P(heads)$ is read "the probability of heads." Any of the 3 forms of the answer given above are valid. We tend to find probabilities using fractions, write them as decimals, and say them as percentages.

b) A balanced die has six sides that are all equally likely to show up on top. So we get:

$$P(\text{die is a 4}) = \frac{1}{6} \approx 0.1667 = 16.67\%$$

When it becomes necessary to round a probability, we generally use 4 decimal places.

c) This one is a little different than the previous two. The six sides of the die have the numbers 1, 2, 3, 4, 5, and 6 on them. So three of the sides, 2, 4, and 6 would all result in an even number being shown. So we get:

$$P(\text{die is a even}) = \frac{3}{6} = \frac{1}{2} = 0.5 = 50\%$$

d) I don't know! There are many possible outcomes to a Josh Hamilton plate appearance. He could hit a home run, walk, be hit by a pitch, singe, double, triple, fly out, ground out, foul out, strike out, etc. These possibilities are not equally likely, so I can't just count them and produce a fraction as in the above examples.

Sometimes people attempt to use past performance to estimate probabilities for questions like this, but the probabilities are based on samples. This means such answers are merely estimates of the true probabilities.

Part (d) above may seem worrisome, however, in statistics, we are not worried about that type of probability question. Our focus will be on ones more like parts (a), (b), and (c) where the possible outcomes are equally likely. Questions like those in parts (a), (b), and (c) fall into the realm of **classical probability**, while questions like the one in part (d) do not. We are most interested in the questions where the possibilities are equally likely because when we take a simple random sample, each possible sample of a given size is equally likely to be the one chosen.

Now that we have worked through a few examples, let's look at the key definitions needed for basic probability.

Definitions: *Experiment, Simple Outcomes, Events, Sample Space, and Classical Probability.*

Experiment: The activity involving randomness about which we will ask probability questions. For example: rolling a die or flipping a coin.

Simple Outcomes: A simple outcome is an outcome that can only occur in one way. For example: Rolling a 4 on a die is a simple outcome because only one side of the die has a 4 on it. However, rolling an even number is not simple because three sides of the die produce that event.

Event: Any collection of simple outcomes. It could be as many outcomes as all, as few as none, or anywhere in between. It is common to let a single capital letter represent an event.

Sample Space: The set of all possible simple outcomes for an experiment.

Classical Probability: Classical probability applies to experiments where each simple outcome is equally likely to occur. If we are in a situation where each simple outcome is equally likely to occur, then the probability of an event E is given by:

$$P(E) = \frac{f}{N} \; ;$$

Where f is the number of ways the event can occur and N is the total number of outcomes that are possible. Notice that $P(E)$ is the generic notation for "the probability of an event, E."

Formats: There are three standard forms for probabilities: fractions, decimals, and percents. Typically these are used as follows.
- We usually think about and calculate probability using fractions.
- We usually write probabilities in decimal form.
- We typically communicate the answer to people using percentages.

Rounding Rule: When rounding a probability, you should use at least 4 decimal places.

Example 5.1: *Selecting Marbles from a Jar*

A jar contains 274 marbles made up of a mixture of purple, blue, green, orange, red, and yellow. The frequencies for the colors are shown below.

Color	Frequency
Purple	37
Blue	40
Green	52
Orange	61
Red	35
Yellow	49
	274

How does probability apply to random sampling?

Suppose that we will randomly select one marble from the jar.

a) Is the event that a red marble is chosen a simple event? Explain.

b)   What are the simple events in this experiment? How many simple events are possible?

c)   Find the probability that the marble selected is red, that is, find $P(\text{red})$.

d)   Find $P(\text{not green})$

e)   Find $P(\text{black})$

f)   Interpret your answer to part (c) in terms of percentages.

Solution:

a)   No! A simple outcome is one that can only occur 1 way. There are 35 different red marbles. If any one of those is selected, then the color red will have occurred.

b)   Each individual marble represents a possible simple event. So, the number of simple events is the same as the number of marbles in the jar. We have 274 simple events possible for this experiment.

c)   We simply divide the number of red marbles by the number of marbles and get:

$$P(\text{red}) = \frac{35}{274} \approx 0.1277$$

d)   There are two ways to do this one. If it is not green, then it must be purple, blue, orange, red, or yellow. So we add all of these up and divide by the total. This gives us:

$$P(\text{not green}) = \frac{37 + 40 + 61 + 35 + 49}{274} = \frac{222}{274} \approx 0.8102$$

The other way to do this problem is to just subtract the greens from the total and not worry about what the other colors are. Using this method we get:

$$P(\text{not green}) = \frac{274 - 52}{274} = \frac{222}{274} \approx 0.8102$$

> **Key Concept:** *Using Subtraction*
>
> If you will be adding up more than half of the possibilities, then you should usually consider subtraction from the total instead.

e)   This one is a bit tricky, but very easy. There are no black marbles in the jar, so we get:

$$P(\text{black}) = \frac{0}{274} = 0$$

> **Key Concept:** *Impossible Events*
>
> If an event has a probability of zero then it is referred to as an impossible event. However, if you are asked for the probability, you must give the number zero rather than the word impossible.

f)   The probability of red was 0.1277. This means that there is a 12.77% chance that a randomly selected marble will be a red one.

Hopefully, the calculations we have been making above seemed familiar to you. They should have reminded you of calculating relative frequencies from Chapter 2. When you have a finite set of possibilities, this is always the case and it is summarized as follows.

> **)int to Remember:** *Probabilities vs. Relative Frequencies*
>
> When we have a finite set of possible outcomes, calculating a probability is always the same as calculating a population relative frequency.
>
> *Probability = Population Relative Frequency*

Even though calculating a probability is the same as calculating a population relative frequency, these two quantities do not mean exactly the same thing. This is vital to remember when interpreting a probability. We will now explore the meaning of probability.

MEANING OF PROBABILITY: *What does it tell us?*

We have now seen a few examples of how to calculate basic classical probabilities. However, an important question still remains: What does a probability tell us? If the probability of a coin showing heads is 50%, then if I toss a coin will I get half a head? Of course not! If I toss a coin 10 times, does this tell me that I will get half or 5 heads? Still the answer is no. 5 heads would be the most likely outcome to tossing a coin 10 times, but really, anything could happen. So is this probability worthless? No. Probability tells us the expected long term relative frequency of an event. If the chance of heads is 50%, then in the long run heads should show up *about* half of the time. Let's take a look at this visually. The graph shown below tracks the relative frequency of heads (on the vertical axis) versus the number of times the coin has been tossed (on the horizontal axis).

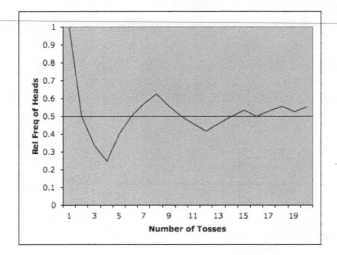
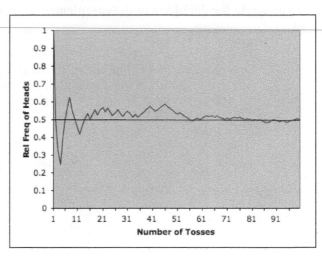

Notice that, for only 20 tosses (above left), the graph strays far from the 50% line quite often. However, for 100 tosses (above right), after the initial chaos the graph seems to be settling in around the 50% line.

From this we conclude that probability is not very useful for predicting the result of a single toss or even a few tosses, because the effects of random variation are large in small samples. However, in the long run the effects of random variation are reduced and the relative frequency of our event should be approaching the probability of the event. As we move forward, it is always important to remember to interpret probability as a long-term relative frequency.

> **Point to Remember:** *Interpreting Probability*
>
> Probability of an event should always be interpreted as the long-term relative frequency of the event. Because of random variation, the relative frequency after a small sample might be far from the actual probability. However, as the sample size increases, the relative frequency of the event will tend to get closer to the probability.

VENN DIAGRAMS: *A way to visualize new probability ideas*

As we introduce new types of probability ideas, it is often useful to have a visual representation of the ideas being presented. A common tool for accomplishing this goal is called a **Venn diagram**. Let's define this new diagram and then we will use it to introduce a new probability concept.

Definition: *Venn Diagram*

> **Venn Diagram:** A graph that includes a box, representing the sample space, with discs, representing events, drawn inside the box. A simple example for the event E is shown below.

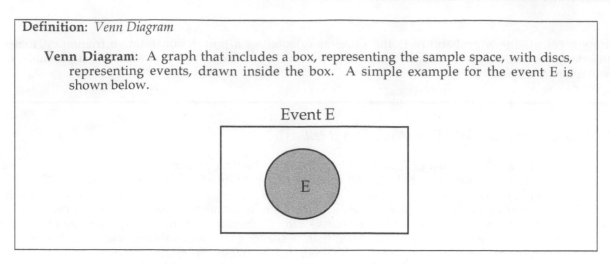

One of the best uses of a Venn diagram is to illustrate a new probability definition. We will use a Venn Diagram here to illustrate the definition of the **complement** of an event.

Definition: *Complement of an Event*

> **Complement of E:** The complement of event E is the event that E does not occur. We also refer to the complement of E as the event (not E). In the graph below, the event (not E) is represented by the shaded area. So (not E) is everything in the sample space, except for those things in E.

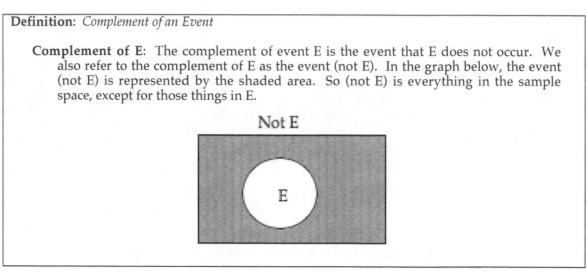

We are going to look at an example to see how complements work, but this example is going to involve questions about a standard deck of playing cards. So, for those of you who are not familiar with them, here they are followed by a little bit of basic information and terminology.

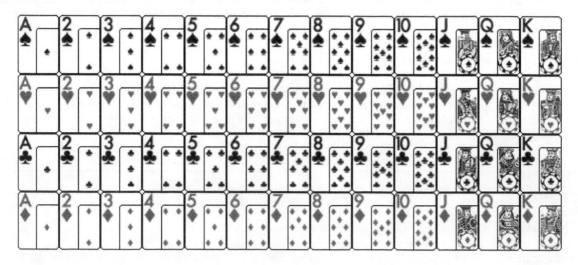

A standard deck of cards contains 52 cards. There are 4 of each of the denominations: Ace, 5, Jack, Queen, King, etc. There are 13 cards of each suit: Spades, Hearts, Clubs, and Diamonds. The Jack, Queen, and King are commonly called face cards.

Example 5.2: *Pick a Card, Any Card*

Consider a deck of 52 playing cards. Our experiment will be to randomly select one of the cards. Consider the events listed below and then find the requested probabilities.

Is it likely that a magician would guess our card by pure luck?

Let   A = the event that the card chosen is the King of clubs
      B = the event that the card chosen is a King
      C = the event that the card chosen is a club
      D = the card chosen is a face card

a) $P(A)$ b) $P(B)$ c) $P(C)$ d) $P(D)$ e) $P(not\ D)$

Solution:

a)   When you specify a suit and a denomination, then there is only one card that will satisfy the description. So we get:

$$P(A) = P(\text{King of Clubs}) = \frac{1}{52} \approx 0.0192$$

b)   There are 4 of any specific denomination of card, so we get: $P(B) = \frac{4}{52} = \frac{1}{13} \approx 0.0769$

c)   There are 13 of any specific suit, so we get: $P(C) = \frac{13}{52} = \frac{1}{4} = 0.25$

d)   Recall that the face cards are Jacks, Queens, and Kings. The deck contains 4 of each denomination, so we get:

$$P(D) = P(\text{Jack, Queen, or King}) = \frac{4+4+4}{52} = \frac{12}{52} \approx 0.2308$$

Notice that 12/52 could be reduced, but it would still be considered a messy fraction, so we go straight to a decimal approximation.

e)   There are two ways to answer this question. The first is to consider what it means to be (not D). This means that it is not a face card. The cards that are not face cards are: Aces, 2's, 3's, 4's, 5's, 6's, 7's, 8's, 9's, Tens. There are 4 of each of those ten options, so we get:

$$P(\text{not } D) = \frac{4+4+4+4+4+4+4+4+4+4}{52} = \frac{4(10)}{52} = \frac{40}{52} \approx 0.7692$$

The second way to do this is to not worry about which cards are not face cards, rather just subtract away all the face cards from the total number of cards. This produces:

$$P(\text{not } D) = \frac{52-12}{52} = \frac{40}{52} \approx 0.7692$$

While both of the above methods are considered acceptable, the second one is usually preferred. We will refine our technique on this type of problem in the next section.

Earlier, we stated that calculating probability is the same as calculating a population frequency. The example shows how we can take advantage of this fact.

Example 5.3: *Single-Payer Health Care*

In recent years, there has been a lot of discussion about reforming the U.S. health care system. One option would be to have all Americans enrolled in the same insurance plan, where the federal government provides coverage for everyone. According to an Oct. 2011 Rasmussen poll, the support for a single-payer plan among American adults is as shown in the table below.

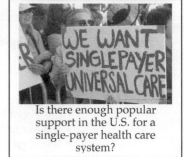

Is there enough popular support in the U.S. for a single-payer health care system?

Opinion	Relative Frequency
Favor a Single-Payer Plan	0.35
Oppose a Single-Payer Plan	0.49
Undecided	0.16
Total	1.00

Suppose that we were to randomly select an adult American at that time. We will define the events as follows:

A = the person favors a single-payer plan
B = the person opposes a single-payer plan
C = the person is undecided

a) Use notation to write the probability that the person favors a single-payer plan and then find the probability.

b) Use notation to express the probability that the person selected does not favor a single-payer plan and find that probability.

Solution:

a) The notation is straightforward. The question is describing event A, so we write $P(A)$.

   Normally, we would now count the number of items in A, and divide by the number in the sample space, but this information is not given. However, we know that this same calculation is used to calculate the population relative frequency. Because the table is claiming to represent all Americans, we can use the relative frequency from the table in place of the probability. Therefore, we get the following: $P(A) = 0.35$.

b) The word 'not' indicates that we should use the complement this time. So the notation is $P(not\ A)$.

   Once again, we will use the relative frequencies for Americans in place of the probability. Because this is the complement, we will count all Americans except those that favor a single-payer plan. That means we will count both those that oppose and those that are undecided. So, we get $P(not\ A) = 0.49 + 0.16 = 0.65$.

> **Caution:** *Complement vs. Opposite*
>
> A common mistake is to find the opposite when asked to find (not A). The opposite of favoring is to oppose. However, the complement is all other options to favoring.

CONTINGENCY TABLES: *Probability questions involving two variables*

A contingency table is designed to simultaneously show and summarize the data obtained for two variables for a sample or population of interest. These tables will be more common when we get to later chapters, but they can also be very useful for illustrating probability ideas. Let's look at an example.

Example 5.4: *Education Level and Voter Participation*

The table below lists the education level together with voting status in the 2004 elections for the 221,461,000 Adult Americans. The frequencies listed are in thousands. The data is based information from the U.S. Census Bureau. The labels in parentheses are the event notation for each event. For example, E1 represents the event that the person has no high school diploma.

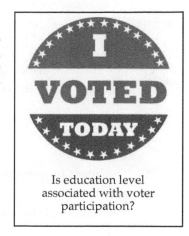

Is education level associated with voter participation?

	Voted in 2004 (V1)	Did Not Vote in 2004 (V2)	Total
No high School Diploma (E1)	12,774	20,345	33,119
High school graduate only (E2)	39,554	30,614	70,168
Some college, or associate degree (E3)	38,622	17,243	55,865
Bachelor's Degree or higher (E4)	50,209	12,100	62,309
Total	141,159	80,302	221,461

Suppose that a person was randomly selected from these adults at that time. Write each of the following probability questions using event notation and then find the requested probability.

a) The probability that the person selected is a High School graduate only.

b) The probability that the person selected voted in 2004.

c) The probability that the person selected does not have a Bachelor's Degree or higher.

d) If we were to randomly sample 1000 American adults at this time, then how many of them should we expect to have voted in 2004? Explain.

Solution:

a) The event described is E2, so the notation is $P(E2)$. To calculate this probability, we need to know two things. How many simple outcomes are possible for this experiment? That would be the grand total, 221,461. And, how many simple outcomes meet the description of E2. That would be the total for the row containing E2, or 70,168. We now simply divide these to get our answer.

$$P(E2) = \frac{70,168}{221,461} \approx 0.3168$$

The frequencies are given in thousands in this table, so the real calculation would be: $P(E2) = \dfrac{70,168,000}{221,461,000} \approx 0.3168$. Notice that the extra zeros on the top and bottom of the fraction cancel out and we get the same answer.

> **Key Concept**: *Adjusted Units*
>
> We do not need to make any adjustment to our probability calculations when working with adjusted units. The adjustment in the numerator and the denominator will always cancel out.

b) The words here describe event V1, so the notation is $P(V1)$. This time we use a column total rather than a row total and we get.

$$P(V1) = \frac{141,159}{221,461} \approx 0.6374$$

c) The event described is $(\text{not } E4)$, so the notation is $P(\text{not } E4)$. The easiest way to do this is to subtract away the 62,309 items in E4 that we do not want from the total number of adult Americans. So our answer is:

$$P(\text{not } E4) = \frac{221,461 - 62,309}{221,461} = \frac{159,152}{221,461} \approx 0.7186$$

d) The event in question is V1. The probability of an event represents the long-term relative frequency of that event. In part (b), we calculated $P(V1) \approx 0.6374$. So, we expect about 63.74% of the 1,000 randomly selected people to have voted. Calculating this out, we get

$$1000 * 0.6374 = 637.4$$

Therefore, we would expect about 637.4 voters in the 1,000 randomly selected American adults.

WRAP SESSION: *Examining a more difficult probability question*

We will now consider a final example to practice some of the methods and terminology learned so far in this section.

Example 5.5: *The sum of two rolled dice*

Suppose that two balanced dice are rolled.

a) List all possible simple outcomes for this experiment.

b) Suppose we are interested in the sum of the two dice. Make a chart listing the possible sums from all possible simple outcomes.

What is the chance or rolling a lucky sum of 7?

c) Find $P(\text{sum is } 7)$

d) Find $P(\text{sum is less than } 7)$

e) Find $P(\text{sum is not } 9)$

f) Suppose that the dice are rolled 50,000 times. How many times should we expect to see a sum of 7? Explain.

Solution:

a) The simple outcomes to this experiment are the faces that show on top of the two dice. One possible simple outcome would be: the first die is a 5 and the second die is a 2. Let's write this outcome as an ordered pair. So we get (5, 2). Now, let's write all possible simple outcomes using this ordered pair notation, so that, the first number represents the first die and the second number represents the second die. Also, let's work systematically. We will list all possible simple outcomes where the first die is a 1 and then all where the first die is a 2 and so on. Here is the list:

(1, 1)	(1, 2)	(1, 3)	(1, 4)	(1, 5)	(1, 6)
(2, 1)	(2, 2)	(2, 3)	(2, 4)	(2, 5)	(2, 6)
(3, 1)	(3, 2)	(3, 3)	(3, 4)	(3, 5)	(3, 6)
(4, 1)	(4, 2)	(4, 3)	(4, 4)	(4, 5)	(4, 6)
(5, 1)	(5, 2)	(5, 3)	(5, 4)	(5, 5)	(5, 6)
(6, 1)	(6, 2)	(6, 3)	(6, 4)	(6, 5)	(6, 6)

Sometimes people object that by including both (2, 5) and (5, 2) (and other similar pairs) I am counting the same roll twice. After all, both represent the event that we ended up with a 2 and a 5. This last statement is true, but ending up with a 2 and a 5 is not a simple outcome because there are two ways that it can occur. The 2 could be either on the first die or the second die. This is sometimes easier to understand if you imagine that the two dice are different colors. It would clearly be different outcomes if the blue die is the 2 one time, but the next time the red die is a 2.

b)   As the directions indicate, the best way to list these sums is a chart. We will put the numbers from one of the dice across the top of the chart and the numbers from the other down the side. Then, in the body of the table, we will list the sums that correspond to the numbers from the left and above our current cell.

	1	2	3	4	5	6
1	2	3	4	5	6	7
2	3	4	5	6	7	8
3	4	5	6	7	8	9
4	5	6	7	8	9	10
5	6	7	8	9	10	11
6	7	8	9	10	11	12

$\longleftarrow$ $3+6$

c)   We say in part (a) that there are 36 possible simple outcomes. We see in the chart from part (b) that there are 6 different ways to get a sum of 7. So our answer is:

$$P(\text{sum is } 7) = \frac{6}{36} = \frac{1}{6} \approx 0.1667$$

Key Concept: *Making the Chart*

While it is possible to answer this question without the chart from part (b), that can be difficult. Therefore, even if I had not been asked to make the chart as a stand-alone question, I would have made it anyway.

d)   We just need to look at the chart above and find all the sums less than seven. They are highlighted below.

	1	2	3	4	5	6
1	2	3	4	5	6	7
2	3	4	5	6	7	8
3	4	5	6	7	8	9
4	5	6	7	8	9	10
5	6	7	8	9	10	11
6	7	8	9	10	11	12

We have highlighted 15 outcomes that meet the description, so we get:

$$P(\text{sum is less than } 7) = \frac{15}{36} \approx 0.4167$$

e)   The simplest way to answer this one is to subtract the four 9's from the total. This yields:

$$P(\text{sum is not } 9) = \frac{36-4}{36} = \frac{32}{36} = \frac{8}{9} \approx 0.8889$$

f) From part (c), we know that $P(\text{sum is } 7) = \dfrac{1}{6}$. The probability of an event represents the long-term relative frequency of that event. So, we expect about 1/6 of the 50,000 rolls of the dice to have a sum of 7. Calculating this out, we get

$$50000 * \frac{1}{6} \approx 8333.33$$

Therefore, we would expect about 8333.33 of the 50,000 rolls of the dice to produce a sum of 7.

THE FUNDAMENTAL RULE OF COUNTING:

In the previous example, we found that when you roll two dice, each with 6 sides, and look at all the possible combinations of outcomes, there are 36 outcomes possible. This result is a special case of one of the most important counting principals in probability. This counting rule is stated in the following Point to Remember.

> **Point to Remember**: *The Fundamental Rule of counting*
>
> **The Fundamental Rule of Counting**: If experiment A has m possible simple outcomes and experiment B has n possible simple outcomes, then if we look at the combined results of these experiment, there are $m \cdot n$ possible combinations of simple outcomes.

This rule can be used in cases where multiple dice are rolled, multiple coins are flipped, and other similar repetitions are performed. We will also see in upcoming sections that it is also very useful when we repeatedly sample items from a finite population.

Now, let's move to some exercises.

Exercise Set 5.1

Concept Review: Review the definitions and concepts from this section by filling in the blanks for each of the following.

1) Classical probability applies to situations where each simple outcome is _____ likely to occur.

2) A simple outcome is one that can only occur in _____ way.

3) Calculating probability is the same as calculating a _____ relative frequency.

4) When we try to interpret probability, we should always think of it as the _____ _____ relative frequency.

5) The complement of event E is the event that E does _____ occur. It is often best to use _____ when calculating complements.

6) The Fundamental Rule of Counting states that when there are m outcomes to one experiment and n outcomes to another experiment, then we must _____ m and n when calculating the total number of possible outcomes created by combining the two experiments.

Applications: Practice the concepts learned in this section within the context of real world applications.

7) Consider the experiment where a single m&m is randomly chosen from a bowl made up of the following well mixed m&m's.

Color	Frequency
Brown	11
Yellow	12
Red	10
Blue	23
Orange	17
Green	14
Total	87

Determine each of the following.
a) P(Yellow)
b) P(Orange)
c) P(*not* Green)

8) A large lecture course has 252 students enrolled. They were asked in a survey to state their eye color. The results are shown below.

Color	Frequency
Brown	96
Blue	66
Green	42
Hazel	28
Amber	17
Gray	3
Total	252

Suppose that a student is randomly selected from this class and his or her eye color is noted. Determine each of the following.
a) P(Brown)
b) P(Hazel)
c) P(*not* Blue)

9) The table below shows the breakdown by class level of all the students at a large University.

Grade level	Rel Freq
Freshman	0.2954
Sophomore	0.2730
Junior	0.2342
Senior	0.1974
Total	1.0000

Suppose that a student is selected at random. Determine each of the following.
a) P(Sophomore)
b) P(Senior)
c) P(not a Freshman)
d) If we were to randomly select 500 students from this University, about how many Freshmen would we expect to get?

10) The table below shows the breakdown by blood type for all Americans.

Blood Type	Rel Freq
O+	0.374
A+	0.357
B+	0.085
AB+	0.034
O-	0.066
A-	0.063
B-	0.015
AB-	0.006
Total	1.000

Suppose that an American is selected at random and his or her blood type is noted. Determine each of the following.
a) P(AB+)
b) P(negative blood type)
c) P(not type A)
d) If we were to randomly select 1200 Americans, about how many would we expect to have type O+ blood?

11) Consider the experiment where a single fair die is rolled and the face up number is noted. Consider the following events:
    A = the number is a 4
    B = the number is odd
    C = the number is ≥ 3
Find:
a) $P(A)$
b) $P(B)$
c) $P(C)$
d) $P(not\ A)$
e) Interpret the answer to part (c).

12) Consider the experiment where a single fair die is rolled and the face up number is noted. Consider the following events:
    A = the number is a 5
    B = the number is even
    C = the number is < 3
Find:
a) $P(A)$
b) $P(B)$
c) $P(C)$
d) $P(not\ C)$
e) Interpret the answer to part (c).

13) Consider the experiment where a single card is randomly chosen from a standard deck of cards. Consider the following events:
    A = the card is a 7
    B = the card is a diamond
    C = the card is a face card
Find:
a) $P(A)$
b) $P(B)$
c) $P(C)$
d) $P(not\ B)$
e) Interpret the answer to part (c).

14) Consider the experiment where a single card is randomly chosen from a standard deck of cards. Consider the following events:
    A = the card is an Ace
    B = the card is a spade
    C = the card is a between 4 and 9 inclusive
Find:
a) $P(A)$
b) $P(B)$
c) $P(C)$
d) $P(not\ C)$
e) Interpret the answer to part (c).

15) The following table shows a cross classification of the party affiliation and annual income level for all the registered voters in a small town.

	Dem A1	Rep A2	Other A3	Total
0 - < $25K B1	805	873	168	1846
$25K - < $50K B2	1562	1611	370	3543
$50K - < $100K B3	1177	1284	275	2736
$100K+ B4	375	425	70	870
Total	3919	4193	883	8995

Suppose that a registered voter is chosen at random. Express each of the following using event notation and determine the probability that the person selected:
a)   is a Republican.
b)   earns $100K or more per year.
c)   is not a Democrat.

16) A car dealership sold 425 new vehicles last quarter. The following table shows a cross classification of the cost of each vehicle with the vehicle type.

	SUV V1	Sedan V2	Truck V3	Total
0 -< 25K C1	28	75	23	126
25K -< 35K C2	53	50	25	128
35K -< 45K C3	41	20	18	79
45K+ C4	40	48	4	92
Total	162	193	70	425

Suppose that a sales file is chosen at random from the above possibilities. Express each of the following using event notation and determine the probability that the vehicle sold:
a)   was an SUV.
b)   cost less than 35K.
c)   was not truck.

17) A 2011 survey asked 1,005 Americans if they believed that the laws covering the sale of firearms should be made more strict, less strict, or kept as they are now. The responses are summarized below together with the region of the country that the respondent is from. (Data is based on a Gallup poll.)

	More A1	Less A2	Keep A3	Total
East R1	184	120	36	340
Midwest R2	56	78	17	151
South R3	79	101	18	198
West R4	139	136	41	316
Total	458	435	112	1005

Suppose that one of these respondents is chosen at random from the above group. Express each of the following using event notation and determine the probability that the person selected:
a)   is from the East.
b)   favors More strict gun laws.
c)   is not from the South.

18) A 2010 Gallup Poll was looking to examine the relationship between religious beliefs and opinions on terrorism. They surveyed 2,482 American adults and asked them the question "Some people think that for an individual person or a small group of persons to target and kill civilians is sometimes justified, while others think that kind of violence is never justified. Which is your opinion?" The participants could choose from Never, Sometimes, and Depends. The responses are cross classified below with the religion of the respondent. (The mix of religious beliefs was not representative of the U.S. mixture.)

	Never A1	Sometimes A2	Depends A3	Total
Muslim R1	421	52	2	475
Protestant R2	481	174	20	675
Catholic R3	310	116	10	436
Jewish R1	243	72	11	326
Mormon R2	192	46	4	242
No Religion R3	249	75	4	328
Total	1896	535	51	2482

Suppose that one these respondents is chosen at random from the above group. Express each of the following using event notation and determine the probability that the person selected:
a)   is a Muslim.
b)   answered 'Sometimes'.
c)   did not answer 'Never'.

19) Suppose two fair dice are rolled. Determine:
   a) P(sum is 5)
   b) P(sum > 7)
   c) P(doubles are rolled)
   d) P(sum is 2, 3, or 12)
   e) If we rolled these dice 600 times, about how many times should we expect the sum to be 5?

20) In the board game "13 Dead End Drive", the players roll 2 six sided dice. However, each die has the numbers 2, 3, 3, 4, 4, 5 on them rather than the standard numbering. Suppose these two dice are rolled and determine:
   a) P(sum is 8)
   b) P(sum < 7)
   c) P(doubles are rolled)
   d) P(exactly one of the dice shows an odd number)
   e) If we rolled these dice 900 times, about how many times should we expect the sum to be 8?

21) A skateboard company let's you make a custom board by choosing your deck (the board) from 6 choices and your wheel set-up from 4 choices. The prices of the decks are $49, $49, $59, $69, $79, and $79. The prices for the wheel set-ups are $39, $49, $54, and $70. Suppose that an indecisive customer randomly chooses the deck and wheel set-up. Determine:
   a) P(total price is $118)
   b) P(total price is ≤ $98)
   c) P(the deck and wheel set-ups cost the same amount)
   d) P(the price is between $90 and $125)
   e) If 400 customers were to randomly choose their boards in such a fashion, about how many times would the total price be $118?

22) A poker player has 4 casino chips in his left pocket valued at $1, $2, $3, and $5. In his right pocket, he has 5 casino chips with values of $1, $1, $2, $3, and $5. Suppose that he randomly selects a chip from each pocket. Determine:
   a) P(sum is $4)
   b) P(Sum ≤ $6)
   c) P(the sum is even)
   d) P(both chips have an even value)
   e) If this process were repeated 450 times, about how many times should we expect the sum to be at most $6?

Section 5.2 – Basic Rules of Probability

The need for probability rules arises when we start constructing new events that are combinations of other events. The most common occurrence of this is the use of the word **AND** or **OR** as a connector between two or more events. We will begin our discussion by defining these events and then we will move on to asking probability questions involving them. We will see that, if you understand the definitions well, you usually do not need special probability rules to help you answer the questions. However, some problems are easier with the rules or require the rules. Here are the relevant definitions.

Definitions: *The AND and OR events*

AND: (A & B) denotes the event that both A and B happen during the experiment. The order is unimportant. So (A & B) is exactly the same as (B & A). This is illustrated visually in the Venn diagram below.

A and B

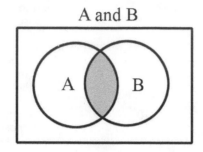

In Words: In mathematical language we would say that the new event (A & B) is the *intersection* of the previous two events. In more everyday language, we would say that the new event (A & B) is the *overlap* of the possible outcomes of the two individual events.

OR: (A or B) denotes the event that either A or B or both occur. So we say that (A or B) has occurred if the simple outcome is just in A, just in B, or even if it is the overlap of the two. Visually this is as shown below by the shaded area in the Venn diagram. Again, order of the events is not important here.

A or B

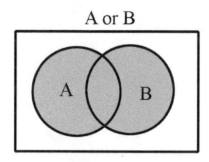

In Words: In mathematical terminology, we would say that the event (A or B) represents the union of the two events. In more everyday language, we could say that for an OR to occur, *at least one* of the events must occur.

Caution: It is a common misconception that items in the overlap should not be included in the OR. However, these items must be included to properly translate the OR statement.

Let's return to the playing card example and see how this works in that context.

Example 5.6: *Pick a Card, Any Card (Revisited)*

Consider a deck of 52 playing cards. Our experiment will be to randomly select one of the cards. Consider the events listed below and then find the requested probabilities.

Can one card satisfy two different events at the same time?

> Let   A = the event that the card chosen is the King of clubs
>   B = the event that the card chosen is a King
>   C = the event that the card chosen is a club
>   D = the card chosen is a face card

a) $P(C \ \& \ D)$

b) $P(C \text{ or } D)$

c) $P(D \ \& \ C)$

d) $P(D \text{ or } C)$

Solution:

a) The key here is to think about the definition and the visual. For the AND to occur, we need a card that meets *both* of the two event descriptions. That is, it must lie in the *overlap* of the two descriptions. So we need a card that is both a club and a face card. The only cards that have both of these characteristics are the jack of clubs, the queen of clubs, and the king of clubs. So we get:

$$P(C \ \& \ D) = \frac{3}{52} \approx 0.0577$$

b) Again, we focus on the definition and the visual. We want any card that meets *at least one* of the two descriptions. I find that the easiest way to accomplish this is to count all of the cards that meet the first description, and then count any cards that meet the second description, but have not been counted yet. So first I count the 13 clubs, and then I consider any face cards that are not clubs. This provides 3 more jacks (the jack of spades, jack of diamonds, and the jack of hearts), 3 more queens, and 3 more kings. So we get:

> **Caution:** *Avoid double counting*
>
> The most common mistake made here is to count all 13 of the clubs and then add all 12 of the face cards (4 jacks, 4 queens, and 4 kings). The problem with this is that the 3 cards in the overlap now get counted twice. We do want to count the overlap, but we never want to double count the same simple outcome.

$$P(C \text{ or } D) = \frac{13+3+3+3}{52} = \frac{22}{52} \approx 0.4231$$

c) In the definition of AND, we mentioned that the order of the two events does not matter. Therefore, we get the same answer here as we did in part (a):

$$P(D \ \& \ C) = \frac{3}{52} \approx 0.0577$$

d) Just as the order does not matter in an AND question, the same is true for an OR. While we could just repeat the answer from part (b), I will show you the logic of the OR again, but this time in the other order. So, I will count all of the items from D, the 12 face cards (4 jacks, 4 queens, 4 kings). Next, I add in anything from C that I have not counted yet. This adds in the 10 spades that remain after the face cards are removed.

$$P(D \text{ or } C) = \frac{12+10}{52} = \frac{22}{52} \approx 0.4231$$

CONTINGENCY TABLES: *Focusing on the concepts behind AND and OR*

We will now continue working with ANDs and ORs, but we will look at them in the context of a contingency table. This setting will help us to really consider visually what we mean when we say that an AND means overlap and that for an OR we want to keep anything that meets either event description. Let's return to the example concerning education level and voter participation.

Example 5.7: *Education Level and Voter Participation (Revisited)*

The table below lists the education level together with voting status in the 2004 elections for the 221,461,000 Adult Americans. The frequencies listed are in thousands. The data is based on information from the U.S. Census Bureau. The labels in parentheses are the event notation for each event. For example, E1 represents the event that the person has no high school diploma.

Is education level associated with voter participation?

	Voted in 2004 (V1)	Did Not Vote in 2004 (V2)	Total
No high School Diploma (E1)	12,774	20,345	33,119
High school graduate only (E2)	39,554	30,614	70,168
Some college, or associate degree (E3)	38,622	17,243	55,865
Bachelor's Degree or higher (E4)	50,209	12,100	62,309
Total	141,159	80,302	221,461

Suppose that a person was randomly selected from these adults at that time. Write each of the following probability questions using event notation and then find the requested probability.

a) The probability that the person selected has no high school diploma and voted in the 2004 elections.

b) The probability that the person selected has no high school diploma or voted in the 2004 elections.

Solution:

a) The key word in the description is the word 'AND'. So, the notation for this question would be:
$P(E1 \ \& \ V1)$. The best way to do this problem is to think visually about what an 'AND' means. We need the *overlap* of the row E1 and the column V1. That would be the cell containing 12,774 people (in thousands). See the circled part of the chart that follows.

	Voted in 2004 (V1)	Did Not Vote in 2004 (V2)	Total
No high School Diploma (E1)	12,774	20,345	33,119
High school graduate only (E2)	39,554	30,614	70,168
Some college, or associate degree (E3)	38,622	17,243	55,865
Bachelor's Degree or higher (E4)	50,209	12,100	62,309
Total	141,159	80,302	221,461

Because we are looking for the overlap, we only count those things in the overlap of the shaded row and column. So we get:

$$P(E1 \ \& \ V1) = \frac{12,774}{221,461} \approx 0.0577$$

b) This is very similar to part (a), however, this time the key word is 'OR'. So, this time we want anything that meets at least one of the descriptions given. Our visual is that we want anything that is shaded, whether it is in the overlap or not. So we have a total of 5 cells shaded (see above). This gives us:

$$P(E1 \ or \ V1) = \frac{12,774 + 39,554 + 38,622 + 50,209 + 20,345}{221,461} = \frac{161,504}{221,461} \approx 0.7293$$

Another option is to use the totals to help shorten our calculations. The first 4 numbers are already totaled for us in the table, so our work could be written in a shorter form as:

$$P(E1 \ or \ V1) = \frac{141,159 + 20,345}{221,461} = \frac{161,504}{221,461} \approx 0.7293 \ .$$

Notice that we don't use the total for both E1 and V1 because that would double count the overlapping cell. So, we used the total for the V1 column and then just added in the one *new* cell from the E1 row.

MUTUALLY EXCLUSIVE EVENTS: *When the events do not overlap*

The thing that made part (b) of the last example tricky was the need to be careful not to count the overlapping cell twice. If the events E1 and V1 did not overlap at all, this would have made the question much simpler. Events that do not overlap are, in fact, so much easier to work with that we have a special definition to describe them.

Definition: *Mutually Exclusive Events*

Mutually Exclusive Events: Two events are considered to be mutually exclusive if it is impossible for them to occur simultaneously. This means that they would have no overlap. A set of three or more events is known as a mutually exclusive set of events if no two of them can occur simultaneously. The Venn diagrams below show some examples of events that are mutually exclusive and also some events that are not.

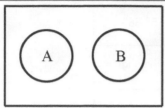

A and B do not overlap, so it is impossible that the two events could occur simultaneously. Thus A & B are mutually exclusive (Mutually Exclusive)

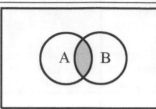

A and B do overlap, so it is possible that both events could occur simultaneously. Thus A & B are not mutually exclusive. (NOT Mutually Exclusive)

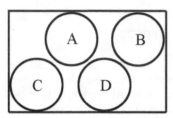

The set of events: A, B, C, D is a mutually exclusive group because no two of the events can occur simultaneously.

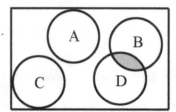

The set of events: A, B, C, D is not a mutually exclusive group because events B & D can occur simultaneously.

Let's take a look at an example that practices these definitions as well as illustrates the usefulness of having mutually exclusive events.

Example 5.8: *Flossing*

100 students were asked, "How many days per week do you floss your teeth?" Their responses are listed in the table below.

Are students flossing as much as they should?

# of days flossing	0	1	2	3	4	5	6	7
Frequency	13	3	5	7	12	16	23	21

Suppose that our experiment is to randomly select one of these 100 people. Let's define a few events for this experiment. Let

A = the event the person selected does not floss
B = the event the person flosses daily
C = the event the person flosses at least 4 days per week
D = the event the person flosses between 2 and 5 days per week, inclusive

a) List the possible numbers of days per week that meet the description for each of the events.

b) List all the mutually exclusive groups of events.

c) Find $P(C \ \& \ D)$

d) Find $P(C \text{ or } D)$

e) Find $P(A \text{ or } C)$

f) $P(A \text{ or } B \text{ or } D)$

g) $P(A \text{ or } B \text{ or } C \text{ or } D)$

Solution:

a) Listing the events as lists of numbers makes it much easier to think about the answers to AND or OR questions. It also makes it easier to see which groups of events are mutually exclusive. We will use the roster form of set notation to accomplish this task.

> A = the person selected does not floss = {0}
> B = the person flosses daily = {7}
> C = the person flosses at least 4 days per week. = {4, 5, 6, 7}
> D = the person flosses between 2 and 5 days per week, inclusive = {2, 3, 4, 5}

b) First, I will list all pairs that are mutually exclusive. Remember: this means that the two sets will have nothing in common.

> A & B,   A & C,   A & D,   B & D

The only other grouping of events that is mutually exclusive is the group A, B, & D

So, the mutually exclusive groups are {AB, AC, AD, BD, ABD}.

c) Recall that & means overlap. So we just look at what numbers are in the overlap, or intersection, of these two events.

> C = {4, 5, 6, 7} and D = {2, 3, 4, 5} $\Rightarrow$ (C & D) = {4, 5}

Therefore, to find the requested probability, we simply need to count the number of people who flossed either 4 or 5 days per week and divide by the total of 100. We get:

$$P(C \text{ \& } D) = P(\{4,5\}) = \frac{12+16}{100} = 0.28$$

d) Remember that OR translates to "at least one" of the events occurs. In the Venn diagram for an OR we shaded both circles including the overlap. The best way to think of this is to shade all of the first event and then shade anything from the second event that has not yet been shaded. Let's apply this idea to the table above. So for (C or D), we will begin by shading all the cells that meet the description C = {4, 5, 6, 7}

# of days flossing	0	1	2	3	4	5	6	7
Frequency	13	3	5	7	12	16	23	21

Now we shade any cells from D = {2, 3, 4, 5} that we have not shaded already. This adds {2, 3} to our list.

# of days flossing	0	1	2	3	4	5	6	7
Frequency	13	3	5	7	12	16	23	21

Now we count all the people corresponding to the shaded cells. This yields:

$$P(C \text{ or } D) = P(\{2,3,4,5,6,7\}) = \frac{5+7+12+16+23+21}{100} = 0.84$$

Because more than half of the cells are shaded, it would actually be a bit faster to just subtract the one we don't want from the total. Removing {0, 1} yields:

$$P(C \text{ or } D) = \frac{100-13-3}{100} = 0.84$$

e) This one is actually easier because the events are mutually exclusive. This means that we can just shade each one, count all shaded cells, and not have to worry about anything being double counted.

# of days flossing	0	1	2	3	4	5	6	7
Frequency	13	3	5	7	12	16	23	21

So we get: $P(A \text{ or } C) = \dfrac{13+12+16+23+21}{100} = 0.85$ OR $P(A \text{ or } C) = \dfrac{100-3-5-7}{100} = 0.85$

f) This is just like the last example, only it has one more event. We will once again shade all the cells that meet the description of our events, this time A, B, or D. This yields:

# of days flossing	0	1	2	3	4	5	6	7
Frequency	13	3	5	7	12	16	23	21

$$P(A \text{ or } B \text{ or } D) = \frac{13+5+7+12+16+21}{100} = 0.74$$

OR $P(A \text{ or } B \text{ or } D) = \dfrac{100-3-23}{100} = 0.74$

Key Concept: *No Overlap*

When calculating 'OR' probabilities for mutually exclusive events, we don't have to worry about double counting anything in the overlap of the events, because there is no overlap. This makes this type much easier.

g) This is not a mutually exclusive group of events. Whenever you are working on an OR question involving events that overlap, we should stick with the Venn diagram strategy. Start by counting all of the items from the first event and then keep adding any new items from the events that follow. So, we start with event A, {0}. Then we add in all of the items from B that are new: {7}. Now, add in anything from C that is new. We already have the 7, so we add in {4, 5, 6}. Finally, the only new items from event D are {2, 3}. Putting this all together, we want {0, 2, 3, 4, 5, 6, 7}.

Key Concept: *With Overlap*

When calculating 'OR' probabilities for overlapping events, we have to worry about double counting anything in the overlap of the events. The best way to avoid this is to start with everything from the first event and then only add in new items from the remaining events.

# of days flossing	0	1	2	3	4	5	6	7
Frequency	13	3	5	7	12	16	23	21

$$P(A \text{ or } B \text{ or } C \text{ or } D) = \frac{100-3}{100} = 0.97$$

THE SPECIAL ADDITION RULE: *A Rule that Takes Advantage of no Overlap*

In the last example, we noted that it is much easier to do OR type probabilities if the events in question are mutually exclusive. This is true because when events have no overlap, there is no worry about double counting. We take advantage of this fact in the following probability rule.

Point to Remember: *The Special Addition Rule*

The Special Addition Rule: If A & B are a pair of mutually exclusive events, then:

$$P(A \text{ or } B) = P(A) + P(B)$$

Extended Version: If A, B, C, ... is a mutually exclusive group of events, then:

$$P(A \text{ or } B \text{ or } C \text{ or } \ldots) = P(A) + P(B) + P(C) + \ldots$$

While it is easier to work with mutually exclusive events, you might feel that it would be a rare situation to have many events with none of them overlapping each other. However, there is one situation that is very common where this does happen. The situation is one where the events are defined to be the different classes in a grouped data table. Let's take a look at such an example.

Example 5.9: *Final Exam Scores*

The final exam scores (out of 100 points possible) for a group of statistics students are shown grouped in the table below. Each class has been represented by the event letter as listed in the table.

How likely is it that a randomly selected student will pass the final exam?

Event	Classes	Relative Freq
A	90 – 99	0.3488
B	80 – 89	0.1628
C	70 – 79	0.2093
D	60 – 69	0.0930
F	50 – 59	0.1163
G	40 – 49	0.0465
H	30 – 39	0.0000
I	20 – 29	0.0233
		1.0000

Suppose that a student from this group is selected at random. Write each of the following using event notation and then find the requested probability.

a) The probability that the student received an A grade. That is, they scored at least a 90.

b) The probability that the student passed the exam. That is, they scored at least a 70.

c) The probability that the student failed the exam. That is, they scored no higher than a 59.

Solution:

a) The notation for this is simple. We wish to find $P(A)$. At first glance, it may seem that we do not have enough information to find this probability. We are not told how many students we are choosing from or how many received a score of at least 90. However, we can use the fact that the probability of an event is always the same value as the population relative frequency of that event. Because the population relative frequencies are provided, we can use them in place of the probabilities. So we get:

$$P(A) = 0.3488$$

b) For the student to score at least a 70, they would have to be in event A, B, or C. So we need to find $P(A \text{ or } B \text{ or } C)$. Because the events are all mutually exclusive, we can use the Special Addition Rule.

$$P(A \text{ or } B \text{ or } C) = P(A) + P(B) + P(C) = 0.3488 + 0.1628 + 0.2093 = 0.7209$$

c) For the student to score no higher than a 59, they would have to be in event F, G, H, or I. Again, these are mutually exclusive, so we get:

$$P(F \text{ or } G \text{ or } H \text{ or } I) = P(F) + P(G) + P(H) + P(I) = 0.1163 + 0.0465 + 0.0000 + 0.0233 = 0.1861$$

THE COMPLEMENT RULE: *Sometimes subtraction is the better option*

The Special Addition Rule is useful for events like those in the previous example, but it also leads us to another equally important formula called the **Complement Rule**. Let's take a look at where this new rule comes from. Consider the following.

Any event either happens or it doesn't happen, therefore $P(E \text{ or } (\text{not } E)) = 1$. But it is not possible for an event and it's complement to occur simultaneously, this means that E and (not E) are mutually exclusive events, so we can apply the Special Addition Rule to the equation above and we get:

$$P(E \text{ or } (\text{not } E)) = 1 \Rightarrow P(E) + P(\text{not } E) = 1.$$

Now if we use a little algebra and subtract $P(E)$ from both sides of the equation, we get:

$$P(\text{not } E) = 1 - P(E).$$

Alternatively, we could start with $P(E) + P(\text{not } E) = 1$ and subtract $P(\text{not } E)$ from both sides of the equation. This would yield:

$$P(E) = 1 - P(\text{not } E)$$

The two results reached above are what we call the **Complement Rule**. We summarize this rule in the following point to remember.

Point to Remember: *The Complement Rule*

The Complement Rule: For any event E and its complement (not E):

$$P(\text{not } E) = 1 - P(E) \quad \text{and} \quad P(E) = 1 - P(\text{not } E)$$

In words: The probability of any event can always be found by subtracting the probability of its complement from 1.

Let's examine the usefulness of this by returning to our table of final exam scores.

Example 5.10: *Final Exam Scores (Continued . . .)*

The final exam scores (out of 100 points possible) for a group of statistics students are shown grouped in the table below. Each class has been represented by the event letter as listed in the table below.

Event	Score	Relative Freq
A	90 – 99	0.3488
B	80 – 89	0.1628
C	70 – 79	0.2093
D	60 – 69	0.0930
F	50 – 59	0.1163
G	40 – 49	0.0465
H	30 – 39	0.0000
I	20 – 29	0.0233
		1.0000

How likely is it that a randomly selected student will pass the final exam?

Suppose that a student from this group is selected at random. Write each of the following using event notation and then find the requested probability.

a) The probability that the student did not receive an A grade. That is, they scored less than 90 points on the exam.

b) The probability that the student scored at least a 50.

Solution:

a)   If the student scored less than 90 points on the exam, then B, C, D, F, G, H, or I has occurred. So we could calculate the probability as follows.

$$P(B \text{ or } C \text{ or } D \text{ or } F \text{ or } G \text{ or } H \text{ or } I) = 0.1628 + 0.2093 + 0.0930 + 0.1163 + 0.0465 + 0.0000 + 0.0233 = 0.6512$$

While this method certainly works. It would be much easier to use the Complement Rule. Because we want everything except for event A. We could say that our answer is:

$$P(\text{not } A) = 1 - P(A) = 1 - 0.3488 = 0.6512$$

b) If the student scored at least a 50, then we want A, B, C, D, and F, but we could also say that we don't want G, H, or I. Using the Complement Rule, we just subtract away what we don't want from 1 as shown below.

$$P(A \text{ or } B \text{ or } C \text{ or } D \text{ or } F) = 1 - P(G \text{ or } H \text{ or } I) = 1 - P(G) - P(H) - P(I) = 1 - 0.0465 - 0.0000 - 0.0233 = 0.9302$$

Using the Complement Rule here allowed us to subtract two things (because 1 of the 3 was zero) rather than adding together 5. Neither way is hard, but the Complement Rule was a bit shorter.

THE GENERAL ADDITION RULE: *A Rule that Helps Us Avoid Double Counting*

We saw how the Special Addition Rule can be useful when dealing with mutually exclusive events, but what if the events are not mutually exclusive. Let's look at an OR question from Example 5.8 and see what happens if we try to apply the Special Addition Rule.

Using the table:

# of days flossing	0	1	2	3	4	5	6	7
Frequency	13	3	5	7	12	16	23	21

And the events:

C = the person flosses at least 4 days per week. = {4, 5, 6, 7}
D = the person flosses between 2 and 5 days per week, inclusive = {2, 3, 4, 5}

Let's try to find $P(C \text{ or } D)$ using the Special Addition Rule (despite the fact that C and D are not mutually exclusive!) Using the rule, we get:

$$P(C \text{ or } D) = P(C) + P(D) = \frac{12+16+23+21}{100} + \frac{5+7+12+16}{100} = \frac{72}{100} + \frac{40}{100} = \frac{112}{100} = 1.12$$

Clearly this can't be the correct answer. Not only is it different from what we got in Example 5.8, but the answer is greater than 1, so it is not a valid answer for a probability question. So, what went wrong? The answer is fairly simple. When we calculated $P(C)$ we counted the 12 people who floss 4 days per week and the 16 people who floss 5 days per week, but then we counted those same people again when we calculated $P(D)$. By adding the two results together, we effectively double counted those 28 people. When you do an 'OR', you should count the people in the overlap, but you don't want to double count them. We could fix this problem by subtracting the probability of the overlap at the end. This would look like this:

$$P(C \text{ or } D) = P(C) + P(D) - P(C \ \& \ D) = \frac{72}{100} + \frac{40}{100} - \frac{28}{100} = \frac{84}{100} = 0.84$$

This is the same answer we obtained in Example 5.8, part (d). This new method is not as fast as the way we did it back in Example 5.8, but it will always work. In fact, it is our next Point to Remember.

Point to Remember: *The General Addition Rule*

The General Addition Rule: If A & B are any pair of events, then:

$$P(A \text{ or } B) = P(A) + P(B) - P(A \ \& \ B)$$

Key Concept: The reason we subtract $P(A \ \& \ B)$ is not because we don't want the overlap when calculating an 'OR'. It's just that, in adding the probability of the individual events, we double counted the overlap, so we must subtract out the extra copy.

In the discussion preceding the above Point to Remember, we noted that using the formula wasn't as easy as the simple counting methods we had used previously to solve 'OR' type questions. When you have the choice between using the General Addition Rule and simple counting techniques, this usually is true. However, there are some situations where we don't have enough information to simply count up the desired outcomes and divide. In such cases, the rule will become the preferable method of solution. Here is an example of such a problem.

Example 5.11: *An Abstract Probability Question*

Suppose that $P(A) = 0.5608$, $P(B) = 0.4870$, and $P(A \text{ \& } B) = 0.2535$.

a) Find $P(A \text{ or } B)$

b) Are A and B mutually exclusive events? Explain.

Solution:

a) In this case, it is hard to answer this question by simply thinking about what an 'OR' means and then using counting techniques. We don't know what the experiment is or what A and B stand for. We don't even know how many outcomes make up the sample space. Situations like this are a good spot to apply probability formulas. We begin by writing down the General Addition Rule.

$$P(A \text{ or } B) = P(A) + P(B) - P(A \text{ \& } B)$$

This formula is perfect for the goal of this problem. The desired result is by itself on one side of the equation and we know the values of the 3 probabilities on the other side. So, we simply plug in the known values and simplify:

$$P(A \text{ or } B) = 0.5608 + 0.4870 - 0.2535 = 0.7943$$

b) There are two ways to answer this question. The first is to use the Special Addition Rule. A and B are mutually exclusive if and only if $P(A \text{ or } B) = P(A) + P(B)$. So, if this formula holds, then they are mutually exclusive events. If it does not hold, then they are not mutually exclusive events.

$$0.7943 \overset{?}{=} 0.5608 + 0.4870, \ \ 0.7943 \neq 1.0478 \Rightarrow \text{NO! A and B are not mutually exclusive events.}$$

The second way is much simpler. A and B are mutually exclusive if and only if it is impossible for the two events to occur simultaneously. If A and B occur simultaneously, then we would say that $(A \text{ \& } B)$ has occurred. So we simply investigate $P(A \text{ \& } B)$. This value was given at the beginning of the problem, so we get:

$$P(A \text{ \& } B) = 0.2535 \neq 0 \Rightarrow \text{A and B can occur simultaneously, thus A \& B are not mutually exclusive.}$$

The fact that A & B are not mutually exclusive. does not affect our answer to part (a) because we used the General Addition Rule, which does not depend on any special conditions.

> **Point to Remember**: *Checking for Mutually Exclusive Events*
>
> A & B are mutually exclusive events if and only if $P(A \text{ \& } B) = 0$
>
> **Note**: This rule is useful for checking to see if two events are mutually exclusive or not.

Example 5.12: *A twist on the General Addition Rule*

Suppose that $P(E) = 0.2316$, $P(F) = 0.3894$, and $P(E \text{ or } F) = 0.6210$.

a) Find $P(E \text{ \& } F)$

b) Are E and F mutually exclusive events? Explain.

c) Find $P(\text{not } E)$.

Solution:

a) It may not be as obvious as last time, but once again we will solve this problem by using the General Addition Rule. Despite the fact that we came up with that formula to help us find the probability of 'OR' events, we can use any formula to find any of its pieces, provided that we know the values of all the other pieces. Before we can use the formula, we must note that the A and B in the formula are merely placeholders. The formula is just as valid with any other letters substituted in.

$$P(A \text{ or } B) = P(A) + P(B) - P(A \& B) \implies P(E \text{ or } F) = P(E) + P(F) - P(E \& F)$$

We will now substitute in all known quantities and then solve for the desired probability.

$$0.6210 = 0.2316 + 0.3894 - P(E \& F)$$

> Subtracting 0.6210 from both sides and adding $P(E \& F)$ to both sides

$$\implies P(E \& F) = 0.2316 + 0.3894 - 0.6210$$

$$\implies P(E \& F) = 0$$

b) Yes, because $P(E \& F) = 0$, we know that E and F are mutually exclusive.

c) We use the complement rule for this one.

$$P(\text{not } E) = 1 - P(E) = 1 - 0.2316 = 0.76814$$

> **Caution:** *A common mistake*
>
> When working with only two events. It is common for people to think that (not E) has to be event F. This does not have to be the case.

WRAP SESSION: *Probability Rules with a Contingency Table*

Example 5.13: *Health Insurance and Smoking Habits*

A December 2011 Gallup poll investigated the link between having health insurance and various health related behaviors. The poll consisted of a random sample of 199,672 adults, aged 18 and older, living in all 50 U.S. states and the District of Columbia. The data below is based on this poll.

	Covered by health Insurance (C1)	Not covered by health Insurance (C2)	Total
Smoke (B1)	32,722	11,568	42,290
Do Not Smoke (B2)	134,484	20,898	155,382
Total	167,206	32,466	199,672

Are smoking status and health care coverage status related?

Suppose that a person is randomly selected from these adults.

a) Express the probability that the adult selected smokes or is not covered by health insurance using probability notation. Find this probability using the General Addition Rule.

b)   Now find $P(B1 \text{ or } C2)$ using simple counting and the idea that 'OR' mean at least one of the events occurs.

c)   Which method seems to be the better way to do this problem, the General Addition Rule or the old method of just counting the outcomes? Explain.

d)   Are the events that the person Smokes and the person is covered by health insurance mutually exclusive? Explain.

e)   If we were to randomly select 4,000 of the participants in this study, about how many of those selected should we expect to covered by health insurance?

Solution:

a)   We will use the row total to find $P(B1)$ and the column total to find $P(C2)$. We then use the overlap of this row and column to find $P(B1 \text{ \& } C2)$. Finally we put it all together using the General Addition Rule.

$$P(B1 \text{ or } C2) = P(B1) + P(C2) - P(B1 \text{ \& } C2) = \frac{42,290}{199,672} + \frac{32,466}{199,672} - \frac{11,568}{199,672} = \frac{63,188}{199,672} \approx 0.3165$$

b)   For this method, we just shade everything in B1 and then anything in C2 that we haven't shaded yet, and then we add all the shaded cells together to get the numerator. See the shading in the table below.

	Covered by health Insurance (C1)	Not covered by health Insurance (C2)	Total
Smoke (B1)	32,722	11,568	42,290
Do Not Smoke (B2)	134,484	20,898	155,382
Total	167,206	32,466	199,672

$$P(B1 \text{ or } C2) = \frac{42,290 + 20,898}{199,672} = \frac{63,188}{199,672} \approx 0.3165$$

c)   The simple counting way used in part (b) seems better because you only have to calculate one probability. To use the General Addition Rule, we had to find three separate probabilities and then put them all together using the rule.

d)   If these events were mutually exclusive, then it would be impossible for them to occur simultaneously. So, we check the cell that holds the overlap of Smoking (B1) and having health insurance (C1).

$$P(B1 \text{ \& } C1) = \frac{32,722}{199,672} \approx 0.1639 \neq 0 \quad \Rightarrow \quad \text{B1 and C2 are not mutually exclusive events.}$$

e)   Covered by health insurance is event C1 and $P(C1) = \frac{167206}{199672} \approx 0.8374 = 83.74\%$. This tells us the expected long term relative frequency of this event. So, we expect about 83.74% of those selected to be covered by health insurance. Calculating this, we get: $(0.8374) * 4000 = 3349.6 \approx 3350$. So we expect about 3,350 of the 4,000 people selected to have health insurance.

Let's practice what we have learned with some exercises.

Exercise Set 5.2

Concept Review: Review the definitions and concepts from this section by filling in the blanks for each of the following.

23) For an 'AND' event to occur, _____ of the individual events must occur. Visually, we think of an 'AND' as the _____ of two events.

24) For an 'OR' event to occur, ____ _____ one of the listed events must occur. The best way to calculate an 'OR' probability is to count all of the items from the first event and then only add in the _____ items from the other event.

25) If two events cannot occur simultaneously, then they are _____ _____ .

26) The _____ Addition Rule can only be used if the events are mutually exclusive.

27) When calculating an 'OR' probability, you need to be very careful not to _____ count the items in the overlap of the two events.

28) The best time to use the Complement Rule is when you realize that you are about to add up more than _____ of the total possibilities.

Mechanics: Practice using the formulas learned in this section on some abstract questions before moving on to the real life applications.

29) Suppose $P(A)=0.3425$, $P(B)=0.5283$, and $P(A\&B)=0.2367$. Find:
a) $P(A \text{ or } B)$
b) $P(\text{not } A)$
c) Are A & B mutually Exclusive? Explain.

30) Suppose $P(A)=0.6316$, $P(B)=0.1812$, and $P(A\&B)=0.0984$. Find:
a) $P(A \text{ or } B)$
b) $P(\text{not } A)$
c) Are A & B mutually Exclusive? Explain.

31) Suppose $P(C)=0.5877$, $P(D)=0.3111$, and $P(C \text{ or } D)=0.8988$. Find:
a) $P(C \& D)$
b) $P(\text{not } (C \& D))$
c) Are C & D mutually exclusive? Explain.

32) Suppose $P(C)=0.2514$, $P(D)=0.5582$, and $P(C \text{ or } D)=0.8096$. Find:
a) $P(C \& D)$
b) $P(\text{not } (C \& D))$
c) Are C & D mutually exclusive? Explain.

33) Suppose $P(E)=0.7052$, $P(E \& F)=0.3975$, and $P(E \text{ or } F)=0.9918$. Find:
a) $P(F)$
b) $P(\text{not } (E \text{ or } F))$

34) Suppose $P(F)=0.4650$, $P(E \& F)=0.1128$, and $P(E \text{ or } F)=0.5014$. Find:
a) $P(E)$
b) $P(\text{not } (E \& F))$

Applications: Practice the concepts learned in this section within the context of real world applications.

35) The following table shows a cross classification of the party affiliation and annual income level for all the registered voters in a small town.

	Dem A1	Rep A2	Other A3	Total
0 - < $25K B1	805	873	168	1846
$25K - < $50K B2	1562	1611	370	3543
$50K - < $100K B3	1177	1284	275	2736
$100K+ B4	375	425	70	870
Total	3919	4193	883	8995

Suppose that a registered voter from this town is chosen at random. Write each of the following in probability notation and then evaluate:

a) Probability the person is a Democrat who earns $100K+ per year.
b) Probability the person is a Republican or earns $50K - < $100K per year.
c) Probability the person is not registered as Other.
d) Are A2 and B1 mutually exclusive events? Explain.

36) A car dealership sold 425 new vehicles last quarter. The following table shows a cross classification of the cost of each vehicle with the vehicle type.

	SUV V1	Sedan V2	Truck V3	Total
0-< 25K C1	28	75	23	126
25K-< 35K C2	53	50	25	128
35K-< 45K C3	41	20	18	79
45K+ C4	40	48	4	92
Total	162	193	70	425

Suppose that a new vehicle is chosen at random from the above group. Write each of the following in probability notation and then evaluate:

a) Probability the vehicle is an SUV that costs less than $25K.
b) Probability the vehicle is a Sedan or costs at least $45K.
c) Probability the vehicle is not a Truck.
d) Are C4 and V3 mutually exclusive events? Explain.

37) A 2011 survey asked 1,005 Americans if they believed that the laws covering the sale of firearms should be made more strict, less strict, or kept as they are now. The responses are summarized below together with the region of the country that the respondent is from. (Data is based on a Gallup poll.)

	More A1	Less A2	Keep A3	Total
East R1	184	120	36	340
Midwest R2	56	78	17	151
South R3	79	101	18	198
West R4	139	136	41	316
Total	458	435	112	1005

Suppose that one these respondents is chosen at random from the above group. Express each of the following using event notation and determine the probability that the person selected:

a) is from the West and favors More strict gun laws.
b) is from the South or is in favor of Keeping the laws as they are now.
c) is not from the Midwest and favors Less strict gun laws.
d) If we randomly selected 100 of the people from this group, about how many of them would you expect to favor More strict gun laws?

38) A 2010 Gallup Poll was looking to examine the relationship between religious beliefs and opinions on terrorism. They surveyed 2,482 American adults and asked them the question "Some people think that for an individual person or a small group of persons to target and kill civilians is sometimes justified, while others think that kind of violence is never justified. Which is your opinion?" The participants could choose from Never, Sometimes, and Depends. The responses are cross classified below with the religion of the respondent. (The mix of religious beliefs was not representative of the U.S. mixture.)

	Never A1	Sometimes A2	Depends A3	Total
Muslim R1	421	52	2	475
Protestant R2	481	174	20	675
Catholic R3	310	116	10	436
Jewish R1	243	72	11	326
Mormon R2	192	46	4	242
No Religion R3	249	75	4	328
Total	1896	535	51	2482

Suppose that one of these respondents is chosen at random from the above group. Express each of the following using event notation and determine the probability that the person selected:

a) has No Religion and thinks that such violence is Sometimes justified.
b) is Protestant or thinks that such violence is Never justified.
c) is not Catholic and feels that it Depends.

39) The following chart shows the frequencies for the different scores on the Chapter 5 homework assignment for a statistics class with 44 students.

Hw Score	0	1	2	3	4	5
Frequency	1	1	5	13	14	10

Consider the events listed below and suppose one of these students scores is picked at random.
A = the score is a 5
B = the score is no more than 4
C = the score is at least 3
D = the score is less than 3.

a) List the possible scores that meet the description for each of the events.
b) List all the mutually exclusive groups of events.
c) $P(B \ \& \ C)$
d) $P(B \text{ or } C)$
e) $P(B \ \& \ D)$
f) $P(B \text{ or } D)$

40) The following chart shows the number of goals scored by the losing hockey team in 47 NHL games.

Number of Goals	0	1	2	3	4
Frequency	8	19	15	4	1

Consider the events listed below and suppose one of these games is picked at random.
A = the number of goals is 0.
B = the number of goals is more than 1.
C = the number of goals is at most 3
D = the number of goals is less than 2.

a) List the possible number of goals that meet the description for each of the events.
b) List all the mutually exclusive groups of events.
c) $P(B \ \& \ C)$
d) $P(B \text{ or } C)$
e) $P(C \ \& \ D)$
f) $P(C \text{ or } D)$

41) The author surveyed 96 of his statistics students during the Spring 2012 semester. They were asked how many movies they saw in the theater over the Winter break. The results are shown below.

# of Movies	0	1	2	3	4	5	6 +
Frequency	32	33	12	11	4	2	2

Consider the events listed below and suppose one of these students is picked at random.
A = the number of movies is at least 2.
B = the number of movies is more than 3.
C = the number of movies is less than 2.
D = the number of movies is from 3 to 5.

a) Find $P(B \ \& \ D)$
b) Find $P(B \text{ or } D)$
c) Find $P((not \ A) \ \& \ D)$
d) Find $P(B \text{ or } C \text{ or } D)$

42) In January 2012, the author surveyed 74 of his car owning statistics students. They were asked how many times they had personally opened the hood of the car during the previous semester. The results are shown below.

# of Opens	0	1	2	3	4	5	6	7 +
Frequency	30	6	15	5	2	3	3	10

Consider the events listed below and suppose one of these students is picked at random.
A = the number of hood opens is at most 4.
B = the number of hood opens is less than 3.
C = the number of hood opens is more than 4.
D = the number of hood opens is from 4 to 6.

a) Find $P(C \ \& \ D)$
b) Find $P(C \text{ or } D)$
c) Find $P((not \ D) \ \& \ C)$
d) Find $P(A \text{ or } B \text{ or } D)$

43) Consider the experiment where a single m&m is randomly chosen from a bowl made up of the following well mixed m&m's.

Color	Frequency
Brown	11
Yellow	12
Red	10
Blue	23
Orange	17
Green	14
Total	87

Determine each of the following.
a) P(Red or Blue)
b) P(Green or Orange)
c) P(Brown and Yellow)

44) Consider the experiment where a single student is chosen from a large lecture course that has 252 students enrolled and the eye color of the student selected is noted. The eye colors of the students are shown below.

Color	Frequency
Brown	96
Blue	66
Green	42
Hazel	28
Amber	17
Gray	3
Total	252

Determine each of the following.
a) P(Brown or Green)
b) P(Amber or Gray)
c) P(Blue and Hazel)

45) According to a 2011 Gallup poll, the religious preference for Americans is as shown in the chart below.

Preference	Rel Freq
Protestant	0.525
Catholic	0.236
Mormon	0.019
Jewish	0.016
Muslim	0.005
Other	0.024
None/Atheist	0.150
No Response	0.025
Total	1.000

Suppose that an American is randomly selected and asked to state a choice for religious preference. Determine each of the following.

a) The probability that the person states that they are Protestant or Catholic.
b) The probability that the person states that they are Jewish and Muslim.
c) The probability that the person does not state that they are in the None/Atheist category.

46) In May 2006, a Gallup poll asked Americans "Which comes closest to describing you: you are convinced that God exists; you think God probably exists (but have a little doubt); you think God probably exists (but you have a lot of doubt); you think God probably does not exist (but you are not sure); or you are convinced that God doest not exist. The relative frequencies for Americans, based on this poll, are shown in the table below.

Does God Exist?	Rel Freq
Convinced God Exists	0.7343
Probably Exists (little doubt)	0.1408
Probably Exists (lot of doubt)	0.0461
Probably Not (but not sure)	0.0362
Convinced Not	0.0275
No Opinion	0.0151
Total	1.0000

Suppose that an American was to be randomly selected at that time and asked to answer the question. Determine each of the following.

a) The probability that the person states that God Exists (but they have a lot of doubt) or have a stronger belief.
b) The probability that the person states that they are Convinced that God does not exist and they have no opinion on the matter.
c) The probability that the person is not Convinced that God exists.

47) Suppose two standard fair dice are rolled. Determine:
a) P(sum is even or sum > 9)
b) P(sum is even & sum > 9)
c) P(doubles are rolled or sum < 6)
d) P(doubles are rolled & sum < 6)

48) In the board game "13 Dead End Drive", the players roll 2 six sided dice. However, each die has the numbers 2, 3, 3, 4, 4, 5 on them rather than the standard numbering. Suppose these two dice are rolled and determine:
a) P(sum is even or sum ≤ 8)
b) P(sum is even & sum ≤ 8)
c) P(doubles are rolled or sum > 6)
d) P(doubles are rolled & sum > 6)

49) A skateboard company let's you make a custom board by choosing your deck (the board) from 6 choices and your wheel set-up from 4 choices. The prices of the decks are $49, $49, $59, $69, $79, and $79. The prices for the wheel set-ups are $39, $49, $54, and $70. Suppose that an indecisive customer randomly chooses the deck and wheel set-up. Determine:
a) The probability that the deck is more than $60 and the wheel set-up is less than $60.
b) The probability that the deck is more than $60 or the wheel set-up is less than $60.
c) The probability that the deck is at least $50 or the total price is over $115.
d) The probability that the deck is at least $50 and the total price is over $115.

50) A poker player has 4 casino chips in his left pocket valued at $1, $2, $3, and $5. In his right pocket, he has 5 casino chips with values of $1, $1, $2, $3, and $5. Suppose that he randomly selects a chip from each pocket. Determine:
a) P(sum is odd or sum < $6)
b) P(sum is odd & sum < $6)
c) P(the chips are the same value or sum > $6)
d) P(the chips are the same value & sum > $6)

51) In the poker game, Texas Hold'em, players try to make the best possible 5 card poker hand using their two hole cards and 5 shared community cards. Consider the situation shown below:

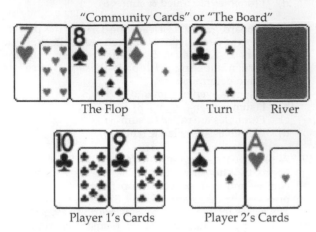

Player 2 is currently ahead with three Aces. Player 1 only has a ten high. However, player 1 can still win. If the remaining mystery card is a 6 or a Jack, then player 1 will win the hand with a straight (5 cards that are consecutive.)

a) What is the probability that player 1 will win the hand?
b) Given that it is not possible for the players to end up tied, what is the probability that player 2 will hang on and win the hand?

52) In the poker game, Texas Hold'em, players try to make the best possible 5 card poker hand using their two hole cards and 5 shared community cards. Consider the situation shown below:

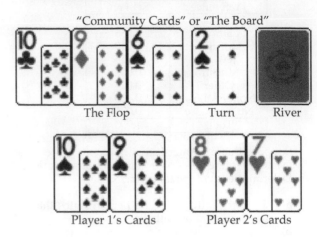

Player 1 currently has 2 pair, but player 2 is leading with a straight (5 consecutive cards). However, player 1 can still if the remaining mystery card in a Ten or a 9. Player 1 can also win if the remaining mystery card is another spade.

a) Determine the probability that the remaining mystery card will be a 10 or a 9.
b) Determine the probability that the remaining mystery card will be a spade.
c) Given that part (a) and part (b) are the only ways that Player 1 can win the hand, determine the overall probability that player 1 will win the hand.

Section 5.3 – Conditional Probability and Independence

In this section, we will be looking at new definitions that can affect the way we calculate probabilities. The first one arises in situations where you are given extra information that can allow you to reduce the size of your sample space. The second one has to do with situations where the extra information has no effect on the answer to the probability question. The first situation is known as **conditional probability** and it is defined as follows.

Definition: *Conditional Probability*

Conditional Probability: A conditional probability question is one where you are asked to find the probability that one event will occur given that another event has occurred. The notation for this is $P(A \mid B)$. The vertical line is read "given". Thus $P(A \mid B)$ is translated "the probability that A will occur given that B has occurred."

Let's take a look at a few simple examples to see how this works.

Example 5.14: *Rolling a fair die*

Consider the experiment where a fair die is rolled. Write each of the following using probability notation and then find the requested probability.

How does partial knowledge of the roll of a die affect probability calculations?

a)   The probability that the die lands with the 3 side face up.

b)   The probability that the die landed with the 3 side face up given that it landed showing an odd number.

c)   The probability that the die landed with the 3 side face up given that it landed showing an even number.

d)   The probability that the die landed showing an odd number given that it landed showing a 2 or higher.

e)   The probability that the die landed showing a 2 or higher given that it landed showing an odd number.

Solution:

a)   This one is not a conditional probability. It can be written as $P(\text{die shows a 3})$. We answer this just like all questions from Section 5.1. First we think about how many simple outcomes make up the sample space. The die has 6 sides: {1, 2, 3, 4, 5, 6}. Then, we think about how many of these outcomes meet our description, just one, the 3. Finally, we make the fraction to find the probability.

$$P(\text{die shows a 3}) = \frac{1}{6} \approx 0.1667$$

b)   Because we are given the extra information that the die landed showing an odd number, this one is a conditional probability. The notation for this would be:

$$P(\text{die shows a 3} \mid \text{die shows an odd number})$$

So, when we think about the possible outcomes, rather than {1, 2, 3, 4, 5, 6}, only the odd numbers should be considered. So our sample space becomes {1, 3, 5}. Considering this reduced sample space, how many times does the number 3 occur? Just once. So we get:

$$P(\text{die shows a 3} \mid \text{die shows an odd number}) = \frac{1}{3} \approx 0.3333$$

c) This one is also conditional. We are given the extra information the die landed showing an even number.
    The notation for this would be:

$$P(\text{die shows a 3} \mid \text{die shows an even number})$$

So, given this extra information, our set of possible outcomes becomes {2, 4, 6}. Considering this reduced sample space, how many times does the number 3 occur? Zero! So we get:

$$P(\text{die shows a 3} \mid \text{die shows an even number}) = \frac{0}{3} = 0$$

> **Key Concept**: *New Sample Space*
>
> When calculating conditional probability, you should begin by considering the given. You then reduce the sample space, or set of possible outcomes, to whatever is described in the given. You then answer the probability question using only this reduced set of outcomes.

d) This time the given is that the die landed showing a 2 or higher. So our new sample space is {2, 3, 4, 5, 6}. Now, using this set of possibilities, we answer the question "What is the probability of getting an odd number?" So how many odd numbers are there in our new set of 5 possibilities? There are two, the 3 and the 5. So we get:

$$\{ \cancel{1}, 2, \textcircled{3}, 4, \textcircled{5}, 6 \}$$

$$P(\text{die shows an odd number} \mid \text{die shows a number 2 or higher}) = \frac{2}{5} = 0.4$$

> **Caution:** Even though a die has 3 odd numbers on it, we can only count the 2 that meet the description in the given. The 1 was removed when we were told that the die shows a number 2 or higher.

e) This time, the given is that the die landed showing an odd number. So our new sample space is {1, 3, 5}. Of those possibilities, how many are 2 or higher? Two of them are, the 3 and the 5. So we get:

$$P(\text{die shows a number 2 or higher} \mid \text{die shows an odd number}) = \frac{2}{3} \approx 0.6667$$

> **Key Concept**: *Order Matters for Conditional Probability*
>
> Notice that parts (d) and (e) above are the same except for the order of the two events. Despite the similarity in the questions, the answers are different. This is a typical result for conditional probabilities. Mathematically, we would say that conditional probability is not commutative. That is: $P(A \mid B) \neq P(B \mid A)$

In all of the conditional probabilities calculated in the previous example, the key to making each of them a simple counting problem was to consider the given to be the new sample space for the probability question. This is extremely important and worth making a point to remember.

> **Point to Remember**: *Conditional Probability Changes the Sample Space*
>
> When finding the value of a conditional probability, the key is to make the given the new sample space. So for $P(A \mid B)$ we want to consider the outcomes in event B to be our new sample space.
>
> The implication of this is as follows: When calculating $P(A \mid B)$, we must answer the question "Out of the outcomes in B, how many also satisfy A?"

Let's use this idea in another example. This one involves a contingency table.

Example 5.15: *Education Level and Voter Participation (Revisited)*

The table below lists the education level together with voting status in the 2004 elections for the 221,461,000 Adult Americans. The frequencies listed are in thousands. The data is based information from the U.S. Census Bureau. The labels in parentheses are the event notation for each event. For example, E1 represents the event that the person has no high school diploma.

Does having a Bachelor's Degree or higher make it more likely that you will vote in an election?

	Voted in 2004 (V1)	Did Not Vote in 2004 (V2)	Total
No high School Diploma (E1)	12,774	20,345	33,119
High school graduate only (E2)	39,554	30,614	70,168
Some college, or associate degree (E3)	38,622	17,243	55,865
Bachelor's Degree or higher (E4)	50,209	12,100	62,309
Total	141,159	80,302	221,461

Suppose that a person was randomly selected from these adults at that time. Write each of the following probability questions using event notation and then find the requested probability.

a) The probability that the person selected voted in 2004.

b) The probability that the person selected voted in 2004 given that they have a Bachelor's degree or higher.

c) The probability that the person selected has a Bachelor's degree or higher given that they voted in 2004.

d) Is it fair to say that getting a Bachelor's degree causes people to be more likely to vote? Explain.

Solution:

a) There is no condition given in this first question. We simply want $P(V1)$. So we divide the number of people in V1 by the total number of people in the table. This yields:

$$P(V1) = \frac{141,159}{221,461} \approx 0.6374$$

b) This time we are given that they have a Bachelor's or higher, so we want $P(V1 \mid E4)$. We need to make this given the sample space for this question, so we only want to use the numbers in the E4 row of the table. (See the circled row on the table on the following page).

If we focus our attention on the row for E4, we see that there are a total of 62,309 possible people to choose from. Of those 62,309, we see that 50,209 of them voted in the 2004 election. So we get:

$$P(V1 \mid E4) = \frac{50,209}{62,309} \approx 0.8058$$

	Voted in 2004 (V1)	Did Not Vote in 2004 (V2)	Total
No high School Diploma (E1)	12,774	20,345	33,119
High school graduate only (E2)	39,554	30,614	70,168
Some college, or associate degree (E3)	38,622	17,243	55,865
Bachelor's Degree or higher (E4)	50,209	12,100	62,309
Total	141,159	80,302	221,461

Notice that the numerator does not include all 141,159 people that voted in 2004. Because we were told the person selected has a Bachelor's degree or higher, if we use the 141,159 people, we will be counting some people who are not possible (because their education level is other than a Bachelor's or higher.)

c) This time we are given that they voted in 2004, so we want $P(E4 \mid V1)$. We need to make this given the sample space for this question, so we only want to use the numbers is the V1 column of the table. (See the shaded column in the table above.) If we focus our attention on the column for V1, we see that there are a total of 141,159 people that voted in 2004, 50,209 of which have a Bachelor's degree or higher. So we get:

$$P(E4 \mid V1) = \frac{50,209}{141,159} \approx 0.3557$$

d) From parts (a) and (b), we see that if a person from this group has a Bachelor's degree or higher, then the probability that they voted in 2004 is 80.58%, compared to 63.74% for the whole group. This might make it tempting to say that getting the degree causes the increased probability for voting. However, we must keep in mind that this is an observational study, so we can only show that getting the degree is associated with higher voting probability. In observational studies, we must always worry about confounding variables such as income level that might be affecting both variables.

THE CONDITIONAL PROBABILITY RULE: *A formula for computing conditional probability*

We have seen in the previous section that it is usually best to use counting rather than probability rules to answer probability questions. However, there are situations when using a rule is the best option. Because of this, we will now develop a **Conditional Probability Rule**. This rule actually comes from the counting idea of making the given the new sample space that has been discussed in the previous examples in this section.

Let's take a look at this idea visually using a Venn diagram and see if the visual can lead us to a probability rule. We will try to develop a rule to help us find $P(B \mid A)$. As discussed previously, we should make the given our new sample space. So rather than considering all the possible outcomes to the experiment, we will only consider those that make up event A. See the shaded region below in the Venn Diagram that follows (on the left.)

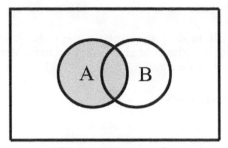

The given becomes the
new sample space.

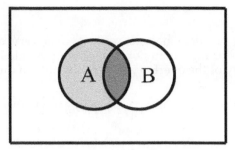

We only count the part of B that
lies in the new sample space, A.

Now, considering only the shaded outcomes in A, we would then count the number of outcomes that are also in event B. However, if you know that the outcome is in event A, then the only way for B to happen is if the outcome is in the overlap, (A and B). (See the darker shaded region in the figure above on the right.) So using the counting methods for conditional probability, we see that the denominator would be the number of outcomes in A and the numerator would be the number of outcomes in the overlap, (A and B). So we get:

$$P(B \mid A) = \frac{n(A \ \& \ B)}{n(A)}$$

where $n(A)$ is the number of outcomes in event A and $n(A \text{ and } B)$ is the number of outcomes in event (A and B). This is almost the conditional probability rule. However, probability rules always tell you how to get one probability using other probabilities. Currently our equation tells us how to get our result by counting outcomes. However, if we let N represent the total number of outcomes in the original sample space, then we can convert the numerator and denominator to probabilities by dividing them by N.

$$P(B \mid A) = \frac{n(A \ \& \ B)}{n(A)} = \frac{\dfrac{n(A \ \& \ B)}{N}}{\dfrac{n(A)}{N}} = \frac{P(A \ \& \ B)}{P(A)}$$

These results are summarized in the following point to remember.

Point to Remember: *Conditional Probability Rule*

The Conditional Probability Rule: $P(B \mid A) = \dfrac{P(A \ \& \ B)}{P(A)}$

In words: A conditional probability can be found by dividing the probability of the overlap by the probability of the given.

Let's take a look at Algebraic example to see how this new rule works.

Example 5.16: *An Abstract Use of the Conditional Probability Rule*

Given that $P(C) = 0.5248$, $P(D) = 0.4111$, and $P(C \ \& \ D) = 0.3095$, find:

a) $P(C \mid D)$ b) $P(D \mid C)$

Solution:

a) Because this problem has no context, it is very difficult to do by counting. We don't know what the experiment is or how many outcomes are possible. However, the rule should still work. We simply divide the probability of the overlap by the probability of the given. So we get:

$$P(C \mid D) = \frac{P(C \ \& \ D)}{P(D)} = \frac{0.3095}{0.4111} \approx 0.7529$$

b) This is almost the same question, but because the given is now event C, we must put that in our denominator. The numerator is still the overlap of the two events. The order of events is not important for the overlap.

$$P(D \mid C) = \frac{P(C \ \& \ D)}{P(C)} = \frac{0.3095}{0.5248} \approx 0.5897$$

THE GENERAL MULTIPLICATION RULE: *A rule for sampling without replacement*

The Conditional Probability Rule can be used for abstract algebraic problems like the previous example. However, the real power of the Conditional Probability Rule is that we can use it to generate the even more useful **General Multiplication Rule**. The job of the General Multiplication Rule is to help us solve difficult 'AND' type questions. Because the Conditional Probability Rule has an 'AND' in it, we can use algebra to solve for the 'AND' probability and we will have our new rule. The algebra work is shown below.

$$P(B \mid A) = \frac{P(A \ \& \ B)}{P(A)} \ \Rightarrow \ P(A) \cdot P(B \mid A) = \frac{P(A \ \& \ B)}{P(A)} \cdot P(A) \ \Rightarrow \ P(A) \cdot P(B \mid A) = P(A \ \& \ B)$$

$$\Rightarrow \ P(A \ \& \ B) = P(A) \cdot P(B \mid A)$$

This new rearranged version of the conditional probability rule is known as the **General Multiplication Rule**.

> **Point to Remember**: *General Multiplication Rule*
>
> **The General Multiplication Rule:** $P(A \ \& \ B) = P(A) \cdot P(B \mid A)$
>
> *In words*:   The probability that two events will both occur can be found by multiplying the probability of the first event by the probability of the second event given the first.

We learned in previous sections that to find $P(A \ \& \ B)$, we can simply count the number of outcomes that fall in the overlap of the two events. For that reason, it might seem strange that we would use a probability formula that requires us to calculate two probabilities rather than just find the probability of the overlap directly. However, situations arise where the full sample space is not given and, therefore, the overlap can be difficult to determine.

Let's take a look at an example that illustrates the usefulness of this new formula.

Example 5.17: *Selecting Multiple Marbles from a Jar (without replacement)*

A jar contains 274 marbles made up of a mixture of purple, blue, green, orange, red, and yellow. Event letters have been written after each color in the table. The frequencies for the colors are shown below.

Color	Frequency
Purple (P)	37
Blue (B)	40
Green (G)	52
Orange (O)	61
Red (R)	35
Yellow (Y)	49
	274

How does probability apply to random sampling of multiple items without replacement?

Suppose 2 marbles are randomly selected without replacement. Write each of the following events using probability notation and then find the indicated probability.

a) The probability that both of the marbles chosen are Red.

b) The probability that a Green is chosen and then a Yellow is chosen.

c) The probability that a Blue and an Orange are chosen.

d) Suppose we choose 3 marbles rather than 2. Find the probability that a Green is chosen followed by an Orange, followed by a Yellow.

e) Suppose we choose 4 without replacement. Find the probability that they are all Green.

Solution:

a) We will write this event as $(R_1 \ \& \ R_2)$, where the subscript number indicates the order in which the picks were made. So R_1 indicates that the first marble chosen was red and R_2 indicates that the second marble was red. So we want to find $P(R_1 \ \& \ R_2)$. Because this is an AND question, we can apply the General Multiplication Rule.

$$P(R_1 \ \& \ R_2) = P(R_1) \cdot P(R_2 \mid R_1)$$

> **Key Concept**: *Subscripts for Order*
>
> When sampling multiple items without replacement, it can be helpful to use subscripts on the events to indicate the order in which they were selected. For example, if we write R_2, then we are indicating that we picked a red marble on the second selection.

The key to setting up the formula here is to make sure that the individual probability, $P(R_1)$, matches the given event in the conditional probability. Also, the individual probability should always be the first pick. Now let's do the computation. Finding $P(R_1)$ is straightforward. There are 274 marbles in the jar and 35 of them are red. Finding $P(R_2 \mid R_1)$ just requires us to modify our sample space. Because we are given that the first marble picked is red, we know that only 34 red marbles remain. Also, because one marble has been removed from the jar, only 273 marbles remain altogether. Putting all this into the formula yields:

$$P(R_1 \ \& \ R_2) = P(R_1) \cdot P(R_2 \mid R_1) = \frac{35}{274} \cdot \frac{34}{273} = \frac{1190}{74802} \approx 0.0159$$

Previously we mentioned that it would be better in many cases to just count the possibilities rather than using probability formulas. However, as can be seen by the fractional form of our answer, there are 74,802 possible outcomes to consider, and they are not listed in a table for us. Do we want to list them all out to aid in the count or just apply the General Multiplication Rule?

> **Caution:** *Order is Important in the General Multiplication Rule*
>
> Technically, we could also use the formula
>
> $$P(R_1 \text{ \& } R_2) = P(R_2) \cdot P(R_1 \mid R_2).$$
>
> However, finding the two pieces required by the formula can be very difficult. How do we find $P(R_2)$ if we don't know which marble was removed on the first pick? When calculating $P(R_1 \mid R_2)$, we have to wonder how the second pick coming out red affects the first pick. These things can be done, but they are not nearly as simple as the order we used to get the answer above.

b) The sentence structure indicates that a Green was first and a Yellow was second. Therefore, we are looking for $P(G_1 \text{ \& } Y_2)$. Applying the General Multiplication Rule yields:

$$P(G_1 \text{ \& } Y_2) = P(G_1) \cdot P(Y_2 \mid G_1) = \frac{52}{274} \cdot \frac{49}{273} \approx 0.0341$$

When calculating the second probability fraction, we reduced the denominator to 273 because a marble had already been chosen. However, we did not reduce the number of yellows because we were given that the chosen marble was green rather than yellow.

c) This time the sentence does not indicate order. A blue and an Orange means exactly the same as an Orange and a Blue. If no order is specified, we must consider all possible orders when calculating the probability. So our notation would be:

$$P(B \text{ \& } O) = P((B_1 \text{ \& } O_2) \text{ or } (O_1 \text{ \& } B_2))$$

When choosing two marbles it is impossible for both of the possible orders to occur simultaneously. This means that the objects of our OR are mutually exclusive, and thus, we can use the Special Addition Rule to solve this. So we get:

$$P(B \text{ \& } O) = P((B_1 \text{ \& } O_2) \text{ or } (O_1 \text{ \& } B_2)) = P(B_1 \text{ \& } O_2) + P(O_1 \text{ \& } B_2)$$

Finally we apply the General Multiplication Rule to the AND questions to get our answer.

$$P(B_1 \text{ \& } O_2) + P(O_1 \text{ \& } B_2) = P(O_1) \cdot P(B_2 \mid O_1) + P(B_1) \cdot P(O_2 \mid B_1)$$

$$= \frac{61}{274} \cdot \frac{40}{273} + \frac{40}{274} \cdot \frac{61}{273} \approx 0.0652$$

This work above may look very complicated, however, with practice, these become very fast problems to do. After getting used to these computations, most people go straight to the multiplication of fractions and skip all of the notation. We also must remember that, if there are many mutually exclusive ways something can happen, we just add together the probabilities for all the different possibilities.

d) Choosing 3 marbles rather than 2 is actually an easy adjustment. When we apply the General Multiplication Rule, the notation looks messy, but we simply multiply the probability of the choices in order, assuming that previous picks were as listed. So if we want $P(G_1 \text{ \& } O_2 \text{ \& } Y_3)$, then we find apply the General Multiplication Rule as follows.

$$P(G_1 \text{ \& } O_2 \text{ \& } Y_3) = P(G_1) \cdot P(O_2 \mid G_1) \cdot P(Y_3 \mid (G_1 \text{ \& } O_2)) = \frac{52}{274} \cdot \frac{61}{273} \cdot \frac{49}{272} \approx 0.0076$$

e)   This time we want all 4 to be Green, so the notation is $P(G_1 \text{ \& } G_2 \text{ \& } G_3 \text{ \& } G_4)$. Applying the General Multiplication Rule simply means to multiply the probability of each choice, always assuming we have been taking greens out of the jar. This yields:

$$P(G_1 \text{ \& } G_2 \text{ \& } G_3 \text{ \& } G_4) = \frac{52}{274} \cdot \frac{51}{273} \cdot \frac{50}{272} \cdot \frac{49}{271} \approx 0.0012$$

STATISTICAL INDEPENDENCE: *When the given has no effect*

So far in this section we have been studying conditional probabilities. Sometimes, when we are told that one event occurs, it has no effect on the probability that the other event will occur. Such events are considered to be statistically independent events. We will see that knowing events are independent can greatly simplify probability calculations. Let's look at the formal definition of statistical independence and then some examples.

> **Definition**: *Statistical Independence*
>
> **Statistical Independence** (or independence): Event B is considered to be independent of event A if and only if knowing event A has occurred has no effect on the probability that event B will occur. Using notation, we state this as:
>
> $$P(B \mid A) = P(B)$$
>
> **Dependent**: If two events are not independent, then we say they are dependent.

Example 5.18: *Health Insurance and Smoking Habits (Revisited)*

A December 2011 Gallup poll investigated the link between having health insurance and various health related behaviors. The poll consisted of a random sample of 199,672 adults, aged 18 and older, living in all 50 U.S. states and the District of Columbia. The data below is based on this poll.

Are those with health insurance less likely to smoke than those without it?

	Covered by health Insurance (C1)	Not covered by health Insurance (C2)	Total
Smoke (B1)	32,722	11,568	42,290
Do Not Smoke (B2)	134,484	20,898	155,382
Total	167,206	32,466	199,672

Suppose that a person is randomly selected from these adults.

a)   Is the event that the person smokes independent of the event that they are Covered by health insurance?

b)   If the events are dependent, then who is more likely to smoke, someone with health insurance or someone without it?

Solution:

a) The events in question are smoking, event B1, and being covered by health insurance, event C1. To answer this question we just check to see if $P(B1 \mid C1) = P(B1)$. We will start by finding the answers to these two probability questions. $P(B1)$ is not a conditional probability question, so we will just use the row total over the grand total.

$$P(B1) = \frac{42{,}290}{199{,}672} \approx 0.2118$$

Next, we find $P(B1 \mid C1)$. For this one, the event C1 becomes the new sample space. Therefore, we only use numbers from the C1 column to calculate the probability. The denominator will be the total number of items in the C1 column, and the numerator will only be the part of that column that is in the B1 row.

$$P(B1 \mid C1) = \frac{32{,}722}{167{,}206} \approx 0.1957$$

We are now ready to check for independence. If the events are independent, then $P(B1 \mid C1) = P(B1)$.

$$P(B1 \mid C1) \overset{?}{=} P(B1)$$

$$0.1957 \neq 0.2118 \implies P(B1 \mid C1) \neq P(B1) \implies$$

B1 and C1 are not independent.. So, we can say that the event a person smokes is dependent on the event that the person has health insurance.

> **Key Concept:** *Dependence*
>
> When we state that one event is dependent on another, we just mean that knowing one event occurs affects the probability that the other will occur. We are not stating that knowing one determines the other.

b) Part (a) shows us that these events are dependent and that $P(B1 \mid C1) \approx 0.1957$. Now, we will calculate the probability that a randomly selected person from this group will be a smoker given that they do not have health insurance.

$$P(B1 \mid C2) = \frac{11{,}568}{32{,}466} \approx 0.3563$$

So, it appears that someone without health insurance is almost twice as likely to smoke as someone who does have health insurance. The sad irony of this is that the smoker is more likely to have expensive health care needs.

Let's investigate the idea of independence with another example.

Example 5.19: *A coin flip together with the roll of a die*

Consider an experiment where we toss a coin and roll a die and examine the results for the two objects together.

Do the results of a die and a coin affect each other?

a)   List all possible simple outcomes to this experiment.

b)   Is getting heads on the coin independent of rolling a 3 on the die.

c)   Is getting heads on the coin mutually exclusive of rolling a 3 on the die.

Solution:

a) Because there are 6 simple outcomes to rolling a die and 2 simple outcomes to flipping a coin, the Fundamental Rule of Counting tells us that there should be $6 \times 2 = 12$ simple outcomes when we do these two experiments together. We will list them below using an H for heads, a T for tails, and just listing the number for the die.

	1	2	3	4	5	6
Heads	H1	H2	H3	H4	H5	H6
Tails	T1	T2	T3	T4	T5	T6

b) To answer this, we want to calculate the probability of heads on the coin with and without the condition that the roll of the die was a 3. So we want to see if $P(\text{heads} \mid \text{die is a 3}) \overset{?}{=} P(\text{heads})$.

We will begin with the probability of heads. There is no condition or given on this question, so our denominator will be all 12 simple outcomes. Of those 12, the 6 outcomes in the first row of the table all have heads occurring. So we get:

$$P(\text{heads}) = \frac{6}{12} = \frac{1}{2} = 0.5$$

For $P(\text{heads} \mid \text{die is a 3})$, we will only consider the two simple outcomes in the given column or the die resulting in a 3.

$$P(\text{heads} \mid \text{die is a 3}) = \frac{1}{2} = 0.5$$

Because the two results are the same, we have $P(\text{heads} \mid \text{die is a 3}) = P(\text{heads}) \Rightarrow$ heads on the coin and a 3 on this die are independent of each other.

c) The events are mutually exclusive if and only if $P[\text{heads} \ \& \ (\text{die is a 3})] = 0$. To calculate the probability of an AND we look at the overlap between the heads row and the 3 column. From the table, we can see that 1 of the 12 outcomes of the experiment was H3. This shows us that it is possible for the two to occur simultaneously.

$$P[\text{heads} \ \& \ (\text{die is a 3})] = \frac{1}{12} \neq 0 \Rightarrow$$

Heads and a 3 are NOT mutually exclusive events.

> **Caution:** *Independent vs. Mutually Exclusive Events*
>
> It is a common point of confusion to think that events being independent and mutually exclusive mean the same thing. Notice that these two events are independent, but they are not mutually exclusive.

THE SPECIAL MULTIPLICATION RULE: *If the events are independent . . .*

The **Special Multiplication Rule** is a special case of the General Multiplication Rule. It applies to independent events. It can be derived from applying the definition of independent events to the General Multiplication Rule. Recall the General Multiplication Rule states that $P(A \ \& \ B) = P(A) \cdot P(B \mid A)$. However, if A and B are independent events, then $P(B \mid A) = P(B)$. Putting these together we get the following. If A & B are independent events, then:

$$P(A\ \&\ B)=P(A)\cdot P(B\ |\ A)\overset{*}{=}P(A)\cdot P(B)\Rightarrow P(A\ \&\ B)=P(A)\cdot P(B)$$

The equal sign with the * above it is only valid for independent events. This new rule is summarized and expanded in the following Point to Remember.

Point to Remember: *Special Multiplication Rule*

If A & B are independent events, then $P(A\ \&\ B)=P(A)\cdot P(B)$

Extended Version: If the events A, B, C, . . . are all independent events, then

$$P(A\ \&\ B\ \&\ C\ \&\ \ldots)\ =\ P(A)\cdot P(B)\cdot P(C)\cdot\ \ldots$$

In Words: If you know that events are independent and you want to calculate an 'AND' type probability involving them, then you can just calculate the individual probabilities and multiply them together.

Example 5.20: *Applying the Special Multiplication Rule*

As was illustrated in the last example, the results of rolling a balanced die and tossing a fair coin are independent events. Similarly, the results of several rolls of a balanced die are independent of each other as are the results of several tosses of a fair coin. Given this, determine:

a) The probability that a coin would be tossed and a die rolled and the results would be heads and a 5.

b) The probability that 4 coins would be tossed and all would show heads.

c) The probability that three dice would be rolled and all show a 5.

Solution:

a) Because these two events are independent, we will use the Special Multiplication Rule.

$$P(\text{heads}\ \&\ 5)=P(\text{heads})\cdot P(5)=\frac{1}{2}\cdot\frac{1}{6}=\frac{1}{12}\approx 0.0833$$

b) Again independence allows the use of the Special Multiplication Rule.

$$P(H_1\ \&\ H_2\ \&\ H_3\ \&\ H_4)=P(H_1)\cdot P(H_2)\cdot P(H_3)\cdot P(H_4)=\left(\frac{1}{2}\right)^4=\frac{1}{16}=0.0625$$

c) $P(5_1\ \&\ 5_2\ \&\ 5_3)=P(5_1)\cdot P(5_2)\cdot P(5_3)=\left(\frac{1}{6}\right)^3\approx 0.0046$

We have seen many new definitions and rules in this section. It is now time to sort them out by practicing on some exercises.

Exercise Set 5.3

Concept Review: Review the definitions and concepts from this section by filling in the blanks for each of the following.

53) When you do a conditional probability problem, the given becomes the new _____ _____.

54) When calculating conditional probabilities using the Conditional Probability Rule, the numerator is the probability of the _____ of the two events and the denominator is the probability of the _____.

55) If two events are independent, then one event occurring doesn't _____ whether or not the other one will occur.

56) If you want to use the Special Multiplication Rule, then the events in question must be _____ of each other.

Mechanics: Practice using the formulas learned in this section on some abstract questions before moving on to the real life applications.

57) The contingency table below cross classifies two variables for a probability experiment.

	A1	A2	A3	Total
B1	434	244	221	899
B2	270	362	388	1020
B3	406	427	220	1053
B4	286	389	365	1040
Total	1396	1422	1194	4012

a) Find $P(A2 \mid B3)$.

b) Find $P(A2)$.

c) Are the events A2 and B3 independent events? Explain using the answer to parts (a) and (b).

d) Are the events A3 and B1 independent events? Explain.

✓ 58) The contingency table below cross classifies two variables for a probability experiment.

	A1	A2	A3	Total
B1	9375	14375	1250	25000
B2	7125	10925	950	19000
B3	3000	4600	400	8000
B4	10500	16100	1400	28000
Total	30000	46000	4000	80000

a) Find $P(A1 \mid B1)$.

b) Find $P(A1)$.

c) Are the events A1 and B1 independent events? Explain using the answer to parts (a) and (b).

d) Are the events A2 and B2 independent events? Explain.

59) The contingency table below cross classifies two variables for a probability experiment.

	D1	D2	Total
C1	105	63	168
C2	177	224	401
C3	243	28	271
Total	525	315	840

a) Are the events C1 and D2 independent events? Explain.

b) Are the events C3 and D2 independent events? Explain.

60) The contingency table below cross classifies two variables for a probability experiment.

	D1	D2	Total
C1	264	513	777
C2	437	598	1035
C3	762	891	1653
Total	1463	2002	3465

a) Are the events C1 and D1 independent events? Explain.

b) Are the events C2 and D2 independent events? Explain.

61) Suppose that $P(A) = 0.415$, $P(B) = 0.388$, and $P(A \& B) = 0.222$. Determine each of the following.

a) $P(A|B)$
b) $P(B|A)$
c) Are A and B independent events? Explain.
d) Are A and B mutually exclusive events? Explain.

62) Suppose that $P(E) = 0.250$, $P(F) = 0.460$, and $P(E \& F) = 0.115$. Determine each of the following.

a) $P(E|F)$
b) $P(F|E)$
c) Are E and F independent events? Explain.
d) Are E and F mutually exclusive events? Explain.

63) Suppose that E & F are independent events and that $P(E) = 0.3891$ and $P(F) = 0.6742$. Find:

a) $P(E \text{ and } F)$
b) Are E and F mutually exclusive? Explain.
c) Explain why two mutually exclusive events typically are not independent.

64) Suppose that A & B are independent events and that $P(A) = 0.1194$ and $P(B) = 0.2010$.

a) $P(A \text{ and } B)$
b) Are A and B mutually exclusive? Explain.
c) Find $P(A \text{ or } B)$.

Applications: Practice the concepts learned in this section within the context of real world applications.

65) The following table shows a cross classification of the party affiliation and annual income level for all the registered voters in a certain city.

	Dem A1	Rep A2	Other A3	Total
0 - < $25K B1	805	873	168	1846
$25K - < $50K B2	1562	1611	370	3543
$50K - < $100K B3	1177	1284	275	2736
$100K+ B4	375	425	70	870
Total	3919	4193	883	8995

Suppose that a registered voter is chosen at random. Write each of the following in probability notation and then evaluate:

a) The probability that the person is a Democrat.
b) The probability that the person selected is a Democrat given they earn less than $25K per year.
c) Is the event that the person selected is a Democrat independent of the event that the person selected earns less than $25K per year? Explain.
d) Is the event that the person selected is a Republican independent of the event that the person earns $100K+ per year? Explain.

66) The following table shows a cross classification of the cost of a new vehicle with the type of new vehicle.

	SUV V1	Sedan V2	Truck V3	Total
0 -< 25K C1	28	75	23	126
25K -< 35K C2	53	50	25	128
35K -< 45K C3	41	20	18	79
45K+ C4	40	48	4	92
Total	162	193	70	425

Suppose that a new vehicle is chosen at random from the above possibilities. Write each of the following in probability notation and then evaluate:

a) Probability the vehicle a truck.
b) Probability the vehicle is a truck given that it cost $45K or more.
c) Is the event that the vehicle selected is a truck independent of the event that the vehicle selected costs $45K or more? Explain.
d) Are C3 and V1 independent events? Explain.

67) A 2011 survey asked 1,005 Americans if they believed that the laws covering the sale of firearms should be made more strict, less strict, or kept as they are now. The responses are summarized below together with the region of the country that the respondent is from. (Data is based on a Gallup poll.)

	More A1	Less A2	Keep A3	Total
East R1	184	120	36	340
Midwest R2	56	78	17	151
South R3	79	101	18	198
West R4	139	136	41	316
Total	458	435	112	1005

Suppose that one of these respondents is chosen at random from the above group.

a) Is the event that the respondent believes that gun control laws should be less strict independent of the event that they are from the South? Explain.
b) Is the event that the respondent believes that gun control laws should be kept about the same independent of the event that they are from the East? Explain.
c) Use conditional probabilities to see which region of the country is most likely to produce a respondent that favors stricter gun laws and which region is least likely to produce such a respondent.

68) A 2010 Gallup Poll was looking to examine the relationship between religious beliefs and opinions on terrorism. They surveyed 2,482 American adults and asked them the question "Some people think that for an individual person or a small group of persons to target and kill civilians is sometimes justified, while others think that kind of violence is never justified. Which is your opinion?" The participants could choose from Never, Sometimes, and Depends. The responses are cross classified below with the religion of the respondent. (The mix of religious beliefs was not representative of the U.S. mixture.)

	Never A1	Sometimes A2	Depends A3	Total
Muslim R1	421	52	2	475
Protestant R2	481	174	20	675
Catholic R3	310	116	10	436
Jewish R4	243	72	11	326
Mormon R5	192	46	4	242
No Religion R6	249	75	4	328
Total	1896	535	51	2482

Suppose that one these respondents is chosen at random from the above group.

a) Is the event that the respondent believes that such violence is never justified independent of the event that the respondent is a Muslim? Explain.
b) Is the event that the respondent believes that it depends on the situation independent of the event that the respondent is a Mormon? Explain.
c) Use conditional probabilities to see which religious beliefs is most likely to produce a respondent that such violence is sometimes justified and which is least likely to produce such a respondent.

69) The following chart shows the frequencies for the different scores on the Chapter 5 homework assignment for a statistics class with 44 students.

Hw Score	0	1	2	3	4	5
Frequency	1	1	5	13	14	10

Consider the events listed below and suppose one of these students scores is picked at random.
A = the score is a 5
B = the score is no more than 4
C = the score is at least 3
D = the score is less than 3.

a) Find $P(D|B)$.
b) Find $P(B|D)$.
c) Find $P(B|C)$.
d) Are events B and C independent? Explain.
e) Are events A and D mutually exclusive? Explain.
f) Are events A and D independent? Explain.

70) The following chart shows the number of goals scored by the losing hockey team in 47 NHL games.

Number of Goals	0	1	2	3	4
Frequency	8	19	15	4	1

Consider the events listed below and suppose one of these games is picked at random.
A = the number of goals is 0.
B = the number of goals is more than 1.
C = the number of goals is at most 3.
D = the number of goals is less than 2.

a) Find $P(C|B)$.
b) Find $P(B|C)$.
c) Find $P(C|D)$.
d) Are events C and D independent? Explain.
e) Are events B and D mutually exclusive? Explain.
f) Are events B and D independent? Explain.

71) The author surveyed 96 of his statistics students during the Spring 2012 semester. They were asked how many movies they saw in the theater over the Winter break. The results are shown below.

# of Movies	0	1	2	3	4	5	6 +
Frequency	32	33	12	11	4	2	2

Consider the events listed below and suppose one of these students is picked at random.
A = the number of movies is at least 2.
B = the number of movies is more than 3.
C = the number of movies is less than 2.
D = the number of movies is from 3 to 5.

a) Find $P(A \mid B)$.

b) Find $P(C \mid D)$.

c) Are events B and D independent? Explain.
d) Suppose that two of these students are randomly chosen without replacement. Determine the probability that neither of them saw a movie.

72) In January 2012, the author surveyed 74 of his car owning statistics students. They were asked how many times they had personally opened the hood of the car during the previous semester. The results are shown below.

# of Opens	0	1	2	3	4	5	6	7 +
Frequency	30	6	15	5	2	3	3	10

Consider the events listed below and suppose one of these students is picked at random.
A = the number of hood opens is at most 4.
B = the number of hood opens is less than 3.
C = the number of hood opens is more than 4.
D = the number of hood opens is from 4 to 6.

a) Find $P(B \mid A)$.

b) Find $P(D \mid C)$.

c) Are events B and C independent? Explain.
d) Suppose that two of these students are randomly chosen without replacement. Determine the probability that neither of them opened the hood.

73) Consider the experiment where two m&m's are randomly chosen without replacement from a bowl made up of the following well mixed m&m's.

Color	Frequency
Brown	11
Yellow	12
Red	10
Blue	23
Orange	17
Green	14
Total	87

Determine each of the following.
a) the probability of a Red followed by a Yellow.
b) the probability that both are Green.
c) the probability that one is Brown and the other is Blue.
d) Suppose 4 are chosen without replacement. What is the chance that all 4 will be Orange?

74) Consider the experiment where two students are chosen, without replacement, from a large lecture course that has 252 students enrolled and the eye color of the students selected is noted. The eye colors of the students are shown below.

Color	Frequency
Brown	96
Blue	66
Green	42
Hazel	28
Amber	17
Gray	3
Total	252

Determine each of the following.
a) the probability of Brown eyes followed by Green eyes.
b) the probability that both people have green eyes.
c) the probability that one has Hazel eyes and the other has Amber.
d) Suppose 4 are chosen without replacement. What is the chance that all 4 will have green eyes?

75) According to a 2011 Gallup poll, the religious preference for Americans is as shown in the chart below.

Preference	Rel Freq
Protestant	0.525
Catholic	0.236
Mormon	0.019
Jewish	0.016
Muslim	0.005
Other	0.024
None/Atheist	0.150
No Response	0.025
Total	1.000

Suppose that we are randomly choosing two Americans at this time and asking them to state a choice for religious preference. Suppose that the sampling is being done with replacement. This means that each selection will be independent of the other selections. Determine each of the following.

a) The probability that both of those selected will be Catholic.
b) The probability that the first person selected is Jewish and the second is in the None/Atheist category.
c) The probability that the one of the people selected is Jewish and the other is in the None/Atheist category.
d) Suppose that 5 people are to be selected with replacement. Find the probability that all 5 will be Protestant.

76) In May 2006, a Gallup poll asked Americans "Which comes closest to describing you: you are convinced that God exists; you think God probably exists (but have a little doubt); you think God probably exists (but you have a lot of doubt); you think God probably does not exist (but you are not sure); or you are convinced that God doest not exist. The relative frequencies for Americans, based on this poll, are shown in the table below.

Does God Exist?	Rel Freq
Convinced God Exists	0.7343
Probably Exists (little doubt)	0.1408
Probably Exists (lot of doubt)	0.0461
Probably Not (but not sure)	0.0362
Convinced Not	0.0275
No Opinion	0.0151
Total	1.0000

Suppose that we are randomly choosing two Americans at this time and asking them to answer the question. Suppose that the sampling is being done with replacement. This means that each selection will be independent of the other selections. Determine each of the following.

a) The probability that both of those selected will believe that God probably exists (with little doubt.)

b) The probability that the first person selected is convinced that God does exist and the second is convinced that God does not exist.

c) The probability that one of the people selected is convinced that God does exist and the other is convinced that God does not exist.

d) Suppose that 8 people are to be selected with replacement. Find the probability that all 8 will be convinced that God exists.

77) Suppose a fair die is rolled 4 times.

a) What is the chance it will show the number 6 on all 4 rolls?

b) What is the chance it will show the same number on all 4 rolls?

78) Suppose a player observes 3 plays of roulette. Note: A roulette wheel has 18 red numbers, 18 black numbers, and 2 green numbers. The results of different plays on a roulette wheel are independent of one another.

a) What is the chance the ball will land in a red slot all 3 plays?

b) What is the chance the ball will land in the same color slot all three plays?

c) What is the chance the ball will not land in the same color all three times? (Hint: use your answer to part (b) rather than computing this directly.)

d) What is the chance the 4th play will result in a red number, given the first 3 plays were all black?

79) Suppose two standard fair dice are rolled. A chart listing the sums from all possible simple outcomes is shown below. Use the chart to determine:

	1	2	3	4	5	6
1	2	3	4	5	6	7
2	3	4	5	6	7	8
3	4	5	6	7	8	9
4	5	6	7	8	9	10
5	6	7	8	9	10	11
6	7	8	9	10	11	12

a) $P(\text{sum is odd} \mid \text{at least one die is odd})$

b) Are the events that the sum is odd and the event that at least one of the dice is odd independent events? Explain.

c) Are the events that sum is at least 7 independent from the event that at least one of the dice showed a 4 or higher? Explain.

d) Suppose that we were to roll the two dice three separate times. Assuming that these three rolls would be independent of each other, what is the probability that we would roll doubles all three times?

80) In the board game "13 Dead End Drive", the players roll 2 six sided dice. However, each die has the numbers 2, 3, 3, 4, 4, 5 on them rather than the standard numbering. Suppose these two dice are rolled together. A chart listing the sums from all possible simple outcomes is shown below. Use the chart to determine:

	2	3	3	4	4	5
2	4	5	5	6	6	7
3	5	6	6	7	7	8
3	5	6	6	7	7	8
4	6	7	7	8	8	9
4	6	7	7	8	8	9
5	7	8	8	9	9	10

a) $P(\text{sum is even} \mid \text{at least one die is even})$

b) Are the events that the sum is even and the event that at least one of the dice is even independent events? Explain.

c) Are the events that sum is at most 7 independent from the event that at least one of the dice showed a 3 or lower? Explain.

d) Suppose that we were to roll the two dice three separate times. Assuming that these three rolls would be independent of each other, what is the probability that we would roll doubles all three times?

81) In the game of Texas Hold'em, players try to make the best possible 5 card poker hand using their two hole cards and 5 shared community cards. Consider the situation shown below:

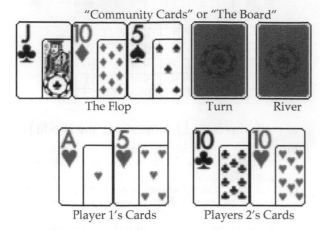

Player 1 has a pair of 5's and is behind Player 2 who has 3 of a kind with tens. There are still a few ways for Player 1 to win, but it will require both of the remaining cards. If the next two cards are both 5's, then Player 1 will have 4 fives, which will beat your Player 2's full house. If the next two cards are both Aces, then Player 1 will win with a better full house than Player 2. If the next two cards are a king and a queen, then Player 1 will win with a straight.

a) What is the chance that the two remaining mystery cards will both be 5's and Player 1 will win this hand with a four of a kind?
b) What is the chance that the two remaining mystery cards will both be aces and Player 1 will win with a better full house?
c) What is the chance that the two remaining mystery cards will be a King and a Queen (in either order) and Player 1 will win with a straight?
d) Given that Player 1 can only win by one of the three mutually exclusive ways described above, what is the overall chance Player 1 will win this hand?

82) In the game of Texas Hold'em, players try to make the best possible 5 card poker hand using their two hole cards and 5 shared community cards. Consider the situation shown below:

Player 2 has a set of Queens. Player 1 only has King high, so Player 1 is currently behind in the hand. However, it is still possible for Player 1 to win. If one of the two remaining mystery cards is a 9 or an Ace, Player 1 will have a straight. However, even if Player 1 is lucky enough to have that happen, if the other card pairs one of the community cards (including the turn card), then Player 2 will have a full house or a 4 of a kind.

a) What is the chance that the next mystery card will be an Ace or a 9 and give Player 1 the lead and the final card will not pair one of the community cards to make a full house or a 4 of a kind for Player 2?
b) What is the chance that the next mystery card will help neither of the players and that Player 1 will win with an Ace or a 9 on the final card?
c) Given that Player 1 can only win by one of the three mutually exclusive ways described above, what is the overall chance Player 1 will win this hand?

Section 5.4 – Discrete Random Variables

In this section, we want to learn how to connect the probability theory we are learning with the descriptive statistics we worked on in Chapter 3. In particular, we would like to learn how to answer "would it be unusual if?" type questions for probability experiments. Following the lead of Chapter 3, we would need to find z-scores to answer such questions. However, this requires us to know means and standard deviations. To get these, we need to introduce something known as a **random variable**. First, we will explore the notation and usefulness of **random variables**. Later, we will learn how to find the mean and standard deviation of these **random variables**. Let's begin with a definition. All of the random variables in this chapter will be discrete. We will examine some continuous random variables in Chapter 6.

Definitions: *Discrete Random Variables*

Random Variable: A random variable is a variable whose value depends on chance.

Discrete Random Variable: A discrete random variable is a random variable whose possibilities form a discrete set (gaps exist between any two possibilities). Discrete random variables often come from counting.

Example: We could roll a fair die and let X equal the number that lands face up. The value of the variable depends on chance, because each time we roll the die, the face that shows is a random event.

Notation: If X equals the number that lands face up on the roll of a fair die, then we would denote the probability that the die is a 4 as $P(X = 4)$. If this is the only random variable we are using, we may shorten this to $P(4)$.

When we are working with a discrete random variable, it is common to create a table that lists all the possible values the variable can take on together with the probability of each of these values. Making this table makes it easier to answer probability questions that may come later. This table is called the **probability distribution** for the variable. This table is very similar to a relative frequency distribution like the ones we made in Chapter 2. In Chapter 2, we often turned these tables in to relative frequency histograms. In this chapter, we will make a similar graph for the probabilities called a **probability histogram**. The definitions are shown below.

Definitions: *Probability Distribution and Probability Histograms for Discrete Random Variables*

Probability Distribution: A probability distribution for a discrete random variable is a table that lists each of the possible values of the random variable together with the probabilities for each of those values. Except for rounding error, the sum of the probabilities should equal 1, $\sum P(x) = 1$.

Probability Histogram: This is a histogram where we make a bar for each possible value for the random variable and the height represents the probability for that value. Because each bar represents a single value, the bars go from half mark to half mark.

Once we find the probability distribution and make a probability histogram for a discrete random variable, we can then begin to spot patterns in random events and event talk about distribution shape as we did back in Chapter 2.

Let's look at an example.

Example 5.21: *Number of Rooms in new homes*

A developer is building a new subdivision consisting of 179 homes. There are several different models of new homes in the development with varying numbers of rooms in the houses. The chart below gives the frequency of homes for each number of rooms possible.

Total # of rooms	7	8	9	10	11	12	13	14
Frequency	19	27	35	33	25	19	15	6

Suppose one of the homes in this development is selected at random. Let X = the number of rooms in the selected home.

How can a random variable help us examine home sizes?

a)   Use random variable notation to express the probability that the home selected has exactly 8 rooms. Then, find this probability using the information from the chart above.

b)   Find the probability distribution for the random variable X.

c)   Construct a probability histogram for X.

d)   What is the best name for the shape of the distribution of X seen in the histogram? Explain.

e)   Interpret the fact that the bar for a 9-room home is the tallest bar.

Solution:

a)   Because X is the number of rooms in the selected home, we can write $P(X = 8)$. Because there is only one random variable in a problem, we could also just write $P(8)$. To find this probability, we simply use the information from the table above and divide the number of houses with 8 rooms by the total number of houses.

$$P(X = 8) = P(8) = \frac{27}{179} \approx 0.1508$$

b)   First, we must decide what the possible values of this variable are. The homes range from 7 rooms to 14 rooms, so X could take on any integer value from 7 to 14. Or we could say $X \in \{7, 8, 9, 10, 11, 12, 13, 14\}$

We would then want to find the probabilities for all of these values and assemble the information into a chart. We already calculated the probability for X = 8 above. So, here is what we know so far.

x	7	8	9	10	11	12	13	14
$P(X = x)$		0.1508						

Now, we compute the probabilities for all the other values of x in a similar fashion and then fill in the table.

$$P(X = 7) = \frac{19}{179} \approx 0.1061 \qquad P(X = 9) = \frac{35}{179} \approx 0.1955 \qquad P(X = 10) = \frac{33}{179} \approx 0.1844 \quad \text{etc.}$$

x	7	8	9	10	11	12	13	14
$P(X = x)$	0.1061	0.1508	0.1955	0.1844	0.1397	0.1061	0.0838	0.0335

c)   You should have noticed that making the probability distribution involved the same type of calculations as making the relative frequencies in a grouped data table. So, not surprisingly, making a probability histogram for this data set is the same as making a relative frequency histogram in Section 2.2. The only real difference is that the height of the bars is labeled as a probability rather than a relative frequency.

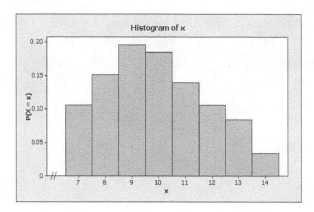

A probability distribution groups a discrete random variable as single value grouping. Therefore, the bars go from half mark to half mark.

d) The tallest bar is for 9 rooms. There are only two bars to the left, but there are 5 bars to the right forming a bit of a tail. Because of this, I would say this variable has a slightly right-skewed distribution shape.

e) Because the height of the bar represents probability, I would say that the fact that the bar for 9 rooms is the tallest means that if I were to randomly select one of these homes, the most likely number of rooms would be 9.

> **Key Concept:** *Interpreting*
>
> In the past we would have said that the fact that 9 is the tallest bar means that there are more nine room homes than any other size. Now, for probability, this height represents a higher chance of being selected.

Let's take a look at one more example to illustrate the usefulness of random variable notation and to examine a few possible variations. We will also use this example to review some of the probability calculations from the previous sections.

Example 5.22: *Ratings for the Ms. Pac-Man App*

Most online retailers give customers an opportunity to rate the items they purchase. This is true for Applications purchased from the Apple I-Tunes store. At the time of this writing, the App, Ms. Pac-Man had received thousands of customer reviews. Suppose we randomly selected one of the customers that had rated this app and we let Y = the rating given by this customer. The probability distribution for the possible ratings is shown in the chart below.

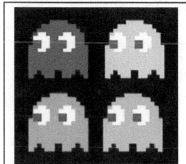

y	1	2	3	4	5
$P(Y = y)$	0.1988	0.0802	0.1256	0.1437	0.4517

How likely is it that a randomly selected reviewer would give Ms. Pac-Man 5 stars?

Assume that we randomly selected one of the Ms. Pac-Man reviews.

a) Express using probability notation and then find the probability that the rating is at least 3 stars.

b) Find $P(2 \leq Y < 4)$.

c) Find $P(Y \geq 2)$.

d) Find $P(Y \geq 2 \mid Y < 4)$.

Solution:

a) One of the advantages of using a random variable notation is that is makes it easy to reduce many probability questions into very short and simple notation. In this case, the phrase "at least 3 stars" translates into greater than or equal to 3. This problem is using the letter Y to represent the variable rather than using the standard

X. This choice is somewhat arbitrary, but it does not affect any of the work that we will do, So we get $P(Y \geq 3)$. This means that Y could be 3 or 4 or 5. The probabilities for each of these possibilities are listed in the probability distribution table. These are mutually exclusive options, so we use the Special Addition Rule and get:

$$P(Y \geq 3) = P(3) + P(4) + P(5) = 0.1256 + 0.1437 + 0.4517 = 0.7210$$

b) For $P(2 \leq Y < 4)$, the 2 is included, but the 4 is not, so we get:

$$P(2 \leq Y < 4) = P(2 \text{ or } 3) = 0.0802 + 0.1256 = 0.2058$$

c) For this one it is best to use the Complement Rule and subtract away the values we don't want. Because we want everything 2 stars and above, we will subtract out $P(1)$.

$$P(Y \geq 2) = 1 - P(1) = 1 - 0.1988 = 0.8012$$

d) The conditional probability rule states that $P(B \mid A) = \dfrac{P(A \text{ \& } B)}{P(A)}$. Translating this to our question, we get:

$P(Y \geq 2 \mid Y < 4) = \dfrac{P(Y \geq 2 \text{ \& } Y < 4)}{P(Y < 4)}$. To be in the overlap of the two events described in the numerator, Y would have to be a 3 or 4. This yields:

$$\frac{P(Y \geq 2 \text{ \& } Y < 4)}{P(Y < 4)} = \frac{P(2 \text{ or } 3)}{P(1 \text{ or } 2 \text{ or } 3)} = \frac{0.0802 + 0.1256}{0.1988 + 0.0802 + 0.1256} = \frac{0.2058}{0.4046} \approx 0.5087$$

Now that we have completed a couple of examples, there are a few key concepts worth making a note of.

Key Concepts: *Choice of Variable Letter and a Remark about the Notation*

    Choosing a Letter for the variable: The standard letter used for a discrete random variable is X. However, this is somewhat arbitrary and we are free to choose other variables such as the Y used in the example above. Changing the variable has no effect on the way we solve the problem. Starting with Chapter 7, it will be common for us to use other letters or symbols for our random variables and we should remember that this does not change how we work with them.

    Notation: In the previous two examples, we made probability distributions and labeled the probability row using $P(X = x)$ and $P(Y = y)$. This is fairly standard notation, but the use of both the lower and upper case letter can be confusing. The upper case letter is generally used to represent our variable and the lower case letter is used as a placeholder for specific values the variable might take on.

THE MEAN AND STANDARD DEVIATION OF DISCRETE RANDOM VARIABLES:

While it is true that random variable notation makes it simpler to express the events we are working with, that is not the main reason why we use random variables. The more important thing about random variables is that using them allows us to find the mean and standard deviation for random events. This, in turn, allows us to think about what the expected range of the outcomes might be, and it helps us decide whether or not a given outcome should be considered unusual or not.

The formulas for the mean and standard deviation can be generated from the formulas for the population mean and standard deviation of grouped data sets. Let's begin by obtaining the formula for the **mean of a discrete random variable**.

Recall from Section 3.4: $\mu = \dfrac{\sum xf}{N}$ is the formula for the population mean for grouped data. We then apply the distributive property to move the division inside of the sum. This yields $\dfrac{\sum xf}{N} = \sum \dfrac{xf}{N}$. Next we separate out the factor of $\dfrac{f}{N}$ which gives us $\sum \dfrac{xf}{N} = \sum x \cdot \dfrac{f}{N}$. And finally, we recognize that $\dfrac{f}{N}$ is the population relative frequency of x and, therefore, is equal to $P(X = x)$. Making this substitution gives us $\sum x \cdot \dfrac{f}{N} = \sum x \cdot P(X = x)$. Putting this all together we get the following.

$$\mu = \frac{\sum xf}{N} = \sum \frac{xf}{N} = \sum x \cdot \frac{f}{N} = \sum x \cdot P(X = x)$$

This last expression is our formula for the mean of a discrete random variable. Rather than using the symbol μ for this, we will use the symbol μ_x. The subscript of x tells us that we are working with the mean of a random variable rather than the mean of a population. So we have:

$$\mu_x = \sum x \cdot P(X = x)$$

Next, we follow the same steps to convert the formula for the population standard deviation of grouped data into one for the **standard deviation of a discrete random variable**. The conversion goes as follows.

$$\sigma = \sqrt{\frac{\sum (x - \mu)^2 \cdot f}{N}} = \sqrt{\sum \frac{(x - \mu)^2 \cdot f}{N}} = \sqrt{\sum (x - \mu)^2 \cdot \frac{f}{N}} = \sqrt{\sum (x - \mu)^2 \cdot P(X = x)}$$

Substituting μ_x for μ and σ_x for σ yields: $\sigma_x = \sqrt{\sum (x - \mu_x)^2 \cdot P(X = x)}$

The definitions and formulas are shown below.

Definition: *Mean, Standard Deviation, and Variance for Discrete Random Variables*

If X is a discrete random variable, then we can find its **mean**, μ_x, and its **standard deviation**, σ_x, using the following formulas.

$$\mu_x = \sum x \cdot P(X = x) \quad \text{OR} \quad \mu_x = \sum x \cdot P(x)$$

$$\sigma_x = \sqrt{\sum (x - \mu_x)^2 \cdot P(X = x)} \quad \text{OR} \quad \sigma_x = \sqrt{\sum (x - \mu_x)^2 \cdot P(x)}$$

We also define the **variance** as: $\sigma_x^2 = \sum (x - \mu_x)^2 \cdot P(x)$

Of course, we will practice calculating these formulas with some examples. However, the more important item for us to learn is how to use and interpret these numbers. These ideas are presented in the following Point to Remember.

Point to Remember: *Interpretation of the Mean and Standard Deviation of Random Variables*

- μ_x represents the expected mean for the values of x obtained after a large number of trials of the random experiment. Because of this, μ_x is often called the **expected value** or **expectation**.
- σ_x represents the expected standard deviation for the values of x obtained after a large number of trials of the experiment.
- The two values can be combined together to calculate z-scores for various values of the variable or to find the expected range for the variable. (See the formulas below.)
- In any single run of our experiment, we expect the value of the random variable to lie within two standard deviations of the mean and we consider it to be an **unusual** or rare outcome when it does not.

$$\text{z-score: } z = \frac{x - \mu_x}{\sigma_x} \qquad \text{Expected Range: between } \mu_x - 2\sigma_x \text{ and } \mu_x + 2\sigma_x$$

Let's take a look at an example to see how these new values are calculated and interpreted in the context of an application.

Example 5.23: *Number of Rooms in new homes (Revisited)*

A developer is building a new subdivision consisting of 179 homes. There are several different models of new homes in the development with varying numbers of rooms in the houses. Suppose one of the homes in this development is selected at random. Let X = the number of rooms in the selected home. The probability distribution for X is as shown below.

Can we know how many rooms we should expect from a randomly selected home?

x	7	8	9	10	11	12	13	14
$P(X = x)$	0.1061	0.1508	0.1955	0.1844	0.1397	0.1061	0.0838	0.0335

a) Find the mean of the random variable X.

b) Interpret μ_x.

c) Find the standard deviation of the random variable X.

d) Interpret σ_x.

e) Would it be unusual if we randomly selected a home from this subdivision and it had 7 rooms? Explain.

f) What is the expected range for the number of rooms in a randomly selected home?

Solution:

a) We will answer this question by making a table. We need columns for the values of x, for $P(x)$ and for the product $x \cdot P(x)$. First, we just fill in the given values for x, and $P(x)$. Next we fill in the column for $x \cdot P(x)$ by multiplying across the rows. The work for a few of the rows is as shown to the right of the table

x	$P(x)$	$x \cdot P(x)$
7	0.1061	0.7427
8	0.1508	1.2064
9	0.1955	1.7595
10	0.1844	1.844
11	0.1397	1.5367
12	0.1061	1.2732
13	0.0838	1.0894
14	0.0335	0.469
	0.9999	9.9209

$x \cdot P(x) = 8 * 0.1508 = 1.2064$

$x \cdot P(x) = 12 * 0.1061 = 1.2732$

The mean of the random variable is given by the sum of the values of $x \cdot P(x)$. This value has been filled into the table above, so we get:

$$\mu_x = \sum x \cdot P(x) = 9.9209$$

b) When we interpret probability, we are supposed to interpret it as the expected long-term relative frequency of the event. When we interpret the mean of a random variable, we will also look for a long-term interpretation. We say that μ_x represents the expected mean of the values obtained for the random variable after a large number of trials. So, for this particular problem, we give the following interpretation.

If we randomly select a large number of homes from this development, then we expect the average number of rooms for the selected homes to be about 9.9209.

c) To calculate the standard deviation, we need to add a new column to our table. Because $\sigma_x = \sqrt{\sum (x - \mu_x)^2 \cdot P(x)}$, we need to add a $(x - \mu_x)^2 \cdot P(x)$ column. See table below.

x	$P(x)$	$x \cdot P(x)$	$(x - \mu_x)^2 \cdot P(x)$
7	0.1061	0.7427	0.905209
8	0.1508	1.2064	0.556430
9	0.1955	1.7595	0.165795
10	0.1844	1.844	0.001154
11	0.1397	1.5367	0.162675
12	0.1061	1.2732	0.458634
13	0.0838	1.0894	0.794496
14	0.0335	0.469	0.557408
	0.9999	9.9209	3.60180

$(8 - 9.9209)^2 * 0.1508 = 0.556430$

$(12 - 9.9209)^2 * 0.1061 = 0.458634$

With this column filled in and summed up, we are ready to complete our calculation of σ_x.

$$\sigma_x = \sqrt{\sum (x - \mu_x)^2 \cdot P(x)} = \sqrt{3.60180} \approx 1.8978$$

d) Our interpretation would be very similar to the one given in part (b) where we took a long-term approach to the interpretation.

If we randomly select a large number of homes from this development, then we expect the standard deviation for the number of rooms for the selected homes to be about 1.8978.

e) This question shows us the most important use of the mean and standard deviation of a random variable. We can use them to compute a z-score for 7 rooms and then we can use that z-score to answer this question.

$$z = \frac{x - \mu_x}{\sigma_x} = \frac{7 - 9.9209}{1.8978} \approx -1.539$$

This tells us that it would not be unusual if the home we selected had 7 rooms, because 7 rooms is less than 2 standard deviations below the mean.

f) To state an expected range, we first find the two-standard-deviation boundaries.

$$\mu_x - 2\sigma_x = 9.9209 - 2 * 1.8978 = 6.1253 \quad \text{and} \quad \mu_x + 2\sigma_x = 9.9209 + 2 * 1.8978 = 13.7165$$

The smallest value of the random variable that lies between these two values is 7 rooms and the largest value that lies between them is 13 rooms. Therefore, is we were to randomly select one of the homes from this development, we would expect the number of rooms to be somewhere from 7 to 13 rooms and we would consider it to be unusual if it was not.

Caution: *Do NOT round the endpoints for an expected range*

It is a common mistake to round the boundaries of an expected range to the nearest integer. If we did this for the example above, then we would conclude that the expected range was from 6 to 14 rooms. However, because 13.7165 is two standard deviations above the mean, 14 rooms would be more than two standard deviations above the mean, and thus, unusual. We didn't round the boundary down to 13 either, we simply considered the largest and smallest values of the random variable that lie *between* the two calculated boundaries.

WRAP SESSION: *Putting it all together*

Let's take a look at one more example to review most of what we have learned in this section about discrete random variables. In this example,

Example 5.24: *Jury Selection*

Suppose that a jury of 12 is to be selected from a pool of 50 prospective jury members. The jury pool consists of 21 women and 29 men. Let Y = the number of women selected to the jury. If the all the members of the jury pool were equally likely to be selected to the jury, then the probability distribution for Y would be as shown below.

Can we use random variables to determine if there was a gender bias in jury selection?

y	$P(Y = y)$
0	0.000427
1	0.005985
2	0.034648
3	0.109720
4	0.211603
5	0.261618
6	0.212328
7	0.113747
8	0.039811
9	0.008847
10	0.001180
11	0.000084
12	0.000002
	1.000000

Assume that the members of the jury pool all had an equal chance at being selected for the jury.

a) Use random variable notation to express the probability that the selected jury would contain at least 10 women. Then, find this probability using the information from the chart above.

b) Construct a probability histogram for the discrete random variable, Y.

c) What distribution name best describes the shape of the histogram? Explain.

d) Calculate the mean and standard deviation of the discrete random variable, Y.

e) Would you consider it to be unusual if the jury contained 10 or more women? Explain.

f) Determine the expected range for the values of Y. That is, what number of women on the jury would not be considered an unusual outcome?

g) Determine the probability that the number of women on the jury would lie in the expected range. Does this answer agree with the Empirical Rule? Explain.

h) Suppose that when the jury selection was completed, the jury actually contained 10 women. Would you consider that to be convincing evidence that those selecting the juror were biased towards selecting women jurors or is it plausible that this 10-woman jury was just the result of random variation? Explain.

Solution:

a) The phrase "at least" indicates the use of greater than or equal symbol. So, we get $P(Y \geq 10)$. The different values of Y are mutually exclusive, so this is calculated as follows.

$$P(Y \geq 10) = P(10 \text{ or } 11 \text{ or } 12) = P(10) + P(11) + P(12)$$

$$= 0.001180 + 0.000084 + 0.000002 = 0.001266$$

b) We will make this in the same way as a relative frequency histogram; only we will label the vertical scale as probability. Each value of the variable will get its own histogram bar, so this will be single value grouping. This means that the bars will go from half mark to half mark. The graph is shown below.

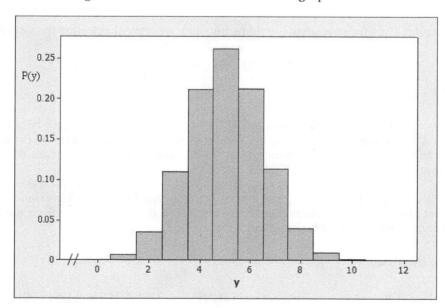

c) This graph appears to be roughly symmetric with a center peak and tails on each side. For these reasons, I would say that bell-shaped is the best description for the distribution of this random variable.

d)   The fact that our random variable is Y rather than X has no effect on how we do the work on this problem. We simply replace the x's by y's in the formula. We will make a table to find the sums that we need. First, we will use the formula $\mu_y = \sum y \cdot P(y)$ to find the mean and then we will use this result to complete the final column of the table.

y	$P(y)$	$y \cdot P(y)$	$(y - \mu_y)^2 \cdot P(y)$
0	0.000427	0	0.010846
1	0.005985	0.005985	0.097685
2	0.034648	0.069296	0.320203
3	0.109720	0.329160	0.456610
4	0.211603	0.846412	0.228869
5	0.261618	1.308090	0.000419
6	0.212328	1.273968	0.195682
7	0.113747	0.796229	0.436971
8	0.039811	0.318488	0.348808
9	0.008847	0.079623	0.138735
10	0.001180	0.011800	0.029030
11	0.000084	0.000924	0.002984
12	0.000002	0.000024	0.000097
	1.0001	5.039999	2.266939

$$\mu_y = \sum y \cdot P(y) = 5.039999$$

$$(3 - 5.039999)^2 * 0.109720$$

$$(10 - 5.039999)^2 * 0.001180$$

Applying the formula for the standard deviation of a random variable to this info, we get:

$$\sigma_y = \sqrt{\sum (y - \mu_y)^2 \cdot P(y)} = \sqrt{2.266939} \approx 1.5056$$

So, we have $\mu_y = 5.039999$ and $\sigma_y \approx 1.5056$.

Technology Tip: *Speeding up the process*

The TI-83 and TI-84 are capable of doing most of this process for you. Enter the y values into L1 and the values of $P(y)$ into L2. Then choose STAT > CALC > 1-Var Stats L1, L2 and press ENTER.

e)   Because we are asked if 10 or more women would be unusual, we should calculate the z-score for 10.

$$z = \frac{x - \mu_y}{\sigma_y} = \frac{10 - 5.039999}{1.5056} \approx 3.294$$

To have 10 women on this jury would be unusual (if they were randomly selected), because 10 is more than 2 standard deviations above the mean. In fact, this would be very unusual because 10 is more than 3 standard deviations above the mean. 11 and 12 women would be further above the mean, so they would also be considered very unusual results.

f)   To be in the expected range, the variable must take on a value that lies within two standard deviations of the mean. We will first calculate the numbers that are two standard deviations away from the mean, and then list all values of the random variable that lie between them.

Lower Boundary: $\mu_y - 2 \cdot \sigma_y = 5.039999 - 2 * 1.5056 = 2.028799$

Upper Boundary: $\mu_y + 2 \cdot \sigma_y = 5.039999 + 2 * 1.5056 = 8.051199$

The smallest possibility in this range is 3 and the largest is 8. So, if the jury were randomly selected we would have expected anywhere from 3 to 8 women to be on the jury.

g) Translating into symbols, we want $P(3 \le Y \le 8)$. So, we will just add up the mutually exclusive values of the random variable that meet this description.

$$P(3 \le Y \le 8) = P(3) + P(4) + P(5) + P(6) + P(7) + P(8)$$

$$0.109720 + 0.211603 + 0.261618 + 0.212328 + 0.113747 + 0.039811 = 0.948827$$

The empirical rule for bell-shaped distributions states that we expect about 95% of our data to lie within 2 standard deviations of the mean. For a random variable, we would convert this relative frequency prediction to a probability estimate. Because 95% corresponds to a probability of 0.95, and because we got 0.948827 for this bell-shaped distribution, I would say this does agree with the Empirical Rule.

h) In a random process, when our result is not the same as the expected value, our first instinct should be to think that this difference is just due to random variation. We would stick with this explanation if our result was within the expected range and had more than a 5% chance of occurring due to random variation. However, a jury of 10 women is not in the expected range. It is in fact over three standard deviations away from the mean. And the probability of this occurring just due to random variation was calculated to only be 0.001266 or 0.1266%.

For all of the above reasons, even though random variation is still a possible explanation for having so many women on the jury, it does not seem like a plausible one. There seems to be convincing evidence that those choosing the jury were biased towards choosing women.

> **Reality Check:**
>
> Jury selection is not actually a random process at all. The defense tries to select jurors that will be sympathetic to their clients and the prosecution attempts to get jurors that will be likely to convict. One or both of these two sides might favor women jurors in a particular trial.

The Empirical Rule discussion in part (h) above is familiar material from Chapter 3. However, it is also important enough that we will translate it all for discrete random variables in the following Point to Remember.

Point to Remember: *The Empirical Rule for Roughly Bell-Shaped Random Variables*

In Chapter 3, we learned the Empirical Rule. It specified the percentages of data we should expect to find within 1, 2, or 3 standard deviations of the mean. These percentages represented relative frequencies, which in turn are the same value as the probabilities for our discrete random variables. Translating what we learned to probability we get the following. If the distribution of our random variable is roughly bell shaped, then:
- We expect there to be about a 68% chance that our experiment will result in a value for the random variable that lies within 1 standard deviation of the mean.
- We expect there to be about a 95% chance that our experiment will result in a value for the random variable that lies within 2 standard deviations of the mean.
- We expect there to be about a 99.7% chance that our experiment will result in a value for the random variable that lies within 3 standard deviations of the mean.

In Symbols:

$$P(\mu_x - \sigma_x < X < \mu_x - \sigma_x) \approx 0.68$$
$$P(\mu_x - 2\sigma_x < X < \mu_x - 2\sigma_x) \approx 0.95$$
$$P(\mu_x - 3\sigma_x < X < \mu_x - 3\sigma_x) \approx 0.997$$

There are a few things that we should keep in mind for the Empirical Rule.
- We are not always dealing with perfectly or even roughly bell-shaped distributions. So, we need to understand that we may be off quite a bit from the above numbers.
- Statisticians usually consider an event to be unusual if it is in the extreme 5% of the possibilities. Therefore, we consider an outcome to be unusual if it lands more than 2 standard deviations away from the mean.

It is now time to practice what we have learned with some exercises.

Exercise Set 5.4

<u>Concept Review</u>: Review the definitions and concepts from this section by filling in the blanks for each of the following.

83) A random variable is a numerical quantity whose value depends on _____ .

84) When we are asked to find the probability distribution for a discrete random variable, we should make a _____ that lists the possible values of the variable together with their _____ .

85) Probability histograms are basically the same as a _____ frequency histogram from Chapter 3. The bars are done for single values. Therefore, they are drawn from _____ mark to _____ mark.

86) For frequency and relative frequency histograms, we interpreted the tallest bar to be the class with the most data in it For a probability histogram, we interpret the tallest bar to represent the value of the _____ that has the greatest _____ of occurring.

87) The mean of a random variable is also called the _____ value.

88) μ_x and σ_x tell us the expected mean and standard deviation after a _____ number of trials.

89) If you are asked if a specific value of a random variable is unusual, then you should calculate the _____ for that data value. We consider outcomes to be unusual if they lie more than _____ standard deviations away from the _____ .

90) The expected range consists of the possible outcomes that lie within _____ standard deviations of the mean.

<u>Applications</u>: Practice the concepts learned in this section within the context of real world applications.

91) The following chart shows the frequencies for the different scores on the chapter 5 homework assignment for a statistics class with 44 students.

Hw Score	0	1	2	3	4	5
Frequency	1	1	5	13	14	10

Let X = the score on this assignment for a randomly selected student from the class.

a) Find $P(X=4)$.
b) Find the probability distribution of X.
c) Find $P(X \le 3)$.
d) Create a probability histogram for X.
e) What distribution shape best describes this random variable? Explain.

92) The following chart shows the number of goals scored by the losing hockey team in 47 NHL games.

Number of Goals	0	1	2	3	4
Frequency	8	19	15	4	1

Let Y = the number of goals for the losing team if we were to randomly select one of the games from the chart.

a) Find $P(Y=2)$.
b) Find the probability distribution of Y.
c) Find $P(Y \ge 1)$.
d) Create a probability histogram for Y.
e) What distribution shape best describes this random variable? Explain.

93) The author surveyed 96 of his statistics students during the Spring 2012 semester. They were asked how many movies they saw in the theater over the Winter break. The results are shown below.

# of Movies	0	1	2	3	4	5	6
Frequency	32	33	12	11	4	2	2

Suppose we will randomly select one of these students. Let Y = the number of movies seen by the selected student during the Winter break.

a) Find $P(Y=1)$.
b) Find the probability distribution of Y.
c) Find $P(Y \ge 1)$.
d) Create a probability histogram for Y.
e) What distribution shape best describes this random variable? Explain.

94) In January 2012, the author surveyed 65 of his car owning statistics students. They were asked how many times they had personally opened the hood of the car during the previous semester. The results are shown below.

# of Opens	0	1	2	3	4	5	6	7
Frequency	30	6	15	5	2	3	3	1

Suppose one of these students is randomly selected. Let X = the number of times that they had opened their car hood.

a) Find $P(X=2)$.
b) Find the probability distribution of X.
c) Find $P(X \le 2)$.
d) Create a probability histogram for X.
e) What distribution shape best describes this random variable? Explain.

95) Suppose two standard fair dice are rolled. A chart listing the sums from all possible simple outcomes is shown below.

	1	2	3	4	5	6
1	2	3	4	5	6	7
2	3	4	5	6	7	8
3	4	5	6	7	8	9
4	5	6	7	8	9	10
5	6	7	8	9	10	11
6	7	8	9	10	11	12

Let X = the sum of the two dice.

a) Find the probability distribution of X.
b) Write using random variable notation and then find the probability. The sum of the dice is at least 6.
c) Write using random variable notation and then find the probability. The sum of the dice is at least 10 or at most 3.
d) Write using random variable notation and then find the probability. The sum of the dice is at least 7 given that it is at most 10.

96) In the board game "13 Dead End Drive", the players roll 2 six sided dice. However, each die has the numbers 2, 3, 3, 4, 4, 5 on them rather than the standard numbering. Suppose these two dice are rolled together. A chart listing the sums from all possible simple outcomes is shown below.

	2	3	3	4	4	5
2	4	5	5	6	6	7
3	5	6	6	7	7	8
3	5	6	6	7	7	8
4	6	7	7	8	8	9
4	6	7	7	8	8	9
5	7	8	8	9	9	10

Let Y = the sum of the two dice.

a) Find the probability distribution of Y.
b) Write using random variable notation and then find the probability. The sum of the dice is at most 6.
c) Write using random variable notation and then find the probability. The sum of the dice is at least 8 or at most 5.
d) Write using random variable notation and then find the probability. The sum of the dice is at most 8 given that it is at least 6.

97) A skateboard company let's you make a custom board by choosing your deck (the board) from 6 choices and your wheel set-up from 4 choices. The prices of the decks are $49, $49, $59, $69, $79, and $79. The prices for the wheel set-ups are $39, $49, $54, and $70. Suppose that an indecisive customer randomly chooses the deck and wheel set-up.

Let Y = the total price for the two parts.

a) Find the probability distribution of Y.
b) Write using random variable notation and then find the probability. The total price is at least $100
c) Write using random variable notation and then find the probability. The total price is at least $90 and at most $120
d) Write using random variable notation and then find the probability. The total price is at least $120 given that the total is at least $100.

98) A poker player has 4 casino chips in his left pocket valued at $1, $2, $3, and $5. In his right pocket, he has 5 casino chips with values of $1, $1, $2, $3, and $5. Suppose that he randomly selects a chip from each pocket.

Let X = the sum of the two casino chips.

a) Find the probability distribution of X.
b) Write using random variable notation and then find the probability. The sum of the chips is less than $7.
c) Write using random variable notation and then find the probability. The sum of the two chips is more than $4 and less than $8.
d) Write using random variable notation and then find the probability. The sum of the two chips is less than $5 given that is at most $7.

99) A class of 41 statistics students was asked to rate the "fairness of grading" for their statistics instructor. They rated the instructor from 1 (not fair at all) to 10 (totally fair). Suppose we let X = the rating given by a randomly selected student from the class. The probability dist for X is shown below.

x	P(x)
1	0.0488
2	0.0244
3	0.0000
4	0.0000
5	0.0976
6	0.1707
7	0.1463
8	0.1463
9	0.2927
10	0.0732

Write each of the following events using random variable notation and then find the probability.

a) the student gives the instructor a rating of 9.
b) the person gives the instructor a rating of at least 6.
c) the student gives the instructor a rating of at least 5 but less than 9.
d) the student gives the instructor a rating less than 7 given they gave a rating of at least 5.

100) Suppose Y = the number of people waiting in line at a certain fast food restaurant at 10 a.m. The probability distribution for Y is shown in the table below.

y	P(y)
0	0.2906
1	0.2372
2	0.1688
3	0.1384
4	0.0920
5	0.0534
6	0.0169
7	0.0027

Suppose we observe the line at the restaurant on a randomly selected day at 10 a.m. Write each of the following events using random variable notation and then find the probability.

a) the number of people in line is 5
b) the number of people in line is more than 2.
c) the number of people in line is between 2 and 4 (inclusive).
d) the number of people in line is at least 3 given that it is no more than 4.

101) College Statistics students were surveyed and asked how many hours (rounded to the nearest half an hour) they had exercised the previous day. If we let Y = the amount of exercise for one of these students, then the probability distribution for Y is as shown below.

y	P(y)
0	0.5052
0.5	0.1443
1	0.1546
1.5	0.0412
2	0.0825
2.5	0.0207
3	0.0309
3.5	0.0103
4	0.0103

a) Find μ_y.

b) Find σ_y.

c) Should we consider it to be unusual if we randomly select a student and that student had exercised 2 hours the previous day? Use a z-score to explain.

d) What is the expected range for the amount of exercise per day for Statistics students?

102) A California resident buys 8 quick pick lottery tickets for the state's Fantasy 5 game. To win, a player must match at least two of five numbers picked from 1 to 39. If we let X = the number of winning tickets, then the probability distribution for X is as follows.

x	P(x)
0	0.3798
1	0.3909
2	0.1760
3	0.0453
4	0.0073
5	0.0007
6	0.0000
7	0.0000
8	0.0000

a) Find μ_x.
b) Find σ_x.
c) Should a player consider himself to be unusually lucky if he wins on at least 4 out of the 8 tickets? Use a z-score to explain.
d) What is the expected range for the number of wins in the 8 plays?

103) In exercise (91), we found the probability distribution for X, where X = the chapter 5 hw score for a randomly selected stat student from a certain class of 44 students. The distribution was as shown below.

x	P(x)
0	0.0227
1	0.0227
2	0.1136
3	0.2955
4	0.3182
5	0.2273

a) Find the expected value of X
b) Interpret μ_x.
c) Find the standard deviation of X.
d) What is probability that X will lie within 1 standard deviation of its mean?
e) What is the probability that X will lie within 2 standard deviations of its mean?

104) In exercise (92), we found the probability distribution for Y, where Y = the number of goals for the losing team if we randomly chose from a given set of 47 NHL games. The distribution was as shown below.

y	P(y)
0	0.1702
1	0.4043
2	0.3191
3	0.0851
4	0.0213

a) Find μ_y.

b) Find σ_y.

c) Should a team that scored 3 goals and still lost the game consider that to be an unusual event? Use a z-score to explain.

d) What is the expected range for the number of goals scored by a randomly selected losing team?

105) In exercise (97), we found the probability distribution for Y, where Y = the total price for the two parts of a custom skateboard. The distribution was as shown below.

y	P(y)
88	0.0833
98	0.1250
103	0.0833
108	0.0833
113	0.0417
118	0.1250
119	0.0833
123	0.0417
128	0.0833
129	0.0417
133	0.0833
139	0.0417
149	0.0833

a) Find the expected value of Y.

b) Interpret μ_y.

c) Find the standard deviation of Y.

d) What is the probability that Y will lie within 1 standard deviation of its mean?

e) What is the probability that Y will lie within 2 standard deviations of its mean?

f) Do the probabilities from parts (d) and (e) agree with the Empirical Rule? Explain.

106) In exercise (98), we found the probability distribution for X, where X = the sum of the two chip values from a poker player's pocket. The distribution was as shown below.

x	P(x)
2	0.10
3	0.15
4	0.20
5	0.10
6	0.20
7	0.10
8	0.10
10	0.05

a) Find the expected value of X.

b) Interpret μ_x.

c) Find the standard deviation of X.

d) What is the probability that X will lie within 1 standard deviation of its mean?

e) What is the probability that X will lie within 2 standard deviations of its mean?

f) Do the probabilities from parts (d) and (e) agree with the Empirical Rule? Explain.

107) During the first few weeks after Avocado Freddy's Restaurant opened its doors in Hayward, CA, the number of burritos sold per day was tracked. The number of burritos per day, X, was a discrete random variable with $\mu_x = 93.57$ and $\sigma_x = 15.058$.

a) Find the expected range for X.

b) Assume that the number of burritos per day is roughly bell-shaped. What is the approximate probability that a randomly selected day will have a number of burritos sold outside of the expected range?

c) Assume that the number of burritos per day is roughly bell-shaped. What range for the number of burritos sold per day should have about a 68% chance of happening on a randomly selected day?

d) After a few months of being open for business, a day was randomly selected and the number of burritos sold that day was found to be 152. Is it plausible that this is just a random variation from the mean of the first few weeks or is it strong evidence that business is getting better? Explain.

108) An Amateur golfer has been playing regularly for several years. Her score for any given day is a discrete random variable X, with $\mu_x = 82.71$ and $\sigma_x = 5.7197$.

a) Find the expected range for X.
b) Assume that her scores are roughly bell-shaped. What is the approximate probability that a randomly selected round would have a score outside of the expected range?
c) Assume that her scores are roughly bell-shaped. What range for the scores should have about a 68% chance of happening on a randomly selected day?
d) Recently, she decided to take lessons for a few months. On a randomly selected day after the lessons were over, she played and had a score of 75 for the round. Is it plausible that this is just a random variation from her normal average or is it strong evidence that lessons have lowered her scores? Explain.

109) A Stat teacher is playing a game of Texas Hold'em. Suppose that he is holding the following cards.

Let Y = the number of aces and/or kings that show up in the 5 community cards (or "board") to match the teacher's cards. The probability distribution of Y is as follows.

y	P(y)
0	0.5126
1	0.3844
2	0.0938
3	0.0089
4	0.0003
5	0.0000

a) Find μ_y.
b) Find σ_y.
c) Would it be unusual if the "board" contained 3 cards that matched the teacher's holdings? Use a z-score to explain.
d) What is the expected range for the number of cards on the flop that will match the teacher's cards?

110) During a televised poker game, professional poker player Phil Hellmuth and amateur Ernest Wiggins played each other in a somewhat famous hand of poker. The cards and chances of winning the hand were as shown below.

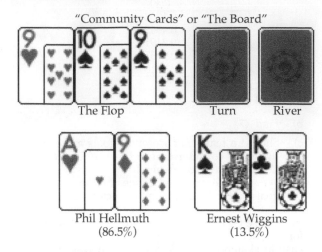

"Community Cards" or "The Board"

The Flop   Turn   River

Phil Hellmuth   Ernest Wiggins
(86.5%)   (13.5%)

Suppose that they decided to play out the last two mystery cards four separate times. Let Y = the number of times out of the four that the amateur Wiggins would win the hand. The probability distribution of Y is as follows.

y	P(y)
0	0.5598
1	0.3495
2	0.0818
3	0.0085
4	0.0003

a) Find μ_y.
b) Find σ_y.
c) Would it be unusual if Ernest Wiggins won 3 or more of the four plays of this hand? Use a z-score to explain.
d) What is the expected range for the number of wins for Ernest in the 4 plays of the hand?
e) Ernest in fact won 3 of the 4 plays of the last two cards. Is it plausible that this was just luck for Ernest or should we suspect that something "fishy" was going on? Explain.

Section 5.5 – The Binomial Distribution

In this section, we will be exploring the **binomial distribution**. The "bi" in binomial stands for two. The binomial distribution often can be used to describe experiments where there are two possible outcomes. Before we can begin discussing this distribution, we need to learn a new mathematical computation known as binomial coefficients or combinations. The name binomial coefficients comes from pre-calculus where they provide the coefficients of the expansion of $(a+b)^n$. In the statistics setting, We prefer to call them combinations because they tell us how many different combinations of x items can be chosen from a set of n items. Let's look at the definition of this new term.

Definition: *Combinations (or Binomial Coefficients)*

Combinations (or Binomial Coefficients): The number of possible combinations of x items chosen from a group of n items (if order does not matter) is given by $\binom{n}{x}$ (read "n choose x"). Combinations can be calculated using the formula:

$$\binom{n}{x} = \frac{n!}{x!(n-x)!}$$

where $n! = n(n-1)(n-2) \cdot \ldots \cdot 3 \cdot 2 \cdot 1$ and $0! = 1$ ($n!$ is read "n factorial".)

Technology Note: Calculating combinations using factorials can be a bit messy and time consuming. Examples will be shown below, but most calculators have a built in function to calculate combinations directly. Check your instruction manual.

Let's take a look at how combinations are calculated.

Example 5.25: *Calculating Combinations*

a) Compute $\binom{9}{3}$ b) Compute $\binom{9}{6}$ c) Compute $\binom{9}{9}$ d) Compute $\binom{9}{0}$

Solution:

a) We will compute this problem and the ones that follow using the factorial formulas given above.

$$\binom{9}{3} = \frac{9!}{3!(9-3)!} = \frac{9!}{3!6!} = \frac{9 \cdot 8 \cdot 7 \cdot 6 \cdot 5 \cdot 4 \cdot 3 \cdot 2 \cdot 1}{3 \cdot 2 \cdot 1 \cdot 6 \cdot 5 \cdot 4 \cdot 3 \cdot 2 \cdot 1} = \frac{9 \cdot 8 \cdot 7}{3 \cdot 2 \cdot 1} = 84$$

b) We will compute this one in the same fashion as the last one.

$$\binom{9}{6} = \frac{9!}{6!(9-6)!} = \frac{9!}{6!3!} = \frac{9 \cdot 8 \cdot 7 \cdot 6 \cdot 5 \cdot 4 \cdot 3 \cdot 2 \cdot 1}{6 \cdot 5 \cdot 4 \cdot 3 \cdot 2 \cdot 1 \cdot 3 \cdot 2 \cdot 1} = \frac{9 \cdot 8 \cdot 7}{3 \cdot 2 \cdot 1} = 84$$

The mathematical reason why parts (a) and (b) have the same answer is simple. The two are the same numbers except for the order of the multiplication in the denominator. This result should not be a surprise. Intuitively, if you have a group of 9 items, then any time you choose 3 of them, you are really separating the 9 items into a group of 3 and a group of 6. So, for every group of 3 that is possible, there is a corresponding group of 6 as well. Combinations count the number of groups possible.

c) Even though we can calculate this one using the formula, we really should be able to answer it intuitively. The only way to choose 9 items from a group of 9 is to choose the whole group. Therefore, the answer should be 1. Verifying on the calculator we get:

$$\binom{9}{9} = \frac{9!}{9!(9-9)!} = \frac{9!}{9!0!} = \frac{9!}{9!\cdot 1} = \frac{9!}{9!} = 1$$

d) This one is not as clear intuitively. However, based on the answers to (a) and (b), we should expect that we would get the same answer as part (c). Let's check this using the formula:

$$\binom{9}{0} = \frac{9!}{0!(9-0)!} = \frac{9!}{0!9!} = \frac{9!}{1\cdot 9!} = \frac{9!}{9!} = 1$$

We will now summarize the key concepts learned in the above example.

Key Concepts: *Special Situations for Combinations*

- $\binom{n}{x}$ and $\binom{n}{n-x}$ will always be equal. Just like we saw for $\binom{9}{3}$ and $\binom{9}{6}$.

- $\binom{n}{n}=1$ and $\binom{n}{0}=1$. Just like we saw for $\binom{9}{9}$ and $\binom{9}{0}$.

Now that we have practiced calculating combinations, it is time to practice using them to answer a counting question.

Example 5.26: *Practicing Counting with Combinations*

a) If order doesn't matter, how many ways can you choose 2 items from a group of 6?

b) Verify the answer to part (a) by listing all possible groups of two letters that can be chosen from the letters A, B, C, D, E, F.

c) If order doesn't matter, how many possible juries of 12 could be chosen from a pool of 68 people?

Solution:

a) It is the job of combinations to answer questions just like this. So, the number of ways of choosing 2 items from a group of 6 is given by $\binom{6}{2}$. Let's make the calculations:

$$\binom{6}{2} = \frac{6!}{2!(6-2)!} = \frac{6!}{2!4!} = \frac{6\cdot 5\cdot 4\cdot 3\cdot 2\cdot 1}{2\cdot 1\cdot 4\cdot 3\cdot 2\cdot 1} = \frac{6\cdot 5}{2\cdot 1} = 15$$

So our conclusion is that there are 15 ways to choose 2 items from 6, if order doesn't matter.

b) Order does not matter, so we will not list AB and BA, rather we will just list AB. The set of all possible pairs of this type are as follows.

$$AB, AC, AD, AE, AF, BC, BD, BE, BF, CD, CE, CF, DE, DF, EF$$

Note that there are 15 possible pairs of letters just as we computed in part (a).

c) The answer would be the number of ways of choosing 12 items from a group of 68, or $\binom{68}{12}$. Using the formulas we get:

$$\binom{68}{12} = \frac{68!}{12!(68-12)!} = \frac{68!}{12!56!} = 7.282025623E12$$

At first, this answer seems strange. We see 7.282 and we might wonder how the number of possibilities could be so small or more importantly, how could it be a decimal. The key to this answer is understanding the E12 at the end of the answer. The E12 is scientific notation and the 12 stands for the exponent on 10. So we get:

$$\binom{68}{12} = 7.282025623 \times 10^{12} = 7,282,025,623,000 \text{ different juries are possible.}$$

This next example will show us the type of two-outcome experiment that will lead to the use of combinations.

Example 5.27: *Repeated Plays of Roulette*

Suppose that a gambler plays the game of roulette 4 times, betting on the color black each time. Note: A roulette wheel has 38 slots that are equally likely to have the ball land in them. There are 18 red slots, 18 black slots, and 2 green slots. Individual plays of the game are independent of one another.

What are your chances of winning if you repeatedly bet on the color black in the game of roulette?

a) Suppose that WWLL means the player wins the first 2 times and loses the last 2 times. List all the possible outcomes that can result in 4 such plays of the game.

b) Determine an expression for the probability of each of the outcomes.

c) Let X = the number of wins in the 4 plays. Find $P(X=3)$.

d) Determine the probability distribution of X.

Solution:

a) Because there are two possible outcomes to each play (a win or a loss), there should be $2\times2\times2\times2=16$ different outcomes that are possible (from the Fundamental Rule of Counting). If we can come up with that many that are distinct, then we have accomplished our task.

WWWW, WWWL, WWLW, WLWW, LWWW, WWLL, WLWL, LWWL, WLLW, LWLW, LLWW, WLLL, LWLL, LLWL, LLLW, LLLL.

Key Concept: *Use Patterns*

The key to listing all possible outcomes is to have a pattern. In the work to the left, we listed all outcomes with 4 wins, and then moved to 3 wins, and so on. If you don't use a pattern, then it is very easy to miss something.

b) The probability of a win on any one play is found by dividing the number of black slots by the total number of slots. If we let p equal the probability of a win on any one play, then we get: $p = \dfrac{18}{38}$. If we let q equal the probability of a loss and use the Complement Rule, then we get: $q = 1 - \dfrac{18}{38} = \dfrac{20}{38}$. The key to answering this question is the fact that the individual plays are independent of each other. So, using the Special Multiplication Rule we get results such as the following.

$$P(WWWW) = P(W_1 \text{ \& } W_2 \text{ \& } W_3 \text{ \& } W_4) = P(W_1) \cdot P(W_2) \cdot P(W_3) \cdot P(W_4) = p \cdot p \cdot p \cdot p = p^4$$

$$P(WWWL) = P(W_1 \text{ \& } W_2 \text{ \& } W_3 \text{ \& } L_4) = P(W_1) \cdot P(W_2) \cdot P(W_3) \cdot P(L_4) = p \cdot p \cdot p \cdot q = p^3 q$$

$$P(WLWW) = P(W_1 \text{ \& } L_2 \text{ \& } W_3 \text{ \& } W_4) = P(W_1) \cdot P(L_2) \cdot P(W_3) \cdot P(W_4) = p \cdot q \cdot p \cdot p = p^3 q$$

If we have 3 wins and 1 loss, the answer is the same despite the location of the loss in the order of the four plays.

The chart below shows the answers we would get if we continue in the above fashion for all 16 different possible outcomes to this experiment.

Outcome	Probability
WWWW	$p \cdot p \cdot p \cdot p = p^4$
WWWL	$p \cdot p \cdot p \cdot q = p^3 q$
WWLW	$p \cdot p \cdot q \cdot p = p^3 q$
WLWW	$p \cdot q \cdot p \cdot p = p^3 q$
LWWW	$q \cdot p \cdot p \cdot p = p^3 q$
WWLL	$p \cdot p \cdot q \cdot q = p^2 q^2$
WLWL	$p \cdot q \cdot p \cdot q = p^2 q^2$
LWWL	$q \cdot p \cdot p \cdot q = p^2 q^2$
WLLW	$p \cdot q \cdot q \cdot p = p^2 q^2$
LWLW	$q \cdot p \cdot q \cdot p = p^2 q^2$
LLWW	$q \cdot q \cdot p \cdot p = p^2 q^2$
WLLL	$p \cdot q \cdot q \cdot q = pq^3$
LWLL	$q \cdot p \cdot q \cdot q = pq^3$
LLWL	$q \cdot q \cdot p \cdot q = pq^3$
LLLW	$q \cdot q \cdot q \cdot p = pq^3$
LLLL	$q \cdot q \cdot q \cdot q = q^4$

For simplicity, I have left the probabilities listed in terms of p and q. We will fill in the actual numbers in the parts to come.

c) $P(X = 3) = P(WWWL \text{ or } WWLW \text{ or } WLWW \text{ or } LWWW)$. Because these are mutually exclusive possibilities, we can use the Special Addition Rule. This produces:

$$P(X = 3) = P(WWWL) + P(WWLW) + P(WLWW) + P(LWWW) = p^3 q + p^3 q + p^3 q + p^3 q = 4p^3 q$$

Now we substitute $p = \dfrac{18}{38}$ and $q = \dfrac{20}{38}$ into this expression to obtain our final answer.

$$P(3) = 4p^3 q = 4 \cdot \left(\frac{18}{38} \right)^3 \left(\frac{20}{38} \right) \approx 0.2238$$

The key thing to notice here is that when there are many outcomes that meet the description and each has the same probability, then we can just multiply the probability of one of the outcomes by the number of outcomes meeting the description. We will take advantage of this fact to speed up our work on part (d).

d) The probability distribution of X is a table listing all possible values of X together with the probabilities for those values. We have already found this probability for X = 3. We now need to find them for X = 0, X = 1, X = 2, X = 4.

$$P(X=0) = P(LLLL) = q \cdot q \cdot q \cdot q = q^4 = \left(\frac{20}{38}\right)^4 \approx 0.0767$$

The chart shows 4 outcomes that produce one win, so we get:

$$P(X=1) = 4 \cdot P(WLLL) = 4pq^3 = 4 \cdot \left(\frac{18}{38}\right) \cdot \left(\frac{20}{38}\right)^3 \approx 0.2762$$

The chart shows 6 outcomes that produce two wins, so we get:

$$P(X=2) = 6 \cdot P(WWLL) = 6p^2q^2 = 6 \cdot \left(\frac{18}{38}\right)^2 \left(\frac{20}{38}\right)^2 \approx 0.3729$$

The chart shows only 1 outcome that produces 4 wins, so we get:

$$P(X=4) = P(WWWW) = p^4 = \left(\frac{18}{38}\right)^4 \approx 0.0503$$

Putting all these answers into a table produces the desired probability distribution.

x	$P(X=x)$
0	0.0767
1	0.2762
2	0.3729
3	0.2238
4	0.0503
	0.9999

The total for the probability column is supposed to be 1. However, due to the fact that we rounded all of our answers, we ended up slightly lower than 1. This is fairly normal.

DEVELOPING A FORMULA: *When listing the outcomes becomes unreasonable*

The technique used to answer the questions above works fine when there are only 4 plays of the game. However, suppose that we played 11 times rather than 4. Would we still want to use the same technique to find the probability of 4 wins in the 11 plays? Let's try to figure out a better method for this new scenario.

We could approach this question in a manner similar to the one used to find all the probabilities for 4 plays. However, the difficulty with this is that there is a large number of ways to win 4 times in 11 plays. Two of them are WWWWLLLLLLL and WWLLLWLLLLW, but there are many others. Listing all of these would prove to be a difficult task (there are in fact 330 such possibilities!) While it might be quite a job to list them all, finding the probability of each is not hard at all. Because each possibility would have four wins and seven losses, the probability for each different outcome would be p^4q^7. If there really are 330 such ways then the answer to this question would come from adding those 330 probabilities together or, better yet, just multiplying one of them by 330. This yields:

$$P(4 \text{ wins in } 11 \text{ plays}) = 330 p^4 q^7 = 330 \cdot \left(\frac{18}{38}\right)^4 \left(\frac{20}{38}\right)^7 \approx 0.1859$$

The big question here is "how do we find the 330 without listing all the possibilities?"

The trick is to consider the 11 plays as blanks where we need to choose 4 of them to place the wins. We would then fill in the other 7 with the losses. So the question becomes:

> For the 11 blanks listed in the box below, how many ways are there to choose 4 of them to fill in with W's?

___   ___   ___   ___   ___   ___   ___   ___   ___   ___   ___

When put in these terms, we should see that the answer comes from using combinations. The number of ways of choosing 4 blanks from the 11 is given by "11 choose 4".

$$\binom{11}{4} = \frac{11!}{4! \cdot 7!} = 330$$

Putting all of this together we see that the answer to the probability of 4 wins in 11 plays is given by:

$$P(4 \text{ wins in } 11 \text{ plays}) = \binom{11}{4} \cdot p^4 q^7 = \binom{11}{4} \cdot \left(\frac{18}{38}\right)^4 \left(\frac{20}{38}\right)^7 \approx 0.1859$$

THE BINOMIAL PROBABILITY FORMULA: *A Simpler Way*

The goal now is to generalize the work we did in the preceding discussion in such a way, that we could just jump straight to the final line of work and get our answer without spending time making charts and listing possibilities. In the preceding discussion, we saw that, to get the probability of 4 wins in eleven plays, we needed to count 11 choose 4 ways and then multiply that by the chance of a win 4 times and by the chance of a loss 7 times. So if we let the number of plays be n, let X = the number of wins in the n plays, let p = the probability of a win, and q = the probability of a loss, then we get the following. The probability of x wins in n plays is given by n choose x multiplied by p raised to the x and q raised to n − x (n − x represents what remains after the x wins are taken away from the n plays). In symbols we get the following:

$$P(X = x) = \binom{n}{x} \cdot p^x q^{n-x}$$

This discussion and formula are summarized in the following Point to Remember.

Point to Remember: *Procedure for using the Binomial Probability Formula*

The Binomial Probability Formula: If we are conducting an experiment where there are two possible outcomes, success or failure, and the experiment is repeated n times, then if we let X = the number of successes in the n trials, then the probabilities can be found using the formula:

$$P(X = x) = \binom{n}{x} \cdot p^x q^{n-x} \quad \text{where}$$

$p = P(\text{success in any 1 try})$ and $q = P(\text{failure in any 1 try}) = 1 - p$

REQUIREMENTS: The above formula can be used if the experiment meets the following conditions:
- The n trials must have only 2 complementary outcomes (success and failure).
- The trials must be identical and independent.
- The probability of success, p, must remain the same from trial to trial.

Technology: Most graphing calculators and software packages have the ability to calculate the formula quickly and easily. In the remaining examples, we will simply write the formula and then show the answer. At the end of this section, you will find instructions for computing this formula using various technologies.

Let's practice this new procedure by returning to a roulette example.

Example 5.28: *Roulette (Using the new formula)*

Suppose that a gambler plays roulette 7 times, betting $1 on black each time. Let X = the number of times the ball lands in a black slot during the 7 trials.

a) Identify a success.

b) Determine n, p, and q.

c) Find $P(X = 4)$.

d) Find the probability that the gambler wins $3. (Note: When he wins, he will win $1. When he loses, he loses $1.)

What are the chances of winning money at roulette if you play several times?

e) Find the probability that you will win money. (He will have to win more plays than he loses.)

f) Determine the probability that he will lose money.

Solution:

| Key Concept: *Identifying a success* |

a) Because we have let X = the number of times the ball lands in a black slot during the seven trials, a success will be any try where the ball lands in a black slot.

When we identify a success, we don't try to look for what appears to be a good event. We must identify whatever event is being counted by our random variable, even if it seems like a negative outcome.

b) *n* is the number of trials. We are playing roulette 7 times, so $n = 7$.

p is the probability of a success in 1 trial. There are 18 black numbers out of 38. So, we get $p = \dfrac{18}{38}$.

q is the probability of failure and it can be found using the complement rule: $q = 1 - p = \dfrac{20}{38}$

c)   We can use the binomial formula for this one.

$$P(X = x) = \binom{n}{x} \cdot p^x q^{n-x} \Rightarrow P(X = 4) = \binom{7}{4} \cdot \left(\frac{18}{38}\right)^4 \left(\frac{20}{38}\right)^3 \approx 0.2569$$

> **Technology Tip:**
>
> You can find detailed instructions for making this calculation with various technologies at the end of this section.

d)   To win \$3, he would need 5 wins out of the 7 tries. This is because, in the 5 wins, he wins \$5 and, in the 2 losses, he loses \$2. So, he ends up with \$5 – \$2 = \$3.

$$P(\text{winning } \$3) = P(X = 5) = \binom{7}{5} \cdot \left(\frac{18}{38}\right)^5 \left(\frac{20}{38}\right)^2 \approx 0.1387$$

e)   To win money, he needs to win more times than he loses, so we get:

$$P(\text{winning money}) = P(X \geq 4) = P(4) + P(5) + P(6) + P(7)$$

$$P(X = 6) = \binom{7}{6} \cdot \left(\frac{18}{38}\right)^6 \left(\frac{20}{38}\right)^1 \approx 0.0416 \quad \text{and} \quad P(X = 7) = \binom{7}{7} \cdot \left(\frac{18}{38}\right)^7 \left(\frac{20}{38}\right)^0 = \left(\frac{18}{38}\right)^7 \approx 0.0054$$

$$\Rightarrow P(\text{winning money}) \approx 0.2569 + 0.1387 + 0.0416 + 0.0054 = 0.4426$$

f)   With an odd number of plays, it is not possible to break even, so losing money is the complement of winning money. So, rather than using the binomial formula several times, we can just apply the complement rule.

$$P(\text{losing money}) = 1 - P(\text{winning money}) \approx 1 - 0.4426 = 0.5574$$

> **Reality Check:** *Is roulette a good investment for your money?*
>
> The chance of a player winning money in a single play of roulette by betting on black is $\frac{18}{38} \approx 0.4737$. By playing 7 times rather than just one, the player will lower their chance of winning down to 0.4426. When gambling in a casino (where players are always at a disadvantage), the more times you play, the lower your chance of winning money.
>
> Because your chance of winning money in a single play of Roulette is less than 50%, playing roulette is not a good investment. If you decide to play many times, it gets even worse. Never consider playing a casino game to be an investment. If you play, then you will be at a disadvantage and you will be gambling, not investing.

SAMPLING APPLICATIONS: *Applying the Binomial Formula to Sampling Situations*

The gambling applications are interesting, but the goal of the course is to learn inferential statistics. So, it's time to try to apply what we are learning to applications where we are taking random samples from populations. The type of populations we will apply the binomial formula to are called **two-category populations**.

> **Definition:** *Two-Category Populations*
>
> **Two-Category Populations:** In two-category populations, every item is identified by either having or not having some specified characteristic. Those having the characteristic are considered *successes* and those without it are considered *failures*.
>
> **Caution:** It is common for people to look for and count negative outcomes. For example, we might count the number of plane crashes in 1,000,000 flights or the number of falls in 25 snowboarding jumps.

Our goal will be to figure out the probability of having x successes in a sample of size n. This language should suggest that we would want to use the binomial probability formula to answer such questions. However, there is a problem. The typical method of sampling is sampling without replacement and that method violates some of the requirements of using the formula. Let's take a look at two examples that illustrates both the problem and the solution.

Example 5.29: *Choosing Marbles (Small Population)*

Suppose that we have a jar containing 20 marbles. 8 of the marbles are blue and 12 of the marbles are red. Suppose that 3 marbles are to be selected.

a) If 3 marbles are chosen with replacement, find the probability that all 3 will be blue.

b) If 3 marbles are chosen without replacement, find the probability that all 3 will be blue.

Solution:

How does sampling with and without replacement affect the probability of success when choosing from a small population?

a) Because the sampling is done with replacement, the probability of selecting a blue stays constant for all the draws. We can also say that, because the marbles are replaced after they are selected, that the later selections are not affected by the previous ones. This means that the picks are independent trials. Therefore, the Special Multiplication Rule can be used.

$$P(\text{all 3 are blue}) = P(B_1 \ \& \ B_2 \ \& \ B_3) = P(B_1) \cdot P(B_2) \cdot P(B_3) = \left(\frac{8}{20}\right) \cdot \left(\frac{8}{20}\right) \cdot \left(\frac{8}{20}\right) = 0.064$$

b) If the marbles are being selected without replacement, then the later selections are affected by the previous ones. This means the picks are not independent. Therefore, we must use the General Multiplication Rule and condition later picks on the previous ones.

$$P(\text{all 3 are blue}) = P(B_1 \ \& \ B_2 \ \& \ B_3) = \left(\frac{8}{20}\right) \cdot \left(\frac{7}{19}\right) \cdot \left(\frac{6}{18}\right) \approx 0.0491$$

When we choose the marbles without replacement, we lose two of our requirements for using the binomial formula. The trials are not independent and the probability of a success (blue) is not constant from trial to trial. The change caused a substantial difference between the two answers from parts (a) and (b) above. In this next example, we will see how this changes if we are working with a larger population.

Example 5.30: *Choosing Marbles (Large Population)*

This time, suppose that we have a jar containing 20,000 marbles. 8,000 of the marbles are blue and 12,000 of the marbles are red. Suppose that 3 marbles are to be selected.

a) If 3 marbles are chosen with replacement, find the probability that all 3 will be blue.

b) If 3 marbles are chosen without replacement, find the probability that all 3 will be blue.

Solution:

a) This question is just like part (a) from the previous example, except that the size of the population is larger. We use the Special Multiplication Rule due to the sampling with replacement.

$$P(\text{all 3 are blue}) = P(B_1 \ \& \ B_2 \ \& \ B_3) = \left(\frac{8000}{20000}\right) \cdot \left(\frac{8000}{20000}\right) \cdot \left(\frac{8000}{20000}\right) = 0.064$$

b) This time we are sampling without replacement, so we are back to the General Multiplication Rule.

$$P(\text{all 3 are blue}) = P(B_1 \ \& \ B_2 \ \& \ B_3) = \left(\frac{8000}{20000}\right) \cdot \left(\frac{7999}{19999}\right) \cdot \left(\frac{7998}{19998}\right) \approx 0.0640$$

In Example 5.30, we see that, despite the lack of independence of selections, we got approximately the same answer either way, when rounded to 4 decimal places. This seems to indicate that, under certain conditions, we may still be able to use the binomial formula for problems where the sampling is done without replacement.

> **'oint to Remember**: *The Binomial formula and sampling without replacement.*
>
> Sampling without replacement violates the requirements of independence of trials and a constant probability of success that are listed for using the binomial formula. However, if the sample size is less than 5% of the population size, then this violation usually has an insignificant effect on the answers, so:
>
> When X = the number of successes in a sample of size n, even if the sampling is done without replacement, X will still have approximately the binomial distribution provided that our sample size is less than 5% of the population size. Thus, in these cases, we can use the binomial probability formula to calculate the probabilities of X.

Let's see how this works with a real world example.

Example 5.31: *Are doctors hiding their mistakes?*

"Your x-ray showed a broken rib, but we fixed it with Photoshop."

According to a February 2012 LA Times article, about 20% of doctors admit that, in the last year, they had withheld information about medical mistakes from their patients. Suppose that we randomly selected 15 doctors at that time. Let X = the number of the doctors that would admit that, in the last year, they had withheld information about medical mistakes from their patients.

a) Discuss the requirements for using the binomial formula to find probabilities for the values of X.

b) Find $P(X = 2)$.

c) Find the probability that at least 3 of the doctors sampled had withheld such information.

d) Find $P(X \geq 8)$.

e) Would it be unusual if more than half of those sampled had withheld such information? Explain using your answer to part (d).

Solution:

a) There are only two complementary outcomes. The doctor selected did withhold such information (a success) or the doctor did not (a failure). The trials are identical. Each doctor sampled is asked whether or not they have withheld information about a medical mistake from their patients.

The problems arise with the other two requirements. Because sampling is done without replacement, the trials are not independent, and the probability of success will change from trial to trial. However, the sample size of 15 is most likely less than 5% of the population size.

$$n = 15 = 0.05 * 300$$

Therefore, assuming that there are more than 300 doctors in the population, we can still use the binomial formula to get good approximations of the desired probabilities.

b) Because this problem is about success (withheld mistakes) and failure (did not withhold), we need to determine n, p, and q. n is the number of trials, which, in this case, is the sample size. So $n = 15$. p is the chance that a randomly selected doctor would have withheld such information. This would be the same as the population relative frequency, so $p = 0.20$. q is the complementary probability, and thus, $q = 1 - p = 1 - 0.20 = 0.80$. We can now apply the binomial probability formula.

$$P(X = x) = \binom{n}{x} \cdot p^x q^{n-x} \implies P(X = 2) = \binom{15}{2} \cdot (0.20)^2 (0.80)^{13} \approx 0.2309$$

c) At least 3 successes translates to $P(X \geq 3)$. If we did this directly we would use the Special Addition Rule and say that:

$$P(X \geq 3) = P(3) + P(4) + \ldots + P(15)$$

Doing the problem this way would require us to use the binomial probability formula 13 times. While this is a reasonable task, it would be much easier if we use the Complement Rule. This would produce:

$$P(X \geq 3) = 1 - P(X \leq 2) = 1 - P(0) - P(1) - P(2)$$

We already have $P(2)$ from part (b). So we calculate the other two.

$$P(X = 1) = \binom{15}{1} \cdot (0.20)^1 (0.80)^{14} \approx 0.1319 \quad \text{and}$$

$$P(X = 0) = \binom{15}{0} (0.20)^0 (0.80)^{15} \approx 0.0352$$

> **Caution:** *Remember P(0)*
>
> It is a common mistake for people to forget about the probability of zero successes when working with success failure problems. Zero successes is always an option.

$$\implies P(X \geq 3) = 1 - P(0) - P(1) - P(2) \approx 1 - 0.0352 - 0.1319 - 0.2309 = 0.6020$$

d) We should probably just do this directly by using the Special Addition Rule.

$$P(X \geq 8) = P(8) + P(9) + P(10) + P(11) + P(12) + P(13) + P(14) + P(15)$$

$$P(8) = \binom{15}{8} \cdot (0.20)^8 (0.80)^7 \approx 0.0035$$

Calculating the rest of the probabilities as shown above for $P(8)$, we get the following.

$$P(X \geq 8) \approx 0.0035 + 0.0007 + 0.0001 + 0.0000 + 0.0000 + 0.0000 + 0.0000 + 0.0000 = 0.0043$$

e)   More than half of 15 doctors translates to 8 or more. In part (d), we found $P(X \geq 8) \approx 0.0043$. If the probability of something extreme happening due to chance is less than 5%, we generally consider it to be an unusual outcome. The probability of more than half of the doctors withholding such a mistake is much lower than 5%, so we would consider this to be unusual.

In the past, whenever we were asked whether or not something was unusual, we answered this by calculating a z-score. However, this requires us to know the mean and standard deviation of our random variable. If we wish to find these quantities for the doctor problem, we must first use the binomial probability formula to find the probability distribution of X and then we could use the techniques learned in Section 5.4 to find the mean and standard deviation of the random variable. This is possible, but it is also a lot of work. There is a much shorter way to find the mean and standard deviation for binomial distributions and we will explore that next.

THE MEAN AND STANDARD DEVIATION OF BINOMIAL RANDOM VARIABLES:

This next example is designed to help us discover shortcut formulas for the mean and standard deviation of binomial random variables. Once we learn these formulas, we will use them on all future questions concerning binomial distributions (success/failure problems).

Example 5.32: *Exploring mean and standard deviation for a binomial random variable*

Suppose that X is a binomial random variable with $n = 5$, $p = 0.3$, and $q = 0.7$.

a)   Determine the probability distribution for X.

b)   Determine the mean and standard deviation of X using the methods of Section 5.4.

c)   Compare the results from part (b) with the quantities np and $\sqrt{npq}$.

Solution:

a)   X can take on any value from 0 to 5. We can find the probabilities for each of these using the binomial probability formula. Then, we will assemble the information into a table.

$$P(X = 0) = \binom{5}{0} \cdot (0.3)^0 (0.7)^5 = 0.16807 \quad ; \quad P(X = 1) = \binom{5}{1} \cdot (0.3)^1 (0.7)^4 = 0.36015$$

$$P(X = 2) = \binom{5}{2} \cdot (0.3)^2 (0.7)^3 = 0.30870 \quad ; \quad P(X = 3) = \binom{5}{3} \cdot (0.3)^3 (0.7)^2 = 0.13230$$

$$P(X = 4) = \binom{5}{4} \cdot (0.3)^4 (0.7)^1 = 0.02835 \quad ; \quad P(X = 5) = \binom{5}{5} \cdot (0.3)^5 (0.7)^0 = 0.00243$$

x	$P(x)$
0	0.16807
1	0.36015
2	0.30870
3	0.13230
4	0.02835
5	0.00243
	1.00000

Rounding Note: *Exact Answers*

Even though we usually use 4 decimal places for probabilities, 5 decimal places were used on this problem to get exact answers and to remove rounding error from the process.

b) We will now add a $x \cdot P(x)$ column to help us find the mean, μ_x. We will then use μ_x to fill in the $(x - \mu_x)^2 \cdot P(x)$ column.

x	$P(x)$	$x \cdot P(x)$	$(x-\mu_x)^2 \cdot P(x)$
0	0.16807	0.00000	0.3781575
1	0.36015	0.36015	0.0900375
2	0.30870	0.61740	0.0771750
3	0.13230	0.39690	0.2976750
4	0.02835	0.11340	0.1771875
5	0.00243	0.01215	0.0297675
	1.00000	1.5	1.05

$$\mu_x = \sum x \cdot P(x) = 1.5$$

We can now find the standard deviation, $\sigma_x = \sqrt{\sum(x-\mu_x)^2 \cdot P(x)} = \sqrt{1.05} \approx 1.0247$.

c) $np = 5(0.3) = 1.5$ which equals the value of μ_x found above.

$\sqrt{npq} = \sqrt{5(0.3)(0.7)} = \sqrt{1.05} \approx 1.0247$ which equals the value of σ_x found above.

The fact that $\mu_x = np$ and $\sigma_x = \sqrt{npq}$ for this binomial distribution is not a coincidence. In fact, it will be true for all binomial distributions (success/failure problems). The results are summarized below.

Point to Remember: *The Mean and Standard Deviation of Binomial Random Variables*

If the random variable X has a *binomial* distribution, then we can always use the following shortcut formulas for calculating the mean and standard deviation for the random variable.

$$\mu_x = np \quad \text{and} \quad \sigma_x = \sqrt{npq}$$

Caution: These formulas are great because they allow us to calculate the mean and standard deviation of a binomial random variable without having to make the entire probability distribution table first. However, these formulas can only be used for binomials random variables. We will still have to use the tables and formulas as done in the previous example for other types of discrete random variables.

WRAP SESSION: *Looking for change in a binomial distribution*

Let's take a look at one final example to practice all the ideas learned in this section.

Example 5.33: *Vacation Time*

An August 2007 study of American workers found that 78.6% of them are either completely or somewhat satisfied with the amount of vacation time they receive. Suppose that we randomly sample 25 American workers, without replacement, and let X = the number of them that say they are either completely or somewhat satisfied with the amount of vacation time they receive.

a) What kind of probability distribution does the random variable X have?

b) Find $P(X = 20)$.

Are Americans satisfied with the amount of vacation time they have?

c) Find the probability that at most 22 of them will say that they are either completely or somewhat satisfied with the amount of vacation time they receive.

d) Determine the mean and standard deviation of the random variable.

e) Would it be unusual if less than half of them reported that they are either completely or somewhat satisfied with the amount of vacation time they receive? Explain.

f) What is the expected range for this random variable?

g) Suppose that a present day sample of 25 Americans is taken and we find that less than half of those sampled state that they are either completely or somewhat satisfied with the amount of vacation time they receive. Would you say that it is plausible that nothing has changed on this topic with Americans, but that this low amount is just due to random variation, or should this low number be considered convincing evidence that the current percentage of Americans that are either completely or somewhat satisfied with the amount of vacation time they receive is now lower than 78.6%? Explain.

Solution:

a) This is a success/failure problem and even though the sampling is done without replacement, I am confident that 25 workers is less than 5% of the American workforce. So, X will have approximately the binomial distribution. For this problem, a success is that a randomly selected worker says that they are either completely or somewhat satisfied with the amount of vacation time they receive.

We are sampling 25 people and asking them each to answer this question, so $n = 25$.

78.6% of the population we are choosing from feels this way, so $p = 0.786$. Thus, $q = 1 - 0.786 = 0.214$.

b) $P(X = x) = \binom{n}{x} \cdot p^x q^{n-x} \Rightarrow P(X = 20) = \binom{25}{20} \cdot (0.786)^{20} (0.214)^5 \approx 0.1931$

c) At most 22 translates to: $P(X \le 22)$. We have two options for calculating this probability. We could use the binomial probability formula to calculate all the probabilities for X from 0 to 22 and then add them up, or we could use the Complement Rule and just subtract the ones we don't want from 1. The latter option is a lot less work.

$$P(X \le 22) = 1 - P(23) - P(24) - P(25) \approx 1 - 0.0540 - 0.0165 - 0.0024 = 0.9271$$

d) Thankfully this is a binomial distribution, so we can use the shortcut formulas! (Otherwise, we would have to calculate all 26 probabilities from $P(0)$ to $P(25)$ and then use them to complete the table.)

$$\mu_x = np = 25(0.786) = 19.65 \quad \text{and} \quad \sigma_x = \sqrt{npq} = \sqrt{25 * 0.786 * 0.214} \approx 2.0506$$

e) Because we are asked "would it be unusual if?", we will begin by calculating a z-score. Less than half of them would mean X ≤ 12, so we will calculate the z-score for 12.

$$z = \frac{x - \mu_x}{\sigma_x} \approx \frac{12 - 19.65}{2.0506} \approx -3.731$$

We see from this z-score that having only 12 people respond this way would be very unusual as 12 is more than 3 standard deviations below the mean. If it were less than 12 people, then it would be even more unusual.

> **Key Concept**: *Unusual Range?*
>
> When asked if a range of possibilities would be unusual, the answer must be yes for all numbers in the range for us to answer YES to the question. Otherwise, if any number in the range is not unusual, then we would say NO for the range.

f) Any values that lie within 2 standard deviations of the mean would be in the expected range. So we begin by computing the boundary values.

$$\mu_x - 2\sigma_x = 19.65 - 2(2.0506) \approx 15.55 \quad \text{and}$$

$$\mu_x + 2\sigma_x = 19.65 + 2(2.0506) \approx 23.75$$

So if $15.55 < X < 23.75$, then X would be in the expected range. Because X can only be whole numbers in this application, we say that the expected range is anywhere from 16 to 23 people.

> **Caution:** *Don't Round!*
>
> These numbers where chosen because 16 was the smallest whole number in the range and 23 was the largest. If we rounded the 23.75 up to 24, then we would be including a number that was more than 2 standard deviations away from the mean.

g) We know from part (e) that if the true percentage of Americans that were either completely or somewhat satisfied with the amount of vacation time they receive had not changed from 2007, then it would be very unusual for less than half of those in a sample of size 25 to respond this way. Because our current sample is said to have less than half of the people expressing satisfaction with their vacation time, it does not seem plausible that they number has stayed the same. Therefore, we should conclude that this would be convincing evidence that Americans are not currently as satisfied with the amount of vacation time they receive as they were in 2007.

TECHNOLOGY SECTION: *Calculating Binomial Probabilities with Various Technologies*

This section will show you how to use various technologies to calculate probabilities for binomial random variables. For the TI 84, there are also instructions for computing combinations. For each technology, we will be computing $P(X = 4)$ for a binomial random variable with $n = 11$, $p = 0.37$, and $q = 0.63$.

TI 84:

On the TI 84, you have a choice between entering the entire formula or using a built in calculation tool. Both procedures are shown below.

Entering the entire formula: $\binom{11}{4} \cdot (0.37)^4 (0.63)^7$

1. Type in the 11 and then choose MATH > PRB > nCr and press ENTER.
2. Now type the 4 (this completes the combination, but we will enter the rest on the same line.)
3. Now type times ($\times$) followed by (0.37)^4 times ($\times$) (0.63)^7.
4. Press ENTER. (See the screen shots to the right.)

Using the built in calculation tool:

1. Choose DISTR > binompdf(> then press ENTER.
2. Enter the values of n, p, and x separated by commas.
3. Close the parentheses and press ENTER. (See the screen shots to the right.)

Using either procedure, we get:

$$P(X = 4) = \binom{11}{4} \cdot (0.37)^4 (0.63)^7 \approx 0.2436$$

STATCRUNCH:

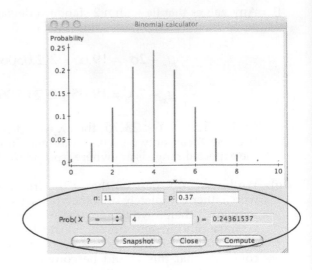

1. Choose Stat > Calculators > Binomial
2. Enter the values of n and p in the appropriate text boxes.
3. Use the pull down menu to choose '='.
4. Enter the value of X = 4 into the text box.
5. Click Compute.

Thus, we get: $P(X=4) = \binom{11}{4} \cdot (0.37)^4 (0.63)^7 \approx 0.2436$

MINITAB:

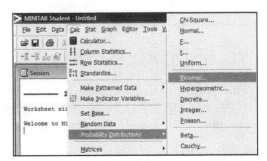

1. Choose Calc > Prob Distributions > Binomial
2. Click the probability radio button.
3. Enter 11 in the number of trials text box and 0.37 in the probability of success text box.
4. Click the input constant radio button and enter 4.
5. Click OK.

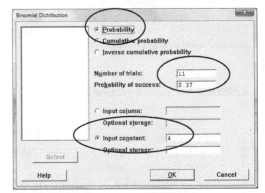

```
Probability Density Function

Binomial with n = 11 and p = 0.37

x   P( X = x )
4     0.243615
```

The result is: $P(X=4) = \binom{11}{4} \cdot (0.37)^4 (0.63)^7 \approx 0.2436$

EXCEL:

1. Click in any cell.
2. Click in the f_x box.
3. Type "=BINOMDIST(4,11,0.37,0)".
   Note: The zero at the end specifies '=' for $P(X=4)$. Use a one at the end to specify '≤' and get $P(X \le 4)$.
4. Press enter to get the result.

The result is:

$$P(X=4) = \binom{11}{4} \cdot (0.37)^4 (0.63)^7 \approx 0.2436$$

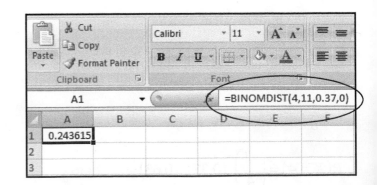

Exercise Set 5.5

Concept Review: Review the definitions and concepts from this section by filling in the blanks for each of the following.

111) $\binom{n}{x}$ represents the number of ways of _____ x objects from a set of n objects.

112) An n, p, q problem is officially known as having the _____ distribution. These problems are about counting the number of _____ in many trials.

113) In the binomial formula, $\binom{n}{x}$ represent the number of different possible _____ for the success and the failures.

114) In a two-category population, a success is defined as the item you are _____ . Successes are sometimes positive outcomes and sometimes they are _____ outcomes.

115) When we apply the binomial formula to situations where sampling is done without _____ , we need to make sure that our sample size is less than ____ % of the population size.

116) The shortcut formulas for the mean and standard deviation of a binomial random variable are as follows. $\mu_x =$ _____ and $\sigma_x =$ _____ .

Mechanics: Practice using the formulas and calculations learned in this section on some abstract questions before moving on to the real life applications.

117) Calculate each of the following:

a) $\binom{7}{5}$ b) $\binom{7}{2}$

c) $\binom{15}{1}$ d) $\binom{15}{15}$

118) Calculate each of the following:

a) $\binom{8}{3}$ b) $\binom{8}{5}$

c) $\binom{9}{0}$ d) $\binom{9}{1}$

119) Suppose that X is a random variable with the binomial distribution with $n=6$ and $p=0.73$.
a) Find $P(X=4)$.
b) Find the probability distribution of X.
c) Construct a probability histogram for X.
d) What distribution shape best describes this random variable? Explain.
e) Use the shortcut formulas to find μ_x and σ_x.

120) Suppose that X is a random variable with the binomial distribution with $n=7$ and $p=0.28$.
a) Find $P(X=2)$.
b) Find the probability distribution of X.
c) Construct a probability histogram for X.
d) What distribution shape best describes this random variable? Explain.
e) Use the shortcut formulas to find μ_x and σ_x.

121) Suppose that X is a random variable with the binomial distribution with $n=11$ and $p=0.563$.
a) Find $P(X=8)$.
b) Find the probability distribution of X.
c) Construct a probability histogram for X.
d) What distribution shape best describes this random variable? Explain.
e) Use the shortcut formulas to find μ_x and σ_x.

122) Suppose that X is a random variable with the binomial distribution with $n=12$ and $p=0.471$.
a) Find $P(X=10)$.
b) Find the probability distribution of X.
c) Construct a probability histogram for X.
d) What distribution shape best describes this random variable? Explain.
e) Use the shortcut formulas to find μ_x and σ_x.

Applications: Practice the concepts learned in this section within the context of real world applications.

123) If 20 people are in a room and everyone shakes hands with everyone, then how many handshakes take place?

124) A reality TV show takes 18 people and randomly splits them into two teams of 9. How many different combinations are possible for one of the teams of 9 people?

125) A coin is tossed 3 times. One possible outcome would be heads first, tails second, and heads third. We would write this outcome as HTH.
   a) List all the possible outcomes (including the one shown above).
   b) Find the probability of each outcome.
   c) Find the probability that the 3 tosses will result in 2 heads followed by a tail.
   d) Find the probability that the 3 tosses will result in 2 heads and a tail.
   e) Let X = the number of heads in the 3 tosses. Determine the probability distribution of X using your answer to part (b).
   f) Find μ_x and σ_x using your answer to part (e) and the tables and formulas method from Section 5.4.

126) A person plays roulette 4 times betting on Red each time. Recall: there are 18 red numbers, 18 black numbers, and 2 green numbers. We will let X = the number of wins in the 4 plays. One possible outcome would be win the first two and lose the last 2, this would be listed as WWLL and would produce the value X = 2.
   a) List all the possible outcomes (including the one shown above).
   b) Find the probability of each outcome.
   c) Find the probability that the 4 plays will result in 2 wins followed by 2 losses.
   d) Find the probability that the 4 plays will result in 2 wins and 2 losses.
   e) Determine the probability distribution of X using your answer to part (b).
   f) Find μ_x and σ_x using your answer to part (e) and the tables and formulas method from Section 5.4.

127) A coin is tossed 3 times. Let X = the number of heads in the three tosses.
   a) Determine n, p, and q.
   b) Determine the probability distribution of X using the binomial probability formula.
   c) Find μ_x and σ_x using the shortcut formulas from this section.

128) A person plays roulette 4 times betting on Red each time. Recall: there are 18 red numbers, 18 black numbers, and 2 green numbers. We will let X = the number of wins in the 4 plays.
   a) Determine n, p, and q.
   b) Determine the probability distribution of X using the binomial probability formula.
   c) Find μ_x and σ_x using the shortcut formulas from this section.

129) In October of 2011, shortly after the Occupy Wall Street movement got started, a Rasmussen poll estimated that 33% of Americans approved of the movement. Suppose a random sample of 8 Americans was taken at that time and we let X = the number who approved of the occupy wall street movement.
   a) Determine n, p, and q.
   b) Find the probability that the first 3 people selected would approve of the movement and the last 5 would not.
   c) Find the probability that 3 of the people selected would approve of the movement and 5 would not.
   d) Determine the probability distribution of X using the binomial probability formula.
   e) Find μ_x and σ_x using the shortcut formulas from this section.

130) On September 4, 2011, a Real Clear Politics poll estimated that 44.8% of likely voters would vote for Barack Obama against the Republican nominee the next year in the general election. Suppose we took a random sample of 7 registered voters at that time and let X = the number who said they would vote for Obama in the next year's election.
   a) Determine n, p, and q.
   b) Find the probability that the first 5 of the 7 people would say they would vote for Obama.
   c) Find the probability that 5 of those selected would say they would vote for Obama and 2 would not.
   d) Determine the probability distribution of X using the binomial probability formula.
   e) Find μ_x and σ_x using the shortcut formulas from this section.

131) A city has a population of 1,349,856 people. 11.43% of them are left-handed. Suppose that we randomly selected 9 of them and let X = the number of those selected that are left-handed.
   a) Determine the probability distribution of X.
   b) Construct a probability histogram for X.
   c) What distribution shape best describes this random variable? Explain.
   d) Calculate μ_x and σ_x.
   e) Find the probability that the number of lefties selected would lie within 1 standard deviation of the mean.
   f) Discuss how your answer to part (e) compares with the Empirical Rule.

132) Comparative psychologist Damian Scarf of the University of Otago in New Zealand trained pigeons to peck clusters of items in ascending numerical order. After a year of training, the pigeons were doing this correctly about 74% of the time. Suppose that we had one of these pigeons answer 10 such questions and let X = the number of questions answered correctly.
a) Determine the probability distribution of X.
b) Construct a probability histogram for X.
c) What distribution shape best describes this random variable? Explain.
d) Calculate μ_x and σ_x.
e) Find the probability that the number of correct answers would lie within 1 standard deviation of the mean.
f) Discuss how your answer to part (e) compares with the Empirical Rule.

133) A September 2011 Rasmussen study found that 72% of Americans had gone to a cookout that summer. Suppose that we randomly sampled 40 Americans at that time and let X = the number that had been to a cookout.
a) Calculate the probability that exactly 30 of them had been to a cookout that summer.
b) Calculate $P(25 < X \le 30)$.
c) Calculate μ_x and σ_x.
d) Would it be considered unusual if the number that had been to a cookout was at most 25 people? Explain.
e) Find the expected range for the number of people out of the 40 selected that would have been to a cookout that summer.

134) A December 2009 article by the FINRA Investor Education Foundation reported that 54% of Americans said that in the last year, they had always paid off their credit cards in full. Suppose that we randomly sampled 37 Americans at that time and let X = the number that had always paid off their credit cards in full during the past year.
a) Calculate the probability that exactly 20 of them had paid off their credit cards in full during the past year.
b) Calculate $P(15 \le X < 20)$.
c) Calculate μ_x and σ_x.
d) Would it be considered unusual if the number that had paid off their cards in full was at least 25 people? Explain.
e) Find the expected range for the number of people out of the 37 selected that would have always paid off their credit cards in full during the past year.

135) According to 2008 data from the CDC, 10% of non-smokers had not been to a dentist in at least five years. Suppose that we randomly selected 48 non-smokers and let X = the number that had not been to the dentist in at least 5 years.
a) Calculate $P(X = 10)$.
b) Calculate $P(X \ge 3)$.
c) Calculate μ_x and σ_x.
d) Would it be considered unusual if 10 or more of those selected had not been to the dentist in at least 5 years? Explain.
e) Suppose that we randomly sampled 48 smokers and found that 10 of them had not been to the dentist in at least 5 years. Would you say that it seems plausible that 10% of smokers have not been to the dentist in at least 5 years and that this higher number is just due to random variation? Or would you consider this to be strong evidence that the percentage of smokers that have not visited the dentist for at least 5 years is higher than it is for non-smokers? Explain.

136) According to a July 2011 New York Times article, "A History of College Grade Inflation", only 15% of the grades given to college students in 1960 were A grades. Suppose that we randomly selected 42 college students from 1960 and let X = the number that had received an A grade in a randomly selected course.
a) Calculate $P(X = 18)$.
b) Calculate $P(X \ge 3)$.
c) Calculate μ_x and σ_x.
d) Would it be considered unusual if 18 or more of those selected had received A grades in the specified course? Explain.
e) Suppose that we randomly sampled 42 college students from 2012 and found that 18 of them had received A grades in a specified course. Would you say that it seems plausible that 15% of college grades are still A's and that this higher number is just due to random variation? Or would you consider this to be strong evidence that the percentage of grades given in college courses has increased since 1960? Explain.

137) 62.5% of the students who complete statistics class at Chabot College are female. Suppose we randomly select 25 students who completed statistics at Chabot. Let X = the number of those selected that are female.
a) Find $P(X = 12)$.
b) Find $P(11 \le X < 15)$.
c) Find $P(X \le 22)$.
d) Find and interpret μ_x.
e) Find σ_x.
f) Would it be unusual if 20 of those selected were female? Explain using a z-score.
g) What is the expected range for the number of female students in the sample?

138) According to the Nielson Media Group, the highest rated Super Bowl ever was the game in 1982 between San Francisco and Cincinnati. Nielson estimates that 49.1% of households watched that game. Suppose that at that time we sampled 18 households that had TVs and we let X = the number that said they watched that Super Bowl.

a) Find $P(X=5)$.

b) Find $P(7<X\le 11)$.

c) Find $P(X>4)$.

d) Find and interpret μ_x.

e) Find σ_x.

f) Would it be unusual if none of those selected watched that game? Explain using a z-score.

g) What is the expected range for the number of households in the sample that watched?

139) The best pair of starting cards to have in the game of Texas Hold'em is pocket Aces or AA. If this hand is up against another player holding 87 suited (an 8 and 7 of the same suit), then the player with the Aces will win 76.8% of the time (assuming both hands commit to play to the end without folding).

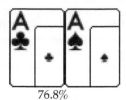 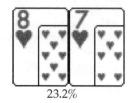

76.8%   23.2%

Suppose these hands are matched up with each other 11 times and we let X = the number of wins for the Aces.

a) Find $P(X\ge 8)$.

b) Find μ_x and σ_x.

c) Would it be unusual if the Aces won every time? Explain using a z-score.

d) What is the expected range for the number of wins for the Aces?

Suppose these hands are matched up with each other 101 times and we let X = the number of wins for the Aces.

e) Find μ_x and σ_x.

f) Would it be unusual if the Aces won every time? Explain using a z-score.

g) What is the expected range for the number of wins for the Aces?

h) Should a player who starts the hand holding two Aces feel cheated if they do not win the hand? Explain.

140) In the game of Texas Hold'em, a pocket pair versus two bigger cards is considered a classic race because the two hands have almost the same chance of winning. An example of such cards is shown below with their chances of winning.

 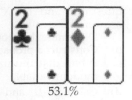

46.9%   53.1%

Suppose these hands are matched up with each other 11 times and we let X = the number of wins for the Ace/King hand.

a) Find the chance that the Ace/King hand will win over half the time. $P(X\ge 6)$.

b) Find μ_x and σ_x.

c) Would it be unusual if the Ace/King won at least 6 times? Explain using a z-score.

d) What is the expected range for the number of wins for the Ace/King?

Suppose these hands are matched up with each other 1001 times and we let X = the number of wins for the Ace / King hand.

e) Find μ_x and σ_x.

f) Would it be unusual if the Ace/King won at least 501 times? Explain using a z-score.

g) What is the expected range for the number of wins for the Ace/King?

h) Would you say that this is a fair race? Explain.

Chapter Problem – The Art of the Chase

For most of the history of poker, it was seen as a game of luck played by gamblers. In 1986, professional poker player, Billy Baxter sued the U.S. government for a tax refund claiming that his poker playing should be seen as a business entitled to deductions for expenses, travel costs etc. Baxter was successful in his case arguing that his profits were not the result of luck, but skill. One of the findings of the court was "The money, once bet, would have produced no income without the application of Baxter's skills." Since this time, most of those familiar with poker will concede that skill does play a roll in poker success. After that, a new debate was opened up: Is the primary skill needed to be successful the psychological ability to "read" people or is the primary skill the application of mathematics?

Does statistical and mathematical knowledge win out over luck or psychology in poker?

Until around 2003, most people would have argued the psychological people reading skills were more important than the math. However, around that time, many people began playing poker against others on online poker sites. On these sites, you had no visual or audio contact with your opponent. Because of this, many players started spending more time studying the mathematical and statistical strategies that could be used in poker. These players soon rose to the top of the professional poker player ranks. Now, virtually all professional poker players understand that mathematical and statistical analysis can greatly improve their results.

In this problem, we will use the skills we have learned in this chapter to get a glimpse at how probability and expected values help poker players make better decisions.

In the game of Texas Hold'em, it is common to be confident that you are behind in the hand, but to still need to decide whether or not to call a bet. You might still call because you are hoping to get a card that will put you ahead by the end. This is known as drawing or chasing. In this problem, we will use the knowledge we have gained in this chapter to fully analyze a chasing situation in Texas Hold'em. So here is the scenario. A professional poker player is playing no limit Texas Hold'em. Before the flop, he has a pair of Kings.

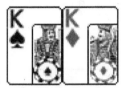

The Pro's Cards

Let's suppose that before the flop he bet $100 and one opponent called the $100 and all other players folded leaving an extra $30 in blinds in the pot. This made the pot have a total of $230 in it. The Flop comes as follows.

"Community Cards"

The Flop   Turn   River

This seems like a good flop for the professional player. Unless his opponent has two hearts for a flush, he has the best hand. He is somewhat afraid that his opponent might have one heart and could make a flush and beat him if another heart comes on the next card, the "turn". He decides that he needs to make a big bet to keep his opponent from catching up with him. He bets the size of the pot $230. Without hesitation, his opponent moves her remaining $600 "all-in". $230 of this amount is a call of the professional's bet; the other $370 represents a raise that the pro must call if he wishes to stay in the hand. The pot now has $1060 in it and, if the pro wishes to stay in the hand, he will now have to put in an additional $370, otherwise he must fold his hand. There will be no further betting if the pro calls because his opponent is "all-in".

Now that his opponent has quickly put all her money in the pot, the pro is convinced that she must have two hearts for a flush. (Which two hearts she has is actually irrelevant, but let's say it is the Ace and the Jack of hearts.)

The Opponent's Cards

So, the pro is sure that his opponent has a better hand. Should he cut his losses, fold the hand, and save the $370 for a better time? Or should he call and hope to get lucky and make a full house or 4-of-a-kind, snatching victory from the jaws of defeat? There are two cards left to come. The pro will win if one or both of the next two cards creates a pair in the community cards. So, he needs to do some math to decide what to do here. The first thing that the professional player needs to know is his chances of winning the hand. The exact calculations are a bit too messy for most players to do at the table. However, most good players have tricks to estimate their chances quickly or they have common situations like this one memorized. The chances for each player are as follows:

34.44%   65.56%

Now that he knows his chance of winning the hand, he needs to decide if it makes sense to call. To make this decision, he needs to calculate the expected value of a call. If the expected value is positive, then calling would be profitable in the long run. If the expected value is negative, then calling would lose money in the long run. We will let X = the amount of money won or lost as a result of his call. If he calls and wins the hand, he will win $1060, but if he calls and loses, then his call costs him an extra $370 that he would have saved if he folded. Let's do the math for him.

1) a) Complete the table below.

	x	$P(x)$	$x \cdot P(x)$
We call & win	1060	0.3444	
We call & lose	-370	0.6556	
		1.0000	

    b) Find and interpret the expected value of the variable.
    c) Should the poker pro make this call? Explain.

Now, let's see why this decision makes sense. We should always analyze probability by looking at the long run. Let's suppose that the professional finds himself in this situation 10 times and called every time. Let Y = the number of wins in the 10 times.

2) a) Determine μ_y and σ_y.
    b) Determine the expected range for the number of wins in the 10 tries.
    c) If he won the minimum number of times from part (b) how much would he win or lose?
    d) If he won the maximum number of times from part (b) how much would he win or lose?
    e) Does calling in this situation mean that he *expects* to see a profit after 10 such hands? Explain.

3) Repeat (a-e) of part (2) if Y = the number of wins in 1000 such situations.

Chapter 5: Technology Project

Use the technology of your choice to complete the problems below.

1) In this problem we will simulate rolling a using the "Die Simulator" application from the StatSims folder.
   a) Enter your name in the textbox provided and change the sample size to 600.
   B) If this is a fair die, then what would you expect the count to be for each number after 600 rolls?
   C) If this is a fair die, then what would you expect the percent to be for each number after 600 rolls?
   d) Click 'Roll Once' a few times and then click 'Automatic' to finish the 600 rolls.
   e) Use "ALT / PrintScreen" to copy then window and then paste it to word. Use Re-Draw if needed.
   F) Which number's count was furthest from what you expected? How many was it off by?
   G) Which number's percent was furthest from what you expected? How much was the percent off by?
   H) Click 'Clear'. Change the sample size to 600000 (Do not use comma in 600,000). How, if at all, does this change affect the expected counts and percents for each number? Click the 'Automatic' button.
   i) Use "ALT / PrintScreen" to copy the window and then paste it to word.
   J) Which number's count was furthest from what you expected? How many was it off by?
   K) Which number's percent was furthest from what you expected? How much was the percent off by?
   L) What shape would you say the histogram has taken on? Explain.

2) This problem uses statistical software to calculate the mean and standard deviation of a random variable.
   a) Enter or load the y-values from exercise (100) from Section 5.4 into one column & and enter the probabilities into another, then name them "y" and "P(y)".
   b) Have the software create a new $y \cdot P(y)$ column by using the two columns you entered.
   C) Use your software package to find the sum of this new column. What does this sum represent?
   d) Have the software create a new $(y - \mu_y)^2 \cdot P(y)$ column.
   e) Use the software to find the sum of this new column.
   F) Now take the square root of this sum. What does this answer represent in terms of the random variable?

3) This problem will use the "Multiple Coin Simulator" application from the StatSims folder.
   a) Enter you name in the textbox provided. Choose 20 coins from the pull down menu. Enter 1000000 for the number of flips of the coins. (Do not use commas when entering the 1000000.)
   b) Click the 'Flip Once' button and few times and then click the 'Automatic' button to finish the 1,000,000 flips of the 20 coins.
   c) Use "ALT / PrintScreen" to copy then window and then paste it to word. Use Refresh if needed.
   D) What name best describes the shape of the histogram's distribution?
   E) Use the formula from Section 5.5 to calculate the theoretical probability of getting 15 heads when tossing 20 fair coins. (Hint: What are the values of n, p, and q for this problem?) Compare your answer to the value in the chart.
   F) Would it be unusual to get 17 heads when tossing 20 fair coins? Explain using a z-score for 17.
   G) How many times did your 20 coins come up showing 17 heads? Does this contradict your answer to part (F)? Explain.
   H) If you tossed a coin 20 times and it showed heads 17 or more times, would you consider this convincing evidence that the coin was biased or would you just attribute the large number of heads to random variation? Explain.

4) Now we will use statistical software to calculate the theoretical probabilities for the 20 coins from problem (3).
   a) Use your statistical package to find the probability of 15 heads when flipping 20 fair coins.
   b) Use your statistical package to find $P(X \le 15)$.
   C) Use your answer from part (b) to find $P(X \ge 16)$. Show your work.
   D) (*Challenge*) Determine $P(8 \le X \le 16)$ by using results from your statistical package. This will usually require two calculations on the software and you may still have to do some work by hand. Show your work on the final calculation by writing out what you are doing using probability notation and then plug in the numbers from the calculator to get your final answer.

Chapter 5: Chapter Review

Section 5.1: Classical Probability and Notation

- An experiment is the activity involving randomness about which we will ask probability questions.
- A simple outcome is an outcome that can only occur in one way.
- An event is any collection of simple outcomes. It could be as many outcomes as all, as few as none, or anywhere in between.
- The sample space for an experiment is the set of all possible simple outcomes.
- Classical probability applies to experiments where each simple outcome is equally likely to occur.
- We usually write probabilities in decimal form and use at least 4 decimal places if we are rounding.
- If you are adding more than half of the possibilities, consider subtracting from the total instead.
- An event that has a probability of zero is referred to as an impossible event.
- When we have a set of finite possibilities, calculating probability is the same as calculating a population relative frequency.
- The probability of an event should be interpreted as the long-term relative frequency of that event.
- Random variation typically causes the relative frequency of an event to be slightly different than the true probability. As the number of trials gets larger, this difference tends to get smaller.
- Venn diagrams are useful for illustrating probability experiments and definitions. We use a box to represent the sample space and discs to represent events.
- The complement of and event E (not E) is the event that E does not occur.
- The complement of an event is not usually the same thing as the opposite of the event.
- If it is reasonable to do quickly, making a chart of all possible outcomes to an experiment can make probability calculations much easier.
- The Fundamental Rule of Counting states that, if experiment A has m possible simple outcomes and experiment B has n possible simple outcomes, then if we look at the combined results of these two experiments, then there are $m \cdot n$ possible simple outcomes.

Section 5.2: Basic Rules of Probability

- $(A \,\&\, B)$ is the event that *both* A and B happen during the experiment. Visually this is the overlap of the two events. Order does not matter for an AND statement.
- $(A \text{ or } B)$ is the event that *at least one* of the two events occurs. Visually, we want all of one and only the *new* outcomes from the other.
- OR's do include the overlap, but be careful not to double count the overlap.
- Two events are considered mutually exclusive if it is impossible for the overlap to occur.
- For a larger group of events to be considered mutually exclusive, it must be impossible for any overlaps to occur among any of the events in the group.
- A common way to get a large number of mutually exclusive events is to let each of the classes in a grouped data table represent an event.
- If asked if two events are mutually exclusive, check to see if $P(A \,\&\, B) = 0$.
- The Special Addition Rule: If event A and event B are mutually exclusive, then
  $P(A \text{ or } B) = P(A) + P(B)$.
- The Complement Rule: $P(\text{not } E) = 1 - P(E)$ and $P(E) = 1 - P(\text{not } E)$
- The General Addition Rule: $P(A \text{ or } B) = P(A) + P(B) - P(A \,\&\, B)$
- The General Addition Rule has a built in correction for double counting the overlap.

Section 5.3: Conditional Probability and Independence

- A conditional probability question is one where you are asked to find the probability that one event will occur given that another event has occurred.
- $P(A\mid B)$ is read as "the probability of A *given* B."
- When calculating a conditional probability you should consider the *given* to be the new sample space for the experiment.
- The order is important for conditional probability. In general, $P(A\mid B) \neq P(B\mid A)$.
- When calculating $P(A\mid B)$, we must answer the question "Out of the outcomes in B, how many also satisfy A?"
- The Conditional Probability Rule: $P(B\mid A) = \dfrac{P(A\ \&\ B)}{P(A)}$. In words, a conditional probability can be found by dividing the probability of the overlap by the probability of the given.
- The General Multiplication Rule: $P(A\ \&\ B) = P(A) \cdot P(B\mid A)$. In words, the probability that two events will both occur can be found by multiplying the probability of the first event by the probability of the second event *given* the first.
- When making multiple picks with or without replacement, it is useful to use subscripts to indicate the order in which the events occurred.
- For two events to be statistically independent means that knowing that event A has occurred has no effect on the probability that event B will occur. In symbols: $P(B\mid A) = P(B)$.
- If two events are mutually exclusive, that does not mean that they are independent.
- The Special Multiplication Rule: If A and B are independent events, then $P(A\ \&\ B) = P(A) \cdot P(B)$.
- If you know that events are independent, then use $P(A\ \&\ B) = P(A) \cdot P(B)$.
- If you are asked if two events are independent, then check to see if $P(B\mid A) = P(B)$.

Section 5.4: Discrete Random Variables

- A random variable is a variable whose value depends on chance.
- A discrete random variable is a random variable whose possibilities form a discrete set. Discrete random variables often come from counting.
- A probability distribution for a discrete random variable is a table that lists each of the possible values of the random variable together with the probabilities for each of those values.
- A probability histogram is one where we draw a bar for each possible value for the random variable and the height represents the probability for that value. The bars are drawn from half mark to half mark.
- In a probability histogram, a tall bar represents a high chance of the value occurring.
- The mean of a discrete random variable is given by: $\mu_x = \sum x \cdot P(x)$.
- μ_x represents the expected mean for the values of x obtained after a large number of trials of the experiment. μ_x is often referred to as the expected value.
- The standard deviation of a discrete random variable is given by: $\sigma_x = \sqrt{\sum (x - \mu_x)^2 \cdot P(x)}$.
- σ_x allows us calculate z-scores and expected range to separate the expected from the unusual.
- Do not round the boundaries when calculating an expected range. Rather, choose the smallest and largest values of the random variable that lie within these boundaries.

Section 5.5: The Binomial Distribution

- $\binom{n}{x}$ tells us the number of possible combinations of x items chosen from a group of n items.

- The binomial formula states that the probability of x successes in n trials of a repeated experiment is given by the formula: $P(X = x) = \binom{n}{x} \cdot p^x q^{n-x}$.

- p is the probability of a success in any single trial of the experiment. $q = 1 - p$

- In the binomial formula, the $\binom{n}{x}$ has the job of counting all of the different possible orders for the specified number of successes and failures.

- In a two-category population, a success is defined by seeing the event that is being counted.

- The binomial formula can still be used when the sampling is done without replacement provided that the sample size is at most 5% of the population size.

- For a binomial distribution, we can use shortcut formulas for the mean and standard deviation. The shortcut formulas are $\mu_x = np$ and $\sigma_x = \sqrt{npq}$.

- If we are asked if it would be unusual for a random variable to land in a specified range, we only answer yes if the *entire* range of possibilities would be considered unusual.

Review Diagrams:

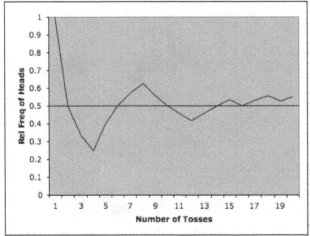
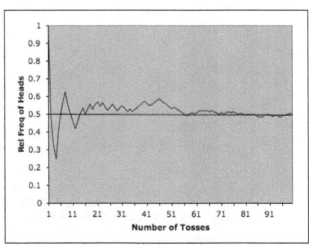

Probability tells us the long-term relative frequency of an event. In the short run, random variation can cause the relative frequency to be quite different than the actual probability.

The complement of an event is made up of everything not included in the original event. The complement does not mean the opposite, it means everything possible except for the original event.

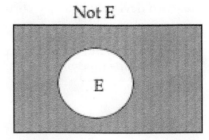

A and B

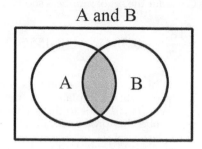

$(A \& B)$ is the event that *both* A and B happen during the experiment. Visually this is the overlap of the two events. Order does not matter for an AND statement.

A or B

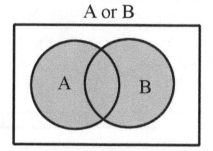

$(A \text{ or } B)$ is the event that *at least one* of the two events occurs. Visually, we want all of one and only the *new* outcomes from the other.

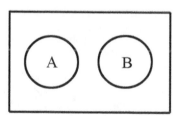

Two events are considered mutually exclusive if it is impossible for the overlap to occur.

Conditional probability: $P(B \mid A)$

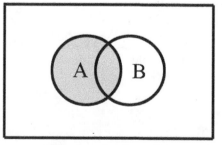

The given becomes the new sample space.

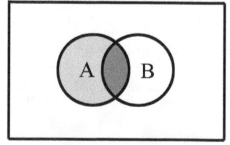

We only count the part of B that lies in the new sample space, A.

Chapter 5: Review Exercises

1) Consider the set of numbers shown below.

$$\left\{ \frac{18}{37},\ -0.5841,\ \frac{7}{2},\ 0.455543,\ 1.604 \right\}$$

   a) Which of the numbers above cannot be probabilities? Explain.
   b) Why is it useful to think about this while doing probability problems?

2) A preschool has 138 children that attend. The director is interested in the question "What is the probability that a randomly selected child from the preschool is allergic to peanuts?"
   a) What is the experiment?
   b) What is the sample space?
   c) What is the event that she is interested in?

3) The table below shows the artists contained in one of the play lists on a student's phone together with the number of songs by each artist.

Artist	Frequency
Linkin Park	17
Rihanna	8
Keith Urban	5
Switchfoot	11
	41

Suppose that random play is chosen for this playlist. (This will be sampling without replacement.) Find the probability that:

   a) The song played will be by Rihanna.
   b) The song will be by Keith Urban or Switchfoot.
   c) The song will not be by Linkin Park.
   d) The first two songs will include one by Switchfoot and one by Linkin Park.
   e) The first two songs are by the same artist.
   f) The first 4 songs will all be by Linkin Park.

4) A large fish tank contains a total of 39 fish. The types and frequencies of the fish are shown in the chart below.

Type	Guppy	Molly	Goldfish	Danio
Frequency	9	13	5	11

Suppose that two fish will be randomly selected without replacement from the tank. Determine the probability that:

   a) The first fish selected will be a Goldfish.
   b) The first fish selected will be a Molly or a Danio.
   c) The first fish selected will not be a Guppy.
   d) One of the fish is a Danio and one is a Guppy.
   e) The two fish are both the same type.
   f) If four fish are chosen without replacement, what is the probability that they will all be Danios?

5) Suppose I asked my daughter to clean up her room and tell her I will reward her with two randomly selected coins from my pocket if she does a good job. In my pocket, I have 2 quarters, a dime, a nickel, and 2 pennies. Let X = the total value, in decimal $, of the two coins selected.

   a) Determine the probability distribution of X.
       Hint: make a chart like for the sum of two dice, but remember that we can't give her the same coin twice.
   b) Find $P(X \geq 0.15)$.
   c) Find $P(X > 0.25\ \&\ X < 0.50)$.
   d) $P(X > 0.25\ \text{or}\ X < 0.10)$.
   e) Find $P(X \geq 0.15|\ \text{at least 1 penny is chosen})$.
   f) Find the values of μ_x and σ_x.

   Note: $\sum x^2 = 0.06665041$

   g) Find the expected range for the amount she will get paid.

6) A sales representative attends a convention in Las Vegas. They decide to go to a buffet dinner and then to see a show. She is considering 5 different buffets with costs of $20, $25, $30, $40, and $50. She is considering 4 shows with ticket costs of $30, $50, $50, and $80. Being in Vegas has put her in a gambling mood and she decides to randomly select one of the buffets and one of the shows. Let X = the total cost of her dinner and show.

   a) Determine the probability distribution of X.
   b) Her company has given her $75 to cover her expenses for the evening. Determine the probability that she will go over this limit.
   c) Find $P(X \geq \$60\ \&\ X < \$100)$.
   d) Find $P(X \geq \$95\ \text{or}\ X < \$75)$.
   e) Find the probability that her total will be more than $75 given that she spent at least $50 on the show.
   f) Find the values of μ_x and σ_x.

   Note: $\sum x^2 = 7745$

   g) Would it be unusual for her to spend $100? Explain.

7) Consider the contingency table shown below and suppose that one item is selected at random.

	B1	B2	B3	Total
A1			184	
A2		152	149	400
A3	216	190	207	613
A4		203	148	502
Total	552	760	688	2000

a) Fill in the blanks.
b) Find $P(A1)$.
c) Find $P(A3 \ \& \ B1)$.
d) Find $P(A4 \text{ or not } B2)$.
e) Find $P(B2 \mid A2)$.
f) Are A2 and B2 independent? Explain.
g) Are A4 and B3 independent? Explain.

8) Consider the contingency table shown below and suppose that one item is selected at random.

	T1	T2	T3	Total
R1	77	45	76	198
R2			118	
R3		23	66	134
Total		170	260	748

a) Fill in the blanks.
b) Find $P(T2)$.
c) Find $P(R1 \ \& \ T3)$.
d) Find $P(R2 \text{ or } T1 \text{ or } T3)$.
e) Find $P(R3 \mid T3)$.
f) Are R3 and T3 independent? Explain.
g) Are R1 and T2 independent? Explain.

9) A group of 58 students were asked how many hours they spent studying for their second statistics exam. Their responses, rounded to the nearest hour, are summarized in the table below.

Hours	0	1	2	3	4	5	6	7	8	9
Freq	2	3	4	9	10	12	8	6	3	1

Consider the events listed below and suppose one of these students is picked at random.
A = The student did not study.
B = The student studied for at least 5 hours.
C = The student studied for less than 4 hours.
D = The student studied 2 to 5 hours.
E = The student studied between 3 and 8 hours.

a) List all mutually exclusive groups of events.
b) Determine $P(D \ \& \ E)$.
c) Determine $P(D \text{ or } E)$.
d) Determine $P(A \text{ or } B \text{ or } C)$.
e) Find $P(B \mid E)$.
f) Are events B and E independent? Explain.

10) A small business has 29 employees. The table below summarizes the number of sick days taken last year by the employees.

Sick Days	0	1	2	3	4	5	7	10
Freq	4	8	6	4	3	2	1	1

Consider the events listed below and suppose one of these employees is picked at random.
A = The employee never took a sick day.
B = The employee was out sick at most twice.
C = The employee was out sick more than 4 times.
D = The employee was out sick 2 to 5 days.
E = The employee was out sick 4 to 8 days.

a) List all mutually exclusive groups of events.
b) Determine $P(C \ \& \ D)$.
c) Determine $P(C \text{ or } D)$.
d) Determine $P(A \text{ or } D \text{ or } E)$.
e) Find $P(D \mid E)$.
f) Are events D and E independent? Explain.

11) According to 2013 estimates, the age breakdown in the United States was as shown in the table below.

Event	Age	Rel Freq
A	0 – < 10	0.1309
B	10 – < 20	0.1384
C	20 – < 30	0.1371
D	30 – < 40	0.1295
E	40 – < 50	0.1412
F	50 – < 65	0.1927
G	65 and over	0.1302
		1.0000

Consider the experiment where a person is randomly selected from the United States at that time and the person's age is noted. Express each the following using probability and event notation and then find the requested probability.
a)   The person selected is in their twenties.
b)   The person selected is less than 30 years old.
c)   The person selected is at least 20 years old.
d)   The person's age is at least 30, but less than 65.

12) A large group of statistics students were asked to state their GPAs. Their responses are summarized in the chart below.

Event	GPA	Rel Freq
A	1.5 – < 2.0	0.0313
B	2.0 – < 2.5	0.0833
C	2.5 – < 3.0	0.1667
D	3.0 – < 3.5	0.4479
E	3.5 – < 4.0	0.2291
F	4.0	0.0417
		1.0000

Consider the experiment where one of these stat students is randomly selected and their GPA is noted. Express each the following using probability and event notation and then find the requested probability.
a)   The student selected had a GPA of 4.0.
b)   The student selected had a GPA less than 3.0.
c)   The student selected had at least a 2.0 GPA.
d)   The student's GPA was at least 2.0, but less than 3.5.

13) Suppose that $P(C) = 0.4128$, $P(D) = 0.7355$, and $P(C \& D) = 0.3389$.
a)   Find $P(C \text{ or } D)$.
b)   Find $P(\text{not } D)$.
c)   Find $P(C \mid D)$.
d)   Find $P(D \mid C)$.

14) Suppose that $P(C) = 0.3553$, $P(D) = 0.6844$, and $P(C \text{ or } D) = 0.7799$.
a)   Find $P(C \& D)$.
b)   Find $P(\text{not } C)$.
c)   Find $P(C \mid D)$.
d)   Find $P(D \mid C)$.

15) Suppose that E & F are independent and $P(E) = \frac{3}{4}$ and $P(F) = \frac{5}{8}$, Find:
a) $P(E \& F)$.
b) $P(E \text{ or } F)$.
c)   Are E & F mutually exclusive? Explain.

16) Suppose $P(A) = \frac{1}{4}$ $P(B) = \frac{1}{2}$ and $P(A \text{ or } B) = \frac{3}{4}$.
a)   Find $P(A \& B)$. Are A & B mutually exclusive? Explain.
b)   Find $P(A \mid B)$. Are A & B independent? Explain.

17) As of March 2015, Stephen Curry of the Golden State Warriors was a 89.7% free throw shooter. He also makes 46.9% of his field goal attempts and 43.6% of his 3-point shots. Suppose that Stephen Curry attempted four field goals, three 3-pointers, and two free throws, in that order. Assume the results of the shots are independent.
a)   What is the probability that he would make all of those shots?
b)   What is the probability that he would miss all of those shots?
c)   What is the probability that he would miss at least one of those shots?

18) Suppose that two coins are flipped and 3 dice are rolled.
a)   What is the probability that both coins come up heads and all the dice come up 4?
b)   What is the probability that both coins show the same side and all 3 dice show the same number?

19) Suppose that Y = the number of people in line at the checkout stand of a small hardware store at any given time during store hours. The probability distribution for Y is shown below.

y	P(Y = y)
0	0.1737
1	0.2209
2	0.1839
3	0.1384
4	0.1037
5	0.0810
6	0.0552
7	0.0301
8	0.0131

Suppose we observe the line at the hardware store on a randomly selected time. Write each of the following events using random variable notation and then find the probability.
a) the number of people in line is more than 2.
b) the number of people in line is between 2 and 4 (inclusive).
c) Create a probability histogram for Y.
d) What distribution shape best describes this random variable?
e) Find μ_y and σ_y. Note: $\sum y^2 = 10.1868$
f) Find and interpret the expected range for the random variable Y.

20) Suppose that we randomly select the champion of the men's NCAA basketball tournament from the years 1979 through 2014. Let Z = the seed number for the champion selected. The probability distribution for Z is shown below.

z	P(Z = z)
1	0.5556
2	0.1667
3	0.1389
4	0.0278
5	0.0000
6	0.0556
7	0.0278
8	0.0278

Write each of the following events using random variable notation and then find the probability.
a) the champion's seed is more than 4.
b) the champion's seed is between 3 and 6 (inclusive).
c) Create a probability histogram for Z.
d) What distribution shape best describes this random variable?
e) Find μ_z and σ_z. Note: $\sum z^2 = 8.0603$
f) Find and interpret the expected range for the random variable Z.

21) In a certain city, 32.9% of the households have at least 1 HDTV. Suppose that we randomly select 15 households and let X = the number of households that have at least 1 HDTV.
a) Find $P(X = 6)$.
b) Find $P(4 \le X < 8)$.
c) Find the probability that at least 2 of the households have at least 1 HDTV.
d) Find μ_x and σ_x.
e) Should it be considered unusual if at least 10 of the 15 randomly selected households from this city have at least 1 HDTV? Explain.

22) 87.9% of college students carry a cell phone with them on campus. Suppose 9 college students are randomly selected. Let X = then number of those selected that were carrying their cell phone with them.
a) Find $P(X = 7)$.
b) Find $P(5 < X \le 8)$.
c) Find the probability that less than 8 of the students selected were carrying their cell phones.
d) Find μ_x and σ_x.
e) Find the expected range for the number of students out of 9 that would be carrying their cell phones.

23) Identify whether or not each of the following is a binomial random variable and briefly explain your reasoning.

a) Let X = the weight of a randomly selected ripe apple.
b) Let X = the number of defective light bulbs in a sample of 1000 light bulbs.
c) Let X = the number of times the sum of two dice is larger than 9 out of 80 rolls of the dice.
d) Let X = the sum of two rolled dice.
e) Why is it so important to recognize a binomial random variable when you have one?

Chapter 6 - The Normal Distribution

Chapter Problem: *A Tie for Olympic Downhill Gold*

During the 2014 Winter Olympics in Sochi, Russia, something surprising happened in one of the women's downhill skiing events. For the first time in Olympic history, an Alpine skiing race ended in a tie. Two skiers, Tina Maze of Slovenia and Dominique Gisin of Switzerland, both finished with a time of 1 minutes and 41.57 seconds and both women were awarded the gold medal. It is natural for people to wonder, "What is the chance of that?" However, because it has never happened before, the past relative frequency of a tie is not useful in calculating this probability. Coincidently, both of these women had previously been involved in a tie for the lead in other non-Olympic events. At the end of this chapter, we will return to this situation and use the tools we will have learned to attempt to estimate the chance of such a tie occurring.

What is the chance that an Olympic downhill race will end in a tie?

Introduction:

In Chapter 5, we studied probability for discrete random variables. There were a finite number of possibilities that our variables could take on. In this chapter, we are turning our attention towards continuous random variables, like race times, where there are infinitely many possible values that our variable can take on. This means that finding probability by counting possibilities will no longer make sense and we need a new method for finding probabilities. We can get a hint as to what this method will be by examining the probability histogram from a binomial random variable from Ch 5 (see below).

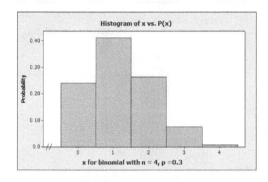

In Chapter 5, we learned to use a formula to calculate the probability for a binomial random variable. In this chapter, it is useful to notice that the probability for any value of a binomial variable is equal to the area of the corresponding histogram bar for that value. This is due to the fact that the bars are all 1 unit wide.

$$Area = base \cdot height = 1 \cdot height = 1 \cdot P(x) = P(x)$$

This relationship between area and probability is crucial for working with continuous random variables.

For continuous variables, we will rely on the strategy of using area underneath a curve to represent probability. There are many situations that arise in statistical studies where the distribution of the data set involved is bell-shaped. In fact, such situations are so common, that bell-shaped distributions are known as normal distributions. Normal distributions are common when dealing with the heights, weights, lengths, etc. of mature things occurring in nature. It also can come up when dealing with large sets of standardized test scores. And perhaps more importantly, normal distributions come up in many situations involving sample means and sample proportions that we will study later in the inferential statistics portion of the text. In this chapter we will see how to find and use the area underneath a bell-shaped curve for probability applications.

The goal of this chapter will be to learn some of the important properties of normal distributions, to find the area underneath them, to find boundaries for known areas, and to use these results to solve applications. We will explore how normal distributions can be used to estimate probabilities for some binomial distributions. This is useful in situations where n is large and using the binomial formula becomes difficult. And finally, we will learn how to examine sample data and assess whether or not it is a reasonable possibility that the sample data came from a normally distributed population. We will explore these ideas in the following sections:

Let's get started.

Section 6.1 – Introducing the Normal Distribution

In this chapter, we will focus our attention on using the area underneath certain bell-shaped curves, known as **normal curves**, to help us answer probability and percentage questions about many commonly occurring variables. We will begin this discussion by formally defining normal curves and learning some of their basic properties.

> **Definitions**: *Normal Curves and Normal Distributions*
>
> **Normal Curves**: A special class of bell-shaped curves.
>
> **Normal Distributions**: A population or a random variable is called normally distributed if it has the shape of a normal curve.

Let's begin with an informal example that illustrates how normal curves can be useful in answering many important questions. The graph below shows the relative frequency histogram for the heights of all 9,727 10-yr-old boys in a small county in California. The heights of the boys are measured in inches.

Ignoring the smooth curve that is drawn in, hopefully, you can still see that the histogram is roughly bell-shaped. The smooth curve is the best fitting normal curve for the data set. We will now explore the connection between the smooth normal curve and the relative frequency distribution for the 10-yr-old boys.

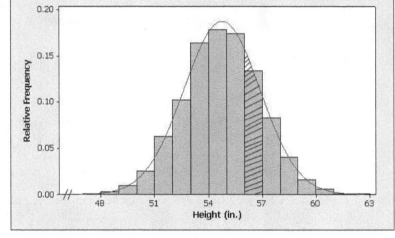

Let's focus on the boys who have heights between 56 and 57 inches tall. Notice the following about the area of that histogram bar (or any of the bars for that matter.)

$$\text{Area of Bar} = (\text{Base})(\text{height}) =$$
$$b \cdot h = 1 \cdot h = h = \text{Relative Frequency}$$

So the first important thing to notice is that the area of the histogram bar in question has a base that is 1 unit wide and that causes the area of the bar to be equal to its height, which is the relative frequency of 10-yr-old boys in that height range.

Now, let's switch our attention to the area under the smooth normal curve that has been shaded with the slashed lines. If we focus on just the area under the curve from 56 to 57, we should notice the following:

Area under the curve ≈ area of the histogram bar.

Notice that this is not a perfect match, but it does appear that the extra bit of shading on the upper left roughly makes up for the upper right corner of the histogram bar, which is not shaded. Combining the discussions of the area under the curve and the area of the bars, we see the following fact about the relative frequency for 10-yr-old boys with heights between 56 and 57 inches tall:

Relative Frequency = Area of histogram bar ≈ area under the curve between 56 and 57.

So, from this, we conclude that we can use area under normal curves to approximate population relative frequencies for normal populations. Recall from Chapter 5 that we stated that population relative frequency is equal to the corresponding probability for a given event. So, if X is the height of a 10-yr-old boy selected at random, we could also make the following statement.

P(56 < X < 57) = Population Relative Frequency ≈ area under the curve between 56 and 57.

So, we see that we have a connection between area under a normal curve and the population relative frequency or the probability of an event. This relationship is summarized as follows:

Points to Remember: *Uses for Area Under a Normal Curve*

- If a population is approximately normally distributed, then:

    Population Relative Frequency ≈ area under the normal curve

- If a random variable is approximately normally distributed, then:

    Probability ≈ area under the normal curve

Because it appears we will be able to make important use of the area under normal curves, we will now move to a more in-depth study of normal curves in general.

NORMAL CURVES: *Learning the Basic Properties*

Once a curve has been classified as normal, it can be completely determined by two parameters: the mean, μ, and the standard deviation, σ, of the curve. If you know these two numbers for a normal curve, you can figure out anything else you need to know about the distribution.

Let's look at the sketch of a typical normal distribution, with mean, μ, and standard deviation, σ, and see what properties we notice.

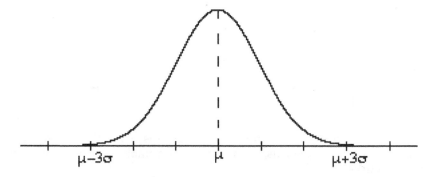

One feature that should be obvious is the bell shape, but let's look at some of the other key features that might not be as easily noticed.

The left and right hand sides of the curve are mirror images of each other, which indicates that the curve is symmetric. All symmetric curves have their symmetry about the mean, μ, of the curve.

It appears that the graph actually stops on the left and right side, but this in not true. The curve actually has the x-axis as a horizontal asymptote on each side. This means that the graph goes on forever in each direction with the height approaching closer to zero the further out on the curve we go.

While it is true that the graph extends forever in each direction, almost all of the area lies between the values $\mu - 3\sigma$ and $\mu + 3\sigma$. This follows from the Empirical Rule, which states that about 99.7% of the data in bell-shaped data sets lie within 3 standard deviations of the mean.

Because the area under the curve will be used to approximate relative frequencies and probabilities, it should not come as a surprise to learn that the total area under the curve is equal to 1.

The following Point to Remember summarizes these properties.

Point to Remember: *Basic Properties of Normal Curves*

The Basic Properties of a normal curve are as follows:
- The total area under a normal curve is always equal to 1.
- All normal curves are symmetric about their mean, μ.
- Normal curves extend indefinitely in both directions and the height approaches zero on each side.
- Almost all of the area under a normal curve lies between $\mu - 3\sigma$ & $\mu + 3\sigma$

Now let's try sketching a few specific curves.

Example 6.1: *Getting familiar with the properties of normal curves*

Sketch the graph of the normal distribution with a mean of 10 and a standard deviation of 2. Illustrate as many of the properties of normal curves as possible.

Solution:

The following is the completed sketch followed by some discussion of the order in which things would usually be done.

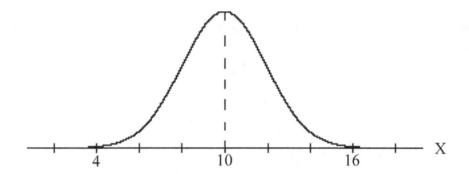

The first thing you should do when drawing your normal curve is draw the horizontal axis. Next, draw the normal curve by starting out parallel to the axis, then rise up, and finally return to the axis. Remember that the goal is to create a bell-shaped curve.

Once the curve is drawn, you then begin labeling the axis. First, drop down from the peak of the curve and label that location of the number line as the mean, which in this case is 10. Then go to the spots on the left and right side where the graph seems to disappear and label them with the numbers that represent three standard deviations away from the mean.

$$\mu - 3\sigma = 10 - 3(2) = 4 \text{ and } \mu + 3\sigma = 10 + 3(2) = 16$$

Finally, label the axis with an X (unless your normally distributed variable happens to be some other letter).

> **Key Concepts**: *Notes about sketching normal curves*
>
> Keep the following thoughts in mind when you are sketching the graph of a normal curve:
> - It is much harder to label the axis first and then draw the curve. Always start by drawing the curve first and then labeling its key features.
> - The peak of the curve will always occur at the mean, μ.
> - The visible edges of the curve occur roughly at $\mu - 3\sigma$ & $\mu + 3\sigma$.
> - We do not typically draw a vertical (or y-axis) when drawing a normal curve. Because of this, it is not possible to show that the area is equal to 1 in our sketch.

Example 6.2: *Examining the affects of the standard deviation*

a) Sketch the graph of the normal distribution with a mean of 15 and a standard deviation of 3. Label the axis below the peak and at the visible edges of the normal curve.

b) On the same axis, sketch the graph of the normal distribution with a mean of 15 and a standard deviation of 2. Label the axis below the peak and at the visible edges of the curve for this one as well.

c) Discuss the similarities and differences that you notice.

Solution:

a)

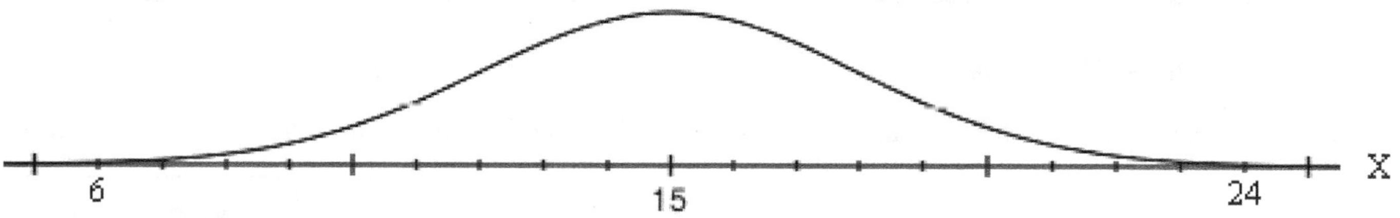

The peak is located directly above the mean of 15 and then the curve has flattened and blended in with the x-axis about 3 standard deviations from the mean. The calculations for the visible edges are shown below.

$$\mu - 3\sigma = 15 - 3(3) = 6 \quad \& \quad \mu + 3\sigma = 15 + 3(3) = 24$$

b)

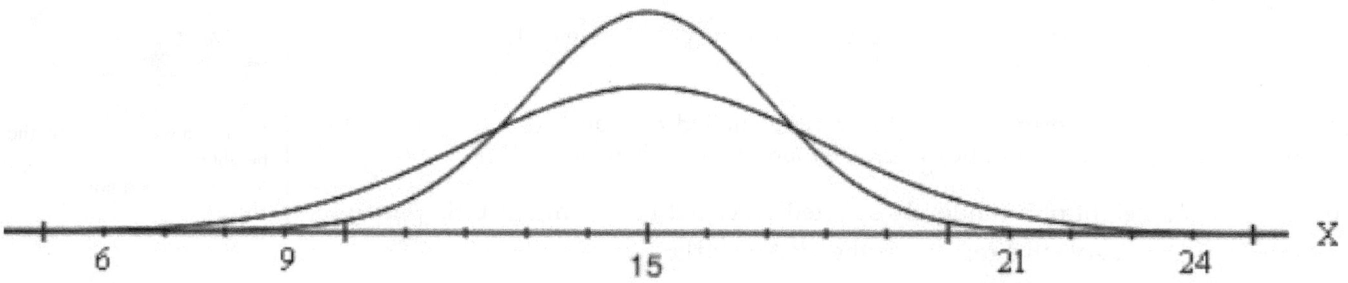

The peak is still at the mean of 15, but this time the curve flattens and blends in with the x-axis at 9 and 21. In order to preserve the area of 1, this new narrower curve must also be a little taller than the first one.

$$\mu - 3\sigma = 15 - 3(2) = 9 \quad \& \quad \mu + 3\sigma = 15 + 3(2) = 21$$

c)   The similarities are the bell shape and the symmetry about the mean, 15.   The peak is at the same location because the mean is the same. Another similarity that is important is that the total area under each curve is 1.

The fact that the area is 1 under each curve contributes to a difference we see in the curves. The smaller standard deviation for the second curve caused it to have most of its area in a narrower range, but because the area is fixed, the curve had to have a higher peak to make up for this.

The change in shape that we saw in the example above is worth a little further discussion. The standard deviation of a curve measures the spread of the data in the distribution. The larger the standard deviation of a normal curve, the more spread out or wider it becomes. However, because the area under a normal curve is always equal to 1, a wider curve must also be shorter to keep the area constant. This is also true in the reverse order. If the standard deviation becomes smaller, then the curve will become narrower, and thus taller. The exact height is not important, but recognizing the give and take between width and height of the curve is crucial. This relationship is summarized in the following Point to Remember.

> **Point to Remember**: *The relationship between the height and width of a normal curve*
>
> Here are a few things to keep in mind regarding the standard deviation of a normal curve and the shape of the curve.
> - The standard deviation measures the spread of a data set and directly affects the width of the normal curve.
> - Because the total area under a normal curve is fixed at 1, changing the standard deviation will indirectly affect the height also.
> - A larger standard deviation creates a wider and shorter normal curve.
> - A smaller standard deviation creates a narrower and taller normal curve.

APPLICATIONS OF AREA: *Using Area to Represent Percentages and Probabilities*

Now that we have learned a little bit about normal curves, let's look at an example to see how area under a normal curve can be helpful in answering questions about real world applications.

Example 6.3: *Heights of 10-year-old boys*

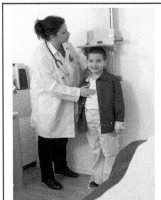

Consider the heights of all 10-yr-old boys in the United States.   Suppose that those heights are approximately normally distributed with $\mu = 54.75$ inches and $\sigma = 2.125$ inches.

a)   Sketch the normal curve for this data set. Label the axis below the peak and at the visible edges of the normal curve.

b)   Shade the area under the curve that represents the percentage of 10-yr-old boys that are more than 54.75 inches tall.

c)   Use properties of normal curves to find the shaded area and then use that to find the percentage of 10-yr-old boys that are more than 54.75 inches tall.

What can we learn about the height of 10-year-old boys from the area under a normal curve?

d)   Let X = the height of a randomly selected 10-yr old boy from the U.S. Shade the area under the curve that represents the $P(X < 50)$.

e)   Based on your picture, make a guess at the amount of area that is shaded. How does that relate to $P(X < 50)$?

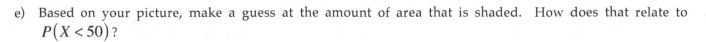

Solution:

a) The mean is right below the peak of the curve and visible edges of the curve disappear about 3 standard deviations away from the mean. We calculate the flattening out points as follows:

$$\mu - 3\sigma = 54.75 - 3(2.125) = 48.375 \quad \& \quad \mu + 3\sigma = 54.75 + 3(2.125) = 61.125$$

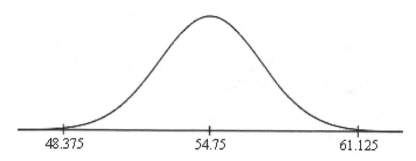

b) Because they want the boys that are more than 54.75 inches tall, we will shade the area to the right of 54.75 inches on our picture.

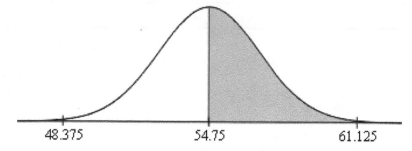

c) Two properties come into play when finding this area. First, we know that the total area under a normal curve is equal to 1. Second, we know that all normal curves are symmetric about their mean. Therefore, when we find the area to the right of the mean for a normal curve, this will always be exactly half of the total area. This means that the shaded area is 0.5. This shaded area is equivalent to the relative frequency of boys taller than 54.75 inches. To convert this to a percentage, we simply multiply by 100%.

$$0.5 * 100\% = 50\% \text{ of the boys are more than 54.75 inches tall.}$$

d) Because we want $P(X < 50)$, we should place 50 in the appropriate spot on the number line and then shade the area to the left of 50. Because they have labeled the variable as X, we should label the horizontal axis in the same way.

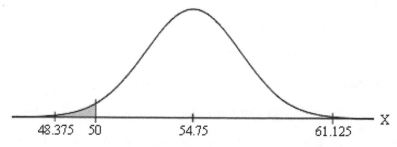

e) There are two methods that can be used to estimate the area. We can just do a best guess based on the look of our graph or we can use the Empirical Rule from Chapter 3 to help us make a better estimate.

Method 1: The total amount of area under the curve is 1. It looks like less than 5% of the total area is shaded. As a rough guess, I will say it looks like about 3% of the area is shaded. So, I guess the area is 0.03.

Method 2: 50 inches is roughly 2 standard deviations below the mean. The Empirical Rule for bell-shaped data states that roughly 95% of bell-shaped data lies within 2 standard deviations of the mean. This leaves 5% of the data to be equally split on the two sides. Therefore, the area to the left of 50 inches is probably about 2.5% of the area or 0.025.

Because this is just an estimate, either answer is fine. $P(X < 50) \approx 0.025$

At this point, it is important to point out that we do not have to be experts at estimating the area under curves either by eye or using the Empirical Rule. In the next two sections, we will learn how to find exact values for these areas using technology. However, even though technology can find these areas, it is useful to have a rough estimate of the answer. Such estimates help confirm correct answers and these estimates also help catch mistakes.

Key Concept: *The Empirical Rule can be applied to area under a normal curve*

Despite the fact that the Empirical Rule for Bell-Shaped data was given for us to estimate percentages of a data set in Chapter 3, it can be used here to estimate area under a normal curve. Remember, for normal distributions, the relative frequency (the decimal form of the percentage) is equivalent to the area under the corresponding normal curve.

WRAP SESSION: *Starting from a Graph of the Distribution*

Let's look at one last example to practice the ideas learned so far and to see how things are different if we begin with a graph of the distribution rather than a description in words.

Example 6.4: *Blood Sugar Levels*

Typically when blood sugar levels are measured, the patient is asked to fast for at least 8 hours before the blood is drawn for testing. Suppose that the graph shown below represents the distribution of the post fasting blood sugar level for a certain population of adults. The blood sugar level is measured in milligrams per deciliter. Use the graph to answer each the questions below.

Can a normal curve help us predict the percentage of adults at risk for type II diabetes?

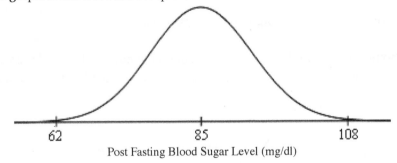

Post Fasting Blood Sugar Level (mg/dl)

a)   What kind of distribution do post fasting blood sugar levels appear to take on?

b)   Use the graph to estimate the mean and standard deviation for these post fasting blood sugar levels.

c)   A post fasting blood sugar level above 100 mg/dl is a risk factor for Type II Diabetes. Use the graph to estimate the percentage of adults that have this risk factor. Shade the appropriate corresponding area on the graph.

d)   If Y = the post fasting blood sugar level for a randomly selected adult from this population, estimate $P(80 < Y < 90)$. Shade the appropriate corresponding area on the graph.

Solution:

a) Based on the bell-shape shown for the distribution, it seems reasonable that the post fasting blood sugar levels are approximately normally distributed.

b) The mean should be located right below the peak of the graph. Based on the labeling on the graph, it appears that the mean is 85 mg/dl.

The spots where the visible edges of the curve disappear should be about 3 standard deviations from the mean. The two locations on the graph where this happens are at 62 and 108. The difference between either of these two values and the mean is 23 mg/dl $(108 - 85 = 23)$. Because this value of 23 represents a distance of 3 standard deviations, we can divide this amount be three to approximate the standard deviation.

$$\text{Standard Deviation} = \sigma \approx \frac{23}{3} \approx 7.6667 \text{ mg/dl}$$

c) The first step is to shade this region on the graph to get a visual representation of the area. Because they stated that they want the percentage of the adults that are above 100, we should shade the area to the right of 100 mg/dl on the graph. Exact placement of the 100 is not required, but we should take care to notice that 100 is closer to 108 than it is to 85 and to place it accordingly.

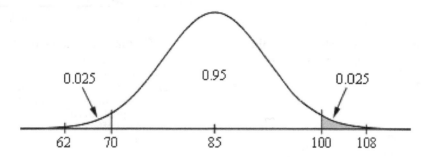

This area appears to be pretty small, probably less than 5% of the total. Also, 100 is 15 mg/dl above the mean and this represents about two standard deviations. Therefore, we can also use the Empirical Rule to fine tune our estimate. About 95% of the area (or an area of 0.95) lies within two standard deviations of the mean. This leaves a leftover area of about 0.05. Only half of this would be on the right hand side. Thus the area above 100 is approximately 0.025. Converting to a percentage, we would estimate that about 2.5% of this adult population has the risk factor of a post fasting blood sugar level over 100 mg/dl.

d) We begin by adding the numbers 80 and 90 to our number line and then shading the area between them. Exact placement of these numbers is not needed, but we should notice that they are much closer to the center of 85 than they are to the edges, 62 and 108. Because they are using Y for the variable, we should label the horizontal axis in the same way.

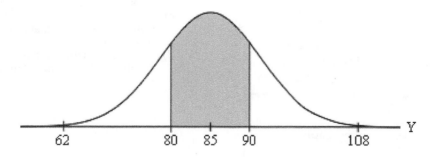

Just using a rough visual estimate, it appears that about half of the total area is shaded. This fits well with an estimate based on the Empirical Rule. 80 mg/dl and 90 mg/dl are both 5 mg/dl away from the mean. This is less that 1 standard deviation from the mean. According to the Empirical rule, the area within 1 standard deviation of the mean should be about 0.68 (or 68%). Because we have shaded an area that extends less than

1 standard deviation in each direction, we should expect the area to be smaller than 0.68. Our initial estimate of 0.50 fits this description, so we should go with that.

$$P(80 < Y < 90) \approx 0.50$$

It is important to remember that in the next two sections of this chapter, we will be learning how to find such areas exactly. Because of this, we should not be concerned that we are currently only getting rough estimates of the areas. These estimates will be good enough to check our work in these later sections.

Time to practice with some exercises.

Exercise Set 6.1:

Concept Review: Review the definitions and concepts from this section by filling in the blanks for each of the following.

1) Normal distributions are _____ - shaped.

2) If a population is normally distributed, then the area under the corresponding normal curve can be used to approximate _____ _____
 _____ .

3) If a random variable is normally distributed, then the area under the corresponding normal curve can be used to approximate _____ for the random variable.

4) 4 properties of normal curves.
   a) Total area under the curve is ___ .
   b) Curve is symmetric about its _____ .
   c) Curve extends _____ in both directions and the height approaches _____ on each side.
   d) Almost all of the area lies between _____ and _____ .

5) If σ becomes larger, then the normal curve becomes shorter and _____ . If σ becomes smaller, then the normal curve becomes _____ and _____ .

6) The Empirical Rule was originally given for percentages and bell-shaped distributions, but it can also be used now to estimate _____ under _____ curves.

Mechanics: Practice working with normal distributions before moving on to applications.

7) Together on the same axis, sketch the graphs of:
   a) The normal curve with $\mu = 10$ and $\sigma = 2$.
   b) The normal curve with $\mu = 12$ and $\sigma = 3$.
   c) How did the increase in standard deviation affect the graph of the curve?

8) Together on the same axis, sketch the graphs of:
   a) The normal curve with $\mu = 22$ and $\sigma = 7$.
   b) The normal curve with $\mu = 18$ and $\sigma = 4$.
   c) How did the decrease in standard deviation affect the graph of the curve?

9) Consider the normal curve shown below.

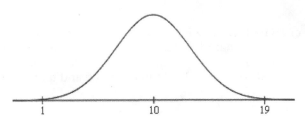

   a) Estimate the values of μ and σ.
   b) If we were to change the mean to 15, what effect would that have on the graph of the curve?
   c) If we were to change the standard deviation to 6, what effect would that have on the graph of the original curve?
   d) What effect would either of these changes have on the total area under the curve?

10) Consider the normal curve shown below.

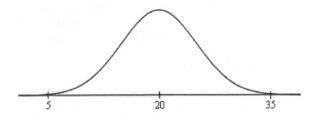

   a) Estimate the values of μ and σ.
   b) If we were to change the mean to 11, what effect would that have on the graph of the curve?
   c) If we were to change the standard deviation to 2, what effect would that have on the graph of the original curve?
   d) What effect would either of these changes have on the total area under the curve?

Applications: Practice the ideas learned in this section within the context of real world applications.

11) The lengths of adult female green anacondas are normally distributed with a mean length of 24.1 feet and a standard deviation of 2.307 feet.
   a) Sketch the normal curve for this population. Label the axis below the peak and at the visible edges of the normal curve.
   b) Shade the area under the normal curve that corresponds to the percentage of female green anacondas with lengths between 19 and 29 feet long.
   c) Use your graph and/or the Empirical Rule to estimate the percentage of female green anacondas with lengths between 19 and 29 feet long.

12) The amount of rice that goes into the bags of rice produced by a certain company is normally distributed with a mean of 5 pounds and a standard deviation of 0.142 lbs.
   a) Sketch the curve for the distribution of the weights of these rice bags. Label the axis below the peak and at the visible edges of the normal curve.
   b) Shade the area under the normal curve that corresponds to the percentage of rice bags with weights between 4.85 and 5.15 lbs.
   c) Use your graph and/or the Empirical Rule to estimate the percentage of rice bags with weights between 4.85 and 5.15 lbs.

13) The TI-84 Plus C, color calculator, comes with a rechargeable lithium-polymer battery. The lasting time for a fully charged battery is normally distributed with a mean of 7.5 hours and a standard deviation of 1.273 hours.
   a) Sketch the curve for the distribution of the battery lasting times. Label the axis below the peak and at the visible edges of the normal curve.
   b) Shade the area under the normal curve that corresponds to the percentage of fully charged batteries that would last less than 5 hours.
   c) Use your graph and/or the Empirical Rule to estimate percentage of fully charged batteries that would last less than 5 hours.

14) The amount of time that Tim Duncan of the San Antonio Spurs takes between free throws is a normally distributed variable with a mean of 9.5 seconds and a standard deviation of 0.5 seconds.
   a) Sketch the curve for the distribution of the amount of time between free throws for Tim Duncan. Label the axis below the peak and at the visible edges of the normal curve.
   b) It is against the rules to take more than 10 seconds between free throws. Shade the area under the normal curve that corresponds to the percentage of time that Tim violates this rule.
   c) Use your graph and/or the Empirical Rule to estimate the percentage of the time that Tim violates this rule.

15) The high temperature in Death Valley during the month of July is a normally distributed random variable with $\mu_x = 115$ and $\sigma_x = 7.062$.
   Let X = the high temperature for a randomly selected day in July.
   a) Sketch the normal curve for X. Label the axis below the peak and at the visible edges of the normal curve.
   b) Shade the area under the normal curve that corresponds to $P(X > 110)$.
   c) Use your graph and/or the Empirical Rule to estimate $P(X > 110)$.

16) The rainfall total in Hayward, CA during the month of January is a normally distributed random variable with $\mu_x = 4.3$ inches and $\sigma_x = 1.077$.
   Let X = the rainfall total for a randomly selected January in Hayward.
   a) Sketch the normal curve for X. Label the axis below the peak and at the visible edges of the normal curve.
   b) Shade the area under the normal curve that corresponds to $P(X < 6)$.
   c) Use your graph and/or the Empirical Rule to estimate $P(X < 6)$.

17) Kevin works at a bike shop. One of his tasks is to assemble bikes. The time it takes him to fully assemble a bike is a normally distributed random variable with $\mu_Y = 21.3$ minutes and $\sigma_Y = 3.0972$ minutes. Let Y = the time it takes Kevin to assemble a randomly selected bike.
   a) Sketch the normal curve for Y. Label the axis below the peak and at the visible edges of the normal curve.
   b) Shade the area under the normal curve that corresponds to $P(Y < 15 \text{ or } Y > 25)$.
   c) Use your graph and/or the Empirical Rule to estimate $P(Y < 15 \text{ or } Y > 25)$.

18) The systolic blood pressure, the pressure in the arteries when the heart beat fills them with blood, is a normally distributed random variable with $\mu_Y = 115$ and $\sigma_Y = 15$. Systolic readings below 90 are considered low blood pressure and readings over 140 are considered high blood pressure.
   Let Y = the systolic blood pressure in for a randomly selected adult.
   a) Sketch the normal curve for Y. Label the axis below the peak and at the visible edges of the normal curve.
   b) Shade the area under the normal curve that corresponds to $P(Y < 90 \text{ or } Y > 140)$.
   c) Use your graph and/or the Empirical Rule to estimate $P(Y < 90 \text{ or } Y > 140)$.

Section 6.2 - The Standard Normal Curve

In the previous section, we learned that area under a normal curve can be used to represent relative frequencies for normally distributed populations and that this area can also be used to represent probabilities for normally distributed random variables. However, in the previous section, we were only able to estimate these areas by examining the graph or by using the Empirical Rule. In this section, we want to learn to use technology to accurately find the values under a special normal curve called the **Standard Normal Curve**. In the next section of the book, we will learn how to use the areas under the Standard Normal Curve to find areas under any normal curve. This will then allow us to start working on real world applications. Let's start by defining the Standard Normal Curve.

Definition: *The Standard Normal Curve*

Standard Normal Curve: The normal curve with $\mu = 0$ and $\sigma = 1$ is known as the Standard Normal Curve.

Soon, we will learn to use technology to find the area under this special normal curve, but first, let's start by taking a quick look at a sketch of the Standard Normal Curve.

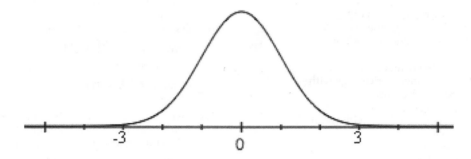

Like all normal curves, the Standard Normal Curve is centered its mean. So this means that the peak of the curve occurs at $\mu = 0$ and the visible edges of the curve disappear about three standard deviations away from the mean at –3 and 3.

$$\mu - 3\sigma = 0 - 3(1) = -3 \quad \& \quad \mu + 3\sigma = 0 + 3(1) = 3$$

Now for the big question: Why do they call this one the *Standard* Normal distribution? Is it the standard situation for the mean of a data set to be 0 or for its standard deviation to be 1? No! So where does the name come from? Why is this one so special?

To answer these questions, let's look at an example.

Example 6.5: *Examining the z-scores for the Standard Normal Curve*

Let X = a randomly selected value from the Standard Normal distribution:

a)   Find the z-score for $X = 3$.

b)   Find the z-score for $X = -2.5$.

c)   Find the z-score for an arbitrary X-value.

d)   What does this tell us about the numbers on the axis of the standard normal curve?

Solution:

Here is a sketch of the standard normal curve with all the indicated values that we wish to find z-scores for.

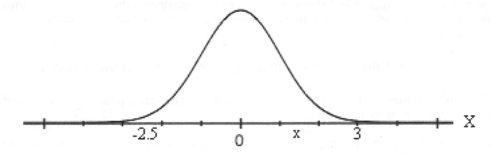

a) z-score for $X = 3$: $z = \dfrac{x - \mu}{\sigma} = \dfrac{3 - 0}{1} = 3$

b) z-score for $X = -2.5$: $z = \dfrac{x - \mu}{\sigma} = \dfrac{-2.5 - 0}{1} = -2.5$

c) z-score for an arbitrary X-value (or for $X = x$): $z = \dfrac{x - \mu}{\sigma} = \dfrac{x - 0}{1} = x$

d) The fact that, even for an arbitrary X-value, we always end up back where we started when we calculate a z-score means that we must have been starting with z-scores in the first place! This means that the values on the axis for the Standard Normal Curve are actually values of Z rather than values of X. Because of this, we should label the axis on the Standard Normal Curve as the z-axis as shown below.

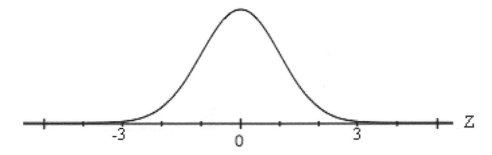

In Chapter 3, we learned that the process of finding z-scores is known as standardizing a variable. So the Standard Normal Curve represents the standardized version of a normal curve and that is where it gets its name.

> **Point to Remember:** *The Standard Normal Curve represents z-scores*
>
> The Standard Normal Curve represents the z-scores for data from other normally distributed random variables. Therefore, the units for Z are the number of standard deviations away from the mean.

The goal of this section is to find accurate values for various areas under the Standard Normal Curve. However, to find these areas accurately by hand requires the use of Calculus. Worse news is that it requires a very messy and tedious estimation formula known as Simpson's Rule from Calculus. So, rather than teach you the Calculus method for finding these areas, we will define a function that represents these areas and then we will learn to use various forms of technology to evaluate this new function. That way, we can let the technology be responsible for the tedious calculations that go with the estimation formula from Calculus. Let's define this new area finding function.

Definition: *The NormalCdf function*

> **normalcdf:** When we want to find an area under the Standard Normal Curve, we will use the *normalcdf* function and technology to accomplish this goal. We enter the lower z-score boundary and the upper z-score boundary and the function provides the area that lies between these two boundaries under the Standard Normal Curve. The structure is as follows:
>
> $$normalcdf(\text{lower } z\text{ - }score, \ \text{upper } z\text{ - }score) \longrightarrow \text{Area Between}$$
>
> *Rounding Rule*: Unless otherwise specified, it will be standard procedure to round areas under curves to 4 decimal places.
>
> Caution: Even though technology is good at finding these areas, it is only as good as our typing skills. It is common to have a 'typo' when using this command. Always have a good sketch of the area before you go to the calculator. Try to estimate the area in your head visually as a check on the technology.

Let's look at a quick example that illustrates the structure of this new function and after that we will see how to evaluate the function using various forms of technology.

Example 6.6: *Learning the structure of the normalcdf function*

Find the area under the Standard Normal Curve between the boundaries $Z = -1.5$ and $Z = 2.3$.

Solution:

Let's begin by looking at a sketch of the area we are trying to find.

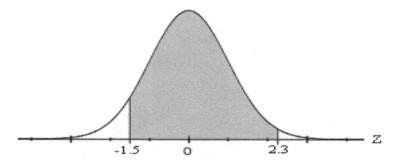

So how do we find the value of such an area? It's not a rectangle, triangle, circle, or any nice shape for which we know an area formula. In the previous section, we estimated this area visually or with the aid of the Empirical Rule. Let's give that a quick try. Given that the total area under the curve is one, we could try to visually estimate the area that is not shaded on each side and then subtract that away from the total area of 1.

From the Empirical rule, we know that the area to the left of $Z = -2$ is approximately 0.025, the total unshaded area on the left appears to be a little more than twice the size of the area to the left of $Z = -2$. Let's call the unshaded area on the left 0.06. Similarly, we estimate the area to the right of $Z = 2$ to be about 0.025, but not all of that area is unshaded, perhaps the part that remains past $Z = 2.3$ is about 0.015. Based on all this, we have a visual estimate as follows:

$$Area \approx 1 - 0.06 - 0.015 = 0.925$$

This feels like a well-reasoned and decent estimate of the area. However, it is still just an estimate. If we wanted to use technology to give us a more accurate estimate, we would use technology to evaluate the new normalcdf function. The structure of this new function for this area would be as follows.

$$Area = normalcdf(\text{lower z-score, upper z-score}) = normalcdf(-1.5, 2.3)$$

If we use technology to evaluate this function, we get: $Area = normalcdf(-1.5, 2.3) \approx 0.9225$.

The good news is that our estimate was pretty close to the correct amount of area. However, it is both easier and more accurate to get the answer using technology and normalcdf. Let's see how this is done with various forms of technology.

USING TECHNOLOGY: *Calculating normalcdf with various technologies*

Let's see how to evaluate $normalcdf(-1.5, 2.3)$ to find the area under the Standard Normal Curve between $Z = -1.5$ and $Z = 2.3$ using four common forms of technology.

TI-84:

1. From the DISTR (distribution) menu, choose "normalcdf(". DISTR is located above the "VARS" key. This will put "normalcdf(" on the home screen.
2. Enter the lower boundary z-score, then a comma, then the upper boundary z-score. See the screen shots below.
3. Press the Enter key to get the desired area. Round your answer to 4 decimal places.

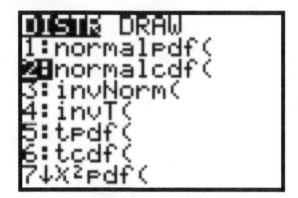
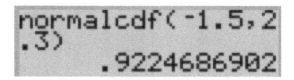

So, we get: Area ≈ 0.9225

Note: On some models of the TI-84 you must enter a value for the mean and standard deviation also. Enter $\mu = 0$ and $\sigma = 1$ to ensure that your area is from the Standard Normal Curve.

STATCRUNCH:

1. Choose Stat > Calculators > Normal
2. At the top of the window it says "Standard" and "Between". Click on "Between".
3. Enter 0 for the mean and 1 for the Std. Dev. (This makes it the Standard Normal Curve.)
4. Enter the lower boundary z-score in the left side of the probability parentheses and the upper z-score boundary in the right ride of the probability parentheses.
5. Click "Compute" and the area will be shown to the right of the equal sign. Round your answer to 4 decimal places.

So, we get: Area ≈ 0.9225

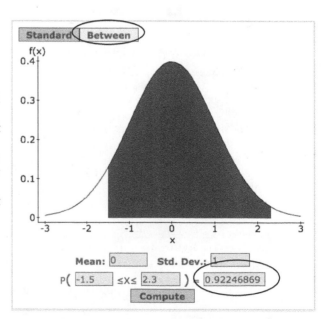

EXCEL:

1. Click in any of the cells in the worksheet.
2. Click in the f_x box.
3. Type in "=NORMDIST(-1.5, 0, 1, TRUE)" and press ENTER. (Notes: Don't type the quotes, but you must type the equal sign.) The first number is your z-score boundary, the next two are a mean of 0 and a standard deviation of 1 (Standard Normal), and the TRUE indicates that you want area.
4. The area to the left of this z-score will be shown in that cell.
5. Click in another cell and then click in the f_x box.
6. This time, type in "NORMDIST(2.3, 0, 1, TRUE)" and press enter.
7. This gives you the area to the left of your other z-score boundary.
8. To get the area between your two z-scores you must subtract the smaller area from the larger. Round your answer to 4 decimal places.

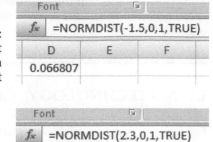

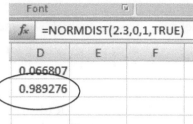

So, we get: Area $= 0.989276 - 0.066807 \approx 0.9225$

MINITAB:

1. Enter your two z-scores into C1 (or any column).
2. From the Calc Menu, choose Probability Distribution, and click on Normal . . .
3. In the pop-up window: Select "Cumulative Probability"; make sure the mean is 0 and the standard deviation is 1 (Standard Normal Curve); Select "Input columns" and enter c1 in that box. Click OK.
4. Minitab will give you the area to the left of your two z-scores.
5. To get the area between your two z-scores you must subtract the smaller value from the larger. Round your answer to 4 decimal places.

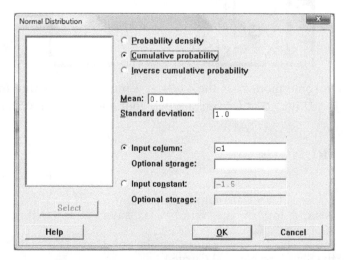

So, we get: Area $= 0.989276 - 0.066807 \approx 0.9225$

USING THE NORMALCDF FUNCTION: *Practicing the technology*

The previous example has basically shown us what we need to know about using this function, but there are still a few twists worth looking at. We will now explore these in the following example.

Example 6.7: *More Practice and Dealing with Infinity*

For the Standard Normal Curve, find each of the following:

a)   The area under the curve between $Z = 0.64$ and $Z = 2.17$

b)   The area to the right of $Z = -1.74$

c)   The area to the left of $Z = -2.01$

d)   The area to the right of $Z = 4.05$

e)   The area to the left of 4.05

Solution:

a)   First the sketch:

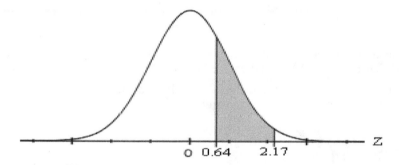

From the sketch, I notice that the amount of area is less than half of the area, so the answer should be less than 0.5. Turning to technology we get: Area = $normalcdf(0.64, 2.17) \approx 0.2461$

b)   Again, we start with a sketch.

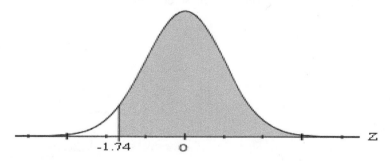

This time we notice that all of the right side is shaded as well as much of the left side. We should expect that we have most of the area and will get an answer close to 1. A reasonable estimate might be 0.95.

This time, we have a new issue to deal with. The lower boundary is –1.74, but there is no upper boundary. The area extends to the right forever. In such cases, we say that the upper boundary is positive infinity, but how do we enter infinity into our technology? There is no '∞' key for most forms of technology used for statistics. However, because almost all of the area under the Standard Normal Curve lies between –3 and 3, we can use any very large number in place of infinity. One of the largest numbers possible on most calculators is a 1 followed by 99 zeros, or 1×10^{99}. Whenever we need to use ∞ in a calculation, we will simply substitute 1×10^{99}. We will miss the area beyond 1×10^{99}, but it is almost too small to measure (in fact, the area is less than 1×10^{-99}). Any number substantially larger than 3 will do the trick. If you have trouble entering 1×10^{99} into your technology, you could just use the number 100 and you should get the same answer. The screen shot below shows how this would look on the TI-84.

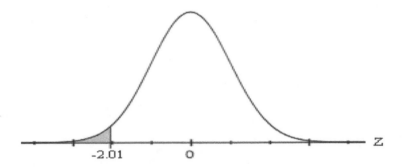

$$\text{Area} = normalcdf(-1.74, \infty) \approx 0.9591$$

c)   The sketch:

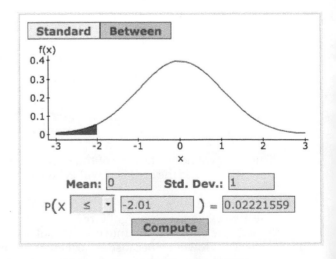

This time, we should notice that very little area is shaded and, therefore, we expect a fairly small answer (meaning much closer to 0 than 1.) Based on the Empirical Rule, we might expect the area to be around 0.025. Because our lower boundary is $-\infty$, we will use -1×10^{99} as our lower boundary (similar to using 1×10^{99} in place of ∞ in the previous example.) So we get:

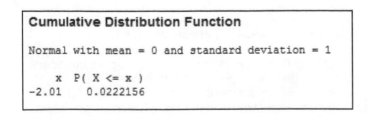

$$\text{Area} = normalcdf(-\infty, -2.01) \approx 0.0222$$

MINITAB/EXCEL/STATCRUNCH USERS: Both Minitab and Excel always give the area to the left of your z-score. So those two versions of technology are perfect for this question. On StatCrunch, choose Standard rather than between to get a quick answer. See the screen shots below.

d) The sketch:

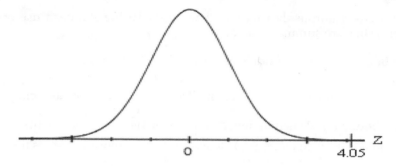

Notice that no visible area can be seen as shaded. That is because, to the right of 4.05, the graph has already blended in (visually) with the z-axis. This would seem to indicate a very small answer. Because there is no upper boundary, we will use positive infinity as our upper boundary. Using technology, we get:

$$\text{Area} = = normalcdf(4.05, \infty) \approx 2.562E - 5$$

If we just look at the 2.562, we have an answer that does not make sense. First of all, it's greater than 1, which is not possible for the area under a normal curve (total area is 1). Secondly, we were expecting a very small answer, not a large one. The key to interpreting the answer is the E –5 at the end of the number. This is the technologies version of scientific notation and it means $\times 10^{-5}$. So our answer becomes:

$$\text{Area} \approx 2.562E - 5 = 2.562 \times 10^{-5} = 0.00002562$$

But, we usually round our area answers to 4 decimal places, so we end up with:

$$\text{Area} \approx 0.0000$$

When the area you get is small enough so that it rounds to 0.0000 to 4 decimal places, you should write all the zeros rather than just saying 0. When we see an answer of 0, we think there is no area under the curve to the right of 4.05, but, in fact, the area is just very small. This idea is conveyed by writing ≈ 0.0000, which indicates that the area is just too small to show up in the first 4 decimal places.

e) Sketch:

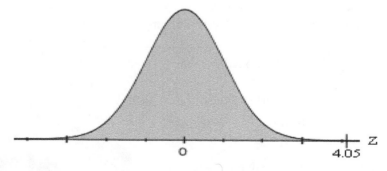

This time, we notice that all the visible area is shaded, so we should expect an answer that is extremely close to 1. Because our region has no lower boundary, we will use negative infinity as our lower boundary.

$$\text{Area} = normalcdf(-\infty, 4.05) \approx 0.9999743783 \approx 1.0000$$

Similar to the previous example, we want to write our answer as 1.0000 rather than 1. This indicates that the area rounds to 1 when written to 4 decimal places, rather than that the answer is exactly 1. We don't really have all the area, just almost all of it.

Key Concepts: *Dealing with missing boundaries and tricky areas*

The previous example showed us a few twists on the standard use of the *normalcdf* function. They are summarized below:

No left boundary: When finding an area to the left of a z-score, there is no lower boundary. In such cases, we will use -1×10^{99} to represent $-\infty$ as the left boundary in the *normalcdf* function. (**Note:** -100 works just as well.)

No right boundary: When finding an area to the right of a z-score, there is no upper boundary. In such cases, we will use 1×10^{99} to represent ∞ as the right boundary in the *normalcdf* function. (**Note:** -100 works just as well.)

Small answers: When the area you get is small enough so that it rounds to 0.0000 to 4 decimal places, you should write all the zeros rather than just saying 0. When we see an answer of 0, we think there is no area under the curve to the right of our boundary, but, in fact, the area is just very small. This idea is conveyed by writing ≈ 0.0000, which indicates that the area is just too small to show up in the first 4 decimal places.

Large answers: Similar to the previous statement, we want to write our big answers as 1.0000 rather than 1. This indicates the area rounds to 1 when written to 4 decimal places, rather than that the answer is 1. We don't really have all the area, just almost all of it.

Extra Decimal Places: Even though it will be standard practice for us to write all area using 4 decimal places as shown above, there may be times where more accuracy is desired and more decimal places are specifically requested. This is most often important when the area found is close to zero or to 1. Sometimes knowing the chance is very small is not good enough and we need to write out many decimal places to show the actual values. The directions will always request this when it is required in this text.

CALCULATOR TIP: *Storing* 1×10^{99} *in the variable I*

After a while, you might get tired of typing 1×10^{99} in your calculator so many times. One way to make this a bit easier is to store this value in the variable I on your graphing calculator. See the procedure shown below.

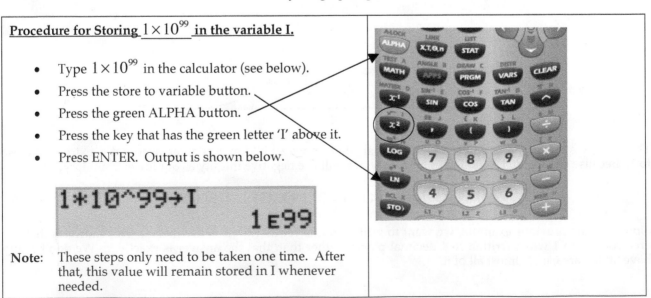

Procedure for Storing 1×10^{99} **in the variable I.**

- Type 1×10^{99} in the calculator (see below).
- Press the store to variable button.
- Press the green ALPHA button.
- Press the key that has the green letter 'I' above it.
- Press ENTER. Output is shown below.

```
1*10^99→I
              1ᴇ99
```

Note: These steps only need to be taken one time. After that, this value will remain stored in I whenever needed.

You can now use I when your upper boundary is ∞. You can also use –I when your lower boundary is –∞.

IMPORTANT AREAS: *Three areas you might want to memorize*

There are a few area questions that can be asked that are especially important. In this next example, we will look at those area questions.

Example 6.8: *Thinking about the units on a z-curve*

Find the area under the Standard Normal Curve between the boundaries:

a) $Z = -1$ and $Z = 1$

b) $Z = -2$ and $Z = 2$

c) $Z = -3$ and $Z = 3$

d) Discuss the reason that these areas should be considered important.

Solution:

a) Sketch:

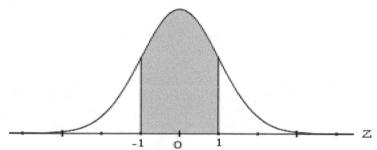

It looks like we may have a bit more than half of the curve shaded, but it's a little hard to tell. So we go to the calculator and we get:

$$\text{Area} = = normalcdf(-1,\ 1) \approx 0.6827$$

b) Sketch:

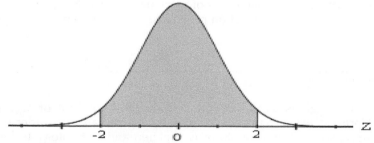

This time, it appears that we have most of the area shaded. So, our answer should be near 1. On the calculator we get:

$$\text{Area} = = normalcdf(-2,\ 2) \approx 0.9545$$

c)   Sketch:

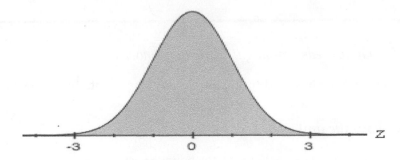

This time, it appears that almost all of the visible area has been shaded, so we should be even closer to 1 than on the previous question. On the calculator we get:

$$Area = = normalcdf(-3, 3) \approx 0.9973$$

d)   To understand the reason why these areas are important, we need to remember what the units are on the z-axis. The units are the number of standard deviations away from the mean.

This means, when we find the area between –1 and 1 to be 0.6827, we are learning that, for a normal curve, the percentage of data that lies within 1 standard deviation of the mean is approx. 68.27%.

Extending this idea to parts (b) and (c), we can say that 95.45% of normal data lies within 2 standard deviations of the mean and 99.73% of the normal data values lies within 3 standard deviations of the mean.

If Z is a random variable that has the Standard Normal Distribution, then we could state similar results using probability notation.

In Chapter 3, we learned the Empirical Rule for Bell-shaped distributions, which told us the rough amount of data that would lie within 1, 2, or 3 standard deviations of the mean. What we have done above is very similar. We will return to this idea in Section 6.3 and state an updated version of the Empirical Rule for Normal distributions. Because these areas will be considered important in future sections, it is good to become familiar with them.

WORKING BACKWARDS: *What to do when we start with an area*

In all of the problems we have worked so far, we were given boundaries and asked to find the area under the Standard Normal Curve. The questions often come to us in the reverse order. That is, sometimes we are given areas under the Standard Normal Curve, and then we are asked to find the boundaries that trap the described areas. In this section we will just practice the mechanics of working backwards, but in the next section we will see that this skill is needed for many important application problems. Let's begin by defining **invNorm**, our function that helps us work backwards.

> **Definition:** *The invNorm Function*
>
> **invNorm:** invNorm gives us the z-score with a given amount of area (under the Standard Normal Curve) to its left. When we are given an area under the Standard Normal Curve, we will use the *invNorm* function and technology to help find the desired z-score. The input to this function is always the area to the left of a z-score boundary. The function then provides the z-score boundary. The "inv" stands for inverse. An inverse function does the opposite of the original function, or you might say that it works backwards. The structure is as follows:
>
> $$invNorm(\text{Area to the Left}) \longrightarrow z-score$$

USING TECHNOLOGY: *Calculating invNorm with various technologies*

Let's see how to evaluate *invNorm*(0.2500) to find the z-score boundary for the Standard Normal Curve so that the area to the left of the z-score is 0.2500. We will look at this using four common forms of technology.

TI-84:

1. From the DISTR (distribution) menu, choose "invNorm(". This will put "invNorm(" on the home screen.
2. Enter the area to the LEFT of the desired z-score. See the screen shot below.
3. Press the Enter key to get the desired area. Round your answer to exactly 3 decimal places.

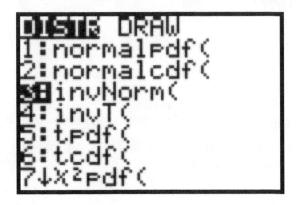

So, we get: $Z = invNorm(0.2500) \approx -0.674$

Note: On some models of the TI-84 you must enter a value for the mean and standard deviation also. Enter $\mu = 0$ and $\sigma = 1$ to ensure that you are getting a z-score for the Standard Normal Curve.

STATCRUNCH:

1. Choose Stat > Calculators > Normal
2. At the top of the window it says "Standard" and "Between". Click on Standard.
3. Enter 0 for the mean and 1 for the Std. Dev. (This makes it the Standard Normal curve.)
4. Make sure that the probability inequality shows "≤".
5. Enter the area to the LEFT in the box following the equal sign.
6. Click "Compute" and the z-score will be shown inside the box inside of the parentheses. Round your answer to 4 decimal places.

   So, we get: $Z = invNorm(0.2500) \approx -0.674$

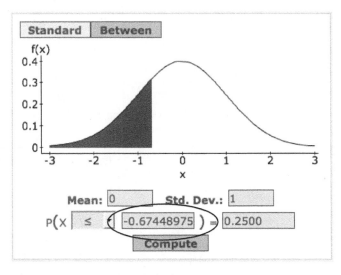

EXCEL:

1. Click in any of the cells in the worksheet.
2. Click in the f_x box.
3. Type in "NORMINV(0.2500, 0, 1)" and press ENTER. (Notes: Don't type the quotes, but you must type the equal sign.) The first number is area to the LEFT. The next two are a mean of 0 and a standard deviation of 1 (Standard Normal).
4. The z-score with area 02500 will be shown in the selected cell.
5. Round your answer to 4 decimal places.

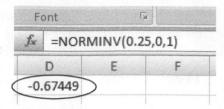

So, we get: $Z = invNorm(0.2500) \approx -0.674$

MINITAB:

1. From the Calc Menu, choose Probability Distribution, and click on Normal . . .
2. In the pop-up window: Select "Inverse cumulative Probability"; make sure the mean is 0 and the standard deviation is 1 (Standard Normal Curve).
3. Select "Input Constant" and then enter the area to the LEFT of the desired z-score. Click OK.
4. Minitab will give you the z-score with the desired area to the LEFT.
5. Round your answer to 4 decimal places.

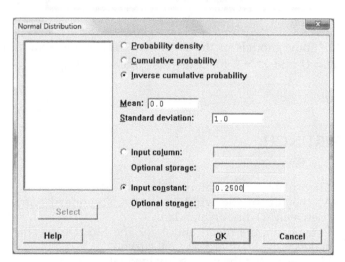

Inverse Cumulative Distribution Function

Normal with mean = 0 and standard deviation = 1

```
P( X <= x )          x
      0.25  -0.674490
```

So, we get: $Z = invNorm(0.2500) \approx -0.674$

Now that we see the basics of how technology is used for evaluating values of invNorm, let's look at an example to see how this works with some slight variations to the question.

Example 6.9: *Using invNorm to solve various working backwards questions*

For the Standard Normal Curve:

a)   Find the z-score that has an area of 0.7804 to its left.

b)   Find the z-score that has an area of 0.1092 to its left.

c)   Find the z-score that has area 0.0581 to its right.

d)   Find the two z-scores that trap an area of 0.95 between them with equal outside areas.

Solution:

a)   As before, it is good to start off with a sketch. To do this is a little tougher than before, because we don't know exactly where to draw the boundary of the shaded area. The boundary is what we are trying to find. In the previous examples, our graph helped us estimate the answer. In this type of problem, we must roughly estimate the answer to draw our sketch.

So here is the key. 0.7804 is a lot of area. We say this because it is more than half of the total area under the Standard Normal Curve. The only way we could have more than half of the data to our left, is if our boundary is somewhere on the right hand side. So, our picture should be roughly as follows:

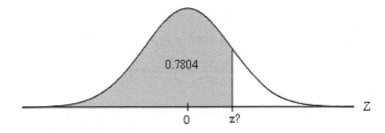

We know that the value of z we are looking for is somewhere to the right of zero, but we are not sure exactly where. That is why it is shown on the picture as z? To find its location will again require the use of the technology, but this time, because we are starting with an area and looking for the boundary, we need to use our new function, invNorm. The structure of this function is invNorm(area to the left) and it will give us the boundary. Because we are finding a z-score, we will round our answer using 3 decimal places. For this problem we get:

$$Z = invNorm(0.7804) \approx 0.774$$

So our completed sketch would be as follows:

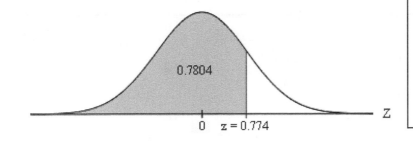

> **Key Concept**: *Sketches for finding z*
>
> When you first draw the sketch, you should only think about whether the boundary is to the left or the right of zero. Do not try to place the boundary perfectly. Finding the perfect spot is the job of the invNorm command.

b)   Find the z-score that has an area of 0.1092 to its left.

Again, we will begin with a sketch. This time, the area to our left is less than half of the total area. In order for this to be the case, the boundary we are looking for must be on the left side of zero. Here is a rough sketch.

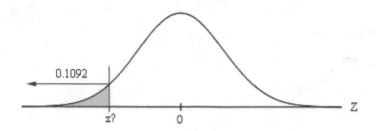

> **Key Concept**: *Placement of Area*
>
> It is usually more convenient to show the area on top of an arrow as in the above sketch, than to try to squeeze the number into our small shaded area where it might be hard to read.

Again, we turn to technology and the invNorm function for the final answer.

$$Z = invNorm(0.1092) \approx -1.231$$

c)   Find the z-score that has area 0.0581 to its right.

Again, the area is a small number representing far less than half of the total area. To have such a small amount of area to our right, the boundary we are looking for must be on the right.

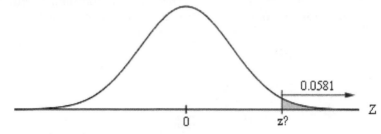

Before we turn to technology, we must notice something very important. The area we were given is an area to the right, not an area to the left. The invNorm function expects us to provide an area to the left and that is what we must do. We find the area to the left using the complement rule:

Area to the left $=$ 1 – area to the right $=$ 1 – 0.0581 $=$ 0.9419

It's a good idea to put this value on our sketch as well.

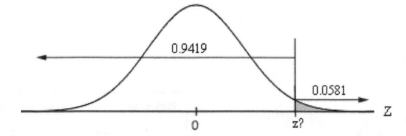

> **Key Concept**: *Areas to the Right*
>
> When you are given an area to the right, you must always subtract from 1 to get the area to the left before going to the invNorm function.

Now, we turn to technology with this area to the left and get:

$$Z = invNorm(0.9419) \approx 1.571$$

d)   Find the two z-scores that trap an area of 0.95 between them with equal outside areas.

If the area in the middle is 0.95, then that leaves 1 − 0.95 = 0.05 as the amount of area left over. This area is to be split evenly for the two outside areas, so each outside area should be 0.05/2 = 0.025 as shown in the sketch below.

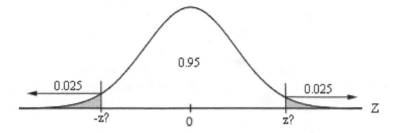

0.95

0.025   0.025

-z?   0   z?

Key Concept: *Areas in the Middle*

When finding two z-score that trap a specified area between them with equal outside areas, you can just find one and then use symmetry to get the other.

Notice that the two boundaries have been labeled as −z and z. This is due to the fact that we have equal outside areas and that the Standard Normal Distribution is symmetric about its mean, 0. This means that we can really just find one of the two boundaries and the other will just have the opposite sign. Because we already have the area to the left of −z labeled on our picture, it is probably a little easier to start with that one.

$$-Z = invNorm(0.025) \approx -1.960$$

Thus, by symmetry, we also have $Z = 1.960$. So the two z-values that trap an area of 0.95 between them with equal outside areas are $-Z = -1.960$ and $Z = 1.960$.

The previous example showed us how to use the invNorm function to work backwards with a Standard Normal Curve. We do this so often, that there is a special notation for asking such questions. That notation is shown below.

Definition: *Special notation for finding a z-score with a specified area to its right*

z_α: (read z subscript α or z sub α) is the z-score, or boundary, that has area α to its right. (α is read as 'alpha'.)

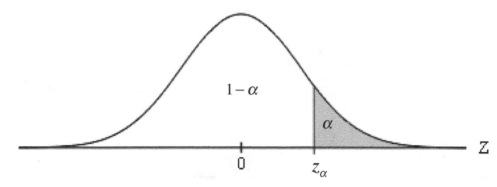

$1 - \alpha$

α

0   z_α

Caution: Even though this special notation focuses on areas to the right of the z-score boundary, we must remember to enter the area to the left of the boundary when using the invNorm function. Always draw a sketch and remember to find the area to the left by subtracting from the total area of 1.

$$z_\alpha = invNorm(1 - \alpha)$$

Let's look at a quick example to practice the notation.

Example 6.10: *Practicing with the z_α notation*

a) Find $z_{0.10}$

b) Find $z_{0.85}$

Solution:

a) To be successful at this type of question, we must understand the notation. When we are asked to find $z_{0.10}$, we are being asked to find the z-score that has area 0.10 to its right. To have a small amount of area to our right, the boundary we are looking for must be on the right. As before, when given an area on the right, we subtract from 1 to find the area to the left.

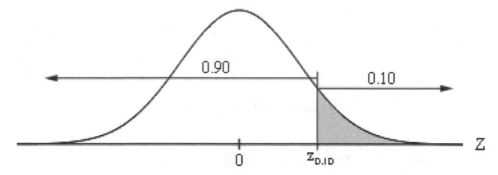

Using technology, we get: $z_{0.10} = invNorm(0.90) \approx 1.282$

b) $z_{0.85}$ is the z-score with area 0.85 to its right. This is a large amount of area, so the z-score must be on the left and the area to its left would be $1 - 0.85 = 0.15$.

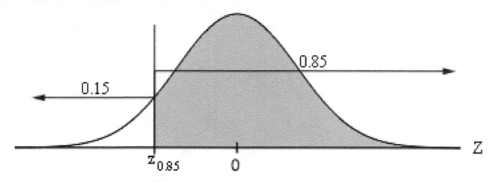

Using technology, we get: $z_{0.85} = invNorm(0.15) \approx -1.036$

WRAP SESSION: *Probability Notation*

The area under a normal curve can also give us the probabilities for a normal random variable. Therefore, many of the area questions we have asked in this section, could also be posed using probability notation.

In this final example, we will examine questions using probability notation and we will also review the concepts of AND and OR probabilities from Chapter 5.

Example 6.11: *Using Area to Answer Probability Questions*

Suppose that Z is a random variable with the Standard Normal Distribution. Find each of the following:

a) $P(Z > 1.588)$

b) $P(Z > -1.3 \ \& \ Z < 2.6)$

c) $P(Z < 0.76 \ \text{OR} \ Z > 1.25)$

d) If $P(Z > k) = 0.10$, then find k.

Solution:

a) In Section 6.1, we stated that the probability for a normally distributed random variable could be found by finding the corresponding area under the corresponding normal curve. So, $P(Z > 1.588)$ becomes the area to the right of $Z = 1.588$ under the Standard Normal Curve.

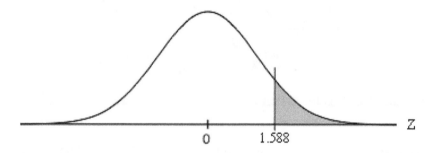

This appears to be a fairly small amount of area. It is much closer to 0 than 1. We are back to finding area again, so this calls for the normalcdf function.

$$P(Z > 1.588) = Area = normalcdf(1.588, \infty) \approx 0.0561$$

b) $P(Z > -1.3 \ \& \ Z < 2.6)$ is the overlap of the two areas requested. This becomes the area between $Z = -1.3$ and $Z = 2.6$ (see the graph below).

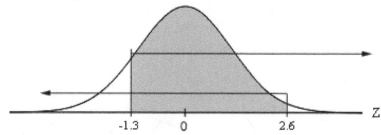

Much of the total area under the curve is shaded, so I expect an answer closer to 1 than to 0.

$$P(Z > -1.3 \ \& \ Z < 2.6) = P(-1.3 < Z < 2.6) = normalcdf(-1.3, 2.6) \approx 0.8985$$

c)   Notice that the two inequalities in $P(Z < 0.76 \ \text{OR} \ Z > 1.25)$ do not overlap in the graph below.

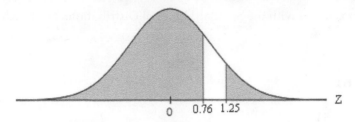

This means that we can apply the special addition rule: $P(A \ \text{OR} \ B) = P(A) + P(B)$

So we get: $P(Z < 0.76 \ \text{OR} \ Z > 1.25) = P(Z < 0.76) + P(Z > 1.25)$

We can now work on each piece using the normalcdf function.

$$P(Z < 0.76) = normalcdf(-\infty, \ 0.76) \approx 0.7764$$

$$P(Z > 1.25) = normalcdf(1.25, \ \infty) \approx 0.1056$$

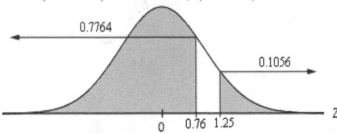

Therefore: $P(Z < 0.76 \ \text{OR} \ Z > 1.25) = P(Z < 0.76) + P(Z > 1.25) \approx 0.7764 + 0.1056 = 0.8820$

Another acceptable approach to this problem would have been to find the area between $Z = 0.76$ and $Z = 1.25$, and then subtract that middle area from 1. While not as direct an approach, it would be faster.

d)   The key to finding the k in $P(Z > k) = 0.10$ is to realize that, because we know that answer to the probability question, we already know the area. The value of k represents a boundary on the Standard Normal Curve that has area 0.10 to its right. Because we know the area and are looking for the boundary, this is a working backwards question and requires the use of the invNorm function. Because the 0.10 is the $P(Z > k)$, that means that 0.10 is the area to the right of k. We must find the area to the left of k using the complement rule and then we can use invNorm to find the value of k.

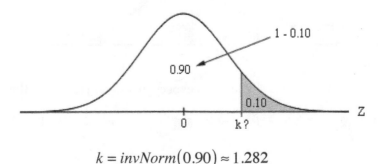

$$k = invNorm(0.90) \approx 1.282$$

Let's practice these new ideas with a few exercises.

Exercise Set 6.2

Concept Review: Review the definitions and concepts from this section by filling in the blanks for each of the following.

19) The Standard Normal Curve is the normal curve with a mean of ____ and a standard deviation of ____ .

20) The Standard Normal Curve represents the _____ from other normal curves. Therefore, the units are measured in the number of _____ _____ from the mean.

21) When using the normalcdf function, we must enter both the _____ z-score _____ and the _____ z-score _____ of the region.

22) When using the invNorm function, we only need to enter the area on the _____ of the boundary we are seeking.

23) z_α tells us that there is an area of ____ to the _____ of the Z we are looking for.

24) If the region we are finding the area of has no lower boundary, then we use ____ as our lower boundary. If the region we are finding the area of has no upper boundary, then we use ____ as our upper boundary.

Mechanics: Practice using the technology to work with the Standard Normal Curve. Use either the normalcdf function or the invNorm function for each of the following. Include a sketch with each area, probability, or z-score to be found.

25) For the Standard Normal Curve, find each of the following:
   a) The area between Z = -0.62 and Z = 2.77
   b) The area between –2 and 2
   c) The area to the left of Z = 2.103
   d) The area to the right of 1.45

26) For the Standard Normal Curve, find each of the following:
   a) The area between Z = 1.657 and Z = 2.501
   b) The area between –3 and 3
   c) The area to the left of Z = -1.505
   d) The area to the right of 0.559

27) For the Standard Normal Curve, find each of the following.
   a) The area between -4.01 and 4.56
   b) The area to the left of -4.592
   c) The area to the right of 5.672

28) For the Standard Normal Curve, find each of the following.
   a) The area between 4.085 and 5.993
   b) The area to the right of -4.399
   c) The area to the left of 7.851

29) If the random variable Z has the Standard Normal distribution, then find:
   a) $P(-1.32 < Z < -0.47)$
   b) $P(Z < -1.751)$
   c) $P(Z > -2.04)$

30) If the random variable Z has the Standard Normal distribution, then find:
   a) $P(-2.470 < Z < -1.095)$
   b) $P(Z < 2.68)$
   c) $P(Z > 1.904)$

31) If the random variable Z has the Standard Normal distribution, then find:
   a) $P(Z < 1.04 \text{ OR } Z > 1.89)$
   b) $P(Z < 2 \text{ \& } Z > 1)$
   c) If $P(Z < k) = 0.65$, find k.

32) If the random variable Z has the Standard Normal distribution, then find:
   a) $P(Z < 2.506 \text{ OR } Z > -0.853)$
   b) $P(Z < -0.308 \text{ \& } Z > 1.662)$
   c) If $P(Z > k) = 0.20$, find k.

33) For the Standard Normal Curve, find each of the following.
   a) The z-score with area 0.1234 to its left.
   b) The z-score with area 0.9876 to its left.
   c) The z-score with area 0.025 to its right.
   d) The two z-scores that trap an area of 0.90 between them with equal outside areas.

34) For the Standard Normal Curve, find each of the following.
   a) The z-score with area 0.7735 to its left.
   b) The z-score with area 0.2567 to its left.
   c) The z-score with area 0.005 to its right.
   d) The two z-scores that trap an area of 0.80 between them with equal outside areas.

35) For the Standard Normal Curve, find:
   a) $z_{0.01}$
   b) $z_{0.05}$
   c) $z_{0.80}$

36) For the Standard Normal Curve, find:
   a) $z_{0.025}$
   b) $z_{0.005}$
   c) $z_{0.90}$

Section 6.3 – Applications of Normal Distributions

In the previous section, we learned how to use the normalcdf function and the invNorm function to work with areas under the Standard Normal Curve. We also learned that the Standard Normal Curve represents the z-scores from other normal curves. In this section, we wish to expand on this connection between a typical normal curve and the Standard Normal Curve. This will allow us to start using the area under normal curves to answer real world questions. The key to this is learning that we can use z-scores to move an area question from any normal curve to the Standard Normal Curve without changing the desired area. This fact is illustrated in the following Point to Remember.

Point to Remember: *Standardizing does not alter the area we are finding*

The area that lies between two boundaries 'A' and 'B' under a normal curve is equal to the area under the Standard Normal Curve that lies between the z-scores for the original boundaries. See graphs below.

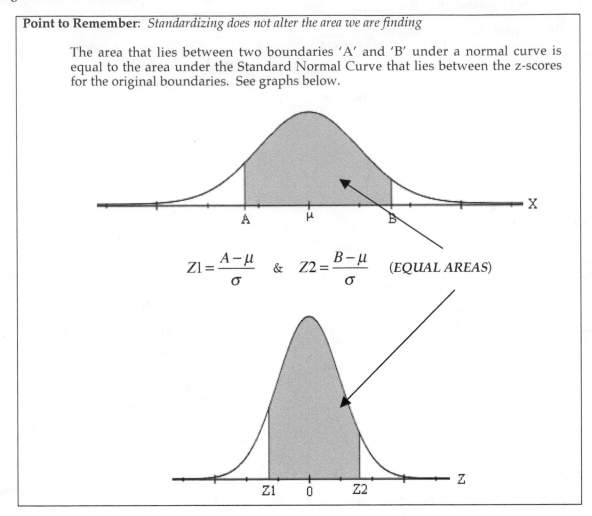

$$Z1 = \frac{A-\mu}{\sigma} \quad \& \quad Z2 = \frac{B-\mu}{\sigma} \quad (EQUAL\ AREAS)$$

The goal of this section is to take what we learned in the previous section and combine it with the fact stated above to find areas under any normal curve, not just the Standard Normal Curve. Let's look at an example to see how this works.

Example 6.12: *Practicing Transforming Area from One Curve to the Standard Normal Curve*

Consider the normal curve with mean $\mu = 73.1$ and standard deviation $\sigma = 8.019$. Let X be a boundary for this curve.

a) Find the area to the left of $X = 80$.

b) Find the area between $X = 65$ and $X = 85$.

Solution:

a) First, we will sketch the area to be found.

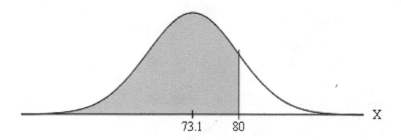

> **Key Concept:** *Labeling the axis*
>
> The axis is labeled with an X rather than a Z, because this is just *a* normal curve, not *the* Standard Normal Curve.

Next, we will use the idea that the area under any normal curve is equal to the corresponding area under the Standard Normal Curve. The correspondence between the two curves is given by the z-score formula. So, specifically, we can say that the area to the left of 80 for this normal curve is equal to the area to the left of the z-score of 80 under the Standard Normal Curve. So we need to find the z-score for $X = 80$.

$$z = \frac{80 - 73.1}{8.019} \approx 0.860$$

So now the task becomes that of finding the area to the left of z = 0.860 under the Standard Normal Curve. Let's look at that sketch.

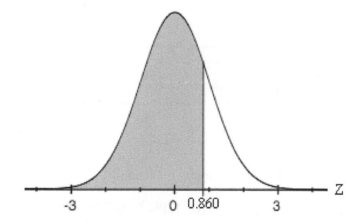

Now we can find this area using the *normalcdf* function.

$$\text{Area} = normalcdf\left(-\infty,\ 0.860\right) \approx 0.8051$$

From the Point to Remember on the previous page, we know that this area we found on the Standard Normal Curve is equal to the area we were looking for on the original normal curve. Visually, we are saying:

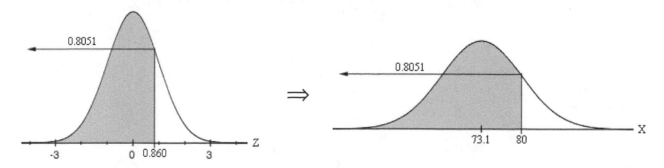

While we could always draw both a sketch for the original normal curve, X, and the Standard Normal curve, Z, we usually like to do all of our work on a single sketch. To do this we just put the z-scores below the x values they correspond to. Then, even though we find our area for the z-curve, we show it on the picture for the x-curve. We will use a single sketch for the rest of this example and for future problems similar to it.

b) Area between $X = 65$ and $X = 85$. Start with a sketch.

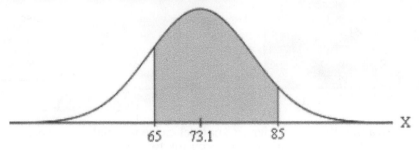

Now we find the z-scores for each x.

$$z = \frac{65 - 73.1}{8.019} \approx -1.010 \quad \text{and} \quad z = \frac{85 - 73.1}{8.019} \approx 1.484$$

We add those to our sketch.

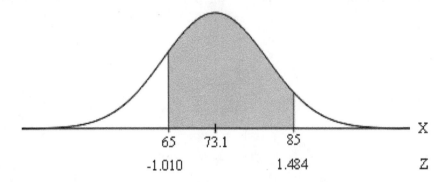

And then finally we find the area using the normalcdf function and technology.

$$\text{Area} = normalcdf\left(-1.010,\ 1.484\right) \approx 0.7748$$

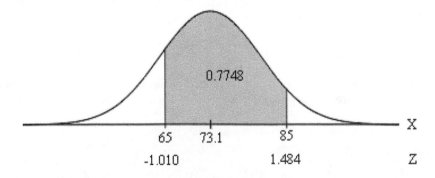

We will usually illustrate all of our work on a single sketch. We used three this time just to show the progression.

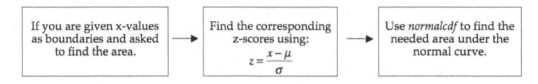

Point to Remember: *Procedure for finding the area under a normal curve*

Do each of the following steps when finding area under a normal curve.
- Sketch the normal curve and label the mean and the x boundaries. Shade the region you are finding the area of.
- Calculate the z-scores for all x boundaries and label these z-scores on the sketch just below the corresponding x-values.
- Use normalcdf(lower boundary, upper boundary) with your z-scores to find the area you need.
- Show your answer on the sketch.

| If you are given x-values as boundaries and asked to find the area. | → | Find the corresponding z-scores using: $z = \dfrac{x - \mu}{\sigma}$ | → | Use *normalcdf* to find the needed area under the normal curve. |

APPLICATIONS: *Using Area Under a Normal Curve to find Percentages*

Recall from Section 6.1 that, if a population is normally distributed, then the relative frequencies for that population can be found by using the corresponding areas under the corresponding normal curve. This next example looks at the details of that process.

Example 6.13: *Heights of 10-yr-old Boys (Revisited)*

Consider the heights of all 10-yr-old boys in the United States. Suppose that those heights are approximately normally distributed with $\mu = 54.75$ inches and $\sigma = 2.125$ inches.

a) In order to ride alone on the *Autopia* ride at Disneyland, a child must be at least 54 inches tall. Determine the percentage of 10-yr old boys who are tall enough to ride this ride alone.

b) What percentage of the 10-yr-old boys have heights that lie within 1 standard deviations of the mean?

Mickey is tall enough to ride *Autopia* alone. What percentage of 10-yr-old boys are tall enough to do the same?

c) What percentage of the 10-yr-old boys have heights that lie within 2 standard deviations of the mean?

d) Without doing any work, can you state the percentage of the 10-yr-old boys who have heights that lie within 3 standard deviations of the mean? Explain your reasoning.

Solution:

a) The first task here is translation. In order for someone to ride alone on *Autopia*, they must be at least 54 inches tall. Therefore, we want to find the percentage of 10-yr-old boys that are at 54 inches tall. To find the percentage requested, we will need to find the corresponding area under a normal curve. This area represents relative frequency, which we will then convert to a percentage. We begin by sketching the area to be found. Because of the phrase "at least 54", we will shade the area to the right of 54 inches on our graph.

In addition to labeling the boundary of 54 inches on our graph, we also need to compute the z-score for 54 and show that below the initial x-value of 54. After we have the z-score, we can then use the normalcdf function to find the desired area. See the steps and graph below.

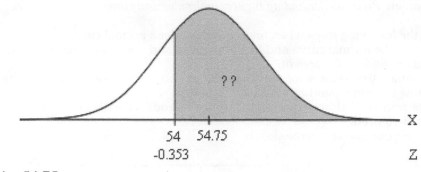

$$z = \frac{54 - 54.75}{2.125} \approx -0.353 \quad \Rightarrow \quad \text{Area} = normalcdf(-0.353, \infty) \approx 0.6380 = 63.80\%$$

So, 63.80% of 10-yr old boys should be tall enough to ride alone on *Autopia* at Disneyland.

b) This problem is a little different, in that we are not told specific x-values. Instead, we are just told to find the area within 1 standard deviation of the mean. If you think about it carefully, you will realize that the x-values do not need to be determined to answer this question, but we will find them this time for clarity.

The two x-values that are 1 standard deviation away from the mean are found as follows.

$$x_1 = \mu - \sigma = 54.75 - 2.125 = 52.625 \quad \& \quad x_2 = \mu + \sigma = 54.75 + 2.125 = 56.875$$

Now we compute the z-scores for each of these x-values.

$$z_1 = \frac{52.625 - 54.75}{2.125} = -1.000 \quad \& \quad z_2 = \frac{56.875 - 54.75}{2.125} = 1.000$$

We should now see, why it was unnecessary to find the actual x-values. Recall that the units on z-scores are the number of standard deviations away from the mean. So, of course, the x-value that is 1 standard deviation below the mean would have a z = -1 and the x-value that is 1 standard deviation above the mean would have a z = 1.

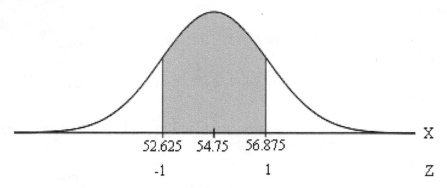

The relative frequency / area can be found using normalcdf.

$$\text{Area} = normalcdf(-1, 1) \approx 0.6827 = 68.27\%$$

This answer should be familiar from the previous section. Do you recognize it?

c) Because we are looking for the percentage that lies within 2 standard deviations of the mean, the z-scores needed will be z = –2 and z = 2. So we can draw a quick sketch and then jump right to finding the area with the normalcdf function.

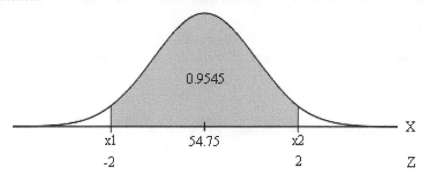

Area = $normalcdf(-2, 2) \approx 0.9545 = 95.45\%$

It was not necessary to find the exact x-values, because we use z-scores to find area and we know the z-scores based on the number of standard deviations away from the mean that the x-values are.

d) If we want the percentage of data that lies within 3 standard deviations of the mean, then our z-scores would be z = -3 and z = 3. In the previous section we discussed the important areas between –1 and 1, -2 and 2, and between –3 and 3. The answers to parts (b) and (c) matched up with these important areas and I would expect this one to do the same.

Area $\approx 0.9973 = 99.73\%$

In Section 3.5 we learned the Empirical Rule for bell-shaped distributions. That rule gave us approximations for the percentage of a data set that was expected within 1, 2, or 3 standard deviations from the mean. In that version of the rule, we gave rough estimates of those percentages, but if we know that the data set we are dealing with is normally distributed, then we can be very specific with our percentages. The results are summarized below.

Point to Remember: *Empirical Rule for Normal Populations*

For a normally distributed population, you will find that:

*   68.27% of the data will lie within 1 standard deviation of the mean.

*   95.45% of the data will lie within 2 standard deviations of the mean.

*   99.73% of the data will lie within 3 standard deviations of the mean.

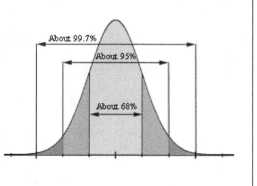

WORKING BACKWARDS: *Going from an area to an x-value*

We saw in the previous section, that sometimes you are given an area and asked to find a boundary. We will now explore how such situations are dealt with for general normal distributions.

Example 6.14: *A discussion of working backwards*

Consider the normal curve with a mean $\mu = 17.1$ and standard deviation $\sigma = 4.934$.

a) Find the x-value that has area 0.18 to its right.

b) Find the 2 x-values that divide the curve into a middle area of 0.90 and equal outside areas.

Solution:

a) We begin with a sketch. Notice that 0.18 is less than half of the area under the curve. If less than half of the area is to the right of our x-value, then our x-value must also be on the right.

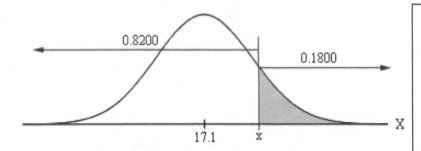

> **Caution:** *Areas vs. z-scores*
>
> Even though the area to the right was given as 0.18, it can be useful to write it as 0.1800 on the picture. Consistently writing areas using 4 decimal places and z-scores with 3 decimal places can help avoid getting the two types of numbers mixed up.

We must remember that the invNorm function requires us to provide the area to the left, rather than the area to the right, when working backwards. The area to the left is found by subtracting 0.18 from 1.

We now turn to the invNorm function and input the area to the left.

$$invNorm(0.82) \approx 0.915$$

So what have we just found? It can't be the x-value we want because it is smaller than the mean of 17.1. Recall that the job of invNorm is to give us the z-score with area 0.82 to its left under the Standard Normal Curve. So we have z = 0.915 and we must find the x-value that corresponds to it. There are two ways to accomplish this.

The first and easiest is to just consider what the units are for z-scores. A z-score of 0.915 tells us that the x-value we want is 0.915 standard deviations above the mean. To find this value we simply take the mean and add 0.915 times the standard deviation to it as follows.

$$x = \mu + 0.915\sigma = 17.1 + 0.915 * 4.934 = 21.61461$$

So the x-value that has area 0.18 to its right is 21.61461. See the updated sketch below.

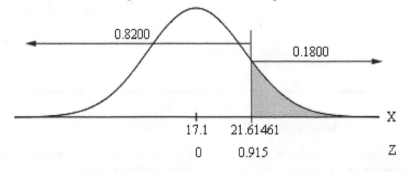

The other way we can get from the z-score to an x-value is more algebraic. The idea is to take the z-score formula and solve it for x as follows:

$$z = \frac{x-\mu}{\sigma} \implies z \cdot \sigma = x - \mu \implies x = \mu + z\sigma$$

This is known as the destandardizing formula. Using it on this problem we get:

$$x = \mu + z\sigma = \mu + 0.915\sigma = 17.1 + 0.915(4.934) = 21.61461$$

We get the same answer whether we use the units on z-scores or the formula to find our x-value. Choose the method that works the best for you.

b) We begin with a sketch. If the area in the middle is 0.90 with equal outside areas, then the outside areas must each equal 0.05.

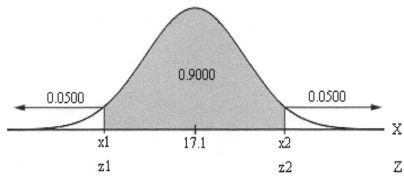

We use the invNorm function to find z1. We can then use symmetry to get z2.

$$z1 = invNorm(0.0500) \approx -1.645 \implies z2 \approx 1.645$$

$$x1 = \mu + z\sigma = 17.1 + (-1.645)(4.934) = 8.98357$$

$$x2 = \mu + z\sigma = 17.1 + 1.645(4.934) = 25.21643$$

Key Concept: *To add or subtract?*

Even though the destandardizing formula has a '+' sign in it, if your z-score is negative, then it becomes a subtraction.

So the two x-values that trap a middle area of 0.90 with equal outside areas are 8.98357 and 25.21643.

Point to Remember: *Procedure for finding x-values for a normal curve when areas are given*

Use the steps below when you are given an area for a normal curve and need to find the corresponding x-value boundaries.

- Sketch the normal curve and label the mean. Show the given area and the x boundaries you are looking for. These boundaries will be shown as unknowns and you just place them roughly where you think they will end up.
- Use the invNorm(area to the left) function to find the z-score that corresponds to the x-value you are looking for.
- Use the destandardizing formula $x = \mu + z\sigma$ to find the x-value you need.
- Put your answer on the sketch.

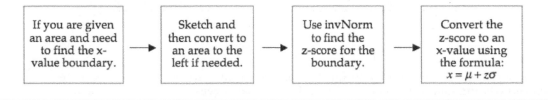

Example 6.15: *Finding Quartiles and Percentiles for Car Tires*

A tire manufacturer makes a tire that has a mean tread life of about 48,000 miles. Suppose that the tread lifetimes for the tires are normally distributed with a standard deviation of about 5000 miles.

a) How long would a tire have to last to be in the longest lasting 20% of the tires made by this manufacturer?

b) Find the Quartiles for the tread life of this brand of tire.

c) Find and interpret the 90th percentile, P_{90}.

d) If they wanted to set a mileage for the Warranty on these tires, where should they set that value if they only want to replace the worst 5% of the tires for their customers?

How can a normal distribution help us set up the tire warranty for a company?

Solution:

a) For a normally distributed population, percentages are equal to the area under the corresponding normal curve. So, we are being asked to find the x-value with area 0.20 to its right. Because the area to the right is less than half, the x-value we are looking for must be on the right hand side. Here's the sketch:

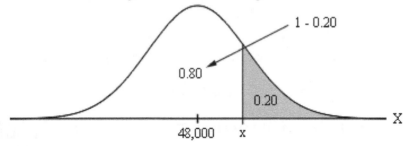

Even though we are asked about the area to the right, we must subtract that 0.20 from 1 to get the area on the left. Area to the left is what we must have to use the invNorm function to find our z-score. Finally, we convert the z-score to a mileage for the tires.

$$z = invNorm(0.8000) \approx 0.842 \Rightarrow x = \mu + z\sigma = 48,000 + 0.842(5,000) = 52,210$$

So, a tire must last for more than 52,210 miles to be in the longest lasting 20% of the tires.

b) Finding the quartiles is also a working backwards question, because quartiles divide a data set into 4 equal parts. In other words, they divide the data set into 4 sections, each containing 25% of the data. For normal curves, percentages are equivalent to areas under the curve. Here is a sketch:

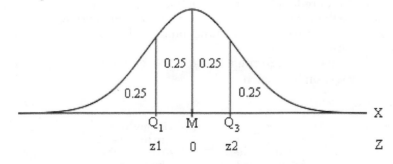

Notice that only the z-scores for Q_1 and Q_3 are unknown. The z-score for M is 0, because the mean has half of the data below it and half of the data above it. For normal curves, the mean and median are always the same value. We should also note that the z1 and z2 will be opposites due to symmetry. So really, we only need to use the invNorm function once on this problem.

$$z1 = invNorm(0.25) \approx -0.674 \quad \Rightarrow \quad z2 = 0.674$$

$$Q_1 = \mu - z\sigma = 48,000 - 0.674(5,000) = 44,630 \quad \& \quad Q_3 = \mu + z\sigma = 48,000 + 0.674(5,000) = 51,370$$

So the quartiles are: $Q_1 = 44,630$ miles, $M = 48,000$ miles, $Q_3 = 51,370$ miles.

c)   In Chapter 3, we learned that a percentile is a number that has a given percentage of the data below it. Therefore, P_{90} has 90% of the tire lifetimes below it. So, we are looking for the x-value with area 0.90 to its left. Because we have more than half of the area to the left, P_{90} must be on the right side of the graph.

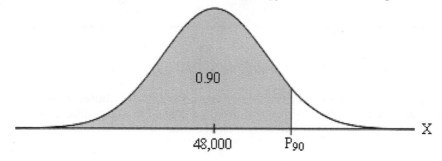

The z-score is given by: $z = invNorm(0.90) \approx 1.282$

So, $P_{90} = x = \mu + z\sigma = 48,000 + 1.282 * 5,000 = 54,410$ miles.

Interpretation: 90% of the tires of this type manufactured by this company have tread lifetimes that are *less than* 54,410 miles.

d)   Because they only want the warranty to cover the worst 5% of the tires, we are looking for an amount of miles that would have 5% of the tires to its left and the other 95% of the tires to its right. Converting this to area, we get the picture below. We will then use invNorm to find the z-score and convert that to a tread life.

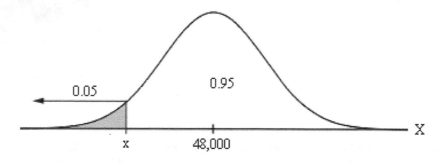

$$z = invNorm(0.05) \approx -1.645 \quad \Rightarrow \quad x = 48,000 - 1.645 * 5,000 = 39,775$$

If we want exactly 5% of the tires to be eligible for replacement under this warranty, we would set the warranty at 39,775 miles. You have probably noticed that warranties are usually set at nicer numbers, so the company might end up being generous and decide to set the warranty at 40,000 miles instead.

Point to Remember: *Procedure for finding percentiles for a normal curve*

Use the steps below to find percentiles for normal distributions.

- Sketch the normal curve and label the mean.
- The percentile number *always* represents the area to the left of the percentile, x-value, that you are looking for.
- Use the invNorm(area to the left) function to find the z-score that corresponds to the percentile, x-value, you are looking for.
- Use the destandardizing formula $x = \mu + z\sigma$ to find the percentile, x-value, that you need.
- Show your answer on the sketch.
- Interpret the percentile by stating that the given percentage of the data lies below, or is smaller, or is less than, etc. than the percentile you found.

WRAP SESSION: *Working with Normal Random Variables*

The final setting we need to look at in this section is that of a normally distributed random variable. We stated in Section 6.1, that if a variable is normally distributed, then we could answer probability questions using the area under the corresponding normal curve. We will now look at an example of this situation.

Example 6.16: *Oh fudge! Holiday Weight Gain*

In September 2014, the results of a survey conducted by Forza Supplements were released. The study found that December is the worst month for weight gain with people gaining on average about 4 pounds during that month. Let X = the amount of weight gained in December for a randomly selected person. Suppose that the amount of weight gain is normally distributed with $\mu_X = 4.1$ and $\sigma_X = 2.83$.

a) Find and interpret: $P(X < 0)$

b) Find and interpret: $P(X \le 10 \mid X > 5)$

c) Find and interpret: P_{10}

Is it possible to lose weight in December despite all of the holiday temptations?

d) Find: $P(\mu_x - 2\sigma_x < X < \mu_x + 2\sigma_x)$

Solution:

a) Finding probabilities is just like finding the percentages questions in previous examples. We are simply trying to find an area given certain x-value boundaries. For this one, that boundary is at $X = 0$. We want to find the area to the left. So, we will begin with a z-score and then calculate the area using normalcdf.

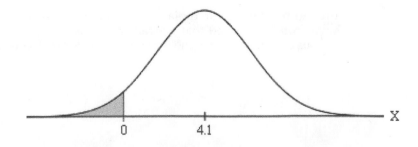

$$z = \frac{x - \mu_X}{\sigma_x} = \frac{0 - 4.1}{2.83} \approx -1.449 \implies P(X < 0) = Area = normalcdf(-\infty, -1.449) \approx 0.0737$$

Interpretation: If $X < 0$, then this means the amount of weight gained is negative. This would mean that the person would have lost weight. So, there is a 7.37% chance that a randomly selected person will actually lose some weight during the holiday month of December.

b) To find $P(X \le 10 \mid X > 5)$ we will use the Conditional Probability Rule from Section 5.3.

$$P(A \mid B) = \frac{P(A \& B)}{P(B)} \implies P(X \le 10 \mid X > 5) = \frac{P(X \le 10 \ \& \ X > 5)}{P(X > 5)}$$

So we must calculate these last two probabilities and then substitute them into the formula.

The fact that one of the inequality symbols is a strict inequality '>' and the other one, '≤', is inclusive (it includes the possibility of equals) does not matter when working with a continuous random variable. The only difference is whether or not we include the endpoints when computing the area. But the area above a single point equals zero, so it does not matter whether the endpoints are included or not.

Let's begin with $P(X > 5)$. Here's the sketch.

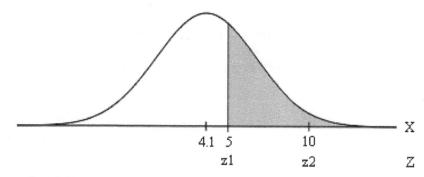

$$z1 = \frac{5 - 4.1}{2.83} \approx 0.318 \implies P(X > 5) = normalcdf(0.318, \infty) \approx 0.3752$$

Now we turn to $P(X \le 10 \ \& \ X > 5)$. For an '&' question, we want the overlap of $X \le 10 \ \& \ X > 5$, which is the area between these two boundaries (see sketch below). We already found the z-score for 10 in part (a).

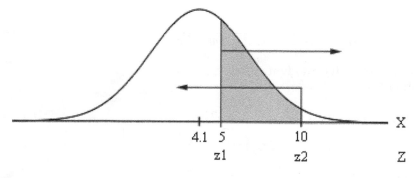

$$z2 = \frac{10 - 4.1}{2.83} \approx 2.085 \implies P(X \le 10 \ \& \ X > 5) = normalcdf(0.318, 2.085) \approx 0.3567$$

Finally, putting it all together, we get:

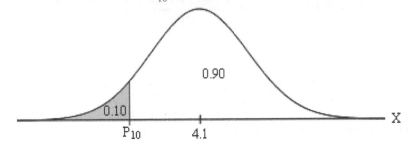

$$P(X \le 10 \mid X > 5) = \frac{P(X \le 10 \ \& \ X > 5)}{P(X > 5)} = \frac{0.3567}{0.3752} \approx 0.9507$$

Interpretation: Given that we know that a person has gained more than 5 pounds during December, the chance that they have gained no more than 10 pounds is about 95.07%.

c)   Recall that the 10 in P_{10} is giving us the area to the left of the x-value we are looking for. This is a small amount of area to the left, so P_{10} must be on the left side of the mean.

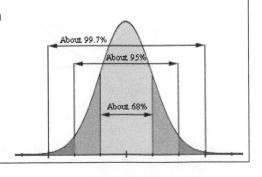

Key Concept: *Percentiles for RV's*

When interpreting percentiles for random variables, it is more appropriate to refer to a percent chance, rather than a percentage of the data set.

The z on the sketch comes from: $z = invNorm(0.10) \approx -1.282$. To find P_{10}, we now just apply the destandardizing formula.

$$P_{10} = x = \mu + z\sigma = 4.1 - 1.282 * 2.83 \approx 0.472$$

Interpretation: There is a 10% chance that a randomly selected person will gain less than 0.472 pounds during the holiday month of December.

d)   The key to finding $P(\mu_x - 2\sigma_x < X < \mu_x + 2\sigma_x)$ is noticing that, in words, this is asking us the probability that a randomly selected person will gain an amount of weight that lies within 2 standard deviations of the mean weight gain for December. For a normally distributed variable this should have an answer of 0.9545 (from the Empirical Rule).

So, $P(\mu_x - 2\sigma_x < X < \mu_x + 2\sigma_x) \approx 0.9545$

The Empirical Rule given in this section was actually for the relative frequencies of a normal population. However, in Chapter 5, we stated that probabilities are always equal to the corresponding population relative frequency, so it is valid to apply the Empirical Rule to this problem or to any other normally distributed random variable. Part (d) of the example above illustrated the Empirical Rule for Normal Random Variables. This rule is officially stated below.

Point to Remember: *Empirical Rule for Normal Random Variables*

For a normally distributed random variable, X, you will always find that:

- $P(\mu_x - \sigma_x < X < \mu_x + \sigma_x) = 0.6827$

- $P(\mu_x - 2\sigma_x < X < \mu_x + 2\sigma_x) = 0.9545$

- $P(\mu_x - 3\sigma_x < X < \mu_x + 3\sigma_x) = 0.9973$

The previous example also contained a discussion of what to do if our endpoints are included or not. The results of that discussion are summarized as follows.

Key Concept: *Does it matter whether or not the endpoints are included?*

For normally distributed variables (or any continuous variable for that matter), it does not matter whether you are finding a strict inequality or an inclusive one. So if X is a normally distributed random variable, then the following equality statements are true.

$$P(X > k) = P(X \geq k) \quad \& \quad P(X < k) = P(X \leq k)$$

Let's practice what we have learned with some exercises.

Exercise Set 6.3

Concept Review: Review the definitions and concepts from this section by filling in the blanks for each of the following.

37) We convert areas under normal curves to area under the Standard Normal Curve by calculating the _____ for the x-value boundaries of the region of interest.

38) The empirical rule for _____ populations states that 68.27% of the data lies within ____ standard deviation of the mean, _____ % lies within 2 standard deviations of the mean, and _____ % lies within 3 standard deviations of the mean.

39) If an x-value has a z-score of 1.57, then that x-value is 1.57 _____ _____ _____ the _____ .

40) The 74th percentile, or P$_{74}$, is the x-value that has an area of _____ to its _____ .

Mechanics: Practice using technology and the *normalcdf* and *invNorm* functions to solve each of the following. Find the z-scores before using the *normalcdf* function. Use the *invNorm* function to find z-scores. Show sketches with all *normalcdf* or *invNorm* functions.

41) Consider the normal distribution with $\mu = 19$ and $\sigma = 5.3$.
   a) Determine the area between 15 and 25.
   b) Determine the area to the right of 20.
   c) Determine the area to the left of 10.

42) Consider the normal distribution with $\mu = 185.4$ and $\sigma = 27.2$.
   a) Determine the area between 200 and 225.
   b) Determine the area to the right of 175.
   c) Determine the area to the left of 214.

43) Consider the normal distribution with $\mu = 51.05$ and $\sigma = 14.09$.
   a) Determine the x-value with area 0.10 to its right.
   b) Determine the x-value with area 0.60 to its left.
   c) Determine the two x-values that trap an area of 0.90 between them with equal outside areas.

44) Consider the normal distribution with $\mu = 3.1416$ and $\sigma = 0.827$.
   a) Determine the x-value with area 0.20 to its left.
   b) Determine the x-value with area 0.95 to its right.
   c) Determine the two x-values that trap an area of 0.99 between them with equal outside areas.

45) The random variable X is normally distributed with $\mu_x = 58.19$ and $\sigma_x = 16.51$.
   a) Find $P(X > 50)$
   b) Find $P(X < 60 \text{ or } X > 75)$
   c) Find the quartiles.

46) The random variable X is normally distributed with $\mu_x = 8.169$ and $\sigma_x = 3.513$.
   a) Find $P(X < 5)$
   b) Find $P(X > 9 \ \& \ X < 15)$
   c) Find the quartiles.

47) The random variable Y is normally distributed with $\mu_Y = 12.07$ and $\sigma_Y = 0.23055$.
   a) Find $P(Y > 12 \ \& \ Y < 12.5)$
   b) Find $P(Y < 12.5 \mid Y > 12)$

48) The random variable Y is normally distributed with $\mu_Y = 502.7$ and $\sigma_Y = 99.067$.
   a) Find $P(Y < 400 \text{ or } Y > 700)$
   b) Find $P(Y > 500 \mid Y < 600)$

Applications: Practice the ideas learned in this section within the context of real world applications.

49) The heights of 5-yr old girls in the U.S. are normally distributed with a mean of 42.56 inches and a standard deviation of 1.573 inches.
   a) What percentage of the girls have heights between 40 and 45 inches tall?
   b) In order to ride the white water rafting ride at *California Adventure*, a child must be at least 42 inches tall. What percentage of 5-yr old girls can ride the ride?
   c) Find and interpret the 10th percentile for the heights of 5-yr old girls in the U.S.
   d) Determine the quartiles for the heights of the 5-yr old girls.

50) The lasting times for the batteries used in a portable DVD player are normally distributed with a mean of 5.5 hours and a standard deviation of 0.819 hours.
   a) What percentage of the batteries will last between 4 and 7 hours?
   b) In order to last through the duration of a common flight the batteries must last at least 5 hours. What percentage of the batteries will last that long?
   c) Find and interpret the 90th percentile for the lasting times of these batteries.
   d) Determine the quartiles for the batteries.

51) The lengths of adult female green anacondas are normally distributed with a mean length of 24.1 feet and a standard deviation of 2.307 feet.
   a) Determine the percentage of adult female green anacondas that are longer than 30 feet in length.
   b) What percentage of these snakes have length between 22 and 26 feet?
   c) How long would one of these snakes have to be in order to be considered in the longest 1% of adult female green anacondas?
   d) Determine the quartiles for the lengths of adult female green anacondas.

52) The amount of calories in a popular brand of all beef frank is normally distributed with a mean of 180 calories and a standard deviation of 6.833 calories.
   a) Determine the percentage of these beef franks that contain less than 170 calories.
   b) What percentage of these franks have between 180 and 200 calories?
   c) How many calories would one of these franks have to contain in order to be considered in the top 5% of calories contained?
   d) Determine the quartiles for the number of calories contained in these beef franks.

53) The TI-84 Plus C, color calculator, comes with a rechargeable lithium-polymer battery. The lasting time for a fully charged battery is normally distributed with a mean of 7.5 hours and a standard deviation of 1.273 hours.
   a) Determine the percentage of fully charged batteries that would last less than 5 hours.
   b) Determine the percentage of fully charged batteries that would last more than 6 hour, but less than 9 hours.
   c) How fast would the batteries have to go dead in order to be in the worst 10% of the batteries?
   d) Find and interpret the 80th percentile for the calculator batteries.

54) The amount of time that Tim Duncan of the San Antonio Spurs takes between free throws is a normally distributed variable with a mean of 9.5 seconds and a standard deviation of 0.5 seconds.
   a) It is against the rules to take more than 10 seconds between free throws. Determine the percentage of time that Tim violates this rule.
   b) Determine the percentage of time that he takes less than 9 seconds or more than 11 seconds between free throws.
   c) How much time could he take in between free throws for it to be considered to be in the slowest 2% of times?
   d) Find and interpret the 30th percentile for his time between free throws.

55) Kevin works at a bike shop. One of his tasks is to assemble bikes. The time it takes him to fully assemble a bike is a normally distributed random variable with $\mu_Y = 21.3$ minutes and $\sigma_Y = 3.0972$ minutes. Let Y = the time it takes Kevin to assemble a randomly selected bike.
   a) Find and interpret $P(Y < 20)$.
   b) Find and interpret $P(Y < 15 \text{ or } Y > 25)$.
   c) If $P(Y > k) = 0.85$, then find k.
   d) Find and interpret the 65th percentile for the bike assembly times.

56) The systolic blood pressure, the pressure in the arteries when the heart beat fills them with blood, is a normally distributed random variable with $\mu_Y = 115$ and $\sigma_Y = 15$. Systolic readings below 90 are considered low blood pressure and readings over 140 are considered high blood pressure. Let Y = the systolic blood pressure in for a randomly selected adult.
   a) Find and interpret $P(Y > 140)$.
   b) Find and interpret $P(Y > 90 \text{ & } Y < 140)$.
   c) If $P(Y > k) = 0.20$, then find k.
   d) Find and interpret the 10th percentile for the systolic readings adults.

57) The high temperature in Death Valley during the month of July is a normally distributed random variable with $\mu_x = 115$ and $\sigma_x = 7.062$. Let X = the high temperature for a randomly selected day in July.

a) Find and interpret $P(X > 100^\circ)$.

b) Find and interpret $P(95^\circ < X \le 105^\circ)$.

c) Find and interpret the 20th percentile for high temperatures in July.

d) Find and interpret $P(X \le 120^\circ \mid x > 100^\circ)$.

58) The rainfall total in Hayward, CA during the month of January is a normally distributed random variable with $\mu_x = 4.3$ inches and $\sigma_x = 1.077$. Let X = the rainfall total for a randomly selected January in Hayward.

a) Find and interpret $P(X < 5)$.

b) Find and interpret $P(X \le 2 \;\&\; X < 3)$.

c) Find and interpret $P(X \le 2 \mid x < 3)$.

d) Find and interpret the 99th percentile for rainfall total in Hayward during the month of January.

59) The normal body temperature, T, for humans is normally distributed with a mean of $\mu_T = 98.2^\circ F$ and a standard deviation of $\sigma_T = 0.352^\circ F$.

Suppose 40 humans are randomly selected and their temperatures are taken. Let X = the number with temperatures below 98°F.

a) What is the distribution of X? Give details.

b) Would it be considered unusual if none of those selected had temperatures below 98°F? Explain.

60) The amount of rice, R, that goes into the bags of rice produced by a certain company is normally distributed with a mean of $\mu_R = 5$ pounds and a standard deviation of $\sigma_R = 0.142$ lbs. Suppose 38 bags are randomly selected and weighed. Let X = the number with weights below 4.8 lbs.

a) What is the distribution of X? Give details.

b) Would it be considered unusual if none of those selected had weights below 4.8 lbs.? Explain.

61) Refer to exercise (49) and fill in the blanks using the empirical rule.

a) 68.27% of 5-yr old girls in the U.S. have heights between _____ and _____ in.

b) 95.45% of 5-yr old girls in the U.S. have heights between _____ and _____ in.

c) 99.73% of 5-yr old girls in the U.S. have heights between _____ and _____ in.

d) 90% of 5-yr old girls in the U.S. have heights between _____ and _____ in.

62) Refer to exercise (51) and fill in the blanks using the empirical rule.

a) 68.27% of adult female green anacondas have lengths between _____ and _____ ft.

b) 95.45% of adult female green anacondas have lengths between _____ and _____ ft.

c) 99.73% of adult female green anacondas have lengths between _____ and _____ ft.

d) 80% of adult female green anacondas have lengths between _____ and _____ ft.

Section 6.4 - Approximating the Binomial Distribution

In Chapter 5, we were introduced to the Binomial Formula for finding probabilities for success/failure problems. As useful as this formula can be, there are also times were it can become difficult or impractical to use. The following discussion example will illustrate such a situation. After we see what the trouble is, we will then turn to the normal distribution in search of a practical solution.

Discussion Example: *Exploring the difficulty with the binomial distribution*

A study released in June 2006, showed that 66% of the fans of "The Sopranos" believe that organized crime groups like the Sopranos do exist. Suppose a random sample of 827 fans of the "The Sopranos" is taken. Let X = the number of fans who believe that organized crime groups like the Sopranos do exist.

a) Find the probability that exactly 550 of those sampled believe that organized crime groups like the Sopranos do exist.

b) Find the probability that the number that believe organized crime groups like the Sopranos do exist is somewhere between 525 and 575, inclusive.

c) Find the probability that at least 520 of those selected believe that organized crime groups like the Sopranos do exist.

Solution:

a) At first glance this should seem like a very easy question. A success has been defined as a person selected believing that organized crime groups like the Sopranos do exist, and then X counts the number of successes. This indicated that this is a binomial distribution (or n, p, q problem). In symbols their question becomes: $P(X = 550)$. We would start by finding the values of n, p, and q.

n = 827 (the number of trials)   p = 0.66 (probability of success on a given trial)

q = 1 – p = 0.34 (probability of a failure on a given trial)

So, we use the binomial formula: $P(X = x) = \binom{n}{x} p^x q^{n-x}$ and get:

$$P(X = 550) = \binom{827}{550}(0.66)^{550}(0.34)^{277}$$

This seems straight forward until you try to calculate this value. On the TI-84, I get:

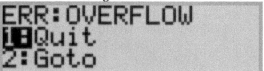

It certainly should be possible to get 550 successes in 827 tries, so the answer should be between 0 and 1. So why the overflow? The reason is that $\binom{827}{550}$ is a number over 100 digits long, and this number by itself produces the overflow on the calculator.

So, what we have is a technology problem. The TI-84 can't handle numbers longer than 100 digits. However, the TI 86/89/92 can. So, one solution is for everyone to go out and buy a new calculator. However, if the value of n is larger than in this problem, we may end up with overflow problems on other calculators as well. In addition to the problem of overflow, we will encounter another type of difficulty in parts (b) and (c). Despite the fact that we have not yet solved this question, let's move to parts (b) and (c) and look at the difficulties that arise there.

b) Suppose that you have purchased a new calculator that can handle more digits without getting an overflow error. Translating the question from part (b) into symbols we get: $P(525 \leq X \leq 575)$. We would use the special addition rule to work on this problem.

$$P(525 \leq X \leq 575) = P(525) + P(526) + \ldots + P(575)$$

This means, we would have to add together 51 probabilities to answer the original question. That may not seem that bad, until you realize that to get each probability involves the use of the binomial formula. So we have:

$$P(525 \leq X \leq 575) = \binom{827}{525}(0.66)^{525}(0.34)^{302} + \binom{827}{526}(0.66)^{526}(0.34)^{301} + \ldots + \binom{827}{575}(0.66)^{575}(0.34)^{252}$$

So now, even if you had a calculator that could handle the calculation, you are still faced with a lot of work. And if you think you might be willing to do that work, consider part (c).

c) In symbols this one becomes: $P(X \geq 520)$. And to find it we would calculate:

$$P(X \geq 520) = \binom{827}{520}(0.66)^{520}(0.34)^{307} + \binom{827}{521}(0.66)^{521}(0.34)^{306} + \ldots + \binom{827}{827}(0.66)^{827}(0.34)^{0}$$

This means using the formula 308 times and then adding all the results together. That could easily ruin your weekend.

Even though we know a technique for doing this problem, we either run into problems with technology or excessive workload. We should hope that there is a better way, and there is! We will leave this problem unsolved for now, discuss the better method, and then return to this problem.

The following is a probability histogram for the binomial distribution we were just working with. It should give a hint as to how we will tackle this problem.

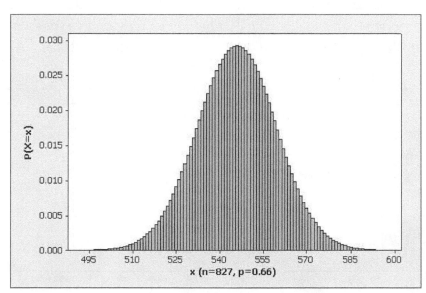

It should be fairly easy to recognize the shape of this distribution. It is, without a doubt, bell-shaped. This means that, even though it is a binomial distribution, it may also be approximately normally distributed. This means that we should be able to find approximations for the probabilities we were looking for in the previous example by finding areas under an appropriate normal curve. Before we return to that example, let's take a look at some other binomial distributions and try to learn what we need to know from them.

All of the graphs below are probability histograms of binomial distributions.

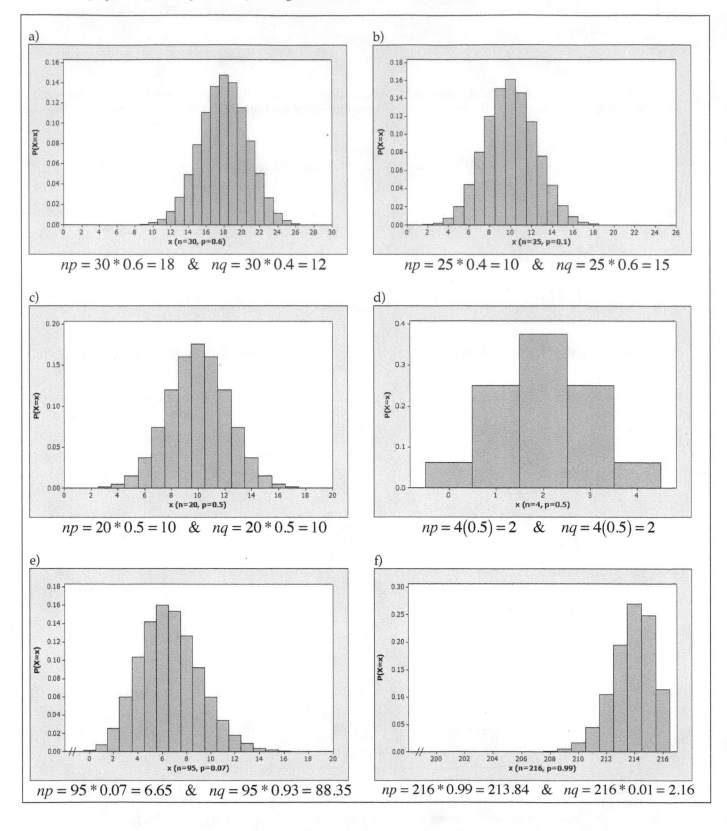

Here are some properties worth noting:

- Some of these binomial distributions seem approximately normal, but some do not. Graphs (a), (b), and (c) seem to clearly be bell-shaped. Graph (e) appears right skewed and graph (f) appears to be left skewed. Graph (d) is a little bit tough to categorize. It is symmetric, but it probably does not have enough bars to take on a shape as complicated as a bell.

  It may seem fine to make the decision about whether or not a binomial distribution is approximately normal by looking at its probability histogram. However, to do this you must calculate the probabilities for all the x-values and this is precisely the task that is giving us difficulty. So we need another way to make this decision. While we will not show the details here, it has been determined that a binomial distribution will have a decent bell shape histogram provided that both $n \cdot p$ and $n \cdot q$ are at least 10. If you look at the values of $n \cdot p$ and $n \cdot q$ provided just below each graph, you will see that for the ones that look normal $n \cdot p$ and $n \cdot q$ are both at least 10, but if it doesn't look bell-shaped, then at least one of these products will be less than 10.

- Because all of the histogram bars have a width of 1, their area equals their height which equals the probability for that value of x. Thus, when we are trying to find the probability, we could try to find the area of the histogram bar instead.

- Because this is single value grouping, each histogram bar starts and ends at a 1/2 mark. For example, the histogram bar for 6 in graph (c) starts at 5.5 and ends at 6.5.

So here is the idea. If a binomial distribution has a bell-shape, then we can find the probabilities for this distribution by using the area under the appropriate normal curve to estimate the area of a histogram bar, which is equal to the probability for that value of x.

Let's discuss the details by returning to the example we got stuck on at the beginning of this section.

Example 6.17: *Discovering a solution to the binomial distribution difficulties*

A study released in June 2006, showed that 66% of the fans of "The Sopranos" believe that organized crime groups like the Sopranos do exist. Suppose a random sample of 827 fans of the "The Sopranos" is taken. Let X = the number who believe that organized crime groups like the Sopranos do exist.

a) Find the probability that exactly 550 of those sampled believe that organized crime groups like the Sopranos do exist.

b) Find the probability that the number that believe organized crime groups like the Sopranos do exist is somewhere between 525 and 575, inclusive.

c) Find the probability that at least 520 of those selected believe that organized crime groups like the Sopranos do exist.

Solution:

a) We are trying to find $P(X = 550)$. We saw this histogram for binomial distribution and it looked like it had a very good bell-shape. However, let's check the numerical requirements for having a bell-shape anyways. Recall: n = 827, p = 0.66, q = 0.34.

$$np = 827(0.66) = 545.82 \geq 5 \quad \& \quad nq = 827(0.34) = 281.18 \geq 5$$

Notice that these two numbers were not just bigger than 5, they were way bigger. This means that a normal distribution should provide a very good approximation for this particular binomial distribution.

So we should be able to find $P(X = 550)$ by using the area under the appropriate normal curve that corresponds to the area of the histogram bar for x = 550. But which normal curve is the appropriate normal curve to use? Recall that a normal curve is completely determined by its mean and standard deviation. So we should use the normal curve where the mean and standard deviation match that of this binomial distribution. So, from the formulas from Section 5.5, we get.

$$\mu_x = np = 827(0.66) = 545.82 \quad \& \quad \sigma_x = \sqrt{npq} = \sqrt{827(0.66)(0.34)} \approx 13.623$$

Now, the histogram bar we are working on starts at 549.5 and ends at 550.5, so these will be the boundaries for the area we are trying to find. Here's the sketch.

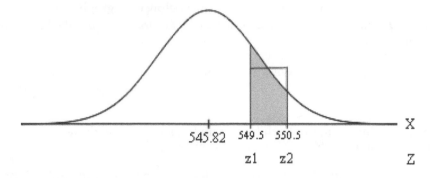

Notice that the area shaded under the normal curve is roughly the same as the area of the histogram bar we are looking for. We now find the z-score for each of the x-values.

$$z1 = \frac{549.5 - 545.82}{13.623} \approx 0.270 \quad \&$$

$$z2 = \frac{550.5 - 545.82}{13.623} \approx 0.344$$

Next we use the normalcdf function to find the area under the curve:

$$P(X = 550) \approx normalcdf(0.270, \ 0.344) \approx 0.0282$$

Key Concept: *Approx. vs. Exact*

The answer we found is an approximation. The exact answer using a calculator that doesn't have the overflow problem is:

$$P(X = 550) = \binom{827}{550}(0.66)^{550}(0.34)^{277}$$

≈ 0.0280. So, the answer we obtained from the normal approximation method is very good.

The size of the histogram bar was exaggerated greatly to make room for all of the labeling that was needed.

b) Next we are trying to find $P(525 \le X \le 575)$. We are trying to find the area of all the histogram bars from x = 525 to x = 575, but the bar for x = 525 begins at 524.5 and the bar for x = 575 ends at 575.5, so we will use 524.5 and 575.5 as the boundaries for our region under the normal curve. Here's the sketch.

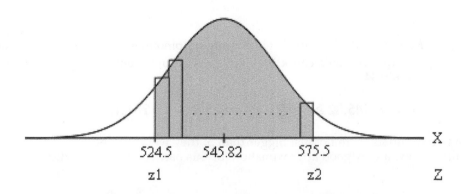

Because the bars are connected, we do not need to find their areas individually, we just start at the beginning of the first bar, and stop and the end of the last bar. Let's find the z's.

$$z1 = \frac{524.5 - 545.82}{13.623} \approx -1.565 \quad \&$$

$$z2 = \frac{575.5 - 545.82}{13.623} \approx 2.179$$

$$P(525 \le X \le 575) \approx$$

$$normalcdf(-1.565, 2.179) \approx 0.9265$$

> **Key Concept**: *Approx. vs. Exact*
>
> Using the binomial distribution to find the exact answer for this one yields: $P(525 \le X \le 575) \approx 0.9265$. So in this case, the normal approximation yields the same answer as the binomial distribution to 4 decimal places.

Only a few bars were shown on the graph. It is not necessary to show them all or even any of them. However, it is usually a good idea to show the first and last bars to help think about the boundary of your region.

c) Finally, we wish to find $P(X \ge 520)$. For this one, we wish to start at the histogram bar for x = 520 and also include all bars to the right of that one. This bar starts at 519.5, so that will be the lower boundary of our region.

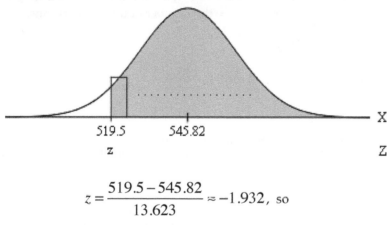

> **Key Concepts**: *Approx. vs. Exact and a bar for 827?*
>
> Using the binomial formula 307 times and adding the results together yields:
>
> $P(X \ge 520) \approx 0.9727$.
>
> So, once again the normal approximation is providing a very good answer without all the work and difficulties with technology.
>
> It could be argued that because n = 827, we need to stop our area at the end of that bar, which would be at 827.5. However, if your binomial distribution is really approximately normal, then the amount of the area beyond the last bar should be negligible.

$$z = \frac{519.5 - 545.82}{13.623} \approx -1.932, \text{ so}$$

$$P(X \ge 520) \approx normalcdf(-1.932, \infty) \approx 0.9733$$

Even though part (c) seemed like the most difficult problem to do when we first looked at this problem. Now that we are using the technique of the normal approximation, it was actually the easiest as it only required one z-score.

The following procedure summarizing the requirements needed and the steps used to approximate probabilities for a binomial distribution by using area under a normal curve.

Point to Remember: *Procedure for obtaining a normal approximation for binomial probabilities*

Requirements: A binomial distribution can be approximated by area under a normal curve provided that $np \geq 10$ **AND** $nq \geq 10$.

Procedure:
- Determine n, p, q
- Calculate $\mu_x = np$ and $\sigma_x = \sqrt{npq}$
- Sketch the normal curve and indicate the area to be found. Remember: we are estimating the area of histogram bars, so your boundaries need to represent the start and end of those bars. This means that your boundaries will always be at the half marks.
- Calculate z-score(s) needed by using μ_x and σ_x.
- Use the *normalcdf* command to find the required area.

Example 6.18: *Working with 2 random variables in one problem*

The amount of soda that a certain company's filling machine puts in each can is a normally distributed random variable with mean $\mu = 12.04$ and a standard deviation $\sigma = 0.0391$. The cans are supposed to contain 12 ounces each. Suppose a random sample of 300 cans is taken. Let X = the number of under filled cans.

a) Use the normal approximation method to find $P(X > 50)$

b) Verify that it is acceptable to use the normal approximation for this problem.

Solution:

a) The key to this problem is to notice the definition of the random variable. We have defined an under filled can to be a success, and then we are counting how many times it occurs out of 300 trials. This means we have a binomial distribution (n, p, q problem.).

Determine n, p, and q.

We are checking 300 cans so, n = 300. p is the probability of a randomly selected can being under filled. This value is not given, but, because the amount of soda per can is a normally distributed variable, we can find p using the techniques from Section 6.3. Let's let Y = the amount of soda per can. We want the area to the left of 12 under the normal curve with $\mu_Y = 12.04$ and $\sigma_Y = 0.0391$. So we start with a sketch.

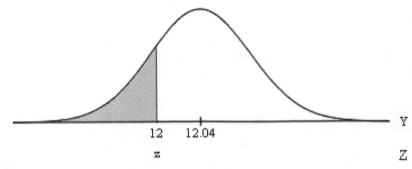

$$z = \frac{12 - 12.04}{0.0391} \approx -1.023 \Rightarrow p = normalcdf(-\infty, \; -1.023) \approx 0.1532 \; \Rightarrow q = 1 - p = 0.8468$$

The normal distribution used in step 1 was critical for finding the value of p. However, now that we know p, we will no longer need this normal distribution.

Even though finding the $P(X > 50)$ is an n, p, q question, because the value of n is large, it will be easiest to use the normal approximation method to find the desired probability.

Calculate $\mu_x = np$ **and** $\sigma_x = \sqrt{npq}$

$$\mu_x = np = 300(0.1532) = 45.96 \quad \& \quad \sigma_x = \sqrt{npq} = \sqrt{300(0.1532)(0.8468)} \approx 6.2385$$

Sketch.

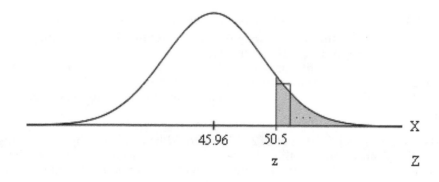

Notice that because we want $P(X > 50)$ we do NOT include the bar for 50, but start with the bar for 51. The bar for 51 begins at 50.5, so that is the boundary we are using.

We are using a different normal curve this time, because we are working with a different variable. When trying to calculate the probability of a success, the variable used was the amount of soda in a randomly selected can, Y. Now, to find $P(X > 50)$, the variable was the number of under filled cans out of 300, X.

We can now find the desired area using z-scores and normalcdf.

$$z = \frac{50.5 - 45.96}{6.2385} \approx 0.728 \Rightarrow P(X > 50) \approx$$

$$normalcdf(0.728, \infty) \approx 0.2333$$

> **Caution:** *Should we use half marks?*
>
> It may seem strange that we used 50.5 when finding $P(X > 50)$, but we used 12 when finding $P(Y < 12)$. There is a good reason for this and it is discussed in the looking deeper section following the example.

b) To verify that the normal approximation is an acceptable way to solve this problem, we must check to see if the requirements for using that method have been satisfied.

$$np = 300(0.1532) = 40.56 \geq 10 \quad \text{and} \quad nq = 300(0.8468) = 259.04 \geq 10$$

Because both of these quantities are at least 10, the requirements have been met, and it was appropriate to use the normal approximation procedure to solve this problem.

LOOKING DEEPER: *Why do we use 1/2 marks in some cases but not others?*

The answer to this question is short and simple, but that doesn't mean it can't be confusing.

We do NOT need half marks when working with a continuous variable and a normal curve, but we DO need them when we work with a discrete variable and use a normal curve.

Any variable that is truly normally distributed is a continuous variable. Certainly, the amount of soda in a can was a continuous variable. When we are asked for the chance that a randomly selected can contains less than 12 ounces, if we used 11.5, we would be missing cans that contained 11.8 ounces (even though this is less than 12 and should be included.) Recall that it is OK to include the 12, because, it is mathematically impossible for a can to contain exactly 12 ounces.

When we worked on $P(X > 50)$, we used 50.5 because X represented the number of cans out of 300 that were under filled, a discrete variable. (You might have 48 or 49 cans under filled, but it is not possible that it would be a number like 48.7619 cans.) The random variable in this case was not normally distributed, however, it was approximately normally distributed. To fit this discrete binomial variable under our continuous normal curve, we had to focus on the area of histogram bars to get the correct area, and these bars start and end at the 1/2 marks. Using these 1/2 marks when approximating a binomial distribution with a normal distribution is referred to as the **continuity correction**.

While the best understanding of this question of 1/2 marks should be answered by considering whether we have a continuous variable or a discrete one, in this chapter you could also just focus on whether the variable is normally distributed to begin with (no 1/2 marks) or did it start off as a binomial distribution (use 1/2 marks.)

Exercise Set 6.4

Concept Review: Review the definitions and concepts by filling in the blanks for each of the following.

63) We approximate binomial probabilities using the area of the _____ bars. To do this accurately, we must use _____ marks as the boundaries of the region we find the area of.

64) If $np \geq$ ____ and $nq \geq$ ____ , then a binomial distribution is considered to be approximately _____ .

Mechanics: Practice using the normal approximation before moving on to applications.

65) Suppose that X is a binomial random variable with n = 340 and p = 0.894.
   a) Verify that the normal approximation to a binomial can be used on this problem.
   b) Approximate $P(X = 300)$.
   c) Approximate $P(300 \leq X < 310)$.
   d) Approximate $P(X > 290)$.

66) Suppose that X is a binomial random variable with n = 1191 and p = 0.226.
   a) Verify that the normal approximation to a binomial can be used on this problem.
   b) Approximate $P(250 < X \leq 300)$.
   c) Approximate $P(X \leq 250)$.

Applications: Practice the ideas learned in this section in the context of real world applications.

67) In April of 2004, it was estimated that 60.7% of the California adult population opposed a voucher system for education. A poll was taken of 1,329 random adult Californians at that time. Let X = the number of them that oppose a voucher system.
   a) Approximate the probability that exactly 800 of those surveyed oppose a voucher system.
   b) Approximate the probability that at least 750 of those surveyed oppose a voucher system.

68) A player is repeatedly betting $1 on the color red in roulette. Recall: A roulette wheel has 18 Red, 18 black, and 2 green numbers.
   a) What is the probability that the player will be "ahead" after 1 play of the game? That is, find $P(\text{Red})$.
   b) Approximate the probability that the player will be "ahead" after 101 plays of the game. That is, find $P(X \geq 51)$, where X is the number of wins in 101 plays.
   c) Approximate the probability that the player will be "ahead" after 1001 plays of the game. (Hint: to be "ahead" you must win more than half of the time. See part (b) above.)
   d) What does this show you about your chance of winning at roulette?

69) The best pair of starting cards to have in the game of Texas Hold'em is pocket Aces or AA. If this hand is up against another player holding 87 suited (an 8 and 7 of the same suit), then the player with the Aces will win 76.8% of the time (assuming both hands commit to play to the end before the flop).

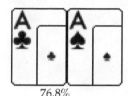 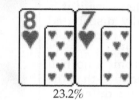

| 76.8% | 23.2% |

Suppose these hands are matched up with each other 100 times and we let X = the number of wins for the Aces.
a) Verify that the normal approximation to a binomial can be used on this problem.
b) Approximate $P(X < 80)$
c) Approximate $P(X \geq 90)$
d) What would be the expected range for the number of wins for the two Aces?

70) A pocket pair versus two over cards is considered a classic race because the two hands have almost the same chance of winning. An example of such cards is shown below with their chances of winning.

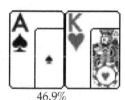 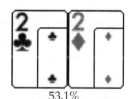

| 46.9% | 53.1% |

Suppose these hands are matched up with each other 100 times and we let X = the number of wins for the Ace/King hand.
a) Verify that the normal approximation to a binomial can be used on this problem.
b) Approximate $P(45 \leq X \leq 55)$
c) Approximate $P(X < 50)$
d) What would be the expected range for the number of wins for the Ace/King hand?

✓ 71) The battery life, B, on an Apple I-pod is a normally distributed variable with a mean of $\mu_B = 11.74$ hours and a standard deviation of $\sigma_B = 0.7833$ hours. 200 I-pods are randomly selected and their battery lifetime is recorded. Let X = the number of I-pods with batteries that last longer than 12 hours.
a) Determine the distribution of X.
b) Approximate $P(X > 100)$

72) The gestation period, G, for kittens (of house cats) is a normally distributed variable with a mean of $\mu_G = 65.4$ days and a standard deviation of $\sigma_G = 0.7925$ days. 127 pregnant house cats are randomly selected and their gestation time is recorded. Let X = the number of cats with pregnancies that last less than 65 days.
a) Determine the distribution of X.
b) Approximate $P(X \leq 30)$

Section 6.5 – Assessing Normality

In this chapter, we have learned how to use area to represent relative frequencies and probabilities when we are working with a normal distribution, but how do we know if the population is really normal or not? In this section we will explore the process of testing a sample to see if it is reasonable to believe that the sample comes from a normally distributed population, or at least an approximately normally distributed population. One issue that we need to be aware of with this process is that we can't actually use sample data to prove that our data came from a normal population. What we will try to do is find convincing evidence that the sample did not come from a normal population by examining the differences between our sample and what is expected from data that comes from a normally distributed population. If we find large enough differences between our data and normal data, then we will be convinced that our population is not normally distributed. However, if the differences are smaller enough, then we will decide that it is a *reasonable possibility* that our data came from a normal population. This may not sound like a very strong result, but it is often good enough for the work we will be doing in the coming chapters.

Can we use area under a normal curve to estimate the percentage of great white sharks that are more than 20 ft long? It depends on whether or not the lengths of those sharks are normally distributed.

One simple way to test for the normality of a population is to make a histogram for the sample data. If you have a large sample and it has a histogram that looks nothing like a bell shape, then you can be confident that the population is not even approximately normal. However, we learned in Chapter 2, that, if the sample is small, then it is hard to determine the shape of the population with any certainty. If the histogram for the sample data does look roughly bell-shaped, then we cannot reject the idea that the population is normal. This procedure for assessing normality with a histogram is given below.

)int to Remember: *Procedure for using a histogram to assess normality*

The steps below can be used to attempt to decide whether or not sample data you have collected was drawn from a normally distributed population.

- Create a histogram for the sample. This can be done by hand or preferably using technology.
- If the histogram is not at least roughly bell-shaped, then you should conclude that the sample did not come from a normal population.
- If the histogram is roughly bell-shaped, then you can conclude that there is a reasonable possibility that the sample was taken from a normal population.

Warnings: There are a few things to worry about when using this procedure.

- If the sample size is small, the histogram might not have enough data for a clear shape to emerge. With small samples, random variation has a large effect on the graph.
- For very small samples, the histogram will almost never present a clear bell-shape. This can cause us to conclude that a population is not normally distributed even in the cases when the population is actually normally distributed.
- Even when you have a large enough sample size for random variation to have a smaller effect and for a clear shape to emerge, there can still be disagreement among different people as to what constitutes roughly bell-shaped histogram.

Let's look at an example to see how this works and where the difficulties lie.

Example 6.19: *Using a Histogram to Assess Normality*

Histograms are shown below for four different samples. Each sample was randomly selected from an unknown population. Use the histograms provided and the procedure above to assess the normality of each of the populations from which the data was randomly selected.

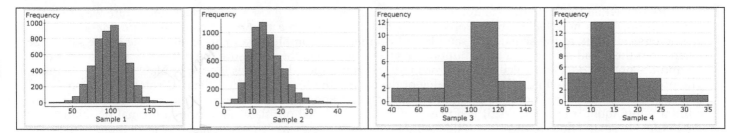

a) What can you conclude about the normality of the distribution of the population that sample 1 was selected from? Are you confident in this answer? (**Note**: Sample 1 has a size of 5000 pieces of data.)

b) What can you conclude about the normality of the distribution of the population that sample 2 was selected from? Are you confident in this answer? (**Note**: Sample 2 has a size of 6000 pieces of data.)

c) What can you conclude about the normality of the distribution of the population that sample 3 was selected from? Are you confident in this answer? (**Note**: Sample 3 has a size of 25 pieces of data.)

d) What can you conclude about the normality of the distribution of the population that sample 4 was selected from? Are you confident in this answer? (**Note**: Sample 4 has a size of 30 pieces of data.)

Solution:

a) The histogram for sample 1 appears to be at least roughly bell-shaped. That tells us that there is a reasonable possibility that the sample was taken from a normally distributed population. Because the sample size is large, $n = 5,000$, I feel fairly confident in this answer. The lack of symmetry near the peak is a small concern, but the differences from a bell-shape seem small enough that they might just be the result of random variation in the sample.

b) The histogram for sample 2 appears to be right-skewed. This is convincing evidence that the sample was NOT taken from a normally distributed population. Because the sample size is large, $n = 6,000$, I feel very confident in this answer. The lack of symmetry in the tails is too large for us to believe that the population is actually normal and that the lack of symmetry is just the result of random variation in the sample.

c) The histogram for sample 3 appears to be left-skewed. This provides some evidence that the sample was NOT taken from a normally distributed population. However, because the sample size is small, $n = 25$, I am not very confident in this answer. In small samples, random variation is still having a large effect on the shape we see in our sample data. The lack of symmetry in the tails might just be the result of random variation in the sample.

d) The histogram for sample 4 appears to be right-skewed. This provides some evidence that the sample was NOT taken from a normally distributed population. However, because the sample size is small, $n = 30$, I am not very confident in this answer. In small samples, random variation is still having a large effect on the shape we see in our sample data. The lack of symmetry in the tails might just be the result of random variation in the sample.

In the example above, we were not told the true distribution of the populations our samples were taken from. However, it turns out that the histograms from both parts (a) and (c) were both based on samples that were drawn from the same population and that population was actually normally distributed. With a large sample, we correctly and confidently identified the population as normally distributed, but with the small sample we incorrectly decided that the population was not normally distributed. The failure to reach the correct conclusion with a small sample is a drawback of using the histogram method. The histograms from both parts (b) and (d) were also based on samples drawn from the same population. In those two cases, the population was right-skewed. We made the correct decision on both of these parts, but we were still not very confident in our decision when the sample size was small. This turns out to be a big problem, because, in future chapters, we will be most concerned with assessing the normality of the population when we are dealing with very small samples like those in parts (c) and (d) above.

For the cases when the histogram is not giving a clear conclusion, we need a more black and white way to make our decision. This new technique involves using technology to do a numerical analysis of our data set. The technology will look at the size of our sample and compare our sample data to an ideal sample of the same size taken from the Standard Normal Distribution. The technology will then measure the difference between our data set and the normal data and calculate the probability of seeing such differences if our population is really normal. The probability calculated is called the **P-value** of the test. If the P-value is large, that indicates we are looking at differences that have a high chance of occurring just due to random variation even if our sample is taken from a normal population. In such cases, it is a reasonable possibility that our data came from a normal population. If the P-value is small enough, then it is unlikely that we would see such differences just due to random variation if our data really came from a normal population. In such cases, we would conclude that our population did not come from a normal population. The words large enough and small enough are vague, so we will need a cut-off to help us make decisions. The standard value used as a cut-off is 0.05. So if our P-value is less than or equal to 0.05, then we will conclude that our sample is not from a normal population.

With the histogram method of assessing normality, we had trouble with small samples. This was partially due to the fact that it is hard to get a bell-shape histogram from a small sample even if the population actually is normally distributed. With the P-value method, we sometimes have the opposite problem. For small samples, we will often get a P-value larger than 0.05, even when the population is not actually normally distributed. This P-value will cause us to conclude that there is a reasonable possibility that our population is normally distributed. Because this is a common problem with the P-value method, it is important that we never conclude that the population IS normal, but rather than it is a *reasonable possibility* that it is normal.

Point to Remember: *Procedure for using a P-value to assess normality*

P-value: Our random sample will probably never look exactly like an ideal sample from a normal distribution. When we see the differences between our data and normal data, we have two possible conclusions.
- Maybe our sample data did not come from a normal population and that is why we see the difference we do.
- Maybe our sample data really did come from a normal population, but it just doesn't look quite the same due to random variation.
- The P-value is the probability that, if our sample really came from a normal population, we would have seen differences at least as big as we observed between our data and the ideal normal sample of the same size.

Procedure and Conclusions for the P-value method:

- Use software such as StatCrunch or Minitab to find the P-value. This is normally referred to as a "Normality Test" by the software.
- If the P-value is less than or equal to 0.05, then conclude that sample did not come from a normal population. (Our data looks too different from an ideal normal sample for the differences to reasonably just be random variation.)
- If the P-value is greater than 0.05, then conclude that there is a reasonable possibility that the sample was taken from a normal population. (Our data looks enough like an ideal normal sample for the differences to reasonably just be random variation.)

Warning: The P-value method cannot prove that our sample was taken from a normally distributed population. When your P-value is larger than 0.05 it only means that there is a reasonable possibility that your sample came from a normally distributed population. Be careful with your wording.

Example 6.20: *Testing Normality using the P-value Method*

The StatCrunch output below shows the results of using technology to run normality tests on the same four sample data sets that we investigated in the previous example. Use the P-values provided to assess the normality of the population each sample was drawn from.

Anderson-Darling goodness-of-fit results:

Variable	n	Stat	P-Value
Sample 1	5000	0.61135336	0.1119

Anderson-Darling goodness-of-fit results:

Variable	n	Stat	P-Value
Sample 2	6000	35.986758	<0.0001

Anderson-Darling goodness-of-fit results:

Variable	n	Stat	P-Value
Sample 3	25	0.70115695	0.0588

Anderson-Darling goodness-of-fit results:

Variable	n	Stat	P-Value
Sample 4	30	0.94667849	0.0144

a) What can you conclude about the distribution of the population that sample 1 was selected from?

b) What can you conclude about the distribution of the population that sample 2 was selected from?

c) What can you conclude about the distribution of the population that sample 3 was selected from?

d) What can you conclude about the distribution of the population that sample 4 was selected from?

Solution:

a) For sample 1, the output shows a P-value of 0.1119. Because $0.1119 > 0.05$, we conclude that there is a reasonable possibility that sample 1 was taken from a normally distributed population.

b) For sample 2, the output shows a P-value < 0.0001. We are not told the exact size of the P-value, but we do know that it is very small, smaller than 0.0001. Because $\text{P-value} < 0.0001 \leq 0.05$, we conclude that we have convincing evidence that sample 2 was NOT taken from a normally distributed population.

c) For sample 3, the output shows a P-value of 0.0588. Because $0.0588 > 0.05$, we conclude that there is a reasonable possibility that sample 3 was taken from a normally distributed population.

d) For sample 4, the output shows a P-value of 0.0144. Because $0.0144 \leq 0.05$, we conclude that we have convincing evidence that sample 4 was NOT taken from a normally distributed population.

Recall from the discussion after Example 6.19, the population for samples (1) and (3) was normally distributed and the population for samples (2) and (4) was right-skewed. It is worth noting that, unlike the histogram method, the P-value method reached the correct conclusion all four times, even for the small samples.

WRAP SESSION: *Putting it all together*

Now that we have an idea of how to determine whether or not it is reasonable to assume that a population is normally distributed, let's take a look at an example from beginning to end. We will first test a data set to see if it is plausible for it to have been drawn from a normal population. We will then see the types of calculations we would be able to make and we will examine the concerns we might have about our answers.

Example 6.21: *Investigating the length of California's great white sharks*

In July 2014, an article was published in the Orange County Register that claimed that the population of great white sharks off of the coast of California was estimated to have a size of about 2,400 sharks. Suppose that a random sample of 57 mature great white sharks off of the California were observed and measured. The histogram and P-value below represent the lengths, in feet, of these 57 mature great white sharks.

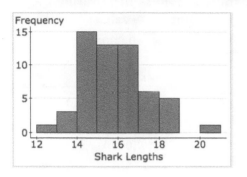

Anderson-Darling goodness-of-fit results:			
Variable	**n**	**Stat**	**P-Value**
Shark Lengths	57	0.305605	0.5561

How big are the great white sharks that swim off of the coast of California?

a)   Based on the histogram, what do you conclude about the normality of the population of mature great white sharks off of the California coast? Explain.

b)   Based on the P-value, what do you conclude about the normality of the population of mature great white sharks off of the California coast? Explain.

c)   Suppose that this sample of 57 mature great white had a mean of 15.84 feet and a standard deviation of 1.6087 feet. Estimate the percentage of California's mature great white sharks that are at least 20 feet long.

d)   Estimate and interpret the 90th percentile for the length of California's mature great white sharks.

e)   What concerns would we have about the accuracy of the estimates made in parts (c) and (d) above? Explain.

Solution:

a)   The histogram for the great white shark lengths appears to either be bell-shaped or possibly slightly right-skewed. Because the sample size is fairly small, $n = 57$, it is hard to be certain of the true shape of the population. However, it is a reasonable possibility that the population is normally distributed.

b)   The output shows a P-value of 0.5561. Because $0.5561 > 0.05$, we conclude that there is a reasonable possibility that sample of great whites was taken from a normally distributed population.

c)   Because parts (a) and (b) tell us that it is a reasonable possibility that the population is normally distributed, we will use the area under a normal curve to answer this question. We will use the mean and standard deviation calculated from the sample data for our normal curve.

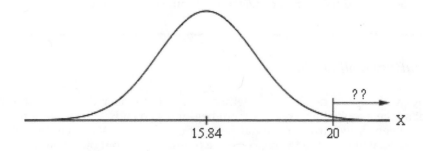

$$z = \frac{20 - 15.84}{1.6087} \approx 2.586 \quad \Rightarrow \quad \text{Area} = normalcdf(2.586, \infty) \approx 0.0049 = 0.49\%$$

So, we would estimate that about 0.49% of the mature great white sharks that swim off of California's coast are at least 20 feet long..

d) Recall, P_{90} has 90% of the shark lengths below it. So, we are looking for the x-value with area 0.90 to its left. Because we have more than half of the area to the left, P_{90} must be on the right side of the graph.

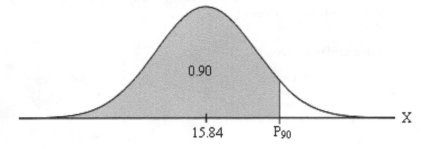

The z-score is given by: $z = invNorm(0.90) \approx 1.282$

So, $P_{90} = x \approx \bar{x} + 1.282 \cdot s = 15.84 + 1.282 * 1.6087 \approx 17.902$ feet.

Interpretation: 90% of the mature great white sharks off of the coast of California are *shorter than* 17.902 feet long and the other 10% of those sharks are longer than 17.902 feet.

e) There are two main concerns and they both arrive from the fact that we are making our calculations based off of sample data. Firstly, we are using the mean and standard deviation from our sample when working with the normal curve. Because these values are from a fairly small random sample, they will not be perfect estimates of the true mean and standard deviation for the sharks. Secondly, we are not sure based on parts (a) and (b) that the shark lengths are normally distributed. We only found that it was a reasonable possibility that the population is normal. If the population is not actually normally distributed, then that will bring in even more error to the estimates that we have made.

Caution: *We can't prove that the population is normal!*

It is important to remember that when we the sample produces a bell-shaped histogram or a P-value that is at least 0.05, this tells us that there is a *reasonable possibility* that the population is normal. It is a very common mistake for people to state that the population *is* normal after seeing a roughly bell-shaped histogram or a large P-value from the sample data. It is not possible with these types of tests to prove that the population is normal. Therefore, we need to be careful and only state that there is a reasonable possibility that the population in normal in such cases.

Let's practice what we have learned with some exercises.

Exercise Set 6.5

<u>Concept Review</u>: Review the definitions and concepts by filling in the blanks for each of the following.

73) If the histogram for your sample data is roughly bell-shaped, then you can conclude that there is a _____ _____ that your sample was taken from a _____ distributed population.

74) If the histogram for your sample data is not roughly bell-shaped, then you can be confident that your sample is _____ taken from a normal population. Your confidence will drop for _____ sample sizes.

75) If the P-value ___ _____ , then you can conclude that your sample data did not come from a normally distributed population. The difference between your data and an ideal normal sample are too _____ to just be the result of _____ _____ .

76) If the P-value ___ _____ , then you can conclude that there is a reasonable possibility that your sample data was taken from a normally distributed population. The difference between your data and an ideal normal sample are _____ enough to just be the result of _____ _____ .

<u>Mechanics</u>: Practice the mechanics of assessing normality before moving on to applications.

77) A histogram and a P-value are given below to help assess the normality of a random sample of size, $n = 1,573$, taken from an unknown population.

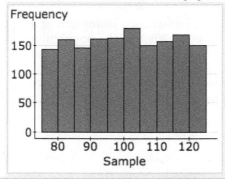

Anderson-Darling goodness-of-fit results:

Variable	n	Stat	P-Value
Sample	1573	16.109985	<0.0001

a) Based on the histogram, what do you conclude about the normality of the population? Explain.
b) Based on the P-value, what do you conclude about the normality of the population? Explain.
c) If your conclusions on parts (a) and (b) agree, how confident are you in your conclusion. If the conclusions do not agree, which one do you trust more? Explain.

78) A histogram and a P-value are given below to help assess the normality of a random sample of size, $n = 1,912$, taken from an unknown population.

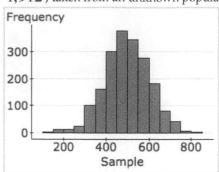

Anderson-Darling goodness-of-fit results:

Variable	n	Stat	P-Value
Sample	1912	0.30374287	0.5718

a) Based on the histogram, what do you conclude about the normality of the population? Explain.
b) Based on the P-value, what do you conclude about the normality of the population? Explain.
c) If your conclusions on parts (a) and (b) agree, how confident are you in your conclusion. If the conclusions do not agree, which one do you trust more? Explain.

79) A histogram and a P-value are given below to help assess the normality of a random sample of size, $n = 73$, taken from an unknown population.

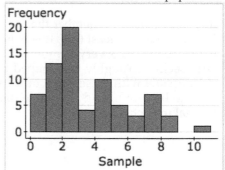

Anderson-Darling goodness-of-fit results:

Variable	n	Stat	P-Value
Sample	73	1.8317668	<0.0001

a) Based on the histogram, what do you conclude about the normality of the population? Explain.
b) Based on the P-value, what do you conclude about the normality of the population? Explain.
c) If your conclusions on parts (a) and (b) agree, how confident are you in your conclusion. If the conclusions do not agree, which one do you trust more? Explain.

80) A histogram and a P-value are given below to help assess the normality of a random sample of size, $n = 67$, taken from an unknown population.

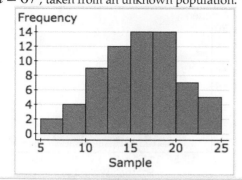

Anderson-Darling goodness-of-fit results:

Variable	n	Stat	P-Value
Sample	67	0.15528127	0.9535

a) Based on the histogram, what do you conclude about the normality of the population? Explain.
b) Based on the P-value, what do you conclude about the normality of the population? Explain.
c) If your conclusions on parts (a) and (b) agree, how confident are you in your conclusion. If the conclusions do not agree, which one do you trust more? Explain.

81) A histogram and a P-value are given below to help assess the normality of a random sample of size, $n = 22$, taken from an unknown population.

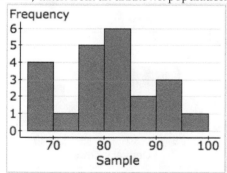

Anderson-Darling goodness-of-fit results:

Variable	n	Stat	P-Value
Sample	22	0.16953606	0.9229

a) Based on the histogram, what do you conclude about the normality of the population? Explain.
b) Based on the P-value, what do you conclude about the normality of the population? Explain.
c) If your conclusions on parts (a) and (b) agree, how confident are you in your conclusion. If the conclusions do not agree, which one do you trust more? Explain.

82) A histogram and a P-value are given below to help assess the normality of a random sample of size, $n = 19$, taken from an unknown population.

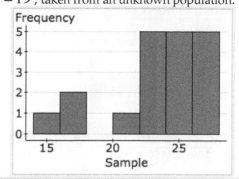

Anderson-Darling goodness-of-fit results:

Variable	n	Stat	P-Value
Sample	19	1.0875719	0.0057

a) Based on the histogram, what do you conclude about the normality of the population? Explain.
b) Based on the P-value, what do you conclude about the normality of the population? Explain.
c) If your conclusions on parts (a) and (b) agree, how confident are you in your conclusion. If the conclusions do not agree, which one do you trust more? Explain.

Applications: Practice the ideas learned in this section in the context of real world applications.

83) A researcher is investigating the weights of the populations of mature platypuses. The histogram and P-value below represent the weights for a random sample of 154 platypuses, measured in pounds.

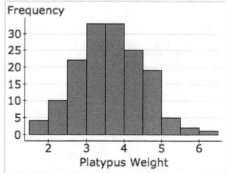

Anderson-Darling goodness-of-fit results:

Variable	n	Stat	P-Value
Platypus Weight	154	0.27227029	0.6657

a) Based on the histogram, what do you conclude about the normality of the population? Explain.
b) Based on the P-value, what do you conclude about the normality of the population? Explain.
c) Would it be reasonable to use a normal curve to estimate the percentage of platypuses in the population that have weights between 2 pounds and 5 pounds? Explain.

84) The histogram and P-value below represent the total
     cholesterol numbers for a random sample of 59 adults
     from the U.S. aged 20 or older, measured in mg/dL.
     (Based on data from CDC.gov)

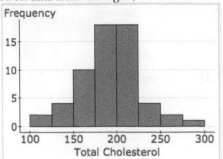

Anderson-Darling goodness-of-fit results:

Variable	n	Stat	P-Value
Total Cholesterol	59	0.34948566	0.4626

a) Based on the histogram, what do you conclude
    about the normality of the population? Explain.
b) Based on the P-value, what do you conclude
    about the normality of the population? Explain.
c) Would it be reasonable to use a normal curve to
    estimate the percentage of adults in the
    population that have total cholesterol numbers
    higher than 240 mg/dL? Explain.

85) The histogram and P-value below represent the base
     annual salaries for a random sample of 73 Major
     League Baseball players from the 2014 season.
     (Based on data from ESPN.com)

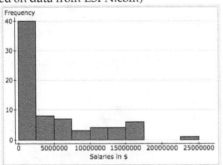

Anderson-Darling goodness-of-fit results:

Variable	n	Stat	P-Value
Salaries in $	73	6.551167	<0.0001

a) Based on the histogram, what do you conclude
    about the normality of the population? Explain.
b) Based on the P-value, what do you conclude
    about the normality of the population? Explain.
c) Would it be reasonable to use a normal curve to
    estimate the percentage of all MLB players that
    have total base salaries higher than $10,000,000?
    Explain.

86) The histogram and P-value below represent the
     weight, in ounces, for a random sample of 127 NCAA
     game used footballs.

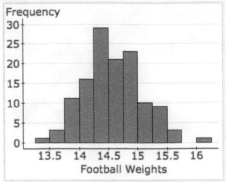

Anderson-Darling goodness-of-fit results:

Variable	n	Stat	P-Value
Football Weights	127	0.29857256	0.5815

a) Based on the histogram, what do you conclude
    about the normality of the population? Explain.
b) Based on the P-value, what do you conclude
    about the normality of the population? Explain.
c) Would it be reasonable to use a normal curve to
    estimate the percentage of all NCAA footballs
    that have weights in the regulation range from 14
    to 15 ounces? Explain.

87) The histogram and P-value below represent the
     delivery time, in minutes, for a random sample of 29
     pizza deliveries to a statistics student's home.

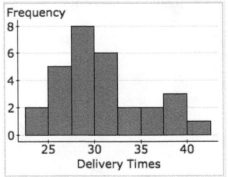

Anderson-Darling goodness-of-fit results:

Variable	n	Stat	P-Value
Delivery Times	29	0.67910244	0.0682

a) Based on the histogram, what do you conclude
    about the normality of the population? Explain.
b) Based on the P-value, what do you conclude
    about the normality of the population? Explain.
c) Would it be reasonable to use a normal curve to
    estimate the probability that a randomly selected
    pizza order for this student would arrive in less
    than 30 minutes time? Explain.

88) A statistics test was given to thousands of students. The histogram and P-value below represent a random sample of 33 students that took this test.

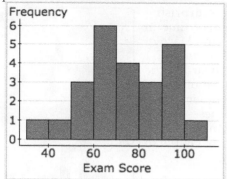

Anderson-Darling goodness-of-fit results:

Variable	n	Stat	P-Value
Exam Score	33	0.42239259	0.3033

a) Based on the histogram, what do you conclude about the normality of the population? Explain.
b) Based on the P-value, what do you conclude about the normality of the population? Explain.
c) Would it be reasonable to use a normal curve to estimate the probability of a randomly selected student scoring at least 70 points on this exam? Explain.

89) Refer to the Platypus weight data from Exercise (83). Suppose that the sample produced a mean of $\bar{x} \approx 3.64$ pounds and a standard deviation of $s \approx 0.87399$ pounds.
a) Estimate the percentage of all platypuses that weigh more than 5 pounds.
b) Estimate the 40th percentile for platypus weights.
c) Interpret the 40th percentile.
d) What concerns should you have about the accuracy of your estimates made in parts (a) and (b) above. Explain.

90) Refer to the football weight data from Exercise (86). Suppose that the sample produced a mean of $\bar{x} \approx 14.58$ ounces and a standard deviation of $s \approx 0.49242$ ounces.
a) Estimate the percentage of all NCAA game used footballs that weigh less than 15 ounces.
b) Estimate the 10th percentile for NCAA game used football weights.
c) Interpret the 10th percentile.
d) What concerns should you have about the accuracy of your estimates made in parts (a) and (b) above. Explain.

Chapter Problem: A Tie for Olympic Downhill Gold

During the 2014 Winter Olympics in Sochi, Russia, something surprising happened in one of the women's downhill skiing events. For the first time in Olympic history, an Alpine skiing race ended in a tie. Two skiers, Tina Maze of Slovenia and Dominique Gisin of Switzerland, both finished with a time of 1 minute 41.57 seconds (or 101.57 seconds) and both women were awarded the gold medal. It is natural for people to wonder "What is the chance of that?" However, because it has never happened before, the past relative frequency of a tie is not useful in calculating this probability. Coincidently, both of these women had previously been involved in a tie for the lead in other non-Olympic events. In this chapter problem, we will make some attempts at using a normal curve to try to estimate the chance of such a tie.

What is the chance that an Olympic downhill race will end in a tie?

Let's start the process with some of the facts from the race. Thirty-five women competed in the finals of this downhill event. In such events, it is rare for one of the bottom qualifiers to compete for the medals. Because of this, we will focus on the top 22 racers out of the 35. These 22 women all finished within 2 seconds of the winner. For these 22 women, the mean race time was 102.604 seconds with a standard deviation of 0.623314 seconds. Dominique Gisin set the winning time with 3 women yet to race. Tina Maze was the last competitor to race and tied for the gold medal. We will investigate the chances of a tie in a few ways, but we will begin by deciding whether or not it seems appropriate to use a normal curve to help us with our estimates.

a) The first task is to look at the race time for the top 22 skiers. If we consider this to be a random sample of the times the skiers had the potential to achieve, then it is our goal to determine if that population of potential race times is normally distributed. The histogram and normal test P-value are shown below for the race times of the top 22 women. Use the histogram and or the P-value from the sample to assess the normality of the population.

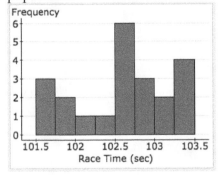

Anderson-Darling goodness-of-fit results:
Where: Row < 22.5

Variable	n	Stat	P-Value
Race Time (sec)	22	0.55846564	0.1315

b) Dominique Gisin finished with a time of 101.57 seconds. However her time was rounded to the nearest hundredth of a second. This means that any time between 101.565 and 101.575 would have also been rounded to a tying time of 101.57 seconds. Use a normal curve with a mean of 102.604 seconds and a standard deviation of 0.623314 seconds (based off of our sample of 22 race times) to estimate the probability that the final racer, Tina Maze, would achieve a time between 101.565 and 101.575 and tie Dominique Gisin for the gold medal.

c) There were actually 3 women left to race after Gisin. What is the probability that at least 1 of them would have tied her? Hint: Use the complement rule and your answer from part (b).

d) Perhaps any of the women that finished within 2 seconds of Gisin had a chance to tie her. There were 21 such competitors. What is the chance that at least 1 of those 21 women would have tied her?

e) Both of these women had previously been involved in ties for the win in non-Olympic downhill races. Does this surprise you? Explain using your answers to parts (b), (c), and (d).

Chapter 6 - Technology Project

1) This problem will use the "Normal Distributions" application from the StatSims folder.

    a) Enter your name in the textbox provided.
    b) Click on the "Identify" tab. The purple graph is the Standard Normal Curve. Take guesses at the mean and standard deviation of the red curve shown. Enter the guesses in the boxes provided.
    c) Press the "Guess" button to check your answers and to see your curve. The curve matching your guesses will be shown in green. You may try two more times to improve the match between your green curve and the target red curve.
    d) If after three tries the output below your name says "Nice Job!", then use "ALT / PrintScreen" to copy this window to your report. If the output says "Too much Error", then click new and try again.
    E) Write out with the blanks filled in: "The mean of a normal curve affects where the _____ of the curve is located. The standard deviation directly affects how _____ the curve is and indirectly affects the _____ of the graph."

2) This problem will also use the "Normal Distributions" application from the StatSims folder. The amount of annual rainfall in a certain city has a normal distribution with mean 25 inches and st dev 5.34 inches. Let X = the amount of rainfall in a randomly selected year. Choose from the CDF & InvCDF to find the following:

    a) Enter your name in the textbox provided.
    B) Use the CDF tab to find $P(x \leq 28)$. **Note:** You should enter x-values rather than z-scores. Make sure that you enter the mean and standard deviation as well. Use "ALT / PrintScreen" to copy the window and then paste it to word. Use the Calculate button to redraw the graph if needed. Circle the answer on the printout.
    C) Use the CDF tab to find $P(x > 21)$. Use "ALT / PrintScreen" to copy the window and then paste it to your report. Circle the answer on the printout.
    D) Use the CDF tab to find $P(15 < x \leq 30)$. Use "ALT / PrintScreen" to copy the window and then paste it to your report. Circle the answer on the printout.
    E) Use the InvCDF tab to find the 85th percentile. Make sure that you remember to enter the mean and standard deviation in the textboxes provided. Use "ALT / PrintScreen" to copy and paste to your report. Handwrite the answer for the 85th percentile in the appropriate spot on the graph (after you have printed the report).
    F) Interpret the 85th percentile by filling in the blanks. _____ % of the years in this city have _____ totals that are _____ _____ _____ .
    G) Use InvCDF to find the x value with area 0.384 to its right. Hint: InvCDF never works with areas on the right, so you will need to make an adjustment. Use "ALT / PrintScreen" to copy and paste to your report. Circle the answer on the printout.
    H) Label the area 0.384 on the graph from part (G) on the print out.

3) This problem will use Technology to check a random sample to see if it is reasonable that it came from a normally distributed population.

    a) Use your Statistics software to generate a random sample of size 87 from a binomial population with n = 514 and p = 0.67.
    b) Use the software to create a histogram for the sample data. Copy the histogram to your report.
    c) Use the software to conduct a normal test to find a P-value. Copy the results to your report.
    d) Based on the histogram and the P-value, what conclusion would you draw about the normality of the population the random sample was taken from? Explain. (Hint: See Section 6.5 guidance.)

Chapter 6: Chapter Review

Section 6.1: Introducing the Normal Distribution

- Normal curves are a special type of bell-shaped curves.
- A variable or population is normally distributed if it has the shape of one of these special bell-shaped curves.
- If a population is approximately normally distributed, then area under a normal curve can be used as an approximation for relative frequencies for the population.
- If a random variable is approximately normally distributed, then area under a normal curve can be used as an approximation for probabilities for that variable.
- The total area under a normal curve is always equal to 1.
- A normal curve is symmetric about its mean, μ.
- Normal curves extend indefinitely in both direction and the height approaches zero on each side.
- Almost all of the area lies between $\mu - 3\sigma$ and $\mu + 3\sigma$.
- The standard deviation affects the width of a normal curve. If σ gets larger, then the curve gets wider. If σ gets smaller, then the curve gets narrower.
- Because the total area is fixed at 1, a wider curve is shorter in the center and a narrower curve is taller in the center.

Section 6.2: Area under the Standard Normal Curve

- The standard normal curve is the normal curve with $\mu = 0$ and $\sigma = 1$.
- The standard normal curve represents the z-scores from any other normal distribution.
- The units on the standard normal curve are the number of standard deviations away from the mean.
- We will use technology to find areas under the standard normal curve.
- We will let *normalcdf*(A, B) represent the area under the standard normal curve between the values A and B. A and B are z-scores.
- If we are finding the area of a region that does not have an upper boundary, then we use ∞ as the upper boundary.
- If we are finding the area of a region that does not have a lower boundary, then we use $-\infty$ as the lower boundary.
- For most technologies, we will just enter a larger number such as 1×10^{99} in place of ∞.
- Unless otherwise indicated in a problem, we will round areas to four decimal places. If the first four decimal places will all be zeros, then we write, $Area \approx 0.0000$.
- Even though we will use technology to find the areas we need, we should still draw a sketch of the region and attempt to estimate the area in our head. This will help us catch entry mistakes on our technology.
- If we are given an area and asked to find boundaries for the associated region under the curve, then we consider this to be working backwards.
- We will let *invNorm*(0.1754) represent the z-score with an area of 0.1754 to its left. We will use technology to find such areas.
- The invNorm function will always assume that you are entering the area to the left. If you are given an area to the right or a middle area, then you must adjust it to an area to the left before using the invNorm function.
- z_α represents the z-score with area α to its right.
- If we are told that the random variable z has the standard normal distribution, then we find probabilities for the variable using the corresponding area under the standard normal curve.

Section 6.3: Areas Under Any Normal Curve

- We can transform an area under any normal curve to an area under the standard normal curve by calculating the z-scores from the boundaries of the original normal curve to obtain the boundaries on the standard normal curve.
- When we transform an area from a normal curve to the standard normal curve, the area is not changed.
- To find the area under a normal curve, we must first use z-scores to convert the area to the standard normal curve.
- Even though we are technically moving the area to a new curve, we usually just show the z-scores for the boundaries of our region underneath the original x-value boundaries.
- If we are asked to find a relative frequency for a normally distributed population, then we will approximate this using the corresponding area under the normal curve.
- If we are asked to find a probability for a normally distributed random variable, then we will approximate this using the corresponding area under the normal curve.
- **Empirical Rule** for a normal population: 68.27% of the data will lie within 1 standard deviation of the mean, 95.45% of the data will lie within 2 standard deviations of the mean, and 99.73% of the data will lie within 3 standard deviations of the mean.
- **Empirical Rule** for a normally distributed random variable, X: $P(\mu - \sigma < X < \mu + \sigma) = 0.6827$,

  $P(\mu - 2\sigma < X < \mu + 2\sigma) = 0.9545$, and $P(\mu - 3\sigma < X < \mu + 3\sigma) = 0.9973$.
- Problems where an area is given and we need to find the x-value(s) that correspond to this area are considered to be working backwards problems.
- When working backwards to find a boundary, we must enter an area to the left into invNorm to find the z-score. We then convert this z-score back to an x-value.
- A z-score of 1.645 indicates that we need an x-value that is 1.645 standard deviations above the mean. Therefore, $x = \mu + 1.645\sigma$.
- A z-score of −1.960 indicates that we need an x-value that is 1.960 standard deviations below the mean. Therefore, $x = \mu - 1.960\sigma$.
- In general, we can use the formula $x = \mu + z \cdot \sigma$ to convert our z-scores to x-values when we are working backwards.
- Quartiles divide a data set into 4 equal parts. To find the quartiles for a normal distribution, we divide the area under the curve into four sections that each have an area of 0.25 and then we work backwards to find the boundaries that make this area split happen.
- When finding a percentile, the percentile number always tells us the area to the left of the boundary we are looking for. For example, P_{73} is the 73rd percentile and it is the x-value with an area of 0.73 to its left.
- When interpreting a percentile, we always talk about the percentage of the data that is less than the boundary that corresponds to the percentile.
- Any variable that is truly normally distributed will be a continuous variable. When calculating probabilities for continuous variables, it does not matter whether or not the boundaries are included.
- Never adjust the boundaries for a probability when working with a continuous random variable.

Section 6.4: Approximating the Binomial Distribution

- Binomial random variables with a large number of trials can cause overflow problems with technology. They can also be very time consuming to compute exactly.
- Many binomial random variables with a large number of trials are approximately normally distributed.
- If $n \cdot p \geq 10$ and $n \cdot q \geq 10$, then we can assume that the binomial distribution is approximately normally distributed.
- Binomial random variables are discrete and normal distributions are for continuous random variables. Because of this, we need to make what is called the continuity correction when approximating probabilities for a binomial random variable using area under a normal curve.
- We make the continuity correction by finding the area that corresponds to the histogram bars for the binomial random variable. Recall: the histogram bars for a binomial random variable go from half mark to half mark. For example, the histogram bar for $P(X = 48)$ starts at 47.5 and ends at 48.5.
- Always draw the histogram bars for your boundary numbers on your graph and then use the graph to help you make the half mark adjustments.
- Recall: we calculate the mean and standard deviation for a binomial random variable using the shortcut formulas $\mu_x = n \cdot p$ and $\sigma_x = \sqrt{n \cdot p \cdot q}$.

Section 6.5: Assessing Normality

- A histogram of sample data can be helpful in assessing the normality of the corresponding population.
- If the histogram is not at least roughly bell-shaped, then you should conclude that the sample did not come from a normal population.
- If the histogram is roughly bell-shaped, then you can conclude that there is a reasonable possibility that the sample was taken from a normal population.
- Histograms require a large sample size to reveal a clear bell-shaped pattern.
- The P-value method for assessing normality is better when your sample size is small.
- We use technology to find our P-value.
- The P-value is the probability that, if our sample really came from a normal population, we would have seen differences at least as big as we observed between our data and the ideal normal sample of the same size.
- If the P-value is less than or equal to 0.05, then conclude that sample did not come from a normal population. (Our data looks too different from an ideal normal sample for the differences to reasonably just be random variation.)
- If the P-value is greater than 0.05, then conclude that there is a reasonable possibility that the sample was taken from a normal population. (Our data looks enough like an ideal normal sample for the differences to reasonably just be random variation.)
- The P-value method cannot prove that our sample was taken from a normally distributed population. When your P-value is larger than 0.05 it only means that there is a reasonably possibility that your sample came from a normally distributed population.

Review Diagrams:

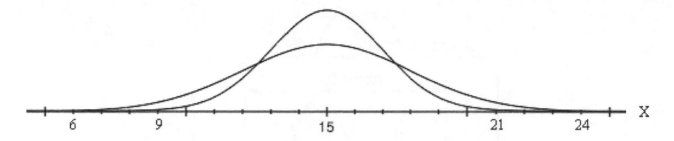

- Normal curves are symmetric about their mean (15 for the above curves).
- The standard deviation directly affects the width of the curve. A small standard deviation makes a narrow curve and a large standard deviation makes a wide one.
- Because the total area under each normal curve is 1, a wider curve is a shorter curve and a narrower curve is taller in the center.

The area that lies between two boundaries 'A' and 'B' under a normal curve is equal to the area under the standard normal curve that lies between the z-scores for the original boundaries. See graphs below.

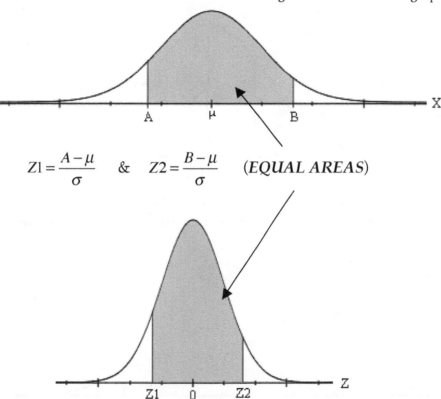

$$Z1 = \frac{A - \mu}{\sigma} \quad \& \quad Z2 = \frac{B - \mu}{\sigma} \quad (EQUAL\ AREAS)$$

The Empirical Rule for Normal Curves

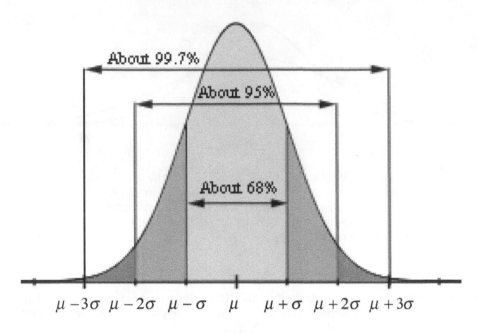

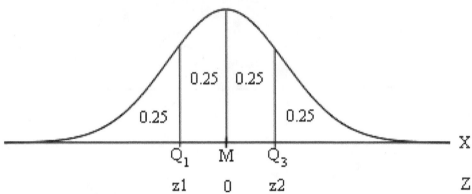

Quartiles are x-values that divide the area under the curve into 4 equal parts.

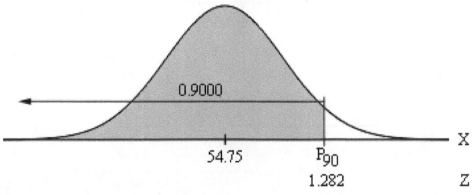

P_{90} is the x-value that has 90% of the data below it. So it is the x-value with area 0.90 to its left. That is more than half of the area to the left, so P_{90} must be on the right.

Finding area is working forwards. We do this when asked to find a percentage, relative frequency, probability, or area for a normal distribution.

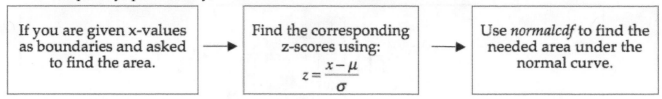

If you are given x-values as boundaries and asked to find the area. → Find the corresponding z-scores using: $z = \dfrac{x - \mu}{\sigma}$ → Use *normalcdf* to find the needed area under the normal curve.

Finding a boundary is working backwards. We do this when asked to find a boundary, an x-value, a percentile, or quartiles for a normal distribution.

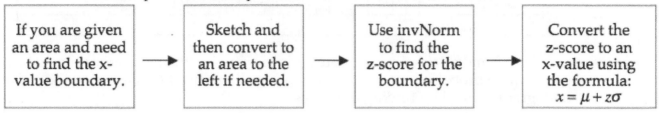

If you are given an area and need to find the x-value boundary. → Sketch and then convert to an area to the left if needed. → Use invNorm to find the z-score for the boundary. → Convert the z-score to an x-value using the formula: $x = \mu + z\sigma$

Normal Approximation to a Binomial Distribution:

If $np \geq 10$ and $nq \geq 10$, then the binomial is approximately normal.

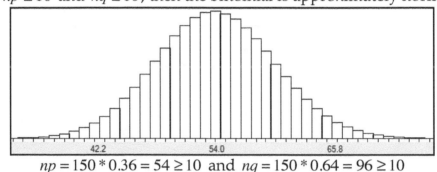

$np = 150 * 0.36 = 54 \geq 10$ and $nq = 150 * 0.64 = 96 \geq 10$

If $np < 10$ or $nq < 10$, then the binomial is NOT approximately normal.

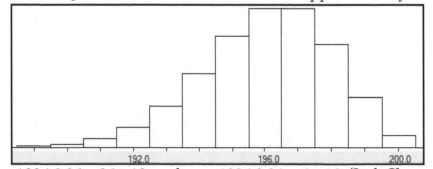

$np = 100 * 0.96 = 96 \geq 10$ and $nq = 100 * 0.04 = 4 < 10$ (Left-Skewed!)

The Continuity Correction:

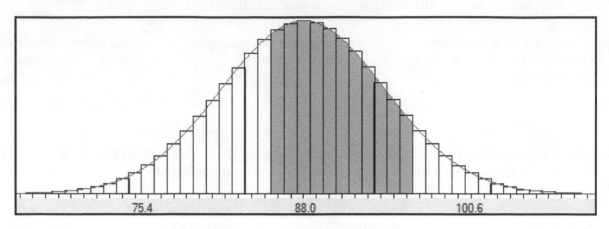

Binomial random variables are discrete and we are using the continuous normal curve to approximate probabilities. For this to work well, we need to use the boundaries of the histogram bars when finding our areas.

For example: To find $P(86 \leq X < 97)$ we want to include the bar for 86, so we begin our area at the left side of that histogram bar, 85.5. We do not want to include the bar for 97, so we would end our area at when the bar for 96 ends and the bar for 97 begins, at 96.5.

Chapter 6: Review Exercises

Mechanics: The following exercises will help you review the mechanics of the calculations learned in this chapter.

1) Together on the same axis, sketch the graphs of the normal curve with:
   a) $\mu = 9$ and $\sigma = 2$
   b) $\mu = 10.5$ and $\sigma = 1.3$

2) Together on the same axis, sketch the graphs of the normal curve with:
   a) $\mu = 14$ and $\sigma = 3$
   b) $\mu = 19.4$ and $\sigma = 4.9$

3) For the standard normal curve, find each of the following.
   a) The area between –2.601 and 1.098.
   b) The area to the right of 2.034.
   c) The area to the left of 1.908.
   d) The z-value with an area of 0.67 to its right.
   e) The two z-scores that trap an area of 0.70 between them with equal outside areas.

4) For the standard normal curve, find each of the following.
   a) The area between 1.031 and 2.852.
   b) The area to the right of –1.655.
   c) The area to the left of –0.856.
   d) The z-value with an area of 0.37 to its right.
   e) The two z-scores that trap an area of 0.88 between them with equal outside areas.

5) If the random variable z has the standard normal distribution, then find:
   a) $P(-1.933 < z \leq -0.805)$
   b) $P(z < 1.621 \text{ OR } z > 2.557)$
   c) $z_{0.18}$

6) If the random variable z has the standard normal distribution, then find:
   a) $P(0.555 \leq z < 2.009)$
   b) $P(z < -1.681 \text{ OR } z > 0.957)$
   c) $z_{0.77}$

7) Consider the normal distribution with $\mu = 118$ and $\sigma = 22.091$.
   a) Determine the area between 90 and 130.
   b) Determine the area to the right of 100.
   c) Determine the x-values that trap an area of 0.60 between them with equal outside areas.

8) Consider the normal distribution with $\mu = 27$ and $\sigma = 2.3899$.
   a) Determine the area between 25 and 30.
   b) Determine the area to the right of 30.
   c) Determine the x-values that trap an area of 0.75 between them with equal outside areas.

9) The random variable X is normally distributed with $\mu_x = 8.02$ and $\sigma_x = 0.51085$.
   a) $P(X < 8.907)$
   b) $P(X > 7 \text{ and } X \leq 9)$
   c) $P(X > 7 \mid X \leq 9)$
   d) P_{85}

10) The random variable X is normally distributed with $\mu_x = 5642.7$ and $\sigma_x = 988.07$.
   a) $P(X \geq 4500)$
   b) $P(X > 5000 \text{ and } X \leq 7000)$
   c) $P(X > 5000 \mid X \leq 7000)$
   d) P_{63}

11) Suppose that X is a binomial random variable with $n = 517$ and $p = 0.318$.
   a) Verify that the normal approximation to a binomial can be used on this problem.
   b) Approximate $P(X = 170)$.
   c) Approximate $P(150 < X \leq 170)$.

12) Suppose that X is a binomial random variable with $n = 775$ and $p = 0.592$.
   a) Verify that the normal approximation to a binomial can be used on this problem.
   b) Approximate $P(X = 450)$.
   c) Approximate $P(470 \leq X < 500)$.

Applications: Apply the concepts learned in this chapter to the following applications. Use technology where appropriate.

13) The lengths of mature rainbow trout are normally distributed with a mean of 24.3 inches and a standard deviation of 5.581 inches.

    a) Find the percentage of mature rainbow trout that are longer than 30 inches.
    b) Determine the quartiles for the lengths of mature rainbow trout.
    c) Find the 98th percentile for the lengths of mature rainbow trout.
    d) Interpret the 98th percentile for mature rainbow trout.

14) The weights of adult coyotes are normally distributed with a mean weight of 30.5 pounds and a standard deviation of 7.75 pounds.

    a) What percentage of adult coyotes weigh less than 40 pounds?
    b) Determine the quartiles for the weights of adult coyotes.
    c) Find the 90th percentile for adult coyote weights.
    d) Interpret the 90th percentile for adult coyote weights.

15) The flight time for a commercial airliner for a nonstop flight from Los Angeles, CA to Boston, MA is normally distributed with a mean of 5.31 hours and a standard deviation of 0.249 hours.

    a) What percentage of the flights take between 5.25 and 5.5 hours to complete?
    b) Fill in the blanks: The middle 95.45% of flight times are between _____ and _____ hours long.
    c) Fill in the blanks: The middle 80% of flight times are between _____ and _____ hours long.

16) The time it takes the author of this text to solve a Rubik's Cube is normally distributed with a mean of 1.94 minutes and a standard deviation of 0.461 minutes.

    a) What percentage of the attempts at solving the puzzle take between 1 and 3 minutes?
    b) Fill in the blanks: The middle 68.27% of the solve times are between _____ and _____ minutes long.
    c) Fill in the blanks: The middle 75% of the solve times are between _____ and _____ minutes long.

17) The lap speed, Y in seconds, for a particular car at a local racetrack is a normally distributed random variable with $\mu_y = 57.83$ and $\sigma_y = 2.8093$. Suppose a lap is randomly selected for this car.

    a) Find $P(55 \le Y < 60)$.
    b) Find $P(Y < 60 \text{ or } Y \ge 65)$.
    c) Find $P(Y \ge 55 \mid Y < 60)$.
    d) Find k, if $P(Y > k) = 0.05$.

18) The average annual snowfall total for Kirkwood Ski Resort, Y in inches, is a normally distributed random variable with $\mu_y = 603.8$ and $\sigma_y = 152.83$. Suppose a year is randomly selected for this resort.

    a) Find $P(550 < Y \le 700)$.
    b) Find $P(Y < 500 \text{ or } Y \ge 750)$.
    c) Find $P(Y \ge 500 \mid Y \le 750)$.
    d) Find k, if $P(Y \le k) = 0.15$.

19) At a certain financial institution, about 39.1% of all home loan applications are rejected. Let X = the number of loans applications that are rejected in a random sample of size 480. Use the normal approximation to find each of the following.

    a) $P(X = 200)$
    b) The probability that at least 200 applications are rejected.
    c) Verify that we have met the requirements for using the normal approximation.

20) The weight, W, in pounds, of an ostrich egg is a normally distributed variable with $\mu_w = 3.1$ pounds and $\sigma_w = 0.519$ pounds. Suppose that we randomly select 350 ostrich eggs and let X = the number of the eggs that weight less than 2.75 pounds.

    a) Determine the distribution of X. Give the details.
    b) What is the expected range for X?
    c) Use the normal approximation method to estimate the probability that at least 100 of the eggs weigh less than 2.75 pounds.

21) The histogram and P-value below represent the number of apps downloaded from Apple, in millions, for a random sample of 37 days from 2012. The data is based on information from an article by bgr.com.

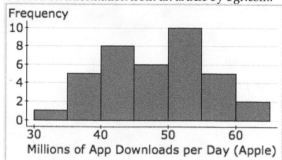

Anderson-Darling goodness-of-fit results:

Variable	n	Stat	P-Value
App Downloads	37	0.30076427	0.5625

Note: $\bar{x} \approx 48.46$, $s \approx 7.7767$

a) Based on the histogram, what do you conclude about the normality of the population? Explain.
b) Based on the P-value, what do you conclude about the normality of the population? Explain.
c) Estimate the percentage of days in 2012 where the number of downloads/day exceeded 55 million.
d) Estimate the 65th Percentile for the number of app downloads per day from Apple in 2012.
e) Interpret the 65th percentile.
f) What concerns should you have about the accuracy of your estimates made in parts (c) and (d) above? Explain.

22) The histogram and P-value below represent the annual car insurance cost, in dollars, for a random sample of 20 college students.

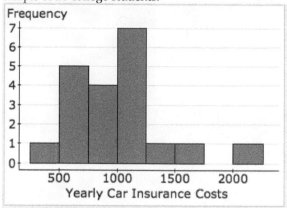

Anderson-Darling goodness-of-fit results:

Variable	n	Stat	P-Value
Car Insurance	20	0.51532276	0.1684

Note: $\bar{x} \approx 996.5$, $s \approx 405.40$

a) Based on the histogram, what do you conclude about the normality of the population? Explain.
b) Based on the P-value, what do you conclude about the normality of the population? Explain.
c) Estimate the percentage of college students that pay less than $1200 per year for car insurance.
d) Estimate the 20th Percentile for the annual car insurance costs of college students.
e) Interpret the 20th percentile.
f) What concerns should you have about the accuracy of your estimates made in parts (c) and (d) above? Explain.

Chapter 7 – Sampling Distributions

Chapter Problem: *To Catch a Thief*

Suppose that a company produces a standard size can of soda. This means that the cans are labeled as containing 12 fluid ounces of soda. When the volume for the cans is labeled, the amount labeled is understood to be the mean amount in all such cans. Suppose that a consumer group believed that the company was cheating their customers by, on average, under filling the cans. How could the consumer group use a random sample to evaluate the soda company's claim? How effective would sampling be in evaluating the company's claim? If the company cheats a little, will they get caught? If the company cheats by a lot, would they get caught then?

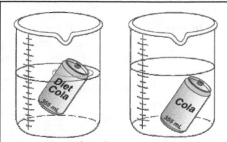

If we accept that the amount of soda in cans will vary, then is there a way to use a random sample to decide if we are being cheated?

In this chapter, we will learn the tools needed to answer such a question. We will return to this problem at the end of the chapter when we are properly equipped to answer the questions.

Introduction:

In this chapter, we will begin to bridge the gap between the descriptive statistics and probability we have learned so far and inferential statistics. Recall, from Chapter 1, that inferential statistics is the process of drawing conclusion about a population, based on information obtained from a sample. Learning inferential statistics is the main goal of an introductory statistics course.

For example, we may wish to know what percentage of Americans approve of the job the President of the U.S. is doing. We might want to estimate what percentage of Americans watched the most recent Super Bowl. Or we may try to estimate the probability of heads on a newly minted coin that we suspect is not fair. All of these topics are about probabilities or percentages, but we may also be interested in similar information regarding a population mean. Perhaps we want to know the average lasting time for a newly designed light bulb or maybe we want to estimate the average energy output for a newly designed solar panel.

In all of the situations described above, it is impractical or impossible to collect census data from the entire population to find the true answer to our question. Sometimes, as with light bulbs, the process of collecting data can destroy the item being studied. In other cases where data collection is not destructive, like asking someone if they watched the Super Bowl, it is often time consuming and expensive to ask everyone, and this provides another deterrent to taking a census.

So what shall we do? The simple answer is: We will only use a sample from the population of interest to obtain an estimate for the targeted population value. We might ask a random sample of 1000 Americans if they approve of the job the President is doing. We might flip the coin 800 times and calculate the percentage of heads in the sample. We might test 100 of the new light bulbs and find the average lifetime for the sample.

However, to really say we are doing inferential statistics, there is much more to it than that. We will need to face the fact that estimates from samples have errors. And then we will need to learn how to predict how much error there will be. In this chapter, we will examine the relationship between estimates from samples and the population quantities that we are trying to estimate. To do a good job with this, we will have to learn the distribution for the sample proportion and the sample mean.

We will examine all of the ideas mentioned above and more in the following sections:

Let's get started.

Section 7.1 – The Mean and Standard Deviation of the Sample Proportion, $\hat{p}$

In this section, we will focus on estimating the value of a population percentage, **population proportion**, or the true probability of some event. The process is nearly identical for all three of these variations. And, in all three cases, we will want to use a **sample proportion** as our estimate. We begin by defining these new terms.

Definitions: *Population Proportion and Sample Proportion*

Population Proportion, p: A population proportion is the ratio of the number of data values in a population that have a desired trait to the size of the population. If having the desired trait is considered to be a success, the p can be thought of the proportion of successes in the population. The symbol for the population proportion is p.

Sample Proportion, $\hat{p}$: A sample proportion is the ratio of the number of data values in a sample that have a desired trait to the size of the sample. The symbol for the sample proportion is $\hat{p}$ (read as "p-hat"). $\hat{p}$ is calculated as shown below.

$$\hat{p} = \frac{x}{n} \text{ , where } x \text{ is the number of successes in a sample of size } n$$

When a value is calculated from a sample for the purpose of estimating a population quantity, we refer to the sample value as a **statistic**. The population quantity we are trying to estimate is often referred to as the **parameter** of interest. And, because the statistic represents a single number guess at the parameter, we refer to the statistic as a **point estimate** of that parameter. The formal definitions of these new terms are shown below.

Definitions: *Parameters, Statistics, and Point Estimates*

Parameter: A quantity that describes a population value. For example, a population mean, μ, a population standard deviation, σ, and a population proportion, p, are all considered parameters.

Statistic: A quantity that describes a sample value, typically with the goal of estimating a parameter. For example, a sample mean, $\overline{x}$, a sample standard deviation, s, and a sample proportion, $\hat{p}$, are all considered statistics.

Point Estimate: A single value (statistic), calculated from a sample, which will be used to estimate a parameter for the population being sampled. Examples:
- $\overline{x}$ is a point estimate for μ.
- s is a point estimate for σ.
- $\hat{p}$ is a point estimate for p.

It is worth noting that you are taking a class that is called statistics rather than parameters. This is because most of our work in a statistics course is based off of data that is collected from a sample. The statistic can be known once the sample is taken, but we can only make estimates of the parameter.

SAMPLING ERROR: *Dealing with the fact that point estimates are usually wrong!*

In the introduction to this chapter, I stated that if we use a statistic from a sample to estimate a parameter from the population, then we would have to face the fact that we would get errors. This error results from the fact that our samples are chosen randomly and that means the value we get for the statistic will vary. As a result of this random variation, the statistic often has a different value than the parameter. This difference is referred to as sampling error. We define this below for proportions and will define it for means in Section 7.3.

Definitions: *Sampling Error (for proportions)*

Sampling Error: Sampling error is the difference that results from using an estimate obtained from a sample (a statistic) rather than a census value to estimate a population quantity (a parameter).

Sampling Error for Proportions: When we are trying to estimate a population proportion, p, we use the statistic $\hat{p}$ as our estimate. The sampling error is the absolute value of the difference between these two quantities. The error is expressed below in symbolic form.

$$\text{Sampling Error} = |\hat{p} - p|$$

Let's take a look at an example to illustrate these definitions.

Example 7.1: *Exploring the Definitions*

A coin is tossed 319 times in an effort to estimate the true probability of heads (proportion of times that it will produce heads in the long run) for this coin. Assume that the coin is fair (true probability of heads is 0.5) and answer the following questions.

a) Find the point estimate and sampling error if the 319 tosses result in 164 heads.

b) Find the point estimate and sampling error if the 319 tosses result in 151 heads.

c) Suppose we will be satisfied with our estimate if the sampling error is less than 0.02, what range of sample proportions would be considered acceptable?

d) What is the probability that we will have no sampling error in our estimate? Explain.

Solution:

a) Because we are trying to estimate the true probability (or true proportion of heads, p) for this coin, we will use the statistic $\hat{p}$ as our point estimate. Based on the sample data, we get:

$$\hat{p} = \frac{x}{n} = \frac{164}{319} \approx 0.5141$$

To find the sampling error, we calculate the difference between this value and the true proportion, 0.5.

$$\text{Sampling Error} \approx |0.5141 - 0.5| = 0.0141$$

b) This time, our point estimate is $\hat{p} = \frac{x}{n} = \frac{151}{319} \approx 0.4734$.

Using this, we find the sampling error $\approx |0.4734 - 0.5| = 0.0266$.

c) If we will be satisfied with our estimate if the sampling error is less than 0.02, then the boundaries between acceptable values and unacceptable ones would lie 0.02 away (on either side) from the true proportion of 0.5. This translates as follows:

$$|\hat{p} - p| < 0.02 \implies |\hat{p} - 0.50| < 0.02 \implies 0.48 < \hat{p} < 0.52$$

This means that will be satisfied with our estimate as long as it was between 0.48 and 0.52.

d) The only way that we get no sampling error is if our point estimate, $\hat{p}$, is equal to the parameter, p. In symbols, this translates to $P(\hat{p} = p)$ or $P(\hat{p} = 0.50)$. In this case, because our sample consists of 319 tosses, there is no number of heads that will produce a sample proportion equal to 0.50. Therefore, $P(\hat{p} = 0.50) = 0$.

The result of part (d) above is interesting. It points out that in the situation described above, it is actually impossible to get a correct estimate for the exact probability of heads for this coin when using a sample of size 319. This would be the case for any odd sized sample, no matter how large it was. If we tossed the coin an even number of times, then it would be possible to get an estimate from a sample that was correct, but the chance is not very good. Suppose that we tossed the coin 500 times to get our estimate, if the coin showed heads exactly 250 times, then we would have no sampling error. However, the chance of this occurring is actually quite small. Here is the probability calculated using the binomial formula from Section 5.5.

$$P(\hat{p} = 0.50) = P(250 \text{ heads}) = \binom{500}{250}(0.5)^{250}(0.5)^{250} \approx 0.0357$$

So, what we should learn from this is that it is often impossible to avoid sample error, and even when you can get the right answer, the chance of no error is still quite small. So, when we make estimates based on samples we need to expect there to be sampling error. This is summarized in the following point to remember.

> **Point to Remember:** *Expect Sample Estimates to have Error*
>
> When we use a statistic from a sample to estimate a population parameter, it is often impossible to get the answer exactly right. When it is possible to get an estimate that is exactly correct, it is still very unlikely. For our current work with proportions, we summarize this by saying that the probability of no sampling error is approximately zero. In symbols:
>
> $$P(\hat{p} = p) \approx 0$$

Because sampling error is hard to avoid, the goal is to learn how to control it and that is what we will look at next. The graphs below show the running proportion of successes in two random samples as they were collected. The horizontal axis represents the number of trials completed in the sample and the vertical axis is the relative frequency of success up to that point. The dashed line represents the true probability (or the population proportion).

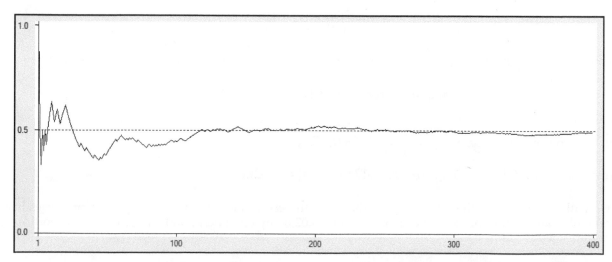

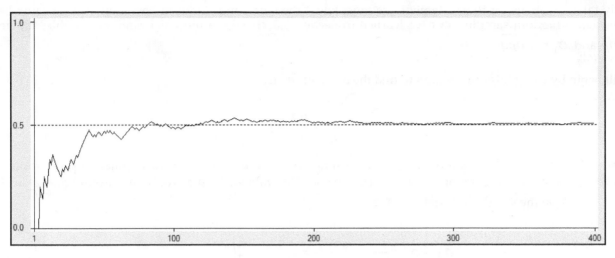

Notice that while the sample size is smaller, the sample proportion varies quite a bit and is often far from the true population proportion. However, as more and more trials occur, the variation in the sample proportion tends to get smaller and the sample proportion starts to stay closer to the true proportion. Both of these traits are important to sampling error and can be predicted by the mean and standard deviation of the sample proportion, $\hat{p}$. Finding formulas for these quantities is our next task.

THE MEAN AND STANDARD DEVIATION OF $\hat{p}$: *Can Sampling Error be Predicted?*

We are about to attempt to find the mean and standard deviation of the sample proportion, $\hat{p}$. However, in the past, we only did this for data sets or random variables, so how does this apply to $\hat{p}$. The simple answer is, $\hat{p}$ is a random variable. In Chapter 5, we learned that a random variable is a quantity whose value depends on chance. How does this apply to $\hat{p}$? Chance enters into this calculation the moment we take a random sample. If you toss a coin 100 times and then calculate the proportion of heads, then you are finding a value for $\hat{p}$ from a sample of size 100. However, if you do it again, you will likely have different results in the sample and arrive at a different value for $\hat{p}$. Because the value of $\hat{p}$ depends on the sample we use, and because our sample is randomly chosen, $\hat{p}$ is a random variable. Therefore it makes sense to attempt to find the mean and standard deviation for $\hat{p}$. As we do this, we will rely on what we learned about binomial distributions in Section 5.5.

The key to discovering the mean and standard deviation of $\hat{p}$ is to focus on the fact that $\hat{p}$ is the ratio of data values with the desired attribute in the sample. A data value that has the desired attribute is referred to as a success. This mention of the term success should remind you of the binomial distribution from Section 5.5. That section dealt with success/failure problems. The difference here is that we are dealing with the proportion of success in our sample, $\hat{p}$, rather than the number of successes in our sample, x. These two quantities are certainly related. In fact, the formula for the sample proportion is as follows:

$$\hat{p} = \frac{x}{n} \; ; \; \text{where } x \text{ is the number of successes in the sample and } n \text{ is the sample size.}$$

To use this fact to determine the distribution of $\hat{p}$, we just need to know one important fact. It is stated as follows:

If the random variable x is divided by a constant, n, then the new random variable created by this division will have a mean and standard deviation equal to $\dfrac{\mu_x}{n}$ and $\dfrac{\sigma_x}{n}$ respectively.

To fully take advantage of this statement, we must know the mean and standard deviation of x, the number of successes in a random sample. But we learned in Section 5.5, that for a binomial random variable, x, we get $\mu_x = np$ and $\sigma_x = \sqrt{npq}$.

We will begin by using this information to find the mean of $\hat{p}$, $\mu_{\hat{p}}$.

$$\mu_{\hat{p}} = \mu_{\frac{x}{n}} = \frac{\mu_x}{n} = \frac{np}{n} = p$$

In words, this says that the mean of all possible sample proportions is equal to the population proportion. This makes $\hat{p}$ a good point estimate for p, because all the possible values of $\hat{p}$ are centered around the value of p. Now let's work on the standard deviation, $\sigma_{\hat{p}}$.

$$\sigma_{\hat{p}} = \sigma_{\frac{x}{n}} = \frac{\sigma_x}{n} = \frac{\sqrt{npq}}{n} = \sqrt{\frac{npq}{n^2}} = \sqrt{\frac{pq}{n}}$$

The important thing to notice is that the sample size is in the denominator of the result. This means that as our sample size increases, the standard deviation of the possible values of $\hat{p}$ decreases. This tells us that, for larger sample sizes, the possible values of our point estimate, $\hat{p}$, are getting closer and closer to their mean, which is p, the parameter we are trying to estimate. Awesome!

These results are summarized in the following Point to Remember.

Point to Remember: *Theorem 7.1 (The mean and standard deviation of $\hat{p}$)*

If we take a random sample of size n from a population where the proportion of successes is p, then the mean and standard deviation of the random variable $\hat{p}$ will be:

$$\mu_{\hat{p}} = p \text{ and } \sigma_{\hat{p}} = \sqrt{\frac{pq}{n}}.$$

Example 7.2: *Practicing the new formulas*

Suppose that the true proportion of successes in our population is 73.24%.

a) Determine the mean and standard deviation for all possible sample proportions from samples of size 50.

b) Determine the mean and standard deviation for all possible sample proportions from samples of size 175.

c) What effect did increasing the sample size have on the mean of the sample proportions, $\mu_{\hat{p}}$?

f) What effect did increasing the sample size have on the standard deviation of the sample proportions, $\sigma_{\hat{p}}$?

Solution:

a) The first thing to note is that the proportion of successes in the population is p. Therefore, we can say that $p = 73.24\% = 0.7324$. We now use the value of p to get q: $q = 1 - p = 0.2676$. The sample size is stated as 50, so we have $n = 50$.

Now, we will simply apply the formulas from Theorem 7.1 above. So, we get:

$$\mu_{\hat{p}} = p = 0.7324 \quad \text{and} \quad \sigma_{\hat{p}} = \sqrt{\frac{pq}{n}} = \sqrt{\frac{0.7324 * 0.2676}{50}} \approx 0.062608$$

b) We will again use the same formulas, but this time with a sample size of $n = 175$.

$$\mu_{\hat{p}} = p = 0.7324 \quad \text{and} \quad \sigma_{\hat{p}} = \sqrt{\frac{pq}{n}} = \sqrt{\frac{0.7324 * 0.2676}{175}} \approx 0.033466$$

c) The sample size change has no effect at all on the calculation of $\mu_{\hat{p}}$. This should have been expected because the sample size is not involved in the formula: $\mu_{\hat{p}} = p$.

d) Increasing the sample size produced a smaller value for the standard deviation of $\sigma_{\hat{p}}$. This is due to the fact that the sample size is in the denominator of the formula: $\sigma_{\hat{p}} = \sqrt{\frac{pq}{n}}$.

BACK TO SAMPLING ERROR: *How do these new formulas help us predict sampling error?*

Now that we have had a little bit of practice using the formulas for the mean and standard deviation of the sample proportion, we want to learn how to use the formulas to help us predict the sampling error that we will usually get when we use $\hat{p}$ as a point estimate for p. To accomplish this goal, we will use the idea that the expected range for any random variable is from two standard deviations below the mean to two standard deviations above the mean. Consider the following:

Suppose that a random sample of size n, is taken from a population where the proportion of items with a desired attribute (the successes) is p. Because $\hat{p}$ is a random variable, we can state that we expect $\hat{p}$ to lie within two standard deviations of its mean. In symbols, this is stated as follows:

$$\mu_{\hat{p}} - 2\sigma_{\hat{p}} < \hat{p} < \mu_{\hat{p}} + 2\sigma_{\hat{p}}$$

Now the goal becomes to get the sampling error, $|\hat{p} - p|$, to show up in this formula. This requires a bit of Algebra. We begin the process by substituting for $\mu_{\hat{p}}$.

$$\mu_{\hat{p}} - 2\sigma_{\hat{p}} < \hat{p} < \mu_{\hat{p}} + 2\sigma_{\hat{p}} \implies p - 2\sigma_{\hat{p}} < \hat{p} < p + 2\sigma_{\hat{p}}$$

$$\implies -2\sigma_{\hat{p}} < \hat{p} - p < +2\sigma_{\hat{p}} \implies |\hat{p} - p| < 2\sigma_{\hat{p}}$$

The work above shows us that we expect the sampling error when estimating p by $\hat{p}$ to be less than $2\sigma_{\hat{p}}$. We can also state this in a different form by substituting for $\sigma_{\hat{p}}$. This allows to also state that we

expect the sampling error to be less than $2\sqrt{\frac{pq}{n}}$.

The preceding discussion is summarized in the following definitions.

Definitions: *Expected Error and Standard Error when estimating p by using $\hat{p}$*

Expected Error for $\hat{p}$: The expected error tells us how much error to expect when we use $\hat{p}$ to estimate p. In words, we expect our sampling error to be less than 2 standard deviations of our point estimate. In symbols, we get the following.

$$\text{Expected Error} < 2\sigma_{\hat{p}} \quad \text{OR} \quad \text{Expected Error} < 2\sqrt{\frac{pq}{n}}$$

Note: We might get sampling error larger than these formulas predict, but because that would mean that $\hat{p}$ was more than two standard deviations away from its mean , such occurrences would be considered unusual.

Standard Error for $\hat{p}$: Because we use $\sigma_{\hat{p}}$ to help us calculate what type of estimation errors are considered expected and which errors are considered unusual, it is common to refer to $\sigma_{\hat{p}} = \sqrt{\frac{pq}{n}}$ as the expected error for $\hat{p}$.

Let's practice this new definition with an example and explore why all this is useful for estimating a population proportion.

Example 7.3: *College Grads working for others*

According to an October 2011 Gallup Poll, 73% of college graduates were working full time for an Employer (as opposed to working part time or being self employed). Assuming that 73% is the true population proportion, answer each of the following questions about estimating this value using a random sample.

a) For a random sample of size $n = 233$, find the values for $\mu_{\hat{p}}$ and $\sigma_{\hat{p}}$.

b) If we use the sample proportion, $\hat{p}$, to estimate the true population proportion, what is the expected error of the estimate?

c) If the sample size is increased to $n = 1014$, what effect, if any, will this have on the expected sampling error?

d) If the sample size is $n = 1593$, would it be unusual for our sample proportion to be $\hat{p} = 0.7037$? Explain.

Solution:

a) The population proportion for this trait is 73%. So, we have $p = 0.73$ and $q = 1 - p = 0.27$. We now apply the formulas from Theorem 7.1 and get the following.

$$\mu_{\hat{p}} = p = 0.73 \quad \text{and} \quad \sigma_{\hat{p}} = \sqrt{\frac{pq}{n}} = \sqrt{\frac{0.73 * 0.27}{233}} \approx 0.029085$$

b) The expected error is less than 2 standard deviations of $\hat{p}$. This tells us that we expect the sampling error to be as shown below.

$$|\hat{p} - p| < 2\sqrt{\frac{pq}{n}} \approx 2 * 0.029085 = 0.05817$$

In words: Even though we expect error in a sample estimate, we expect that our sample proportion will not miss the true proportion by more than 0.05817.

c) The sample size change affects the value of $\sigma_{\hat{p}}$ and therefore, it will also affect our expected error. The calculations are as follows.

$$\text{Expected Error} < 2\sqrt{\frac{pq}{n}} \approx 2 * \sqrt{\frac{0.73 * 0.27}{1014}} = 0.027884$$

d) Typically, when we are asked whether a given value of a random variable is unusual, we use a z-score to help us answer the question. This remains true when our random variable is $\hat{p}$. To accomplish this goal, we must find the values of $\mu_{\hat{p}}$ and $\sigma_{\hat{p}}$.

$$\mu_{\hat{p}} = p = 0.73 \quad \text{and} \quad \sigma_{\hat{p}} = \sqrt{\frac{pq}{n}} = \sqrt{\frac{0.73 * 0.27}{1593}} \approx 0.011123$$

We can now move on to the z-score:

$$z = \frac{\hat{p} - \mu_{\hat{p}}}{\sigma_{\hat{p}}} \approx \frac{0.7037 - 0.73}{0.011123} \approx -2.364$$

Yes. A sample proportion of 0.7037 would be considered unusual, because it is more than 2 standard deviations below its mean.

The examples and theorems that we have explored so far have presented with a lot of new and important information. The key points are listed in the following Point to Remember.

int to Remember: *Relating our new formulas to inferential statistics*

Three very important facts have just been illustrated that are very good news for estimating p by a value of $\hat{p}$ from a randomly chosen sample.

1) $\mu_{\hat{p}} = p$ is good news for estimating because it means that all of our guesses, $\hat{p}$'s, are centered around the value we are trying to estimate, p.

2) Added good news comes from the statement that $\sigma_{\hat{p}} = \sqrt{\dfrac{pq}{n}}$, because this tells us that all the $\hat{p}$'s will get closer to their center (p) as the sample size we choose increases. Recall: We expect most of a data set to lie within 2 standard deviations of its mean.

3) Thus, if we increase our sample size, we will make all the $\hat{p}$'s get closer to p and that means the specific $\hat{p}$ we randomly choose will probably be a good estimate of p.

Summary: It would be unusual for the sampling error to exceed $2\sqrt{\dfrac{pq}{n}}$, so our expected error decreases as our sample size increases.

So far, all of the examples that we have explored have been about estimating a population proportion. We can also apply what we have learned when trying to estimate the probability for a random event. We will conclude this section with such an example.

WRAP SESSION: *Applying what we have learned to probabilities*

Example 7.4: *Testing the dice in a game of Craps*

Craps is one of the most popular table games in casinos. The game is centered around rolling two dice and noting the sum. The most important sum in this game is 7. If we are working with a pair of fair dice, then we learned in Chapter 5 that the probability of rolling a 7 is given by: $P(\text{Sum} = 7) = \dfrac{6}{36} = \dfrac{1}{6} \approx 0.1667$

Can we use a sample of dice rolls to estimate the true probability of rolling a sum of 7?

a) Suppose that we will use a random sample of 578 rolls of the dice to get a point estimate for the true probability of rolling a sum of 7. Assuming that the dice are fair and balanced, then determine the mean and standard deviation for the possible values of the sample proportion that we could get.

b) What is the expected range for the possible values of the sample proportions.

c) If we use the sample proportion of 7's for an estimate of the true probability that the sum will equal 7 for these dice, then what is the expected error for the estimate.

d) Suppose that a sample of size 578 is obtained and the number of times the sum equals 7 is 125 times. Calculate the point estimate for the true probability that the sum will equal 7 for these dice.

e) Is it likely that this point estimate is exactly equal to the true probability that the sum will equal 7 for these dice? Explain.

f) If these were really fair dice, then would it be unusual to get a point estimate such as ours from part (d)? Explain.

g) Based on our point estimate and the answer to part (f), would you say that these dice are probably fair and that the difference between this result and the true probability is just the result of random sampling error or do you suspect that these dice are not fair. Explain.

Solution:

a) Because the sample proportion is $\hat{p}$, we are being asked to find the values of $\mu_{\hat{p}}$ and $\sigma_{\hat{p}}$. Assuming that the dice are fair and balanced, then $p = P(\text{Sum} = 7) = \dfrac{6}{36} = \dfrac{1}{6} \approx 0.1667$. So, we get:

$$\mu_{\hat{p}} = p = \frac{1}{6} \approx 0.1667 \quad \text{and} \quad \sigma_{\hat{p}} = \sqrt{\frac{pq}{n}} = \sqrt{\frac{0.1667 * 0.8333}{578}} \approx 0.015503$$

b) We expect any random variable to lie within two standard deviations of its mean. So, we get:

$$\mu_{\hat{p}} - 2\sigma_{\hat{p}} < \hat{p} < \mu_{\hat{p}} + 2\sigma_{\hat{p}} \implies 0.1667 - 2 * 0.0155 < \hat{p} < 0.1667 + 2 * 0.0155$$

$$\implies 0.1357 < \hat{p} < 0.1977$$

Therefore, the expected range for our sample proportion is anywhere between 0.1357 and 0.1977.

c) For the expected error, we use the formula: $|\hat{p} - p| < 2\sigma_{\hat{p}} \approx 2 * 0.0155 = 0.0310$. So we expect our sample proportion to be within 0.0310 of the true probability that the sum will equal 7 for these dice.

d) When estimating the true probability, p, we should use the sample proportion, $\hat{p}$, as our estimate.

$$\hat{p} = \frac{x}{n} = \frac{125}{578} \approx 0.2163$$

e) No. We stated earlier in this section that $P(\hat{p} = p) \approx 0$.

f) We can see that this would in fact be unusual, because our point estimate, $\hat{p} \approx 0.2163$, does not lie in the expected range. We can and will confirm that with a z-score.

$$z = \frac{\hat{p} - \mu_{\hat{p}}}{\sigma_{\hat{p}}} \approx \frac{0.2163 - 0.1667}{0.015503} \approx 3.199$$

So, yes if this were a fair and balanced pair of dice, then 0.2163 would in fact be a very unusual sample proportion, because it is more than 3 standard deviations above the mean.

g) Typically, our default explanation for the sampling error we obtain is that it is merely random variation. However, in this case it would be very unusual for that to be the case. The large amount of sampling error should cause us to suspect that these dice are, in fact, not fair and balanced, but rather biased towards having a sum of 7.

Time to practice all that we have learned with some exercises.

Exercise Set 7.1:

Concept Review: Review the definitions and concepts from this section by filling in the blanks for each of the following.

1) The sample proportion is $\hat{p} = \dfrac{x}{n}$, where x is the number of _____ in the sample of size n.

2) A parameter is a quantity that describes a _____ value. A statistic is a quantity that describes a _____ value.

3) A point estimate is a single value calculated from a _____ and used to estimate a _____ quantity.

4) Sampling Error is the _____ that results from using an estimate obtained from a _____ rather than a census to estimate a population quantity.

5) The probability of obtaining the exact value of a population parameter by using a point estimate from a random sample is usually approximately equal to _____ .

6) We expect our sampling error to be less than _____ standard deviations of our point _____ .

7) In words, $\mu_{\hat{p}} = p$ says that if we find the average of all possible _____ proportions, then the result is the _____ proportion.

8) $\sigma_{\hat{p}} = \sqrt{\dfrac{pq}{n}}$ is good news because it tells us that the higher the sample size, the closer the possible values of ___ get to the population proportion, ___ .

Mechanics: Practice the calculations needed for this section before moving on to the real world applications.

9) Suppose that we are taking a random sample of size 438 from a population where the true proportion of successes is 0.5744. Suppose that our sample contained 251 successes.

   a) Find the value of the point estimate.
   b) Find the sampling error for this point estimate.
   c) Suppose that we will be satisfied as long as our estimate has sampling error of 0.03 or less. What range of sample proportions would be considered acceptable?
   d) What is the probability that we will have no sampling error? Explain.

10) Suppose that we are taking a random sample of size 771 from a population where the true proportion of successes is 0.4171. Suppose that our sample contained 325 successes.

   a) Find the value of the point estimate.
   b) Find the sampling error for this point estimate.
   c) Suppose that we will be satisfied as long as our estimate has sampling error of 0.04 or less. What range of sample proportions would be considered acceptable?
   d) What is the probability that we will have no sampling error? Explain.

11) Suppose that the true proportion of successes in our population is 28.64%.

   a) Determine the mean and standard deviation of all possible sample proportions from samples of size 188.
   b) Determine the mean and standard deviation of all possible sample proportions from samples of size 913.

12) Suppose that the true proportion of successes in our population is 85.68%.

   a) Determine the mean and standard deviation of all possible sample proportions from samples of size 277.
   b) Determine the mean and standard deviation of all possible sample proportions from samples of size 1073.

13) Suppose that the true proportion of successes in our population is 71.06%.

   a) Determine the mean and standard deviation of all possible sample proportions from samples of size 449.
   b) Determine the expected error for a point estimate from a sample of size 449.
   c) Would it be considered unusual if a sample of size 449 produced a sample proportion of 66.82%? Explain.

14) Suppose that the true proportion of successes in our population is 39.81%.

   a) Determine the mean and standard deviation of all possible sample proportions from samples of size 685.
   b) Determine the expected error for a point estimate from a sample of size 685.
   c) Would it be considered unusual if a sample of size 685 produced a sample proportion of 46.57%? Explain.

Applications: Practice the ideas learned in this section within the context of real world applications.

15) According to a September 2011 Rasmussen study, 46% of Americans were planning to get a flu shot before the upcoming flu season. Suppose that a random sample of size 539 was taken at that time and those polled were asked if they planned on getting a flu shot.
   a) Find the mean and standard deviation for all possible sample proportions that we might obtain from our random sample of size 539.
   b) Is it likely that our sample will produce a sample proportion that is exactly equal to the true population proportion? Explain.
   c) How much error should we expect to get if we used the sample proportion obtained as a point estimate for the true population proportion?
   d) If the sample contained 235 people that said they were going to get a flu shot, then what would be our point estimate for the population proportion?
   e) Would the point estimate from part (d) be considered unusual? Explain.

16) According to an October 2011 Rasmussen study, 61% of Americans think that the U.S. should celebrate Columbus Day. Suppose that a random sample of size 659 was taken at that time and those polled were asked if they thought that the U.S. should celebrate Columbus Day.
   a) Find the mean and standard deviation for all possible sample proportions that we might obtain from our random sample of size 659.
   b) Is it likely that our sample will produce a sample proportion that is exactly equal to the true population proportion? Explain.
   c) How much error should we expect to get if we used the sample proportion obtained as a point estimate for the true population proportion?
   d) If the sample contained 418 people that said they thought that the U.S. should still celebrate Columbus Day, then what would be our point estimate for the population proportion?
   e) Would the point estimate from part (d) be considered unusual? Explain.

17) According to an October 2011 Gallup poll, 62% of Americans say that they would amend the U.S. Constitution to replace Electoral College system for electing presidents with a popular vote system. Suppose that a random sample of size 1,018 was taken at that time and those polled were asked if they supported a change to a popular vote.
   a) Find the mean and standard deviation for all possible sample proportions that we might obtain from our random sample of size 1,018.
   b) Would it be considered unusual if 66.31% of those surveyed supported a change to a popular vote? Explain.
   c) Would it be considered unusual if 59.72% of those surveyed supported a change to a popular vote? Explain.
   d) What is the expected range for the proportion of people in our sample that would support a change to a popular vote?

18) According to an October 2011 Rasmussen, 71% of Americans say that volunteering serves their community more than entering politics. Suppose that a random sample of size 891 was taken at that time and those polled were asked if they thought volunteering was better.
   a) Find the mean and standard deviation for all possible sample proportions that we might obtain from our random sample of size 891.
   b) Would it be considered unusual if 73.29% of those surveyed thought volunteering was better? Explain.
   c) Would it be considered unusual if 64.76% of those surveyed thought volunteering was better? Explain.
   d) What is the expected range for the proportion of people in our sample that think volunteering is better?

19) A roulette wheel has 18 red numbers, 18 black numbers, and 2 green numbers. Suppose that we are planning on observing 583 spins of such a wheel. We are interested in estimating the true proportion of reds for this roulette wheel.
   a) Assuming that the wheel is fair, find the mean and standard deviation for all possible sample proportions that we might obtain from our random sample of size 583.
   b) Suppose that the ball landed in a red slot 292 times in the sample of 583 spins. What would be our point estimate for the true probability of reds for this wheel?
   c) If the wheel were fair, would you consider the point estimate from part (b) to be unusual? Explain.
   d) How much sampling error does this represent?
   e) Based on your answer to part (c), would you tend to think that this sampling error is just random variation or do you think it is strong evidence that the wheel is actually not fair? Explain.

20) A statistics student was suspicious that her local meteorologist was not very good at predicting the weather. She noted 175 times when the meteorologist stated that there was an 80% chance of rain the next day. The student then noted the number of times it ended up raining the next day.
   a) Assuming that the meteorologist is accurate, find the mean and standard deviation for all possible sample proportions of rainy days that the student might obtain from her random sample of size 175.
   b) Suppose that it actually rained on 123 of the 175 observed days. What would be our point estimate for the true chance of rain on those days?
   c) If the meteorologist were accurate, would you consider the point estimate from part (b) to be unusual? Explain.
   d) How much sampling error does this represent?
   e) Based on your answer to part (c), would you tend to think that this sampling error is just random variation or do you think it is strong evidence that the meteorologist is not accurate? Explain.

Section 7.2 – The Sampling Distribution of $\hat{p}$

In the previous section, we learned the mean and standard deviation of the sample proportion, $\hat{p}$. We saw that this allowed us to learn quite a bit about how point estimates work and how much sampling error is expected when using a point estimate. However, there was one key piece of information that was missing in that section. While it is useful to know how much sampling error to expect, we would also like to know the probability that our sampling error will be a certain size. In order to calculate probabilities involving the sample proportion, we must first know what kind of distribution $\hat{p}$ has. In the previous section, we used the binomial distribution for the number of successes to help us determine the mean and standard deviation for the sample proportion of successes. We now want to continue along that line of thinking and use the common shape of the binomial distribution, to help use determine the likely shape of the sample proportion, $\hat{p}$. The following fact will be helpful in doing this work.

> *If the random variable x is divided by a constant, n, then the new random variable created by this division will have the same type of distribution as x, but the mean and standard deviation of the new distribution will be equal to $\dfrac{\mu_x}{n}$ and $\dfrac{\sigma_x}{n}$ respectively.*

In Section 6.4, we learned that a binomial random variable, x, will be approximately normal provided that both $np \geq 10$ and $nq \geq 10$. Combining this with the fact above, we can assume that under these same conditions, $\hat{p}$ will also be approximately normally distributed. This discussion is summarized in the following theorem.

Point to Remember: *Theorem 7.2 (The sampling distribution of $\hat{p}$)*

If we take a random sample of size n from a population where the proportion of successes is p and if both $np \geq 10$ and $nq \geq 10$, then the random variable $\hat{p}$ will be approximately normally distributed with $\mu_{\hat{p}} = p$ and $\sigma_{\hat{p}} = \sqrt{\dfrac{pq}{n}}$.

Let's look at an example that practices the mechanics of this new theorem.

THEORY IN ACTION: *The Implications of Theorem 7.2*

Let's take a look at an example that illustrates the ideas presented so far.

Example 7.5: *Practicing the Mechanics of Theorem 7.2*

Suppose that a random sample is taken from a population where the proportion of successes in the population is 0.732.

a) For samples of size 50, determine the distribution of the possible values of $\hat{p}$.

b) For samples of size 50, determine $P(\hat{p} > 0.80)$

c) For samples of size 500, determine the distribution of the possible values of $\hat{p}$.

d) For samples of size 500, determine $P(\hat{p} > 0.80)$

Solution:

a) To conclude that $\hat{p}$ is normally distributed, we must verify that $np \geq 10$ and $nq \geq 10$. For this part, we are told that $n = 50$. We are also told that the proportion of success is 0.732, thus we know that $p = 0.732$. So, $q = 1 - p = 1 - 0.732 = 0.268$. So we are now ready to verify the requirement:

$$np = 50(0.732) = 36.6 \geq 10 \quad \text{and} \quad nq = 50(0.268) = 13.4 \geq 10$$

This verifies that $\hat{p}$ is normally distributed. Now we must investigate which normal distribution it is specifically. So we need the mean and standard deviation of $\hat{p}$.

$$\mu_{\hat{p}} = p = 0.732 \quad \text{and} \quad \sigma_{\hat{p}} = \sqrt{\frac{pq}{n}} = \sqrt{\frac{0.732 * 0.268}{50}} \approx 0.062638$$

So we conclude that the possible values of $\hat{p}$ are normally distributed with $\mu_{\hat{p}} = 0.732$ and $\sigma_{\hat{p}} \approx 0.062638$.

b) Now that we know we are working with a normal distribution, this becomes a Chapter 6, area under a normal curve, question. Here is the sketch.

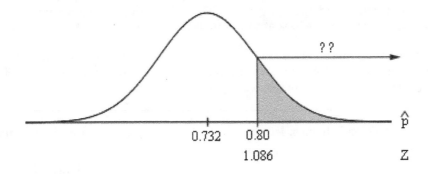

So we find the z-score: $z = \dfrac{0.80 - 0.732}{0.062638} \approx 1.086$ and then we turn to technology for the area.

$$P(\hat{p} > 0.80) \approx normalcdf(1.086, \infty) \approx 0.1387$$

c) The only change from part (a) is the sample size, so this will be very similar to the work above.

$$np = 500(0.732) = 366 \geq 10 \quad \text{and} \quad nq = 500(0.268) = 134 \geq 10$$

This verifies that $\hat{p}$ is normally distributed. Now we must investigate which normal distribution it is specifically. So we need the mean and standard deviation of $\hat{p}$.

$$\mu_{\hat{p}} = p = 0.732 \quad \text{and} \quad \sigma_{\hat{p}} = \sqrt{\frac{pq}{n}} = \sqrt{\frac{0.732 * 0.268}{500}} \approx 0.019808$$

So we conclude that $\hat{p}$ is normally distributed with $\mu_{\hat{p}} = 0.732$ and $\sigma_{\hat{p}} \approx 0.019808$.

d) Because we have a new standard deviation, the graph looks different (see below), but the work is the same.

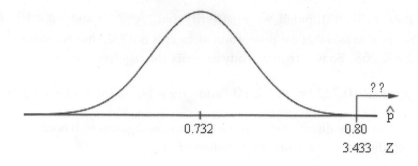

$$z = \frac{0.80 - 0.732}{0.019808} \approx 3.433 \quad \Rightarrow \quad P(\hat{p} > 0.80) = normalcdf(3.433, \infty) \approx 2.985E - 4 \approx 0.0003$$

This last question illustrates a couple things worth noting.

Key Concepts: *The effect of the sample size and dealing with Scientific Notation*

    Sample Size: The change in sample size affected the standard deviation. This had a big effect on our z-score and thus our area. This change will have an important and desired consequence when we look at sampling error.

    Scientific Notation: Very small areas often come out in scientific notation. The E-4 tells us to move our decimal 4 places to the left. So, $2.985E - 4$ becomes 0.0002985 which, when rounded to 4 decimal places, becomes 0.0003.

Now that we have practiced the mechanics, let's take a look at an application and consider how knowing the distribution of $\hat{p}$ can be helpful when considering sampling error.

Example 7.6: *Estimating Suffering During a Crisis*

In 2011, Greece was dealing with a debt crisis and the government was introducing austerity measures to public employees and recipients of government programs. Polling at that time found that 25% of the Greeks rated their lives so poorly that they considered themselves to be "suffering". Suppose that a random sample of 281 Greeks will be sampled and asked whether or not they considered themselves to be "suffering".

How accurately can we estimate the "suffering" of the Greeks during the 2011 debt crisis?

a) Determine the distribution of all possible sample proportions.

b) Determine the probability that the sample proportion from a sample of 281 Greeks will have a sampling error of less than 0.03.

c) Determine the probability that the sample proportion from a sample of 281 Greeks will have a sampling error of less than 0.05.

d) Give a logical explanation for why the probability was larger in part (c) than it was in part (b).

e) Determine the distribution of all possible sample proportions for samples of size 1,081.

f) Determine the probability that the sample proportion from a sample of 1,081 Greeks will have a sampling error of less than 0.03.

g) In part (c), we saw that we could increase our chance of getting an acceptable answer allowing more sampling error. In part (f), we saw that we can also increase our chance of getting an acceptable answer by increasing our sample size. Which method do you think is the better way to increase the chance of obtaining an acceptable estimate? Explain your reasoning.

Solution:

a) To determine the distribution of all possible sample proportions, $\hat{p}$, we must first check the value of np and nq. They state that the sample size will be 281, so $n = 281$. At the time of the sample, 25% of the Greeks considered themselves to be suffering, so $p = 0.25$. Therefore, $np = 281 * 0.25 = 70.25 \geq 10$ and $nq = 281 * 0.75 = 210.7 \geq 10$. Therefore, we know that $\hat{p}$ is approximately normally distributed. This is a good start, but it does not fully answer the question we were asked. There are infinitely many normal distributions. We need to specify which one we will be working with by stating the mean and standard deviation of $\hat{p}$.

$$\mu_{\hat{p}} = p = 0.25 \quad \text{and} \quad \sigma_{\hat{p}} = \sqrt{\frac{pq}{n}} = \sqrt{\frac{0.25 * 0.75}{281}} \approx 0.025831$$

So we conclude that the possible values of $\hat{p}$ are normally distributed with $\mu_{\hat{p}} = 0.25$ and $\sigma_{\hat{p}} \approx 0.025831$.

b) Sampling error is the distance between our point estimate, $\hat{p}$, and the true population proportion, p. So, the first thing to do is to translate the question into probability notation.

$$P\left(|\hat{p} - p| < 0.03\right) = P\left(|\hat{p} - 0.25| < 0.03\right) = P\left(-0.03 < \hat{p} - 0.25 < 0.03\right) = P\left(0.22 < \hat{p} < 0.28\right)$$

Translating the question into probability notation correctly is often the toughest part. Because $\hat{p}$ is normally distributed, we can now simply answer the question by finding the appropriate area under a normal curve.

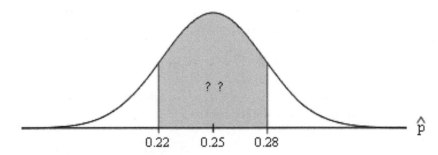

We now compute the z-scores for the two boundaries using the formula: $z = \dfrac{\hat{p} - \mu_{\hat{p}}}{\sigma_{\hat{p}}}$

$$z_1 = \frac{0.22 - 0.25}{0.025831} \approx -1.161 \quad \text{and} \quad z_2 = \frac{0.28 - 0.25}{0.025831} \approx 1.161$$

Finally, we turn to technology to find the area.

$$P(0.22 < \hat{p} < 0.28) = normalcdf(-1.161, 1.161) \approx 0.7544$$

c) We have changed the amount of sampling error that is acceptable. This changes our translation as follows.

$$P(|\hat{p} - p| < 0.05) = P(|\hat{p} - 0.25| < 0.05) = P(-0.05 < \hat{p} - 0.25 < 0.05) = P(0.20 < \hat{p} < 0.30)$$

Now we answer the question by finding the appropriate area under a normal curve.

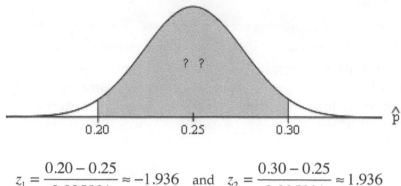

$$z_1 = \frac{0.20 - 0.25}{0.025831} \approx -1.936 \quad \text{and} \quad z_2 = \frac{0.30 - 0.25}{0.025831} \approx 1.936$$

Finally, we turn to technology to find the area.

$$P(0.20 < \hat{p} < 0.30) = normalcdf(-1.936, \ 1.936) \approx 0.9471$$

d) It makes sense that we have a better chance of obtaining an acceptable estimate when we increase the amount of sampling error allowed, because essentially this means that we are lowering our standards. If we will accept more error in our estimate, then any estimate that was satisfactory under the old standard still works. However, we are now also willing to accept some estimates that just missed the 0.03 sampling error threshold, but that will meet the new, looser standard of 0.05. Accepting a higher amount of error means that we accept a larger number of point estimates. This, in turn, means that we have a higher probability of obtaining an acceptable estimate.

e) Because the requirement for $\hat{p}$ to be normally distributed was met with a sample size of 281, it should certainly also be met when the sample size increases to 1,081. However, we will still go ahead and verify this.

$$np = 1081 * 0.25 = 270.25 \geq 10 \quad \text{and} \quad nq = 1081 * 0.75 = 810.75 \geq 10$$

This verifies that $\hat{p}$ is normally distributed. Now we must investigate which normal distribution it is specifically. So we need the mean and standard deviation of $\hat{p}$.

$$\mu_{\hat{p}} = p = 0.25 \quad \text{and} \quad \sigma_{\hat{p}} = \sqrt{\frac{pq}{n}} = \sqrt{\frac{0.25 * 0.75}{1081}} \approx 0.013170$$

So we conclude that the possible values of $\hat{p}$ are normally distributed with $\mu_{\hat{p}} = 0.25$ and $\sigma_{\hat{p}} \approx 0.013170$.

f)   The translation is the same as in part (b), so we are once again looking for $P(0.22 < \hat{p} < 0.28)$.

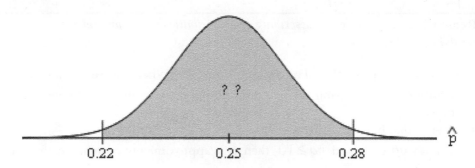

Even though this is essentially the same question as before, we are now working with a different standard deviation. Therefore, we will get different z-scores and a different area.

$$z_1 = \frac{0.22 - 0.25}{0.013170} \approx -2.278 \quad \text{and} \quad z_2 = \frac{0.28 - 0.25}{0.013170} \approx 2.278$$

Finally, we turn to technology to find the area.

$$P(0.22 < \hat{p} < 0.28) = normalcdf(-2.278, 2.278) \approx 0.9773$$

g)   While it is true that increasing the amount of error that we are willing to accept increases our chances of obtaining an acceptable point estimate, this is in essence lowering our standards. The more we lower our standards, the less people will want to hire us to make estimates for them. On the other hand, if we raise the sample size, then by collecting more data we can produce better estimates without having to lower our standards. Generally, raising the sample size is preferred over lowering the standards. An exception to this can occur if the cost of increasing the sample size is prohibitive.

The answer to question (g) above is an important one for us to remember for the rest of this course. The key points are summarized below.

Key Concept: *Increasing the chance of obtaining an acceptable point estimate.*

Lower Your Standards: If you are able to lower your standards, by increasing the amount of error that is considered acceptable, then you will have a higher probability of obtaining an acceptable point estimate from your random sample. A few things to consider . . .
- This might make sense if your standards were originally set extremely high. Maybe lowering them a little will still produce estimates generally considered accurate.
- If you lower your standards too much, no one will want to hire you to make estimates for them.
- It is common that you will not set the standard. The person who hires you will. In such cases, this decision is out of your hands.

Increase your Sample Size: If you increase your sample size, then you will have a higher probability of obtaining an acceptable point estimate from your random sample. A few things to consider . . .
- Increasing the sample size is often easy and not too expensive. In such cases, this is a good option.
- Raising your sample size allows you to maintain a high standard.
- We generally will choose raising our sample size rather than increasing the amount of error that is consider acceptable.

The previous example showed us that calculating the probability that we will get a specified amount of sampling error is simply a question of finding the appropriate area under a normal curve. However, this is often quite difficult for students to do. The following point to remember shows the procedure to use to answer such questions.

Point to Remember: *Procedure for describing the distribution of $\hat{p}$ and calculating sampling error probabilities.*

Distribution of the possible sample proportions, $\hat{p}$: When we are asked to determine the distribution of the possible sample proportions, $\hat{p}$, we must do 4 things to fully answer the question.

- Verify that both $np \geq 10$ and $nq \geq 10$.
- If both $np \geq 10$ and $nq \geq 10$, then $\hat{p}$ is approximately normally distributed.
- Calculate the mean of the possible sample proportions, $\mu_{\hat{p}} = p$.
- Calculate the standard deviation of the possible sample proportions, $\sigma_{\hat{p}} = \sqrt{\dfrac{pq}{n}}$.

Translating Sampling Error Questions: If we are asked to find the probability that tl sampling error when using the point estimate $\hat{p}$, then add and subtract the allowed sampling error from the true population proportion.

In symbols: The probability that the sampling error is less than E is translated as:

$$P\left(p - E < \hat{p} < p + E\right)$$

We conclude this section with one final example where we examine these ideas in the context of estimating the probability of an event.

WRAP SESSION: *Applying what we have learned to probabilities*

Example 7.7: *Estimating Free Throw Probability*

The free throw percentage for a professional basketball player is supposed to represent the true probability that the player will make a given free throw. However, the free throw percentage is always based on a sample of free throws from the player. Therefore, there is likely error when using this sample percentage as the true probability that this player will make a free throw. Suppose that the true probability that LeBron James will make a free throw is 76.3%. Suppose that we will use a random sample of 317 free throw attempts by LeBron to estimate his true free throw percentage.

How accurately can we estimate the probability of making a free throw using sample data?

a) What is the sampling distribution for the possible sample proportions we might obtain?

b) What is the probability that our sampling error will be less than 0.05?

c) If LeBron's true free throw probability is actually 76.3%, what is the chance that he will make less than 75% of his free throws over a sample of 317 attempts?

d) If LeBron did actually make less than 75% of his free throws in the sample of 317 attempts, would you say that was probably just the result of random variation or would you say that the sample result would be convincing evidence that LeBron's true free throw percentage was actually lower than 76.3%? Explain.

Solution:

a) First, we need to find n, p, and q. The sample size is 317 free throws, so $n = 317$. We are told to assume that the true probability of LeBron making a free throw is 76.3%, so $p = 0.763$. Finally, $q = 1 - p = 0.237$. We can now check to see if the sample proportions are approximately normal.

$$np = 317 * 0.763 = 241.871 \geq 10 \quad \text{and} \quad nq = 317 * 0.237 = 75.129 \geq 10$$

This tells us that $\hat{p}$ is approximately normal, so we should also find the mean and standard deviation of $\hat{p}$.

$$\mu_{\hat{p}} = p = 0.763 \quad \text{and} \quad \sigma_{\hat{p}} = \sqrt{\frac{pq}{n}} = \sqrt{\frac{0.763 * 0.237}{317}} \approx 0.023884$$

So, we can say that $\hat{p}$ is approximately normally distributed with $\mu_{\hat{p}} = 0.763$ and $\sigma_{\hat{p}} \approx 0.023884$.

b) We begin by translating the question into probability notation. We add and subtract the desired sampling error from the true proportion as shown below.

$$P(0.763 - 0.05 < \hat{p} < 0.763 + 0.05) = P(0.713 < \hat{p} < 0.813)$$

Next we sketch the area that we are looking for under the appropriate normal curve. We find the z-scores and then we calculate the desired area.

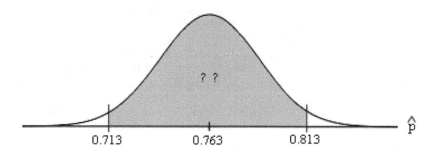

$$z_1 = \frac{0.713 - 0.763}{0.023884} \approx -2.093 \quad \text{and} \quad z_2 = \frac{0.813 - 0.763}{0.023884} \approx 2.093$$

$$P(0.713 < \hat{p} < 0.813) = normalcdf(-2.093, 2.093) \approx 0.9637$$

c) We will begin by translating the question into probability notation, $P(\hat{p} < 0.75)$.

Next we sketch the area that we are looking for under the appropriate normal curve. We find the z-score and then we calculate the desired area.

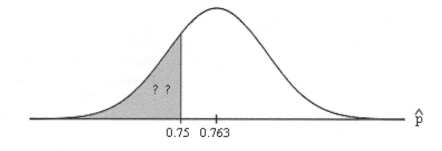

$$z = \frac{0.75 - 0.763}{0.023884} \approx -0.544 \quad \text{and} \quad P(\hat{p} < 0.75) = normalcdf(-\infty, -0.544) \approx 0.2933$$

d) In statistics, our default explanation for the differences between sample values and what we believe to be the truth is that these differences are just due to random variation. We will believe this unless the probability of such differences being due to random variation gets too low (typically defined as a 5% cutoff). In part (c), we saw that there is a 29.33% chance that a 76.3% free throw shooter would make less than 75% of their free throws just due to random chance (or an unlucky run). Because this chance is more than 5%, we consider that to be a plausible explanation for why LeBron shot this lower percentage over this stretch of 317 free throws. Therefore, we will not be convinced that he has gotten worse at shooting free throws, rather we will stick with the default explanation that it is just a decrease caused by random variation. (We will explore this idea in much greater detail in Chapter 9.)

The question answered in part (d) of the example above is one of the most important types of questions that we ask in statistics. The method for deciding between the two choices is summarized in the following point to remember.

Point to Remember: *Deciding whether or not random variation is a plausible explanation*

When data is obtained from a random sample, it almost never produces the exact results that we were expecting. The default explanation for why this happens is random variation from the random sampling process. We typically continue to believe this explanation is plausible as long as there is more than a 5% chance of the difference being due to random variation.

- If the difference between our sample result and the expected result has more than a 5% chance of occurring due to random chance, then we say it is plausible to believe that random variation is the explanation for this difference.
- If the difference between our sample result and the expected result has less than a 5% chance of occurring due to random chance, then we feel that another explanation should be sought out. We say that the sample is providing convincing evidence that random variation is not the best explanation.

Note: 5% is the most commonly used cutoff for making this decision, but sometimes people use 1% or 10% as well. This will be discussed in greater detail in Chapter 9.

Time to practice what we have learned in this section with some Exercises.

Exercise Set 7.2:

Concept Review: Review the definitions and concepts from this section by filling in the blanks for each of the following.

21) If $np \geq$ ____ and $nq \geq$ ____ , then $\hat{p}$ will be approximately _____ distributed.

22) To fully describe the sampling distribution of $\hat{p}$ we must state the type of distribution and we must also provide the _____ and _____ _____ .

Mechanics: Practice the calculations needed for this section before moving on to the real world applications.

✓ 23) Suppose that a random sample of size 200 will be taken from a population where the proportion of data having a given attribute is 0.784.

a) Determine the distribution of the possible values of $\hat{p}$.

b) Determine $P(\hat{p} > 0.75)$.

c) Determine the probability that $\hat{p}$ will be within 0.05 of the true population proportion.

24) Suppose that a random sample of size 250 will be taken from a population where the proportion of data having a given attribute is 0.338.

   a) Determine the distribution of the possible values of $\hat{p}$.

   b) Determine $P(\hat{p} < 0.30)$.

   c) Determine the probability that $\hat{p}$ will be within 0.03 of the population proportion.

25) Suppose that a random sample of size 487 will be taken from a population where the proportion of successes is 0.5446.

   a) Determine the distribution of all possible values of the sample proportion.

   b) Determine $P(\hat{p} < 0.60)$.

   c) Determine the probability the sampling error for the point estimate will be less than 0.04.

26) Suppose that a random sample of size 391 will be taken from a population where the proportion of successes is 0.8307.

   a) Determine the distribution of all possible values of the sample proportion.

   b) Determine $P(\hat{p} > 0.90)$.

   c) Determine the probability the sampling error for the point estimate will be less than 0.025.

27) Suppose that a random sample of size 600 will be taken from a population where 37% of the population has a given attribute.

   a) Determine the distribution of the possible values of $\hat{p}$.

   b) Determine $P(\hat{p} < 0.35 \text{ or } \hat{p} > 0.40)$

   c) Determine $P(\hat{p} < 0.35 | \hat{p} \leq 0.40)$

28) Suppose that a random sample of size 500 will be taken from a population were 54.4% of the population has a given attribute.

   a) Determine the distribution of the possible values of $\hat{p}$.

   b) Determine $P(\hat{p} > 0.50 \text{ \& } \hat{p} < 0.60)$

   c) Determine $P(\hat{p} \geq 0.50 | \hat{p} < 0.60)$

Applications: Practice the ideas learned in this section within the context of real world applications.

$\sqrt{}$29) According to a September 2011 Rasmussen poll, just 33% of Americans took a summer vacation during 2011. Suppose that we did not know this value and we were hired to take a sample and estimate the true proportion of Americans that took a vacation during summer 2011. We will take a random sample of size 444 to estimate this value.

   a) Determine the distribution of the possible values we might get for $\hat{p}$.

   b) Suppose the person hiring us to do the estimate will only be satisfied if our sampling error is less than 0.025. What is the chance that our sample will yield a satisfactory estimate?

   c) Suppose the person hiring us to do the estimate will only be satisfied if our sampling error is less than 0.05. What is the chance that our sample will yield a satisfactory estimate?

   d) Give a logical explanation for why the probability was higher when the larger amount of sampling error was allowed.

30) According to an October 2011 Rasmussen poll, 54% of Americans see government bailouts as bad for the country. Suppose that a politician was unaware of this number and hired us to estimate the true proportion of Americans that see government bailouts as bad for the country. We will take a random sample of size 761 adults to estimate this value.

   a) Determine the distribution of the possible values we might get for $\hat{p}$.

   b) Suppose the politician hiring us to do the estimate will only be satisfied if our sampling error is less than 0.015. What is the chance that our sample will yield a satisfactory estimate?

   c) Suppose the politician hiring us to do the estimate will only be satisfied if our sampling error is less than 0.03. What is the chance that our sample will yield a satisfactory estimate?

   d) Give a logical explanation for why the probability was higher when the larger amount of sampling error was allowed.

31) Shortly after Steve Jobs' death in 2011, a Rasmussen poll showed that 48% of Americans think that Apple will remain on the cutting edge of technology. Suppose that Apple was unaware of this number and hired us to estimate the true proportion of Americans that believed Apple would remain on the cutting edge despite Jobs' death. Suppose Apple will only be satisfied with our estimate provided that the sampling error is less than 2 percentage points.

a) If we plan on making the estimate using a random sample of 580 Americans, then determine the distribution of the possible values we might get for $\hat{p}$.

b) What is the probability that our sample will yield a satisfactory estimate?

c) What change could we make to increase our chance of getting a satisfactory estimate?

d) Suppose that we increase our sample size to 1,095 homeowners. Determine the distribution of the possible values we might then get for $\hat{p}$.

e) With the new sample size of 1,095, what is the probability that our sample will yield a satisfactory estimate?

32) According to an October 2011 Rasmussen poll, 34% of Americans say that their home is worth less than what they still owe. Suppose that a bank was unaware of this number and hired us to estimate the true proportion of Americans with homes worth less than what they still owe. The bank will be satisfied with our estimate provided that the sampling error is less than 4 percentage points.

a) If we plan on making the estimate using a random sample of 357 homeowners, then determine the distribution of the possible values we might get for $\hat{p}$.

b) What is the probability that our sample will yield a satisfactory estimate?

c) What chance could we make to increase our chance of getting a satisfactory estimate?

d) Suppose that we increase our sample size to 657 homeowners. Determine the distribution of the possible values we might then get for $\hat{p}$.

e) With the new sample size of 657, what is the probability that our sample will yield a satisfactory estimate?

33) In October 2011, one of the demands of the Occupy Wall Street protestors was for the forgiveness of the nearly $1 trillion worth of student loans. Suppose that we plan to take a random sample of 394 Americans and ask if they support the forgiving of these student loans. (According to a Rasmussen study, only 21% of Americans support this.)

a) What is the distribution of the sample proportions that are possible?

b) What is the chance that the sampling error will be less than 3 percentage points?

c) What change would you recommend in the sampling process to increase the chance that the sampling error would be less than 3 percentage points?

d) If we increased the sample size to 1,215 Americans, then what is the chance that the sampling error will be less than 3 percentage points?

34) When a certain pasta company bags and produces its bags of spaghetti, 5.7% of the pieces of spaghetti end up getting broken. Suppose that 200 pieces of spaghetti that have been bagged are randomly selected and that the number of broken pieces is counted.

a) What is the distribution of the sample proportions that are possible?

b) What is the chance that the sampling error will be less than 1 percentage point?

c) What change would you recommend in the sampling process to increase the chance that the sampling error would be less than 1 percentage point?

d) If we increased the sample size to 1000 pieces, then what is the chance that the sampling error will be less than 1 percentage point?

35) Suppose that a fair coin is to be tossed 150 times for the purpose of estimating the true proportion of times it will land heads face up.

a) Determine the distribution of the possible values of the point estimate.

b) Assuming that the coin is fair, determine the probability that the proportion of heads in the sample would be less than 40%.

c) If the 150 tosses do produce less than 40% heads, would you say that this is just the result of random variation in the sample or would you say that this indicates that the coin is biased towards tails? Explain.

36) In sports betting, a line is placed on a game that gives a person making a random choice a 50% chance of winning their bet. However, you must bet $11 to win $10. This means a player must win 11 times out of every 21 plays to break even. (11 wins times $10 gives $110 won. 10 losses at $11 each total $110 lost.). Assume that a player makes 250 sports bets, betting $11 each time.

   a) Determine the distribution of the possible samples proportions of wins (assume the gambler makes a random choice of which team to bet on.)
   b) Determine the probability of such a gambler being ahead (winning money) on the 250 bets.
   c) If a gambler is ahead after 250 such bets, would you say that this indicates that they are making skillful choices rather than just having random luck? Explain.

37) The best pair of starting cards to have in the game of Texas Hold'em is pocket Aces. If this hand is up against another player holding 87 suited (an 8 and 7 of the same suit), then the player with the Aces will win 76.8% of the time (assuming both hands commit to play to the end before the flop).

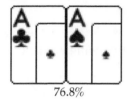
76.8%   23.2%

Suppose a player tracks the results of 73 such match ups and keeps track of the proportion of the time that the Aces beat the 87 suited.

   a) Determine the distribution of the possible sample proportions.
   b) Should the player consider herself unusually unlucky if she only wins 70% of the time or less with the aces? Explain.
   c) What is the chance of winning 70% of the time or less with the aces?

38) The second best pair of starting cards to have in the game of Texas Hold'em is pocket Kings. If this hand is up against another player holding AK suited (an Ace and King of the same suit), then the player with the Kings will win 66.03% of the time (assuming both hands commit to play to the end before the flop).

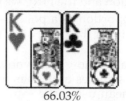
66.03%   33.97%

Suppose a player tracks the results of 149 such match ups and keeps track of the proportion of the time that the Kings beat the AK suited.

   a) Determine the distribution of the possible sample proportions.
   b) Should the player consider himself unusually lucky if he wins 75% of the time or more with the kings? Explain.
   c) What is the chance of winning 75% of the time or more with the kings?

7.3 - The Mean and Standard Deviation of the Sample Mean, $\bar{x}$

In the previous two sections, we were interested in using $\hat{p}$ as a point estimate for the true population proportion, p. In this section and the next, we will shift our focus to estimating the mean of a population. Just as we used the sample proportion as a point estimate for the population proportion, we will now use the sample mean, $\bar{x}$, as a point estimate for the population mean, μ.

We will begin by investigating how this works for an extremely small population. We do this so that there is a small number of possible samples and, therefore, we can look at everything that could happen when we try to estimate the population mean using the sample mean. We will then take what we learn and generalize it into ideas that can later be applied to large populations.

Example 7.8: *Considering $\bar{x}$ as a random variable*

Consider the population consisting of the exam scores for 5 students from a very small statistics class.

67	76	83	89	93

a)   Determine the mean of this population.

b)   List all possible samples of size 2 that could be obtained from the population.

c)   Find the mean for each of the samples from part (b).

d)   Determine the probability that the mean from a randomly selected sample of size two will be exactly equal to the population mean. That is, find $P(\bar{x} = \mu)$.

Solution:

a) $\mu = \dfrac{\sum x}{5} = \dfrac{408}{5} = 81.6$

b)   When finding all samples of size 2, it is useful to know ahead of time how many there should be. This is given to us by using combinations. From 5 values we will be choosing 2, so we get $\dbinom{5}{2} = 10$.

67, 76	67, 83	67, 89	67, 93	76, 83	76, 89	76, 93	83, 89	83, 93	89, 93

c)   Let's organize this into a table. Find each sample mean using $\bar{x} = \dfrac{\sum x}{2}$.

Sample	67, 76	67, 83	67, 89	67, 93	76, 83	76, 89	76, 93	83, 89	83, 93	89, 93
$\bar{x}$	71.5	75	78	80	79.5	82.5	84.5	86	88	91

d)   Because we will choose our samples using the procedure of simple random selection, every sample of a given size will be equally likely to be the one chosen. Because we have 10 possible samples of size 2, each one will have a 1/10 or 0.1 chance of being chosen. However, none of the sample means equals the population mean of 81.6, so

$$P(\bar{x} = \mu) = P(\bar{x} = 81.6) = \frac{0}{10} = 0$$

A couple of useful things emerged while we were solving the problem above. The first one is that the value of $\bar{x}$ depends on the sample we randomly choose. The fact that the value of $\bar{x}$ depends on chance makes it a random variable. The second thing to notice is that we had no chance of getting the value of the true mean from a single sample. Therefore, we were certain to have sampling error when using $\bar{x}$ as our point estimate. This is typically the case when estimating a population mean. These facts are summarized below.

Key Concepts: *Expect sampling error from the random variable $\bar{x}$*

     Two important facts are important to consider when estimating μ by a value of $\bar{x}$ from a randomly chosen sample.
- $\bar{x}$ is a random variable and, therefore, all the formulas pertaining to random variables apply to $\bar{x}$.
- It is typical for $P(\bar{x} = \mu) \approx 0$.

Because we now know that we should expect sampling error when using $\bar{x}$ as a point estimate for μ, we want to have a method of determining just how much sampling error we should expect. Just as was the case for sample proportions, it will be helpful to learn formulas for the mean and standard deviation of $\bar{x}$. We will now explore this idea.

Example 7.9: *Investigating the mean and standard deviation of $\bar{x}$*

Let's return to the population of all five test scores from a small statistics class. This is the population we worked with in the previous example. In that example we found all possible sample means from samples of size 2 along with the corresponding sample means. The population, samples, and sample means are shown below.

Population:

67	76	83	89	93

Sample	67, 76	67, 83	67, 89	67, 93	76, 83	76, 89	76, 93	83, 89	83, 93	89, 93
$\bar{x}$	71.5	75	78	80	79.5	82.5	84.5	86	88	91

a) Determine the mean and standard deviation of the population.

b) Determine the mean of all possible values of $\bar{x}$ from samples of size 2.

c) Determine the standard deviation of all possible values of $\bar{x}$ from samples of size 2.

Solution:

a) We will use technology to find the population mean and standard deviation. From the TI-84 output shown, we get: $\mu = 81.6$ and $\sigma \approx 9.28655$

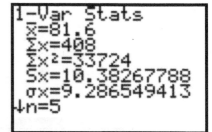

     Recall: The TI-84 shows the value for the mean as $\bar{x}$, but, because this is population data that we are working with, we label the mean as μ.

b) We noted in Example 7.8 that $\bar{x}$ is a random variable. And in this case, due to the finite number of samples possible, it is a discrete random variable. Therefore, when we are asked to find the mean of all possible values of $\bar{x}$, we can use the formulas we learned in Section 5.4 to accomplish this task. We also noted in Example 7.8 that, because there are 10 possible sample of size 2, each sample mean has a 1/10 or 0.1 probability of occurring.

     Recall: $\mu_x = \sum x P(x)$ is the formula for the mean of a random variable x. Our variable has a different name so we simply substitute the $\bar{x}$ in place of x, just as we would if our variable was y or some other letter. So we will use: $\mu_{\bar{x}} = \sum \bar{x} P(\bar{x})$. This is usually best accomplished by completing a table.

Sample	$\bar{x}$	$P(\bar{x})$	$\bar{x} \cdot P(\bar{x})$
67, 76	71.5	0.1	7.15
67, 83	75	0.1	7.5
67, 89	78	0.1	7.8
67, 93	79.5	0.1	7.95
76, 83	80	0.1	8
76, 89	82.5	0.1	8.25
76, 93	84.5	0.1	8.45
83, 89	86	0.1	8.6
83, 93	88	0.1	8.8
89, 93	91	0.1	9.1
		1.0	81.6

$$\bar{x} \cdot P(\bar{x}) = 82.5 * 0.1 = 8.25$$

So, for samples of size 2, we get: $\mu_{\bar{x}} = \sum \bar{x}P(\bar{x}) = 81.6$

c)   We now move on to the standard deviation of our random variable $\bar{x}$. From Section 5.4 we know $\sigma_x = \sqrt{\sum (x - \mu_x)^2 P(x)}$. Substituting $\bar{x}$ for x, we get $\sigma_{\bar{x}} = \sqrt{\sum (\bar{x} - \mu_{\bar{x}})^2 P(\bar{x})}$. Again a table would be useful. We will add the $(\bar{x} - \mu_{\bar{x}})^2 P(\bar{x})$ column to the table above.

$\bar{x}$	$P(\bar{x})$	$\bar{x} \cdot P(\bar{x})$	$(\bar{x} - \mu_{\bar{x}})^2 P(\bar{x})$
71.5	0.1	7.15	10.201
75	0.1	7.5	4.356
78	0.1	7.8	1.296
79.5	0.1	7.95	0.441
80	0.1	8	0.256
82.5	0.1	8.25	0.081
84.5	0.1	8.45	0.841
86	0.1	8.6	1.936
88	0.1	8.8	4.096
91	0.1	9.1	8.836
	1.0	81.6	32.34

$$(78 - 81.6)^2 * 0.1 = 1.296$$

So we get: $\sigma_{\bar{x}} = \sqrt{\sum (\bar{x} - \mu_{\bar{x}})^2 P(\bar{x})} = \sqrt{32.34} \approx 5.6868$

Notice that the mean of all possible sample means of size 2 turned out to be equal to the mean of the population. In symbols: $\mu_{\bar{x}} = \mu$ Is this just a coincidence? No. It turns out this will always be the case.

Notice that the standard deviation of the sample means, $\sigma_{\bar{x}}$, turned out to be smaller than the standard deviation of the population. We should wonder if there is a formula that can predict this value. It turns out that $\sigma_{\bar{x}}$ can always be found using the formula: $\sigma_{\bar{x}} = \dfrac{\sigma}{\sqrt{n}} \sqrt{\dfrac{N-n}{N-1}}$

Example 7.10: *Testing the Standard deviation formula*

Once again, we will consider the extremely small population consisting of 5 statistics test scores.

Population: | 67 | 76 | 83 | 89 | 93 |

Verify that the formula $\sigma_{\bar{x}} = \dfrac{\sigma}{\sqrt{n}} \sqrt{\dfrac{N-n}{N-1}}$ works for the sample means from samples of size 2.

Solution:

Recall: N is the population size. In this case, $N = 5$. From the previous example we know that $\sigma \approx 9.28655$.

$n = 2$, so we get $\sigma_{\bar{x}} = \dfrac{\sigma}{\sqrt{n}} \sqrt{\dfrac{N-n}{N-1}} \approx \dfrac{9.28655}{\sqrt{2}} \sqrt{\dfrac{5-2}{5-1}} = \dfrac{9.28655}{\sqrt{2}} \sqrt{\dfrac{3}{4}} \approx 5.6868$

This value does match the answer obtained by using tables and discrete random variable formula in Example 7.9.

SIMPLIFYING THE CALCULATION OF $\sigma_{\bar{x}}$:

While this formula for $\sigma_{\bar{x}}$ is a great improvement over using tables and formulas from Section 5.4, it is still more complicated than it needs to be in most real life applications. In most real life applications, the sample size is often relatively small compared to the size of the population. For example we might take a sample of 50 Americans from a population of around 300,000,000 Americans. In such cases, the $\sqrt{\dfrac{N-n}{N-1}}$ part of the formula is really not necessary. This is illustrated below.

$$\sigma_{\bar{x}} = \dfrac{\sigma}{\sqrt{n}} \sqrt{\dfrac{N-n}{N-1}} = \dfrac{\sigma}{\sqrt{n}} \sqrt{\dfrac{300,000,000-50}{300,000,000-1}} = \dfrac{\sigma}{\sqrt{n}} \sqrt{\dfrac{299,999,950}{299,999,999}} \approx$$

$$\dfrac{\sigma}{\sqrt{n}} \sqrt{0.999999837} \approx \dfrac{\sigma}{\sqrt{n}} \sqrt{1} = \dfrac{\sigma}{\sqrt{n}} \cdot 1 = \dfrac{\sigma}{\sqrt{n}}$$

So in most real life applications, we get very accurate values for $\sigma_{\bar{x}}$ by using the simpler formula:

$$\sigma_{\bar{x}} \approx \dfrac{\sigma}{\sqrt{n}}$$

The following Point to Remember summarizes the results of our discussion.

Point to Remember: *Formulas for the mean and standard deviation of $\overline{x}$*

Theorem 7.3: If a sample of size n is taken from a population with a mean of μ and a standard deviation of σ, then the mean and standard deviation for all possible sample means are given by the formulas:

$$\mu_{\overline{x}} = \mu \qquad \text{and} \qquad \sigma_{\overline{x}} \approx \frac{\sigma}{\sqrt{n}}$$

In Words: The mean of all possible sample means of a given sample size is always equal to the mean of the population being sampled. The standard deviation of all possible sample means of a given sample size is approximately equal to the standard deviation of the population divided by the square root of the sample size.

Let's practice these new formulas with a quick example.

Example 7.11: *Practicing the mechanics of Theorem 7.3*

Suppose that a population has a mean of 78 and a standard deviation of 19.2.

a) Determine the mean and standard deviation for all possible sample means from samples of size 20.

b) Determine the mean and standard deviation for all possible sample means from samples of size 40.

c) Determine the mean and standard deviation for all possible sample means from samples of size 400.

d) What effect did increasing the sample size have on the mean of the sample means?

e) What effect did increasing the sample size have on the standard deviation of the sample means.

Solution:

a) We will simply apply the formulas we just learned above, so we get:

$$\mu_{\overline{x}} = \mu = 78 \quad \text{and} \quad \sigma_{\overline{x}} \approx \frac{\sigma}{\sqrt{n}} = \frac{19.2}{\sqrt{20}} \approx 4.2933$$

b) Again, we use the same formulas only this time n = 40.

$$\mu_{\overline{x}} = \mu = 78 \quad \text{and} \quad \sigma_{\overline{x}} \approx \frac{\sigma}{\sqrt{n}} = \frac{19.2}{\sqrt{40}} \approx 3.0358$$

c) This time we use n = 400.

$$\mu_{\overline{x}} = \mu = 78 \quad \text{and} \quad \sigma_{\overline{x}} \approx \frac{\sigma}{\sqrt{n}} = \frac{19.2}{\sqrt{400}} = 0.96$$

Rounding Note:

It was acceptable to only use 2 decimal places for this last $\sigma_{\overline{x}}$ because it was an exact value.

d) The size of the sample has no effect on the answer for $\mu_{\overline{x}}$.

e) The larger the sample size, the smaller the value of $\sigma_{\overline{x}}$. This is due to the n in the denominator of that formula.

BACK TO SAMPLING ERROR: *How do these new formulas help us predict sampling error?*

We will now return our discussion back to sampling error. We want to see what effect the formulas we have just learned have on the error we get when trying to estimate the population mean by the sample mean from a randomly selected sample. This will be similar to our results for proportions from Section 7.1.

Suppose that a random sample of size n, is taken from a population with a mean of μ and a standard deviation of σ. Because $\bar{x}$ is a random variable, we can state that we expect $\bar{x}$ to lie within two standard deviations of its mean. In symbols, this is stated as follows:

$$\mu_{\bar{x}} - 2\sigma_{\bar{x}} < \bar{x} < \mu_{\bar{x}} + 2\sigma_{\bar{x}}$$

Now the goal becomes to get the sampling error, $\left|\bar{x} - \mu\right|$, to show up in this formula. This requires a bit of Algebra. We begin the process by substituting for $\mu_{\bar{x}}$.

$$\mu_{\bar{x}} - 2\sigma_{\bar{x}} < \bar{x} < \mu_{\bar{x}} + 2\sigma_{\bar{x}} \implies \mu - 2\sigma_{\bar{x}} < \bar{x} < \mu + 2\sigma_{\bar{x}}$$

$$\implies -2\sigma_{\bar{x}} < \bar{x} - \mu < +2\sigma_{\bar{x}} \implies \left|\bar{x} - \mu\right| < 2\sigma_{\bar{x}}$$

The work above shows us that we expect the sampling error when estimating μ by $\bar{x}$ to be less than $2\sigma_{\bar{x}}$. We can also state this in a different form by substituting for $\sigma_{\bar{x}}$. This allows to also state that we expect the sampling error to be less than $2\dfrac{\sigma}{\sqrt{n}}$.

The discussion above is summarized in the following definitions.

Definitions: *Sampling Error, Expected Error, and Standard Error when estimating μ by using $\bar{x}$*

Sampling Error for $\bar{x}$: The sampling error when estimating μ by $\bar{x}$ is given by the absolute value of the difference between these two quantities. In symbols,

$$\text{Sampling Error} = \left|\bar{x} - \mu\right|$$

Expected Error for $\bar{x}$: The expected error tells us how much error to expect when we use $\bar{x}$ to estimate μ. In words, we expect our sampling error to be less than 2 standard deviations of our point estimate. In symbols, we get the following.

$$\text{Expected Error} < 2\sigma_{\bar{x}} \quad \text{OR} \quad \text{Expected Error} < 2\dfrac{\sigma}{\sqrt{n}}$$

Note: It is possible that we will get sampling error larger than these formulas predict, but because that would mean that $\bar{x}$ was more than two standard deviations away from its mean, such occurrences would be considered unusual.

Standard Error for $\bar{x}$: Because we use $\sigma_{\bar{x}}$ to help use calculate what type of estimation errors are considered expected and which errors are considered unusual, it is common to refer to $\sigma_{\bar{x}} \approx \dfrac{\sigma}{\sqrt{n}}$ as the expected error for $\bar{x}$.

Example 7.12: *Estimating the Carbs in an Energy Bar*

Clif bars have a mean of 45 grams of carbs. Assume that the standard deviation
for the amount of carbs in Clif bars is 2.47 grams.

a) Suppose that we will take a random sample of size 10 Clif bars. Determine
the mean and standard deviation of the possible values of $\bar{x}$.

b) If you used the mean from a random sample of 10 Clif bars to estimate the
mean amount of carbs for all Clif bars, how much error would you expect?
Explain.

How much sampling error should
we expect when estimating the carbs
in an energy bar?

c) For samples of size 50, determine the mean and standard deviation of $\bar{x}$.

d) If you used the mean from a random sample of 50 energy bars to estimate the mean amount of carbs for all
the energy bars, how much error would you expect? Explain.

e) Is it possible that you would get more than 0.6896 carbs in error when using the mean from a random sample
of size 50? Explain.

Solution:

Before we answer the specific questions, let's begin by summarizing the information given. Though not
specifically stated, it seems that the mean and standard deviation given are for all the bars of this brand and are
therefore population values. So we have.

$$\mu = 45 \text{ and } \sigma = 2.47$$

a) This question can be answered simply by substituting into the formulas just developed. Because $n = 10$, we
get:

$$\mu_{\bar{x}} = \mu = 45 \text{ and } \sigma_{\bar{x}} \approx \frac{2.47}{\sqrt{10}} \approx 0.78108$$

b) We will use the expected error formula from the previous page. We must remember that when we calculate
the expected range we have to use the mean and standard deviation of $\bar{x}$ (for samples of size 10) in our
calculation.

$$\text{Expected Error} = |\bar{x} - \mu| < 2\sigma_{\bar{x}} = 2(0.78108) = 1.56216$$

So we can say that if we used the mean from a random sample of 10 Clif bars to estimate the mean amount of
carbs for all the energy bars, our expected error would be less than 1.56216 carbs.

c) This time $n = 50$, so we get:

$$\mu_{\bar{x}} = \mu = 45 \text{ and } \sigma_{\bar{x}} \approx \frac{2.47}{\sqrt{50}} \approx 0.34931$$

d) Remember, we must calculate the expected error using the standard deviation of $\bar{x}$ (for samples of size 50) in
our calculation.

$$\text{Expected Error} = |\bar{x} - \mu| < 2\sigma_{\bar{x}} = 2(0.34931) = 0.68962$$

So we can say that if you used the mean from a random sample of 50 energy bars to estimate the mean
amount of carbs for all the energy bars, you expect the error to be less than 0.68962 carbs.

e) It is possible that we would get more error than 0.68962 carbs, however, that would mean that the value of $\bar{x}$ we obtained from our sample would have been more than 2 standard deviations away from its mean. That is possible, but it would be unusual.

One of the most important facts to notice from the previous example is that increasing our sample size from 10 to 50 made the expected error in our estimate smaller.

Point to Remember: Three very important facts have just been illustrated that are very good news for estimating μ by a value of $\bar{x}$ from a randomly chosen sample.

- $\mu_{\bar{x}} = \mu$ is good news for estimating because it means that all of our guesses ($\bar{x}$'s) are centered around the value we are trying to estimate (μ).

- Added good news comes from the statement that $\sigma_{\bar{x}} \approx \dfrac{\sigma}{\sqrt{n}}$, because this tells us that all the $\bar{x}$'s will get closer to their center (μ) as the sample size we choose increases. Recall: We expect most of a data set to lie within 2 standard deviations of its mean.

- Thus, if we increase our sample size, we will make all the $\bar{x}$'s get closer to μ and that means the specific $\bar{x}$ we randomly choose will probably be a good estimate of μ.

Summary: It would be unusual for sampling the error to exceed $2\dfrac{\sigma}{\sqrt{n}}$, so our expected error decreases as our sample size increases.

WRAP SESSION: *Thinking about sample size and accuracy of our estimate*

Example 7.13: *Mean Home Price for a City*

Suppose the prices of all new homes in a certain city have a mean of $578,948 with a standard deviation of $158,724.

How much error should we expected when estimating the mean home price for a city?

a) For samples of size 37, determine the mean and standard deviation of all possible values of $\bar{x}$.

b) If the mean from a random sample of 37 new homes was used to estimate the average cost of all new homes, would it be unusual for the estimate to be off by more than $25,000? Explain.

c) What would be the expected (not unusual) range for the estimate of the mean cost of all new homes using the mean from a sample of size 37 as your estimate?

d) What would be the expected range for the total value of 37 randomly selected homes from this city?

e) What recommendation would you give those collecting the sample, if it is important that their estimate be within $25,000 of the true mean? Explain the reason for your answer.

f) What sample size would be needed so that we would expect our estimate to be within $25,000 of the true mean?

g) Can we calculate the probability that the error obtained when estimating the mean of all homes by the mean of a sample of size 37 would be less than $25,000?

Solution:

a) Summarizing the information given, we see that $\mu = 578{,}948$, $\sigma = 158{,}724$, and $n = 37$. We can now use the formulas derived earlier to determine the mean and standard deviation of $\overline{x}$.

$$\mu_{\overline{x}} = \mu = \$578{,}948 \text{ and } \sigma_{\overline{x}} \approx \frac{\sigma}{\sqrt{n}} = \frac{158724}{\sqrt{37}} \approx \$26{,}094$$

b) For the estimate to be off by more than $25,000, it would have to land outside of the interval from $553,948 and $603,948. (Note: these numbers come from calculating the expression $\mu \pm 25000$.) Because this is a question about whether or not such values would be unusual, it is appropriate to calculate z-scores for these values. Because these are values of $\overline{x}$, we must be careful to use the standard deviation of $\overline{x}$ when calculating the z-scores.

$$z_1 = \frac{\overline{x} - \mu_{\overline{x}}}{\sigma_{\overline{x}}} = \frac{553948 - 578948}{26094} \approx -0.958 \text{ and } z_2 = \frac{\overline{x} - \mu_{\overline{x}}}{\sigma_{\overline{x}}} = \frac{603948 - 578948}{26094} \approx 0.958$$

For an estimate to be off by more than $25,000, it would only have to be more than 0.96 standard deviations away from the mean. So it is definitely possible to have an $\overline{x}$ that is more than $25,000 away from the true mean an yet less than 2 standard deviations away from the true mean, therefore it would not be unusual to get such a value. (**Note**: The result of part (b) could also have been quickly stated by noticing that the error mentioned, $25,000, was less than the value of the standard deviation of $\overline{x}$.)

c) For the estimate to not be considered unusual, it would need to lie within two standard deviations of its mean. So we calculate as follows:

$$\mu_{\overline{x}} \pm 2\sigma_{\overline{x}} = 578948 \pm 2(26094) \text{ which gives the interval } (526760, 631136)$$

So when estimating the average cost of all new homes using the mean from a sample of size 37, we would expect to get an estimate somewhere between $526,760 and $631,136.

> **Key Concept**: *The true mean*
>
> While it is most accurate to state that we expect $\overline{x}$ to be within two standard deviations of *its* mean. We often just say that we expect $\overline{x}$ to be within two standard deviations of the true mean. We can say this because $\mu_{\overline{x}} = \mu$.

d) In part (c) above, we said that the expected range for the sample average was: $\$526{,}760 < \overline{x} < \$631{,}1360$. To answer the question about the expected total value of the homes, we must remember that $\overline{x} = \frac{\sum x}{n} = \frac{\sum x}{37}$. If we multiply all three parts of the inequality by the sample size of 37, this will yield an expected range for the total value.

$$\$526{,}760 < \frac{\sum x}{37} < \$631{,}1360 \Rightarrow 37 \cdot \$526{,}760 < 37 \cdot \frac{\sum x}{37} < 30 \cdot \$631{,}136 \Rightarrow \$19{,}490{,}120 < \sum x < \$23{,}352{,}032$$

Therefore, we can say that we should expect the total value from a random sample of 37 homes to be somewhere between $19,490,120 and $23,353,032.

e) I would suggest that they take a sample of a size larger than 37 new homes when calculating their estimate. We see from part (b) that it would not be considered unusual for the estimate from a sample of size 37 to be more than $25,000 off. We also see from part (c) that the expected range for the estimate includes values that are more than $50,000 away from the true mean.

Increasing the sample size should be effective in fixing these problems, because a larger sample size will create a smaller value for $\sigma_{\overline{x}}$. This in turn would make the z-scores above larger, making an error of more than $25,000 more unusual. Similarly, making $\sigma_{\overline{x}}$ smaller would reduce the expected error of the estimate, making it more likely that the estimate would be within $25,000.

f) The expected error of an estimate is given by $2\dfrac{\sigma}{\sqrt{n}}$. So, we want $2\dfrac{\sigma}{\sqrt{n}} \le 25000$. It's just a matter of substituting for σ and then doing some algebra.

> **Key Concept:** *Rounding Note*
>
> It may seem that a number like 161.24 should be rounded down, however, if we round down, we lower the denominator of our expected error and actually get an expected error larger than $25,000.

$$2 \cdot \frac{158724}{\sqrt{n}} \le 25000 \;\Rightarrow\; 2(158724) \le 25000\sqrt{n}$$

$$\Rightarrow\; \sqrt{n} \ge \frac{2(158724)}{25000} \;\Rightarrow\; n \ge \left(\frac{2(158724)}{25000}\right)^2 \approx 161.24$$

Because we can't have a decimal sample size, we should round up and recommend a sample size of 162, so that our expected error will be less than $25,000.

g) Let's begin by rephrasing the probability question using symbols.

$$P(578948 - 25000 < \bar{x} < 578948 + 25000) = P(553948 < \bar{x} < 603948)$$

or, using the z-scores calculated above in part (b), we could state this as: $P(-0.958 < z < 0.958)$

I would like to find the answer to this probability question by using the area under the standard normal curve between -0.958 and 0.958, but this can only be done if z has the standard normal distribution and that would only be the case if $\bar{x}$ has a normal distribution. The problem is, we do not know if that is the case or not!

The best we can do at this point is to give an estimate based on the general empirical rule. Because we know that for most data sets 50% to 80% of the data lies within 1 standard deviation of the mean, we can estimate that the chance of our estimate being within $25,000 of the true mean is probably somewhere between 0.50 and 0.80.

The vague answer we just gave in part (g) is not what someone who was paying us to do this statistical analysis of new home prices would expect. If we want our work to be more professional, then we better learn how to give a more precise statement of the probabilities involved here. We will learn how to do that in the next section. In part (d), we saw that knowing information about the sample mean, also helps us estimate the sample total. The technique used in part (d) is summarized below.

> **Key Concepts:** *Using $\bar{x}$ to estimate the total in a random sample*
>
> In this section, we have focused our attention on better understanding the nature of sample means. However, because the sample mean is calculated by dividing the total of the sample by the sample size, we can also use what we have learned to estimate the size of a sample total. We can find the sample total by multiplying the sample mean by the sample size as shown below.
>
> $$\bar{x} = \frac{\sum x}{n} \;\Rightarrow\; \sum x = n \cdot \bar{x}$$

It's time to practice what we have learned with some exercises.

Exercise Set 7.3:

Concept Review: Review the definitions and concepts from this section by filling in the blanks for each of the following.

39) $\mu_{\bar{x}} = \mu$ tells us that $\bar{x}$ is a random variable and that if you average all possible values of the _____ mean, then the result equals the _____ mean.

40) $\sigma_{\bar{x}} \approx \dfrac{\sigma}{\sqrt{n}}$ is good news because it tells us that the higher the sample size, the closer the possible values of ____ get to the population _____ .

41) While it is true that $\mu_{\bar{x}} = \mu$, it is also typically the case that $P(\bar{x} = \mu) \approx$ _____ .

42) When we estimate μ by using $\bar{x}$ as a point estimate, we expect the sampling error to be less than _____ or _____ .

Mechanics: Practice the calculations needed for this section before moving on to the real world applications.

43) Consider the population consisting of:

   84   92   105   121

   a) Determine the mean and standard deviation of this population.
   b) List all possible samples of size 2 that could be obtained from the population.
   c) Find the mean for each of the samples from part (b).
   d) Use formulas from Section 5.4 and the methods from Example 7.9 to find the mean and standard deviation for all possible values of $\bar{x}$ from samples of size 2.
   e) Verify that the formula $\sigma_{\bar{x}} = \dfrac{\sigma}{\sqrt{n}}\sqrt{\dfrac{N-n}{N-1}}$ yields the same result as you obtained in part (d).

44) Consider the population consisting of:

   12   16   19   20   22   27

   a) Determine the mean and standard deviation of this population.
   b) List all possible samples of size 5 that could be obtained from the population.
   c) Find the mean for each of the samples from part (b).
   d) Use formulas from Section 5.4 and the methods from Example 7.9 to find the mean and standard deviation for all possible values of $\bar{x}$ from samples of size 5.
   e) Verify that the formula $\sigma_{\bar{x}} = \dfrac{\sigma}{\sqrt{n}}\sqrt{\dfrac{N-n}{N-1}}$ yields the same result as you obtained in part (d).

45) Suppose that a population has a mean of 112 and a standard deviation of 38.2.

   a) Determine the mean and standard deviation for all possible sample means from samples of size 10.
   b) Determine the mean and standard deviation for all possible sample means from samples of size 30.
   c) What effect did increasing the sample size have on the mean of the sample means?
   d) What effect did increasing the sample size have on the standard deviation of the sample means?

46) Suppose that a population has a mean of 37.8 and a standard deviation of 9.805.

   a) Determine the mean and standard deviation for all possible sample means from samples of size 15.
   b) Determine the mean and standard deviation for all possible sample means from samples of size 50.
   c) What effect did increasing the sample size have on the mean of the sample means?
   d) What effect did increasing the sample size have on the standard deviation of the sample means?

47) Suppose that a population has a mean of 12.05 and a standard deviation of 0.10553.

   a) Determine the mean and standard deviation for all possible values of $\bar{x}$ from samples of size 21.
   b) Determine the expected error that we will get when using $\bar{x}$ as a point estimate for μ.
   c) Determine the mean and standard deviation for all possible values of $\bar{x}$ from samples of size 77.
   d) For this new sample size of 77, determine the expected error that we will get when using $\bar{x}$ as a point estimate for μ.
   e) Give a logical explanation for why we expect less error when the sample size is increased.

48) Suppose that a population has a mean of 127.97 and a standard deviation of 13.008.

    a) Determine the mean and standard deviation for all possible values of $\overline{x}$ from samples of size 17.

    b) Determine the expected error that we will get when using $\overline{x}$ as a point estimate for μ.

    c) Determine the mean and standard deviation for all possible values of $\overline{x}$ from samples of size 106.

    d) For this new sample size of 106, determine the expected error that we will get when using $\overline{x}$ as a point estimate for μ.

    e) Give a logical explanation for why we expect less error when the sample size is increased.

Applications: Practice the ideas learned in this section within the context of real world applications.

49) Suppose that mature Chihuahuas have a mean weight of 4.95 pounds with a standard deviation of 0.825 pounds. We are interested in estimating this mean weight using a random sample.

    a) For samples of size 8, determine the mean and standard deviation of the possible values of $\overline{x}$.

    b) If you used the mean weight from a random sample of 8 Chihuahuas to estimate the mean weight for all such Chihuahuas, how much error would you expect? Explain.

    c) Would it be unusual if your estimate from (b) was off by more than 0.5 lbs? Explain.

    d) For samples of size 25, determine the mean and standard deviation of the possible values of $\overline{x}$.

    e) If you used the mean weight from a random sample of 25 Chihuahuas to estimate the mean weight for all such Chihuahuas, how much error would you expect? Explain.

    f) For $n = 25$, would it be unusual if your estimate was off by more than 0.5 lbs? Explain.

50) Suppose that NBA player Kobe Bryant's true average points per game is 25.3 with a standard deviation of 8.133 points. We are interested in estimating his true mean points per game using a random sample.

    a) For samples of size 17, determine the mean and standard deviation of the possible values of $\overline{x}$.

    b) If you used the mean points from a random sample of 17 games to estimate the mean scoring average for all his games, how much error would you expect? Explain.

    c) Would it be unusual if your estimate from (b) was off by more than 3 points? Explain.

    d) For samples of size 82, determine the mean and standard deviation of the possible values of $\overline{x}$.

    e) If you used the mean points from a random sample of 82 games to estimate the mean scoring average for all his games, how much error would you expect? Explain.

    f) For $n = 82$, would it be unusual if your estimate was off by more than 3 points? Explain.

51) Suppose the monthly dining out expenses for a family of 5 has a mean of $559.71 with a standard deviation of $229.24. Consider trying to estimate this mean using a random sample.

    a) Determine the mean and standard deviation for all possible sample means from samples of size 12.

    b) What is the expected error when using the mean from a random sample of size 12 months as your estimate?

    c) What would be the expected (not unusual) range for the estimate of the true mean monthly expense using the mean from a random sample of size 12 as your estimate?

    d) What would be the expected range for the total amount of dining out expenses for this family from 12 randomly selected months?

    e) Suppose that we used the mean from a random sample of 12 such months to estimate the mean of all months for this family, would it be unusual for the sampling error to be over $75? Explain.

52) The purchase price for all 55-inch HDTV's sold have a mean of $1282 and a standard deviation of $305.19. Consider trying to estimate this mean using a random sample.

    a) Determine the mean and standard deviation for all possible sample means from samples of size 20.

    b) What is the expected error when using the mean from a random sample of size 20 as your estimate?

    c) What would be the expected (not unusual) range for the estimate of the mean purchase price of all the HDTV's using the mean from a random sample of size 20 as your estimate?

    d) What would be the expected range for the total purchase price for a random sample of 20 recently sold 55-inch HDTV's?

    e) Suppose that we used the mean from a random sample of 20 such HDTV's to estimate the mean of all such HDTV's, would it be unusual for the error to be over $100? Explain.

53) In problem (49), if you wanted the expected sampling error to be less than 0.25 lbs, how big of a sample should you use to make your estimate?

54) In problem (52), if you wanted the expected sampling error to be less than $50, how big of a sample should you use to make your estimate?

55) The Nissan Leaf is an all electric car. Suppose that the 2011 Nissan Leaf claims an average of 99 miles per charge with a standard deviation of 12.33 miles. We are unsure if these claims are true and decide to estimate the true average miles per charge using a random sample of 30 such cars.

a) For samples of size 30, determine the mean and standard deviation of all possible values of the sample mean. Assume the mileage claims about the Nissan Leaf are true.

b) Suppose that our sample of 30 Leafs produced a mean of 96.2 miles per charge. If Nissan's mileage claims are true, would that be considered an unusual value for our point estimate? Explain.

c) Would you say that a point estimate of 96.2 miles per charge is strong evidence that the true average is less than 99 miles, or is it plausible that this difference from the claimed 99 miles was just random variation? Explain.

d) Suppose that our sample of 30 Leafs produced a mean of 93.1 miles per charge. If Nissan's mileage claims are true, would that be considered an unusual value for our point estimate? Explain.

e) Would you say that a point estimate of 93.1 miles per charge is strong evidence that the true average is less than 99 miles, or is it plausible that this difference from the claimed 99 miles was just random variation? Explain.

56) A statistics teacher is trying to lose weight and is counting his calories. He is trying to average 500 calories for breakfast. Assume that the standard deviation is 265 calories. He decides to estimate his true average calories at breakfast using a random sample of 40 breakfasts.

a) For samples of size 40, determine the mean and standard deviation of all possible values of the sample mean. Assume the true average is 500 calories.

b) Suppose that his sample of 40 breakfasts produced a mean of 545.2 calories per breakfast. If his true mean breakfast calories is 500, would that be considered an unusual value for his point estimate? Explain.

c) Would you say that a point estimate of 545.2 calories per breakfast is strong evidence that the true average is more than 500 calories, or is it plausible that this difference from the claimed 500 calories is just random variation? Explain.

d) Suppose that his sample of 40 breakfasts produced a mean of 645.2 calories per breakfast. If his true mean breakfast calories is 500, would that be considered an unusual value for his point estimate? Explain.

e) Would you say that a point estimate of 645.2 calories per breakfast is strong evidence that the true average is more than 500 calories, or is it plausible that this difference from the claimed 500 calories is just random variation? Explain.

Section 7.4 - The Sampling Distribution of $\bar{x}$

In the previous section, we ended our discussion by asking a probability question involving $\bar{x}$. We mentioned that it would have been desirable to answer the question using the area under a normal curve. However, we could not do that because we only knew the mean and standard deviation of $\bar{x}$. We did not know the shape of $\bar{x}$'s distribution. In this section, we will give two conditions, either of which, will tell us that $\bar{x}$ is normally distributed. The first one, given in the following point to remember, depends on the distribution of the population.

Point to Remember: *Theorem 7.4 (Normal Population $\Rightarrow$ Normal $\bar{x}$)*

If the population we are sampling from is normally distributed with mean μ and standard deviation σ, then for *any* given sample size, $\bar{x}$ will also be normally distributed with mean $\mu_{\bar{x}} = \mu$ and standard deviation $\sigma_{\bar{x}} \approx \dfrac{\sigma}{\sqrt{n}}$.

This tells us that, if we are sampling from a normal population, then we can use area under a normal curve to answer probability questions involving $\bar{x}$. The graphs below show the distributions of a normal curve with a mean of 15 and a standard deviation of 3 followed by the graphs of $\bar{x}$ for samples of sizes n = 7, n = 20, n = 33. The graph of the population was formed by making a histogram for 10,000 randomly selected data values from the population. The graphs of $\bar{x}$ were formed by making histograms for the values of $\bar{x}$ for 10,000 different samples of the indicated size taken from the initial normal population.

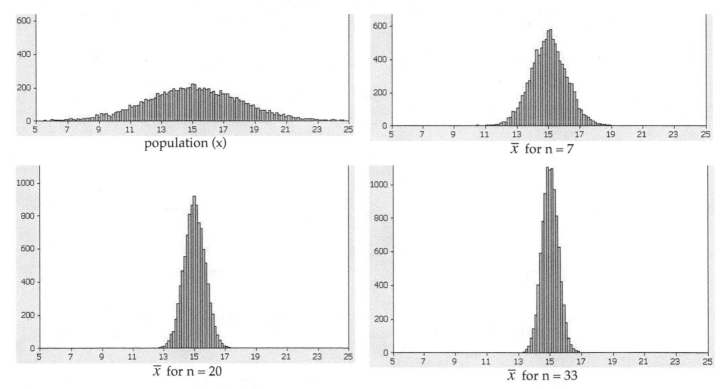

The Graphs above illustrate a few things worth noting:

- None of the preceding graphs appear to have perfect bell shapes. This is because they are obtained from a histogram of 10,000 randomly selected members. The random variation from sampling makes the graphs a little rough, however, with 10,000 pieces of data, the graphs do reflect the shape of the population from which the 10,000 data pieces were drawn.
- In all but the first graph, the 10,000 data values each represent the mean of a sample or an $\bar{x}$. Therefore, those histograms are revealing the shape of the set of all $\bar{x}$'s, not the original population.

- In every case we see a pretty good bell shape. The reason the shape is not identical for each one is that the increasing sample size is causing the standard deviation of the $\bar{x}$'s to decrease. This results in a narrower and taller curve.
- As discussed in the previous section, we see that as the sample size increases, the values of $\bar{x}$ are moving closer to the population mean μ.

Let's see how this theorem works in an example.

Example 7.14: *Applying Theorem 7.4*

Suppose that we are working with a normal population with a mean of 28.19 and a standard deviation of 6.9461.

a) For samples of size 21, determine the distribution of all possible values of $\bar{x}$.

b) Find $P(\bar{x} > 27.2)$

c) Find $P(29 < \bar{x} \le 30)$

Solution:

a) Because the population is said to be normally distributed, we can apply theorem 7.4 and say that $\bar{x}$ is also normally distributed. We can also apply the formulas from Section 7.3 and say that:

$$\mu_{\bar{x}} = \mu = 28.19 \quad \text{and} \quad \sigma_{\bar{x}} \approx \frac{\sigma}{\sqrt{n}} = \frac{6.9461}{\sqrt{21}} \approx 1.5158$$

So, putting it all together, we say that $\bar{x}$ is normally distributed with $\mu_{\bar{x}} = 28.19$ and $\sigma_{\bar{x}} \approx 1.5158$.

b) Because part (a) tells us that $\bar{x}$ is normally distributed, we can use an area under a normal curve to answer this question. So at this point, the work becomes very similar to what we did in Chapter 6. We will begin with a sketch of the curve to be used and the area to be found.

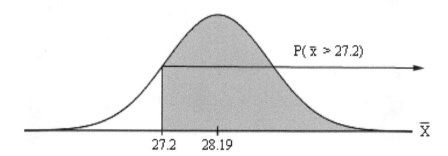

Notice that the axis is labeled with $\bar{x}$ rather than just an x, because this is a probability question about $\bar{x}$. This also reminds us that, when we calculate our z-score, we must use the mean and standard deviation of $\bar{x}$ rather than of the original population. So, we get:

$$z = \frac{\bar{x} - \mu_{\bar{x}}}{\sigma_{\bar{x}}} = \frac{27.2 - 28.19}{1.5158} \approx -0.653$$

The probability we need is the area to the right of this value under the standard normal curve. We can find that using the normalcdf command and technology.

$$P(\bar{x} > 27.2) = normalcdf(-0.653, \infty) \approx 0.7431$$

c) This is very similar to part (b) only we have two boundaries instead of just one. See the sketch below.

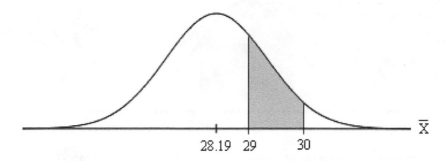

We now find the z-scores and the area as we did in part (b).

$$z_1 = \frac{29 - 28.19}{1.5158} \approx 0.534 \quad \text{and} \quad z_2 = \frac{30 - 28.19}{1.5158} \approx 1.194$$

So, $P(29 < \bar{x} \le 30) = normalcdf(0.534, 1.194) \approx 0.1804$.

> **Caution:** *Calculating the z-score*
>
> The key to finding probabilities for $\bar{x}$ using area under a normal curve is remembering to use $\sigma_{\bar{x}}$ when calculating the z-scores. Other than that, the work is just like what we did in chapter 6.

Let's move to an example that references a specific application.

Example 7.15: *Estimating the Heights of Adult Women*

Suppose the heights of adult women are normally distributed with a mean of 64.3 inches and a standard deviation of 2.5529 inches.

a) For samples of size 10, determine the distribution of all possible values of $\bar{x}$.

b) Determine the probability that the mean height from a sample of size 10 women will have a sampling error of less that 0.5 inches.

c) If it is important to you that your point estimate of the average height of all adult women be within 0.5 inch of the actual value, then is a sample of size 10 large enough? Explain.

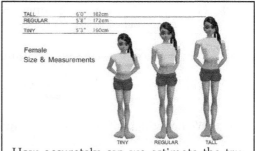

How accurately can we estimate the true mean height for adult women using a random sample?

d) For samples of size 120, determine the distribution of all possible values of $\bar{x}$.

e) Determine the probability that the mean height from a sample of size 120 women would be within 0.5 inches of the population mean height of 64.3 inches.

Solution:

a) Because the population we are sampling from is normally distributed, we can say that $\bar{x}$ will be normally distributed with $\mu_{\bar{x}} = \mu = 64.3$ and $\sigma_{\bar{x}} \approx \frac{\sigma}{\sqrt{n}} = \frac{2.5529}{\sqrt{10}} \approx 0.80730$.

b) First, let's translate this question into symbols. For the sampling error to be less than 0.5 inches, we need our sample mean to be within 0.5 inches of the population mean. So we need the sample mean to be somewhere between 0.5 below the true mean to 0.5 above the true mean. So, we get:

$$P(\mu - 0.5 < \bar{x} < \mu + 0.5) = P(64.3 - 0.5 < \bar{x} < 64.3 + 0.5) = P(63.8 < \bar{x} < 64.8)$$

Now, because in part (a) we determined that $\bar{x}$ is normally distributed, we can find this probability by finding the following area under the normal curve specified in part (a).

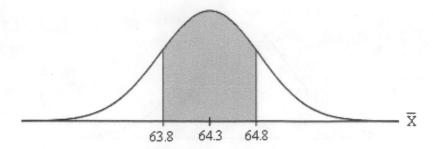

The next step is to compute z-scores (remember to use $\sigma_{\bar{x}}$ for $n = 10$ rather than σ.)

$$z_1 = \frac{63.8 - 64.3}{0.80730} \approx -0.619 \quad \text{and} \quad z_2 = \frac{64.8 - 64.3}{0.80730} \approx 0.619$$

We now turn to technology and the normalcdf command.

$$P(63.8 < \bar{x} < 64.8) = normalcdf(-0.619,\ 0.619) \approx 0.4641$$

So there is a 46.41% chance that the sampling error when using the sample mean height from a sample of 10 women to estimate the population mean height of all women will be less than 0.5 inches.

c) No, a 46.41% chance of getting a satisfactory answer does not seem high enough. If it is important for us to be within 0.5 inches, then we probably want to have that happen most of the time, not a mere 46.41% of the time.

d) We still have a normally distributed population. The only change here from part (a) is the sample size. So, $\bar{x}$ will be normally distributed with $\mu_{\bar{x}} = \mu = 64.3$ and $\sigma_{\bar{x}} \approx \frac{\sigma}{\sqrt{n}} = \frac{2.5529}{\sqrt{120}} \approx 0.23305$.

e) We are still answering the same question as in part (b):

$$P(\mu - 0.5 < \bar{x} < \mu + 0.5) = P(64.3 - 0.5 < \bar{x} < 64.3 + 0.5) = P(63.8 < \bar{x} < 64.8)$$

And we will still answer it by using the area under a normal curve. However, due to the change in sample size we are now dealing with a different standard deviation.

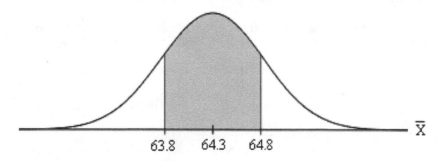

The next step is to compute z-scores. However, we must remember that, because our sample size has changed, the standard deviation of $\bar{x}$ has also changed. So we must use the new standard deviation calculated in part (d):

$$z_1 = \frac{63.8 - 64.3}{0.23305} \approx -2.145 \quad \text{and} \quad z_2 = \frac{64.8 - 64.3}{0.23305} \approx 2.145$$

We again turn to technology and the normalcdf command.

$$P(63.8 < \bar{x} < 64.8) = normalcdf(-2.145, 2.145) \approx 0.9680$$

So there is a 96.8% chance that the mean height from a sample of 120 women would be within 0.5 inches of the population mean height of all women.

Even though we drew the same picture for parts (b) and (e), in reality, because the standard deviation of $\bar{x}$ was smaller, the curve was taller and narrower. That is why the area increased even though the height boundaries were unchanged.

> **Key Concept:** *Improving the chance of a satisfactory result*
>
> By increasing the sample size from 10 to 120 women, we greatly increased our chances of getting a satisfactory result for our estimate of the population mean.

LARGE SAMPLES: *Another way to know that $\bar{x}$ is normally distributed*

Now, let's return to the example involving home prices from the Section 7.3, Example 7.13, part (f). We were told that in a certain city, the prices have a mean of $578,948 with a standard deviation of $158,724 and then we were asked:

> What is the probability that the error obtained when estimating the mean of all homes by the mean of a sample of size 37 would be less than $25,000?

Recall: We were unable to answer this question because we did not know the distribution of $\bar{x}$. Does Theorem 7.4 solve this problem for us? Unfortunately, no it doesn't. We are still stuck because we are not told that the population is normal. In fact, home prices tend to be right-skewed, so we can be confident that we do not have a normal population. However, it turns out that we can solve this problem, but the key is not the distribution of the population, rather it is the size of the sample we are working with. The theorem that follows opens the door to completing this problem.

> **Point to Remember:** *Theorem 7.5 (Big Sample $\Rightarrow$ Normal $\bar{x}$)*
>
> *The Central Limit Theorem (CLT)* If we take a large sample from a population with mean μ and standard deviation σ, then $\bar{x}$ will be normally distributed with mean $\mu_{\bar{x}} = \mu$ and standard deviation $\sigma_{\bar{x}} \approx \dfrac{\sigma}{\sqrt{n}}$. If the sample size if large enough, this is true regardless of the shape of the distribution of the population. (See notes below.)
>
> - If $n \geq 30$, then $\bar{x}$ will be normally distributed regardless of the population's distribution.
> - If $15 \leq n < 30$, then $\bar{x}$ will be normally distributed as long as the population is not severely skewed. A sample containing outliers is often an indication of a skewed population.
> - If $n < 15$, then we return to Theorem 7.4 and require a normally distributed population.

The graphs shown that follow illustrate how increasing sample sizes affect the distribution of $\bar{x}$. We see the distributions of a Uniform population with mean 5 and a severely right-skewed population with mean 4 followed by the graphs of $\bar{x}$ for samples of sizes n = 7, n = 20, n = 33. The graphs of the populations were formed by making a histogram for 10,000 randomly selected data values from each population. The graphs of $\bar{x}$ were formed by making histograms for the values of $\bar{x}$ for 10,000 different samples of the indicated size taken from the initial populations.

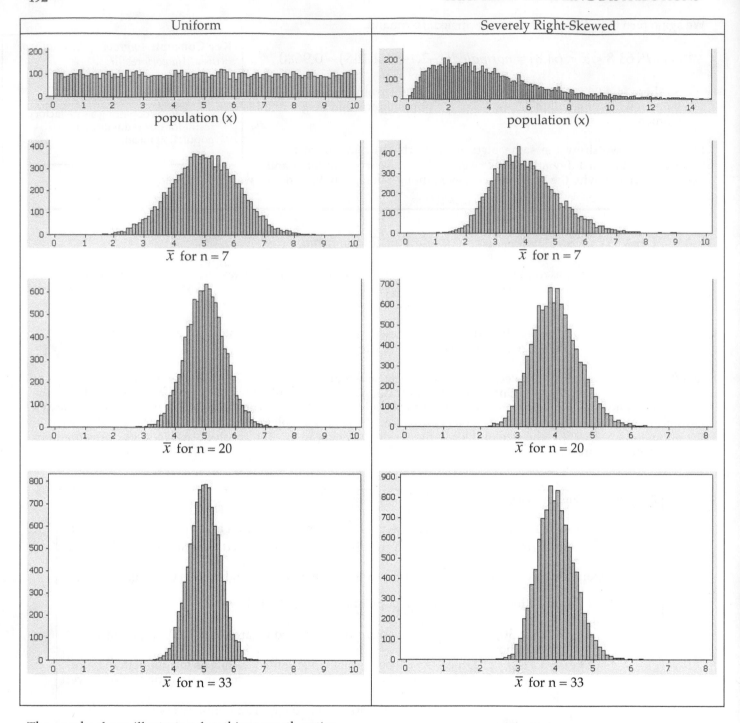

The graphs above illustrate a few things worth noting:

- The initial populations are clearly not bell-shaped.
- For n = 7, because uniform distributions are not skewed, the $\bar{x}$'s from the uniform population are producing a roughly bell-shaped distribution curve. However, the severely right-skewed population still seems to be producing right-skewed $\bar{x}$'s.
- For n = 20, the uniform distribution is now producing a nice bell-shaped curve for $\bar{x}$. However, the distribution for the $\bar{x}$'s from the severely right-skewed population still shows signs of being right-skewed, though it clearly is becoming more bell-shaped.
- For n = 33, both the populations are now producing bell-shaped distributions for $\bar{x}$. Hints of the right-skewed population still show up for the $\bar{x}$'s from that population, however, the shape of $\bar{x}$ is now close enough to normal that it could give decent probability approximations for $\bar{x}$.

Example 7.16: *Applying the Central Limit Theorem*

Suppose that we are working with a population with a mean of 14.88 and a standard deviation of 9.0507.

a) Determine the distribution for the possible values of $\bar{x}$ for a sample of size 50.

b) Find $P(\bar{x} > 15)$.

c) Find $P\left(\sum x < 675\right)$.

d) What is the distribution of the population?

Solution:

a) Because the sample size is $50 \geq 30$, we can apply the CLT and say that $\bar{x}$ is normally distributed. We can also apply the formulas from Section 7.3 and say that:

$$\mu_{\bar{x}} = \mu = 14.88 \quad \text{and} \quad \sigma_{\bar{x}} \approx \frac{\sigma}{\sqrt{n}} = \frac{9.0507}{\sqrt{50}} \approx 1.2800$$

So, putting it all together, we say that $\bar{x}$ is normally distributed with $\mu_{\bar{x}} = 14.88$ and $\sigma_{\bar{x}} \approx 1.2800$.

b) Because part (a) tells us that $\bar{x}$ is normally distributed, we can use an area under a normal curve to answer this question. We will begin with a sketch of the curve to be used and the area to be found.

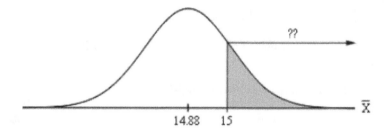

For the z-score we get:

$$z = \frac{\bar{x} - \mu_{\bar{x}}}{\sigma_{\bar{x}}} = \frac{15 - 14.88}{1.2800} \approx 0.094$$

The probability we need is the area to the right of this value under the standard normal curve. We can find that using the normalcdf command and technology.

So, $P(\bar{x} > 15) = normalcdf(0.094, \infty) \approx 0.4626$.

c) Questions about $\sum x$ can quickly be converted to questions about $\bar{x}$ by simply dividing by the sample size, $n = 50$. So, the question becomes : $P\left(\sum x < 675\right) = P\left(\dfrac{\sum x}{50} < \dfrac{675}{50}\right) = P(\bar{x} < 13.5)$. We can now solve this new problem using the area under the appropriate normal curve. We begin with a sketch.

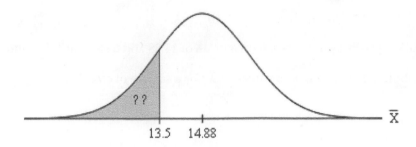

13.5   14.88

For the z-score we get: $z = \dfrac{\bar{x} - \mu_{\bar{x}}}{\sigma_{\bar{x}}} = \dfrac{13.5 - 14.88}{1.2800} \approx -1.078$

The probability we need is the area to the left of this value under the standard normal curve. We can find that using the normalcdf command and technology.

$P\left(\sum x < 675\right) = P\left(\bar{x} < 13.5\right) = normalcdf\left(-\infty, -1.078\right) \approx 0.1405$.

> **Caution:** *What becomes normal?*
>
> It is important to note that large sample sizes do not change the shape of the population to normal. Large samples create a normal distribution shape in the set of all possible $\bar{x}$'s from samples of that size drawn from the population.

d) The population distribution is not stated in the original problem and it remains an unknown. A large sample does not change the shape of the population.

Let's now return to the probability questions that had us stumped at the end of Section 7.3.

Example 7.17: *Sampling Error for Home Prices*

The prices of all new homes in a certain town have a mean of $578,948 with a standard deviation of $158,724.

a) What is the distribution of the population in this problem?

b) For samples of size 37, determine the sampling distribution of $\bar{x}$.

c) If we were to randomly select 37 new homes from this town, what is the probability that the total price of the 37 homes would exceed $20,000,000?

How much error should we expected when estimating the mean home price for a city?

d) What is the probability that the error obtained when estimating the mean of all homes by the mean of a sample of size 37 would be less than $25,000?

e) If we increase the sample size from 37 to 100, what will happen to the probability that the error obtained when estimating the mean of all homes by $\bar{x}$ will be less than $25,000?

Solution:

a) The distribution of the population is not stated. Variables based on price, often are right-skewed, so that would be my guess about this population, but that is just speculation.

b) Because the sample size is $37 \geq 30$, we can apply the CLT and say that $\bar{x}$ is normally distributed (regardless of the distribution of the population). We can also apply the formulas from Section 7.3 and say that:

$$\mu_{\bar{x}} = \mu = 578{,}948 \quad \text{and} \quad \sigma_{\bar{x}} \approx \frac{\sigma}{\sqrt{n}} = \frac{158{,}724}{\sqrt{37}} \approx 26{,}094$$

So, putting it all together, we say that the possible values of $\bar{x}$ are normally distributed with $\mu_{\bar{x}} = 578{,}948$ and $\sigma_{\bar{x}} \approx 26{,}094$.

c) This is a question about a sample total, $\sum x$. So, we will begin by converting it to a question about $\bar{x}$.

$$P\left(\sum x > 20,000,000\right) = P\left(\frac{\sum x}{37} > \frac{20,000,000}{37}\right) \approx P(\bar{x} > 540,541)$$

Because part (b) tells us that $\bar{x}$ is normally distributed, we can use an area under a normal curve to answer this question. We will begin with a sketch of the curve to be used and the area to be found.

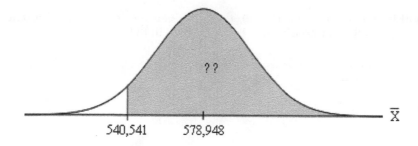

For the z-score we get: $z = \dfrac{\bar{x} - \mu_{\bar{x}}}{\sigma_{\bar{x}}} = \dfrac{540,541 - 578948}{26094} \approx -1.510$

The probability we need is the area to the right of this value under the standard normal curve. We can find that using the normalcdf command and technology.

So, $P\left(\sum x > 20,000,000\right) \approx P(\bar{x} > 540,541) = normalcdf\left(-1.510, \infty\right) \approx 0.9345$

d) Let's begin by rephrasing the question in symbols.

$$P(578948 - 25000 < \bar{x} < 578948 + 25000) = P(553948 < \bar{x} < 603948)$$

Again, we will use an area under a normal curve to answer this question. We will begin with a sketch of the curve to be used and the area to be found.

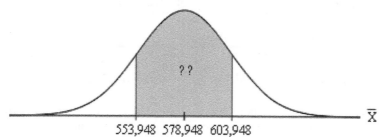

For the z-scores we get:

$$z1 = \frac{\bar{x} - \mu_{\bar{x}}}{\sigma_{\bar{x}}} = \frac{553,948 - 578948}{26094} \approx -0.958 \text{ and } z2 = \frac{\bar{x} - \mu_{\bar{x}}}{\sigma_{\bar{x}}} = \frac{603,948 - 578948}{26094} \approx 0.958$$

The probability we need is the area between these two values under the standard normal curve. We can find that using the normalcdf command and technology.

So, $P(553948 < \bar{x} < 603948) = normalcdf\left(-0.958, 0.958\right) \approx 0.6619$

e) Because $n = 100 \geq 30$, we will still have a normally distributed $\bar{x}$ (by the CLT). In symbols, the question remains the same.

$$P(578948 - 25000 < \bar{x} < 578948 + 25000) = P(553948 < \bar{x} < 603948)$$

However, we are now working with a different standard deviation for $\bar{x}$.

$$\sigma_{\bar{x}} \approx \frac{\sigma}{\sqrt{n}} = \frac{158{,}724}{\sqrt{100}} = 15{,}872.4$$

The basic sketch will be the same as in part (c), though because our standard deviation is now smaller, the curve will be narrower, and the boundaries will be further out in the tails.

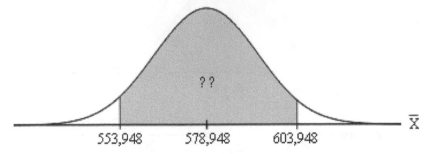

For the z-scores we now get:

$$z_1 = \frac{\bar{x} - \mu_{\bar{x}}}{\sigma_{\bar{x}}} = \frac{553{,}948 - 578948}{15{,}872.4} \approx -1.575 \quad \text{and} \quad z_2 = \frac{\bar{x} - \mu_{\bar{x}}}{\sigma_{\bar{x}}} = \frac{603{,}948 - 578948}{15{,}872.4} \approx 1.575$$

The probability we need is the area between these two values under the standard normal curve. We can find that using the normalcdf command on the TI-84.

So, $P(553948 < \bar{x} < 603948) = normalcdf(-1.575,\ 1.575) \approx 0.8847$

Increasing the sample size from 37 to 100 increased our chance of getting sample error of less than $25,000 from 66.19% chance to a 88.47% chance. If less than $25,000 is considered an acceptable amount of error, then we have reduced our chance of getting an unacceptable amount of error from 33.91% (using the complement rule 1 − 0.6619 = 0.3391) to 11.53% (1 − 0.8847 = 0.1153).

LOOKING DEEPER: *Why does the central limit theorem work?*

While the proof of the Central Limit Theorem is not appropriate for an introductory course, the reasons behind it are not that hard to understand. To see the ideas in action, let's take a look at the theorem applied to the uniform from 0 to 10 distribution. Recall, the uniform distribution is one where all possible numbers are equally likely to occur. The shape of the population is flat or horizontal. The graph of the population is shown below.

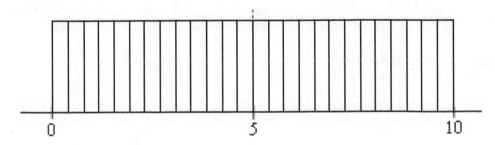

Now, suppose we take a sample of size 33 from this distribution. The shape of the sample should approximate the shape of the population, so the 33 values should be scattered somewhat evenly (or uniformly) throughout the range from 0 to 10. The graph below shows such a sample, represented by the 33 purple circles. Notice that these values are spread out somewhat uniformly from 0 to 10, just like the population they were drawn from.

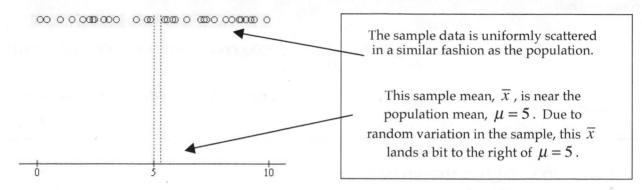

The sample data is uniformly scattered in a similar fashion as the population.

This sample mean, $\overline{x}$, is near the population mean, $\mu = 5$. Due to random variation in the sample, this $\overline{x}$ lands a bit to the right of $\mu = 5$.

Now, because the sample values are spread evenly throughout the range from 0 to 10, where will the sample mean, $\overline{x}$, end up? It should be in the middle (or center). Certainly, it is possible that with a random sample, we might get a few more value showing up on the right side of the population mean than on the left. This might result in an $\overline{x}$ that falls slightly to the right the population mean of 5. However, it is still roughly in the center. You might argue: But it is random, so maybe 20 out of the 33 values sampled will be to the right of the population mean. Perhaps even 25 out of 33 or even 33 out of 33 on the right side of the population mean is possible. The response is: Yes, these things are possible, but the more unbalanced a sample you are looking for, the more unlikely it is to happen. Therefore, the further you get from the population mean of 5, the less likely it is that a sample will create a value of $\overline{x}$ that falls there.

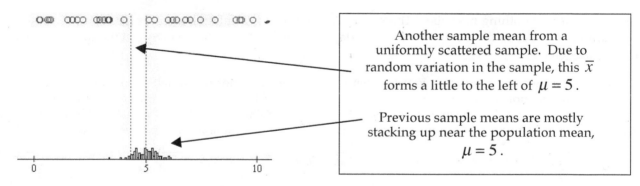

Another sample mean from a uniformly scattered sample. Due to random variation in the sample, this $\overline{x}$ forms a little to the left of $\mu = 5$.

Previous sample means are mostly stacking up near the population mean, $\mu = 5$.

In the distribution of the values of $\overline{x}$, this fact shows up in that the highest part of the curve is at the number 5 and the height decreases as you move to the left or the right. The histogram shown represents nearly a million values of $\overline{x}$ from nearly a million different random samples from the population, uniform 0 to 10. This many $\overline{x}$'s should give us a good sense of the actual distribution of $\overline{x}$ for samples of size 33.

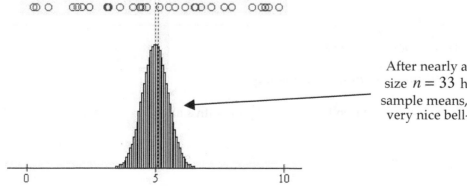

After nearly a million samples of size $n = 33$ have been taken, the sample means, $\overline{x}'s$, are forming a very nice bell-shaped histogram.

Note: No values of $\bar{x}$ can be seen between 0 and 1 on the graph. Why not? Is it possible to get a value of $\bar{x}$ to lie there? Yes it is possible, but extremely unlikely. One way you could get such a value of $\bar{x}$ would be if all 33 of your data values were between 0 and 1. There is a 10% chance that any randomly selected value from the uniform 0 to 10 distribution would lie between 0 and 1. We want all 33 to lie in this region. The chance of that is computed below.

$$P\left(\text{All 33 values of x are below 1}\right) = \left(\frac{1}{10}\right)^{33} = 0.000000000000000000000000000000001$$

With this probability in mind, perhaps it isn't at all shocking that we have no values of $\bar{x}$ on the far left side of the graph!

THE STANDARDIZED VERSION OF $\bar{x}$

As we have seen in previous chapters, the way we standardize a variable is to convert it from its normal units to the number of standard deviations away from its mean. This is always accomplished by using a z-score formula. The same is true with values of $\bar{x}$, but it is worth a special mention here because the formula looks a little different and we will use it a lot. The standardized version of $\bar{x}$ is given by:

$$z = \frac{\bar{x} - \mu_{\bar{x}}}{\sigma_{\bar{x}}} \Rightarrow z \approx \frac{\bar{x} - \mu}{\sigma / \sqrt{n}}$$

In a way, there is nothing new about these formulas, but when calculating z-scores for $\bar{x}$, we always need to be careful to remember to divide by the standard deviation of $\bar{x}$ ($\sigma_{\bar{x}}$) rather than by just the standard deviation of the population (σ).

The other point worth mentioning is that when you standardize a normal variable, you always get a z-score that has the standard normal distribution. That means that any theorem that guarantees us a normal $\bar{x}$, is also guaranteeing us a standard normal z (for $\bar{x}$). The following point to remember summarizes the conditions under which $\bar{x}$ will be normal and, therefore, under which z will have the standard normal distribution.

> **Point to Remember:** *Three ways to know that $\bar{x}$ is normally distributed.*
>
> - The population is normal $\Rightarrow$ $\bar{x}$ is normal (*regardless of the sample size*)
> - Sample size $n \geq 30$ $\Rightarrow$ $\bar{x}$ is normal (*regardless of population's shape*)
> - Sample size $15 \leq n < 30$ *and* population not severely skewed $\Rightarrow$ $\bar{x}$ is normal
>
> **Note:** If your sample does not meet any of the three conditions listed above, then $\bar{x}$'s distribution is unknown.

Let's take a moment to explore these ideas in an example.

Example 7.18: *Working with the standardized version of $\bar{x}$*

Suppose that a sample of size $n = 50$ is taken from a population with a mean, $\mu = 30.4$, and a standard deviation, $\sigma = 5.8$.

a) What is the distribution $\bar{x}$?

b) Find $P\left(\mu - \dfrac{\sigma}{\sqrt{n}} < \bar{x} < \mu + \dfrac{\sigma}{\sqrt{n}}\right)$

c)   Find $P\left(\mu - 3\dfrac{\sigma}{\sqrt{n}} < \bar{x} < \mu + 3\dfrac{\sigma}{\sqrt{n}}\right)$

d)   Determine the standardized version of $\bar{x}$, and state its distribution.

Solution:

a)   Because $n = 50 \geq 30$, we know (by the CLT) that $\bar{x}$ is normally distributed regardless of the distribution of the population. We are not done yet, because we still need to know the mean and standard deviation of $\bar{x}$. The formulas from Section 7.3 help us with that.

$$\mu_{\bar{x}} = \mu = 30.4 \quad \text{and} \quad \sigma_{\bar{x}} \approx \frac{\sigma}{\sqrt{n}} = \frac{5.8}{\sqrt{50}} \approx 0.82024$$

So, we can say that the possible values of $\bar{x}$ are normally distributed with $\mu_{\bar{x}} = 30.4$ and $\sigma_{\bar{x}} \approx 0.82024$

b)   The only real work here is translation. $P\left(\mu - \dfrac{\sigma}{\sqrt{n}} < \bar{x} < \mu + \dfrac{\sigma}{\sqrt{n}}\right)$ can be translated "the probability that $\bar{x}$

lies within 1 standard deviation of its mean. Because $\bar{x}$ is normally distributed, we can answer this using the empirical rule for normally distributed variables. From Section 6.3 we know that for any normally distributed random variable, x:

$$P(\mu_x - \sigma_x < x < \mu_x + \sigma_x) \approx 0.6827$$

This is true for any normally distributed random variable, including our $\bar{x}$ from this problem. So substituting $\bar{x}$ for x we get:

$$P(\mu_{\bar{x}} - \sigma_{\bar{x}} < \bar{x} < \mu_{\bar{x}} + \sigma_{\bar{x}}) \approx 0.6827 \Rightarrow P\left(\mu - \frac{\sigma}{\sqrt{n}} < \bar{x} < \mu + \frac{\sigma}{\sqrt{n}}\right) \approx 0.6827$$

c)   This is just like part (b) except that we need to use the value from the empirical rule for the chance that a normally distributed random variable will lie within 3 standard deviations of the mean rather that 1. So we get:

$$P(\mu_{\bar{x}} - 3\sigma_{\bar{x}} < \bar{x} < \mu_{\bar{x}} + 3\sigma_{\bar{x}}) \approx 0.9973 \Rightarrow P\left(\mu - 3\frac{\sigma}{\sqrt{n}} < \bar{x} < \mu + 3\frac{\sigma}{\sqrt{n}}\right) \approx 0.9973$$

d)   To determine the standardized version, z, of $\bar{x}$, we simply use the z-score formula for $\bar{x}$. This gives us:

$$z = \frac{\bar{x} - \mu_{\bar{x}}}{\sigma_{\bar{x}}} \approx \frac{\bar{x} - \mu}{\sigma / \sqrt{n}} = \frac{\bar{x} - 30.4}{5.8 / \sqrt{50}} \approx \frac{\bar{x} - 30.4}{0.82024}$$

Because $\bar{x}$ is normally distributed, z will have the standard normal distribution.

It may seem strange that we do not come up with a specific number for z, but this is not the z-score for a specific value of $\bar{x}$, rather it is a formula for converting any $\bar{x}$ to its corresponding z-score. That is why the $\bar{x}$ remains as a placeholder in the formula.

WRAP SESSION: *Looking Forward to Inferential Statistics*

Let's take a look at one final example to practice and expand the ideas covered so far.

Example 7.19: *Estimating the Mean Commission*

A large pharmaceutical company pays its sales representatives on commission. The income of individual sales reps varies quite a bit, but the average monthly income for all the reps is thought to be $4,582 with a standard deviation of $3,107. Suppose a random sample of 45 sales reps is taken and we obtain the monthly income for each.

a) What is the distribution for the $\bar{x}$'s that are possible for this sample size? Explain.

How accurately can we estimate the mean sales commission for a pharmaceutical sales representative?

b) If the sample mean from the 45 selected sales reps is used as a point estimate for the mean of the population, then what is the expected sampling error?

c) What is the chance that the sampling error would exceed the expected amount from part (b)?

d) For a sample of size 45 determine $P(\bar{x} \geq 5912)$

e) Suppose the sample mean for the 45 reps is $5,912, does this indicate that the mean for all such reps might not be $4,582 as previously thought? Explain.

Solution:

a) Because n = 45 ≥ 30, we know that $\bar{x}$ is normally distributed (by the CLT). As always, we must specify the mean and standard deviation for the normal distribution.

$$\mu_{\bar{x}} = \mu = 4582 \quad \text{and} \quad \sigma_{\bar{x}} \approx \frac{\sigma}{\sqrt{n}} = \frac{3107}{\sqrt{45}} \approx 463.16$$

So, we say that $\bar{x}$ is normally distributed with $\mu_{\bar{x}} = \$4582$ and $\sigma_{\bar{x}} \approx \$463.16$

b) We always expect a random variable to be within 2 standard deviations of its mean. So here, we expect $\bar{x}$ to be within $2\sigma_{\bar{x}}$ of μ. So, substituting in the relevant numbers, we can say we expect $\bar{x}$ to lie within 2(463.16) = $926.32 of the true mean monthly income for the sales reps. So, we conclude that our expected error is less than $926.32.

c) For any normally distributed random variable, we have a 95.45% chance of being within 2 standard deviations of the mean. This $\bar{x}$ is normally distributed, so that percent applies here as well. However, we were asked the chance that our error would exceed the expected amount, so we must use the complement rule. The chance that the sampling error will exceed $926.32 is:

$$1 - 0.9545 = 0.0455 = 4.55\%$$

d) Because $\bar{x}$ is normally distributed, this is a fairly straightforward process. We just need to find the area to the right of \$5912. Let's begin with a sketch.

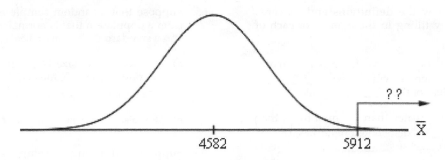

The z-score for \$5912 is given by $z = \dfrac{\bar{x} - \mu_{\bar{x}}}{\sigma_{\bar{x}}} \approx \dfrac{5912 - 4582}{463.16} \approx 3.049$ and it is shown on the graph above.

Notice that with such a large z-score, the area in question is very small. Let's use the normalcdf function and technology to find it.

$$P(\bar{x} \geq 5912) = normalcdf(3.049, \infty) \approx 0.0011 = 0.11\% \text{ chance}$$

e) Part (d) gives us the insight we need for this question. First of all, if the true mean for all the sales reps is really \$4512, then it would be very unusual to get a mean of \$5912 for a sample of 45 reps. We can say this, because the z-score for \$5912 is 3.049. We can quantify what we mean by unusual in this case, because we calculated the chance of getting a sample mean that large or larger to be only 0.11% if the true mean is really \$4582. So we are faced with two choices.

Choice 1: The true mean of the population really is \$4582 as thought, but we got a larger sample mean just due to random variation.

Choice 2: The population mean is actually larger than the previously thought value of \$4582.

We are generally willing to accept difference from an expected mean as being due to random variation provided that there is more than a 5% chance of seeing such a difference just due to random variation. However, if choice 1 is the truth, then it would be very unlikely (0.11% chance) that we would see a value of $\bar{x}$ that is \$5912 or larger. If choice 2 is the truth, then such a value for $\bar{x}$ would not be as unexpected. Because we did, in fact, see such a large value of $\bar{x}$, I feel this does indicate that the mean for all such reps might not be \$4,582 as previously thought. (We will explore questions such as this one is much greater detail in Chapter 9.)

Time to practice what we have learned with some exercises.

Exercise Set 7.4:

Concept Review: Review the definitions and concepts from this section by filling in the blanks for each of the following.

57) If our sample is taken from a normal _____ , then $\bar{x}$ will also be _____ distributed, regardless of the _____ size.

58) If our sample size is greater than or equal to 30, then $\bar{x}$ will be _____ distributed regardless of the distribution of the original _____ . This is the statement of the _____ _____ Theorem.

59) If the sample size is $15 \le n < 30$, and if the population is not severely _____ , then ___ will be normal.

60) *True or False*? If our sample size is greater than or equal to 30, the population will become normal.

61) When calculating z-scores involving sample means, make sure that you use the standard deviation of ___ rather than the _____ standard deviation.

62) Typically, the best way to increase your chance of obtaining a satisfactory estimate of the population mean is to increase your _____ _____ .

Mechanics: Practice the calculations needed for this section before moving on to the real world applications.

63) Suppose that a random sample is going to be taken from a population that has a mean of 153.7 and a standard deviation of 16.973.
   a) For a randomly selected item, find
   $$P(147 < x \le 155).$$
   b) For samples of size 85, what is the distribution of all possible sample means? Explain.
   c) For $n = 85$, determine $P(147 < \bar{x} \le 155)$.

64) Suppose that a random sample is going to be taken from a population that has a mean of 31.09 and a standard deviation of 14.2.
   a) For a randomly selected item, find
   $$P(30 \le x < 35).$$
   b) For samples of size 47, what is the distribution of all possible sample means? Explain.
   c) For $n = 47$, determine $P(30 \le \bar{x} < 35)$.

65) Suppose that a random sample is going to be taken from a population that is normal with a mean of 23.88 and a standard deviation of 3.561.

   a) For samples of size 14, what is the distribution of all possible sample means? Explain.
   b) For a sample of size 14, determine $P(\bar{x} < 22)$.
   c) For a sample of size 14, find $P\left(\sum x \ge 322\right)$.

66) Suppose that a random sample is going to be taken from a population that is normal with a mean of 287.55 and a standard deviation of 40.57.

   a) For samples of size 23, what is the distribution of all possible sample means? Explain.
   b) For a sample of size 23, determine $P(\bar{x} > 275)$.
   c) For a sample of size 23, find $P\left(\sum x \le 6463\right)$.

67) Suppose that a random sample is going to be taken from a Uniform population with a mean of 36.74 and a standard deviation of 5.0807.

   a) For samples of size 19, what is the distribution for all possible values of $\bar{x}$? Explain.
   b) Determine that the probability that the sampling error from a sample of size 19 will be less than 2.
   c) Determine that the probability that the sampling error from a sample of size 19 will be less than 3.

68) Suppose that a random sample is going to be taken from a population that is severely right-skewed with a mean of 5.07 and a standard deviation of 14.864.

   a) For samples of size 107, what is the distribution for all possible values of $\bar{x}$? Explain.
   b) Determine that the probability that the sampling error from a sample of size 107 will be less than 2.5.
   c) Suppose we increased our sample size to 210. Determine that the probability that the sampling error from a sample of size 107 will be less than 2.5.

Applications: Practice the ideas learned in this section within the context of real world applications.

69) A company produces cans of minestrone soup. They state that the number of calories per can is a normally distributed variable with a mean of 200 and a standard deviation of 10.48.

   a) For a random sample of size 15, what is the distribution of all possible sample means? Explain.
   b) For a random sample of size 15, determine the probability that the mean of the sample is more than 210 calories.
   c) Find the probability that the sampling error from a random sample of 15 cans will be less than 5 calories.

70) A pest control company uses a certain pesticide as a perimeter barrier for residential customers. The pesticide has a mean effectiveness time of 37.8 days with a standard deviation of 7.8 days. Suppose that a random sample of 50 homes is chosen and the effectiveness time is measured for each application of the pesticide.

 a) What is the distribution for possible samples means? Explain.
 b) Determine the probability that the sample mean obtained will be less than 40 days.
 c) Determine the probability that the sampling error from a sample of 50 homes will be less than 3 days.

71) The scores for an amateur league bowler are slightly right skewed with a mean of 185 and a standard deviation of 15 points. Suppose that a league official is unaware of this, but plans to use a random sample of size 28 games to estimate this player's true average score.

 a) What is the distribution of all possible sample means? Explain.
 b) Suppose that the sampling error will be considered acceptable as long as it is less than 5 points. Determine the probability that the sampling error will be acceptable.
 c) Repeat part (b) if the acceptable level of sampling error is 10 points.
 d) Determine the probability that the total for the 28 randomly selected games is at least 5000.
 e) Give a logical explanation for why we had a higher chance of getting an acceptable amount of error in part (c) compared to part (b).

72) The wingspans of adult female bald eagles are normally distributed with a mean of 84.5 inches and a standard deviation of 2.75 inches. A researcher unaware of this fact plans on estimating the wingspan of adult female bald eagles using the mean from a random sample of size 23 as a point estimate.

 a) What is the distribution of all possible sample means? Explain.
 b) Suppose that the sampling error will be considered acceptable as long as it is less than 1 inch. Determine the probability that the sampling error will be acceptable.
 c) Repeat part (b) if the acceptable level of sampling error is 2 inches.
 d) Give a logical explanation for why we had a higher chance of getting an acceptable amount of error in part (c) compared to part (b).

73) On March 12th, 2007, the national average for a gallon of regular unleaded gasoline was $2.559 with a standard deviation of $0.3427. Suppose that we take a random sample of 45 gas stations and use the sample mean as a point estimate for the population mean national gas price.

 a) What is the distribution of all possible sample means? Explain.
 b) Suppose that the sampling error will be considered acceptable as long as it is less than $0.05. Determine the probability that the sampling error will be acceptable.
 c) Suppose that our point estimate will be computed from a sample of size 500 rather than of 45. Determine the probability that the sampling error would be less than $0.05.
 d) Give a logical explanation for why we have a higher chance of getting an acceptable amount of error when we increase our sample size.

74) In February 2010, Twitter reported that its users were averaging 50 million tweets per day. Assume that the standard deviation was 10 million tweets. Suppose that a tech reporter was attempting to estimate this number around that time using the mean from a random sample of size 35 days.

 a) What is the distribution of all possible sample means? Explain.
 b) Suppose that the sampling error will be considered acceptable as long as it is less than 2.5 million tweets. Determine the probability that the sampling error will be acceptable.
 c) Suppose that our point estimate will be computed from a sample of size 90 days rather than of 35. Determine the probability that the sampling error would be less than 2.5 million tweets.
 d) Give a logical explanation for why we have a higher chance of getting an acceptable amount of error when we increase our sample size.
 e) Determine the probability that the total number of tweets for 35 randomly selected days from that time period would be less than 1.9 billion tweets.

75) A statistics teacher has been teaching introductory statistics for years. She knows that the average score on her final exam is 82.7 points with a standard deviation of 12.584. Suppose that she is going to use a random sample of 43 students to estimate this mean.

a) What is the distribution of all possible sample means for our sample of 43 students? Explain.

b) Assuming that the true mean and standard deviation remain as described above, determine the probability that the sample of 43 students will produce a mean score on the final of 80 points or less.

c) If the sample of 43 students does produce a mean final exam score of 80 points, would you say that is strong evidence that something has changed and her true average is now less than 82.7 points, or is it plausible that this difference from the stated 82.7 is just random variation? Explain using your answer to part (b).

d) Assuming that the true mean and standard deviation remain as described above, determine the probability that the sample of 43 students will produce a mean score on the final of 76 points or less.

e) If the sample of 43 students does produce a mean final exam score of 76 points, would you say that is strong evidence that something has changed and her true average is now less than 82.7 points, or is it plausible that this difference from the stated 82.7 is just random variation? Explain using your answer to part (d).

76) Tim Lincecum is a Cy Young Award winning pitcher. Suppose that his true mean ERA per game is 2.98 with a standard deviation of 2.0335. We want to estimate his current mean ERA per game based on a sample of 31 games.

a) What is the distribution of all possible sample means for our sample of size 31 games? Explain.

b) Assuming that Tim's true mean and standard deviation remain as described above, determine the probability that the sample of 31 games will produce a mean ERA of 3.44 or higher.

c) If the sample of 31 games does produce a mean ERA of 3.44, would you say that is strong evidence that Tim's true average ERA is more than 2.98, or is it plausible that this difference from the stated 2.98 is just random variation? Explain using your answer to part (b).

d) Assuming that Tim's true mean and standard deviation remain as described above, determine the probability that the sample of 31 games will produce a mean ERA of 4.05 or higher.

e) If the sample of 31 games does produce a mean ERA of 4.05, would you say that is strong evidence that Tim's true average ERA is more than 2.98, or is it plausible that this difference from the stated 2.98 is just random variation? Explain using your answer to part (d).

Chapter Problem: To Catch a Thief

Directions: Read through the story below and answer the questions that arise.

A company produces a standard size can of soda. This means they are labeled as containing 12 fluid ounces. When the volume for the cans is put on the label, the amount is understood to be the mean amount for all such cans. Suppose that the standard deviation for *all* the cans this company produces is known to be 0.2306 oz.

A consumer group is suspicious that this company might be trying to save a little money by, on average, under filling their cans. They decide to test the company's claim about the cans containing, on average, 12 ounces. They start by obtaining a random sample of 40 cans of the soda and measuring the contents in each can and then using the mean of this sample as a point estimate for the mean of all the cans.

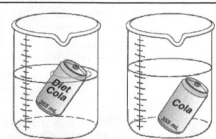

If we accept that the amount of soda in cans will vary, then is there a way to use a random sample to decide if we are being cheated?

a) If they decided to accuse the company of cheating their customers provided that the point estimate is less than 12 ounces, then what is the chance they will make a false accusation, assuming that the company actually fills the cans with an average of 12 ounces? In symbols, find $P(\bar{x} < 12 \mid \mu = 12)$.

b) Does your answer to part (a) require that the population be normally distributed? Explain.

The consumer group would not like to take such a high risk of making a false accusation, so they decide that they will only accuse the company of under filling their cans if their point estimate is less than 11.9 ounces.

c) If the soda company really does produce an average amount of 12 ounces, what is the chance that the consumer group will make a false accusation under their new criteria? Find $P(\bar{x} < 11.9 \mid \mu = 12)$. Do you think this is a low enough chance of making a false accusation?

Suppose the soda company actually puts only 11.95 ounces in their cans, on average, figuring it will save them money, and the cautious consumer group will be afraid to falsely accuse them of under filling.

d) With this new assumption about the soda company, what is the chance that the cautious consumer group will get a point estimate that does lead to a correct accusation that company is under filling their cans? Do you think the soda company will get away with it?
Hint: you must find $P(\bar{x} < 11.9 \mid \mu = 11.95)$

e) See what happens to your answer to part (d) if the soda company only puts 11.85 ounces, on average in their cans? *Hint*: now you must find $P(\bar{x} < 11.9 \mid \mu = 11.85)$. Do you think the soda company will get away with it?

f) See what happens to your answer to part (d) if the soda company only puts 11.6 ounces, on average in their cans? Do you think the soda company will get away with it?

g) Can a sample of only 40 cans really provide enough evidence to catch a cheating company? Explain.

Chapter 7: Technology Project

1) For this problem, we will use the application 'Proportion Sim' from the StatSims folder.
   a) Enter your name into the textbox on the upper right of the window. Enter 893 for the number of trials (this is our sample size) and 0.753 in the textbox for the true probability of a success (this is the population proportion).
   B) Completely determine the distribution of the possible sample proportions. Show work.
   C) Calculate the probability that $\hat{p}$ will lie within 0.03 of the true probability (or proportion). Do this using your answer to part (B). (Show your work and include a sketch of the graph used.)
   d) Enter 0.783 in the textbox for the observed proportion of successes (this represents a sampling error of 3% or 0.03). Click the Automatic button and let it run until you have at least 1,000,000 samples taken, then click the pause button.
   e) Use the ALT / PRINT SCREEN keys to copy and paste this window to your report.
   F) The red portions of the graph represent the values of $\hat{p}$ that lie more than 0.03 away from the true proportion. The percentage of $\hat{p}$'s that landed in each of these tails is shown in the output. Subtract these percentages from 100% to determine the percentage of the $\hat{p}$'s that actually landed within 0.03 of the true proportion. This represents the percentage of your $\hat{p}$'s that landed in the black region of the graph.
   G) Did you get the shape for the $\hat{p}$'s that you expected? Do the values of the mean and standard deviation of these sample proportions listed in the windows *exactly* match what you calculated in parts (B)? Was there a difference between your answers to parts (C) and (F)?
   H) Why are things not exactly matching up with your expectations? **Choose one of the following explanations for the differences in part (G):** Are the differences small enough so that random variation is a reasonable explanation for the differences? Or are the differences so big that you would consider it strong evidence that something has gone wrong?

2) This problem uses the application 'Central Limit Theorem' from the StatSims folder.
   a) Enter your name into the textbox on the upper right of the window. Enter a sample size of 17 and select a Uniform Population. Enter a population mean of 20 and a population standard deviation of 5.
   B) Write out with the blanks filled in: Because ____ $\leq n =$ _____ < _____ and the population has a _____ distribution (which is symmetric and not skewed at all), I would expect that the _____ would be normally distributed.
   C) Calculate the mean and standard deviation for all possible sample means of samples of size 17. Use formulas from Section 7.3 and the population mean and standard deviation given in part (a) above.
   d) Click automatic. Once the number of samples reaches at least 3,000,000 click pause and the draw curve button.
   e) Use the ALT / PRINT SCREEN keys to copy and paste this window to your report.
   F) Did you roughly get the shape for the $\bar{x}$'s that you expected? Do the values of the mean and standard deviation of these sample means listed in the windows roughly match what you calculated in part (C)? What is the best explanation for the differences between your theoretical calculations and the results of the simulation?
   G) Write out with the blanks filled in: The following three facts were illustrated: Because the mean of my $\bar{x}$ values was _____ , which is close to 20, we have illustrated the formula $\mu_{\bar{x}} = \mu$; Because the standard deviation of my 3,000,000+ values of $\bar{x}$ was _____ , which is close to 1.2127, we have illustrated the formula $\sigma_{\bar{x}} \approx$ _____ ; Also, despite the fact the distribution of the _____ was not normal, the possible values of ____ were normally distributed (because _____ $\leq n <$ _____ and the population was not _____ _____). These three facts illustrate Theorem 7.___ .

Chapter 7: Chapter Review

Section 7.1: The Mean and Standard Deviation of the Sample Proportion, $\hat{p}$

- The population proportion, p, is the true proportion of successes in the population.
- The sample proportion, $\hat{p}$, is the proportion of successes in a sample.
- $\hat{p} = \dfrac{x}{n}$ where x is the number of successes in a sample of size n.
- A Parameter is the general name given to a population quantity. For example: p, μ, and σ are all parameters.
- A Statistics in the general name given to a quantity computed from sample data. For example: $\hat{p}$, $\bar{x}$, and s are all statistics.
- A point estimate is the name given to a statistic that is used as an estimate for a parameter.
- $\hat{p}$ is a point estimate for p. $\bar{x}$ is a point estimate for μ. s is a point estimate for σ.
- Sampling error is the difference between a point estimate and the corresponding parameter. For example: if $\hat{p}$ is used as a point estimate for p, then the sampling error is given by $|\hat{p} - p|$.
- When we make estimates using a sample, we expect there to be sampling error. In fact, it is often impossible to get the exact right answer for the population value using a sample. $P(\hat{p} = p) \approx 0$ and $P(\bar{x} = \mu) \approx 0$.
- The average of all possible sample proportions for a given sample size is the population proportion. $\mu_{\hat{p}} = p$
- The standard deviation of all possible sample proportions for a given sample size is given by $\sigma_{\hat{p}} = \sqrt{\dfrac{pq}{n}}$.
- We expect the value of $\hat{p}$ to be within 2 standard deviations of the true population proportion, p. In symbols: $|\hat{p} - p| < 2\sigma_{\hat{p}}$ or $|\hat{p} - p| < 2\sqrt{\dfrac{pq}{n}}$
- The expected error formula above show us that we expect to have less error in our estimates as the sample size gets larger.

Section 7.2: The Sampling Distribution of $\hat{p}$

- If $np \geq 10$ and $nq \geq 10$, then $\hat{p}$ will be approximately normally distributed.
- If you are willing to accept more sampling error, then it will be more likely that you will get an acceptable estimate from your random sample. This is considered to be lowering your standards.
- A better way to increase your chance of obtaining an acceptable estimate from a random sample is to increase the sample size.
- To calculate the probability that your sampling error will be less than some amount, E, you should calculate the following: $P(p - E < \hat{p} < p + E)$.
- If the difference between our sample result and the expected result has more than a 5% chance of occurring due to random chance, then we say it is reasonable to believe that random variation is the explanation for this difference.
- If the difference between our sample result and the expected result has less than a 5% chance of occurring due to random chance, then we feel that another explanation should be sought out. We say that the sample is providing convincing evidence that random variation is not a reasonable explanation.

Section 7.3: The Mean and Standard Deviation of the Sample Mean, $\overline{x}$

- $\overline{x}$ is a random variable and, therefore, all the formulas pertaining to random variables apply to $\overline{x}$.
- It is typical for $P(\overline{x} = \mu) \approx 0$.
- If a sample of size n will be taken from a population with a mean of μ and a standard deviation of σ,

  then for the random variable $\overline{x}$, we get: $\mu_{\overline{x}} = \mu$ and $\sigma_{\overline{x}} \approx \dfrac{\sigma}{\sqrt{n}}$.

- We expect the value of $\overline{x}$ to be within 2 standard deviations of the true population mean, μ. In

  symbols: $|\overline{x} - \mu| < 2\sigma_{\overline{x}}$ or $|\overline{x} - \mu| < 2\dfrac{\sigma}{\sqrt{n}}$

- We may in fact get sample error larger than indicated above. However, this would mean that $\overline{x}$ was more than two standard deviations away from its mean, which would be unusual.
- The formulas for expected error above show us that we expect less error when we increase the sample size.

Section 7.4: The Sampling Distribution of $\overline{x}$

- If we take our samples from a normal population, then the random variable $\overline{x}$ will also be normally distributed.
- When we calculate a z-score for a value of $\overline{x}$, we must make sure that we divide by $\sigma_{\overline{x}}$ rather than σ.
- The Central Limit Theorem tells us that the larger our sample size, the more normally distributed the random variable $\overline{x}$ tends to be.
- **Large Samples**: If $n \geq 30$, then $\overline{x}$ will be normally distributed regardless of the population's distribution.
- **Medium Samples**: If $15 \leq n < 30$, then $\overline{x}$ will be normally distributed as long as the population is not severely skewed. A sample containing outliers is often an indication of a skewed population.
- **Small Samples**: If $n < 15$, then we return to Theorem 7.4 and require a normally distributed population.
- Large samples do not change the shape of the population to normal. Large samples create a normal distribution shape in the set of all possible $\overline{x}$'s from samples of that size drawn from the population.

- The standardized version of $\overline{x}$ is given by the formula: $z = \dfrac{\overline{x} - \mu}{\sigma_{\overline{x}}}$ or $z = \dfrac{\overline{x} - \mu}{\sigma/\sqrt{n}}$

Review Diagrams:

The values that we get for the sample proportion, $\hat{p}$, vary from sample to sample. Therefore, $\hat{p}$ is a random variable. The distribution of $\hat{p}$ depends on the value of n, p, and q.

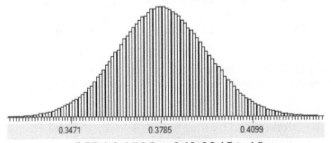

$$np = 957 * 0.3785 = 362.2245 \geq 10 \text{ and}$$
$$nq = 957 * 0.6215 = 594.7755 \geq 10 \quad \Rightarrow$$
$$\hat{p} \text{ is approximately normal.}$$

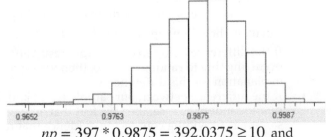

$$np = 397 * 0.9875 = 392.0375 \geq 10 \text{ and}$$
$$nq = 397 * 0.0125 = 4.9625 < 10 \quad \Rightarrow$$
$$\hat{p} \text{ is NOT approximately normal.}$$

The values that we get for the sample mean, $\overline{x}$, vary from sample to sample. Therefore, $\overline{x}$ is a random variable. The distribution of $\overline{x}$ depends on the both the distribution of the population and the size of the sample.

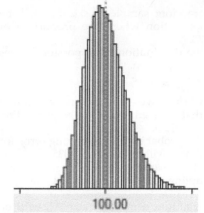

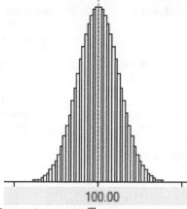

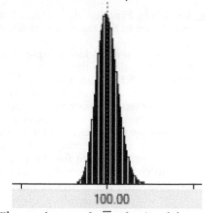

The values of $\overline{x}$ obtained from samples of size 20 from a severely right-skewed population appear to be a little bit right-skewed rather than approximately normal.

The values of $\overline{x}$ obtained from samples of size 20 from a uniform population appear to be approximately normal. This happens because the population is symmetric rather than severely skewed.

The values of $\overline{x}$ obtained from samples of size 67 from a severely right-skewed population appear to be approximately normal. This happens because the sample size is larger than 30.

The larger the sample size, the smaller the standard deviation of our point estimates. This means that there will be a higher percentage of point estimates with an acceptable amount of sampling error.

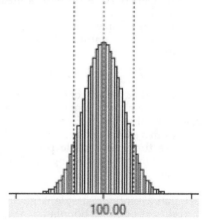

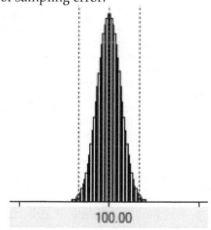

Using a sample size of 20, 86.33% of the point estimates had an acceptable amount of sampling error.

When the sample size was raised to 60, the standard deviation became smaller. This made the point estimates form a narrower and taller curve. This time, 99.04% of the point estimates had an acceptable amount of sampling error.

Chapter 7 – Review Exercises

Mechanics: Practice the calculations needed before moving on to the real world applications.

1) Suppose that a random sample of size 19 will be taken from a population that is severely left-skewed with a mean of 185.1 and a standard deviation of 39.055.
   a) Determine the mean of all possible sample means obtained from samples of size 19.
   b) Determine the standard deviation of all possible sample means obtained from samples of size 19.
   c) If you used the mean from a sample of size 19 as a point estimate for the population mean, how much sampling error would you expect?
   d) Suppose the point estimate was $\bar{x} = 179.6$. How much sampling error does this estimate have?

2) Suppose that a random sample of size 12 will be taken from a population that is U-shaped with a mean of 17.82 and a standard deviation of 5.6607.
   a) Determine the mean of all possible sample means obtained from samples of size 12.
   b) Determine the standard deviation of all possible sample means obtained from samples of size 12.
   c) If you used the mean from a sample of size 12 as a point estimate for the population mean, how much sampling error would you expect?
   d) Suppose the point estimate was $\bar{x} = 19.33$. How much sampling error does this estimate have?

3) Suppose that a random sample of size 57 will be taken from a two-category population where the true probability of a success is 0.9144.
   a) Determine the mean of all possible sample proportions obtained from samples of size 57.
   b) Determine the standard deviation of all possible sample proportions from samples of size 57.
   c) If you used the proportion from a sample of size 57 as a point estimate for the true population proportion, how much sampling error would you expect?
   d) Suppose the sample contained 54 successes. How much sampling error does this estimate have?

4) Suppose that a random sample of size 107 will be taken from a two-category population where the true probability of a success is 0.0763.
   a) Determine the mean of all possible sample proportions obtained from samples of size 107.
   b) Determine the standard deviation of all possible sample proportions from samples of size 107.
   c) If you used the proportion from a sample of size 107 as a point estimate for the true population proportion, how much sampling error would you expect?
   d) Suppose the sample contained 5 successes. How much sampling error does this estimate have?

5) Suppose that a random sample of size 618 will be taken from a population where the proportion of successes is 0.3773.
   a) Determine the distribution of all possible values of the sample proportion.
   b) Determine $P(\hat{p} > 0.35)$.
   c) Is it likely that we will obtain a sample proportion that is exactly equal to the population proportion? Explain.
   d) Determine the probability the sampling error for the point estimate will be less than 0.035.
   e) Suppose that our sample contains 256 successes. Find the sampling error for the point estimate.

6) Suppose that a random sample of size 372 will be taken from a population where the proportion of successes is 0.6107.
   a) Determine the distribution of all possible values of the sample proportion.
   b) Determine $P(\hat{p} \leq 0.65)$.
   c) Is it likely that we will obtain a sample proportion that is exactly equal to the population proportion? Explain.
   d) Determine the probability the sampling error for the point estimate will be less than 0.03.
   e) Suppose that our sample contains 211 successes. Find the sampling error for the point estimate.

7) Suppose that a random sample is going to be taken from a U-Shaped population with a mean of 306.74 and a standard deviation of 53.807.
   a) For samples of size 26, what is the distribution for all possible values of the sample mean? Explain.
   b) Determine $P\left(\sum x \leq 8320\right)$.
   c) Is it likely that we will obtain a sample mean that is exactly equal to the population mean? Explain.
   d) Determine that the probability that the sampling error from a sample of size 26 will be less than 20.
   e) Suppose that our sample produces a mean of 298.54. Find the sampling error for the point estimate.

8) Suppose that a random sample is going to be taken from a right-exponential population with a mean of 8.621 and a standard deviation of 5.3391.
   a) For samples of size 82, what is the distribution for all possible values of the sample mean? Explain.
   b) Determine $P\left(\sum x > 656\right)$.
   c) Is it likely that we will obtain a sample mean that is exactly equal to the population mean? Explain.
   d) Determine that the probability that the sampling error from a sample of size 82 will be less than 1.25.
   e) Suppose that our sample produces a mean of 9.803. Find the sampling error for the point estimate.

Applications: Practice the ideas learned in this chapter within the context of real world applications.

9) In 2010, the mean summer vacation spending for families of 4 was $4019.77 with a standard deviation of $2861.82. A travel magazine is planning on estimating the average summer vacation spending for families of 4 by using the mean from a random sample of size 152. They will consider it acceptable if their estimate is within $250 of the true mean.
   a) What is the distribution of all possible sample means? Explain.
   b) How much sampling error should they expect from their point estimate?
   c) Determine the probability that their sample of size 152 will result in a point estimate with an acceptable amount of sampling error.
   d) What is the best method for increasing the chance of obtaining an acceptable estimate?
   e) If they increased their sample size to 677 families of 4, then what would be the probability that their sample will result in a point estimate with an acceptable amount of sampling error?
   f) Determine the probability that the total summer vacation spending for a random sample of 152 families of size 4 would be less than $550,000.

10) In 2011, Americans, on average, consumed 47.3 gallons of soda per year with a standard deviation of 30.581 gallons. A health organization wants to estimate the average annual soda consumption for Americans by using a random sample of size 214. They will consider it acceptable if their estimate is within 1.5 gallons of the true mean.
   a) What is the distribution of all possible sample means? Explain.
   b) How much sampling error should they expect from their point estimate?
   c) Determine the probability that their sample of size 214 will result in a point estimate with an acceptable amount of sampling error.
   d) What is the best method for increasing the chance of obtaining an acceptable estimate?
   e) If they increased their sample size to 1674 individuals, then what would be the probability that their sample will result in a point estimate with an acceptable amount of sampling error?
   f) Determine the probability that the total soda consumption per year for 214 randomly selected American would be at least 10,000 gallons.

11) Binge drinking is defined as consuming four or more drinks for women and five or more drinks for men on an occasion. According to a 2012 CDC study, about 12.67% of American adults binge drink on a regular basis. Suppose that at that time, health researchers want to estimate the percentage of adult Americans that binge drink using a sample of 491 people. They will consider it acceptable if their estimate is within 3% of the true percentage.
   a) What is the distribution of all possible sample proportions? Explain.
   b) How much sampling error should they expect from their point estimate?
   c) Determine the probability that their sample of size 491 will result in a point estimate with an acceptable amount of sampling error.
   d) What is the best method for increasing the chance of obtaining an acceptable estimate?
   e) If they increased their sample size to 1291 individuals, then what would be the probability that their sample will result in a point estimate with an acceptable amount of sampling error?

12) In a 2002 article published by the Chronicle of Higher Education, it was reported that 2.7% of college students had falsely claimed that their grandmother had died as an excuse for late schoolwork. Suppose that a statistics teacher at this time was going to take a sample of 513 students with the goal of estimating the true proportion of all college students that had falsely used this excuse. Suppose that he will consider it acceptable if his estimate is within 0.5% of the true proportion.
   a) What is the distribution of all possible sample proportions? Explain.
   b) How much sampling error should he expect from their point estimate?
   c) Determine the probability that his sample of size 513 will result in a point estimate with an acceptable amount of sampling error.
   d) What is the best method for increasing the chance of obtaining an acceptable estimate?
   e) If he increased his sample size to 1485 college students, then what would be the probability that his sample will result in a point estimate with an acceptable amount of sampling error?

13) According to a Gallup poll, 36% of Americans favor legalizing the use of marijuana in 2006. Suppose that this study is to be repeated today using a sample of 1,005 Americans.

a) Assuming that the true proportion of Americans is still the same as it was in 2006, what is the distribution of all possible sample proportions for samples of size 1,005?

b) Assuming that the true proportion of Americans is still the same as it was in 2006, what is the probability that the sample proportion obtained would be at least 50%?

c) If the sample of 1,005 adults did in fact produce a sample proportion of at least 50%, would you say that is strong evidence that the true proportion of Americans that favor legalizing the use of marijuana has increased from the 2006 level , or is it plausible that this difference from the 36% of 2006 is just random variation in the sample? Explain using your answer from part (b).

14) A 2012 study of users of online dating websites revealed that the mean time spent by women to evaluate if a profile was a match was 84 seconds with a standard deviation of 73.2 seconds (based on an article published by the onlinedatingpost.com). Suppose a sample of 37 male users of such services is taken at the same time for the purpose of estimating the true mean time spent by male users to evaluate if a profile was a match.

a) Assuming that the true mean time and standard deviation for male users is the same as it was for the female users, what is the distribution of all possible sample means for samples of size 37?

b) Assuming that the true mean time and standard deviation for male users is the same as it was for the female users, what is the probability that the sample mean obtained would be less than 70 seconds?

c) If the sample of 37 male users did in fact produce a sample mean less than 70 seconds, would you say that is strong evidence that the true mean time spent by male users to evaluate if a profile was a match was less than the 84 seconds for female users, or is it plausible that this difference from the 84 seconds for the women is just random variation in the sample? Explain using your answer from part (b).

Chapter 8 – Confidence Intervals

Chapter Problem: *Simulating the NBA Draft Lottery*

Every year, the NBA holds a draft where new players to the league are chosen by the teams. Traditionally, the team with the worst record during the previous season would get the first pick. In 1985, to avoid having teams purposely lose games in order to pick first the next season, the league instituted a lottery to determine the draft order. All teams that miss the playoffs the previous season are entered into this lottery. Initially, all of these teams had an equal chance at the 1st pick, the 2nd pick, and so on. Eventually the league decided that it would be a more fair system if the teams that lost more games had a better chance at getting one of the first draft choices. The league has tweaked this system over the years and is currently using a fairly complicated method of determining draft order.

The NBA uses a rather complicated lottery system to determine the first 14 picks in their draft. Can we use Statistics to estimate the probabilities involved?

As of 2013, there are 14 teams that miss the playoffs each year and enter the draft lottery. The lottery consists of 14 balls numbered from 1 to 14. Four of these balls are randomly chosen. Using the combinations we learned in Section 5.5, we can compute that there are 1001 different groups of four numbers that can be chosen. To simplify the numbers, the league has decided that no team will be assigned the combination of 11, 12, 13, and 14. If those balls are chosen, they are thrown back and they choose four new ones. The remaining 1000 combinations are then assigned to the teams participating in the draft lottery. The table shown to the right shows the number of combinations given to each team based on the team's record during the previous season.

Teams Record During the Previous Season	Number of Lottery Ball Combinations Assigned	Probability of Receiving the #1 Draft Choice
Worst Record	250	0.250
2nd Worst Record	199	0.199
3rd Worst Record	156	0.156
4th Worst Record	119	0.119
5th Worst Record	88	0.088
6th Worst Record	63	0.063
7th Worst Record	43	0.043
8th Worst Record	28	0.028
9th Worst Record	17	0.017
10th Worst Record	11	0.011
11th Worst Record	8	0.008
12th Worst Record	7	0.007
13th Worst Record	6	0.006
14th Worst Record	5	0.005

The lottery system makes it straightforward to figure out any teams chances of getting the #1 draft choice. However, after that, it gets quite complicated. Once the #1 choice is decided, they draw again to decide who will get the #2 choice as well as the #3 choice (no team can be chosen more than once). After that, the remaining teams are assigned the 4th pick thru the 14th pick, based on their records during the previous season starting with the worst remaining record getting the 4th pick and continuing on to the best remaining record picking 14th. One of the more complicated questions this method produces is: What is the chance that a given team will get the 3rd pick in the draft. This is tricky because the answer depends on which teams were chosen to pick 1st and 2nd. In fact, the system is so complicated, that, when it was first introduced, people decided to answer such questions using computer simulations of the lottery rather than actually doing the calculations.

At the end of this chapter, we will return to this problem and attempt to use the results of such a simulation to answer the question. The simulation results will allow us to get an estimate for the true probability, but even if we run the simulation a large number of times, we know from Chapter 7 that the result from the simulation will not be the exact answer. In this chapter, we will learn how to use the results of the computer simulation to give a reasonable answer to this challenging probability question.

Introduction:

In the previous chapter, we explored the process of estimating population proportions and population means using sample proportions and sample means. However, the strange reality of that chapter was that we talked about estimating the population quantities when they were already known. Surely it should seem strange to estimate a quantity when you already know its value. In that chapter, we were just learning how the sample estimates were related to the corresponding population quantities. In this chapter, we will remove the training wheels (of knowing the population quantities) and learn how to make estimates for population proportions and population means when they are unknown.

We will begin by trying to estimate unknown population proportions. We will then move on to apply the same theory to the estimation of population means. For each of these topics we will investigate how the accuracy of our estimate is affected by the sample size. These topics will be pursued in the following sections.

Let's get started.

Section 8.1 – Confidence Intervals for the Population Proportion, p

There are many situations where it is desirable to know the true proportion of a population that has a certain attribute, but it is not usually practical to take a census to find the value. For example, we may be interested in determining the percentage of a population that has brown eyes. Or perhaps a candidate for public office would like to poll the voters one month before an election to see what percentage of the voters are planning to vote for the candidate. Also, because a probability represents the long-term proportion of times an event will occur, we might also want to use the techniques learned in this section to estimate difficult probabilities. In these cases where it is not practical to find the true proportion by taking a census, it may still be possible to estimate the desired quantity using the proportion from a random sample.

In the previous chapter, we learned that the best strategy for estimating a population quantity (a parameter) was to use the corresponding sample value (a statistic) as a point estimate. Let's begin with a brief example that shows how this is different when the population proportion is unknown.

Are Americans Confident in U.S. Public Schools? (*Discussion Example*)

In June 2011, a poll was conducted by the Gallup organization investigating whether or not Americans were confident in the public school system. Of the 1,020 adults surveyed, 348 expressed confidence in the U.S. public school system.

Are Americans satisfied with the job being done by the U.S. public school system?

a)   Use the data from the survey to find a point estimate for the true proportion of Americans adults that are confident in the U.S. public school system.

b)   How likely is it that your estimate from part (a) is exactly equal to the true proportion for all American Adults? Explain.

c)   How much sampling error do we expect in our estimate from part (a).

Solution:

a)   To estimate the population proportion, we should use the corresponding sample proportion, $\hat{p}$.

$$\hat{p} = \frac{x}{n} = \frac{348}{1020} \approx 0.3412$$

b)   In chapter 7, we learned that it is usually impossible or very unlikely that our sample value will be exactly equal to the corresponding population value. Using probability notation, we would say: $P(\hat{p} = p) \approx 0$.

c) In Chapter 7, we learned that the expected sampling error when estimating p by $\hat{p}$ is less than two standard deviations of $\hat{p}$. However, we don't know the true proportion of American adults that have confidence in the system, so we cannot calculate this value.

The example above shows us the beginning strategy for estimating population proportions, but it also points out some obstacles that we will need to overcome. The fact that our sample estimate is almost certainly wrong is troubling. It is hard to image that people would be satisfied with our work, if all we could tell them was that our estimate was almost certainly incorrect. We will need to come up with an estimate that has a reasonable chance of being correct.

While it is true that our estimate is almost certainly not correct, we also learned in Chapter 7 that it was probably within 2 standard deviations of $\hat{p}$ away from p. We will now seek to use this fact more fully than we did in Chapter 7.

CONFIDENCE INTERVALS: *Why being close is actually useful.*

In order to take full advantage of the fact that $\hat{p}$ is usually close to p, we need to switch from making **point estimates** to making **confidence interval estimates**. Here are the relevant definitions.

> **Definitions:** *Confidence Intervals and the Confidence Level*
>
> **Confidence Interval**: A confidence interval is an interval of numbers that we claim contains the population parameter being estimated. The interval is based on a point estimate and is given with a percentage that states how confident we are the interval contains the parameter.
>
> **Confidence Level**: The confidence percentage given with these intervals is known as the confidence level. The general notation for confidence level is $(1-\alpha) \cdot 100\%$. The most commonly used confidence level is 95%, with 90% and 99% also frequently used.
>
> *Example*: A 95% confidence level would have $1 - \alpha = 0.95$ and $\alpha = 0.05$. This means that, if we constructed 100 confidence intervals using 100 random samples, we would expect about 95 of them to contain the true population parameter and we would expect about 5 of them to fail to capture the true population parameter.

To come up with a confidence interval estimate, we need to take full advantage of the information we learned about the distribution of $\hat{p}$ in chapter 7. We learned that, if $np \geq 10$ and $nq \geq 10$, then $\hat{p}$ is approximately

normally distributed with $\mu_{\hat{p}} = p$ and $\sigma_{\hat{p}} = \sqrt{\dfrac{pq}{n}}$. We will now use algebra and these facts from Chapter 7 to

derive a formula we can use to compute confidence intervals for population proportions. It will be our goal to use nice confidence levels like 95%, but for now, we will start out using the familiar 95.45% from the Empirical Rule.

If $\hat{p}$ is approximately normally distributed, then the Empirical Rule yields the following:

$$P(\mu_{\hat{p}} - 2\sigma_{\hat{p}} < \hat{p} < \mu_{\hat{p}} + 2\sigma_{\hat{p}}) = 0.9545$$

The next step in developing a confidence interval is to make the substitutions: $\mu_{\hat{p}} = p$ and $\sigma_{\hat{p}} = \sqrt{\dfrac{pq}{n}}$. This

yields:

$$P\left(p-2\sqrt{\frac{pq}{n}}<\hat{p}<p+2\sqrt{\frac{pq}{n}}\right)=0.9545$$

The good news at this point is that we have a statement involving an interval that we are 95.45% confident is true. The problem is that this interval has $\hat{p}$ in the middle. We want an interval that is based on $\hat{p}$ that is likely to contain p. To obtain this goal, we will simply perform some algebraic operations to rearrange the inequality so that p is in the middle rather than $\hat{p}$. The algebra steps have been omitted, but the results are shown below.

$$P\left(\hat{p}-2\sqrt{\frac{pq}{n}}<p<\hat{p}+2\sqrt{\frac{pq}{n}}\right)=0.9545$$

One problem still remains with this formula. We are trying to estimate the value of p, but we need this value to calculate our standard deviation, $\sqrt{\frac{pq}{n}}$. It is actually possible to use more complicated algebra steps to remedy this problem, but the standard solution to this problem is to substitute our statistic $\hat{p}$ in place of the unknown parameter p.

$$P\left(\hat{p}-2\sqrt{\frac{pq}{n}}<p<\hat{p}+2\sqrt{\frac{pq}{n}}\right)=0.9545 \Rightarrow P\left(\hat{p}-2\sqrt{\frac{\hat{p}\hat{q}}{n}}<p<\hat{p}+2\sqrt{\frac{\hat{p}\hat{q}}{n}}\right)\approx0.9545$$

We now have an interval that will be true for 95.45% of all possible sample proportions and this interval states that the population proportion, p, will lie somewhere between $\hat{p}-2\sqrt{\frac{\hat{p}\hat{q}}{n}}$ and $\hat{p}+2\sqrt{\frac{\hat{p}\hat{q}}{n}}$. Notice that this interval is based on our point estimate, $\hat{p}$, because we are claiming that in 95.45% of our random samples it will be true that p will lie within $2\sqrt{\frac{\hat{p}\hat{q}}{n}}$ of $\hat{p}$.

Finally, for us to verify that it is appropriate to use the normal distribution for $\hat{p}$, we are supposed to check that $np \geq 10$ and $nq \geq 10$. However, the values of both p and q are unknown. Therefore, when we are verifying that $\hat{p}$ is approximately normally distributed, we will substitute $\hat{p}$ in place of p. This yields the following:

$$np \approx n\hat{p} = n\frac{x}{n} = x \text{ and similarly: } nq \approx n\hat{q} = n(1-\hat{p}) = n - n\hat{p} = n - n\frac{x}{n} = n - x$$

We will use these substitute values for np and nq when checking our requirements. Let's try all of this out by returning to the example about Americans confidence in public schools.

Example 8.1: *Are Americans Confident in U.S. Public Schools?*

In June 2011, a poll was conducted by the Gallup organization investigating whether or not Americans were confident in the public school system. Of the 1,020 adults surveyed, 348 expressed confidence in the U.S. public school system.

Are Americans satisfied with the job being done by the U.S. public school system?

a) Find a 95.45% confidence interval estimate for the true proportion of Americans adults that are confident in the U.S. public school system.

b) Interpret the interval in terms of the application.

c) Comment on the requirements.

d) Does the confidence interval we found really contain the true proportion of American adults that are confident in the U.S. public school system? Explain.

Solution:

a) We will use the formula $P\left(\hat{p}-2\sqrt{\dfrac{\hat{p}\hat{q}}{n}}<p<\hat{p}+2\sqrt{\dfrac{\hat{p}\hat{q}}{n}}\right)\approx 0.9545$ to accomplish this goal. We have the following information from the Gallup poll.

$$n=1020 \text{ and } \hat{p}=\frac{x}{n}=\frac{348}{1020}\approx 0.3412 \Rightarrow \hat{q}=1-\hat{p}\approx 0.6588$$

Plugging these values into the formula we get: $P\left(\hat{p}-2\sqrt{\dfrac{\hat{p}\hat{q}}{n}}<p<\hat{p}+2\sqrt{\dfrac{\hat{p}\hat{q}}{n}}\right)\approx 0.9545 \Rightarrow$

$$P\left(0.3412-2\sqrt{\frac{0.3412*0.6588}{1020}}<p<0.3412+2\sqrt{\frac{0.3412*0.6588}{1020}}\right)\approx 0.9545$$

$$\Rightarrow P(0.3412-0.0297<p<0.3412+0.0297)\approx 0.9545$$

$$\Rightarrow P(0.3115<p<0.3709)\approx 0.9545$$

Finally, because this is called a confidence interval, we will write our answer using interval notation.

$$p\in(0.3115,\ 0.3709)$$

b) We are 95.45% confident that the true proportion of American adults that are confident in the U.S. public school system is somewhere between 31.15% and 37.09%.

c) Because np and nq are not available, we will substitute the values $n\hat{p}=x$ and $n\hat{q}=n-x$ in their places.

The number of successes in our sample is given by $x=348\geq 10$. And the number of failures in our sample is given by
$n-x=1020-348=672\geq 10$. Therefore, it appears that $\hat{p}$ is normally distributed, so we are justified in using a formula based on the Empirical Rule for normally distributed variables.

> **Caution:** *A Common mistake in Interpreting Confidence Intervals*
>
> A common mistake made when interpreting a confidence interval is making the statement about the sample proportion rather than about the population proportion.
>
> *Example:* "I am 95.45% confident that the proportion of the 1020 American adults surveyed that are confident in the U.S. public school system is somewhere between 31.15% and 37.09%
>
> *Problem:* First of all, it was not our job to estimate the location of the sample proportion; it was our job to estimate the location of the population proportion. Secondly, the sample proportion for the 1020 people surveyed was 0.3412 and we should be 100% confident that 0.3412 is somewhere between 0.3115 and 0.3709.

d) Because our interval is based on a random sample, we do not know for sure whether or not the interval contains the true population proportion, p. However, we say that we are 95.45% confident that it does. This reflects the idea that 95.45% of all random samples we could have possibly chosen would have produced an interval that contained the true value of p. So, we know it is likely that the interval does contain the true value of p.

LOOKING DEEPER: *Does the interval always contain the true value of p?*

In the previous example, we said that we are 95.45% confident that our interval contained the population proportion, but what does that really tell us? After all, the population proportion is not a random variable that will be in this particular interval sometimes when we look, but not at other times. The 95.45% probability really applies to the random variable $\hat{p}$. Our initial probability statement was that we would get a value of $\hat{p}$ that lies within 2 standard deviations of p. If we get such a $\hat{p}$, then our eventual interval will, in fact, contain the population proportion, p. That means that, before we get our sample, we could say that there is a 95.45% chance that we will end up with an interval that contains p. Once we pick a sample, we are now destined to either get an interval that does contain p or one that does not. It is not possible for the particular interval we find to contain p at some moments in time, but not others.

So how should we interpret it when we say we are 95.45% confident that our interval contains the true population proportion? The answer, like always for probability, is that we should interpret that number as a long-term relative frequency. It tells us that if we compute 95.45% confidence intervals on a regular basis, then in the long run, 95.45% of the intervals we create will have really contained the proportion we were estimating and the other 4.55% of the intervals we computed, will have missed their target. For any particular interval, we know it would be unusual if it does not contain the mean, but it is always possible that it does not. Let's examine how this might play out.

Suppose that we assign 20 different people the task of selecting a random sample to estimate the population proportion. Each of them will take their own random sample, compute their own sample proportion, and compute their own 95.45% confidence interval. Will they all obtain intervals that contain the true population proportion? Let's take a look at a simulation of such an experiment. Let's suppose that the true population proportion is $p = 0.63$. The table that follows shows the 20 different sample proportions along with the 20 different intervals. It also lists how many of the sample proportion were exactly equal to the population proportion and how many of the confidence intervals contained the population proportion. Let's take a look at how good of a job each sample did at estimating the population proportion.

Sample proportion, $\hat{p}$	Does $\hat{p} = p$? Recall: $p = 0.63$	95.45% Confidence Interval	Dashed line represents $p = 0.63$	Does the interval contain $p = 0.63$?
0.6767	No	(0.6057, 0.7476)		Yes
0.5988	No	(0.5245, 0.6731)		Yes
0.6287	No	(0.5555, 0.7020)		Yes
0.6587	No	(0.5868, 0.7306)		Yes
0.7126	No	(0.6439, 0.7812)		No
0.6227	No	(0.5492, 0.6963)		Yes
0.6707	No	(0.5994, 0.7419)		Yes
0.5689	No	(0.4938, 0.6440)		Yes
0.5928	No	(0.5183, 0.6673)		Yes
0.6227	No	(0.5492, 0.6963)		Yes
0.6467	No	(0.5742, 0.7192)		Yes
0.6587	No	(0.5868, 0.7306)		Yes
0.6647	No	(0.5931, 0.7363)		Yes
0.5809	No	(0.5060, 0.6557)		Yes
0.5809	No	(0.5060, 0.6557)		Yes
0.6647	No	(0.5931, 0.7363)		Yes
0.6767	No	(0.6057, 0.7476)		Yes
0.6826	No	(0.6120, 0.7532)		Yes
0.6107	No	(0.5368, 0.6847)		Yes
0.6647	No	(0.5931, 0.7363)		Yes

Notice that not a single one of the $\hat{p}$'s is exactly equal to the population proportion, p. This is not surprising. Recall from chapter 7, we learned that $P(\hat{p} = p) \approx 0$. However, almost all of the 95.45% confidence intervals do contain the population proportion, 0.63. However, one of the intervals is (0.6439, 0.7812) and all the numbers in that interval are larger than the true population proportion, 0.63. Sometimes people wonder "What did that person do wrong when finding his confidence interval?" The answer is, he probably did nothing wrong. When we construct 95.45% confidence intervals, we only expect 95.45% of them to contain the correct answer. For 20 intervals, we expect about $0.9545(20) = 19.09 \approx 19$ of them to contain the true population proportion, and that is exactly what happened in our simulation.

If we must blame someone or something, then the blame is on the variation that occurs with a random sample. Because the sample is taken randomly, there will be times when our sample proportion, $\hat{p}$, is far enough away from the population proportion that, even when we extend left and right to make our interval, we still do not reach out far enough to get an interval that contains the true proportion. So, we can blame the fact that one of our intervals missed the target on luck, but we should not call it bad luck. When you do your work with 95.45% confidence, you should not expect to be correct 100% of the time.

Key Concept: *Confidence Level vs. Successful Captures*

The confidence level for a confidence interval tells us the percentage of times we will successfully capture the true population proportion if we were to repeat the sampling and estimating process over a long period of tries. Unlike a point estimate that has almost no chance of being equal to the true population proportion, a confidence interval is likely to contain the true proportion on any one try and we can predict roughly how many successes we will get in the long run when using the confidence level.

CHANGING THE CONFIDENCE LEVEL: *Moving to 90%, 95%, or 99% confidence*

Because our confidence level can be used to predict what percentage of our intervals will, in the long run, contain the true population proportion, we may wish to raise or lower this level from time to time, depending on our needs. So the question arises, what will happen to our confidence interval formula, if we change our confidence level? Let's look at a few specific questions.

Q1. What will happen to the formula $P\left(\hat{p} - 2\sqrt{\dfrac{\hat{p}\hat{q}}{n}} < p < \hat{p} + 2\sqrt{\dfrac{\hat{p}\hat{q}}{n}} \right) \approx 0.9545$, if we change our confidence

level to 99.73%?

The answer to this is fairly simple and comes from the Empirical Rule for normally distributed random variables. 95.45% is the chance that the normally distributed variable, $\bar{x}$, would lie within two standard

deviations of its mean. The two standard deviations piece of our formula was represented by $2\sqrt{\dfrac{\hat{p}\hat{q}}{n}}$.

Because 99.73% is the chance that a normally distributed random variable will lie within 3 standard deviations of its mean, we simply change the 2 in the formula to a 3. So we get the new formula:

$$P\left(\hat{p} - 3\sqrt{\dfrac{\hat{p}\hat{q}}{n}} < p < \hat{p} + 3\sqrt{\dfrac{\hat{p}\hat{q}}{n}} \right) \approx 0.9973$$

Q2. What will happen to the formula $P\left(\hat{p}-2\sqrt{\dfrac{\hat{p}\hat{q}}{n}}<p<\hat{p}+2\sqrt{\dfrac{\hat{p}\hat{q}}{n}}\right)\approx 0.9545$, if we change our confidence level to 68.27%?

This is very similar to question 1. Only this time, we are using 68.27% which is the chance that a normally distributed random variable will lie within 1 standard deviation of its mean, so this time, we replace the 2 in the formula by a 1. This yields:

$$P\left(\hat{p}-1\sqrt{\dfrac{\hat{p}\hat{q}}{n}}<p<\hat{p}+1\sqrt{\dfrac{\hat{p}\hat{q}}{n}}\right)\approx 0.6827 \;\Rightarrow\; P\left(\hat{p}-\sqrt{\dfrac{\hat{p}\hat{q}}{n}}<p<\hat{p}+\sqrt{\dfrac{\hat{p}\hat{q}}{n}}\right)\approx 0.6827$$

Q3. What will happen to the formula $P\left(\hat{p}-2\sqrt{\dfrac{\hat{p}\hat{q}}{n}}<p<\hat{p}+2\sqrt{\dfrac{\hat{p}\hat{q}}{n}}\right)\approx 0.9545$, if we change our confidence level to 95%?

This one is similar to, but more complicated than the previous questions. 95% is not a standard Empirical Rule percentage. However, the goal is still the same as before. We must replace the 2 in the formula by a new number of standard deviations away from the mean, or z-score, so that the probability, or area under the standard normal curve, will be 0.95. This is just a working backwards question similar to those in Section 6.2.

The first step is to draw a sketch of the normal curve and then use invNorm to determine the z-score we need.

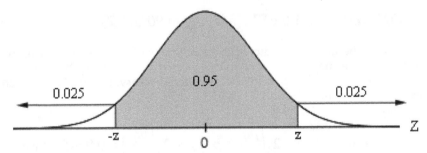

Because we want there to be a 95% chance that $\hat{p}$ will lie within z standard deviations of the true proportion, we put an area of 0.95 in the middle with equal outside areas. We can then use invNorm and technology to find the value of –z. We simply enter the area to the left of –z as follows.

$$\text{InvNorm}(0.025)\approx -1.960$$

By symmetry, we get that $z\approx 1.960$. Thus, to get the desired 95% confidence, we simply replace the 2 in the formula by 1.960. This yields:

$$P\left(\hat{p}-1.960\sqrt{\dfrac{\hat{p}\hat{q}}{n}}<p<\hat{p}+1.960\sqrt{\dfrac{\hat{p}\hat{q}}{n}}\right)\approx 0.95$$

So, in general, to be able to specify the desired confidence level, $(1-\alpha)\cdot 100\%$, we must replace the 2 in the original formula by a new z-score we will call z^*. z^* must be such that the are under the standard normal curve between $-z^*$ and z^* is equal to the desired confidence level, $1-\alpha$.

$$P\left(\hat{p}-z^*\sqrt{\dfrac{\hat{p}\hat{q}}{n}}<p<\hat{p}+z^*\sqrt{\dfrac{\hat{p}\hat{q}}{n}}\right)=1-\alpha$$

These steps are summarized in the following point to remember.

Point to Remember: *Finding the correct z-score.*

As we change our confidence level, we simply pick the value of z^*, such that our confidence level area is trapped between the values of $-z^*$ and z^*. This is accomplished by taking the following steps:

- Draw a sketch of the standard normal curve. Put the desired confidence area in the middle with equal outside areas.
- Compute the outside areas by subtracting the middle area from 1 and then dividing the result by 2.
- Use invNorm and technology on this tail area to find the value of $-z^*$. z^* is the positive version of this number.

The procedure for applying this theory is shown in the following point to remember.

Point to Remember: *Procedure for finding confidence intervals for the population proportion, p.*

Requirement: $n\hat{p} \geq 10$ and $n\hat{q} \geq 10$ or equivalently $x \geq 10$ and $n - x \geq 10$. *In words:* We must have at least 10 successes and at least 10 failures in our sample. If these requirements are met, then we know that $\hat{p}$ has an approximately normal distribution.

Steps: We complete the steps below to create our confidence intervals.

- *Point Estimate:* We begin by calculating the sample proportion using the formula $\hat{p} = \dfrac{x}{n}$. Sometimes the value of $\hat{p}$ is given in the problem as a sample percentage.
- *z-score:* For a confidence level of $(1-\alpha) \cdot 100\%$, sketch the standard normal curve and use invNorm to determine the two z values that trap an area of $1-\alpha$ in the middle with equal outside areas. The positive value is represented by the symbol z^*.
- *Endpoints:* Calculate the endpoints of the confidence interval using the formula:

$$\hat{p} \pm z^* \cdot \sqrt{\frac{\hat{p}\hat{q}}{n}}$$

- *Interval:* The confidence interval is written in the form

$$p \in \left(\hat{p} - z^* \cdot \sqrt{\frac{\hat{p}\hat{q}}{n}}, \ \hat{p} + z^* \cdot \sqrt{\frac{\hat{p}\hat{q}}{n}} \right)$$

Rounding Rule: The boundaries on the confidence interval should be written with the same number of decimal places as were used in $\hat{p}$.

Let's put this new theory into practice with another example.

Example 8.2: *Can money buy happiness?*

In November of 2005, the Pew Research Center conducted a survey of Americans to find out whether or not they were happy. The survey found that 34% of Americans reported themselves to be "Very Happy." The survey also broke down these results based on the income level of the participants. Of the 312 Americans earning $100,000 or more per year, 152 of them reported that they were "Very Happy." Use the results of this survey to answer each of the following questions.

Can money buy happiness?

a) Use the sample data to find a point estimate for the true proportion of all Americans that earn $100,000 or more per year that consider themselves to be "Very Happy."

b) Compute a 99% confidence interval for the true proportion of all Americans that earn $100,000 or more per year that consider themselves to be "Very Happy."

c) Interpret this interval in terms of the application.

d) Comment on the requirements.

e) Can we say with 99% confidence that the percentage of top wage earners that are "Very Happy" is higher than the 34% for Americans in general? Explain using the confidence interval from part (b).

f) We know that the point estimate found in part (a) is unlikely to be exactly equal to the true proportion of all Americans that earn $100,000 or more per year that consider themselves to be "Very Happy." How close do you think the point estimate was to the true proportion? Explain.

g) Suppose that, in November 2005, there were 23,940,000 Americans that earned $100,000 or more per year. Use your answer to part (b) to determine a 99% confidence interval for the true number of those 23,940,000 Americans that consider themselves to be "Very Happy."

Solution:

a) The point estimate for the population proportion, p, is the sample proportion, $\hat{p}$. Because our sample contained 152 successes in 312 the surveyed, we get the following.

$$\hat{p} = \frac{x}{n} = \frac{152}{312} \approx 0.4872$$

b) Our confidence interval will come from the formula:

$$P\left(\hat{p} - z^* \cdot \sqrt{\frac{\hat{p}\hat{q}}{n}} < p < \hat{p} + z^* \cdot \sqrt{\frac{\hat{p}\hat{q}}{n}}\right) = 1 - \alpha$$

We already determined that $\hat{p} \approx 0.4872$, so $\hat{q} = 1 - \hat{p} \approx 1 - 0.4872 = 0.5128$. We also know that the sample size was 312, so n = 312. The only unknown left in our formula is z^*. We can find this value by finding the two z-values on the standard normal curve that trap an area of 99% between them. Let's draw a quick sketch and then find the desired values using invNorm and technology.

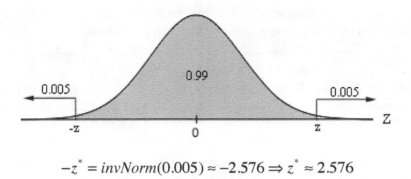

$$-z^* = invNorm(0.005) \approx -2.576 \Rightarrow z^* \approx 2.576$$

With an area in the tail of 0.005, we see that $z^* = 2.576$. We can now find the boundaries of our confidence interval by plugging our known values into $\hat{p} \pm z^* \cdot \sqrt{\dfrac{\hat{p}\hat{q}}{n}}$.

$$\hat{p} \pm z^* \cdot \sqrt{\frac{\hat{p}\hat{q}}{n}} \approx 0.4872 \pm 2.576\sqrt{\frac{0.4872 * 0.5128}{312}} = 0.4872 \pm 0.0729 \Rightarrow p \in (0.4143,\ 0.5601)$$

c) We are 99% confident that the true proportion of all Americans that earn $100,000 or more per year that consider themselves to be "Very Happy" is somewhere between 41.43% and 56.01%.

> **Key Concept:** *Using Percentages*
>
> Despite the fact that this problem is about proportions, it is common to use the percent form when interpreting the confidence interval.

d) We need at least 10 successes and at least 10 failures to meet the requirements for computing a confidence interval for a population proportion.

$x = 152 \geq 10$ and $n - x = 312 - 152 = 160 \geq 10$. So, this tells us that $\hat{p}$ is approximately normally distributed and, therefore, the requirements have been met.

e) If $p \in (0.4143,\ 0.5601) \Rightarrow p > 0.34 \Rightarrow$ Yes, we are 99% confident that the percentage of top wage earners that are "Very Happy" is higher than the 34% for Americans in general.

f) We learned in Chapter 7 that there is almost no chance that the sample proportion, 48.72% is exactly equal to the true population proportion. However, after we added and subtracted 0.0729 to form our interval, we were then 99% confident that we had the true proportion. This must mean that we are confident that our point estimate was within 7.29% of the truth.

g) If we write our answer to part (b) using inequalities, we would say that we are 99% confident that $0.4143 < p < 0.5601$. Recall that p represents the proportion of successes in the population. Therefore,

$p = \dfrac{x}{N}$, where x is the total number of successes in the population. If we multiply all three parts of our inequality by the population size, $N = 23,940,000$, this would give us the requested interval. The work is shown below.

$$0.4143 < \frac{x}{N} < 0.5601 \Rightarrow 0.4143(23,940,000) < \frac{x}{N} \cdot N < 0.5601(23,940,000) \Rightarrow$$

$$9,918,342 < x < 13,408,794$$

In words, we are 99% confident that the true number of the 23,940,000 Americans that make at least $100,000 per year that are "Very Happy" is somewhere between 9,918,342 and 13, 408,794 of those Americans.

Part (f) above points out that in order to move from a point estimate that has essentially no chance of being correct to a confidence interval that is very likely to contain the true population proportion, we had to give ourselves some margin for error by adding and subtracting the 0.0729 from our point estimate. Because of this, the ± piece in a confidence interval calculation is known as the **margin of error**.

Definition: *Margin or Error*

Margin of Error: The quantity that is subtracted and added from the point estimate to form a confidence interval is known as the margin of error, E. For confidence intervals involving proportions, the formula for margin of error is as shown below.

$$E = z^* \cdot \sqrt{\frac{\hat{p}\hat{q}}{n}}$$

WRAP SESSION: *A case where a confidence interval does not answer the key question*

Let's take a look at one final example to practice the ideas presented so far and to see another variation on interpreting a confidence interval.

Example 8.3: *Estimating an NBA player's free throw percentage*

Shaquille O'Neal is widely regarded as one of the greatest NBA players of all time. However, he is not regarded in this manner because of his free throw shooting ability. In fact, it was a common strategy for opposing teams to purposely foul him near the end of games so that he would have to shoot free throws. After a long and successful basketball career, Shaq ended up making 5,935 of 11,252 of his free throw attempts. For this problem, we will assume that Shaq's 11,252 attempts represent a random sample of his true potential at the free throw line.

It was always an adventure when Shaquille O'Neal shot a free throw. With every made or missed free throw, his free throw percentage changed. How can we estimate the true probability that he would make one?

a) Use Shaq's free throw data to compute a 90% confidence interval for the true probability of him making any given free throw.

b) Comment on the requirements.

c) What is the margin of error for this interval?

d) Compute a 95% confidence interval for the true probability of Shaq making any given free throw.

e) What effect did raising the confidence level have on the margin of error and on the interval itself?

f) Can we say with 95% confidence that Shaq had a better than 52% chance of making a given free throw? Explain.

Solution:

a) At first glance, this question might appear quite different than the ones addressed in the previous two examples. However, because a probability tells us the long-term proportion of tries that result in our event occurring, we can use the proportion procedure to estimate probabilities as well.

$$n = 11,252, \quad \hat{p} = \frac{x}{n} = \frac{5935}{11252} = 0.5275 \Rightarrow \hat{q} = 1 - 0.5275 = 0.4725$$

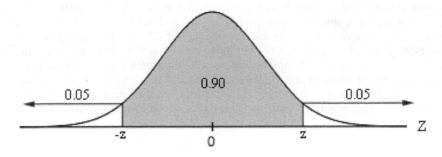

$$-z^* = invNorm(0.05) \approx -1.645 \Rightarrow z^* \approx 1.645$$

$$\hat{p} \pm z^* \cdot \sqrt{\frac{\hat{p}\hat{q}}{n}} \approx 0.5275 \pm 1.645\sqrt{\frac{0.5275 * 0.4725}{11252}} = 0.5275 \pm 0.0077 \Rightarrow p \in (0.5198,\ 0.5352)$$

b) $x = 5935 \geq 10$ and $n - x = 11252 - 5935 = 5317 \geq 10$, thus, the requirements have been met.

c) The margin of error is the $\pm$ piece in our calculation in part (a). Thus, $E \approx 0.0077$.

d) Changing the confidence level has no effect on our point estimate, but it will affect our margin of error by changing the z-score.

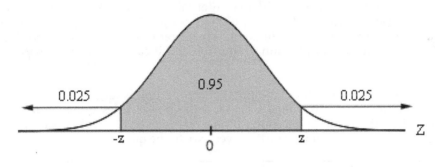

$$-z^* = invNorm(0.025) \approx -1.960 \Rightarrow z^* \approx 1.960$$

$$\hat{p} \pm z^* \cdot \sqrt{\frac{\hat{p}\hat{q}}{n}} \approx 0.5275 \pm 1.960\sqrt{\frac{0.5275 * 0.4725}{11252}} = 0.5275 \pm 0.0092 \Rightarrow p \in (0.5183,\ 0.5367)$$

e) The larger confidence level caused us to get a larger z-score. In turn, this z-score caused us to get a larger margin of error. This larger margin of error created a wider confidence interval.

f) No, $p \in (0.5183,\ 0.5367) \Rightarrow p$ could be less than 52%, for example, 51.9% is in the interval. The fact that 51.9% is in the interval means that it is a reasonable possibility for the true value of p. Therefore, we cannot be confident that the true probability of Shaq making a free throw was greater than 52%.

In the above example, we saw that increasing the confidence level resulted in a wider confidence interval. It actually makes sense that we would need a wider interval to be 95% confident than to be 90% confident in our answer. If we were 90% confident with the first interval, then to gain more confidence that our interval contains the population proportion, we need to add extra possibilities for the population proportion by expanding our interval. This widening of the confidence interval is no coincidence. It will always happen. Consider the following analogy.

If you try to catch a butterfly in your hand, it is very difficult. The butterfly seems to follow an unpredictable flight pattern, and you are trying to catch it with a relatively small hand. This means that you have to move your hand to just the right place at just the right time to catch the butterfly. However, it is easy to catch a butterfly if you use a net. If you have a net with a two-foot diameter, then you can try to swing the net so that the butterfly is right in the middle of the opening. It's alright if you miss by a little, because the net gives you some margin for error. As long as your aim is off by less than 1 foot, then two-foot diameter of the net will still allow you to catch the butterfly. If you want to have a better chance at catching the butterfly, you could simply make your net bigger.

Key Concept: *Confidence level vs. the length of a confidence interval*

For a fixed sample size, the larger your confidence level the wider your confidence interval will be and vice versa.

"If you want to have a better chance at catching a butterfly, then you need to make your net bigger."

The Wrap Session Example also illustrated the following:

Key Concept: *Using confidence intervals to answer questions about the parameter*

Reasonable Possibilities: The confidence interval provides us with a list of the reasonable possibilities for the population proportion. No special attention should be given to the point estimate in the center of the interval. There is only one true value for the population proportion and it can be anywhere within our interval.

Yes or No? To be confident that the population proportion is larger (or smaller) than a given value, the entire range of reasonable possibilities must be larger (or smaller) than the value in question. If any value in the interval fails to meet the requested condition, then we must answer 'No' to the question.

Now let's move on to some exercises.

Exercise Set 8.1

Concept Review: Review the definitions and concepts from this section by filling in the blanks for each of the following.

1) When estimating a population proportion, our point estimate will be the _____ _____ .

2) Because we do not expect our point estimate to be correct, we add and subtract an amount from it to form a confidence interval. The amount added and subtracted is referred to as the _____ of _____ .

3) When we expand our estimate to a confidence interval, the confidence percentage stated is known as the confidence _____ .

4) When we say we are 95% (or some other %) confident that our interval contains the population proportion, this means that in the _____ _____ , about 95% of such intervals will contain the true population proportion.

5) The requirement for finding a confidence interval for a proportion is that $n\hat{p} \geq$ ____ and $n\hat{q} \geq$ ____ . Or, equivalently, we can verify that we have at least 10 _____ and at least 10 _____ .

6) For a fixed sample size, the higher the confidence level, the _____ the interval and vice versa.

7) The procedure learned in this section is designed to find confidence intervals for population proportions, but it can also be used to find confidence intervals for _____ and _____ .

8) A confidence interval provides us with a list of the _____ possibilities for the population proportion.

9) To be confident that the population proportion is larger than a given value, the _____ range of reasonable possibilities must be _____ than the value in question.

10) If any value in the interval fails to meet a requested condition, then we cannot be _____ that the true proportion meets the condition.

Mechanics: Practice the calculations needed for confidence interval estimates of population proportions before moving on to the real world applications.

11) Suppose a random sample of size 561 produced 200 items with the desired attribute.
   a) Determine a point estimate for the population proportion of items with the desired attribute.
   b) Compute a 68.27% confidence interval for the true population proportion.
   c) Compute a 95.45% confidence interval.
   d) Compute a 99.73% confidence interval.
   e) What effect did increasing the confidence level have on the confidence interval?

12) Suppose a random sample of size 947 produced 146 items with the desired attribute.
   a) Determine a point estimate for the population proportion of items with the desired attribute.
   b) Compute a 68.27% confidence interval for the true population proportion.
   c) Compute a 95.45% confidence interval.
   d) Compute a 99.73% confidence interval.
   e) What effect did increasing the confidence level have on the confidence interval?

13) Suppose a random sample of size 318 produced 197 items with the desired attribute.
   a) Determine a point estimate for the population proportion of items with the desired attribute.
   b) Determine a 95% confidence interval for the population proportion.
   c) What was the margin of error for your point estimate?

14) Suppose a random sample of size 588 produced 497 items with the desired attribute.
   a) Determine a point estimate for the population proportion of items with the desired attribute.
   b) Determine a 95% confidence interval for the population proportion.
   c) What was the margin of error for your point estimate?

15) Suppose that in a random sample of 613 items, 34.42% had the desired attribute.
   a) Determine a 90% confidence interval for the population proportion.
   b) Comment on the requirements for finding the above interval.

16) Suppose that in a random sample of 294 items, 87.41% had the desired attribute.
   a) Determine a 99% confidence interval for the population proportion.
   b) Comment on the requirements for finding the above interval.

Applications: Practice the ideas learned in this section within the context of real world applications.

17) In June 2011, a random sample of 40,104 children revealed that 3,195 of the children had food allergies (data is based on an Associated Press article).
   a) Use the data to compute a point estimate for the true proportion of children that have food allergies.
   b) What is the probability that this point estimate is exactly equal to the true population proportion? Explain.
   c) Determine a 95% confidence interval for the true proportion of children that have food allergies.
   d) Comment on the requirements for finding the above interval.

18) According to a 2009 study of 396,316 Americans conducted by the CDC, 128,803 of those studied reported that they usually ate fruit 2 or more times per day.
   a) Use the data to compute a point estimate for the true proportion of Americans that usually eat fruit 2 or more times per day.
   b) What is the probability that this point estimate is exactly equal to the true population proportion? Explain.
   c) Determine a 90% confidence interval for the true proportion of Americans that usually eat fruit 2 or more times per day.
   d) Comment on the requirements for finding the above interval.

19) Shortly after being elected Governor of Wisconsin, Scott Walker was the center of national controversy after leading the charge to limit the state's public employees' ability to collectively bargain. After the changes were voted into law in June 2011, a University of Wisconsin poll showed that 206 of 556 Wisconsin residents approved of the way that Scott Walker was handling his job as Governor.

   a) Determine a point estimate for the proportion of all Wisconsin residents who approve of the job the governor is doing.
   b) Determine a 99% confidence interval for the true proportion of registered voters in Wisconsin who approve of the job the governor is doing.
   c) At the 99% confidence level, how close do you think your point estimate is to the true population proportion? Explain.
   d) Interpret the interval in terms of the application using percentages.

20) During the early stages of the primaries for the 2012 Presidential election in the U.S., a poll taken by Rasmussen Reports asked 3500 likely voters whether they expected to vote for the eventual Republican Candidate or the Incumbent, Obama. 1408 of those surveyed stated that they expected to vote for Obama.

   a) Use the data to determine a point estimate for the true proportion of all likely voters who would expect to vote for Obama in the 2012 election.
   b) Determine a 95% confidence interval for the true proportion of likely voters who would expect to vote for Obama in the 2012 election.
   c) At the 95% confidence level, how close do you think your point estimate is to the true population proportion? Explain.
   d) Interpret the interval in terms of the application using percentages.

21) Suppose that a random sample of 2,077 video game players revealed that 41.79% of the players were female. Data is based on a 2011 report by the Entertainment Software Association.

   a) Comment on the requirements for finding a confidence interval for the true proportion of video game players that are female.
   b) Use the data provided to calculate a 90% confidence interval for the true proportion of video game players that are female.
   c) Interpret the interval in terms of the application using percentages.

22) In August 2011, 1500 Americans were surveyed and asked to rate economic conditions in the country as "excellent", "good", "only fair", or "poor." Of the 1500 surveyed, 53.93% rated the economic conditions in the U.S. as "poor."

   a) Comment on the requirements for finding a confidence interval for the true proportion of Americans that would rate the economic conditions in the U.S. as "poor."
   b) Use the data provided to calculate a 99% confidence interval for the true proportion of Americans that would rate the economic conditions in the U.S. as "poor."
   c) Interpret the interval in terms of the application using percentages.

23) Before California's texting ban went into effect in January 2009, about 1.4 percent of drivers on average were observed texting or manipulating an electronic device (such as a smart phone) at any point in time behind the wheel. In July 2011, a survey of 1,200 drivers revealed that 49 of them manipulating an electronic device while driving. (Based on an Auto Club study.)

   a) Find a 95% confidence interval for the true proportion of drivers that are manipulating an electronic device while driving.
   b) Can we be 95% confident that the true proportion of drivers that are manipulating an electronic device while driving is higher than it was before the ban? Explain using your answer to part (a).
   c) Do you suspect that the ban caused more people to start texting or can you think of other possible confounding variables? Explain.

24) A random sample of 273 Chicago area specialty doctors' offices were called and asked to book an appointment for a new patient child on Medicare. 180 of those offices refused to see the child. At that same time specialty doctors were refusing 11% of privately insured children. (Based on a 2011 article from the New England Journal of Medicine.)

   a) Find a 90% confidence interval for the true proportion of Chicago area specialty doctors that would refuse to accept a new child patient on Medicare.
   b) Can we be 90% confident that the true proportion of Chicago area specialty doctors that would refuse to accept a new child patient on Medicare.is higher than the refusal rate for privately insured patients? Explain using your answer to part (a).
   c) Do you suspect that being on Medicare causes you to be more likely to be refused an appointment with a specialty doctor or can you think of other possible confounding variables? Explain.

25) In March 2014, a survey of 8,210 public high school students from the Atlantic Canadian Region revealed that 62.17% of them reported having at least one energy drink in the previous year. (Based on a study from the University of Waterloo.)

a) Comment on the requirements for finding a confidence interval for the true population proportion.

b) Find a 90% confidence interval for the true proportion of high school students in the Atlantic Canadian Region that had consumed an energy drink in the previous year.

c) Can we be 90% confident that more than half of high school students in the Atlantic Canadian Region that had consumed an energy drink in the previous year? Explain using your answer to part (b).

d) Suppose that, in March 2014, there were a total of 740,000 high school students in the Atlantic Canadian Region. Use your answer to part (b) to determine a 90% confidence interval for the true number of those 740,000 high school students that would report that they had at least one energy drink in the previous year.

e) Explain why it might not be appropriate to extend these results to all high school students in North America.

26) A professional sports bettor kept a record of 500 randomly chosen sports bets that resulted in a win or a loss (no ties). The records show that he won 56.80% of the 500 bets.

a) Comment on the requirements for finding a confidence interval for the true population proportion.

b) Find a 99% confidence interval for the true proportion of bets this gambler would be expected to win. (This would represent the gamblers long term probability of picking a winner rather than a loser.)

c) Based on your answer to part (b), can you say with 99% confidence that the gambler's chance of winning a bet is greater than 50%? Explain.

d) Based on your answer to part (b), can you say with 99% confidence that the gambler's chance of winning a bet is greater than 11/21? Explain. (Note: a sports better must have a chance of winning greater than 11/21 in order to expect to win money in the long run.)

27) The IRS admitted that between 2010 and 2012 it targeted tax-exempt groups for extra scrutiny and that the vast majority of those were conservative groups. In February 2014, a Fox News Poll surveyed 1,006 registered voters and asked them if they felt that this was an example of corruption at the IRS. 647 of those surveyed said that they did feel this way.

a) Comment on the requirements for finding a confidence interval for the true population proportion.

b) Find a 95% confidence interval for the true proportion of all registered voters in the U.S. at that time that would have said that they felt this targeting was an example of corruption at the IRS.

c) Can we be 95% confident that less than 2/3 of all registered voters in the U.S. at that time would have said that they felt this targeting was an example of corruption at the IRS? Explain using your answer to part (b).

d) Suppose that, in February 2014, there were 147,000,000 registered voters. Use your answer to part (b) to determine a 95% confidence interval for the true number of those 147,000,000 registered voters that would have said that they felt this targeting was an example of corruption at the IRS.

28) In 2012, a random sample of 1,380 people living in North America showed that 1,085 of them were Internet users. (Based on data from *Internet World Stats*.)

a) Comment on the requirements for finding a confidence interval for the true population proportion.

b) Find a 99% confidence interval for the true proportion of all people who live in North America that use the Internet.

c) Can we be 99% confident that more than 3/4 of those living in North America are Internet users? Explain using your answer to part (b).

d) Suppose that, in 2012, there were 495,000,000 people living in North America. Use your answer to part (b) to determine a 99% confidence interval for the true number of those 495,000,000 people that use the Internet.

29) When testing new medications, those conducting the study must worry about the placebo effect, where people report feeling better just because they are taking a medication, not because the medication is actually working. They must also worry about what is called the nocebo effect. The nocebo affect is reporting a side effect when taking a medication, even though the medication, in fact, does not cause that side effect. One study on the nocebo effect found that, in a random sample of 184 people classified as allergic to penicillin, 90.5% could actually take penicillin without an adverse reaction.

a) Determine a 95% confidence interval for the true population proportion of those classified as allergic to penicillin that actually can take the drug without an adverse reaction.

b) Interpret the interval in terms of the application.

30) A Fox News poll released in September of 2011, showed that 51.04% of 911 randomly sampled adult Americans believed that it was at least somewhat likely that there will be "major political uprisings" in the U.S. in the next 10 years.

a) Determine a 99% confidence interval for the true proportion of adult Americans that believe that it is at least somewhat likely that there will be "major political uprisings" in the U.S. in the next 10 years.

b) Interpret the interval in terms of the application using percentages.

c) Suppose that, in September 2011, there were 238,000,000 adult Americans. Use your answer to part (b) to determine a 99% confidence interval for the true number of those 238,000,000 adult Americans that believed that it was at least somewhat likely that there would be "major political uprisings" in the U.S. in the next 10 years.

31) A statistics instructor asks each of his 40 students to flip a quarter 100 times and record the number of heads in the 100 tosses. The most heads obtained by any of the students was 62.

a) Based on this student's sample data, compute a 95% confidence interval for the true proportion of heads for this student's coin.

b) Based on the interval obtained in part (a), can we say with 95% confidence that this student's coin has a greater than 50% chance of showing heads on any flip?

c) Criticize the sampling method and discuss possible biases that could be caused by this method of obtaining our data.

d) Do you think this coin truly is biased towards heads? Explain.

32) A statistics instructor asks each of her 45 students to roll a die 100 times and record the number of times each of the 6 faces ended up on top. The most unusual result obtained by any student was a die that only showed the number 2 six times in the 100 rolls.

a) Based on this student's sample data, compute a 95% confidence interval for the true proportion of 2's for this student's die.

b) Based on the interval obtained in part (a), can we say with 95% confidence that this student's die has less than a 1/6 chance of showing a 2 face up on any given roll?

c) Criticize the sampling method and discuss possible biases that could be caused by this method of obtaining our data.

d) Do you think this die is truly biased against the number 2? Explain.

Section 8.2 – Sample Size Considerations for Estimating Proportions

In the previous section we learned how to identify the margin of error when computing a confidence interval. This is useful; however, we don't just want to be able to identify the margin of error, we want to be able to control its size. In the wrap session at the end of the previous section, we saw that increasing the confidence level increased the margin of error. Therefore, it makes sense that if we lower the confidence level, then we would decrease the margin of error. This is true; however, it is undesirable to lower our confidence level below 90%. So, we need another option for decreasing the margin of error. A better way to decrease the margin of error in our estimates is to increase the sample size. We can determine the appropriate sample size by solving the margin of error formula for n. Using algebra we can show the following.

$$E = z^* \cdot \sqrt{\frac{\hat{p}\hat{q}}{n}} \;\Rightarrow\; n = \hat{p}\hat{q} \cdot \left(\frac{z^*}{E}\right)^2 \;\Rightarrow\; n = \hat{p}(1-\hat{p}) \cdot \left(\frac{z^*}{E}\right)^2$$

The good news is, we have successfully solved for n. However, the bad news is that it may not be practical to use this formula because solving for the sample size implies that we don't have a sample yet. That means that we won't have a value for the sample proportion, $\hat{p}$. Also, we should remember from Chapter 7 that the original value in that spot in the formula was actually p, not $\hat{p}$. But, of course, we do not know the population proportion either. So, what do we do? As strange as it may seem, the standard procedure is to take a guess at the value of p and plug that in. We let p_g represent the guessed value of p. Substituting that into the above formula yields:

$$n = p_g(1-p_g) \cdot \left(\frac{z^*}{E}\right)^2$$

Now that we have the formula for sample size, we need a good method of coming up with a guess for p. The key thing to think about when making our guess is that we never want to end up with a sample size that is too small. If our sample size is too small, then we will end up with a margin of error that is too big. If our sample size is higher than needed, then the margin of error will be smaller than requested, and it would be unusual to get in trouble for not having enough error in our estimate. The following discussion shows us how to pick p_g in such a way as to ensure that we do not get a sample size that is too small.

We want to think of $n = p_g(1-p_g) \cdot \left(\frac{z^*}{E}\right)^2$ as a function where the input is p_g and the output is n. For any specific problem we are working on, the desired margin of error, E, and the value of $z_{\alpha/2}$ are fixed. Thus, for the purpose of finding the value of p_g that maximizes the output n, we can make the substitution $A = \left(\frac{z^*}{E}\right)^2$ to simplify our equation. Note: because of the square, $A > 0$. So, we get:

$$n = p_g(1-p_g) \cdot \left(\frac{z^*}{E}\right)^2 \;\Rightarrow\; n = p_g(1-p_g) \cdot A \;\Rightarrow\; n = Ap_g(1-p_g) \;\Rightarrow\; n = Ap_g - Ap_g^2 \;\Rightarrow\; n = -Ap_g^2 + Ap_g$$

We should recognize this last equation from algebra. It is the equation of a parabola. Because the coefficient of the squared term is negative (-A), this will be a parabola that opens down. This means that it has an input that creates a maximum output. For these variables, that means there is a value of p_g that creates the largest possible value of n. The graph of this function is shown below.

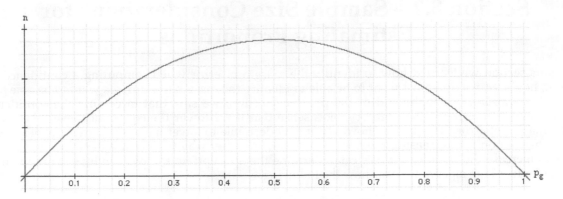

Because the graph has its intercepts at $p_g = 0$ and $p_g = 1$, the vertex occurs when $p_g = 0.5$. So, we see from the graph, that we need our biggest sample size when $p_g = 0.5$ and the farther the value of p_g gets from 0.5, the smaller the sample size we need. Because we never want a sample size that is too small, there are two implications to this. The first is that, when we have a range of reasonable possibilities for p_g, we should use the one that is closest to 0.5. The second implication is that, if we have no reasonable guess for the value of p_g, then we should use the guess $p_g = 0.5$. Let's take a look at an example to see how this works.

Example 8.4: *Making a conservative guess at the true value of p*

Suppose that we are going to calculate the sample size needed to ensure a margin of error of at most E for a confidence interval for a population proportion. If past experience with the topic tells us that it is reasonable to believe that p is somewhere in the intervals given below, then for each one, specify the best conservative guess for p for use in the sample size formula.

a) $p \in (0.2, 0.3)$

b) $p \in (0.67, 0.77)$.

c) $p \in (0.417, 0.535)$

d) $p \in [0, 1]$

Solution:

a) We always want to choose the value of p, from the interval given, in such a way as to guarantee that we do not get a sample size that is too small. Let's look at the interval $p \in (0.2, 0.3)$ on the graph from the discussion above.

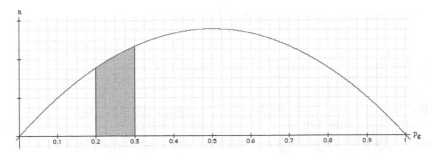

We see that in this interval, the highest value of n occurs when we make the guess $p_g = 0.3$. Because we do not want a value of n that is too small, $p_g = 0.3$ is the correct conservative guess to make.

Technically, the value 0.3 was not in our interval. It was just the boundary. Because this is just a guess anyway, it is acceptable, and standard practice, to guess a boundary value.

b) Let's look at $p \in (0.67, 0.77)$ on the graph.

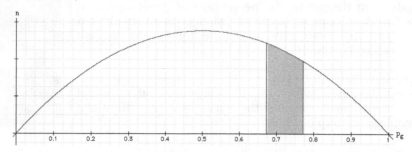

This time, the highest possible value of n occurs at the left side of the interval. So our conservative guess will be $p_g = 0.67$.

c) Now let's look at $p \in (0.417, 0.535)$ on this graph.

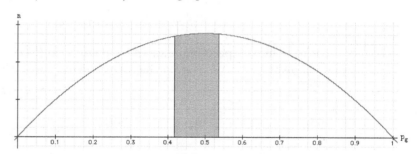

This time, the highest possible value of n, does not occur at the left endpoint or the right endpoint of the interval. The highest value of n occurs inside the interval when $p_g = 0.5$. So, our conservative guess this time will be $p_g = 0.5$.

d) This one is just like the previous one. The interval spans the entire set of possibilities. The highest possible n always comes from using $p_g = 0.5$. Because that value is in this interval, we will use it again.

The formula for calculating sample size for proportions as well as the strategy for guessing at the value of p are summarized in the following point to remember.

Point to Remember: *Estimating the sample size needed to obtain a requested margin of error.*

The minimum sample size needed to get a margin of error of at most E is given by the formula:

$$n = p_g \left(1 - p_g\right) \cdot \left(\frac{z^*}{E}\right)^2 \quad ; \text{ where } p_g \text{ is a guess at the value of p.}$$

Consider each of the following points when determining the sample size:
- If you have an interval of reasonable possibilities for the value of p. Use the value from the interval that is closest to 0.5 as your guess at p.
- If you have no idea what would be a reasonable guess at the value of p, then guess 0.5.
- To ensure that our sample size is never to small, we always round up rather than down.

Let's look at how all of these ideas work in a specific example.

Example 8.5: *Congressional Approval Rating*

Periodically, polling is done to determine the percentage of Americans that approve of the job being done by Congress. Typically, such polls are conducted using a 95% confidence level. It is also common for the pollsters to desire a margin of error of about 3 percentage points.

a) Determine the sample size that will be required to get margin of error of at most 3 percentage points when estimating the congressional approval rating at the 95% confidence level. Assume this survey will take place at a time when no reasonable guess at p is known.

b) Once again, determine the sample size that will be required to get margin of error of at most 3 percentage points when estimating the congressional approval rating at the 95% confidence level. This time, assume that it is reasonable to believe that $p \in (0.25,\ 0.35)$.

How big of a sample size should we take to gauge the approval rating of the U.S. Congress?

Solution:

a) Because they want a margin of error of at most 3 percentage points, we will use $E = 0.03$. We are told that we have no reasonable guess at the value of p. Whenever this happens, we use $p_g = 0.5$. Finally, we need to find the z-score that corresponds to 95% confidence.

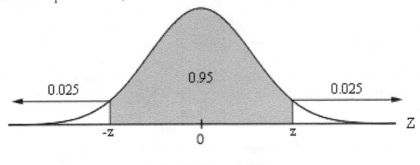

$$-z = invNorm(0.025) \approx -1.960 \ \Rightarrow \ z \approx 1.960$$

Plugging all of this into our formula for determining sample size, we get the following:

$$n = p_g\left(1 - p_g\right) \cdot \left(\frac{z^*}{E}\right)^2 = 0.5\left(1 - 0.5\right)\left(\frac{1.960}{0.03}\right)^2$$

| Caution: *Changing to Decimal Form* |
| It is vital that you change the 3% to 0.03 before making your calculation. |

$$= 0.5 * 0.5 \left(\frac{1.960}{0.03}\right)^2 \approx 1067.11$$

We are always supposed to round up the value of n, so we need a sample size of at least 1068 people.

b) This time, we are told that we are confident that $p \in (0.25, 0.35)$. In such cases, we should choose our guess at p by picking the value from the interval that is closest to 0.5. So, we will use $p_g = 0.35$.

$$n = p_g (1 - p_g) \cdot \left(\frac{z^*}{E} \right)^2 = 0.35(1 - 0.35) \left(\frac{1.960}{0.03} \right)^2$$

$$= 0.35 * 0.65 \left(\frac{1.960}{0.03} \right)^2 \approx 971.07$$

> **Key Concept:** *Benefit of a Guess*
>
> Notice that by making a guess of the true value of p, we will now use a smaller sample size. This should save us time and money!

We always round up, so we will take a sample of 972 people for our survey.

Time to practice with some exercises:

Exercise Set 8.2

Concept Review: Review the definitions and concepts from this section by filling in the blanks for each of the following.

33) When we increase our sample size, it _____ the margin of error.

34) When calculating sample size requirements, we always round n _____ to the next whole number.

35) When determining the sample size required to obtain a desired margin of error in proportion problems, we must _____ at the value of the population proportion.

36) If we have no previous information to help us make a guess at the value of the population proportion, then we should use _____ as our guess.

Mechanics: Practice the calculations needed for determining the sample size required to obtain a specified margin of error for a confidence interval estimate of population proportions before moving on to the real world applications.

37) If recent work produced the given confidence interval for p, then what should we use as a conservative guess for the value of p when computing sample size?

  a) $p \in (0.358, 0.444)$

  b) $p \in (0.764, 0.810)$

  c) $p \in (0.457, 0.561)$

38) If recent work produced the given confidence interval for p, then what should we use as a conservative guess for the value of p when computing sample size?

  a) $p \in (0.212, 0.282)$

  b) $p \in (0.484, 0.590)$

  c) $p \in (0.647, 0.709)$

39) Suppose we want to find a 90% confidence interval for a population proportion. Determine the sample size required to produce a margin of error of at most 3 percentage points if:
  a) We have reason to believe that the population proportion is somewhere between 0.34 and 0.58.
  b) We have reason to believe that the population proportion is smaller than 0.34.

40) Suppose we want to find a 99% confidence interval for a population proportion. Determine the sample size required to produce a margin of error of at most 2.5 percentage points if:
  a) We have reason to believe that the population proportion is at least 0.42.
  b) We have reason to believe that the population proportion is greater than 0.64.

41) Suppose that, from a previous sample, we were 95% confident that the true population proportion was in the interval $(0.7582, 0.8216)$.
  a) Use the confidence interval to determine the point estimate, $\hat{p}$, and the margin of error, E, for the previous study.
  b) Determine the sample size required to produce a margin of error of at most 1.5 percentage points.
  c) Suppose that a sample of the size found in part (b) is taken and produces 2381 items with the desired attributed. Determine the new 95% confidence interval based on this data.
  d) Did your new margin of error exactly match the one specified in part (b)? Discuss briefly.

42) Suppose that, from a previous sample, we were 95% confident that the true population proportion was in the interval $(0.0622, 0.1844)$.
   a) Use the confidence interval to determine the point estimate, $\hat{p}$, and the margin of error, E, for the previous study.
   b) Determine the sample size required to produce a margin of error of at most 4 percentage points.
   c) Suppose that a sample of the size found in part (b) is taken and produces 65 items with the desired attributed. Determine the new 95% confidence interval based on this data.
   d) Did your new margin of error exactly match the one specified in part (b)? Discuss briefly.

Applications: Practice the ideas learned in this section within the context of real world applications.

43) Suppose we want to conduct a study to estimate the percentage of cell phone users who support laws requiring "hands free" driving. If we want to find a 99% confidence interval, determine the sample size required to produce a margin of error of at most 5 percentage points if:
   a) We have no idea what proportion of cell phone users support such laws.
   b) We have reason to believe that more than 70% of cell phone users support such "hands free" laws.

44) Suppose we want to conduct a study to estimate the percentage of snowboarders (as opposed to skiers) at resorts in America. If we want to find a 90% confidence interval, determine the sample size required to produce a margin of error of at most 3.5 percentage points if:
   a) We have no idea what proportion of American riders are snowboarders.
   b) We have reason to believe that less than 35% of all the riders at American resorts are snowboarders.

45) Suppose we want to conduct a study to estimate the percentage of college students who obtain their news via the Internet. If we want to find a 95% confidence interval, determine the sample size required to produce a margin of error of at most 3 percentage points if:
   a) We have no idea what proportion of college students obtain their news via the Internet.
   b) We have reason to believe that more than 80% of all college students obtain their news via the Internet.

46) Suppose we want to conduct a study to estimate the percentage of American workers that consider themselves to be poor. If we want to find a 95% confidence interval, determine the sample size required to produce a margin of error of at most 1.5 percentage points if:
   a) We have no idea what proportion of American workers that consider themselves to be poor.
   b) We have reason to believe that less than 15% of all American workers consider themselves to be poor.

47) In Exercise (19) from Section 8.1, we found that the proportion of registered voters that approved of the job Scott Walker was doing as Governor of Wisconsin was somewhere between 31.77% and 42.33%. Our confidence level was 99%.
   a) Use this interval to make a conservative guess for the population proportion and determine the sample size we would need to lower the margin of error to 2 percentage points.
   b) Suppose that political upheaval made us feel as though we could no longer trust our previous interval. What sample size would then be required to ensure that a new poll would have a margin of error of at most 2 percentage points?

48) In Exercise (26) from Section 8.1 we saw that the 99% confidence interval for the proportion of bets the sports gambler would be expected to win was from 51.09% to 62.51%.
   a) Use this interval to make a conservative guess for the population proportion and determine the sample size we would need to lower the margin of error to 1 percentage point.
   b) Suppose that we were doing this study for a different gambler that we have no information about. What sample size would then be required to ensure that our study would have a margin of error of at most 1 percentage point?

49) In Exercise (21) from Section 8.1, we found that the proportion video game players that are female was somewhere between 40.01% and 43.57%. Our confidence level was 90%.
   a) Use this interval to make a conservative guess for the population proportion and determine the sample size we would need to lower the margin of error to 1 percentage point.
   b) Suppose that changes in games and society made us no longer trust our previous interval. What sample size would then be required to ensure that a new survey would have a margin of error of at most 1 percentage point?

50) In Exercise (24) from Section 8.1 we saw that the 90% confidence interval for the proportion of Chicago area specialty doctors that would refuse to accept a new child patient on Medicare was from 61.21% to 70.65%.
   a) Use this interval to make a conservative guess for the population proportion and determine the sample size we would need to lower the margin of error to 3 percentage points.
   b) Suppose that we were doing this study for a different city that we have no information about. What sample size would then be required to ensure that our study would have a margin of error of at most 3 percentage points?

Section 8.3 – Confidence Intervals for the Population Mean, μ

In this section, we will continue with the topic of confidence intervals; however, we will switch from confidence intervals for population proportions to confidence intervals for population means. This will allow us to compute confidence interval estimates for such things as the mean lifetime for a new brand of light bulb, or the mean sodium content for a brand of potato chips. We will begin with a brief discussion of the needed theory and then we will move to some examples.

In Section 7.4, we learned that, if we take a random sample of size n from a population with a mean of μ and a standard deviations of σ, then the sample mean, $\bar{x}$, is approximately normally distributed (provided that the population is normal or that the sample size is large) with $\mu_{\bar{x}} = \mu$ and $\sigma_{\bar{x}} \approx \dfrac{\sigma}{\sqrt{n}}$. From this we can conclude

that $z = \dfrac{\bar{x} - \mu}{\sigma/\sqrt{n}}$ will have the standard normal distribution. And, in turn, this implies that

$$P\left(\mu - z^* \cdot \frac{\sigma}{\sqrt{n}} < \bar{x} < \mu + z^* \cdot \frac{\sigma}{\sqrt{n}} \right) = 1 - \alpha,$$ where the area between $-z^*$ and z^* under the standard normal

curve equals $1 - \alpha$. To arrive at our formula for confidence intervals for population means, we will now use algebra to solve this last inequality for μ. The result of the algebra work is shown below.

$$P\left(\mu - z^* \cdot \frac{\sigma}{\sqrt{n}} < \bar{x} < \mu + z^* \cdot \frac{\sigma}{\sqrt{n}} \right) = 1 - \alpha \;\Rightarrow\; P\left(\bar{x} - z^* \cdot \frac{\sigma}{\sqrt{n}} < \mu < \bar{x} + z^* \cdot \frac{\sigma}{\sqrt{n}} \right) = 1 - \alpha$$

If we knew the value of the population standard deviation, σ, then we could use the formula above to compute confidence intervals for population means. However, it is not realistic to know the value of the population standard deviation, σ, in situations where you don't know the population mean, μ. Recall from Section 3.3 that you must use μ when computing σ. We had a similar problem to this in Section 8.1 when our initial formula for a confidence interval for population proportions, required us to already know the true value of p. In that section, we solved this problem by substituting the sample proportion, $\hat{p}$, in its place. Here, we will seek a similar solution to our current problem. Because the population standard deviation, σ, will not be known, we will substitute the sample standard deviation, s, in its place. When we are computing a confidence interval, we always take a sample to get our point estimate, $\bar{x}$. While we are computing the sample mean, it would be easy to use the sample to get the value of s as well.

> **Key Concept:** *dealing with an unknown* σ
>
> The formula:
>
> $$\sigma = \sqrt{\frac{\sum (x - \mu)^2}{N}}$$ shows us that it is not
>
> realistic for us to know the value of σ when we are estimating the value of μ.

So, the initial solution to this problem is simple. If you don't know the population standard deviation σ, then replace it by the sample standard deviation, s. This will be the best solution to the problem, but it does have consequences. In Section 8.1, when we replaced p by $\hat{p}$, the sampling error was negligible because we were multiplying $\hat{p}$ with $1 - \hat{p}$ and most of the error canceled out. However, in this section, no such cancellation of sampling error will occur. Therefore, if the value of s turns out to be smaller than the true value of σ, then our confidence interval will be narrower than it really should be. This narrower interval is more likely to miss the value of the true mean. This means that such a replacement will hurt our confidence. The following graphs illustrate how the varying sample standard deviations in different samples affect the length of our intervals. This, in turn, causes us to miss the true mean more often than we should.

In the graph below, the population standard deviation is known and used to compute all the intervals. Because we always used the same value for the standard deviation, all of our 80% confidence Intervals have the same width.

In the graph below, the population standard deviation was assumed to be unknown. Therefore, we used the sample standard deviation to compute our 80% confidence intervals. Because the sample standard deviation varied from sample to sample, so did the width of our intervals. This variation of width caused us to miss the true mean of 20 more often than expected.

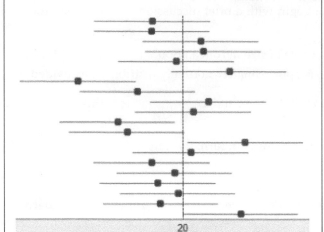

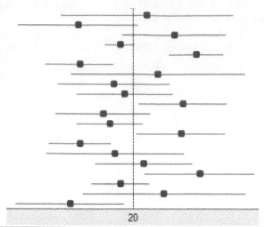

What adjustment could we make to our interval to regain the lost confidence? We learned in Section 8.1 that by increasing the length of our confidence interval, we could increase our level of confidence. Therefore, if we replace the population standard deviation, σ, by an estimate, s, then to make up for the uncertainty this introduces, we must make our interval a bit wider.

The big question now is, how do we decide exactly how much to lengthen our confidence interval? The answer to this question is solved for us by the student t variable and the **student t-distribution**. Let's learn about this new variable and distribution and then we will return to the topic of confidence intervals.

THE STUDENT's t DISTRIBUTION: *The adjustment for using s in place of σ*

Recall: The standardized version of $\bar{x}$ is given by it's z-score formula. Thus, the standardized version of $\bar{x}$ is $z = \dfrac{\bar{x} - \mu}{\sigma / \sqrt{n}}$. If $\bar{x}$ is normally distributed, then z will have the standard normal distribution. However, if we replace σ by s, then more uncertainty is introduced into the calculation and we no longer would have the standard normal distribution. It turns out that replacing the σ in $\dfrac{\bar{x} - \mu}{\sigma / \sqrt{n}}$ by s, changes the distribution of this variable to what is known as a **Student's t-distribution**. So, rather than calling the calculation a z-score, we will now refer to it as a t-score. The formula for a t-score is $t = \dfrac{\bar{x} - \mu}{s / \sqrt{n}}$. The following point to remember summarizes this discussion.

Definition: *The Student's t-distribution.*

Student's t distribution: If $\bar{x}$ is normally distributed, then the variable $t = \dfrac{\bar{x} - \mu}{s / \sqrt{n}}$

will have the Student t-distribution with $n - 1$ degrees of freedom, or $df = n - 1$.

The scary thing about this new information is that it implies that we need to learn a whole new distribution to take the place of the standard normal distribution. Worse yet, we have to learn many different t-distributions, because for every different sample size, there is a different t-distribution. This is not actually as bad as it sounds. The t-distribution is very similar to the standard normal distribution and, in some cases, it can even be easier to work with. Let's take a look at some t-distributions together with the standard normal distribution and discuss their properties.

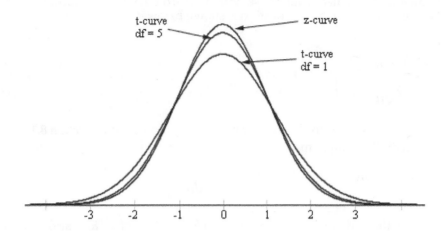

We can see from the graphs above that t-curves share much in common with the standard normal curve, but there are some differences as well. The following is a list of the properties of t-curves that are similar to the z-curve and also those that are different.

Point to Remember: *Properties of the t-distribution*

Properties similar to the standard normal curve:
- The total area under a t-curve is equal to 1. This is required for any probability distribution curve.
- The curve is symmetric about 0.
- The curve extends indefinitely in both directions and the height approaches zero on each side.

Properties different from the standard normal curve:
- There are many t-curves, rather than just 1.
- t-curves are shorter in the center and thus taller in the tails. This means that we must go farther out in a t-curve than for the standard normal curve to capture any specified amount of area. This will eventually result in the wider confidence intervals that we need.

Additional property: The larger the degrees of freedom, or df, the more t-curves look like the standard normal curve. As our sample size, and thus our df, increases, our confidence in s as an estimate of σ also increases. Thus, it is not necessary to make as large of an adjustment to the width of our confidence interval.

Now it's time to take a look at how this change from the standard normal curve to the t-distribution will affect the work we do in computing confidence intervals.

Let's suppose that $\bar{x}$ is normally distributed. This means that $t = \dfrac{\bar{x} - \mu}{s/\sqrt{n}}$ has the Student's t-distribution with

$df = n - 1$. Further suppose that the area between $-t^{*}$ and t^{*} under the t-curve with $df = n - 1$ equals $1 - \alpha$.

Then, in symbols, we could write $P\left(-t^* < \dfrac{\overline{x} - \mu}{s/\sqrt{n}} < t^*\right) = 1 - \alpha$. Our goal is to use algebra to rearrange this

formula so that μ is isolated in the middle. This would give us a formula that could be used to find confidence intervals for population means even when using the sample standard deviation, s, rather than the population standard deviation, σ. The result of such algebra steps is shown below.

$$P\left(-t^* < \frac{\overline{x} - \mu}{s/\sqrt{n}} < t^*\right) = 1 - \alpha \;\Rightarrow\; P\left(\overline{x} - t^* \cdot \frac{s}{\sqrt{n}} < \mu < \overline{x} + t^* \cdot \frac{s}{\sqrt{n}}\right) = 1 - \alpha$$

The formula shown above is very similar to the one developed for proportions in Section 8.1. To find the population mean, we start with the sample mean, $\overline{x}$. Because we know this will not give us the exact right

answer, we must give ourselves some margin for error, $\pm\, t^* \cdot \dfrac{s}{\sqrt{n}}$.

It would appear that, the new thing we need to learn is how to find values of t^* for various confidence levels, $1 - \alpha$. Just as we used the invNorm function to find z^* in Section 8.1, we will now introduce the **invT** functions to help use find the value of t^* needed here.

FINDING t^* USING invT: *How is it different form invNorm?*

> **Definition:** *invT* and t_α
>
> **invT:** The invT function allows us to find a t-score with a given area to its left. The structure of the function is shown below.
>
> invT(Area to the left of t, df) → t-score
>
> The two inputs to the function are the desired area to the left of the t-score and the degrees of freedom. The function returns the t-score that achieves this.
>
> **Note:** Instructions for calculating the value of this function using various forms of technology are given at the end of this section. Tables for finding t-scores are also provided in the appendix.
>
> t_α: t_α is the t-value that has area α to its right. For example, $t_{0.025}$ has an area of 0.025 to its right.

The example below shows how to use invT to find t-scores that we will often need for confidence intervals involving the mean.

Example 8.6: *Practicing the use of invT*

Use the invT function to find each of the following values. Illustrate each with a graph.

a) $t_{0.05}$ if df = 7.

b) $t_{0.05}$ if df = 27.

c) $t_{0.025}$ if n = 24.

d) $t_{0.005}$ if n = 71.

Solution:

a) $t_{0.05}$ is the spot on the number line for the t-curve that has an area of 0.05 to its right. By symmetry, $-t_{0.05}$ would have an area of 0.05 to its left. That leaves an area of 0.90 to lie between these two values. See the graph below.

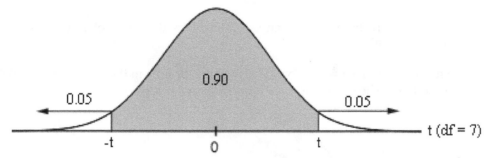

Finding these two values of t is a working backwards question. When we wanted to do this for the standard normal curve, we used the invNorm function. For the t-distribution, we will use the invT function. The function gives the value of t given a specified amount of area to the left and the df. The structure of the function is:

invT(area to the left of t, df)

Because the area to the left of –t is specified on our graph, we will find that value and then use symmetry to find the value of t. So, we get:

$$-t = invT\left(0.05,\ 7\right) \approx -1.895 \quad \Rightarrow \quad t_{0.05} = t \approx 1.895$$

> **Key Concept**: *How t is related to a confidence interval*
>
> As can be seen from the area in the middle of our curve, this is the value of $t_{\alpha/2}$ that would be needed for finding a 90% confidence interval if df = 7.

b) This is identical to the last one, except that the *df* has changed. So, we have the following.

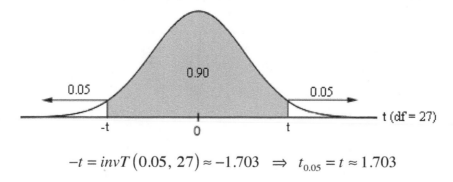

$$-t = invT\left(0.05,\ 27\right) \approx -1.703 \quad \Rightarrow \quad t_{0.05} = t \approx 1.703$$

Because the df is larger this time, we have a taller and narrower t-curve, this means that we didn't have to go out as far as in part (a) to capture the area of 0.90 in the middle.

c) This one is similar to the ones above with a couple of key changes. First, we are looking for $t_{0.025}$, so we have different areas in the tails and thus in the center. Also, we are given the sample size, n, rather than the degrees of freedom, df. This is easily remedied because the $df = n-1$. Thus we have $df = n-1 = 24-1 = 23$. The graph and structure are shown below.

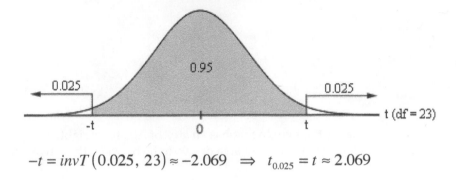

$$-t = invT(0.025, 23) \approx -2.069 \quad \Rightarrow \quad t_{0.025} = t \approx 2.069$$

Based on the area in the center, this time we can say that this is the value of t^* that we would use if we wanted a 95% confidence interval.

d) Because $n = 71$, we have $df = n-1 = 71-1 = 70$. This time the area in the tails is given as 0.005, so the area in the middle will be 0.99. The graph and structure are shown below.

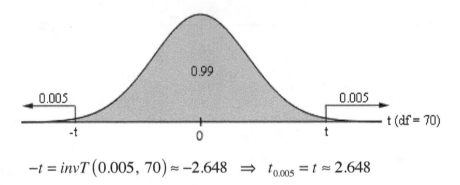

$$-t = invT(0.005, 70) \approx -2.648 \quad \Rightarrow \quad t_{0.005} = t \approx 2.648$$

> **Caution:** *We must find the df when n is provided*
>
> It may seem tricky that we were given the value of n, rather than the value of the df. However, we should consider this, we don't really even know what the degrees of freedom are, but we do know that n represents the sample size. Thus, we are usually going to know n and we will use it to find the df. The meaning of degrees of freedom is explained in more detail in Chapter 10.

BACK TO CONFIDENCE INTERVALS:

We saw earlier, that if $\bar{x}$ is normally distributed, then $P\left(\bar{x} - t^* \cdot \dfrac{s}{\sqrt{n}} < \mu < \bar{x} + t^* \cdot \dfrac{s}{\sqrt{n}}\right) = 1 - \alpha$. We now

know how to find the values of t^* using invT, so we are ready to compute confidence intervals again. Our new procedure is shown in the following point to remember.

Point to Remember: *Procedure for finding confidence intervals for μ when σ is unknown.*

Requirements: In order to use the t distribution to find the value of t^*, $\bar{x}$ must be normally distributed. So we need at least one of the following conditions to be true:

- The sample size is large ($n \geq 30$)
- The population is normally distributed.
- $15 \leq n < 30$ and the population is not severely skewed.

Steps: We complete the steps below to create our confidence intervals.

- *Point Estimate*: Calculate $\bar{x}$ and s from the sample using technology (if they are not already given.)
- *t-score*: For a confidence level of $(1 - \alpha) \cdot 100\%$, sketch the t-curve with $df = n - 1$ and use invT to determine the two t values, $\pm t^*$, that trap an area of $1 - \alpha$ in the middle with equal outside areas.
- *Endpoints*: Calculate the endpoints of the confidence interval using the formula:

$$\bar{x} \pm t^* \cdot \frac{s}{\sqrt{n}}$$

- *Interval*: The confidence interval is written $\mu \in \left(\bar{x} - t^* \cdot \dfrac{s}{\sqrt{n}}, \bar{x} + t^* \cdot \dfrac{s}{\sqrt{n}}\right)$.

Rounding Rule: The boundaries on the confidence interval should be written with the same number of decimal places as were used in $\bar{x}$.

When we were working with proportions, we saw that the margin of error was the amount added and subtracted from the point estimate. This remains true when working with means.

Definition: *Margin of Error (for estimating population means)*

Margin of Error: The margin of error when working with means is the amount added and subtracted from the sample mean, $\bar{x}$.

$$E = t^* \cdot \frac{s}{\sqrt{n}}$$

Let's take a look at an example.

Example 8.7: *Estimating the mean depth of the snow pack in Lake Tahoe*

A ski and snowboard resort in Lake Tahoe wants to estimate the mean depth of their snow pack. They randomly chose 41 locations on the mountain and measured the depth of the snow in each location. The sample yielded a mean of 67.53 inches with a standard deviation of 22.98 inches.

a) Comment on the requirements for calculating a confidence interval for the mean depth of the snow pack at the resort.

b) Compute a 95% confidence interval for the mean depth of the snow pack at this resort.

How accurate of an estimate of the true mean snow depth at a Tahoe resort can be found using a random sample of 41 measurements?

c) What was the margin of error for this interval?

d) Interpret the interval in terms of the application.

e) Based on the interval from part (b), can we say with 95% confidence that the average snow pack at this resort exceeds 60 inches? Explain.

Solution:

a) $n = 41 \geq 30 \Rightarrow \bar{x}$ is normally distributed. Therefore, the requirements have been met.

b)   The mean and standard deviation are provided by the problem, so we do not have to calculate them ourselves. Let's summarize the information given. The mean and standard deviation provided are stated as coming from the random sample, thus we have:

$$\bar{x} = 67.53, \ s = 22.98, \ n = 41$$

Because the value of σ is unknown in this example, we will be computing a t-interval. So, we must find the value of $t_{\alpha/2}$ needed for 95% confidence. $df = n - 1 = 41 - 1 = 40$. Let's look at the graph.

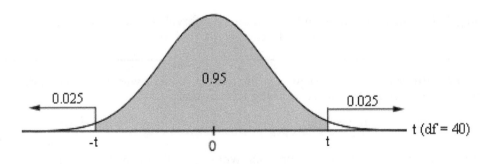

$$-t = invT(0.025, 40) \approx -2.021 \ \Rightarrow \ t_{0.025} = t \approx 2.021$$

$$\bar{x} \pm t^* \cdot \frac{s}{\sqrt{n}} = 67.53 \pm 2.021 \cdot \frac{22.98}{\sqrt{41}} = 67.53 \pm 7.25 \ \Rightarrow \ \mu \in (60.28, \ 74.78)$$

c)   The piece we add and subtract from the point estimate is the margin of error. Looking at the work above, we see that $E = 7.25$.

d)   We are 95% confident that the true mean depth of the snow pack at this resort is somewhere between 60.28 inches and 74.48 inches.

e)   Yes. $\mu \in (60.28, \ 74.78) \Rightarrow \mu > 60$. We are 95% confident that the mean depth of the snow pack is somewhere in the interval and that implies it is greater than 60.28 inches. Therefore, it must also be greater than 60 inches.

WRAP SESSION: *A medium sized sample with data provided*

Example 8.8: *Estimating the profits of a poker player*

A professional poker player is trying to estimate her average monthly income. She obtains a random sample of 18 of her poker sessions and notes the amount won in each session (losing sessions have negative amounts listed). The sample data is shown below. The amounts are in dollars. A boxplot of the data is shown below the data set.

Are 18 sessions of poker enough to distinguish a lucky player from a skillful one?

665	-399	564	524	997	153	-26	1455	824
234	643	274	-157	846	583	647	559	168

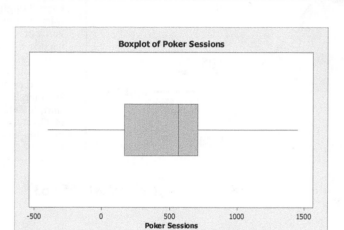

a) Use the boxplot to discuss whether or not the requirements have been met for computing a confidence interval for the true mean of this data set.

b) Compute a 90% confidence interval for the true long-term mean amount won per session.

c) Based on the interval from part (b), can we say with 90% confidence that she is, on average, a winning player? Explain.

d) Based on the interval from part (b), can we say with 90% confidence that her average win per session exceeds $400? Explain.

e) Suppose that this sample was taken from a population consisting of 847 poker sessions. Use your answer to part (b) to determine a 90% confidence interval for the total amount of winnings for those 847 poker sessions.

Solution:

a) Because $15 \leq n = 18 < 30$, we require that the population we are sampling from is not severely skewed. In the boxplot shown above, we see that the right whisker is slightly longer than the left whisker. However, the left side of the box is a little wider than the right side. These differences could easily just be random variation in such a small sample. While it might be possible that the population is skewed slightly, the roughly symmetric look and the lack of outliers in the boxplot are compelling evidence that the population is not severely skewed. I am convinced that the requirements are met.

b) This time, we are not given the values of the mean and standard deviation, so we must find them using the sample data. We can accomplish this using the technology of our choice. A screen shot from a TI-84 is shown to the right.

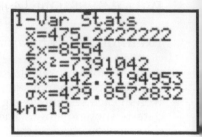

Because we entered sample data, we must use the value of s rather than σ. So, we have:

$$\bar{x} = 475.22, \ s = 442.32, \ n = 18 \Rightarrow df = 17$$

Because σ is unknown, this will be a t-interval. So we must find the value of t^* needed for a 90% confidence level. The graph is shown below.

0.90

0.05   0.05

-t   0   t   t (df = 17)

$$-t = invT(0.05, \ 17) \approx -1.740 \ \Rightarrow \ t_{0.05} = t \approx 1.740$$

Caution: s or σ ?

Even though the calculator output shows a value of σ, it cannot be used in our calculations. This would only truly be the value of σ if we had entered population data. We merely entered sample data, so the value of σ on the screen is meaningless and must be ignored.

$$\bar{x} \pm t^* \cdot \frac{s}{\sqrt{n}} = 475.22 \pm 1.740 \cdot \frac{442.32}{\sqrt{18}} = 475.22 \pm 181.41 \ \Rightarrow \ \mu \in (293.81, \ 656.63)$$

> **Caution:** *Another misinterpretation to avoid*
>
> Sometimes people will misinterpret a confidence interval for the mean by stating "90% of the poker player's sessions will result in winnings between \$293.81 and \$656.63. It is important to remember that the interval is not for the individual sessions, but for the true mean of all of her sessions. In fact, only 6 of the 18 sessions in the sample were in this range.

c) Yes we can. If $\mu \in (293.81, \ 656.63) \Rightarrow \mu > 293.81 \Rightarrow \mu > 0$. We are confident that her average winnings are somewhere between \$293.81 and \$656.63 per session. Any amount in this range is positive and, therefore, tells us that she is, on average, a winning player.

d) No we cannot. If $\mu \in (293.81, \ 656.63) \Rightarrow \mu$ could be less than \$400. For example, it could be \$350, because that is one of the reasonable possibilities for μ contained in the interval.

e) In part (b), we estimated that $293.81 < \mu < 656.63$. Because $\mu = \dfrac{\sum x}{N}$, we can find $\sum x$ by multiplying by the population size, $N = 847$. $293.81 \cdot (847) < \mu \cdot N < 656.63 \cdot (847) \Rightarrow$ We are 90% confident that the total winnings for the 847 sessions is somewhere between \$248,857.07 and \$556,165.61.

> **Key Concept:** *What a confidence interval tells us about the true population mean*
>
> A confidence interval provides us with a list of the reasonable possibilities for the true value of the population mean. In order to be confident that the true mean is greater (or less than) a specific value, the entire set of possibilities from the interval must be greater than (or less than) the specified values. In part (d) of the example above, we were not stating that the player's mean profit does not exceed \$400. In fact, it could be a value like \$650, because it is in the interval. We are stating that we can not be confident it is greater than \$400.

USING TECHNOLOGY: *Calculating the value of invT using various technologies*

In this section, we introduced the invT function for finding the t-scores needed for confidence intervals for population means. We will now learn how to calculate the value of invT using various technologies. A table for doing the same thing is available in the appendix in the back of the text. The examples below will all attempt to find the value of $t_{0.025}$ with $n = 24 \Rightarrow df = 24 - 1 = 23$. This is the t-score that would be needed for a 95% confidence interval. The graph is shown below.

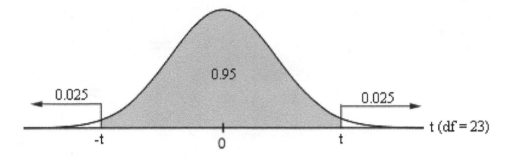

MINITAB:

1. From the Calc Menu, choose Probability Distributions, and click on t . . .
2. Click on the Inverse cumulative probability circle. Enter the degrees of freedom. Click on Input constant and enter the area in the left tail. Click OK.
3. The output will be the t-score on the left. (Even though it is labeled as an 'x')
4. Change to a positive value and round to 3 decimal places.

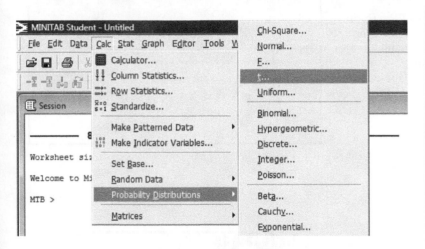

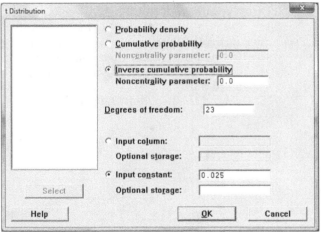

Inverse Cumulative Distribution Function

Student's t distribution with 23 DF

```
P( X <= x )          x
     0.025   -2.06866
```

Thus we have $-t_{0.025} \approx -2.069$ and $t_{0.025} \approx 2.069$.

STATCRUNCH:

1. Choose Stat > Calculators > T
2. Enter the DF in the box provided. Enter the tail area of 0.025 in the box after the '=' sign. Change the symbol in the menu from '<=' to '=>'. Click Compute.
3. The t-score will be in the box shown circled below.
4. You should already have the positive value, but you still need to round to 3 decimal places.

Thus we have $t_{0.025} \approx 2.069$.

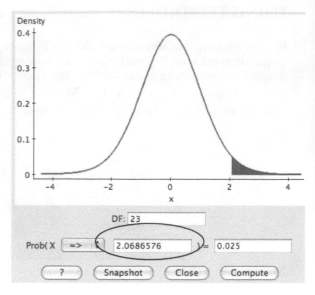

EXCEL:

1. Click in any of the cells in the worksheet.
2. Click in the f_x box.
3. Type in "= TINV(0.05,23)" and press ENTER. (Notes: Don't type the quotes, but you must type the equal sign. IMPORTANT: You must enter the total area of the two tails rather than just one of the tails.)
4. The positive t-score will be entered into the cell you started in.
5. Round the t-score to 3 decimal places.

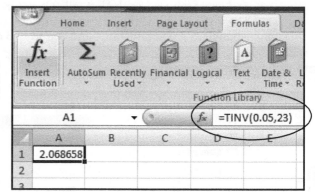

TI 84:

1. From the DISTR menu, choose invT(
2. Enter the tail area, followed by the df.
3. The output is the negative t-score on the left.
4. Change to a positive value and round to 3 decimal places.

Thus we have $-t_{0.025} \approx -2.069$ and $t_{0.025} \approx 2.069$.

NOTE: The TI-83 does not have the invT(function built in. It can be programmed to do this or TI-83 users will need to use the tables provided in the appendix to find t-scores for confidence intervals.

Exercise Set 8.3

Concept Review: Review the definitions and concepts from this section by filling in the blanks for each of the following.

51) t-curves are similar in shape to the z-curve except that they tend to be _____ and _____ .

52) There are many different t-curves. Each curve has its own degree of freedom. The formula for finding the degrees of freedom is $df =$ _____ .

53) As the df increases, t-curves look more and more like the _____ _____ curve.

54) We must use a t-curve when σ is _____ and we have replaced it with ____ .

55) When using the invT function, we must always enter the area to the _____ of the t-score we are looking for.

56) The requirements for the confidence interval are designed to make sure that _____ is normally distributed. This ensures that our _____ level is accurate.

57) A confidence interval provides us with a list of the _____ _____ for the true value of the population mean.

58) *True or False*: If a claimed value for the population mean is in our confidence interval, then we can be confident that the claimed value is correct.

Mechanics: Practice the calculations needed for confidence interval estimates of population means before moving on to the real world applications.

59) Use invT or invNorm together with technology or the t-table to find each of the following:
   a) $t_{0.05}$ if df = 19
   b) $t_{0.05}$ if df = 29
   c) $t_{0.01}$ if df = 13
   d) $z_{0.005}$

60) Use invT or invNorm together with technology or the t-table to find each of the following:
   a) $t_{0.025}$ if df = 13
   b) $t_{0.025}$ if df = 50
   c) $t_{0.005}$ if df = 22
   d) $z_{0.05}$

61) Use invT or invNorm together with technology or the t-table to find each of the following:
   a) $t_{0.025}$ if n = 23
   b) $t_{0.1}$ if n = 76
   c) $t_{0.05}$ if n = 31
   d) $z_{0.01}$ if n = 111

62) Use invT or invNorm together with technology or the t-table to find each of the following:
   a) $t_{0.005}$ if n = 17
   b) $t_{0.01}$ if n = 101
   c) $t_{0.025}$ if n = 57
   d) $z_{0.10}$ if n = 215

63) Suppose a random sample of size 76 produced a mean of 18.93 and a standard deviation of 4.078.
   a) Comment on the requirements for finding a confidence interval for the population mean.
   b) Determine a 95% confidence interval for the population mean.
   c) What was the margin of error for your point estimate?

64) Suppose a random sample of size 25 produced a mean of 87.4 with a standard deviation of 13.88.
   a) Comment on the requirements for finding a confidence interval for the population mean.
   b) Determine a 90% confidence interval for the population mean.
   c) What was the margin of error for your point estimate?

65) Suppose a random sample of size 19 produced a mean of 36.025 with a standard deviation of 9.0707.
   a) Comment on the requirements for finding a confidence interval for the population mean.
   b) Determine a 99% confidence interval for the population mean.
   c) What was the margin of error for your point estimate?

66) Suppose a random sample of size 101 produced a mean of 1907.42 and a standard deviation of 204.57.
   a) Comment on the requirements for finding a confidence interval for the population mean.
   b) Determine a 95% confidence interval for the population mean.
   c) What was the margin of error for your point estimate?

Applications: Practice the ideas learned in this section within the context of real world applications.

67) A manufacturer has produced a new type of battery to be used in portable Blu-ray players. They tested the batteries in a random sample of 36 of their Blu-ray players. The sample produced a mean of 5.62 hours with a standard deviation of 1.0639 hours.
   a) Comment on the requirements for finding a confidence interval for the mean.
   b) Compute a 95% confidence interval for the true average lasting time of the battery in all of the companies portable Blu-ray players.
   c) Interpret the interval in terms of the application.

68) A study was conducted to estimate the average cost of a new statistics textbook from a college bookstore. A random sample of 60 new stat books from college books stores produced a mean of $112.95 with a standard deviation of $24.06.
   a) Comment on the requirements for finding a confidence interval for the mean.
   b) Compute a 90% confidence interval for the average cost of all new stat textbooks from college bookstores.
   c) Interpret the interval in terms of the application.

69) A developmental psychologist is interested in the cognitive development of children born as twins. It is known that the IQ's of 9-year-old children is normally distributed with an average of 100 points. The psychologist obtains a random sample of 28 nine-year-olds that are part of a pair of twins. He gives them a standard IQ test and finds the mean score to be 94.286 with a standard deviation of 9.37. Assume that the IQs for twins are normally distributed.
   a) Comment on the requirements for finding a confidence interval for the mean.
   b) Compute a 99% confidence interval for the true mean IQ of 9-year-old twins.
   c) Interpret the interval in terms of the application.
   d) Can we say with 99% confidence, based on the interval from part (b), that the mean IQ of 9-year-old twins is less than 100? Explain.

70) For the 2008-2009 academic year, the average cost of tuition and fees at public 4-year colleges was $6590 (based on information published by The College Board). In an attempt to balance their budgets, many states were considering raising their tuition and fees. The following year, a random sample of 21 4-year public colleges produced an average of $7020 for tuition and fees with a standard deviation of $3100. Assume that the tuitions for all public 4-year colleges are slightly right skewed.
   a) Comment on the requirements for finding a confidence interval for the mean.
   b) Compute a 95% confidence interval for the true mean cost of tuition and fees at public 4-year colleges.
   c) Interpret the interval in terms of the application.
   d) Can we say with 95% confidence, based on the interval from part (b), that the mean cost of tuition and fees at public 4-year colleges is more than $6590? Explain.

71) A manufacturer has built a new hybrid SUV and needs to estimate the average gas consumption for city driving conditions. They tested 12 of the vehicles in city driving conditions and obtained the following sample for the gas mileage for each vehicle.

36.04	36.31	33.24	35.75	31.75	33.43
37.25	34.11	35.11	35.48	33.83	32.58

Note: $\sum x^2 = 14{,}374.4076$

   a) Use the normal probability plot for the sample data shown below to comment on the requirements of finding a confidence interval for the mean.

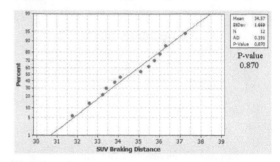

   b) Compute a 99% confidence interval for the true mean city gas mileage for all such hybrid SUVs.
   c) Can we say with 99% confidence, based on the interval from part (b), that the true mean city gas mileage for all such hybrid SUVs is less than 35 mpg? Explain.

72) A study was conducted on the sleep habits of Koala bears. A random sample of 18 Koalas was monitored over a 24 hour period and the following times, in hours, were obtained for the amount of sleep for each during that period.

19.9	19.7	19.4	19.3	19.8	18.8
19.4	19.2	19.5	20.1	19.7	19.3
19.3	20.3	19.7	19.4	20.2	19.3

Note: $\sum x^2 = 6897.83$

   a) Use the boxplot of the sample data shown below to comment on the requirements for finding a confidence interval for the mean.

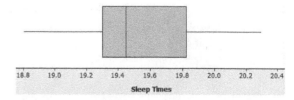

   b) Compute a 95% confidence interval for the mean number of hours of sleep per day for Koala bears.
   c) Can we say with 95% confidence, based on the interval from part (b), that the mean number of hours of sleep per day is less than 20 hours per day? Explain.

73) The points scored by the winning teams in a sample of 48 games played during the 2007 NFL season are shown below.

20	22	51	10	21	22	31	37	33	8
29	13	26	20	20	31	23	32	28	10
27	30	21	49	38	25	19	35	38	38
20	41	16	22	48	27	13	30	34	20
33	31	27	17	42	44	38	38		

Note: $\bar{x} \approx 28.1$, $s \approx 10.488$

a) Comment on the requirements for finding a confidence interval for the mean.
b) Compute a 90% confidence interval for the mean points scored by the winning teams during the 2007 NFL season.
c) Can we say with 90% confidence, based on the interval from part (b), that the mean points scored by the winning teams during the 2007 NFL season is more than 25 points? Explain.
d) There were 256 games played during the 2007 NFL season. Use your answer to part (b) to determine a 90% confidence interval for the true total number of points scored by the winning teams during that season.

74) A researcher wants to conduct a new study determine the average gestation time for house cats. A random sample of 11 pregnant cats was taken and produced the following gestation times, in days.

64.3	65.5	64.7	65.9	67.0	66.8
64.6	65.5	65.7	66.9	65.7	

Note: $\sum x^2 = 47,476.88$

a) Use the normal probability plot for the sample data shown below to comment on the requirements of finding a confidence interval for the mean.

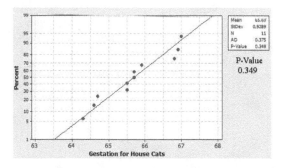

b) Compute a 95% confidence interval for the true mean gestation time for house cats.
c) Suppose past studies have shown that the gestation time for house cats is 65.5 days. Can we say with 95% confidence, based on the interval from part (b), that the true mean gestation time for house cats is actually different than the 65.5 days found in previous studies? Explain.

75) The owner of "Everything Grows", a plant business in Danville, CA wishes to increase traffic to the company's website. To accomplish this goal, he paid for a search engine optimization. Before this took place, the website was averaging 16.67 hits per day. A random sample of 18 days after the optimization was completed had the following number of hits:

27	37	33	11	32	5
31	6	11	23	22	29
13	9	33	21	35	37

Note: $\bar{x} \approx 23.0556$, $s \approx 11.2065$

a) Use the boxplot of the sample data shown below to comment on the requirements for finding a confidence interval for the mean.

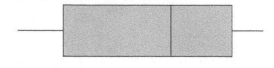

b) Compute a 95% confidence interval for the mean number of hits per day after the optimization.
c) Can we say with 95% confidence, based on the interval from part (b), that the mean number of hits per day was higher after the optimization than it was before? Explain.
d) Use your answer to part (b) to determine a 95% confidence interval for the true total number of hits during the 365 days following the optimization.

76) The list prices of a sample of 39 homes (5+ bedrooms) from Malibu, CA in March 2013 are shown below. All prices shown are in $1000s.

4910	5250	8995	8500	6990	3095
8995	1695	2699	5995	2195	1600
16750	16995	4875	4700	2195	7750
1495	14500	6495	5495	6511	795
7995	8700	5395	3350	14500	11950
2695	3575	995	5500	5850	5750
10650	2150	6495			

Note: $\bar{x} \approx 6282.692$, $s \approx 4224.139$

a) Comment on the requirements for finding a confidence interval for the mean.
b) Compute a 95% confidence interval for the mean list price of all 5+ bedroom homes in Malibu in March 2013.
c) Can we say with 95% confidence, based on the interval from part (b), that the mean list price is more than 5 million dollars? Explain.
d) There were 340 such homes for sale in Malibu at that time. Use your answer to part (b) to determine a 95% confidence interval for the true total amount for the list prices of those 340 homes.

77) Because of their heavier weights, the braking distance for SUVs tends to be further than it is for cars. To help alleviate this problem a tire maker has produced a new tread design that they believe will help shorten the stopping distance for the heavier SUVs. A random sample of 10 SUVs with the new tires is tested and the average 60 mph braking distance for the sample is found to be 131.7 feet with a standard deviation of 4.5007 feet.

a) Comment on the requirements for finding a confidence interval for the mean.
b) Compute a 90% confidence interval for the mean 60 mph braking distance for SUVs using these new tires.
c) Suppose that it is known that the average stopping distance for cars traveling at 60 mph is 130 ft. Can we say with 90% confidence, based on the interval from part (b), that the mean 60 mph braking distance for SUVs using these new tires is greater than the mean for cars? Explain.
d) Suppose that the tire company purposely chose all lightweight SUVs for this test. How, if it all would that change the way we view these results?

78) In 2009, the Average number of movies seen in the theater by people living in the U.S. and Canada was 4 per year. During that same time, a random sample of 14 statistics students produced an average of 6.32 movies seen per year with a standard deviation of 3.437 movies seen per year.

a) Comment on the requirements for finding a confidence interval for the mean.
b) Compute a 95% confidence interval for the mean number of movies seen per year for statistics students.
c) Can we say with 95% confidence, based on the interval from part (b), that the mean number of movies seen per year for statistics students is greater than the 2009 average for people living in the U.S. and Canada? Explain.
d) Suppose that there were 750,000 statistics students at that time. Use your answer to part (b) to determine a 95% confidence interval for the true total number of movies seen that year by those 750,000 students.
e) Suppose that all of these students were from the same statistics class. How, if at all, would that change the way we view these results?

79) A study was conducted in April 2013 to estimate the average late season price of snowboard bindings. A random sample of 28 bindings produced a mean price of $88.75 with a standard deviation of $35.43. Assume that the prices for all the snowboard bindings is somewhat skewed to the right.

a) Comment on the requirements for finding a confidence interval for the mean price of all such bindings.
b) Compute a 95% confidence interval for the mean price of all the bindings in April 2013
c) Interpret the interval in terms of the application.
d) Can we say with 95% confidence, based on the interval from part (b), that the true mean price for snowboard bindings in April 2013 was less than $100? Explain.
e) Suppose that all of the bindings used in this sample were from the same store. How, if at all, would that change the way we view these results?

80) The eggs sold in grocery stores come in a variety of sizes. Three common sizes that are sold are large, extra large, and jumbo. A consumer is curious what the mean weight is for eggs classified as extra large. The consumer obtains a random sample of 24 eggs labeled as extra large. The sampled eggs yield a mean of 2.2286 ounces with a standard deviation of 0.06904 ounces. Assume that the weights for extra large eggs form a roughly symmetric distribution.

a) Comment on the requirements for finding a confidence interval for the mean weight of extra large eggs.
b) Compute a 99% confidence interval for the true mean weight of extra large eggs.
c) Interpret the interval in terms of the application.
d) Can we say with 99% confidence, based on the interval from part (b), that the true mean weight of extra large eggs differs from 2.25 ounces? Explain.
e) Suppose that all 24 of these eggs were obtained by randomly choosing just 2 cartons of 12 eggs each. How, if at all, would that change the way we view these results?

Section 8.4 – Sample Size Considerations for Estimating Means

In the previous section, we learned how to find a confidence interval estimate of a population mean. Part of computing this interval involved calculating the margin of error. Now, we turn to the question of determining the sample size needed to shrink the margin of error down to a desired size. In Section 8.2, we accomplished this goal for proportions by solving the margin or error formula for n. We will follow a similar path when working with means. The result of the algebra is shown below.

$$E = t^* \cdot \frac{s}{\sqrt{n}} \quad \Rightarrow \quad n = \left(\frac{t^* \cdot s}{E}\right)^2$$

The above formula would work fine, but it requires us to know the sample standard deviation, s. Because we are trying to determine the sample size to use in our study, it will be common for us to not have a sample yet. This means that we will also not have a value for the sample standard deviation, s. In such cases, we will use a guess at the population standard deviation, σ. The Empirical Rule tells us that we expect most of the data set to lie within 2 standard deviations of the mean. Therefore, we expect the minimum to be about 2 standard deviations below the mean and the maximum to be about 2 standard deviations above the mean. So we expect the maximum and minimum to be about 4 standard deviations apart. The work is shown below.

$$\max \approx \mu + 2\sigma \text{ and } \min \approx \mu - 2\sigma$$

$$\Rightarrow \quad \max - \min \approx (\mu + 2\sigma) - (\mu - 2\sigma) = \mu + 2\sigma - \mu + 2\sigma = 4\sigma$$

$$\Rightarrow \quad \max - \min \approx 4\sigma \quad \Rightarrow \quad \frac{\max - \min}{4} \approx \frac{4\sigma}{4} \quad \Rightarrow \quad \sigma \approx \frac{\max - \min}{4}$$

In cases where we do not have a sample, we cannot use a t-score, because we don't know that sample size, and thus the df. When estimating the required sample size using a guess at the population standard deviation, we will use z-scores in our formula. The above discussion is summarized in the following Point to Remember.

Point to Remember: *Estimating the sample size needed to obtain a requested margin of error.*

The minimum sample size needed to get a margin of error of at most E is calculated by using one of the following two formulas:

If you have a recent sample, then use: $n = \left(\dfrac{t^* \cdot s}{E}\right)^2$ where $df = n - 1$

If no sample is available, then use: $n = \left(\dfrac{z^* \cdot \sigma_g}{E}\right)^2$ where $\sigma_g = \dfrac{\max - \min}{4}$

Consider the following points when determining the sample size.
- To ensure that our sample size is never too small, we always round up rather than down.
- If using the value of s from a recent sample, then the df for the t-score is found using the size of your recent sample.

Example 8.9: *Sample Size needed for Lake Tahoe Snow Pack*

In Example 8.7, we found a confidence interval for the mean depth of the snow pack at a Lake Tahoe winter resort. Using 95% confidence, we found:

$$\bar{x} \pm t^* \cdot \frac{s}{\sqrt{n}} = 67.53 \pm 2.021 \cdot \frac{22.98}{\sqrt{41}}$$

$$= 67.53 \pm 7.25 \implies \mu \in (60.28, \ 74.78)$$

How large of a sample size is needed to get an estimate of the mean snow pack that is accurate to within 5 inches?

Suppose that it was decided that the margin of error was too large and that we have been requested to do the study again, but that we needed to get a margin of error of at most 5 inches.

a)   Use the information from the previous sample to help determine the sample size required to ensure a margin of error of at most 5 inches.

b)   Suppose that we knew from the beginning that we wanted a margin of error of at most 5 inches. Assuming that we estimated that the snow depth varied from a low of 10 inches to a max of 120 inches, what sample size would be needed to get the desired margin of error?

Solution:

a)   Because we have a previous sample to work with, we will use the formula $n = \left(\dfrac{t^* \cdot s}{E} \right)^2$ for this one. We can see from the work shown above that $t_{0.025} = 2.021$ and $s = 22.98$. We are asked to ensure a margin of error of at most 5 inches, so we will use $E = 5$.

Caution: *Which value of E to use*

When working with a previous sample, be careful not to use the old margin of error. Doing this will just return the previous sample size.

$$n = \left(\frac{t^* \cdot s}{E} \right)^2 = \left(\frac{2.021 * 22.98}{5} \right)^2 \approx 86.28 \implies n = 87$$

Notice that we round the sample size up to 87 rather than down to the nearer 86. Better to have a sample size that is too big than one that is too small.

b)   Assuming that we had no previous sample to work with, we would use the formula $n = \left(\dfrac{z^* \cdot \sigma_g}{E} \right)^2$. This means that we must find the values of $z_{\alpha/2}$ and σ_g. We are working at the 95% confidence level.

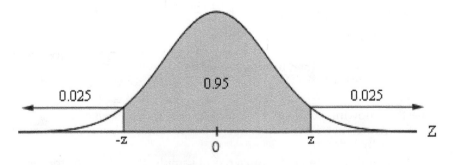

$$-z = invNorm(0.025) \approx -1.960 \implies z \approx 1.960$$

We will use the estimated minimum depth of 10 inches and the estimated maximum depth of 120 inches to estimate the standard deviation.

$$\sigma_g = \frac{\text{max}-\text{min}}{4} = \frac{120-10}{4} = 27.5$$

Finally, we know that it is desired that $E = 5$. Plugging into the formula yields:

$$n = \left(\frac{z^* \cdot \sigma_g}{E}\right)^2 = \left(\frac{1.960 * 27.5}{5}\right)^2 \approx 116.21 \Rightarrow n = 117$$

In this case, we would advise them to take a random sample of 117 snow depth measurements.

WRAP SESSION: *An example with data provided*

Example 8.10: *Estimating the Range for a Baby Monitor*

A company that manufactures baby monitors is trying to estimate the average range for their newest model monitor. They would like to obtain a 90% confidence interval estimate with a margin of error of at most 1.5 feet. Suppose that preliminary testing of 16 such monitors in different homes revealed the following ranges, in feet.

What is the average effective range for a baby monitor?

| 66.7 | 77.7 | 83.5 | 82.2 | 85.5 | 93.8 | 85.0 | 67.6 |
| 90.2 | 88.9 | 93.7 | 86.2 | 93.2 | 70.1 | 67.7 | 79.5 |

a) Take advantage of the preliminary sample to determine the minimum sample size that should be used in the next study to obtain the desired margin of error of at most 1.5 feet.

b) Suppose that those doing the preliminary research only told us that they estimated the minimum range to be about 60 feet and that the maximum to be about 100 feet. Use this information to help determine the minimum sample size that could be used to obtain the desired margin of error of at most 1.5 feet.

Solution:

a) To take advantage of the preliminary sample, we need to know the mean and standard deviation from this sample of 16 baby monitors. We should employ technology to help us with this. StatCrunch output is shown below.

Summary statistics:

Column	Mean	Std. Dev.
Monitor Range	81.96875	9.556409

From this output, we now see that $s \approx 9.5564$. Based on the requested error, we will use $E = 1.5$. The sample size was 16, so when finding the t-score, we will use $df = 16 - 1 = 15$.

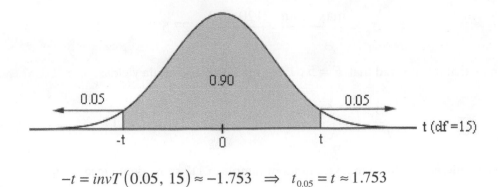

$$-t = invT\left(0.05,\ 15\right) \approx -1.753 \quad \Rightarrow \quad t_{0.05} = t \approx 1.753$$

Plugging all of this information into the formula, we get the following:

$$n = \left(\frac{t^* \cdot s}{E}\right)^2 = \left(\frac{1.753 * 9.5564}{1.5}\right)^2 \approx 124.73 \quad \Rightarrow \quad n = 125$$

So, it appears that we would want to test a sample of at least 125 baby monitors to estimate the mean range.

b) Assuming that we had no previous sample to work with, we would use the formula $n = \left(\dfrac{z^* \cdot \sigma_g}{E}\right)^2$. This

means that we must find the values of z^* and σ_g. We are working at the 90% confidence level.

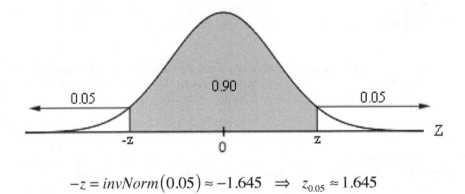

$$-z = invNorm\left(0.05\right) \approx -1.645 \quad \Rightarrow \quad z_{0.05} \approx 1.645$$

We will use the estimated minimum range of 60 feet and the estimated maximum range of 100 feet to take a guess at the standard deviation.

$$\sigma_g = \frac{max - min}{4} = \frac{100 - 60}{4} = 10$$

Finally, we know that it is desired that $E = 1.5$. Plugging into the formula yields:

$$n = \left(\frac{z^* \cdot \sigma_g}{E}\right)^2 = \left(\frac{1.645 * 10}{1.5}\right)^2 \approx 120.27 \quad \Rightarrow \quad n = 121$$

In this case, we would advise them to take a random sample of at least 121 baby monitors.

Let's practice these ideas with some exercises.

Exercise Set 8.4

Concept Review: Review the definitions and concepts from this section by filling in the blanks for each of the following.

81) When we increase our sample size, it _____ the margin of error.

82) When calculating sample size requirements, we always round n _____ to the next whole number.

83) If a recent sample is available, then we should use ___ in place of the unknown value of σ. In such cases we will use a ___ -score in the formula for sample size.

84) If no recent sample is available, then we should use $\sigma_g = \dfrac{\text{max} - \text{min}}{4}$ in place of the unknown value of σ. In such cases we will use a ___ -score in the formula for sample size.

Mechanics: Practice the calculations needed for confidence interval estimates of population means before moving on to the real world applications.

85) Suppose we will be computing a 95% confidence interval for a population that has a standard deviation of 18.952.
   a) What sample size will be required to have a margin of error of at most 2.5?
   b) If we decide we need an even smaller margin of error, what effect will that have on the sample size required?
   c) What sample size will be required to have a margin of error of at most 1.25?

86) Suppose we will be computing a 99% confidence interval for a population that has a standard deviation of 3.083.
   a) What sample size will be required to have a margin of error of at most 0.5?
   b) If we decide we need an even smaller margin of error, what effect will that have on the sample size required?
   c) What sample size will be required to have a margin of error of at most 0.1?

87) Suppose we will be computing a 90% confidence interval for a population mean and that a recent sample of size 23 produced a standard deviation of 13.608. What sample size will be required to have a margin of error of at most 1.25?

88) Suppose we will be computing a 95% confidence interval for a population mean and that a recent sample of size 31 produced a standard deviation of 35.552. What sample size will be required to have a margin of error of at most 4?

89) Suppose that we will be computing a 99% confidence interval for a population mean and that we estimate the minimum for this population to be about 20 and the maximum to be about 100.
   a) Use the given estimates of the maximum and minimum population values to guess at the value of σ.
   b) Calculate the minimum sample size required if we want our confidence interval to have a margin of error of at most 3.25.

90) Suppose that we will be computing a 90% confidence interval for a population mean and that we estimate the minimum for this population to be about 0 and the maximum to be about 1500.
   a) Use the given estimates of the maximum and minimum population values to guess at the value of σ.
   b) Calculate the minimum sample size required if we want our confidence interval to have a margin of error of at most 25.

91) Suppose that, from a previous sample, we were 98% confident that the true population mean was in the interval $(84.57, \ 91.83)$.
   a) Use the confidence interval to determine the point estimate, $\overline{x}$, and the margin of error, E, for the previous study.
   b) Suppose that we increased the sample size to reduce the margin of error to 1.50. Is it possible to determine the new confidence interval from the information we have? Explain.
   c) Suppose that the new sample produced a mean of 86.49. Determine the new 98% confidence interval based on this information.

92) Suppose that, from a previous sample, we were 98% confident that the true population mean was in the interval $(6.812, \ 7.444)$.
   a) Use the confidence interval to determine the point estimate, $\overline{x}$, and the margin of error, E, for the previous study.
   b) Suppose that we increased the sample size to reduce the margin of error to 0.250. Is it possible to determine the new confidence interval from the information we have? Explain.
   c) Suppose that the new sample produced a mean of 7.388. Determine the new 98% confidence interval based on this information.

Applications: Practice the ideas learned in this section within the context of real world applications.

93) In a certain grove of giant sequoias, the standard deviation for the height of the mature trees is known to be $\sigma = 26$ ft.
   a) What sample size would be required to produce a 99% confidence interval for the mean height of the trees in this grove with a margin of error of at most 5 feet?
   b) If a sample of this size is taken and produces a point estimate of 218.9 feet, what would be the 99% confidence interval?

94) Suppose that the standard deviation for the heights of mature male giraffes is known to be $\sigma = 0.703$ ft.
   a) What sample size would be required to produce a 95% confidence interval for the mean height of mature males giraffes with a margin of error of at most 0.25 feet?
   b) If a sample of this size is taken and produces a point estimate of 17.075 feet, what would be the 95% confidence interval?

95) A recent sample of adult humpback whales produced the following lengths, in feet:

43.2	44.1	47.9	52.0	40.2
45.4	43.5	42.7	40.6	41.3

   Note: $\sum x^2 = 19{,}556.25$

   a) Use the sample data provided to calculate an estimate for the value of σ.
   b) If we want a margin of error of 0.5 feet or less, then determine the sample size required to compute a 90% confidence interval for the mean length of all adult humpbacks.

96) A recent sample of pregnant house cats produced the following gestation times, in days:

64.3	65.5	64.7	65.9	67.0	66.8
64.6	65.5	65.7	66.9	65.7	

   Note: $\sum x^2 = 47{,}476.88$

   a) Use the sample data provided to calculate an estimate for the value of σ.
   b) If we want a margin of error of 0.25 days or less, then determine the sample size required to compute a 99% confidence interval for the mean gestation time for all pregnant house cats.

97) A fast food chain is introducing a new burger. It is required that they provide the mean number of calories for these burgers. In a preliminary sample of 31 such burgers, they found a standard deviation of 18.3 calories.

   a) If they need to compute a 95% confidence interval for the true mean number of calories per burger with a margin of error of at most 5 calories, what sample size is required?
   b) What sample size would they need if the margin of error had to be at most 2 calories?

98) A company has just produced a new smart phone with a large display screen. They want to make a claim about the average battery life under typical use conditions. In a preliminary sample involving 10 such phones, they found a standard deviation of 0.758 hours for the battery life.

   a) If they need to compute a 90% confidence interval for the true mean number of hours of battery life under typical use conditions with a margin of error of at most 0.10 hours, what sample size is required?
   b) What sample size would they need if the margin of error had to be at most 0.05 hours?

99) Suppose that we would like to conduct a study to estimate the mean price of gas in the San Francisco bay area. Our knowledge of the area tells us that reasonable values for the maximum and minimum prices for regular unleaded are $3.18/gal and $3.75/gal.

   a) Use the given estimates of the maximum and minimum gas prices to guess at the value of σ.
   b) Determine the sample size needed to estimate the average price of regular unleaded in the area with a margin of error of at most $0.05 at the 99% confidence level.
   c) Determine the sample size needed to estimate the average price of regular unleaded in the area with a margin of error of at most $0.03 at the 99% confidence level.

100) Suppose that we would like to conduct a study to estimate the mean price of homes in a certain small town. Our knowledge of the area tells us that reasonable values for the maximum and minimum prices for these homes are $275,000 and $1,500,000.

   a) Use the given estimates of the maximum and minimum home prices to guess at the value of σ.
   b) Determine the sample size needed to estimate the average price of the homes in this town with a margin of error of at most $25,000 at the 90% confidence level.
   c) Determine the sample size needed to estimate the average price of the homes in this town with a margin of error of at most $10,000 at the 90% confidence level.

101) A scuba diver wishes to estimate the average dive time for dives at a depth of 60 ft. Based on experience she estimates that she can usually stay at that depth for at least 25 minutes and at most 55 minutes depending on the conditions.

   a) Use the given estimates of the maximum and minimum dive times to guess at the value of σ.
   b) Determine the sample size needed to estimate the mean dive time at this depth with a margin of error of at most 2.5 minutes at the 90% confidence level.
   c) Determine the sample size needed to estimate the mean dive time at this depth with a margin of error of at most 2.5 minutes at the 99% confidence level.

102) A recreation poker player wants to estimate his average profit or loss per 100 hands played. Based on experience, he remembers losing as much as $300 over 100 hands and winning as much as $450 over 100 hands.

    a) Use the given estimates of the maximum and minimum profit to guess at the value of σ. (Hint: a loss should be considered as a *negative* value for profit.)

    b) Determine the sample size needed to estimate the mean profit per 100 hands for this player with a margin of error of at most $5 at the 90% confidence level.

    c) Determine the sample size needed to estimate the mean profit per 100 hands for this player with a margin of error of at most $5 at the 99% confidence level.

Chapter Problem: *Simulating the NBA Draft Lottery*

Every year, the NBA holds a draft where new players to the league are chosen by the teams. Traditionally, the team with the worst record during the previous season would get the first pick. In 1985, to avoid having teams purposely lose games in order to pick first the next season, the league instituted a lottery to determine the draft order. All teams that miss the playoffs the previous season are entered into this lottery. Initially, all of these teams had an equal chance at the 1st pick, the 2nd pick, and so on. Eventually the league decided that it would be a more fair system if the teams that lost more games had a better chance at getting one of the first draft choices. The league has tweaked this system over the years and is currently using a fairly complicated method of determining draft order.

What is the probability that the team with the 5th worst record will end up with the 3rd overall draft choice in the NBA draft?

As of 2013, there are 14 teams that miss the playoffs each year and enter the draft lottery. The lottery consists of 14 balls numbered from 1 to 14. Four of these balls are randomly chosen. Using the combinations we learned in Section 5.5, we can compute that there are 1001 different groups of four numbers that can be chosen. To simplify the numbers, the league has decided that no team will be assigned the combination of 11, 12, 13, and 14. If those balls are chosen, they are thrown back and they choose four new ones. The remaining 1000 combinations are then assigned to the teams participating in the draft lottery. The table shown to the right shows the number of combinations given to each team based on the team's record during the previous season.

Teams Record During the Previous Season	Number of Lottery Ball Combinations Assigned	Probability of Receiving the #1 Draft Choice
Worst Record	250	0.250
2nd Worst Record	199	0.199
3rd Worst Record	156	0.156
4th Worst Record	119	0.119
5th Worst Record	88	0.088
6th Worst Record	63	0.063
7th Worst Record	43	0.043
8th Worst Record	28	0.028
9th Worst Record	17	0.017
10th Worst Record	11	0.011
11th Worst Record	8	0.008
12th Worst Record	7	0.007
13th Worst Record	6	0.006
14th Worst Record	5	0.005

The lottery system makes it straightforward to figure out any teams chances of getting the #1 draft choice. However, after that, it gets quite complicated. Once the #1 choice is decided, they draw again to decide who will get the #2 choice as well as the #3 choice (no team can be chosen more than once). After that, the remaining teams are assigned the 4th pick thru the 14th pick, based on their records during the previous season starting with the worst remaining record getting the 4th pick and continuing on to the best remaining record picking 14th. One of the more complicated questions this method produces is: What is the chance that a given team will get the 3rd pick in the draft. This is tricky because the answer depends on which teams were chosen to pick 1st and 2nd. In fact, the system is so complicated, that, when it was first introduced, people decided to answer such questions using computer simulations of the lottery rather than actually doing the calculations.

In this Chapter Problem, we will attempt to use the results of such a simulation to determine the probability that the team with the 5th worst record will end up with the 3rd overall draft choice. The simulation results will allow us to get an estimate for the true probability, but even if we run the simulation a large number of times, we know from Chapter 7 that the result from the simulation will not be the exact answer. However, we can use the point estimate from the simulation and the procedures we learned in this chapter to calculate a confidence interval for the true chance of such an event.

The first thing to note is that we will be using a confidence interval for proportions to answer this question. Probabilities represent the true proportion of times an event will occur in the long run. We can use the results of the simulation to represent a sample of many trials of the NBA draft lottery. From the simulation, we can find the proportion of times in the simulated lotteries that the team with the fifth worst record will end up with the 3rd overall draft choice. The first step of this process is to decide how many simulations of the lottery should make up our sample (this will be the number of times the simulation should run.)

a) *Determining the minimum sample size*: Because the team with the 5th worst record only has 88 combinations out of 1000, let's say that it's reasonable to assume that the probability will end up being smaller than 20%. Use this assumption to decide the minimum sample size we would need to get an estimate for the probability that has a margin of error of less than 0.1% using a confidence level of 99%.

Continued on the next page →

The chart below shows the results of running the simulation 1,533,484 times. You may notice that we ran the simulation more times than was required by our answer to part (a). There is no harm in having an extra large sample size. The information in this chart should be used to answer the questions that follow.

Draft choice order for the team with the 5th worst record:	# of times this occurred in the simulation:
1	132,127
2	143,672
3	167,904
4	0
5	402,153
6	550,506
7	130,820
8	6302
9	0
10	0
11	0
12	0
13	0
14	0
	1,533,484

Reading the Chart:

This chart indicates that out of 1,533,484 simulations of the lottery, we noticed 6302 of them resulted in the team with the 5th worst record ending up with the 8th overall draft choice.

b) *Getting a Point Estimate*: Determine the proportion of times, in the simulation, that the team with the 5th worst record ended up with the 3rd overall draft choice. Write your answer as a fraction first and then using 6 decimal places. Hint: You must use the numbers from the chart. The decimal form of the answer is given in the back of the book. Check it before continuing.

c) Is it likely that the sample proportion from part (b), before rounding, is exactly equal to the actual probability of the team with the 5th worst record ending up with the 3rd overall draft choice? Explain.

d) *Computing the Confidence Interval Estimate*: Use your answer to part (b) to determine a 99% confidence interval for the actual probability of the team with the 5th worst record ending up with the 3rd overall draft choice.

e) Interpret the interval from part (d) in terms of this application.

f) Can we say with 99% confidence that the exact probability of the team with the 5th worst record ending up with the 3rd overall draft choice is less than 11%? Explain.

g) Using work similar to parts (b) and (d) above, determine a 99% confidence interval for the actual probability of the team with the 5th worst record ending up with the 5th overall draft choice.

h) Can we say with 99% confidence that the exact probability of the team with the 5th worst record ending up with the 5th overall draft choice is larger than 25%? Explain.

Chapter 8: Technology Project

Use the technology of your choice to complete problem 1.

1) The goal of this exercise is to become familiar with using technology to compute a confidence interval for a given data set.
   a) Enter and name the data from exercise (72), Section 8.3 into your statistics application.
   B) Explain why we cannot use z-scores for confidence intervals for population means.
   C) Comment on the requirements for computing an interval for this data set.
   d) Use your statistics application to create a modified boxplot for the data set.
   E) Use the boxplot to help discuss whether or not the requirement for finding a confidence interval for the mean has actually been met. Explain in detail.
   f) Use your statistics application to create a 95% confidence interval. (Note: Some technologies do not write the answer in confidence interval form. Rather, they just list the two endpoints of the interval. If this is the case for your statistics application, then write your interval in the standard interval format.)
   G) Interpret the interval in words.
   H) Can we say with 95% confidence, based on the interval from part (H), that the mean sleep time for all Koalas is greater than 19.5 hours? Explain.

2) This one uses the application "Confidence Interval Sim - Means" from the textbook webpage.
   a) Select a Normal distribution for the population. Enter 13 for the sample size, 975 for the number of trials, and set the confidence level to 95%.
   B) Have the requirements been met for finding a confidence interval for the true mean? Explain in detail.
   C) How many of the 975 confidence intervals do you expect to contain the true mean? Show Work.
   d) Click the "Compute 1" button several times until you see at least one interval that does not contain the true mean. Pay attention to the relationship between the YES and NO in the interval tracker and the graph shown at the bottom. Now click "Automatic" to finish the 975 trials.
   E) Use the scroll bar on the interval tracker to make sure the window shows an interval marked with a NO. Highlight this interval and explain in detail why it was marked as NO.
   F) Use the "Percent containing the true Mean" output to determine how many of your 975 intervals actually contained the true mean. Show work.

3) This one uses the application "Birthday Simulator" located in the StatSims folder. In this problem, we will attempting to estimate the chance that at least 10 people in a group of 32 will be involved in a birthday match.
   a) Enter your name in the textbox provided. Enter 32 for the group size.
   B) Suppose that it is reasonable to assume that the true probability of at least 10 matches is less than 1%. Calculate the minimum sample size needed to estimate the probability with a margin of error of less than 0.1% using a 99% confidence level. Enter this sample size in the Number of simulations box. Show work and handwrite the math.
   C) Click the Simulate 1 button to simulate counting the number of people involved in a birthday match in a group of 32 people. How many people in this group of 32 were involved in a birthday match?
   d) Click the automatic button to run the simulation the required number of times.
   E) Use the Summary of all Simulations and the total Number of Simulations to determine the proportion of times, in this simulation, we had at least 10 people involved in matching birthdays. Write your answer as a fraction first and then using 6 decimal places.
   F) Is it likely that the sample proportion from part (E), before rounding, is exactly equal to the actual probability of having at least 10 people out of 32 involved in matching birthdays? Explain.
   G) Use your answer to part (E) to determine a 99% confidence interval for the actual probability of having at least 10 people out of 32 involved in matching birthdays. Show your work and handwrite the math.
   H) Interpret the interval from part (G) in terms of this application.

Chapter 8: Chapter Review

Section 8.1: Confidence Intervals for the Population Proportion, p

- The point estimate for a population proportion is the sample proportion, $\hat{p}$
- There is typically little or no chance that our point estimate, $\hat{p}$, will be exactly equal to the population proportion, p.
- A confidence interval is an interval of numbers that we claim contains the population parameter being estimated. This interval is based on the point estimate obtained from a sample.
- The amount we add and subtract for our point estimate to create our confidence interval is called the margin of error.
- The confidence percentage that we give with a confidence interval is called the confidence level.
- Our confidence level tells us the percentage of samples that will produce a confidence interval that actually does contain the population proportion we are seeking.
- If we are 95% confident in our interval, then in the long run, 95% of such intervals will contain the true population proportion.
- To adjust our confidence level, we must change the z-score used in the computations.
- The requirement for computing a confidence interval for a population proportions is that we must have at least 10 successes and at least 10 failures in our sample data.
- For a fixed sample size, the higher the confidence level, the wider the interval and vice versa.
- The procedure for finding a confidence interval for a population proportion can also be used to find a confidence interval for a population percentage or for estimating the true probability of an event based on a large sample of trials.
- The confidence interval is providing us with a list of the reasonable possibilities for the true value of the population proportion.
- If a specific desired value for the population proportion lies in the interval, then it is a reasonable possibility that the specific value is the true population proportion. However, if a specific desired value for the population proportion is in the interval, then that does not prove that this is the true population proportion.
- If a specific desired value for the population proportion does not lie in our confidence interval, then we are confident that this value is not the true population proportion.
- The endpoints for the confidence interval for a population proportion are calculated using the formula:

$$\hat{p} \pm z^{*} \cdot \sqrt{\frac{\hat{p}\hat{q}}{n}}$$

Section 8.2: Sample Size Considerations for Estimating Proportions

- If we increase our sample size, then our margin of error will decrease.
- When calculating sample size requirements, we always round n up to the next whole number.
- Because we do not know the true population proportion and we do not yet have a sample proportion, we must guess at the true population proportion when estimating sample size.
- The formula for calculating the needed samples size is: $n = p_{g}\left(1 - p_{g}\right) \cdot \left(\frac{z^{*}}{E}\right)^{2}$; where p_{g} is a guess at the value of the true population proportion, p.
- If we have no previous information to help us make a guess at the value of the population proportion, then we should use a guess of 0.5 when calculating sample size.
- If we have a range of reasonable possibilities for the true population proportion, then we should use the value closest to 0.5 when calculating the sample size.
- Caution: Don't forget to change your margin of error from percent to decimal before calculating sample size.

Section 8.3: Confidence Intervals for the Population Mean, μ

- Because it is not realistic for us to know the population standard deviation, σ, we will use the sample standard deviation, s, in its place.
- Because using s introduces more random variation into the process, we must expand our confidence interval by using t-scores rather than z-scores in our confidence intervals.
- t-curves are similar in shape to the z-curve except that they tend to be shorter and wider.
- There are many different t-curves. Each curve has its own degree of freedom. The formula for degrees of freedom is $df = n - 1$.

- As the df increases, t-curves look more and more like the standard normal curve, the z–curve.
- When using the invT function, we must always enter the area to the left of the t-score we are looking for. (The opposite is true if you are using the t-tables from the appendix.)
- The requirements for the confidence interval are designed to make sure that $\bar{x}$ is normally distributed. This ensures that our confidence level is accurate.
- We require at least one of the following conditions to be true before computing a confidence interval for the mean: The sample size is large ($n \geq 30$); The population is normally distributed; $15 \leq n < 30$ and the population is not severely skewed.
- A confidence interval for the mean provides us with a list of the reasonable possibilities for the true value of the population mean.
- The margin of error and the boundaries for our confidence interval should be written using the same number of decimal places as were used in the point estimate, $\bar{x}$.
- The endpoints for the confidence interval for a population mean are calculated using the formula:

$$\bar{x} \pm t^* \cdot \frac{s}{\sqrt{n}}$$

Section 8.4: Sample Size Considerations for Estimating Means

- Because we do not know the true value for the population standard deviation, we must attempt to estimate it somehow.
- If a recent sample is available, then use the sample standard deviation, s, together with a t-score where the df is calculated using the size of the recent sample. The formula is $n = \left(\frac{t^* \cdot s}{E} \right)^2$.

- When working with a previous sample, be careful not to use the old margin of error in the formula. This will just lead us back to the old sample size.
- If no recent sample is available, then we should use a guess at the population standard deviation given by $\sigma_g = \frac{\text{max} - \text{min}}{4}$, where we are making reasonable guesses at the maximum and minimum data values in the population.

- When using a guess at the population standard deviation, the formula becomes $n = \left(\frac{z^* \cdot \sigma_g}{E} \right)^2$.

- The formula $\sigma_g = \frac{\text{max} - \text{min}}{4}$ tends to overestimate the true value of σ. This means our sample size usually comes out bigger than needed, but better too big of a sample than a sample that is too small.

Review Diagrams:

Sample proportion, $\hat{p}$	Does $\hat{p} = p$? Recall: $p = 0.63$	95.45% Confidence Interval	Dashed line represents $p = 0.63$	Does the interval contain $p = 0.63$?
0.6767	No	(0.6057, 0.7476)		Yes
0.5988	No	(0.5245, 0.6731)		Yes
0.6287	No	(0.5555, 0.7020)		Yes
0.6587	No	(0.5868, 0.7306)		Yes
0.7126	No	(0.6439, 0.7812)		No
0.6227	No	(0.5492, 0.6963)		Yes
0.6707	No	(0.5994, 0.7419)		Yes
0.5689	No	(0.4938, 0.6440)		Yes
0.5928	No	(0.5183, 0.6673)		Yes
0.6227	No	(0.5492, 0.6963)		Yes
0.6467	No	(0.5742, 0.7192)		Yes
0.6587	No	(0.5868, 0.7306)		Yes
0.6647	No	(0.5931, 0.7363)		Yes
0.5809	No	(0.5060, 0.6557)		Yes
0.5809	No	(0.5060, 0.6557)		Yes
0.6647	No	(0.5931, 0.7363)		Yes
0.6767	No	(0.6057, 0.7476)		Yes
0.6826	No	(0.6120, 0.7532)		Yes
0.6107	No	(0.5368, 0.6847)		Yes
0.6647	No	(0.5931, 0.7363)		Yes

The confidence level tells the percentage of time we expect to obtain a confidence interval that actually does contain the true population proportion.

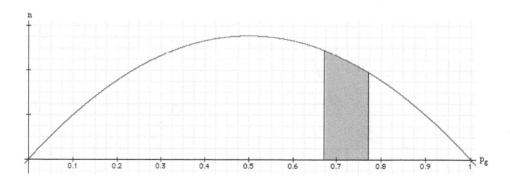

The closer the true population proportion is to 0.5, the larger the sample size that is required to obtain the desired margin of error.

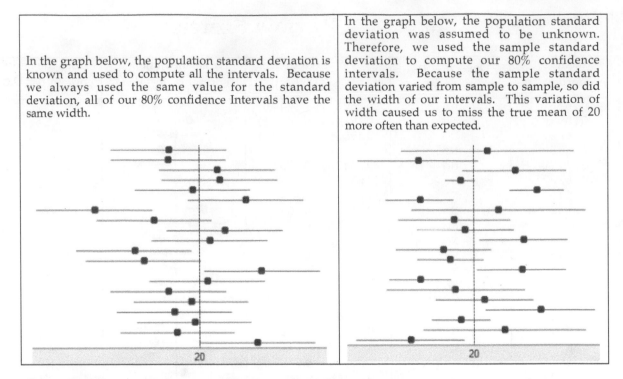

In the graph below, the population standard deviation is known and used to compute all the intervals. Because we always used the same value for the standard deviation, all of our 80% confidence Intervals have the same width.

In the graph below, the population standard deviation was assumed to be unknown. Therefore, we used the sample standard deviation to compute our 80% confidence intervals. Because the sample standard deviation varied from sample to sample, so did the width of our intervals. This variation of width caused us to miss the true mean of 20 more often than expected.

Because using s introduces more random variation into the process, we must expand our confidence interval by using t-scores rather than z-scores in our confidence intervals.

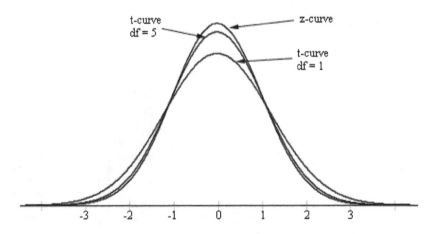

t-curves are similar in shape to the z-curve except that they tend to be shorter and wider. There are many different t-curves. Each curve has its own degree of freedom. The formula for degrees of freedom is $df = n - 1$. As the df increases, t-curves look more and more like the standard normal curve, the z–curve.

Chapter 8: Review Exercises

Mechanics: The following exercises will help you review the mechanics of the calculations learned in this chapter.

1) Suppose a random sample of size 495 produced 179 items with the desired attribute.
   a) Determine a point estimate for the population proportion of items with the desired attribute.
   b) Comment on the requirements for finding a confidence interval for the true population proportion.
   c) Determine a 95% confidence interval for the population proportion.
   d) What was the margin of error for your point estimate?

2) Suppose a random sample of size 76 produced a mean of 107.42 and a standard deviation of 20.575.
   a) Comment on the requirements for finding a confidence interval for the population mean.
   b) Determine a 99% confidence interval for the population mean.
   c) What was the margin of error for your point estimate?

3) Suppose a random sample of size 14 produced a mean of 47.4 with a standard deviation of 6.8258.
   a) Comment on the requirements for finding a confidence interval for the population mean.
   b) Determine a 90% confidence interval for the population mean.

4) Suppose that, in a random sample of size 1195, 68.87% of the items had the desired attribute.
   a) Comment on the requirements for finding a confidence interval for the true population proportion.
   b) Determine a 98% confidence interval for the population proportion.

5) Suppose we will be computing a 95% confidence interval for a population mean and that a recent sample of size 46 produced a standard deviation of 50.772. What sample size will be required to have a margin of error of at most 2.5?

6) Suppose we want to find a 90% confidence interval for a population proportion. Determine the sample size required to produce a margin of error of at most 3 percentage points if:
   a) We have reason to believe that the population proportion is somewhere between 0.68 and 0.82.
   b) We have reason to believe that the population proportion is greater than 0.85.

7) Suppose we want to find a 99% confidence interval for a population proportion. Determine the sample size required to produce a margin of error of at most 1.5 percentage points if:
   a) We have reason to believe that the population proportion is at least 0.30.
   b) We have reason to believe that the population proportion is greater than 0.60.

8) Suppose that we will be computing a 98% confidence interval for a population mean and that we estimate the minimum for this population to be about 300 and the maximum to be about 700.
   a) Use the given estimates of the maximum and minimum population values to guess at the value of σ.
   b) Calculate the minimum sample size required if we want our confidence interval to have a margin of error of at most 20.

Applications: Apply the concepts learned in this chapter to the following applications. Use technology where appropriate.

9) A 2011 study asked 60,000 college students from the U.S. to select their ideal employers. Among these students, Google showed up in the top 5 for 32,148 of them.

   a) Use the data to determine a point estimate for the true proportion of all students that would put Google in their top 5 list of ideal employers.
   b) Determine a 99% confidence interval for the true proportion of all students that would put Google in their top 5 list of ideal employers.
   c) At the 99% confidence level, how close do you think your point estimate is to the true population proportion? Explain.
   d) Interpret the interval in terms of the application using percentages.
   e) Suppose that, in 2011, there were 21,000,000 college students in the U.S. Use your answer to part (b) to determine a 99% confidence interval for the true number of those 21,000,000 students would put Google in their top 5 list of ideal employers.

10) Ten years after the attacks on America on 9/11/2001, a CBS News / NY Times Poll reported that 23.09% of 1,165 adults interviewed said that they are more cautious now than they were ahead of the attacks.

   a) Comment on the requirements for finding a confidence interval for the true proportion of Americans that are more cautious now than they were ahead of the attacks.
   b) Use the data provided to calculate a 95% confidence interval for the true proportion of Americans that are more cautious now than they were ahead of the attacks.
   c) What was the margin of error for your estimate?
   d) Interpret the interval in terms of the application using percentages.
   e) Suppose that, in 2011, there were 238,000,000 adult Americans. Use your answer to part (b) to determine a 95% confidence interval for the true number of those 238,000,000 adult Americans that believed that they were more cautious now than they were ahead of the attacks.

11) A study was conducted to estimate the amount of sugar in people's diets. Suppose that people's sugar intakes form a right-skewed data set. A random sample of 6100 adults from the U.S. was taken and their daily intake of added sugar was recorded. The sample produced a mean intake of added sugar of 21.4 teaspoons per day with a standard deviation of 10.3 teaspoons (based on a 2010 study at Emory University).

   a) Comment on the requirements for finding a confidence interval for the true mean daily sugar consumption for U.S. adults.
   b) Compute a 95% confidence interval for the true mean daily sugar consumption for U.S. adults.
   c) Interpret the interval in terms of the application.
   d) Can we say with 95% confidence, based on the interval from part (b), that the true mean daily sugar consumption for U.S. adults is higher than the recommended 8 teaspoons per day? Explain.
   e) What was the margin of error for your estimate?
   f) Suppose that there were 238,000,000 adults in the U.S. at that time. Use your answer to part (b) to determine a 95% confidence interval for the true total amount of sugar consumed per day by those adults.

12) A random sample of 14 adults that consume about 1 serving of potatoes per day was selected and their weights were recorded over a 4-year period. The weight gains, in pounds, for the 14 participants are shown below. (The data below is based on a 2011 Harvard study.)

3.41	7.27	-1.52	10.61	7.28	3.93
-0.43	3.61	2.34	13.26	3.43	5.31
2.17	3.97				

Note: $\sum x^2 = 502.7578$

   a) Use the normal probability plot for the sample data shown below to comment on the requirements of finding a confidence interval for the mean.

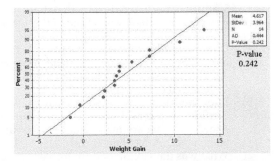

   b) Compute a 99% confidence interval for the true mean 4-year weight gain for adults that consume about 1 serving of potatoes per day.
   c) Interpret the interval in terms of the application.
   d) Typically, adults gain about 3.35 pounds over a 4-year period. Can we say with 99% confidence, based on the interval from part (b), that the true mean 4-year weight gain for adults that consume about 1 serving of potatoes per day is higher than what is typically expect for an adult over that time span? Explain.

   e) What sample size would be required to reduce the margin of error for this estimate down to 0.75 pounds?
   f) Suppose that there were 15,000,000 adults that consume about 1 serving of potatoes per day. Use your answer to part (b) to determine a 99% confidence interval for the true total amount of weight gain for those 15,000,000 adults over a 4-year period.

13) In 2011, McGill University in Montreal conducted a study to see if the amount of pain experienced by a baby while blood was drawn is reduced if the baby was being held in skin-to-skin contact by a parent. Babies were held in skin-to-skin contact with mom or dad while the blood was drawn and the pain of the baby was rated using visual cues on a scale from a low of 0 to a high of 21. Data for a random sample of 25 such blood draws is shown below.

11	8	11	8	12
7	12	8	4	7
11	12	6	11	7
8	9	11	7	12
5	6	9	4	10

Note: $\sum x^2 = 2,024$

   a) Use the boxplot of the sample data shown below to comment on the requirements for finding a confidence interval for the mean.

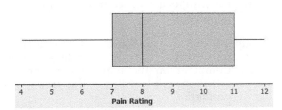

   b) Compute a 90% confidence interval for the true mean pain rating for babies having blood drawn while being held in skin-to-skin contact by a parent.
   c) Research has found that babies having blood drawn while lying in an incubator (rather than being held) experience an average pain rating of 12. Can we say with 90% confidence, based on the interval from part (b), that the mean pain rating for babies having blood drawn while being held in skin-to-skin contact by a parent is lower than 12? Explain.
   d) What sample size would be required to reduce the margin of error for this estimate down to 0.5?

14) The author of this text played 51 hands of poker against 8 computer-simulated opponents. The number of chips won or lost (losses shown as negatives) for each of the 51 hands is shown in the table below.

-1	0	0	-53	0	0	0	0	-3
-1	0	0	-142	0	0	0	-3	-1
0	0	0	0	-3	-1	0	0	85
0	0	0	307	0	-3	-1	0	-42
24	0	0	0	-3	-80	0	0	162
0	0	0	-3	-1	0			

Note: $\bar{x} \approx 4.647$, $s \approx 56.283$

a) Comment on the requirements for finding a confidence interval for the mean.
b) Compute a 95% confidence interval for the true mean chips per hand that the author would win or lose per hand in the long run against these computer-simulated opponents.
c) Interpret the interval in terms of the application.
d) Can we say with 95% confidence, based on the interval from part (b), that the true mean chips per hand that the author would win or lose per hand in the long run against these computer-simulated opponents is positive? Explain.
e) What sample size would be required to reduce the margin of error for this estimate down to 2 chips per hand?

15) A study was conducted to examine the effect of napping on retention. 12 subjects were asked to memorize 15 pairs of cards showing pictures of animals and everyday objects. The subjects were asked to take a quick nap and then they returned to be quizzed on the cards. Of the 180 questions given, 85% were correctly answered after the nap. (Based on a study conducted by the University of Lubeck in Germany.)

a) Comment on the requirements for finding a confidence interval for the true population proportion of correct answers after a nap.
b) Find a 95% confidence interval for the true proportion correct answers that people would get right on this quiz after taking a brief nap.
c) In a similar study, it was found that people tend to get about 60% of these questions correct if time passes after studying, but without a nap. Can we be 95% confident that the true proportion of correct answers after a nap is higher than 60%? Explain using your answer to part (b).
d) Use the interval from part (b) to make a conservative guess for the population proportion and determine the sample size we would need to lower the margin of error to at most 3 percentage points.
e) Suppose that we wanted to test the effect of odor pairing with retention. Assuming we had no guess at what proportion of quiz questions would be answered correctly, what sample size would we need so that such a study would have a margin of error of at most 3 percentage points?

16) A poll was taken in 2010 of 1,098 Americans who purchase "green" products. The results showed that 575 of those surveyed agreed with the statement "global warming or climate change is occurring and it is primarily caused by human activity."

a) Comment on the requirements for finding a confidence interval for the population proportion of "green" consumers who would agree with the above statement.
b) Find a 99% confidence interval for the true proportion of all "green" consumers who agree that "global warming or climate change is occurring and it is primarily caused by human activity."
c) A year earlier, it was found that 58% of "green" consumers agreed with the statement. Can we be 99% confident that the true proportion of all "green" consumers who agree that "global warming or climate change is occurring and it is primarily caused by human activity" has decreased from 58%? Explain using your answer to part (b).
d) Use the interval from part (b) to make a conservative guess for the population proportion and determine the sample size we would need to lower the margin of error to at most 1.5 percentage points.
e) Suppose that we wanted to ask this question again in two years. Given that people's opinion may change in that time, what sample size would we need so that such a study would have a margin of error of at most 1.5 percentage points?

Chapter 9 - Testing Hypotheses

Chapter Problem: *Are pregnant women at higher than normal risk of death due to contraction of the H1N1 (Swine Flu) virus?*

In April of 2010, the *Los Angeles Times* reported that the death rates from H1N1 flu were higher among pregnant women. The article pointed out that during the 5-month peak of the outbreak, "5% of H1N1 deaths were among pregnant women although they account for only 1% of the population." The article goes on to say that "the research leaves no doubt about the value of H1N1 flu vaccination for all pregnant women."

The question we want to tackle in this chapter is this: Does the data really show that pregnant women are at a higher risk of death due to H1N1 or could the higher death rate that was observed during the 5-month period of the outbreak simply be the result of random chance? In this chapter, we will explore the necessary tools to answer this and many other questions. We will then return to solve the H1N1 question in the chapter problem at the end of the chapter.

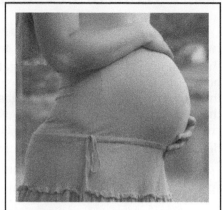

Should pregnant women be encouraged to get the H1N1 vaccination?

Introduction:

In Chapter 8, we introduced methods for estimating the value of a population parameter. In this chapter we will look at this idea from a different perspective. Rather than making an estimate, we will look at situations where a value has already been claimed for the population parameter and we will try to test the claim. In rough terms, we will test claims by taking random samples and comparing our observed results with what we would expect to see if the initial claims were true. The larger the difference between the observed and expected results, the more we will lean towards rejecting the initial claim. Large differences are less likely to be the result of random variation.

Before we can fully understand this new topic, we need to carefully define some terms and learn how to decide how large the difference between observed and expected values must be before we can reject the initial claim. We will then look at the details of testing claims involving means and proportions. We will pursue these goals in the following sections:

Section 9.1   Definitions and Notation
Section 9.2   Testing a Population Proportion, p
Section 9.3   Testing a Population Mean, μ

Let's get started.

Section 9.1 - Definitions & Notation

SETTING UP THE CLAIMS TO BE TESTED:

We will begin our study of hypothesis testing by learning how to write out the hypotheses involved. There are two hypotheses involved in every test. The first one is called the **null hypothesis** and it is denoted H_o. This is the statement we are trying to gather evidence against. The null hypothesis will always state that the population mean or proportion is equal to some specific value. This value might be the mean amount of calories in a hot dog, or the mean price of gas in a neighboring state, or the proportion of voters that approve of the job the President is doing. If no obvious claimed value for the population mean or proportion can be found, we will choose one to use as a default. The other hypothesis is referred to as the **alternative hypothesis** and is denoted, H_1. This is the statement that we will try to gather evidence for during the test. It is also what we will believe if we reject H_o. This hypothesis is more general than the null in that it does not claim any specific value for the population mean or proportion.

Definitions: *The null and alternative hypotheses*

Null Hypothesis: This hypothesis, H_o, sets a specific claimed value for the population mean or proportion. This value could be claimed, old, comparable, or just a default. This hypothesis must always be written using an equal sign. For tests involving the mean or proportion, this always takes the forms shown below.

$$H_o : \mu = \mu_0, \text{ where } \mu_0 \text{ represents the claimed value for the population mean.}$$

$$H_o : p = p_0, \text{ where } p_0 \text{ represents the claimed value for the population proportion.}$$

Alternative Hypothesis: The alternative hypothesis, H_1, is the claim about the population mean or proportion that we will try to show is true by using our sample data as evidence. The testing process seeks to gather evidence that supports this claim. This claim does not include equality. The three possible forms of the alternative hypothesis are shown below.

For Means: $H_1 : \mu > \mu_0,$ $H_1 : \mu < \mu_0,$ $H_1 : \mu \neq \mu_0$

For Proportions: $H_1 : p > p_0,$ $H_1 : p < p_0,$ $H_1 : p \neq p_0$

We introduced this chapter by discussing a situation where we want to test whether or not pregnant women were at a higher risk of death due to the H1N1 virus. Because pregnant women make up 1% of the total population, we would normally expect about 1% of H1N1 deaths to be among pregnant women. This claim contains the idea of equality because it states that we expect the death rate to be equal to 1%. Therefore, this 1% value would be used in the null hypothesis. The alternative hypothesis would be that the death rate is higher than the expected 1%. If the alternative hypothesis is true, then no specific death rate is expected. In symbols, we would write:

> **Caution:** While it is true that the testing process always attempts to gather evidence for H_1 and against H_o, that does not always mean that we are hoping that the hypothesis test shows H_o to be false. For example, we are really hoping that pregnant women are at a higher risk of death from the H1N1 virus. This will be discussed more in later examples.

$$H_o : p = 0.01 \text{ and } H_1 : p > 0.01$$

For now, we will leave the example of the pregnant women and develop the idea of the null and alternative hypotheses further in the context of other applications. Let's consider the following situation concerning the national unemployment rate in the U.S.

Unemployment Rate *(Set up phase)*

In March 2012, the Bureau of Labor Statistics reported that the national unemployment rate for the U.S. was at 8.2%. The unemployment rate is calculated by dividing the number of unemployed workers by the total labor force. A political pollster believes that the government's method of calculating this rate is inaccurate. He wants to conduct a hypothesis test using a random sample of size 1,001 from the total labor force to show that the true unemployment rate is actually higher than claimed by the Bureau of Labor Statistics.

Is the true unemployment rate higher than what is claimed?

What would be used as the null and alternative hypotheses?

When developing the two hypotheses, we should always begin by searching for some number that is either an old, claimed, or comparable value for the population mean or proportion in question. For this situation, we are looking at the unemployment rate, which is a percentage or proportion. The Bureau of Labor Statistics *claims* that the rate is 8.2%. The null hypothesis always includes a specific number that the population proportion might be **equal** to. So, this indicates that the null hypothesis, or H_o, should be:

H_o : the true unemployment rate is **equal** to 8.2%. Or $H_o : p = 0.082$

We now turn our attention to finding the alternative hypothesis, or H_1. When writing this hypothesis, we look for a statement, other than equality, about how the population proportion in this application compares to the specific value listed in H_o. The key phrase is that the political pollster believes that the true unemployment rate "is actually higher than claimed by the Bureau." Because "higher than" suggests inequality, it will be used in our alternative hypothesis.

H_1 : the population proportion of unemployed workers is higher than 8.2%. Or $H_1 : p > 0.082$

The final answer to this question is written in the form:
$$H_o : p = 0.082$$
$$H_1 : p > 0.082$$

Point to Remember: *A strategy for writing* H_o *and* H_1

- H_o must always be written with an equal sign. Look for a specific number that can be used as a default value for μ or p. This is usually a claimed, old, comparable, or default value.

- H_1 is the claim we are trying to show is true. Look for a word in the problem that indicates an alternative to equality that someone is seeking evidence for: decreased, exceeds, differs from, etc. H_1 can never include the possibility of equality.

THE LOGIC OF A HYPOTHESIS TEST:

In the previous example, we saw how to set up the hypotheses for the employment situation. We will now try to get a glimpse at the logic of a hypothesis test by answering the following question: Once the hypotheses are set up, how would we try to show that the true proportion of unemployed workers is actually higher than 8.2%?

To gather evidence supporting H_1, we select a random sample from the population and calculate the sample proportion, $\hat{p}$. Suppose that in our sample of the workforce we found that $\hat{p} = 0.1591$, then, because this value is larger than 0.082, we would have evidence that supports the claim that $p > 0.082$. The big question is, does this value provide enough evidence to convince us beyond a reasonable doubt that $p > 0.082$. We know from Chapter 7 that, even if $p = 0.082$, it is still possible that we would get a value larger than 0.082 simply due to the random variation in our sample. We also know from Chapter 7 that it is very reasonable to attribute a difference from the expected 0.082 to random variation if the difference is less than one standard deviation of $\hat{p}$. However, if the difference was more than three standard deviations of $\hat{p}$, then it would seem very unlikely that such a large difference was due to random variation. In such cases, we would consider this very large difference between our sample value and the expected 0.082 to be strong evidence against H_o and in support of H_1. For this sample size, let's assume that $\sigma_{\hat{p}} \approx 0.00867$. Then we should be convinced that $p > 0.082$, because our $\hat{p}$ of 0.1591 is more than 3 standard deviations away from the claimed value, $p = 0.082$. This very large difference between $\hat{p}$ and 0.082 is unlikely to be the result of random variation and should be considered very strong evidence supporting the claim that $p > 0.082$.

But what if our sample produced $\hat{p} = 0.0891$? Despite the fact that the sample proportion is higher than 0.082, we should not be convinced that $p > 0.082$. The sample proportion, $\hat{p}$, is supposed to be close to the population proportion, p and this value of $\hat{p} = 0.0891$ seems to be very close to the claimed value, 0.082. These two values are less than one standard deviation of $\hat{p}$ apart from each other. Such a small difference could easily just be the result of random variation in our sample. Therefore, it seems like it is a reasonable possibility that the true p could be equal to 0.082. To feel convinced that H_o is false, we would need to see a value of $\hat{p}$ that is not just to the right of p, but also unusually far to the right of p.

We know from Chapter 7, that as long as $np \geq 10$ and $nq \geq 10$, then $\hat{p}$ will be approximately normally distributed. If H_o is true, then the claimed population proportion from H_o would be in the center of the graph. If our value of $\hat{p}$ is unusually far to the right of p, then it will lie in the right tail of the curve. For this reason we say that this is a **right-tailed test**.

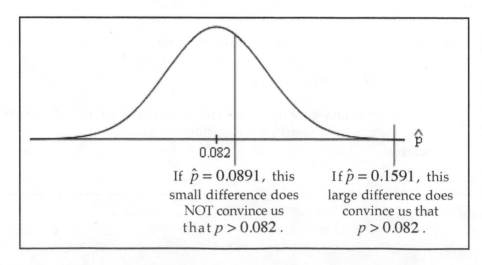

The preceding discussion introduced the idea of a right-tailed test. The other possibilities are a **left-tailed** test or a **two-tailed** test. The definitions of all three types are as follows:

Definition: *Left-tailed, right-tailed, and two-tailed tests*

To decide whether a hypothesis test should be considered left-tailed, right-tailed, or two-tailed, we should always look at the symbol used in the alternative hypothesis, H_1. This shows us which tail the sample mean or proportion would have to lie in to provide strong evidence in support of H_1.

- If $H_1 : \mu < \mu_0$ or $H_1 : p < p_0$, then it is a **left-tailed test**.
- If $H_1 : \mu > \mu_0$ or $H_1 : p > p_0$, then it is a **right-tailed test**.
- If $H_1 : \mu \neq \mu_0$ or $H_1 : p \neq p_0$, then it is a **two-tailed test**.

Now that we have discussed the logic behind setting up the null and alternative hypotheses and the basic strategy for attempting to show H_1, let's look at a few more examples to practice the ideas that we have learned.

Example 9.1: *Changing attendance at Disney's Magic Kingdom? (Set up phase)*

During 2003, it is reported that 14 million people visited Disney's Magic Kingdom in Orlando, Florida (Source: MouseBuzz.com). This represents an average daily attendance of about 38,356 people. Since then, the U.S. economy has fallen on hard times. This may have hurt the park as people try to cutback on their spending. However, it is possible that this could help the park as people choose a vacation to Disney World over a trip to Europe or a cruise in the Caribbean. A travel magazine wants to use a hypothesis test to see if the average daily attendance at Disney's Magic Kingdom has changed from the 2003 level. Assume that $\sigma_{\bar{x}} \approx 1{,}333$.

Does the economy affect the attendance at theme parks?

a) Determine the null and alternative hypotheses.

b) Identify the test as left-tailed, right-tailed, or two-tailed.

c) Provide two different examples of sample means that should be considered strong evidence in support of H_1 and would probably lead to the rejection of H_0.

d) Provide an example of a sample mean that should be considered weak evidence in support of H_1, but probably would NOT lead to the rejection of H_0.

Solution:

a) The first thing to note is that this test concerns an average or mean, rather than a percentage or proportion. The problem states that the average daily attendance for 2003 was 38,356 people. Because this is a specific value that the mean used to be equal to, we will use this value in our null hypothesis. So we start with $H_o : \mu = 38{,}356$. To find the alternative hypothesis, we need to read for a key word or phrase indicating the direction of the test. The key phrase in the problem is that the travel magazine wants to know if the average daily attendance "has changed from the 2003 level." The word "changed" does not indicate a direction. So, we need to use a symbol that includes all possible values of the mean that are different than 38,356. The appropriate symbol is the "not equal to" symbol. So, we get $H_1 : \mu \neq 38{,}356$.

$$H_o : \mu = 38{,}356$$
Our final answer is:
$$H_1 : \mu \neq 38{,}356$$

b) To determine whether a test is left-tailed, right-tailed, or two-tailed, we can simply look at the symbol used in the alternative hypothesis, H_1. Because H_1 uses the symbol '$\neq$', we would consider this to be a two-tailed test.

c) For a two-tailed test, evidence against H_0 and in support of H_1 occurs when we get a value of $\bar{x}$ that lands either to the right or the left of the claimed value 38,356. For this to be considered strong enough evidence to convince us that we should reject H_0, we would want the values to be unusually far to the left or right of the claimed value of 38,356. Values of $\bar{x}$ that are more than three standard deviations of $\bar{x}$ away from 38,356 would work. For example, if $\bar{x} = 32{,}000$, or if $\bar{x} = 45{,}000$, then these large differences from 38,356 should convince us that $\mu \neq 38{,}356$. It is very unlikely that such a large difference is just the result of random variation.

d) Our evidence would be considered weak evidence against H_0 if it could easily just be the result of random variation. Values of $\bar{x}$ that fall within one standard deviation of the claimed 38,356 would work. For example, $\bar{x} = 38{,}400$, provides evidence against H_0, but the small difference from the claimed 38,356 makes the evidence too weak to lead to the rejection of H_0.

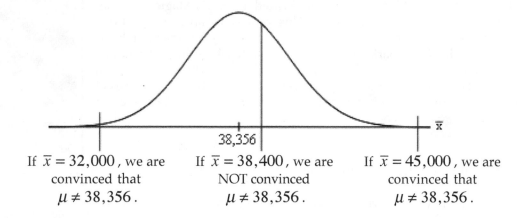

If $\bar{x} = 32{,}000$, we are convinced that $\mu \neq 38{,}356$.   If $\bar{x} = 38{,}400$, we are NOT convinced that $\mu \neq 38{,}356$.   If $\bar{x} = 45{,}000$, we are convinced that $\mu \neq 38{,}356$.

Point to Remember: *Strong and Weak Evidence against H_0*

Strong Evidence: Sample values that are unusually far away from the claimed value in H_0 are considered strong evidence against H_0 because it is unlikely that such differences are just the result of random variation in the sample. Such value would lead to the rejection of H_0. The sample value must also be on the side indicated in the alternative hypothesis to be considered strong evidence.

Weak Evidence: Sample values that are considered close to the value claimed in H_0 could easily just be different from the claimed value due to random variation. Such values would not lead to the rejection of H_0.

Let's look at another example:

Example 9.2: *Keeping the pitch counts down? (Set up phase)*

In the early years of professional baseball, pitchers would routinely pitch all 9 innings of a game. In fact, some pitchers would continue on even if the game went to extra innings. In the modern game, pitchers' valuable arms are often protected by management by not letting them continue after too many pitches are thrown. Research has shown that the risk of injury increases dramatically after 110 pitches. A study is going to be conducted to try to show that the average pitch count for major league starting pitchers is less than 110 pitches. Assume that $\sigma_{\bar{x}} \approx 3.8455$.

Are the pitch counts kept lower now that star pitchers make such high salaries?

a) Determine the null and alternative hypotheses.

b) Identify the test as left-tailed, right-tailed, or two-tailed.

c) If the sample mean is 108.9 pitches, would that be strong enough evidence to reject H_0? Explain.

d) If the sample mean is 91.5 pitches, would that be strong enough evidence to reject H_0? Explain.

Solution:

a) As always, we begin with '=' in H_o. There really is no claimed value for the average number of pitches in this problem. However, because we are trying to show that the average is less than 110 we will begin with a default of $H_o : \mu = 110$. To set up the alternative hypothesis, we want to find wording that indicates the direction we are trying to show is true. The key phrase here is "less than 110" which indicates that we should use a '<' symbol in H_1. So we get:

$$H_o : \mu = 110$$
$$H_1 : \mu < 110$$

b) Because we used the symbol '<' in H_1, this would be considered a left-tailed test.

c) If $\bar{x} = 108.9$, then this would be considered weak evidence against H_0. This value is less than 1 standard deviation of $\bar{x}$ below the claimed value of 110 and could easily just be caused by random variation. In such cases, we would NOT Reject H_0.

d) If $\bar{x} = 91.5$, then this would be considered very strong evidence against H_0. This value is more than 3 standard deviations of $\bar{x}$ below the claimed value of 110 and it is very unlikely that such a large difference was caused by random variation. In such cases, we would Reject H_0.

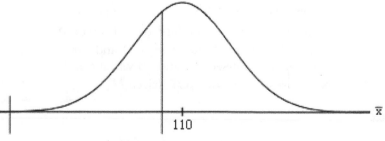

If $\bar{x} = 91.5$, we are convinced that $\mu < 110$.

If $\bar{x} = 108.9$, we are NOT convinced $\mu < 110$.

Let's practice setting up the claims with one more example.

Example 9.3: *Is the Honeymoon Over? (Set-up Phase)*

In January 2009, it was estimated that President Obama had an approval rating of 62%. After 8 months in office, there had been a stimulus bill passed, bailouts of banks and automakers, and health care reform had been proposed. Many of these actions met with criticism from the people. A pollster wants to conduct a hypothesis test to see if the President's true approval rating has fallen below the 50% mark after 8 months in office. Assume that $\sigma_{\hat{p}} \approx 0.015$.

Has the President's approval rating now fallen below 50%?

a) Determine the null and alternative hypothesis for her test.

b) Identify the test as left-tailed, right-tailed, or two-tailed.

c) If the sample proportion is 0.3823, would that be strong enough evidence to reject H_0? Explain.

d) If the sample proportion is 0.4952, would that be strong enough evidence to reject H_0? Explain.

Solution:

a) As always, we begin with '=' in H_o. Also, this problem deals with a percentage or proportion rather than means, so we will use p rather than μ in H_o and H_1. We will let p be the true proportion of Americans that approve of the job that the President is doing. Because we are trying to show that the percentage has fallen below 50%, we will start with a default claim $H_o: p = 0.50$. The word "below" indicates a less than, so we will use the '<' symbol in H_1.

$$H_o: p = 0.50$$
$$H_1: p < 0.50$$

b) Because we used the symbol '<' in H_1, this would be considered a left-tailed test.

c) If $\hat{p} = 0.3823$, then this would be considered very strong evidence against H_0. This value is more than 3 standard deviations of $\hat{p}$ below the claimed value of 0.50 and it is very unlikely that such a large difference was caused by random variation. In such cases, we would Reject H_0.

d) If $\hat{p} = 0.4952$, then this would be considered weak evidence against H_0. This value is less than 1 standard deviation of $\hat{p}$ below the claimed value of 0.50 and could easily just be caused by random variation. In such cases, we would NOT Reject H_0.

If $\hat{p} = 0.3823$, we are convinced that $p < 0.50$.

If $\hat{p} = 0.4952$, we are NOT convinced that $p < 0.50$.

CONCLUSIONS AND ERRORS: *Thinking about what can go wrong*

To perform a hypothesis test, we eventually have to reach some conclusions. There are two conclusions possible for every test we perform:

1) Reject H_o (If we have strong enough evidence supporting H_1)
2) Do Not Reject H_o (If we don't have enough evidence to support H_1)

Because we use sample data to reach our conclusions, sometimes we will be correct and sometimes we will make errors. In most cases, we will not be sure whether we are correct or not. We cannot evaluate our decision unless we know the exact value for the population mean, μ, or the population proportion, p. Remember, to determine the exact value for μ or p, we would need to take a census and this is rarely done. Let's examine the possibilities by considering the hypotheses from the unemployment rate discussion.

> **Caution:** *Never accept H_o.*
>
> The process of hypothesis testing only allows us to gather evidence in support of H_1 and against H_o, so we can attempt to show that H_1 is true and that H_o is false. The process does not gather evidence to support H_o, so we will never come to the conclusion "accept H_o".

Recall the claims about the unemployment rate were:
$$H_o : p = 0.082$$
$$H_1 : p > 0.082$$

Suppose that the unemployment rate really was 8.2%. That is, assume H_o is true. Hopefully our sample would provide little or no evidence supporting H_1 and we would not reject H_o. This would be a correct decision. However, even when H_o is true, bad luck in the random sampling process could provide us with data that provides strong evidence for H_1. If this happened and we rejected H_o, then we would be making an error. In this case, we would be claiming that the true unemployment rate was greater than 8.2% when that was in fact not true. This type of error is considered very serious and we will refer to it as a **type I error**.

Now, let's suppose that the true unemployment rate is actually higher than 8.2%. Note this means that H_o is false. We would hope that our sample would provide strong evidence supporting H_1 and then we would reject H_o. This would be a correct decision. However, even when H_o is false, it can be hard to provide enough evidence to be convinced that H_1 is true. When this happens, we will usually play it safe and not reject H_o (because we are afraid of making a type I error). In that case, we would fail to show that the true unemployment rate is higher than 8.2%, when it really is. When we Do Not Reject H_o when it is in fact false, we make what is called a **type II error**.

Key Concept: *The lesser of two evils.*

While type I error is usually considered more serious, both kinds of error are to be avoided if possible. Some cases do exist where a type II error is considered more serious by most people. But, when we have reasonable doubt as to what the truth actually is, we will make the decision that avoids the possibility of a type I error.

Definitions: *Type I and Type II Errors*

1) **Type I error:** Rejecting H_o, when it is in fact true.
2) **Type II error:** Not Rejecting H_o, when it is in fact false.

The following table summarizes the possible situations and results of a hypothesis test:

	H_o is True	H_o is False
Reject H_o	Type I error	Correct decision
Do Not Reject H_o	Correct decision	Type II error

LOOKING DEEPER: *When neither claim seems to be true (A tricky case)*

When conducting a left-tailed or right-tailed test, we can occasionally find ourselves in a tricky situation. Consider the "unemployment" example where the claims were $H_o : p = 0.082$ and $H_1 : p > 0.082$. Now, suppose that the true unemployment rate is 8.1%, that is, suppose $p = 0.081$. This is a tricky case, because technically, $H_o : p = 0.082$ is a false claim. If H_o is false, then it would seem that we would want to reject H_o. However, we stated earlier that we should only Reject H_o if we found enough evidence to convince us that H_1 is true. The problem is, if $p = 0.081$, then $H_1 : p > 0.082$ is also false. If both claims are false, then no matter what decision we make it would be hard to consider it a correct decision. This is a confusing situation, but it is not very common, and there is a simple way to handle it.

In this example, the political pollster was attempting to show that the true unemployment rate was higher than the 8.2% claimed by the Bureau of Labor Statistics. If the true unemployment rate is not higher than 8.2%, then because the pollster's claim is false, we will consider the default claim H_o, to be true. The following explains how this would play out in terms of the chart above.

Suppose that the true unemployment proportion is 0.081, but an unlucky random sample produced enough evidence to show that $p > 0.082$. Based on this sample evidence, we would then decide to reject H_o. However, this would clearly have to be considered an error, because if the truth is that $p = 0.081$, then $H_1 : p > 0.082$ was false. This would mean that we made an error by rejecting H_o. This sounds like the definition of a type I error. Based on the table, this is consistent with considering H_o being a true claim.

Alternatively, suppose that our sample did not produce enough evidence to show that $p > 0.082$. Based on this lack of evidence, we would not reject H_o. Given that the unemployment rate is, in fact, not higher than 8.2%, this seems like it would be a correct decision. Based on the table, this is also consistent with considering H_o being a true claim.

> **Point to Remember**: *One of the claims is always considered to be true.*
>
> If the true value of μ or p reveals that H_1 is false, then H_o is always considered to be true for the purpose of determining whether we have made a type I error, type II error, or a correct decision. For the purpose of deciding if H_0 should be considered true, if we have $H_1 : p > 0.082$, think of H_0 including all other possibilities. That is, think of it as $H_o : p \leq 0.082$.

We will see this demonstrated in one of the later examples in this section.

COMPARING HYPOTHESIS TESTING TO A COURT TRIAL: *Learning from the similarities.*

We can make many useful analogies between a hypothesis test and a courtroom trial. We will consider the null hypothesis to be the defendant's claim and the alternative hypothesis to be the prosecutor's claim in the trial. Using the notation of this chapter we would say the following.

H_o : The defendant is innocent.

H_1 : The defendant is guilty.

Let's consider type I and type II errors in this new setting. A type I error is rejecting the null when it is true. The analogy to the courtroom would be finding an innocent defendant guilty. This is considered the most serious error that a trial could result in. Therefore, many of the laws involved in trials are aimed at preventing this error. In a similar way, we will construct the rules of hypothesis tests in such a way as to minimize the risk of making this type of error.

The other type of error that could be made in a hypothesis test is a type II error. That is to not reject the null when it is false. In the courtroom, this would happen if the jury acquits a guilty defendant. This is considered to be a bad thing, but generally not as bad as convicting someone who is innocent. In the courtroom, if the jury is unsure whether the defendant is guilty or innocent, they are told that they should write not guilty on their ballots. That way, if they make a mistake, it will be a type II error.

Similarly, we do not wish to make any type of error during a hypothesis test. However, if an error is going to happen, we would rather it be a type II error than the more serious type I error. As we progress through this chapter, we will continue to use this analogy to help make sense of hypothesis testing.

IDENTIFYING ERRORS AND CORRECT DECISIONS: *If we somehow learned the truth*

We will see in the next section that when we make the key decision of whether to reject H_o or not, we always consider the risk of making a type I error. Because of this, it is important to be able to recognize when a decision is a type I error, a type II error, or a correct decision. The following examples demonstrate how this is done.

Example 9.4: *Changing attendance at Disney's Magic Kingdom? (Revisited)*

Consider the Magic Kingdom attendance question from Example 9.1. Recall that we were doing a two-tailed test where $H_o : \mu = 38,356$ and $H_1 : \mu \neq 38,356$.

a) Suppose the magazine's research does provide enough evidence to show that the true average daily attendance for the park has changed from the 38,256 from 2003. What decision should they make regarding H_o?

b) Suppose the magazine's research does not provide enough evidence to show that the true average daily attendance for the park has changed from the 38,256 from 2003. What decision should they make regarding H_o?

c) Suppose that it was later determined that the true average daily attendance for the park was 39,000 people. Classify the decision from part (a) as a type I error, type II error, or correct decision.

d) Suppose that it was later determined that the true average daily attendance for the park was 39,000 people. Classify the decision from part (b) as a type I error, type II error, or correct decision.

Solution:

a) Because it is stated that we had enough evidence to show that the true average daily attendance for the park has changed from 38,356, this means that the magazine is convinced that $H_1 : \mu \neq 38,356$ is true, so the magazine would reject $H_o : \mu = 38,356$.

b) Because it is stated that we did not have enough evidence to show that the true average daily attendance for the park has changed from 38,356, this means that the magazine is not convinced that $H_1 : \mu \neq 38,356$ is true, so the magazine would NOT reject $H_o : \mu = 38,356$.

c) Because they tell us that the true mean is 39,000 people, we know the following fact.

$$\mu = 39,000 \Rightarrow H_o : \mu = 38,356 \text{ is a false claim.}$$

Combining this with the answer to part (a), we reach the following conclusion. The magazine rejected H_o, when it was in fact false. Therefore, they made a correct decision.

d) In part (b), we decided that the magazine would not reject $H_o : \mu = 38,356$. But we now know from the given information that H_o is false. Therefore, by not rejecting H_o when it was in fact false, the magazine has made a type II error.

Let's look at one more example of this type to illustrate how to handle the tricky situation mentioned in the Looking Deeper feature earlier in this section.

Example 9.5: *Keeping the pitch counts down? (Revisited)*

Consider the pitch counts from Example 9.2. Recall that we were doing a left-tailed test where $H_o : \mu = 110$ pitches and $H_1 : \mu < 110$ pitches.

a) Suppose that the study's data provides enough evidence to show that the true average pitch count is less than 110 pitches per start. What decision should they make regarding H_o?

b) Suppose that the study's data does not provide enough evidence to show that the true average pitch count is less than 110 pitches per start. What decision should they make regarding H_o?

c) Suppose that it was later determined that the true average pitch count was 111 pitches per start. Classify the decision from part (a) as a type I error, type II error, or correct decision.

d) Suppose that it was later determined that the true average pitch count was 111 pitches per start. Classify the decision from part (b) as a type I error, type II error, or correct decision.

Solution:

Given: Because $\mu = 111 \Rightarrow H_1 : \mu < 110$ is false. In a single-tailed test, if H_1 is false, then H_o is considered to be true.

a) Because it is stated that there was enough evidence to show that the true average pitch count is less than 110 pitches per start, this means that we are convinced that $H_1 : \mu < 110$ is true, so we would reject $H_o : \mu = 110$.

b) Because it is stated that there was not enough evidence to show that the true average pitch count is less than 110 pitches per start, this means that we are not convinced that $H_1 : \mu < 110$ is true, so we would NOT reject $H_o : \mu = 110$.

c) Because they tell us that the true mean is 111 pitches, we know the following fact.

$\mu = 111 \Rightarrow H_1 : \mu < 110$ is a false claim. In a single tailed test, if H_1 is false, then H_o is considered to be true.

Combining this with the answer to part (a), we reach the following conclusion. We rejected H_o, when it was in fact true. Therefore, they made a Type I Error.

d) In part (b), we decided that we would not reject $H_o : \mu = 110$. But we now know from the given information that H_o was true. Therefore, by not rejecting H_o when it was in fact true, we have made a correct decision.

WRAP SESSION: *Interpreting the possible conclusions.*

Finally, not only is it important to recognize whether you have made a type I error, a type II error, or a correct decision, but you should also be able to explain to people, in plain language, what each of those mean. The following example shows how this is done.

Example 9.6: *Is the Honeymoon Over? (Revisited)*

Consider the approval rating test from Example 9.3.

The hypotheses were stated as:
$$H_o : p = 0.50$$
$$H_1 : p < 0.50$$

a) Using everyday language, explain what it would mean, in terms of evidence and the application, for those conducting the test to make a type I error.

b) Using everyday language, explain what it would mean, in terms of evidence and the application, for those conducting the test to make a type II error.

c) Using everyday language, explain what it would mean, in terms of evidence and the application, for those conducting the test to make a correct decision.

Solution:

a) In the language of hypothesis testing, a type I error would be rejecting H_o when it was in fact true. Translating this into plain language and in terms of the evidence yields the following. Those conducting the test would make a type I error if they had enough evidence to show that the proportion of Americans that approve of the President is lower than 0.50, when in fact it is not lower.

b) In the language of hypothesis testing, a type II error would be not rejecting H_o when it was in fact false. Translating this into plain language in terms of the evidence yields the following: Those conducting the test would make a type II error if they did not get enough evidence to show that the true proportion of Americans that approve of the President is lower than 0.50, when in fact it is lower.

c) There are two types of correct decisions that could be made depending on whether or not the proportion is less than 50%. One possibility would be if they get enough evidence to show that the proportion of Americans that approve of the President is lower than 0.50, when in fact it is lower. The other would be failing to get enough evidence to show that the proportion of Americans that approve of the President is lower than 0.50, when in fact it is not lower.

> **Key Concept**: *Use plain language.*
>
> When explaining what it means to make an error or correct decision, it is best to just explain what the conclusion is and what the true situation is. Do not clutter the explanation with statistical terms like Reject or Null that most people are not familiar with.

LOOKING DEEPER: *Why do we use a subscript of '0' on null hypothesis, H_o, and a '1' for the alternative, H_1?*

Using a subscript of zero on a variable is very common in sciences such as physics and chemistry. When it is used in these areas the zero stands for at time zero. For example, if 'v' is the velocity of an observed object, then v_0 is the velocity at time zero, or the initial velocity. If T stands for the temperature of a solution, then T_0 stands for the temperature at the start of the experiment, or the initial temperature.

Borrowing from the sciences, we could say that another name for the null hypothesis would be the initial hypothesis. The name is not commonly used in statistics, but it is actually easier to understand. The null hypothesis is our starting point in doing a hypothesis test. We must always begin by stating a value that μ or p could be equal to. Because this is our starting point, it is the initial hypothesis.

So, why was the name 'null hypothesis' chosen? Another word for null could be default. It is often the case that the null hypothesis is not actually being claimed by anybody. However, to show a $<$, $>$, or $\neq$ type of alternative hypothesis, we must always put it up against an "equal" to value. When no "equal to" claim is around, we write one to use as a default or null.

Time to put this into practice with some exercises.

Exercise Set 9.1

Concept Review: Review the definitions and concepts from this section by filling in the blanks for each of the following.

1) H_o must always be written using an _____ sign.

2) The specific value used in H_o is usually an old, _____ , comparable, or _____ value for the mean or proportion.

3) A type I error occurs if we _____ H_o when it is in fact a _____ statement.

4) A type II error occurs if we _____ H_o when it is in fact a _____ statement.

Mechanics: Practice identifying the type of test based on the statement of the alternative hypothesis:

(5 – 12) Identify each of the following as a left-tailed, right-tailed, or two-tailed test.

5) $H_0 : \mu = 12$
     $H_1 : \mu > 12$

6) $H_0 : \mu = 6.8$
     $H_1 : \mu \neq 6.8$

7) $H_0 : \mu = 20.83$
     $H_1 : \mu < 20.83$

8) $H_0 : \mu = 24$
     $H_1 : \mu < 24$

9) $H_0 : p = 0.52$
     $H_1 : p \neq 0.52$

10) $H_0 : p = 0.85$
     $H_1 : p > 0.85$

11) $H_0 : p = 0.3827$
     $H_1 : p > 0.3827$

12) $H_0 : p = 0.1485$
     $H_1 : p < 0.1485$

Applications: Practice the ideas learned in this section within the context of a real world application.

13) On October 2, 2008, the auto toll on the Golden Gate Bridge was increased from $5 to $6. This hike was expected to raise revenue, but if it causes people to avoid the bridge, then revenue could in fact decrease. Before the hike, the average daily revenue from the bridge tolls was $234,018. A study is to be conducted to see if the average daily revenue has changed since the toll hike. Assume $\sigma_{\bar{x}} \approx \$6,700$.
   a) Determine the appropriate null and alternative hypotheses for this test.
   b) Is this a left-tailed, right-tailed, or two-tailed test?
   c) If the sample mean was found to be $240,000, would that be considered strong enough evidence to Reject H_0? Explain.

14) In October of 2007, the average credit score for all existing borrowers for FHA home loans was 633. After that time the housing market crashed in response to many homeowners defaulting on their loans resulting in foreclosure on their homes. Two years later, a real estate group wants to see if the average credit score has changed from the October 2007 level. Assume $\sigma_{\bar{x}} \approx 5.25$.
   a) Determine the appropriate null and alternative hypotheses for this test.
   b) Is this a left-tailed, right-tailed, or two-tailed test?
   c) If the sample mean was found to be 650.7, would that be considered strong enough evidence to Reject H_0? Explain.

15) The owner of "Everything Grows", a plant business in Danville, CA wishes to increase traffic to the company's website. To accomplish this goal, he paid for a search engine optimization. Before this took place, the website was averaging 16.67 hits per day. He wishes to see if the average has increased after the optimization. Assume $\sigma_{\bar{x}} \approx 2.64$ hits.
   a) Determine the appropriate null and alternative hypotheses for this test.
   b) Is this a left-tailed, right-tailed, or two-tailed test?
   c) If the sample mean was found to be 25.4 hits, would that be considered strong enough evidence to Reject H_0? Explain.

16) A company produces a wall mount for large size HDTVs. The box claims that the wall mount can safely hold weights up to 200 pounds. The company does not want to risk being sued due to the failure of one of their wall mounts, so they routinely perform strength tests on them. They want to be on the safe side, so in these tests, they check to see if the average failure weight for the wall mounts is less than 250 pounds. Assume $\sigma_{\bar{x}} \approx 3.511$ lbs.
   a) Determine the appropriate null and alternative hypotheses for this test.
   b) Is this a left-tailed, right-tailed, or two-tailed test?
   c) If the sample mean was found to be 247.8 lbs., would that be considered strong enough evidence to Reject H_0? Explain.

17) In 2007, according to the National Institute on Drug Abuse, 31.72% of 12th graders had abused marijuana the prior year. Since then, efforts such as anti-drug education programs have been implemented to deter drug use. Suppose they want to do a test this year to see if the true percentage of the current 12th graders that abused marijuana during the last year has decreased from the 2007 level. Assume $\sigma_{\hat{p}} \approx 0.0251$.
   a) Determine the appropriate null and alternative hypotheses for this test.
   b) Is this a left-tailed, right-tailed, or two-tailed test?
   c) If the sample proportion was found to be 0.3052, would that be considered strong enough evidence to Reject H_0? Explain.

18) Studies have shown that only 28% of Americans that live in states without hands-free laws use a hands-free device when talking on a cell phone while driving. A researcher is interested in doing a test to see if this percentage is higher in states that have laws requiring the use of hands-free devices while driving. Assume $\sigma_{\hat{p}} \approx 0.0199$.

a) Determine the appropriate null and alternative hypotheses for this test.
b) Is this a left-tailed, right-tailed, or two-tailed test?
c) If the sample proportion was found to be 0.2981, would that be considered strong enough evidence to Reject H_0? Explain.

19) For the winter of 2008, the Everglades National Park reported that 32% of the park's U.S. visitors were from the state of Florida. A park official wants to do a test during the following spring to see if the percentage of the U.S. visitors from Florida is different during that season. Assume $\sigma_{\hat{p}} \approx 0.0153$.

a) Determine the appropriate null and alternative hypotheses for this test.
b) Is this a left-tailed, right-tailed, or two-tailed test?
c) If the sample proportion was found to be 0.2711, would that be considered strong enough evidence to Reject H_0? Explain.

20) A lottery official has become concerned that one of the 51 balls used to determine the winning numbers is being selected more often than it should be. He plans on conducting a hypothesis test to see if this number has a higher than normal probability of being selected. Assume $\sigma_{\hat{p}} \approx 0.0053$.

a) Determine the appropriate null and alternative hypotheses for this test.
b) Is this a left-tailed, right-tailed, or two-tailed test?
c) If the sample proportion was found to be 0.0410, would that be considered strong enough evidence to Reject H_0? Explain.

21) A Gallup study in January 2008 found that 25.1% of Americans were considered obese. In June 2010, they decided to conduct a new study to see if the current percentage of Americans that are considered obese has increased since 2008. Assume $\sigma_{\hat{p}} \approx 0.0108$.

a) Determine the appropriate null and alternative hypotheses for this test.
b) Is this a left-tailed, right-tailed, or two-tailed test?
c) Provide an example of a sample proportion that should be considered strong evidence in support of H_1 and would probably lead to rejecting H_0.

22) Research reveals that 52.7% of community college students who take a statistics class pass on the first attempt. A statistics instructor wants to perform a test to see if this percentage is lower among students that do not complete their technology projects. Assume $\sigma_{\hat{p}} \approx 0.0233$.

a) Determine the appropriate null and alternative hypotheses for this test.
b) Is this a left-tailed, right-tailed, or two-tailed test?
c) Provide an example of a sample proportion that should be considered strong evidence in support of H_1 and would probably lead to rejecting H_0.

23) A test is to be conducted to investigate the fairness of a certain die. There is a concern that the number 4 is not showing up the proper proportion of the time. Assume $\sigma_{\hat{p}} \approx 0.0088$.

a) Determine the appropriate null and alternative hypotheses for this test.
b) Is this a left-tailed, right-tailed, or two-tailed test?
c) Provide an example of a sample proportion that should be considered weak evidence in support of H_1 and would probably not lead to rejecting H_0.

24) Egg farmers try to find and remove all cracked eggs from the processing line before they are packaged for shipping. However, human testers are only able to detect about 85.8% of cracked eggs, so some always get into the cartons. One egg company considers it acceptable if no more than 4% of the eggs in the cartons are cracked. As part of the quality control process, they wish to use random sampling to test if the percentage of cracked eggs making it into the cartons today is at an unacceptable level. Assume $\sigma_{\hat{p}} \approx 0.0052$.

a) Determine the appropriate null and alternative hypotheses for this test.
b) Is this a left-tailed, right-tailed, or two-tailed test?
c) Provide an example of a sample proportion that should be considered weak evidence in support of H_1 and would probably not lead to rejecting H_0.

25) Studies have shown that the average braking distance for SUVs is about 15 feet further than for cars. To help alleviate this problem a tire maker has produced a new tread design that they believe will help the heavier SUVs stop over a shorter distance. It is known that the average stopping distance for cars traveling at 60 mph is 130 ft. The tire maker wants to perform a hypothesis test to show that the true mean braking distance from 60 mph for SUVs with the new tires is less than the average for cars. Assume $\sigma_{\bar{x}} \approx 2.8751$ ft.

a) Determine the appropriate null and alternative hypotheses for this test.
b) Is this a left-tailed, right-tailed, or two-tailed test?
c) Provide an example of a sample mean that should be considered strong evidence in support of H_1 and would probably lead to rejecting H_0.

26) MouseWaits is an I-phone app that provides wait times for the rides at Disneyland. One day in April 2010, the app showed a wait time for Space Mountain of 55 minutes. A guest wants to perform a hypothesis test to see if the true mean wait time differs from the reported 55 minutes. Assume $\sigma_{\bar{x}} \approx 1.4522$ minutes.

a) Determine the appropriate null and alternative hypotheses for this test.
b) Is this a left-tailed, right-tailed, or two-tailed test?
c) Provide an example of a sample mean that should be considered strong evidence in support of H_1 and would probably lead to rejecting H_0.

27) A caller to a sports talk radio show claims that the mean score for winning teams in the NFL must be higher than 25 points. A statistician listening to the program decides to perform a hypothesis test to see if the caller is correct. Assume $\sigma_{\bar{x}} \approx 2.53$ points.
   a) Determine the appropriate null and alternative hypotheses for this test.
   b) Is this a left-tailed, right-tailed, or two-tailed test?
   c) Provide an example of a sample mean that should be considered weak evidence in support of H_1 and would probably not lead to rejecting H_0.

28) People in California generally feel that they are being charged a higher price for gas than people living in other areas of the country. In August 2009, a nationwide study showed that the average price for a gallon of gas in the U.S. was \$3.097/gal. A California newspaper wanted to perform a hypothesis test to determine if the average price in California was higher than the nationwide average. Assume $\sigma_{\bar{x}} \approx \$0.034$.
   a) Determine the appropriate null and alternative hypotheses for this test.
   b) Is this a left-tailed, right-tailed, or two-tailed test?
   c) Provide an example of a sample mean that should be considered weak evidence in support of H_1 and would probably not lead to rejecting H_0.

29) Refer to exercise (17) concerning marijuana abuse.
   a) Suppose the sample data provides insufficient evidence to show that the true proportion of current 12th graders that have abused marijuana has decreased from the 2007 level. What decision should they make regarding H_0?
   b) Suppose the sample data provides enough evidence to show that the true proportion of current 12th graders that have abused marijuana has decreased from the 2007 level. What decision should they make regarding H_0?
   c) Suppose that it was later determined that the true proportion of the current 12th graders that have abused marijuana is 31.72%. Classify the decision from part (a) as a type I error, a type II error, or a correct decision.
   d) Suppose that it was later determined that the true proportion of the current 12th graders that have abused marijuana is 31.72%. Classify the decision from part (b) as a type I error, a type II error, or a correct decision.

30) Refer to exercise (14) concerning credit scores.
   a) Suppose the real estate group's research provides insufficient evidence to show that the average credit score for FHA borrowers has changed from what it was before the crash. What decision should they make regarding H_0?
   b) Suppose the real estate group's research provides enough evidence to show that the average credit score for FHA borrowers has changed from what it was before the crash. What decision should they make regarding H_0?
   c) Suppose that it was later determined that the true average credit score at the time of the study is 693. Classify the decision from part (a) as a type I error, a type II error, or a correct decision.

d) Suppose that it was later determined that the true average credit score at the time of the study is 693. Classify the decision from part (a) as a type I error, a type II error, or a correct decision.

31) Refer to exercise (27) concerning NFL scores.
   a) Suppose the statistician's sample provides insufficient evidence to show that the true mean score for the winning teams in the NFL is higher than 25 points. What decision should they make regarding H_0?
   b) Suppose that it was later determined that the true mean score for the winning teams in the NFL is 24.7 points. Classify the decision from part (a) as a type I error, a type II error, or a correct decision.

32) Refer to exercise (20) concerning a lottery ball.
   a) Assume the official's sample data provides enough evidence to show that the true probability for the suspected number is higher than the normal probability of being selected. What decision should they make regarding H_0?
   b) Suppose that it was later determined that the true proportion or probability for the suspected number is 0.0187. Classify the decision from part (a) as a type I error, a type II error, or a correct decision.

33) Refer to exercise (21) and explain using everyday language what it would mean, in terms of the application and evidence, for the tire maker to make:
   a) A type I error
   b) A type II error
   c) A correct decision

34) Refer to exercise (22) and explain using everyday language what it would mean, in terms of the application and evidence, for the statistics teacher to make:
   a) A type I error
   b) A type II error
   c) A correct decision

35) Refer to exercise (13) and explain using everyday language what it would mean, in terms of the application and evidence, for those studying the bridge to make:
   a) A type I error
   b) A type II error
   c) A correct decision

36) Refer to exercise (26) and explain using everyday language what it would mean, in terms of the application and evidence, for the egg farmers to make:
   a) A type I error
   b) A type II error
   c) A correct decision

Section 9.2 – Testing the population proportion, p

Even though we have practiced setting up hypothesis tests and have thought about the logic and possible conclusions, we have not actually performed a full hypothesis test yet. Let's look at a full run through of a hypothesis test and we will carefully define and examine the new terms and ideas that arise. As we did with confidence intervals, we will begin with tests of proportions and then move on to tests of the mean in the next section. Let's see how a full test works by returning to the political pollster's test on the unemployment rate.

Unemployment Rate (Discussion of the full test)

We will use the unemployment rate example, so let's start by restating the scenario along with some additional information.

Is the true unemployment rate higher than the Bureau of Labor Statistics claims it is?

In March 2012, the Bureau of Labor Statistics reported that the national unemployment rate for the U.S. was at 8.2%. The unemployment rate is calculated by dividing the number of unemployed workers by the total labor force. A political pollster believes that the government's method of calculating this rate is inaccurate. To gather evidence, the pollster takes a random sample of 1,097 people from the total workforce and finds that 116 of them are unemployed. Use this data to conduct a hypothesis test to see if the true unemployment rate is actually higher than claimed by the Bureau of Labor Statistics.

In this text we will perform a hypothesis test in three phases: Set Up the Test, Gather and Weigh the Evidence, and Make Decisions and State Conclusions. Let's get started with the Set Up the Test phase.

SET UP THE TEST:

The set up phase of a hypothesis test happens before any data is collected or analyzed. The first part of this phase is stating the null and alternative hypotheses. We already accomplished this task for this problem in the previous section. Because the political pollster wants to show that the average is "higher than" the claimed 8.2%, we came up with the following.

$$H_o : p = 0.082$$
$$H_1 : p > 0.082$$

The second part of the set up the test phase is determining the **significance level** of the test. We have learned that statistics from a random sample are almost always different from the true parameter due to random variation.   So, in a hypothesis test, when our sample statistic is different from the initial claimed value of the parameter, we must try to decide whether or not it is reasonable to believe that this difference is just due to random variation. The significance level sets a boundary for how unlikely it must be that the difference was due to random variation before we switch to believing the alternative hypothesis rather than the null hypothesis.   Also, because hypothesis tests attempt to make conclusions about the population based on evidence obtained from sample data, there is always a risk of making errors in these conclusions. In particular, as we enter a hypothesis test, we must accept some risk of making a type I error. The significance level also tells us the maximum risk we are willing to take of making type I error. The significance level is denoted by the Greek letter α. It is common to use 5% for the significance level. We will also see some other possible values later in the section. Let's finish this phase of the test by clearly stating our significance level.

$$\alpha = 0.05$$

Definition: *Significance Level*

    Significance Level: The significance level of a hypothesis test, denoted by α, is the maximum risk of a type I error that we are willing to take. Symbolically, this is stated as $\alpha = P(\text{making a type I error} \mid H_o \text{ is true})$. The "tester" chooses the significance level of a hypothesis test before data is collected and will use it as a cut-off for deciding whether or not to reject H_o.

Once the test has been set up, we move to the second phase of a hypothesis test. In this phase, we will collect sample data, summarize it into a number that helps us see if the data supports the alternative hypothesis, and then we calculate how likely or unlikely it would be to see such data if the null hypothesis were true. Let's run through this phase by continuing with the unemployment problem.

GATHER AND WEIGH THE EVIDENCE:

We need to examine our sample data and determine if it provides enough evidence to reject H_o. Remember that we are generally more worried about making a type I error than a type II error. We can only make a type I error if H_o is true, so we will start by assuming that H_o is true and only reject H_0 if we are confident that this assumption was faulty. When we assume H_0 is true, we are assuming that $p = 0.082$.

If $p = 0.082$, then we would expect our sample to produce a value of $\hat{p}$ that is "close" to 0.082. We know that, due to random variation, sample proportions rarely are exactly equal to their corresponding population proportions, so some difference between $\hat{p}$ and 0.082 would be expected. However, if we get a value far higher than 0.082, then we will have to give up our assumption that $p = 0.082$. Another way of saying far higher might be to say that $\hat{p}$ is unusually high. When we hear the word unusual, this should inspire us to calculate a z-score, and that is precisely what we will do. Because we will be calculating a z-score for $\hat{p}$, we will use the following formula from Chapter 7.

$$z = \frac{\hat{p} - \mu_{\hat{p}}}{\sigma_{\hat{p}}} = \frac{\hat{p} - p}{\sqrt{\dfrac{p \cdot q}{n}}}$$

To use this formula we need to know the values of both $\hat{p}$ and p. To find $\hat{p}$, we just use our sample data. The problem states that 116 of the 1,097 people sampled were unemployed. So, we get the following:

$$\hat{p} = \frac{x}{n} = \frac{116}{1097} \approx 0.1057$$

The value of p presents more of a problem for us. We are doing this hypothesis test because we don't know the true value for p. However, we do know that H_o claims that $p = 0.082$, so we will use that value when we calculate our z-score. Using the claimed value makes sense for two reasons. The first is that we conduct hypothesis tests using the assumption of innocence. That is, we assume that H_o is true until we get strong evidence to the contrary. Secondly, we are trying to decide if our value of $\hat{p}$ is unusually far above the claimed value of p, so it makes sense that we begin our z-score calculation by taking the difference between $\hat{p}$ and the claimed proportion. So we get the following:

$$z = \frac{\hat{p} - p_0}{\sqrt{\dfrac{p_0 \cdot q_0}{n}}} = \frac{0.1057 - 0.082}{\sqrt{\dfrac{0.082 * 0.918}{1097}}} \approx 2.861$$

The value we have just calculated is known as the **test statistic** in this hypothesis test. Using the Empirical Rule from Chapter 3, we can now state that the sample proportion of 0.1057 is unusually far above the claimed proportion of 0.082. We can state this because our z-score shows us that 0.1057 is more than 2 standard deviations above the claimed proportion.

Definition: *The Test Statistic*

Test Statistic: The test statistic is a value obtained from the sample that is used to determine whether or not we have enough evidence to reject H_o. You might think that we would use $\hat{p}$ for this purpose, but it is not always obvious from $\hat{p}$ whether or not we have an unusually large difference from p, so we use $z = \dfrac{\hat{p} - p_0}{\sqrt{\dfrac{p_0 \cdot q_0}{n}}}$ as our test statistic.

Note: The p_0 in the test statistic is the specific value for the population proportion that was claimed in H_o. If H_o were true, then we expect $\hat{p}$ to be near p_0. (Because we learned in Chapter 7 that most values of $\hat{p}$ are near the true value of the population proportion.) Therefore, if H_o were true, then we would expect the test statistic to be near zero.

Soon, we must choose between the following two conclusions.

- H_o is true and $p = 0.082$, but, due to random variation in our sample, we still ended up with a sample proportion of 0.1057. (This could be the case, but the z-score shows that it would be unusual.)
- H_o is false and $p > 0.082$, and this is the reason we ended up with a sample proportion of 0.1057. (Given that the true proportion is usually close to the sample proportion, but the claimed proportion in this case is unusually far away from the sample proportion, this seems like the best choice.)

Based on the two options given above, and, because our sample proportion is unusually far above the claimed proportion, it seems like we should reject H_o and believe H_1. However, if we reject H_o, then there is always the possibility that H_o is true and that we are making a type I error. Before we take that risk, we should determine how big of a risk it actually is.

In essence, it all comes down to the following question: What is the probability of getting a value of $\hat{p}$ as high or higher than what we saw in this sample, if the true population proportion, p, really is 0.082? Stated symbolically: Find $P(\hat{p} \geq 0.1057 \mid p = 0.082)$.

To answer this question we need to know the probability distribution for $\hat{p}$. In Section 7.2, we learned that, provided that $np \geq 10$ and $nq \geq 10$, $\hat{p}$ will be approximately normally distributed with $\mu_{\hat{p}} = p$ and $\sigma_{\hat{p}} = \sqrt{\dfrac{p \cdot q}{n}}$. Once again, because we do not know the true values for p and q, we will substitute the claimed values p_0 and q_0. First, let's verify that $\hat{p}$ is approximately normal.

$$np_0 = 1097 * 0.082 = 89.954 \geq 10 \quad \text{and} \quad nq_0 = 1097 * 0.918 = 1007.046 \geq 10$$

This tells us that $\hat{p}$ is approximately normally distributed, and therefore, we can find $P(\hat{p} \geq 0.1057 \mid p = 0.082)$ by using the area to the right of 0.1057 under the appropriate normal curve. See the illustration below.

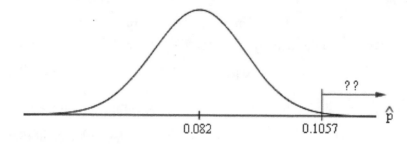

The vertical line shows the location of our sample proportion on the normal curve based on the assumption that $p = 0.082$. This appears to be "far" from the claimed proportion, but we will calculate the probability of getting such a sample proportion to see how unusual it really is.

To calculate the area under a normal curve, we must first find the z-score. However, this is just our test statistic from the previous step in the process, so we have $z \approx 2.861$.

Next we use technology and $normalcdf(2.861, \infty)$ to find the area to the right of z.
We find area $normalcdf(2.861, \infty) \approx 0.0021$. This value is known as the **P-value** in a hypothesis test.

The above calculations show us that, if $p = 0.082$, then the probability of getting a value for $\hat{p}$ as large or larger as the one in our sample is only 0.0021.

Definition: *P-Value*

P-Value: The P-value of a test statistic is the probability of seeing a value of the test statistic that is at least as inconsistent with H_o as our test statistic, given that H_o is true. To be inconsistent with H_o, the sample proportion must be in the direction specified in H_1. This probability is calculated with the assumption that p is equal to the specific value in H_o.

Note: In the previous example, we found the area to the right of our test statistic because we were performing a right-tailed test.

We are now ready for the final phase of the hypothesis test. We need to decide whether or not to reject H_0, and we must state our conclusion in words using plain language.

DECISIONS AND CONCLUSIONS:

We have to choose between one of the following possibilities:

- Maybe H_o is true and, due to random variation, we were unusually unlucky in our sample, or
- Maybe H_o is false and that is why we got the sample proportion as high as we did.

The first possibility is very unlikely. There is only a 0.0021 chance of something like that happening. So we will probably go with option 2 and believe that the reason we saw such a high value for the sample proportion was because the true population proportion is really higher than 0.082. However, if we do decide to Reject H_0, then we will be taking a 0.21% risk of making a type I error. This is less than the maximum risk we were willing to take of making a type I error, $\alpha = 0.05$. Therefore, because the risk of a type I error is acceptably low, we will take the risk by deciding to:

$$\text{Reject } H_o.$$

Finally, we end the test by stating the conclusion in words using plain language.

The data provided enough evidence, at the 5% significance level, to show that the true unemployment rate for the U.S. in March of 2012 was higher than the reported 8.2%.

Key Concept: *The risk of a type I error.*

We use the normal distribution of $\hat{p}$ to determine how "unlikely" it is that we would get a sample proportion like ours just due to random variation if H_o is true. If this probability is "small enough", then we reject H_o. However, in the above example, when we rejected H_0, it was possible we made a type I error. But, there was only about a 0.20% chance of getting a sample proportion like we did if H_o is true. We are willing to take that small risk and reject H_o.

UNDERSTANDING THE P-VALUE AND SIGNIFICANCE LEVEL: *What do they tell us?*

The P-value is a key player in a hypothesis test. Ultimately, it was compared to the significance level and that comparison was used to help us decide whether or not to Reject H_0. As important as this number is, it is also a bit difficult to understand. Therefore, we will now spend a little time here attempting to better understand what information the P-value tells us.

If the P-value is 0.10, then that means that there is a 10% chance of seeing a value of the test statistic as far away from p_0 as our value was if H_o really is a true claim. If we were to Reject H_o every time we had a P-value as low as 10%, then we must keep in mind that when we are testing claims that are true, we will still get such P-values 10% of the time. That means, that in the long run, we would end up rejecting 10% of the true claims that we come across. Because of this, we state the following important idea.

Point to Remember: *P-Value as risk of making a type I error*

Because the P-value tells us the percentage of true claims we would reject in the long run, we consider the P-value to be the actual risk of making a type I error that we would be taking, *IF* we decide to reject H_o.

The information above would be very helpful in deciding whether or not to reject H_o as long as it was clear whether the risk of making a type I error was "small" or "large". This is where the significance level, α, comes in. Recall: the significance level is the maximum risk that we are willing to take of making a type I error.

The most commonly used value for α is 0.05. When $\alpha = 0.05$, we are willing to take no higher than a 5% risk of making a type I error. This means that we are willing to accept the consequences of rejecting a true null hypothesis 1 out of every 20 times we test a null that was actually true. If this value of α seems small to you, keep in mind that we consider a type I error to be a very serious thing, and increasing the value of α would mean making more type I errors. If, on the other hand, you think that this value of α is too big, then you need to realize that if we make this value too small, then it will be hard to reject any claims, including false ones. This would cause us to make more type II errors.

Point to Remember: *The logic of the P-value*

- If the P-value is "large", then that means there would be a good chance of seeing a value of the test statistic like ours even if H_o is true. So, it is a reasonable possibility that H_o could be true. That means we have poor evidence against H_o, and it would not be wise to reject it.
- If the P-value is "small", then that means that it would be very unlikely to see a value of the test statistic like ours if H_o is true. We know that we did in fact get our test statistic, so that causes us to doubt that H_o is true. So we have strong evidence against H_o, and it would be wise to reject it.

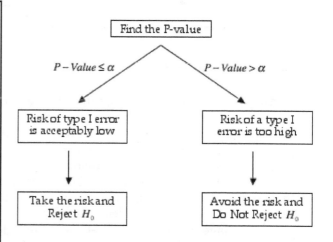

Now that we have discussed a complete run through of a hypothesis test and defined all of the important new definitions, we will now summarize the procedure for performing a complete test of a hypothesis for a population proportion. The process shown here will be repeated in various forms as we continue to perform hypothesis tests in the remaining sections of the text. It is important that you work on understanding the concepts behind each of the phases and steps of a hypothesis test that are presented here.

Procedure for performing a hypothesis test for p

Requirement: The normal distribution can be used to find the P-value provided that $\hat{p}$ is approximately normally distributed. We check this by verifying that $np_o \geq 10$ and $n(1-p_o) \geq 10$.

Phases: We perform the hypothesis test by completing three phases:

SET UP THE TEST:
- Determine H_o and H_1.
- Decide on the significance level, α.

GATHER AND WEIGH THE EVIDENCE:
- Calculate the test statistic: $z = \dfrac{\hat{p}-p_o}{\sqrt{\dfrac{p_o(1-p_o)}{n}}} = \dfrac{\hat{p}-p_o}{\sqrt{\dfrac{p_o q_o}{n}}}$ (Use 3 decimal places)
- Determine the P-value using the normalcdf function.

DECISIONS AND CONCLUSIONS:
- If P-value $\leq \alpha$, then Reject H_o, otherwise Do Not Reject H_o (P-value $> \alpha$).
- State the conclusion of the test in plain language using the words of the application.

Let's give this procedure a try in a formal example.

Example 9.7: *Is Global Warming exaggerated?*

During the past decade, the Gallup organization has tracked the percentage of Americans that feel that global warming is exaggerated. In 2004, this percentage was 38%. Since then, there have been many efforts to bring awareness about global warming, but there were also leaked e-mails revealing that some scientists had attempted to hide the decline in some temperature readings during recent decades. These events as well as others may have caused the percentage of Americans that feel that global warming is exaggerated to change. Suppose that a recent sample of 517 Americans revealed that 211 of them believed that global warming has been exaggerated.

Is skepticism about global warming on the rise?

a) Does the data provide enough evidence, at the 5% significance level, to show that the percentage of Americans that believe that global warming is exaggerated has changed from the 2004 level of 38%?
b) Comment of the requirements for the hypothesis test.
c) Discuss the possibility that we have made a type I or type II error.

Solution:

a) SET UP THE TEST:

Determine H_o & H_1. As always, we begin with '=' in H_o. Also, this problem deals with a percentage or proportion rather than means, so we will use p rather than μ in H_o and H_1. We will let p be the true proportion of Americans that believe global warming is exaggerated. Because we are trying to show that the percentage has changed from the 2004 level of 38%, we will start with a default claim $H_o : p = 0.38$. The word "changed" does not indicate a direction, so this will be a two-tailed test.

$$H_o : p = 0.38$$
$$H_1 : p \neq 0.38$$

Determine the Significance Level. This is given as 5%, so $\alpha = 0.05$. (Thus, we are willing to take up to a 5% risk of making a type I error on this problem.)

GATHER AND WEIGH THE EVIDENCE:

Calculate the Test Statistic. Recall: $\hat{p} = \dfrac{x}{n}$ where x is the number of successes in n trials. Thus

$\hat{p} = \dfrac{x}{n} = \dfrac{211}{517} \approx 0.4081$. Also, the claimed value is $p_0 = 0.38 \Rightarrow q_0 = 1 - p_0 = 0.62$. So, we get:

$$z = \frac{\hat{p} - p_0}{\sqrt{\dfrac{p_0 \cdot q_0}{n}}} = \frac{0.4081 - 0.38}{\sqrt{\dfrac{(0.38)(0.62)}{517}}} \approx 1.316.$$

The real value of p should be close to $\hat{p}$, our test statistic shows that the claimed value is 1.316 standard deviations away from $\hat{p}$. So, it is difficult to decide at this time if the claimed value could be the true value. The P-value will help us make this decision.

Calculate the P-value. As long as the requirements have been met (we will examine this in part (b) of this example), then our test statistic has approximately the standard normal distribution. This is a two-tailed test, so according to the definition of P-value, we see that we need to find the probability of being at least as far away from 0.38, in either direction as our 0.4081 was. In terms of the test statistic, this becomes: find $P(z < -1.316 \text{ OR } z > 1.316)$.

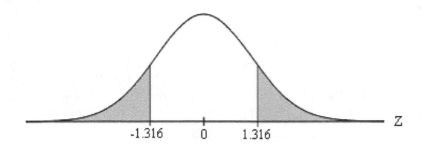

Notice that there is symmetry to the shaded area, so we can simply find the area of one side and then double it. The area to the right of $z = 1.316$ can be found using *normalcdf*$(1.316, \infty)$, and it is 0.0941. Therefore the total area, and thus the P-value, is given by: P-value $= 2 \cdot (0.0941) = 0.1882$.

DECISIONS AND CONCLUSIONS:

Reject H_o or Do Not Reject H_o. The P-value tells us that, if H_o is true, there is an 18.82% chance of getting a sample proportion as far away as our 40.81% just due to the random variation in our sample. Therefore, if we reject H_o, then we will be taking an 18.82% risk of making a type I error. So, because the P-value > 0.05, we Do Not Reject H_o. The risk of making a type I error is approximately 18.82% and this is an unacceptably high risk.

State the Conclusion in Words. At the 5% significance level, the data did not provide enough evidence to show that the percentage of Americans that believe global warming is exaggerated has exceeded the 2004 peak of 38%.

Key Concept: *Stating the Conclusion in Words*

When stating the conclusion in words, always refer to whether or not there was enough evidence to support H_1.

b) The requirement for $\hat{p}$ to be approximately normally distributed is that $np_0 \geq 10$ and $nq_0 \geq 10$. If H_o is true, then the true percentage is 38%, so we use $p_o = 0.38$. For this example, $np_o = 517 * 0.38 = 196.46 \geq 10$ and $nq_0 = 517 * 0.62 = 320.54 \geq 10$, so the requirement has been met.

c) Because we did not reject H_o, it is not possible that we have made a type I error, but it is possible that we have made a type II error. This will be the case if it turns out that H_o was actually false.

Key Concept: *When to check the requirements*

Since we need to know what H_o says in order to check the requirements for hypothesis tests, we must always complete at least the "set up the test" phase of the hypothesis test before checking the requirements.

As stated previously, the P-value of a hypothesis test is very important, but it can also be difficult to fully understand. Because of that, I now offer another look at how we should interpret the P-value from the preceding example.

Key Concept: *What we mean by the risk of a type I error*

When we say we would be taking an 18.82% risk of making a type I error, that mean that if we were to reject with this amount of evidence, then, in the long run, we woul end up rejecting 18.82% of the true claims we test.

The previous example also pointed out how to deal with a P-value when conducting a two-tailed test. Here is the logic behind the doubling of the area in such cases.

Key Concept: *Two-tailed tests and P-values*

For a two-tailed test, evidence for the H_1 can be found on either side of the claimed mean. Therefore we consider the area on both sides of the normal curve that is as fa away from zero as our test statistic. This means that the P-value is twice what w might have initially thought it would be. However, this makes sense, because with a two-tailed test, there are two ways to get unlucky and make a type I error.

The following Points to Remember summarize all the different scenarios for calculating P-values and for using them to decide whether or not to Reject H_0.

Point to Remember: *Finding P-values*

- For a left-tailed test, the P-value is the area to the left of your test statistic.

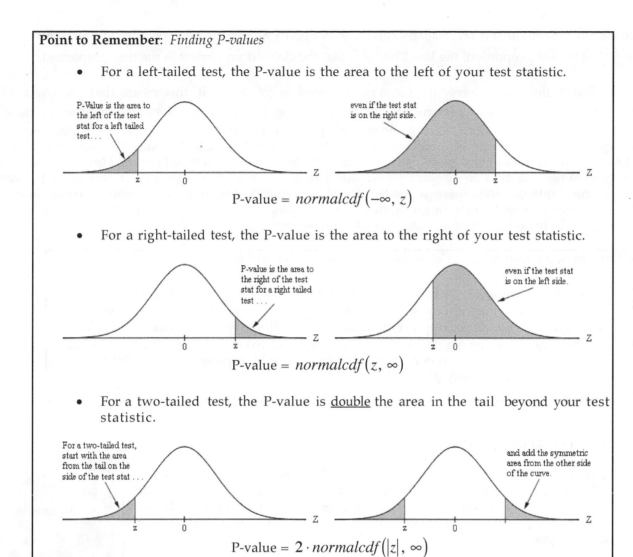

P-value = *normalcdf* $(-\infty, z)$

- For a right-tailed test, the P-value is the area to the right of your test statistic.

P-value = *normalcdf* (z, ∞)

- For a two-tailed test, the P-value is <u>double</u> the area in the tail beyond your test statistic.

P-value = $2 \cdot$ *normalcdf* $(|z|, \infty)$

Point to Remember: *Using P-values to make a decision*

- If P-value $\leq \alpha$, then Reject H_o (Risk of type I error is acceptable)
- If P-value $> \alpha$, then Do Not Reject H_o (Risk of making type I error is too high)

GOING BACK TO COURT: *An explanation for risking a type I error*

It is useful at this point to make more comparisons between hypothesis testing and a courtroom trial. In a trial, the defendant is presumed innocent until proven guilty. In a hypothesis test, we make all of our calculations based on the assumption that H_o is true. In the courtroom, the defendant is only convicted if the jury feels convinced beyond a reasonable doubt that the defendant is guilty. In hypothesis testing, we only reject H_o if our P-value is smaller than a predetermined significance level. In either situation, this would happen if there is a large amount of evidence to support the case. In a hypothesis test, evidence consists of seeing a test statistic that is far away from the claimed value of the proportion. The further away the test statistic is, the more evidence we have. Remember from Chapters 7 and 8, $\hat{p}$ is usually near the true proportion, p. So, the further $\hat{p}$ is from the claimed proportion, the less likely it is that the claimed proportion is the true proportion.

Finally, we stated that a commonly used significance level is 5% and that this means that we reject H_o roughly 1 out of every 20 times we perform a test where H_o is true. If you put this same risk into the courtroom, you would convict roughly 1 out of every 20 innocent people who were put on trial. This should point out the need to keep α small. At this point, people sometimes think it would be better to make α much smaller, say 0.000001%. This indeed would be a great idea if we were only concerned about type I errors. However, the only way to be sure to never convict an innocent person would be to never convict anybody. If this strategy were employed in the courtroom, then there would be no need to even bother with a trial. Also, if no one is ever convicted, then every time there is a guilty defendant on trial, the jury would make the mistake of not convicting them. In hypothesis testing, this means the following:

Point to Remember: *The relationship between type I and type II error*

The risk of making a type II error is denoted by β. As α gets smaller, β, gets larger. That means that if we decrease the acceptable risk of making a type I error, α, then as a result, the risk of making a type II error, β, will increase and vice versa. The probability of making a type II error can only be calculated if we know the true value of the population proportion or mean in question. We will explore this idea further in this chapter's technology project.

Example 9.8: *Is the Honeymoon Over?*

In January 2009, it was estimated that President Obama had an approval rating of 62%. After 8 months in office, there had been a stimulus bill passed, bailouts of banks and automakers, and health care reform had been proposed. In September of 2009, a Rasmussen poll of 1500 likely voters showed that 46.33% of those polled approved of the job he was doing as president.

a) Does the data provide enough evidence, at the 1% significance level, to show that the true percentage of all likely voters who approve of the president's job performance has fallen below 50%?

b) Comment on the requirements for performing the hypothesis test.

Has the President's approval rating fallen below 50%?

Solution:

a) SET UP THE TEST:

Determine H_o & H_1. This problem is about a percentage, so we will use p rather than μ. As always, we start with '=' in H_o. Because we want to see if the approval rating has fallen below 50%, as a default, we will start with $H_o : p = 0.5$. The key phrase here is "fallen below" which indicates a left-tailed test.

$$H_o : p = 0.5$$
$$H_1 : p < 0.5$$

Determine the Significance Level. Significance level is 1%, so $\alpha = 0.01$. (This means that we are willing to take up to a 1% risk of making a type I error.)

GATHER AND WEIGH THE EVIDENCE:

Calculate the Test Statistic. Typically we expect to calculate the value of $\hat{p}$ using the formula $\hat{p} = \dfrac{x}{n}$. However, in this problem, they have provided us with the sample percentage rather than the number of successes. This means that we are already given the value of $\hat{p}$, 0.4633. So our test statistic is:

$$z = \frac{0.4633 - 0.50}{\sqrt{\dfrac{(0.50)(0.50)}{1500}}} \approx -2.843$$

This tells us that the claimed proportion is 2.843 standard deviations away from $\hat{p}$. This would be unusual for the true proportion. So, we will most likely reject H_o.

Calculate the P-value. Because H_1 contains the '<' symbol, this will be a left tailed test. Therefore, the P-Value is the area to the left of the test stat. Using $normalcdf(-\infty, -2.843)$ we get,

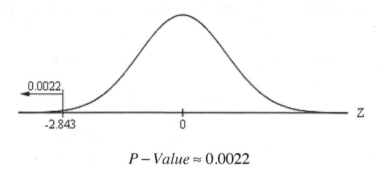

$$P - Value \approx 0.0022$$

> **Key Concept:** *Understanding the P-value*
>
> A P-value of 0.0022 tells us that if we reject here, then in the long run we will end up rejecting 0.22% of the true claims we face. Because our significance level of 1% tells us that we are willing to take up to a 1% risk of making a type I error, we are OK with that.

DECISIONS AND CONLUSIONS:

Reject H_o or Do Not Reject H_o. The P-value tells us that, if we reject H_o, then we will be taking a 0.22% risk of making a type I error. Because the P-value ≤ 0.01, we Reject H_o (acceptable risk of making a type I error.)

State the Conclusion in Words. The data provided enough evidence, at the 1% significance level, to show that the true percentage of people who approve of the job President Obama is doing has fallen below 50%.

b) Because the default claimed approval rating was 50%, we know that $p_o = 0.50$. From this we get $np_o = 1500(0.50) = 750 \geq 10$ and $nq_o = 1500(0.50) = 750 \geq 10$, so the requirement has been met.

> **Caution:** *A common mistake made when checking the requirements*
>
> When checking the requirements and when working inside the square root in the test statistic, be sure that you use p_o rather than $\hat{p}$. This is different from what was done for confidence intervals in Section 8.1. The reason for this is that we are making the "assumption of innocence" here and, therefore, p_o is the most appropriate replacement for p. However, in Section 8.1, no claim had been made and the only replacement available for p was $\hat{p}$.
>
> *Calculation Tip*: It is usually easier to make your calculations if you determine q_o before you check the requirement or calculate the test statistic.

THE CONFIDENCE INTERVAL PERSPECTIVE OF A TEST: *Another way to look at it.*

Here is another way to look at how we are making our decision in a hypothesis test. In Chapter 8, we centered our confidence intervals around $\hat{p}$. We did this because we know that $\hat{p}$ is expected to be near the true value of p. Therefore, we suspect that there is a good chance that the true value of p is near our value of $\hat{p}$. This leads us to the following two cases in a hypothesis test:

CASE I: If $\hat{p}$ is near the claimed value for the proportion, p_0, then because we suspect that p is also near $\hat{p}$, it is a reasonable possibility that p_0 might be the true value p. This would mean that H_o might be a true claim and, therefore, it would be unwise to reject it.

CASE II: If $\hat{p}$ is not near the claimed value for the proportion, p_0, then because we suspect that p is near $\hat{p}$, it is likely that p_0 is not the true value p. This would mean that H_o is probably a false claim and, therefore, it would be wise to reject it.

Let's explore this through a couple of examples:

Example 9.9: *Is Global Warming Exaggerated? (The confidence interval perspective)*

a) Use the data from **Example 9.7** to compute a 95% confidence interval for the true proportion of Americans that feel that global warming is exaggerated.

b) Explain how the interval we obtain agrees with the decision reached in the hypothesis test performed in **Example 9.7**.

Solution:

a) This is a confidence interval for a proportion. So, we will use the formula $\hat{p} \pm z^* \sqrt{\dfrac{\hat{p}\hat{q}}{n}}$.

Compute $\hat{p}$. In Example 9.7 we saw that $\hat{p} = \dfrac{x}{n} = \dfrac{211}{517} \approx 0.4081$. Therefore, $\hat{q} = 1 - \hat{p} = 0.5919$.

Find the z-scores. Because the confidence level is 95%, we use a middle area of 0.95 and 0.025 on each side.

$$-z^* = invNorm(0.025) \approx -1.960 \Rightarrow z^* \approx 1.960$$

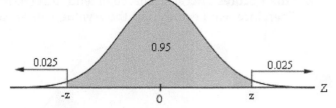

Calculate the Interval. $\hat{p} \pm z^* \sqrt{\dfrac{\hat{p}\hat{q}}{n}} = 0.4081 \pm 1.960 \sqrt{\dfrac{0.4081 * 0.5919}{517}} = 0.4081 \pm 0.0424$

$\Rightarrow p \in (0.3657, \ 0.4505)$. This means that we are 95% confident that the true value for the population proportion is somewhere between 0.3657 and 0.4505.

b) The interval claims that p is between 0.3657 and 0.4505. That means that it is possible that p is equal to 0.38. If $p = 0.38$, then $H_o : p = 0.38$ is a true claim. Because it seems reasonable that H_o could be true, we should not reject it. In symbols:

If $p \in (0.3657, \ 0.4505) \Rightarrow p$ could be $0.38 \Rightarrow H_o : p = 0.38$ could be true $\Rightarrow$ Do not Reject H_o

---

Key Concepts: *Meaning of decision and best order*

When the question refers to the decision made in a hypothesis test, the reference is always to the choice of Reject H_o or Do Not Reject H_o.

While it is possible to show that the interval result agrees with the hypothesis test by starting with the decision to Reject or Not Reject H_o and going to the confidence interval, it is usually easiest to go from the interval to the decision as shown above.

Example 9.10: *Is the Honeymoon Over? (The confidence interval perspective)*

a) Using the data from **Example 9.8**, compute a 98% confidence interval for the true percentage of all likely voters who approved of the President's job performance in September 2009.

b) Explain how the answer to part a) agrees with the results of the test performed in **Example 9.8**.

c) Would you say that our decision in part a) of **Example 9.8** was a type I error, a type II error or a correct decision? Explain.

Solution:

a) Because this is a proportion problem, we will use the formula: $\hat{p} \pm z^* \sqrt{\dfrac{\hat{p}\hat{q}}{n}}$

Calculate $\hat{p}$. In the previous example, we saw that $\hat{p} = 0.4633$ and thus $\hat{q} = 1 - \hat{p} = 0.5367$

Find the z-scores. Because the confidence level is 98%, the area in the middle is 0.98 with 0.01 on each side. Therefore, we need to find the z-value with area 0.01 to its right.

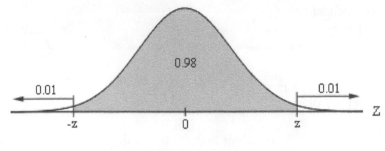

0.98

0.01   0.01

-z   0   z   Z

> **Key Concept**: *Choosing the confidence level to match a single-tailed test*
>
> Because the hypothesis test was left-tailed, we need the area $\alpha = 0.01$ to be in a single side of the graph for the confidence interval. Recall: Confidence intervals are equivalent to two-tailed hypothesis tests.

$$-z^* = invNorm(0.01) \approx -2.326 \Rightarrow z^* \approx 2.326$$

Calculate the Interval. Substituting into the formula we get the following.

$$\hat{p} \pm z^* \sqrt{\frac{\hat{p}\hat{q}}{n}} = 0.4633 \pm 2.326 \sqrt{\frac{(0.4633)(0.5367)}{1500}} = 0.4633 \pm 0.0299 \text{ or } p \in (0.4334, \ 0.4932)$$

So we are 98% confident that the true proportion of all likely voters who approved of the President's job performance in September 2009 is somewhere between 43.34% and 49.32%.

b) The interval claims that p is somewhere between 0.4334 and 0.4932. If p is anywhere in that interval, then p is less than 0.50. If $p < 0.50$, then H_o is a false claim. Because we are confident that H_o is false, we should reject it. In symbols:

$$\text{If } p \in (0.4334, \ 0.4932) \Rightarrow p < 0.50 \Rightarrow H_o : p = 0.50 \text{ is false} \Rightarrow \text{Reject } H_o$$

c) The fact that the decision from the test and the confidence interval agree does not help us answer this question. Whether we have made an error or a correct decision, the decision from the test and the interval should agree because they are based on the same sample. We are just looking at the same question using two different methods. That being said, let's look at the answer to the question.

In the test, we rejected H_o. However, we still do not know whether or not H_o is a true claim. We can rule out a type II error because we rejected H_o. If H_o turns out to be true, then we have made a type I error. We perceive the risk of a type I error to be only 0.22%. If H_o turns out to be false, then we have made a correct decision.

WRAP SESSION: *When the claimed proportion seems to be missing*

There is one more important twist that can show up in hypothesis tests about population proportions. Let's examine this twist with one final example.

Example 9.11: *Testing the balance of the 1962 penny*

A friend claims that the 1962 penny is not an evenly balanced coin. They claim that, if you spin it repeatedly and let it slow and fall on one side, it will not turn out to be a fair coin. I spun a 1962 penny 100 times and it came up heads 22 times.

Is the 1962 coin unbalanced?

a) Does this provide enough evidence, at the 5% significance level, to show that my 1962 penny is not evenly balanced?
b) Discuss the requirements for performing the hypothesis test.
c) Criticize the way the data was collected.

Solution:

a) SET UP THE TEST:

Determine H_o & H_1. As always, we begin with '=' in H_o. Also, this problem deals with proportions rather than means, so we will use p rather than μ in H_o and H_1. We will let p be the true proportion of heads for this coin. If the coin is evenly balanced, then we expect the proportion of heads to be 50% or 0.5. So, we will start with $H_o : p = 0.5$. There is no direction clearly indicated in the claims and "not evenly balanced" could mean more than 50% or less than 50% heads, so this will be a two-tailed test.

$$H_o : p = 0.5$$
$$H_1 : p \neq 0.5$$

Determine the Significance Level. This is given as 5%, so $\alpha = 0.05$. (Thus, we are willing to take up to a 5% risk of making a type I error on this problem.)

GATHER AND WEIGH THE EVIDENCE:

Calculate the Test Statistic. The coin showed heads 22 out of the 100 spins.

Thus $\hat{p} = \dfrac{x}{n} = \dfrac{22}{100} = 0.22$, so $z \doteq \dfrac{0.22 - 0.5}{\sqrt{\dfrac{(0.5)(0.5)}{100}}} = -5.600$.

```
(0.22-0.5)/√(0.5
*0.5/100)
              -5.6
```

The real value of p should be close to $\hat{p}$, but our test statistic shows that the claimed value is 5.600 standard deviations away from $\hat{p}$. So, it is extremely unlikely that the claimed value is the true value.

Calculate the P-value. This is a two-tailed test, so in addition to finding the area to the left of –5.600, we must also find the area to the right of 5.600. We will accomplish this by finding the area to the right of 5.600 and doubling it.

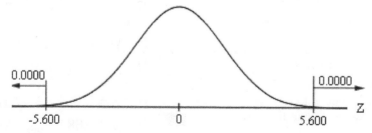

P-Value $= 2 * normalcdf(5.600, \infty) \approx 0.0000$

DECISIONS AND CONCLUSIONS:

Reject H_o or Do Not Reject H_o. If we reject H_o, then we will be taking almost no risk of making a type I error. So, because the P-value ≤ 0.05, we Reject H_o. The risk of making a type I error is approximately 0.00% and this, of course, is an acceptable risk.

State the Conclusion in Words. At the 5% significance level, the data provided enough evidence to show that my 1962 penny is not evenly balanced. (This agrees with my friend's theory about the 1962 penny.)

b) If my 1962 penny is evenly balanced then it would come up heads 50% of the time so, $p_o = 0.5$. For this example, $np_o = 100(0.5) = 50 \geq 10$ and $n(1 - p_o) = 100(1 - 0.5) = 50 \geq 10$, so the requirement has been met.

c) Rather than spinning 100 different 1962 pennies, we spun the same penny 100 times. This leaves us wondering whether the problem is with the 1962 penny in general, or just this specific penny that I tested.

Key Concept: *Choosing p_0 when it appears to be missing.*

If you are performing a hypothesis test involving proportions and no numerical value is given in the problem for the claimed proportion, then the value must typically be computed using the probability of the event in question under normal conditions.

Let's practice these ideas with some exercises.

Exercise Set 9.2

Concept Review: Review the definitions and concepts from this section by filling in the blanks for each of the following.

37) The significance level is the probability we will make a type ___ error if H_o is in fact _____ . We interpret it as the maximum _____ we are willing to take of making a type___ error.

38) The P-value is the chance of seeing a test statistic as inconsistent with the claimed proportion as the one from our_____ if H_o is in fact true. We interpret it as the actual _____ we would be taking of making a type I error if we decide to _____ H_o .

39) The test statistic is a value obtained from the _____ that is used to determine whether or not we have enough _____ to reject H_o .

40) The more inconsistent the test statistic is with the claimed value of the proportion, the more _____ we have _____ H_o .

41) When calculating the P-value for a two tailed test, we must remember to _____ the area in the tail.

42) If the P-value is less than or equal to α, then we _____ H_o because we feel that the risk of making a type ___ error is _____ .

43) $\hat{p}$ is the symbol for the _____ proportion. p is the symbol for the _____ proportion. p_0 is the symbol for the _____ proportion.

44) We use p when we are working with proportions, but we also use it for _____ & _____ .

45) In a proportion test, evidence consists of a large _____ between $\hat{p}$ and ____ .

46) *True or False?* If $\alpha = 0.10$, then, in the long run, we will end up rejecting 10% of the claims we test. (Explain.)

Mechanics: Practice the calculations needed for hypothesis testing before working on real world applications.

(47 – 52) a) Calculate the value of the test statistic.
b) Determine the P-value for the test statistic you have calculated.
c) State whether or not you would reject H_o if the significance level is 5%.

47) $H_o : p = 0.63$; $x = 446,$ $H_1 : p < 0.63$ $n = 768$

48) $H_o : p = 0.24$; $x = 50,$ $H_1 : p > 0.24$ $n = 136$

49) $H_o : p = 0.084$; $\hat{p} = 0.061,$ $H_1 : p \neq 0.084$ $n = 255$

50) $H_o : p = 0.703$; $\hat{p} = 0.632,$ $H_1 : p \neq 0.703$ $n = 600$

51)
$$H_o : p = 0.50 \quad x = 219,$$
$$H_1 : p > 0.50 \quad ; \quad n = 518$$

52)
$$H_o : p = 0.82 \quad x = 277,$$
$$H_1 : p < 0.82 \quad ; \quad n = 316$$

Applications: Practice the ideas learned in this section within the context of a real world application.

53) In 2007, according to the National Institute on Drug Abuse, 31.72% of 12th graders had abused marijuana the prior year. Since then, efforts such as anti-drug education programs have been implemented to deter drug use. A current sample of 218 twelfth graders indicated that 64 of them abused marijuana in the last year.
 a) Perform a hypothesis test, at the 5% significance level, to determine if the true percentage of the current 12th graders that abused marijuana during the last year has decreased from the 2007 percentage.
 b) Comment on the requirements for the test.

54) According to the Nielsen Media Group, 9.12% of households with televisions tuned in to watch the season 7 finale of *American Idol*. The next season a sample of 468 families with TVs showed that 39 of them watched the season 8 finale.
 a) Does the above sample indicate, at the 10% significance level, that the true percentage of viewers was different in season 8?
 b) Comment on the requirements for the test.

55) For the winter of 2008, the Everglades National Park reported that 32% of the park's U.S. visitors were from the state of Florida. A random sample of 499 U.S. visitors during the spring contained 225 Floridians.
 a) Does the data provide enough evidence, at the 1% significance level, to show that the true percentage of the U.S. visitors from Florida was different in the spring?
 b) Comment on the requirements for the test.

56) In April 2010, the Gallup organization reported that 76% of Europeans stated that they were satisfied with the quality of the air in the city where they live. At that same time a sample of 1015 people living in the Americas (North & South combined) contained 755 people that were satisfied with the air quality in the city where they live.
 a) Does the data provide enough evidence, at the 5% significance level, to show that the true percentage of those in the Americas that are satisfied with their air quality is different than in Europe?
 b) Comment on the requirements for the test.

57) A Gallup study in January 2008 found that 25.1% of Americans were considered obese. In June 2010, a random sample of 784 Americans contained 209 that were considered obese.
 a) Does the data provide enough evidence, at the 10% significance level, to show that the true percentage of Americans that are considered obese has increased since 2008?
 b) Discuss the possibility that you have made a type I or Type II error in part (a).
 c) Comment on the requirements for the test.

58) Statistics reveal that 52.7% of community college students who take a statistics class pass the statistics class. A random sample of 73 students, who did not do their computer projects, produced only 10 who passed.
 a) Does this data provide enough evidence, at the 10% significance level, to show that those not doing the computer projects have a lower chance of passing the class?
 b) Discuss the possibility that you have made a type I or Type II error in part (a).
 c) Comment on the requirements for the test.

59) A candidate for mayor in a large city is running against several other candidates. Unless the candidate receives a majority of the votes, there will be a run-off election. One day before the election, a poll was taken from a random sample of 493 likely voters and it was determined that 50.7% of those polled were planning to vote for the candidate.
 a) At the 10% significance level, can we say that the candidate will win without a run-off election?
 b) Discuss the possibility that you have made a type I or type II error in part (a).
 c) Comment on the requirements for the test.

60) Egg farmers try to find and remove all cracked eggs from the processing line before they are packaged for shipping. However, human testers are only able to detect about 85.8% of cracked eggs, so some always get into the cartons. One egg company considers it acceptable if no more than 4% of the eggs in the cartons are cracked. As part of the quality control process they chose and tested 288 eggs that were in the cartons ready to be shipped. 7.29% of the eggs in the sample were found to be cracked.
 a) Does this provide enough evidence, at the 10% significance level, to show that the testers are currently allowing an unacceptable proportion of cracked eggs to make it into the cartons?
 b) Discuss the possibility that you have made a type I or type II error in part (a).
 c) Comment on the requirements for the test.

61) Studies have shown that among people wanting to migrate to a new country permanently, the top destination region in the world is North America. 60% of those desiring to migrate to the United States have at least a high school education. In a 2009 Gallup poll, a random sample of 400 people wishing to migrate to Canada revealed that 311 of them had at least a high school education.
 a) Does the data provide enough evidence, at the 5% significance level, to show that the true percentage of those wishing to migrate to Canada that have at least a high school education is different than for those wishing to migrate to the United States?
 b) What appears to be the case about the education level of those wishing to migrate to Canada as compared to those wishing to migrate to the U.S.?

62) In 2009, the Tea Party movement began in the U.S. The group got a large amount of attention from the press when they began rallying against President Obama's health care reform plan. In April 2010, CBS News conducted a poll to try to learn more about Tea Party members. At that time, it was known that 25% of Americans were college graduates. The CBS News poll found that 584 of the 1580 Tea Party members sampled were college graduates.
a) Does the data provide enough evidence, at the 1% significance level, to show that the true percentage of Tea Party members that are college grads is different than for Americans overall?
b) What appears to be the case about the education level of Tea Party members?

63) A study conducted in April 2008 found that 47% of Americans have high-speed internet access at home. At that same time a sample of 314 San Francisco Bay Area residents found that 76.11% of them had high-speed internet access at home.
a) Does this provide enough evidence, at the 1% significance level, to show that the true proportion of people with high-speed internet access is higher in the Bay Area than for the nation as a whole?
b) Suppose that we later learned that the true proportion of people in the Bay Area with high-speed internet access at home was in fact 68%, then in part (a) did we make a type I error, a type II error, or a correct decision? Explain.

64) Studies have shown that only 28% of Americans use a hands-free device when talking on a cell phone while driving. A recent sample of 126 people who live in states with laws requiring the use of a hands-free device found that 54.76% of them use such a device when talking while driving.
a) Does this provide enough evidence, at the 5% significance level, to show that the true proportion of people using a hands-free device is higher in states with laws that require them?
b) Suppose that the true proportion of people using hands-free devices in the states where the law requires them is 54%, then in part (a) did we make a type I error, a type II error, or a correct decision? Explain.

65) A test is to being conducted to investigate the fairness of a certain die. There is a concern that the number 4 is not showing up the proper proportion of the time. The die was rolled 450 times and the number 4 came up 60 times.
a) At the 10% significance level, does this provide enough evidence to show that the number 4 is not showing up the proper proportion of the time?
b) Suppose that the true probability of 4's for this particular die is actually 15.8%, then in part (a) did we make a type I error, a type II error, or a correct decision? Explain.

66) A gambler studying the game of Roulette has come up with the following theory. He believes that if the color black comes up three times in a row, then red will be more likely than normal on the next spin of the wheel. He tries this theory out in the casino and bets on the color red only after the color black comes up 3 consecutive times. After 112 such plays, he has won 58 times.
a) Does this data provide enough evidence, at the 5% significance level, to show that his theory is correct?
b) Suppose that the true probability of red in this situation is actually 47.37%, then in part (a) did we make a type I error, a type II error, or a correct decision? Explain.

67) An online poker player feels like he is losing too much for it just to be bad luck. He is suspicious that the poker site is fixing the hands to take his money. He knows that when he goes all in with pocket aces against another player that he should win at least 80% of the time. He keeps records on 50 such hands and finds that he only won on 31 of those hands.
a) Does this data provide enough evidence, at the 5% significance level, to show that his true winning percentage with aces on this poker site will be less than 80%?
b) Does this show that this site is fixed? Explain. Would you recommend that this player stop playing at this site?

68) A lottery official has become concerned that one of the 51 balls used to determine the winning numbers is being selected more often than it should be. The official draws 500 lottery balls with replacement and finds that the number in question came up 14 times.
a) At the 5% significance level, does this indicate that this number has a higher than normal probability of being selected?
b) If you knew what number had been tested, would you be wise to choose this number when playing the lottery? Explain.

69) Refer to Exercise (55).
a) Compute an 99% confidence interval for the true percentage of American Everglade visitors during the Spring of 2008 that were from Florida.
b) Explain how the answer to part a) agrees with the decision of the test performed in exercise (55).

70) Refer to Exercise (56).
a) Compute an 95% confidence interval for the true percentage of those in the Americas that are satisfied with their air quality.
b) Explain how the answer to part a) agrees with the results of the test performed in exercise (56).

71) Refer to Exercise (59).
a) Compute an 80% confidence interval for the true percentage of voters who will vote for the candidate.
b) Explain how the answer to part a) agrees with the decision of the test performed in exercise (59).

72) Refer to Exercise (60).
a) Compute an 90% confidence interval for the true percentage of cracked eggs in the current shipment.
b) Explain how the answer to part a) agrees with the results of the test performed in exercise (60).

73) Refer to Exercise (63).
   a) Compute an 98% confidence interval for the true percentage of Bay Area residents who have high-speed internet access at home.
   b) Explain how the answer to part a) agrees with the decision of the test performed in exercise (63).

74) Refer to Exercise (66).
   a) Compute an 90% confidence interval for the true probability of red after three blacks in a row.
   b) Explain how the answer to part a) agrees with the results of the test performed in exercise (66).

Section 9.3 – Testing the Population Mean, μ

In this section, we will switch from testing claims about a population proportion, p, to testing claims about a population mean, μ. This change will not affect the logic of a hypothesis test at all. However, there will be a few small changes made to the mechanics of the process. The first difference we notice occurs when we set up the hypotheses. Because the test concerns a population mean, we will use μ rather than p when writing our null and alternative hypotheses. The bigger change occurs when we compute our test statistic. Because we will be testing a population mean, μ, we will use the sample mean, $\bar{x}$, in our attempt to gather evidence against H_o. This means that we will base our test statistic on the z-score formula for $\bar{x}$ rather than the one for $\hat{p}$. Recall from Chapter 7:

$$z = \frac{\bar{x} - \mu}{\sigma / \sqrt{n}}$$

Ideally, we would use this to get our test statistic. However, we must recall from Chapter 8 that it is unrealistic to require the use of σ when calculating a confidence interval for μ. This is still the case for hypothesis tests. We are doing the test because we don't know the population mean, μ, and calculating σ requires the use of μ, $\sigma = \sqrt{\dfrac{\sum (x - \mu)^2}{N}}$. Just as we did in Chapter 8, we will deal with this problem by substituting the value of the sample standard deviation, s, in place of the population standard deviation, σ.

Recall from Chapter 8 that, provided $\bar{x}$ is normally distributed, $t = \dfrac{\bar{x} - \mu}{s / \sqrt{n}}$ has the t-distribution with $n - 1$ degrees of freedom. That means if we substitute s for σ in our test statistic, then we will have a test statistic with the t-distribution rather than the standard normal distribution. The only part of our procedure that will be affected by this change is the calculation of the P-value. Because our test statistic will be a t-score rather than a z-score, we will need to introduce a new *tcdf* function to use instead of the *normalcdf* function. This function is almost identical to the *normalcdf* except that it requires us to also enter the degrees of freedom. We will briefly show how this new function works in the following example and we will explore it further after the first example is finished. At the end of the section, step-by-step instructions for using *tcdf* with several technology options will be provided.

Let's look at an example:

Example 9.12: *Taxi in Times for San Francisco International Airport*

According to the *Bureau of Transportation Statistics* (BTS) (September 2009), the average time from landing to gate for commercial airlines at San Francisco International Airport (SFO) is 6.38 minutes. Suppose a travel magazine doubts this claim and decides to test it. They randomly select 51 flights and record the "Taxi-In" times. These flights yield a mean of 7.47 minutes with a standard deviation of 3.8229 minutes.

Does it take longer to "taxi in" at SFO than claimed by officials?

a) Comment on the requirements for performing a hypothesis test on the mean "taxi-in" time for SFO.

b) Does the data provide enough evidence, at the 5% significance level, to show that the true average "taxi-in" time for SFO is actually more than 6.38 minutes.

Solution:

a) **REQUIREMENTS:** Because the sample size is $n = 51 \geq 30$, we know from the Central Limit Theorem that $\overline{x}$ is normally distributed. Therefore, the requirements have been met.

b) **SET UP THE TEST:**

Determine H_o & H_1. As always, we will begin with '=' in H_o. The BTS claims that the mean is 6.38 minutes, so we will start with $H_o : \mu = 6.38$. The key here is that we are trying to show that the mean is "actually more" than 6.38 minutes. So we get the following:

$$H_o : \mu = 6.38$$
$$H_1 : \mu > 6.38$$

Determine the Significance Level. This is given as 5%, so $\alpha = 0.05$. (This tells us that we are willing to take up to a 5% risk of making a type I error on this problem.)

GATHER AND WEIGH THE EVIDENCE:

Calculate the Test Statistic. Because σ is unknown, we will need to use t as our test statistic.

$$t = \frac{\overline{x} - \mu_o}{s / \sqrt{n}} = \frac{7.47 - 6.38}{3.8229 / \sqrt{51}} \approx 2.036$$

For large samples, t-scores give us the same sense of whether or not a value is unusual as z-scores do. Therefore, because the claimed value of the mean, 6.38, is unusually far away from $\overline{x}$, it is unlikely that 6.38 is the true mean of the population.

Calculate the P-value. Because H_1 contains the '>' symbol, this is a right tailed test, so we need to determine how likely it is to get a value for our test statistic as large or larger than 2.036 if the mean actually was 6.38. Because we have a large sample, t has the t-distribution with df = 51 - 1 = 50. So, we need to find the area to the right of 2.036 under the appropriate t-curve.

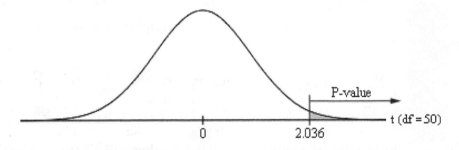

To find this area, we will define a *tcdf* function. The *tcdf* function works just like the *normalcdf* function except that you must provide the degrees of freedom along with the lower and upper boundaries of the region. The structure of the new function is *tcdf*(lower boundary, upper boundary, df).

So, P-value $= tcdf(2.036, \infty, 50) \approx 0.0235$

DECISIONS AND CONCLUSIONS:

Reject H_o or Do Not Reject H_o. The P-value tells us that, if we decide to reject H_o, then we will be taking a 2.35% risk of making a type I error. Therefore, because the P-value < 0.05, we should **Reject** H_o (acceptable risk).

State the Conclusion in Words. The data provides enough evidence, at the 5% significance level, to show that the true average "taxi in" time for SFO is actually more than 6.38 minutes.

> **Key Concept:** *s in place of σ, means a t-score rather than a z-score*
>
> When σ is unknown, we must use *s* in it's place. This results in a test statistic that is a t value rather than a z value. However, this merely means that we need to use the *tcdf* function rather than the *normalcdf* function.

FINDING P-VALUES USING TCDF: *How is it different from normalcdf?*

Example 9.12 showed us how to find the P-value for a right-tailed test. The following example will show us how to handle the left-tailed and two-tailed cases. These examples only show how the *tcdf* function is used for this purpose. At the end of this section, different technology options for calculating *tcdf* will be presented.

Example 9.13: *Practicing the test statistic and P-value with the tcdf function*

For each of the cases below, assume that the significance level is 5%, and then calculate the test statistic, find the P-value, and decide whether or not to Reject H_o.

a) $\begin{array}{l} H_o : \mu = 10 \\ H_1 : \mu < 10 \end{array}$; $\begin{array}{l} \bar{x} = 9.34,\ n = 32, \\ s = 2.1653 \end{array}$

b) $\begin{array}{l} H_o : \mu = 50 \\ H_1 : \mu \neq 50 \end{array}$; $\begin{array}{l} \bar{x} = 50.614,\ n = 20, \\ s = 3.1416 \end{array}$

Solutions:

a) **Calculate the Test Statistic.** Because we are forced to use the sample standard deviation, *s*, rather than σ, we must calculate a t-score.

$$t = \frac{9.34 - 10}{2.1653 / \sqrt{32}} \approx -1.724$$

```
(9.34-10)/(2.165
3/√(32))
            -1.724252438
```

Calculate the P-value. Because this is a left-tailed test, the P-value will be the area to the left of -1.724 or the $P(t < -1.724)$. Remember that you must consider the df when working with t values and $df = n - 1 = 32 - 1 = 31$.

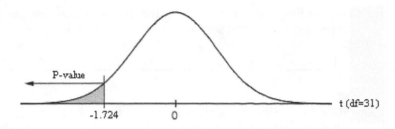

$$\text{P-value} = tcdf(-\infty, -1.724, 31) \approx 0.0473$$

Reject H_o or Do Not Reject H_o. Because the P-value $< \alpha$, our risk of a type I error is acceptably low, so we Reject H_o

b) **Calculate the Test Statistic.** Because we are using s, this will again be a t-score.

$$t = \frac{50.614 - 50}{3.1416 / \sqrt{20}} \approx 0.874$$

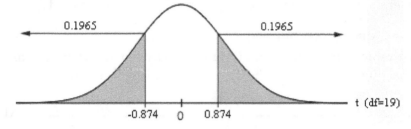

Calculate the P-value. Recall that with a two-tailed test, we need to find the chance of being as far away from zero, in either direction, as our test statistic was. So we need to find the area to the right of 0.874 and also the area to the left of -0.874 or $P(t < -0.874 \text{ or } t > 0.874)$. We have $df = 20 - 1 = 19$ for this one.

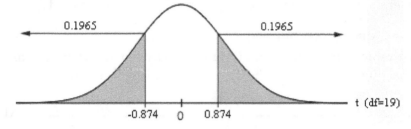

The area on the right hand side is found using $tcdf(0.874, \infty, 19) \approx 0.1965$. The area on the left is the same by symmetry. The P-value is the total of these two areas, so the P-value = 0.3930.

Reject H_o or Do Not Reject H_o. Because the P-value $> \alpha$, our risk of a type I error is too high, so we **Do Not Reject H_o**

The following Point to Remember summarizes what we have learned about the new tcdf function.

Definition: *the tcdf function*

The *tcdf* function allows us to find needed areas under various t-curves. The structure for the function is:

$$tcdf(\text{lower boundary}, \text{upper boundary}, df)$$

Note: Instructions for making this calculation using various technologies are shown at the end of this section.

Now that we have practiced finding the P-values using the *tcdf* function, we are ready to return to the full hypothesis test process. The procedure for this section is summarized as follows.

Procedure for performing a hypothesis test for μ :

Requirements: In order to use the t distribution to find the P-value, $\overline{x}$ must be normally distributed. So we need at least one of the following conditions to be true:

- The sample size is large $(n \geq 30)$
- The population is normally distributed.
- $15 \leq n < 30$ and the population is not severely skewed.

Phases: We perform the hypothesis test by completing three phases:

SET UP THE TEST:
- Determine H_o and H_1 .
- Decide on the significance level, α .

GATHER AND WEIGH THE EVIDENCE:
- Calculate the test statistic: $t = \dfrac{\overline{x} - \mu_o}{s/\sqrt{n}}$ (Use 3 decimal places)
- Determine the P-value using the *tcdf* function with $df = n - 1$.

DECISIONS AND CONCLUSIONS:
- If P-value $\leq \alpha$, then Reject H_o , otherwise Do Not Reject H_o (P-value $> \alpha$).
- State the conclusion of the test in plain language using the words of the application.

LOOKING DEEPER: *What is the job of a test statistic?*

At first glance it may seem like our test statistic has changed drastically from what it was in Section 9.2. However, if we look closer at the details, we will see that, in terms of the ideas involved, it is virtually the same.

In Section 9.2, the numerator was $\hat{p} - p_o$. The $\hat{p}$ was the value of the proportion observed in our sample and the p_o was the claimed value of the proportion from H_o . In this section, the numerator is $\overline{x} - \mu_o$. The $\overline{x}$ is the observed value of the mean from the sample and the μ_o is the claimed value for the population mean from H_o . In each case, the numerator consists of the value observed in the sample minus the value claimed for the population in H_o .

In Section 9.2, the denominator was $\sqrt{\dfrac{p_o q_o}{n}}$. This was intended as an approximation for the standard deviation of $\hat{p}$. In this section, the denominator is $s/\sqrt{n}$ and this is an approximation for the standard deviation of $\overline{x}$. So in general, we could say that in both of the tests of this chapter, the test statistic is:

$$\text{test stat} = \frac{(\text{observed sample value}) - (\text{value expected if } H_o \text{ is true})}{\text{standard deviation of the sample value}}$$

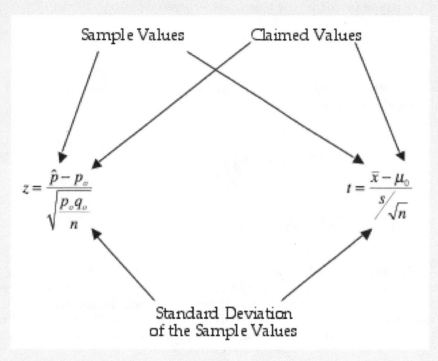

Sample Values   Claimed Values

$$z = \frac{\hat{p} - p_o}{\sqrt{\dfrac{p_o q_o}{n}}} \qquad\qquad t = \frac{\bar{x} - \mu_o}{s / \sqrt{n}}$$

Standard Deviation
of the Sample Values

So, in general, test statistics calculate the number of standard deviations apart a claimed value of the population parameter is away from the observed sample value of that same quantity.

Let's practice the new procedure with another example.

Example 9.14: *Changing attendance at Disney's Magic Kingdom?*

During 2003, it is reported that 14 million people visited Disney's Magic Kingdom in Orlando, Florida (Source: MouseBuzz.com). This represents an average daily attendance of about 38,356 people. Since then, the U.S. economy has fallen on tough times. This may have hurt the park as people try to cutback on their spending. However, it is possible that this could help the park as people choose a vacation to Disney World over a trip to Europe or a cruise in the Caribbean. A travel magazine wants to look into possible changes in the attendance. To investigate this, a writer from the magazine obtains a random sample of 28 days from the park during the last year. The attendance figures are shown in the chart below.

Does the economy affect the attendance at theme parks?

16,571	51,245	25,400	53,950	31,107	35,459
18,843	21,272	79,850	68,278	45,982	56,815
39,888	41,008	34,734	46,753	49,869	43,916
59,463	42,831	55,722	27,654	47,490	
37,332	34,042	25,321	52,738	35,483	

a) Have the requirements been met for performing a hypothesis test of the mean? Explain.

b) Perform a hypothesis test, using a 10% significance level, to determine if the average daily attendance has changed from the 2003 level.

c) Should we conclude that the true mean difference has changed from the 2003 value? Explain.

d) Suppose that, at the time of this sample, the true value of the mean was actually 39,866 people per day. In part (b), did we make a type I error, a type II error, or a correct decision? Explain.

Solution:

a) Because $15 \leq n = 28 < 30$, we need a population that is not severely skewed. To check this, we will take a look at the boxplot for this data set.

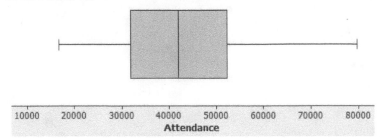

The two halves of the box are roughly symmetric. The right whisker is about twice as long as the left whisker. This indicates that the population might be somewhat right-skewed. However, we would need a larger imbalance between the whiskers, possibly with outliers, before we would conclude that the population was severely skewed to the right. With a sample size of 28, the lack of obvious signs of the population being severely skewed indicates that we are probably safe to proceed with the hypothesis test.

b) SET UP THE TEST:

Determine the Null and Alternative Hypotheses. As always, we begin with '=' in H_o. In 2003, the average daily attendance was 38,356 people. So, we begin with $H_o : \mu = 38,356$. The key word to help us here is the word "changed" and we get the following:

$$H_o : \mu = 38,356$$
$$H_1 : \mu \neq 38,356 \qquad \text{(Two-tailed test)}$$

Determine the Significance Level. This is given in this problem as 10%, so $\alpha = 0.10$. (This means that we are willing to take up to a 10% risk of making a type I error on this problem.)

GATHER AND WEIGH THE EVIDENCE:

Calculate the Test Statistic. We use the formula: $t = \dfrac{\bar{x} - \mu_0}{s / \sqrt{n}}$

Summary statistics:

Column	n	Mean	Std. dev.
Attendance	28	42107.714	14948.52

We know from H_o that $\mu_0 = 38,356$. Also, the sample size is given as $n = 28$. We can use technology to find $\bar{x}$ and s from the sample data. Using the StatCrunch output to the right, we get:

$$\bar{x} \approx 42,107.714 \text{ and } s \approx 14,948.52$$

$$t = \frac{\bar{x} - \mu_0}{s / \sqrt{n}} = \frac{42,107.714 - 38,356}{14,948.52 / \sqrt{28}} \approx 1.328$$

Procedural Note: *When we are given data rather than the sample mean.*

If data is provided rather than the sample mean, then we can use the data and technology to find the sample mean and the sample standard deviation.

It does not seem unusual for our $\bar{x}$ to be 1.328 student deviations away from the claimed mean of 38,365 even if H_o is true. Probably we will not reject H_o, but this t-score is in the gray area, so let's check the P-value to be sure.

Calculate the P-value. Examining the definition of P-value, we see that we need to find the probability of being at least as far away from 38,356, in either direction, as 42,107.7 is. In terms of the test statistic, this becomes: find $P(t < -1.328 \text{ OR } t > 1.328)$. We will use $df = n - 1 = 28 - 1 = 27$.

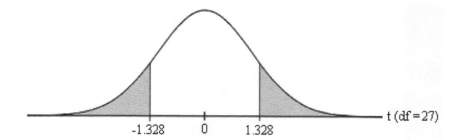

The shaded area shows all possible values of the test statistic that are at least as far away from the zero as our test statistic was. It appears that, even if H_o is true, there is a reasonable chance of the test statistic landing in the shaded area. The P-value will tell us how high of a chance it actually is.

Notice that there is symmetry to the shaded area, so we can simply find the area of one side and then double it. The area to the right of $t = 1.328$ can be found using $tcdf(1.328, \infty, 27)$, and it is 0.0976. Therefore the total area, and thus the P-value, is given by: P-value $= 2 \cdot (0.0976) = 0.1952$.

DECISIONS AND CONCLUSIONS:

Reject H_o or Do Not Reject H_o. Above we saw that the P-value = 0.1952. That means that there would be a reasonable chance, 19.52%, of getting a sample mean like ours due to random variation, even if H_o was actually true. Therefore, we should not be convinced that H_0 is false. In fact, if we decide to reject H_o, then we would be taking a 19.52% risk of making a type I error. In this problem, we stated that we would not take the risk of making a type I error if it was higher than 10%. Therefore, because $0.1952 > 0.10$, we **do not reject H_o**.

> **Caution**: *the importance of doubling the P-value for two-tailed tests*
>
> If we had forgotten to double the area when finding the P-value, we would have Rejected H_o and we would not have been aware of the actual risk we were taking of making a type I error.

State the Conclusion in Words (using plain language): At the 10% significance level, the data did not provide enough evidence to show that the true average daily attendance at the Magic Kingdom park has changed since 2003.

c) We did get a different average attendance from our sample than the claimed value of 38,356 people. However, the difference was small enough that there is a 19.52% chance of seeing such a difference just due to the random variation expected in a sample, even if the average daily attendance has not changed. So while we did see a difference in the mean attendance of our sample, it was not large enough to be convinced that the population mean has changed.

d) $\mu = 39,866 \Rightarrow H_o : \mu = 38,356$ is false. In the test, we decided to Not Reject H_o. Thus we have not rejected a false claim and have made a type II error.

THE CONFIDENCE INTERVAL PERSPECTIVE OF A TEST: *Another way to look at it.*

As we saw in Section 9.2, confidence intervals can give us another way to look at why we made the decision we did in a hypothesis test. Let's examine this again with the t-distribution.

Example 9.15: *Changing attendance at Disney's Magic Kingdom? (A confidence interval perspective)*

a) Use the data from **Example 9.14** to compute a 90% confidence interval for the true mean daily attendance at the Magic Kingdom Park.

b) Explain how the interval we obtain agrees with the decision reached in the hypothesis test performed in **Example 9.14**.

Solution:

a) Because this is an interval for a mean, we will use the formula $\bar{x} \pm t^{*} \cdot \dfrac{s}{\sqrt{n}}$.

Calculate $\bar{x}$ and s. In example 9.14 we saw that $\bar{x} \approx 42{,}107.7$ and $s \approx 14{,}948.5$

Find the t-scores. Because the confidence level is 90%, we put a middle area of 0.90 and 0.05 on each side.

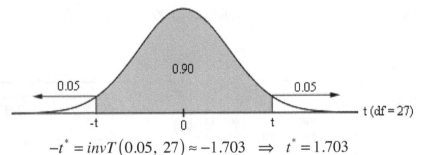

Key Concept: *Picking the confidence level*

Confidence intervals are equivalent to two-tailed hypothesis tests. So, when the hypothesis test has a significance level of $\alpha = 0.10$, the area in the middle of the confidence interval graph is $1 - \alpha = 0.90$. The $\alpha = 0.10$ is divided among the two tails.

$$-t^{*} = invT(0.05,\ 27) \approx -1.703 \quad \Rightarrow \quad t^{*} = 1.703$$

Calculate the Interval. $42107.7 \pm 1.703 \cdot \dfrac{14948.5}{\sqrt{28}} = 42107.7 \pm 4811.0$ or $\mu \in (37296.7,\ 46918.7)$.

This means that we are 90% confident that the true value for the population mean is somewhere between 37.296.7 and 46,918.7 people per day.

b) The interval claims that μ is between 37.296.7 and 46,918.7. That means that it is a reasonable possibility that μ is equal to 38,356. If $\mu = 38{,}356$, then $H_o : \mu = 38{,}356$ is a true claim. Because it is a reasonable possibility that H_o could be true, we should not reject it. In symbols:

If $\mu \in (37296.7,\ 46918.7) \Rightarrow \mu$ could be $38{,}356 \Rightarrow H_o : \mu = 38{,}356$ could be true $\Rightarrow$ Do not Reject H_o

PRACTICAL SIGNIFICANCE: *Does the difference really matter to anyone?*

In this chapter, we have learned that we reject H_0 when the difference between our sample value and the claimed value is large enough to create a P-value smaller than the significance level. Such differences our said to be **statistically significant**. However, just because the difference is large enough to cause us to reject H_0 does not mean that the difference is large enough that people will care about it. A difference that is large enough that people who care about it is said to be **practically significant**.

Definition: *Statistical Significance vs. Practical Significance*

Statistical Significance: If the difference between the sample value and the claimed value is large enough to lead to the rejection of H_0, then we say that the difference is statistically significant. We feel that there is strong evidence that such differences are not the result of random variation.

Practical Significance: If the difference between the sample value and the claimed value is large enough that matters to those working with variables in question, then we say the difference is practically significant.

Note: No difference should ever be considered practically significant if it is not statistically significant. Lack of statistical significance means that the difference may just be the result of random variation in the sample and the difference might not really exist in the population at all.

Example 9.16: *Does a cargo box hurt your gas mileage?*

A growing family has decided that they need more room for their belongings when the go on road trips. Rather than buying a bigger car, they decide to purchase a cargo box for their SUV. After purchasing and attaching the cargo box, they become concerned that the box might be hurting their gas mileage. They know that without the cargo box, their SUV averages 17.9 miles per gallon on road trips. They kept track of the gas mileage on 31 trips after the cargo box was attached. The sample of 31 trips yielded $\bar{x} \approx 17.57$ and $s \approx 0.61107$.

Cargo boxes provide extra storage, but do you end up paying a high price in extra gas use?

a) Does the data provide enough evidence, at the 5% significance level, to show that the true average mileage with the cargo box attached is lower than it was before they attached it?

b) Would you say that the difference with the cargo box on was statistically significant? Explain.

c) Would you say that the difference with the cargo box on was practically significant? Explain.

Solution:

a) SET UP THE TEST:

Determine H_o **&** H_1. As always, we begin with '=' in H_o. Before adding the cargo box, the average mileage was 17.9 mpg. So, we will have $H_o : \mu = 17.9$. The key phrase here is "lower than it was before" which indicates a left-tailed test.

$$H_o : \mu = 17.9$$
$$H_1 : \mu < 17.9$$

Determine the Significance Level. The significance level is given as 5%, so $\alpha = 0.05$. (Thus, we are willing to take up to a 5% risk of making a type I error on this problem.)

GATHER AND WEIGH THE EVIDENCE:

Calculate the Test Statistic. Because σ is unknown, we will need to use t as our test statistic. The sample size was 31 and produced $\bar{x} \approx 17.57$ and $s \approx 0.61107$.

$$t = \frac{\bar{x} - \mu_o}{s / \sqrt{n}} = \frac{17.57 - 17.9}{0.61107 / \sqrt{31}} \approx -3.007$$

This tells us that the old value of the mean, 17.9 mpg, is 3.007 "student-t" deviations away from our $\bar{x}$. This is considered very unusual, so we expect that we will end up rejecting H_o. The P-value should confirm this suspicion.

Calculate the P-value. Because H_1 contains the '<' symbol, this is a left-tailed test, so we need to find the area to the left of our test statistic. We have $df = 31 - 1 = 30$ for this one.

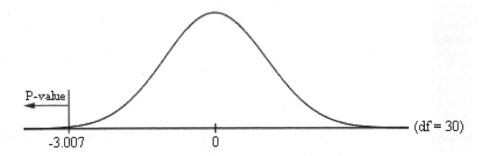

P-value = $tcdf(-\infty, -3.007, 30) \approx 0.0026$.

If adding the cargo box did not change the mileage, there would only be a 0.26% chance of getting a test statistic this far to the left. It seems unlikely that the mileage is still 17.9 mpg.

DECISIONS AND CONCLUSIONS:

Reject H_o or Do Not Reject H_o. The P-value tells us that, if we decide to reject H_o, we will be taking a 0.26% risk of making a type I error. Therefore, because the P-value < 0.05, we Reject H_o (acceptable risk of making a type I error).

State the Conclusion in Words. The data does provide enough evidence, at the 5% significance level, to show that true average mileage for the SUV is lower after adding the cargo box.

b) The P-value was lower than the significance level. So, yes, difference in the mileage between our sample value and the old value is statistically significant. By this we mean that there is not a very good chance that the lower mileage in our sample is simply due to the random variation in the sample.

c) This is somewhat of an opinion question, but the difference between the sample value and the mean without the cargo box is pretty small, $17.9 - 17.57 = 0.33$ mpg. If the family really needs the extra space, it is probably better to add the cargo box and deal with slightly lower mileage. This is especially true if the other option would be to buy a larger SUV. I would say that this difference does not appear to be practically significant.

WRAP SESSION: *A left-tailed, small sample case*

Example 9.17: *Keeping the pitch counts down?*

In the early years of professional baseball, pitchers would routinely pitch the whole 9 innings of a game. In fact, some pitchers would continue on even if the game went to extra innings. In the modern game, pitchers valuable arms are often protected by management by not letting them continue after too many pitches are thrown. Research has shown that the risk of injury increases dramatically after 110 pitches. The following is the ending pitch count for the starting pitchers from 13 games where the pitcher was removed after completing at least 5 innings and keeping the opponents to 3 or less runs. (This removes situations where the pitcher was removed early because of poor performance rather than for safety reasons.)

Are the pitch counts kept lower now that star pitchers make such high salaries?

| 101 | 91 | 102 | 98 | 109 | 102 | 111 |
| 97 | 107 | 106 | 114 | 108 | 103 | |

a) Does the data provide enough evidence, at the 1% significance level, to show that the average pitch count for major league starting pitchers in less than 110 pitches?

b) Comment on the requirements.

c) Does this show that pitchers are being removed earlier than in past years to protect their valuable arms? Explain.

d) Compute a 98% confidence interval for the true mean pitch count for major league starting pitchers.

e) Explain how the interval from part (d) agrees with the decision reached in the hypothesis test in part (a).

Solution:

a) SET UP THE TEST:

Determine H_o & H_1. As always, we begin with '=' in H_o. There really is no claimed value for the average number of pitches in this problem. However, because we are trying to show that the average is less than 110, we will begin with a default of $H_o : \mu = 110$. The key phrase here is "less than 110" which indicates a left-tailed test.

$$H_o : \mu = 110$$
$$H_1 : \mu < 110$$

Determine the Significance Level. The significance level is given as 1%, so $\alpha = 0.01$. (Thus, we are willing to take up to a 1% risk of making a type I error on this problem.)

GATHER AND WEIGH THE EVIDENCE:

Calculate the Test Statistic. Because σ is unknown, we will need to use t as our test statistic. We can use technology to find the mean and standard deviation for the sample data. The StatCrunch output to the right yields $\bar{x} \approx 103.769$ and $s \approx 6.2869$. The sample size was 13, so we get:

Summary statistics:

Column	n	Mean	Std. dev.
Pitches	13	103.76923	6.2869421

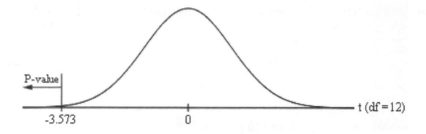

$$t = \frac{\bar{x} - \mu_o}{s/\sqrt{n}} = \frac{103.769 - 110}{6.2869/\sqrt{13}} \approx -3.573$$

This tells us that the claimed value of the mean, 110 pitches, is 3.573 "student-t" deviations away from our $\bar{x}$. This is considered very unusual, so we expect that we will end up rejecting H_o. The P-value should confirm this suspicion.

Calculate the P-value. Because H_1 contains the '<' symbol, this is a left-tailed test, so we need to find the area to the left of our test statistic. We have df = 13 - 1 = 12 for this one.

P-value = $tcdf(-\infty, -3.573, 12) \approx 0.0019$.

If we are willing to reject with this level of evidence, then, in the long run, we will reject 0.19% of the true claims that we face.

DECISIONS AND CONCLUSIONS:

Reject H_o or Do Not Reject H_o. The P-value tells us that, if we decide to reject H_o, we will be taking a 0.19% risk of making a type I error. Therefore, because the P-value < 0.01, we Reject H_o (acceptable risk of making a type I error).

State the Conclusion in Words. The data does provide enough evidence, at the 1% significance level, to show that average pitch count for major league starting pitchers is less than 110 pitches.

b) Because $n = 13 < 15$, we need the population to be normally distributed. We can't show that we have a normal population, but we can check to see if there is evidence that it is not normal. A normal probability plot from Minitab is shown to the right.

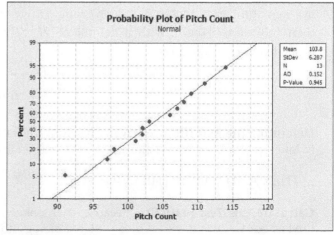

Because the P-value from the probability plot is 0.945 > 0.05, we can conclude that a normal population is a reasonable possibility. Even though this does not show that we have a normal population, the fact that it "passes" the test means that it is a reasonable possibility that the requirements have been met.

c) We have shown that the average pitch count for major league starting pitchers is less than 110 pitches. However, we cannot tell why this is done just by looking at the data. After all, this is an observational study, not a controlled experiment. We shall leave it to sports radio talk show hosts to speculate as to why this is done.

d) Because this is a confidence interval for a mean, we will use the formula $\bar{x} \pm t^* \cdot \dfrac{s}{\sqrt{n}}$.

Calculate $\bar{x}$ **and s.** In our work above, we saw that $\bar{x} \approx 103.769$ and $s \approx 6.2869$.

Find the t-scores. Because the confidence level is 98%, we put a middle area of 0.98 and 0.01 on each side. We then use technology to find the t-scores we need.

Key Concept: *Picking the confidence level*

Confidence intervals are equivalent to two-tailed hypothesis tests. So, when the hypothesis test is single tailed and has a significance level of $\alpha = 0.01$, the area in each single tail of the graph is $\alpha = 0.01$. This leaves $1 - 2\alpha = 0.98$ for the middle portion of the graph.

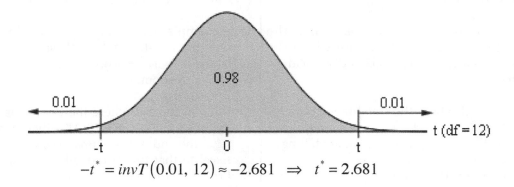

$$-t^* = invT(0.01, 12) \approx -2.681 \quad \Rightarrow \quad t^* = 2.681$$

Calculate the Interval. $103.769 \pm 2.681 \cdot \dfrac{6.2869}{\sqrt{13}} = 103.769 \pm 4.675$ or $\mu \in (99.094, 108.444)$. This means that we are 98% confident that the true value for the population mean is somewhere between 99.094 and 108.444 pitches per start.

e) The interval claims that μ is between 99.094 and 108.444. That means that we are confident that μ is less than 110 pitches. If $\mu < 110$, then $H_o : \mu = 110$ is a false claim and $H_1 : \mu < 110$ is a true claim. Because we are confident that H_o is False, we should reject it. In symbols:

$$\text{If } \mu \in (99.094, 108.444) \Rightarrow \mu < 110 \Rightarrow H_o : \mu = 110 \text{ is False} \Rightarrow \text{Reject } H_o$$

Caution: *Make sure you are on the correct side*

When you are using a confidence interval to confirm the decision made in a hypothesis test, make sure that your confidence interval is on the side of the claimed mean that agrees with H_1. Consider this. In the example above, if our confidence interval work had produced $\mu \in (112.4, 118.8)$, this would have been be a little tricky to interpret. Even though $\mu \in (112.4, 118.8) \Rightarrow \mu \neq 110$, it still would not be correct to Reject $H_o : \mu = 110$. We should only Reject H_o when we have strong evidence that H_1 is true. However, $\mu \in (112.4, 118.8) \Rightarrow H_1 : \mu < 110$ is False. This is the opposite of what we were trying to prove. In order to Reject H_o, our data must support H_1.

TECHNOLOGY SECTION: *Finding areas under t-curves with different technologies*

This section provides a quick tutorial on how to find area under a t-curve for the TI-83/84, Microsoft Excel, Minitab, and StatCrunch.

EXCEL:

To find areas under a t-curve in Microsoft Excel you will make use of the TDIST function. This function can be used to find the area to the right of a positive test statistic under a specified t-curve. Examples for different P-value situations are shown below. The structure for TDIST is:

TDIST(t-score, degrees of freedom, number of tails)

P-value for a two-tailed test:	**P-value for a one-tailed test:**
This example shows how you would find the P-value in a two-tailed hypothesis test where the test statistic was a t-score of 1.953 and we had 34 degrees of freedom.	This example shows how you would find the P-value in a one-tailed hypothesis test where the test statistic was a t-score of 2.553 and we had 20 degrees of freedom.
1. Click in the cell where the P-value is desired. 2. Type "=TDIST(1.953, 34, 2)". By entering the '2' at the end of the expression, we are telling Excel to double the area. 3. Press Enter to see the result.	1. Click in the cell where the P-value is desired. 2. Type "=TDIST(2.553, 20, 1)". By entering the '1' at the end of the expression, we are telling Excel to that this is a one-tailed test. 3. Press Enter to see the result.
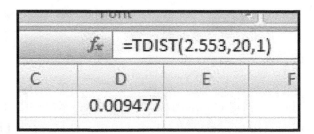	
Note: Excel insists on a positive value for the t-score. If you have a negative value for the test stat, just enter the positive value and that will still work due to the symmetry of t-curves.	**Note**: Excel insists on a positive value for the t-score. The answer above is the area to the right of a positive test statistic (appropriate for a right-tailed test). If you are doing a left-tailed test and have a negative t-score, then you will need to enter the positive value, but the answer will still be correct due to the symmetry of t-curves.

TI-83/84:

The tcdf function on the TI-83/84 works almost identically to what is presented in the reading in this section. Just like the normalcdf function from Chapter 6, tcdf is found under the distribution (DISTR) menu. The structure of the function is:

$$\text{tcdf(lower boundary, upper boundary, df)}$$

If the lower boundary is " $-\infty$ ", then use " -1×10^{99} " as the lower boundary.

If the upper boundary is " ∞ ", then use " 1×10^{99} " as the upper boundary.

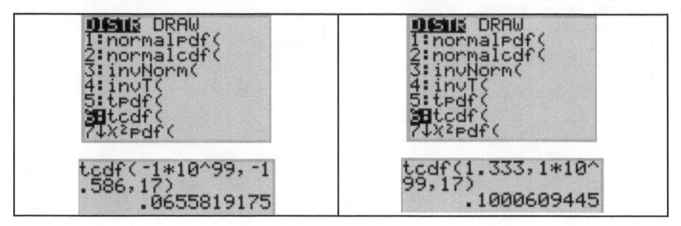

Tech Tip: Recall from chapter 6 that you can store the value 1×10^{99} in the variable I.

STATCRUNCH:

To find areas under a t-curve in StatCrunch you will make use of one of the calculators in the STAT menu. From the STATCRUNCH window choose STAT > Calculators > T. This will open the t-distribution calculator in StatCrunch. Examples for area to the left and right are shown below.

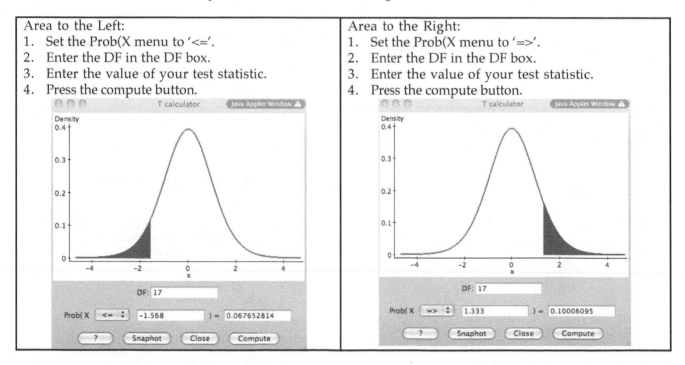

MINITAB:

Minitab only gives areas to the left. So, if you need an area to the right, you must first find the area to the left and then subtract from 1. Directions and screen shots are shown below.

Area to the Left:	Area to the Right:
1. Choose CALC > Probability Dist > t . . .	1. Choose CALC > Probability Dist > t . . .
2. Select 'Cumulative probability'.	2. Select 'Cumulative probability'.
3. Enter the DF in the textbox.	3. Enter the DF in the textbox.
4. Check 'Input Constant:' and enter your test statistic.	4. Check 'Input Constant:' and enter your test statistic.
5. Press OK.	5. Press OK.
	6. Subtract the Minitab result from 1.

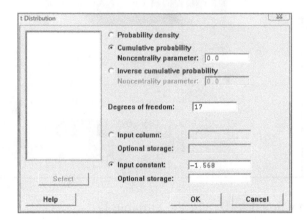

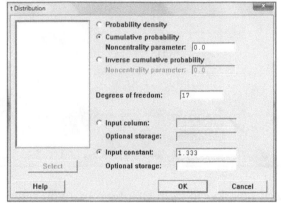

Cumulative Distribution Function

Student's t distribution with 17 DF

```
    x   P( X <= x )
-1.568    0.0676528
```

Cumulative Distribution Function

Student's t distribution with 17 DF

```
    x   P( X <= x )
1.333    0.899939
```

Area to the left is given above as 0.0676528

Area to the Right = 1 − 0.899939 = 0.100061

Exercise Set 9.3

Concept Review: Review the definitions and concepts from this section by filling in the blanks for each of the following.

75) We use t-scores rather than z-scores whenever σ is _____ and replaced by ___ .

76) $\bar{x}$ is the _____ mean, μ is the _____ mean, and μ_o is the _____ mean.

77) In a test of the mean, evidence consists of a large _____ between _____ and μ_o.

78) In general, evidence in a hypothesis test comes from seeing large differences between what we observed in the _____ and what we expected to see if H_o was _____ .

Mechanics: Practice the calculations needed for hypothesis testing before working on real world applications.

(79 – 84) a) Calculate the value of the test statistic.
   b) Determine the P-value for the test statistic you have calculated.
   c) State whether or not you would reject H_o if the significance level was 5%.

79) $H_o : \mu = 41$ $\bar{x} = 42.66, n = 22,$
    $H_1 : \mu > 41$; $s = 4.4524$

80) $H_o : \mu = 6.6$ $\bar{x} = 6.34, n = 15,$
    $H_1 : \mu < 6.6$; $s = 1.2705$

81) $H_o : \mu = 21.8$ $\bar{x} = 21.074, n = 37,$
    $H_1 : \mu \neq 21.8$; $s = 2.805$

82) $H_o : \mu = 200$ $\bar{x} = 273.3, n = 92,$
    $H_1 : \mu \neq 200$; $s = 41.833$

83) $H_o : \mu = 18.3$ $\bar{x} = 18.90, n = 42,$
    $H_1 : \mu < 18.3$; $s = 0.8557$

84) $H_o : \mu = 1.05$ $\bar{x} = 0.953, n = 58,$
    $H_1 : \mu > 1.05$; $s = 0.27422$

Applications: Practice the ideas learned in this section within the context of a real world application.

85) In September 2009, the author of this text hiked to the top of Half-Dome from the Yosemite Valley floor. It took him about 5.5 hours to reach the top. He decided to perform a hypothesis test to see if the average time it takes hikers to make the journey to the top is different than his. He collected a sample of 14 randomly selected Half-Dome hikers and asked them how long it took them to reach the top. The sample yielded a mean of 4.91 hours with a standard deviation of 1.682 hours.
   a) Does the data provide enough evidence, at the 10% significance level, to show that the true average time to the top for hikers is different than 5.5 hours?
   b) Comment on the requirements of the hypothesis test.

86) As of June 2010, there had been a total of 20 perfect games pitched in Major league baseball. This means that every batter the pitcher faced during a 9-inning game made an out. Only 17 of the 20 perfect games have known pitch counts. A sports fan is interested in determining if during a perfect game, the pitcher throws fewer pitchers per batter than normal. The average number of pitches per batter in major league baseball is known to be about 3.9. Using the 17 perfect games with known pitch counts as the sample, we get a mean of 3.765 pitches/ batter with a standard deviation of 0.46572.
   a) Does the data provide enough evidence, at the 5% significance level, to show that the true average pitches per batter in a perfect game is less than the normal 3.9 pitches per batter?
   b) Comment on the requirements of the hypothesis test.

87) On October 2, 2008, the auto toll on the Golden Gate Bridge was increased from $5 to $6. This hike was expected to raise revenue, but if it causes people to avoid the bridge, then revenue could in fact decrease. Before the hike, the average daily revenue from the bridge tolls was $234,018. A few months after the change was made, a random sample of 30 days was chosen and the average revenue per day was found to be $249,931 with a standard deviation of $36,713.
   a) Perform a hypothesis test, at the 5% significance level, to determine if the average daily revenue has changed since the toll hike.
   b) Comment on the requirements for the hypothesis test.

88) *Lost Coast Forest Products* produces small bundles of wood to sell at campgrounds. The bundles of wood are labeled as containing 18 pounds. However, due to the small number of pieces of firewood they contain, the actual weight in each bundle varies a bit. Suppose that a random sample of 40 such bundles is obtained and produces a mean of 17.3 pounds with a standard deviation of 2.4308 pounds.

   a) Perform a hypothesis test, at the 5% significance level, to see if the true average for such bundles is different than the 18 pounds on the label.
   b) Comment on the requirements of the test.

89) In January of 2010, the average number of hours on Facebook per month for users was 7 (Source: Nielsen). A statistics teacher wonders if that number is different for the students at her school. She collects a random sample of 250 Facebook users and surveys them on their Facebook habits. The sample produces a mean of 10.77 hours with a standard deviation of 6.793 hours.
   a) Does the data provide enough evidence, at the 5% significance level, to show that the true mean hours per month for students at the statistics teacher's school is different than for all users?
   b) Comment on the requirements of the hypothesis test.
   c) If students are claiming that they do not have enough free time to complete their assignments, does this indicate that they may actually just need to budget their time better? Explain.

90) In-n-Out Burger is a very popular "fast food" restaurant on the west coast. In fact, it is so popular that, during peak times, the drive thru lines can become 20 to 30 cars long. A statistics student wants to see if, during peak times, the average drive thru wait time is greater than 10 minutes. He collects a random sample of 12 cars during peak times and finds the average wait time to be 11.72 minutes with a standard deviation of 4.5922 minutes.
   a) Does the data provide enough evidence, at the 1% significance level, to show that the true mean drive thru wait time during peak hours is more than 10 minutes?
   b) Comment on the requirements of the hypothesis test.
   c) Can we conclude that the mean is actually not more than 10 minutes? Explain.

91) The Subway website lists the number of calories in a 6 inch Super Turkey Breast sub as 333. A consumer watchdog group believes that the true average is actually higher than this. To test their theory they obtain a random sample of 14 such sandwiches and have the calorie content analyzed. The sample yields the following calorie data:

321	342	345	314	332	333	339
354	339	338	322	355	356	332

Note: $\sum x^2 = 1,594,810$

   a) Perform a hypothesis test to see if the sandwiches contain, on average, more calories than claimed. Use $\alpha = 0.01$
   b) Use the normal probability plot for the sample data shown below to comment on the requirements of the test.

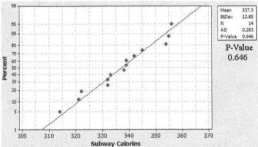

   c) Should the consumer watchdog group accuse Subway of false advertising? Explain.

92) The California Energy Commission claims that 25% of the heating and cooling cost in residential homes is wasted on air leaking out of the ducts. A random sample of 20 homes that recently had leaks in their ducts repaired is taken and their energy costs are measured for one year. The average energy cost for all residential homes in this area was $2578/year. The yearly cost for the sample of 20 homes is shown below.

2374	3821	1240	1268	3297	2058	1630
3374	5022	726	3054	2699	2272	3184
1909	1102	3323	1849	1875	562	

Note: $\bar{x} = 2331.95$, $s \approx 1137.36$

   a) Does the data provide enough evidence, at the 5% significance level, to show that the true mean energy costs for homes that have had their ducts repaired is less than the town average?

   b) Use the boxplot of the sample data shown below to comment on the requirements of the hypothesis test.

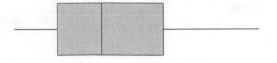

   c) Does it appear that getting your ducts repaired is effective in lowering your energy costs? Explain.

93) A national restaurant chain is considering introducing a new menu with higher prices. They are hoping that such a change will increase revenue. However, they are also concerned that by raising prices during tough economic times, they might lose customers. They decide to test out the new menus in one of their locations before putting them out nationally. The average daily revenue for that restaurant was $15,470 per day with the old prices. A sample of 40 days with the new menus produced mean daily revenue of $14,312 with a standard deviation of $2419.
   a) Perform a hypothesis test, at the 5% significance level, to determine if the true average daily revenue has changed with the new menu prices.
   b) Comment on the requirements of the hypothesis test.
   c) Would you recommend to the chain that they roll out these new menus nationally? Explain.
   d) Discuss the possibility that you have made a type I or type II error.

94) In July of 2006, the average price of a 5+ bedroom house in Malibu, CA was known to be about 7 million dollars. After that time, a crisis erupted in the home loan industry resulting in many people losing their homes in foreclosures. A realtor wants to see if this crisis has resulted in a lower average price in April 2008. She randomly selected 39 Five+ bedroom homes for sale in Malibu and found the average price for those homes to be $6,282,670 with a standard deviation of $4,224,100.
   a) Perform a hypothesis test, at the 5% significance level, to determine if the true mean price is lower than it was in July 2006.
   b) Comment on the requirements of the hypothesis test.
   c) Discuss the possibility that you have made a type I or type II error.

95) MouseWaits is an I-phone app that provides wait times for the rides at Disneyland. One day in April 2010, the app showed a wait time for Space Mountain of 55 minutes. At that time a random sample of 11 guests provided the following wait times in minutes.

63	64	68	62	46	50
51	73	49	68	62	

Note: $\sum x^2 = 39,948$

a) Does the data provide enough evidence, at the 10% significance level, to show that the true mean wait time differs from the reported 55 minutes.

b) Use the normal probability plot for the sample data shown below to comment on the requirements of the hypothesis test.

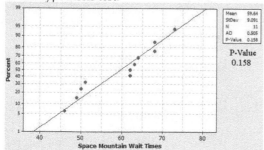

c) Discuss the possibility that you have made a type I or type II error.

96) The average time for a person to get over a cold is about 6 days. Zicam is a product that claims that it can shorten the duration of a cold. A random sample of 24 cold sufferers is given the product at the onset of their colds and the time it takes to get over the cold is recorded. The results are shown below (based on data from the Cleveland Clinic Zicam Study).

4.2	3.3	4.0	3.0	4.2	5.2	5.7	3.8
3.6	5.2	3.3	4.0	5.1	4.6	3.0	4.4
4.3	4.2	4.1	4.8	3.8	5.7	4.8	3.8

Note: $\bar{x} \approx 4.2542$, $s \approx 0.76895$

a) Does the data provide enough evidence, at the 1% significance level, to show that the true mean recovery time with Zicam is less than normal.

b) Use the boxplot of the sample data shown below to comment on the requirements of the test.

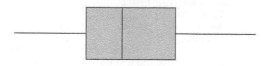

c) Discuss the possibility that you have made a type I or type II error.

97) The owner of "Everything Grows", a plant business in Danville, CA wishes to increase traffic to the company's website. To accomplish this goal, he paid for a search engine optimization. Before this took place, the website was averaging 16.67 hits per day. He wishes to see if the average has increased after the optimization. A random sample of 18 days after the optimization was completed had the following number of hits:

27	37	33	11	32	5
31	6	11	23	22	29
13	9	33	21	35	37

Note: $\bar{x} \approx 23.0556$, $s \approx 11.2065$

a) Perform a hypothesis test to see if the true average number of hits has increased since the optimization. Use $\alpha = 0.01$.

b) Use the boxplot of the sample data shown below to comment on the requirements of the hypothesis test.

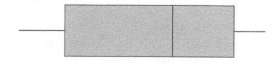

c) Would you consider the difference between the sample mean and the claimed mean to be statistically significant, practically significant, both, or neither? Explain.

d) Discuss the possibility that you have made a type I or type II error.

98) A company produces a wall mount for large size HDTVs. The box claims that the wall mount can safely hold weights up to 200 pounds. The company does not want to risk being sued due to the failure of one of their wall mounts, so they routinely perform strength tests on them. They want to be on the safe side, so in these tests, they will consider it a problem if the average failure weight for the wall mounts is less than 250 pounds. In a recent test, they randomly chose 30 wall mounts and increased the amount of weight on them until they failed. The failure weights, in pounds, are listed below.

253	245	258	238	221	248
263	255	265	270	222	245
237	226	223	244	217	212
249	273	231	247	243	276
228	260	229	221	242	263

Note: $\bar{x} \approx 243.467$, $s \approx 17.817$

a) Perform a hypothesis test, at the 5% significance level, to see if the true average failure weight for the wall mounts is less than 250 pounds.

b) Comment on the requirements for the hypothesis test.

c) Would you consider the difference between the sample mean and the claimed mean to be statistically significant, practically significant, both, or neither? Explain.

d) Discuss the possibility that you have made a type I or type II error.

99) Because coins get damaged, lost, etc., new coins are made and put into circulation on a regular basis. I suspected that because of this, nickels would be, on average, less than 15 years old. In September 2009, I went through my loose change and found 30 nickels. The year of mint for those nickels were as shown below.

2008	1977	1974	1989	1980	2004
1976	1990	1976	2000	1994	1980
2007	1999	1981	1982	2000	2005
1995	1974	1990	2006	2002	1980
1990	1974	1999	2005	1988	1999

Note: $\bar{x} = 1990.8$, $s \approx 11.601$

a) Does the data provide enough evidence, at the 1% significance level, to show that the true average year of mint for nickels in circulation is greater than 1993?

b) Comment on the requirements for the test.

c) Suppose that the true value of the mean is actually 1994.2, then in part (a), did we make a type I error, a type II error, or a correct decision? Explain.

d) Would you consider the difference between the sample mean and the claimed mean to be statistically significant, practically significant, both, or neither? Explain.

100) *Campbell's* produces cans of soup that are labeled as containing 10.75 ounces. The company routinely performs hypothesis tests on its own product to try to detect if its filling machine is malfunctioning. Suppose that a recent sample of 32 cans of soup produced the following weights in ounces.

10.78	10.74	10.81	10.79	10.85	10.69
10.76	10.88	10.81	11.03	10.77	10.77
10.86	10.70	10.70	10.75	10.73	10.85
10.67	10.96	10.78	10.66	10.66	10.68
10.77	10.75	10.73	10.77	10.72	10.67
10.83	10.79				

Note: $\bar{x} \approx 10.7722$, $s \approx 0.084309$

a) Perform a hypothesis test, at the 5% significance level, to determine if the filling machine is, on average, filling the cans with an incorrect amount.

b) Comment on the requirements of the test.

c) Suppose that the true value of the mean is actually 10.76 oz., then in part (a), did we make a type I error, a type II error, or a correct decision? Explain.

d) Would you consider the difference between the sample mean and the claimed mean to be statistically significant, practically significant, both, or neither? Explain.

101) It is widely believed that health care costs have been rising at an unacceptable rate. In 2005, the average cost of health care premiums for an individual with a job-based health care plan was $3991 per year. A news website wants to show that the costs have increased dramatically since then. In 2007, they obtained a random sample of 60 individuals from the U.S. who have a job-based health care plan. The sample produced an average cost of $5311 per year with a standard deviation of $1195.

a) Perform a hypothesis test, at the 5% significance level, to show that the true average cost has increased from the 2005 level.

b) Comment on the requirements of the test.

c) Suppose that the true mean value for individual job-based coverage is $4250/year, then in part (a), did we make a type I error, a type II error, or a correct decision? Explain.

d) Would you consider the difference between the sample mean and the claimed mean to be statistically significant, practically significant, both, or neither? Explain.

102) The price of snowboarding equipment generally falls dramatically as the season comes to a close. During January of 2008, the average price for a new pair of snowboard bindings was $138. A snowboarder statistics student wants to conduct a study to see if the average price of such bindings in April of 2008 has fallen below $100. A random sample of 28 snowboard bindings produced a mean price of $88.75 with a standard deviation of $35.43.

a) Perform a test to see if the true average price has fallen below $100. Use $\alpha = 0.10$

b) Comment on the requirements of the test.

c) Suppose that the true mean price for the bindings is $102, then in part (a), did we make a type I error, a type II error, or a correct decision. Explain.

103) Refer to Exercise (91).

a) Compute a 98% confidence interval for the true average number of calories for Subway 6-inch Super Turkey Breast subs.

b) Explain how the answer to part a) agrees with the results of the test performed in exercise (91).

104) Refer to Exercise (88).

a) Compute a 95% confidence interval for the true average weight of the wood bundles.

b) Explain how the answer to part a) agrees with the results of the test performed in exercise (88).

105) Refer to Exercise (93).

a) Compute a 95% confidence interval for the true average daily revenue with the new menus.

b) Explain how the answer to part a) agrees with the results of the test performed in exercise (93).

106) Refer to Exercise (94).

a) Compute a 90% confidence interval for the true mean price of the homes in 2008.

b) Explain how the answer to part a) agrees with the results of the test performed in exercise (94).

107) Refer to Exercise (101).

a) Compute a 98% confidence interval for the true average cost of individual job-based health care coverage.

b) Explain how the answer to part a) agrees with the results of the test performed in exercise (101).

108) Refer to Exercise (102).

a) Compute an 95% confidence interval for the true mean price of the bindings in April 2008.

b) Explain how the answer to part a) agrees with the results of the test performed in exercise (102).

Chapter Problem: Pregnancy and the H1N1 Flu Virus

Are pregnant women at higher than normal risk of death due to contraction of the H1N1 (Swine Flu) virus?

In April of 2010, the *Los Angeles Times* reported that the death rates from H1N1 flu were higher among pregnant women. The article pointed out that during the 5-month peak of the outbreak, "5% of H1N1 deaths were among pregnant women although they account for only 1% of the population." The article goes on to say that "the research leaves no doubt about the value of H1N1 flu vaccination for all pregnant women."

The question we want to tackle in this chapter problem is this: Does the data really show that pregnant women are at a higher risk of death due to H1N1 or could the higher death rate that was observed during the 5-month period of the outbreak simply be the result of random chance?

a) Complete the "Set up the Test" phase using a 5% significance level. Assume that we wish to show that the proportion of pregnant women among the swine flu deaths is greater than the proportion of pregnant women in the overall population.

b) The details of the research stated that 30 pregnant women died of swine flu during the 5-month peak of the outbreak. Use the fact that this was 5% of the total deaths to determine the total number of swine flu deaths during that period. This will be our sample size for completing the test.

c) Complete the "Gather and Weigh the Evidence" phase of the test.

d) Complete the "Decisions and Conclusions" phase of the test.

e) Comment on the requirements.

f) Would you say that the article is justified when it says "the research leaves no doubt about the value of H1N1 flu vaccination for all pregnant women"? Explain.

g) Compute a 90% confidence interval for the true proportion of pregnant women among the swine flu deaths.

h) Explain how the answer to part (g) agrees with the decision of the test in part (d) above.

i) Does the agreement between parts (d) and (g) prove that we have made a correct decision in this hypothesis test? Explain.

Chapter 9: Technology Project

1) Use the technology of your choice to perform a hypothesis test.
   a) Enter and name (or LOAD) the data from Exercise (6), Ch 9 Review Exercises.
   B) Using only the sample size given in the problem, comment on the requirements for performing the test.
   c) Use the technology to perform a normality test on the sample data. Paste the results into your report.
   D) Use the results of the normality test to help discuss whether or not the requirement for performing the hypothesis test has actually been met. Explain in detail. (See Chapter 6, Section 5 for the guidelines.)
   E) Write out steps 1 & 2 for the hypothesis test requested in the problem.
   f) Use the technology to find the test statistic and P-value for the hypothesis test.
   g) Copy and paste the results to your report.
   H) Write out the Decision and Conclusion of the hypothesis test in your report.
   I) If the true mean number of questions per day for Giselle was somehow found to be 450 questions, then have we made a type I error, type II error, or a correct decision? Explain in detail.

2) This one uses the application "Hyp Test Sim - Props" located in the StatSims folder. We will test the claims: $H_0 : p = 0.4737$ & $H_1 : p \neq 0.4737$.
   a) Enter you name in the textbox provided. Based on the claims written above, fill in the box for the claimed proportion and select the type of test. Set the significance level to 10%. Enter 0.4737 for the true proportion. Use 1087 for the sample size, and 7777 for the number of trials.
   B) Have the requirements been met for doing this test? Explain and show work.
   C) If we reject H_0, would that be a correct decision or a type I error? Explain by writing out the following with the blanks filled in. The true value of p is _____ $\Rightarrow H_0 : p = 0.4737$ is a _____ claim $\Rightarrow$ Rejecting it would be a _____
   D) If we perform the test 7777 times, how many rejections would you expect to see? Explain / Show work. Write your answer as a decimal. (Hint: the probability of rejecting for this test is shown above the graph.)
   e) Now click "Automatic" to simulate the 7777 trials. Use "ALT / PrtSc" to copy and paste to your report.
   F) How many times did you actually end up Rejecting H_0? Show your work. Show your decimal answer and also an answer rounded to the nearest integer.

3) The one also uses the application "Hyp Test Sim - Means" located in the StatSims folder. A soda company claims to have an average of 12 ounces in their cans. Their filling machine has a standard deviation of 0.23 ounces. They routinely perform a hypothesis test to see if the true average is different than the 12 ounces labeled on the cans. We want to investigate the power of their test. Assume that the test is done at the 5% significance level using a sample of 40 cans. The **POWER** of a hypothesis test is defined as the probability that the hypothesis test will reject a false claim.
   A) Write out steps 1 & 2 for the hypothesis test requested in the problem.
   b) Enter your name in the textbox provided. Based on the information given above, fill in the claimed mean, the type of test, the significance level, the sample size and standard deviation. Set the population type to left-skewed.
   C) Comment on the requirements for performing this test.
   d) Suppose that the machine is actually underfilling the cans by 0.05 ounces. Enter the true mean that corresponds to this in the appropriate box. Enter 1000 for the number of trials and then click the Automatic button to carry out the tests. Use "ALT / PrintScreen" to copy and paste to your report.
   E) Find and circle the power of the test on the output screen.
   F) Click the Clear button. Suppose that the company was only concerned about underfilling the cans. Make the appropriate change in the simulator and write down the new power number.
   G) Further suppose that the company was willing to take up to a 10% risk of making a type I error Make the appropriate change in the simulator and write down the new power number.
   H) Now use trial and error to determine the minimum sample size needed to increase the power to at least 85%. Write down the minimum sample size on the printout.

Chapter 9: Chapter Review

Section 9.1: Definitions and Notation

- In this chapter, the null hypothesis, H_o, must always be written using an equals sign, "=".
- The null hypothesis, H_o, cannot be shown to be true. We either reject H_o or we do not reject H_o, but we never accept H_o.
- A type I error is rejecting H_o when it is in fact true.
- A type II error is not rejecting H_o when it is in fact false.
- The direction of the symbol in H_1 tells us whether we have a left-tailed test ($H_1 : \mu <$), a right-tailed test ($H_1 : \mu >$), or a two-tailed test ($H_1 : \mu \neq$).
- Sample values that are unusually far away from the claimed value in H_0 are considered strong evidence against H_0 because it is unlikely that such differences are just the result of random variation in the sample. Such values would most likely lead to the rejection of H_0.
- Sample values that are considered close to the value claimed in H_0 could easily just be different from the claimed value due to random variation. Such values would not lead to the rejection of H_0.

Section 9.2: Testing the Population Proportion, p

- The significance level is the maximum risk of making a type I error that we are willing to take. If H_o is true, then this tells us the long-term percentage of times we will reject H_o.
- The test statistic is the value we obtain from the sample that measures the size of the difference between the sample value and the claimed value. In this chapter, the test statistic is always a z-score or a t-score.
- The P-value is the probability of seeing a value of the test statistic that is at least as inconsistent with H_o as our test statistic, given that H_o is true. We interpret it as the risk we would be taking of making a type I error if we reject H_o with our current evidence.
- Because of the assumption of innocence, we calculate the test statistic and the P-value assuming that μ equals the claimed value from H_o.
- If σ is known, then our test statistic is a z-score and our P-value will be calculated using the normalcdf function.
- For a two-tailed test, we must double the area in the tail on the side where our test statistic lies.
- If P-value $\leq \alpha$, then we do Reject H_o. We do this because we perceive the risk of making a type I error to be acceptably low.
- If P-value $> \alpha$, then we Do Not Reject H_o. We perceive the risk of making a type I error to be too high to take.
- The decision step is always about rejecting or not rejecting the null hypothesis, H_o.
- When we state the conclusion in words, we always discuss whether we had or did not have enough evidence to show the statement in H_1.
- To perform a hypothesis test concerning the mean, you must have a sample size of at least 30, a normal population, or if $15 \leq n < 30$, then the population cannot be severely skewed.
- When comparing a confidence interval to a hypothesis test, there are two possibilities. If the claimed value lies in the interval, then it is a reasonable possibility that H_o is true, so we do not reject H_o. If the claimed value does not lie in the interval, then we are confident that H_o is false, and so we reject H_o.
- If the hypothesis test is about a proportion, percentage, or probability, then we are doing a test about p rather than μ.

Section 9.2: Testing the Population Proportion, p (Continued ...)

- If the number of successes in the sample is given, then we must calculate the sample proportion using the formula $\hat{p} = {x}/{n}$.
- If the percentage of successes from the sample is given, then we have been given the sample proportion. Just change it to a decimal when labeling $\hat{p}$.
- The test statistic for a proportion problem will always be a z-score. Therefore, we will always find the P-value using normalcdf. Caution: Make sure that you use p_o in the denominator rather than $\hat{p}$. This is the opposite of Chapter 8.
- If there doesn't seem to be any obvious value for the claimed proportion, p_o, then you should use the probability of the event in question under normal conditions.
- The requirements for a test of population proportion is that $\hat{p}$ is approximately normally distributed. We check this by verifying that both $np_o \geq 10$ and $n(1 - p_o) \geq 10$. Caution: Make sure that you use p_o in the calculation rather than $\hat{p}$. This is the opposite of Chapter 8.

Section 9.3: Testing the Population Mean, μ

- If σ is unknown, then we will use the sample standard deviation, s, in its place. This means that our test statistic is a t-score and our P-value will be calculated using the tcdf function with $df = n - 1$.
- If we are given sample data rather than the sample mean and standard deviation, then we will use the data to calculate the values of $\bar{x}$ and s.
- The requirements for a t-test are the same as for a z-test. To perform a hypothesis test concerning the mean, you must have a sample size of at least 30, or a normal population, or if $15 \leq n < 30$, then the population cannot be severely skewed.
- If the difference between the sample value and the claimed value is large enough to lead to the rejection of H_0, then we say that the difference is statistically significant. We feel that there is strong evidence that such differences are not the result of random variation.
- If the difference between the sample value and the claimed value is large enough that matters to those working with variables in question, then we say the difference is practically significant.
- No difference should ever be considered practically significant if it is not statistically significant.

Review Diagrams:

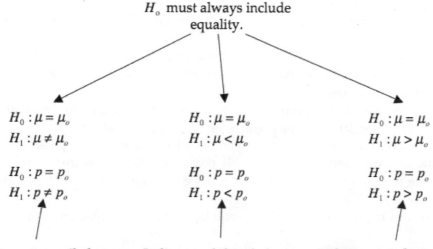

H_o must always include equality.

$H_0 : \mu = \mu_o$
$H_1 : \mu \neq \mu_o$

$H_0 : \mu = \mu_o$
$H_1 : \mu < \mu_o$

$H_0 : \mu = \mu_o$
$H_1 : \mu > \mu_o$

$H_0 : p = p_o$
$H_1 : p \neq p_o$

$H_0 : p = p_o$
$H_1 : p < p_o$

$H_0 : p = p_o$
$H_1 : p > p_o$

Indicates a two-tailed test   Indicates a left-tailed test   Indicates a right-tailed test

	H_o is True	H_o is False
Reject H_o	Type I error	Correct decision
Do Not Reject H_o	Correct decision	Type II error

If the problem is about a mean,
then use this one.

If about a proportion,
then use this one.

$$t = \frac{\bar{x} - \mu_o}{s / \sqrt{n}}$$

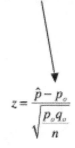

$$z = \frac{\hat{p} - p_o}{\sqrt{\dfrac{p_o q_o}{n}}}$$

Tests of the mean always
use t-scores because it is
not realistic to know σ.

Proportion problems
always require a z-score.

Find the P-value

$P - Value \leq \alpha$

$P - Value > \alpha$

Risk of type I error
is acceptably low

Risk of a type I
error is too high

Take the risk and
Reject H_o

Avoid the risk and
Do Not Reject H_o

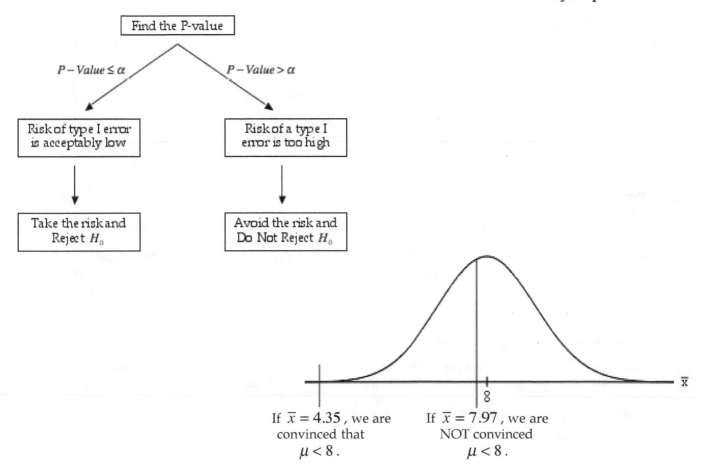

If $\bar{x} = 4.35$, we are
convinced that
$\mu < 8$.

If $\bar{x} = 7.97$, we are
NOT convinced
$\mu < 8$.

Point to Remember: *Finding P-values*

- For a left-tailed test, the P-value is the area to the left of your test statistic.

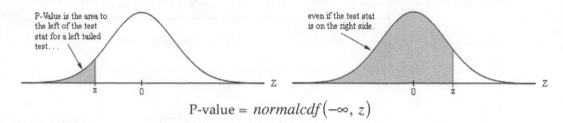

$$\text{P-value} = normalcdf(-\infty, z)$$

- For a right-tailed test, the P-value is the area to the right of your test statistic.

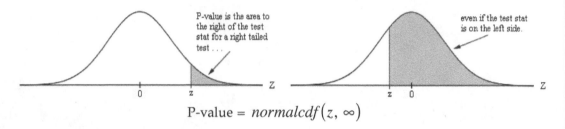

$$\text{P-value} = normalcdf(z, \infty)$$

- For a two-tailed test, the P-value is <u>double</u> the area in the tail beyond your test statistic.

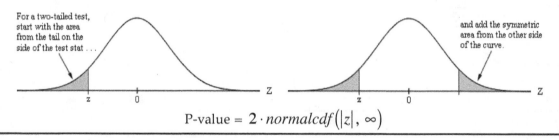

$$\text{P-value} = 2 \cdot normalcdf(|z|, \infty)$$

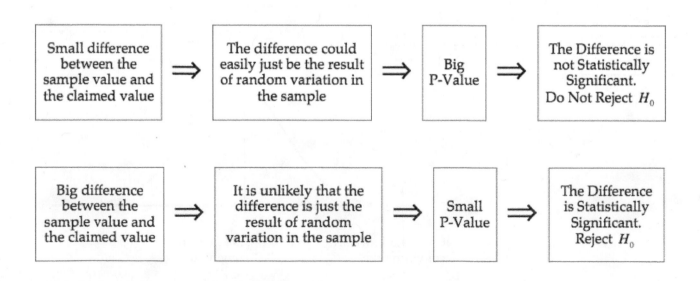

| Small difference between the sample value and the claimed value | $\Rightarrow$ | The difference could easily just be the result of random variation in the sample | $\Rightarrow$ | Big P-Value | $\Rightarrow$ | The Difference is not Statistically Significant. Do Not Reject H_0 |

| Big difference between the sample value and the claimed value | $\Rightarrow$ | It is unlikely that the difference is just the result of random variation in the sample | $\Rightarrow$ | Small P-Value | $\Rightarrow$ | The Difference is Statistically Significant. Reject H_0 |

Chapter 9: Review Exercises

(1-4) a) Calculate the value of the test statistic.
       b) Determine the P-value for the test statistic you have calculated.
       c) State whether or not you would reject H_o if the significance level was 5%.

1) $H_o : \mu = 14$ $\bar{x} = 11.58,\ n = 38,$
    $H_1 : \mu < 14$; $s = 5.8762$

2) $H_o : p = 0.85$ $\hat{p} = 0.9117,$
    $H_1 : p < 0.85$; $n = 452$

3) $H_o : p = 0.3566$ $x = 235,$
    $H_1 : p > 0.3566$; $n = 612$

4) $H_o : \mu = 100$ $\bar{x} = 114.81,\ n = 19,$
    $H_1 : \mu \neq 100$; $s = 24.055$

5) A marriage counselor suspects that, in more than half of all marriages, women do the bills. Suppose that in a random sample of 519 married couples, it is determined that the women do the bills in 291 of them.

   a) Does the data provide enough evidence, at the 10% significance level, to show that the women do the bills in more than half of all married couples.
   b) Comment on the requirements for the test.
   c) Discuss the possibility that we have made a type I error or a type II error on this problem.

6) Child researchers state that the average 4-yr old asks about 400 questions per day. The author suspected that his 4-yr old daughter Giselle was above average in this category. He randomly chose 12 days and counted the number of questions she asked on those days. The data was as shown below.

| 481 | 549 | 435 | 380 | 345 | 373 |
| 477 | 474 | 378 | 513 | 528 | 397 |

   Note: $\sum x^2 = 2,419,192$

   a) Does the data provide enough evidence, at the 5% significance level, to show that Giselle's true average number of questions per day is greater than 400?
   b) Use the normal probability plot for the data shown below to comment on the requirements of the test.

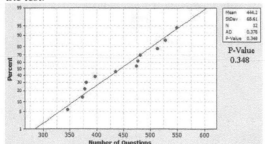

   c) Explain what it would mean, in terms of the evidence and the application, to make a type I error on this problem.

7) It is commonly accepted that adults should get about 8 hours of sleep per night, but does that apply to teenagers as well? A random sample of 28 teenagers was obtained and the number of hours they slept on a Friday night to Saturday morning was recorded. The sample produced a mean of 9.33 hours with a standard deviation of 1.6985 hours.
   a) Does the data provide enough evidence, at the 1% significance level, to show that the true mean Friday to Saturday sleep time for teenagers is greater than 8 hours?
   b) Comment on the requirements for the test.
   c) If it turns out that the true mean amount of sleep for teenagers is 9.1 hours, have we made a type I error, type II error, or a correct decision in part (a)? Explain.

8) Studies have shown that 71% of American drivers can drive a stick shift. A professor believes that this percentage is lower for the students at his University. He obtains a random sample of 250 students and determines that 65.2% of them can drive a stick.
   a) Does the data provide enough evidence, at the 1% significance level to show that the proportion of students at this university that can drive a stick is less than 71%?
   b) Comment on the requirements for the test.
   c) Does this show that there is no difference between the percentage of college students at this university that can drive a stick and the percentage for all Americans? Explain.

9) During a major league baseball game, the baseball is often replaced. This usually happens because a ball is hit into the crowd or because it becomes overly damaged. It is stated that the average lifespan of a major league baseball is 7 pitches. A random sample of 14 balls was observed in college baseball games. The lifetimes of the balls are shown below.

| 3 | 9 | 1 | 9 | 19 | 16 | 1 |
| 6 | 10 | 7 | 13 | 11 | 5 | 9 |

   Note: $\sum x^2 = 1371$

   a) Perform a test to see if the average lifetime for a college baseball is different than for major league baseball. Use $\alpha = 0.10$.
   b) Use the normal probability plot for the data shown below to comment on the requirements of the test.

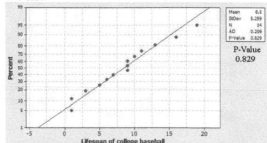

   c) Discuss the possibility that we have made a type I error or a type II error on this problem.

10) It is traditionally stated that the average body temperature for humans is 98.6 degrees Fahrenheit. It is commonly believed that the true mean percentage is actually lower than that. A random sample of 23 people had their temperatures taken and the temperatures, in degrees Fahrenheit, are shown below.

97.5	99.7	100.0	98.4	97.6	96.5
97.9	98.0	97.8	98.9	98.3	96.4
97.8	98.1	97.1	98.2	97.9	97.8
96.4	98.0	97.6	99.1	98.7	

Note: $\bar{x} \approx 97.987$, $s \approx 0.91914$

a) Does the data provide enough evidence, at the 10% significance level to show that the true mean body temperature for humans is less than what is traditionally stated?

b) Use the boxplot for the data shown below to comment on the requirements of the test.

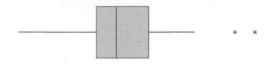

Body Temperatures

c) It turns out that the true mean body temperature for humans is 98.2 degrees. Given this information, have we made a type I error, type II error, or a correct decision in part (a)? Explain.

11) It is said that the average American drinks 65 ounces of coffee per week. A statistics student feels that, during finals week, college students exceed this amount. She collects data from a random sample of 40 college students during finals week and finds a mean coffee consumptions of 90.54 ounces with a standard deviation of 68.422 ounces.

a) Does this data provide enough evidence, at the 5% significance level, to show that the true average coffee consumption for college students during finals week exceeds the national average?

b) Explain what it would mean, in terms of the application and evidence, for us to make a type II error on this problem.

12) People generally accept that when you flip a coin, it will come up heads about 50% of the time. But, what if you spin it rather than flip it? I picked 3 randomly chosen nickels minted in 1990 and spun them repeatedly keeping track of how often they settled showing the heads side up. After a total of 147 spins, the heads side was up 94 times.

a) Does the data provide enough evidence, at the 5% significance level, to show that the true percentage of heads for these coins is not 50%?

b) Comment on the requirements for the test.

c) Explain what it would mean, in terms of the evidence and the application, to make a type I error on this problem.

d) Would you consider the difference between the sample proportion and the claimed proportion to be statistically significant, practically significant, both, or neither? Explain.

13) During the campaign for the 2008 U.S. Presidential election, one of the issues was whether the solution to the U.S. dependency on foreign oil was more drilling in the U.S. or increased energy conservation efforts. Candidate Barack Obama suggested that people should routinely check their tire pressure to help conserve gasoline. To see if this would indeed work, the idea was tested on a random sample of 16 cars. With properly inflated tires, the true average gas mileage for these cars was known to be 23.8 mpg. Next, 10 psi was removed from all the tires. With this lowered tire pressure, the mileage for the 16 cars was found to be as follows:

27.8	26.7	25.5	24.8	13.3	22.1	25.8	23.8
28.4	21.5	19.4	19.5	15.0	16.1	17.7	14.7

Note: $\bar{x} \approx 21.381$, $s \approx 4.9859$

a) Perform a test to see if the change has reduced the average gas mileage for cars with lowered tire pressure. Use $\alpha = 0.10$

b) Use the boxplot for the data shown below to comment on the requirements of the test.

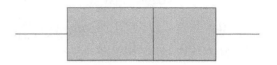

Gas Mileages

c) Does this data support the idea that keeping your tire inflated to the proper level will help conserve gas? Explain using the ideas of statistical significance and practical significance.

d) Explain what it would mean, in terms of the application and evidence, for us to make a type I error on this problem.

14) The average IQ for all people is known to be 100. A recent article claimed that a person's IQ is a good predictor of what occupational group they will end up in. A random sample of 14 factory packers and sorters were given an IQ test. The sample produced a mean IQ of 90.8 and a standard deviation of 9.37.

a) Does this data provide enough evidence, at the 10% significance level, to show that the true average IQ for factory packers and sorters is less than the average IQ for all people?

b) Comment on the requirements.

c) Explain what it would mean, in terms of the application and evidence, for us to make a correct decision on this problem.

d) Would you consider the difference between the sample mean and the claimed mean to be statistically significant, practically significant, both, or neither? Explain.

15) In 1965, 54.1% of the adult population of the U.S. were smokers. By 2004, that number had dropped to 25.6%. Since that time, more laws have been passed banning smoking in most public areas. Suppose that a recent sample of 713 adults contained 24.26% smokers.
   a) Perform a hypothesis test at the 5% significance level, to see if it appears that the percentage of smokers in the adult population has decreased since 2004.
   b) Does part (a) tell us that recent laws have had no effect in deterring people to smoke? Explain.
   c) Would you consider the difference between the sample proportion and the claimed proportion to be statistically significant, practically significant, both, or neither? Explain.

16) In Spring of 2008 mobile subscribers sent and received an average of 357 text messages per month. During that same time period, a sample of 58 college students produced a monthly average of 812.3 texts with a standard deviation of 408.15.
   a) Does the data provide enough evidence, at the 1% significance level, to show that college students text, on average, more than mobile users in general?
   b) What effect do you think this result would imply about a survey of adults in the U.S. that required respondents to text in their responses?

17) Refer to Exercise (15) above.
   a) Compute a 90% confidence interval for the true proportion of smokers in the adult population of the U.S.
   b) Explain how the answer to part a) agrees with the results of the test performed in exercise (15).

18) Refer to Exercise (16) above.
   a) Compute a 98% confidence interval for the true mean number of texts per month for college students during Spring 2008.
   b) Explain how the answer to part a) agrees with the results of the test performed in exercise (16).

19) Refer to Exercise (13) above.
   a) Compute an 80% confidence interval for the true average gas mileage for cars with lowered tire pressure.
   b) Explain how the answer to part a) agrees with the results of the test performed in exercise (13).

20) Refer to Exercise (8) above.
   a) Compute a 98% confidence interval for the true proportion of students at the university that can drive a stick.
   b) Explain how the answer to part a) agrees with the results of the test performed in exercise (8).

Chapter 10 - Tests using the Chi-Square Distribution

Chapter Problem: *Does increased parental support for college result in lower grades?*

In January 2013, Laura Hamilton of the University of California at Merced released a study about the relationship between parental support for college and students grades. The study was titled "More Is More or More Is Less?" In an article discussing this study printed by *Inside Higher Ed*, it was stated that "the students least likely to excel are those who receive essentially blank checks for college expenses." This research is contrary to the common belief that children of wealthy parents have an advantage at school.

Is the amount of financial support students receive from parents related to the grades the students receive?

At the end of this chapter, we will use sample data to test if there really is a link between parental support and student grades. We will also investigate whether the classic view that wealthy students have an advantage or the new theory that such students have lower grades seems more likely.

Introduction:

In this chapter we will study some hypothesis testing topics that require the use of a distribution other than the Standard Normal and Student's t distributions. Consider the following situations:

The *Equal Justice Initiative* is trying to gather evidence that there is racial bias in the California criminal justice system. They want to show that the racial/ethnic distribution of those incarcerated does not match the racial/ethnic distribution of the state.

A news organization wants to determine whether or not people's support for the government monitoring emails depends on their political affiliation.

A manufacturer of a medical pump needs to make sure that the pump not only is averaging the correct supply of medicine, but it also needs to make sure that it never deviates substantially from the target amount. To check the consistency of such a pump, they will perform a test on a sample of pumps to ensure that the standard deviation is less than 1.5 CCs per hour.

All of the above situations seem like reasonable situations in which to perform a hypothesis test. However, the appropriate test statistics in each of these cases turns out to have a distribution other than the Standard Normal or Student's t-distribution. Therefore, we will need to learn how to work with a new distribution called the Chi-Square distribution to perform the appropriate hypothesis tests. We will investigate and use this new distribution in the following sections:

Section 10.1	Introducing the Chi-Square Distribution
Section 10.2	Chi-Square Goodness-of-Fit Tests
Section 10.3	Chi-Square Test of Independence
Section 10.4	Inferences for the Population Standard Deviation, σ

Let's get started.

Section 10.1 - Introducing the Chi-Square Distribution

The first thing that should be pointed out is that there are actually many Chi-Square distributions. Just like for the t-distribution, a Chi-Square distribution is determined by the number of degrees of freedom. Also, we will usually use the Greek symbol for the letter chi (χ) when we refer to the Chi-Square (χ^2) distribution. The following are all graphs of χ^2 curves with various degrees of freedom.

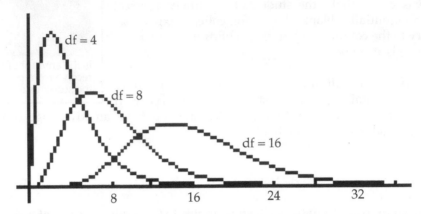

Let's make a few observations about the χ^2 curves shown above. The first thing that may catch your attention is that these curves are right skewed rather than the symmetric bell-shape that we are used to seeing from normal curves and Student's t-curves. You may also notice that a vertical axis has been drawn in as well as the standard horizontal number line. This primary reason that this vertical axis is shown is to mark the location of the number zero on the number line. These curves start at zero and extend indefinitely to the right. These curves do not extend into the negative side of the horizontal axis. You should also notice that the shape of these curves varies depending on the number of degrees of freedom. Smaller df's produce taller more severely right-skewed graphs. Larger df's flatten out and become less skewed and begin to resemble bell-shaped normal curves. As was true with normal and Student t-curves, the area under these curves will represent probability. This means that the total area under the different curves is always equal to 1.

There is another important property that is not obvious from the graphs. The mean of a χ^2 curve is equal to its degree of freedom. Previously, in Chapter 3, we stated that for a right skewed distribution, the mean would fall to the right of the mode, or peak, of the curve. This will be helpful for us to know when sketching graphs and finding P-values. All of these properties are summarized in the following Point to Remember.

Point to Remember: *Properties of χ^2 Curves*

The Basic Properties of a χ^2 curve are as follows:

- The total area under a χ^2 curve is always equal to 1.
- χ^2 curves are right skewed. They are NOT symmetric.
- χ^2 curves start at zero and extend indefinitely to the right while the height of the curve approaches zero.
- As the degrees of freedom increase, the shape of a χ^2 curve begins to look more and more like a normal curve.
- The mean of a χ^2 curve is equal to its degree of freedom.
- The peak of the curve will occur slightly before the χ^2 value corresponding to the number of degrees of freedom.

During the course of this chapter, we will be performing hypothesis tests as well as calculating confidence intervals. For the hypothesis tests, we will need to be able to calculate P-values by finding the area to either the right or left of a test statistic. When we turn to confidence intervals, it will be important for us to start with a confidence percentage and convert that to an area. From that area we will need to work backwards to find lower and upper boundaries. We will begin with a discussion of how to find areas to the right or left of a given Chi-Square value, χ^2.

Definition: $\chi^2 cdf$

$\chi^2 cdf$: This function will give us a way of expressing the area of a region between two boundaries underneath a Chi-Square curve with a given number of degrees of freedom, df. This function will represent the area between a lower boundary and an upper boundary. The structure is as shown below.

$$\chi^2 cdf(\text{lower boundary}, \text{upper boundary}, df)$$

Note: Instructions for calculating the value of this function using various forms of technology are given at the end of this section.

It turns out that it is rare to want the area between two boundaries for a χ^2-curve. It is more likely to need the area to the right or the left of a single boundary. Let's begin with an example finding areas to the right.

Example 10.1: *Sketching χ^2 Curves and Finding Areas to the Right*

Draw a sketch of each of the following and then use the $\chi^2 cdf$ function and technology to find the area to the right of each of the following values of χ^2 :

a) Find the area to the right of $\chi^2 = 17.5$ with $df = 12$.

b) Find the area to the right of $\chi^2 = 13.7$ with $df = 18$.

c) Find the area to the right of $\chi^2 = 23$ with $df = 7$.

Solution:

a) We begin by drawing a sketch of the curve. Draw a horizontal and a vertical axis. Start drawing the curve from the origin. Rise up quickly and drop down to the axis slowly to create a longer tail on the right. This creates the right-skewed look we need. Put a tick mark on the horizontal axis just to the right of the peak. Label this using the df of 12. The graph starts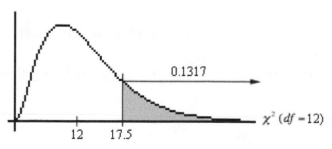
at 0 and we have now labeled 12. This should give us a decent sense of where 17.5 goes on the graph. We can now label that spot on the graph and then shade the desired area to the right. Because there is no upper boundary for our shaded region, we will use ∞ as the upper boundary. Using technology, we get:

$$\text{Area} = \chi^2 cdf(17.5, \infty, 12) \approx 0.1317$$

b) This time we have a $df = 18$. Therefore, we will label a tick mark just to the right of the peak as 18. This means that the value we have been given, 13.7, lies between the start of the curve and the mean of 18. The area to the right can be found using:

$$\text{Area} = \chi^2 cdf(13.7, \infty, 18) \approx 0.7484$$

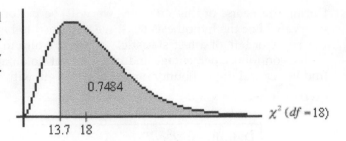

c) This time we have a $df = 7$. Therefore, we will label a tick mark just to the right of the peak as 7. This means that the value we have been given, 23, lies far out in the right tail of the curve. The area to the right can be found using:

$$\text{Area} = \chi^2 cdf(23, \infty, 7) \approx 0.0017$$

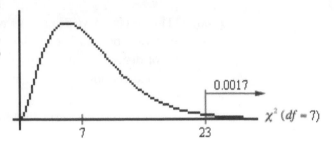

Key Concept: *Using the df to draw better sketches*

Knowing that the *df* occurs just after the peak on the curve helps us to know where to place the boundary we are working with. It also gives us a rough idea of what the area will be. A rough estimate of the area helps us to catch errors when using the technology to find the area.

Most of the hypothesis tests in this chapter turn out to be right-tailed tests. Because of this, finding areas to the right as we did above is the most important skill we need when working with χ^2 curves. However, when we perform hypothesis tests on a population standard deviation, σ, we will also need to be able to find areas to the left of a given boundary. The following example illustrates how this is done.

Example 10.2: *Sketching χ^2 Curves and Finding Areas to the Left*

Draw a sketch of each of the following and then use the $\chi^2 cdf$ function and technology to find the area to the left of each of the following values of χ^2:

a) Find the area to the left of $\chi^2 = 7.492$ with $df = 5$.

b) Find the area to the left of $\chi^2 = 6.309$ with $df = 9$.

Solution:

a) We have a $df = 5$. Therefore, we will label a tick mark just to the right of the peak as 5. This means that the value we have been given, 7.492, lies to the right of the peak as well. Notice that, because the curve does not extend indefinitely to the left, we will use zero as our lower boundary rather than using $-\infty$.

$$\text{Area} = \chi^2 cdf(0,\ 7.492,\ 5) \approx 0.8135$$

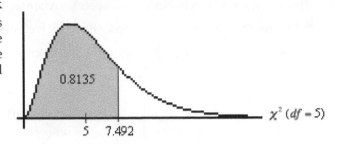

b) This time we have a $df = 9$. Therefore, we will label a tick mark just to the right of the peak as 9. This means that the value we have been given, 6.309, would lie between the starting point of zero and our tick mark at 9. The area to the left can be found using:

$$\text{Area} = \chi^2 cdf(0,\ 6.309,\ 9) \approx 0.2914$$

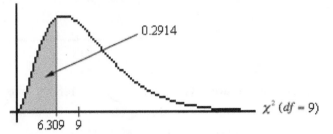

WORKING BACKWARDS: *When you know an area and are finding the Chi-Square boundary*

Finding area to the right or left of a given value will be useful for finding P-values in hypothesis tests. However, to find confidence intervals, we will need to learn how to work backwards. We need a function that can tell use the χ^2 value that has a given area to its left. We will call this the $inv\chi^2$ function.

Definition: $inv\chi^2$

$inv\chi^2$: This function will give us a way of find the χ^2 value that has a given amount of area to its left. The structure is as shown below.

$$inv\chi^2 (\text{area to the left}, df)$$

Note: Instructions for calculating the value of this function using various forms of technology or using tables are given at the end of this section.

Let's practice this new function with an example.

Example 10.3: *Working backwards from areas to χ^2 boundaries using $inv\chi^2$*

a) Find the χ^2 value that has an area of 0.05 to its left for a χ^2 curve with $df = 12$.

b) Find the χ^2 value that has an area of 0.01 to its right for a χ^2 curve with $df = 15$.

c) Find the two χ^2 values that have an area of 0.95 between them with the remaining area divided equally among the tails for a χ^2 curve with $df = 23$.

Solution:

a) It's always good to begin with a sketch. After we sketch the right-skewed shape, we should place the *df* of 12, just to the right of the peak. Because we only want a small amount of area to the left of our χ^2 value, we should indicate the χ^2 value we are looking for on the left side of our graph between 0 and 12.

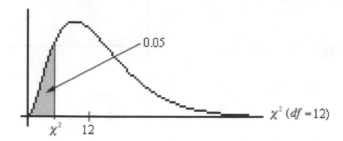

Because we are given the area to the left, this is set up perfectly for using the $inv\chi^2$ function. So, we get the following.

$$\chi^2 = inv\chi^2 \left(\text{area to the left}, df \right) = inv\chi^2 \left(0.05, 12 \right) \approx 5.226$$

b) We should place the *df* of 15, just to the right of the peak. Because we only want a small amount of area to the right of our χ^2 value, we should indicate the χ^2 value we are looking for on the right side of our graph between 15 and the tail of the curve.

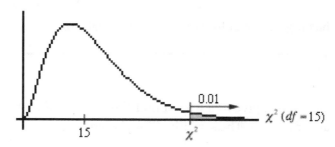

Because we are given the area to the right, we must subtract this from 1 to find the needed area to the left. This will set us up for using the $inv\chi^2$ function. So, we get the following.

$$1 - 0.01 = 0.99 \quad \Rightarrow \quad \chi^2 = inv\chi^2 \left(\text{area to the left}, df \right) = inv\chi^2 \left(0.99, 15 \right) \approx 30.578$$

c) We should place the *df* of 23, just to the right of the peak. Because we want most of the area between our two values, we should indicate the left value χ_L^2 on the left near zero on our graph. We should indicate the right value χ_R^2 on the right near the tail of our graph.

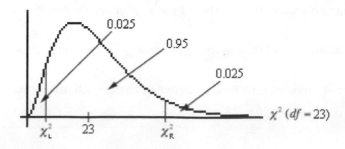

Because the area in the middle is 0.95, we have 0.05 left over. Dividing that among the two outside portions gives us an area of 0.025 on each side. We will then compute our values as follows.

$$\chi_L^2 = inv\chi^2 \left(\text{area to the left}, df \right) = inv\chi^2 \left(0.025, 23 \right) \approx 11.689$$

$$1 - 0.025 = 0.975 \quad \Rightarrow \quad \chi_R^2 = inv\chi^2 \left(\text{area to the left}, df \right) = inv\chi^2 \left(0.975, 23 \right) \approx 38.076$$

Caution: *Chi-Square Curves Lack Symmetry*

Because a Chi-Square curve is right-skewed rather than symmetric, we must find the left boundary, χ_L^2, and then right boundary, χ_R^2, separately. We cannot just use the first one to find the second one as we did for z-scores and t-scores.

USING TECHNOLOGY: *Finding values of $\chi^2 cdf$ and $inv\chi^2$ with various technologies*

This section will show you how to use various technologies to calculate values of $\chi^2 cdf$ and $inv\chi^2$. For each technology, we will be computing $\chi^2 cdf \left(17.5, \infty, 12 \right)$ and $inv\chi^2 \left(0.99, 15 \right)$.

EXCEL:

Excel only gives area to the right automatically. So, using $\chi^2 cdf$ will be fairly straightforward. When finding $inv\chi^2$, you must subtract from 1 to provide the area to the right rather than the area to the left. Directions and screen shots are shown below.

Calculating $\chi^2 cdf \left(17.5, \infty, 12 \right)$:	Calculating $inv\chi^2 \left(0.99, 15 \right)$:
1. Click in the cell where you want to store the answer.	1. Click in the cell where you want to store the answer.
2. Type "=CHIDIST(17.5,12)".	2. Subtract the area to the left from 1 to determine the area to the right.
3. Press Enter to see the result.	3. Type "=CHIINV(0.01,15)". **Note:** we are entering the area to the right rather than the area to the left.
	4. Press Enter to see the result.

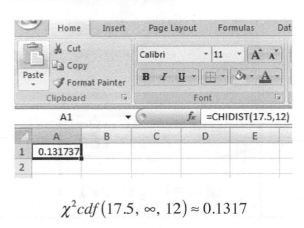

$$\chi^2 cdf \left(17.5, \infty, 12 \right) \approx 0.1317$$

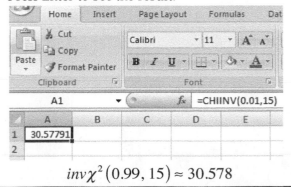

$$inv\chi^2 \left(0.99, 15 \right) \approx 30.578$$

TI-83/84:

$\chi^2 cdf$ works almost identically to what is presented in the reading in this section. It is also, very similar to the $tcdf$ function used in Section 9.3. We will be using the "$\chi^2 cdf($" option found in the DISTR menu. The structure of the function is:

$$\chi^2 cdf \left(\text{lower boundary}, \text{upper boundary}, df\right)$$

If the upper boundary is "∞", then use "1×10^{99}" as the upper boundary.

$inv\chi^2$: Unfortunately, this function is not built into the TI-83 or TI-84. However, with just a few steps, we can create this function using the calculator's SOLVER function located at the bottom of the MATH menu. See the steps and screenshots shown below on the right.

Calculating $\chi^2 cdf \left(17.5, \infty, 12\right)$:	Calculating $inv\chi^2 \left(0.99, 15\right)$:
1. Choose DISTR	1. Choose MATH > Solver...
2. Choose $\chi^2 cdf($	2. Where it lists eqn: 0 =, complete the equation as
3. Fill in with the needed boundaries and df.	$0 = \chi^2 cdf \left(0, X, D\right) - A$
	3. Press enter.
	4. Enter 15 for the D, 0.99 for the A.
	5. Use the arrow keys to move to the X line.
	6. Press the ALPHA key and then SOLVE (Enter Key).

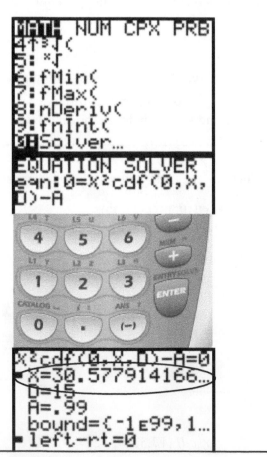

MINITAB:

Minitab only gives areas to the left. So, if you need an area to the right, you must first find the area to the left and then subtract from 1. Directions and screen shots are shown below.

Calculating $\chi^2 cdf(17.5, \infty, 12)$:	Calculating $inv\chi^2(0.99, 15)$:
1. Choose CALC > Probability Dist > Chi-Square …	1. Choose CALC > Probability Dist > Chi-Square …
2. Select 'Cumulative probability'.	2. Select 'Inverse cumulative probability'.
3. Enter the DF in the textbox.	3. Enter the DF in the textbox.
4. Check 'Input Constant:' and enter your boundary value.	4. Check 'Input Constant:' and enter the area to the left.
5. Click OK.	5. Click OK.
6. Because Minitab gives the area to the left, subtract from 1.	

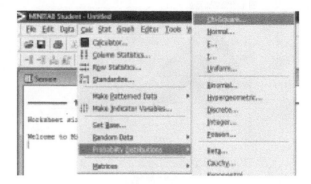

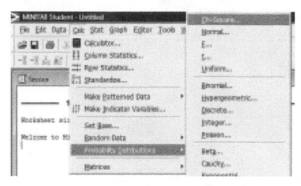

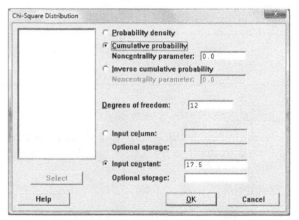

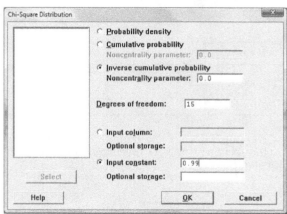

Cumulative Distribution Function

```
Chi-Square with 12 DF

    x   P( X <= x )
  17.5    0.868263
```

$\chi^2 cdf(17.5, \infty, 12) \approx 1 - 0.8683 = 0.1317$

Inverse Cumulative Distribution Function

```
Chi-Square with 15 DF

P( X <= x )        x
   0.99        30.5779
```

$inv\chi^2(0.99, 15) \approx 30.578$

STATCRUNCH:

To find values of $\chi^2 cdf$ and $inv\chi^2$, we will use one of the calculators found in the STAT menu. From the STATCRUNCH window choose STAT > Calculators > Chi-Square. This will open the Chi-Square calculator in StatCrunch. Examples for both $\chi^2 cdf$ and $inv\chi^2$ are shown below.

Calculating $\chi^2 cdf\left(17.5,\ \infty,\ 12\right)$:	Calculating $inv\chi^2\left(0.99,15\right)$:
1. Set the P(X menu to "≥".	1. Set the P(X menu to "≤".
2. Enter the $df = 12$ in the DF box.	2. Enter the $df = 15$ in the DF box.
3. Enter your left boundary of 17.5 in the box following the "≥" symbol.	3. Enter the area to the left of 0.99 in the box following the "=" sign.
4. Press the Compute button.	4. Press the Compute button.
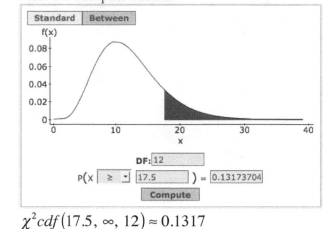	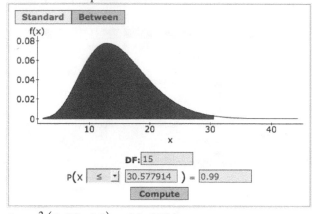
$\chi^2 cdf\left(17.5,\ \infty,\ 12\right) \approx 0.1317$	$inv\chi^2\left(0.99,15\right) \approx 30.578$

Exercise Set 10.1

Concept Review: Review the definitions and concepts from this section by filling in the blanks for each of the following.

1) χ^2 curves are _____ skewed. They are NOT _____ .

2) χ^2 curves start at _____ and extend indefinitely to the _____ while the height of the curves approach zero.

3) The peak of the curve will occur slightly _____ the χ^2 value corresponding to the number of degrees of _____ .

4) When using the $\chi^2 cdf$ function, we input left and right _____ as well as the ____ and the function gives us _____ as an output.

5) When using the $inv\chi^2$ function, we input the _____ to the _____ and the function give us the _____ boundary as an output.

6) When finding the boundaries that trap a specified amount of area in the middle, we must compute the left and right hand boundaries _____ because of the lack of _____ in the graph.

Mechanics: Practice using technology to work with χ^2 curves. Use either the $\chi^2 cdf$ function or the $inv\chi^2$ function for each of the following. Include a sketch with each problem.

7) Find the requested area for the indicated Chi-Square curve.
a) df = 10; area to the right of 14.76
b) df =5; area to the right of 8.3
c) df = 6; area to the right of 6

8) Find the requested area for the indicated Chi-Square curve.
a) df = 17; area to the right of 11.6
b) df = 15; area to the right of 33.8
c) df = 4; area to the right of 4

9) Find the requested area for the indicated Chi-Square curve.
a) to the right of 2.5 for a df = 6
b) to the right of 20.741 for a df = 4.
c) to the right of 3.744 for a df = 21.

10) Find the requested area for the indicated Chi-Square curve.
a) to the right of 4.7 for a df = 8
b) to the right of 5.104 for a df = 28
c) to the right of 17.044 for a df = 3

11) Find the requested area for the indicated Chi-Square curve.
   a) df = 4; area to the left of 5.61
   b) df =9; area to the left of 8.344
   c) df = 11; area to the left of 11

12) Find the requested area for the indicated Chi-Square curve.
   a) df = 7; area to the left of 5.322
   b) df = 10; area to the left of 13.707
   c) df = 8; area to the left of 8

13) Find the requested area for the indicated Chi-Square curve.
   a) to the left of 13.005 for a df = 12
   b) to the left of 18.504 for a df = 3.
   c) to the left of 2.899 for a df = 19.

14) Find the requested area for the indicated Chi-Square curve.
   a) to the left of 8.077 for a df = 5
   b) to the left of 4.881 for a df = 23
   c) to the left of 26.888 for a df = 7

15) Find the requested Chi-Square boundary for the indicated Chi-Square curve.
   a) df = 14; area to the left equals 0.90
   b) df =10; area to the left equals 0.01

16) Find the requested Chi-Square boundary for the indicated Chi-Square curve.
   a) df = 5; area to the left equals 0.05
   b) df =7; area to the left equals 0.99

17) Find the requested Chi-Square boundary for the indicated Chi-Square curve.
   a) df = 6; area to the right equals 0.005
   b) df =17; area to the right equals 0.95

18) Find the requested Chi-Square boundary for the indicated Chi-Square curve.
   a) df = 11; area to the right equals 0.10
   b) df =9; area to the right equals 0.995

19) Find the requested Chi-Square boundaries for the indicated Chi-Square curve.
   a) df = 5; area between the boundaries equals 0.90
   b) df = 35; area between the boundaries equals 0.95

20) Find the requested Chi-Square boundaries for the indicated Chi-Square curve.
   a) df = 12; area between the boundaries equals 0.99
   b) df = 50; area between the boundaries equals 0.80

Section 10.2 - Chi-Square Goodness-of-Fit Tests

We now return to the topic of hypothesis testing. The goal in this section is to test whether or not the percentage distribution for a population is the same as some claimed distribution. This is very similar to the tests of a population proportion done in Section 9.2 except that here we will have more categories than just success and failure. We will once again be using the now familiar 3-phase process. Because the main ideas will be the same as Chapter 9, we will begin with an example and discuss the modifications to the process as we work through the example.

Testing for Racial Bias in Incarceration Rates: (*Discussion Example*)

According to an article published on the web page of the *Equal Justice Initiative*, "Racial discrimination remains a dominant feature of criminal justice in the United States". Is it possible to verify or refute such claims using data and hypothesis testing? The first chart below shows the distribution of the population of California by racial/ethnic makeup. The second chart shows the racial/ethnic makeup of a random sample of 547 recently incarcerated Californians.

Is there a racial bias in California incarceration rates?

California Population:

White	Latino	Black	Other
40.1%	37.6%	5.8%	16.5%

Sample Frequencies:

White	Latino	Black	Other
147	210	155	35

Does the data from the recent random sample provide enough evidence, at the 5% significance level, to show that the true racial/ethnic distribution for all recently incarcerated Californians differs from the racial/ethnic makeup of the overall population in that state.

Solution:

SET UP THE TEST:

Determine H_o and H_1. Recall from Chapter 9 that the null should always include the idea of equality. We are being asked to show that the true racial/ethnic distribution "differs", so this must be the alternative. To include the ideas of equality, H_o will be written using the phrase "is the same as" rather than the "differs" from the alternative. Because we are working with many categories in this chapter, rather than only success and failure, it is simpler to write H_o and H_1 using words rather than symbols. This is what we will do on all problems in this section.

> H_o: The true racial/ethnic distribution for all recently incarcerated Californians is the same as the racial/ethnic makeup of the overall population in the state.
>
> H_1: The true racial/ethnic distribution for all recently incarcerated Californians differs from the racial/ethnic makeup of the overall population in the state.

Determine the significance level. This is given as 5%, so $\alpha = 0.05$. (Thus, we are willing to take up to a 5% risk of making a type I error in this problem.)

GATHER AND WEIGH THE EVIDENCE:

Calculate the test statistic. This is where things start to look quite a bit different from the test statistics we used in Chapter 9, but the ideas used are actually very similar. Our goal is to examine how different what we saw in our sample is from what we would expect to see if H_o is true. What we actually see are the observed frequencies from the sample. If H_o is true, then we would expect to see frequencies that match up with the percentages given for the whole California population. For example, for the general California population, the percentage for "White" is 40.1%. So, if H_o is true, we would expect 40.1% of our sample of 547 recent incarcerations to be white. So we calculate 40.1% of 547 or $547 * 0.401 = 219.347$. This is the expected frequency (denoted E) for "White". We now do this for all the ethnicities in the chart. At this point, it will be useful to make a table to organize our work.

Ethnic Group	Observed Freq. (O)	Claimed (p)	Expected Freq. ($E = n \cdot p$)
White	147	0.401	$547 * 0.401 = 219.347$
Latino	210	0.376	$547 * 0.376 = 205.672$
Black	155	0.058	$547 * 0.058 = 31.726$
Other	35	0.165	$547 * 0.165 = 90.255$
	547	1.00	547

In the work above table, we introduced two new terms, **Observed Frequency** and **Expected Frequency**. Let's take a moment to define those new terms.

Definitions: *Observed and Expected Frequencies*

Observed Frequencies: Observed frequencies, denoted by the (O) column, are the frequencies obtained for each category when the random sample is collected.

Expected Frequencies: Expected frequencies, denoted by the (E) column, are the frequencies that we expect to see in each category from the sample if H_o is a true claim. They are calculated using the formula $E = n \cdot p$. You should recognize this formula from the mean (or *expected value*) of a binomial random variable. The n is the sample size and the p, which will usually vary from row to row, is the percentage that would apply if H_o is a true claim.

Note: The total for the 'E' column should be the same as for the 'O' column. Use this as a check your work.

The chart is a good start, but we need to start looking at the "difference" between what we saw, (O), and what we expected to see, (E). So the next step would be a simple subtraction, O - E.

Ethnic Group	O	E	O - E
White	147	219.347	$147 - 219.347 = -72.347$
Latino	210	205.672	$210 - 205.672 = 4.328$
Black	155	31.726	$155 - 31.726 = 123.274$
Other	35	90.255	$35 - 90.255 = -55.255$
	547	547	0

We would like to get add these differences to see if there is a large total difference. But even though differences existed, when we sum them, we get zero. This will happen every time on every problem, because the negative differences always have the same total as the positive ones. To avoid this problem, we will square each difference to make it positive before we add them up. So, we will now add an $(O - E)^2$ column to our table.

Ethnic Group	O	E	O - E	$(O-E)^2$
White	147	219.347	-72.347	5234.088
Latino	210	205.672	4.328	18.732
Black	155	31.726	123.274	15196.479
Other	35	90.255	-55.255	3053.115
	547	547	0	

You might expect us to total this new column, but that would not actually be useful at this time. Think about this. If you tossed a coin 1,000,000 times you would expect 500,000 heads, but you would not be surprised if you missed that total by 50. However, if you tossed the coin 100 times, you would expect 50 heads and you would be shocked if you missed that by 50. After all, this would mean all heads or all tails in 100 tosses and we know that would be extremely unlikely. So, the point to this aside is that, when judging whether or not you have a big difference, it is important to take into consideration the size of the number you were expecting.

Now the question becomes "How do we take the expected size into consideration?" Consider this, when calculating the test statistic for a test of a population mean, after we have taken the difference, $\bar{x} - \mu_o$, we then divided by the standard deviation of $\bar{x}$ to *standardize* the difference. In the same way, we will divide our $(O-E)^2$ by E to *standardize* it before we find our sum. Let's finish off that table!

Ethnic Group	O	E	O - E	$(O-E)^2$	$\dfrac{(O-E)^2}{E}$
White	147	219.347	-72.347	5234.088	23.862
Latino	210	205.672	4.328	18.732	0.091
Black	155	31.726	123.274	15196.479	478.991
Other	35	90.255	-55.255	3053.115	33.828
	547	547	0		536.772

Congratulations! You have just finished off a very long test statistic calculation. The sum we just found is our test statistic and we denote it χ^2. So our result for this step is:

$$\chi^2 = \sum \frac{(O-E)^2}{E} \approx 536.772$$

It is important to note that this is NOT a z-score or a t-score that we have found and thus we CANNOT use the Empirical Rule to decide whether or not it is unusual. Also, while this was a lengthy process, in future problems, we can reduce our work by skipping the $(O-E)$ and $(O-E)^2$ columns as they do not produce sums that we use.

Calculate the P-value. We begin by thinking about what we would expect to get for our test statistic if H_o were actually true. Ideally, if H_o is true then we would expect our observed frequencies to be the same as or near the expected frequencies. If this were the case, then our $\frac{(O-E)^2}{E}$'s would be very close to zero, and thus our test statistic would be very near zero. So, the further away from zero our test statistic is, the more evidence we have to support H_1. Also, because we squared all of the differences, our test statistic can only be on the right side of zero. This means that we are doing a right-tailed test. We now want to calculate the P-value, which would be the probability of being as far or farther to the right as our test statistic was from zero, if H_o is true. To do this we need to know the distribution of our test statistic. The following Point to Remember will give us this critical piece of information.

> **Point to Remember**: *The distribution of the Chi-Square Test Statistic*
>
> If the random sample is taken from a population whose percentage distribution is the same as the one claimed in H_o and all expected frequencies are at least 5, then the test statistic, $\chi^2 = \sum \dfrac{(O-E)^2}{E}$ has the Chi-Square distribution with $df = k-1$, where k is the number of categories in the table.

Therefore, the P-value we need is the area to the right of our test statistic, $\chi^2 \approx 536.772$, using $df = 4-1 = 3$. Notice that the *df* occurs just after the peak of the curve. This means that in reality, our test statistic is much farther to the right than it has been shown below.

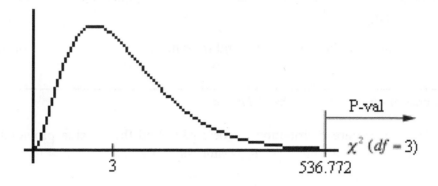

$$P - value = \chi^2 cdf\left(536.722,\ \infty,\ 3\right) \approx 0.0000$$

This P-value tells us that, if H_0 is true, there is almost no chance of seeing a test statistic this large just due to random variation. Therefore, our test statistic provided a large amount of evidence against H_0.

DECISIONS AND CONCLUSIONS:

Reject H_o or Do Not Reject H_o. The P-value tells us that, if we decide to Reject H_o, then we would be taking almost no risk of making a type I error. So, because the P-value ≤ 0.05, we Reject H_o. The risk of making a type I error is practically zero and, therefore, acceptably low.

State the conclusion in words. The data provided enough evidence, at the 5% significance level, to show that the true racial/ethnic distribution for all recently incarcerated California prisoners is different from the distribution for Californians in general.

> **Key Concepts**: *A few differences from previous hypothesis tests*
>
> - The null and alternative hypotheses are always stated in words for a Goodness-of-fit test.
> - H_o always contains a phrase denoting equals, such as "is the same as".
> - H_1 always contains the idea of a difference or change.
> - The χ^2 test statistic is not a z-score or a t-score and should not be interpreted as one.
> - Because of the squaring step used in calculating the test statistic, all goodness-of-fit tests are **right-tailed**, even though the "differs from" wording suggests a two-tailed test.

Is the fact that we were able to Reject H_o proof that there is racial bias in the California justice system?

No, while the data did provide convincing evidence that the true racial/ethnic distribution for all incarcerated California prisoners is different from the distribution for Californians in general, the hypothesis test does not tell us why this difference has occurred. We are convinced that the difference we saw was not just due to random variation, but we don't know if the cause is racial bias, economic conditions, cultural differences, etc.

Where the requirements met for using the Chi-Square distribution?

Yes. For success / failure problems, we required that both np and nq be at least 10 so that $\hat{p}$ will have a normal distribution. Similar to this, in Chi-Square Goodness-of-fit tests, we require that the values of $E = np$ for every category be at least 5. The smallest expected frequency we had was for "Black" and it was 31.726, well over the required 5.

The following Procedure summarizes the requirements and steps needed to do a Goodness-of-fit test.

Procedure for performing a χ^2 Goodness-of-Fit test:

Requirements: The Chi-Square distribution can be used to find the P-value provided that the expected frequency for all categories is greater than or equal to 5. $E = np \geq 5$ for every category.

Phases: We perform the hypothesis test by completing three phases:

SET UP THE TEST:
- Determine H_o and H_1 (this is done in words).
- Decide on the significance level, α.

GATHER AND WEIGH THE EVIDENCE:

- Make a table to calculate the test statistic: $\chi^2 = \sum \dfrac{(O-E)^2}{E}$ (Use 3 decimal places)

- Find the P-value using χ^2cdf command with $df = k-1$.

DECISIONS AND CONCLUSIONS:
- Reject H_o or Do Not Reject H_o.
- State the conclusion of the test in plain language using the words of the application.

Notes:
- $E = np$ and 'p' is percentage/probability/relative frequency for each category that applies if H_o is true.
- 'k' is the number of categories.

Now that we've gone through the process in detail, let's practice this new procedure with another example. This time we will not need such a detailed explanation. This should allow us to see a somewhat streamlined process compared to our first example.

Example 10.4: *Unions in the Workplace*

According to a 2013 Fox News Article, "Unions Suffer Steep Decline in Membership", the percentage of workers that are members of or are represented by unions at work has been shrinking since it's peak in the 1950s. In 2011, the state of Wisconsin was in the news for laws modifying public employee unions' ability to negotiate contracts. The first table below shows the distribution of the level of union involvement by workers in Wisconsin in 2011. The second table shows the union involvement by 1,009 workers in Wisconsin in a 2013 random sample.

Is the distribution of union membership changing?

Level of Union Involvement	2011 Wisconsin Percentages	2013 Random Sample in Wisconsin
Union Member	13.3%	113
Represented by Union	14.1%	121
Non Union Worker	72.6%	775

a) Does the data suggest, at the 1% significance level, that the true distribution of Union involvement for current Wisconsin workers has changed from what it was in 2011?

b) Comment on the requirements.

c) Discuss the possibility that we have made a type I or type II error.

Solution:

a) SET UP THE TEST:

Determine H_0 and H_1. The phrase "has changed from" does not include the possibility of equality. Therefore, this phrase will be used in H_1 and we will use the phrase "has remained the same as" which denotes equality in H_0.

> H_o: The true distribution of 2013 Union involvement for current Wisconsin workers has remained the same as it was in 2011.
> H_1: The true distribution of 2013 Union involvement for current Wisconsin workers has changed from what it was in 2011.

Determine the Significance Level. This is given as 1%, so $\alpha = 0.01$. (Thus, we are willing to take up to a 1% risk of making a type I error on this problem.)

GATHER AND WEIGH THE EVIDENCE:

Calculate the test statistic. For a Goodness-of-fit test, we need to make a table to find our test statistic. The values of the observed frequencies, O, come from the sample data. The values of p come from converting the 2011 percentages to decimal form. These are used to calculate the frequencies we would expect to see if H_0 was a true claim. We calculate the expected frequencies, E, using the formula $E = np$. The completed table is shown below with the work for a couple of the numbers shown to the right of the table.

Level of Union Involvement	O	p	E = np	$\frac{(O-E)^2}{E}$
Union Member	113	0.133	134.2	3.348
Represented by Union	121	0.141	142.27	3.180
Non Union Worker	775	0.726	732.53	2.462
Totals:	1009	1.000	1009	8.990

$$\frac{(113-134.2)^2}{134.2} \approx 3.348$$

$$1009 * 0.726 = 732.53$$

The test statistic is $\chi^2 = \sum \dfrac{(O-E)^2}{E} \approx 8.990$

Calculate the P-value. All Goodness-of-fit tests are right tailed, so we want to find the area to the right of our test statistic. We have 3 categories, so we have $df = k - 1 = 3 - 1 = 2$. The sketch is shown below. Technology is used to find the needed area.

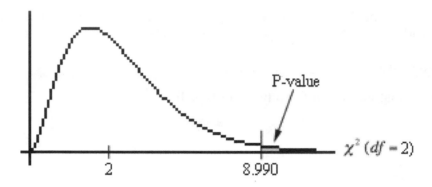

$$P - value = \chi^2 cdf\left(8.990,\ \infty,\ 2\right) \approx 0.0112$$

DECISIONS AND CONCLUSIONS:

Reject H_o or Do Not Reject H_o. The P-value tells us that, if we decide to Reject H_o, then we would be taking a 1.12% risk of making a type I error. So, because the P-value ≥ 0.01, we Do Not Reject H_o. The risk of making a type I error is a little higher than we are willing to take this time.

State the conclusion in words. The data did not provide enough evidence, at the 1% significance level, to show that the true distribution of 2013 Union involvement for current Wisconsin workers has changed from what it was in 2011.

b)   All three of our expected frequencies were well over 5. Therefore, the requirements have been met.

c)   A type I error is not possible, because we did not reject H_o. It is possible that we have made a type II error, and this will be the case if it turns out that H_o is, in fact, false. The chance of a type II error can not be computed. It is worth noting that our P-value was almost small enough to Reject H_0. In fact, if this test had been done at the standard 5% significance level, then we would have Rejected H_0. This is reason to be more concerned than usual that a type II error may have occurred.

In both of the examples we have seen so far, the expected percentages were provided in a table. Let's look at one final example where the expected percentages seem to be missing and see how that should be handled.

WRAP SESSION: *A case where the percentages seem to be missing*

Example 10.5: *Testing the Randomness of a Test-Generator*

A teacher wishes to check the randomness of an exam generating software package. The software creates multiple-choice exams and claims that the correct answers will be randomly assigned to one of the 5 choices: A, B, C, D, or E. To check the software, the teacher generated a 40-question exam and noted the number of times each letter was assigned the correct answer. The results were as follows:

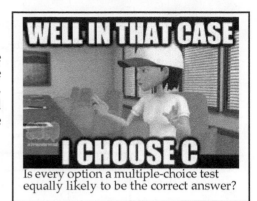

Is every option a multiple-choice test equally likely to be the correct answer?

Correct Answer	A	B	C	D	E
Frequency	7	10	12	9	2

a) Does the data provide enough evidence, at the 10% significance level, to show that the software is not using simple random selection to assign the correct answers to a letter?

b) Which categories provided the most and least evidence against H_o?

c) If you were a student taking an exam generated by this software and you had to guess at an answer, how would the results of this hypothesis test affect your choice?

d) Comment on the requirements.

Solution:

a) SET UP THE TEST:

Determine H_0 and H_1. The phrase "is not using" does not include the possibility of equality. Therefore, this phrase will be used in H_1 and we will use the phrase "is using" which denotes equality in H_0.

H_o : The software is using simple random selection to assign the correct answers to a letter.

H_1 : The software is not using simple random selection to assign the correct answers to a letter.

Determine the Significance Level. This is given as 10%, so $\alpha = 0.10$. (Thus, we are willing to take up to a 10% risk of making a type I error on this problem.)

GATHER AND WEIGH THE EVIDENCE:

Calculate the test statistic. For a goodness-of-fit test we need to make a table to find our test statistic. The values of the observed frequencies, O, come from the frequencies for the different letters assigned a correct answer on the 40-question test.

Typically, we would look for the values of p to be provided in a table. However, this time, no such table was given. When no values of p are given, we need to figure them out by reading H_o. Recall that 'E' stands for the frequencies we would "expect" to get if H_o is a true claim. In this case, if H_o is true, then the software is using simple random selection to assign the correct answer to a letter. If this is true, then each of the five letters would be equally likely to be the one chosen. Because there are 5 categories, the value of p for each one is given by:

> **Key Concept**: *If no percentages are given*
>
> If no percentages are given to use for the values of p, then determine the values for p by considering what the probability of each category would be if Ho turns out to be true.

$$p = \frac{1}{5} = 0.2 = 20\%$$

We now calculate the expected frequencies, E, using the formula $E = np$. So, for each possible correct answer, we have the following: $E = np = 40 * 0.2 = 8$. The completed table is shown below.

Correct Answer	O	p	E	$\dfrac{(O-E)^2}{E}$
A	7	0.2	8	0.125
B	10	0.2	8	0.500
C	12	0.2	8	2.000
D	9	0.2	8	0.125
E	2	0.2	8	4.500
Totals:	40		40	7.250

The test statistic is $\chi^2 = \sum \dfrac{(O-E)^2}{E} \approx 7.250$

Calculate the P-value. All Goodness-of-fit tests are right tailed, so we want to find the area to the right of our test statistic. We have 5 categories, so we have $df = k - 1 = 5 - 1 = 4$. The sketch is shown below. Technology is used to find the needed area.

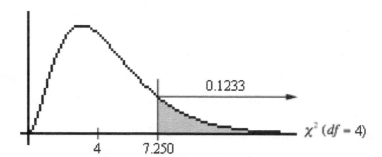

$$P - value = \chi^2 cdf(7.250, \infty, 4) \approx 0.1233$$

DECISIONS AND CONCLUSIONS:

Reject H_o or Do Not Reject H_o. The P-value tells us that, if we decide to Reject H_o, then we would be taking a 12.33% risk of making a type I error. So, because the P-value ≥ 0.10, we Do Not Reject H_o. The risk of making a type I error is a little higher than we are willing to take this time.

State the conclusion in words. The data did not provide enough evidence, at the 10% significance level, to show that the software is not using simple random selection to assign the correct answers to a letter.

b) Recall: In a χ^2 test, the larger the value of χ^2, the more evidence you have against H_o. So, to answer this question we look at the size of the individual values of $\dfrac{(O-E)^2}{E}$. The larger these values are the more evidence they give us, and the smaller they are the less evidence they provide. So in this example the largest value of $\dfrac{(O-E)^2}{E}$ came from the category 'letter E' (4.500) and the smallest values came from the categories 'letter A' and 'letter D' (0.125 each).

c) Strictly speaking, we did not have enough evidence to show that each letter is not equally likely, so our guess would be unaffected by this hypothesis test. However, this was a close call, and most of the evidence against equally likely came from 'letter C' and 'letter E'. So, if I were guessing, I would avoid 'letter E' (which came up 6 less times than expected) and lean towards 'letter C' (which came up 4 more times than expected).

d) All of expected frequencies, $E's$, where at least 5. So, the requirements have been met.

> **Caution:** *Requirements are a check of Expected Frequencies not Observed Frequencies*
>
> In the example above, the observed frequency for the letter 'E' choice was only 2. Because this frequency is less than 5, you might have been temped to say, in part (d), that the requirements were not met. However, the requirements state that we need $E \geq 5$ for all categories. It is not a problem if an Observed frequency, O, is less than 5.

LOOKING DEEPER: *Just what is* $\dfrac{(O-E)^2}{E}$ *calculating anyway?*

It is helpful to our understanding of why we reject H_o or not, to know that each of the individual values of $\dfrac{(O-E)^2}{E}$ can be thought of as similar to a z-score for that category. This means that by looking at this value, we can tell if any of the categories produced an unusually large difference between the observed and expected frequencies.

For example, in the previous problem, the largest value of $\dfrac{(O-E)^2}{E}$ that we saw was 4.500, the next largest was 2.000 and all the other values were less than 1. If we think of these as individual values as being similar to z-scores, then we could say that most of the differences we saw were small enough to be the kind of normal difference produced by taking a random sample and 2 categories produced a difference large enough to be considered unusual.

To be able to reject H_o in one of these problems, you need to average differences that are near unusual. So, we need to be getting values for $\dfrac{(O-E)^2}{E}$ that average out to about 2. This means that it will typically take a value of $\sum \dfrac{(O-E)^2}{E}$ that is about 2 times the degrees of freedom to be able to reject H_o. (Because df = # categories – 1)

In the previous problem we would have needed a value of about $2(5-1) = 8$ in order to reject. We obtained a test stat of 7.250. So, because our test statistic was a little less than twice the df, it is not surprising that we did not quite get a P-value small enough to allow us to Reject H_o.

> **Key Concepts**: *Consider the size of the difference in every category*
>
> - Even though the χ^2 test statistic is not a z-score, the individual values of $\dfrac{(O-E)^2}{E}$ can be thought of as similar to z-scores.
> - In a χ^2 test, it usually takes a test statistic about 2 times the size of the df to reject H_o. This should not be considered to be a rule, rather it just gives us an early idea of whether or not we are headed towards Rejecting H_o.

Let's practice what we have learned with some exercises.

Exercise Set 10.2

Concept Review: Review the definitions and concepts from this section by filling in the blanks for each of the following.

21) When calculating the test statistic for a goodness-of-fit test, the 'O' stands for the _____ frequency and the values of 'O' are obtained from the _____ .

22) When calculating the test statistics for a Goodness-of-fit test, the 'E' stands for the _____ frequency. These are the frequencies we expect to see if H_o is _____ .

23) The degrees of freedom for a Goodness-of-fit test is given by the formula $df = k - 1$, where the k stands for the number of _____ .

24) The individual values of $\dfrac{(O-E)^2}{E}$ can be thought of as being similar to _____ . The larger these values get, the more _____ we have against H_o.

25) H_o must always include a phrase like 'is the same as', 'has not changed', etc. This is because H_o must always include the possibility of _____ .

26) Because of the _____ step in calculating the test statistic, all Goodness-of-fit tests are _____ tailed.

27) The requirement for a Goodness-of-fit test is that all _____ frequencies must be at least ___ .

28) If no percentages are given to help us calculate the expected frequencies, then we will substitute the _____ for each category that would apply if H_o was _____ .

Applications: Practice the ideas learned in this section within the context of real world applications.

29) Colleges are often interested in seeing how the success rates of student athletes compare to the success rates for all students. The table below presents the relative frequency distribution for three categories for all students at Chabot College in Hayward, CA.

Passing (A, B, or C)	Not Passing (D or F)	Withdrawal
0.665	0.120	0.215

a) Use the observed frequencies from a sample of 61 current student athletes at Chabot (listed in the following table) to determine, at the 1% significance level, if the true success rates for student athletes are different from those of all the students.

Passing (A, B, or C)	Not Passing (D or F)	Withdrawal
43	10	8

b) Comment on the requirements for doing the Goodness-of-fit test.

30) In September 2008, A Gallup survey estimated the percentage of adults in the United States that would identify themselves with a certain political affiliation. The percentages from 2008 are shown below.

Democrat	35.07%
Republican	32.33%
Independent	30.57%
Other	2.03%

In November 2013, a random sample of 439 American adults were asked to identify their political affiliation. The results are shown below.

Democrat	122
Republican	100
Independent	201
Other	16

a) Does the data provide enough evidence, at the 5% significance level, to show that the true distribution of political party affiliations in the U.S. is different from what it was in September 2008?

b) Comment on the requirements for doing the Goodness-of-fit test.

31) In 2010, the current ethnic distribution in the United States was as follows:

White	Black	Asian	Hispanic	Other
63.7%	12.2%	4.7%	16.4%	3.0%

At that time, a random sample of 500 heart attack deaths in the U.S. produced the following ethnic breakdown.

White	Black	Asian	Hispanic	Other
333	62	23	71	11

a) Does the data provide enough evidence, at the 5% significance level, to show that the true ethnic distribution among heart attack victims is different than the ethnic distribution in the U.S.?
b) Comment on the requirements.
c) What, if anything, does this data tell us about the relationship between ethnicity and heart attacks?
d) Discuss the possibility that you have made a type I error or a type II error.

32) A study conducted in Hong Kong during the year 2000 produced the distribution of blood types shown below. The last column shows the frequencies from a recent random sample of 377 Hong Kong residents.

Blood Type	2000 Percentages	Current Sample Frequencies
O+	39.8%	148
A+	25.6%	102
B+	26.9%	97
Other	7.7%	30

a) Does the data suggest, at the 10% significance level, that the true distribution of Hong Kong's blood types has changed since 2000?
b) Comment on the requirements.
c) Given that only 0.6% of people in Hong Kong had negative blood types in 2000 and 7.1% had type AB+, explain why all 4 negative blood types were combined with the AB+ rather than showing all 8 blood types.
d) What, if anything, does this data tell us about how and why blood types in Hong Kong are changing over time?
e) Discuss the possibility that you have made a type I error or a type II error.

33) A study was conducted in a U.S. state before it enacted laws requiring the use of a hands-free device for drivers talking on a cell phone. The residents were asked how often they talked on a cell phone while driving without using a hands-free device. The percentages for the state's residents are shown in the table below. The last column shows the frequencies from a random sample of 518 residents taken 1 year after the law went into effect.

Cell calls without hands-free?	Percentages before the law	Frequencies after the law in effect
Always	48.1%	158
Sometimes	30.6%	170
Never	21.3%	190

a) Does the data suggest, at the 1% significance level, that the true distribution of the use of hands-free devices changed after the law went into effect?
b) Comment on the requirements.
c) Which category above provided the most and least evidence in support of the alternative hypothesis? Explain.
d) What, if anything, does this data tell us about how and why hands free use has changed since the laws were past?

34) The table below shows the percentage of T-shirts sold by size in 1985 together with the frequencies for the number of each size sold in a random sample of 760 recent purchases.

T-shirt Size	1985 Percentages	Frequencies in the sample
Small	12.8%	86
Medium	30.2%	211
Large	35.4%	255
X-Large	15.9%	130
XX-Large	5.7%	78

a) Does the data suggest, at the 5% significance level, that the current distribution of the T-shirt sizes is different than it was in 1985?
b) Comment on the requirements.
c) Which category above provided the most and least evidence in support of the alternative hypothesis? Explain.
d) What, if anything, does this data tell us about how and why T-shirt purchases are changing over time?

35) A gambler suspects that the colors on a roulette wheel are not showing up in the proper proportions. He observes 250 plays of the game and sees the following frequencies for each of the colors on the wheel.

Red	Black	Green
99	140	11

a) Perform a test at, the 1% significance level, to determine if the colors on a roulette wheel are not showing up in the proper proportions. Recall that the wheel has 18 red, 18 black, and 2 green numbers.
b) If you were a gambler, how if at all, would the results of this test affect the way that you played this game? Explain.
c) Explain why you could not do this test if you only observed 90 plays of the game.

36) A student suspects that a die is not fair. To test her suspicions she rolls the die 150 times and gets the following frequencies for each of the numbers on the die.

# on die	1	2	3	4	5	6
Freq.	30	22	12	28	23	35

a) Perform a test at, the 1% significance level, to determine if the die is not fair.
b) If you were the student, would you now have any doubts about the fairness of the die? Explain.
c) If we increased the sample size, would we be more likely to Reject H_o? Explain.

37) According to the m&m web site (May 2007), the color distribution for their candy varies depending on the type of m&m you buy. The color distribution claimed by the web site for milk chocolate m&m's is shown in the chart below. A statistics student scooped 117 m&m's out of a large bag of milk chocolate m&m's. The color counts for the student's sample are also shown below.

Color	Claimed Percentage	Color Counts from Sample
Brown	13%	26
Yellow	14%	13
Red	13%	21
Blue	24%	11
Orange	20%	21
Green	16%	25

a) Does the data provide enough evidence, at the 10% significance level, to show that the true distribution of colors of all the candy in the bag is not as claimed by the web site?
b) Would taking a larger scoop for the sample make it more likely that we would reject the claimed percentages? Explain.
c) In terms of this application and evidence, explain what it would have meant for us to make a type I error.
d) In terms of this application and evidence, explain what it would have meant for us to make a type II error.

38) A teacher asked 76 students to randomly pick a natural number (in their heads) from 1 to 5 (inclusive). The table below shows the frequencies obtained for each of the numbers.

# picked	1	2	3	4	5
Freq.	8	14	24	21	9

a) Does the data provide enough evidence, at the 5% significance level, to show that the students' version of random selection is not the same as simple random sampling?
b) In terms of this application and evidence, explain what it would have meant for us to make a type I error.
c) In terms of this application and evidence, explain what it would have meant for us to make a type II error.

39) In 2013, the MythBusters investigated whether bathroom stalls were used equally or if people preferred some stall locations over others. To test this, they put counting devices on the bathroom stall doors in a public restroom that had 4 stalls. They numbered the stalls from 1 to 4, with stall 1 closest to the door and stall 4 the furthest from the door. The counts from their sample of 119 uses are shown below.

Stall Number	1	2	3	4
Freq.	23	38	34	24

a) Does the data provide enough evidence, at the 5% significance level, to show that the true distribution of the use of the stalls is something other than uniform?
b) The myth they were testing was that stall number 1 gets the most use and should be avoided (for other less used and cleaner stalls). Would you consider that myth Confirmed, Plausible, or Busted? Explain.

40) Percentages of Marijuana use by teens in 2008 are shown in the table below together with frequencies from a 2011 sample of 819 teen conducted by The Partnership at Drugfree.org. In both cases, teens were asked if they had used marijuana in the last month, during the last year (but not in the last month), every in their life (but not in the last year), or never.

Used	2008 Percentage	2011 Sample frequencies
Last Month	19%	223
Last Year	12%	99
Ever	8%	65
Never	61%	432

a) Does the data provide enough evidence, at the 1% significance level, to show that the true 2011 distribution of marijuana use is different than it was in 2008.
b) What, if anything, does this data tell us about how and why teen marijuana used changed over this 3-year period?

Section 10.3 - Chi-Square Test of Independence

We will now turn our attention to a new type of test known as a Test of Independence. For example, we may want to determine if a person's skill at parking depends on the person's gender or we might want to investigate whether the way people feel about the NSA collecting phone call data depends on their political party affiliation. Except for a few minor changes, this process is extremely similar to the Goodness-of-fit test from Section 10.2. So, once again, we will dive right into an example and discuss the changes needed as we work through the hypothesis test.

Testing for Differences in Parking Skill by Gender: (*Discussion Example*)

A 2012 study attempted to determine if there were differences in parking skill based on gender. The researchers monitored parking lots across Great Britain and scored a person's parking ability based on factors such as speed at finding a space, speed at parking, how well the car was lined up between the lines, etc. Each driver was given a score, out of 20 possible points, and the driver's gender was noted. The data below summarizes the results for a random sample of 582 drivers.

Is the ability to skillfully park a car independent of the gender of the driver?

Parking Score

Gender	0 – 5 P1	6 – 10 P2	11 – 15 P3	16 – 20 P4	Totals
Female G1	9	63	157	50	279
Male G2	7	89	169	38	303
Totals	16	152	326	88	582

Does the sample data provide enough evidence, at the 5% significance level, to show that the parking score is dependent on the gender of the driver?

Solution:

SET UP THE TEST:

Determine H_o **and** H_1. The key thing to think about here is that, when you do a hypothesis test, you always compare what happened in the sample to what you expect to happen if H_o is true. Also, we know that H_o should contain the idea of equality. If we make H_o state that parking score and gender are independent, then we have some probability rules that state certain quantities should be **equal**. There are no equality properties for dependence! Therefore, we state are null and alternative hypotheses as follows:

H_o: The parking score is independent of the driver's gender.

H_1: The parking score is dependent on the driver's gender.

Determine the significance level. This is given as 5%, so $\alpha = 0.05$.

GATHER AND WEIGH THE EVIDENCE:

Calculate the test statistic. Just as in Goodness-of-fit tests, our test statistic will once again be $\chi^2 = \sum \dfrac{(O-E)^2}{E}$. The 'O' still represents the observed frequencies, which are the frequencies given in our chart of sample data, and the 'E' still represents the frequencies we expect to get if H_o is true. So the thing we need to explore is the following. What do we expect to happen if the parking score and gender are independent of each other? Let's begin by looking at one specific cell in the chart. Consider the cell for a parking score from $0-5$ for a female driver. In symbols we are looking at the cell (G1 & P1). Note: the observed frequency for this cell is 9. We will once again start with the formula $E = np$ and this time we will think of the 'p' as probability.

Recall from Chapter 5, that if A and B are independent, then $P(A \ \& \ B) = P(A) \cdot P(B)$. Therefore, when we calculate the 'p' for this cell, we will use $p = P(G1 \ \& \ P1) = P(G1) \cdot P(P1)$. We don't know the actual values for $P(G1)$ and $P(P1)$, but we can approximate them using the relative frequencies from the sample data. Working with the numbers from the contingency table above we see that:

$$P(G1) \approx \frac{279}{582} \quad \& \quad P(P1) \approx \frac{16}{582}$$

So, $E = np = 582 \cdot P(G1 \ \& \ P1) \overset{*}{=} 582 \cdot P(G1) \cdot P(P1) \approx 582 \cdot \dfrac{279}{582} \cdot \dfrac{16}{582} = \dfrac{279 \cdot 16}{582} \approx 7.67$

This provides us with our expected frequency for the first cell of the table. Note the '$\overset{*}{=}$' marks the step where we assumed H_o was true and used the Special Multiplication Rule for independent events. Let's repeat the process to find the value of E for the cell (G2 & P3). We get:

$$P(G2) \approx \frac{303}{582} \quad \& \quad P(P3) \approx \frac{326}{582}$$

So, $E = np = 582 \cdot P(G2 \ \& \ P3) \overset{*}{=} 582 \cdot P(G2) \cdot P(P3) \approx 582 \cdot \dfrac{303}{582} \cdot \dfrac{326}{582} = \dfrac{303 \cdot 326}{582} \approx 169.72$

In both of the previous calculations, we should see the following pattern developing. When we calculate E, the formula always simplifies to $E = \dfrac{R \cdot C}{n}$, where R is the total for the row the cell is in and C is the column total for the column the cell is in. Using this, we can quickly compute more values of E for the table.

$$(G1 \ \& \ P2): \ E = \frac{279 \cdot 152}{582} \approx 72.87 \qquad\qquad (G2 \ \& \ P4): \ E = \frac{303 \cdot 88}{582} \approx 45.81$$

We want to organize our observed and expected frequencies together so that we can compute $\chi^2 = \sum \dfrac{(O-E)^2}{E}$. Because we already have a two-dimensional table, we need to do this a little differently that for a Goodness-of-fit test. We will simply insert each expected frequency (E) into the table cells with the observed frequencies (O) by writing the E's below the O's and we will put the E's in parentheses so that we know which is which. The table below shows this for our current data set.

Parking Score

Gender	0 – 5 P1	6 – 10 P2	11 – 15 P3	16 – 20 P4	Totals
Female G1	9 (7.67)	63 (72.87)	157 (156.28)	50 (42.19)	279
Male G2	7 (8.33)	89 (79.13)	169 (169.72)	38 (45.81)	303
Totals	16	152	326	88	582

The remaining Expected frequencies shown above were all calculated using the formula $E = \dfrac{R \cdot C}{n}$ as shown in the work above the table. We do not compute expected frequencies for the totals because they do not represent combinations of gender together with a parking score.

Next we need to start computing $\dfrac{(O-E)^2}{E}$ for each of the cells. This is done exactly as it was for the Goodness-of-fit. So, for the first cell, we have $\dfrac{(9-7.67)^2}{7.67} \approx 0.231$. Continuing in this fashion and then adding all the values we get:

$$\chi^2 = \sum \frac{(O-E)^2}{E} \approx 0.231 + 1.337 + 0.003 + 1.446 +$$
$$0.212 + 1.231 + 0.003 + 1.332 = 5.795$$

The pieces of the sum have been organized so that each term is in the same position as the corresponding cell. That is 1.332 is in row 2, column 4 and, therefore, represents $\dfrac{(O-E)^2}{E}$ for the cell (G2 & P4).

Calculate the P-value. As in the previous section, if H_o were actually true, then we would expect our test statistic to be near 0. And again, because we squared all of the differences, our test statistic can only be on the right side of zero. This means that we are doing a right-tailed test. We now want to calculate the P-value, which would be the probability of the test statistic landing as far or farther to the right as our test statistic was from zero, if H_o is true. To do this we need to know the distribution of our test statistic. The following Point to Remember will give us this critical piece of information.

> **Point to Remember**: *Distribution of χ^2 in a Test of Independence*
>
> If the sample is taken from a population where the two variables in question are truly independent and, if all expected frequencies are at least 5, then the test statistic, $\chi^2 = \sum \dfrac{(O-E)^2}{E}$ has the Chi-Square distribution with $df = (r-1)(c-1)$, where r is the number of row categories and c is the number of column categories in the table.

We now want to find the area to the right of our test statistic, $\chi^2 \approx 5.795$, using $df = (2-1)(4-1) = 3$. A sketch of the desired area and the P-value calculation are shown below.

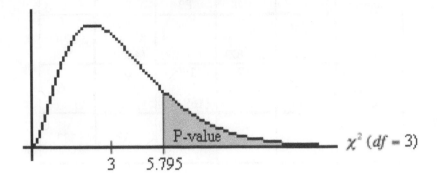

$$P - value = \chi^2 cdf\left(5.795,\ \infty,\ 3\right) \approx 0.1220$$

DECISIONS AND CONCLUSIONS:

Reject H_o or Do Not Reject H_o. The P-value tells us that, if we decide to Reject H_o, then we would be taking a 12.20% risk of making a type I error. Because the P-value > 0.05, we Do Not Reject H_o. The risk of making a type I error is a little higher than we are willing to take this time. We can also interpret the P-value as telling us that If H_o were true, then there would be a 12.20% chance of seeing differences like we did in our table just due to random variation.

State the conclusion in words. The data did not provide enough evidence, at the 5% significance level, to show that the parking score is dependent on the driver's gender.

Were the Requirements met on the above hypothesis test?

Yes. All of the expected frequencies were at least 5, so the requirements were met for this test.

So, which gender is better at parking cars?

Based on this data, we cannot conclusively answer this question. By deciding not to reject H_o, we are stating that it is reasonable to believe that gender and parking skills are not related. In the sample data, it looks like the women scored a bit better. A higher percentage of women than men had scores in the highest range. A lower percentage of women than men had scores in the lowest point range. However, our test showed that these differences are small enough that it is reasonable to believe that gender is not a factor and that the differences are just the result of random variation in the sampling process.

Is parking skill independent of gender?

It is important to note that the alternative hypothesis is that the variables are dependent and that this is what we are trying to prove. The procedure is called a test of independence only because we are challenging independence. Because independence is the null hypothesis we make no attempt to gather evidence to support it and, therefore, we **CANNOT** use this test to prove that two variables are independent!

Here are a few points worth noting from our discussion example.

Key Concepts: *Lessons learned from our first example*

- The null and alternative hypotheses are always stated in words for a test of independence.
- H_o always contains the idea of independence.
- H_1 always contains the idea of dependence.
- Expected frequencies are based on the assumption of independence and the Special Multiplication Rule: $P(A \ \& \ B) = P(A) \cdot P(B)$
- Because of the squaring process, all independence tests are **right-tailed**.
- Degrees of Freedom are based on (#rows - 1)(#columns - 1) rather than on the number of categories. $df = (r-1)(c-1)$
- This type of test can show dependence, but it cannot show independence.

The following procedure summarizes the requirements and phases needed to do a Chi-Square Test of Independence.

Procedure for performing a χ^2 Independence test:

Requirements: The Chi-Square distribution can be used to find the P-value provided that the expected frequency for all cells is greater than or equal to 5. $E \geq 5$ for every cell.

Phases: We perform the hypothesis test by completing three phases:

SET UP THE TEST:
- Determine H_o and H_1 (this is done in words).
- Decide on the significance level, α.

GATHER AND WEIGH THE EVIDENCE:

- Make a table to calculate the test statistic: $\chi^2 = \sum \dfrac{(O-E)^2}{E}$ (Use 3 decimal places)

- Find the P-value using χ^2cdf command with $df = (r-1)(c-1)$

DECISIONS AND CONCLUSIONS:
- Reject H_o or Do Not Reject H_o.
- State the conclusion of the test in plain language using the words of the application.

Notes:

- $E = \dfrac{R \cdot C}{n}$, R = Row total , C = Column total.

- r is the number of row categories and c is the number of column categories.

FURTHER EXPLORATION: *Where is the evidence?*

Example 10.6: *Identifying the cells that provide the most and least evidence for* H_1

In the preceding discussion example, which of the cells in the table provided the most and which provided the least evidence that the parking score is dependent on the driver's gender.

Solution:

Answering this is fairly simple. The greater our test statistic is, the more evidence we have to show dependence. So we merely examine the contribution each cell made to the overall test statistic.

The smallest contribution was 0.003. This value occurred in both the cells for female and male drivers scoring from 11 to 15 points on the parking test. These values are so small, because the observed frequencies of 157 and 169 were very close to the frequency we would have expected if the two variables had been independent. If you consider the 0.003 as similar to a z-score, then this is a very normal difference to see if the variables are independent. These two cells provided almost no evidence to support dependence.

The largest contribution, 1.446, came from the cell that represented female drivers scoring from 16 to 20 points on the parking test. This value is larger because the observed frequency of 50 is a bit different than the expected frequency of 42.19. If you consider the 1.446 as similar to a z-score, then we see that it would be a mild surprise to see such a difference if the variables were independent. Because even our largest contribution to the test statistic did not register as unusual, it is not surprising that we did not have enough evidence to Reject H_o.

WRAP SESSION: *One last look at the process*

Example 10.7: *Privacy Rights vs. National Security*

In 2013, a private contractor, Edward Snowden, that was working for the NSA leaked information that the U.S. government was collecting phone call and email information from U.S. citizens. After this news became publicly known, a poll was taken by the Pew Research Center concerning these issues. One of the questions asked was "Should government be able to monitor emails if it might prevent future terror attacks?" The responses of the 1,004 people surveyed are shown below grouped by both response and political party affiliation.

Is a person's feeling about the NSA monitoring emails dependent on the person's political affiliation?

Response to Survey

Party	Yes	No	Undecided	Totals
Republican	173	201	14	388
Democrat	219	178	18	415
Independent	76	121	4	201
Totals	468	500	36	1,004

a) Does the data provide enough evidence, at the 10% significance level, that the answers to this question are associated with people's political party association?

b) Which cells in the table provided the most and least evidence against H_o?

c) If you found an association between the response to the question and the party affiliation of the respondents, then which party members are most and least likely to support the monitoring of emails for national security purposes?

d) Comment on the requirements for performing the test of independence.

Solution:

a) SET UP THE TEST:

Determine H_o and H_1. In our discussion example, we stated that H_o should always contain the idea of independence and H_1 should always contain the idea of dependence. They use different words in this problem, but associated has the idea of connected, related, or dependent. Therefore, we state are null and alternative hypotheses as follows:

H_o: People's responses are not associated with their political party affiliation.

H_1: People's responses are associated with their political party affiliation.

Determine the significance level. This is given as 10%, so $\alpha = 0.10$.

GATHER AND WEIGH THE EVIDENCE:

Calculate the test statistic. We begin by filling in the expected frequencies for the table using the formula $E = \dfrac{R \cdot C}{n}$ and get the following:

Response to Survey

Party	Yes	No	Undecided	Totals
Republican	173 (180.86)	201 (193.23)	14 (13.91)	388
Democrat	219 (193.45)	178 (206.67)	18 (14.88)	415
Independent	76 (93.69)	121 (100.10)	4 (7.21)	201
Totals	468	500	36	1,004

$$E = \frac{R \cdot C}{n} = \frac{415 * 36}{1004} \approx 14.88$$

$$\frac{(O-E)^2}{E} = \frac{(18-14.88)^2}{14.88} \approx 0.654$$

The test statistic is $\chi^2 = \sum \dfrac{(O-E)^2}{E} \approx$ $0.342 + 0.312 + 0.001 +$

$3.375 + 3.977 + 0.654 +$

$3.340 + 4.364 + 1.429 = 17.794$

Calculate the P-value. $df = (3-1)(3-1) = 4$. A sketch and the P-value calculation are shown below.

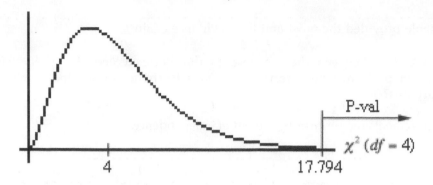

$$P - value = \chi^2 cdf(17.794, \infty, 4) \approx 0.0014$$

DECISIONS AND CONCLUSIONS:

Reject H_o or Do Not Reject H_o. Because the P-value $\leq$ 0.10, we Reject H_o. The risk of making a type I error is small enough that we are willing to take it.

State the conclusion in words. The data did provide enough evidence, at the 10% significance level, to show that people's responses are associated with their political party affiliation.

> **Key Concept:** *Association*
>
> In this problem the words "associated with" take the place of the words "dependent upon" and "not associated with" replaces "independent of". This is fairly common wording in a test of independence.

b) The most evidence against independence came from the cell "Response is NO and party is Independent". The value of $\dfrac{(O-E)^2}{E}$ for that cell was 4.364. Thinking of this as being similar to a z-score, it is very unusual value to get if H_o is true. The least evidence against independence came from the cell "Undecided and Republican". The value of $\dfrac{(O-E)^2}{E}$ for that cell was only 0.001. Thinking of this as being similar to a z-score, it is a very normal value to get if H_o is true.

c) This question is really not statistical in nature. We simply need to calculate the percentage of each political party surveyed who support email monitoring.

$$\text{Republicans: } \frac{173}{388} \approx 0.4459 = 44.59\%$$

$$\text{Democrats: } \frac{219}{415} \approx 0.5277 = 52.77\%$$

$$\text{Independent: } \frac{76}{201} \approx 0.3781 = 37.81\%$$

So, we see that Democrats are the most likely to support the email monitoring and Independents are the least likely to support email monitoring.

d) REQUIREMENTS: All of the expected frequencies are at least 5, so the requirements have been met. Note: There was an observed frequency of 4, but this is fine because the requirement is about expected frequencies.

Technology Tip: *Speeding up the calculations*

With most forms of statistics technology, it is possible to speed up the computations of the values of $\frac{(O-E)^2}{E}$ by entering in all of your observed frequencies and all of your expected frequencies and then you can have the technology compute all of the values of $\frac{(O-E)^2}{E}$ at once. See Appendix A for directions on doing this with the TI-84 Calculator.

LOOKING DEEPER: *What are degrees of freedom anyway?*

Having seen degrees of freedom defined in many different ways at this point, you may be wondering what degrees of freedom are and why the formulas for computing them keep changing. I will now attempt to give you some insight into this topic. Degrees of freedom are best understood by looking at the χ^2 tests from this chapter.

Let's begin by looking at a Goodness-of-fit test and asking this question: How many categories have to change for us to say that the distribution has changed? It is common for people to say the answer is one, but let's think about that. If the percentage in one category has gone up, then the percentage in another category must have gone down (because we always have a total of 100%). So the minimum number of categories that would have to change is actually two.

Turning this around, we see the following. If all of the categories except for one have stayed the same, then the last category must have stayed the same as well. In fact, if you know what changes have occurred in all the categories except for one, then you could figure out what the change was in that category using the fact that the total is 100%. So you could say, if there are k categories, then $k-1$ of them are free to experience change, but the last one's fate is determined by those other $k-1$ categories. This is why we say that there are $k-1$ degrees of freedom in a Goodness-of-fit test.

When we examine the Test of Independence, we see that the formula for degrees of freedom there is similarly motivated. Let's consider the table from our last example.

Response to Survey

Party	Yes	No	Undecided	Totals
Republican	173 (180.86)	201 (193.23)	14 (13.91)	388
Democrat	219 (193.45)	178 (206.67)	18 (14.88)	415
Independent	76 (93.69)	121 (100.10)	4 (7.21)	201
Totals	468	500	36	1,004

Notice that for any row or column, the sum of the O's and the E's are both the same and that $\sum(O-E)=0$ for any row or column. This means that if you knew the difference between the observed and expected frequencies for all but one cell in any row or column, then you could use that information to find the difference in the remaining cell in that same row or column.

In other words, if r is the number of rows, then in any row, $r-1$ of the cells have the freedom to change, but the last one is determined by the first $r-1$. Similarly, if c is the number of columns, then in any column, $(c-1)$ of the cells have the freedom to change, but the last one is determined by the first $c-1$. Thus the total number of cells with the freedom to change is given by $(r-1)(c-1)$. This is why we say that in a test of independence $df=(r-1)(c-1)$.

Hopefully, this adds a little insight into where these formulas for df come from and that you no longer view them as randomly changing from test to test.

It's time to practice what you have learned with some exercises.

Exercise Set 10.3

Concept Review: Review the definitions and concepts from this section by filling in the blanks for each of the following.

41) For a Chi-square test of independence, the degrees of freedom is given by the formula $df=(r-1)(c-1)$, where r is the number of ____ categories and c is the number of _____ categories.

42) In the test statistic for a chi-square Test of Independence, the 'E' stands for the frequency we expect if H_o is _____ . This means that they are calculated under the assumption that the variables in question are _____ .

43) H_o must always include a phrase like 'is independent of' or '_____ associated with' because the probability formulas for independence have an _____ sign in them and H_o must always include _____ .

44) Despite the name, a Test of Independence can only show that the variables are _____ . This test cannot show that the variables are _____ .

Applications: Practice the ideas learned in this section within the context of real world applications.

45) In October 2013, Americans were able to start signing up for health insurance coverage through government exchanges. During this phase of the rollout of the Affordable Care Act (or Obamacare), many people experienced trouble with the government website and others received cancellation notices from their current insurance company. In November 2013, a Fox News poll of 1,006 randomly selected registered voters asked people if they thought that the health care law should be thrown out, fixed, or left alone. Their responses are shown below together with their political party affiliation. (Based on summary results from the poll.)

Opinion of the Health Care Law

	Throw it out	Fix it	Keep it as is	Totals
Democ	83	288	65	436
Repub	320	93	32	445
Indep	60	53	12	125
Totals	463	434	109	1006

a) Does the data indicate, at the 5% significance level, that American's opinion of the health care law is dependent on their political affiliation?
b) Comment on the requirements.
c) Based on the results of this test, which political group appears to be most likely to support throwing out the health care law? Explain.

46) In April 2006, a random sample of 900 Americans were asked if they thought it was appropriate for retired military generals to criticize the secretary of defense during a time of war. The table below shows their responses cross-classified with their political affiliation. Sample is based on a Fox News Poll.

Appropriate to criticize?

	Yes	No	Don't Know	Totals
Repub	149	257	8	414
Democ	275	93	19	387
Indep	63	32	4	99
Totals	487	382	31	900

a) Perform a hypothesis test to determine if the responses are dependent on the political affiliation of the respondent. Use a 5% significance level.
b) Comment on the requirements.
c) Based on the results of this test, which political group appears to be most likely to support the generals criticizing the secretary of defense? Explain.

47) The table below represents a sample of 688 college students. The data is cross-classified by the time of year the students were born and their coffee drinking habits.

How often do you drink coffee?

	Daily	Sometimes	Never	Totals
Autumn	32	79	47	158
Winter	45	95	49	189
Spring	39	87	71	197
Summer	24	72	48	144
Totals	140	333	215	688

a) Does it appear that the level of coffee drinking of college students is dependent on the season in which they were born? Use a 10% significance level.
b) Comment on the requirements.
c) Discuss the possibility that you have made a type I or type II error.

48) The following table shows the cross classification by age and number of accidents as the driver for a recent sample of 153 college students.

Number of accidents in the last 3 years

	0	1	2+	Totals
Under 21 yrs	39	19	26	84
21 - under 25	26	11	8	45
25 yrs and over	18	4	2	24
Totals	83	34	36	153

a) Perform a hypothesis test to determine if the number of accidents in the last 3 years is dependent on the age of the student. Use a 5% significance level.
b) Comment on the requirements
c) Discuss the possibility that you have made a type I or type II error.

49) The current energy crisis has created some conflicts between those who want to develop additional sources of energy and those who are afraid that doing so will harm the environment. A random sample of 1182 Americans was taken and they were asked which should take priority, the need to develop additional energy sources or protecting the environment? Their responses, cross-classified with their political affiliation, are listed below.

Which takes priority?

	Energy	Environ	Don't Know	Totals
Repub	261	228	55	544
Democ	148	297	51	496
Indep	43	78	21	142
Totals	452	603	127	1,182

a) Does the data provide sufficient evidence, at the 5% significance level, to show that Americans' priority between creating additional energy sources and protecting the environment is dependent on their political affiliation?
b) Which cell provided the most and which cell provided the least evidence in support for the alternative hypothesis?
c) Based on the results of this test, which political group appears to be most likely to say that the Environment takes first priority? Explain.
d) Show the work for the calculation of the expected frequency, E, for the square for Republicans that put Energy as top priority. Use the formula $E = np$ and the assumption of independence as shown in calculating the test statistic in the discussion example.

50) In some states, there have been efforts to pass propositions that would give parents whose children attend private school a government voucher to help pay the costs of this private education. The voucher is a portion of the tax dollars that would normally support that child's public school education. The table below contains the results of a random sample of 1,329 adults who were asked whether or not they support the idea of School Vouchers. Their answers are cross-classified with their child's education status.

Status of Children in School

	Children in Public School	Children in Private School	No Children in School	Totals
Support Vouchers	166	32	281	479
Oppose Vouchers	251	20	536	807
Undecided	8	1	34	43
Totals	425	53	851	1,329

a) Does it appear that the person's response is dependent on the status of their children? Use a 10% significance level.
b) Comment on the requirements.
c) Based on the results of this test, which parental status group appears to be most likely to support voucher programs? Explain.
d) Show the work for the calculation of the expected frequency, E, for the square for Children in public school and parents Support vouchers. Use the formula E=np and the assumption of independence as shown in calculating the test statistic in the discussion example.

51) The following table cross classifies a random sample of 513 Americans by using their education level and their smoking habits. Sample data is based on a 2011 CDC study.

Smoking Status

	Smoke	Don't Smoke	Totals
No High school Diploma	20	52	72
High School Only	53	168	221
Some College	25	92	117
Bachelor's or Higher	9	94	103
Totals	107	406	513

a) Does the data provide sufficient evidence, at the 5% significance level, to show that a person's smoking status is dependent on their education level?
b) Based on the results of this test, which education level appears to be most likely to smoke? Explain.
c) Discuss the possibility that you have made a type I or type II error.

52) The table below cross-classifies how often people talk on their cell phones while driving with the region of the country they live in. The random sample of 1574 adults is based on a 2006 Harris Poll.

How often do you talk on a cell phone while driving?

	All the time	Sometimes	Never	Totals
East	16	240	149	405
Mid-West	28	330	113	471
South	19	162	54	235
West	19	310	134	463
Totals	82	1042	450	1574

a) Perform a hypothesis test to determine if the cell phone habits are dependent on the region of the country. Use a 1% significance level.
b) Based on the results of this test, which region of the country appears to be most likely to never talk on a cell phone while driving? Explain.
c) Discuss the possibility that you have made a type I or type II error.

53) In 2006, the NFL began playing some of their games during the season on Thursday nights. This often means that a team plays on a short rest and recovery time having just played 4 days earlier on Sunday. Many are concerned that playing on short rest might lead to an increase in injuries. The data below cross-classifies the number of injury stoppages during games with the day the game was played on. The data below shows the number of injuries for a team in each of the games played during the 2012 season.

Game Day

Injuries	Thursday	Not Thursday	Totals
0	8	55	63
1	12	81	93
2+	10	66	76
Totals	30	202	232

a) Does the data provide sufficient evidence, at the 5% significance level, to show that the number of injuries a team has during a game is dependent on the day of the week they were playing?
b) Comment on the requirements.
c) Does the 2012 data provide any evidence to support the idea that Thursday games are more dangerous for players? Explain.

54) The hometown fans of a superstar baseball player feel that the player does not perform as well at the plate when there are runners on base. The data below shows the results of his at bats this year cross-classified with the number of runners on base. (At bats resulting in a walk have been excluded.)

Number of runners on base

	0	1	2	3	Totals
Out	157	128	87	25	397
Single	57	50	20	10	137
Extra Bases	19	20	27	8	74
Totals	233	198	134	43	608

a) Suppose that we consider this year's at bats to be a random sample of the superstar's true potential at the plate. Does the data indicate, at the 10% significance level, that the player's performance is dependent on the number of runners on base at the time of the at bat?
b) Comment on the requirements.
c) What would you say to the fans who voiced the concern that the player was under performing with runners on base?

55) Many roulette players believe that if a certain color does not have the ball land in it on 1 play of the game, then it is more likely to land there on the next play of the game. A statistician decided to research this idea by observing 2000 plays of a game of roulette. The results are shown below where the columns represent the color on the previous play and the row represents the color that occurred during the current play of the game.

Color on previous play

	Red	Black	Green	Totals
Red	465	441	55	961
Black	454	413	46	913
Green	69	51	6	126
Totals	988	905	107	2000

a) Perform a hypothesis test to determine if the color that the ball lands in on a given play of the game is dependent on the color it landed in on the previous play of the game. Use a 5% significance level.
b) Do you think we have made an error or a correct decision? Explain.

56) Consider the experiment where we toss a coin and roll and die. This experiment was repeated 500 times and the results of the experiment have been cross-classified in the table below. Note: the first cell represents the fact that 41 times, out of the 500 runs of the experiment, heads showed on the coin at the same time that a 1 was rolled on the die.

Number showing on the Die

	1	2	3	4	5	6	Totals
Heads	41	49	43	39	47	36	255
Tails	37	37	48	43	48	32	245
Totals	78	86	91	82	95	68	500

a) Perform a hypothesis test to determine if the side that shows on a coin is dependent on the number that is rolled on the die. Use a 10% significance level.
b) Do you think we have made an error or a correct decision? Explain.

Section 10.4 – Inferences for a Population Standard Deviation, σ

In Chapter 8, we computed confidence intervals for the population proportion, p, and for the population mean, μ. In Chapter 9, we performed hypothesis tests involving the same two quantities. Another population quantity that we are interested in computing confidence intervals and hypothesis tests for is the population standard deviation, σ. The population standard deviation measures the amount of variation in a population. This quantity can be important for measuring the consistency in a manufacturing process and for measuring the variation in many other situations. The reason that we waited until now to perform inferences involving this quantity is because such inferences require use of the Chi-Square distribution. We were not introduced to this type of distribution until the beginning of this chapter.

The inferential procedures we learned involving p and μ required us to know the distribution of the two random variables $\hat{p}$ and $\bar{x}$. In Chapter 7, we learned that under certain conditions, those two random variables were approximately normally distributed. In this section we will be using the random variable s as our estimate of σ. The following Point to Remember provides the distribution information we need about the random variable s.

> **Point to Remember**: *A Chi-Square distribution involving the random variable s*
>
> If a random sample of size n is taken from an approximately normally distributed population, then the random variable $\chi^2 = \dfrac{(n-1)s^2}{\sigma^2}$ has the Chi-Square distribution with $n-1$ degrees of freedom, $df = n-1$.

In this section, we will see how knowing the distribution of this quantity can help us compute confidence intervals for the population standard deviation, σ. We will also see how this allows us to perform hypothesis tests involving σ.

CONFIDENCE INTERVAL FOR σ: *Developing the Formula*

Suppose that the two values χ_L^2 and χ_R^2 separate the area under the Chi-Square distribution with $df = n-1$ into a middle area of $1-\alpha$ and equal outside areas (See the diagram to the right). If $\dfrac{(n-1)s^2}{\sigma^2}$ has the Chi-Square distribution with degrees of freedom, $df = n-1$, then we get the following result.

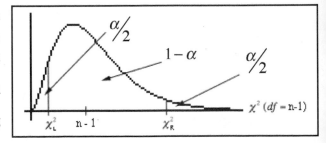

$$P\left(\chi_L^2 < \frac{(n-1)s^2}{\sigma^2} < \chi_R^2 \right) = 1-\alpha$$

If we use algebra to solve this inequality for σ, we get the following.

$$P\left(\sqrt{\frac{(n-1)s^2}{\chi_R^2}} < \sigma < \sqrt{\frac{(n-1)s^2}{\chi_L^2}} \right) = 1-\alpha$$

Notice that the result above gives us a range of possible values that we are $(1-\alpha) \cdot 100\%$ confident contains the true population standard deviation, σ. From this last formula, we get our procedure for finding a confidence interval for σ. This procedure is summarized in the following Point to Remember.

Point to Remember: *Procedure for Computing a Confidence Interval for* σ

Requirements: In order to use the Chi-Square distribution to find the values of χ_L^2 and χ_R^2, our sample must have been randomly chosen from a Normally distributed population.

Steps: We complete the steps below to create our confidence interval.

- *Point Estimate*: Calculate the sample standard deviation, s, by using the sample data and technology (unless the value of s is provided in the problem.)

- χ^2 *values*: For a confidence level of $(1-\alpha) \cdot 100\%$, sketch the Chi-Square curve with $df = n-1$ and use $inv\chi^2$ to determine the two Chi-Square values, χ_L^2 and χ_R^2, that trap are area of $1-\alpha$ in the middle with equal outside areas.

- *Endpoints*: Calculate the two endpoints of the confidence interval using the two formulas shown below.

$$\text{Left Endpoint} = \sqrt{\frac{(n-1)s^2}{\chi_R^2}} \quad \text{and} \quad \text{Right Endpoint} = \sqrt{\frac{(n-1)s^2}{\chi_L^2}}$$

- *Interval*: The confidence interval is written $\sigma \in \left(\sqrt{\frac{(n-1)s^2}{\chi_R^2}}, \sqrt{\frac{(n-1)s^2}{\chi_L^2}} \right)$.

Cautions: A few of things to be careful of during this process.

- Because χ^2 curves are right-skewed rather than symmetric, we must find two separate Chi-Square values χ_L^2 and χ_R^2 to calculate the endpoints of our confidence interval. We can't just use one endpoint to help us find the other one.

- The algebra used to solve our original inequality for σ caused the value of χ_R^2 to end up in the left endpoint and for the value χ_L^2 to end up in the right endpoint. This may seem counterintuitive, so be careful here.

- If the population is not at least approximately normal, then this can cause our confidence level to have large differences from the true percentage of the time that our intervals actually capture σ. Because of this, we should use technology to help assess the normality of our sample rather than just hoping that the population is approximately normal.

Now that we have developed the procedure, let's look at an application of confidence intervals for a population standard deviation, σ.

Example 10.8: *Investigating the consistency of an IV pump*

A consultant is testing the consistency of a medical IV pump. Not only is it important that the pump deliver the correct mean amount of medication, but it is also very important that it deliver the medication with only a small amount of variation. A pump that has too much variation can at times be delivering levels of medication that are ineffective or unsafe for the patient. The consultant is testing a pump that is supposed to deliver 20 cc of medication per hour. A sample of 8 test runs of the pump produced the following data in CCs per hour.

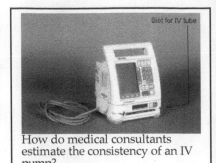

How do medical consultants estimate the consistency of an IV pump?

| 20.99 | 18.32 | 19.36 | 20.60 | 19.06 | 17.68 | 20.15 | 21.33 |

a) Have the requirements been met for finding a confidence interval for σ? Explain.

b) Determine a 90% confidence interval for the true standard deviation for the rate at which this IV pump delivers medication to patients.

c) Interpret this interval in terms of the application.

d) Suppose that, for use of this device to be approved, it must have a standard deviation that is less than 10% of the targeted mean. Can we be 90% confident that this pump will be approved? Explain using your interval from part (a).

Solution:

a) We need the sample to have been taken from a normally distributed population. It is difficult to be sure of this with such a small sample, but we can use technology to see if it is at least reasonable to believe that the population is normal. The P-value from a StatCrunch normality test on the sample is shown on the right.

Because the P-value $= 0.8589 > 0.05$, it is a reasonable possibility that this sample was taken from an approximately normally distributed population. We can proceed with the confidence interval.

Anderson-Darling goodness-of-fit results:

Variable	n	Stat	P-Value
IV Pump Rate	8	0.18680568	0.8589

b) *Point Estimate*: We begin by using technology to find the sample standard deviation, $s \approx 1.3007$.

χ^2 *values*: Now we need to use technology and $inv\chi^2$ to determine the two values, χ_L^2 and χ_R^2, that trap an area of 0.90 in the middle with equal areas on the outside. We will use the Chi-Square curve with $df = n - 1 = 8 - 1 = 7$.

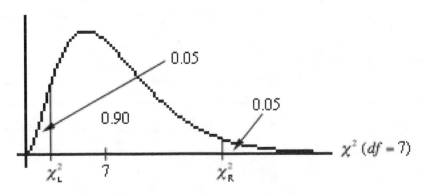

$$\chi_L^2 = inv\chi^2(0.05, 7) \approx 2.167 \quad \text{and} \quad \chi_R^2 = inv\chi^2(0.95, 7) \approx 14.067$$

Endpoints: Now we use these two Chi-Square values to help us find the endpoints of our interval.

$$\text{Left Endpoint} = \sqrt{\frac{(n-1)s^2}{\chi_R^2}} = \sqrt{\frac{7*(1.3007)^2}{14.067}} \approx 0.9175$$

$$\text{Right Endpoint} = \sqrt{\frac{(n-1)s^2}{\chi_L^2}} = \sqrt{\frac{7*(1.3007)^2}{2.167}} \approx 2.3377$$

Interval: The confidence interval is: $\sigma \in (0.9175, \; 2.3377)$

c) We are 90% confident that the true population standard deviation for the rate at which this pump delivers medication to the patient is somewhere between 0.9175 cc/hour and 2.3377 cc/hour.

d) No, if $\sigma \in (0.9175, \; 2.3377)$, then that means that σ could be 2.25 cc/hr. Dividing this by the targeted mean of 20 cc/hr shows us that the population standard deviation could be more than 10% of the targeted mean.

$$\frac{2.25}{20} = 0.1125 = 11.25\% > 10\%$$

HYPOTHESIS TESTS INVOLVING σ: *Determining the Test Statistic and the P-value Logic*

In the last part of the example above, we were trying to see if we were 90% confident that the true population standard deviation was less than 10% of 20 cc/hr. In other words, we wanted to see if we could find strong evidence that the value of σ was less than 2 cc/hr. Based on this alternative wording, it might have been appropriate to perform a hypothesis test rather than to compute a confidence interval. As we have seen in previous sections, the key to performing a hypothesis test is to determine an appropriate test statistic and then to determine how to find the P-value for the hypothesis test.

When testing a claim about the population standard deviation, σ, our null hypothesis will be $H_0 : \sigma = \sigma_0$, where σ_0 represents the claimed value of the population standard deviation.. We will use the test statistic $\chi^2 = \frac{(n-1)s^2}{\sigma_0^2}$. If H_0 is true, then χ^2 will have the Chi-Square distribution with $df = n-1$. Also, if H_0 is true, then we should get a value of s that is close to the value of σ. If these two values are equal, then we get: $\chi^2 = \frac{(n-1)s^2}{\sigma_0^2} = \frac{(n-1)\sigma_0^2}{\sigma_0^2} = n-1$.

From this, we can say that the further we land to the right of $n-1$, the more evidence we have that $\sigma > \sigma_0$. The further we land to the left of $n-1$, the more evidence we have that $\sigma < \sigma_0$.

These facts will be the basis for computing the P-value for hypothesis tests involving, σ. The procedure is summarized in the following procedure box.

Procedure for performing a hypothesis test for a population standard deviation, σ

Requirements: The Chi-Square distribution can be used to find the P-value provided that the population is approximately normally distributed.

Phases: We perform the hypothesis test by completing three phases:

SET UP THE TEST:
- Determine H_o and H_1.
- Decide on the significance level, α.

GATHER AND WEIGH THE EVIDENCE:

- Calculate the test statistic: $\chi^2 = \dfrac{(n-1)s^2}{\sigma_0^2}$ (Use 3 decimal places)

- Find the P-value using χ^2cdf command with $df = n - 1$. (See notes below.)

DECISIONS AND CONCLUSIONS:
- Reject H_o or Do Not Reject H_o.
- State the conclusion of the test in plain language using the words of the application.

Notes about finding the P-value:
- If $H_1 : \sigma > \sigma_0$, then it is a right-tailed test. The P-value is the area to the right of the test statistic.
- If $H_1 : \sigma < \sigma_0$, then it is a left-tailed test. The P-value is the area to the left of the test statistic.
- If $H_1 : \sigma \neq \sigma_0$, then it is a two-tailed test. Find either the area to left or to the right of your test statistic, whichever is smaller. A sketch will make this clear in most cases. The P-value is double the smaller area.

Example 10.9: *Consistency in Commission Income*

A real estate agent has been making a good income for the last 5 years selling homes. However, there is a lot of variability in his income. If the agent sells two homes in a month, he can make as much as $30,000. But, it is also common for the agent to have a month where no homes are sold. In those months, he makes no money. The agent knows that for full-time real estate agents in his city, the mean monthly income is $10,558 with a standard deviation of $12,892. This particular agent is considering starting a family and feels that it is important to reduce the variability in his income. He has heard that people in car sales can make just as much money, but that the monthly income is more consistent. He takes a random

Can a real estate agent achieve a more consistent income by switching to selling cars for a living?

sample of 12 people who sell cars full-time for a living. He looks at the income for a randomly selected month for each of these people. The 12 monthly income amounts, in dollars, from this sample are shown below.

11,052	9,116	14,694	16,581	5,573	13,581	2,521	12,178	13,473	970	4,220	21,677

a) Have the requirements been met for performing a hypothesis test on σ? Explain.

b) Does the data provide enough evidence, at the 10% significance level, to show that the true standard deviation for the monthly income selling cars full-time in this city is less than it is for selling homes?

Solution:

a) We need the sample to have been taken from a normally distributed population. It is difficult to be sure of this with a small sample, but we can use technology to see if it is at least reasonable to believe that the population is normal. The P-value from a StatCrunch normality test on the sample is shown below.

Because the P-value $= 0.7802 > 0.05$, it is a reasonable possibility that this sample was taken from an approximately normally distributed population. We can proceed with the hypothesis test.

Anderson-Darling goodness-of-fit results:

Variable	n	Stat	P-Value
Commission	12	0.22158512	0.7802

b) SET UP THE TEST:

Determine H_o **&** H_1. In hypothesis tests involving σ, we begin with '=' in H_o. We are told that the standard deviation for real estate agents' monthly income is $\sigma = 12,892$. So, we will have $H_0 : \sigma = 12,892$. For H_1, the key phrase is "less than it is for selling homes" which indicates a left-tailed test.

$$H_0 : \sigma = 12,892$$

$$H_1 : \sigma < 12,892$$

Determine the Significance Level. The significance level is given as 10%, so $\alpha = 0.10$. (Thus, we are willing to take up to a 10% risk of making a type I error on this problem.)

GATHER AND WEIGH THE EVIDENCE:

Calculate the Test Statistic. We will use technology to find the needed sample standard deviation. The sample size was 12 and produced $s \approx 6186.85$.

Summary statistics:

Column	n	Std. dev.
Commission	12	6186.8533

$$\chi^2 = \frac{(n-1)s^2}{\sigma_0^2} = \frac{11(6186.85)^2}{(12892)^2} \approx 2.533$$

Calculate the P-value. Because H_1 contains the '<' symbol, this is a left-tailed test. So, we need to find the area to the left of our test statistic. We have $df = n - 1 = 12 - 1 = 11$ for this one.

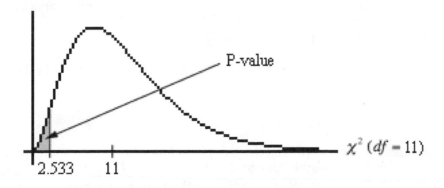

P-value $= \chi^2 cdf (0,\ 2.533,\ 11) \approx 0.0044$.

If the variability in car sales income was the same as for home sales, there would only be a 0.44% chance of getting a test statistic this far to the left. It seems likely that the standard deviation is less than $12,892.

DECISIONS AND CONCLUSIONS:

Reject H_o or Do Not Reject H_o. The P-value tells us that, if we decide to reject H_o, we will be taking a 0.44% risk of making a type I error. Therefore, because the P-value < 0.10, we Reject H_o (acceptable risk of making a type I error).

State the Conclusion in Words. The data does provide enough evidence, at the 10% significance level, to show that true standard deviation for the monthly income selling cars full-time in this city is less than it is for selling homes.

WRAP SESSION: *Comparing the Confidence Interval and the Hypothesis Test*

Example 10.10: *Variation in Action Movie Budgets*

Based on the data from www.the-numbers.com, it is estimated that the mean production budget for all movies of all types is $30,700,901 with a standard deviation of $39,101,021. A film student is interested in investigating if the standard deviation for the budgets of films from the action Genre is different than it is for all types of movies combined. To investigate this, the student randomly selects 16 action movies and records their production budgets. The sample yields a mean of $44,593,750 and a standard deviation of $28,230,727. The student also used technology to perform a normality test on the data and the output from that test is shown below to the right.

Is the amount of variation in action movies different than for all movie genres combined?

a) Using the normality test output to the right, comment on the requirements for finding a confidence interval for the population standard deviation and for performing a hypothesis test involving the population standard deviation.

Anderson-Darling goodness-of-fit results:

Variable	n	Stat	P-Value
Action Budgets	16	0.27738229	0.6038

b) Does the sample data provide enough evidence, at the 5% significance level, to show that the true population standard deviation for action movies is different than the population standard deviation for all movies genres combined?

c) Determine a 95% confidence interval for the true population standard deviation for action movies.

d) Interpret the interval from part (c) in terms of the application.

e) Explain how the confidence interval from part (c) agrees with the decision made in the hypothesis test in part (b).

Solution:

a) For both of the procedures described, we need the sample to have been taken from a normally distributed population. We can use the technology output to decide if it is at least reasonable to believe that the population is normal. Because the P-value $= 0.6038 > 0.05$, it is a reasonable possibility that this sample was taken from an approximately normally distributed population. We can proceed with the hypothesis test and the confidence interval.

b) SET UP THE TEST:

Determine H_o & H_1. In hypothesis tests involving σ, we begin with '=' in H_o. We are told that the standard deviation for the production budgets of all movie types is $\sigma = 39,101,021$. So, we will have $H_0 : \sigma = 39,101,021$. For H_1, the key phrase is "different than the population standard deviation" which indicates a two-tailed test.

$$H_0 : \sigma = 39,101,021$$
$$H_1 : \sigma \neq 39,101,021$$

Determine the Significance Level. The significance level is given as 5%, so $\alpha = 0.05$. (Thus, we are willing to take up to a 5% risk of making a type I error on this problem.)

GATHER AND WEIGH THE EVIDENCE:

Calculate the Test Statistic. The sample size was 16 and produced $s = 28,230,727$.

$$\chi^2 = \frac{(n-1)s^2}{\sigma_0^2} = \frac{15(28,230,727)^2}{(39,101,021)^2} \approx 7.819$$

Calculate the P-value. Because H_1 contains the '$\neq$' symbol, this is a two-tailed test. So, because our test statistic falls on the left side of our sketch, we need to find the area to the left of our test statistic and then double it. We have $df = n - 1 = 16 - 1 = 15$ for this one.

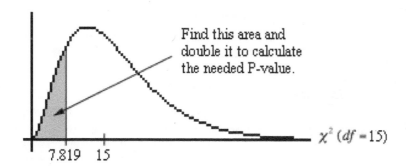

Find this area and double it to calculate the needed P-value.

$\chi^2 (df = 15)$

7.819   15

> **Caution:** *Doubling for two-tailed tests*
>
> When finding the P-value for two tailed tests, you need to double the smaller of the two area on either side of your test statistic. The sketch of the graph should be helpful in determining which area to find. If you ever get a P-value larger than 1, this is a clear indicator that you have done something wrong. Most likely, this has happened because you found the area on the wrong side of your test statistic.

P-value $= 2 \cdot \chi^2 cdf (0, \ 7.819, \ 15) \approx 0.1383$.

This P-value tells us that if the true standard deviation for action movies was really the same as it is for all genres combined, then there would still be a 13.83% chance of getting a test statistic at least as inconsistent with H_o as our test statistic. It seems like there is a reasonable possibility that the true standard deviation for action movies could be the same as the standard deviation for all genres combined.

DECISIONS AND CONCLUSIONS:

Reject H_o or Do Not Reject H_o. The P-value tells us that, if we decide to reject H_o, we will be taking a 13.83% risk of making a type I error. Therefore, because the P-value > 0.05, we Do Not Reject H_o (too high of a risk of making a type I error).

State the Conclusion in Words. The data does not provide enough evidence, at the 5% significance level, to show that true standard deviation for action movies is different than the population standard deviation for all movies genres combined.

c) *Point Estimate*: We were given the sample standard deviation, $s = 28{,}230{,}727$.

χ^2 *values*: Now we need to use technology and $inv\chi^2$ to determine the two values, χ_L^2 and χ_R^2, that trap an area of 0.95 in the middle with equal areas on the outside. We will use the Chi-Square curve with $df = n - 1 = 16 - 1 = 15$.

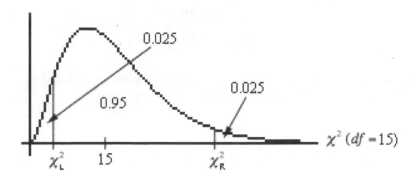

$$\chi_L^2 = inv\chi^2\left(0.025,\ 15\right) \approx 6.262 \quad \text{and} \quad \chi_R^2 = inv\chi^2\left(0.975,\ 15\right) \approx 27.488$$

Endpoints: Now we use these two Chi-Square values to help us find the endpoints of our interval.

$$\text{Left Endpoint} = \sqrt{\frac{(n-1)s^2}{\chi_R^2}} = \sqrt{\frac{15 * (28{,}230{,}727)^2}{27.488}} \approx 20{,}854{,}324$$

$$\text{Right Endpoint} = \sqrt{\frac{(n-1)s^2}{\chi_R^2}} = \sqrt{\frac{15 * (28{,}230{,}727)^2}{6.262}} \approx 43{,}692{,}929$$

Interval: The confidence interval is: $\sigma \in \left(20{,}854{,}324\ ,\ 43{,}692{,}929\right)$

d) We are 95% confident that the true population standard deviation for action movies is somewhere between $20,854,324 and $43,692,929.

e) *In words*: Because we are confident that the population standard deviation for action movies is somewhere between $20,854,324 and $43,692,929, it is a reasonable possibility that the population standard deviation for action movies could be equal to $39,101,021. This means that it is a reasonable possibility that H_o could be true. Therefore, we should not reject H_o. This agrees with the decision from the hypothesis test.

In Symbols: If $\sigma \in \left(20{,}854{,}324\ ,\ 43{,}692{,}929\right) \implies \sigma$ could be 39,101,021. $\implies H_0 : \sigma = 39{,}101{,}021$ could be true. $\implies$ We should not reject H_o. This agrees with the decision from the hypothesis test.

It's time to practice what you have learned with some exercises.

Exercise Set 10.4:

Concept Review: Review the definitions and concepts from this section by filling in the blanks for each of the following.

57) When computing confidence intervals for σ, or when performing hypothesis tests on the value of σ, we use the _____ distribution with df = _____.

58) In order to use the Chi-Square distribution for inferences involving σ, it is important that our sample be taken from a population that is _____ distributed.

59) Because χ^2 curves are _____ rather than _____, we must find two separate Chi-Square values when computing the endpoints of our confidence interval.

60) For two-tailed tests of , we must find either the area to the left or to the right of our test statistic, whichever is _____ . The P-value is _____ the smaller area.

Mechanics: Practice the calculations needed for confidence intervals and hypothesis tests involving σ before working on real world applications.

61) A random sample of size 19 is taken from a population that is normally distributed. The sample produces a standard deviation of 157.26. Determine a 99% confidence interval for the true population standard deviation.

62) A random sample of size 31 is taken from a population that is normally distributed. The sample produces a standard deviation of 2.8033. Determine a 95% confidence interval for the true population standard deviation.

63) A random sample of size 41 is taken from a population that is normally distributed. The sample produces a standard deviation of 5.7709. Determine a 90% confidence interval for the true population standard deviation.

64) A random sample of size 13 is taken from a population that is normally distributed. The sample produces a standard deviation of 2085.4. Determine a 99% confidence interval for the true population standard deviation.

65) A random sample of size 28 is taken from a population that is normally distributed. The sample produces a standard deviation of 9.9448. The hypotheses and significance level for the test are given below.

$$H_0 : \sigma = 15$$
$$H_1 : \sigma < 15 \quad ; \quad \alpha = 0.05$$

a) Compute the value of the test statistic.
b) Determine the P-value for the test.
c) Decide whether or not to Reject H_0.

66) A random sample of size 17 is taken from a population that is normally distributed. The sample produces a standard deviation of 27.177. The hypotheses and significance level for the test are given below.

$$H_0 : \sigma = 25$$
$$H_1 : \sigma > 25 \quad ; \quad \alpha = 0.05$$

a) Compute the value of the test statistic.
b) Determine the P-value for the test.
c) Decide whether or not to Reject H_0.

67) A random sample of size 14 is taken from a population that is normally distributed. The sample produces a standard deviation of 17.095. The hypotheses and significance level for the test are given below.

$$H_0 : \sigma = 18$$
$$H_1 : \sigma \neq 18 \quad ; \quad \alpha = 0.05$$

a) Compute the value of the test statistic.
b) Determine the P-value for the test.
c) Decide whether or not to Reject H_0.

68) A random sample of size 29 is taken from a population that is normally distributed. The sample produces a standard deviation of 0.053358. The hypotheses and significance level for the test are given below.

$$H_0 : \sigma = 0.025$$
$$H_1 : \sigma \neq 0.025 \quad ; \quad \alpha = 0.05$$

a) Compute the value of the test statistic.
b) Determine the P-value for the test.
c) Decide whether or not to Reject H_0.

Applications: Practice the ideas learned in this section within the context of real world applications.

69) A dieter kept track of the number of calories eaten per day over a 4-month period during which the dieter lost 15 pounds. The number of calories eaten per day is shown below together with the technology output of a normality test on the data set.

2028	2357	2301	2317	2700	2254
3271	2983	2159	2048	1742	2488
2071	1568	2094	1927		

Note: $\sum x^2 = 85,225,692$

Anderson-Darling goodness-of-fit results:

Variable	n	Stat	P-Value
Calories	16	0.41504678	0.2946

a) Use the output of the normality test to comment on the requirements for finding a confidence interval for the standard deviation during this 4-month time period.
b) Determine a 95% confidence interval for the true standard deviation for the number of calories eaten per day during this 4-month period.
c) Interpret the interval in terms of the application.
d) During the 1-year prior to going on this diet, this person's daily calorie intake had a standard deviation of 750 calories per day. Can we say with 95% confidence that this person consumed a more consistent number of calories per day while on the diet? Explain using your interval from part (b).

70) A mountain biker keeps track of his cycling data using the app *Bike Tracks* on his phone. He regularly rides the same route near his house. He randomly chose 11 rides and noted the top speed, in miles per hour, for each of the rides. The data is shown below together with the technology output of a normality test on the speeds.

| 38.7 | 39.8 | 38.0 | 40.1 | 39.1 | 37.6 |
| 41.0 | 41.6 | 36.8 | 41.1 | 38.2 | |

Note: $\sum x^2 = 16,990.56$

Anderson-Darling goodness-of-fit results:

Variable	n	Stat	P-Value
Top Speed	11	0.20174682	0.8374

a) Use the output of the normality test to comment on the requirements for finding a confidence interval for the standard deviation of the top speeds for bike rides on this route.
b) Determine a 90% confidence interval for the true standard deviation for the top speeds by this rider on this particular route.
c) Interpret the interval in terms of the application.
d) Can we say with 90% confidence that the population standard deviation for the top speeds for this rider on this route exceeds 1 mph? Explain using your interval from part (b).

71) A computer programmer lived most of her life in San Francisco where the daily high temperature has a mean of about 63.8 $^\circ F$ with a standard deviation of about 10.8 $^\circ F$. When she retired, she moved to Toronto. A systematic random sample from her first year in Toronto yielded the following daily high temperatures, measured in degrees Fahrenheit. The technology output of a normality test on the temperatures is shown as well.

| 30 | 32 | 41 | 54 | 64 | 75 |
| 81 | 79 | 70 | 57 | 46 | 36 |

Note: $\sum x^2 = 40,605$

Anderson-Darling goodness-of-fit results:

Variable	n	Stat	P-Value
Toronto High Temps	12	0.28885097	0.5522

a) Use the output of the normality test to comment on the requirements for performing a hypothesis test for the true standard deviation of the daily high temperatures in Toronto.
b) Does the data provide enough evidence, at the 1% significance level, to show that the true standard deviation of daily high temperatures is higher in Toronto than it is in San Francisco?
c) Suppose this person likes to experience large changes in the weather. Which city is the better fit for this? Explain using your answer to part (b).

72) A recreational poker player typically plays Texas Hold'em in a cash game format. His records reveal that he averages a profit of $42.50 per session with a standard deviation of $221.14. Recently he has decided to try playing in tournaments instead of cash game. His profit, in dollars, from a random sample of 10 tournaments is shown below. The technology output of a normality test on the tournament results is shown as well.

| 5 | -30 | 26 | 217 | 115 |
| -30 | -60 | 136 | 90 | -25 |

Note: $\sum x^2 = 93,636$

Anderson-Darling goodness-of-fit results:

Variable	n	Stat	P-Value
Tournament Profit	10	0.41477319	0.2682

a) Use the output of the normality test to comment on the requirements for performing a hypothesis test for the true standard deviation of the tournament profit amounts.
b) Does the data provide enough evidence, at the 10% significance level, to show that the true standard deviation of this player's tournament profits will differ from the standard deviation of his cash game profits?
c) The means from the two styles of playing poker seem similar. Use the results of your hypothesis test to explain why this player might prefer playing tournament poker rather than cash games.

73) The owner of a diner knows from the receipts that her servers' average tip from dinner customers is $8.57 per table with a standard deviation of $4.75 per table. She has one server who seems to get more complaints than the other servers, but also receives more praise from customers than the other servers. A random sample of 41 receipts for this server yields a mean tip per table of $9.25 with a standard deviation of $5.14.

   a) Comment on the requirements for computing a confidence interval or for performing a hypothesis test for the true standard deviation of the dinner tips for this one server.
   b) Does the data provide enough evidence, at the 5% significance level, to show that the true standard deviation of this server's dinner tips is greater than the standard deviation of the combined tips for all the servers?
   c) Determine a 90% confidence interval for the true standard deviation for the dinner tips received by this server.
   d) Explain how the confidence interval from part (c) agrees with the decision made in the hypothesis test in part (b).
   e) The owner believed that, because of the diverse reviews on this server, this server's tips would have a larger standard deviation than the other servers. Was the owner correct, incorrect, or we can't tell? Explain.

74) A restaurant owner is training a new bartender. When making drinks, the size of a "shot "of alcohol is supposed to be 1.5 ounces. The owner wants the trainee to not only pour the correct amount on average, but to also do so consistently. The owner will feel that the trainee is ready to work unsupervised when the standard deviation of the shots is less than 0.1 ounces. The owner tests the trainee on a random sample of 25 shot pours and finds a mean of 1.52 ounces with a standard deviation of 0.083 ounces.

   a) Comment on the requirements for computing a confidence interval or for performing a hypothesis test for the true standard deviation of the shot pours for this trainee.
   b) Does the data provide enough evidence, at the 1% significance level, to show that the true standard deviation of this trainee's shot pours is less than 0.1 ounces?
   c) Determine a 98% confidence interval for the true standard deviation of this trainee's shot pours.
   d) Explain how the confidence interval from part (c) agrees with the decision made in the hypothesis test in part (b).
   e) What will have to change for this trainee to pass this test and be declared ready?

75) A movie theater has 6 ticket windows. Traditionally they have had customers form 6 lines, one at each window. Under this system, on Friday nights between 6 PM and 9 PM, they had an average customer wait time of 10.37 minutes with a standard deviation of 4.477 minutes. The owner has decided to try switching to a single line system where the person at the front of the line is then directed to the next available ticket window. A random sample of 61 customers had their wait times recorded on a Friday night between 6 PM and 9 PM. The sample had a mean weight time of 9.65 minutes with a standard deviation of 2.85 minutes.

   a) Comment on the requirements for computing a confidence interval or for performing a hypothesis test for the true standard deviation of the Friday night wait times.
   b) Does the data provide enough evidence, at the 10% significance level, to show that the true standard deviation of the Friday night wait times is different for the single line system than it was for the multiple line system?
   c) Determine a 90% confidence interval for the true standard deviation of the single line wait times.
   d) Explain how the confidence interval from part (c) agrees with the decision made in the hypothesis test in part (b).
   e) Would you recommend that the owner stick with the single line system? Why or why not?

76) The songs in Billboard's Hot 100 list for 2014 had a mean duration of 224.83 seconds with a standard deviation of 31.528 seconds. A fan of metal music feels that there is more variation in the style of music that he likes. He takes a random sample of 20 popular metal songs from 2014 and finds a mean duration of 256.3 seconds with a standard deviation of 43.780 seconds.

   a) Comment on the requirements for computing a confidence interval or for performing a hypothesis test for the true standard deviation of the duration of metal songs.
   b) Does the data provide enough evidence, at the 5% significance level, to show that the true standard deviation of the duration of metal songs is different than from the popular songs from the Hot 100 list from 2014?
   c) Determine a 95% confidence interval for the true standard deviation of the duration of metal songs.
   d) Explain how the confidence interval from part (c) agrees with the decision made in the hypothesis test in part (b).
   e) Would you say that this metal music fan was correct in his theory, wrong in his theory, or we can't tell? Explain.

Chapter Problem: Parental Support of College Costs

Does increased parental support for college result in lower grades?

In January 2013, Laura Hamilton of the University of California at Merced released a study about the relationship between parental support for college and students grades. The study was titled "More Is More or More Is Less?" In an article discussing this study printed by *Inside Higher Ed*, it was stated that "the students least likely to excel are those who receive essentially blank checks for college expenses." This research is contrary to the common belief that children of wealthy parents have an advantage at school.

Is the amount of financial support students receive from parents related to the grades the students receive?

A sample of 10,870 college students were asked to provide the amount of financial support their parents gave them last year for college together with their GPA's for that year. The data collected is summarized in the contingency table shown below. (Data below was simulated based on the facts of the Merced study.)

	College GPA			
Support	0.00 thru less than 2.00	2.00 thru less than 3.00	3.00 thru 4.00	Totals
$0 – $3999	651	1180	3420	5251
$4000 – $11,999	517	913	2176	3606
$12,000 and above	300	505	1208	2013
Totals	1468	2598	6804	10,870

a) Does the data provide enough evidence, at the 5% significance level, to show that student GPA's are dependent on the amount of financial support provided by the parents? Show all phases for the appropriate hypothesis test.

b) Comment on the requirements for the test.

c) Based on the sample data, which level of support produced the highest percentage of students in the 3.0 to 4.0 GPA category? Show work.

d) Based on the sample data, which level of support produced the highest percentage of students in the below 2.0 GPA category? Show work.

e) Is it reasonable to believe that the lower grades among those with higher financial support are just the result of random variation in the sample data? Explain.

f) Does this show that financial support from the parents is directly causing the students to perform worse in college? Explain.

g) What other lurking/confounding variables might be contributing to this relationship? Explain.

Chapter 10 - Technology Project

1)   Load the data from Exercise (34), Section 10.2 into StatCrunch.
    A) Write down the null and alternative hypotheses and the significance level for this hypothesis test. Label as steps 1 and 2.
    b) Choose Data > Compute Expression and then in the expression box, enter the expression '760 * p' to compute the expected frequencies. (Don't type the quotes and make sure to use a lower case 'p'.) Enter the name 'Expected' as the column label. Click compute. If you are struggling with this part, then you can just compute all of the expected frequencies by hand and then enter them in yourself.
    c) Adjust the size of the window, so that only the data and the name of the data set are in view. Use "ALT / PrintScreen" to copy the window and then paste it to your report (better yet, use the snipping tool).
    d) Calculate the test statistic and P-value by doing the following. Choose Stat > Goodness of fit > Chi Square Test. Choose appropriate columns for observed and expected and then click calculate.
    e) Use "ALT / PrintScreen" to copy the window and then paste it to your report.
    F) Circle and label steps 3 & 4 on the printout.
    G) Write steps 5 & 6 on the printout.

2) a) Load the data from Exercise (46) from Section 10.3 into StatCrunch.
    B) Write down the null and alternative hypotheses and the significance level for this hypothesis test. Label as steps 1 and 2.
    c) Calculate the test statistic and P-value by doing the following. Choose Stat > Tables > Contingency > With Summary. Select the data columns and indicate the column for the Row labels and then click Next. Check Expected Count and Chi-Square (Contributions) and then click Calculate.
    d) Use "ALT / PrintScreen" to copy the window and then paste it to your report.
    E) Circle and label steps 3 & 4 on the printout.
    F) Write steps 5 & 6 on the printout.

3) In this problem we will be investigating whether or not the results of a rolled die and a flipped coin are independent events or not.
    A) Write out steps 1 & 2 on the printout. Use a 50% sig level. (Aren't we statistical daredevils!)
    b) Run the application "Coin – Dice" which is located in the StatSims folder (This program will not work unless you have downloaded the folder and unzipped it). Enter your name in the name box. Enter 2000 for the number of flips / rolls. Click the FLIP/ROLL button several times to get a feel for what is happening. Click the AUTOMATIC button to complete the 2000 flip / rolls. (Use "ALT / PrintScreen" to copy the window and then paste it to your report when finished.)
    c) Load the data set "Ch 10 – Davis – CoinDice" into StatCrunch.
    d) Replace the zeros in the worksheet with the frequencies from your simulation in part (b) above.
    e) Use a screen capture tool like the "Snipping Tool" (Windows) or "Grab" (Mac) to capture the data entered in the StatCrunch Worksheet. Try to just capture the portion of the screen containing the data and labels. Copy and Paste this screen capture into your report.
    f) Calculate the test statistic and P-value by doing the following. Choose Stat > Tables > Contingency > With Summary. Select the data columns (1 thru 6) and indicate the column for the Row labels and then click Next. Check Expected Count and Chi-Square and then click Calculate.
    g) Use "ALT / PrintScreen" to copy the window and then paste it to your report.
    H) Circle and label steps 3 & 4 on the printout.
    I) Write steps 5 & 6 on the printout.
    J) Fill in the Blanks. In reality, the results of the coin and die do not affect each other. Therefore, H_o is _____ , and in part (H), I _____ H_o. Therefore, I have made a _____.

Chapter 10: Chapter Review

Section 10.1: Introducing the Chi-Square Distribution

- The total area under a χ^2 curve is always equal to 1.
- χ^2 curves are right skewed. They are NOT symmetric.
- χ^2 curves start at zero and extend indefinitely to the right while the height of the curve approaches zero.
- As the degrees of freedom increase, the shape of a χ^2 curve begins to look more and more like a normal curve.
- The mean of a χ^2 curve is equal to its degree of freedom.
- The peak of the curve will occur slightly before the χ^2 value corresponding to the number of degrees of freedom.
- We use $\chi^2 cdf$ find the area under a Chi-Square curve. The structure is:

  $\chi^2 cdf \left(\text{lower boundary}, \text{upper boundary}, df \right)$.

- We use $inv\chi^2$ to find boundaries on a Chi-Square curve. The structure is: $inv\chi^2 \left(\text{area to the left}, df \right)$.
- Because a Chi-Square curve is right-skewed rather than symmetric, we must find the left boundary, χ_L^2, and then right boundary, χ_R^2, separately.

Section 10.2: Chi-Square Goodness-of-Fit Tests

- The null and alternative hypotheses are always stated in words for a Goodness-of-fit test.
- H_o always contains a phrase denoting equals, such as "is the same as".
- H_1 always contains the idea of a difference or change.
- The test statistic is $\chi^2 = \sum \dfrac{(O-E)^2}{E}$, where $df = k-1$, where k is the number of categories in the table.
- Even though the χ^2 test statistic is not a z-score, the individual values of $\dfrac{(O-E)^2}{E}$ can be thought of as similar to z-scores.
- In a χ^2 test, it usually takes a test statistic about 2 times the df to reject H_o.
- Observed frequencies, O's, are the frequencies for each category in the sample.
- Expected frequencies, E's, are the frequencies that we expect to see in each category from the sample if H_o is a true claim.
- $E = n \cdot p$, where p the percentage (or probability) that would apply if H_o is a true claim.
- If no percentages are given to use for the values of p, then determine the values for p by considering what the probability of each category would be if Ho turns out to be true.
- Requirements for a Goodness-of-Fit Test: $E = np \geq 5$ for every category.
- Because of the squaring step used in calculating the test statistic, all goodness-of-fit tests are **right-tailed**, even though the "differs from" wording suggests a two-tailed test.

Section 10.3: Chi-Square Test of Independence

- H_o always contains the idea of independence.
- H_1 always contains the idea of dependence.
- Sometimes the words "associated with" take the place of the words "dependent upon" and "not associated with" replaces "independent of".
- The test statistic is $\chi^2 = \sum \dfrac{(O-E)^2}{E}$, where $df = (r-1)(c-1)$, where r is the number of row categories and c is the number of column categories.
- Expected frequencies are based on the assumption of independence and the Special Multiplication Rule: $P(A \,\&\, B) = P(A) \cdot P(B)$.
- Shortcut formula: $E = \dfrac{R \cdot C}{n}$, R = Row total, C = Column total.
- Requirements for a Goodness-of-Fit Test: $E \geq 5$ for every cell.
- Because of the squaring process, all independence tests are **right-tailed**.

Section 10.4: Inferences for the Population Standard Deviation, σ

- Requirements for both confidence intervals and hypothesis tests involving σ are the same. We must have a normally distributed population.
- The left endpoint of the confidence interval is given by $\sqrt{\dfrac{(n-1)s^2}{\chi_R^2}}$ and the right endpoint is given by $\sqrt{\dfrac{(n-1)s^2}{\chi_L^2}}$.
- Because χ^2 curves are right-skewed rather than symmetric, we must find two separate Chi-Square values χ_L^2 and χ_R^2 to calculate the endpoints of our confidence interval. We can't just use one endpoint to help us find the other one.
- The algebra used to solve our original inequality for σ caused the value of χ_R^2 to end up in the left endpoint and for the value χ_L^2 to end up in the right endpoint.
- For a confidence level of $(1-\alpha) \cdot 100\%$, sketch the Chi-Square curve with $df = n-1$ and use $inv\chi^2$ to determine the two Chi-Square values, χ_L^2 and χ_R^2, that trap are area of $1-\alpha$ in the middle with equal outside areas.
- We are back to symbols for the hypotheses. $H_0 : \sigma = \sigma_0$
- The test statistic is $\chi^2 = \dfrac{(n-1)s^2}{\sigma_0^2}$.
- If $H_1 : \sigma > \sigma_0$, then it is a right-tailed test. The P-value is the area to the right of the test statistic.
- If $H_1 : \sigma < \sigma_0$, then it is a left-tailed test. The P-value is the area to the left of the test statistic.
- If $H_1 : \sigma \neq \sigma_0$, then it is a two-tailed test. Find either the area to left or to the right of your test statistic, whichever is smaller. A sketch will make this clear in most cases. The P-value is double the smaller area.

Chapter 10 – Review Exercises

1) A professional football player grew up in a rural area in the Midwest and now lives in a large city where he plays as a running back. The distribution of the education level of people in the city where he plays football is shown below.

No High School Diploma	High School Only	Some College	Bachelor's Degree or Higher
16.58%	34.54%	27.87%	21.01%

The education level for a recent random sample of 400 people from his hometown is shown in the table below.

No High School Diploma	High School Only	Some College	Bachelor's Degree or Higher
32	219	91	58

a) Does the data show, at the 10% significance level, that the distribution of education levels in his home town is different than in the city where he plays football?
b) Comment on the requirements.
c) Discuss the possibility that you have made a type I error or a type II error.
d) Which education category provided the most evidence against H_0? Explain.

2) A gambler is monitoring a craps game in a casino and keeping track of the results of the dice he rolls. After observing 185 rolls, he has observed the following frequencies for the listed sums:

Sum:	2,3,12	7,11	4,5,6,8,9,10
Frequency:	24	51	110

a) Does the data presented above provide enough evidence, at the 1% significance level, to show that the dice are not producing these sums in the proper proportions?
b) Comment on the requirements.
c) Explain what it would mean in terms of this application and evidence for the gambler to make a type I error.
d) Explain what it would mean in terms of this application and evidence for the gambler to make a type II error.

3) In December 2003, 1150 randomly selected people were asked: "Do you think it would be a good idea or a bad idea to ban all religious holidays from schools in the U.S.?" Their responses are shown below, cross-classified with their political affiliation.

	Dem	Rep	Ind	Totals
Good Idea	62	36	18	116
Bad Idea	417	446	103	966
Good & Bad	21	10	5	36
Not Sure	15	15	2	32
Totals	515	507	128	1150

a) Does the data provide enough evidence, at the 5% significance level, to show that people's opinion on this matter is dependent on their political affiliation?
b) Comment on the requirements.
c) Show the work for the calculation of the expected frequency for the Democrat and Good Idea cell using the formula $E = np$ and the assumption that H_0 is true.

4) A January 2012 story in the Vancouver Sun had the headline "Android user more likely to have sex on first date." The story then went on to report details of a study of Canadian singles. Among other things, the survey asked respondents what type of phone they had and whether or not they had ever had sex on a first date. The data below is based on that study.

	Android	iPhone	BlackBerry	Totals
Sex on first date	185	311	51	547
No sex on first date	150	314	57	521
Totals	335	625	108	1068

a) Does the data provide enough evidence, at the 5% significance level to show that the type of phone a person has is dependent on whether or not the person has had sex on the first date?
b) Comment on the requirements.
c) Would you say that the headline was justified? Explain.

5) During the 2014-2015 skiing and snowboarding season, the mean price of a lift ticket in the U.S. was $65.81 with a standard deviation of $25.91. A California snowboarder is confident that the mean price for a ticket is higher in California, but they are not sure about the standard deviation of the prices. The snowboarder obtained a random sample of 12 California resorts and found the lift ticket prices. The California sample data is shown below. (National and California data is based off of information from OnTheSnow.com.) The output from a StatCrunch normality test is shown as well.

49	95	64	89	69	67
39	80	124	59	120	58

Note: $\sum x^2 = 77,235$

Anderson-Darling goodness-of-fit results:

Variable	n	Stat	P-Value
CA Prices	12	0.36099647	0.3842

a) Use the output of the normality test to comment on the requirements for computing a confidence interval or for performing a hypothesis test for the true standard deviation of the California lift ticket prices.
b) Does the data provide enough evidence, at the 5% significance level, to show that the true standard deviation of the California lift ticket prices is different than the standard deviation for the prices for the whole U.S.?
c) Determine a 95% confidence interval for the true standard deviation of the California lift ticket prices.
d) Interpret the interval in terms of the application.
e) Explain how the confidence interval from part (c) agrees with the decision made in the hypothesis test in part (b).
f) Based on the results from the hypothesis test, is the true standard deviation for California lift ticket prices the same as for the U.S., different than for the U.S., or we can't tell for sure? Explain.

6) A candy manufacturer produces bags of salt water taffy for sale in coastal gift stores. The bags are labeled as containing about 40 pieces of taffy. The company will be happy with the consistency in the filling process as long as the standard deviation is not larger than 1.25 pieces of taffy per bag. A random sample of 23 bags of their salt water taffy was taken. The number of pieces of taffy in each bag was counted and the results are listed in the following table.

45	40	42	38	40	42
40	43	38	39	41	40
42	40	38	42	41	41
44	40	37	41	42	

Note: $\sum x^2 = 38,176$

Anderson-Darling goodness-of-fit results:

Variable	n	Stat	P-Value
Taffy Count	23	0.41608962	0.3057

a) Use the output of the normality test to comment on the requirements for computing a confidence interval or for performing a hypothesis test for the true standard deviation of the number of pieces of taffy per bag.
b) Does the data provide enough evidence, at the 1% significance level, to show that the true standard deviation of the number of pieces of taffy per bag is larger than 1.25 pieces?
c) Determine a 98% confidence interval of the true standard deviation of the number of pieces taffy per bag.
d) Interpret the interval in terms of the application.
e) Explain how the confidence interval from part (c) agrees with the decision made in the hypothesis test in part (b).
f) Based on the results from the hypothesis test, is the true standard deviation for the number of pieces per bag at an acceptable level, at an unacceptable level, or we can't tell? Explain.

Chapter 11 – Two Population Studies

In many of the hypothesis tests performed in the previous sections, we were testing a claim about how the mean (or proportion) of one data set compared to the mean (or proportion) of some other comparable population. We compared the mean gas price in the San Francisco Bay area to the statewide average in California. We compared the average weight of tomatoes grown with and without a growth supplement. We compared the passing rates of statistics students who do their computer projects with the passing rates of those who do not. In such problems, we should ask the following questions: How is it that we know the population mean for the whole state of California, but yet we do not know the population mean for the Bay Area? Isn't the Bay Area part of California? Why would someone growing tomatoes keep track of the weights of all of their tomatoes last year? Is it fair to compare last year to this year and give the credit for any change to the growth supplement? Maybe this year had better weather for tomato growth. Was the research that shows the population proportion of those who pass statistics classes obtained during the same semester as the data for those not doing computer projects? If not, is that a fair comparison.

In any of the examples mentioned above, it would be much more realistic to assume we could get sample values from each of the two populations in question rather than having a census and thus a population mean (or proportion) from one of them. In this chapter we will explore inferential techniques for comparing the means or proportions of two populations based on information obtained from samples from those populations. We will be looking at both confidence intervals and hypothesis tests. There are many different methods that can be explored on this topic. We will focus on three of the most commonly used hypothesis tests. We will explore these ideas in the following sections:

Section 11.1	Inferences from Paired Samples
Section 11.2	Inferences from Independent Samples
Section 11.3	Two-Sample Inferences for Proportions

Section 11.1 - Inferences from Paired Samples

In many situations where we are interested in comparing the means of two populations, the populations are closely related in some manner. When this is the case, it is often true that we can choose a single sample and use it to obtain the sample data we need to study both populations. We do this by obtaining two pieces of data from each sampled item. By collecting data in this fashion, we are creating a natural pairing with each piece of sample data from one population with each piece of sample data from the other population. So while we only selected one random sample, we used it to get two paired samples from the two populations of interest. The situations listed below are all good candidates for using this paired sample technique.

Testing subjects reaction time before and after they consume alcohol.

Comparing the weight of people before and after a New Year's weight loss resolution.

Comparing the writing ability of students before and after they take a composition class.

We will explore the examples listed above and many others as we work through this section. Let's jump right in and look at the study involving reaction time before and after alcohol consumption.

Example 11.1:

A researcher is interested in the effects of alcohol on reaction time. She obtains a random sample of 16 people and tests their reaction time by having them place their hand on a table near a button. When they hear an audio signal, they are to lift their hand off the table and press the button as quickly as possible. The time from the signal to the pressing of the button is measured. The group is then asked to consume 4 beers over a 90-minute time interval and then the reaction time test is repeated. The researcher is hoping to establish that excessive alcohol consumption has an adverse effect on reaction time. The reaction times for the 16 subjects before and after the alcohol are shown below. The data is paired, so the times above and below each other are for the same person. The times are measured in milliseconds. 250 milliseconds equal one fourth of a second.

Before beers	221	124	259	184	216	223	208	136
After beers	244	143	274	165	238	243	251	123

Before beers	178	198	215	229	288	165	237	161
After beers	189	198	225	242	295	221	264	235

a) Perform a hypothesis test, at the 5% significance level, to see if we can conclude that people, on average, react slower after drinking four beers in 90 minutes.

b) Comment on the requirements.

Solution:

a) Because this is a hypothesis test, we will carry out the familiar 6 step process, making adjustments as necessary to adapt to our current situation.

STEP 1: Determine H_o & H_1. A key change in this step is that neither hypothesis will contain any specific numbers. Rather, the hypotheses will make statements about the relative size of the two population means in question. Also, let's say population 1 is the reaction times before beer and population 2 is the reaction times after beer. The key phrase for setting up the hypotheses is "conclude that people, on average, react slower after drinking four beers." Reacting slower means that the reaction time before the beers is shorter than the reaction time after the beers. This idea needs to be reflected in our statement of the alternative hypothesis. So we get:

$$H_o : \mu_1 = \mu_2$$
$$H_1 : \mu_1 < \mu_2$$

Note 1: When we do two population problems, it is common to use numbering subscripts to reference which values go with which populations. We stated above that population 1 is the reaction times before beer and population 2 is the reaction times after beer.

STEP 2: The significance level is given as 5%, so $\alpha = 0.05$.

STEP 3: Because we are interested in comparing the means of the two populations, it makes sense that we would start gathering evidence by comparing the two sample means. However, we want to take advantage of the fact that the data comes to us in pairs. To do this, we will make a new set of data consisting of the differences between the before and after times for the subjects. The new data set is shown in the table that follows.

Before times (x)	After times (y)	Differences ($d = x - y$)
221	244	-23
124	143	-19
259	274	-15
184	165	19
216	238	-22
223	243	-20
208	251	-43
136	123	13
178	189	-11
198	198	0
215	225	-10
229	242	-13
288	295	-7
165	221	-56
237	264	-27
161	235	-74

Note 2: A negative difference represents a slower reaction time after alcohol for the subject, a positive difference represents a fast reaction time for the subject, and a difference of zero means that the subject had the same reaction time.

Because most of the reaction times are negative, we definitely have some evidence that the alcohol is slowing down people's reaction times. However, we need to know if it is enough evidence to show that, on average, people have slower reaction times after consuming alcohol. To work in this direction, we next compute the average of these sample differences. As we work further, it will probably be useful to know the standard deviation of the sample differences as well. The screen shots below show the work on the TI-84 to find the desired quantities.

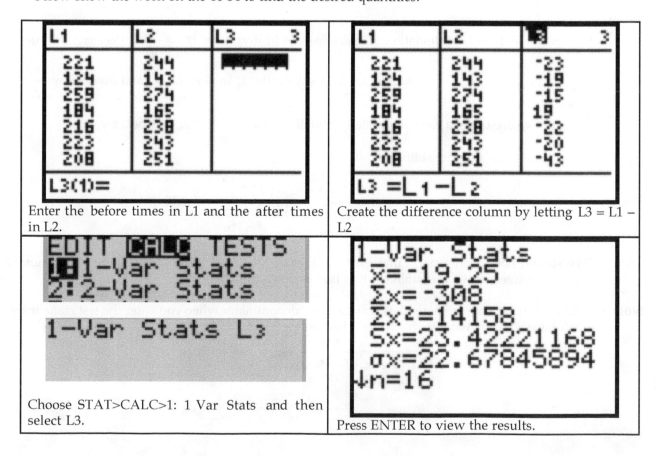

Enter the before times in L1 and the after times in L2.

Create the difference column by letting L3 = L1 − L2

Choose STAT>CALC>1: 1 Var Stats and then select L3.

Press ENTER to view the results.

So, the mean and the standard deviation for the difference are:

$$\bar{d} = -19.25 \text{ and } s_d \approx 23.422$$

Note 3:   Despite the fact that the calculator describes the results as $\bar{x}$ and s, we know that this sample data represented differences, d, so we use $\bar{d}$ and s_d.

Looking at the mean of the sample differences, we see that the value is negative. So we know that, in our sample, people reacted faster, on average, before consuming the beer than they did after. This provides some evidence that beer slows people average reaction time, but we need to compute our test statistic and eventually our p-value to see if the difference is significant enough to show that the same relationship exists in the general population.

The pattern in all of the test statistics (involving means) that we have computed is shown below.

$$\text{test stat} = \frac{(\text{sample value}) - (\text{expected value})}{(\text{standard deviation of sample value})}$$

For this type of test we will use the following:

Sample value: $\bar{d}$

Expected Value: The words expected value imply that we would use the difference we expect to see if H_o is true. So we will use 0. This is because, if the equals part of H_o is true, then we expect $\mu_1 = \mu_2$ and thus we would expect to see no difference in the average reaction time.

Standard deviation: Ideally we would divide by $\sigma_{\bar{d}} \approx \dfrac{\sigma_d}{\sqrt{n}}$. Because σ is usually not available, we will substitute s_d in place of σ_d and divided by $\dfrac{s_d}{\sqrt{n}}$.

Because we are using a sample standard deviation, our test statistic will be a t-value.

So our test statistic is:

$$t = \frac{\bar{d} - 0}{s_d / \sqrt{n}} = \frac{-19.25}{23.422 / \sqrt{16}} \approx -3.288$$

We should note at this point that, with a t value below -3, this seems like a very unusually big average difference, so it is unlikely that it is the result of chance.

Note 4:   Make sure that you use parentheses around the denominator when you enter the test statistic into your calculator. This is what it should look like on the TI-84:

```
-19.25/(23.422/√
(16))
            -3.287507472
```

STEP 4:   As noted in step 3, because we are using a sample standard deviation, our test statistic is a t-value. If the values of $\overline{d}$ are normally distributed (we will investigate this in part b), then our test statistic will have the t-distribution with $df = n-1$.

Because our sample size is 16, we get $df = n-1 = 16-1 = 15$.

We see from H_1 that this is a left-tailed test. So we need to find the area to the left of our test statistic, $t \approx -3.288$, under the t-curve with 15 degrees of freedom.

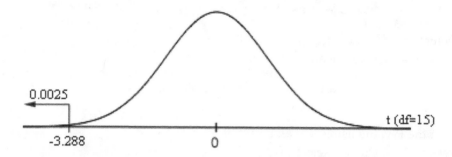

Using the TI-84 to find the area to the right we get: $tcdf(-\infty, -3.288, 15) \approx 0.0025$
So, our p-value ≈ 0.0025.

STEP 5:   We see that our p-value is very small, certainly smaller than our significance level. Therefore, with an acceptably small risk of making a type I error, we Reject H_o.

STEP 6:   We had enough evidence, at the 5% significance level, to show that people, on average, react slower after drinking four beers in 90 minutes.

b) To calculate the p-value used in step 4, we need to know that the possible value of $\overline{d}$ are approximately normally distributed. The rules are the same for any sample average, whether we choose to call it $\overline{x}$ or $\overline{d}$ is irrelevant. Because $15 \le n = 16 < 30$, we must hope that the differences in the population are not severely skewed.

The steps taken in this example are summarized in the following procedure:

Procedure for performing the paired t-test for two population means from dependent samples:

Requirements:

1) The samples must consist of naturally paired data.

2) The differences must meet at least one of the following:
   a) Sample size needs to be large ($n \geq 30$)
   b) The differences in the population need to be normally distributed.
   c) $15 \leq n < 30$ and the population differences are not severely skewed.

Steps:

1) Determine H_o and H_1.
2) Decide on the significance level, α.
3) Calculate the test statistic (Use 3 decimal places): $t = \dfrac{\bar{d}}{s_d / \sqrt{n}}$
4) Find the P-value using tcdf and $df = n - 1$
5) Reject H_o or Do Not Reject H_o.
6) State the conclusion of the test in words.

CONFIDENCE INTERVALS:

We can also use the ideas explored so far to find a confidence interval for the value of the difference between the two population means, $\mu_1 - \mu_2$.

The typical formula for a confidence interval takes the form:

(Sample Value) $\pm$ (z-score)(Standard Deviation of Sample Value)

In the paired sample case this would be: $\bar{d} \pm z^* \dfrac{\sigma_d}{\sqrt{n}}$

Of course, we will switch from σ to s, so this formula becomes: $\bar{d} \pm t^* \dfrac{s_d}{\sqrt{n}}$

This new formula and the procedure that goes with it are summarized as follows:

> **Procedure for calculating a paired t-interval for the difference between two population means** $(\mu_1 - \mu_2)$ **from dependent samples:**
>
> **Requirements:**
>
>   1) The samples must consist of naturally paired data.
>
>   2) The differences must meet at least one of the following:
>   a) Sample size needs to be large ($n \geq 30$)
>   b) The differences in the population need to be normally distributed.
>   c) $15 \leq n < 30$ and the population differences are not severely skewed.
>
> **Steps:**
>
>   1) Calculate the paired differences, d, from the sample data.
>   2) Calculate the mean and standard deviation of the sample differences, if they are not given.
>   3) For a confidence level of $1 - \alpha$, use the t-table to find t^* with $df = n - 1$
>
>   4) The confidence interval for $(\mu_1 - \mu_2)$ is given by $\bar{d} \pm t^* \dfrac{s_d}{\sqrt{n}}$

Let's try this out by returning to the reaction time example and looking at it as a confidence interval rather than a hypothesis test.

Example 11.2:

A researcher is interested in the effects of alcohol on reaction time. She obtains a random sample of 16 people and tests their reaction time by having them place their hand on a table near a button. When they hear an audio signal, they are to lift their hand off the table and press the button as quickly as possible. The time from the signal to the pressing of the button is measured. The group is then asked to consume 4 beers over a 90-minute time interval and then the reaction time test is repeated. The reaction times for the 16 subjects before and after the alcohol are shown below. The data is paired, so the times above and below each other are for the same person. The times are measured in milliseconds. 250 milliseconds equal one fourth of a second.

Before beers	221	124	259	184	216	223	208	136
After beers	244	143	274	165	238	243	251	123

Before beers	178	198	215	229	288	165	237	161
After beers	189	198	225	242	295	221	264	235

a) Compute a 90% confidence interval for the difference between the average reaction times, $\mu_1 - \mu_2$, of all people before and after drinking 4 beers in 90 minutes.

b) Interpret the interval in terms of the application.

c) Explain how the interval obtained in this problem agrees with the decision reached in the hypothesis test in the previous example.

Solution:

a) Much of the work of this problem has already been done for us in the previous example. We have computed the needed differences along with the mean and standard deviation of those differences. We need only find our t-value and then we can start into the formula.

Because we are asked to find a 90% confidence interval, the area in the middle will be 0.90. That leaves 0.10 remaining and when we split that between the two tails, we get an area in the tail of 0.05. We then look that up using df = $16 - 1 = 15$ and we get the value: $t_{0.05} = 1.753$.

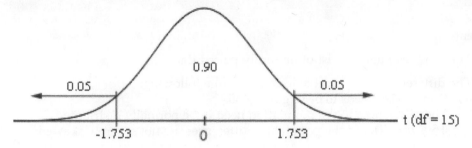

With that, we are ready to jump into the formula:

$$\bar{d} \pm t^* \frac{s_d}{\sqrt{n}} = -19.25 \pm 1.753 \frac{23.422}{\sqrt{16}} \approx -19.25 \pm 10.26 \Rightarrow \mu_1 - \mu_2 \in (-29.51, \ -8.99)$$

b)   A straight forward interpretation would be: "I am 90% confident that difference between the mean reaction time before drinking and after drinking alcohol is somewhere between –29.51 milliseconds and –8.99 milliseconds."

Note 1:   This interpretation follows the pattern we learned in chapter 8, but it is not very good. The negative is confusing and it is not clearly stated whether the alcohol increased or decreased the average reaction time. So an improved interpretation would be:

"I am 90% confident that the average reaction time after drinking 4 beers in 90 minutes is somewhere between 8.99 and 29.51 milliseconds slower than the average reaction time before the alcohol was consumed."

Note 2:   We know that the average reaction time is slower after alcohol because $\mu_1 - \mu_2$ will only come out negative if $\mu_1 < \mu_2$.

c)   If $\mu_1 - \mu_2$ is somewhere between –29.51 and –8.99, then we know that $\mu_1 - \mu_2$ is negative. If $\mu_1 - \mu_2$ is negative, then it must be that μ_1 is smaller than μ_2. This would suggest that $H_a : \mu_1 < \mu_2$ is true and that $H_o : \mu_1 = \mu_2$ is a false. If H_o is false, then it should be rejected, and that is in fact what we decided to do in our hypothesis test in the previous example. In symbols:

If $\mu_1 - \mu_2 \in (-29.51, \ -8.99) \Rightarrow \mu_1 - \mu_2 < 0 \Rightarrow \mu_1 < \mu_2 \Rightarrow H_1 : \mu_1 < \mu_2$ is true and $H_o : \mu_1 = \mu_2$ is false $\Rightarrow$ Reject H_o

---

WRAP SESSION:

Let's practice these ideas with one more example.

Example 11.3:

A doctor wants to conduct a study to determine if there is a difference between the average weights of people who make a new year's resolution to lose weight one year after they begin their weight loss efforts. She obtained a random sample of 24 people that were making weight loss resolutions and weighed them on Jan 1, 2007. She weighed the same people again on Jan 1, 2008. The paired weights of the people are shown in the tables below.

Jan 1, 2007	221	271	277	196	252	266	239	130
Jan 1, 2008	226	270	265	194	271	245	227	120

Jan 1, 2007	159	235	212	190	234	183	238	198
Jan 1, 2008	153	245	212	201	217	194	238	192

Jan 1, 2007	174	201	171	194	182	242	202	217
Jan 1, 2008	170	194	177	183	199	224	195	214

Note: $\sum d^2 = 2816$

a) Comment on the requirements for conducting a hypothesis test or computing a confidence interval involving the before and after weights.

b) Does the data provide enough evidence, at the 5% significance level, to show that there will be a difference between the average weights of people at the time of their resolutions and one year later?

c) Determine a 95% confidence interval for the difference between the average weights of people at the time of their resolutions and one year later.

d) Interpret the interval in terms of the application.

e) Explain how the interval obtained in part (C) agrees with the decision reached in the hypothesis test from part (b).

Solution:

a) This is naturally paired data in that we have the weights for each person before and after the year of the weight loss resolution. Because $15 \leq n = 24 < 30$, we must hope that the weight differences in the population are not severely skewed.

Note 1: One way to check that the population weight differences are not severely skewed would be to make a dotplot of boxplot for the sample differences and check them for severe skewness or outliers.

b) This sounds like a hypothesis test for paired data, so let's run through the 6-step process.

STEP 1: The key phrase here is "difference between the average weights of people at the time of their resolutions and one year later". Because the word difference does not indicate a direction, this will be a two-tailed test. Let population 1 be the weights before beginning a weight loss attempt and population 2 be the weights 1 year later. The hypotheses are as follows.

$$H_o : \mu_1 = \mu_2$$
$$H_1 : \mu_1 \neq \mu_2$$

STEP 2: $\alpha = 0.05$. We are willing to take up to a 5% risk of making a type I error.

STEP 3:   Because the test statistic formula is $t = \dfrac{\overline{d}}{s_d/\sqrt{n}}$, we need to find the difference between the 2007 weights and the 2008 weights. After that, we can use the TI-84 to find the mean and standard deviation of these differences. The table for the difference is shown below followed by the mean and standard deviation.

2007 Weight (x)	2008 Weight (y)	Differences ($d = x - y$)
221	226	-5
271	270	1
277	265	12
196	194	2
252	271	-19
266	245	21
239	227	12
130	120	10
159	153	6
235	245	-10
212	212	0
190	201	-11
234	217	17
183	194	-11
238	238	0
198	192	6
174	170	4
201	194	7
171	177	-6
194	183	11
182	199	-17
242	224	18
202	195	7
217	214	3

$$\overline{d} \approx 2.417 \text{ and } s_d \approx 10.786$$

So our test statistic becomes: $t = \dfrac{\overline{d}}{s_d/\sqrt{n}} = \dfrac{2.417}{10.786/\sqrt{24}} \approx 1.098$

Note 2:   The value $\sum d^2 = 2816$ was given to check your data entry on the TI-84.

I don't expect this test statistic to lead to rejection, but let's check the p-value.

STEP 4:   The sample size is 24, so we get $df = n - 1 = 23$. This is a two-tailed test, so we need to find the area in the tail beyond our test statistic and then double it.

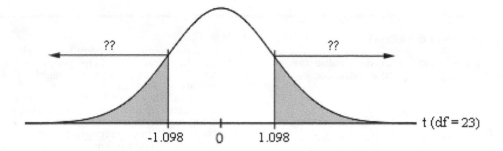

Using the calculator we get: p-value = $2 * tcdf(1.098, \infty, 23) \approx 0.2836$

So, if we decide to Reject H_o, then we would be taking a 28.36% risk of making a type I error. This is too high, so we:

STEP 5:   Do Not Reject H_o (too risky)

STEP 6:   There was not enough evidence, at the 5% significance level, to show that there will be a difference between the average weights of people at the time of their resolutions and one year later.

c)   Because we are asked to find a 95% confidence interval, the area in the middle will be 0.95. That leaves 0.05 remaining and when we split that between the two tails, we get an area in the tail of 0.025. We then look that up using df = 24 – 1 = 23 and we get the value: $t_{0.025} = 2.069$.

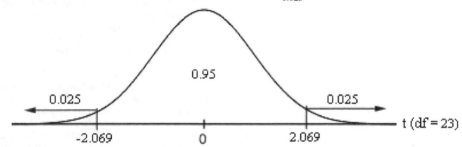

With that, we are ready to jump into the formula:

$$\bar{d} \pm t^* \frac{s_d}{\sqrt{n}} = 2.417 \pm 2.069 \frac{10.786}{\sqrt{24}} \approx 2.417 \pm 4.555 \Rightarrow \mu_1 - \mu_2 \in (-2.138,\ 6.972)$$

d)   A negative difference represents a weight gain and a positive difference represents a weight loss. So we get:

"I am 95% confident that the difference between the average weights of people at the time of their resolutions and one year later is somewhere between 2.138 lbs. gained and 6.972 lbs. lost."

e)   If $\mu_1 - \mu_2$ is somewhere between –2.138 and 6.972, then $\mu_1 - \mu_2$ could be zero. If $\mu_1 - \mu_2$ could be zero, then μ_1 could be equal to μ_2. This would suggest that $H_o : \mu_1 = \mu_2$ could be a true statement. If it could be true, then it should not be rejected and that is in fact what we decided in our hypothesis test in part (b). In symbols:

If $\mu_1 - \mu_2 \in (-2.138,\ 6.972) \Rightarrow \mu_1 - \mu_2$ could be 0 $\Rightarrow \mu_1$ could equal $\mu_2 \Rightarrow H_o : \mu_1 = \mu_2$ could be true $\Rightarrow$ Do Not Reject H_o

Exercise Set 11.1

(1-2) Fill in the blanks for each of the following.

1) A sample contains paired data if each data value for one variable naturally _____ to a value for the other variable.

2) $\mu_1 - \mu_2 < 0 \Rightarrow \mu_1$ is _____ than μ_2.

   $\mu_1 - \mu_2 > 0 \Rightarrow \mu_1$ is _____ than μ_2.

(3-6) a) Calculate the value of the test stat.
       b) Find the P-value.
       c) State whether or not you would reject H_o if the significance level was 5%.

3) $H_o : \mu_1 = \mu_2$;
   $H_1 : \mu_1 > \mu_2$

   $n = 12$, $\bar{d} = 14.25$, $s_d = 31.185$

4) $H_o : \mu_1 = \mu_2$;
   $H_1 : \mu_1 < \mu_2$

   $n = 19$, $\bar{d} = -5.861$, $s_d = 7.8515$

5) $H_o : \mu_1 = \mu_2$;
   $H_1 : \mu_1 \neq \mu_2$

   $n = 40$, $\bar{d} = -22.88$, $s_d = 61.007$

6) $H_o : \mu_1 = \mu_2$;
   $H_1 : \mu_1 > \mu_2$

   $n = 26$, $\bar{d} = 7.832$, $s_d = 35.822$

7) A pharmaceutical company has developed a new drug that they feel will lower the level of bad cholesterol in patients who take it. They obtained a random sample of 14 patients who had dangerously high levels of bad cholesterol. They measured their cholesterol levels before they started treatment with the drug and measured it again 4 months later. The paired results are shown below.

Before	After	Before	After
172	165	148	114
153	120	150	97
147	133	193	129
183	166	181	118
184	95	174	118
146	102	136	79
130	94	187	96

Note: $\sum d^2 = 39,472$

a) Does the data show, at the 5% significance level, that the drug will lower, on average, the level of bad cholesterol in patients who take it?
b) Compute a 90% confidence interval for the difference in the mean levels of bad cholesterol before and after the treatment.
c) Interpret the interval in terms of the application.
d) Explain how the interval from part (b) agrees with the decision reached in part (a).
e) Comment on the requirements.

8) A pharmaceutical company has developed a new drug that they feel will help people who suffer from insomnia get more sleep per night. They obtained a random sample of 18 patients who suffer from insomnia. They recorded the number of hours sleep for the patients on two randomly selected nights. For one of the nights, they were given a placebo and on the other night they were given the drug. The paired results are shown below.

Placebo	Drug	Placebo	Drug
5.5	7.2	4.2	5.6
5.6	7.1	4.5	6.3
3.8	4.9	5.5	5.3
3.4	5.1	5.1	5.4
5.4	6.0	5.0	5.7
4.6	3.4	3.6	5.1
3.9	6.1	4.7	5.8
5.7	6.2	3.1	7.6
4.2	5.7	4.7	5.0

Note: $\sum d^2 = 48$

a) Does the data show, at the 1% significance level, that the drug will increase, on average, the number of hours of sleep per night for patients who take it?
b) Compute a 98% confidence interval for the difference in the mean number of hours of sleep with and without the drug.
c) Interpret the interval in terms of the application.
d) Explain how the interval from part (b) agrees with the decision reached in part (a).
e) Comment on the requirements.

9) The Pebble Beach Pro-Am golf tournament is actually held on three golf courses. The two less famous courses used are called Poppy Hills and Spyglass Hill. The paired scores for the Poppy Hills (PH – population 1) course and the Spyglass Hill (SH – population 2) course are shown below for a random sample of 12 pro golfers during the 2008 event.

PH	SH	PH	SH
74	69	71	75
71	69	76	73
74	70	75	74
71	71	73	74
74	72	76	78
75	72	76	78

Note: $\sum d^2 = 93$

a) Does the data show, at the 10% significance level, that there is a difference in average score at the two courses for professional players?
b) Compute a 90% confidence interval for the difference in the mean scores for pros at the two golf courses.
c) Interpret the interval in terms of the application.
d) Explain how the interval from part (b) agrees with the decision reached in part (a).
e) Comment on the requirements.
f) In the decision in part (a), did we make a type I error, a type II error, or a correct decision? Explain.

10) The U.S. Open golf event is generally played on very difficult golf courses. To increase the difficulty level, they don't water the greens during the tournament. This should make the course become more difficult during each round of play. The paired scores for a random sample of 16 players during Rd 1 (Pop 1) and Rd 2 (Pop 2) of the 2007 event are shown in the table below.

Rd. 1	Rd. 2	Rd. 1	Rd. 2	Rd. 1	Rd. 2
69	69	72	72	71	76
72	72	71	74	71	74
73	72	76	74	72	72
72	80	73	73	71	73
73	75	73	81	72	73

Note: $\sum d^2 = 185$

a) Does the data provide enough evidence, at the 1% significance level, to show that the average score for all the players was lower in Round 1 than Round 2 that year?
b) Compute a 98% confidence interval for the difference in the mean scores for all players during round 1 and round 2 of that event.
c) Interpret the interval in terms of the application.
d) Explain how the interval from part (b) agrees with the decision reached in part (a).
e) Comment on the requirements.
f) In the decision in part (a), did we make a type I error, a type II error, or a correct decision? Explain.

11) A large timeshare company in Hawaii noticed that they seemed to be selling fewer units than in the past. At the end of a slow summer month, the company decided to test out a new incentive plan. They offered bonuses to any of their sales associates who produced an increase in sales the following month. After the end of the first incentive month, they randomly selected the records for 31 of their sales associates and compared the number of units sold in the month prior to the bonus plan (Population 1) to the number of units sold during the first month of the plan (Population 2). The paired sample produced the following statistics.

$$n = 31 \ , \ \bar{d} \approx -0.226 \ , \ s_d \approx 1.820$$

a) Does the data provide enough evidence, at the 5% significance level, to show that the average number of units sold for all the sales personnel was higher the month after the incentive plan than they were the month before the plan?
b) Compute a 90% confidence interval for the difference in average sales for all the personnel the month before the incentive plan and the month after the plan.
c) Interpret the interval in terms of the application.
d) Explain how the interval from part (b) agrees with the decision reached in part (a).
e) Comment on the requirements.
f) If the true difference between the means was $\mu_1 - \mu_2 = 0.53$, then did we make a type I error, a type II error, or a correct decision? Explain.

12) The author of a poker book wanted to show that his book could improve the performance of most self-taught poker players. He obtained a random sample of 46 poker players who had never read a poker book, but played poker on a regular basis. He had them record their profit for 100 hours of play. If they lost money, then they would record that as a negative amount. He then had them read his book and attempt to employ the strategies at the poker table. He had them record the profit (or loss) for the next 100 hours of play after having read the book. The paired sample produced the following statistics. The profits/losses prior to reading the book are population 1 and those after reading the book are population 2.

$$n = 46 \ , \ \bar{d} \approx -\$68.27 \ , \ s_d \approx \$163.88$$

a) Does the data provide enough evidence, at the 5% significance level, to show that players, on average, will do better after having read the book?
b) Compute a 90% confidence interval for the difference in average profit for all self-taught players who read this book.
c) Interpret the interval in terms of the application.
d) Explain how the interval from part (b) agrees with the decision reached in part (a).
e) Comment on the requirements.
f) If the true difference between the means was $\mu_1 - \mu_2 = -\$30.75$, then did we make a type I error, a type II error, or a correct decision? Explain.

13) Several sections of an introductory Algebra class are being taught with the aid of computerized instruction. Students are given a quiz at the end of each chapter that they are required to pass. If they fail the first attempt, then they must attempt a computer generated practice quiz online again and again until they pass it. Once they have passed the practice quiz, they are then allowed to retake the real quiz (a similar version to the first one). A random sample of 25 students that failed a quiz, but eventually retook it, was obtained. Let scores on a first failed attempt be population 1, and the scores on a subsequent retake after passing a practice quiz be population 2. The sample produced the following statistics.

$$n = 25 \ , \ \bar{d} \approx -18.12 \ , \ s_d \approx 11.322$$

a) Does the data provide enough evidence, at the 1% significance level, to show that students, on average, will do better after having passed the practice quiz?
b) Compute a 98% confidence interval for the difference in average score for all students on the first and second attempt of the chapter quiz.
c) Interpret the interval in terms of the application.
d) Explain how the interval from part (b) agrees with the decision reached in part (a).
e) Comment on the requirements.
f) Explain, in terms of the application and evidence, what it would mean to make a type I error on this problem.
g) Explain, in terms of the application and evidence, what it would mean to make a type II error on this problem.

14) One of the goals of a freshman composition course is to reduce the number of major errors that students make when writing an essay. Let the number of major errors on a first essay of the semester be population 1, and the number of major errors on the final essay of the semester be population 2. A random sample of 89 students who recently completed a freshman composition course was obtained, and the number of major mistakes on their first and last essays was recorded. The sample produced the following statistics.

$$n = 89 \ , \ \bar{d} \approx 1.35 \ , \ s_d \approx 1.8062$$

a) Does the data provide enough evidence, at the 10% significance level, to show that students, on average, will make less major mistakes on their last essay than on their first essay?

b) Compute a 80% confidence interval for the difference in average number of major mistakes for all students on the first and last essay during the course.

c) Interpret the interval in terms of the application.

d) Explain how the interval from part (b) agrees with the decision reached in part (a).

e) Comment on the requirements.

f) Explain, in terms of the application and evidence, what it would mean to make a type I error on this problem.

g) Explain, in terms of the application and evidence, what it would mean to make a type II error on this problem.

Section 11.2 – Inferences from Independent Samples

In the previous section we looked at inferences for the difference between two population means using a sample containing matched pairs of data. However, there are many cases when we have two independently obtained samples from the two populations of interest, and therefore, the data values are not paired. In fact, the samples might not even be the same size.

In this situation, if we want to compute confidence intervals or perform hypothesis tests that seek to compare the relative size of two population means, we need a to compute a single value from the samples that can be used to determine the relative size of the sample means. The simplest way to get that information is to look a t the difference between the two sample means, $\bar{x}_1 - \bar{x}_2$ where $\bar{x}_1$ is the mean of sample 1 and $\bar{x}_2$ is the mean of sample 2. If this difference is negative, then the second number must have been larger. If the difference is positive, then the first number must have been larger. And, finally, if the difference is zero, then the two sample means must have been equal.

To make the needed probability calculations for any confidence intervals or hypothesis tests, we need to know the distribution of this new random variable, $\bar{x}_1 - \bar{x}_2$.

Distribution and standardized version of $\bar{x}_1 - \bar{x}_2$:

If $\bar{x}_1$ & $\bar{x}_2$ are both normally distributed, then $\bar{x}_1 - \bar{x}_2$ is also normally distributed with:

$$\mu_{\bar{x}_1 - \bar{x}_2} = \mu_1 - \mu_2 \quad \& \quad \sigma_{\bar{x}_1 - \bar{x}_2} = \sqrt{\frac{\sigma_1^2}{n_1} + \frac{\sigma_2^2}{n_2}}$$

And from this, we could say the standardized version of $\bar{x}_1 - \bar{x}_2$ is:

$$z = \frac{(\bar{x}_1 - \bar{x}_2) - (\mu_1 - \mu_2)}{\sqrt{\frac{\sigma_1^2}{n_1} + \frac{\sigma_2^2}{n_2}}}$$

Let's explore these ideas in more detail by working through an example.

Example 11.4:

Edith is growing tomatoes in her garden. She has decided to test a new growth supplement on some of her tomato plants to see if it increases the average weight of the tomatoes produced. She randomly chooses half of her tomato plants and uses the growth supplement on those plants, but not on the other half of the plants. She then randomly selected 15 of the tomatoes grown on the plants with the supplement and then selects another independent sample of 18 tomatoes from the plants where the supplement was not used. The samples obtained yielded the following tomato weights in ounces:

Sample 1 - Growth Supplement					Sample 2 - No Supplement					
6.56	6.89	7.28	7.04	7.34	6.70	6.39	6.97	6.33	7.02	6.90
7.57	7.15	7.01	7.41	7.25	6.10	6.96	7.10	6.44	7.31	7.42
6.80	7.66	7.69	6.51	8.20	6.60	6.81	6.66	7.25	6.42	6.81

a) Does the data provide enough evidence, at the 5% significance level, to show that the supplement produces larger tomatoes, on average, than tomatoes grown without the supplement.

b) Comment on the requirements.

Solution:

a) As is always the case, this will be a six step process.

STEP 1:   Determine H_o & H_1. A key change in this step is that neither hypothesis will contain any specific numbers. Rather, the hypotheses will make statements about the relative size of the two population means in question. The key phrase for setting up the hypotheses is "show that the supplement produces larger tomatoes, on average, than tomatoes grown without the supplement." This phrase needs to be reflected in our statement of the alternative hypothesis. So we get:

$$H_o : \mu_1 = \mu_2$$
$$H_1 : \mu_1 > \mu_2$$

Note: When we do two sample problems, it is common to use numbering subscripts to reference which values go with which populations. When doing this, it is vital that you have specified which number goes with which population. Notice, when the data was given, it was specified that "1" goes with supplement and "2" goes without.

STEP 2:   The significance level is given as 5%, so $\alpha = 0.05$.

STEP 3:   Because we are interested in comparing the means of the two populations, it makes sense that we would start gathering evidence by comparing the two sample means. These need to be calculated from the sample. While we are at it, we might as well find the sample standard deviations. I imagine we will have a need for them soon. We will number the sample means and standard deviations so that we know which sample they came from.

Sample 1 (Supplement) produces: $\bar{x}_1 = 7.224$ & $s_1 \approx 0.4519$

Sample 2 (No Supplement) produces: $\bar{x}_2 \approx 6.788$ & $s_2 \approx 0.3654$

Looking at the sample means, we see that the sample mean for the supplement tomatoes is larger than sample mean for those without the supplement. This provides some evidence that the supplement is effective, but we need to compute our test statistic and eventually our p-value to see if the difference is significant enough to show that the same relationship exists in the population means.

The pattern in all of the test statistics (involving means) we have computed is shown below:

$$\text{test stat} = \frac{(\text{sample value}) - (\text{expected value})}{(\text{standard deviation of sample value})}$$

For this type of test we will use the following:

Sample value: $\bar{x}_1 - \bar{x}_2$

Expected Value: The words expected value imply that we would use the mean of our sample value under the assumption that H_o is true. So will use 0. This is because, if the equals part of H_o is true, then we expect $\mu_1 = \mu_2$ and thus $\mu_{\bar{x}_1 - \bar{x}_2} = \mu_1 - \mu_2 = 0$.

Standard deviation: $\sigma_{\bar{x}_1-\bar{x}_2} = \sqrt{\dfrac{\sigma_1^2}{n_1}+\dfrac{\sigma_2^2}{n_2}}$, However, it is not realistic to expect that we will know the values of the standard deviations of the two populations in question. As we have done in the past, we will substitute the sample standard deviations in their place. Like in previous cases using s, rather than σ, will change our test statistic from a z to a t. So we will use:

$$\sigma_{\bar{x}_1-\bar{x}_2} \approx \sqrt{\dfrac{s_1^2}{n_1}+\dfrac{s_2^2}{n_2}}.$$

So our test statistic is:

$$t = \dfrac{(\bar{x}_1-\bar{x}_2)-0}{\sqrt{s_1^2/n_1+s_2^2/n_2}} = \dfrac{\bar{x}_1-\bar{x}_2}{\sqrt{s_1^2/n_1+s_2^2/n_2}} = \dfrac{7.224-6.788}{\sqrt{\dfrac{(0.4519)^2}{15}+\dfrac{(0.3654)^2}{18}}} \approx 3.006$$

We should note at this point that, with a t value of over 3, this seems like an unusually big difference between the sample means for it to be the result of chance.

Note: This test statistic can be a little intimidating to enter into your calculator. This is what it should look like on the TI-84:

```
(7.224-6.788)/√(
0.4519²/15+0.365
4²/18)
           3.006406082
```

STEP 4: As noted in step 3, because we are using sample standard deviations, our test statistic is a t-value. To proceed further we need the following information:

Distribution of the studentized version of $\bar{x}_1-\bar{x}_2$:

Suppose $\bar{x}_1$ & $\bar{x}_2$ are both normally distributed. Then the random variable:

$$t = \dfrac{(\bar{x}_1-\bar{x}_2)-(\mu_1-\mu_2)}{\sqrt{s_1^2/n_1+s_2^2/n_2}}$$

has approximately the t-distribution with $df = \dfrac{\left(s_1^2/n_1+s_2^2/n_2\right)^2}{\dfrac{\left(s_1^2/n_1\right)^2}{n_1-1}+\dfrac{\left(s_2^2/n_2\right)^2}{n_2-1}}$

(round down to an integer)

So to get our P-value we need to first calculate our degrees of freedom using the above formula.

$$df = \frac{\left((0.4519)^2/15 + (0.3654)^2/18\right)^2}{\dfrac{\left((0.4519)^2/15\right)^2}{15-1} + \dfrac{\left((0.3654)^2/18\right)^2}{18-1}} \approx 26.84 \qquad \text{So we will use df} = 26$$

Note 2:   On the TI-84, we would enter this scary formula as:

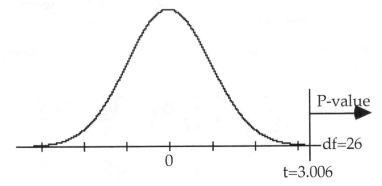

```
(0.4519²/15+0.36
54²/18)²/((0.451
9²/15)²/14+(0.36
54²/18)²/17)
          26.84806328
```

So, back to the p-value, we see from H_1 that this is a right tailed test. So we need to find the area to the right of our test statistic, t = 3.006, under the t-curve with 26 degrees of freedom.

P-value

df=26

0

t=3.006

Using the TI-84 to find the area to the right we get: $tcdf(3.006, \infty, 26) \approx 0.0029$
So our p-value ≈ 0.0029.

STEP 5:   We see that our p-value is very small, certainly smaller than our significance level. Therefore, with an acceptably small risk of making a type I error, we Reject H_o.

STEP 6:   We had enough evidence, at the 5% significance level, to show that the average weight of tomatoes grown using the supplement is greater than the average of those grown without using the supplement.

b)   As seen in the box above, we need both $\bar{x}_1$ & $\bar{x}_2$ to be normally distributed. Because both of our samples have a size of at least 15, but less than 30, we are left hoping that both samples were taken from populations that are not severely skewed. Our procedure also requires that the samples be independently chosen rather than paired. Certainly, there is no natural pairing between the tomatoes from the two sets of plants.

The steps taken in this example are summarized in the following procedure:

Procedure for performing the nonpooled t-test for two population means from independent samples:

Requirements: Each of the samples must meet at least one of the following:
- a) Sample size needs to be large ($n \geq 30$)
- b) The population needs to be normally distributed.
- c) $15 \leq n < 30$ and the population is not severely skewed.

Steps:

1) Determine H_o and H_1.
2) Decide on the significance level, α.
3) Calculate the test statistic: $t = \dfrac{(\bar{x}_1 - \bar{x}_2)}{\sqrt{s_1^2/n_1 + s_2^2/n_2}}$ (Use 3 decimal places)
4) Find the P-value using tcdf and $df = \dfrac{\left(s_1^2/n_1 + s_2^2/n_2\right)^2}{\dfrac{\left(s_1^2/n_1\right)^2}{n_1 - 1} + \dfrac{\left(s_2^2/n_2\right)^2}{n_2 - 1}}$ (Round Down)

$$\text{\textbf{Note:} } \min\{n_1, n_2\} - 1 \leq df \leq n_1 + n_2 - 2$$

5) Reject H_o or Do Not Reject H_o.
6) State the conclusion of the test in words.

Note: Because the formula for df is so complicated, it is nice have a rough idea of what the answer should be. This is given by the statement that: $\min\{n_1, n_2\} - 1 \leq df \leq n_1 + n_2 - 2$. For the tomato example, this would have told us the following. The df would have been at least one less than the smaller of the two sample sizes. That would have been 15 - 1 or 14 in the last example. And the df will always be no more than the sum of the sample sizes minus 2. This was 15 + 18 -2 or 31 in the last example: Notice: our df was found to be 26 and $14 \leq 26 \leq 31$.

LOOKING DEEPER: *Why is the df formula so complicated?*

In the past, calculating the df was always an extremely simple task. Suddenly, it is quite messy. One would hope that there is a good reason for having such a complicated formulas for the df. Here is the quick story of why such a messy formula is used.

Previously there were two different hypothesis tests to choose from for this sort of problem. One of them assumed that the two population standard deviations were equal. With this assumption, you could imagine that the two samples were working together to give a better estimate of the actual population standard deviations. This was called a pooled test, because it was as if all of your data was pooled together for this purpose. If the data were pooled, then you could add the degrees of freedom, and for that sort of test, the formula was:

$$df = (n_1 - 1) + (n_2 - 1) = n_1 + n_2 - 2$$

This was a fairly simple formula to use, however, it doesn't seem very realistic that the two populations would actually have equal standard deviations. If this assumption was faulty, then your p-values would come out smaller than they should. This would mean your risk of making a type I error was larger than it appeared to be.

The other test, was called a nonpooled test, and it assumed that the two population standard deviations were not equal and, therefore, your estimate of the standard deviation of $\overline{x}_1 - \overline{x}_2$ was only as good as the worse of the estimates of the two population standard deviations. This would be the one from the smaller sample. So, when using this test, you used the df that corresponded to smaller sample. The formula in this case was:

$$df = \min\{n_1, n_2\} - 1$$

The problem with this approach is that, even though population standard deviations are not exactly equal, they are often similar in size. This means that the samples probably were working together, to some extent, in estimating the standard deviation of $\overline{x}_1 - \overline{x}_2$. This means we were using a smaller df than we could have been using. This made our p-values larger than they should have been, which in turn made it harder to reject H_o. Therefore, if H_o was false, then we had an increased chance of making a type II error.

The solution to this problem was to find a formula that used the sample standard deviations to assess how similar the population standard deviations were so that the sample could be partially pooled for the purpose of estimating the standard deviation of $\overline{x}_1 - \overline{x}_2$. The messy formula we are using for the df in this section does exactly that. So the more similar the sample standard deviations are to each other, the closer the df comes to $n_1 + n_2 - 2$, and the more different the sample standard deviations are from each other, the closer the df comes to $\min\{n_1, n_2\} - 1$.

If we are comparing two populations using a hypothesis test, it is common that these populations are similar to each other, so you will notice that, in most problems that we do, the df from our formula produces a df just below $n_1 + n_2 - 2$. When you work through this messy formula, keep this in mind. If we didn't have this formula, then we would be learning two different hypothesis tests, rather than just the one in this section.

CONFIDENCE INTERVALS:

We can also use the ideas explored so far to find a confidence interval for the value of the difference between the two population means, $\mu_1 - \mu_2$.

The typical formula for a confidence interval takes the form:

(Sample Value) $\pm$ (z-score)(Standard Deviation of Sample Value)

In the two sample case this would be: $\left(\overline{x}_1 - \overline{x}_2\right) \pm z^* \sqrt{\dfrac{\sigma_1^2}{n_1} + \dfrac{\sigma_2^2}{n_2}}$

Of course, when we switch from σ to s, this formula becomes: $\left(\overline{x}_1 - \overline{x}_2\right) \pm t^* \sqrt{\dfrac{s_1^2}{n_1} + \dfrac{s_2^2}{n_2}}$

This new formula and the procedure that goes with it are summarized as follows:

> **Procedure for calculating a nonpooled t-interval for the difference between two population means $(\mu_1 - \mu_2)$ from independent samples:**
>
> **Requirements**: Each of the samples must meet at least one of the following:
>   a) Sample size needs to be large ($n \geq 30$)
>   b) The population needs to be normally distributed.
>   c) $15 \leq n < 30$ and the population is not severely skewed.
>
> Steps:
>   1) Calculate the sample means and standard deviations from the two samples. If they are not given.
>   2) For a confidence level of $1 - \alpha$, use the t-table to find t^* with
>
> $$df = \frac{\left(s_1^2/n_1 + s_2^2/n_2\right)^2}{\dfrac{\left(s_1^2/n_1\right)^2}{n_1 - 1} + \dfrac{\left(s_2^2/n_2\right)^2}{n_2 - 1}} \quad \text{(Round Down)}$$
>
>   3) The confidence interval for $(\mu_1 - \mu_2)$ is given by $\left(\bar{x}_1 - \bar{x}_2\right) \pm t^* \sqrt{\dfrac{s_1^2}{n_1} + \dfrac{s_2^2}{n_2}}$

Let's try this out by returning to the tomato example and looking at it as a confidence interval rather than a hypothesis test.

Example 11.5:

Edith is growing tomatoes in her garden. She has decided to test a new growth supplement on some of her tomato plants to see what affect it has on the average weight of the tomatoes produced. She randomly chooses half of her tomato plants and uses the growth supplement on those plants, but not on the other half of the plants. She then randomly selected 15 of the tomatoes grown on the plants with the supplement and then selects another 18 tomatoes from the plants where the supplement was not used. The samples obtained yielded the following tomato weights in ounces:

Sample 1 - Growth Supplement					Sample 2 - No Supplement					
6.56	6.89	7.28	7.04	7.34	6.70	6.39	6.97	6.33	7.02	6.90
7.57	7.15	7.01	7.41	7.25	6.10	6.96	7.10	6.44	7.31	7.42
6.80	7.66	7.69	6.51	8.20	6.60	6.81	6.66	7.25	6.42	6.81

a) Compute a 90% confidence interval for the difference between the average weights, $\mu_1 - \mu_2$, of all tomatoes grown with and without the supplement.
b) Interpret the interval in terms of the application.
c) Explain how the interval obtained in this problem agrees with the decision reached in the hypothesis test in the previous example.

Solution:

a) Much of the work of this problem has already been done for us in the previous example. We have computed the needed means and standard deviations as well as the dreaded degrees of freedom. We need only find our t-value and then we can start into the formula.

Because we are asked to find a 90% confidence interval, the area in the middle will be 0.90. That leaves 0.10 remaining and when we split that between the two tails, we get an area in the tail of 0.05. We then look that up using df = 26 (from previous example) and we get the value: $t_{0.05} = 1.706$.

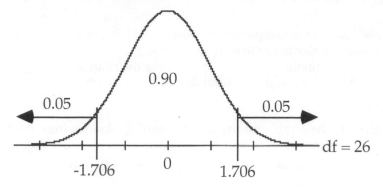

With that, we are ready to jump into the formula:

$$\left(\bar{x}_1 - \bar{x}_2\right) \pm t^* \sqrt{\frac{s_1^2}{n_1} + \frac{s_2^2}{n_2}} = \left(7.224 - 6.788\right) \pm 1.706 \sqrt{\frac{(0.4519)^2}{15} + \frac{(0.3654)^2}{18}} \approx 0.436 \pm 0.247$$

$$\Rightarrow \mu_1 - \mu_2 \in (0.189,\ 0.683)$$

Note 1:   The format for entering the margin of error term is shown in the screen shot below.

```
1.706*√(0.4519²/
15+0.3654²/18)
             .2474103564
```

b)   A straight forward interpretation would be: "I am 90% confident that difference between the mean for tomatoes grown with the supplement and the mean of those grown without it is somewhere between 0.189 ounces and 0.683 ounces."

Note 2:   One problem with making an interpretation like we did here, is that the reader might not be sure what the order of subtraction was between the means, so they may not be sure which mean was larger after reading the statement. So an improved interpretation would be:

"I am 90% confident that the tomatoes grown with the supplement are, on average, somewhere between 0.189 and 0.683 ounces larger than those grown without it."

c)   If $\mu_1 - \mu_2$ is somewhere between 0.189 and 0.683, then we know that $\mu_1 - \mu_2$ is positive. If $\mu_1 - \mu_2$ is positive, then it must be that μ_1 is larger than μ_2. This would suggest that $H_1 : \mu_1 > \mu_2$ is true and $H_o : \mu_1 = \mu_2$ is a false. If H_o is false, then it should be rejected, and that is, in fact, what we decided to do in our hypothesis test in the previous example. In symbols:

If $\mu_1 - \mu_2 \in (0.189,\ 0.683) \Rightarrow \mu_1 - \mu_2 > 0 \Rightarrow \mu_1 > \mu_2 \Rightarrow H_1 : \mu_1 > \mu_2$ is true and $H_o : \mu_1 = \mu_2$ is false $\Rightarrow$ Reject H_o

WRAP SESSION:

Let's practice these ideas with one more example.

Example 11.6:

A pharmaceutical company is concerned that one of its new drugs might produce weight loss as a side effect. They know that people that use the drug tend to lose weight, but they are not sure if that is an effect of the drug or an effect of the illness the drug is treating. Two independent random samples of people with the illness were obtained. The first group was given the new drug; the other group was given a placebo. The weight loss, in pounds, after one month, was recorded for the participants from each group. The following information summarizes the weight loss for each group:

Group 1 (took the new drug): $n_1 = 36$ $\bar{x}_1 = 3.491$ $s_1 = 1.628$

Group 2 (took the placebo): $n_2 = 14$ $\bar{x}_2 = 2.927$ $s_2 = 1.075$

a) Comment on the requirements.

b) Does the data provide enough evidence, at the 5% significance level, to show that there will be a difference between the average weight loss of people who take the new drug and those who don't?

c) Determine a 95% confidence interval for the difference between the average weight loss of people who take the new drug and those who don't.

d) Interpret the interval in terms of the application.

e) Explain how the interval obtained in part (c) agrees with the decision reached in the hypothesis test from part (b).

f) Have we made a type I error, a type II error, or a correct decision? Explain.

g) Should the company be required to warn its customers that the drug causes weight loss? Explain.

Solution:

a) Group 1: Because $n_1 = 36 \geq 30$, we know that $\bar{x}_1$ is normally distributed regardless of the distribution of the population.

   Group 2: However, $n_2 = 14 < 30$, so we are hoping that the population of weight loss values for those with the illness, but not taking the new drug, is normally distributed.

b) The phrasing of this question implies the need for a hypothesis test needs to be done.

STEP 1: $H_o : \mu_1 = \mu_2$ (Because we are only asked if there will be a "difference". No direction is
            $H_1 : \mu_1 \neq \mu_2$

            implied. So, we will do a two-tailed test.)

STEP 2: $\alpha = 0.05$. We are willing to take up to a 5% risk of making a type I error.

STEP 3:   Test Statistic is: $t = \dfrac{\bar{x}_1 - \bar{x}_2}{\sqrt{s_1^2/n_1 + s_2^2/n_2}} = \dfrac{3.491 - 2.927}{\sqrt{\dfrac{(1.628)^2}{36} + \dfrac{(1.075)^2}{14}}} \approx 1.427$

This does not seem to indicate an unusually large difference between the two sample means, but we will check our p-value to make our decision sure.

STEP 4:   Brace yourself. It is time to calculate the degrees of freedom.

$$df = \frac{\left((1.628)^2/36 + (1.075)^2/14\right)^2}{\dfrac{\left((1.628)^2/36\right)^2}{36-1} + \dfrac{\left((1.075)^2/14\right)^2}{14-1}} \approx 35.92 \qquad \text{So we will use df = 35.}$$

Note 1:   This is reasonable value because $\min\{n_1, n_2\} - 1 \le df \le n_1 + n_2 - 2 \Rightarrow 13 \le df \le 48$.

This is a two-tailed test, so we need to find the area in the tail beyond our test statistic and then double it.

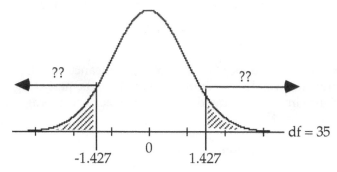

Using the calculator we get: p-value = $2 * tcdf\left(1.427, \infty, 35\right) \approx 0.1624$

So, if we decide to Reject H_o, then we would be taking a 16.24% risk of making a type I error. This is too high, so we:

STEP 5:   Do Not Reject H_o

STEP 6:   There was not enough evidence, at the 5% significance level, to show that there will be a difference between the average weight loss of people who take the new drug and those who don't.

c)   Because we are asked to find a 95% confidence interval, the area in the middle will be 0.95. That leaves 0.05 remaining and when we split that between the two tails, we get an area in the tail of 0.025. We then look that up using df = 35 (calculated in part b) and we get the value: $t_{0.025} = 2.030$.

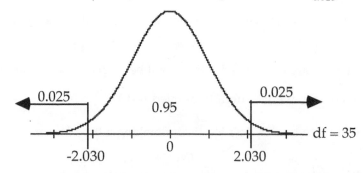

With that, we are ready to jump into the formula:

$$(\bar{x}_1 - \bar{x}_2) \pm t^* \sqrt{\frac{s_1^2}{n_1} + \frac{s_2^2}{n_2}} = (3.491 - 2.927) \pm 2.030 \sqrt{\frac{(1.628)^2}{36} + \frac{(1.075)^2}{14}} \approx 0.564 \pm 0.802$$

$$\Rightarrow \mu_1 - \mu_2 \in (-0.238, \ 1.366)$$

d) We are 90% confident that the average weight loss for those taking the new drug will be somewhere between 1.366 pounds more to 0.238 pounds less than those with the illness that are not taking the drug.

e) If $\mu_1 - \mu_2$ is somewhere between -0.238 and 1.366, then $\mu_1 - \mu_2$ could reasonably be zero. If $\mu_1 - \mu_2$ could be zero, then μ_1 could be equal to μ_2. This would suggest that $H_o : \mu_1 = \mu_2$ could be true. If it is reasonable that H_o could be true, then it should NOT be rejected and, in fact, our decision from part (c) was to Not Reject H_o. In symbols:

If $\mu_1 - \mu_2 \in (-0.238, \ 1.366) \Rightarrow \mu_1 - \mu_2$ could $= 0 \Rightarrow \mu_1$ could $= \mu_2 \Rightarrow H_o : \mu_1 = \mu_2$ could be true
$$\Rightarrow \text{Do Not Reject } H_o$$

Note 2: We are not stating that H_o is true. We are only pointing out that our interval allows for the possibility that it is true, and we do not want to reject a claim if it seems reasonable that it could be true.

f) Because we Did Not Reject H_o, we can rule out a type I error. However, it is possible that we have made a type II error or a correct decision. If it turns out that H_o is true, then by not rejecting it, we would have made a correct decision. On the other hand, if H_o turns out to be false, then by not rejecting it, we have made a type II error.

g) No, because while the samples did show a slightly higher weight loss for those taking the drug, this was not a large enough difference to be convincing that it was due to anything other than the randomness of the sample. A company in such a situation might make a statement like "weight loss by those using this product has not been shown to be significantly different than those taking a placebo."

Exercise Set 11.2

(15-16) Fill in the blanks for each of the following.

15) Independent samples from two populations have no natural _____ from one sample to the other. They might not even have the same sample _____ .

16) Because the df formula in this section is so complicated, it is good to have an _____ of the size of your answer. Use the fact that _____ $\leq df \leq$ _____ to help with this.

(17-20)
a) Calculate the value of the test stat.
b) Find the P-value.
c) State whether or not you would reject H_o if the significance level was 5%.

17) $H_o : \mu_1 = \mu_2$; $H_1 : \mu_1 > \mu_2$

$n_1 = 19$, $\bar{x}_1 = 15.392$, $s_1 = 3.908$

$n_2 = 14$, $\bar{x}_2 = 13.899$, $s_2 = 2.471$

18) $H_o : \mu_1 = \mu_2$; $H_1 : \mu_1 < \mu_2$

$n_1 = 15$, $\bar{x}_1 = 108.07$, $s_1 = 24.851$

$n_2 = 21$, $\bar{x}_2 = 127.57$, $s_2 = 31.652$

19)
$$H_o : \mu_1 = \mu_2$$
$$H_1 : \mu_1 \neq \mu_2 \quad ;$$

$n_1 = 35$, $\bar{x}_1 = 1.537$, $s_1 = 0.5081$

$n_2 = 35$, $\bar{x}_2 = 1.209$, $s_2 = 0.4366$

20)
$$H_o : \mu_1 = \mu_2$$
$$H_1 : \mu_1 > \mu_2 \quad ;$$

$n_1 = 40$, $\bar{x}_1 = 28.445$, $s_1 = 7.909$

$n_2 = 17$, $\bar{x}_2 = 37.771$, $s_2 = 10.873$

21) People in the San Francisco bay area feel that they are being charged a higher price for gas than people living in other areas of the state. A statewide random sample of 60 gas stations produced an average price for a gallon of gas of $3.387/gal with a standard deviation of $0.1625/gal. A random sample of 27 bay area gas stations produced an average price of $3.541/gal with a standard deviation of $0.176/gal.

a) Perform a hypothesis test, at the 5% significance level, to see if the Bay Area (population 1) average is indeed larger than the average price in the entire state (population 2).
b) Compute a 90% confidence interval for the difference between the bay area average price and the statewide average.
c) Interpret the interval in terms of the application.
d) Explain how the interval from part (b) agrees with the decision reached in part (a).
e) Comment on the requirements.
f) For the decision made in part a), discuss the possibility that we made a type I error, a type II error, or a correct decision? Explain.

22) A community college professor was interested in determining if there is a difference between the average GPA of day and night students at his school. He randomly chose samples of both day and night students and obtained their GPAs. The results were as follows:

Day: $n_1 = 40$ $\bar{x}_1 = 2.791$ $s_1 = 0.7464$

Night: $n_2 = 43$ $\bar{x}_2 = 2.699$ $s_2 = 0.8338$

a) Perform the indicated test, at the 1% significance level.
b) Give interpretations of both the significance level and the p-value from part (a) and explain how these interpretations lead you to the decision you made.
c) Compute a 99% confidence interval for the difference between the average GPA of day and night students.
d) Interpret the interval in terms of the application.
e) Explain how the interval from part (c) agrees with the decision reached in part (a).
f) For the decision made in part a), discuss the possibility that we made a type I error, a type II error, or a correct decision? Explain.

23) In a state where a school voucher program has recently been initiated. A review board has been set up to check on the quality of education in public schools vs. private schools. One of the variables they wanted to study was combined SAT scores from the students attending the two types of schools. They chose independent random samples from the two populations and obtained the following results for combined SAT scores.

Public: $n_1 = 126$ $\bar{x}_1 = 1394.6$ $s_1 = 282.75$

Private: $n_2 = 81$ $\bar{x}_2 = 1524.3$ $s_2 = 226.65$

a) Does the data provide enough evidence, at the 5% significance level, to show that there is a difference between the average combined SAT scores of public and private school students?
b) Compute a 95% confidence interval for the difference between the average combined SAT scores of public and private school students.
c) Interpret the interval in terms of the application.
d) Explain how the interval from part (b) agrees with the decision reached in part (a).
e) If the true mean values for the SAT scores are $\mu_1 = 1470.6$ and $\mu_2 = 1480.5$, then, in part (a), did we make a type I error, a type II error, or a correct decision? Explain.

24) A researcher is interested in the average age at which men and women get married in the U.S. He selected independent random samples of 175 women and 150 men and obtained the following results.

Women: $n_1 = 175$ $\bar{x}_1 = 25.13$ $s_1 = 15.291$

Men: $n_2 = 150$ $\bar{x}_2 = 27.31$ $s_2 = 12.085$

a) Does the data provide enough evidence, at the 10% significance level, to show that there is a difference between the average of women and men at the time of marriage?
b) Compute a 90% confidence interval for the difference between the average age of women and men.
c) Interpret the interval in terms of the application.
d) Explain how the interval from part (b) agrees with the decision reached in part (a).
e) If the true mean ages at the time of marriage are $\mu_1 = 24.9$ and $\mu_2 = 27.1$, then, in part (a), did we make a type I error, a type II error, or a correct decision? Explain.

25) A statistics student / snowboarder is interested in comparing the price of an adult lift ticket between California resorts and Colorado resorts. In January 2008, he randomly chose 16 California resorts and 12 Colorado resorts and obtained the following adult lift ticket prices.

California Sample 1	Colorado Sample 2
64	87
59	58
52	87
38	56
53	60
60	45
79	52
62	49
39	87
76	68
52	85
64	56
25	-
73	-
60	-
35	-

Note: $\sum x_1^2 = 53{,}095$ & $\sum x_2^2 = 54{,}922$

a) Does the data provide enough evidence, at the 1% significance level, to show that there is a difference between the average adult lift ticket prices in California and Colorado?
b) Comment on the requirements.
c) Compute a 99% confidence interval for the difference between the average adult lift ticket price in California and Colorado.
d) Interpret the interval in terms of the application.
e) Explain how the interval from part (c) agrees with the decision reached in part (a).

26) A statistics teacher thinks that it is important for students to complete their homework before they take their final exam. To test this theory he collects a random sample of students who recently took the final and separated them into students who completed their last homework assignment and those who did not. He found the following final exam scores for these two groups.

Final Scores - Sample 1: Homework Not Completed		
59	47	58
95	54	76

Final Scores - Sample 2: Homework Completed		
79	98	57
93	95	97
93	95	49
79	69	67
96	87	85

Note: $\sum x_1^2 = 26{,}771$ & $\sum x_2^2 = 105{,}753$

a) Does the data provide enough evidence, at the 5% significance level, to show that students who do not complete their last homework assignment have lower scores, on average, than those who complete their homework?
b) Comment on the requirements.
c) Compute a 90% confidence interval for the difference between the average final exam score of students who do not complete their last homework assignment and those who do.
d) Interpret the interval in terms of the application.
e) Explain how the interval from part (c) agrees with the decision reached in part (a).

Section 11.3 – Two-Sample Inferences for Proportions

In the previous two sections, we examined procedures for comparing the size of two population means by using sample data. Similarly, if we wish to compare the proportion of a certain attribute in two different populations, it is unlikely that we will know true value of the population proportion in either group. Therefore, we will need to use a sample from each population in order to draw conclusions about how the population proportions compare to each other.

In such situations, if we want to compute confidence intervals or perform hypothesis tests that seek to compare the relative size of two population proportions, we need to compute a single value from the samples that can be used to determine the relative size of the sample proportions. The simplest way to get that information is to look at the difference between the two sample proportions, $\hat{p}_1 - \hat{p}_2$ where $\hat{p}_1$ is the proportion of the desired attribute in sample 1 and $\hat{p}_2$ is the proportion of the desired attribute in sample 2. If this difference is negative, then the second number must have been larger. If the difference is positive, then the first number must have been larger. And, finally, if the difference is zero, then the two sample proportions must have been equal.

To make the needed probability calculations for any confidence intervals or hypothesis tests, we need to know the distribution of this new random variable, $\hat{p}_1 - \hat{p}_2$.

Distribution and standardized version of $\hat{p}_1 - \hat{p}_2$:

If $\hat{p}_1$ & $\hat{p}_2$ are both approximately normally distributed, then $\hat{p}_1 - \hat{p}_2$ is also normally distributed with:

$$\mu_{\hat{p}_1 - \hat{p}_2} = p_1 - p_2 \quad \& \quad \sigma_{\hat{p}_1 - \hat{p}_2} = \sqrt{\frac{p_1 q_1}{n_1} + \frac{p_2 q_2}{n_2}}$$

And from this, we could say the standardized version of $\hat{p}_1 - \hat{p}_2$ is:

$$z = \frac{(\hat{p}_1 - \hat{p}_2) - (p_1 - p_2)}{\sqrt{\frac{p_1 q_1}{n_1} + \frac{p_2 q_2}{n_2}}}$$

Let's explore these ideas in more detail by working through an example.

Example 11.7:

Gaining weight during the winter holiday season is a concern for many Americans. A survey conducted early in December 2003 asked a random sample of 518 men and 547 women the following question. "Do you think that you will gain weight over the upcoming holiday period?" 274 of the men and 323 of the women said that they did think they would gain weight.

a) Does the data provide enough evidence, at the 5% significance level, to show that there is a difference in the proportion of all men and women who expected to gain weight over that year's holiday season?

b) Comment on the requirements.

Solution:

a) As this wording implies a hypothesis test, we will do the standard six step process. Before we start on the steps, we should number the two populations. Let's let population 1 be the men and population 2 be the women.

STEP 1: The key word in this problem is "difference". Because this word does not imply a direction, we will do a two-tailed test. Also, this test is about proportions, not means, so our hypotheses will reference values of p rather than μ. The claims are as follows.

$$H_o : p_1 = p_2$$
$$H_1 : p_1 \neq p_2$$

Note 1: Because we do not know the population proportion for men or women, the null and alternative hypotheses do not contain any specific values.

STEP 2: The significance level is given as 5%, so $\alpha = 0.05$.

STEP 3: Because we are interested in comparing the proportion that expect to gain weight in each of the two populations, it makes sense that we would start gathering evidence by comparing the two sample proportions. These need to be calculated from the samples. We will number the sample proportions so that we know which sample they came from.

$$\text{Sample 1 (Men) produces: } \hat{p}_1 = \frac{x_1}{n_1} = \frac{274}{518} \approx 0.5290$$

$$\text{Sample 2 (Women) produces: } \hat{p}_2 = \frac{x_2}{n_2} = \frac{323}{547} \approx 0.5905$$

Note 2: x_1 is the number of successes among the men and x_2 is the number of successes among the women, where a success is the person thinking that they will gain weight over the holidays.

Looking at the sample proportions, we see that the sample proportion for the men is smaller than sample proportion for women. This provides some evidence that the there is a difference between men and women on this issue, but we need to compute a test statistic and eventually a p-value to see if the difference is significant enough to show that this difference also exists in the population proportions.

The pattern in most of the test statistics we have computed is shown below:

$$\text{test stat} = \frac{(\text{sample value}) - (\text{expected value})}{(\text{standard deviation of sample value})}$$

For this type of test we will use the following:

Sample value: $\hat{p}_1 - \hat{p}_2$

Expected Value: The words "expected value" imply that we would use the mean of our sample value under the assumption that H_o is true. So, we will use 0. This is because, if the equal to part of H_o is true, then we expect $p_1 = p_2$ and thus $\mu_{\hat{p}_1 - \hat{p}_2} = p_1 - p_2 = 0$.

Standard deviation: $\sigma_{\hat{p}_1 - \hat{p}_2} = \sqrt{\dfrac{p_1 q_1}{n_1} + \dfrac{p_2 q_2}{n_2}}$, however, we must use the assumption that H_o is true for all parts of the test statistic. So, we will calculate this value assuming that $p_1 = p_2$. If we are assuming the two values are equal, then we could represent each of them using the same variable. Substituting p in place of p_1 and p_2, we get:

$$\sigma_{\hat{p}_1 - \hat{p}_2} = \sqrt{\frac{pq}{n_1} + \frac{pq}{n_2}} = \sqrt{pq\left(\frac{1}{n_1} + \frac{1}{n_2}\right)}.$$

One problem still remains with this standard deviation formula. We do not know the value of p, so we must estimate it. In the past, when we needed to estimate a population proportion, we substituted the sample proportion. This is what we will do here as well. However, we have two samples, not one. So, which one do we use? Because we are calculating the standard deviation under the assumption that $p_1 = p_2$, we will pool the two samples together to provide our estimate of the population proportion. We will call this estimate $\hat{p}_p$, where the subscript of p stands for pooled. To calculate this value, we use the total number of successes, divided by the total sample size. So: $\hat{p}_p = \dfrac{x_1 + x_2}{n_1 + n_2}$. Finally, we substitute this value into our standard deviation formula and get:

$$\sigma_{\hat{p}_1 - \hat{p}_2} \approx \sqrt{\hat{p}_p \hat{q}_p \left(\frac{1}{n_1} + \frac{1}{n_2}\right)}.$$

For these samples, the value of $\hat{p}_p$ is given by:

$$\hat{p}_p = \frac{x_1 + x_2}{n_1 + n_2} = \frac{274 + 323}{518 + 547} = \frac{597}{1065} \approx 0.5606 \Rightarrow \hat{q}_p \approx 1 - 0.5606 = 0.4394$$

So our test statistic is:

$$z = \frac{(\hat{p}_1 - \hat{p}_2) - 0}{\sqrt{\hat{p}_p \hat{q}_p \left(\frac{1}{n_1} + \frac{1}{n_2}\right)}} = \frac{\hat{p}_1 - \hat{p}_2}{\sqrt{\hat{p}_p \hat{q}_p \left(\frac{1}{n_1} + \frac{1}{n_2}\right)}} = \frac{0.5290 - 0.5905}{\sqrt{0.5606 * 0.4394\left(\frac{1}{518} + \frac{1}{547}\right)}} \approx -2.021$$

We should note at this point that, with a z-score below -2, this seems like an unusually big difference between the sample proportions for it to be the result of chance.

Note 3: Recall: Even though we have substituted a sample proportion in place of the population proportion in the standard deviation, it is OK to use z-score because the error in the values of $\hat{p}_p$ and $\hat{q}_p$ roughly cancel each other out when multiplied.

Note 4: This test statistic can be a little intimidating to enter into your calculator. This is what it should look like on the TI-84:

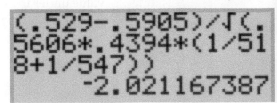

STEP 4: As noted in step 3, our test statistic is a z-value. So, assuming that our test statistic is normally distributed (we will check this in part b), we can use the normalcdf command on the TI-84 to find the p-value. This is a two-tailed test, so we need to find the area beyond our test statistic and then double it.

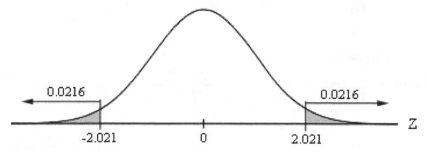

Using the TI-84 to find the area to the right we get:

$normalcdf(2.021, \infty) \approx 0.0216$. So, doubling this we get our p-value ≈ 0.0432.

STEP 5: With a significance level of 5%, this is a very close call. However, our p-value is slightly less than 5%, therefore, with an acceptably small risk of making a type I error, we Reject H_o.

STEP 6: We had enough evidence, at the 5% significance level, to show that the proportion of all men expecting to gain weight over that holiday period was different than the proportion of all women who expected to gain weight over that same time.

b) As seen in the distribution box prior to starting this example, we need both $\hat{p}_1$ & $\hat{p}_2$ to be normally distributed, so that $\hat{p}_1 - \hat{p}_2$ will be normally distributed. We learned in Section 9.2 that we verify normality of a sample proportion by verifying that $np_0 \geq 10$ and $nq_0 \geq 10$. However, in this type of problem, we are given no specific values of p_0 and q_0, so we will substitute the appropriate sample values in their place. The work is as follows:

Men: $n_1 p_0 \approx n_1 \hat{p}_1 = n_1 \dfrac{x_1}{n_1} = x_1 = 274 \geq 10$ & $n_1 q_0 \approx n_1 \hat{q}_1 = n_1 \dfrac{n_1 - x_1}{n_1} = n_1 - x_1 = 244 \geq 10$

Women: $n_2 p_0 \approx n_2 \hat{p}_2 = n_2 \dfrac{x_2}{n_2} = x_2 = 323 \geq 10$ & $n_2 q_0 \approx n_2 \hat{q}_2 = n_2 \dfrac{n_2 - x_2}{n_2} = n_2 - x_2 = 224 \geq 10$

Because all these values are at least 10, we know that $\hat{p}_1$ and $\hat{p}_2$ are normally distributed, and thus, so is $\hat{p}_1 - \hat{p}_2$. This implies that the requirements have been met.

Note 5: The quick check for the requirements could be stated as "we must have at least 10 successes and 5 failures in each of the two samples."

The steps taken in this example are summarized in the following procedure:

Procedure for performing the test for two population proportions:

Requirements: Each of the samples must contain at least 10 successes and at least 10 failures.

Steps:
1) Determine H_o and H_1.
2) Decide on the significance level, α.
3) Calculate the test statistic: $z = \dfrac{\hat{p}_1 - \hat{p}_2}{\sqrt{\hat{p}_p\hat{q}_p\left(\dfrac{1}{n_1} + \dfrac{1}{n_2}\right)}}$, where $\hat{p}_p = \dfrac{x_1 + x_2}{n_1 + n_2}$

(Use 3 decimal places)
4) Find the P-value using normalcdf on the TI-84.
5) Reject H_o or Do Not Reject H_o.
6) State the conclusion of the test in words.

CONFIDENCE INTERVALS:

We can also use the ideas explored so far to find a confidence interval for the value of the difference between the two population proportions, $p_1 - p_2$.

The typical formula for a confidence interval takes the form:

(Sample Value) $\pm$ (z-score)(Standard Deviation of Sample Value)

In the two sample case this would be: $\left(\hat{p}_1 - \hat{p}_2\right) \pm z^*\sqrt{\dfrac{p_1q_1}{n_1} + \dfrac{p_2q_2}{n_2}}$

Of course, we won't know the values of the population proportions, so we will need to substitute the sample proportions: $\left(\hat{p}_1 - \hat{p}_2\right) \pm z^*\sqrt{\dfrac{\hat{p}_1\hat{q}_1}{n_1} + \dfrac{\hat{p}_2\hat{q}_2}{n_2}}$. Because this is not a hypothesis test, we do not have the assumption that $p_1 = p_2$, so we do not pool the successes into a single sample proportion.

This new formula and the procedure that goes with it are summarized as follows:

> **Procedure for calculating a confidence interval for the difference between two population proportions $(p_1 - p_2)$:**
>
> **Requirements**: Each of the samples must contain at least 10 successes and at least 10 failures.
>
> Steps:
> 1) Calculate the sample proportions from the two samples. If they are not given.
> 2) For a confidence level of $1 - \alpha$, use the invNorm to find z^*.
> 3) The confidence interval for $(p_1 - p_2)$ is given by
>
> $$\left(\hat{p}_1 - \hat{p}_2\right) \pm z^* \sqrt{\frac{\hat{p}_1\hat{q}_1}{n_1} + \frac{\hat{p}_2\hat{q}_2}{n_2}}$$

Let's try this out by returning to the previous example and looking at it as a confidence interval rather than a hypothesis test.

Example 11.8:

Gaining weight during the winter holiday season is a concern for many Americans. A survey conducted early in December 2003 asked a random sample of 518 men and 547 women the following question. "Do you think that you will gain weight over the upcoming holiday period?" 274 of the men and 323 of the women said that they did think they would gain weight.

a) Compute a 95% confidence interval for the difference between the proportions of all men and women who thought they would gain weight over that holiday period.

b) Interpret the interval in terms of the application.

c) Explain how the interval obtained in this problem agrees with the decision reached in the hypothesis test in the previous example.

Solution:

a) Much of the work of this problem has already been done for us in the previous example. We have computed the needed sample proportions. We only need to find our z-value and then we can start into the formula.

$$\text{Recall: } \hat{p}_1 = \frac{x_1}{n_1} = \frac{274}{518} \approx 0.5290 \text{ and } \hat{p}_2 = \frac{x_2}{n_2} = \frac{323}{547} \approx 0.5905$$

Because we are asked to find a 95% confidence interval, the area in the middle will be 0.95. That leaves 0.05 remaining and when we split that between the two tails, we get an area in the tail of 0.025. We will then use inverse normal to find the required z-scores.

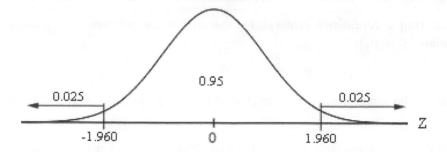

With that, we are ready to jump into the formula:

$$(\hat{p}_1 - \hat{p}_2) \pm z^* \sqrt{\frac{\hat{p}_1 \hat{q}_1}{n_1} + \frac{\hat{p}_2 \hat{q}_2}{n_2}} = (0.5290 - 0.5905) \pm 1.960 \sqrt{\frac{0.5290 * 0.4710}{518} + \frac{0.5905 * 0.4095}{547}}$$

$$= -0.0615 \pm 0.0595 \Rightarrow (p_1 - p_2) \in (-0.1210, \ -0.0020)$$

Note 1:   The format for entering the margin of error term is shown in the screen shot to the right.

```
1.96*√(.529*.471
/518+.5905*.4095
/547)
         .059548764
```

b) The difference in the proportions will only have a negative value if the second number is larger than the first. So, we should include this idea in our interpretation in place of saying the word negative. One possible interpretation is as follows:

> "I am 95% confident that the proportion of all women who think they will gain weight over the holidays is higher than the proportion for men by somewhere between 0.2% and 12.1%."

c) If $p_1 - p_2$ is somewhere between –0.1210 and –0.0020, then we know that $p_1 - p_2$ is negative. If $p_1 - p_2$ is negative, then it must be that p_1 is smaller than p_2. This would suggest that $H_o : p_1 = p_2$ is a false statement. If it is false, then it should be rejected and that is in fact what we decided to do in our hypothesis test in the previous example. In symbols:

$$\text{If } (p_1 - p_2) \in (-0.1210, \ -0.0020) \Rightarrow p_1 - p_2 < 0 \Rightarrow p_1 < p_2 \Rightarrow H_o : p_1 = p_2 \text{ is false} \Rightarrow \text{Reject } H_o$$

WRAP SESSION:

Let's practice these ideas with one more example.

Example 11.9:

A company that makes snowboards and snowboard accessories is trying to decide the best location to spend its marketing budget on the launch of some new products. They have narrowed their choices down to either California or Colorado. They are leaning towards California because the common belief is that Californians are more cutting edge and daring and prefer snowboarding, while Coloradoans are more traditional and prefer skiing. They don't want to finalize this decision without some data to back up this common belief. They obtained a random sample of 1012 visitors to California resorts and 870 visitors to Colorado resorts. They found that, in California (population 1), 458 of the 1012 people sampled preferred snowboarding. In Colorado (population 2), 191 of the 870 people sampled preferred snowboarding.

a) Comment on the requirements for performing a hypothesis test or computing a confidence interval for the population proportions of snowboarders in the two states.

b) Does the data provide enough evidence, at the 5% significance level, to show that the percentage of Californians that prefer snowboarding is higher than the percentage for Coloradoans?

c) Determine a 90% confidence interval for the difference between the proportion of Californians and Coloradoans that prefer snowboarding.

d) Interpret the interval in terms of the application.

e) Explain how the interval obtained in part (c) agrees with the decision reached in the hypothesis test from part (b).

f) Have we made a type I error, a type II error, or a correct decision? Explain.

g) Do you think the company would be justified in choosing California as the focus of marketing dollars for the launch of its new products? Explain.

Solution:

a) The desired attribute in this problem is that the person selected prefers snowboarding, so such a person would be considered a success. We need at least 5 successes and at least 5 failures in each state.

California: 458 success, $1012 - 458 = 554$ failures. These are both well over 10.

Colorado: 191 successes, $870 - 191 = 679$ failures. These are both well over 10.

The requirements have been met.

b) The wording here implies a hypothesis test, so we will complete the standard six step process.

STEP 1: The key idea here is that we want to know if the percentage is higher in California than in Colorado, so this will be a right-tailed test. The claims are as follows:

$$H_o : p_1 = p_2$$
$$H_1 : p_1 > p_2$$

STEP 2: The significance level is given as 5%, so $\alpha = 0.05$.

STEP 3: Before we go to the formula we need to compute the individual sample proportions as well as the pooled sample proportion.

$$\text{Sample 1 (California) produces: } \hat{p}_1 = \frac{x_1}{n_1} = \frac{458}{1012} \approx 0.4526 \Rightarrow \hat{q}_1 = 1 - \hat{p}_1 \approx 0.5474$$

$$\text{Sample 2 (Colorado) produces: } \hat{p}_2 = \frac{x_2}{n_2} = \frac{191}{870} \approx 0.2195 \Rightarrow \hat{q}_2 = 1 - \hat{p}_2 \approx 0.7805$$

$$\text{Pooled Sample: } \hat{p}_p = \frac{x_1 + x_2}{n_1 + n_2} = \frac{458 + 191}{1012 + 870} = \frac{649}{1882} \approx 0.3448 \Rightarrow \hat{q}_p = 1 - \hat{p}_p = 0.6552$$

So our test statistic is:

$$z = \frac{\hat{p}_1 - \hat{p}_2}{\sqrt{\hat{p}_p \hat{q}_p \left(\dfrac{1}{n_1} + \dfrac{1}{n_2} \right)}} = \frac{0.4526 - 0.2195}{\sqrt{0.3448 * 0.6552 \left(\dfrac{1}{1012} + \dfrac{1}{870} \right)}} \approx 10.607$$

Note 1: A z-score over 3 indicates a difference between the sample proportions that would be very unusual to see if the population proportions were equal. Our z-score is way over 3, so it is hard to believe that this difference is due to random chance, but we will check our p-value to verify this.

Note 2: This is what the calculation of the test statistic should look like on the TI-84:

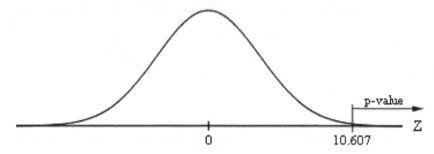

```
(.4526-.2195)/√(
.3448*.6552*(1/1
012+1/870))
        10.60746906
```

STEP 4: Our test statistic is a z-value and this is a right-tailed test. So, we need to find the area to the right of 10.607 under the standard normal curve.

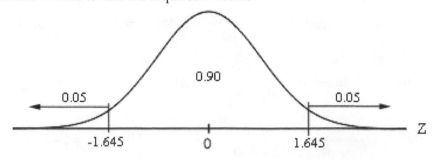

Using the TI-84, we get: P-value = $normalcdf\,(10.607, \infty) \approx 0.0000$.

STEP 5: Our p-value is essentially zero, so certainly it is less than 5%, therefore, with an acceptably small risk of making a type I error, we Reject H_o .

STEP 6: We had enough evidence, at the 5% significance level, to show that the percentage of Californians that prefer snowboarding is higher than the percentage for Coloradoans.

c) Because we are asked to find a 90% confidence interval, the area in the middle will be 0.90. That leaves 0.10 remaining and when we split that between the two tails, we get an area in the tail of 0.05. We will then use inverse normal to find the required z-scores.

With that, we are ready to jump into the formula:

$$\left(\hat{p}_1 - \hat{p}_2\right) \pm z^* \sqrt{\frac{\hat{p}_1 \hat{q}_1}{n_1} + \frac{\hat{p}_2 \hat{q}_2}{n_2}} = \left(0.4526 - 0.2195\right) \pm 1.645 \sqrt{\frac{0.4526 * 0.5474}{1012} + \frac{0.2195 * 0.7805}{870}}$$

$$= 0.2331 \pm 0.0346 \Rightarrow \left(p_1 - p_2\right) \in \left(0.1985,\ 0.2677\right)$$

d) I am 90% confident that the proportion of Californians that prefer snowboarding is somewhere between 19.85% higher to 26.77% higher than for Coloradoans.

e) $\left(p_1 - p_2\right) \in \left(0.1985,\ 0.2677\right) \Rightarrow p_1 - p_2 > 0 \Rightarrow p_1 > p_2 \Rightarrow H_1 : p_1 > p_2$ is true and $H_o : p_1 = p_2$ is false $\Rightarrow$ We should reject H_o. And this is what we did in part (b).

f) Because we rejected H_o, it is possible we have made a type I error. This has only happened if H_o is true. I perceive the risk of this to be almost zero.

g) If they want to launch their new product in an area that has a higher percentage of snowboarders, then spending the money in California certainly seems justified.

It's time to practice with some exercises.

Exercise Set 11.3

(27-28) Fill in the blanks for each of the following.

27) The requirements for two-sample proportion studies are that each _____ must contain at least 10 _____ and at least 10 _____ .

28) $p_1 - p_2 < 0 \Rightarrow p_1$ is _____ than p_2.
$p_1 - p_2 > 0 \Rightarrow p_1$ is _____ than p_2.

(29-32) a)   Calculate the value of the test stat.
b)   Find the P-value.
c)   State whether or not you would reject H_o if the significance level was 5%.

29) $H_o : p_1 = p_2$; $n_1 = 195$, $x_1 = 122$
$H_1 : p_1 > p_2$ $n_2 = 147$, $x_2 = 89$

30) $H_o : p_1 = p_2$; $n_1 = 313$, $x_1 = 97$
$H_1 : p_1 < p_2$ $n_2 = 281$, $x_2 = 118$

31) $H_o : p_1 = p_2$; $n_1 = 675$, $x_1 = 350$
$H_1 : p_1 \neq p_2$ $n_2 = 692$, $x_2 = 309$

32) $H_o : p_1 = p_2$; $n_1 = 912$, $x_1 = 65$
$H_1 : p_1 \neq p_2$ $n_2 = 1081$, $x_2 = 74$.

33) The most common blood type in the world is O+. The proportion of this blood type in different countries can vary quite a bit. For example: In Ireland, 47% of the population has type O+ blood, while in South Korea only 27.4% have this blood type. A random sample of 419 Americans revealed that 157 had type O+ blood. A random sample of 387 Canadians revealed that 151 of them had type O+ blood.

a)   Perform a hypothesis test, at the 5% significance level, to see if the proportion of type O+ blood is different in the U.S. (population 1) and Canada (population 2).
b)   Compute a 95% confidence interval for the difference between the proportion of type O+ blood in the U.S. and in Canada.
c)   Interpret the interval in terms of the application.
d)   Explain how the interval from part (b) agrees with the decision reached in part (a).
e)   Comment on the requirements.
f)   For the decision made in part a), discuss the possibility that we made a type I error, a type II error, or a correct decision? Explain.

34) In June of 2006, a random sample of 1087 Americans was obtained and asked the following question: "Which do you believe is the more important factor in a college education, how much is learned or the reputation of the college?" Among the 384 members of the sample that had a college degree, 306 believed the more important factor was how much is learned. Among the 703 who did not have a college degree, 570 believed that the more important factor was how much is learned.

   a) Perform a hypothesis test, at the 10% significance level, to see if the proportion of those with a degree (population 1) who believe that what is learned is the most important factor differs from the proportion of those without a degree that believe the same thing.
   b) Compute a 90% confidence interval for the difference between the proportion of those with and without a college degree who believe that the most important factor is how much is learned.
   c) Interpret the interval in terms of the application.
   d) Explain how the interval from part (b) agrees with the decision reached in part (a).
   e) Comment on the requirements.
   f) For the decision made in part a), discuss the possibility that we made a type I error, a type II error, or a correct decision? Explain.

35) Studies have shown that driving while talking on a cell phone increases the chance of getting into an accident. Because of this, many states are enacting laws that require the use of a hands-free device if talking on a cell phone while driving. In June 2006, random samples were taken in both states with such laws and states without these laws. In the states with these laws (pop 1), 259 of the 473 people sampled said that they use a hands-free device when driving while on the phone. In states without such a law (pop 2), 235 of the 831 people sampled said that they use a hands-free device when driving while on the phone.

   a) Does the data provide enough evidence, at the 1% significance level, to show that the proportion of people who use hands-free devices is higher in the states that have laws requiring such use?
   b) Compute a 98% confidence interval for the difference between the proportion of hands-free device use between the states with and without laws requiring them.
   c) Interpret the interval in terms of the application.
   d) Explain how the interval from part (b) agrees with the decision reached in part (a).
   e) Comment on the requirements.
   f) Explain in terms of evidence and the application what it would mean to make a type I error in this problem.

36) A random sample of 152 vehicles on the road revealed that 39 of them had drivers talking on a cell phone. A random sample of 74 vehicles that were deemed to have made an unsafe maneuver while driving found that 53 of them had drivers talking on a cell phone.

   a) Does the data provide enough evidence, at the 5% significance level, to show that the proportion of cell phone use by the driver is higher among vehicles making unsafe maneuvers (pop 2) than among the general population of vehicles (pop 1) on the road?
   b) Compute a 90% confidence interval for the difference in the proportion of drivers talking while driving between vehicles in general and those making an unsafe maneuver.
   c) Interpret the interval in terms of the application.
   d) Explain how the interval from part (b) agrees with the decision reached in part (a).
   e) Comment on the requirements.
   f) Explain in terms of evidence and the application what it would mean to make a type I error in this problem.

37) In June 2007, a study was conducted to investigate the prevalence of households that relied solely on cell phones versus households that had landlines. The study revealed that 13.2% of the 258 men sampled and 10.4% of the 241 women sampled lived in a cell phone only household.

   a) Does the data provide enough evidence, at the 10% significance level, to show that there is a difference between the proportion of men and women that live in cell phone only households?
   b) Comment on the requirements.
   c) Compute a 90% confidence interval for the difference between the proportion of men and women that live in cell phone only households.
   d) Interpret the interval in terms of the application.
   e) Explain how the interval from part (c) agrees with the decision reached in part (a).

38) A study conducted in June 2007 found that, in a sample of 117 adults that lived in households that relied solely on cell phones, 68.4% had health insurance. The same study revealed that 84.7% of the 819 adults living in households with landlines had health insurance.

   a) Does the data provide enough evidence, at the 1% significance level, to show that there is a lower proportion of health insurance among adults that live in cell phone only households?
   b) Comment on the requirements.
   c) Compute a 98% confidence interval for the difference in the proportion of adults that have health insurance between those living in cell phone only households and those that have a landline.
   d) Interpret the interval in terms of the application.
   e) Explain how the interval from part (c) agrees with the decision reached in part (a).

Chapter 11 – Review Exercises

1) An automotive magazine tested the breaking distance from 60 to 0 mph for a random sample of cars and SUVs. The results of the samples are shown below. The distances were measured in feet.

   Cars: $n_1 = 12$ $\bar{x}_1 = 134.9$ $s_1 = 6.4904$

   SUVs: $n_2 = 9$ $\bar{x}_2 = 141.4$ $s_2 = 7.2017$

   a) Does the data provide enough evidence, at the 1% significance level, to show that there is a difference between the average breaking distance of cars and SUVs?
   b) Compute a 99% confidence interval for the difference between the average breaking distance of cars and SUVs.
   c) Interpret the interval in terms of the application.
   d) Explain how the interval from part (b) agrees with the decision reached in part (a).
   e) Comment on the requirements.
   f) If the true mean values for the breaking distances are $\mu_1 = 132.8$ and $\mu_2 = 140.5$, then, in part (a), did we make a type I error, a type II error, or a correct decision? Explain.

2) The makers of a new phone with superior text messaging capabilities are trying to decide whether to focus their advertising dollars on people below or above 40 years old. A random sample of 212 cell phone users between the ages of 18 and 39 revealed that 146 of them use text messaging. A random sample of 219 cell phone users between the ages of 40 and 54 revealed that 77 of them use text messaging.

   a) Does the data provide enough evidence, at the 10% significance level, to show that there is a difference between the proportion of text message users among the younger and older age groups?
   b) Comment on the requirements.
   c) Compute a 90% confidence interval for the difference in the proportion of text message users among the younger and older age groups.
   d) Interpret the interval in terms of the application.
   e) Explain how the interval from part (c) agrees with the decision reached in part (a).
   f) What advice would you give the makers of this new product about where to spend their advertising dollars?

3) A statistics student is hooked on playing the drums on the video game *Rock Band*. He often plays each song he is attempting two times. He is interested in investigating the difference in performance between the first try and the second try. The data below shows the percentage of notes correctly played on the first and second attempt for 15 songs randomly selected from the hard level of the game. The data is paired by attempts at a single song.

1st	2nd	1st	2nd	1st	2nd
85	93	98	99	81	81
96	96	96	96	88	93
90	91	96	99	84	87
75	79	91	93	93	95
82	85	83	83	86	89

   Note: $\sum d^2 = 151$

   a) Is there enough evidence, at the 5% significance level to show that the second attempt at a song will be, on average, better than the first attempt?
   b) Compute a 90% confidence interval for the difference in the mean percentage of notes correctly played between the first and second attempt.
   c) Interpret the interval in terms of the application.
   d) Explain how the interval from part (b) agrees with the decision reached in part (a).
   e) Comment on the requirements.
   f) In the decision in part (a), did we make a type I error, a type II error, or a correct decision? Explain.

APPENDIX A - TI Calculator Directions

Chapter 1:

Random Number Generation: The RandInt function is located by choosing MATH > PRB >RandInt(. This produces a random integer between A and B , inclusive. To get integers from A to B, you will need to enter the RandInt(A, B). Press enter repeatedly to get multiple numbers from the same formula.

Ex: To get an integer between 10 and 20 inclusive: RandInt(10,20)

Chapter 2:

Entering Data: Choose STAT > EDIT > Edit .. and you will be taken to the list editor screen. Simply enter data in the desired list. Press ENTER or the down arrow after each number.

Clearing Data: Highlight the heading of the list you want to clear (L1, L2, etc.). Press the CLEAR button and then ENTER. Do NOT push the DEL key, Pushing the DEL key removes the list from the Editor (and actually does not clear it!)

Column Operations / Building Tables: To perform a mathematical operation on all the elements of a list and store the results in a new list, you must do the following.

1. Use the arrow keys to highlight the heading of the list you want to fill with new values. At the bottom of the screen, you will now see something like L2 =
2. Enter the formula you want to use to fill the list. For example: L2 = L1 / 45
3. Press ENTER

Finding the Sum of the Data in a List: Choose LIST (above the STAT key) > MATH > sum(. Then select the list you want the sum of from the key pad. The list names L1, L2, etc. are above the number keys. Use the 2ND to access the list names.

Sorting a Data List: To sort the data in a list, Choose STAT > EDIT > SortA(L1) and press ENTER (Sort Ascending) or Choose STAT > EDIT > SortD(L1) and press ENTER (Sort Descending).

Chapter 3:

Summary Statistics for Raw Data: How to get the mean, standard deviation, median, etc for a raw data set.

1. Enter the data set one number at a time into L1 (or some other list).
2. Choose STAT > CALC > 1-Var Stats and then use the keypad to select L1, and finally press the ENTER key.
3. If you entered sample data, then use $\bar{x}$ for the sample mean and Sx for the sample standard deviation (change the symbol to s .) If you entered population data, then use $\bar{x}$ for the population mean (but change the symbol to μ), and use σx for the population standard deviation (change the symbol to σ .)
4. The Min, Med, and Max will be correct, but Q1 and Q3 use a different formula than this book.

Summary Statistics for Grouped Data: How to get the mean, standard deviation, median, etc for a grouped data set. Same as above, but you must also enter the frequencies into L2 and then choose 1-Var Stats L1, L2 (Both lists must be specified separated by the comma. The comma is the key above the 7 key.)

Chapter 4:

Turning on the r and r^2 feature: The default setting on the TI does not show the values of r and r^2. To change this setting do the following steps. (They only need to be done once.) Choose CATALOG (2ND 0) and then scroll down until the arrow points at DiagnosticOn. Press the ENTER key twice.

Linear Regression, Coefficient of Determination, and Correlation: The following steps will produce all three of the results needed in this chapter.

1. Enter the x-values in List 1 and the y-values in List 2.
2. Choose STAT > CALC > 8:LinReg(a + bx) L1, L2 and press ENTER.
3. To verify $\sum xy$, you must choose STAT > CALC > 2-Var Stats L1, L2 and then scroll down.

Chapter 5:

Calculating Combinations: To calculate combinations you need the nCr function. To get this, press MATH > PRB > nCr.

Ex: To calculate $\begin{pmatrix} 8 \\ 5 \end{pmatrix}$, press 8 nCr 5 ENTER.

Calculating Values for the Binomial Formula: Similar to above, you will need the nCr function from the MATH > PRB menu.

Ex: To Calculate $\begin{pmatrix} 8 \\ 5 \end{pmatrix}(0.72)^5 (0.28)^3$, press 8 nCr 5 * 0.72 ^ 5 * 0.28 ^ 3 ENTER.

Editing the Last Calculation: If you are entering many similar expressions into the calculator, you might want to just edit the last one. After pressing ENTER, press 2ND and then ENTER (This accesses the word ENTRY.). You can then move around with the arrow keys, make changes, and press ENTER to get the new result.

Mean and Standard Deviation for a Discrete Random Variable: How to get the mean, standard deviation:

1. Enter the X-values one number at a time into L1.
2. Enter the probabilities for the X-values into L2.
3. Choose STAT > CALC > 1-Var Stats L1, L2
4. Use the value of $\bar{x}$ for μ_x and the use σx for σ_x.

Chapter 6:

<u>Finding Area Under the Standard Normal Curve</u>: To find the area under the standard normal curve between a given lower boundary and upper boundary, do the following:

1. Choose DISTR (2ND VARS) > normalcdf(

2. Enter the value of the lower boundary (If there is no lower boundary, then enter $-1*10^{99}$.) a comma and then the value of the upper boundary (If there is no upper boundary, then enter $1*10^{99}$.)

Ex: the area between –1.653 and 2.007 is given by: normalcdf(-1.653, 2.007).

Note: It is useful to store the value $1*10^{99}$ into the variable I. Then you can enter –I when there is no lower boundary or I when there is no upper boundary. (See below.)

<u>Storing $1*10^{99}$ in the variable I</u>: This only needs to be done once. Do the following: Type $1*10 \wedge 99$ and then the STO> key and then ALPHA and I. Finally press ENTER. (The STO> key is located 1 key above the ON key. The ALPHA key is green. I is above the 'x^2' key.

<u>Working Backwards</u>: If you need to find a z-score when given area under the curve, do the following steps.

1. Determine the area to the left of the z-score you want. You must always use an area to the left. Make adjustments to the area given if they did not give an area to the left.
2. Choose DISTR > invNorm(
3. Enter the area to the left.
4. Press ENTER.

Ex: To find the z-score with area 0.05 to its left: invNorm(0.05) ENTER

Chapter 9:

<u>Finding P-values using the student t-distribution</u>: These P-values are just areas under the student t-curve, so finding them is very similar to finding area under the standard normal curve in Chapter 6. After sketching the area you need to find, do the following steps.

1. Choose DISTR > tcdf(
2. Enter the lower and upper boundaries of your shaded region. (Use $1*10^{99}$, $-1*10^{99}$, or ALPHA I as needed.)
3. Enter the value for the DF.
4. Press ENTER.

Ex: To find the area to the right of t = 1.873 with df = 17 enter: tcdf(1.873, 1*10 $\wedge$ 99, 17)

Chapter 10:

Finding P-values using the Chi-Square distribution: These P-values are just areas under the χ^2 curve, so finding them is very similar to finding area under the student t-curve in Chapter 9. After sketching the area you need to find, do the following steps.

1. Choose DISTR > χ^2cdf(
2. Enter the lower and upper boundaries of your shaded region. (Use $1*10^{99}$ or ALPHA I for the upper boundary.)
3. Enter the value for the DF.
4. Press ENTER.

Ex: For the area to the right of $\chi^2 = 6.722$ with df = 5 enter: χ^2cdf$\left(6.722, 1*10^{99}, 5\right)$

Working Backwards: If you need to find a χ^2 when given area under the curve, do the following steps.

1. Choose MATH > Solver...
2. Where it lists eqn: 0 =, complete the equation as $0 = \chi^2 cdf(0, X, D) - A$
3. Press enter.
4. Enter the degrees of freedom on the D line and the area to the left on the A line.
5. Use the arrow keys to move to the X line.
6. Press the ALPHA key and then SOLVE (Enter Key).

Computing the values of $\dfrac{(O-E)^2}{E}$: If you have many categories where you need to calculate these values, use these steps to speed up the process.

1. Choose STAT > EDIT > Edit . .
2. Enter all of the observed frequencies, O's, into L1
3. Enter all of the expected frequencies, E's, into L2
4. Use the arrow keys to highlight the heading of the list you want to fill with the Chi-Square contributions (Mini z-scores). At the bottom of the screen, you will now see something like L3 =
5. Enter the formula to fill the list.: L2 = (L1 – L2)^2/L2
6. Press ENTER
7. You can also find the sum of this new column by choosing LIST > MATH > Sum(L3)

Section 1.1:

1) When you are only seeking to organize or summarize your data, this is referred to as <u>descriptive</u> statistics.

2) When you attempt to draw conclusions about the population, based on information you obtained from a sample, that is known as <u>inferential</u> statistics.

3) The group of people or things you wish to state your conclusions about is known as the <u>population</u> .

4) The <u>sample</u> is the part of the population that your data is collected from.

5) a) The population is the entire surface of the resort (all spots on the mountain).
   b) The sample is the 41 locations where the depth measurements were taken.

7) a) All students at the teacher's school.
   b) The 85 students surveyed by the teacher.

9) a) All of the hybrid SUVs of this model type built by this manufacturer.
   b) The 12 vehicles that were tested in city driving conditions.

11) a) the population (we will only be reporting the information to these students)
    b) Descriptive (We are only describing the population.)

13) a) a sample (we are using these 500 likely voters to estimate what all Massachusetts voters will do.)
    b) Inferential (estimating population results based on this sample.)

15) a) the population (We are only talking about Tahoe resorts and we have data from all of them.)
    b) Descriptive (We are only describing the population.)

17) a) Of the 2,077 video game players surveyed, 41.49% of them were female.
    b) Based on the survey of 2,077 video game players, it is estimated that about 41.49% of all video game players are female.

19) a) For this to be descriptive, we should only be describing the results for the first 10 games. "The star player on this basketball team averaged 26.3 points during the first 10 games of the season."
    b) For this to be inferential, we must expand the results beyond the first 10 games. "Based on the first 10 games, we estimate that the star of the local team will average about 26.3 points per game this season."

Section 1.2:

21) An Observational study is one where the researchers simply collect <u>natural</u> data. This type <u>can not</u> show cause and effect.

22) A designed experiment is one where the researchers design and <u>control</u> the experiment. This type <u>can</u> show cause and effect.

23) In a designed experiment, the different values for a variable that will be assigned to the subjects by the experimenter are known as the <u>treatments</u>.

24) In a designed experiment, if neither the participants nor those conducting the experiment are aware of what treatments are given to each participant, then this is known as a <u>double</u> <u>blind</u> experiment.

25) In order to avoid the effects of confounding variables, it is important that we use <u>randomization</u> to assign subjects to either a control or treatment group.

26) In order to make sure that differences between the treatment groups and the control group is not just due to <u>random</u> variation, we need to conduct our experiments using many subjects. This is known as <u>replication</u>.

27) a) Observational. This is a life-long study and to be designed, the researcher would have to control the amount of sleep for the participants for their entire lives.
    b) No, because we can't prove cause and effect in an observational study.
    c) The person's genetics might affect both how long they live and how much sleep they need.

29) a) Designed. The farmer decided whether or not each plant received the fertilizer.
   b) Yes, since it is a designed study.
   c) The soil that the two different treatments are planted in might be different.

31) a) Designed. The teacher randomly split the students into the two groups and required one group to do the homework.
   b) Yes, since it is a designed study.
   c) The students IQ could be a confounder. A smarter student might do the HW because it is easy, but a struggling student might not complete the homework because they don't know how. Randomization should help minimize this problem.

33) a) Observational. If this were designed, then the researcher would have decided how many children each family had.
   b) No, with observational studies, we always have to worry about the effects of confounding variables.
   c) A possible confounding variable might be the IQ of the parents. Those with higher IQs tend to have less children in modern society.

35) a) The treatments are fertilizer or no fertilizer.
   b) The quantity and quality of the tomatoes are both mentioned as possible response variables.
   c) There is replication because the farmer is using a large number of plants in the experiment.
   d) Not really. The farmer seems to know which plants are getting the fertilizer. The plants are unaware, but that is not due to blinding efforts.
   e) The problem does not mention randomizing the treatments. We may still need to worry about the quality of the soil for the two different groups.

37) a) Homework completion required for the test and homework completion not required.
   b) The test scores.
   c) Yes. Many students are assigned to each group.
   d) No. The students are told whether or not homework completion is required and the instructor knows which students are in each group.
   e) The instructor *randomly* split the class into two groups. This should roughly divide any confounding variables evenly between the groups.

39) a) Replication: multiple babies receiving multiple heel sticks.
      Randomization: Even though they didn't actually randomize, they did alternate between mom and dad for the multiple sticks for each baby.
      Treatments: The two treatments were mom holding or dad holding.
   b) The baby's pain reaction might increase or decrease over time. So, if they always had mom do the first half and dad the last half, that could have introduced confounders. The alternation should help here.
   c) Yes. The baby felt significantly less pain when held by mom and this was a well designed study.
   d) They should have explained the risks to the parents and received written consent for participation. The identities of the babies and parents should be kept confidential.

Section 1.3:

41) When you collect data from the entire population of interest, that is known as taking a <u>census</u> . Two disadvantages of this are that it can be <u>destructive</u> or <u>expensive</u> .

42) To minimize our sampling error, we want our samples to be <u>representative</u> rather than biased. This means that the sample contains all the relevant characteristics of the population in the same <u>proportion</u> as they exist in the population.

43) The procedure were each possible sample of a given size is equally likely to be the one chosen is referred to as <u>simple</u> <u>random</u> <u>sample</u> .

44) Sampling error is the result of <u>random</u> variation in our samples. However, the variation decreases as our sample size gets <u>larger</u>. This helps us to get roughly representative samples.

45) Sampling without <u>replacement</u> is a method where after an item is selected, it is <u>NOT</u> returned to the sampling pool.

46) a) Cluster Sampling
    b) Stratified Sampling
    c) Systematic Sampling

47) **TI-84**: On the calculator, choose MATH > PRB > RANDINT(1,20) and then press ENTER 10 times. Repeats are allowed. Answers will vary due to random selection.

StatCrunch: Use DATA > SEQUENCE DATA to enter 1 to 20 in a column. Then choose DATA > SAMPLE COLUMNS and select the column, enter the sample size of 10 and click the "sample with replacement box." Answers will vary due to random selection.

49) **TI-84**: On the calculator, choose MATH > PRB > RANDINT(20,60) and then press ENTER repeatedly. Ignore repeats. Write down results until you have 15 different values. Answers will vary due to random selection.

StatCrunch: Use DATA > SEQUENCE DATA to enter 20 to 60 in a column. Then choose DATA > SAMPLE COLUMNS and select the column, enter the sample size of 15 and make sure that the "sample with replacement box" is NOT checked. Answers will vary due to random selection.

51) STEP 1: $N = 100, n = 12 \Rightarrow \dfrac{100}{12} \approx 8.33 \Rightarrow k = 8$
STEP 2 (**TI-84**): On the calculator, choose MATH > PRB > randInt(1,8). The result is m.

STEP 2 (**StatCrunch**): Use DATA > SEQUENCED DATA to enter 1 to 8 in a column. Then choose DATA > SAMPLE COLUMNS and select the column, and enter a sample size of 1. The result is m.

STEP 3: Sample is:
$m, m + k, m + 2k, \ldots, m + 11k$
Answers will vary due to random selection.

53) STEP 1: $N = 5400, n = 32 \Rightarrow \dfrac{5400}{32} = 168.75 \Rightarrow$
$k = 168$ (We always round down here.)

STEP 2 (**TI-84**): On the calculator, choose MATH > PRB > randInt(1,168). The result is m.

STEP 2 (**StatCrunch**): Use DATA > SEQUENCED DATA to enter 1 to 168 in a column. Then choose DATA > SAMPLE COLUMNS and select the column, and enter a sample size of 1. The result is m.

STEP 3: Sample is:
$m, m + k, m + 2k, \ldots, m + 31k$
Answers will vary due to random selection.

55) a) Let the tables be the clusters.
    b) There are 10 players per table and they need 60 people, so they should choose 6 tables.
    c) The tables are probably numbered from 1 to 50, so choose 6 numbers without replacement using randInt(1 , 50). Then select all the players at the selected table numbers.
    d) A big advantage to the card room would be that they only need to disrupt 6 of their games to accomplish the survey. The disadvantage might be similar responses from people at the same table.

57) a) Dems: $0.517 * 980 = 506.66$
    Reps: $0.431 * 980 = 422.38$
    Other: $0.052 * 980 = 50.96$
    Rounding to the nearest whole number, we get 507 Dems, 422 Reps, and 51 Others.
    b) The advantage of stratifying is that political affiliation, an important characteristic, will be properly represented. The disadvantage is that this may be a bit more of a time consuming and thus expensive sampling process.

59) a) The default method would be to take a simple random sample. Lacking details, I would assume that this is the method that they used.

b) They want to get a good representative sample so they can extend their results to all Americans.

c) As long as they do a good job getting the simple random sample, it should be pretty representative with a large sample of 1000 people. However, random variation will always mean that we don't get perfect answers.

61) a) Since they want to ensure that race is properly represented, they would use the stratified sampling method.

b) People of different races may have different views on racism. Therefore, it is critical to represent these groups properly.

c) This should produce a good representative sample provided that they use a large sample size. As always, random variation in the sample will prevent us from getting perfect answers.

63) a) Choosing all the students from one location on campus will not give all math students an equal chance at being chosen.

b) Students in the math lab are motivated and tend to study more. This sample will probably bias the result towards a higher than actual mean study time.

65) a) People exiting a Starbucks are much more likely to drink beverages that include a shot of espresso than the typical adult.

b) I think the results will be biased towards a high percentage reporting that they drink beverages with a shot of espresso.

c) If she changed the population to all of the customers of this particular Starbuck's, then her results would be more accurate.

Section 1.4:

67) If you are presented with a study that used problematic sampling methods then you should disregard the results.

68) A survey question that has been worded in such a way that it encourages one answer over others is called a loaded question .

69) When those conducting or funding the study have a vested interest in a certain result, this is considered a suspicious source.

70) When a poll is conducted using the method of volunteer sampling, they usually refer to it as a non-scientific study.

71) a) This sounds like volunteer sampling and it should be considered a non-scientific study.

b) People might vote many times for people from their hometown. Therefore, the results might be biased towards people from bigger towns.

73) a) This sounds like attention getting data, because the player waited for data that was surprising or unusual.

b) If you wait until you see data that supports something you wish to prove, your chance of "proving" it increases. If this player has played in over 1000 tournaments and is an average player, then this should happen somewhere in his results.

75) a) This sounds like hand-picking the data. The researcher was throwing out data that did not conform to his theory.

b) By throwing out the data that doesn't support the theory, the remaining data is biased towards supporting the theory.

77) a) Convenience Sampling.

b) People in the author's circle are more likely to agree with the author about the speed limit than people in general.

79) a) Pre-Existing data. She decided to check bias towards "heads" after seeing the results.

b) Random variation can produce more heads or more tails than we expect even for a fair coin. When we only consider the more heads option, we lessen the effect of random variation in our analysis.

81) a) By referring to the execution as "murder", they are encouraging the respondent to say NO to this question.

b) "Do you support the death penalty for those convicted of acts of terrorism?"

83) a) The question begins by telling you why they feel guns are not a good form of self-defense. They are encouraging you to say "No".
   b) A better question might be "Do you feel that gun ownership is an effective form of self-defense?"

85) a) The result of the study states that listening to the radio is beneficial. Not only are we hearing about the study via the radio, but the study was written by someone who sells radio advertising.
   b) No, but the details of this study should be thoroughly investigated if you were going to make an important decision based on these results.

87) a) This source is suspicious because if you believe the study that they are citing, then you would be encouraged to pay for their services.
   b) No, but when the source is suspicious, you may want to go online and investigate this more on your own.

Section 1.5:

89) A variable that takes on non-numeric values is known as a categorical variable.

90) If the variable takes on numeric values, then it is known as a quantitative variable.

91) Quantitative variables whose possible values have gaps between them are known as discrete.

92) Quantitative variables whose possible values do not have gaps between them, but rather form an interval are known as continuous.

93) a) The selected student's favorite beverage
   b) Sarsaparilla
   c) Categorical

95) a) The selected Californian's number of speeding tickets in the last 3 years.
   b) Zero
   c) Quantitative – Discrete

97) a) The height of the selected Giraffe.
   b) 17.3 feet tall
   c) Quantitative – Continuous

99) a) The type of food chosen.
   b) Pizza.
   c) Categorical

101) a) The breaking distance for the selected SUV
    b) 87.4 feet
    c) Quantitative – Continuous

103) a) All adult Americans
    b) The answer to the "simpler tax code" question by the individuals.
    c) Categorical

105) a) All Americans (probably adults)
    b) The weight of the individual Americans
    c) Quantitative – Continuous

107) a) All women at age 70
    b) Treatment 1: Having 1 or 2 drinks per day
       Treatment 2: Having no drinks at all
    c) The treatment variable is the number of drinks which would be quantitative – discrete.
    d) Health at age 70.
    e) Categorical.

Chapter Problem:

a) All adults
b) Designed. The researchers decided which participants took the vitamins and which did not.
c) Treatment 1: taking a multi-vitamin
   Treatment 2: taking a placebo (no vitamin)
d) Occurrence of a serious illness within 6 years of the start of the trial.
e) The researchers used a large sample and randomized the treatment groups. This should roughly split any confounding variables equally between the two groups.

Chapter 1: Review Exercises

1) a) They are the population, because this is the group that the writer wishes to state the conclusions about.
   b) Descriptive statistics.

3) a) All children.
   b) The 1,500 kids involved in the UK study.
   c) Inferential statistics.

5) a) Because they are stating conclusions about people in general, rather than just talking about those in the study, this is inferential statistics.
   b) This time, they only applied the results to the people they collected data from. This is descriptive statistics.

7) a) Observational. The researcher did not control the birth order.
   b) No. Observational studies can only show a link. There may be other variables at play that are not being controlled and are confounding the results.
   c) The amount of time the parents spend with each child is a possible confounding variable.

9) a) This is a designed study because the researchers controlled the choices about the subjects texting activities.
   b) Walking without a phone, walking while reading a long text, walking while composing a text.
   c) The subjects walking form.
   d) Yes, multiple subjects were used, 26 adults.
   e) No. Both the subjects and the researchers new which treatment the subjects were receiving.

11) a) Because the cans are constantly flowing by, the starting point is probably not that important, but we will still randomize the starting point. First we calculate the spacing needed by dividing the population size by the sample size and rounding down. Because 5000 cans go by an hour, we will use 5000 as our population size.

$$\frac{5000}{35} \approx 142.857 \Rightarrow k = 142$$

Next, we would randomly choose a starting can from 1 to 142. Once that can has been chosen, we would choose every 142nd can after that until we had our 35 cans.

b) I will use the TI-84 to randomly select the starting point, m.

$m = randInt(1, 142) = 35$

So, I would start observing the flow and then choose can numbers 35, 177, 319, 461, 603, 745, . . . , 4863. Notice that the spacing between these numbers is 142.
c) We gain the advantage of having a smaller chance of getting a biased sample by spreading out the cans throughout the hour.

12) a) Cluster Sampling
    b) Because the bunches typically contain about 200 bananas, the worker will need 5 bunches to obtain the desired 1000 bananas. He should randomly choose 5 trees and then randomly choose a bunch from each tree.
    c) The advantage is that this will be much faster than randomly selecting 1000 individual bananas. The disadvantage is that the 200 bananas in each bunch might be very similar to each other, thus increasing the chance of a biased sample.

13) a) Dems: $600 * 0.363 = 217.8 \approx 218$
       Repubs: $600 * 0.308 = 184.8 \approx 185$
       Indeps: $600 * 0.329 = 197.4 \approx 197$
    b) The advantage is that political party affiliation is probably an important factor in how people feel about energy independence, and stratifying attempts to get this factor properly represented. Assuming the Rasmussen percentages are correct, the only real disadvantage is that it can be more work for the pollsters.

15) a) This study was based on attention getting data. We only looked at this data because it seemed like a surprising result.
    b) Not necessarily, attention getting data is always biased towards supporting the claim.

16) a) This is a convenience sample because she decided to use her Facebook friends to represent all Facebook users.
    b) Many of her friends will be in a similar age group as her and this may bias her results towards the activity level of her own age group.

17) a) The first version of the question favors the answer "no". The phrase "gun control" is seen by many as contrary to the 2nd amendment of the consitution.

b) The 2nd version seems to favor the answer "yes". To say that a law will be strengthed has an implication that the laws will become better.

19) a) Yes. If they receive their funding from a person that is fighting against voter ID laws, then they might be tempted to reach conclusions that make such laws look bad. However, just because the source is suspicious does not mean that the results are bad. We should just examine their work more carefully.

b) Ideally, we would like to find a source whose funding is not connected to one side of the issue or the other.

21) a) The set of all pitch counts for all starting pitchers in all games in Major League Baseball.

b) Pitch count.

c) 97 pitches.

d) Quantitative – discrete.

22) a) All people (probably adults), not just the people who participated.

b) The amount that the participants are spending.

c) Spending less.

d) Categorical.

23) In order for this to be a designed study, the researcher would have decided which participants were to be concussed. Ethics would preclude the researcher from hitting the subjects in the head!

25) a) The population is not clearly stated, but appears to be older adults.

b) The sample was made up of more than 400,000 healthy men and women between the ages of 50 to 71.

c) The main explanatory variable appears to be the amount of coffee consumed, though gender is also mentioned. The primary response variable is whether or not the subject died during the 13 year window of the study.

d) Amount of coffee consumed would be quantitative-continuous. The gender would be categorical. Death would also be categorical.

e) Observation. The researchers did not control how much coffee people drank, they merely collected data on this.

f) No. In observational studies, we cannot prove cause and effect relationships.

g) The overall health of the subjects could be a confounding variable. A healthier person's system might allow them to confortably drink coffee. However, if a subject became ill, they might be more likely to avoid coffee consumption and also more likely to die.

27) a) Blogging, focusing on social problems, open to comments, control.

b) Yes, the students were randomly assigned to one of six treatment groups.

c) Yes. 161 students participated and we would assume that they were divided roughly evenly into the 6 groups. This would mean more than 20 participants in each of the groups.

d) Level of social anxiety.

e) Yes. This was a designed study rather than an observational study. Therefore, it is reasonable to draw cause and effect conclusions from the study.

f) The participants would give informed written consent to participate. Given that they were high schools students, this should have also included parental consent. The identities of the participants should remain confidential.

28) a) Since the percentages for each group are not given, we must calculate them using fractions. In the population the percentage of households earning less than $25K is given by $\frac{387}{1973} \approx 0.1961 = 19.61\%$. To determine the number of such households, we take this percentage times the sample size. So we get: $\frac{387}{1973} * 50 \approx 9.81$. Similarly for $25K – < $50K we get $\frac{562}{1973} * 50 \approx 14.24$. Rounding these to the nearest integer, we get 10 from less than $25K, 14 from $25K – < $50K.

b) The population is all of the 1,973 households in this town.

c) The sample is the 50 households that were selected in the study.

d) Percentage of gross household income given to charity.

e) 9.3%

f) Quantitative – Continuous

g) Observational. They are simply asking for information that already exists.

h) This would be descriptive because the conclusion is only stated for the 50 households that participated in the survey.

i) This time it would be considered inferential because they are extending the results from the 50 households they surveyed to all of the households in the city.

Section 2.1:

1) The left hand boundary of the class description is called the lower <u>cutpoint</u> and the right hand boundary is called the <u>upper</u> <u>cutpoint</u>.

2) The number of items in each class is known as the <u>frequency</u> of the class.

3) The ratio of the number of items in each class to the total number of items in the data set is known as the <u>relative</u> <u>frequency</u>.

4) The midpoint of a class is the <u>average</u> of the lower and upper cutpoints. This value is often used as a representative for the data values in that class when making computations.

5) The difference between consecutive lower cutpoints is known as the class <u>width</u>.

6) We use the $-<$ symbols when grouping <u>continuous</u> data, but we just use the $-$ symbol alone when grouping <u>discrete</u> data.

7) a)

Points	Frequency	Rel Freq	Midpoints
10 – 14	1	0.0127	12
15 – 19	11	0.1392	17
20 – 24	20	0.2532	22
25 – 29	22	0.2785	27
30 – 34	14	0.1772	32
35 – 39	7	0.0886	37
40 – 44	3	0.0380	42
45 – 49	0	0.0000	47
50 – 54	1	0.0127	52
	79	1.0001	

b) The most commonly occurring class was 25 – 29 points with a frequency of 22. A good representative would be the midpoint, 27.

9) a)

Nickname	Frequency	Rel Freq
Steelers	6	0.1333
49ers	5	0.1111
Cowboys	5	0.1111
Packers	4	0.0889
Raiders	3	0.0667
Redskins	3	0.0667
Patriots	3	0.0667
Giants	3	0.0667
Colts	2	0.0444
Dolphins	2	0.0444
Broncos	2	0.0444
Jets	1	0.0222
Chiefs	1	0.0222
Bears	1	0.0222
Rams	1	0.0222
Ravens	1	0.0222
Buccaneers	1	0.0222
Saints	1	0.0222
	45	0.9998

b) No midpoint is needed because this is categorical data.

c) The Steelers have the most superbowls with 6 wins.

11) a)

# Movies	Frequency	Rel Freq
0	9	0.2903
1	15	0.4839
2	1	0.0323
3	4	0.1290
5	1	0.0323
10	1	0.0323
	31	1.0001

b) Adding up the frequencies for 3 or more movies we get the following:

$$\frac{4+1+1}{31} \approx 0.1935 = 19.35\%$$

13) a)

Labor Time	Frequency	Rel Freq	Midpoints
0 – < 5	1	0.0357	2.5
5 – < 10	7	0.2500	7.5
10 – < 15	4	0.1429	12.5
15 – < 20	9	0.3214	17.5
20 – < 25	5	0.1786	22.5
25 – < 30	1	0.0357	27.5
30 – < 35	1	0.0357	32.5
	28	1.0000	

b) Adding up the first 4 rows, we get:

$$\frac{1+7+4+9}{28} = 0.75 = 75\%$$

15) a)

Time	Freq	Rel Freq	Midpoints
3.5 - < 4.0	1	0.0222	3.75
4.0 - < 4.5	7	0.1556	4.25
4.5 - < 5.0	8	0.1778	4.75
5.0 - < 5.5	7	0.1556	5.25
5.5 - < 6.0	4	0.0889	5.75
6.0 - < 6.5	9	0.2000	6.25
6.5 - < 7.0	5	0.1111	6.75
7.0 - < 7.5	3	0.0667	7.25
7.5 - < 8.0	1	0.0222	7.75
	45	1.0001	

b) Not really only 4 out of 45 or 8.89% lasted that long.

17) a)

Hits	Frequency	Rel Freq	Midpoints
5 – 9	3	0.1667	7
10 – 14	3	0.1667	12
15 – 19	0	0.0000	17
20 – 24	3	0.1667	22
25 – 29	2	0.1111	27
30 – 34	4	0.2222	32
35 – 39	3	0.1667	37
	18	1.0001	

b) $\dfrac{3+2+4+3}{18} \approx 0.6667 = 66.67\%$

c) It's hard to say just based on the percentage from such a small sample of days. Random variation might still be playing a large role here.

19) a)

Score	Frequency	Rel Freq
0	2	0.0465
1	0	0.0000
2	3	0.0698
3	6	0.1395
4	22	0.5116
5	10	0.2326
	43	1.0000

b) All but 5 of the students met the teacher's expectations (or hope). That means that 38 out of 43 or about 88.37% met the expectation. This meets the description of "most of the students", so the teacher is probably satisfied with that.

21) a)

How Serious?	Frequency	Rel Freq
Very	18	0.3830
Somewhat	12	0.2553
Unsure	1	0.0213
Not Too	8	0.1702
Not	8	0.1702
	47	1.0000

b) We should add together the response for Somewhat and Very.

$$\frac{18+12}{47} \approx 0.6383 = 63.83\%$$

c) It is very unlikely that the percentage for all Americans would be the same as for these 47. This is a random sample, but only for a sample of size 47. Random variation will still allow for a lot of sampling error to exist here.

Section 2.2:

23) For a standard histogram, the bars are drawn from lower cutpoint to lower cutpoint . So, unless there is an empty class, there will be no gaps between the bars.

24) When doing a histogram for single value grouping, the bars start and end at half marks.

25) For categorical data, there is no natural flow from one bar to the next, so we do put gaps between the bars.

26) For histograms, we label the number line, but for bar charts, we label the bars .

27) For dotplots, if data values are repeated or if they are very close to each other, then we stack the dots.

28) If an inconsistent scale chops off the bottom of all our bars, this throws off the proportions between the bars. Such graphs can be misleading .

29) a) No. 1000 tosses is a large sample size and should have removed most of the effects of random variation. This graph seems to have a clear pattern, but it is not one where all the numbers are equally likely.

b) I would guess that there would be 4 heads. This makes sense intuitively because it is half of the coins, and 4 is also the tallest bar on our graph.

c) The height of the bar for 6 heads seems to be at about a frequency of 110, for 7 heads about 30 times, and about 7 times for 8 heads. So, I would estimate that about 147 times out of the 1000 tosses resulted in at least 6 heads out of the 8 coins.

31) a) The height of the bar for 20 - < 30 seems to be a little more than half way up between 0.50 and 0.60. So, I would estimate that the relative frequency is about 0.56 and thus 56% of the players are less than 30 years old.

b) There were 366 players left in the tournament at this point, so we get:
$$0.56 * 366 = 204.96 \approx 205$$
Therefore, I would estimate that there were about 205 players below the age of 30 left at this point in the tournament.

c) No. The players that remain at this point are some of the best players. The less skilled players that are out at this point might have mostly been younger or older players.

d) It appears that most of the successful players tend to be on the younger side of the field.

33) a)

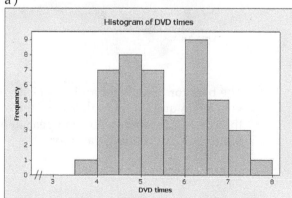

Notes: The bars go from lower cutpoint to lower cutpoint. No gaps exist between the bars. The double slash mark on the horizontal axis indicates a break in scale.

b)

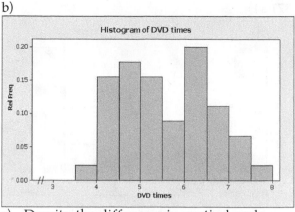

c) Despite the difference in vertical scale, they both give the same visual impression.

35) a)

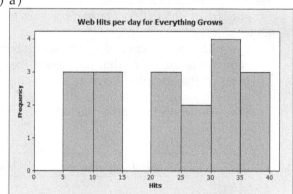

Notes: Even though the data is discrete and the first class is 5 – 9, the bars still go from lower cutpoint to lower cutpoint, so the first bar goes from 5 to 10 (no gaps.) Zero is in its standard location, so we do not need to draw in the double slash mark.

b) Yes. Most of the bars seem to be above 17 hits, including the tallest bar.

√ 37) a)

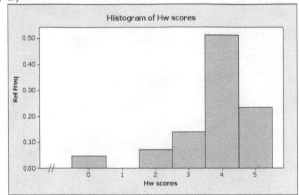

Notes: Because this is single value grouping, the bars are centered around the value of the class. For whole numbers like this, that means the bars go from 1/2 mark to 1/2 mark. The first bar goes from –0.5 to 0.5. The last bar goes from 4.5 to 5.5.

b) I would guess a score of 4. The tallest bar represents the score that happened the most in the sample. What happens in a random sample gives us an estimate of what will happen in the population.

39) a)

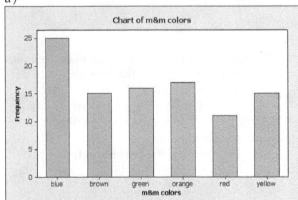

Notes: For categorical data, there is no numbering on the horizontal axis. We just write the description under each bar. Also, for categorical data we put gaps between the bars.

b)

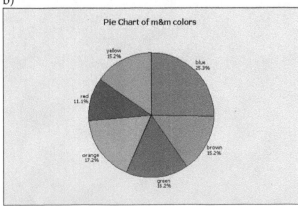

Notes: Start with easy percentages like 25.25% that make up about 1/4 of the graph. Then look for nice sums. For example Yellow plus Red makes up about 25%.

c) 99 m&m's is still considered a pretty small sample size , so the taller bar for blue and the shorter bar for red could possibly just be due to random variation. Yes that does seem reasonable.

d) It is probably a little better to use the bar graph when comparing the heights relative to each other. The pie chart is good for comparing a piece to the whole.

√ 41) a)

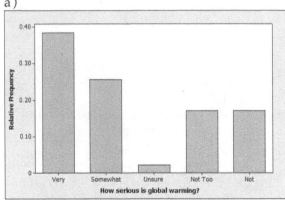

b)

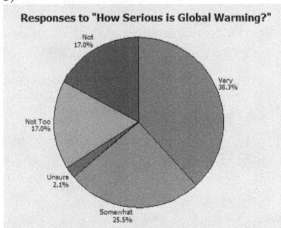

c) The bars for Somewhat and especially for very seem quite a bit higher than the other three bars. These difference appear to be more than just random variation.

43) a)

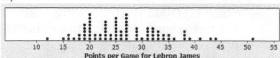

b)   Most of the time, LeBron seems to score
    somewhere between 15 and 35 points. The
    high of 51 points seems like it was an
    unusual occurrence.

45) a)

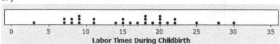

b)   There seem to actually be two gathering
    points for the data. Once around 8 hours
    and one around 19 hours. The data value of
    30.2 hours seems to be a bit unusual in this
    data set.

47) a) The bar for the D's appears to be about 3
         times as tall as the bar for F's. So it seems
         that there are about 3 times as many D's as
         F's in the class.
    b)   There are 6 D's and 4 F's. So the ratio is 6 to
         4 or reduced, 3 to 2. There are actually only
         1.5 times as many D's as F's.
    c)   The bars were truncated. By starting the
         vertical scale at 3, the 0 – 3 part of all the
         bars has been removed.

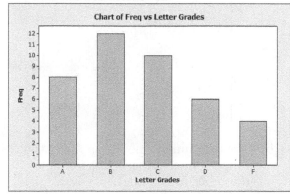

b)   The bar for the D's is now about 1.5 times
    higher than for the F's (which is true to
    the data).

49) a) The bar for the 4th quarter has some height
         to it even though the value for that bar was
         zero. In effect, this means that they
         started all of the bars at a height around –5
         minutes.
    b)

Packers Minutes Trailing by Quarter (during 18 game win streak)

c)   They probably just wanted to make sure
    that there was something visible there so
    that the viewers did not miss the data for
    that quarter.
d)   Since they didn't make bars that were of
    proper proportion, they probably should
    not have made a bar chart at all. Perhaps
    the data should have just been displayed in
    a table.

Section 2.3:

51) Because a stem-and-leaf diagram is interpreted
   like a histogram, it is extremely important
   that we have consistent <u>spacing</u> between the
   numbers.

52) For a standard stem-and-leaf diagram, the
   width of the classes is <u>10</u>. If we use two lines
   per stem, then the width is <u>5</u>.

53) a) 40, 40, 42, 42, 44, 44
    b)   Minutes played is a continuous variable
         (since decimal values are possible). There
         are two line per stem and no special notes
         about the units. So the class descriptions
         are: $0 - <5, 5 - <10, 10 - <15, 15 - <20,$
         $20 - <25, 25 - <30, 30 - <35, 35 - <40,$
         $40 - <45, 45 - <50$
    c)   At least 35 minutes falls into the last three
         rows, so we count the number of items on
         each of these rows.
         $$\frac{7+6+1}{69} \approx 0.2029 = 20.29\%$$

55) a) The note says that the leaf unit is 0.1, this implies that the stem is the ones place. So, we have: 2.5, 2.5, 2.5, 2.6, 2.8

b) GPA is a continuous variable (since many decimal values are possible). There are two line per stem. So the class descriptions are: $1.5 - < 2.0$, $2.0 - < 2.5$, $2.5 - < 3.0$, $3.0 - < 3.5$, $3.5 - < 4.0$, $4.0 - < 4.5$

c) At least a 3.0 falls into the last three rows, so we count the number of items on each of these rows.

$$\frac{16 + 15 + 2}{43} \approx 0.7674 = 76.74\%$$

d) There is no second stem of 4 because we are never supposed to begin or end with an empty class.

57) a)

```
0 | 0000000000000578889
1 | 0022446
2 | 0000000000555
3 | 00
4 | 00
```

b)

```
0 | 00000000000
0 | 578889
1 | 002244
1 | 6
2 | 0000000000
2 | 555
3 | 00
3 |
4 | 00
```

c) I think that two line per stem is a little better. It shows that the two people working 40 hours per week stand apart from the rest of the class. I think it also highlights that there are two high spots.

59) a)

```
 2 | 29
 3 | 7
 4 | 15679
 5 | 04
 6 | 112268
 7 | 23456699
 8 | 0013669
 9 | 013469
10 | 8
```

b) Most of the scores are above 60. Failing scores (below 50) were more rare.

61) a) We will make the leaves the ones digit which is standard. This means that we will just ignore the tenths place that is included in the data set.

```
54 | 79
55 | 2334
55 | 55566677788889
56 | 33344
56 | 56688
57 | 00233444
57 | 8
58 | 0
58 | 8
```

b) Yes. Only 2 of the 41 Big Macs had more than 580 calories.

63) a) We are asked to make the thousands digit the stem and the hundred place the leaves. This means that we will ignore all digits beyond those when making the graph. We should also note the non-standard units.

Note: The leaf unit is the hundreds place

```
 1 | 4
 2 | 779
 3 | 23
 4 | 055
 5 | 3689
 6 | 15669
 7 | 1789
 8 | 1257
 9 | 4
10 | 4
11 |
12 |
13 |
14 | 36
```

b) The two tuition amounts in the $14,000 range both stand far apart from all of all the other universities.

Section 2.4:

65) If the left and right hand sides of a distribution are mirror images of one another, then we refer to that as a <u>symmetric</u> distribution.

66) If a graph has extreme values on one side, but not on the other, then it is referred to as either a left or right <u>skewed</u> distribution.

67) When we look at the graph of sample data, we are not actually trying to determine the shape of the sample, rather we are trying to determine the shape of the distribution of the <u>population</u> from which it was taken.

68) It can be difficult to determine the distribution of the population from sample data if the sample size is too <u>small</u> .

69) a) Right-Skewed or Severely Right-Skewed. Most of the data in the sample is on the left side and the extremes are on the right.
   b) If the sample size was bigger. More sample data gives us a better view of the true population shape.

71) a) Right skewed. The tallest bars are on the left side and the shorter ones are on the right. The tail on the right isn't that long, so this is not really severely skewed.
   b) You would expect that it would be common for a losing team to have few goals and rare for a team to score many goals and still lose.

73) a) Bell-Shaped. This data seems roughly symmetric with the tallest bars in the middle and tails forming on both sides.
   b) Most people expect coin tosses to be heads about half of the time, so it makes sense that 4 heads on 8 coins happens the most. It would seem surprising to me for 8 coins to land all heads or all tails and this was rare in the graph.
   c) The deviations from perfect symmetry are very minor. It is reasonable to believe that such small differences from perfect symmetry are merely due to random variation in the sample.

75) a) Right-Exponential. The tallest bar is on the left and the bars get shorter and shorter as we move to the right.
   b) I don't think you would get a lot of 10 – 16 year olds that were great at poker. Perhaps some from 17 to 19 might be. I think the new bar would be shorter than the one for the 20's. This would change the graph from right-exponential to severely right-skewed.

77) a) Left-Skewed or Severely Left-skewed.. Most students had high GPA's and the lower ones were less frequent. The bar for the low 4's is short, but only a 4.0 gets you in that category.
   b) Because many of these students are ready to transfer, they must have had some success so far in community college. Therefore a good GPA is not surprising.

79) a) Bell-Shaped or Bimodal. Most of the data appears to be in the middle with only a few extremes on each side.
   b) The two high points might be caused by the difference in labor duration for a first time mom vs. a mom have her second or later child. First time moms often have longer labor.

81) We don't talk about the shape of the distribution when working with categorical variables. In some ways the only choices are Uniform or not Uniform. Categorical data can be re-ordered so other shapes usually don't make sense. These answers do not appear to be uniform to me.

83) Probably Severely Right-Skewed. Most people tend to buy the TVs that are cheaper. A few people will pay a lot more for the top of the line models. This shape is common for variables dealing with cash. The extremely rich buy some really expensive items creating tails on the right hand side.

85) My first thought is Bell-Shaped. The heights or lengths of things growing in nature typically form bell shaped data sets. However, because men and women have difference average heights, this will actually end up being a bimodal data set (created by combining the two bell-shapes for the men and women.)

Chapter Problem:

a)

Receipts	Freq	Rel Freq	Mid Pts
300 - < 400	2	0.050	350
400 - < 500	21	0.525	450
500 - < 600	7	0.175	550
600 - < 700	6	0.150	650
700 - < 800	1	0.025	750
800 - < 900	0	0.000	850
900 - < 1000	1	0.025	950
1000 - < 1100	1	0.025	1050
1100 - < 1200	0	0.000	1150
1200 - < 1300	1	0.025	1250
	40	1.000	

Chapter 2: Review Exercises:

1)

a)

Gas Price	Freq	Rel Freq	MidPts
1.60 – < 1.80	1	0.0278	1.70
1.80 – < 2.00	14	0.3889	1.90
2.00 – < 2.20	10	0.2778	2.10
2.20 – < 2.40	6	0.1667	2.30
2.40 – < 2.60	3	0.0833	2.50
2.60 – < 2.80	0	0.0000	2.70
2.80 – < 3.00	1	0.0278	2.90
3.00 – < 3.20	0	0.0000	3.10
3.20 – < 3.40	1	0.0278	3.30
	36	1.0001	

b)

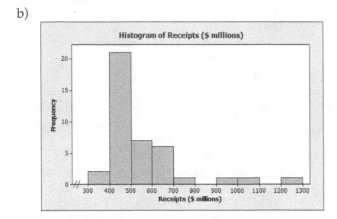

b)

c) I would say that it looks severely right skewed (because the tallest bars are on the left and there is a much longer tail on the right than on the left.)

d) No. This is not a random sample of movies; it is a top 40 list. The histogram of a random sample gives us a hint at the shape of the population, but this is not a random sample.

c) The gas prices appear to have had a severely right skewed distribution. The peak is almost on the far left and there is a long tail to the right.

d) This shows that most gas stations are charging a price that is near the low end, but that a few stations charge much higher prices.

3) a)

Place	Frequency	Rel Freq
1	10	0.3571
2	5	0.1786
3	2	0.0714
4	2	0.0714
5	0	0.0000
6	0	0.0000
7	3	0.1071
8	3	0.1071
9	3	0.1071
	28	0.9998

b)

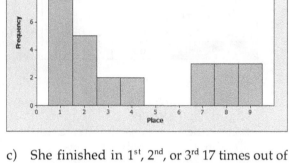

c) She finished in 1st, 2nd, or 3rd 17 times out of 28 tournaments. So she profits in about 60.71% of the tournaments she enters. It is also interesting that when she doesn't make the money, she usually goes out in 7th, 8th, or 9th place.

5) a)

Browser	Frequency	Rel Freq
Chrome	12	0.4286
Explorer	4	0.1429
Firefox	2	0.0714
Safari	10	0.3571
	28	1.0000

b)

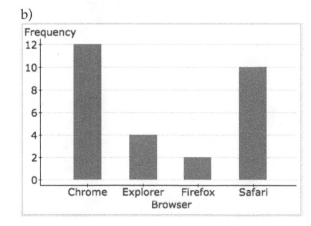

c)

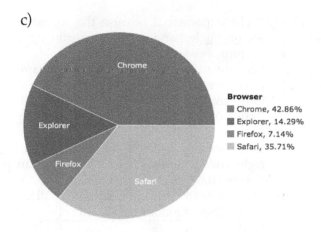

d) It appears that Chrome and Safari are the top choices by far among college students.

7)
a)

Pages	Freq	Rel Freq	Midpoints
40 – 49	6	0.2000	44.5
50 – 59	13	0.4333	54.5
60 – 69	4	0.1333	64.5
70 – 79	3	0.1000	74.5
80 – 89	2	0.0667	84.5
90 – 99	0	0.0000	94.5
100 – 109	1	0.0333	104.5
110 – 119	0	0.0000	114.5
120 – 129	1	0.0333	124.5
	30	0.9999	

b)

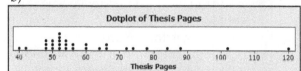

c) Either right-skewed or severely right-skewed because a majority of the data was on the left side with very few on the right, but extremes on the right.

9) a)

```
0 | 00123445666789
1 | 0001111334566789
2 | 0123334449
3 | 111111334
```

b)

```
0 | 0012344
0 | 5666789
1 | 0001111334
1 | 566789
2 | 012333444
2 | 9
3 | 111111334
```

c) I would guess that the wheel is producing a uniform distribution for the numbers. The bars are mostly all the same height.

11) a) Right exponential because the tallest bars are on the left and they get shorter down to nothing as we move to the right.

b) Because this is just a random sample, random variation causes the graph to only look roughly like the population it is drawn from.

13) a) Left-skewed. Most of the data is on the right with on longer tail on the left than on the right.

b) The larger the sample size, the smaller the effect that random variation has on the shape.

15) a) Probably Bell-shaped. The tallest bars are in the center with roughly symmetric tails on each side.

b) A larger sample size would lessen the effects of random variation on the graph. I would expect that if the sample size were increased we would see data fill in the gaps that exist on each side.

17) a) Because we are measuring the distance of a throw, this should be a continuous data set. Based on the bars in the graph, it appears that the width is 5 and that the first class starts at 15. So, the classes would be $15 - < 20, 20 - < 25, \ldots, 55 - < 60$. We can then estimate the heights from the graph to obtain the frequencies. We would then divide to get the relative frequencies and average the cutpoints to find the midpoints for each class. The results are shown below.

Distance	Freq	Rel Freq	Mid Pts
15 – < 20	1	0.0323	17.5
20 – < 25	0	0.0000	22.5
25 – < 30	0	0.0000	27.5
30 – < 35	5	0.1613	32.5
35 – < 40	7	0.2258	37.5
40 – < 45	8	0.2581	42.5
45 – < 50	3	0.0968	47.5
50 – < 55	5	0.1613	52.5
55 – < 60	2	0.0645	57.5
	31	1.0001	

b) I think it would have been better to slide the first bar to the right a bit away from the vertical axis. Because they did not start the horizontal numbering at zero, they should have shown a break in scale.

c) This could be a much weaker competitor, a technical mistake by the athlete, or an error in the data collection process.

19) a) Because the leaf unit is 0.1, that must mean that the stem represents the 1's place.
9.5, 9.5, 9.5, 9.6, 9.6, 9.6, 9.6, 9.7, 9.7, 9.9

b) Because wingspan is a measurement of length, we are using a continuous variable. The first class is the upper 7's and would be represented by $7.5 - < 8.0$.

Wingspan	Freq	Rel Freq	Mid Pts
7.5 – < 8.0	1	0.0154	7.75
8.0 – < 8.5	6	0.0923	8.25
8.5 – < 9.0	21	0.3231	8.75
9.0 – < 9.5	25	0.3846	9.25
9.5 – < 10.0	10	0.1538	9.75
10.0 – < 10.5	2	0.0308	10.25
	65	1.0000	

c) I would say that the wingspans either have a bell-shaped distribution or maybe a slightly left-skewed distribution. Possibly bell-shaped because the two middle rows are the longest with two rows above and below getting shorter as we move away from the peaks. Possibly left-skewed because the longest row is slightly on the right (if the graph is turned sideways).

d) The condors with wingspans of at least 9.5 feet are in the last two rows. There are 12 such birds out of 65.

$$\frac{12}{65} \approx 0.1846 = 18.46\%$$

21) a) Histograms are for quantitative data and bar graphs are for categorical data. Day of the week is categorical data.

b) The days will be the categories. We need to calculate the frequencies by estimating the relative frequencies. For example, the relative frequency for Tuesday appears to be about 0.29. We then use this and the sample size of 45 students to estimate the frequency for this group as follows:

$$freq \approx 45 * 0.29 = 13.05 \approx 13$$

Notice that, because we know the frequency must be a whole number, we rounded the answer to the nearest integer. We continue in a similar fashion to get the rest of the frequencies. We then divide to get the relative frequencies. Midpoints are not appropriate for categorical data.

Day	Freq	Rel Freq
Tuesday	13	0.2889
Wednesday	7	0.1556
Thursday	7	0.1556
Friday	2	0.0444
Saturday	4	0.0889
Sunday	12	0.2667
	45	1.0001

c) Even though Sunday is usually considered the first day of the week, I would leave them as is. Tuesday was the first day students were allowed to take the survey. This order shows that Most students took the survey right away, but there were also a lot of students who waited until the last moment.

d) This can be pulled off of our grouped data table. 16 out of 45 waited until the weekend to complete the survey.

22) a) The bar for Apple appears to be about 7 times higher than the bar for Google. This makes it appear that Apple is about 7 times for valuable.

b) Apple appears to be worth about 337 billion dollars and Google appears to be worth about 175 billion dollars.

$$\frac{337}{175} \approx 1.926$$

So, it appears that Apple was worth about 2 times as much as Google at this time.

c) The graph appears to be truncated. That is, it appears that they started the vertical number at 150 billion, thus chopping off a large piece from the bottom of all the bars.

Section 3.1:

1) $\bar{x}$ is the symbol for the <u>sample</u> mean and μ is the symbol for the <u>population</u> mean.

2) The median of an odd data set is the value in the <u>middle</u> of the ordered list. If the number of values is even, then the median is the <u>mean</u> of the two middle values.

3) L_M stands for the <u>location</u> of the median.

4) The mean is the <u>balancing</u> point of a data set. It balances the total <u>distances</u> of the data on the left with <u>distances</u> on the right. The mean is considered to be the <u>fair</u> share value.

5) The mode is the data value that is <u>repeated</u> the most. If no values are repeated, then we say that there is <u>no mode</u>.

6) Extremes in a data set pull or <u>skew</u> the mean in the direction of the extremes. The median is not affected by extremes. This tells us that the median is <u>resistant</u>.

7) Use the median when you want to separate the data set into a lower <u>half</u> and an upper <u>half</u>. Use the mean if the <u>total</u> is important.

8) The mode is the only appropriate measure of center to use when working with <u>categrorical</u> data.

9) a) $\mu = \dfrac{\sum x}{N} = \dfrac{335}{18} \approx 18.6$

   b) We start by putting the data in order:
   9,14,15,15,16,17,18,18,19,19,19,21,21,22,22, 23,23,24

   $L_M = \dfrac{1}{2}(18+1) = 9.5 \Rightarrow M = \dfrac{19+19}{2} = 19$

   c) Mode: The mode is the most repeated value, so the mode is 19 (repeated 3 times).

11) a) $\mu = \dfrac{\sum x}{N} = \dfrac{644.87}{12} \approx 55.406$

   b) We start by putting the data in order:
   23.45, 26.53, 33.11, 50.64, 58.36, 61.88, 62.68, 63.98, 65.89, 69.75, 72.4, 76.2

   $L_M = \dfrac{1}{2}(12+1) = 6.5 \Rightarrow$

   $M = \dfrac{61.88+62.68}{2} = 62.28$

   c) Mode: because no values in the data set are repeated, there is no mode.

13) a) Mean: It sounds like we have all the games played, so this is population data. So we

   get: $\mu = \dfrac{\sum x}{N} = \dfrac{24}{15} = 1.6$

   b) Median: Start by putting the data in order: {0, 0, 0, 1, 1, 1, 1, 1, 2, 2, 2, 2, 3, 4, 4}. Now use the location formula.

   $L_M = \dfrac{1}{2}(15+1) = 8 \Rightarrow M = 1$

   c) Mode: The mode is the most repeated value, so the mode is 1 (repeated 5 times).

   d) I would use the mean, because I think that the total number of hits would be an important factor in deciding this question.

   e) Because $\mu > M$, this is a right-skewed distribution. The mean has been pulled to the right of the median.

15) a) Mean: This is a random sample of 12 homes, so this is sample data.

   $\bar{x} = \dfrac{\sum x}{n} = \dfrac{2394}{12} = 199.5$

   b) Median: Start by ordering the data set. {104, 117, 134, 152, 172, 172, 198, 214, 236, 263, 274, 358}

   $L_M = \dfrac{1}{2}(12+1) = 6.5 \Rightarrow$

   $M = \dfrac{172+198}{2} = 185$

   c) Mode: The only repeated value is 172. Therefore, we get: Mode = 172

   d) Because $197 is larger than the median in the sample, I would expect that I was in the upper half of bills for this city.

   e) Because $\bar{x} > M$, this is a right-skewed distribution. The mean has been pulled to the right of the median.

17) The prices for a random sample of 16 resorts are given, so we have sample data.

a) $\bar{x} = \dfrac{\sum x}{n} = \dfrac{1053}{16} = 65.8125$

(or $\bar{x} \approx \$65.81$)

b) Start by sorting the data set: {29, 35, 39, 42, 47, 50, 54, 62, 68, 69, 75, 78, 90, 95, 102, 118}

$L_M = \dfrac{1}{2}(16+1) = 8.5 \Rightarrow M = \dfrac{62+68}{2} = 65$

c) Because the mean is so close to the median, this data set is roughly symmetric.

d) I would expect the total cost of the 23 tickets to be about

$23 * 65.8125 \approx \$1513.69$.

19) a) For categorical data, only the mode can be used as a measure of center.

b) The mode is the most repeated value. Vanilla is the mode for this set (repeated 9 times).

c) The most popular flavor of milkshake among this group of 5th graders is vanilla.

21) We are given a random sample of 11 cows, so we have sample data. Remember to sort the data for the median.

a) Mean: $\bar{x} = \dfrac{\sum x}{n} = \dfrac{82{,}837}{11} \approx 7530.64$

b) Median:

$L_M = \dfrac{1}{2}(11+1) = 6 \Rightarrow M = 7667$

c) Because $\bar{x} < M$, this is could be said to be a left-skewed distribution. The mean has been pulled to the left of the median.

d) He should expect the total milk production for the 47 cows to be about

$47 * 7530.64 \approx 353{,}940$ liters per year.

23) The weights for all the passengers in the plane have been given, so we have population data. Remember to sort the data for the median.

a) Mean: $\mu = \dfrac{\sum x}{N} = \dfrac{2623}{18} \approx 145.7$

b) Median: $L_M = \dfrac{1}{2}(18+1) = 9.5 \Rightarrow$

$M = \dfrac{151+155}{2} = 153$

c) Only 7 of the 18 passengers weigh less than 145.7 pounds. $\dfrac{7}{18} \approx 38.89\%$

d) The mean can be used to find the total, but the median cannot. So, the median would be more useful to this airline worker.

25) Data for all of the homes on the street is given, so this is population data.

a) Mean:

$\mu = \dfrac{\sum x}{N} = \dfrac{4597}{9} \approx 510.778 \Rightarrow \$510{,}778$

b) Median: (of sorted data)

$L_M = \dfrac{1}{2}(9+1) = 5 \Rightarrow M = 517 \Rightarrow \$517{,}000$

c) The amount of tax that will be collected is based on the total value of the homes. Therefore, the mean would be more important to the tax collector.

d) Mean:

$\mu = \dfrac{\sum x}{N} = \dfrac{4814}{9} \approx 534.889 \Rightarrow \$534{,}889$

Median: (of sorted data)

$L_M = \dfrac{1}{2}(9+1) = 5 \Rightarrow M = 517 \Rightarrow \$517{,}000$

27) a) Mode. Mode is the only one that works for categorical data. Its job is to find the most common value.

b) The mean. Average income makes sense because all this money is earned by the same person. The result might be helpful in planning a budget.

c) Median. People who hear this result will probably use it to decide whether they are in the top or bottom half of wage earners. If they used the mean, it would be skewed to the right of the middle by people with extremely high incomes.

29) The salaries for all the employees at the flower shop have been provided, so we have population data. Remember to sort the data for the median.

a) Mean: $\mu = \dfrac{\sum x}{N} = \dfrac{172.5}{15} = 11.50$

b) Median: $L_M = \dfrac{1}{2}(15+1) = 8 \Rightarrow$

    $M = 10.25$

c) Mode: The mode is the most repeated value in the data set. In this case the mode is 9.75 (repeated 5 times).

d) Because $\mu > M$, this is a right-skewed distribution.

e) The median would be a good measure for this, because it would at least tell the employees whether they were in the top or bottom half of the salaries.

f) The mean would be good for this because the mean involves the total of the salaries. This total would be important to the owner who pays all the salaries.

g) Changing the max hourly salary would have no effect on the mode or the median (which are resistant to extremes); however, the mean would be pulled higher by the change in the maximum salary. See below.

$$\mu = \frac{\sum x}{N} = \frac{182.5}{15} \approx 12.17$$

Section 3.2:

31) P_{12} is called the 12th percentile and it attempts to have 12% of the data set below it.

32) If $L_{Q_1} = 5.75$, then Q_1 is the mean of the 5th and 6th values in the ordered data set.

33) The five number summary consists of the minimum, Q_1, M, Q_3, and the maximum listed in order.

34) The range of a data set can be found by subtracting the minimum from the maximum.

35) The IQR is found by taking the difference between Q_3 and Q_1. Graphically, it represents the length of the box in our boxplot.

36) The fences lie $1\frac{1}{2}$ box lengths away from the box. Any values that lie outside the fences are considered to be outliers.

37) An outlier that stands apart visually from the rest of the data set is likely to be an error.

38) The whiskers on a modified boxplot extend to the largest and smallest data values that lie within the fences.

39) Use STAT > SortA(L1) to put the data in order.

a) $L_{Q_1} = \dfrac{1}{4}(11+1) = 3 \Rightarrow Q_1 = 19$

    $L_M = \dfrac{1}{2}(11+1) = 6 \Rightarrow M = 24$

    $L_{Q_3} = \dfrac{3}{4}(11+1) = 9 \Rightarrow Q_3 = 26$

b) $L_{P_{28}} = \dfrac{28}{100}(11+1) = 3.36 \Rightarrow$

    $P_{28} = \dfrac{19+21}{2} = 20$

c) {16, 19, 24, 26, 32}

d) $R = 32 - 16 = 16$

41) Use STAT > SortA(L1) to put the data in order.

a) $L_{Q_1} = \dfrac{1}{4}(17+1) = 4.5 \Rightarrow$

    $Q_1 = \dfrac{3.9+4}{2} = 3.95$

    $L_M = \dfrac{1}{2}(17+1) = 9 \Rightarrow M = 5.1$

    $L_{Q_3} = \dfrac{3}{4}(17+1) = 13.5 \Rightarrow$

    $Q_3 = \dfrac{5.5+5.7}{2} = 5.6$

b) $L_{P_{45}} = \dfrac{45}{100}(17+1) = 8.1 \Rightarrow$

    $P_{45} = \dfrac{4.6+5.1}{2} = 4.85$

c) {2.3, 3.95, 5.1, 5.6, 8.1, 8.4}

d) $R = 8.4 - 2.3 = 6.1$

43) Use STAT > SortA(L1) to put the data in order.

a) $L_{P_{43}} = \dfrac{43}{100}(11+1) = 5.16 \Rightarrow$

$P_{43} = \dfrac{900+1200}{2} = 1050$

b) $L_{Q_1} = \dfrac{1}{4}(11+1) = 3 \Rightarrow Q_1 = 600$

$L_M = \dfrac{1}{2}(11+1) = 6 \Rightarrow M = 1200$

$L_{Q_3} = \dfrac{3}{4}(11+1) = 9 \Rightarrow Q_3 = 1400$

5-Num-Sum = {480, 600, 1200, 1400, 2500}

c) $R = 2500 - 480 = 2020$

45) Use STAT > SortA(L1) to put the data in order.

a) $L_{P_{80}} = \dfrac{80}{100}(12+1) = 10.4 \Rightarrow$

$P_{80} = \dfrac{263+274}{2} = 268.5$

b) $L_{Q_1} = \dfrac{1}{4}(12+1) = 3.25 \Rightarrow$

$Q_1 = \dfrac{134+152}{2} = 143$

$L_M = \dfrac{1}{2}(12+1) = 6.5 \Rightarrow$

$M = \dfrac{172+198}{2} = 185$

$L_{Q_3} = \dfrac{3}{4}(12+1) = 9.75 \Rightarrow$

$Q_3 = \dfrac{236+263}{2} = 249.5$

5-Num Sum = $\{104, 143, 185, 249.5, 358\}$

c) $R = 358 - 104 = 254$

47) Sort the data using STAT > SortA(L1)

a) $L_{P_{55}} = \dfrac{55}{100}(23+1) = 13.2 \Rightarrow$

$P_{55} = \dfrac{95+96}{2} = 95.5$

We expect about 55% of the golfers to have scores below 95.5.

Note: We actually have $\dfrac{13}{24} \approx 54.17\%$ of the golfers below 95.5. 55% exactly is not possible with 23 data values.

b) $L_{Q_1} = \dfrac{1}{4}(23+1) = 6 \Rightarrow Q_1 = 88$

$L_M = \dfrac{1}{2}(23+1) = 12 \Rightarrow M = 93$

$L_{Q_3} = \dfrac{3}{4}(23+1) = 18 \Rightarrow Q_3 = 98$

5-num: $\{71, 88, 93, 98, 106\}$

c) $IQR = 98 - 88 = 10$

$\Rightarrow \begin{matrix} LF = 88 - 1.5*10 = 73 \\ UF = 98 + 1.5*10 = 113 \end{matrix}$

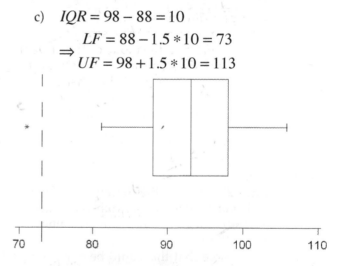

Note: Because 71 is below the lower fence, it is marked as a possible outlier. The left whisker extends to 81, which is the lowest data value within the fences.

d) A score of 71 is a very low score, but not so low that it isn't a reasonable one. This just looks like an unusually good round of golf at this local course.

49) Sort the data using STAT > SortA(L1)

a) $L_{P_{88}} = \dfrac{88}{100}(19+1) = 17.6 \Rightarrow$

$P_{88} = \dfrac{32.8+33}{2} = 32.9$

We expect about 88% of the cars to have gas mileages below 32.9 mpg.

b) $L_{Q_1} = \dfrac{1}{4}(19+1) = 5 \Rightarrow Q_1 = 30.6$

$L_M = \dfrac{1}{2}(19+1) = 10 \Rightarrow M = 31.5$

$L_{Q_3} = \dfrac{3}{4}(19+1) = 15 \Rightarrow Q_3 = 32.5$

5-num: $\{27.4,\ 30.6,\ 31.5,\ 32.5,\ 33.6\}$

c) $IQR = 32.5 - 30.6 = 1.9$

$\Rightarrow \begin{array}{l} LF = 30.6 - 1.5*1.9 = 27.75 \\ UF = 32.5 + 1.5*1.9 = 35.35 \end{array}$

Note: 27.4 is an outlier because it is below the lower fence. The left-whisker extends to 29.1 because it is the smallest value within the fences.

d) It's possible that this could be a mistake in calculating the mileage for that tank of gas. It could also just be unusually poor mileage for that tank. Maybe this trip was all city driving or included driving uphill to the mountains.

51) Sort the data using STAT > SortA(L1)

a) $L_{Q_1} = \dfrac{1}{4}(23+1) = 6 \Rightarrow Q_1 = 11$

$L_M = \dfrac{1}{2}(23+1) = 12 \Rightarrow M = 11.9$

$L_{Q_3} = \dfrac{3}{4}(23+1) = 18 \Rightarrow Q_3 = 12.8$

5-num: $\{9.8,\ 11,\ 11.9,\ 12.8,\ 15.5\}$

b) $IQR = 12.8 - 11 = 1.8$

$\Rightarrow \begin{array}{l} LF = 11 - 1.5*1.8 = 8.3 \\ UF = 12.8 + 1.5*1.8 = 15.5 \end{array}$

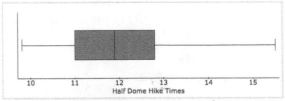

Note: The maximum value is the same as the value of the upper fence. Because, 15.5 is not beyond the upper fence, it is not considered to be an outlier.

c) The two sides of the box are roughly symmetric. However, the right whisker is much longer than the left whisker. Therefore, it appears that Half Dome hike times appear to be right skewed.

d) This time, there are no outliers to discuss.

53) Sort the data using STAT > SortA(L1)

a) $L_{Q_1} = \frac{1}{4}(22+1) = 5.75$

$\Rightarrow Q_1 = \frac{97+101}{2} = 99$

$L_M = \frac{1}{2}(22+1) = 11.5$

$\Rightarrow M = \frac{117+128}{2} = 122.5$

$L_{Q_3} = \frac{3}{4}(22+1) = 17.25$

$\Rightarrow Q_3 = \frac{210+213}{2} = 211.5$

5-num: $\{42,\ 99,\ 122.5,\ 211.5,\ 520\}$

b) $IQR = 211.5 - 99 = 112.5$

$\Rightarrow \begin{array}{l} LF = 99 - 1.5*112.5 = -69.75 \\ UF = 211.5 + 1.5*112.5 = 380.25 \end{array}$

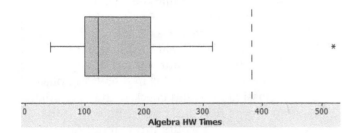

Algebra HW Times

Note: 520 is an outlier because it is above the upper fence. The right-whisker extends to 317 because it is the largest value within the fences.

c) I would say that this is a right-skewed distribution, because the right side of the box is wider than the left side of the box and the right whisker is longer than then left whisker. This is especially true if the outlier on the right is not an error.

d) The outlier is so far to the right of all other data values that it might actually be an error in the data set. If not an error, then it is an unusually large time. Either the student is really slow or maybe they were watching TV and only working during commercials making it take a very long time.

55) Sort the data using STAT > SortA(L1)

a) $L_{Q_1} = \frac{1}{4}(28+1) = 7.25$

$\Rightarrow Q_1 = \frac{5020+5160}{2} = 5090$

$L_M = \frac{1}{2}(28+1) = 14.5$

$\Rightarrow M = \frac{7700+7855}{2} = 7777.5$

$L_{Q_3} = \frac{3}{4}(28+1) = 21.75$

$\Rightarrow Q_3 = \frac{13472+14620}{2} = 14,046$

5-num: {1150, 5090, 7777.5, 14046, 29670}

b) $IQR = 14046 - 5090 = 8956$

$\Rightarrow \begin{array}{l} LF = 5090 - 1.5*8956 = -8344 \\ UF = 14046 + 1.5*9456 = 27480 \end{array}$

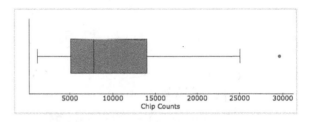

Chip Counts

Note: The software StatCrunch shows outliers using a dot rather than an asterisk.

c) I would say that this is a right-skewed distribution, because the right side of the box is wider than the left side of the box and the right whisker is longer than then left whisker. The outlier on the right also supports the idea that this is right skewed.

d) The fact that the chip stacks shift to a right skewed shape as the tournament progresses tells us that most players end up with lower chip amounts, but that some players are able to have much higher amounts of chips. In financial terms it appears that even though they all start with the same amount, many become poor, but a few become rich, one of them extremely rich.

57) Sort the data using STAT > SortA(L1)

a) $L_{P_{67}} = \dfrac{67}{100}(28+1) = 19.43 \Rightarrow$

$P_{67} = \dfrac{48+48}{2} = 48$

We expect about 67% of people who wear glasses for reading only to have first started wearing them by age 48 years.

b) $L_{Q_1} = \dfrac{1}{4}(28+1) = 7.25$

$\Rightarrow Q_1 = \dfrac{39+40}{2} = 39.5$

$L_M = \dfrac{1}{2}(28+1) = 14.5$

$\Rightarrow M = \dfrac{44+44}{2} = 44$

$L_{Q_3} = \dfrac{3}{4}(28+1) = 21.75$

$\Rightarrow Q_3 = \dfrac{49+49}{2} = 49$

5-num: $\{22,\ 39.5,\ 44,\ 49,\ 53\}$

c) $IQR = 49 - 39.5 = 9.5$

$\Rightarrow\ \begin{aligned}LF &= 39.5 - 1.5*9.5 = 25.25\\ UF &= 49 + 1.5*9.5 = 63.25\end{aligned}$

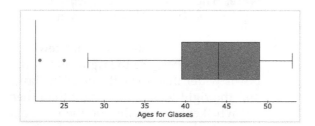

Ages for Glasses

Note: The software StatCrunch shows outliers using dots rather than asterisks.

d) The ages seem to be left skewed. Even though the two sides of the box are about the same width. The whisker on the left is much longer than the whisker on the right.

e) Because neither outlier, 22 or 25, really stands apart from the whisker, they are probably not errors, rather they are just a couple of people who needed glasses for reading at an unusually young age.

59) a) The * furthest to the left would be the min and appears to be about 260. The left side of the box is Q1 and appears to be about 445. The middle line of the box is the median and appears to be about 495. The right side of the box is Q3 and appears to be about 550. Finally, the * furthest to the right is the max and it appears to be about 730. So the five number summary is as shown below.

$\{260,\ 445,\ 495,\ 550,\ 730\}$

b) The graph appears to be roughly symmetric, but the whiskers are quite a bit longer than the sections of the box. This seems most like a bell-shaped distribution.

c) This means that most people are near the mean and that there are extreme scores on both sides.

d) Outliers are either unusual observations or errors. Because these outliers do not really stand far apart from the whiskers, I think they just represent unusually low and high SAT math scores.

61) a) The • represents the value 23.1 from the table. It has been marked this way because it is an outlier.

b) It is not possible for a GPA to be this high, so I must assume that this is an error. It is likely that this value should have been 2.31 and the decimal is in the wrong place.

c) If possible, I would check with this student and try to find the correct number. If that is not possible, I would throw it out rather than guess at the value.

d) If the outlier were 53.1, then this would still be an error for sure. The only real difference for this value is that I would not have any guess as to what went wrong. I would still deal with it in the same manner as discussed above.

63) a) The new tires are those with 10/32 of an inch of tread. Based on the whiskers and the three vertical lines in the box, the five number summary is estimated as follows.

$$\{160, 190, 199, 215, 230\}$$

b) The worn tires are those with 4/32 of an inch of tread. Based on the outlier on the left, the whisker on the right, and the three vertical lines in the box, the five number summary is estimated as follows.

$$\{210, 280, 290, 315, 345\}$$

c) The nearly worn out tires are those with 2/32 of an inch of tread. Based on the outlier on the left, the whisker on the right, and the three vertical lines in the box, the five number summary is estimated as follows.

$$\{275, 325, 365, 400, 455\}$$

d) They do support this theory. For example, the minimum stopping distance for the nearly worn out tires is more than the maximum stopping distance for the new tires.

e) Based on the fact that the shorter the tread the wider the boxplot, it also appears that there is more variation in the stopping distances with worn out tires than there is with new tires.

65) a) Based on the whiskers and the three vertical lines in the box, the five number summary for the Obama states is estimated as follows.

$$\{2.5, 3.4, 4.1, 4.5, 5.7\}$$

b) Based on the whiskers and the three vertical lines in the box, the five number summary for the Romney states is estimated as follows.

$$\{3.5, 4.3, 5.0, 6.4, 10.6\}$$

c) In a way they do. All the numbers in the five number summaries for the Romney states are high than the corresponding values for the Obama states. In addtion, it appears that almost 3/4 of the Romney states give a higher median percentage than the lower 3/4 of the Obama states. However, this data is for the median giving percentages for states that are a mixture of people who voted for both candidates. If these boxplots were separated into Obama voters and Romney voters rather than by states, then the argument would be more compelling. The quote is probably a reach if only based on this state median data.

d) It is interesting that there is an extreme outlier among the Romney states. This value is far enough away from the whisker to be supicious that it could be an error. Also, there is more variation in the median giving percentages of the Romney states compared to the medians from the Obama states.

Section 3.3:

67) The standard deviation measures the amount of variation in a data set.

68) A deviation measures the directed distance from the data value to the mean.

69) Before adding the deviations, we square them to get rid of the negatives. We balance this by taking the square root of the sum.

70) The more spread ot a data set is, the larger its standard deviation will be.

71) σ is the symbol for the population standard deviation and s is the symbol for the sample standard deviation.

72) Variance is the square of the standard deviation.

73) a) $R = \text{max} - \text{min} = 20 - 3 = 17$
b)   This is stated to be population data.

x	$x - \mu$	$(x - \mu)^2$
3	-9.43	88.9249
13	0.57	0.3249
11	-1.43	2.0449
10	-2.43	5.9049
20	7.57	57.3049
18	5.57	31.0249
12	-0.43	0.1849
87	-0.01	185.7143

$$\mu = \frac{\sum x}{N} = \frac{87}{7} \approx 12.43$$

$$\sigma = \sqrt{\frac{\sum (x - \mu)^2}{N}} = \sqrt{\frac{185.7143}{7}} \approx 5.1508$$

75) a) $R = \text{max} - \text{min} = 186.1 - 115.4 = 70.7$
b)   This is stated to be sample data.

x	$x - \bar{x}$	$(x - \bar{x})^2$
151.7	-0.16	0.0256
141.8	-10.06	101.2036
143.9	-7.96	63.3616
115.4	-36.46	1329.3316
184.4	32.54	1058.8516
186.1	34.24	1172.3776
172.9	21.04	442.6816
118.7	-33.16	1099.5856
1214.9	0.02	5267.4188

$$\bar{x} = \frac{\sum x}{n} = \frac{1214.9}{8} \approx 151.86$$

$$s = \sqrt{\frac{\sum (x - \bar{x})^2}{n - 1}} = \sqrt{\frac{5267.4188}{8 - 1}} \approx 27.432$$

77) This is stated to be population data.

a)   Data set I: $\bar{x}_1 = \dfrac{\sum x}{n} = \dfrac{133}{5} = 26.6$ and

$$s_1 = \sqrt{\frac{\sum (x - \bar{x}_1)^2}{n - 1}} = \sqrt{\frac{981.2}{4}} \approx 15.662$$

b)   Data set II: $\bar{x}_2 = \dfrac{\sum x}{n} = \dfrac{283}{5} = 56.6$ and

$$s_2 = \sqrt{\frac{\sum (x - \bar{x}_2)^2}{n - 1}} = \sqrt{\frac{237.2}{4}} \approx 7.7006$$

c)   So, because data set one has the larger standard deviation, it is the set with more overall variation. The larger the standard deviation, the more overall variation a data set has.

79) a) $R = \text{max} - \text{min} = 358 - 104 = 254$
b) We are told that this is a random sample.

x	$x - \bar{x}$	$(x - \bar{x})^2$
274	74.5	5550.25
236	36.5 *	1332.25
172	-27.5 *	756.25
152	-47.5 *	2256.25
104	-95.5	9120.25
117	-82.5	6806.25
134	-65.5 *	4290.25
172	-27.5 *	756.25
214	14.5 *	210.25
198	-1.5 *	2.25
358	158.5	25122.25
263	63.5 *	4032.25
2394	0.0	60235

$$\bar{x} = \frac{2394}{12} = 199.5 \text{ and}$$

$$s = \sqrt{\frac{\sum(x - \bar{x})^2}{n - 1}} = \sqrt{\frac{60235}{12 - 1}} \approx 73.999$$

c) 8 out of the 12 deviations are smaller than 73.999 (marked with a * in the middle column of the table above.) So we get:

$$\frac{8}{12} \approx 66.67\% \text{ of the data values lie}$$

within 1 standard deviation of the mean.

81) a) $R = \text{max} - \text{min} = 598 - 430 = 168$
b) Because we are only attempting to summarize these 9 homes, this is population data.

x	$x - \mu$	$(x - \mu)^2$
525	14.2 *	201.64
523	12.2 *	148.84
517	6.2 *	38.44
461	-49.8	2480.04
598	87.2	7603.84
559	48.2	2323.24
477	-33.8 *	1142.44
430	-80.8	6528.64
507	-3.8 *	14.44
4597	-0.2	20481.56

$$\mu = \frac{4597}{9} \approx 510.8 \text{ and}$$

$$\sigma = \sqrt{\frac{\sum(x - \mu)^2}{N}} = \sqrt{\frac{20481.56}{9}} \approx 47.705$$

c) $\frac{5}{9} \approx 55.56\%$ (See the values marked in the middle column of the table above.)

83) All the siblings from both families are represented here, so these are both sets of population data.

a) The boxplot for the author seems wider from whisker to whisker than for his spouse. This indicates a larger range. Also, the box portion for the author is wider than for the spouse. This indicates that the middle 50% of the ages is also more spread out in the author's family.

b) Author: $\mu_1 = \frac{\sum x}{N} = \frac{359}{7} \approx 51.3$ and

$$\sigma_1 = \sqrt{\frac{\sum(x - \mu_1)^2}{N}} = \sqrt{\frac{209.43}{7}} \approx 5.4698$$

c) Spouse: $\mu_2 = \frac{\sum x}{N} = \frac{240}{7} \approx 34.3$ and

$$\sigma_2 = \sqrt{\frac{\sum(x - \mu_2)^2}{N}} = \sqrt{\frac{125.43}{7}} \approx 4.2330$$

d) So, because the author's family has the larger standard deviation, it is the data set with more overall variation. The larger the standard deviation, the more overall variation a data set has.

85) a) It is stated that these 11 cows represent sample data.

x	$x - \bar{x}$	$(x - \bar{x})^2$
8007	476.4 *	226956.96
8023	492.4	242457.76
7122	-408.6 *	166953.96
7667	136.4 *	18604.96
7577	46.4 *	2152.96
8062	531.4	282385.96
7192	-338.6 *	114649.96
6623	-907.6	823737.76
7894	363.4 *	132059.56
6985	-545.6	297679.36
7685	154.4 *	23839.36
82837	0.4	2331478.56

$$\bar{x} = \frac{82837}{11} \approx 7530.6 \text{ and}$$

$$s = \sqrt{\frac{\sum(x - \bar{x})^2}{n-1}} = \sqrt{\frac{2331478.56}{10}} \approx 482.85$$

b) $\frac{7}{11} \approx 63.64\%$ (see the values marked with a * in the table above.)

c) For this one we look at how many of the deviations, $x - \mu$, are smaller than $2s = 965.7$. Looking at the middle column of the table, we see that all of the values are smaller, so $\frac{11}{11} = 100\%$.

87) a) The problem states that the 16 resorts are sample data.

x	$x - \bar{x}$	$(x - \bar{x})^2$
95	29.19	852.0561
102	36.19	1309.7161
50	-15.81 *	249.9561
75	9.19 *	84.4561
54	-11.81 *	139.4761
68	2.19 *	4.7961
42	-23.81 *	566.9161
118	52.19	2723.7961
69	3.19 *	10.1761
90	24.19 *	585.1561
35	-30.81	949.2561
39	-26.81	718.7761
78	12.19 *	148.5961
47	-18.81 *	353.8161
62	-3.81 *	14.5161
29	-36.81	1354.9761
1053	0.04	10066.4376

$$\bar{x} = \frac{1053}{16} \approx 65.81 \text{ and}$$

$$s = \sqrt{\frac{\sum(x - \bar{x})^2}{n-1}} = \sqrt{\frac{10066.4376}{15}} \approx 25.906$$

b) $\frac{10}{16} = 62.5\%$ (See the values marked with an * in the chart above.)

c) $2s = 51.812 \Rightarrow \frac{15}{16} = 93.75\%$

89) a) $Range = R = 19.75 - 9.75 = 10$

b) We only wish to summarize these 15 salaries, so this is population data.

x	$x - \mu$	$(x - \mu)^2$
9.75	-1.75*	3.0625
12.50	1*	1.0000
10.00	-1.5*	2.2500
10.25	-1.25*	1.5625
9.75	-1.75*	3.0625
9.75	-1.75*	3.0625
11.50	0*	0.0000
19.75	8.25	68.0625
10.25	-1.25*	1.5625
14.00	2.5*	6.2500
9.75	-1.75*	3.0625
11.75	0.25*	0.0625
13.50	2*	4.0000
10.25	-1.25*	1.5625
9.75	-1.75*	3.0625
172.5	0	101.625

$$\mu = \frac{172.5}{15} = 11.50 \text{ and}$$

$$\sigma = \sqrt{\frac{\sum(x - \mu)^2}{N}} = \sqrt{\frac{101.625}{15}} \approx 2.6029$$

c) $\frac{14}{15} \approx 93.33\%$ (See the values marked with an * in the chart above.) Note: This is a larger percentage than we typically expect, but not really a surprise for a small set with an extreme outlier in it.

d) $2\sigma = 5.2058 \Rightarrow \frac{14}{15} \approx 93.33\%$

Section 3.4:

91) When calculating the mean and standard deviation for data that has been grouped into classes, use the <u>midpoint</u> of each class in place of the x-values.

92) When using midpoints for grouped data calculations, all of the answers will be <u>approximations</u>.

93) When counting the number of data values within 1, 2, or 3 standard deviations of the mean for grouped data, remember to count the <u>frequencies</u> for each class rather than counting the <u>number</u> of classes.

94) When computing GPA, the number of <u>units</u> takes the place of the frequencies in all of your calculations.

95) The problem states that this is sample data.

x	f	xf	$(x-\bar{x})^2 f$
1	22	22	28.5912
2	17	34	0.3332
3	10	30	7.3960
4	7	28	24.2172
5	2	10	16.3592
	58	124	76.8968

a) $\bar{x} = \dfrac{\sum xf}{n} = \dfrac{124}{58} \approx 2.14$

b) $s = \sqrt{\dfrac{\sum (x-\bar{x})^2 f}{n-1}} = \sqrt{\dfrac{76.8968}{57}} \approx 1.1615$

97) The problem states that this is population data. We will use the class midpoints for our x-values.

x	f	xf	$(x-\mu)^2 f$
5	7	35	1289.0143
15	10	150	127.4490
25	6	150	248.0694
35	4	140	1079.7796
45	1	45	698.5449
	28	520	3442.8572

a) $\mu = \dfrac{\sum xf}{N} = \dfrac{520}{28} \approx 18.57$

b) $\sigma = \sqrt{\dfrac{\sum (x-\mu)^2 f}{N}} = \sqrt{\dfrac{3442.8572}{28}} \approx 11.089$

99) The problem states that this data is a random sample from Hayward. Also, we will use midpoints for our x-values.

x	f	xf	$(x-\bar{x})^2 f$
1000	14	14000	10765351
1400	6	8400	1364602
1800	8	14400	47309
2200	14	30800	1461511
2800	8	22400	6816909
3800	2	7600	7396627
	52	97600	27852309

a) $\bar{x} = \dfrac{\sum xf}{n} = \dfrac{97600}{52} \approx 1876.9$

b) $s = \sqrt{\dfrac{\sum (x-\bar{x})^2 f}{n-1}} = \sqrt{\dfrac{27852309}{51}} \approx 739.00$

101) Because we are only summarizing the results of the 360 customers we have data for, this will be treated as population data.

x	f	xf	$(x-\mu)^2 f$
5	249	1245	59.7849
4	75	300	19.5075
3	16	48	36.4816
2	12	24	75.6012
1	8	8	98.5608
	360	1625	289.936

a) $\mu = \dfrac{\sum xf}{N} = \dfrac{1625}{360} \approx 4.51$

b) $\sigma = \sqrt{\dfrac{\sum (x-\mu)^2 f}{N}} = \sqrt{\dfrac{289.36}{360}} \approx 0.89654$

103) GPA is calculated like a population mean, but we use the units in place of the frequency.

x	f	xf
4.0	15	60
3.0	37	111
2.0	20	40
1.0	4	4
0.0	3	0
	79	215

$\mu = \dfrac{\sum xf}{N} = \dfrac{215}{79} \approx 2.72$

105) We are only looking to summarize the ages of these employees and we have all of the data for the firm, so this is population data.
   a) Enter the data into L1 and then choose STAT > CALC > 1-Var Stats L1. Remember to verify data entry by checking the value of $\sum x^2$. $\mu \approx 45.2$
   b) $\sigma \approx 11.459$

107) The problem states that this is sample data.
   a) Enter the data set into L1. Choose STAT > CALC > 1 Var Stats L1.
      $\bar{x} \approx 2.135$
   b) $s \approx 0.31974$
   c) Because this was a random sample, the sample mean is a reasonable estimate of what we might average in $/gal as we drive across the country. Therefore, we can multiply this mean by the number of gallons we purchase.
      Cost $\approx 2.135(114.7) \approx \$244.88$

109) We are only looking to summarize the times of these students and we have all of the data for the class, so this is population data.
   a) Enter the data into L1 and then choose STAT > CALC > 1-Var Stats L1. $\mu \approx 156.5$
   b) $\sigma \approx 100.86$

111) The problem states that this is sample data.
   a) STAT > CALC > 1 Var Stats L1 yields
      $\bar{x} \approx 1.48$
   b) $s \approx 2.4396$
   c) We can estimate what this would be for a sample of 47 students by multiplying our sample average with the 47 students.
      Total $\approx 1.48(47) = 69.56$ tickets.
   d) $\begin{aligned} \bar{x} - s &= -0.9596 \\ \bar{x} + s &= 3.9196 \end{aligned} \Rightarrow {}^{23}\!/_{27} \approx 85.19\%$

      Note: We only count values that lie between the boundaries. Therefore, we only count values from 0 to 3. We do not round and include the 4's which are actually more than 1 standard deviation from the mean.

113) We only wish to summarize the chips for the players left in the tournament. This implies that this is population data.
   a) STAT > CALC > 1 Var Stats L1 yields
      $\mu = 10145.75$
   b) $\sigma \approx 6971.01$

c) $\begin{aligned} \mu - \sigma &= 3174.74 \\ \mu + \sigma &= 17116.76 \end{aligned} \Rightarrow \dfrac{28 - 3 - 7}{28} \approx 64.29\%$

   Note: It is often easier to subtract the values outside of the boundaries away from the total.

d) $\begin{aligned} \mu - 2\sigma &= -3796.27 \\ \mu + 2\sigma &= 24087.77 \end{aligned} \Rightarrow \dfrac{28 - 2}{28} \approx 92.86\%$

115) The problem states that this is sample data that will be used to make estimates about all available tickets online.
   a) STAT > CALC > 1 Var Stats L1 yields
      $\bar{x} \approx 199.29$
   b) $s \approx 71.706$
   c) To estimate the total cost for 5 5ickets, we should multiply the average cost of a ticket by 5.
      Total Cost $\approx 5(199.29) = \$996.45$
   d) $\begin{aligned} \bar{x} - s &= 127.584 \\ \bar{x} + s &= 270.996 \end{aligned} \Rightarrow \dfrac{34 - 1 - 6}{34} \approx 79.41\%$

      Note: It is often easier to subtract the values outside of the boundaries from the total.
   e) $\begin{aligned} \bar{x} - 2s &= 55.878 \\ \bar{x} + 2s &= 342.702 \end{aligned} \Rightarrow \dfrac{34 - 0 - 2}{34} \approx 94.12\%$

117) The instructor has times sampled from every quarter mile, but wants to estimate his true average speed. Therefore, this is sample data.
   a) STAT > CALC > 1 Var Stats L1 yields
      $\bar{x} \approx 11.51$
   b) $s \approx 8.9280$
   c) $d = r \cdot t \Rightarrow 5.48 = r(0.86) \Rightarrow$
      $r = \dfrac{5.48}{0.86} \approx 6.37$ mph
   d) By sampling the speed at equal distance intervals, the instructor would oversample the fast speeds and undersample the slow speeds. For example, it takes much more time to climb a hill than to ride down it. Therefore, the climb lowers our average more than the ride down increases it. This means that we should have more speeds sampled from the climb than from the descent to reflect this. But, because the speeds were sampled at equal distances, we have the same amount of data from the climb and from the descent.

119) From exercise (111) we know this is sample data.

a) Enter the number of violations in L1 and the frequencies in L2. Choose STAT > CALC > 1 Var Stats L1, L2. This gives us
$\overline{x} \approx 1.48$

b) $s \approx 2.4396$
Note: This is the same data set as problem (111). It has just been grouped. Therefore, it still only contains one variable, the number of violations. Frequency is not a variable.

c) Because we are using single value grouping, we are using the actual data values to make the computations (rather than using midpoints to guess at the data values).

121) The problem states that this is sample data. We need to use the midpoints as out x-values.
135.5, 138.5, 141.5, 144.5, 147.5, 150.5, 153.5, 156.5

a) Enter the midpoints in L1 and the frequencies in L2. Choose STAT > CALC > 1 Var Stats L1, L2. This gives us
$\overline{x} \approx 145.71$

b) $s \approx 4.2952$

c) $\overline{x} - s = 145.71 - 4.2952 \approx 141.41$
$\overline{x} + s = 145.71 + 4.2952 \approx 150.01$
Now, we count all of the frequencies for all of the midpoints that fall between these two cut-offs.
$$\Rightarrow \frac{16 + 29 + 20}{94} \approx 0.6915 = 69.15\%$$

d) $\overline{x} - 2s = 145.71 - 2*4.2952 \approx 137.12$
$\overline{x} + 2s = 145.71 + 2*4.2952 \approx 154.30$
Once again, we will count all of the frequencies for all of the midpoints that fall between the cut-offs listed above.
$$\Rightarrow \frac{94 - 1 - 2}{94} \approx 0.9681 = 96.81\%$$
Note: It is often easier to subtract the frequencies for the midpoints outside of the boundaries from the total.

123) We have data for all of the players and we just wish to summarize the data. Therefore, this is population data.

a) Determine the midpoint for each of the classes: 20, 24, 28, 32, 36, 40. Enter these values into L1. Enter the frequencies into L2. Choose STAT > CALC > 1 Var Stats L1, L2 and press ENTER.
$\mu \approx 27.13$

b) $\sigma \approx 5.2877$

c) $\mu - \sigma \approx 27.13 - 5.2877 = 21.8423$
$\mu + \sigma \approx 27.13 + 5.2877 = 32.4177$
Now, we count all of the frequencies for all of the midpoints that fall between these two cut-offs.
$$\Rightarrow \frac{119 + 87 + 53}{360} \approx 0.7194 = 71.94\%$$

d) $\mu - 2\sigma \approx 27.13 - 2*5.2877 = 16.5546$
$\mu + 2\sigma \approx 27.13 + 2*5.2877 = 37.7054$
Once again, we will count all of the frequencies for all of the midpoints that fall between the cut-offs listed above.
$$\Rightarrow \frac{57 + 119 + 87 + 53 + 30}{360} \approx 0.9611 = 96.11\%$$

125) GPA is always calculated as a population mean. Enter the grade point values into L1 and the number of units into L2, then choose STAT > CALC > 1-Var Stats L1, L2.
$GPA = \mu \approx 2.81$

Section 3.5:

127) According to the Empirical Rule for bell-shaped data sets, we expect about 68% of the data to lie within 1 standard deviation of the mean, 95% of the data to lie within 2 standard deviations of the mean, and about 99.7% of the data to lie within 3 standard deviations of the mean.

128) If we generalize the Empirical Rule to try to include most data sets, then we say that we expect about 50% to 80% of the data to lie within 1 standard deviation of the mean, 90% to 100% of the data to lie within 2 standard deviations of the mean, and almost 100% of the data to lie within 3 standard deviations of the mean.

129) A data value is considered to be unusual if it is more than $\underline{2}$ standard deviations away from the mean, and it is considered very unusual if it is more than $\underline{3}$ standard deviations away from the mean.

130) A z-score measures the number of standard $\underline{\text{deviations}}$ that a data value is away from the $\underline{\text{mean}}$. When rounding a z-score, always use $\underline{\text{exactly}}$ 3 decimal places.

131) The expected range for data values is anything that lies within $\underline{2}$ standard deviations of the mean.

132) The CV stands for the coefficient of $\underline{\text{variation}}$. It is the $\underline{\text{ratio}}$ of the standard deviation to the mean. The CV is sometimes called the $\underline{\text{variation}}$ percentage.

133) a) $z = \dfrac{x-\mu}{\sigma} = \dfrac{57.8 - 45.34}{13.315} \approx 0.936$

b) Any data values that lie within two standard deviations of the mean. So, we want all the possible values between $\mu - 2\sigma$ and $\mu + 2\sigma$.
$\mu - 2\sigma = 45.34 - 2*13.315 = 18.71$ and $\mu + 2\sigma = 45.34 + 2*13.315 = 71.97$. So the expected range is any data value between 18.71 and 71.97.

c) The data value is 2.071 standard deviations above the mean. Therefore, this is an unusually large data value in this population. The data value is:
$x = 45.34 + 2.071 * 13.315 \approx 72.915$.

135) a) $z = \dfrac{x-\mu}{\sigma} = \dfrac{75 - 150}{29.85} \approx -2.513$

b) Any data values that lie within two standard deviations of the mean. So, we want all the possible values between $\mu - 2\sigma$ and $\mu + 2\sigma$.
$\mu - 2\sigma = 150 - 2*29.85 = 90.3$ and $\mu + 2\sigma = 150 + 2*29.85 = 209.7$.
Because the population only consists of whole numbers we want to go from the small integer larger than 90.3 to the smallest integer less than 209.7. So the expected range is any data value from 91 to 209.

c) The data value is 1.209 standard deviations below the mean. Therefore, this is an expected data value in this population. The data value is:
$x = 150 - 1.209 * 29.85 \approx 113.9$.

137) $CV = \dfrac{\sigma}{\mu} \cdot 100\% = \dfrac{23.055}{187.6} \cdot 100\% \approx 12.29\%$

139) We are given that $\bar{x} \approx 2.135$ and $s \approx 0.31974$

a) $\bar{x} - s \approx 2.135 - 0.31974 = 1.81526$
$\bar{x} + s \approx 2.135 + 0.31974 = 2.45474$
Counting the data values that lie between these two cut-offs yields the following.
$\Rightarrow \dfrac{29}{36} \approx 0.8056 = 80.56\%$

b) $\bar{x} - 2s \approx 2.135 - 2*0.31974 = 1.49552$
$\bar{x} + 2s \approx 2.135 + 2*0.31974 = 2.77448$
$\Rightarrow \dfrac{34}{36} \approx 0.9444 = 94.44\%$

c) $\bar{x} - 3s \approx 2.135 - 3*0.31974 = 1.17578$
$\bar{x} + 3s \approx 2.135 + 3*0.31974 = 3.09422$
$\Rightarrow \dfrac{35}{36} \approx 0.9722 = 97.22\%$

d) The 80.56% just misses the 50% to 80% from the generalized Empirical Rule. This can happen when your data set is extremely skewed and this data set has two extreme values on the right side.
The 94.4% agrees with the 90% to 100% from the generalized Empirical Rule.
The 97.22% is almost 100%. Usually, you should expect 100% of the data from a small data set to be in this range, unless you have outliers, and we do have outliers.

141)   According to the problem, $\mu = 11.8$ and $\sigma = 1.05$.

a) When asked if a specific value is unusual or not, it is best to calculate a z-score.

$$z = \frac{x - \mu}{\sigma} = \frac{13.5 - 11.8}{1.05} \approx 1.619$$

No, it would not be unusual because it is less than 2 standard deviations above the mean. Because it is in the gray area, it would be considered a slow hiking time, but not unusually slow.

b) $z = \frac{x - \mu}{\sigma} = \frac{8 - 11.8}{1.05} \approx -3.619$

Yes, a round trip hiking time of 8 hours would be considered unusual because it is more than 2 standard deviations below the mean. In fact, because it is actually more than 3 standard deviations below the mean, this would be considered an unusually fast round trip hiking time.

c) $\mu - 2\sigma = 11.8 - 2*1.05 = 9.7$ and $\mu + 2\sigma = 11.8 + 2*1.05 = 13.9$. So any round trip hiking time between 9.7 hours and 13.9 hours would be in the expected range.

d) The hike time is 1.308 standard deviations above the mean. Therefore, this is an expected hike time in Half Dome. The actual hike time is:

$$x = 11.8 + 1.308 * 1.05 \approx 13.17 \text{ hours.}$$

143) a) $z = \frac{x - \mu}{\sigma} = \frac{97 - 77}{13.207} \approx 1.514$. No, not really, it is less than 2 standard deviations above the mean.

b) $z = \frac{27 - 77}{13.207} \approx -3.786$. Yes, this would be very unusual as it is more than 3 (almost 4) standard deviations below the mean.

c) $\mu - 2\sigma = 50.586$
$\mu + 2\sigma = 103.414$ $\Rightarrow$ Because the problem states that only whole numbers are possible, the expected range for the test scores would be from 51 to 103.

d) The test score is 2.347 standard deviations below the mean. Therefore, this is an unusually low test score. The actual test score is:

$$x = 77 - 2.347 * 13.207 \approx 46.0$$

145) a) $z = \frac{x - \mu}{\sigma} = \frac{0.300 - 0.270}{0.053} \approx 0.566$.

No, it would not be unusual because it is less than 2 standard deviations above the mean. In fact, because it is less than 1 standard deviation above the mean, this would have been a rather normal batting average for that year.

b) $z = \frac{0.400 - 0.270}{0.053} \approx 2.453$. Yes, it would be unusual, because it is more than 2 standard deviations above the mean.

c) $\mu - 2\sigma = 0.164$
$\mu + 2\sigma = 0.376$ $\Rightarrow$ Any batting average between 0.164 and 0.376 would NOT be considered unusual. This is also the expected range for the batting averages.

d) The batting average is 3.188 standard deviations below the mean. Therefore, this is an unusually low batting average. The actual batting average is:

$$x = 0.270 - 3.188 * 0.053 \approx 0.101$$

147) a) $z = \frac{x - \mu}{\sigma} = \frac{15 - 53}{19.8} \approx -1.919$.

No, it would not be unusual because it is less than 2 standard deviations below the mean. It is almost 2 standard deviations below the mean. So, this would be considered a low number of receptions, but not unusually low.

b) $z = \frac{x - \mu}{\sigma} = \frac{100 - 53}{19.8} \approx 2.374$. Yes, it would be unusual, because it is more than 2 standard deviations above the mean.

c) $\mu - 2\sigma = 13.4$
$\mu + 2\sigma = 92.6$ $\Rightarrow$ Any number of receptions between 13.4 and 92.6 would NOT be considered unusual. Because this is a discrete variable, the expected range would be anything from 14 to 92 recptions.

d) The number of receptions is 0.859 standard deviations above the mean. Therefore, this is a slightly above average number of receptions. The actual number of receptions is: $x = 53 + 0.859 * 19.8 \approx 70.01$. The number of receptions had to have been a whole number. So, it must have been the case that this receiver had 70 receptions.

149) For the Half-Dome hiker's time:
$$z_1 = \frac{x - \mu}{\sigma} = \frac{13.4 - 11.8}{1.05} \approx 1.524$$
For the math student's test score:
$$z_2 = \frac{x - \mu}{\sigma} = \frac{100 - 77}{13.207} \approx 1.742$$
The test score of 100 is the more unusual (rare) value, because the z-scores show that a score of 100 is more standard deviations away from its mean than the hiking time of 13.4 hours.

151) For the baseball player's batting average:
$$z_1 = \frac{x - \mu}{\sigma} = \frac{0.200 - 0.270}{0.053} \approx -1.321$$
For the football player's receptions:
$$z_2 = \frac{x - \mu}{\sigma} = \frac{110 - 53}{19.8} \approx 2.879$$
The 110 receptions is the more unusual (rare), and thus impressive, accomplishment, because the z-scores show that 110 receptions is more standard deviations away from its mean than the 0.200 batting average.

153) According to the problem, for this particular student, $\mu = 3.56$ and $\sigma = 0.493$.
a) $z = \dfrac{x - \mu}{\sigma} = \dfrac{1.0 - 3.56}{0.493} \approx -5.193$
Yes, it would be unusual because it is more than 2 standard deviations below the mean. In fact, it would be very unusual, because it is more than 3 standard deviations below the mean (more than 5 actually).
b) $\mu - 2\sigma = 3.56 - 2 * 0.493 = 2.574$ and $\mu + 2\sigma = 3.56 + 2 * 0.493 = 4.546$.
Because this college does not use the (+/-) grade system, only whole numbers are possible. This means that we expect the grade point value to be from 3.0 to 4.0. So we only would expect A's and B's from this student. Anything else would be unusual.

155) According to the problem, for this particular year, $\mu = 1524.6$ and $\sigma = 2.3595$.
a) $z = \dfrac{2100 - 1524.6}{235.95} \approx 2.439 \Rightarrow$ Yes, with a z-score of 2.439, this score would be considered unusual because it is more than 2 standard deviations above the mean.
b) No. Such a large number of people take the SAT test every year, it would not be strange to have some of them with combined scores that are more than 2 standard deviations above the mean. These scores would be unusually high due to the low percentage of the time that they occur, yet in a large population, they should still occur.

157) a) $CV_1 = \dfrac{s_1}{\overline{x}_1} = \dfrac{0.1035}{12.03} \approx 0.0086 = 0.86\%$
b) $CV_2 = \dfrac{s_2}{\overline{x}_2} = \dfrac{0.2568}{128.15} \approx 0.0020 = 0.20\%$
c) The smaller the CV is, the more consistent the filling machine is. Therefore, the milk filling machine is the more consistent one.

159) They are using samples of 6 times for each pump to find out which pump will be more consistent in the long run. This means that we are working with sample data. Enter data set I into L1 and data set II into L2.
a) STAT > CALC > 1 Var Stats L1 yields $\overline{x}_1 \approx 50.08$ and $s_1 \approx 5.1098$.
b) STAT > CALC > 1 Var Stats L2 yields $\overline{x}_2 \approx 50.23$ and $s_2 \approx 2.4304$.
c) Pump 1 was slightly closer to the target of 50 mg/hour.
d) $CV_1 = \dfrac{s_1}{\overline{x}_1} = \dfrac{5.1098}{50.08} \approx 0.1020 = 10.20\%$,

$CV_2 = \dfrac{s_2}{\overline{x}_2} = \dfrac{2.4304}{50.23} \approx 0.0484 = 4.84\%$
e) The smaller the CV is, the more consistent the pump is. Therefore, Pump 2 is the more consistent pump.
f) Because both pumps have averages that are close to the target of 50 mg/hour, I would recommend Pump 2 because it is more consistent. Large variations in dose are probably not good for the patient.

Chapter Problem:

a) Sort data using STAT > SortA(L1)

$L_{Q_1} = \frac{1}{4}(72+1) = 18.25 \Rightarrow Q_1 = 68$

$L_M = \frac{1}{2}(72+1) = 36.5 \Rightarrow M = 71$

$L_{Q_3} = \frac{3}{4}(72+1) = 54.75$

$\Rightarrow Q_3 = \frac{72+73}{2} = 72.5$

5-number summary: {65, 68, 71, 72.5, 87}
Note: When the two numbers used to calculate a quartile are the same, the quartile has the same value as the original two numbers.

f) The two whiskers both represent the same number of golf scores. The fact that the right whisker is longer tells us that the higher golf scores are more spread out than the lowest ones.

g) We have the scores for all the golfers, so this is population data. Choose STAT > CALC > 1 Var Stats L1. Remember to change the 87 to 78 first. $\mu \approx 70.54$, $\sigma \approx 3.1620$

h) Rory shot a 71 that day.

$z = \frac{71 - 70.54}{3.1620} \approx 0.145 \Rightarrow$ No, in fact, the

positve z-score points out that he shot a higher (worse) than average score that day. The z-score so close to zero also means he shot just a little above average.

j) $\begin{aligned}\mu - 2\sigma &= 64.216 \\ \mu + 2\sigma &= 76.864\end{aligned} \Rightarrow$ The expected range is any

score from 65 to 76.
Note: Because the score of 64 is lower than 64.216, it would be considered unusual. So, it was not counted. The logic is similar for 77.

k) All but the 78, 78, and 79 fell in the expected

range. $\Rightarrow \frac{69}{72} \approx 95.83\%$. This percentage is

consistent with the General Empirical Rule.

Chapter 3: Review Exercises:

1) a) $\bar{x} = \frac{\sum x}{n} = \frac{89}{15} \approx 5.93$

   b) First put the data in order, then use the location to find the median.

   $L_M = \frac{1}{2}(15+1) = 8 \Rightarrow M = 6$

   c) The mode is the most frequently repeated number. Several numbers are repeated, but 10 is repeated the most with 3 occurrences. Mode = 10.

3) Because we have the entire group that we wish to state conclusions about, this is population data.

   a) $R = \max - \min = 46.1 - 8.5 = 37.6$
   b) Mean and Standard Deviation work:

x	$(x-\mu)^2$
46.1	312.405625
24.0	19.580625
8.5	397.005625
28.7	0.075625
26.6	3.330625
28.0	0.180625
29.4	0.950625
36.1	58.905625
227.4	792.435

$\mu = \frac{\sum x}{N} = \frac{227.4}{8} = 28.425$

   c) $\sigma = \sqrt{\frac{\sum(x-\mu)^2}{N}} = \sqrt{\frac{792.435}{8}} \approx 9.9526$

5) We are told that we only wish to summarize this data set. This implies that this is our population of interest.

x	f	xf	$(x-\mu)^2 f$
4	12	48	62.9292
5	23	115	38.2743
6	41	246	3.4481
7	27	189	13.6107
8	18	144	52.6338
9	7	63	51.4087
	128	805	222.3048

   a) $\mu = \frac{\sum xf}{N} = \frac{805}{128} \approx 6.29$

   b) $\sigma = \sqrt{\frac{\sum(x-\mu)^2 f}{N}} = \sqrt{\frac{222.3048}{128}} \approx 1.3179$

7) Begin by putting the data in order.

a) $L_{Q_1} = \dfrac{1}{4}(18+1) = 4.75 \Rightarrow$

$Q_1 = \dfrac{30.7 + 31.6}{2} = 31.15$

$L_M = \dfrac{1}{2}(18+1) = 9.5 \Rightarrow$

$M = \dfrac{42.4 + 47.5}{2} = 44.95$

$L_{Q_3} = \dfrac{3}{4}(18+1) = 14.25 \Rightarrow$

$Q_3 = \dfrac{65 + 70.6}{2} = 67.8$

b) $L_{P_{61}} = \dfrac{61}{100}(18+1) = 11.59 \Rightarrow$

$P_{61} = \dfrac{55.4 + 62.5}{2} = 58.95$

9) a) $z = \dfrac{6000 - 4009.66}{1322.087} \approx 1.505 \Rightarrow$ No, 6000 would not be unusually high, because it is less than 2 standard deviations above the mean.

b) $z = \dfrac{1000 - 4009.66}{1322.087} \approx -2.276 \Rightarrow$ Yes, 1000 would be unusually low, because it is more than 2 standard deviations below the mean.

c) $u - 2\sigma = 4009.66 - 2*1322.087 = 1365.486$
$u + 2\sigma = 4009.66 + 2*1322.087 = 6653.834$
This is a continuous variable, so we will not change these numbers at all. The expected range is between 1365.486 and 6653.834.

11) $CV = \dfrac{s}{\bar{x}} = \dfrac{93.639}{501.6} \approx 0.1867 = 18.67\%$

13) a) $\bar{x} = \dfrac{100}{14} \approx 7.14$

b) $L_M = \dfrac{1}{2}(14+1) = 7.5 \Rightarrow M = 5$

c) The mode is 5 (repeated 3 times).

d) Right-skewed. The mean has been pulled to the right of the median by the extremes on the right.

e) The median. It attempts to separate the lower and upper halves of the data set.

15) Use of technology is suggested on this problem. The wording indicates that this is population data.

a) $R = \max - \min = 7.1 - 0.9 = 6.2$

b) $\mu \approx 3.28$

c) $\sigma \approx 1.6765$

17) Use of technology is suggested on this problem. The wording indicates that this is sample data.

a) $\bar{x} \approx -52.17$

b) $s \approx 189.44$

c) To estimate this, we multiple the 200 sessions by our estimate for the average loss per session, $\bar{x}$. Total Prfoit/Loss
$\approx 200(-52.17) = -10,434$
So, we would expect the gambler to LOSE about $10,434 after 200 sessions.

d) Boundaries: $\bar{x} - s \approx -241.61$ and
$\bar{x} + s \approx 137.27 \Rightarrow \dfrac{23}{30} \approx 76.67\%$

e) Boundaries: $\bar{x} - 2s \approx -431.05$ and
$\bar{x} + 2s \approx 326.71 \Rightarrow \dfrac{28}{30} \approx 93.33\%$

19) The wording suggests that this is sample data. Use of technology is suggested.

a) $\bar{x} \approx 2.97$

b) $s \approx 1.3443$

c) Estimated total TV's for 50 households: about $50(2.97) = 148.5$ TV's.

d) Boundaries: $\bar{x} - s \approx 1.6257$ and
$\bar{x} + s \approx 4.3143 \Rightarrow \dfrac{88 + 147 + 98}{444} = 75\%$

e) Boundaries: $\bar{x} - 2s \approx 0.2814$ and
$\bar{x} + 2s \approx 5.6586$
$\Rightarrow \dfrac{444 - 15 - 12 - 3}{444} \approx 93.24\%$

20) The wording suggests that this is population data. Use of technology is suggested. Use the midpoints as estimates for the x-values.

a) $\mu \approx 4050.40$

b) $\sigma \approx 1813.65$

c) Estimated total ticket sales for 40 days: about $40(4050.40) = 162,016$ tickets.

d) Boundaries: $\mu - \sigma \approx 2236.75$ and $\mu + \sigma \approx 5864.05$

$$\Rightarrow \frac{22 + 45 + 31 + 22}{167} \approx 71.86\%$$

e) Boundaries: $\mu - 2\sigma \approx 423.10$ and $\mu + 2\sigma \approx 7677.70 \Rightarrow \frac{167 - 3}{167} \approx 98.20\%$

21) a) $z = \dfrac{120 - 102.5}{7.3} \approx 2.397$. Yes, 120 points is unusually high for this team because is more than 2 standard deviations above the mean.

b) $z = \dfrac{80 - 102.5}{7.3} \approx -3.082$. Yes, in fact 80 points would be considered very unusual for this team, because 80 points is more than 3 standard deviations below the mean.

c) Lower Boundary: $\mu - 2\sigma = 87.9$

Upper Boundary: $\mu + 2\sigma = 117.1$

Expected range for this team is anywhere between 88 and 117 points.

d) The game score is 2.808 standard deviations above the mean. Therefore, this is an unusually high game score for this team. The actual game score is:

$x = 102.5 + 2.808 * 7.3 \approx 123$ points.

23) a) $CV = \dfrac{s}{\bar{x}} \approx 0.0151 = 1.51\%$

b) No. The CV is a little larger than 1%, so the company either needs to improve the consistency of the machine or lower their requirement.

25) a) $L_{P_{90}} = \dfrac{90}{100}(30 + 1) = 27.9$

$$\Rightarrow P_{90} = \frac{614 + 635}{2} = 624.5$$

b) $L_{Q_1} = \dfrac{1}{4}(30 + 1) = 7.75$

$$\Rightarrow Q_1 = \frac{240 + 280}{2} = 260$$

$L_M = \dfrac{1}{2}(30 + 1) = 15.5$

$$\Rightarrow M = \frac{291 + 319}{2} = 305$$

$L_{Q_3} = \dfrac{3}{4}(30 + 1) = 23.25$

$$\Rightarrow Q_3 = \frac{446 + 483}{2} = 464.5$$

Five Num: {75, 260, 305, 464.5, 915}

c) $IQR = 464.5 - 260 = 204.5$

$UF = 464.5 + 1.5 * 204.5 = 771.25$

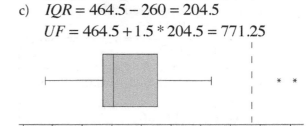

d) Right-skewed. Counting the outliers, we have a much longer whisker on the right side than the left. Also, the right side of the box is wider than the left side of the box.

e) Assuming that these are not errors, it just looks like the author had unusually big breakfasts on these two days.

27) a) The least prepared students are represented by the bottom boxplot. Using the left whisker, the left side of the box, the vertical line in the middle, the right side of the box, and the left whisker, the estimated values of the five number summary are as follows.

$$\{29,\ 32,\ 36,\ 46,\ 64\}$$

b) Same idea as above, but this time we will use the top boxplot for the most prepared students.

$$\{36,\ 60,\ 72,\ 82,\ 101\}$$

c) Yes. According to the boxplots and five number summaries, 3/4 of the most prepared students score 60 or above on the test. This appears to be better than the score of almost all of the least prepared students. The high score for that group is only a 64. The boxplot for the most prepared students also shows that 1/2 of those students scored 72 or higher. No students in the least prepared group scored this high.

Section 4.1:

1) The standard form of a line in statistics is $y = b_0 + b_1 x$, where b_0 is the y-intercept and b_1 is the slope.

2) The x-variable is usually referred to as the predictor or the explanatory variable.

3) The y-variable is usually referred to as the prediction or the response variable.

4) Interpretation of the slope: For each additional unit of the x-value, the y-value is changed by the slope.

5) If (x, y) is an ordered pair in our data set, then we refer to the y as an observed y-value.

6) $\hat{y}$ represents a predicted y-value and it is found by substituting for an x-value in the prediction equation.

7) A scatterplot is a graph where all of the ordered pairs in a data set are graphed.

8) Prediction error is the difference between the observed y-value and the predicted y-value.

9) $x = 0 \Rightarrow y = -5.4 + 3.71(0) = -5.4$
$\Rightarrow (0, \, -5.4)$
$x = 10 \Rightarrow y = -5.4 + 3.71(10) = 31.7$
$\Rightarrow (10, \, 31.7)$

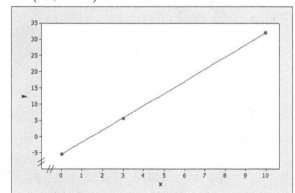

11) $x = 100 \Rightarrow y = -34.56 - 15.85(100)$
$= -1619.56 \Rightarrow (100, \text{-}1619.56)$
$x = 500 \Rightarrow y = -34.56 - 15.85(500)$
$= -7959.56 \Rightarrow (500, \text{-}7959.56)$

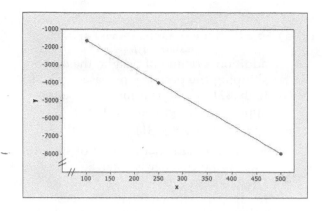

13) a) $b_1 = -250 \Rightarrow \dfrac{\Delta v}{\Delta y} = \dfrac{-\$250}{1yr} \Rightarrow$ For each additional year of age for these color copiers, the price decreases by \$250.

b) $(0 \text{ yr}, \$1500) \Rightarrow$ New copiers of this type are worth \$1500.

c) $y = 2 \Rightarrow v = 1500 - 250(2) = 1000$

So, we estimate that the copier would be worth about \$1000 after 2 years.

d) Pick any other x-values and substitute into the equation to find more values of v.

y	v
1	1250
2	1000
5	250

Plot these points and then connect with a straight line.

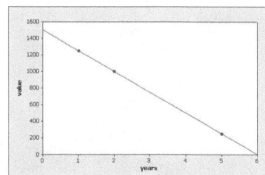

e) This question is not intended to be answered using the equation. Use the graph to answer it. Move on the horizontal axis to 3.5 years. From there, move up until you hit the line. Finally move left to the vertical axis and note the value. Answers will vary. Value $\approx \$625$.

f) $y = 6 \Rightarrow v = 1500 - 250(6) = 0$

Therefore, 6 years is the largest that can make sense. The equation says that the copier will be essentially worthless at this time. If you plug in larger values, then you will get negative values, which do not make sense for this application.

15) a) $b_1 = 2.8 \Rightarrow \dfrac{\Delta c}{\Delta w} = \dfrac{\$2.8}{1\,lb} \Rightarrow$ For each

additional pound of weight, the cost of shipping the package increases by $2.80.

b) (0 lb, $21.05) $\Rightarrow$ This formula does not apply to a weightless package!

c) $w = 14.7 \Rightarrow c = 2.8(14.7) + 21.05 = 62.21$

So, we estimate that the cost of shipping a 14.7 pound package is about $62.21.

d) Even though you can pick any values for w to input into the equation. It is best to pick values on the extreme low and high side.

w	c
1	23.85
19	74.25
14.7	62.21

Plot these 2 additional points and then connect with a straight line.

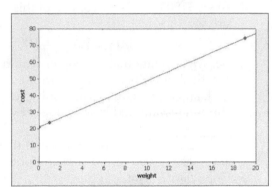

e) Move on the horizontal axis until you reach the value 7, then move up until you hit the line. Finally, move to the left until you hit the vertical axis. Answers will vary. Value $\approx \$40.65$

17) a) $b_1 = 0.19 \Rightarrow \dfrac{\Delta c}{\Delta m} = \dfrac{\$0.19}{1\,mi} \Rightarrow$ For each

additional mile driven, the cost of the moving van rental increases by $0.19.

b) (0 mi., $29.99) $\Rightarrow$ Before we even put any miles on the moving van, we already owe $29.99.

c) Even though you can pick any values for m to input into the equation. It is best to pick values that are spread out among the reasonable possibilities.

m	c
0	29.99
100	48.99
200	67.99

Plot these 3 points and then connect with a straight line.

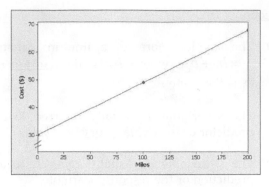

19) a) To do this, we simply plot all the ordered pairs. The fastest time was 75.07 seconds, so I removed the values below 74 from the vertical axis.

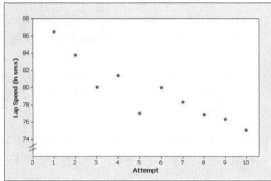

b) We should pick two x-values and plug them in to get the predicted values.

$x = 1 \Rightarrow \hat{y} = 85.443 - 1.0739(1) \approx 84.37$

$\Rightarrow (1,\ 84.37)$

$x = 10 \Rightarrow \hat{y} = 85.443 - 1.0739(10) = 74.704$

$\Rightarrow (10,\ 74.704)$

Plot these points with the scatter and you should see that you get a good fit to the scatterplot.

c) $b_1 = -1.0739 \Rightarrow \dfrac{\Delta \hat{y}}{\Delta x} = \dfrac{-1.0739\ secs}{1\ attempt} \Rightarrow$

For each additional attempt taken at the game, the expected lap time decreases by about 1.07 seconds.

d) First, we need to find the predicted value that goes with x = 3.

$x = 3 \Rightarrow \hat{y} = 85.443 - 1.0739(3) = 82.2213$

$\Rightarrow (3,\ 82.2213)$

Now, we can compute the error.

$e = y - \hat{y} = 80.04 - 82.2213 = -2.1813$

21) a) $x = 67 \Rightarrow \hat{y} = -7.96 + 11.7526(67)$

$= 779.4642 \Rightarrow (67, \ 779.4642)$

So, we estimate that about 779.46 calories would be burned during a 67 minutes long mountain bike ride.

b) $b_1 = 11.7526 \Rightarrow \dfrac{\Delta \hat{y}}{\Delta x} = \dfrac{11.7526 \text{ cals}}{1 \text{ minute}} \Rightarrow$

For each additional minute of ride time, the expected number of calories burned increases by about 11.75 calories.

c) First, we must find the predicted value.

$x = 77 \Rightarrow \hat{y} = -7.96 + 11.7526(77)$

$= 896.9902 \Rightarrow (77, \ 896.9902)$

$e = y - \hat{y} = 844 - 896.9902 = -52.9902$

d) First, we must find the predicted value.

$x = 82 \Rightarrow \hat{y} = -7.96 + 11.7526(82)$

$= 955.7532 \Rightarrow (82, \ 955.7532)$

$e = y - \hat{y} = 1007 - 955.7532 = 51.2468$

23) a) Yes, the line follows the pattern of the data and all of the data values appear to be close to the line.

b) $b_1 = 979.450 \Rightarrow \dfrac{\Delta \hat{y}}{\Delta x} = \dfrac{\$979.45}{1 \text{ year}} \Rightarrow$ For

each additional year that goes by, the expected tuition at Harvard increases by about $979.45.

c) The work for the first residual (or prediction error) is shown below.

$x = 1981 \Rightarrow \hat{y} = -1934953.6 + 979.450(1981)$

$= 5336.85 \Rightarrow (1981, \ 5336.85)$

$e = y - \hat{y} = 6000 - 5336.85 = -663.15$

The work for the other 6 points is similar and the answers are shown below.

x	y	$\hat{y}$	$e = y - \hat{y}$	e^2
1981	6000	5336.85	663.15	439767.92
1985	9800	9254.65	545.35	297406.62
1990	13545	14151.9	-606.9	368327.61
1995	18485	19049.15	-564.15	318265.22
2000	22765	23946.4	-1181.4	1395705.96
2005	28752	28843.65	-91.65	8399.72
2010	34976	33740.9	1235.1	1525472.01
				4353345.06

So, we get: $\sum e^2 \approx 4,353,345.07$

Section 4.2:

25) The best fitting line for a data set is called the regression line.

26) The regression line is the one with the smallest possible sum of squared errors An error is the difference between the height of an actual data point and the height of the line at that same x -value.

27) Linear regression should only be done if a plot of the data values has a roughly linear pattern.

28) When we use a regression equation to make a prediction, we are always predicting the average y-value.

29) It is not wise to make predictions using x-values that are outside of the range of the given data.

30) If the x-value of a data point stands out, then we call it a potentially influential observation . If the y-value of a data point stands out, then we call it an outlier.

31) y stands for the observed y-value of a piece of data. $\bar{y}$ stands for the average of all the y-values in the data set. $\hat{y}$ stands for a predicted y-value using an x-value in the regression equation.

32) When a linear pattern exists for x-values in a certain range, but then begins to change outside of that range, then we refer to this as model breakdown.

33) a) Line B appears a little closer to more of the points.

b) Line A: Values for $\hat{y}$ are obtained by plugging the x values into the equation given for line A.

x	y	$\hat{y}$	$e^2 = (y-\hat{y})^2$
3	21	18	9
5	25	26	1
6	24	30	36
8	30	38	64
8	41	38	9
11	50	50	0
			$\sum e^2 = 119$

Line B: Values for $\hat{y}$ are obtained by plugging the x values into the equation given for line B.

x	y	$\hat{y}$	$e^2 = (y-\hat{y})^2$
3	21	17.5	12.25
5	25	24.5	0.25
6	24	28	16
8	30	35	25
8	41	35	36
11	50	45.5	20.25
			$\sum e^2 = 109.75$

c) Line B is the better fit because it has a smaller sum of squared error than line A.

35) a) First we make a table to find the needed sums.

x	y	$(x-\bar{x})(y-\bar{y})$	$(x-\bar{x})^2$
3	21	41.528	14.694
5	25	12.528	3.361
6	24	6.528	0.694
8	30	-2.139	1.361
8	41	10.694	1.361
11	50	75.694	17.361
41	191	144.833	38.833

Calculator Tips: You can use the calculator to speed up this process. Enter x-values in L1 and the y-values in L2.
Then let L3 = (L1 – 41/6)(L2 – 191/6).
Then let L4 = (L1 – 41/6)^2.

You can also use LIST >MATH > SUM to assist finding the sums.

Note: The calculator keeps track of more digits than I wrote down in the tables. Using the larger number of decimal places produces more accurate values for b_1 and b_0.

$$b_1 = \frac{\sum(x-\bar{x})(y-\bar{y})}{\sum(x-\bar{x})^2} \approx \frac{144.83333}{38.83333} \approx 3.72962$$

$$b_0 = \bar{y} - b_1\bar{x} \approx \frac{191}{6} - 3.729617 * \frac{41}{6} \approx 6.3476$$

$$\hat{y} \approx 6.3476 + 3.7296x$$

b) Values for $\hat{y}$ are obtained by plugging the x values into the regression equation above.

x	y	$\hat{y}$	$e^2 = (y-\hat{y})^2$
3	21	17.536	11.996
5	25	24.996	0.000
6	24	28.725	22.328
8	30	36.184	38.247
8	41	36.184	23.190
11	50	47.373	6.900
			$\sum e^2 \approx 102.66$

Note: notice that $\sum e^2$ is smaller here than from lines A and B in exercise (33).

37) ae)

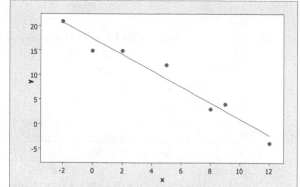

b) Yes. There is a roughly linear pattern to the data set.

c) First we make a table to find the needed sums.

x	y	$(x-\bar{x})(y-\bar{y})$	$(x-\bar{x})^2$
-3	21	-89.265	59.510
0	15	-26.265	22.224
2	15	-15.122	7.367
5	12	0.735	0.082
8	3	-21.122	10.796
9	4	-23.265	18.367
12	-4	-97.837	53.082
33	66	-272.143	171.429

$$b_1 = \frac{\sum(x-\bar{x})(y-\bar{y})}{\sum(x-\bar{x})^2} \approx \frac{-272.143}{171.429} \approx -1.5875$$

$$b_0 = \bar{y} - b_1\bar{x} \approx \frac{66}{7} - (-1.5875) * \frac{33}{7} = 16.9125$$

$$\hat{y} = 16.9125 - 1.5875x$$

d) $\hat{y} = 16.9125 - 1.5875(-2) = 20.0875$

$$\hat{y} = 16.9125 - 1.5875(11) = -0.55$$

41) ae)

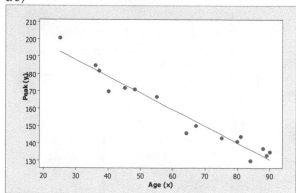

b) Yes. There is a roughly linear pattern to the data set.

39) a) Yes, the data forms a roughly linear pattern.
b) No, there is no pattern at all to the data.
c) No, there is a definite pattern, but it is not linear.

43) ae)

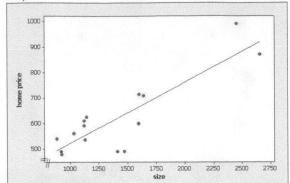

b) Yes, there is a roughly linear pattern to the data.

c) Enter the x-values in L1 and the y-values in L2. Choose STAT > CALC > LinReg(a+bx) L1, L2 and we get:

$$\hat{y} \approx 282.74 + 0.239689x$$

Rounding Note: The prices are given in $1000s, so the $100 place is actually the first decimal place. For example, a home that costs $654,300 would be listed as 654.3. So, since we want 1 decimal place in our predictions, we need at least 2 decimal places in our intercept. Since we want 4 digits in our predictions, we need at least 5 digits in our slope.

d) $\hat{y} \approx 282.74 + 0.239689 * 2200 \approx 810.1$

$= \$810,100$, yes, 2200 sq ft is within the range of the known home sizes in our data set.

e) Pick x values near the min and max of the given data values. Plug them into the regression equation.

x	$\hat{y}$	
1000	522.4	Plot these 2 points and
2500	882.0	then connect with a straight line. See line in part (a).

f) 3400 sq ft is larger than any of the homes in our data set. The model may break down for homes of that size.

g) $\dfrac{\Delta \hat{y}}{\Delta x} = \dfrac{0.240(\$1000)}{1 \text{ ft}^2} = \dfrac{\$240}{1 \text{ ft}^2} \Rightarrow$ For each additional sq ft, the average price of the homes increases by $240.

h) The two big homes in the data set are useful, because they allow us to make predictions for the price of homes between 1637 sq. ft. and 2452 sq. ft. without extrapolating. They show us that the model does not break down in this region.

45) a) Yes. There is a roughly linear pattern to the data set.

b) Enter the x-values in L1 and the y-values in L2. Choose STAT > CALC > LinReg(a+bx) L1, L2 and we get:

$$\hat{y} \approx 199.19 - 29.544x$$

Rounding Note: A large prediction rounded to the nearest tenth of a win might be 101.9. So, since we want one decimal place for our predictions, we need at least 2 decimal places in our intercept. Since we want 4 digits in our predictions, we need at least 5 digits in our slope.

c) $\hat{y} \approx 199.19 - 29.544 * 4.11 \approx 77.8$. If an American league team had an ERA of 4.11 that year, we would have expected that average number of wins to be about 77.8.

d) $\dfrac{\Delta \hat{y}}{\Delta x} = \dfrac{-29.544 \text{ wins}}{1} \Rightarrow$ For each additional unit higher on the ERA, the average number of wins for the team decreases by about 29.544.

e) I would say that the ordered pair (3.98, 63) for the White Sox is the best candidate to be called an outlier. The 63 wins seems too low for an ERA of 3.98.

f) The best candidate to be called a PIO is the ordered pair (4.79, 51) for the Astros. There is a noticeable gap between the ERA for the Astros and the next closest team.

47) a) Enter the x-values in L1 and the y-values in L2. Choose STAT > CALC > LinReg(a+bx) L1, L2 and we get:

$\hat{y} \approx -18.74 + 1.110118x$

Rounding Note: A large prediction rounded to the nearest 0.1 thousand barrels per day might be 10.100.5. So, because we want one decimal place for our predictions, we need at least 2 decimal places in our intercept. Since we want 6 digits in our predictions, we need at least 7 digits in our slope.

b) $\dfrac{\Delta \hat{y}}{\Delta x} = \dfrac{1.110 \text{ thousand barrels/day}}{\$1 \text{ Billion}} =$

$\dfrac{1,110 \text{ barrels/day}}{\$1 \text{ Billion}} \Rightarrow$ For each additional $1 Billion of GDP, the average oil consumption for the country increases by 1,110 barrels per day.

c) The value that seems to stand out the most is the ordered pair (16245, 19150) for the USA. This data value is a PIO because the GDP is so much higher than the next closest country. However, it is not an outlier, because the data point still falls in the overall linear pattern of the data set.

d) It is best not to use this equation to predict the oil consumption for a country because this data set is not a random sample of all countries. It is a top 30 list. A top 30 list is not a respresentative sample and should not be used to make predictions.

49) a) A linear regression does seem appropriate because there is a roughly linear pattern to the data set.

b) Enter the x-values in L1 and the y-values in L2. Choose STAT > CALC > LinReg(a+bx) L1, L2 and we get:

$\hat{y} \approx 71.90 + 268.42x$

Rounding Note: A large prediction rounded to the nearest tenth of a second might be 285.7. So, because we want one decimal place for our predictions, we need at least 2 decimal places in our intercept. Because we want 4 digits in our predictions, we need at least 5 digits in our slope.

c) $\hat{y} \approx 71.90 + 268.42 * 0.98 \approx 335.0$ seconds. This means that we would predict that the averge heating time for 0.98 L of water would be about 335.0 seconds.

d) $\dfrac{\Delta \hat{y}}{\Delta x} = \dfrac{268.42 \text{ seconds}}{1 \text{ Liter}} \Rightarrow$ For each additional liter of water in the pot, the average heatings time for the water increases by 268.42 seconds.

e) While not that unusual, the ordered pair (1.20, 406) could be considered a PIO because there is a noticeable gap between the 1.20 L of water and the next closest value of 1.04 L.

51) a) Enter the x-values (the miles) in L1 and the y-values (the price) in L2. Choose STAT > CALC > LinReg(a+bx) L1, L2 and we get:

$\hat{y} \approx 282.848 - 0.00210945x$

Rounding Note: The prices are given in $100s, so the $1 place is actually the second decimal place. For example, a car that sold for $12,345 would be listed as 123.45. So, since we want 2 decimal places in our predictions, we need at least 3 decimal places in our intercept. Since we want 5 digits in our predictions, we need at least 6 digits in our slope.

b) $\hat{y} \approx 282.848 - 0.00210945 * 35000$

$\approx 209.02 = \$20,902$, yes 35000 is within the range of the known mileages in our data set.

c) 120000 miles is more miles than any of the cars in our data set. The model might break down for mileages this large.

d) $b_1 \approx -0.0021 \Rightarrow \dfrac{\Delta \hat{y}}{\Delta x} = \dfrac{-\$0.21}{1 \text{ mile}} \Rightarrow$ For each additional mile, the average price of a mustang GT convertible decreases by $0.21.

e) If the ordered pair (70000, 250) were added to the data set, then it would be an outlier. This would be an unusually high price for a Mustang with so many miles on it.

f) If the ordered pair (110000, 51) were added to the data set, then this would be a PIO. This car would have a lot more miles on it than any of the other cars in the data set.

Section 4.3:

53) r^2 is called the coefficient of <u>determination</u>.

54) $\sum(y-\bar{y})^2$ represents the total squared error if we used the <u>average</u> y-value to make our estimates rather than the linear <u>regression</u> equation.

55) $\sum(y-\hat{y})^2$ represents the total squared error if we used the linear <u>regression</u> equation to make predictions.

56) $\dfrac{\sum(y-\bar{y})^2-\sum(y-\hat{y})^2}{\sum(y-\bar{y})^2}$ represents the

<u>percent</u> reduction in squared error when we make predictions by using the x-value in the regression equation rather than just always using the overall average y-value to make our predictions.

57) If r^2 is near 0, then we fear that the regression is <u>not useful</u>.

58) If r^2 is near 1, then the regression is <u>very useful</u>.

59) $r^2 = \dfrac{\sum(y-\bar{y})^2-\sum(y-\hat{y})^2}{\sum(y-\bar{y})^2}$

$\approx \dfrac{239.855-73.805}{239.855} \approx 0.6923$

61) a) $y-\bar{y}$ is represented on the graph by the vertical distance from each data point to the horizontal line. Estimates for each $y-\bar{y}$ are shown on the graph below.

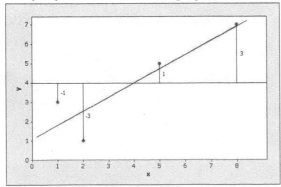

$\sum(y-\bar{y})^2 = (-1)^2 + (-3)^2 + 1^2 + 3^2 = 20$

b) $y-\hat{y}$ is represented on the graph by the vertical distance from each data point to the regression line. Estimates for each $y-\hat{y}$ are shown on the graph below.

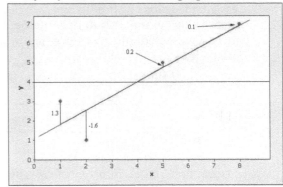

$\sum(y-\hat{y})^2 \approx 1.3^2 + (-1.6)^2 + 0.2^2 + 0.1^2 = 4.3$

c) $r^2 = \dfrac{\sum(y-\bar{y})^2-\sum(y-\hat{y})^2}{\sum(y-\bar{y})^2} \approx \dfrac{20-4.3}{20} = 0.785$

63) We will begin by find the value of $\bar{y}$.

$\bar{y} = \dfrac{\sum y}{n} = \dfrac{191}{6} \approx 31.83$

Using technology we find the regression equation, $\hat{y} \approx 6.34764 + 3.7296x$. We will substitute the x-values into this equation to find the values of $\hat{y}$ used in the table below.

x	y	$\hat{y}$	$(y-\bar{y})^2$	$(y-\hat{y})^2$
3	21	17.54	117.29	12.00
5	25	25.00	46.65	0.00
6	24	28.73	61.31	22.33
8	30	36.18	3.35	38.25
8	41	36.18	84.09	23.19
11	50	47.37	330.15	6.90
	191		642.83	102.67

$r^2 = \dfrac{\sum(y-\bar{y})^2-\sum(y-\hat{y})^2}{\sum(y-\bar{y})^2} \Rightarrow$

$r^2 \approx \dfrac{642.83-102.67}{642.83} \approx 0.8403$

65) a) Yes. The data seems to have a strong linear pattern. It appears that the prediction errors will be small using the line.

   b) We will begin by find the value of $\bar{y}$.

$$\bar{y} = \frac{\sum y}{n} = \frac{134{,}323}{7} = 19{,}189$$

Using technology we find the regression equation, $\hat{y} \approx -1934953.6 + 979.450x$. We will substitute the x-values into this equation to find the values of $\hat{y}$ used in the table below.

x	y	$\hat{y}$	$(y-\bar{y})^2$	$(y-\hat{y})^2$
1981	6000	5337	173949721	439768
1985	9800	9255	88153321	297407
1990	13545	14152	31854736	368328
1995	18485	19049	495616	318265
2000	22765	23946	12787776	1395706
2005	28752	28844	91450969	8400
2010	34976	33741	249229369	1525472
	134323		647921508	4353346

$$r^2 = \frac{\sum(y-\bar{y})^2 - \sum(y-\hat{y})^2}{\sum(y-\bar{y})^2} \Rightarrow$$

$$r^2 \approx \frac{647921508 - 4353346}{647921508} \approx 0.9933$$

   c) Yes. I looked like the regression would be very useful and I found that using regression removes 99.33% of the squared prediction error. That seems very useful indeed.

67) a) Yes. The data seems to have a roughly linear downward trend that follows this line pretty well. It appears that we will get less prediction error using this line than we would if we used the horizontal mean line.

   b) Enter the x-values in L1 and the y-values in L2. Choose STAT > CALC > LinReg(a+bx) L1, L2. If r^2 does not show in the output, see directions for turning "diagnostic on" in section 4.3 of the book. $r^2 \approx 0.8239$

   c) We get a 82.39% reduction in squared error when we use the attempt number in the regression equation to predict the lap time rather than just always using the average lap time as our prediction.

   d) Yes. By using regression, we removed 82.39% of the squared prediction error.

69) a) Enter the x-values in L1 and the y-values in L2. Choose STAT > CALC > LinReg(a+bx) L1, L2. If r^2 does not show in the output, see directions for turning "diagnostic on" in section 4.3 of the book. $r^2 \approx 0.7481$

   b) We get a 74.81% reduction in squared error when we use the size of the home in the linear regression equation to predict the home price rather than just always using the average home price to make our predictions.

   c) 74.81% of the variation in home prices can be explained by using the size of the home in the regression equation.

   d) Yes. By using regression, we removed 74.81% of the squared prediction error.

71) a) Enter the x-values in L1 and the y-values in L2. Choose STAT > CALC > LinReg(a+bx) L1, L2. $r^2 \approx 0.9726$

   b) We get a 97.26% reduction in squared error when we use the ride in the linear regression equation to predict the calories burned rather than just always using the average calories burned to make our predictions.

   c) 97.26% of the variation in calories burned can be explained by using the ride time in the regression equation.

   d) Yes. By using regression, we removed 97.26% of the squared prediction error.

73) a) Enter the x-values in L1 and the y-values in L2. Choose STAT > CALC > LinReg(a+bx) L1, L2. $r^2 \approx 0.3240$

b) The ordered pair (10.2, 1000) is the best candidate because it does not fit the linear pattern. The price seems too high even for a 10.2 megapixel camera.

c) $r^2 \approx 0.0335$

d) Yes. r^2 is now only about 1/10 the size it used to be.

e) If this was the only SLR camera in the sample, then perhaps this camera isn't really part of our target population. I think it is best to remove it.

We get a 3.35% reduction in squared error when we use the number of mega pixels in the linear regression equation to predict the price rather than just always using the average price to make our predictions.
OR
3.35% of the variation in price can be explained by using the number of mega pixels in the regression equation.

f) Not really. The amount of squared prediction error removed in the sample is very small at 3.35%. In fact, this is so close to zero, that we should fear that this equation is not useful at all for making predictions about the population.

75) a) The pattern seems rough with a few outliers, but there does seem to be a roughly linear pattern to the data. This should mean that we will improve our predictions of the number of medals by using the countries population as a predictor.

b) Enter the x-values in L1 and the y-values in L2. Choose STAT > CALC > LinReg(a+bx) L1, L2. $r^2 \approx 0.3739$

c) We get a 37.39% reduction in squared error when we use the population in the linear regression equation to predict the number of medals won rather than just always using the average number of medals won to make our predictions.
OR
37.39% of the variation in the number of medals won can be explained by using the population in the regression equation.

d) No. It turns out that China is both a PIO and an outlier. It would have been nice to see such a problematic data value when deciding if regression would be helpful.

e) No, this was not a random sample it was the top 24 medal winning countries. Top 24 lists ususually are not representative of the population.

Section 4.4:

77) r is known as the linear <u>correlation</u> coefficient.

78) The linear correlation coefficient always has the same sign as the <u>slope</u> of the regression line.

79) If r is close to 1, then there is a <u>strong positive</u> linear correlation between the <u>variables</u>.

80) A positive correlation (or <u>association</u>) means that as the x-value gets larger, the y-value gets <u>larger</u>.

81) If r is close to -1, then there is a <u>strong negative</u> linear correlation between the <u>variables</u>.

82) A negative correlation (or <u>association</u>) means that as the x-value gets larger, the y-value gets <u>smaller</u>.

83) If r is close to 0, then there is <u>weak</u> if any <u>linear</u> correlation between the variables.

84) A strong correlation does not always indicate a <u>cause</u> and effect relationship between the two variables. It is possible that there are other <u>lurking</u> variables that are affecting the variables under consideration in the study.

85) The regression line always passes through the point $(\overline{x}, \overline{y})$.

86) If an ordered pair is to the upper right or lower left of the mean lines, then it makes a <u>positive</u> contribution to the linear correlation. If the ordered pair is on one or both of the mean lines, then the contribution to the linear correlation is <u>zero</u>.

87) a) There is an upward pattern to the data, so we should guess a positive value. There is a very strong linear pattern. Answers will vary.

b) Enter the x-values in L1 and the y-values in L2. Choose STAT > CALC > LinReg(a+bx) L1, L2. If r does not show in the output, see directions for turning "diagnostic on" in section 4.3 of the book. $r \approx 0.9862$

c) There is a strong positive linear correlation between the ride time and calories burned.

d) Since a longer ride will usually require more exertion by the rider, I think it is likely to be the main cause.

89) a) There is an upward pattern to the data, so we should guess a positive value. There is a decent, but not great linear pattern. Answers will vary.

b) Enter the x-values in L1 and the y-values in L2. Choose STAT > CALC > LinReg(a+bx) L1, L2. If r does not show in the output, see directions for turning "diagnostic on" in section 4.3 of the book. $r \approx 0.8649$

c) There is a strong positive linear correlation between the size and price of homes.

d) There are 4 homes to the upper right of the mean lines and 7 homes to the lower left. This would be 11 out of 15, or 73.33%.

e) The ordered pairs that appear to be PIO's are (2659, 870) and (2452, 991). These two homes are much larger than the rest of the homes in the sample. When they are removed, we get $r \approx 0.5460$.

f) If we are interested in predicting the average price of homes that are between 1637 sq. ft. and 2452 sq. ft., then we should keep these values in the data set. Otherwise, they should be removed.

91) a) There is an upward trend to the data, so we should guess a positive value. Also, the linear pattern seems fairly strong. *Answers will vary.*

b) Enter the x-values in L1 and the y-values in L2. Choose STAT > CALC > LinReg(a+bx) L1, L2. $r \approx 0.8958$

c) There appears to be a strong positive linear correlation between the gas price and the HEV sales.

d) Not necessarily. We must remember that this is just an observational study. Therefore, the strong correlation that we see does not prove a cause and effect relationship between the two variables.

e) A lurking variable that may be affecting the HEV sales is time itself. It takes time for a new idea to catch on and HEV's seem to be gaining in popularity over time.

93) a) There is a downward pattern to the data, so we should guess a negative value. There seems to be a pretty strong linear pattern. Answers will vary.

b) Enter the x-values in L1 and the y-values in L2. Choose STAT > CALC > LinReg(a+bx) L1, L2. $r \approx -0.8792$

c) There is a strong negative linear correlation between the mileage and price of the mustangs.

d) There are 4 cars to the upper left of the mean lines and 5 to the lower right. This is 9 out of 12, or 75%.

e) I do suspect that putting more miles on a car does cause it to go down if value. People are generally not willing to pay as much for a car that has a lot of miles on it.

f) Other lurking variables that are affecting the price of the car might be age, features, and condition of paint, upholstery, etc.

95) a) There is a downward pattern to the data, so we should guess a negative value. There seems to be a somewhat strong linear pattern. *Answers will vary.*

b) Enter the x-values in L1 and the y-values in L2. Choose STAT > CALC > LinReg(a+bx) L1, L2. $r \approx -0.8383$

c) There is a strong negative linear correlation between the ERA and the number of wins for a team.

d) I would say that pitchers with high ERA's are part of the cause of losses. If your team gives up a lot of runs, it is harder to win.

e) Other lurking variables that affect the number of wins might be the batting averages of the team, the number of homeruns, the defensive ability of the other players, teams speed, etc.

97) a) Enter the x-values in L1 and the y-values in L2. Choose STAT > CALC > LinReg(a+bx) L1, L2. $r \approx 0.5692$

b) The ordered pair (10.2, 1000) appears to be an outlier. That camera seems to cost much more than any of the others, even for a camera with 10.2 megapixels.

c) If this was the only SLR camera in the sample, then perhaps this camera isn't really part of our target population. I think it is best to remove it.

d) $r \approx 0.1831$

e) Yes, the correlation is now only about 1/3 the size it used to be.

f) Assuming you are not planning on buying an SLR camera, then I would say not really. With the SLR removed, the correlation is so small that it might just represent random variation in the sample.

g) Other lurking variables that may be affecting the price of the camera would be features such as zoom, optional video, etc.

Chapter Problem:

a) Yes. The pattern is not really strong, but there does seem to be a roughly linear pattern to the data set.

b) I would say that (0.7, 117) is an outlier because that child had a higher IQ than we would have expected given the child's dietary score.

c) I would say that (-2.8, 95) is a bit of a PIO. This child's dietary score is quite a bit lower than any of the other children in the sample.

d) $\hat{y} \approx 101.215 + 1.7539x$

Rounding Note: A large prediction rounded to the nearest tenth of an IQ point might be 105.7. So, since we want one decimal place for our predictions, we need at least 2 decimal places in our intercept (I decided to put 3, but extra is acceptable). Since we want 4 digits in our predictions, we need at least 5 digits in our slope.

f) A dietary score of 4.2 is much higher than the dietary score for any of the children in our sample. The model might break down for dietary scores that high. This would be an extrapolation and should be avoided.

h) $b_1 \approx 1.7539 \Rightarrow \dfrac{\Delta\hat{y}}{\Delta x} = \dfrac{1.7539 \text{ IQ pts}}{1 \text{ (dietary score)}} \Rightarrow$ For each additional point increase in dietary score, we expect the average IQ at age 8.5 to increase by about 1.7539 IQ points.

i) $r^2 \approx 0.1333 \Rightarrow$ We get a 13.33% reduction in squared error when we use a child's dietary score at age 3 in the linear regression equation to predict the IQ at age 8, rather than just always using the average IQ at age 8 as our prediction.

Chapter 4: Review Exercises

1) It is best to use x-values that are far apart from one another. Given the range of $1 \le x \le 5$, it is best to substitute $x = 1$ and $x = 5$.

$x = 1 \Rightarrow y = 15.4 - 2.71*1 = 12.69$

$\Rightarrow (1, 12.69)$

$x = 5 \Rightarrow y = 15.4 - 2.71*5 = 1.85$

$\Rightarrow (5, 1.85)$

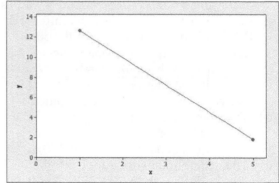

3) a)

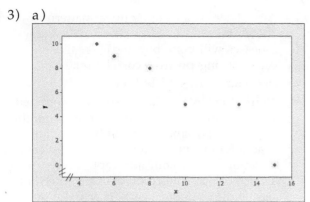

b) Yes, there is a roughly linear pattern to the scatterplot of the data set.

c) First we make a table to find the needed sums.

x	y	$(x-\bar{x})(y-\bar{y})$	$(x-\bar{x})^2$
5	10	-17.24985	20.25
6	9	-9.91655	12.25
8	8	-2.74995	2.25
10	5	-0.58335	0.25
13	5	-4.08345	12.25
15	0	-33.91685	30.25
57	37	-68.5	77.5

$$\bar{x} = \frac{\sum x}{n} = \frac{57}{6} = 9.5 \;;$$

$$\bar{y} = \frac{\sum y}{n} = \frac{37}{6} = 6.1667$$

$$b_1 = \frac{\sum(x-\bar{x})(y-\bar{y})}{\sum(x-\bar{x})^2} = \frac{-68.5}{77.5} \approx -0.88387$$

$$b_0 = \bar{y} - b_1\bar{x} \approx \frac{37}{6} - (-0.88387) * \frac{57}{6} \approx 14.563$$

$$\hat{y} \approx 14.563 - 0.88387x$$

d) Values for $\hat{y}$ are obtained by substituting the x values into the regression equation above.

x	y	$\hat{y}$	$e^2 = (y-\hat{y})^2$
5	10	10.144	0.0206
6	9	9.260	0.0675
8	8	7.492	0.2580
10	5	5.724	0.5246
13	5	3.073	3.7145
15	0	1.305	1.7029
			$\sum e^2 \approx 6.2881$

5) a) $\sum(y-\bar{y})^2$ represents the sum of squared errors for this data set if we always use the overall average y-value to make our predictions.

b) $\sum(y-\hat{y})^2$ represents the sum of squared errors for this data set if we always use the x-value in the regression equation to make our predictions.

c) $r^2 = \dfrac{877.331 - 108.468}{877.331} \approx 0.8764$

7) a) $b_1 = 15.99 \Rightarrow \dfrac{\Delta C}{\Delta G} = \dfrac{\$15.99}{1 \text{ guest}} \Rightarrow$ For each additional guest at the banquet, the cost of increases by \$15.99.

b) $C = 99 + 15.99 * 124 = \$2081.76$

c)

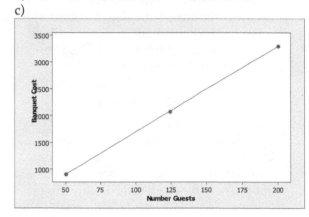

9) a) $\hat{y} = -2.76 + 6.1010 * 100 = 607.34$ Kilowatt-hours/ day.

b) $b_1 = 6.1010 \Rightarrow \dfrac{\Delta\hat{y}}{\Delta x} = \dfrac{6.1010 \text{ kW-h/day}}{1 \text{ m}^2} \Rightarrow$ For each additional square meter of solar panels installed, the average energy output per day increases by about 6.1010 kilowatt-hours.

c) $\sum e^2 \approx 5641.73$

11) ae)

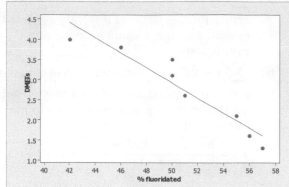

b)   Yes. There is a roughly linear pattern to the data set.

c) $\hat{y} \approx 12.285 - 0.1874x$

Rounding Note: A large prediction rounded to the nearest hundredth of a tooth might be 3.93. So, since we want two decimal places for our predictions, we need at least 3 decimal places in our intercept. Since we want 3 digits in our predictions, we need at least 4 digits in our slope.

d) $\hat{y} \approx 12.285 - 0.1874 * 42 \approx 4.41$ DMFT's

f) $b_1 = -0.1874 \Rightarrow \dfrac{\Delta\hat{y}}{\Delta x} = \dfrac{-0.1874 \text{ DMFTs}}{1\%} \Rightarrow$ For each additional percentage of the population that is drinking fluoridated water, the average number of DMFT's decreases by about 0.1874.

g)   Sure. This data shows that as the percentage of people in the U.S. that were drinking fluoridated water increased, the average number of DMFT's decreased. However, this is an observational study and we should not confuse support with cause and effect.

h)   Perhaps from 1968 to 1991 there was also more of a focus put on good dental hygiene. Perhaps this is just the result of more kids brushing their teeth.

13) a)   Yes. There is a roughly linear pattern to the data.

b)   Guesses will vary, but this looks like a fairly strong positive correlation.

c) $\hat{y} \approx 185.2075 + 13.9604x$

Rounding Note: A large prediction rounded to the nearest hundredth of a calorie might be 753.93. So, since we want two decimal places for our predictions, we need at least 3 decimal places in our intercept. Since we want 5 digits in our predictions, we need at least 6 digits in our slope. (I actually put one extra on each, but extra doesn't hurt!)

d) $r \approx 0.9325$ and $r^2 \approx 0.8695$

e) $b_1 = 13.96 \Rightarrow \dfrac{\Delta\hat{y}}{\Delta x} = \dfrac{13.96 \text{ Calories}}{1 \text{ gram of fat}} \Rightarrow$ For each additional gram of fat in the chicken sandwich, the average number of calories increases by about 13.96 calories.

f)   There is a strong positive linear correlation between the number of grams of fat in a chicken sandwich and the number of calories in the sandwich.

g)   We get an 86.95% reduction in squared error if we use the number of grams of fat in the regression equation to predict the number of calories in the sandwich rather than just always using the overall average number of calories as our prediction.

h)   Yes. By using regression, we removed 86.95% of the squared prediction error.

15) a) When unemployment is high, I would expect the approval rating will be low. When the unemployment rate is low, I would expect the approval rating would be high. When you are the leader, you often get both the credit and the blame (regardless of whether or not that is fair).

b)

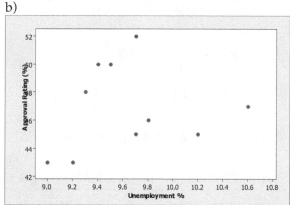

c) This is not a very strong linear pattern at all. However, there does seem to be a bit of a positive trend as we go to the right. Answers will vary.

d) $r \approx 0.1314$ and $r^2 \approx 0.0173$

e) There is weak positive, if any, linear correlation between the unemployment rate and the President's approval rating.

f) We get a 1.73% reduction in squared error if we use the unemployment rate in the linear regression equation to predict the President's approval rating rather than just always using his overall average approval rating as our prediction.

g) Hard to know. It doesn't really make sense to think that higher unemployment rates caused higher approval ratings. This is probably just random variation at work from our sample.

17) a) The ordered pair (5, 58) is a PIO because that student's HW score is much lower than any other students. The instructor might want to remove it because it is a higher exam score than expected for someone who did so little HW. Since this data value is not an error, it should remain in the data set.

b) $\hat{y} = 34.44 + 2.097 * 13 \approx 61.7$ pts   This prediction is wise/reliable because 13 lies within the range of the HW scores in our data set.

c) No. This would be an extrapolation because a HW score of zero is below the lowest HW score in our data set, 5. The pattern we see might not continue to scores as low as zero.

d) $b_1 = 2.097 \Rightarrow \dfrac{\Delta \hat{y}}{\Delta x} = \dfrac{2.097 \text{ Exam pts}}{1 \text{ HW pt}} \Rightarrow$

For each additional homework point earned, the average exam score increases by about 2.097 points.

e) The is a moderately strong positive linear correlation between homework scores and exam scores.

f) We get a 36.39% reduction in squared error when we use a student's homework score in the regression equation to predict the student's exam score rather than just always using the overall average exam score as our prediction.

g) No. This is just an observational study so cause and effect cannot be shown. However, there is a positive correlation. Even though good HW is not a guarantee of good exam scores, it is a good sign. I would prefer to have good HW going into the exam, just in case.

Section 5.1:

1) Classical probability applies to situations where each simple outcome is <u>equally</u> likely to occur.

2) A simple outcome is one that can only occur in <u>one</u> way.

3) Calculating probability is the same as calculating a <u>population</u> relative frequency.

4) When we try to interpret probability, we should always think of it as the <u>long-term</u> relative frequency.

5) The complement of event E is the event that E does <u>NOT</u> occur. It is often best to use <u>subtraction</u> when calculating complements.

6) The Fundamental Rule of Counting states that when there are m outcomes to one experiment and n outcomes to another experiment, then we must <u>multiply</u> m and n when calculating the total number of possible outcomes created by combining the two experiments.

7) a) $P(Yellow) = \dfrac{12}{87} \approx 0.1379$

   b) $P(Orange) = \dfrac{17}{87} \approx 0.1954$

   c) It is often easier to subtract what you don't want from the total rather than counting what you do want.
   $$P(Not\ Green) = \dfrac{87 - 14}{87} \approx 0.8391$$

9) Population relative frequencies have the same value as the corresponding probabilities. So, we can just use the relative frequencies that are given to answer these questions.

   a) $P(Soph) = 0.2730$

   b) $P(Senior) = 0.1974$

   c) For this one, it is easier to subtract away the probability of the event we do not want to occur from the total probability of 1.
   $$P(not\ Freshman) = 1 - 0.2954 = 0.7046$$

d) The probability of getting a freshman is equal to the population relative frequency. This number gives us the expected long-term relative frequency of freshman if we randomly sample.
$$500 * 0.2954 = 147.7$$
Therefore, we expect about 147.7 freshmen in a sample of 500 students.

11) a) $P(A) = \dfrac{1}{6} \approx 0.1667$

   b) $P(B) = P(\{1,3,5\}) = \dfrac{3}{6} = 0.5$

   c) $P(C) = P(\{3,4,5,6\}) = \dfrac{4}{6} \approx 0.6667$

   d) $P(not\ A) = P(\{1,2,3,5,6\}) = \dfrac{5}{6} \approx 0.8333$

   e) In the long run, about 66.67% of the rolls will be greater than or equal to 3.

13) a) There are 4 cards of each denomination, so:
   $$P(A) = \dfrac{4}{52} \approx 0.0769$$

   b) There are 13 cards from each suit, so:
   $$P(B) = \dfrac{13}{52} = 0.25$$

   c) Face cards include Kings, Queens, and Jacks. There are 4 of each of these.
   $$P(C) = \dfrac{4+4+4}{52} \approx 0.2308$$

   d) The best strategy here is just to subtract away the diamonds.
   $$P(not\ B) = \dfrac{52 - 13}{52} = 0.75$$

   e) In the long run, about 23.08% of the time you randomly selected a card, you will get a face card.

15) a) $P(A2) = \dfrac{4193}{8995} \approx 0.4661$

   b) $P(B4) = \dfrac{870}{8995} \approx 0.0967$

   c) $P(not\ A1) = \dfrac{8995 - 3919}{8995} \approx 0.5643$

17) a) $P(R1) = \dfrac{340}{1005} \approx 0.3383$

b) $P(A1) = \dfrac{458}{1005} \approx 0.4557$

c) $P(\text{not } R3) = \dfrac{1005 - 198}{1005} \approx 0.8030$

19) We should begin this problem by making a chart for all of the possible sums when two dice are rolled.

	1	2	3	4	5	6
1	2	3	4	5	6	7
2	3	4	5	6	7	8
3	4	5	6	7	8	9
4	5	6	7	8	9	10
5	6	7	8	9	10	11
6	7	8	9	10	11	12

a) The chart reveals that 36 of the possible combinations of the dice result in a sum of 5.

$$P(\text{Sum is } 5) = \dfrac{4}{36} \approx 0.1111$$

b) $P(\text{Sum} > 7) = P(Sum \in \{8,9,10,11,12\})$

$$= \dfrac{5+4+3+2+1}{36} \approx 0.4167$$

c) Doubles means that both of the dice are the same. We can list the outcomes as an ordered pair. For example, double 3's could be written as (3, 3). So we get:

$P(Doubles) =$

$P(\{(1,1),(2,2),(3,3),(4,4),(5,5),(6,6)\})$

$$= \dfrac{6}{36} \approx 0.1667$$

d) The chart shows 1 sum of two, 2 sums of three, and 1 sum of 12.

$$P(\text{sum is } 2,3, \text{ or } 12) = \dfrac{1+2+1}{36} \approx 0.1111$$

e) The probability from part (a) shows us the expected long-term relative frequency.
$600 * 0.1111 = 66.66$
Therefore, if we rolled the two dice 600 times, we would expect to get about 66.66 sums that were equal to 5.

21) We should begin this problem by making a chart for all of the possible sums for the two different choices.

	39	49	54	70
49	88	98	103	119
49	88	98	103	119
59	98	108	113	129
69	108	118	123	139
79	118	128	133	149
79	118	128	133	149

a) The total of 118 shows up three times.

$$P(\text{sum} = 118) = \dfrac{3}{24} = 0.125$$

b) We would count all sums 98 or smaller. There are only 5 such sums.

$$P(\text{sum} \le 98) = \dfrac{5}{24} \approx 0.2083$$

c) This happens for $49 in two ways. No other price matches are possible.

$$P(\text{same amount}) = \dfrac{2}{24} \approx 0.0833$$

d) The smallest total between $90 and $125 is 98 and the largest is 123.

$$P(90 \le sum \le 125) = \dfrac{14}{24} \approx 0.5833$$

Section 5.2:

23) For an 'AND' event to occur, both of the individual events must occur. Visually, we think of an 'AND' as the overlap of two events.

24) For an 'OR' event to occur, at least one of the listed events must occur. The best way to calculate an 'OR' probability is to count all of the items from the first event and then only add in the new items from the other event.

25) If two events cannot occur simultaneously, then they are mutually exclusive.

26) The Special Addition Rule can only be used if the events are mutually exclusive.

27) When calculating an 'OR' probability, you need to be very careful not to double count the items in the overlap of the two events.

28) The best time to use the Complement Rule is when you realize that you are about to add up more than <u>half</u> of the total possibilities.

29) a) $P(A \text{ or } B) = P(A) + P(B) - P(A \ \& \ B)$
$= 0.3425 + 0.5283 - 0.2367 = 0.6341$

     b) $P(\text{not } A) = 1 - P(A)$
$= 1 - 0.3425 = 0.6575$

     c)   No, $P(A \ \& \ B) = 0.2367 \neq 0$.

31) a) $P(C \text{ or } D) = P(C) + P(D) - P(C \ \& \ D)$
$P(C \ \& \ D) = 0.5877 + 0.3111 - 0.8988$
$P(C \ \& \ D) = 0$

     b) $P(\text{not } (C \ \& \ D)) =$
$1 - P(C \ \& \ D) = 1 - 0 = 1$

     c)   Yes, $P(C \ \& \ D) = 0$.

33) a) $P(E \text{ or } F) = P(E) + P(F) - P(E \ \& \ F)$
$0.9918 = 0.7052 + P(F) - 0.3975$
$P(F) = 0.9918 - 0.7052 + 0.3975$
$P(F) = 0.6841$

     b) $P(\text{not } (E \text{ or } F)) = 1 - P(E \text{ or } F)$
$= 1 - 0.9918 = 0.0082$

35) a)   The phrasing here indicates that we want the person selected to have both of the indicated qualities. That means that this is an AND statement. To find AND probabilities from a table like this, you just need to find the overlap between the indicated row and column.

$$P(\text{A1} \ \& \ \text{B4}) = \frac{375}{8995} \approx 0.0417$$

     b)   This time the language indicated that we are finding A2 OR B3. To compute an OR probability in such a table, count all the values from the first event and add in any NEW values from the other event. See the table below.

	Dem A1	Rep A2	Other A3	Total
0 - < $25K B1	805	873	168	1846
$25K - < $50K B2	1562	1611	370	3543
$50K - < $100K B3	1177	1284	275	2736
$100K+ B4	375	425	70	870
Total	3919	4193	883	8995

You can see that I circled all the items from A2 and then the new stuff from B3. We now add all circled contents.

$$P(\text{A2 or B3}) = \frac{4193 + 1177 + 275}{8995} \approx 0.6276$$

     c) $P(\text{not A3}) = 1 - \dfrac{883}{8995} \approx 0.9018$

     d)   Events A & B are mutually exclusive iff $P(A \ \& \ B) = 0$.

$$P(A2 \ \& \ B1) = \frac{873}{8995} \neq 0 \Rightarrow \text{No, A2 and}$$
B1 are not mutually exclusive.

37) a) The word 'and' indicates that we want $P(R4 \ \& \ A1)$. So, we count the items in the overlap for these two events.

$$P(R4 \ \& \ A1) = \frac{139}{1005} \approx 0.1383$$

b) This time the key word is 'or'. So, we want $P(R3 \text{ or } A3)$. I will use the total for A3 and add in the new cells from R3. See circled cells below.

	More A1	Less A2	Keep A3	Total
East R1	184	120	36	340
Midwest R2	56	78	17	151
South R3	79	101	18	198
West R4	139	136	41	316
Total	458	435	112	1005

$$P(R3 \text{ or } A3) = \frac{112 + 79 + 101}{1005} \approx 0.2905$$

c) Translating into symbols, we get: $P((not \ R2) \ \& \ A2)$. Below, I have shaded the rows corresponding to (not R2) and I have circles the A2 column. We want the overlap of the shaded and circled cells.

	More A1	Less A2	Keep A3	Total
East R1	184	120	36	340
Midwest R2	56	78	17	151
South R3	79	101	18	198
West R4	139	136	41	316
Total	458	435	112	1005

$$P((not \ R2) \ \& \ A2) = \frac{120 + 101 + 136}{1005}$$

$$\approx 0.3552.$$

d) $P(A1) = \dfrac{458}{1005} \approx 0.4557$

$100 * 0.4557 = 45.57$

So, we would expect about 45.57 out of the 100 randomly selected people to favor More strict gun laws.

39) a) $A = \{5\}$, $B = \{0,1,2,3,4\}$, $C = \{3,4,5\}$, $D = \{0,1,2\}$. It would be useful to write these out like this even if the problem did not ask us to.

b) Mutually exclusive pair groups have no overlapping elements at all. The mutually exclusive pairs are A&B , A&D , C&D. There are no larger mutually exclusive groups in this problem.

c) 'AND' means overlap, so we look to see what elements these events have in common.

$$P(B \ \& \ C) = P(\{3,4\}) = \frac{13 + 14}{44} \approx 0.6136$$

d) For an 'OR' problems, take all the elements of the first event {0,1,2,3,4} and also anything new from the second event {5}.

$$P(B \text{ or } C) = P(\{0,1,2,3,4,5\}) = \frac{44}{44} = 1$$

e) The overlapping elements from B and D are {0,1,2}. Because D is completely contained in B, the overlap is D.

$$P(B \ \& \ D) = P(\{0,1,2\}) = \frac{1 + 1 + 5}{44} \approx 0.1591$$

f) For an 'OR', we would normally take everything from B and anything new from D. But D has nothing new to offer. So, in this case, B or D = B.

$$P(B \text{ or } D) = P(\{0,1,2,3,4\}) = \frac{44 - 10}{44} \approx 0.7727$$

41) Even though we were not asked to do so, it is a good idea to list the elements of each event.
$A = \{2,3,4,5,6+\}$, $B = \{4,5,6+\}$, $C = \{0,1\}$, $D = \{3,4,5\}$

a) $P(B \ \& \ D) = P(\{4,5\}) = \dfrac{4 + 2}{96} = 0.0625$

b) $P(B \text{ or } D) = P(\{4,5,6+,3\}) =$
$$\frac{11 + 4 + 2 + 2}{96} \approx 0.1979$$

c) $P((not \ A) \ \& \ D) = P(\{0,1\} \ \& \ \{3,4,5\})$
$$= P(\varnothing) = \frac{0}{96} = 0$$
Note: 'AND' means overlap and these two events have nothing in common.

d) We will count everything from B, then anything new from C, and finally, anything new from D.
$$P(B \text{ or } C \text{ or } D) = P(\{4,5,6+,0,1,3\})$$
$$= \frac{96 - 12}{96} = 0.875 \text{ (Subtracting our '2')}$$

43) a) $P(\text{Red or Blue}) = \dfrac{10+23}{87} \approx 0.3793$

b) $P(\text{Green or Orange}) = \dfrac{14+17}{87} \approx 0.3563$

c) None of the m&m's are more than 1 color.
$$P(\text{Brown \& Yellow}) = \dfrac{0}{87} = 0$$

45) All possibilities seem to be listed and the total is 1.000, so these categories are mutually exclusive, so we can use the Special Addition Rule for all of them.

a) $\text{Prob} = 0.525 + 0.236 = 0.761$

b) Because the categories are mutually exclusive, all 'AND' questions will be impossible. Thus, $\text{Prob} = 0$.

c) Using the Complement Rule:
$\text{Prob} = 1 - 0.150 = 0.850$

47) In problems involving the results of rolling two dice, it is helpful to look at the chart of all possible outcomes.

	1	2	3	4	5	6
1	2	3	4	5	6	7
2	3	4	5	6	7	8
3	4	5	6	7	8	9
4	5	6	7	8	9	10
5	6	7	8	9	10	11
6	7	8	9	10	11	12

a) Since this is an 'OR', first I would count all the even sums. There are 18 of these. Then I would count all of the sums greater than 9 that are not even. This would just be the two rolls resulting in a sum of 11. Then I put these all together.
$$P(\text{sum is even or sum} > 9) = \dfrac{18+2}{36} \approx 0.5556$$

b) For the 'AND', I only want rolls that resulted in both an even sum and a sum > 9.
$$P(\text{sum is even \& sum} > 9) =$$
$$P(\text{sum} \in \{10,12\}) = \dfrac{3+1}{36} \approx 0.1111$$

c) For this one, I would count all the sums less than six and then also count any doubles, I did not have yet.
$$P(\text{sum} < 6 \text{ or doubles}) =$$
$$P(\text{sum} \in \{2,3,4,5\},(3,3),(4,4),(5,5),(6,6))$$
$$= \dfrac{1+2+3+4+4}{36} \approx 0.3889$$
Note: double 1s and double 2s were already counted in the sum is 2 or the sum is 4. We don't want to double count when doing an 'OR' problem.

d) This time, we just want the overlap which is the two rolls just discussed. (1,1) and (2,2) are both doubles and have sums less than 6.
$$P(\text{sum} < 6 \text{ \& doubles}) =$$
$$P(\{(1,1),(2,2)\}) = \dfrac{2}{36} \approx 0.0556$$

49) a) Arranging the prices in a table should be helpful. Because of the word 'and' we want the overlap of the shaded and circled cells below. There are 9 cells in the overlap.
$$\dfrac{9}{24} = 0.375$$

Wheel Set-Ups

	39	49	54	70
49	88	98	103	119
49	88	98	103	119
59	98	108	113	129
69	108	118	123	139
79	118	128	133	149
79	118	128	133	149

Decks

b) This time the key word is 'or', so we should count all the circled items and then any shaded cells that were not already counted in the circle.
$$\dfrac{18+3}{24} = 0.875$$

NEXT PAGE FOR (c) AND (d)

c) The key word here is 'or', so we should count all of the circled and then anything new from the shaded.

$$\frac{16+2}{24}=0.75$$

Wheel Set-Ups

	39	49	54	70
49	88	98	103	119
49	88	98	103	119
Decks 59	98	108	113	129
69	108	118	123	139
79	118	128	133	149
79	118	128	133	149

d) For this one the key word is 'and', so we only want the overlap of the shaded and circled cells above. There are 12 cells shaded among the circled ones.

$$\frac{12}{24}=0.5$$

51) a) We have seen 8 cards, so 44 remain possibilities for the river card. We have seen no 6's and no Jacks, so 4 of each remain in the deck.

$$P(6 \text{ or Jack})=\frac{4+4}{44}\approx 0.1818$$

Therefore, the chance that Player 1 will win the hand is about 18.18%.

b) This is the complement of part (a).
$1-0.1818=0.8182$. So, the chance that Player 2 will win the hand is about 81.82%.

Section 5.3:

53) When you do a conditional probability problem, the given becomes the new <u>sample space</u>.

54) When calculating conditional probabilities using the Conditional Probability Rule, the numerator is the probability of the <u>overlap</u> of the two events and the denominator is the probability of the <u>given</u>.

55) If two events are independent, then one event occurring doesn't <u>affect</u> whether or not the other one will occur.

56) If you want to use the Special Multiplication Rule, then the events in question must be <u>independent</u> of each other.

57) a) We only want to count the part of B3 that is also A2.

	A1	A2	A3	Total
B1	434	244	221	899
B2	270	362	388	1020
B3	406	427	220	1053
B4	286	389	365	1040
Total	1396	1422	1194	4012

$$P(A2 \mid B3)=\frac{427}{1053}\approx 0.4055$$

b) $P(A2)=\frac{1422}{4012}\approx 0.3544$

c) No, $P(A2 \mid B3)\neq P(A2)$.

d) We must repeat all of the work from (a), (b), and (c) for the new events.

$$P(A3 \mid B1)=\frac{221}{899}\approx 0.2458$$

$$P(A3)=\frac{1194}{4012}\approx 0.2976$$

No, $P(A3 \mid B1)\neq P(A3)$.

59) a) We will check this by find the probability of C1 with and without a given of D2.

	D1	D2	Total
C1	105	63	168
C2	177	224	401
C3	243	28	271
Total	525	315	840

$$P(C1 \mid D2)=\frac{63}{315}=0.2$$

$$P(C1)=\frac{168}{840}=0.2$$

Yes, $P(C1 \mid D2)=P(C1)$.

b) We will check this by find the probability of C3 with and without a given of D2.

$$P(C3 \mid D2)=\frac{28}{315}\approx 0.0889$$

$$P(C3)=\frac{271}{840}\approx 0.3226$$

No, $P(C3 \mid D2)\neq P(C3)$.

61) This is an alphabet problem, so we will simply solve it by applying the appropriate formulas.

a) $P(A|B) = \dfrac{P(A \& B)}{P(B)} = \dfrac{0.222}{0.388} \approx 0.5722$

b) $P(B|A) = \dfrac{P(A \& B)}{P(A)} = \dfrac{0.222}{0.415} \approx 0.5349$

c) No, $P(A|B) \neq P(A)$

d) No, $P(A \& B) = 0.222 \neq 0$.

63) This is an alphabet problem, so we will simply solve it by applying the appropriate formulas.

a) Because the problem states that E and F are independent events, we can use the Special Multiplication Rule.

$P(E \& F) = P(E)P(F) =$

$0.3891 * 0.6742 \approx 0.2623$

b) No, $P(E \& F) \neq 0$

c) $P(E \& F) = 0 \Rightarrow P(E|F) = \dfrac{P(E \& F)}{P(F)} = 0$,

so unless $P(E) = 0$, they will not be independent!

65) a) This is not a conditional probability question. Therefore, we use the grand total for the denominator and the total number of democrats for the numerator.

$P(A1) = \dfrac{3919}{8995} \approx 0.4357$

b) This time B1 is the given, so it becomes our new sample space. It's as if the table only contained the following info.

	Dem A1	Rep A2	Other A3	Total
0 - < $25K B1	805	873	168	1846

$P(A1|B1) = \dfrac{805}{1846} \approx 0.4361$

c) No, $P(A1|B1) \neq P(A1)$. It is true that they are not independent because the two probabilities are not exactly equal. However, the difference is very small, so the two variables only have a minor effect on one another.

d) We need to see if conditional probability is different than an individual probability

for these two variables. We will compare $P(A2)$ to $P(A2|B4)$.

$P(A2) = \dfrac{4193}{8995} \approx 0.4661$

	Dem A1	Rep A2	Other A3	Total
$100K+ B4	375	425	70	870

$P(A2|B4) = \dfrac{425}{870} \approx 0.4885$

Since $P(A2|B4) \neq P(A2)$, A2 and B4 are not independent of each other.

67) a) We will check to see if the probability that the person believes the laws should be less strict is affected by them living in the South.

	More A1	Less A2	Keep A3	Total
East R1	184	120	36	340
Midwest R2	56	78	17	151
South R3	79	101	18	198
West R4	139	136	41	316
Total	458	435	112	1005

$P(A2 \mid R3) = \dfrac{101}{198} \approx 0.5101$

$P(A2) = \dfrac{435}{1005} \approx 0.4328$

No, $P(A2 \mid R3) \neq P(A2)$.

b) $P(A3 \mid R1) = \dfrac{36}{340} \approx 0.1059$

$P(A3) = \dfrac{112}{1005} \approx 0.1114$

No, $P(A3 \mid R1) \neq P(A3)$.

NEXT PAGE FOR PART (c)

67) c) $P(A1 \mid R1) = \dfrac{184}{340} \approx 0.5412$

$P(A1 \mid R2) = \dfrac{56}{151} \approx 0.3709$

$P(A1 \mid R3) = \dfrac{79}{198} \approx 0.3990$

$P(A1 \mid R4) = \dfrac{139}{316} \approx 0.4399$

It appears that people in the East are the most likely to favor stricter gun control laws and those in the Midwest are least likely to favor such stricter laws.

69) **Note:** $A = \{5\}$, $B = \{0,1,2,3,4\}$,

$C = \{3,4,5\}$, $D = \{0,1,2\}$.

a) The sample space is reduced to the given B.

Hw Score	0	1	2	3	4	5
Frequency	1	1	5	13	14	10

$P(D|B) = \dfrac{7}{34} \approx 0.2059$

b) This time the sample space is reduced to the event D.

Hw Score	0	1	2	3	4	5
Frequency	1	1	5	13	14	10

We can only count the parts of B that exist in the new sample space.

$P(B|D) = \dfrac{7}{7} = 1$

c) This time the sample space is reduced to the given C.

Hw Score	0	1	2	3	4	5
Frequency	1	1	5	13	14	10

We can only count the part of B that exists in this new reduced sample space.

$P(B|C) = \dfrac{13+14}{37} \approx 0.7297$

d) $P(B) = \dfrac{34}{44} \approx 0.7727 \Rightarrow$

No, $P(B|C) \neq P(B)$

e) $P(A \& D) = P(\{5\} \& \{0,1,2\}) = \dfrac{0}{44} = 0$

The events have no overlap.
Yes, since $P(A \& D) = 0$.

f) $P(A) = \dfrac{10}{44} \approx 0.2273$,

$P(A|D) = 0 \Rightarrow P(A|D) \neq P(A)$
So, no they are not independent.

71) Even though we were not asked to do so, it is a good idea to list the elements of each event.
$A = \{2,3,4,5,6+\}$, $B = \{4,5,6+\}$,

$C = \{0,1\}$, $D = \{3,4,5\}$

a) The sample space is reduced to the given, B.

# of Movies	0	1	2	3	4	5	6+
Frequency	32	33	12	11	4	2	2

$P(A \mid B) = \dfrac{8}{8} = 1$

b) The sample space is reduced to the given, D.

# of Movies	0	1	2	3	4	5	6+
Frequency	32	33	12	11	4	2	2

$P(C \mid D) = \dfrac{0}{17} = 0$

c) We need to compare $P(B \mid D)$ with $P(B)$. So, we will make D the new sample space for the conditional probability.

# of Movies	0	1	2	3	4	5	6+
Frequency	32	33	12	11	4	2	2

$P(B \mid D) = \dfrac{6}{17} \approx 0.3529$,

$P(B) = \dfrac{8}{96} \approx 0.0833$.

$P(B \mid D) \neq P(B) \Rightarrow$ B and D are NOT independent events.

d) Sampling without replacement is a good spot for the General Multiplication Rule. Let's also let E = the event the student did not see a movie.

$P(E_1 \& E_2) = P(E_1) \cdot P(E_2 \mid E_1)$

$= \dfrac{32}{96} \cdot \dfrac{31}{95} \approx 0.1088$

73) a) $P(R1 \ \& \ Y2) = P(R1)P(Y2|R1) =$

$\dfrac{10}{87} * \dfrac{12}{86} \approx 0.0160$

b) $P(G1 \ \& \ G2) = P(G1)P(G2|G1) =$

$\dfrac{14}{87} * \dfrac{13}{86} \approx 0.0243$

c) $P(Br \ \& \ Bl) = P\big((Br_1 \ \& \ Bl_2) \ or \ (Bl_1 \ \& \ Br_2)\big)$

$= \dfrac{11}{87} * \dfrac{23}{86} + \dfrac{23}{87} * \dfrac{11}{86} \approx 0.0676$

d) $P(Or_1 \ \& \ Or_2 \ \& \ Or_3 \ \& \ Or_4) =$

$\dfrac{17}{87} * \dfrac{16}{86} * \dfrac{15}{85} * \dfrac{14}{84} \approx 0.0011$

75) Because the problem states that the different selections are independent, we can use the Special Multiplication Rule to answer any 'AND' type questions.

a) Let's let C = event the person is Catholic.

$P(C_1 \ \& \ C_2) = P(C_1) \cdot P(C_2) =$

$(0.236)^2 \approx 0.0557$

b) Let's use J = Jewish and A = None/Atheist

$P(J_1 \ \& \ A_2) = P(J_1) \cdot P(A_2) =$

$0.016 * 0.150 = 0.0024$

c) This time, no order is specified, so we must add together the probability for both possible orders.

$P(J \ \& \ A) = P\big((J_1 \ \& \ A_2) \ or \ (A_1 \ \& \ J_2)\big)$

$= 0.016 * 0.150 + 0.150 * 0.016 = 0.0048$

d) Let's let P = Protestant and then use the Special Multiplication Rule.

$P(P_1 \ \& \ P_2 \ \& \ P_3 \ \& \ P_4 \ \& \ P_5) = (0.525)^5$

≈ 0.0399

77) The rolls of a die should be independent of one another. So, we can use the special multiplication rule when doing these problems.

a) $P(6 \text{ on all 4 rolls}) =$

$P(6_1) * P(6_2) * P(6_3) * P(6_4) = \left(\dfrac{1}{6}\right)^4$

$\approx 0.0007716 \approx 0.0008$

b) $P(\text{same number on all rolls}) =$

$P(\text{All 1's or All 2's or } \ldots \text{ or All 6's}) =$

$\left(\dfrac{1}{6}\right)^4 + \left(\dfrac{1}{6}\right)^4 + \left(\dfrac{1}{6}\right)^4 + \left(\dfrac{1}{6}\right)^4 + \left(\dfrac{1}{6}\right)^4 + \left(\dfrac{1}{6}\right)^4$

$= 6 * \left(\dfrac{1}{6}\right)^4 \approx 0.0046$

79) a) The given of "at least one die is odd" has been shaded below. We should only count the odd sums from among the shaded choices.

	1	2	3	4	5	6
1	2	3	4	5	6	7
2	3	4	5	6	7	8
3	4	5	6	7	8	9
4	5	6	7	8	9	10
5	6	7	8	9	10	11
6	7	8	9	10	11	12

$\text{Prob} = \dfrac{18}{27} \approx 0.6667$

b) $P(\text{Sum is odd}) = \dfrac{18}{36} = 0.5$. Because this answer is different than with the given in part (a), these two events are NOT independent.

(SEE NEXT PAGE FOR (c) and (d).)

c) We will compare $P(sum \geq 7)$ to

$P(sum \geq 7|$ at least one die showed a 4 or higher$)$.

	1	2	3	4	5	6
1	2	3	4	5	6	7
2	3	4	5	6	7	8
3	4	5	6	7	8	9
4	5	6	7	8	9	10
5	6	7	8	9	10	11
6	7	8	9	10	11	12

All the cells where at least one die was a 4 or higher are shaded. Only these should be considered for the conditional probability.

$P(sum \geq 7|$ at least one 4 or higher$)$

$= \dfrac{21}{27} \approx 0.7778$

$P(sum \geq 7) = \dfrac{21}{36} \approx 0.5833$

Because the given affected the probability answer, they are NOT independent.

d) Let's let D = doubles on a roll of the dice.

$P(D) = \dfrac{6}{36} = \dfrac{1}{6} \approx 0.1667$

$P(D_1 \ \& \ D_2 \ \& \ D_3) = \left(\dfrac{1}{6}\right)^3 \approx 0.0046$

81) We have seen 7 cards, so 45 remain unseen.
   a) We have seen 2 fives, so 2 remain unseen.

   $P(5_{turn} \ \& \ 5_{river}) = \dfrac{2}{45} * \dfrac{1}{44} \approx 0.0010$

   b) We have only seen 1 Ace, so 3 remain.

   $P(A_{turn} \ \& \ A_{river}) = \dfrac{3}{45} * \dfrac{2}{44} \approx 0.0030$

   c) We have seen no Kings or Queens, so all 4 of each remain possible. It doesn't matter which one comes first, so we will consider both orders.

   $P\big((K_{turn} \ \& \ Q_{river}) \ \text{or} \ (Q_{turn} \ \& \ K_{river})\big)$

   $= \dfrac{4}{45} * \dfrac{4}{44} + \dfrac{4}{45} * \dfrac{4}{44} \approx 0.0162$

   d) We have computed all three ways we could win. These ways are mutually exclusive, so we just add them together.

   $P(winning) =$

   $\dfrac{2}{45} * \dfrac{1}{44} + \dfrac{3}{45} * \dfrac{2}{44} + \dfrac{4}{45} * \dfrac{4}{44} + \dfrac{4}{45} * \dfrac{4}{44}$

   ≈ 0.0202

<u>Section 5.4</u>:

83) A random variable is a numerical quantity whose value depends on <u>chance</u>.

84) When we are asked to find the probability distribution for a discrete random variable, we should make a <u>table</u> that lists the possible values of the variable together with their <u>probabilities</u>.

85) Probability histograms are basically the same as a <u>relative</u> frequency histogram from Chapter 3. The bars are done for single values. Therefore, they are drawn from <u>half</u> mark to <u>half</u> mark.

86) For frequency and relative frequency histograms, we interpreted the tallest bar to be the class with the most data in it. For a probability histogram, we interpret the tallest bar to represent the value of the <u>variable</u> that has the greatest <u>chance</u> of occurring.

87) The mean of a random variable is also called the <u>expected</u> value.

88) μ_x and σ_x tell us the expected mean and standard deviation after a <u>large</u> number of trials.

89) If you are asked if a specific value of a random variable is unusual, then you should calculate the <u>z-score</u> for that data value. We consider outcomes to be unusual if they lie more than <u>2</u> standard deviations away from the <u>mean</u>.

90) The expected range consists of the possible outcomes that lie within <u>2</u> standard deviations of the mean.

91) a) $P(X = 4) = \dfrac{14}{44} \approx 0.3182$

b) We find the rest of the probabilities as we did in part (a) and assemble them in a chart.

x	0	1	2	3	4	5
P(x)	0.0227	0.0227	0.1136	0.2955	0.3182	0.2273

c) $P(X \le 3) = 1 - 0.3182 - 0.2273 = 0.4545$

d)

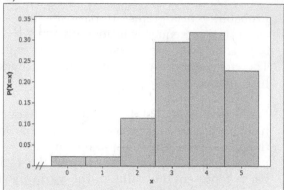

e) Left skewed or severely left-skewed.

93) a) $P(Y = 1) = \dfrac{33}{96} \approx 0.3438$

b) We find the rest of the probabilities as we did in part (a) and assemble them in a chart.

y	0	1	2	3	4	5	6
P(y)	0.3333	0.3438	0.1250	0.1146	0.0417	0.0208	0.0208

c) $P(Y \ge 1) = 1 - P(0) = 1 - 0.3333 = 0.6667$

d)

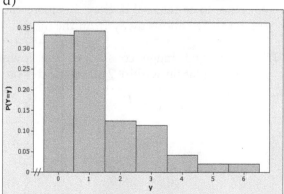

e) Severely Right-skewed.

95) a) We use the 36 outcomes from the chart given to find the probability distribution. For example:

$P(X = 9) = \dfrac{4}{36} \approx 0.1111$

x	$P(x)$
2	0.0278
3	0.0556
4	0.0833
5	0.1111
6	0.1389
7	0.1667
8	0.1389
9	0.1111
10	0.0833
11	0.0556
12	0.0278

b) $P(X \ge 6) = P(6) + \ldots + P(12) \approx 0.7223$

c) $P(X \ge 10 \text{ or } X \le 3) =$
$P(2) + P(3) + P(10) + P(11) + P(12)$
≈ 0.2051

d) $P(X \ge 7 \mid X \le 10) = \dfrac{P(X \ge 7 \ \& \ X \le 10)}{P(X \le 10)}$

$= \dfrac{P(7 \le X \le 10)}{P(X \le 10)} \approx$

$\dfrac{0.1667 + 0.1389 + 0.1111 + 0.0833}{1 - 0.0556 - 0.0278}$

≈ 0.5455

97) a) We should make a chart to show the possible totals for these choices.

Wheel Set-Ups

	39	49	54	70
49	88	98	103	119
49	88	98	103	119
59	98	108	113	129
69	108	118	123	139
79	118	128	133	149
79	118	128	133	149

Decks

Now, we use this chart to find the probabilities. For example:

$$P(Y = 98) = \frac{3}{24} = 0.1250$$

y	$P(y)$
88	0.0833
98	0.1250
103	0.0833
108	0.0833
113	0.0417
118	0.1250
119	0.0833
123	0.0417
128	0.0833
129	0.0417
133	0.0833
139	0.0417
149	0.0833

b) $P(Y \geq 100) \approx 1 - 0.0833 - 0.1250 = 0.7917$

c) $P(Y \geq 90 \ \& \ Y \leq 120) = P(90 \leq Y \leq 120)$
   $\approx 0.1250 + 0.0833 + 0.0833 + 0.0417$
   $+ 0.1250 + 0.0833 = 0.5416$

d) $P(Y \geq 120 | Y \geq 100) = \dfrac{P(Y \geq 120 \ \& \ Y \geq 100)}{P(Y \geq 100)}$

$$= \frac{P(Y \geq 120)}{P(Y \geq 100)} \approx$$

$$\frac{P(123) + P(128) + \ldots + P(149)}{1 - P(88) - P(98)}$$

$$\approx \frac{0.375}{0.7917} \approx 0.4737$$

99) The probabilities for single values are all shown in the chart, so we simply use these to answer the questions.

a) $P(X = 9) = 0.2927$

b) $P(X \geq 6) = 0.1707 + 0.1463 + 0.1463$
   $+ 0.2927 + 0.0732 = 0.8292$

c) $P(5 \leq X < 9) = 0.0976 + 0.1707 +$
   $0.1463 + 0.1463 = 0.5609$

d) For this one, we will use the conditional probability rule.

$$P(X < 7 | X \geq 5) = \frac{P(X < 7 \ \& \ X \geq 5)}{P(X \geq 5)} =$$

$$\frac{P(X = 5 \text{ or } X = 6)}{P(X \geq 5)} = \frac{0.0976 + 0.1707}{1 - 0.0488 - 0.0244}$$

$$\approx 0.2895$$

101) a) $\mu_y = \sum y \cdot P(y)$, so we will make a table to get the needed sum.

y	$P(y)$	$y \cdot P(y)$
0	0.5052	0.00000
0.5	0.1443	0.07215
1	0.1546	0.15460
1.5	0.0412	0.06180
2	0.0825	0.16500
2.5	0.0207	0.05175
3	0.0309	0.09270
3.5	0.0103	0.03605
4	0.0103	0.04120
		0.67525

$$\mu_y = \sum y \cdot P(y) = 0.67525$$

Calculator Method: Enter the y's into L1 and the $P(y)$'s into L2, then choose STAT > CALC > 1-Var Stats L1, L2

b) $\sigma_y = \sqrt{\sum (y - \mu_y)^2 P(y)}$, so we need to add a $(y - \mu_y)^2 P(y)$ column to our table.

y	$P(y)$	$y \cdot P(y)$	$(y - \mu_y)^2 P(y)$
0	0.5052	0.00000	0.230352
0.5	0.1443	0.07215	0.004432
1	0.1546	0.15460	0.016305
1.5	0.0412	0.06180	0.028025
2	0.0825	0.16500	0.144784
2.5	0.0207	0.05175	0.068925
3	0.0309	0.09270	0.166998
3.5	0.0103	0.03605	0.082186
4	0.0103	0.04120	0.113856
		0.67525	0.855863

$$\sigma_y = \sqrt{\sum (y - \mu_y)^2 P(y)} \approx \sqrt{0.855863} \approx 0.92513$$

c) $z = \dfrac{2 - 0.67525}{0.92513} \approx 1.432 \;\Rightarrow\;$ No, this

shows us that 2 hours of exercise lies less than two standard deviations above the mean.

d) We start by calculating the boundaries that are two standard deviations away from the mean.

$\mu_y - 2\sigma_y = -1.17501$ and

$\mu_y + 2\sigma_y = 2.52551$

The smallest value of the variable that lies in this range is 0 and the largest is 2.5. So, the expected range is anywhere from 0 to 2.5 hours of exercise the previous day.

103) a) The expect value is just another name for

$\mu_x \cdot \mu_x = \sum x P(x)$, so we will make a

table to get the needed sum.

x	$P(x)$	$xP(x)$
0	0.0227	0.0000
1	0.0227	0.0227
2	0.1136	0.2272
3	0.2955	0.8865
4	0.3182	1.2728
5	0.2273	1.1365
		3.5457

$\mu_x = \sum x \cdot P(x) = 3.5457$

Calculator Method: Enter the x 's into L1 and the $P(x)$'s into L2, then choose STAT > CALC > 1-Var Stats L1, L2

b) If we randomly selected a large number of HW scores from this class, we would expect the average of the selected scores to be about 3.5457 points.

c) $\sigma_x = \sqrt{\sum(x - \mu_x)^2 P(x)}$, so we need to

add a $(x - \mu_x)^2 P(x)$ column to our table.

x	$P(x)$	$xP(x)$	$(x - \mu_x)^2 P(x)$
0	0.0227	0.0000	0.285384
1	0.0227	0.0227	0.147109
2	0.1136	0.2272	0.271412
3	0.2955	0.8865	0.087996
4	0.3182	1.2728	0.065673
5	0.2273	1.1365	0.480737
		3.5457	1.338311

$\sigma_x = \sqrt{\sum(x - \mu_x)^2 P(x)} = \sqrt{1.338311} \approx 1.1569$

d) $\mu_x - \sigma_x = 2.3888$ and

$\mu_x + \sigma_x = 4.7026 \Rightarrow$ The lowest score we want is a 3 and the highest is a 4. So, we just add those probabilities tog ether.

$P(3 \text{ or } 4) = 0.2955 + 0.3182 = 0.6137$

e) $\mu_x - 2\sigma_x = 1.2319$ and

$\mu_x + 2\sigma_x = 5.8595 \Rightarrow$ The lowest score we want is a 2 and the highest is a 5. So, we just add those probabilities together.

$P(2 \le x \le 5) = 0.9546$

105) a) The expect value is just another name for

$\mu_y \cdot \mu_y = \sum y \cdot P(y)$, so we will make a

table to get the needed sum.

Calculator Method: Enter the y 's into L1 and the $P(y)$'s into L2, then choose STAT > CALC > 1-Var Stats L1, L2

y	$P(y)$	$y \cdot P(y)$
88	0.0833	7.3304
98	0.1250	12.2500
103	0.0833	8.5799
108	0.0833	8.9964
113	0.0417	4.7121
118	0.1250	14.7500
119	0.0833	9.9127
123	0.0417	5.1291
128	0.0833	10.6624
129	0.0417	5.3793
133	0.0833	11.0789
139	0.0417	5.7963
149	0.0833	12.4120
		116.9892

$\mu_y = \sum y \cdot P(y) = 116.9892$

b) If a large number of customers randomly selected a board set-up, then we would expect the average cost of those set-ups to be about \$116.99.

c) $\sigma_y = \sqrt{\sum (y - \mu_y)^2 P(y)}$, so we need to

add a $(y - \mu_y)^2 P(y)$ column to our table.

y	$P(y)$	$y \cdot P(y)$	$(y - \mu_y)^2 P(y)$
88	0.0833	7.3304	70.0031
98	0.1250	12.2500	45.0737
103	0.0833	8.5799	16.3016
108	0.0833	8.9964	6.7311
113	0.0417	4.7121	0.6636
118	0.1250	14.7500	0.1277
119	0.0833	9.9127	0.3368
123	0.0417	5.1291	1.5066
128	0.0833	10.6624	10.0991
129	0.0417	5.3793	6.0156
133	0.0833	11.0789	21.3536
139	0.0417	5.7963	20.2026
149	0.0833	12.4120	85.3568
		116.9892	283.7719

$\sigma_y = \sqrt{\sum (y - \mu_y)^2 P(y)} \approx \sqrt{283.7719} \approx 16.846$

d) $\mu_y - \sigma_y = 100.1432$ and

$\mu_y + \sigma_y = 133.8352 \Rightarrow$ The lowest total we want is a 103 and the highest is a 133. So, we just add those probabilities together.

$P(103 \le Y \le 133) = 0.6667$

e) $\mu_y - 2\sigma_y = 83.2972$ and

$\mu_y + 2\sigma_y = 150.6812 \Rightarrow$ The lowest total we want is a 88 and the highest is a 149. So, we just add those probabilities together.

$P(88 \le Y \le 149) = 1$

f) For bell-shaped random variables, the Empirical Rule says that we should expect about a 68% chance of getting a value that lies within 1 standard deviation of the mean. For this variable, we got a 66.67% chance which is pretty close to that. For 2 standard deviations, the Empirical Rule says that we should expect about a 95% chance. For this variable, we got a 100% chance of getting a value within 2 standard deviations of the mean. This is a bit off, but looking at the probabilities given, it does not appear that this is a bell-shaped distribution.

107) a) First we calculate the 2 standard deviation boundaries. $\mu_x - 2\sigma_x = 63.454$ and

$\mu_x + 2\sigma_x = 123.686 \Rightarrow$ The smallest number of customers in this range would be 64 and the highest would be 123. So, on a randomly selected day, we would expect somewhere between 64 and 123 burritos to be sold.

b) According to the Empirical Rule, there is about a 95% chance that the number of burritos sold will lie within 2 standard deviations of the mean. Using the Complement Rule, there should be about a 5% chance that the number of burritos sold will be outside of this range.

c) This corresponds to a 1 standard deviation range. $\mu_x - \sigma_x = 78.512$ and

$\mu_x + \sigma_x = 108.628 \Rightarrow$ There is about a 68% chance that the number of burritos sold will be somewhere from 79 to 108 on a randomly selected day.

d) If 152 was in the expected range, then we would consider it plausible that this was just a random variation from the old mean of 93.57 customers per day. However, the fact that 152 is outside of this range indicates that there is less than a 5% chance that this is just a random variation. Therefore, we should consider this strong evidence that the mean number of burritos sold is now higher than it used to be.

109) a) $\mu_y = \sum y \cdot P(y)$, so we will make a table to get the needed sum.

y	$P(y)$	$y \cdot P(y)$
0	0.5126	0.0000
1	0.3844	0.3844
2	0.0938	0.1876
3	0.0089	0.0267
4	0.0003	0.0012
5	0.0000	0.0000
		0.5999

$\mu_y = \sum y \cdot P(y) = 0.5999$

Calculator Method: Enter the y's into L1 and the $P(y)$'s into L2, then choose STAT > CALC > 1-Var Stats L1, L2

b) $\sigma_y = \sqrt{\sum (y - \mu_y)^2 P(y)}$, so we need to

add a $(y - \mu_y)^2 P(y)$ column to our table.

y	$P(y)$	$y \cdot P(y)$	$(y - \mu_y)^2 P(y)$
0	0.5126	0.0000	0.184474
1	0.3844	0.3844	0.061535
2	0.0938	0.1876	0.183874
3	0.0089	0.0267	0.051268
4	0.0003	0.0012	0.003468
5	0.0000	0.0000	0.000000
		0.5999	0.484619

$\sigma_y = \sqrt{\sum (y - \mu_y)^2 P(y)} \approx \sqrt{0.484619} \approx 0.69615$

c) $z = \dfrac{3 - 0.5999}{0.69615} \approx 3.448 \implies$ Yes, in fact,

this would be considered very unusual because 3 matching cards would be more than three standard deviations above the mean.

d) We start by calculating the boundaries that are two standard deviations away from the mean.

$\mu_y - 2\sigma_y = -0.7924$ and

$\mu_y + 2\sigma_y = 1.9922 \implies$

The smallest value of the variable that lies in this range is 0 and the largest is 1. So, the expected range is for the board to contain either 0 or 1 cards that match the teacher's cards.

Section 5.5:

111) $\binom{n}{x}$ represents the number of ways of <u>choosing</u> x objects from a set of n objects.

112) An n, p, q problem is officially known as having the <u>binomial</u> distribution. These problems are about counting the number of <u>successes</u> in many trials.

113) In the binomial formula, $\binom{n}{x}$ represent the number of different possible <u>orders</u> for the success and the failures.

114) In a two-category population, a success is defined as the item you are <u>counting</u>. Successes are sometimes positive outcomes and sometimes they are <u>negative</u> outcomes.

115) When we apply the binomial formula to situations where sampling is done without <u>replacement</u>, we need to make sure that our sample size is less than <u>5</u>% of the population size.

116) The shortcut formulas for the mean and standard deviation of a binomial random variable are as follows. $\mu_x = \sum x \cdot P(x)$ and

$\sigma_x = \sqrt{\sum (x - \mu_x)^2 P(x)}$.

117) For combinations, you can skip the factorials (!) and choose MATH > PROB > nCr on the calculator.

a) $\binom{7}{5} = \dfrac{7!}{5! \cdot 2!} = 21$

b) $\binom{7}{2} = \dfrac{7!}{2! \cdot 5!} = 21$

c) $\binom{15}{1} = \dfrac{15!}{1! \cdot 14!} = 15$

d) $\binom{15}{15} = \dfrac{15!}{15! \cdot 0!} = 1$

119) $p = 0.73 \Rightarrow q = 1 - p = 0.27$

a) $P(X = 4) = \binom{6}{4}(0.73)^4(0.27)^2 \approx 0.3105$

b) We now find the other probabilities from 0 to 6 in a similar fashion and organize them into a table. $P(X = 0)$ is shown below.

$$P(X = 0) = \binom{6}{0}(0.73)^0(0.27)^6 \approx 0.0004$$

Calculator tip: Obtain the remaining probabilities by using 2ND ENTER and then editing the previous calculator entry. Or you can enter the x's in L1 and then let L2 = 6 nCr L1*0.73^L1*0.27^(6-L1)

x	$P(x)$
0	0.0004
1	0.0063
2	0.0425
3	0.1531
4	0.3105
5	0.3358
6	0.1513

c)

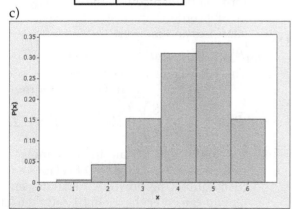

d) Left-skewed

e) $\mu_x = np = 6 * 0.73 = 4.38$,

$\sigma_x = \sqrt{npq} = \sqrt{6 * 0.73 * 0.27} \approx 1.0875$

121) $p = 0.563 \Rightarrow q = 1 - p = 0.437$

a) $P(X = 8) = \binom{11}{8}(0.563)^8(0.437)^3 \approx 0.1390$

b) We now find the other probabilities from 0 to 11 in a similar fashion and organize them into a table. $P(X = 0)$ is shown below.

$$P(X = 0) = \binom{11}{0}(0.563)^0(0.437)^{11} \approx 0.0001$$

Calculator tip: Obtain the remaining probabilities by using 2ND ENTER and then editing the previous calculator entry. Or you can enter the x's in L1 and then let L2 = 11 nCr L1*0.563^L1*0.437^(11-L1)

x	$P(x)$
0	0.0001
1	0.0016
2	0.0101
3	0.0392
4	0.1009
5	0.1820
6	0.2345
7	0.2158
8	0.1390
9	0.0597
10	0.0154
11	0.0018

c)

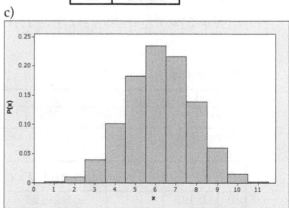

d) Roughly bell-shaped

e) $\mu_x = np = 11 * 0.563 = 6.193$,

$\sigma_x = \sqrt{npq} = \sqrt{11 * 0.563 * 0.437} \approx 1.6451$

123) Handshakes happen between groups of 2. So we need to know the number of groups of 2 possible among 20 people.

So, $\binom{20}{2} = \dfrac{20!}{2! \cdot 18!} = 190$ handshakes.

125) a) The possible outcomes are:

HHH	HHT	HTH	THH	HTT	THT	TTH	TTT

b) The outcomes of coin tosses are independent of each other, so we can use the special multiplication rule to find the probabilities.

Outcomes	Probability
HHH	$0.5 * 0.5 * 0.5 = 0.125$
HHT	$0.5 * 0.5 * 0.5 = 0.125$
HTH	$0.5 * 0.5 * 0.5 = 0.125$
THH	$0.5 * 0.5 * 0.5 = 0.125$
HTT	$0.5 * 0.5 * 0.5 = 0.125$
THT	$0.5 * 0.5 * 0.5 = 0.125$
TTH	$0.5 * 0.5 * 0.5 = 0.125$
TTT	$0.5 * 0.5 * 0.5 = 0.125$

c) $P\left(H_1 \& H_2 \& T_3\right) = 0.5 * 0.5 * 0.5 = 0.125$

d) Since no order is specified, we must consider all possible orders of 2 heads and a tail and add up all their probabilities.

$P(2 \text{ heads} \& 1 \text{ tail}) =$

$P(HHT \text{ or } HTH \text{ or } THH) =$

$0.125 + 0.125 + 0.125 = 3 * 0.125 = 0.375$

e) $P(X = 0) = P(TTT) = (0.5)^3 = 0.125$

$P(X = 1) = P(HTT \text{ or } THT \text{ or } TTH)$

$= 3 * (0.5)^3 = 0.375$

$P(X = 2) = P(HHT \text{ or } HTH \text{ or } THH)$

$= 3 * (0.5)^3 = 0.375$

$P(X = 3) = P(HHH) = (0.5)^3 = 0.125$

x	0	1	2	3
$P(x)$	0.125	0.375	0.375	0.125

f) We need to make a table to get the needed sums.

x	$P(x)$	$xP(x)$	$\left(x-\mu_x\right)^2 P(x)$
0	0.125	0	0.28125
1	0.375	0.375	0.09375
2	0.375	0.750	0.09375
3	0.125	· 0.375	0.28125
		1.5	0.75

$\mu_x = \sum xP(x) = 1.5$ and

$\sigma_x = \sqrt{\sum\left(x-\mu_x\right)^2 P(x)} = \sqrt{0.75} \approx 0.86603$

127) a) $n = 3$, $p = 0.5$, $q = 1 - p = 0.5$

b) $P(X = 0) = q^3 = (0.5)^3 = 0.125$

$P(X = 1) = \binom{3}{1}(0.5)(0.5)^2 = 0.375$

$P(X = 2) = \binom{3}{2}(0.5)^2(0.5) = 0.375$

$P(X = 3) = p^3 = (0.5)^3 = 0.125$

x	0	1	2	3
$P(x)$	0.125	0.375	0.375	0.125

c) $\mu_x = np = 3 * 0.5 = 1.5$,

$\sigma_x = \sqrt{npq} = \sqrt{3 * 0.5 * 0.5} \approx 0.86603$

129) a) We sampled 8 Americans, so $n = 8$. At that time 33% of Americans approved of the movement, so $p = 0.33$. Finally, $q = 1 - p = 0.67$.

b) Because a specific order is specified, we leave off the combination part of the formula (which counts the different possible orders) and just count the number of successes and failures.

$P(sssfffff) = p^3 q^5 = (0.33)^3(0.67)^5 \approx 0.0049$

c) This time, no order is specified, so we do need the combination part of the formula.

$P(X = 3) = \binom{8}{3}(0.33)^3(0.67)^5 \approx 0.2717$

d) **Calculator tip**: Obtain the remaining probabilities by using 2ND ENTER and then editing the previous calculator entry. Or you can enter the x's in L1 and then let L2 = 8 nCr L1*0.33^L1*0.67^(8-L1)

x	$P(x)$
0	0.0406
1	0.1600
2	0.2758
3	0.2717
4	0.1673
5	0.0659
6	0.0162
7	0.0023
8	0.0001

e) $\mu_x = np = 8 * 0.33 = 2.64$

$\sigma_x = \sqrt{npq} = \sqrt{8 * 0.33 * 0.67} \approx 1.3300$

131) Because we are counting the number of lefties out of a sample of 9, this is a success failure problem with $n = 9$, $p = 0.1143$, and $q = 1 - p = 0.8857$.

a) $P(4) = \binom{9}{4}(0.1143)^4(0.8857)^5 \approx 0.0117$

The probabilities for the other values from 0 to 9 are found in a similar fashion and the results are shown below.

x	$P(x)$
0	0.3354
1	0.3896
2	0.2011
3	0.0606
4	0.0117
5	0.0015
6	0.0001
7	0.0000
8	0.0000
9	0.0000

Note: The probabilities for the last 3 are not actually zero, but they are so small that we get all zeros when rounding to 4 decimal places.

b)

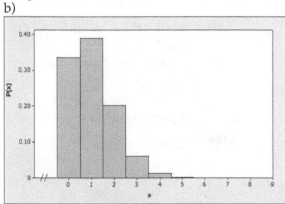

c) I would say this is a severely right-skewed distribution. The tallest bar is near left side and we have a tail to the right.

d) $\mu_x = np = 9 * 0.1143 = 1.0287$

$\sigma_x = \sqrt{npq} = \sqrt{9 * 0.1143 * 0.8857} \approx 0.95453$

e) First, we should find the boundaries.

$\mu_x - \sigma_x = 1.0287 - 0.95453 = 0.07417$

$\mu_x + \sigma_x = 1.0287 + 0.95453 = 1.98323$

The only value of the random variable that lie between these two boundaries is 1, so we get:

$P(\mu_x - \sigma_x < X < \mu_x + \sigma_x) = P(1) = 0.3896$

f) If this were bell-shaped, we would have expected the probability to be around 68%. Even a severely skewed distribution should produce an answer in the 50% to 80% range. Notice that both 0 and 2 were just outside of the 1 standard deviation range. If either had been included, we would have matched up better with the Empirical Rule.

133) Because we are counting the number of successes out of a sample of 40, this is a binomial distribution with $n = 40$, $p = 0.72$, and $q = 1 - p = 0.28$.

a) $P(30) = \binom{40}{30}(0.72)^{30}(0.28)^{10} \approx 0.1318$

b) $P(25 < X \le 30) =$

$P(26) + P(27) + P(28) + P(29) + P(30)$

$\approx 0.0825 + 0.1100 + 0.1313 + 0.1397$

$+ 0.1318 = 0.5953$

c) $\mu_x = np = 40 * 0.72 = 28.8$

$\sigma_x = \sqrt{npq} = \sqrt{40 * 0.72 * 0.28} \approx 2.8397$

d) $z = \dfrac{25 - 28.8}{2.8397} \approx -1.338 \implies$ It would not be unusual, because 25 is less than 2 standard deviations below the mean.

e) First, we should find the boundaries.

$\mu_x - 2\sigma_x = 28.8 - 2 * 2.8397 = 23.1206$

$\mu_x + 2\sigma_x = 28.8 + 2 * 2.8397 = 34.4794$

The values of the random variable that lie between these two boundaries are from 24 to 34. So, we expect anywhere from 24 to 34 of the 40 people sampled to state that they attended a cookout over the summer.

135) Because we are counting the number of successes (not been to the dentist in at least 5 years) out of a sample of 48, this is a binomial distribution with $n = 48$, $p = 0.10$, and $q = 1 - p = 0.90$.

a) $P(10) = \binom{48}{10}(0.10)^{10}(0.90)^{38} \approx 0.0119$

b) $P(X \geq 3) = 1 - P(0) - P(1) - P(2) \approx$
$1 - 0.0064 - 0.0339 - 0.0886 = 0.8711$

c) $\mu_x = np = 48 * 0.10 = 4.8$

    $\sigma_x = \sqrt{npq} = \sqrt{48 * 0.1 * 0.9} \approx 2.0785$

d) $z = \dfrac{10 - 4.8}{2.0785} \approx 2.502 \Rightarrow$ Yes, it would be unusual, because 10 is more than 2 standard deviations above the mean.

e)   If 10 successes had been within 2 standard deviations of the expected value of 4.8, then it would be plausible that the mean for smokers was 4.8 just like for non-smokers. However, because 10 successes is more than 2 standard deviations above 4.8, we should consider this to be strong evidence that the mean for smokers is higher than for non-smokers.

137) $n = 25$, $p = 0.625$, $q = 1 - p = 0.375$

a) $P(X = 12) = \binom{25}{12}(0.625)^{12}(0.375)^{13} \approx 0.0536$

```
25 nCr 12*0.625^
12*0.375^13
            .0535790596
```

b)   **Calculator tip**: Obtain the remaining probabilities by using 2ND ENTER and then editing the previous calculator entry. Or you can enter the x's you need in L1 and then let L2 = 25 nCr L1*0.625^L1*0.375^(25-L1). We then add together the values.
$P(11 \leq X < 15) = P(11) + P(12) + P(13) + P(14)$
$\approx 0.0276 + 0.0536 + 0.0893 + 0.1276$
$= 0.2981$

c) $P(X \leq 22) = 1 - P(23) - P(24) - P(25)$
$\approx 1 - 0.0009 - 0.0001 - 0.0000 = 0.9990$

d) $\mu_x = np = 25 * 0.625 = 15.625$, if we repeatedly selected 25 students and counted the number of females each time, in the long run, the average number of females would be around 15.625.

e) $\sigma_x = \sqrt{npq} = \sqrt{25 * 0.625 * 0.375} \approx 2.4206$

f) $z = \dfrac{20 - 15.625}{2.4206} \approx 1.807 \Rightarrow$ not really, 20 females would be less than 2 standard deviations above the mean.

g) $\mu_x - 2\sigma_x \approx 10.78$ and
$\mu_x + 2\sigma_x \approx 20.47 \Rightarrow$ Anywhere from 11 to 20 females.

139) $n = 11$, $p = 0.768$, $q = 1 - p = 0.232$

a) $P(X \geq 8) = P(8) + P(9) + P(10) + P(11) \approx$

$0.2494 + 0.2752 + 0.1822 + 0.0548$

$= 0.7616$

b) $\mu_x = np = 11 * 0.768 = 8.448$,

$\sigma_x = \sqrt{npq} = \sqrt{11 * 0.768 * 0.232} \approx 1.4000$

c) $z = \dfrac{11 - 8.448}{1.4000} \approx 1.823 \Rightarrow$ not really.

Winning with the Aces all eleven times would still be less than 2 standard deviations above the expected number of wins.

d) $\mu_x - 2\sigma_x \approx 5.648$ and

$\mu_x + 2\sigma_x \approx 11.248 \Rightarrow$ Anywhere from 6 to 11 wins.

e) $\mu_x = np = 101 * 0.768 = 77.568$,

$\sigma_x = \sqrt{npq} = \sqrt{101 * 0.768 * 0.232} \approx 4.2421$

f) $z = \dfrac{101 - 77.568}{4.2421} \approx 5.524 \Rightarrow$ Yes, in fact, winning all 101 hands would be very unusual, because this is more than 3 standard deviations above the mean.

g) $\mu_x - 2\sigma_x \approx 69.0838$ and

$\mu_x + 2\sigma_x \approx 86.0522 \Rightarrow$ Anywhere from 70 to 86 wins are expected.

h) No. They are likely to win with a 76.8% chance, but the chance of losing the hand is 23.2%. We do not consider it unusual when something with more than a 23.2% chance of happening occurs. (We save this distinction for events that have less than a 5% chance of occurring.)

Chapter Problem:

1) a) We simply multiply and find the sum.

	x	$P(x)$	$x \cdot P(x)$
call & win	1060	0.3444	365.064
call & lose	-370	0.6556	-242.572
		1.0000	122.492

b) $\mu_x = 122.492$, in the long run, the poker pro would show an average profit of $122.492 for each time he makes this call in this situation.

c) Yes, in the long run, such calls will be profitable. The outcome of this particular hand is uncertain and, in fact, the poker pro will probably lose in any given situation. However, in the long run, he will win enough of these to make it profitable.

2) $n = 10$, $p = 0.3444$, $q = 1 - p = 0.6556$

a) $\mu_y = np = 10 * 0.3444 = 3.444$,

$\sigma_y = \sqrt{npq} = \sqrt{10 * 0.3444 * 0.6556} \approx 1.5026$

b) $\mu_y - 2\sigma_y \approx 0.4388$ and

$\mu_y + 2\sigma_y \approx 6.4492 \Rightarrow$ Anywhere from 1 to 6 wins are expected.

c) Since he will play ten such hands, if he only wins 1 such hand, then he will lose 9 such hands. In the hand he wins, he would win $1060. In the 9 he loses, he would lose $370 nine times. So, this is represented by $-9 * \$370 = -\$3330$. So, when the ten hands are completed this way, his result is given by: $\$1060 - 9 * \$370 = -\$2270$.

d) If he wins 6 of the ten hands, then he will lose 4. So his overall result for the ten hands would be represented by:

$6 * \$1060 - 4 * \$370 = \$4880$.

Note: After ten plays of making the correct mathematical decision, the poker pro might still lose $2270, but the upside is a possible profit of $4880.

Review Exercises:

1) a) $\left\{-0.5841, \dfrac{7}{2}, 1.604\right\}$ because

probabilities must be between 0 and 1 inclusive. $0 \le P(E) \le 1$

   b) This helps us catch errors. If we get an answer that is negative or larger than 1, we need to look for a mistake in our work.

2) a) The experiment is randomly selecting 1 of the 138 children.
   b) The 138 children that could possibly be selected make up the sample space.
   c) The event of interest is made up of the children at the preschool that are allergic to peanuts.

3) a) $\dfrac{8}{41} \approx 0.1951$

   b) $\dfrac{5+11}{41} = \dfrac{16}{41} \approx 0.3902$

   c) $\dfrac{41-17}{41} = \dfrac{24}{41} \approx 0.5854$

   d) Note: Because no order is specified, we must calculate both possible orders and then add. $\dfrac{11}{41} \cdot \dfrac{17}{40} + \dfrac{17}{41} \cdot \dfrac{11}{40} \approx 0.2280$

   e) Note: It doesn't say which artist, so we must calculate this for all possible artists and then add the results.
   $\dfrac{17}{41} \cdot \dfrac{16}{40} + \dfrac{8}{41} \cdot \dfrac{7}{40} + \dfrac{5}{41} \cdot \dfrac{4}{40} + \dfrac{11}{41} \cdot \dfrac{10}{40} \approx 0.2793$

   f) $\dfrac{17}{41} \cdot \dfrac{16}{40} \cdot \dfrac{15}{39} \cdot \dfrac{14}{38} \approx 0.0235$

5) a) We should make a chart to show all the possible sums. However, since the coins are chosen without replacement, the same exact coin can't be chosen twice. This is why the diagonal is shaded out.

	0.01	0.01	0.05	0.10	0.25	0.25
0.01		0.02	0.06	0.11	0.26	0.26
0.01	0.02		0.06	0.11	0.26	0.26
0.05	0.06	0.06		0.15	0.30	0.30
0.10	0.11	0.11	0.15		0.35	0.35
0.25	0.26	0.26	0.30	0.35		0.50
0.25	0.26	0.26	0.30	0.35	0.50	

Filling in the chart below is just a matter of counting the possible ways a sum can occur. For example,

$$P(X = 0.35) = \dfrac{4}{30} \approx 0.1333 .$$

x	0.02	0.06	0.11	0.15	0.26	0.30	0.35	0.50
P(x)	.0667	.1333	.1333	.0667	.2667	.1333	.1333	.0667

   b) $\dfrac{20}{30} \approx 0.6667$

   c) Recall: '&' means overlap, so
   $P(X > 0.25 \ \& \ X < 0.50)$ becomes
   $P(0.25 < X < 0.50)$. $\dfrac{16}{30} \approx 0.5333$

   d) To computer an 'OR' we should count everything from the first event and then anything new from the second one. So we get $\dfrac{18+6}{30} = 0.8$.

   e) For a conditional probability, we want to make the given the new sample space. There are 18 possibilities where at least 1 penny is chosen and 8 of those are at least 0.15. So, we get $\dfrac{8}{18} \approx 0.4444$.

   f) We should enter the values of x into L1 and the values of $P(x)$ into L2. Then choose STAT > CALC > 1-Var Stats L1, L2 $\mu_x = 0.223337$ and $\sigma_x \approx 0.12950$

   g) $\mu_x - 2\sigma_x \approx -0.035$ and $\mu_x + 2\sigma_x \approx 0.48$. Therefore, anywhere from 0.02 to 0.35 would be in the expected range.

7) a) Use the totals and subtraction to fill in the missing cells.

	B1	B2	B3	Total
A1	86	215	184	485
A2	99	152	149	400
A3	216	190	207	613
A4	151	203	148	502
Total	552	760	688	2000

b) $P(A1) = \dfrac{485}{2000} = 0.2425$

c) We just count the overlap of the two requested events.

$P(A3 \text{ \& } B1) = \dfrac{216}{2000} = 0.1080$

d) For this 'OR' question, I will count all of B1 and B3 (because those are not B2), then add anything new from A4.

$P(A4 \text{ or not } B2) = \dfrac{552 + 688 + 203}{2000} = 0.7215$

e) For this one, the 400 items in the given A2 become our new sample space. Of those 400, 152 of them are B2. So we get $\dfrac{152}{400} = 0.38$.

f) $P(B2) = \dfrac{760}{2000} = 0.38 = P(B2|A2) \Rightarrow$ Yes, they are independent events.

g) We need to find the probabilities with a given and without a given to compare and decide. $P(A4|B3) = \dfrac{148}{688} \approx 0.2151$ and

$P(A4) = \dfrac{502}{2000} = 0.251$. Because

$P(A4|B3) \neq P(A4)$, so NO, they are not independent.

9) a) Even though we are not specifically asked to do so, it is wise to write out numerical lists for each of the events described.
A = {0}
B = {5, 6, 7, 8, 9}   D = {2, 3, 4, 5}
C = {0, 1, 2, 3}   E = {4, 5, 6, 7}
Now we list all groups that have no overlaps at all.
AB, AD, AE, BC, CE
Only the 5 pairs listed are mutually exclusive, no larger groups of events are mutually exclusive.

b) We just want the overlap of the events.

$P(D \text{ \& } E) = P(\{4,5\}) = \dfrac{10 + 12}{58} \approx 0.3793$

c) We will count all of D and then add the new stuff from E.

$P(D \text{ or } E) = P(\{2,3,4,5,6,7\})$

$= \dfrac{4 + 9 + 10 + 12 + 8 + 6}{58} \approx 0.8448$

d) This time, we should count all of A, add the new stuff from B, and then add the new stuff from C.

$P(A \text{ or } B \text{ or } C) = P(\{0,5,6,7,8,9,1,2,3\})$

$= \dfrac{58 - 10}{58} \approx 0.8276$

e) We change our sample space to E.

$P(B \mid E) = \dfrac{26}{36} \approx 0.7222$

f) $P(B) = \dfrac{30}{58} \approx 0.5172$.

Therefore, they are NOT independent, because $P(B \mid E) \neq P(B)$.

11) Because none of the counts are given, we will use the population relative frequencies provided in place of calculating the probabilities ourselves.

a) $P(C) = 0.1371$

b) $P(A \text{ or } B \text{ or } C) =$
$0.1309 + 0.1384 + 0.1371 = 0.4064$

c) $P(C \text{ or } D \text{ or } E \text{ or } F \text{ or } G) =$
$1 - P(A) - P(B) = 1 - 0.1309 - 0.1384$
$= 0.7307$

d) $P(D \text{ or } E \text{ or } F) =$
$0.1295 + 0.1412 + 0.1927 = 0.4634$

13) a) $P(C \text{ or } D) = P(C) + P(D) - P(C \& D)$
    $= 0.4128 + 0.7355 - 0.3389 = 0.8094$

   b) $P(\text{not } D) = 1 - P(D) = 1 - 0.7355 = 0.2645$

   c) $P(C|D) = \dfrac{P(C \& D)}{P(D)} = \dfrac{0.3389}{0.7355} \approx 0.4608$

   d) $P(D|C) = \dfrac{P(C \& D)}{P(C)} = \dfrac{0.3389}{0.4128} \approx 0.8210$

15) a) Because the problem states that E and F are independent. We can use the Special Multiplication Rule.

    $P(E \& F) = P(E) \cdot P(F) = \dfrac{3}{4} \cdot \dfrac{5}{8} = 0.46875$

   b) $P(E \text{ or } F) = P(E) + P(F) - P(E \& F)$

    $= \dfrac{3}{4} + \dfrac{5}{8} - \dfrac{15}{32} = 0.90625$

   c) No, because $P(E \& F) = 0.46875 \neq 0$.

17) a) Because we are told to assume that all these shots are independent, we can use the Special Multiplication Rule.
    $P(FG\ FG\ FG\ FG\ 3P\ 3P\ 3P\ FT\ FT) =$

    $(0.469)^4 (0.436)^3 (0.897)^2 \approx 0.0032$

   b) For this one, we use the Complement Rule to find all needed probabilities.

    $P(\text{Miss FG}) = 1 - 0.469 = 0.531$

    $P(\text{Miss 3P}) = 1 - 0.436 = 0.564$

    $P(\text{Miss FT}) = 1 - 0.897 = 0.103 \implies$

    $(0.531)^4 (0.564)^3 (0.103)^2 \approx 0.0002$

   c) This would be very complicated to calculate directly because there are many different ways to meet this event description. The best plan is to use the Complement Rule.
    $P(\text{Miss at least 1}) = 1 - P(\text{Make them all}) \approx$
    $1 - 0.0032 = 0.9968$

19) a) $P(Y > 2) = 1 - P(0) - P(1) - P(2) =$
    $1 - 0.1737 - 0.2209 - 0.1839 = 0.4215$

   b) $P(2 \leq Y \leq 4) = P(2) + P(3) + P(4) =$
    $0.1839 + 0.1384 + 0.1037 = 0.4260$

   c)

   d) Severely right-skewed.

   e) We should enter the values of y into L1 and the values of $P(y)$ into L2. Then choose STAT > CALC > 1-Var Stats L1, L2
    $\mu_y = 2.4704$ and $\sigma_y \approx 2.0209$

   f) $\mu_y - 2\sigma_y \approx -1.5714$ and
    $\mu_y + 2\sigma_y \approx 6.5122 \implies$ Anywhere from 0 to 6 people.
    If we were to enter the hardware store at a randomly selected time, then we would expect the number of people in line to be somewhere from 0 to 6 people.

21) We are counting the number of successes in 15 households, so this is a binomial distribution with $n = 15$, $p = 0.329$, and $q = 0.671$.

   a) $P(6) = \dbinom{15}{6}(0.329)^6 (0.671)^9 \approx 0.1750$

   b) $P(4 \leq X < 8) = P(4) + P(5) + P(6) + P(7)$
    $= 0.1985 + 0.2142 + 0.1750 + 0.1103 = 0.6980$

   c) $P(X \geq 2) = 1 - P(0) - P(1) \approx$
    $1 - 0.0025 - 0.0185 = 0.9790$

   d) $\mu_x = np = 15 * 0.329 = 4.935$;
    $\sigma_x = \sqrt{npq} = \sqrt{15 * 0.329 * 0.671} \approx 1.8197$

   e) $z = \dfrac{10 - 4.935}{1.8197} \approx 2.783 \implies$ Yes, because 10 is more than 2 standard deviations above the mean. More than 10 would be even more unusual.

23) a) This one is NOT a binomial r.v. because it is the weight of a single apple, not the number of successes out of many.

  b) This one is binomial because it counts the number of successes (defectives) out of many sampled bulbs.

  c) This one is binomial because it counts the number of successes (sums larger than 9) out of 80 rolls.

  d) This one is NOT a binomial r.v. because it is the sum of the dice after one roll, not the number of successes after many rolls.

  e) It is important to recognize a binomial r.v., because these are the n, p, q problems where we must use the "n choose x" formula to calculate probabilities and can use the shortcut formulas for finding the mean and standard deviation.

Section 6.1:

1) Normal distributions are <u>bell</u> - shaped.

2) If a population is normally distributed, then the area under the corresponding normal curve can be used to approximate <u>population</u> <u>relative</u> <u>frequencies</u>.

3) If a random variable is normally distributed, then the area under the corresponding normal curve can be used to approximate <u>probabilities</u> for the random variable.

4) 4 properties of normal curves.
    a) Total area under the curve is <u>1</u>.
    b) Curve is symmetric about its <u>mean</u>.
    c) Curve extends <u>indefinitely</u> in both directions and the height approaches <u>zero</u> on each side.
    d) Almost all of the area lies between $\mu - 3\sigma$ and $\mu + 3\sigma$.

5) If σ becomes larger, then the normal curve becomes shorter and <u>wider</u>. If σ becomes smaller, then the normal curve becomes <u>taller</u> and <u>narrower</u>.

6) The Empirical Rule was originally given for percentages and bell-shaped distributions, but it can also be used now to estimate <u>area</u> under <u>normal</u> curves.

7) a) This curve will be bell-shaped, centered at $\mu = 10$, and flatten out at
    $\mu - 3\sigma = 10 - 3*2 = 4$ and
    $\mu + 3\sigma = 10 + 3*2 = 16$.
    b) This curve will also be bell-shaped, but it will be centered at $\mu = 12$, and will flatten out at $\mu - 3\sigma = 12 - 3*3 = 3$ and $\mu + 3\sigma = 12 + 3*3 = 21$. Because this curve is wider, it will be shorter to maintain the constant area of 1.

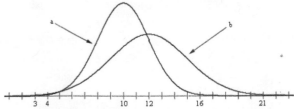

    c) Increasing the standard deviation had the direct effect of making the curve wider which indirectly causes it to get shorter.

9) a) μ should be right below the peak of the graph, so it looks like $\mu = 10$. The spot where the visible edge disappears on the right should be at about $\mu + 3\sigma$.
    $\mu + 3\sigma = 19 \Rightarrow 10 + 3\sigma = 19 \Rightarrow \sigma = 3$
    b) It would not change the shape at all, but the graph would slide 5 units to the right.
    c) If we double σ from 3 to 6, then the graph would become twice as wide and, therefore it would become shorter as well.
    d) Neither of these changes would affect the total area under the curve. The total area under all normal curves is 1, regardless of the values of μ and σ.

11) a) This curve will be centered at $\mu = 24.1$, and will flatten out at
    $\mu - 3\sigma = 24.1 - 3*2.307 = 17.179$ and
    $\mu + 3\sigma = 24.1 + 3*2.307 = 31.021$.

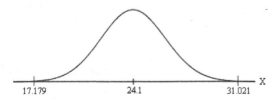

    b) We need the area between 19 and 29.

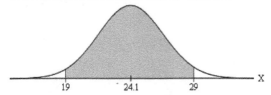

    c) The two boundaries given, 19 and 29 are both about two standard deviations aways from the mean. Based on the Empirical Rule, I would expect this area to about 95% of the area. Therefore, I would estimate that about 95% of female green anacondas are between 19 and 29 feet long.

13) a) This curve will be centered at $\mu = 7.5$, and will flatten out at
$\mu - 3\sigma = 7.5 - 3 * 1.273 = 3.681$ and
$\mu + 3\sigma = 7.5 + 3 * 1.273 = 11.319$.

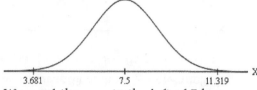

b) We need the area to the left of 5 hours.

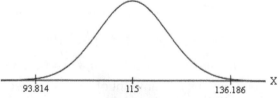

c) 5 hours is about 2 standard deviations below the mean. From the Empirical Rule, we expect about 95% of the area withing 2 standard deviations. The remaining 5% would be split among the two sides. I expect about 2.5% of the batteries to last less than 5 hours.

15) a) This curve will be centered at $\mu_X = 115$, and will flatten out at
$\mu_X - 3\sigma_X = 115 - 3 * 7.062 = 93.814$ and
$\mu_X + 3\sigma_X = 115 + 3 * 7.062 = 136.186$.

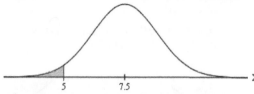

b) We need all the area to the right of 110.

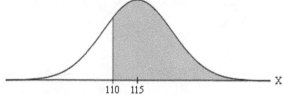

c) 110 is less than one standard deviation away from the mean. According to the Empirical Rule, we would get about 68% of the area within 1 st dev of the mean. That would be 34% on each side. Because 110 is less than 1 st dev away, maybe the area on the left side is about 0.25. We have the entire right half shaded so that is another 0.5 in area. I would guess:
$P(X > 110) \approx 0.75$.

17) a) This curve will be centered at $\mu_Y = 21.3$, and will flatten out at
$\mu_Y - 3\sigma_Y = 21.3 - 3 * 3.0972 = 12.0084$ and
$\mu_Y + 3\sigma_Y = 21.3 + 3 * 3.0972 = 30.5916$.

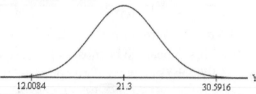

b) We need the total of the area to the left of 15 and also to the right of 25.

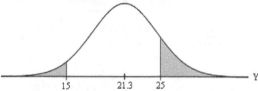

c) 15 is about two st devs to the left, so the area to its left should be about 0.025. 25 is about 1 st dev to the right of the mean, so the area to its right should be about 0.16.
$P(Y < 15 \text{ OR } Y > 25) \approx$
$0.025 + 0.16 = 0.185$

Section 6.2:

19) The Standard Normal Curve is the normal curve with a mean of $\underline{0}$ and a standard deviation of $\underline{1}$.

20) The Standard Normal Curve represents the $\underline{z\text{-}}$ $\underline{scores}$ from other normal curves. Therefore, the units are measured in the number of $\underline{standard}$ $\underline{deviations}$ from the mean.

21) When using the normalcdf function, we must enter both the $\underline{lower}$ z-score $\underline{boundary}$ and the $\underline{upper}$ z-score $\underline{boundary}$ of the region.

22) When using the invNorm command, we only need to enter the area on the $\underline{left}$ of the boundary we are seeking.

23) z_α tells us that there is an area of α to the $\underline{right}$ of the z we are looking for.

24) If the region we are finding the area of has no lower boundary, then we use $-\infty$ as our lower boundary. If the region we are finding the area of has no upper boundary, then we use ∞ as our upper boundary.

25) a) The area appears to be more than half.

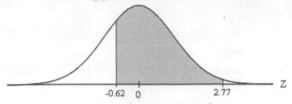

$$Area = normalcdf(-0.62,\ 2.77) \approx 0.7296$$

b) This appears to be most of the area under the curve.

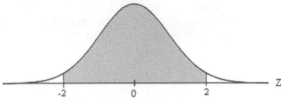

$$Area = normalcdf(-2,\ 2) \approx 0.9545$$

c) Use $-\infty$ for the lower boundary. The area appears close to 1.

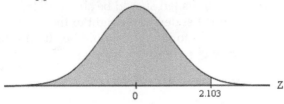

$$Area = normalcdf(-\infty,\ 2.103) \approx 0.9823$$

d) Use ∞ as the upper boundary. The area appears to be small.

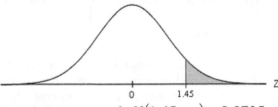

$$Area = normalcdf(1.45,\ \infty) \approx 0.0735$$

27) a) Almost all the area appears to be shaded.

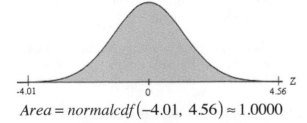

$$Area = normalcdf(-4.01,\ 4.56) \approx 1.0000$$

b) Almost no area is shaded this time. We will use $-\infty$ for the lower boundary.

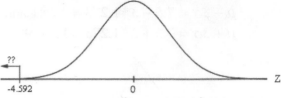

$$Area = normalcdf(-\infty,\ -4.592) \approx 0.0000$$

c) Again, almost no area appears to be shaded. We will use ∞ for the upper boundary.

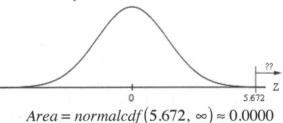

$$Area = normalcdf(5.672,\ \infty) \approx 0.0000$$

29) All probabilities will be found using the corresponding area under the standard normal curve.

a) It appears that far less than half of the area is shaded.

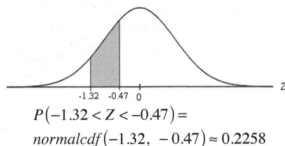

$$P(-1.32 < Z < -0.47) =$$
$$normalcdf(-1.32,\ -0.47) \approx 0.2258$$

b) Only a small amount of area is shaded. We will use $-\infty$ for the lower boundary.

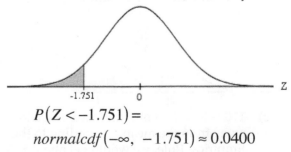

$$P(Z < -1.751) =$$
$$normalcdf(-\infty,\ -1.751) \approx 0.0400$$

c) Most of the area is shaded. We will use ∞ for the upper boundary.

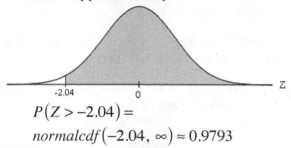

$P(Z > -2.04) =$

$normalcdf(-2.04, \infty) \approx 0.9793$

31) All probabilities will be found using the corresponding area under the standard normal curve.

a) We could find the two shaded area and add, or we could find the unwanted area and subtract from 1.

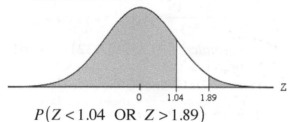

$P(Z < 1.04 \text{ OR } Z > 1.89)$

$1 - normalcdf(1.04, 1.89) \approx$

$1 - 0.1198 = 0.8802$

b) For an AND question, we want the overlap of the two parts. We see in the graph below that the overlap is from 1 to 2.

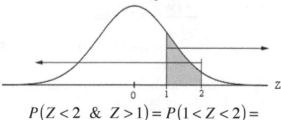

$P(Z < 2 \ \& \ Z > 1) = P(1 < Z < 2) =$

$normalcdf(1, 2) \approx 0.1359$

c) The area to the left of k is 0.65. Because this is a large area, k must be on the right side.

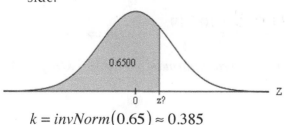

$k = invNorm(0.65) \approx 0.385$

33) Problems that give area and ask for z-scores are working backwards questions and require the use of the invNorm function. **Recall**: we must enter the area to the left in this function.

a) The area to the left is small, so the z-score we need will be on the left side of the graph. Since we are given an area to the left, we can go straight to the invNorm function.

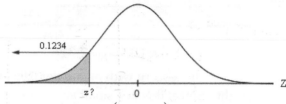

$z = invNorm(0.1234) \approx -1.158$

b) The area to the left is large, so the z-score will be on the right side of the graph.

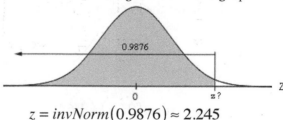

$z = invNorm(0.9876) \approx 2.245$

c) The area to the right is small, so the z will be on the right. Since we are given an area to the right, we must subtract from 1 to get the area on the left.

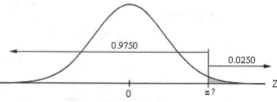

$z = invNorm(0.9750) \approx 1.960$

d) If the area in the middle is 0.90. Then subtracting from 1, we have 0.10 remaining. We divide that equally among the two sides, so we have 0.05 on each side.

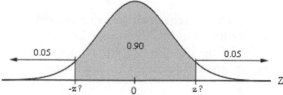

Since we must enter an area on the left, it is easiest to find the negative z first. Then, by symmetry, the other z will be the same, but positive.

$-z = invNorm(0.05) \approx -1.645 \Rightarrow z \approx 1.645$

35) a) $z_{0.01}$ is the z-score with an area of 0.01 to its right. Since, this is a small amount of area to the right, the z is on the right. We subtract from 1 to find the area 0.99 on the left.

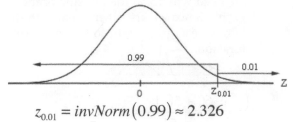

$$z_{0.01} = invNorm(0.99) \approx 2.326$$

b) $z_{0.05}$ is the z-score with an area of 0.05 to its right. Since, this is a small amount of area to the right, the z is on the right. We subtract from 1 to find the area 0.95 on the left.

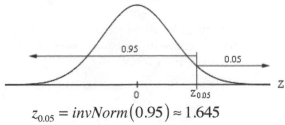

$$z_{0.05} = invNorm(0.95) \approx 1.645$$

c) $z_{0.80}$ is the z-score with an area of 0.80 to its right. Since, this is a large amount of area to the right, the z is on the left. We subtract from 1 to find the area 0.20 on the left.

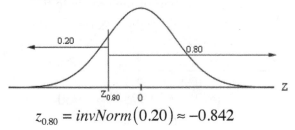

$$z_{0.80} = invNorm(0.20) \approx -0.842$$

Section 6.3:

37) We convert areas under normal curves to area under the Standard Normal Curve by calculating the z-scores for the x-value boundaries of the region of interest.

38) The empirical rule for normal populations states that 68.27% of the data lies within 1 standard deviation of the mean, 95.45 % lies within 2 standard deviations of the mean, and 99.73 % lies within 3 standard deviations of the mean.

39) If an x-value has a z-score of 1.57, then that x-value is 1.57 standard deviations above the mean .

40) The 74th percentile, or P_{74}, is the x-value that has an area of 0.74 to its left .

41) a) We are given x-values, so we need to find z-scores for each of them.

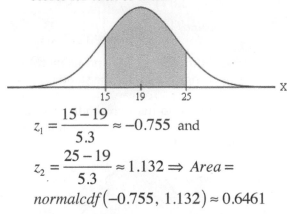

$$z_1 = \frac{15-19}{5.3} \approx -0.755 \text{ and}$$

$$z_2 = \frac{25-19}{5.3} \approx 1.132 \Rightarrow Area =$$

$$normalcdf(-0.755, 1.132) \approx 0.6461$$

b) We begin by finding the z-score for 20. We will use ∞ for the upper boundary.

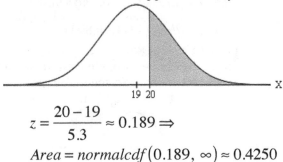

$$z = \frac{20-19}{5.3} \approx 0.189 \Rightarrow$$

$$Area = normalcdf(0.189, \infty) \approx 0.4250$$

c) We will find the z-score for 10 and use $-\infty$ for the lower boundary.

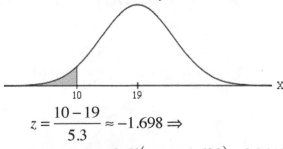

$$z = \frac{10-19}{5.3} \approx -1.698 \Rightarrow$$

$$Area = normalcdf(-\infty, -1.698) \approx 0.0448$$

43) a) The area to the right is small, so the x will be on the right. Sine the area to the right is given, we subtract from 1 to find the area of 0.90 to the left. Since we are working backwards here, we will use invNorm.

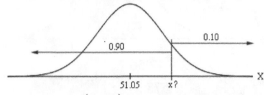

$$z = invNorm(0.90) \approx 1.282 \ \& \ x = \mu + z\sigma$$
$$\Rightarrow x = 51.05 + 1.282 * 14.09 = 69.11338$$

b) The area to the left is large, so the x will be on the right. We now use invNorm to find the z, and then we convert to an x-value.

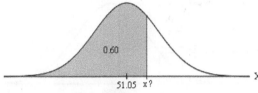

$$z = invNorm(0.60) \approx 0.253 \Rightarrow$$
$$x = 51.05 + 0.253 * 14.09 = 54.61477$$

c) If the middle area is 0.90, then we split the remaining 0.10 to get 0.05 on each side. Because of symmetry, the z on the left and the z on the right will be opposites of each other. Since we have the area to the left of −z on our graph, we will find it first.

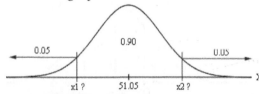

$$-z = invNorm(0.05) \approx -1.645 \Rightarrow z \approx 1.645$$
$$\Rightarrow x_1 = 51.05 - 1.645 * 14.09 = 27.87195,$$
$$\Rightarrow x_2 = 51.05 + 1.645 * 14.09 = 74.22805$$

45) a) The area to the right of 50 will equal the probability we are looking for. We will use ∞ for our upper boundary.

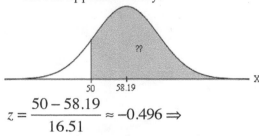

$$z = \frac{50 - 58.19}{16.51} \approx -0.496 \Rightarrow$$
$$Area = normalcdf(-0.496, \ \infty) \approx 0.6901$$

b) We need to find the two shaded areas and add them up, or we could just find the unshaded area and subtract that from one. Either way, we need to find the z-scores first.

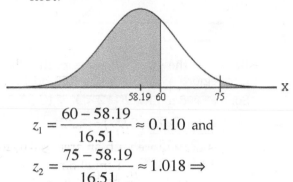

$$z_1 = \frac{60 - 58.19}{16.51} \approx 0.110 \text{ and}$$
$$z_2 = \frac{75 - 58.19}{16.51} \approx 1.018 \Rightarrow$$

Total Shaded Area =
$$1 - normalcdf(0.110, \ 1.018) \approx 0.6981$$

c) The quartiles divide the area under a normal curve into 4 equal parts. That means the area in each part will be 0.25. See the sketch below.

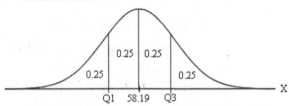

Since half of the area is to the left of the mean and half of the area is to the right, the mean is also the median. To find Q_1 and Q_3, we must first find their z-scores and then convert them to x-values. Because of symmetry, they will have equal but opposite z-scores.

$$-z = invNorm(0.25) \approx -0.674 \Rightarrow z \approx 0.674$$
$$Q_1 = 58.19 - 0.674 * 16.51 \approx 47.06$$
$$Q_2 = M = \mu = 58.19$$
$$Q_3 = 58.19 + 0.674 * 16.51 \approx 69.32$$

47) a) For an 'AND' problem, we need to find the overlap of the two regions.

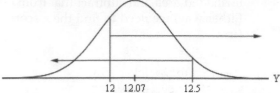

Based on the graph, it appears that the two regions overlap between 12 and 12.5. So, we need to find $P(12 < Y < 12.5)$.

$$z_1 = \frac{12 - 12.07}{0.23055} \approx -0.304 \text{ and}$$

$$z_2 = \frac{12.5 - 12.07}{0.23055} \approx 1.865 \Rightarrow$$

$$P(12 < Y < 12.5) =$$

$$normalcdf(-0.304, 1.865) \approx 0.5883$$

b) For a "given" problem, we need to find

$$P(A|B) = \frac{P(overlap)}{P(given)}. \text{ We found the}$$

overlap for our two events in parts (a). So, we need to find $P(Y > 12)$. We already found the z-score for 12 in part (a).

$$P(Y > 12) = normalcdf(-0.304, \infty) \approx 0.6194$$

$$P(Y < 12.5 \mid Y > 12) = \frac{P(12 < Y < 12.5)}{P(Y > 12)}$$

$$= \frac{0.5883}{0.6194} \approx 0.9498$$

49) $\mu = 42.56$ and $\sigma = 1.573$

a) The decimal form of the percentage will equal the area between 40 and 45.

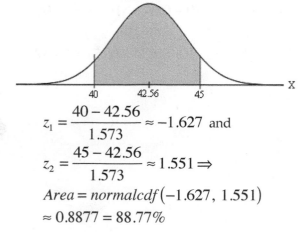

$$z_1 = \frac{40 - 42.56}{1.573} \approx -1.627 \text{ and}$$

$$z_2 = \frac{45 - 42.56}{1.573} \approx 1.551 \Rightarrow$$

$$Area = normalcdf(-1.627, 1.551)$$

$$\approx 0.8877 = 88.77\%$$

b) At least indicates 42 or higher. We will use ∞ for our upper boundary.

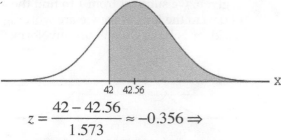

$$z = \frac{42 - 42.56}{1.573} \approx -0.356 \Rightarrow$$

$$Area = normalcdf(-0.356, \infty) \approx 0.6391 = 63.91\%$$

c) The tenth percentile will have an area of 0.10 to its left. Since we know the area and are looking for the boundary, we use invNorm.

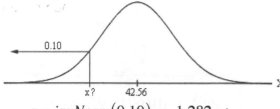

$$z = invNorm(0.10) \approx -1.282 \Rightarrow$$

$$P_{10} = x = 42.56 - 1.282 * 1.573 \approx 40.54$$

Interpretation: 10% of 5-yr old girls have heights below 40.54 inches tall.

d) For a normal curve, the areas under the graph and the z-scores are always the same when finding quartiles.

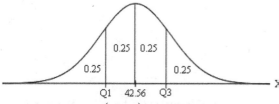

$$-z = invNorm(0.25) \approx -0.674 \Rightarrow z \approx 0.674$$

$$Q_1 = 42.56 - 0.674 * 1.573 \approx 41.50$$

$$Q_2 = M = \mu = 42.56$$

$$Q_3 = 42.56 + 0.674 * 1.573 \approx 43.62$$

51) $\mu = 24.1$ and $\sigma = 2.307$

a) The area to the right of 30 will be the decimal form of the percentage we need. We will use ∞ for our upper boundary.

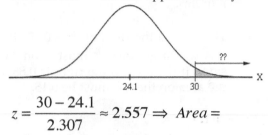

$$z = \frac{30 - 24.1}{2.307} \approx 2.557 \Rightarrow Area =$$

$normalcdf(2.557, \infty) \approx 0.0053 = 0.53\%$

b) Again we will find the area and then convert to a percentage.

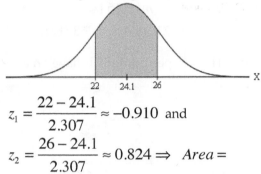

$$z_1 = \frac{22 - 24.1}{2.307} \approx -0.910 \text{ and}$$

$$z_2 = \frac{26 - 24.1}{2.307} \approx 0.824 \Rightarrow Area =$$

$normalcdf(-0.910, 0.824) \approx 0.6136 = 61.36\%$

c) To be in the longest 1% of these snakes, you would have to be a big snake. So, the 1%, or area of 0.01, will be on the right. invNorm works with areas to the left, so we subtract from 1 to get 0.99

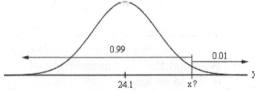

$z = invNorm(0.99) \approx 2.326 \Rightarrow$

$x = 24.1 + 2.326 * 2.307 \approx 29.47$
The snake would have to be at least 29.47 feet long to be in the longest 1%.

d) For a normal curve, the areas under the graph and the z-scores are always the same when finding quartiles.

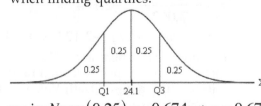

$-z = invNorm(0.25) \approx -0.674 \Rightarrow z \approx 0.674$

$Q_1 = 24.1 - 0.674 * 2.307 \approx 22.545$
$Q_2 = M = \mu = 24.1$
$Q_3 = 24.1 + 0.674 * 2.307 \approx 25.655$

53) $\mu = 7.5$ and $\sigma = 1.273$

a) The area to the left of 5 will be the decimal form of the percentage we need. We will use $-\infty$ for our lower boundary.

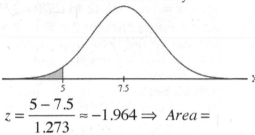

$$z = \frac{5 - 7.5}{1.273} \approx -1.964 \Rightarrow Area =$$

$normalcdf(-\infty, -1.964) \approx 0.0248 = 2.48\%$

b) Again we will find the area and then convert to a percentage. We need the area between 6 and 9 hours.

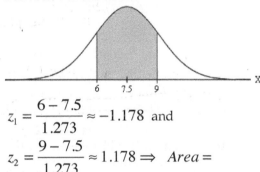

$$z_1 = \frac{6 - 7.5}{1.273} \approx -1.178 \text{ and}$$

$$z_2 = \frac{9 - 7.5}{1.273} \approx 1.178 \Rightarrow Area =$$

$normalcdf(-1.178, 1.178) \approx 0.7612 = 76.12\%$

c) To be in the shortest lasting 10% of these batteries, you would have to be on the left. So, we have an area of 0.10 on the left of the mystery time. We can use the invNorm function to find the z-score.

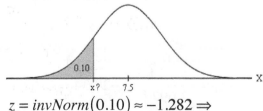

$z = invNorm(0.10) \approx -1.282 \Rightarrow$

$x = 7.5 - 1.282 * 1.273 \approx 5.868$
The batteries would have to go dead in less than 5.868 hours to be considered part of the worst 10% of the batteries.

d) The 80th percentile will have an area of 0.80 to its left.

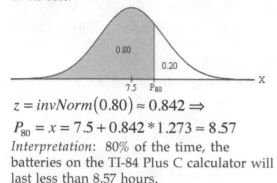

$z = invNorm(0.80) \approx 0.842 \Rightarrow$

$P_{80} = x = 7.5 + 0.842 * 1.273 \approx 8.57$

Interpretation: 80% of the time, the batteries on the TI-84 Plus C calculator will last less than 8.57 hours.

55) All probabilities will be found by using the corresponding area under the normal curve with $\mu_Y = 21.3$ and $\sigma_Y = 3.0972$.

a) For this one, we will need the area to the left of 20.

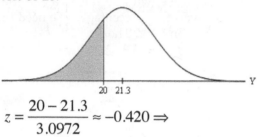

$z = \dfrac{20 - 21.3}{3.0972} \approx -0.420 \Rightarrow$

$normalcdf(-\infty, -0.420) \approx 0.3372$

Interpretation: There is a 33.72% chance that the time it will take Kevin to assemble a randomly selected bike will be less than 20 minutes.

b) As we can see in the sketch below, these two areas do not overlap. Therefore the events are mutually exclusive and we can just add together the probabilities.

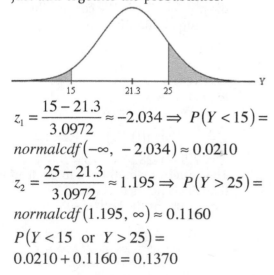

$z_1 = \dfrac{15 - 21.3}{3.0972} \approx -2.034 \Rightarrow P(Y < 15) =$

$normalcdf(-\infty, -2.034) \approx 0.0210$

$z_2 = \dfrac{25 - 21.3}{3.0972} \approx 1.195 \Rightarrow P(Y > 25) =$

$normalcdf(1.195, \infty) \approx 0.1160$

$P(Y < 15 \text{ or } Y > 25) =$

$0.0210 + 0.1160 = 0.1370$

Interpretation: There is a 13.70% chance that the time it will take Kevin to assemble a randomly selected bike will be less than 15 minutes or more than 25 minutes.

c) The area to the right of k is 0.85. Because this is a large area, k must be on the left side. If the area to the right is 0.85, then the area on the left must be 0.15.

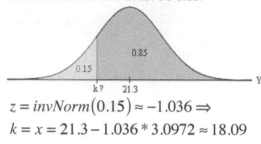

$z = invNorm(0.15) \approx -1.036 \Rightarrow$

$k = x = 21.3 - 1.036 * 3.0972 \approx 18.09$

d) The 65th percentile will have an area of 0.65 to its left.

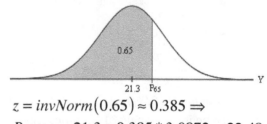

$z = invNorm(0.65) \approx 0.385 \Rightarrow$

$P_{65} = x = 21.3 + 0.385 * 3.0972 \approx 22.49$

Interpretation: There is a 65% chance that it will take less than 22.49 minutes for Kevin to assemble a randomly selected bike.

57) All probabilities will be found by using the corresponding area under the normal curve.

a) We need the area to the right of 100. We will use ∞ for our upper boundary.

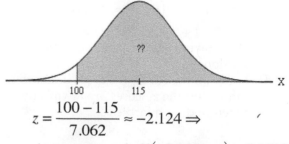

$z = \dfrac{100 - 115}{7.062} \approx -2.124 \Rightarrow$

$Area = normalcdf(-2.124, \infty) \approx 0.9832$

Interpretation: There is a 98.32% chance that the high temperature on a randomly selected July day in Death Valley will be greater than 100° F.

b) This time we need the area between 95 and 105.

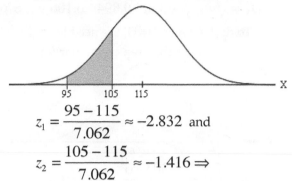

$$z_1 = \frac{95-115}{7.062} \approx -2.832 \text{ and}$$

$$z_2 = \frac{105-115}{7.062} \approx -1.416 \Rightarrow$$

$Area = normalcdf(-2.832, -1.416) \approx 0.0761$

Interpretation: There is a 7.61% chance that the high temperature on a randomly selected July day in Death Valley will be more than 95°, but at most 105° F.

c) The 20th percentile will have an area of 0.20 to its left.

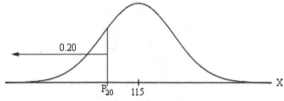

$z = invNorm(0.20) \approx -0.842 \Rightarrow$

$P_{20} = x = 115 - 0.842 * 7.062 \approx 109.05$

Interpretation: 20% of the days in July have a high temperature below 109.05^o F.

d) We will need to use the conditional probability rule for this one.

$$P(X \le 120 | X > 100) =$$

$$\frac{P(X \le 120 \ \& \ X > 100)}{P(X > 100)} = \frac{P(100 < X \le 120)}{P(X > 100)}$$

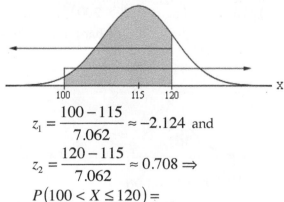

$$z_1 = \frac{100-115}{7.062} \approx -2.124 \text{ and}$$

$$z_2 = \frac{120-115}{7.062} \approx 0.708 \Rightarrow$$

$P(100 < X \le 120) =$

$normalcdf(-2.124, 0.708) \approx 0.7437$

$P(X > 100) =$

$normalcdf(-2.124, \infty) \approx 0.9832 \Rightarrow$

$$P(X \le 120 | X > 100) \approx \frac{0.7437}{0.9832} \approx 0.7564$$

Interpretation: Given that the high temperature on a random July day in Death Valley is more than 100°, there is a 75.64% chance that the high will be no more than 120° F.

59) a) Because X is counting the number of successes in 40 trials, this is a binomial distribution. We also need to find n, p, and q. The value of n = 40 because there are 40 trials. p is the probability of a success and it is not given, but we can figure it out.

$p = P(\text{success in a single trial}) = P(temp < 98)$

The problem tells us that temperature is normally distributed with $\mu_{temp} = 98.2$ and $\sigma_{temp} = 0.352$. So we can find p using area under this curve. We will use $-\infty$ for the lower boundary.

$$z = \frac{98 - 98.2}{0.352} \approx -0.568 \Rightarrow$$

$p = normalcdf(-\infty, -0.568) \approx 0.2850$

X has the binomial distribution with n = 40, p = 0.2850, and q = 1 − p = 0.7150.

b) We should use a z-score to answer this question, but we need to be careful about the details. They are asking if it would be unusual if the number of successes is zero. So, we have to use the mean and standard deviation for X, not for temperature when computing this z-score. First we must find these values.

$\mu_X = np = 40 * 0.2850 = 11.4$

$\sigma_X = \sqrt{npq} = \sqrt{40 * 0.285 * 0.715} \approx 2.8550$

$$z = \frac{0 - 11.4}{2.8550} \approx -3.993 \Rightarrow$$

Yes, $z \approx -3.993 \Rightarrow$ in fact, zero successes is considered very unusual because it is more than 3 standard deviations below the mean.

61) Recall: $\mu = 42.56$ and $\sigma = 1.573$.

a) We should recognize 68.27% from the Empirical Rule as the percentage of data that lies within 1 standard deviation of the mean for normal data sets. $\mu - \sigma = 40.987$ and $\mu + \sigma = 44.133$. So we fill in the blanks with 40.987 and 44.133 in.

b) This time the Empirical Rule tells us to use 2 standard deviations. $\mu - 2\sigma = 39.414$ and $\mu + 2\sigma = 45.706$. So we fill in the blanks with 39.414 and 45.706 in.

c) This time we use 3 standard deviations. $\mu - 3\sigma = 37.841$ and $\mu + 3\sigma = 47.279$. So we fill in the blanks with 37.841 and 47.279 in.

d) 90% is not from the Empirical Rule. So, we must figure out how many standard deviations away from the mean we need by finding the 2 z-scores that trap an area of 0.90 in the middle with equal outside areas.

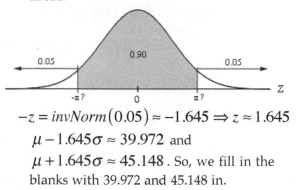

$-z = invNorm(0.05) \approx -1.645 \Rightarrow z \approx 1.645$

$\mu - 1.645\sigma \approx 39.972$ and

$\mu + 1.645\sigma \approx 45.148$. So, we fill in the blanks with 39.972 and 45.148 in.

Section 6.4:

63) We approximate binomial probabilities using the area of the <u>histogram</u> bars. To do this accurately, we must use <u>1/2</u> marks as the boundaries of the region we find the area of.

64) If $np \geq$ <u>10</u> and $nq \geq$ <u>10</u>, then a binomial distribution is considered to be approximately <u>normal</u>.

65) a) $np = 340(0.894) = 303.96 \geq 10$
$nq = 340(0.106) = 36.04 \geq 10$ $\Rightarrow$ This binomial distribution is approx. normal and the requirements have been met.

b) We begin by finding the mean and standard deviation for this binomial variable.

$\mu_X = np = 340 * 0.894 = 303.96$

$\sigma_X = \sqrt{npq} = \sqrt{340 * 0.894 * 0.106} \approx 5.6762$

To find $P(X = 300)$, we need to approximate the area of the bar for 300.

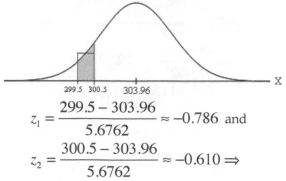

$z_1 = \dfrac{299.5 - 303.96}{5.6762} \approx -0.786$ and

$z_2 = \dfrac{300.5 - 303.96}{5.6762} \approx -0.610 \Rightarrow$

$P(X = 300) \approx normalcdf(-0.786, -0.610) \approx 0.0550$

c) For this one we want to start at the left hand side of the bar for 300 and end at the left hand side of the bar for 310 (since 310 is not included.)

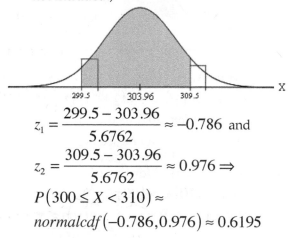

$z_1 = \dfrac{299.5 - 303.96}{5.6762} \approx -0.786$ and

$z_2 = \dfrac{309.5 - 303.96}{5.6762} \approx 0.976 \Rightarrow$

$P(300 \leq X < 310) \approx$

$normalcdf(-0.786, 0.976) \approx 0.6195$

d) To approximate $P(X > 290)$, we want to use the right side of the bar for 290 (since it is not included) as our lower boundary and ∞ as our upper boundary.

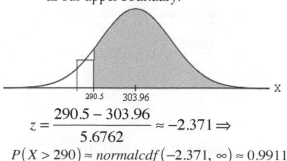

$z = \dfrac{290.5 - 303.96}{5.6762} \approx -2.371 \Rightarrow$

$P(X > 290) \approx normalcdf(-2.371, \infty) \approx 0.9911$

67) This is a binomial distribution with $n = 1329$, $p = 0.607$, and $q = 1 - p = 0.393$. Since we will be using the normal approximation, we need to find the mean and standard deviation.

$$\mu_X = np = 806.703, \ \sigma_X = \sqrt{npq} \approx 17.805$$

a) To approximate this probability, we need to approximate the area of the histogram bar for 800 using the area under the corresponding normal curve.

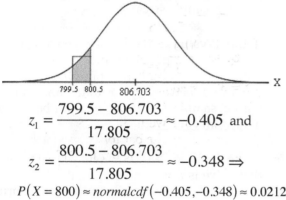

$$z_1 = \frac{799.5 - 806.703}{17.805} \approx -0.405 \text{ and}$$

$$z_2 = \frac{800.5 - 806.703}{17.805} \approx -0.348 \Rightarrow$$

$$P(X = 800) \approx normalcdf(-0.405, -0.348) \approx 0.0212$$

b) At least 750 includes the 750, so this time we want to find $P(X \geq 750)$. We will use 749.5 as our lower boundary (to include the 750) and we will use ∞ as our upper boundary.

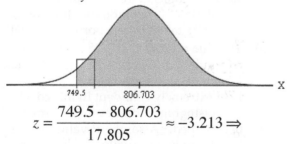

$$z = \frac{749.5 - 806.703}{17.805} \approx -3.213 \Rightarrow$$

$$P(X \geq 750) \approx normalcdf(-3.213, \infty) \approx 0.9993$$

69) This is a binomial distribution with $n = 100$, $p = 0.768$, and $q = 1 - p = 0.232$.

a) $\begin{aligned} np &= 76.8 \geq 10 \\ nq &= 23.2 \geq 10 \end{aligned} \Rightarrow$ This binomial distribution is approx. normal, so the requirements have been met.

b) Before we can use the normal approximation, we must determine the mean and standard deviation.

$$\mu_X = np = 76.8 \text{ and}$$

$$\sigma_X = \sqrt{npq} \approx 4.2211.$$

To find $P(X < 80)$, we will use $-\infty$ as our lower boundary and 79.5 as our upper boundary (since 80 is not included.)

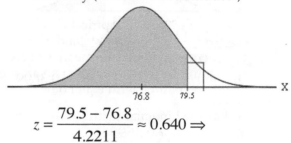

$$z = \frac{79.5 - 76.8}{4.2211} \approx 0.640 \Rightarrow$$

$$P(X < 80) = normalcdf(-\infty, 0.640) \approx 0.7389$$

c) To find $P(X \geq 90)$, we will use 89.5 as our lower boundary (since 90 is included) and we will use ∞ as our upper boundary.

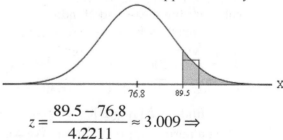

$$z = \frac{89.5 - 76.8}{4.2211} \approx 3.009 \Rightarrow$$

$$P(X \geq 90) \approx normalcdf(3.009, \infty) \approx 0.0013$$

d) $\mu_X - 2\sigma_X \approx 68.4$ and $\mu_X + 2\sigma_X \approx 85.2$, so we expect the two aces to win anywhere from 69 to 85 of the 100 times.

71) a) Because X is a count of the number of successes in 200 trials, this is a binomial distribution. The n is 200, but we need to figure out the value of p from the information provided.

$p = P(\text{success}) = P(Battery > 12)$.

The problem tells us that the battery life, B, is normally distributed with $\mu_B = 11.74$ and $\sigma_B = 0.7833$. Our lower boundary is 12 and we will use $1 \times 10^{99} = I$ for the upper boundary.

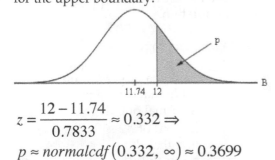

$z = \dfrac{12 - 11.74}{0.7833} \approx 0.332 \Rightarrow$

$p \approx normalcdf(0.332, \infty) \approx 0.3699$

X has the binomial distribution with $n = 200$, $p = 0.3699$, and $q = 1 - p = 0.6301$.

b) The key to this part is to realize we are being asked a probability question about X, therefore we can't use the mean and standard deviation that were given. Those were for battery life, B. We need to calculate the mean and standard deviation for X using n, p, and q.

$\mu_X = np = 200 * 0.3699 = 73.98$ and

$\sigma_X = \sqrt{npq} = \sqrt{200 * 0.3699 * 0.6301} \approx 6.8275$

Now, finding $P(X > 100)$ will be done using a normal approximation. We will use 100.5 as our lower boundary (since 100 is not included), and we will use $1 \times 10^{99} = I$ as our upper boundary.

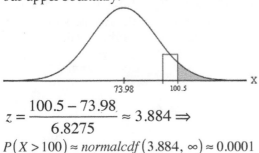

$z = \dfrac{100.5 - 73.98}{6.8275} \approx 3.884 \Rightarrow$

$P(X > 100) \approx normalcdf(3.884, \infty) \approx 0.0001$

Section 6.5:

73) If the histogram for your sample data is roughly bell-shaped, then you can conclude that there is a reasonable possibility that your sample was taken from a normally distributed population.

74) If the histogram for your sample data is not roughly bell-shaped, then you can be confident that your sample is NOT taken from a normal population. Your confidence will drop for smaller sample sizes.

75) If the P-value ≤ 0.05, then you can conclude that your sample data did not come from a normally distributed population. The difference between your data and an ideal normal sample are too large to just be the result of random variation.

76) If the P-value > 0.05, then you can conclude that there is a reasonable possibility that your sample data was taken from a normally distributed population. The difference between your data and an ideal normal sample are small enough to just be the result of random variation.

77) a) This histogram does not look bell-shaped. In fact, it looks more like a uniform population. I conclude that this sample was NOT taken from a normal population.

b) P-value $\approx 0.0000 < 0.05$. Therefore, I conclude that this sample was NOT taken from a normal population.

c) I am extremely confident in this conclusion. The histogram didn't even look roughly bell-shaped. Also, the P-value tells us that there is essentially no chance that our data would have looked like this if it was from a normal population.

79) a) This histogram does not look bell-shaped. It looks more like a right-skewed distribution. I conclude that this sample was NOT taken from a normal population.

   b) P-value $\approx 0.0000 < 0.05$. Therefore, I conclude that this sample was NOT taken from a normal population.

   c) I am confident in this conclusion. The histogram didn't even look roughly bell-shaped. Also, the P-value tells us that there is essentially no chance that our data would have looked like this if it were from a normal population.

81) a) This histogram does look roughly bell-shaped. The peak is in the center and there is equal distance to the two sides. The tall bar on the left seems strange, but that could just be random variation in such a small sample. I conclude that there is a reasonable possibility that this sample was taken from a normal population.

   b) P-value $\approx 0.9229 > 0.05$. Therefore, I conclude that there is a reasonable possibility that this sample was taken from a normal population.

   c) I am reasonbly confident in this conclusion. The histogram had hints of a bell-shape, but also a strange tall bar on the far left. The P-value tells us that there is a large chance that the difference we see between our data and normal data could just be the result of random variation. However, with such a small sample size, the P-value can easily give a false positve for normal.

83) a) This histogram does look roughly bell-shaped. There is also a hint of a right-skew, but that could just be random variation in our sample. I conclude that there is a reasonable possibility that this sample was taken from a normal population.

   b) P-value $\approx 0.6657 > 0.05$. Therefore, I conclude that there is a reasonable possibility that this sample was taken from a normal population.

   c) Yes, both tests above say that it is a reasonable possibility that these weights would be normally distributed. This also makes sense for something growing in nature.

85) a) This histogram does not look bell-shaped. It looks more like a right exponential distribution. I conclude that this sample was NOT taken from a normal population.

   b) P-value $\approx 0.0000 < 0.05$. Therefore, I conclude that this sample was NOT taken from a normal population.

   c) No it does not make sense to use a normal curve for this population. We our confident that this population is not normal. So, areas under a normal curve should not be used to estimate percentage for this population.

87) a) This histogram does not quite look roughly bell-shaped. The peak is on the left side and there is a larger tail on the right side. I conclude that this sample was NOT taken from a normal population.

   b) P-value $\approx 0.0682 > 0.05$. Therefore, I conclude that there is a reasonable possibility that this sample was taken from a normal population.

   c) This is a tough one, because the sample size is small and the two conclusions from parts (a) and (b) disagree with each other. The P-value method is often more reliable, so I would say it is reasonable to estimate the probability using a normal curve. However, we can't be too confident that the probability will be completely accurate.

89) In Exercise (83), we concluded that it would be reasonable to use a normal curve to estimate percentages for the platypus weights. To do this, we need to have the mean and standard deviation for the normal curve. Our best guess at this comes from the sample mean and standard deviation. So, for this exercise, we will use the normal curve with a mean of 3.64 and a standard deviation of 0.87399.

a) To estimate this, we will use the area under the curve to the right of 5 pounds.

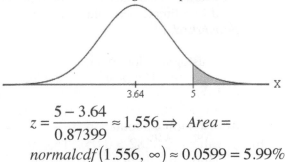

$$z = \frac{5 - 3.64}{0.87399} \approx 1.556 \Rightarrow Area =$$

$$normalcdf(1.556, \infty) \approx 0.0599 = 5.99\%$$

So, we estimate that about 5.99% of all platypuses weigh more than 5 pounds.

b) The 40th percentile will have an area of 0.40 to its left.

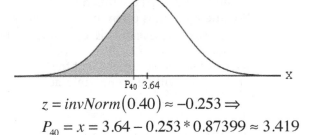

$$z = invNorm(0.40) \approx -0.253 \Rightarrow$$

$$P_{40} = x = 3.64 - 0.253 * 0.87399 \approx 3.419$$

c) *Interpretation*: 40% of all mature platypuses have weights that are less than 3.419 pounds.

d) Unfortunately, there are several things to worry about. We are using sample estimates for the mean and standard deviation of the normal curve. Also, we are not positive that we are working with a normal curve, that is just a reasonable possibility. How accurate our estimates above are depends on how accurately we are estimating the mean and standard deviation and on how close the true distribution is to a normal curve.

Chapter Problem:

a) The histogram shows a hint of bell-shape due to the peak in the center. However, the peaks on the side seem contrary to a bell-shape. P-value $\approx 0.1315 > 0.05$, so there is a decent chance that the differences from bell that we see in our histogram is just due to random variation. I conclude that there is a reasonable possibility that the sample was taken from a normal population.

b) We need to find the area between 101.565 and 101.575.

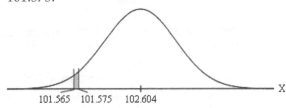

$$z_1 = \frac{101.565 - 102.604}{0.623314} \approx -1.667 \text{ and}$$

$$z_2 = \frac{101.575 - 102.604}{0.623314} \approx -1.651 \Rightarrow$$

$$Area = normalcdf(-1.667, -1.651) \approx 0.0016$$

Based on this area, I would estimate that Tina Maze had about a 0.16% chance of tying Gisin.

c) If we let Y = the number of the remaining three skiers that tie Gisin, then we are looking for $P(Y \geq 1)$. Using the complement rule, we could find $1 - P(Y = 0)$ instead. This is a success failure question, so Y has a binomial distribution with $n = 3$, $p = 0.0016$, and $q = 0.9984$. Using the binomial formula:

$$P(Y = 0) = \binom{3}{0}(0.0016)^0 (0.9984)^3 \approx 0.9952$$

$$1 - P(Y = 0) \approx 1 - 0.9952 = 0.0048.$$

Based on these calculations, if 3 skiers remained, then there is about a 0.48% chance that at least one of them would have tied Gisin for the gold medal.

Chapter 6 - Review Exercises:

1) a) The center of this graph will be at 9 and
   the graph will flatten out at 3 and 15.
   b) This graph will be narrower and taller
   than the one in part (a). It will be centered
   at 10.5 and flatten out around 6.6 and 14.4.

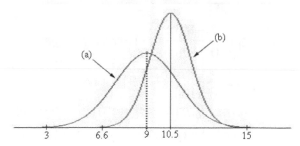

3) a) $normalcdf(-2.601, 1.098) \approx 0.8593$

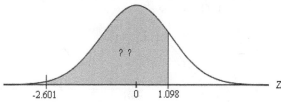

b) $normalcdf(2.034, \infty) \approx 0.0210$

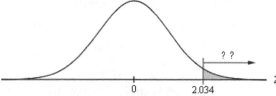

c) $normalcdf(-\infty, 1.908) \approx 0.9718$

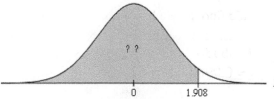

d) Area to the left = $1 - 0.67 = 0.33$.

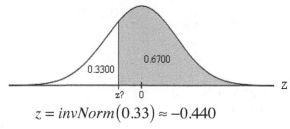

$z = invNorm(0.33) \approx -0.440$

e) A middle area of 0.70 leaves areas of 0.15 in
each tail.

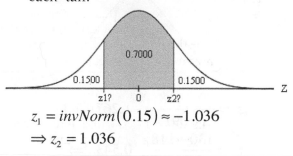

$z_1 = invNorm(0.15) \approx -1.036$

$\Rightarrow z_2 = 1.036$

5) a) $normalcdf(-1.933, -0.805) \approx 0.1838$

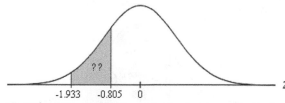

b) The two areas do not overlap, so we find
them separately and then add them
together.

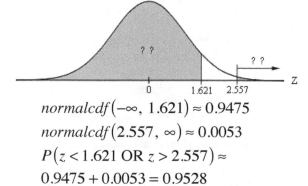

$normalcdf(-\infty, 1.621) \approx 0.9475$

$normalcdf(2.557, \infty) \approx 0.0053$

$P(z < 1.621 \text{ OR } z > 2.557) \approx$

$0.9475 + 0.0053 = 0.9528$

c) $z_{0.18}$ is the z-score with area 0.18 to its
right. So, the area to the left is 0.82.

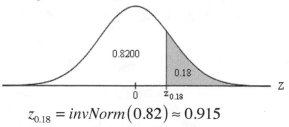

$z_{0.18} = invNorm(0.82) \approx 0.915$

7) a)

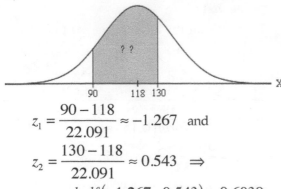

$$z_1 = \frac{90-118}{22.091} \approx -1.267 \quad \text{and}$$

$$z_2 = \frac{130-118}{22.091} \approx 0.543 \quad \Rightarrow$$

$$normalcdf(-1.267,\ 0.543) \approx 0.6039$$

b)

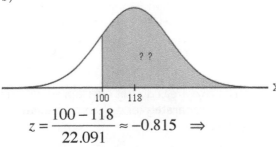

$$z = \frac{100-118}{22.091} \approx -0.815 \quad \Rightarrow$$

$$normalcdf(-0.815,\ \infty) \approx 0.7925$$

c) A middle area of 0.60 leaves areas of 0.20 on each side.

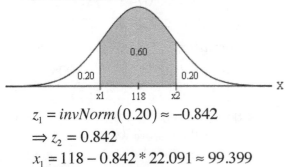

$$z_1 = invNorm(0.20) \approx -0.842$$

$$\Rightarrow z_2 = 0.842$$

$$x_1 = 118 - 0.842 * 22.091 \approx 99.399$$

$$x_2 = 118 + 0.842 * 22.091 \approx 136.601$$

9) a)

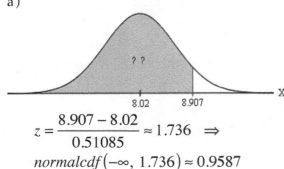

$$z = \frac{8.907-8.02}{0.51085} \approx 1.736 \quad \Rightarrow$$

$$normalcdf(-\infty,\ 1.736) \approx 0.9587$$

b) AND means overlap. So, we need the area between 7 and 9.

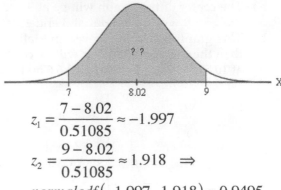

$$z_1 = \frac{7-8.02}{0.51085} \approx -1.997$$

$$z_2 = \frac{9-8.02}{0.51085} \approx 1.918 \quad \Rightarrow$$

$$normalcdf(-1.997,\ 1.918) \approx 0.9495$$

c) Using the conditional probability rule:

$$P(x>7\mid x\le 9) = \frac{P(x>7\ \&\ x\le 9)}{P(x\le 9)}$$

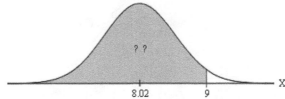

From part (b), we know that

$$P(x>7\ \&\ x\le 9) \approx 0.9495 \quad \text{and}$$

$$P(x\le 9) = normalcdf(-\infty,\ 1.918) \approx 0.9724$$

$$P(x>7\mid x\le 9) = \frac{0.9495}{0.9724} \approx 0.9765$$

d) P_{85} represents the 85th percentile. This is the x-value with area 0.85 to its left.

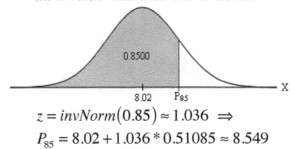

$$z = invNorm(0.85) \approx 1.036 \quad \Rightarrow$$

$$P_{85} = 8.02 + 1.036 * 0.51085 \approx 8.549$$

11) $p = 0.318 \Rightarrow q = 0.682$

a) $np = 517 * 0.318 \geq 10$ and

$nq = 517 * 0.682 \geq 10$. Therefore, this binomial distribution is also approximately normally distributed.

b) The first thing we need to do is find the mean and standard deviation for this distribution. $\mu_x = np = 164.406$ and

$\sigma_x = \sqrt{npq} \approx 10.589$.

Now, we need to find the area that corresponds to the histogram bar for 170.

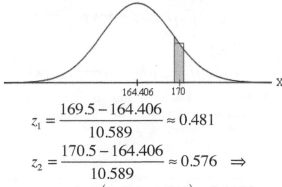

$z_1 = \dfrac{169.5 - 164.406}{10.589} \approx 0.481$

$z_2 = \dfrac{170.5 - 164.406}{10.589} \approx 0.576 \Rightarrow$

$normalcdf(0.481, 0.576) \approx 0.0330$

c) The bar for 150 is not included, so we will start at 150.5. The bar for 170 is included, so we will end at 170.5.

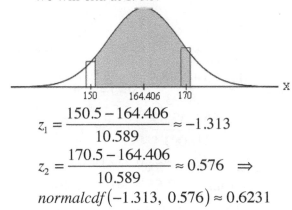

$z_1 = \dfrac{150.5 - 164.406}{10.589} \approx -1.313$

$z_2 = \dfrac{170.5 - 164.406}{10.589} \approx 0.576 \Rightarrow$

$normalcdf(-1.313, 0.576) \approx 0.6231$

13) The population is normal with $\mu = 24.3$ and $\sigma = 5.581$.

a) We want the area to the right of 30.

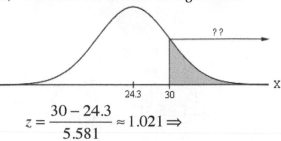

$z = \dfrac{30 - 24.3}{5.581} \approx 1.021 \Rightarrow$

$Area = normalcdf(1.021, \infty) \approx 0.1536$

So, we can say that 15.36% of rainbow trout are longer than 30 inches.

b) The quartiles divide the data set into 4 equal parts. Each of the parts will have an area of 0.25.

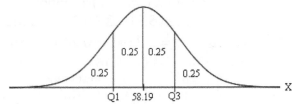

$z_1 = invNorm(0.25) \approx -0.674 \Rightarrow$

$Q_1 = 24.3 - 0.674 * 5.581 \approx 20.5384$

$Q_2 = M = \mu = 24.3$

$z_2 = -z_1 = 0.674 \Rightarrow$

$Q_3 = 24.3 + 0.674 * 5.581 \approx 28.0616$

c) The percentile number gives us the area to the left of the X value we are looking for. So the area to the left is 0.98. See sketch.

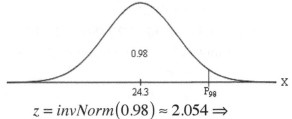

$z = invNorm(0.98) \approx 2.054 \Rightarrow$

$P_{98} = X = 24.3 + 2.054 * 5.581 \approx 35.76$

d) 98% of mature rainbow trout have lengths less than 35.76 inches.

14) a) 88.99%

b) 25.2765, 30.5, 35.7235

c) 40.4355

d) 90% of adult coyotes weigh less than 40.4355 lbs.

15) Normal Dist with $\mu = 5.31$ and $\sigma = 0.249$.

a) We will use the area between 5.25 and 5.5 to find this percentage.

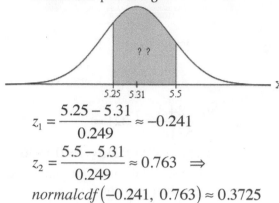

$$z_1 = \frac{5.25 - 5.31}{0.249} \approx -0.241$$

$$z_2 = \frac{5.5 - 5.31}{0.249} \approx 0.763 \implies$$

normalcdf $(-0.241, 0.763) \approx 0.3725$

So, 37.25% of the flights.

b) 95.45% of the area lies within 2 standard deviations for a normal distribution.

$$x_1 = \mu - 2\sigma = 5.31 - 2*0.249 = 4.812$$

$$x_2 = \mu + 2\sigma = 5.31 + 2*0.249 = 5.808$$

The middle 95.45% of flight times are between <u>4.812</u> and <u>5.808</u> hours long.

c) We will want 0.80 in the middle with 0.10 in each of the two tails.

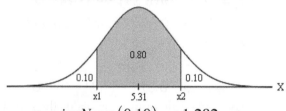

$$z_1 = invNorm(0.10) \approx -1.282 \implies$$

$$x_1 = 5.31 - 1.282 * 0.249 \approx 4.991$$

$$z_2 = -z_1 = 1.282 \implies$$

$$x_2 = 5.31 + 1.282 * 0.249 \approx 5.629$$

The middle 80% of flight times are between <u>4.991</u> and <u>5.629</u> hours long.

17) a) For a normally distributed random variable, we simply use the corresponding area under the normal curve for probability.

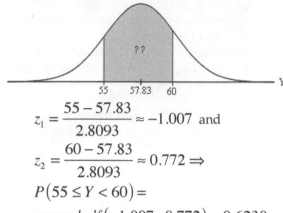

$$z_1 = \frac{55 - 57.83}{2.8093} \approx -1.007 \text{ and}$$

$$z_2 = \frac{60 - 57.83}{2.8093} \approx 0.772 \implies$$

$$P(55 \le Y < 60) =$$

normalcdf $(-1.007, 0.772) \approx 0.6230$

Note: Since Y is a continuous variable, it doesn't matter whether or not the endpoints are included.

b) For an 'OR' question, we want to take all the area from one part and add any new area from the other. Since these two areas are mutually exclusive, we just find the areas and add them together.

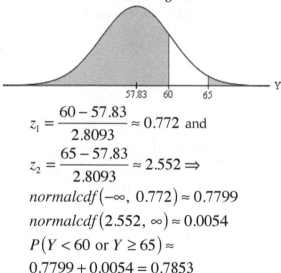

$$z_1 = \frac{60 - 57.83}{2.8093} \approx 0.772 \text{ and}$$

$$z_2 = \frac{65 - 57.83}{2.8093} \approx 2.552 \implies$$

normalcdf $(-\infty, 0.772) \approx 0.7799$

normalcdf $(2.552, \infty) \approx 0.0054$

$$P(Y < 60 \text{ or } Y \ge 65) \approx$$

$$0.7799 + 0.0054 = 0.7853$$

c) For this one, we will use the conditional probability rule. So we get:

$$P(Y \geq 55 | Y < 60) = \frac{P(Y \geq 55 \ \& \ Y < 60)}{P(Y < 60)}$$

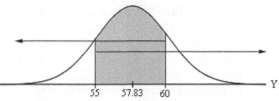

For the '&', we use the overlap from the graph above. So, we want to find

$$P(55 \leq Y < 60)$$

$$= normalcdf(-1.007, \ 0.772) \approx 0.6230.$$

Also, $P(Y < 60) =$

$$normalcdf(-\infty, \ 0.772) \approx 0.7799.$$

So, putting it all together, we get:

$$P(Y \geq 55 | Y < 60) = \frac{P(55 \leq Y < 60)}{P(Y < 60)} \approx$$

$$\frac{0.6230}{0.7799} \approx 0.7988$$

d) This is a working backwards question because we are told that the area to the right of k is 0.05. See sketch that follows.

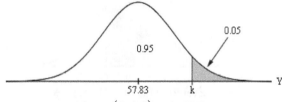

$$z = invNorm(0.95) \approx 1.645 \Rightarrow$$

$$k = 57.83 + 1.645 * 2.8093 \approx 62.45$$

19) We are counting the number of successes in 480 trials, so this is a binomial distribution with $n = 480$, $p = 0.391$, and $q = 0.609$. Since we will be using the normal approximation, we must know the mean and standard deviation.

$$\mu_X = np = 187.68 \text{ and } \sigma_X = \sqrt{npq} \approx 10.691.$$

a) We want to approximate this probability by approximating the area of the histogram bar for 200. See sketch below.

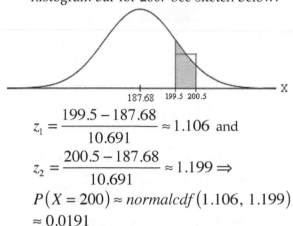

$$z_1 = \frac{199.5 - 187.68}{10.691} \approx 1.106 \text{ and}$$

$$z_2 = \frac{200.5 - 187.68}{10.691} \approx 1.199 \Rightarrow$$

$$P(X = 200) \approx normalcdf(1.106, 1.199)$$

$$\approx 0.0191$$

b) For this one, we want the histogram bar for 200 and all the bars to the right.

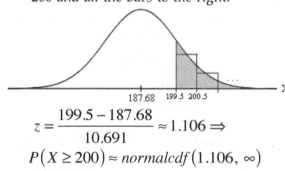

$$z = \frac{199.5 - 187.68}{10.691} \approx 1.106 \Rightarrow$$

$$P(X \geq 200) \approx normalcdf(1.106, \infty)$$

$$\approx 0.1344$$

c) $np = 187.68 \geq 10$ and $nq = 292.32 \geq 10$, so the requirements have been met.

20) a) X represents the number of successes in 350 eggs. So, X has a binomial distribution. The number of trials is n = 350, but the probability of a success is not given. However, they do define a success as a randomly selected egg weighing less than 2.75 pounds. We can find this probability by using the given fact that the ostrich eggs have normally distributed weights. We must find the area to the left of 2.75.

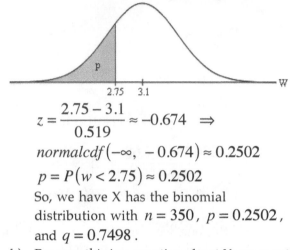

$$z = \frac{2.75 - 3.1}{0.519} \approx -0.674 \implies$$

$normalcdf(-\infty, -0.674) \approx 0.2502$

$p = P(w < 2.75) \approx 0.2502$

So, we have X has the binomial distribution with $n = 350$, $p = 0.2502$, and $q = 0.7498$.

b) Because this is a question about X, we must find the mean and standard deviation of X.

$\mu_x = np = 350 * 0.2502 = 87.57$ and

$\sigma_x = \sqrt{npq} \approx 8.1031$.

$\mu_x - 2\sigma_x = 71.3638$ and

$\mu_x + 2\sigma_x = 103.7762$

Therefore, we would expect somewhere between 72 and 103 of the eggs to weigh less than 2.75 lbs.

c) The phrase at least 100, includes the value of 100. So, we will start at the left side of the bar for 100, or 99.5.

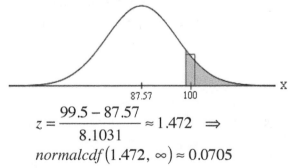

$$z = \frac{99.5 - 87.57}{8.1031} \approx 1.472 \implies$$

$normalcdf(1.472, \infty) \approx 0.0705$

21) a) This histogram does look roughly bell-shaped. I conclude that there is a reasonable possibility that this sample was taken from a normal population.

b) P-value $\approx 0.5625 > 0.05$. Therefore, I conclude that there is a reasonable possibility that this sample was taken from a normal population.

c) To estimate this, we will use the area under the curve to the right of 55 million downloads using a normal curve with a mean of 48.46 and a standard deviation of 7.7767.

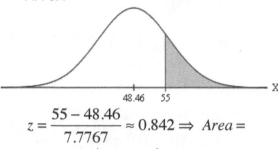

$$z = \frac{55 - 48.46}{7.7767} \approx 0.842 \implies Area =$$

$normalcdf(0.842, \infty) \approx 0.1999 = 19.99\%$

So, we estimate that about 19.99% of all days in 2012 exceeded 55 million app downloads from Apple.

d) The 65th percentile will have an area of 0.65 to its left.

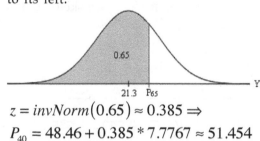

$z = invNorm(0.65) \approx 0.385 \implies$

$P_{40} = 48.46 + 0.385 * 7.7767 \approx 51.454$

e) Interpretation: 65% of all days in 2012 had less than 51.454 million app downloads.

f) We are using sample estimates for the mean and standard deviation of the normal curve. Also, we are not certain that we are working with a normal curve, that is just a reasonable possibility. How accurate our estimates above are depends on how accurately we are estimating the mean and standard deviation and on how close the true distribution is to a normal curve.

Section 7.1:

1) The sample proportion is $\hat{p} = \dfrac{x}{n}$, where x is the number of successes in the sample of size n.

2) A parameter is a quantity that describes a population value. A statistic is a quantity that describes a sample value.

3) A point estimate is a single value calculated from a sample and used to estimate a population quantity.

4) Sampling Error is the difference that results from using an estimate obtained from a sample rather than a census to estimate a population quantity.

5) The probability of obtaining the exact value of a population parameter by using a point estimate from a random sample is usually approximately equal to zero.

6) We expect our sampling error to be less than two standard deviations of our point estimate.

7) In words, $\mu_{\hat{p}} = p$ says that if we find the average of all possible sample proportions, then the result is the population proportion.

8) $\sigma_{\hat{p}} = \sqrt{\dfrac{pq}{n}}$ is good news because it tells us that the higher the sample size, the closer the possible values of $\hat{p}$ get to the population proportion, p.

9) First we should label all the numbers we are given: $n = 438$, $p = 0.5744$, $x = 251$. Next, we find $q = 1 - p = 0.4256$.

a) $\hat{p} = \dfrac{x}{n} = \dfrac{251}{438} \approx 0.5731$

b) $SE = |\hat{p} - p| = |0.5731 - 0.5744| = 0.0013$

c) Anything between $p - 0.03$ and $p + 0.03$ will be acceptable. So, anything between 0.5444 and 0.6044 would be considered acceptable.

d) $P(\hat{p} = p) = 0$

11) We are given: $p = 28.64\% = 0.2864$.

a) $n = 188 \Rightarrow \mu_{\hat{p}} = p = 0.2864$ and
$$\sigma_{\hat{p}} = \sqrt{\dfrac{pq}{n}} = \sqrt{\dfrac{0.2864 * 0.7136}{188}} \approx 0.032971$$

b) $n = 913 \Rightarrow \mu_{\hat{p}} = p = 0.2864$ and
$$\sigma_{\hat{p}} = \sqrt{\dfrac{pq}{n}} = \sqrt{\dfrac{0.2864 * 0.7136}{913}} \approx 0.014962$$

13) We are given: $p = 71.06\% = 0.7106$.

a) $n = 449 \Rightarrow \mu_{\hat{p}} = p = 0.7106$ and
$$\sigma_{\hat{p}} = \sqrt{\dfrac{pq}{n}} = \sqrt{\dfrac{0.7106 * 0.2894}{449}} \approx 0.021401$$

b) $EE < 2\sigma_{\hat{p}} \approx 2 * 0.021401 = 0.042802$

c) $z = \dfrac{\hat{p} - \mu_{\hat{p}}}{\sigma_{\hat{p}}} = \dfrac{0.6682 - 0.7106}{0.021401} \approx -1.981$

No, 0.6682 is just under 2 standard deviations away from its mean, so it is not considered unusual (but it is very close).

15) Givens: $n = 539$; $p = 0.46 \Rightarrow q = 0.54$

a) $\mu_{\hat{p}} = p = 0.46$ and
$$\sigma_{\hat{p}} = \sqrt{\dfrac{pq}{n}} = \sqrt{\dfrac{0.46 * 0.54}{539}} \approx 0.021467$$

b) No, $P(\hat{p} = p) = 0$.

c) $EE < 2\sigma_{\hat{p}} \approx 2 * 0.021467 = 0.042934$

d) $\hat{p} = \dfrac{x}{n} = \dfrac{235}{539} \approx 0.4360$

e) $z = \dfrac{\hat{p} - \mu_{\hat{p}}}{\sigma_{\hat{p}}} = \dfrac{0.4360 - 0.46}{0.021467} \approx -1.118$

No, 0.4360 is less than 2 standard deviations below the mean.

17) Givens: $n = 1018$, $p = 0.62 \Rightarrow q = 0.38$

a) $\mu_{\hat{p}} = p = 0.62$ and

$$\sigma_{\hat{p}} = \sqrt{\frac{pq}{n}} = \sqrt{\frac{0.62 * 0.38}{1018}} \approx 0.015213$$

b) $z = \dfrac{\hat{p} - \mu_{\hat{p}}}{\sigma_{\hat{p}}} = \dfrac{0.6631 - 0.62}{0.015213} \approx 2.833$

Yes, 0.6631 is more than 2 standard deviations above the mean.

c) $z = \dfrac{\hat{p} - \mu_{\hat{p}}}{\sigma_{\hat{p}}} = \dfrac{0.5972 - 0.62}{0.015213} \approx -1.499$

No, 0.5972 is less than 2 standard deviations below the mean.

d) $p - 2\sigma_{\hat{p}} = 0.62 - 2 * 0.015213 = 0.589574$

$p + 2\sigma_{\hat{p}} = 0.62 + 2 * 0.015213 = 0.650426$

Therefore, we expect the sample proportion to be somewhere between 58.96% and 65.04%.

19) Givens: $n = 583$

a) Fair Wheel $\Rightarrow p = \dfrac{18}{38} \approx 0.4737$

$\Rightarrow q = \dfrac{20}{38} \approx 0.5263$

$\mu_{\hat{p}} = p = 0.4737$ and

$$\sigma_{\hat{p}} = \sqrt{\frac{0.4737 * 0.5263}{583}} \approx 0.020679$$

b) $\hat{p} = \dfrac{x}{n} = \dfrac{292}{583} \approx 0.5009$

c) $z = \dfrac{\hat{p} - \mu_{\hat{p}}}{\sigma_{\hat{p}}} = \dfrac{0.5009 - 0.4737}{0.020679} \approx 1.315$

No, 0.5009 is less than 2 standard deviations above the mean.

d) $SE = |\hat{p} - p| = |0.5009 - 0.4737| = 0.0272$

e) Random variation is our default explanation. Because part (c) shows us that it would not be unusual for this point estimate to be the result of random variation if the wheel was fair, we will stick with random variation as our explanation for the sampling error.

Section 7.2:

21) If $np \geq 10$ and $nq \geq 10$, then $\hat{p}$ will be approximately <u>normally</u> distributed.

22) To fully describe the sampling distribution of $\hat{p}$ we must state the type of distribution and we must also provide the <u>mean</u> and <u>standard deviation</u>.

23) $n = 200$, $p = 0.784 \Rightarrow q = 0.216$

a) $np = 156.8 \geq 10$ and $nq = 43.2 \geq 10$, so $\hat{p}$ is normally distributed with

$\mu_{\hat{p}} = p = 0.784$

and $\sigma_{\hat{p}} = \sqrt{\dfrac{0.784 * 0.216}{200}} \approx 0.029098$.

b) We must remember to use $\mu_{\hat{p}}$ and $\sigma_{\hat{p}}$ when calculating z-scores for $\hat{p}$.

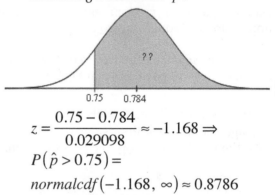

$z = \dfrac{0.75 - 0.784}{0.029098} \approx -1.168 \Rightarrow$

$P(\hat{p} > 0.75) =$

$normalcdf(-1.168, \infty) \approx 0.8786$

c) We want to be within 0.05 of the population proportion. This translates to

$P(0.784 - .05 < \hat{p} < 0.784 + 0.05) =$

$P(0.734 < \hat{p} < 0.834)$.

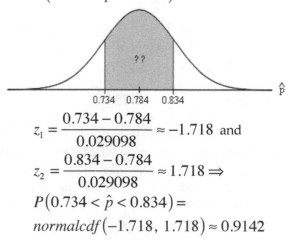

$z_1 = \dfrac{0.734 - 0.784}{0.029098} \approx -1.718$ and

$z_2 = \dfrac{0.834 - 0.784}{0.029098} \approx 1.718 \Rightarrow$

$P(0.734 < \hat{p} < 0.834) =$

$normalcdf(-1.718, 1.718) \approx 0.9142$

25) $n = 487$, $p = 0.5446 \Rightarrow q = 0.4554$

   a) $np \approx 265.22 \geq 10$ and $nq \approx 221.78 \geq 10$, so $\hat{p}$ is normally distributed with

$$\mu_{\hat{p}} = p = 0.5446$$

and $\sigma_{\hat{p}} = \sqrt{\dfrac{0.5446 * 0.4554}{487}} \approx 0.022567$.

   b) We must remember to use $\mu_{\hat{p}}$ and $\sigma_{\hat{p}}$ when calculating z-scores for $\hat{p}$.

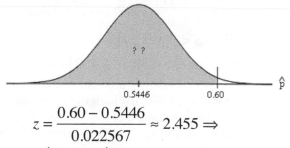

$$z = \dfrac{0.60 - 0.5446}{0.022567} \approx 2.455 \Rightarrow$$

$$P(\hat{p} < 0.60) =$$

$$normalcdf(-\infty,\ 2.455) \approx 0.9930$$

   c) We want to be within 0.04 of the population proportion. This translates to

$$P(0.5446 - .04 < \hat{p} < 0.5446 + 0.04) =$$

$$P(0.5046 < \hat{p} < 0.5846).$$

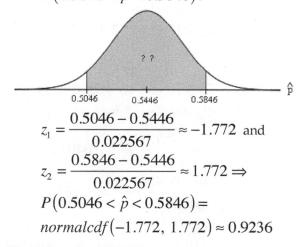

$$z_1 = \dfrac{0.5046 - 0.5446}{0.022567} \approx -1.772 \text{ and}$$

$$z_2 = \dfrac{0.5846 - 0.5446}{0.022567} \approx 1.772 \Rightarrow$$

$$P(0.5046 < \hat{p} < 0.5846) =$$

$$normalcdf(-1.772,\ 1.772) \approx 0.9236$$

27) $n = 600$, $p = 0.37 \Rightarrow q = 0.63$

   a) $np = 222 \geq 10$ and $nq = 378 \geq 10$, so the possible values of $\hat{p}$ are normally distributed with $\mu_{\hat{p}} = p = 0.37$

and $\sigma_{\hat{p}} = \sqrt{\dfrac{0.37 * 0.63}{600}} \approx 0.019710$.

   b) Examining the graph of
$P(\hat{p} < 0.35 \text{ or } \hat{p} > 0.40)$ shown below, we see that the two parts do not overlap.

Therefore, we can find each area separately and then add the two values together.

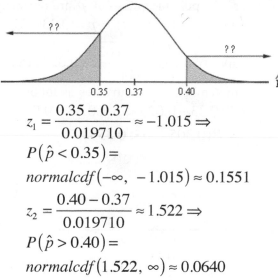

$$z_1 = \dfrac{0.35 - 0.37}{0.019710} \approx -1.015 \Rightarrow$$

$$P(\hat{p} < 0.35) =$$

$$normalcdf(-\infty,\ -1.015) \approx 0.1551$$

$$z_2 = \dfrac{0.40 - 0.37}{0.019710} \approx 1.522 \Rightarrow$$

$$P(\hat{p} > 0.40) =$$

$$normalcdf(1.522,\ \infty) \approx 0.0640$$

Finally, we get our result by adding these two values together.

$$P(\hat{p} < 0.35 \text{ or } \hat{p} > 0.40) \approx$$

$$0.1551 + 0.0640 = 0.2191$$

   c) For this one, we can use the conditional probability rule. $P(A|B) = \dfrac{P(A \ \& \ B)}{P(B)} \Rightarrow$

$$P(\hat{p} < 0.35 | \hat{p} \leq 0.40) =$$

$$\dfrac{P(\hat{p} < 0.35 \ \& \ \hat{p} \leq 0.40)}{P(\hat{p} \leq 0.40)}$$

We can simplify the numerator by noting that & means 'overlap'. Examining the graph below, we see that the overlap is the region to the left of 0.35.

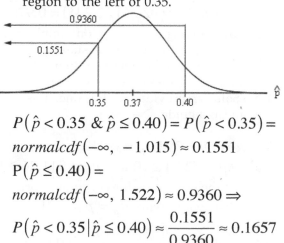

$$P(\hat{p} < 0.35 \ \& \ \hat{p} \leq 0.40) = P(\hat{p} < 0.35) =$$

$$normalcdf(-\infty,\ -1.015) \approx 0.1551$$

$$P(\hat{p} \leq 0.40) =$$

$$normalcdf(-\infty,\ 1.522) \approx 0.9360 \Rightarrow$$

$$P(\hat{p} < 0.35 | \hat{p} \leq 0.40) \approx \dfrac{0.1551}{0.9360} \approx 0.1657$$

29) Givens: $n = 444$, $p = 0.33 \Rightarrow q = 0.67$

    a) $np = 146.52 \geq 10$ and $nq = 297.48 \geq 10$, so the possible values of $\hat{p}$ are normally distributed with $\mu_{\hat{p}} = p = 0.33$

    and $\sigma_{\hat{p}} = \sqrt{\dfrac{0.33 * 0.67}{444}} \approx 0.022315$.

    b) In symbols, this translates as follows:
$$P(0.33 - 0.025 < \hat{p} < 0.33 + 0.025)$$
$$= P(0.305 < \hat{p} < 0.355)$$

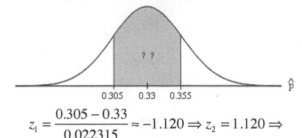

$$z_1 = \frac{0.305 - 0.33}{0.022315} \approx -1.120 \Rightarrow z_2 = 1.120 \Rightarrow$$
$$P(0.305 < \hat{p} < 0.355) =$$
$$normalcdf(-1.120, 1.120) \approx 0.7373$$

    c) In symbols, this translates as follows:
$$P(0.33 - 0.05 < \hat{p} < 0.33 + 0.05)$$
$$= P(0.28 < \hat{p} < 0.38)$$

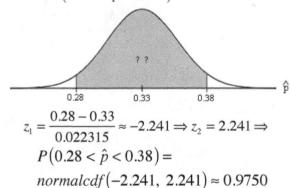

$$z_1 = \frac{0.28 - 0.33}{0.022315} \approx -2.241 \Rightarrow z_2 = 2.241 \Rightarrow$$
$$P(0.28 < \hat{p} < 0.38) =$$
$$normalcdf(-2.241, 2.241) \approx 0.9750$$

    d) By allowing more error, our employer is essentially lowering the standard. A lower standard should be easier to meet.

31) No Solution provided for this one. Use solution to #29 as a guide.

33) Givens: $n = 394$, $p = 0.21 \Rightarrow q = 0.79$

    a) $np = 82.74 \geq 10$ and $nq = 311.26 \geq 10$, so the possible values of $\hat{p}$ are normally distributed with $\mu_{\hat{p}} = p = 0.21$

    and $\sigma_{\hat{p}} = \sqrt{\dfrac{0.21 * 0.79}{394}} \approx 0.020520$.

    b) In symbols, this translates as follows:
$$P(0.21 - 0.03 < \hat{p} < 0.21 + 0.03)$$
$$= P(0.18 < \hat{p} < 0.24)$$

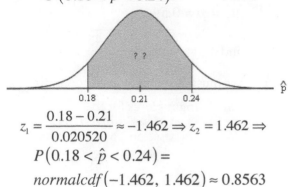

$$z_1 = \frac{0.18 - 0.21}{0.020520} \approx -1.462 \Rightarrow z_2 = 1.462 \Rightarrow$$
$$P(0.18 < \hat{p} < 0.24) =$$
$$normalcdf(-1.462, 1.462) \approx 0.8563$$

    c) It appears that the amount of acceptable error is not going to change. So, we should increase the sample size to increase our chance of getting sampling error less than 3%.

    d) $n = 1215 \Rightarrow$
$$\sigma_{\hat{p}} = \sqrt{\frac{0.21 * 0.79}{1215}} \approx 0.011685$$
$$z_1 = \frac{0.18 - 0.21}{0.011685} \approx -2.567 \Rightarrow z_2 = 2.567 \Rightarrow$$
$$P(0.18 < \hat{p} < 0.24) =$$
$$normalcdf(-2.567, 2.567) \approx 0.9897$$

35) $n = 150$, $p = 0.5 \Rightarrow q = 0.5$

    a) $np = 75 \geq 10$ and $nq = 75 \geq 10$, so $\hat{p}$ is normally distributed with $\mu_{\hat{p}} = p = 0.5$

    and $\sigma_{\hat{p}} = \sqrt{\dfrac{0.5 * 0.5}{150}} \approx 0.040825$.

    b) $z = \dfrac{0.40 - 0.50}{0.040825} \approx -2.449 \Rightarrow$
$$P(\hat{p} < 0.40) \approx 0.0072$$

    c) Because there is less than a 5% chance of this occurring just due to random variation, I would take this to be strong evidence that the coin is biased.

37) $n = 73$, $p = 0.768 \Rightarrow q = 0.232$

a) $np \approx 55 \geq 10$ and $nq \approx 17 \geq 10$, so the possible values of $\hat{p}$ are normally distributed with $\mu_{\hat{p}} = p = 0.768$ and

$$\sigma_{\hat{p}} = \sqrt{\frac{0.768 * 0.232}{73}} \approx 0.049404.$$

b) $z = \dfrac{0.70 - 0.768}{0.049404} \approx -1.376$. No, 70% is less than 2 standard deviations below the expected proportion, so it would not be considered unusual.

c) In symbols this translates to $P(\hat{p} \leq 0.70)$.

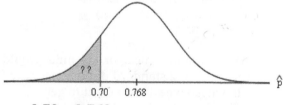

$z = \dfrac{0.70 - 0.768}{0.049404} \approx -1.376 \Rightarrow P(\hat{p} \leq 0.70) =$ $normalcdf(-\infty, -1.376) \approx 0.0844$

Section 7.3:

39) $\mu_{\bar{x}} = \mu$ tells us that $\bar{x}$ is a random variable and that if you average all possible values of the sample mean, then the result equals the population mean.

40) $\sigma_{\bar{x}} \approx \dfrac{\sigma}{\sqrt{n}}$ is good news because it tells us that the higher the sample size, the closer the possible values of $\bar{x}$ get to the population mean.

41) While it is true that $\mu_{\bar{x}} = \mu$, it is also typically the case that $P(\bar{x} = \mu) \approx 0$.

42) When we estimate μ by using $\bar{x}$ as a point estimate, we expect the sampling error to be less than $2\sigma_{\bar{x}}$ or $2\dfrac{\sigma}{\sqrt{n}}$.

43) a) Enter the data into L1 and then choose STAT > CALC > 1-Var Stats L1
$\mu = 100.5$; $\sigma \approx 14.009$

bcd)

Sample	$\bar{x}$	$P(\bar{x})$	$\bar{x} \cdot P(\bar{x})$	$(\bar{x} - \mu_{\bar{x}})^2 P(\bar{x})$
84, 92	88	1/6	14.667	26.0417
84, 105	94.5	1/6	15.75	6
84, 121	102.5	1/6	17.083	0.6667
92, 105	98.5	1/6	16.417	0.6667
92, 121	106.5	1/6	17.75	6
105, 121	113	1/6	18.833	26.0417
			100.5	65.4168

$$\mu_{\bar{x}} = \sum \bar{x} \cdot P(\bar{x}) = 100.5 \ ;$$

$$\sigma_{\bar{x}} = \sqrt{\sum (\bar{x} - \mu_{\bar{x}})^2 P(\bar{x})} = \sqrt{65.4168} \approx 8.0881$$

e) $\sigma_{\bar{x}} = \dfrac{14.009}{\sqrt{2}} \sqrt{\dfrac{4-2}{4-1}} \approx 8.0881$

45) We are given that $\mu = 112$ and $\sigma = 38.2$.

a) $\mu_{\bar{x}} = \mu = 112$; $\sigma_{\bar{x}} \approx \dfrac{38.2}{\sqrt{10}} \approx 12.080$

b) $\mu_{\bar{x}} = \mu = 112$; $\sigma_{\bar{x}} \approx \dfrac{38.2}{\sqrt{30}} \approx 6.9743$

c) None

d) It decreased it. This happens because we are dividing by the square root of the sample size. Larger n, means larger denominator, means small answer.

47) Givens: $\mu = 12.05$, $\sigma = 0.10553$

a) $\mu_{\bar{x}} = \mu = 12.05$;
$$\sigma_{\bar{x}} \approx \dfrac{0.10553}{\sqrt{21}} \approx 0.023029$$

b) $EE < 2\sigma_{\bar{x}} = 2 * 0.023029 = 0.046058$

c) $\mu_{\bar{x}} = \mu = 12.05$;
$$\sigma_{\bar{x}} \approx \dfrac{0.10553}{\sqrt{77}} \approx 0.012026$$

d) $EE < 2\sigma_{\bar{x}} = 2 * 0.012026 = 0.024052$

e) Bigger samples are more representative of the populations they are drawn from. The reason for this is that the amount of random variation in a sample decreases as the sample size increases. This is explained mathematically by the sample size, n, in the denominator of the formula:

$$EE < 2\dfrac{\sigma}{\sqrt{n}}.$$

49) We are given that $\mu = 4.95$ and $\sigma = 0.825$.

 a) $\mu_{\bar{x}} = \mu = 4.95$ and

 $\sigma_{\bar{x}} \approx \dfrac{0.825}{\sqrt{8}} \approx 0.29168$

 b) Expected error is less than $2\sigma_{\bar{x}}$.
 $2\sigma_{\bar{x}} \approx 2 * 0.29168 = 0.58336 \Rightarrow$ The expected error is less than 0.58336 lbs.

 c) Not necessarily. For example, an error of 0.53 lbs would be more than 0.5 lbs yet not unusual because it is smaller than the expected error.

 d) $\mu_{\bar{x}} = \mu = 4.95$ and $\sigma_{\bar{x}} \approx \dfrac{0.825}{\sqrt{25}} = 0.165$

 e) Less than $2\sigma_{\bar{x}} = 0.330$ lbs.

 f) Yes, because $2\sigma_{\bar{x}} \approx 0.330$, that would be an $\bar{x}$ more than 2 standard deviations away from its mean.

51) Givens: $\mu = 559.71$, $\sigma = 229.24$

 a) $\mu_{\bar{x}} = \mu = 559.71$; $\sigma_{\bar{x}} \approx \dfrac{229.24}{\sqrt{12}} \approx 66.176$

 b) $EE < 2\sigma_{\bar{x}} = 2 * 66.176 = 132.352$

 c) $\bar{x}$ should end up within 2 standard deviations of $\bar{x}$ away from the true mean.
 $\mu - 2\sigma_{\bar{x}} = 559.71 - 2 * 66.176 \approx 427.36$
 $\mu + 2\sigma_{\bar{x}} = 559.71 + 2 * 66.176 \approx 692.06$
 So, the expected range for $\bar{x}$ is somewhere between \$427.36 and \$692.06.

 d) In part (c) above, we concluded that we expect $427.36 < \bar{x} < 692.06$. Recall: $\sum x = n \cdot \bar{x}$. So, we should multiply all three parts of the inequality by the sample size of 12: $12(427.36) < 12 \cdot \bar{x} < 12(692.06)$.
 $\Rightarrow$ $\$5{,}128.32 < \sum x < \$8{,}304.72$

 e) $EE < 2\sigma_{\bar{x}} = 2 * 66.176 = 132.352$
 No. \$75 in sampling error is less than expected, so not unusual.

53) $2\sigma_{\bar{x}} < 0.25 \Rightarrow 2\dfrac{0.825}{\sqrt{n}} < 0.25 \Rightarrow$

 $1.65 < 0.25\sqrt{n} \Rightarrow \dfrac{1.65}{0.25} < \sqrt{n} \Rightarrow$

 $n > \left(\dfrac{1.65}{0.25}\right)^2 \approx 43.56$. So we need 44 or more Chihuahuas.

55) Givens: $\mu = 99$, $\sigma = 12.33$, $n = 30$

 a) $\mu_{\bar{x}} = \mu = 99$; $\sigma_{\bar{x}} \approx \dfrac{12.33}{\sqrt{30}} \approx 2.2511$

 b) $z = \dfrac{\bar{x} - \mu_{\bar{x}}}{\sigma_{\bar{x}}} = \dfrac{96.2 - 99}{2.2511} \approx -1.244 \Rightarrow$
 No. A sample mean of 96.2 miles would be less than 2 standard deviations away from the mean we would expect to get.

 c) The default explanation for differences in Statistics is random variation. Because it would not be unusual to get a sample mean of 96.2 just due to random variation, we say that it is plausible that the difference is just due to random variation.

 d) $z = \dfrac{\bar{x} - \mu_{\bar{x}}}{\sigma_{\bar{x}}} = \dfrac{93.1 - 99}{2.2511} \approx -2.621 \Rightarrow$
 Yes. A sample mean of 93.1 miles would be more than 2 standard deviations away from the mean we would expect to get.

 e) The default explanation for differences in Statistics is random variation. However, it would be unusual to get a sample mean of 93.1 just due to random variation, so we will say that we have strong evidence that the true average is actually less than 99 miles.

Section 7.4:

57) If our sample is taken from a normal population, then $\bar{x}$ will also be normally distributed, regardless of the sample size.

58) If our sample size is greater than or equal to 30, then $\bar{x}$ will be normally distributed regardless of the distribution of the original population. This is the statement of the Central Limit Theorem.

59) If the sample size is $15 \le n < 30$, and if the population is not severely skewed, then $\bar{x}$ will be normal.

60) False. A large sample ensures that $\bar{x}$ (not the population) will be normally distributed.

61) When calculating z-scores involving sample means, make sure that you use the standard deviation of $\bar{x}$ rather than the population standard deviation.

62) Typically, the best way to increase your chance of obtaining a satisfactory estimate of the population mean is to increase your <u>sample size</u>.

63) Givens: $\mu = 153.7$, $\sigma = 16.973$

a) $P(147 < x \leq 155)$ is unknown since we don't know the distribution of the population. The distribution of x and the population are always the same.

b) Since $n = 85 \geq 30$, the possible values of $\bar{x}$ are normal with $\mu_{\bar{x}} = \mu = 153.7$ and

$$\sigma_{\bar{x}} \approx \frac{16.973}{\sqrt{85}} \approx 1.8410$$

c) We will use the area under the normal curve for $\bar{x}$ to answer this question.

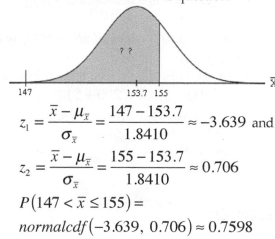

$$z_1 = \frac{\bar{x} - \mu_{\bar{x}}}{\sigma_{\bar{x}}} = \frac{147 - 153.7}{1.8410} \approx -3.639 \text{ and}$$

$$z_2 = \frac{\bar{x} - \mu_{\bar{x}}}{\sigma_{\bar{x}}} = \frac{155 - 153.7}{1.8410} \approx 0.706$$

$$P(147 < \bar{x} \leq 155) =$$

$$normalcdf(-3.639, 0.706) \approx 0.7598$$

Note: When finding a z-scores for $\bar{x}$, make sure that you use $\mu_{\bar{x}}$ and $\sigma_{\bar{x}}$. Also, because $\bar{x}$ is continuous, we do not adjust the endpoints, regardless of whether or not they are included.

65) Givens: $\mu = 23.88$, $\sigma = 3.561$, Normal Pop.

a) Since the population is normal, the possible values of $\bar{x}$ are normal (regardless of the sample size) with $\mu_{\bar{x}} = \mu = 23.88$

and $\sigma_{\bar{x}} \approx \frac{3.561}{\sqrt{14}} \approx 0.95172$.

b) We must use $\mu_{\bar{x}}$ and $\sigma_{\bar{x}}$ to calculate the z-scores.

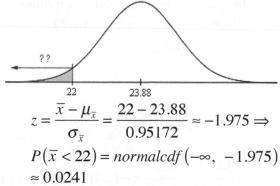

$$z = \frac{\bar{x} - \mu_{\bar{x}}}{\sigma_{\bar{x}}} = \frac{22 - 23.88}{0.95172} \approx -1.975 \Rightarrow$$

$$P(\bar{x} < 22) = normalcdf(-\infty, -1.975)$$

$$\approx 0.0241$$

c) Our first step is to convert this from a question about the sample total to a question about the sample mean. Recall:

$$\bar{x} = \frac{\sum x}{n}. \text{ So we must divide both sides by}$$

the sample size of 14.

$$P\left(\frac{\sum x}{14} \geq \frac{322}{14}\right) = P(\bar{x} \geq 23). \text{ Now we}$$

can find the z-scores and the area needed.

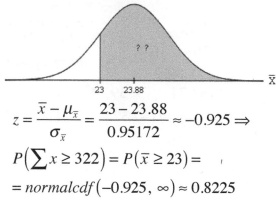

$$z = \frac{\bar{x} - \mu_{\bar{x}}}{\sigma_{\bar{x}}} = \frac{23 - 23.88}{0.95172} \approx -0.925 \Rightarrow$$

$$P\left(\sum x \geq 322\right) = P(\bar{x} \geq 23) =$$

$$= normalcdf(-0.925, \infty) \approx 0.8225$$

67) Givens: $\mu = 36.74$, $\sigma = 5.0807$, Uniform Pop

a) $15 \leq n = 19 < 30$ and we know that the population is uniform, which is not skewed at all. Therefore, $\bar{x}$ is approximately normally distributed with $\mu_{\bar{x}} = \mu = 36.74$ and

$$\sigma_{\bar{x}} \approx \frac{5.0807}{\sqrt{19}} \approx 1.1656.$$

b) In symbols, this translates as follows:

$$P(36.74 - 2 < \bar{x} < 36.74 + 2)$$
$$= P(34.74 < \bar{x} < 38.74)$$

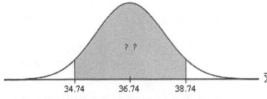

$$z_1 = \frac{34.74 - 36.74}{1.1656} \approx -1.716 \Rightarrow z_2 = 1.716 \Rightarrow$$
$$P(34.74 < \bar{x} < 38.74) =$$
$$normalcdf(-1.716,\ 1.716) \approx 0.9138$$

c) In symbols, this translates as follows:

$$P(36.74 - 3 < \bar{x} < 36.74 + 3)$$
$$= P(33.74 < \bar{x} < 39.74)$$

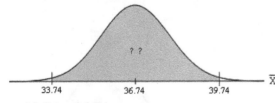

$$z_1 = \frac{33.74 - 36.74}{1.1656} \approx -2.574 \Rightarrow z_2 = 2.574 \Rightarrow$$
$$P(33.74 < \bar{x} < 39.74) =$$
$$normalcdf(-2.574,\ 2.574) \approx 0.9899$$

✓69) The problem states that the population is normal with $\mu = 200$ and $\sigma = 10.48$.

a) Since the population is normal, $\bar{x}$ is normal (regardless of the sample size) with

$$\mu_{\bar{x}} = \mu = 200 \text{ and } \sigma_{\bar{x}} \approx \frac{10.48}{\sqrt{15}} \approx 2.7059$$

b) We must use $\mu_{\bar{x}}$ and $\sigma_{\bar{x}}$ to calculate the z-score.

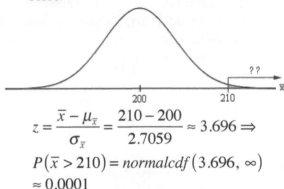

$$z = \frac{\bar{x} - \mu_{\bar{x}}}{\sigma_{\bar{x}}} = \frac{210 - 200}{2.7059} \approx 3.696 \Rightarrow$$
$$P(\bar{x} > 210) = normalcdf(3.696,\ \infty)$$
$$\approx 0.0001$$

c) In symbols, this translates as follows:

$$P(200 - 5 < \bar{x} < 200 + 5)$$
$$= P(195 < \bar{x} < 205)$$

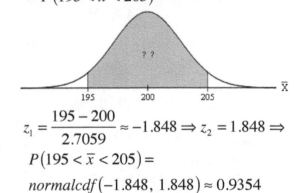

$$z_1 = \frac{195 - 200}{2.7059} \approx -1.848 \Rightarrow z_2 = 1.848 \Rightarrow$$
$$P(195 < \bar{x} < 205) =$$
$$normalcdf(-1.848,\ 1.848) \approx 0.9354$$

71) Givens: $\mu = 185$, $\sigma = 15$, $n = 28$, Slightly Right-Skewed Population

a) $15 \leq n = 28 < 30$ and population is not SEVERELY skewed, so $\bar{x}$ is approx. normally distributed with $\mu_{\bar{x}} = \mu = 185$ and $\sigma_{\bar{x}} \approx \dfrac{15}{\sqrt{28}} \approx 2.8347$.

b) In symbols, this translates as follows:
$$P(185 - 5 < \bar{x} < 185 + 5)$$
$$= P(180 < \bar{x} < 190)$$

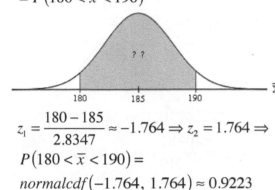

$$z_1 = \frac{180 - 185}{2.8347} \approx -1.764 \Rightarrow z_2 = 1.764 \Rightarrow$$
$$P(180 < \bar{x} < 190) =$$
$$normalcdf(-1.764,\ 1.764) \approx 0.9223$$

c) In symbols, this translates as follows:
$$P(185 - 10 < \bar{x} < 185 + 10)$$
$$= P(175 < \bar{x} < 195)$$

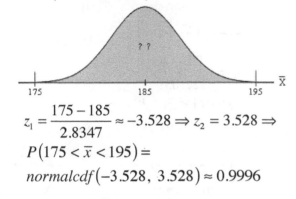

$$z_1 = \frac{175 - 185}{2.8347} \approx -3.528 \Rightarrow z_2 = 3.528 \Rightarrow$$
$$P(175 < \bar{x} < 195) =$$
$$normalcdf(-3.528,\ 3.528) \approx 0.9996$$

d) The first step is to convert this from a question about the total of the sample to a question about the sample mean.
$$P\left(\sum x \geq 5000\right) = P\left(\frac{\sum x}{28} \geq \frac{5000}{28}\right) \approx P(\bar{x} \geq 178.57)$$

$$z = \frac{178.57 - 185}{2.8347} \approx -2.268 \Rightarrow$$
$$P\left(\sum x \geq 5000\right) \approx P(\bar{x} \geq 178.57) =$$
$$normalcdf(-2.268,\ \infty) \approx 0.9883$$

e) By allowing more error, we are essentially lowering the standard. A lower standard should be easier to meet. More samples will now produce acceptable amounts of error.

73) The population has an unknown distribution with $\mu = 2.559$ and $\sigma = 0.3427$.

a) Since $n = 45 \geq 30$, $\bar{x}$ is normal with
$\mu_{\bar{x}} = \mu = 2.559$ and
$$\sigma_{\bar{x}} \approx \frac{0.3427}{\sqrt{45}} \approx 0.051087.$$

b) To say that the sampling error is less than \$0.05 means that the value of $\bar{x}$ lies within \$0.05 of the true mean of the population. So, we are looking for
$$P(\mu - 0.05 < \bar{x} < \mu + 0.05)$$
$$= P(2.509 < \bar{x} < 2.609).$$

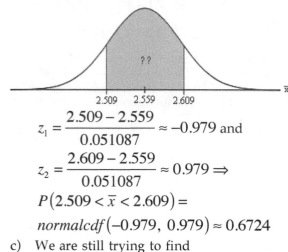

$$z_1 = \frac{2.509 - 2.559}{0.051087} \approx -0.979 \text{ and}$$
$$z_2 = \frac{2.609 - 2.559}{0.051087} \approx 0.979 \Rightarrow$$
$$P(2.509 < \bar{x} < 2.609) =$$
$$normalcdf(-0.979, \ 0.979) \approx 0.6724$$

c) We are still trying to find $P(2.509 < \bar{x} < 2.609)$, but the value of $\sigma_{\bar{x}}$ has changed due to the increased sample size. $\sigma_{\bar{x}} \approx \frac{0.3427}{\sqrt{500}} \approx 0.015326$

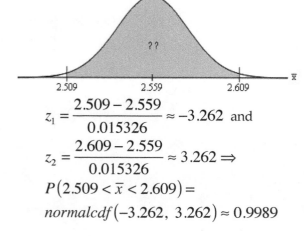

$$z_1 = \frac{2.509 - 2.559}{0.015326} \approx -3.262 \text{ and}$$
$$z_2 = \frac{2.609 - 2.559}{0.015326} \approx 3.262 \Rightarrow$$
$$P(2.509 < \bar{x} < 2.609) =$$
$$normalcdf(-3.262, \ 3.262) \approx 0.9989$$

d) More data should always tend to produce better estimates. The larger sample size decreases the standard deviation of $\bar{x}$. This in turn pushes the possible values of $\bar{x}$ closer to μ, thus giving us a better chance of getting an acceptable amount of error.

75) Givens: $\mu = 82.7$, $\sigma = 12.584$, $n = 43$

a) Since $n = 43 \geq 30$, $\bar{x}$ is normal with
$$\mu_{\bar{x}} = \mu = 82.7 \text{ and } \sigma_{\bar{x}} \approx \frac{12.584}{\sqrt{43}} \approx 1.919.$$

b) In symbols, $P(\bar{x} \leq 80)$.

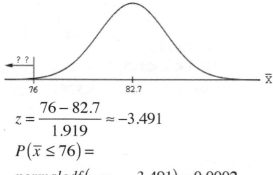

$$z = \frac{80 - 82.7}{1.919} \approx -1.407$$
$$P(\bar{x} \leq 80) =$$
$$normalcdf(-\infty, \ -1.407) \approx 0.0797$$

c) Random variation is our default explanation for such differences. Because there is more than a 5% chance of differences just due to random variation, random variation remains a plausible explanation.

d) In symbols, $P(\bar{x} \leq 76)$.

$$z = \frac{76 - 82.7}{1.919} \approx -3.491$$
$$P(\bar{x} \leq 76) =$$
$$normalcdf(-\infty, \ -3.491) \approx 0.0002$$

e) The chance of the class average being 76 or lower just due to random variation is extremely small, so that is not a very likely explanation. Because of this, we will say that this sample produced strong evidence that something has changed and her true average is now less than 82.7 pts.

Chapter Problem:

The problem states that the standard deviation of all such cans is 0.2306 oz. Because this value is for all the cans, it is the population standard deviation, σ. They say the sample size will be 40 cans, so $n = 40$.

a) $\mu_{\bar{x}} = \mu = 12$ and

$$\sigma_{\bar{x}} \approx \frac{\sigma}{\sqrt{n}} = \frac{0.2306}{\sqrt{40}} \approx 0.036461$$

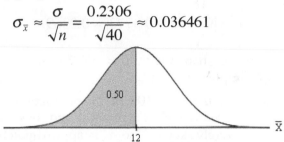

   Since we want exactly the left half of the area under the curve, we know the area is 0.5 without using z-scores or normalcdf.

   $$P(\bar{x} < 12 \mid \mu = 12) = 0.5$$

b) No, since $n = 40 \geq 30$, we know that $\bar{x}$ will be normally distributed regardless of the distribution of the population.

c) $\mu_{\bar{x}}$ and $\sigma_{\bar{x}}$ are the same as in part (a).

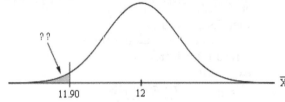

   $$z = \frac{11.9 - 12}{0.036461} \approx -2.743 \Rightarrow P(\bar{x} < 11.9 \mid \mu = 12)$$

   $$= normalcdf(-\infty, -2.743) \approx 0.0030$$

   Since this is less than a 1% chance of making a false accusation, it seems low enough to be acceptable.

d) This time we will use $\mu_{\bar{x}} = \mu = 11.95$.

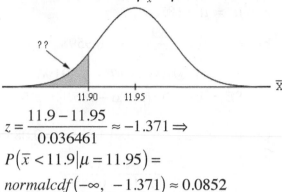

$$z = \frac{11.9 - 11.95}{0.036461} \approx -1.371 \Rightarrow$$

$$P(\bar{x} < 11.9 \mid \mu = 11.95) =$$

$$normalcdf(-\infty, -1.371) \approx 0.0852$$

There is only an 8.52% chance that our sample will provide a sample mean low enough for us to make an accusation against the company. So, even though they are cheating us a little bit, they will probably get away with it.

Review Exercises:

1) Givens: $\mu = 185.1$, $\sigma = 39.055$, $n = 19$

   a) $\mu_{\bar{x}} = \mu = 185.1$

   b) $\sigma_{\bar{x}} \approx \dfrac{\sigma}{\sqrt{n}} = \dfrac{39.055}{\sqrt{19}} \approx 8.9598$

   c) $2\sigma_{\bar{x}} = 17.9196 \Rightarrow EE < 17.9196$

   d) $SE = |\bar{x} - \mu| = |179.6 - 185.1| = 5.5$

3) Givens: $n = 57$, $p = 0.9144 \Rightarrow q = 0.0856$

   a) $\mu_{\hat{p}} = p = 0.9144$

   b) $\sigma_{\hat{p}} = \sqrt{\dfrac{pq}{n}} = \sqrt{\dfrac{0.9144 * 0.0856}{57}} \approx 0.037057$

   c) $2\sigma_{\hat{p}} = 0.074114 \Rightarrow EE < 0.074114$

   d) $\hat{p} = \dfrac{x}{n} = \dfrac{54}{57} \approx 0.9474 \Rightarrow$

      $SE = |\hat{p} - p| = |0.9474 - 0.9144| = 0.0330$

5) $n = 618$, $p = 0.3773$, and $q = 0.6227$.

   a) $np = 618 * 0.3773 \geq 10$ and

      $nq = 618 * 0.6227 \geq 10 \Rightarrow \hat{p}$ is approximately normally distributed with $\mu_{\hat{p}} = p = 0.3773$ and

      $\sigma_{\hat{p}} = \sqrt{\dfrac{pq}{n}} \approx 0.019498$.

   b) $z = \dfrac{0.35 - 0.3773}{0.019498} \approx -1.400 \Rightarrow$

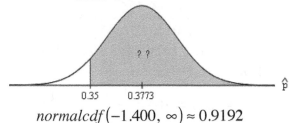

      $normalcdf(-1.400, \infty) \approx 0.9192$

   c) No. $P(\hat{p} = p) \approx 0$.

   d) $P(0.3773 - 0.0350 < \hat{p} < 0.3773 + 0.0350)$

      $= P(0.3423 < \hat{p} < 0.4123)$

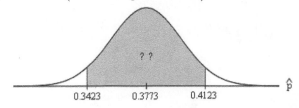

$z_1 = \dfrac{0.3423 - 0.3773}{0.019498} \approx -1.795$

$z_2 = \dfrac{0.4123 - 0.3773}{0.019498} \approx 1.795 \Rightarrow$

$normalcdf(-1.795, 1.795) \approx 0.9273$

   e) $\hat{p} = \dfrac{256}{618} \approx 0.4142 \Rightarrow$

      $E = |0.4142 - 0.3773| = 0.0369$

7) Pop is U-shaped with $\mu = 306.74$ and $\sigma = 53.807$.

   a) $15 \leq n = 26 < 30$ and the population is U-shaped (which is symmetric and thus NOT severely skewed), so $\bar{x}$ is approximately normally distributed with $\mu_{\bar{x}} = \mu = 306.74$ and

      $\sigma_{\bar{x}} \approx \dfrac{\sigma}{\sqrt{n}} = \dfrac{53.807}{\sqrt{26}} \approx 10.552$.

   b) The first step is to convert this from a question about the sample total to a question about the sample mean.

      $P\left(\sum x \leq 8320\right) = P\left(\dfrac{\sum x}{26} \leq \dfrac{8320}{26}\right) = P(\bar{x} \leq 320)$

      $z = \dfrac{320 - 306.74}{10.552} \approx 1.257 \Rightarrow$

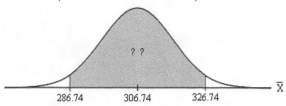

      $P\left(\sum x \leq 8320\right) = P(\bar{x} \leq 320) =$

      $normalcdf(-\infty, 1.257) \approx 0.8956$

   c) No. $P(\bar{x} = \mu) \approx 0$.

   d) $P(306.74 - 20 < \bar{x} < 306.74 + 20)$

      $= P(286.74 < \bar{x} < 326.74)$

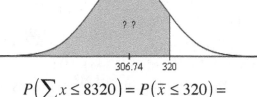

$$z_1 = \frac{286.74 - 306.74}{10.552} \approx -1.895$$

$$z_2 = \frac{326.74 - 306.74}{10.552} \approx 1.895 \Rightarrow$$

$normalcdf(-1.895, 1.895) \approx 0.9419$

e) $\bar{x} = 298.54 \Rightarrow E = |298.54 - 306.74| = 8.2$

9) Population distribution shape is unknown with $\mu = 4019.77$ and $\sigma = 2861.82$.

 a) $n = 152 \geq 30 \Rightarrow \bar{x}$ is normal with $\mu_{\bar{x}} = 4019.77$ and

 $$\sigma_{\bar{x}} \approx \frac{2861.82}{\sqrt{152}} \approx 232.12 .$$

 b) $EE < 2\sigma_{\bar{x}} = 2 * 232.12 = 464.24$
 So, we expect the error to be less than $464.24.

 c) $P(4019.77 - 250 < \bar{x} < 4019.77 + 250)$
 $= P(3769.77 < \bar{x} < 4269.77)$

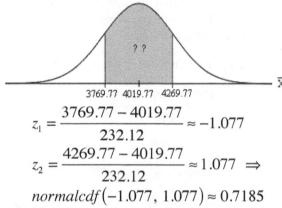

$$z_1 = \frac{3769.77 - 4019.77}{232.12} \approx -1.077$$

$$z_2 = \frac{4269.77 - 4019.77}{232.12} \approx 1.077 \Rightarrow$$

$normalcdf(-1.077, 1.077) \approx 0.7185$

 d) Increase the sample size.

 e) $n = 677 \Rightarrow \sigma_{\bar{x}} \approx \frac{2861.82}{\sqrt{677}} \approx 109.99$

 $$z_1 = \frac{3769.77 - 4019.77}{109.99} \approx -2.273$$

 $$z_2 = \frac{4269.77 - 4019.77}{109.99} \approx 2.273 \Rightarrow$$

 $normalcdf(-2.273, 2.273) \approx 0.9770$

 f) $P\left(\sum x < 550000\right) = P\left(\frac{\sum x}{152} < \frac{550000}{152}\right) \approx$

 $P(\bar{x} < 3618.42)$

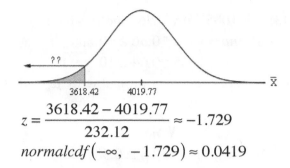

$$z = \frac{3618.42 - 4019.77}{232.12} \approx -1.729$$

$normalcdf(-\infty, -1.729) \approx 0.0419$

11) $n = 491$, $p = 0.1267$, and $q = 0.8733$.

 a) $np = 491 * 0.1267 \geq 10$ and
 $nq = 491 * 0.8733 \geq 10 \Rightarrow \hat{p}$ is
 approximately normal with $\mu_{\hat{p}} = 0.1267$

 and $\sigma_{\hat{p}} = \sqrt{\frac{pq}{n}} \approx 0.015012$.

 b) $EE < 2\sigma_{\hat{p}} = 2 * 0.015012 = 0.030024$
 So, we expect the error to be less than
 0.030024 or 3.0024%.

 c) $P(0.1267 - 0.03 < \hat{p} < 0.1267 + 0.03)$
 $= P(0.0967 < \hat{p} < 0.1567)$

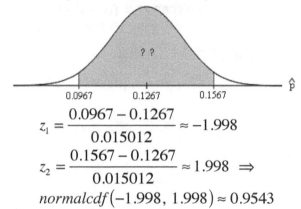

$$z_1 = \frac{0.0967 - 0.1267}{0.015012} \approx -1.998$$

$$z_2 = \frac{0.1567 - 0.1267}{0.015012} \approx 1.998 \Rightarrow$$

$normalcdf(-1.998, 1.998) \approx 0.9543$

 d) Increase the sample size.

 e) $n = 1291 \Rightarrow \sigma_{\hat{p}} = \sqrt{\frac{pq}{n}} \approx 0.0092578$

 $$z_1 = \frac{0.0967 - 0.1267}{0.0092578} \approx -3.241$$

 $$z_2 = \frac{0.1567 - 0.1267}{0.0092578} \approx 3.241 \Rightarrow$$

 $normalcdf(-3.241, 3.241) \approx 0.9988$

13) $n = 1005$, $p = 0.36$, and $q = 0.64$.

   a) $np = 1005 * 0.36 \geq 10$ and

      $nq = 1005 * 0.64 \geq 10 \Rightarrow \hat{p}$ is

      approximately normal with $\mu_{\hat{p}} = 0.36$

      and $\sigma_{\hat{p}} = \sqrt{\dfrac{pq}{n}} \approx 0.015141$.

   b) In symbols, $P(\hat{p} \geq 0.50)$.

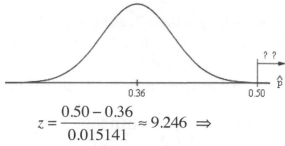

      $z = \dfrac{0.50 - 0.36}{0.015141} \approx 9.246 \Rightarrow$

      $normalcdf(9.046, \infty) \approx 0.0000$

   c) Even though our default explanation for differences from the expected percentage of 36% is random variation, we saw in part (b) that there is almost no chance of this big of a difference being due to random variation. Because the chance of the difference occurring due to random variation is less than 5%, we should now start to believe that the true percentage has increased.

14) $\mu = 84$ and $\sigma = 73.2$

   a) $n = 37 \geq 30 \Rightarrow \bar{x}$ is approximately normal with $\mu_{\bar{x}} = 84$ and

      $\sigma_{\bar{x}} \approx \dfrac{73.2}{\sqrt{37}} \approx 12.034$.

   b) In symbols, $P(\bar{x} < 70)$.

      $z = \dfrac{70 - 84}{12.034} \approx -1.163 \Rightarrow$

      $normalcdf(-\infty, -1.163) \approx 0.1224$

   c) Because there is a 12.24% chance of seeing such a difference from the expected 84 seconds just due to random variation, we will conclude that it is reasonable that this difference is just due to random variation. We conclude this because 12.24% > 5%.

Section 8.1:

1) When estimating a population proportion, our point estimate will be the sample proportion.

2) Because we do not expect our point estimate to be correct, we add and subtract an amount from it to form a confidence interval. The amount added and subtracted is referred to as the margin of error.

3) When we expand our estimate to a confidence interval, the confidence percentage stated is known as the confidence level.

4) When we say we are 95% (or some other %) confident that our interval contains the population proportion, this means that in the long run, about 95% of such intervals will contain the true population proportion.

5) The requirement for finding a confidence interval for a proportion is that $n\hat{p} \geq 10$ and $n\hat{q} \geq 10$. Or, equivalently, we can verify that we have at least 10 successes and at least 10 failures.

6) For a fixed sample size, the higher the confidence level, the wider the interval and vice versa.

7) The procedure learned in this section is designed to find confidence intervals for population proportions, but it can also be used to find confidence intervals for percentages and probabilities.

8) A confidence interval provides us with a list of the reasonable possibilities for the population proportion.

9) To be confident that the population proportion is larger than a given value, the entire range of reasonable possibilities must be larger than the value in question.

10) If any value in the interval fails to meet a requested condition, then we cannot be confident that the true proportion meets the condition.

11) Givens: $n = 561$, $x = 200$

a) $\hat{p} = \dfrac{x}{n} = \dfrac{200}{561} \approx 0.3565$

b) 68.27% confidence $\Rightarrow z^* = 1$.

$$\hat{p} \pm z^* \cdot \sqrt{\dfrac{\hat{p}\hat{q}}{n}} =$$

$$0.3565 \pm 1 \cdot \sqrt{\dfrac{0.3565 * 0.6435}{561}} \approx$$

$$0.3565 \pm 0.0202 \Rightarrow p \in (0.3363, 0.3767)$$

c) 95.45% confidence $\Rightarrow z^* = 2$.

$$\hat{p} \pm z^* \cdot \sqrt{\dfrac{\hat{p}\hat{q}}{n}} =$$

$$0.3565 \pm 2 \cdot \sqrt{\dfrac{0.3565 * 0.6435}{561}} \approx$$

$$0.3565 \pm 0.0404 \Rightarrow p \in (0.3161, 0.3969)$$

d) 99.73% confidence $\Rightarrow z^* = 3$.

$$\hat{p} \pm z^* \cdot \sqrt{\dfrac{\hat{p}\hat{q}}{n}} =$$

$$0.3565 \pm 3 \cdot \sqrt{\dfrac{0.3565 * 0.6435}{561}} \approx$$

$$0.3565 \pm 0.0607 \Rightarrow p \in (0.2958, 0.4172)$$

e) The higher the confidence level, the wider the confidence interval.

13) Givens: $n = 318$, $x = 197$

a) $\hat{p} = \dfrac{197}{318} \approx 0.6195$

b) We need the z-scores for 95% confidence.

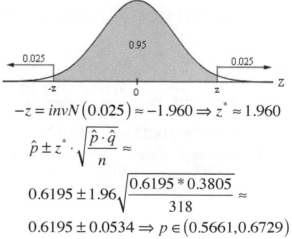

$$-z = invN(0.025) \approx -1.960 \Rightarrow z^* \approx 1.960$$

$$\hat{p} \pm z^* \cdot \sqrt{\dfrac{\hat{p} \cdot \hat{q}}{n}} \approx$$

$$0.6195 \pm 1.96 \sqrt{\dfrac{0.6195 * 0.3805}{318}} \approx$$

$$0.6195 \pm 0.0534 \Rightarrow p \in (0.5661, 0.6729)$$

c) The margin of error is the part we add and subtract to get the boundaries. $E = 0.0534$

15) Givens: $n = 613$, $\hat{p} = 0.3442$

   a) We need the z-scores for 90% confidence.

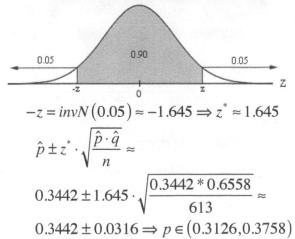

$$-z = invN(0.05) \approx -1.645 \Rightarrow z^* \approx 1.645$$

$$\hat{p} \pm z^* \cdot \sqrt{\frac{\hat{p} \cdot \hat{q}}{n}} \approx$$

$$0.3442 \pm 1.645 \cdot \sqrt{\frac{0.3442 * 0.6558}{613}} \approx$$

$$0.3442 \pm 0.0316 \Rightarrow p \in (0.3126, 0.3758)$$

   b) $n\hat{p} = 613 * 0.3442 \approx 211 \geq 10$ and
$n\hat{q} = 613 * 0.6558 \approx 402 \geq 10$, so the requirements have been met.

17) Givens: $n = 40,104$, $x = 3,195$

   a) $\hat{p} = \dfrac{x}{n} = \dfrac{3195}{40104} \approx 0.0797$

   b) $P(\hat{p} = p) \approx 0$. Due to the random variation in our sample, it is often nearly impossible to get the true proportion exactly correct from a sample.

   c) We need the z-scores for 95% confidence.

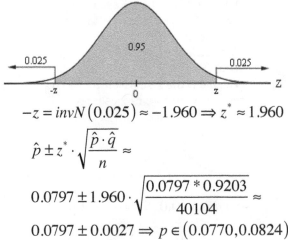

$$-z = invN(0.025) \approx -1.960 \Rightarrow z^* \approx 1.960$$

$$\hat{p} \pm z^* \cdot \sqrt{\frac{\hat{p} \cdot \hat{q}}{n}} \approx$$

$$0.0797 \pm 1.960 \cdot \sqrt{\frac{0.0797 * 0.9203}{40104}} \approx$$

$$0.0797 \pm 0.0027 \Rightarrow p \in (0.0770, 0.0824)$$

   d) Our sample contained 3,195 successes and 36,909 failures. Both of these are way over 10, so the requirements have been met.

19) Givens: $n = 556$ and $x = 206$

   a) $\hat{p} = \dfrac{x}{n} = \dfrac{206}{556} \approx 0.3705$

   b) We need the z-scores for 99% confidence.

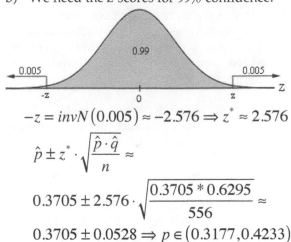

$$-z = invN(0.005) \approx -2.576 \Rightarrow z^* \approx 2.576$$

$$\hat{p} \pm z^* \cdot \sqrt{\frac{\hat{p} \cdot \hat{q}}{n}} \approx$$

$$0.3705 \pm 2.576 \cdot \sqrt{\frac{0.3705 * 0.6295}{556}} \approx$$

$$0.3705 \pm 0.0528 \Rightarrow p \in (0.3177, 0.4233)$$

   c) Just using the point estimate, we have 0% confidence that we have the true proportion. However, when we add and subtract the margin of error, we become 99% confident that we have captured the true proportion. Therefore, we must be 99% confident that the point estimate is within 0.0528 of the true proportion.

   d) We are 99% confident that the true percentage of all Wisconsin residents who approve of the job the Governor is doing is somewhere between 31.77% and 42.33%.

21) Givens: $n = 2,077$, $\hat{p} = 0.4179$

a) $n\hat{p} = 2077 * 0.4179 \approx 868 \geq 10$ and
$n\hat{q} = 2077 * 0.5821 \approx 1209 \geq 10$, so the requirements have been met.

b) We need the z-scores for 90% confidence.

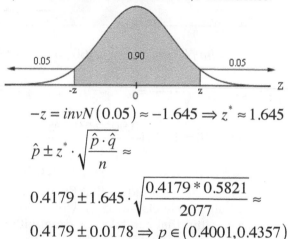

$-z = invN(0.05) \approx -1.645 \Rightarrow z^* \approx 1.645$

$$\hat{p} \pm z^* \cdot \sqrt{\frac{\hat{p} \cdot \hat{q}}{n}} \approx$$

$$0.4179 \pm 1.645 \cdot \sqrt{\frac{0.4179 * 0.5821}{2077}} \approx$$

$$0.4179 \pm 0.0178 \Rightarrow p \in (0.4001, 0.4357)$$

c) We are 90% confident that the true proportion of video game players that are female is somewhere between 40.01% and 43.57%.

23) Givens: $n = 1200$, $x = 49$

a) $\hat{p} = \dfrac{x}{n} = \dfrac{49}{1200} \approx 0.0408$

We need the z-scores for 95% confidence.

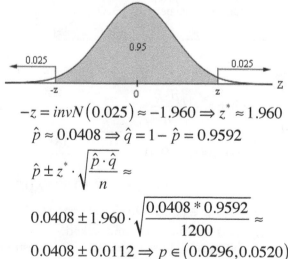

$-z = invN(0.025) \approx -1.960 \Rightarrow z^* \approx 1.960$

$\hat{p} \approx 0.0408 \Rightarrow \hat{q} = 1 - \hat{p} = 0.9592$

$$\hat{p} \pm z^* \cdot \sqrt{\frac{\hat{p} \cdot \hat{q}}{n}} \approx$$

$$0.0408 \pm 1.960 \cdot \sqrt{\frac{0.0408 * 0.9592}{1200}} \approx$$

$$0.0408 \pm 0.0112 \Rightarrow p \in (0.0296, 0.0520)$$

b) Yes, $p \in (0.0296, 0.0520) \Rightarrow p > 0.014$.

c) Personally, being around in California during this time period, I think the increase in the percentage of those manipulating such devices is due to an overall increase in the use of such devices.

25) Givens: $n = 8,210$ and $\hat{p} = 0.6217$

a) $x = n\hat{p} = 8210 * 0.6217 \geq 10$ and
$n - x = n\hat{q} = 8210 * 0.3783 \geq 10$, so the requirements have been met.

b) We need the z-scores for 90% confidence.

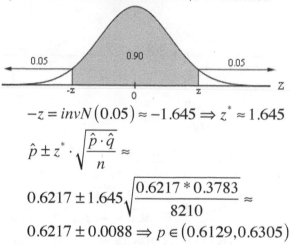

$-z = invN(0.05) \approx -1.645 \Rightarrow z^* \approx 1.645$

$$\hat{p} \pm z^* \cdot \sqrt{\frac{\hat{p} \cdot \hat{q}}{n}} \approx$$

$$0.6217 \pm 1.645 \sqrt{\frac{0.6217 * 0.3783}{8210}} \approx$$

$$0.6217 \pm 0.0088 \Rightarrow p \in (0.6129, 0.6305)$$

c) Yes, $p \in (0.6129, 0.6305) \Rightarrow p > 0.5$

d) To covert from the proportion of successes in the population to the number of successes in the population, we just need to multiply by the population size, $N = 740,000$.
$740000 * 0.6129 = 453,546$ and
$740000 * 0.6305 = 466,570$. Therefore, we are 90% confident that somewhere between 453,546 and 466,570 of the 740,000 Atlantic Canadian Region high school students have consumed an energy drink in the previous year.

e) Our sample was only from high school students in the Atlantic Canadian Region and we have no reason to believe that this region would be representative of all of North America.

27) Givens: $n = 1006$ and $x = 647$

a) $x = 647 \geq 10$ and $n - x = 359 \geq 10$, so the requirements have been met.

b) We need the z-scores for 95% confidence.

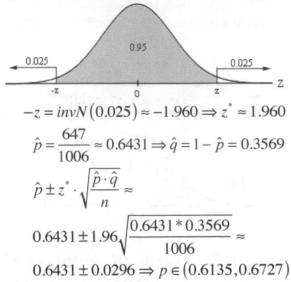

$$-z = invN(0.025) \approx -1.960 \Rightarrow z^* \approx 1.960$$

$$\hat{p} = \frac{647}{1006} \approx 0.6431 \Rightarrow \hat{q} = 1 - \hat{p} = 0.3569$$

$$\hat{p} \pm z^* \cdot \sqrt{\frac{\hat{p} \cdot \hat{q}}{n}} \approx$$

$$0.6431 \pm 1.96 \sqrt{\frac{0.6431 * 0.3569}{1006}} \approx$$

$$0.6431 \pm 0.0296 \Rightarrow p \in (0.6135, 0.6727)$$

c) No, $p \in (0.6135, 0.6727) \Rightarrow$ It is reasonable that p could be 0.67, which is more than 2/3.

d) To covert from the proportion of successes in the population to the number of successes in the population, we just need to multiply by the population size, $N = 147,000,000$.
$147000000 * 0.6135 = 90,184,500$ and
$147000000 * 0.6727 = 98,886,900$.
Therefore, we are 95% confident that somewhere between 90,184,500 and 98,886,900 of the 147,000,000 registered voters would have said that they felt this targeting was an example of corruption at the IRS.

29) Givens: $n = 184$ and $\hat{p} = 0.9050$

a) We need the z-scores for 95% confidence.

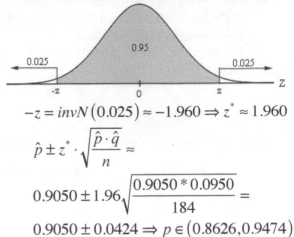

$$-z = invN(0.025) \approx -1.960 \Rightarrow z^* \approx 1.960$$

$$\hat{p} \pm z^* \cdot \sqrt{\frac{\hat{p} \cdot \hat{q}}{n}} \approx$$

$$0.9050 \pm 1.96 \sqrt{\frac{0.9050 * 0.0950}{184}} =$$

$$0.9050 \pm 0.0424 \Rightarrow p \in (0.8626, 0.9474)$$

b) We are 95% confident that the proportion of all people classified as allergic to penicillin that can take the drug without an adverse effect is somewhere between 0.8626 and 0.9474.

31) Givens: $n = 100$, $x = 62$

a) $\hat{p} = \frac{x}{n} = \frac{62}{100} \approx 0.62$

We need the z-scores for 95% confidence.

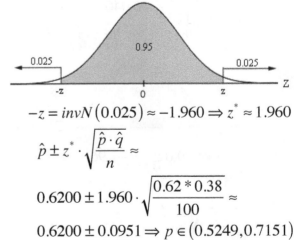

$$-z = invN(0.025) \approx -1.960 \Rightarrow z^* \approx 1.960$$

$$\hat{p} \pm z^* \cdot \sqrt{\frac{\hat{p} \cdot \hat{q}}{n}} \approx$$

$$0.6200 \pm 1.960 \cdot \sqrt{\frac{0.62 * 0.38}{100}} \approx$$

$$0.6200 \pm 0.0951 \Rightarrow p \in (0.5249, 0.7151)$$

b) Yes, $p \in (0.5249, 0.7151) \Rightarrow p > 0.5$

c) This sample was handpicked. We purposely chose the most unusual result out of the 40 experiments in the class.

d) The coin could be biased, but it could also easily just have had so many heads due to random variation. While 62 heads in 100 tosses is considered unusual. It actually took 40 people trying to get this result.

Section 8.2:

33) When we increase our sample size, it <u>decreases</u> the margin of error.

34) When calculating sample size requirements, we always round n <u>up</u> to the next whole number.

35) When determining the sample size required to obtain a desired margin of error in proportion problems, we must <u>guess</u> at the value of the population proportion.

36) If we have no previous information to help us make a guess at the value of the population proportion, then we should use <u>0.5</u> as our guess.

37) When making a guess at the value of p, we always choose the possibility that is closest to 0.5. This way our sample size is never too small.

a) $p \in (0.358, 0.444) \Rightarrow p_g = 0.444$

b) $p \in (0.764, 0.810) \Rightarrow p_g = 0.764$

c) $p \in (0.457, 0.561) \Rightarrow p_g = 0.5$

Note: On the last one, the interval contained the value of 0.5, so that is the closest value in the interval to 0.5.

39) Givens: We want $E = 0.03$ and for a confidence level of 90%, the z-scores are:

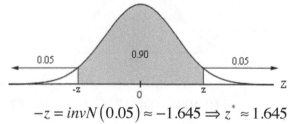

$-z = invN(0.05) \approx -1.645 \Rightarrow z^* \approx 1.645$

a) $p \in (0.34, 0.58) \Rightarrow p_g = 0.5 \Rightarrow$

$$n = p_g \cdot (1 - p_g) \cdot \left(\frac{z^*}{E}\right)^2 =$$

$$0.5 * 0.5 * \left(\frac{1.645}{0.03}\right)^2 \approx 751.67 \Rightarrow n = 752$$

b) $p \in [0, 0.34) \Rightarrow p_g = 0.34 \Rightarrow$

$$n = p_g \cdot (1 - p_g) \cdot \left(\frac{z^*}{E}\right)^2 =$$

$$0.34 * 0.66 * \left(\frac{1.645}{0.03}\right)^2 \approx 674.70 \Rightarrow n = 675$$

41) Givens: $(0.7582, 0.8216)$ and 95% confidence

a) $\hat{p}$ should be directly in the center of the confidence interval. We can average the endpoints to find $\hat{p}$.

$$\hat{p} = \frac{0.7582 + 0.8216}{2} = 0.7899$$

The margin of error is the distance from $\hat{p}$ to either endpoint of the interval.
$E = 0.8216 - 0.7899 = 0.0317$

b) For a confidence level of 95% we get:

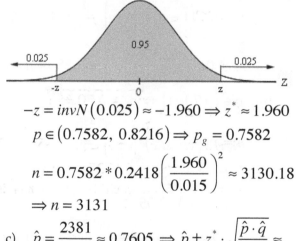

$-z = invN(0.025) \approx -1.960 \Rightarrow z^* \approx 1.960$

$p \in (0.7582, 0.8216) \Rightarrow p_g = 0.7582$

$$n = 0.7582 * 0.2418 \left(\frac{1.960}{0.015}\right)^2 \approx 3130.18$$

$\Rightarrow n = 3131$

c) $\hat{p} = \frac{2381}{3131} \approx 0.7605 \Rightarrow \hat{p} \pm z^* \cdot \sqrt{\frac{\hat{p} \cdot \hat{q}}{n}} \approx$

$$0.7605 \pm 1.96 \sqrt{\frac{0.7605 * 0.2395}{3131}} =$$

$0.7605 \pm 0.0149 \Rightarrow p \in (0.7456, 0.7754)$

d) No it did not match exactly, but it was close. The new margin of error was 0.0149 and it was requested that it be at most 0.015. By choosing $p_g = 0.7582$ we were trying to make sure that our margin of error was not too large. By doing this, sometimes your margin of error will be slightly smaller than requested. This is not a problem.

43) Givens: $E = 0.05$ and for a confidence level of 99%, the z-scores are:

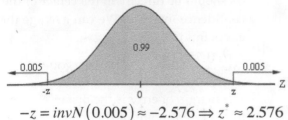

$$-z = invN(0.005) \approx -2.576 \Rightarrow z^* \approx 2.576$$

a) No idea $\Rightarrow p_g = 0.5 \Rightarrow$

$$n = p_g \cdot (1 - p_g) \cdot \left(\frac{z^*}{E}\right)^2 =$$

$$0.5 * 0.5 * \left(\frac{2.576}{0.05}\right)^2 \approx 663.58 \Rightarrow n = 664$$

b) $p \in (0.70, 1] \Rightarrow p_g = 0.70 \Rightarrow$

$$n = p_g \cdot (1 - p_g) \cdot \left(\frac{z^*}{E}\right)^2 =$$

$$0.7 * 0.3 * \left(\frac{2.576}{0.05}\right)^2 \approx 557.41 \Rightarrow n = 558$$

45) Givens: $E = 0.03$ and for a confidence level of 95%, the z-scores are:

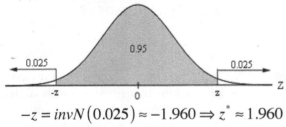

$$-z = invN(0.025) \approx -1.960 \Rightarrow z^* \approx 1.960$$

a) No idea $\Rightarrow p_g = 0.5 \Rightarrow$

$$n = p_g \cdot (1 - p_g) \cdot \left(\frac{z^*}{E}\right)^2 =$$

$$0.5 * 0.5 * \left(\frac{1.960}{0.03}\right)^2 \approx 1067.11 \Rightarrow n = 1068$$

b) $p \in (0.80, 1] \Rightarrow p_g = 0.80 \Rightarrow$

$$n = p_g \cdot (1 - p_g) \cdot \left(\frac{z^*}{E}\right)^2 =$$

$$0.8 * 0.2 * \left(\frac{1.960}{0.03}\right)^2 \approx 682.95 \Rightarrow n = 683$$

47) Let's start by finding the z-scores for 99% confidence.

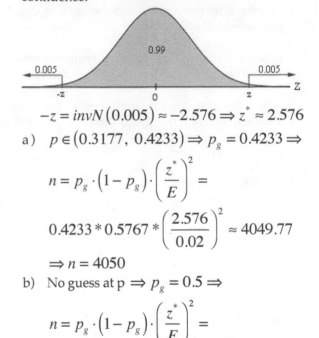

$$-z = invN(0.005) \approx -2.576 \Rightarrow z^* \approx 2.576$$

a) $p \in (0.3177, 0.4233) \Rightarrow p_g = 0.4233 \Rightarrow$

$$n = p_g \cdot (1 - p_g) \cdot \left(\frac{z^*}{E}\right)^2 =$$

$$0.4233 * 0.5767 * \left(\frac{2.576}{0.02}\right)^2 \approx 4049.77$$

$$\Rightarrow n = 4050$$

b) No guess at p $\Rightarrow p_g = 0.5 \Rightarrow$

$$n = p_g \cdot (1 - p_g) \cdot \left(\frac{z^*}{E}\right)^2 =$$

$$0.5 * 0.5 * \left(\frac{2.576}{0.02}\right)^2 = 4147.36 \Rightarrow n = 4148$$

49) Let's start by finding the z-scores for 90% confidence.

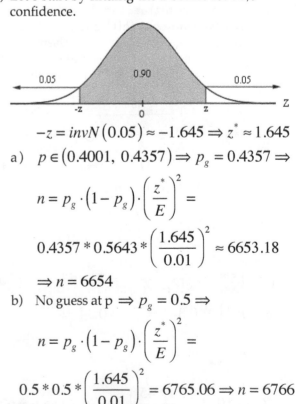

$$-z = invN(0.05) \approx -1.645 \Rightarrow z^* \approx 1.645$$

a) $p \in (0.4001, 0.4357) \Rightarrow p_g = 0.4357 \Rightarrow$

$$n = p_g \cdot (1 - p_g) \cdot \left(\frac{z^*}{E}\right)^2 =$$

$$0.4357 * 0.5643 * \left(\frac{1.645}{0.01}\right)^2 \approx 6653.18$$

$$\Rightarrow n = 6654$$

b) No guess at p $\Rightarrow p_g = 0.5 \Rightarrow$

$$n = p_g \cdot (1 - p_g) \cdot \left(\frac{z^*}{E}\right)^2 =$$

$$0.5 * 0.5 * \left(\frac{1.645}{0.01}\right)^2 = 6765.06 \Rightarrow n = 6766$$

<u>Section 8.3:</u>

51) t-curves are similar in shape to the z-curve except that they tend to be <u>shorter</u> and <u>wider</u>.

52) There are many different t-curves. Each curve has its own degree of freedom. The formula for finding the degrees of freedom is $df = $ <u>n- 1</u>.

53) As the df increases, t-curves look more and more like the <u>standard</u> <u>normal</u> curve.

54) We must use a t-curve when σ is <u>unknown</u> and we have replaced it with <u>s</u>.

55) When using the invT function, we must always enter the area to the <u>left</u> of the t-score we are looking for.

56) The requirements for the confidence interval are designed to make sure that $\bar{x}$ is normally distributed. This ensures that our <u>confidence</u> <u>level</u> is accurate.

57) A confidence interval provides us with a list of the <u>reasonable</u> <u>possibilities</u> for the true value of the population mean.

58) False. The fact that it is in the interval makes it a reasonable possibility, but only 1 of many reasonable possibilities. Therefore, a confidence interval can never make us confident that a specific value is the correct mean.

59) a) $-t_{0.05} = invT(0.05, 19) \approx -1.729 \Rightarrow$

$t_{0.05} \approx 1.729$

b) $-t_{0.05} = invT(0.05, 29) \approx -1.699 \Rightarrow$

$t_{0.05} \approx 1.699$

c) $-t_{0.01} = invT(0.01, 13) \approx -2.650 \Rightarrow$

$t_{0.01} \approx 2.650$

d) $-z_{0.005} = invNorm(0.005) \approx -2.576 \Rightarrow$

$z_{0.005} \approx 2.576$

Note: z-scores do not have a df associated with them.

61) a) $n = 23 \Rightarrow df = 23 - 1 = 22$

$-t_{0.025} = invT(0.025, 22) \approx -2.074 \Rightarrow$

$t_{0.025} \approx 2.074$

b) $n = 76 \Rightarrow df = 76 - 1 = 75$

$-t_{0.1} = invT(0.1, 75) \approx -1.293 \Rightarrow$

$t_{0.1} \approx 1.293$

c) $n = 31 \Rightarrow df = 31 - 1 = 30$

$-t_{0.05} = invT(0.05, 30) \approx -1.697 \Rightarrow$

$t_{0.05} \approx 1.697$

d) $-z_{0.01} = invNorm(0.01) \approx -2.326 \Rightarrow$

$z_{0.01} \approx 2.326$

Note: z-scores do not have a df associated with them, so the sample size is irrelevant.

63) Givens: $n = 76$, $\bar{x} = 18.93$, and $s = 4.078$.

a) Since $n = 76 \geq 30$, the CLT tells us that $\bar{x}$ will be normally distributed. Thus the requirements have been met.

b) We need the t-scores for 95% confidence.

$n = 76 \Rightarrow df = 76 - 1 = 75$

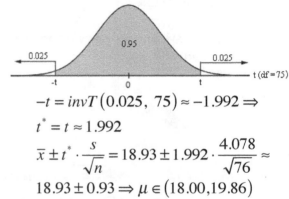

$-t = invT(0.025, 75) \approx -1.992 \Rightarrow$

$t^* = t \approx 1.992$

$\bar{x} \pm t^* \cdot \dfrac{s}{\sqrt{n}} = 18.93 \pm 1.992 \cdot \dfrac{4.078}{\sqrt{76}} \approx$

$18.93 \pm 0.93 \Rightarrow \mu \in (18.00, 19.86)$

c) The margin of error is the part we added and subtracted to get the boundaries, therefore, $E = 0.93$.

65) Givens: $n = 19$, $\bar{x} = 36.025$, $s = 9.0707$

 a) Because $15 \le n = 19 < 30$ and the population is unknown, we must hope that the population is not severely skewed. We need this so that $\bar{x}$ will be normal.

 b) We need the t-scores for 99% confidence with $df = 19 - 1 = 18$.

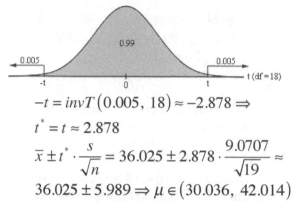

$-t = invT(0.005,\ 18) \approx -2.878 \Rightarrow$

$t^* = t \approx 2.878$

$\bar{x} \pm t^* \cdot \dfrac{s}{\sqrt{n}} = 36.025 \pm 2.878 \cdot \dfrac{9.0707}{\sqrt{19}} \approx$

$36.025 \pm 5.989 \Rightarrow \mu \in (30.036,\ 42.014)$

 c) The margin of error is the part we added and subtracted to get the boundaries, therefore, $E = 5.989$.

67) Givens: $n = 36$, $\bar{x} = 5.62$, and $s = 1.0639$.

 a) Because $n = 36 \ge 30$, the CLT tells us that $\bar{x}$ will be normally distributed. Thus the requirements have been met.

 b) We need the t-scores for 95% confidence with $df = 36 - 1 = 35$.

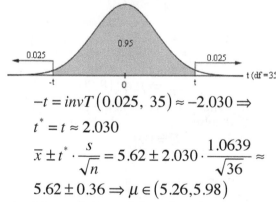

$-t = invT(0.025,\ 35) \approx -2.030 \Rightarrow$

$t^* = t \approx 2.030$

$\bar{x} \pm t^* \cdot \dfrac{s}{\sqrt{n}} = 5.62 \pm 2.030 \cdot \dfrac{1.0639}{\sqrt{36}} \approx$

$5.62 \pm 0.36 \Rightarrow \mu \in (5.26, 5.98)$

 c) We are 95% confident that the true mean duration for the portable Blu-ray player batteries is somewhere between 5.26 and 5.98 hours.

69) Givens: $n = 28$, $\bar{x} = 94.286$, $s = 9.37$.

 a) $15 \le n = 28 < 30$, but the population is known to be normal. Therefore, we know that $\bar{x}$ is normal and the requirements are met.

 b) We need the t-scores for 99% confidence with $df = 28 - 1 = 27$.

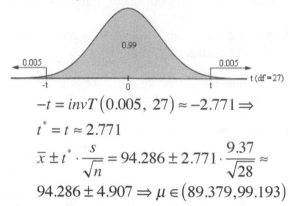

$-t = invT(0.005,\ 27) \approx -2.771 \Rightarrow$

$t^* = t \approx 2.771$

$\bar{x} \pm t^* \cdot \dfrac{s}{\sqrt{n}} = 94.286 \pm 2.771 \cdot \dfrac{9.37}{\sqrt{28}} \approx$

$94.286 \pm 4.907 \Rightarrow \mu \in (89.379, 99.193)$

 c) We are 99% confident that the true mean IQ for 9-year-old twins is somewhere between 89.379 and 99.193 points.

 d) Yes, $\mu \in (89.379, 99.193) \Rightarrow \mu < 100$.

71) a) Because $n = 12 < 15$, we need the mileages for all such SUVs to be a normally distributed population. The P-value from the normtest is greater than 0.05, so it is a reasonable possibility that this population is in fact normal.

 b) We are not given values for the mean or standard deviation, so we will need to compute them from the sample data. Using technology, we get $\bar{x} \approx 34.573$ and $s \approx 1.6685$.
 We need the t-scores for 99% confidence with $df = 12 - 1 = 11$.

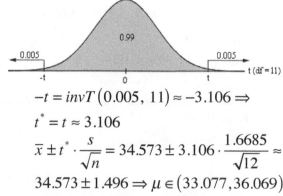

$-t = invT(0.005,\ 11) \approx -3.106 \Rightarrow$

$t^* = t \approx 3.106$

$\bar{x} \pm t^* \cdot \dfrac{s}{\sqrt{n}} = 34.573 \pm 3.106 \cdot \dfrac{1.6685}{\sqrt{12}} \approx$

$34.573 \pm 1.496 \Rightarrow \mu \in (33.077, 36.069)$

 c) No, $\mu \in (33.077, 36.069) \Rightarrow \mu$ could be more than 35. For example, it could be 35 mpg.

73) a) Since $n = 48 \geq 30$, $\bar{x}$ will be normal. Thus, the requirements have been met.

b) We must use the sample data to compute the mean and standard deviation. $\bar{x} \approx 28.1$ and $s \approx 10.488$. We need the t-scores for 90% confidence with $df = 48 - 1 = 47$.

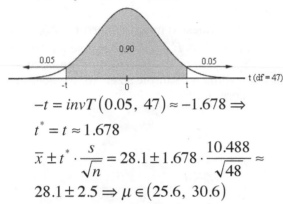

$$-t = invT(0.05,\ 47) \approx -1.678 \Rightarrow$$

$$t^* = t \approx 1.678$$

$$\bar{x} \pm t^* \cdot \frac{s}{\sqrt{n}} = 28.1 \pm 1.678 \cdot \frac{10.488}{\sqrt{48}} \approx$$

$$28.1 \pm 2.5 \Rightarrow \mu \in (25.6,\ 30.6)$$

c) Yes, $\mu \in (25.6,\ 30.6) \Rightarrow \mu > 25$

d) To covert from the population mean to the population total, we just need to multiply by the population size, $N = 256$. $256 * 25.6 = 6553.6$ and $256 * 30.6 = 7833.6$. Therefore, we are 90% confident that the true total number of points scored by the winning teams during that season was somewhere from 6554 points to 7833 points.

75) Givens: $n = 18$, $\bar{x} \approx 23.0556$, $s \approx 11.2065$

a) Since $15 \leq n = 18 < 30$, we need the number of hits for all such days to NOT be from a severely skewed population. The boxplot of the data is roughly symmetric with no outliers. It seems reasonable to assume that the population this sample was drawn from is not severely skewed. Therefore, we will consider the requirements to be met.

b) We need the t-scores for 95% confidence with $df = 18 - 1 = 17$.

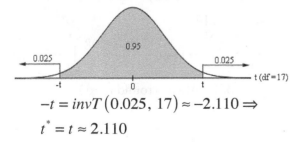

$$-t = invT(0.025,\ 17) \approx -2.110 \Rightarrow$$

$$t^* = t \approx 2.110$$

$$\bar{x} \pm t^* \cdot \frac{s}{\sqrt{n}} = 23.0556 \pm 2.110 \cdot \frac{11.2065}{\sqrt{18}} \approx$$

$$23.0556 \pm 5.5733 \Rightarrow \mu \in (17.4823, 28.6289)$$

c) Yes. The mean number of hits before the optimization was 16.67 hits. $\mu \in (17.4823, 28.6289) \Rightarrow \mu > 16.67$

d) To covert from the population mean to the population total, we just need to multiply by the population size, $N = 365$. $365 * 17.4823 = 6381.0395$ and $365 * 28.6289 = 10,449.5485$. Therefore, we are 95% confident that the true total number of hits during that year is somewhere from 6,382 hits to 10,449 hits.

77) Givens: $n = 10$, $\bar{x} \approx 131.7$, $s \approx 4.5007$

a) Because $n = 10 < 15$ and our population is unknown, we must hope that the population is normal, so that $\bar{x}$ will be normal.

b) We need the t-scores for 90% confidence with $df = 10 - 1 = 9$.

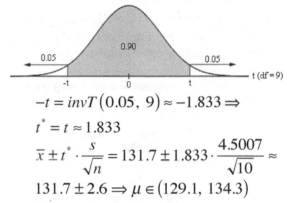

$$-t = invT(0.05,\ 9) \approx -1.833 \Rightarrow$$

$$t^* = t \approx 1.833$$

$$\bar{x} \pm t^* \cdot \frac{s}{\sqrt{n}} = 131.7 \pm 1.833 \cdot \frac{4.5007}{\sqrt{10}} \approx$$

$$131.7 \pm 2.6 \Rightarrow \mu \in (129.1,\ 134.3)$$

c) No, $\mu \in (129.1,\ 134.3) \Rightarrow \mu$ could be less than 130 ft. For example, it could be 129.5 ft, which is less than the mean braking distance for the cars.

d) All the formulas we are working with for this problem assume that we have a random sample. If they only used lightweight SUVs, then it sounds like their sample was handpicked. We could either throw out our results or perhaps we can just be careful to state the conclusion about lightweight SUVs, not SUVs in general.

79) Givens: $n = 28$, $\bar{x} \approx 88.75$, $s \approx 35.43$

  a) $15 \leq n = 28 < 30$ and our population is stated to be somewhat skewed, but not severely skewed. Therefore, $\bar{x}$ will be approximately normal and the requirements are met.

  b)   We need the t-scores for 95% confidence with $df = 28 - 1 = 27$.

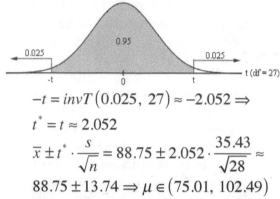

$$-t = invT(0.025, \ 27) \approx -2.052 \Rightarrow$$

$$t^* = t \approx 2.052$$

$$\bar{x} \pm t^* \cdot \frac{s}{\sqrt{n}} = 88.75 \pm 2.052 \cdot \frac{35.43}{\sqrt{28}} \approx$$

$$88.75 \pm 13.74 \Rightarrow \mu \in (75.01, \ 102.49)$$

  c)   We are 95% confident that the true mean late season price for snowboard bindings is somewhere between \$75.01 and \$102.49.

  d)   No, $\mu \in (75.01, \ 102.49) \Rightarrow \mu$ could be more than \$100. For example, it could be \$101, which is more than the specified amount of \$100.

  e)   All the formulas we are working with for this problem assume that we have a random sample. If they only used prices from one store, then it sounds like they used a convenience sample. We could either throw out our results or perhaps we can just be careful to state the conclusion only about the snowboard bindings at this store, not snowboard bindings in general.

Section 8.4:

81) When we increase our sample size, it <u>decreases</u> the margin of error.

82) When calculating sample size requirements, we always round n <u>up</u> to the next whole number.

83) If a recent sample is available, then we should use <u>s</u> in place of the unknown value of σ. In such cases we will use a <u>t</u>-score in the formula for sample size.

84) If no recent sample is available, then we should use $\sigma_g = \dfrac{max - min}{4}$ in place of the unknown value of σ. In such cases we will use a <u>z</u>-score in the formula for sample size.

85) Given: the population standard deviation is $\sigma = 18.952$.

  a)   The requested margin of error is 2.5, so we know that $E = 2.5$. Because we are given the value of σ, we will use the z-score formula for sample size. So, we need the z-scores for 95% confidence.

$$-z = invN(0.025) \approx -1.960 \Rightarrow z^* \approx 1.960$$

$$n = \left(\frac{z^* \sigma}{E}\right)^2 = \left(\frac{1.96 * 18.952}{2.5}\right)^2 \approx 220.77$$

$$\Rightarrow n = 221 \ \text{(Always round up.)}$$

  b)   We will need an even bigger sample.

  c) $n = \left(\dfrac{z^* \sigma}{E}\right)^2 = \left(\dfrac{1.96 * 18.952}{1.25}\right)^2 \approx 883.08$

$$\Rightarrow n = 884 \ \text{(Always round n up.)}$$

87) Givens: $n = 23$, $s \approx 13.608$, $E = 1.25$ Because the standard deviation provided is from a sample, we will use the t-score formula this time. We need the t-scores for 90% confidence with $df = 23 - 1 = 22$.

$$-t = invT(0.05, \ 22) \approx -1.717 \Rightarrow$$

$$t^* = t \approx 1.717$$

$$n = \left(\frac{t^* \cdot s}{E}\right)^2 = \left(\frac{1.717 * 13.608}{1.25}\right)^2 \approx 349.39$$

$$\Rightarrow n = 350 \ \text{(Always round n up.)}$$

89) Givens: $1 - \alpha = 0.99$, min $= 20$, max $= 100$

a) $\sigma_g = \dfrac{\text{max} - \text{min}}{4} = \dfrac{100 - 20}{4} = 20$

b) We want $E = 3.25$ and we need the z-scores for 99% confidence. We use z-scores whenever we are using σ_g.

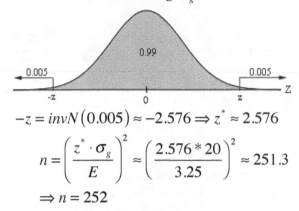

$-z = invN(0.005) \approx -2.576 \Rightarrow z^* \approx 2.576$

$n = \left(\dfrac{z^* \cdot \sigma_g}{E}\right)^2 \approx \left(\dfrac{2.576 * 20}{3.25}\right)^2 \approx 251.3$

$\Rightarrow n = 252$

91) Givens: $(84.57, 91.83)$ and 98% confidence

a) $\bar{x}$ should be directly in the center of the confidence interval. We can average the endpoints to find $\bar{x}$.

$\bar{x} = \dfrac{84.57 + 91.83}{2} = 88.2$

The margin of error is the distance from $\bar{x}$ to either endpoint of the interval.
$E = 91.83 - 88.2 = 3.63$

b) No. We would need to find a new sample and determine the mean from this new sample. It is not reasonable to assume we would get the same value, $\bar{x} = 88.2$, that was obtained in the previous sample.

c) We can get the new interval by adding and subtracting the margin of error from the new point estimate.
$\bar{x} \pm E = 86.49 \pm 1.50 \Rightarrow \mu \in (84.99, 87.99)$

93) Given: We are told that $\sigma = 26$.

a) We use z-scores whenever we know the value of σ. We want 99% confidence.

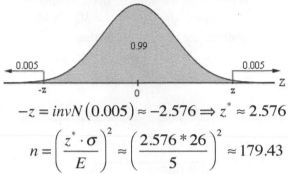

$-z = invN(0.005) \approx -2.576 \Rightarrow z^* \approx 2.576$

$n = \left(\dfrac{z^* \cdot \sigma}{E}\right)^2 \approx \left(\dfrac{2.576 * 26}{5}\right)^2 \approx 179.43$

$\Rightarrow n = 180$ trees need to be sampled.

b) The point estimate is $\bar{x} = 218.9$. This sample size from part (a) should yield $E = 5.0$. We simply add and subtract this from the point estimate to get our interval.
$218.9 \pm 5.0 \Rightarrow \mu \in (213.9, 223.9)$

95) a) The best estimate for σ is the sample standard deviation, s. Using the sample data and technology, we find $s \approx 3.6051$.

b) We need to find our t-scores using a df that is based on the sample used to find s. Therefore, $df = 10 - 1 = 9$. A 90% confidence level is requested.

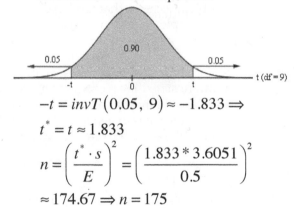

$-t = invT(0.05, 9) \approx -1.833 \Rightarrow$

$t^* = t \approx 1.833$

$n = \left(\dfrac{t^* \cdot s}{E}\right)^2 = \left(\dfrac{1.833 * 3.6051}{0.5}\right)^2$

$\approx 174.67 \Rightarrow n = 175$

97) Givens: With $n = 31$, $s \approx 18.3$.

   a) We need to find our t-scores using a df that is based on the sample used to find s. Therefore, $df = 31 - 1 = 30$. A 95% confidence level is requested.

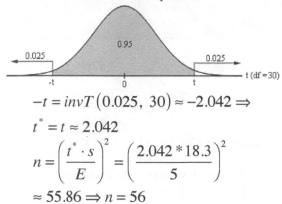

$$-t = invT(0.025, \ 30) \approx -2.042 \Rightarrow$$

$$t^* = t \approx 2.042$$

$$n = \left(\frac{t^* \cdot s}{E}\right)^2 = \left(\frac{2.042 * 18.3}{5}\right)^2$$

$$\approx 55.86 \Rightarrow n = 56$$

   b) Identical to the work above, only this time we want $E = 2$.

$$n = \left(\frac{t^* \cdot s}{E}\right)^2 = \left(\frac{2.042 * 18.3}{2}\right)^2$$

$$\approx 349.10 \Rightarrow n = 350$$

99) Givens: min $= 3.18$, max $= 3.75$

   a) $\sigma_g \approx \dfrac{\text{max} - \text{min}}{4} = \dfrac{3.75 - 3.18}{4} = 0.1425$.

   b) For 99% confidence the z-scores are:

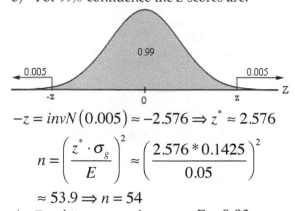

$$-z = invN(0.005) \approx -2.576 \Rightarrow z^* \approx 2.576$$

$$n = \left(\frac{z^* \cdot \sigma_g}{E}\right)^2 \approx \left(\frac{2.576 * 0.1425}{0.05}\right)^2$$

$$\approx 53.9 \Rightarrow n = 54$$

   c) For this one, we change to $E = 0.03$.

$$n = \left(\frac{z^* \cdot \sigma_g}{E}\right)^2 \approx \left(\frac{2.576 * 0.1425}{0.03}\right)^2$$

$$\approx 149.7 \Rightarrow n = 150$$

101) Givens: min $= 25$, max $= 55$

   a) $\sigma_g \approx \dfrac{\text{max} - \text{min}}{4} = \dfrac{55 - 25}{4} = 7.5$.

   b) For 90% confidence the z-scores are:

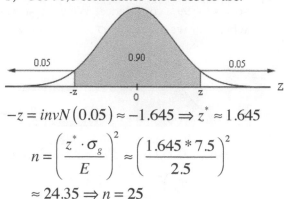

$$-z = invN(0.05) \approx -1.645 \Rightarrow z^* \approx 1.645$$

$$n = \left(\frac{z^* \cdot \sigma_g}{E}\right)^2 \approx \left(\frac{1.645 * 7.5}{2.5}\right)^2$$

$$\approx 24.35 \Rightarrow n = 25$$

   c) For this one, we change to 99% confidence.

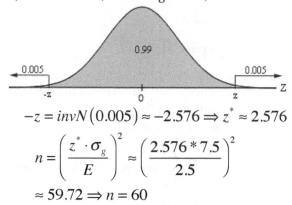

$$-z = invN(0.005) \approx -2.576 \Rightarrow z^* \approx 2.576$$

$$n = \left(\frac{z^* \cdot \sigma_g}{E}\right)^2 \approx \left(\frac{2.576 * 7.5}{2.5}\right)^2$$

$$\approx 59.72 \Rightarrow n = 60$$

Chapter Problem:

a) Given info: $E = 0.1\% = 0.001$.
   Probabilities are proportions, so we also
   need the z-scores for 99% confidence.

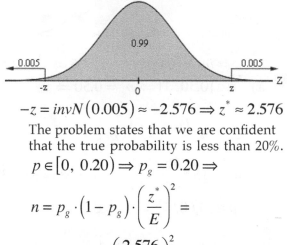

$$-z = invN(0.005) \approx -2.576 \Rightarrow z^* \approx 2.576$$

The problem states that we are confident
that the true probability is less than 20%.

$$p \in [0,\ 0.20) \Rightarrow p_g = 0.20 \Rightarrow$$

$$n = p_g \cdot (1 - p_g) \cdot \left(\frac{z^*}{E}\right)^2 =$$

$$0.20 * 0.80 * \left(\frac{2.576}{0.001}\right)^2 = 1,061,724.16$$

$$\Rightarrow n = 1,061,725$$

b) $\hat{p} = \dfrac{x}{n} = \dfrac{167,904}{1,533,484} \approx 0.109492$

c) No, $P(\hat{p} = p) \approx 0$.

d) $\hat{p} \pm z^* \cdot \sqrt{\dfrac{\hat{p}\hat{q}}{n}} =$

$$0.109492 \pm 2.576 \cdot \sqrt{\frac{0.109492 * 0.890508}{1,533,484}}$$

$$\approx 0.109492 \pm 0.000650 \Rightarrow$$

$$p \in (0.108842,\ 0.110142)$$

e) We are 99% confident that the true
   probability of the team with the 5th worst
   record ending up with the 3rd overall draft
   choice is somewhere between 0.108842 and
   0.110142.

Ch 8: Review Exercises

1) Givens: $x = 179$, $n = 495$

   a) $\hat{p} = \dfrac{x}{n} = \dfrac{179}{495} \approx 0.3616$

   b) Our sample contained 179 successes and 316
      failures. Both of these are at least 10, so
      the requirements have been met.

   c) We need the z-scores for 95% confidence.

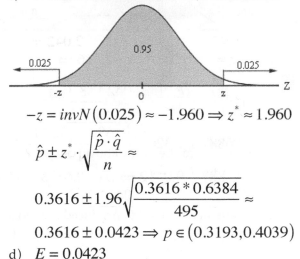

$$-z = invN(0.025) \approx -1.960 \Rightarrow z^* \approx 1.960$$

$$\hat{p} \pm z^* \cdot \sqrt{\frac{\hat{p} \cdot \hat{q}}{n}} \approx$$

$$0.3616 \pm 1.96\sqrt{\frac{0.3616 * 0.6384}{495}} \approx$$

$$0.3616 \pm 0.0423 \Rightarrow p \in (0.3193, 0.4039)$$

   d) $E = 0.0423$

3) Givens: $n = 14$, $\bar{x} = 47.4$, $s = 6.8258$

   a) $n = 14 < 15$ and the population is
      unknown. So we must hope that the
      population is normally distributed so that
      $\bar{x}$ will be normally distributed.

   b) We need the t-scores for 90% confidence
      with $df = 14 - 1 = 13$.

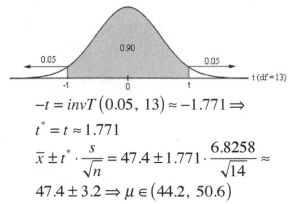

$$-t = invT(0.05, 13) \approx -1.771 \Rightarrow$$

$$t^* = t \approx 1.771$$

$$\bar{x} \pm t^* \cdot \frac{s}{\sqrt{n}} = 47.4 \pm 1.771 \cdot \frac{6.8258}{\sqrt{14}} \approx$$

$$47.4 \pm 3.2 \Rightarrow \mu \in (44.2, 50.6)$$

4) Givens: $n = 1195$, $\hat{p} = 0.6887$

a) $n\hat{p} = 1195 * 0.6887 \approx 823 \geq 10$ and
$n\hat{q} = 1195 * 0.3113 \approx 372 \geq 10$, so the
requirements have been met.

b) We need the z-scores for 98% confidence.

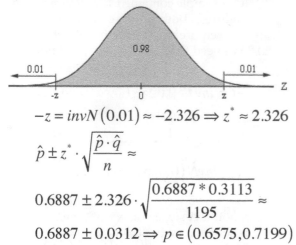

$$-z = invN(0.01) \approx -2.326 \Rightarrow z^* \approx 2.326$$

$$\hat{p} \pm z^* \cdot \sqrt{\frac{\hat{p} \cdot \hat{q}}{n}} \approx$$

$$0.6887 \pm 2.326 \cdot \sqrt{\frac{0.6887 * 0.3113}{1195}} \approx$$

$$0.6887 \pm 0.0312 \Rightarrow p \in (0.6575, 0.7199)$$

5) A sample of size $n = 46$ produced a standard
deviation of $s = 50.772$. We need to find the
t-scores for 95% confidence with
$df = 46 - 1 = 45$.

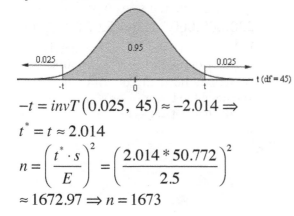

$$-t = invT(0.025, \ 45) \approx -2.014 \Rightarrow$$

$$t^* = t \approx 2.014$$

$$n = \left(\frac{t^* \cdot s}{E} \right)^2 = \left(\frac{2.014 * 50.772}{2.5} \right)^2$$

$$\approx 1672.97 \Rightarrow n = 1673$$

7) Givens: $E = 0.015$ and for a confidence level
of 99%, the z-scores are:

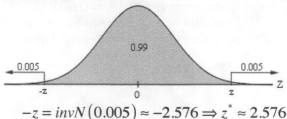

$$-z = invN(0.005) \approx -2.576 \Rightarrow z^* \approx 2.576$$

a) $p \in [0.30, \ 1] \Rightarrow p_g = 0.50 \Rightarrow$

$$n = p_g \cdot (1 - p_g) \cdot \left(\frac{z^*}{E} \right)^2 =$$

$$0.5 * 0.5 * \left(\frac{2.576}{0.015} \right)^2 \approx 7373.08 \Rightarrow n = 7374$$

b) $p \in (0.60, \ 1] \Rightarrow p_g = 0.60 \Rightarrow$

$$n = p_g \cdot (1 - p_g) \cdot \left(\frac{z^*}{E} \right)^2 =$$

$$0.6 * 0.4 * \left(\frac{2.576}{0.015} \right)^2 \approx 7078.16 \Rightarrow n = 7079$$

8) Givens: $1 - \alpha = 0.98$, min = 300, max = 700

a) $\sigma_g = \dfrac{\text{max} - \text{min}}{4} = \dfrac{700 - 300}{4} = 100$

b) We want $E = 20$ and we need the z-scores
for 98% confidence. We use z-scores
whenever we are using σ_g.

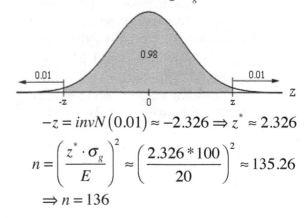

$$-z = invN(0.01) \approx -2.326 \Rightarrow z^* \approx 2.326$$

$$n = \left(\frac{z^* \cdot \sigma_g}{E} \right)^2 \approx \left(\frac{2.326 * 100}{20} \right)^2 \approx 135.26$$

$$\Rightarrow n = 136$$

9) Givens: $n = 60{,}000$ and $x = 32{,}148$

a) $\hat{p} = \dfrac{x}{n} = \dfrac{32148}{60000} = 0.5358$

b) We need the z-scores for 99% confidence.

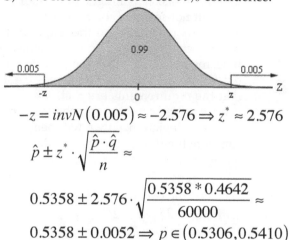

$-z = invN(0.005) \approx -2.576 \Rightarrow z^* \approx 2.576$

$\hat{p} \pm z^* \cdot \sqrt{\dfrac{\hat{p} \cdot \hat{q}}{n}} \approx$

$0.5358 \pm 2.576 \cdot \sqrt{\dfrac{0.5358 * 0.4642}{60000}} \approx$

$0.5358 \pm 0.0052 \Rightarrow p \in (0.5306, 0.5410)$

c) Just using the point estimate, we have 0% confidence that we have the true proportion. However, when we add and subtract the margin of error, we become 99% confident that we have captured the true proportion. Therefore, we must be 99% confident that the point estimate is within 0.0052 of the true proportion.

d) We are 99% confident that the true proportion of all students that would put Google in their top 5 list of ideal employers is somewhere between 53.06% and 54.10%.

e) To covert from the proportion of successes in the population to the number of successes in the population, we just need to multiply by the population size, $N = 21{,}000{,}000$.

$21{,}000{,}000 * 0.5306 = 11{,}142{,}600$ and

$21{,}000{,}000 * 0.5410 = 11{,}361{,}000$.

Therefore, we are 99% confident that somewhere between 11,142,600 and 11,361,000 of the 21,000,000 students would put Google in their top 5 list of ideal employers.

11) Givens: $n = 6100$, $\bar{x} = 21.4$, $s = 10.3$

a) $n = 6100 \geq 30 \Rightarrow \bar{x}$ is normal and the requirements are met.

b) We need the t-scores for 95% confidence with $df = 6100 - 1 = 6099$.

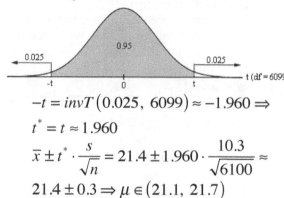

$-t = invT(0.025,\ 6099) \approx -1.960 \Rightarrow$

$t^* = t \approx 1.960$

$\bar{x} \pm t^* \cdot \dfrac{s}{\sqrt{n}} = 21.4 \pm 1.960 \cdot \dfrac{10.3}{\sqrt{6100}} \approx$

$21.4 \pm 0.3 \Rightarrow \mu \in (21.1,\ 21.7)$

c) We are 95% confident that the true mean amount of sugar consumption for U.S. adults is somewhere between 21.1 teaspoons and 21.7 teaspoons.

d) Yes, $\mu \in (21.1,\ 21.7) \Rightarrow \mu > 8$.

e) ± 0.3 teaspoons of sugar

f) To covert from the population mean to the population total, we just need to multiply by the population size, $N = 238{,}000{,}000$.

$238{,}000{,}000 * 21.1 = 5{,}021{,}800{,}000$ and

$238{,}000{,}000 * 21.7 = 5{,}164{,}600{,}000$.

Therefore, we are 95% confident that the true total amount of sugar consumed per day by adult Americans is somewhere between 5,021,800,000 teaspoons per day and 5,164,600,000 teaspoons per day.

12) a) Since $n = 14 < 15$, we need the weight gain for all such people to be a normally distributed population. The P-value from the normtest is greater than 0.05, so it is a reasonable possibility that this population is in fact normal.

b) We are not given values for the mean or standard deviation, so we will need to compute them from the sample data. Using technology, we get $\bar{x} \approx 4.617$ and $s \approx 3.9643$.
We need the t-scores for 99% confidence with $df = 14 - 1 = 13$.

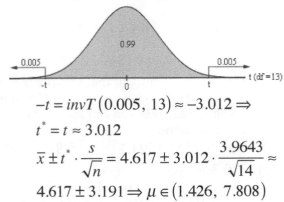

$$-t = invT(0.005, 13) \approx -3.012 \Rightarrow$$

$$t^* = t \approx 3.012$$

$$\bar{x} \pm t^* \cdot \frac{s}{\sqrt{n}} = 4.617 \pm 3.012 \cdot \frac{3.9643}{\sqrt{14}} \approx$$

$$4.617 \pm 3.191 \Rightarrow \mu \in (1.426, \ 7.808)$$

c) We are 99% confident that the true mean weight gain for adults that consume at about 1 serving of potatoes per day is somewhere between 1.426 pounds and 7.808 pounds.

d) No, $\mu \in (1.426, \ 7.808) \Rightarrow \mu$ could be less than 3.35 pounds. For example, it could be only 2 pounds.

e) Because we already have some sample data, we will use the standard deviation and t-score from that sample to make our computation.

$$n = \left(\frac{t^* \cdot s}{E}\right)^2 = \left(\frac{3.012 * 3.9643}{0.75}\right)^2$$

$$\approx 253.47 \Rightarrow n = 254$$

13) a) $15 \leq n = 25 < 30$, so we need the population to not be severely skewed. Based on the boxplot, it does not appear that the population is severely skewed. The left whisker is longer than the right one, but not severely so. Also, the right side of the box is wider than the left, and this contradicts the skew seen in the whiskers. It seems reasonable that the population is not severely skewed. So, it is reasonable that the requirements are met.

b) We are not given values for the mean or standard deviation, so we will need to compute them from the sample data. Using technology, we get $\bar{x} = 8.64$ and $s \approx 2.56385$.
We need the t-scores for 90% confidence with $df = 25 - 1 = 24$.

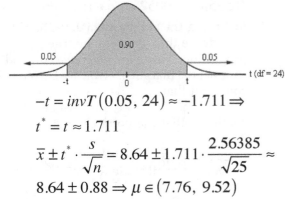

$$-t = invT(0.05, 24) \approx -1.711 \Rightarrow$$

$$t^* = t \approx 1.711$$

$$\bar{x} \pm t^* \cdot \frac{s}{\sqrt{n}} = 8.64 \pm 1.711 \cdot \frac{2.56385}{\sqrt{25}} \approx$$

$$8.64 \pm 0.88 \Rightarrow \mu \in (7.76, \ 9.52)$$

c) Yes, $\mu \in (7.76, \ 9.52) \Rightarrow \mu < 12$.

d) Because we already have some sample data, we will use the standard deviation and t-score from that sample to make our computation.

$$n = \left(\frac{t^* \cdot s}{E}\right)^2 = \left(\frac{1.711 * 2.56385}{0.5}\right)^2$$

$$\approx 76.97 \Rightarrow n = 77$$

15) Givens: $n = 180$, $\hat{p} = 0.8500$

a) $n\hat{p} = 180 * 0.85 \approx 153 \geq 10$ and
$n\hat{q} = 180 * 0.15 \approx 27 \geq 10$, so the
requirements have been met.

b) We need the z-scores for 95% confidence.

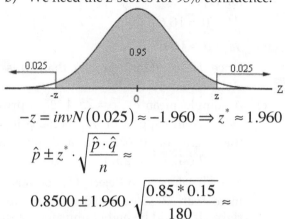

$-z = invN(0.025) \approx -1.960 \Rightarrow z^* \approx 1.960$

$$\hat{p} \pm z^* \cdot \sqrt{\frac{\hat{p} \cdot \hat{q}}{n}} \approx$$

$$0.8500 \pm 1.960 \cdot \sqrt{\frac{0.85 * 0.15}{180}} \approx$$

$$0.8500 \pm 0.0522 \Rightarrow p \in (0.7978, 0.9022)$$

c) Yes. $p \in (0.7978, 0.9022) \Rightarrow p > 0.60$.

d) $p \in (0.7978, 0.9022) \Rightarrow p_g = 0.7978$

$$n = p_g \cdot (1 - p_g) \cdot \left(\frac{z^*}{E}\right)^2 =$$

$$0.7978 * 0.2022 * \left(\frac{1.96}{0.03}\right)^2 \approx 688.56$$

$$\Rightarrow n = 689$$

e) No idea $\Rightarrow p_g = 0.5 \Rightarrow$

$$n = 0.5 * 0.5 \cdot \left(\frac{z^*}{E}\right)^2 =$$

$$0.5 * 0.5 * \left(\frac{1.96}{0.03}\right)^2 \approx 1067.11$$

$$\Rightarrow n = 1068$$

Section 9.1

1) H_o must always be written using an <u>equal</u> sign.

2)   The specific value used in H_o is usually an old, <u>claimed</u>, comparable, or <u>default</u> value for the mean or proportion.

3)   A type I error occurs if we <u>reject</u> H_o when it is in fact a <u>true</u> statement.

4)   A type II error occurs if we <u>do not reject</u> H_o when it is in fact a <u>false</u> statement.

5)   Since H_1 has the '>' symbol, this is a right-tailed test.

7)   Since H_1 has the '<' symbol, this is a left-tailed test.

9)   Since H_1 has the '$\neq$' symbol, this is a two-tailed test.

11) Since H_1 has the '>' symbol, this is a right-tailed test.

13) a)   Before the toll change, the average was $234,018 per day. This old value will be the claimed mean. The key phrase is that "see if the average has **changed** since the toll hike". This word does not indicate a direction, so we will use '$\neq$' for H_1.

$$H_o : \mu = 234{,}018$$

$$H_1 : \mu \neq 234{,}018$$

b)   Since H_1 contains a does not equal, this is a two-tailed test.

c)   A sample mean of $\overline{x} = 240{,}000$ does provide evidence in support of H_1 because it does not equal 234,018. However, this value is less than 1 standard deviation away from 234,018. This makes it weak evidence against H_0. Such a small difference could reasonably be the result of random variation. We should not reject H_0 with this weak evidence.

15) a)   Before the optimization, the average was 16.67 hits per day. This old value will be the claimed mean. The key phrase is that "he wishes to see if the average has **increased**". This indicates a 'greater than' for H_1.

$$H_o : \mu = 16.67$$

$$H_1 : \mu > 16.67$$

b)   Since H_1 contains a greater than, this is a right-tailed test.

c)   A sample mean of $\overline{x} = 25.4$ does provide evidence in support of H_1 because it is to the right of 16.67. In addition, with $\sigma_{\overline{x}} \approx 2.64$, $\overline{x} = 25.4$ would be strong enough evidence to Reject H_0, because it is more than 3 standard deviations to the right. It would be highly unusual for such a big difference to just be the result of random variations.

17) a)   According to the 2007 study, the proportion used to be at 31.72%. We will use that for the specific value in H_0. In the current study, we want to see if this percentage has "decreased". Therefore, we will use the symbol '<' in H_1. We always convert percentages into decimal form when writing the hypotheses.

$$H_0 : p = 0.3172$$

$$H_1 : p < 0.3172$$

b)   Since H_1 contains a less than, this is a left-tailed test.

c) $\sigma_{\hat{p}} \approx 0.0251$ means that $\hat{p} = 0.3052$ would be less than 1 standard deviation below the claimed 0.3172. This evidence would be too weak for us to Reject H_0.

19) a) In winter, the percentage was 32%. We will use that for the specific value in H_0. In the spring, we want to see if this percentage has "changed". Therefore, we will use the symbol '$\neq$' in H_1. We always convert percentages into decimal form when writing the hypotheses.

$H_0 : p = 0.32$

$H_1 : p \neq 0.32$

b) Since H_1 contains '$\neq$', this is a two-tailed test.

c) $\sigma_{\hat{p}} \approx 0.0153$ means that $\hat{p} = 0.2711$ would be more than 3 standard deviations below the claimed 0.32. This evidence should be strong enough for us to Reject H_0.

21) a) According to the 2008 study, the proportion used to be at 25.1%. We will use that for the specific value in H_0. In the 2010 study, they want to see if this percentage has "increased". Therefore, we will use the symbol '$>$' in H_1. We always convert percentages into decimal form when writing the hypotheses.

$H_0 : p = 0.251$

$H_1 : p > 0.251$

b) Since H_1 contains a greater than, this is a right-tailed test.

c) In order to provide evidence, the sample proportion must be to the right of the claimed value. With $\sigma_{\hat{p}} \approx 0.0108$, a value like $\hat{p} = 0.2855$ would be over three standard deviations to the right of the claimed value of 0.251. Such a big difference should be considered strong enough evidence for us to Reject H_0.

23) a) If this were a fair die, then, in the long run, the number 4 would show up 1/6 of the time. We will use the decimal form $\frac{1}{6} \approx 0.1667$ for the specific value in H_0. We want to see if the current proportion is "not proper". Therefore, we will use the symbol '$\neq$' in H_1.

$H_0 : p = 0.1667$
$H_1 : p \neq 0.1667$

b) Since H_1 contains '$\neq$', this is a two-tailed test.

c) In order to provide some evidence against H_0, the sample proportion could be to the left or right of the claimed value. For it to be weak evidence, it cannot be a big difference. With $\sigma_{\hat{p}} \approx 0.0088$, possible values like this for the sample proportion are $\hat{p} = 0.1645$ or $\hat{p} = 0.1682$. These differences would both be less than 1 standard deviation from the claimed 0.1667 and should be considered too small to lead to the rejection of H_0.

25) a) The problem states that the average braking distance for cars is known to be 130 feet. We start out by using 130 feet as a default comparable value for the mean for the SUVs. Since the tire maker wants to show the mean is "**less**" than for cars, we will use a less than symbol in H_1.

$H_o : \mu = 130$

$H_1 : \mu < 130$

b) Since H_1 contains a less than symbol, this is a left-tailed test.

c) In order to provide evidence against H_0, the sample mean must be to the left of the claimed value. With $\sigma_{\bar{x}} \approx 2.8751$, a value like $\bar{x} = 121$ would be over 3 standard deviations to the left of the claimed 130. This should be strong enough evidence to Reject H_0.

27) a) To show the mean is higher than 25 points, we start out by using 25 points as a default comparable value for the mean. Since the caller wants to show the mean is "**higher**" than 25 points, we will use a greater than symbol in H_1.

$H_o : \mu = 25$

$H_1 : \mu > 25$

b) Since H_1 contains a greater than symbol, this is a right-tailed test.

c) In order to provide some evidence against H_0, the sample mean must be to the right of the claimed mean. For it to be weak evidence, it cannot be a big difference. With $\sigma_{\bar{x}} \approx 2.53$, a value like $\bar{x} = 26.1$ is less than 1 standard deviation above the claimed 25 and should be considered too close to lead to the rejection of H_0.

29) a) Because the data provides insufficient evidence for H_1, we will not reject H_0.

 b) Because the data provides enough evidence in support of H_1, we would reject H_0.

 c) If $p = 0.3172$, then $H_0 : p = 0.3172$ is true. In part (a), we decided not to Reject H_0. By not rejecting a true claim, we have made a Correct Decision.

 d) If $p = 0.3172$, then $H_0 : p = 0.3172$ is true. In part (b), we decided to Reject H_0. By rejecting a true claim, we have made a Type I error.

31) a) Because the sample provides insufficient evidence for H_1, we will not reject H_0.

 b) If $\mu = 24.7$, then $H_1 : \mu > 25$ is false and H_0 should be treated as true for the purpose of classifying our decision. In part (a), we decided not to Reject H_0. By not rejecting a true claim, we have made a Correct Decision.

33) a) The tire maker makes a type I error if the data provides enough evidence to show that the true mean braking distance is less than the average for cars, when in fact the mean braking distance is not less than for cars.

 b) The tire maker makes a type II error if the data does not provide enough evidence to show that the true mean braking distance is less than the average for cars, when in fact the mean braking distance is less than for cars.

 c) There are 2 ways that a correct decision could be made. It is a correct decision if the data provides enough evidence to show that the true mean braking distance is less than the average for cars, when in fact the mean braking distance is less than for cars. Or, a correct decision is also made if the data does not provide enough evidence to show that the true mean braking distance is less than the average for cars, when in fact the mean braking distance is not less than for cars.

35) a) Those studying the bridge make a type I error if their data provides enough evidence to show that the average daily revenue has changed, when in fact the average daily revenue has not changed.

 b) Those studying the bridge make a type II error if their data does not provide enough evidence to show that the average daily revenue has changed, when in fact the average daily revenue has changed.

 c) There are 2 ways that a correct decision could be made. Those studying the bridge make a correct decision if their data provides enough evidence to show that the average daily revenue has changed, when in fact the average daily revenue has changed. Or if their data does not provide enough evidence to show that the average daily revenue has changed, when in fact the average daily revenue has not changed.

Section 9.2

37) The significance level is the probability we will make a type I error if H_o is in fact true. We interpret it as the maximum risk we are willing to take of making a type I error.

38) The P-value is the chance of seeing a test statistic as inconsistent with the claimed proportion as the one from our sample if H_o is in fact true. We interpret it as the actual risk we would be taking of making a type I error if we decide to reject H_o.

39) The test statistic is a value obtained from the sample that is used to determine whether or not we have enough evidence to reject H_o.

40) The more inconsistent the test statistic is with the claimed value of the proportion, the more evidence we have against H_o.

41) When calculating the P-value for a two-tailed test, we must remember to double the area in the tail.

42) If the p-value is less than or equal to α, then we reject H_o because we feel that the risk of making a type I error is acceptable.

43) $\hat{p}$ is the symbol for the <u>sample</u> proportion. p is the symbol for the <u>population</u> proportion. p_0 is the symbol for the <u>claimed</u> proportion.

44) We use p when we are working with proportions, but we also use it for <u>percentages</u> & <u>probabilities</u>.

45) In a proportion test, evidence consists of a large <u>difference</u> between $\hat{p}$ and p_0.

46) False. In the long run, we will end up rejecting 10% of the true claims we test. Hopefully, we will reject far more than 10% of the false ones.

47) a) $\hat{p} = \dfrac{x}{n} = \dfrac{446}{768} \approx 0.5807 \Rightarrow$

$z = \dfrac{0.5807 - 0.63}{\sqrt{\dfrac{0.63 * 0.37}{768}}} \approx -2.830$

b) $H_1 : p < 0.63 \Rightarrow$ This is a left-tailed test.

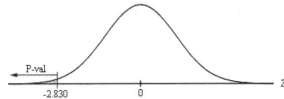

$P - val = normalcdf(-\infty, \ -2.830)$

≈ 0.0023

c) $P - val \approx 0.0023 \le \alpha \Rightarrow$ Reject H_o

(Acceptable risk of making a type I error)

49) a) $z = \dfrac{0.061 - 0.084}{\sqrt{\dfrac{0.084 * 0.916}{255}}} \approx -1.324$

b) $H_1 : p \ne 0.084 \Rightarrow$ This is a two-tailed test.

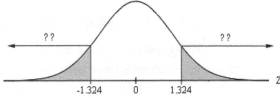

$P - val = 2 * normalcdf(1.324, \ \infty)$

≈ 0.1855

c) $P - val \approx 0.1855 > \alpha \Rightarrow$ Do Not Reject H_o

(Risk of a type I error is too high)

51) a) $\hat{p} = \dfrac{x}{n} = \dfrac{219}{518} \approx 0.4228 \Rightarrow$

$z = \dfrac{0.4228 - 0.50}{\sqrt{\dfrac{0.50 * 0.50}{518}}} \approx -3.514$

b) $H_1 : p > 0.50 \Rightarrow$ This is a right-tailed test.

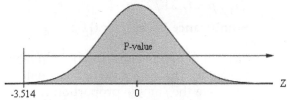

$P - val = normalcdf(-3.514, \ \infty) \approx 0.9998$

c) $P - val \approx 0.9998 > \alpha \Rightarrow$ Do Not Reject H_o

(Risk of a type I error is too high)

53) a) SET UP THE TEST:

Determine H_o and H_1: In 2007, the percentage of abusers was reported to be 31.72%. We will use this value as a default for the claimed proportion. They want to see percentage has "decreased" in the current population.

$H_o : p = 0.3172$

$H_1 : p < 0.3172$

Significance Level: $\alpha = 0.05$

GATHER AND WEIGH THE EVIDENCE:
Calculate the test statistic: We will calculate the sample proportion from the given data. So we

have $\hat{p} = \dfrac{x}{n} = \dfrac{64}{218} \approx 0.2936$.

$z = \dfrac{0.2936 - 0.3172}{\sqrt{\dfrac{0.3172 * 0.6828}{218}}} \approx -0.749$

Calculate the P-value: $H_1 : p < 0.3172 \Rightarrow$ This is a left-tailed test.

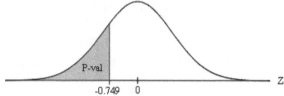

$P - val = normalcdf\left(-\infty,\ -0.749\right) \approx 0.2269$

DECISIONS AND CONCLUSIONS:
Decision: $P - val \approx 0.2269 > \alpha \Rightarrow$ Do Not Reject H_o (too risky).

Conclusion: The data did not provide enough evidence, at the 5% significance level, to show that the true percentage of the current 12th graders that abused marijuana during the last year has decreased from the 2007 percentage.

b) $np_o = 218 * 0.3172 = 69.1496 \geq 10$

$nq_o = 218 * 0.6828 = 148.8504 \geq 10$

$\Rightarrow$ the requirements have been met

---

55) a) SET UP THE TEST:

Determine H_o and H_1: In the winter of 2008, the percentage of visitors that were Floridians was reported to be 32%. We will use this value as a default for the claimed proportion. They want to see percentage is "**different**" in the Spring.

$H_o : p = 0.32$

$H_1 : p \neq 0.32$

Significance Level: $\alpha = 0.01$

GATHER AND WEIGH THE EVIDENCE:
Calculate the test statistic: We will calculate the sample proportion from the given data. So we have

$\hat{p} = \dfrac{x}{n} = \dfrac{225}{499} \approx 0.4509$.

$z = \dfrac{0.4509 - 0.32}{\sqrt{\dfrac{0.32 * 0.68}{499}}} \approx 6.268$

Calculate the P-value: $H_1 : p \neq 0.32 \Rightarrow$ This is a two-tailed test.

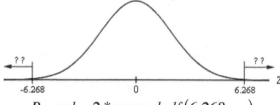

$P - val = 2 * normalcdf\left(6.268,\ \infty\right)$
≈ 0.0000

DECISIONS AND CONCLUSIONS:
Decision: $P - val \approx 0.0000 \leq \alpha \Rightarrow$ Reject H_o (acceptable risk).

Conclusion: The data did provide enough evidence, at the 1% significance level, to show that the true percentage of the U.S. visitors from Florida was different in the spring.

b) $np_o = 499(0.32) = 159.68 \geq 10$

$nq_o = 499(0.68) = 339.32 \geq 10$

$\Rightarrow$ the requirements have been met

57) a) SET UP THE TEST:
Determine H_o and H_1: In 2008, the percentage of Americans considered obese was reported to be 25.1%. We will use this value as a default for the claimed proportion. We want to see percentage has "**increased**" in 2009.

$H_o : p = 0.251$

$H_1 : p > 0.251$

Significance Level: $\alpha = 0.10$

GATHER AND WEIGH THE EVIDENCE:
Calculate the test statistic: We will calculate the sample proportion from the given data. So we have

$\hat{p} = \dfrac{x}{n} = \dfrac{209}{784} \approx 0.2666$.

$z = \dfrac{0.2666 - 0.251}{\sqrt{\dfrac{0.251 * 0.749}{784}}} \approx 1.007$

Calculate the P-value: $H_1 : p > 0.251 \Rightarrow$ This is a right-tailed test.

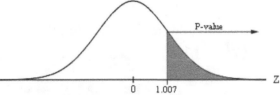

$P - val = normalcdf(1.007, \infty)$

≈ 0.1570

DECISIONS AND CONCLUSIONS:
Decision: $P - val \approx 0.1570 > \alpha \Rightarrow$ Do Not Reject H_o (Risk of a type I error is too high).
Conclusion: The data did not provide enough evidence, at the 10% significance level, to show that the true percentage of obese Americans has increased from the 2008 level.

b) We did not reject H_o, so a type I is not possible, but if H_o is actually false, then we have made a type II error.

c) $np_o = 784(0.251) = 196.784 \geq 10$

$nq_o = 784(0.749) = 587.216 \geq 10$

$\Rightarrow$ the requirements have been met

59) Givens: $n = 493$, $\hat{p} = 0.507$
   a) SET UP THE TEST:
Determine H_o and H_1: A "majority" means more than half or greater than 0.5.

$H_o : p = 0.5$

$H_1 : p > 0.5$

Significance Level: $\alpha = 0.10$

GATHER AND WEIGH THE EVIDENCE:
Calculate the test statistic:

$z = \dfrac{0.507 - 0.50}{\sqrt{\dfrac{0.50 * 0.50}{493}}} \approx 0.311$

Calculate the P-value: $H_1 : p > 0.50 \Rightarrow$ This is a right-tailed test.

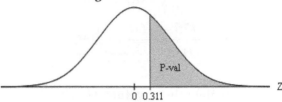

$P - val = normalcdf(0.311, \infty)$

≈ 0.3779

DECISIONS AND CONCLUSIONS:
Decision: $P - val \approx 0.3779 > \alpha \Rightarrow$ Do Not Reject H_o (Too Risky)
Conclusion: The data does not provide enough evidence, at the 10% significance level, to show that the candidate will win without a run-off election.

b) Since we did not reject the null hypothesis, it is not possible that we have made a type I error. However, a type II error is possible. This would be a type II error if it turns out that H_o is in fact false.

c) $np_o = 493(0.5) = 246.5 \geq 10$

$nq_o = 493(0.5) = 246.5 \geq 10$

$\Rightarrow$ the requirements have been met

61) a) SET UP THE TEST:

Determine H_o and H_1: It is reported that 60% of those wishing to migrate to the U.S. have at least a high school education. We will use this value as a default for the claimed proportion. We want to see if the percentage for Canada is "**different**".

$H_o : p = 0.60$

$H_1 : p \neq 0.60$

Significance Level: $\alpha = 0.05$

GATHER AND WEIGH THE EVIDENCE:
Calculate the test statistic: We will calculate the sample proportion from the given data. So we have

$$\hat{p} = \frac{x}{n} = \frac{311}{400} = 0.7775 .$$

$$z = \frac{0.7775 - 0.60}{\sqrt{\dfrac{0.60 * 0.40}{400}}} \approx 7.246$$

Calculate the P-value: $H_1 : p \neq 0.60 \Rightarrow$ This is a two-tailed test.

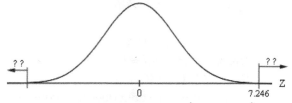

$P - val = 2 * normalcdf(7.246, \infty)$

≈ 0.0000

DECISIONS AND CONCLUSIONS:
Decision: $P - val \approx 0.0000 \leq \alpha \Rightarrow$ Reject H_o (acceptable risk).

Conclusion: The data did provide enough evidence, at the 5% significance level, to show that the true percentage of those wishing to migrate to Canada that have at least a high school education is different than the 60% for the U.S.

b) Since our sample percentage for Canada was unusually far to the right of the U.S. percentage, I would assume that the percentage of those wishing to migrate to Canada that have at least a high school education is higher than for the U.S.

63) Givens: Comparable proportion is 0.47, $\hat{p} = 0.7611$

a) SET UP THE TEST:

Determine H_o and H_1: We want to show that the proportion is "higher" in the bay area.

$H_o : p = 0.47$

$H_1 : p > 0.47$

Significance Level: $\alpha = 0.01$

GATHER AND WEIGH THE EVIDENCE:
Calculate the test statistic:

$$z = \frac{0.7611 - 0.47}{\sqrt{\dfrac{0.47 * 0.53}{314}}} \approx 10.335$$

Calculate the P-value: $H_1 : p > 0.47 \Rightarrow$ This is a right-tailed test.

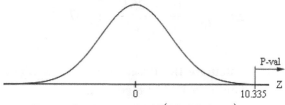

$P - val = normalcdf(10.335, \infty)$

Entering this in the calculator, we get:

```
normalcdf(10.335
,1*10^99)
    2.49976914E-25
```

The E-**25** indicates that we must move the decimal 25 places to the left. Since we normally round P-values to 4 decimal places, we get . $P - val \approx 0.0000$

DECISIONS AND CONCLUSIONS:
Decision: $P - val \approx 0.0000 \leq \alpha \Rightarrow$ Reject H_o (Acceptable risk of making a type I error)

Conclusion: The data does provide enough evidence, at the 1% significance level, to show that the proportion of people with high-speed internet access at home is higher than for the nation as a whole.

b) $p = 0.68 \Rightarrow H_o : p = 0.47$ is false $\Rightarrow$ Rejecting H_o was a correct decision.

65) Givens: $n = 450$, $x = 60$. No value for p seems to be claimed, but if the die is fair, then the number 4 would show up $1/6$ of the time or approximately 16.67% of the time.

a) SET UP THE TEST:

Determine H_o and H_1: The phrases "not fair" and not showing up the "proper proportion" of times do not indicate a direction. So, we get

$$H_o : p = 0.1667$$
$$H_1 : p \neq 0.1667$$

Significance Level: $\alpha = 0.10$

GATHER AND WEIGH THE EVIDENCE:
Calculate the test statistic:

$$\hat{p} = \frac{x}{n} = \frac{60}{450} \approx 0.1333 \Rightarrow$$

$$z = \frac{0.1333 - 0.1667}{\sqrt{\dfrac{0.1667 * 0.8333}{450}}} \approx -1.901$$

Calculate the P-value:

$H_1 : p \neq 0.1667 \Rightarrow$ This is a two-tailed test.

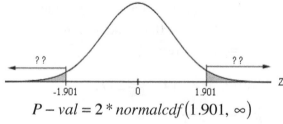

$$P - val = 2 * normalcdf(1.901, \infty)$$
$$\approx 0.0573$$

DECISIONS AND CONCLUSIONS:
Decision: $P - val \approx 0.0573 \leq \alpha \Rightarrow$ Reject H_o (Acceptable risk of making a type I error)
Conclusion: The data provided enough evidence, at the 10% significance level, to show that the die is not fair.

b) $p = 0.158 \Rightarrow H_0 : p = 0.1667$ is false. In part (a), we Rejected H_0. Putting these two facts together, we have a made a correct decision.

67) a) SET UP THE TEST:

Determine H_o and H_1: It is stated that the pocket aces should win at least 80% of the time. Because the phrase at least contains the idea of "equality", we will use 80% as a default for the claimed proportion. The poker player wants to see percentage has **"less than"** 80%.

$$H_o : p = 0.80$$

$$H_1 : p < 0.80$$

Significance Level: $\alpha = 0.05$

GATHER AND WEIGH THE EVIDENCE:
Calculate the test statistic: We will calculate the sample proportion from the given data. So we have

$$\hat{p} = \frac{x}{n} = \frac{31}{50} = 0.62 .$$

$$z = \frac{0.62 - 0.80}{\sqrt{\dfrac{0.80 * 0.20}{50}}} \approx -3.182$$

Calculate the P-value: $H_1 : p < 0.80 \Rightarrow$ This is a left-tailed test.

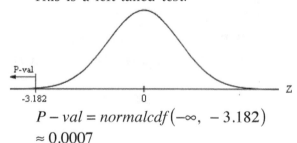

$$P - val = normalcdf(-\infty, -3.182)$$
$$\approx 0.0007$$

DECISIONS AND CONCLUSIONS:
Decision: $P - val \approx 0.0007 \leq \alpha \Rightarrow$ Reject H_o (acceptable risk).
Conclusion: The data did provide enough evidence, at the 5% significance level, to show that the true winning percentage with aces on this poker site will be less than 80%.

b) No, it is possible that the player has just gotten very unlucky in these 50 hands. The P-value tells us that, even if the site is fair, there is still a 0.07% chance of losing this much. However, because it is so unlikely that this would happen by chance, I would recommend that the player stop playing at this site.

69) Given: $\hat{p} = \dfrac{x}{n} = \dfrac{225}{499} \approx 0.4509$

a) We need the z-scores for 99% confidence.

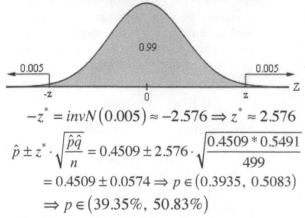

$$-z^* = invN(0.005) \approx -2.576 \Rightarrow z^* \approx 2.576$$

$$\hat{p} \pm z^* \cdot \sqrt{\dfrac{\hat{p}\hat{q}}{n}} = 0.4509 \pm 2.576 \cdot \sqrt{\dfrac{0.4509 * 0.5491}{499}}$$

$$= 0.4509 \pm 0.0574 \Rightarrow p \in (0.3935, 0.5083)$$

$$\Rightarrow p \in (39.35\%, 50.83\%)$$

b) We are 99% confident that the true percentage of American Everglade visitors during the spring of 2008 that were from Florida is somewhere between 39.35% and 50.83%. Therefore, we are confident that the percentage is different than the 32% from winter 2008. So, we should reject $H_o : p = 0.32$.

In symbols:

If $p \in (0.3935, 0.5083) \Rightarrow p \neq 0.32$

$\Rightarrow H_o : p = 0.32$ is False $\Rightarrow$ reject H_o

71) Givens: $n = 493$, $\hat{p} = 0.507$

a) We need the z-scores for 80% confidence.

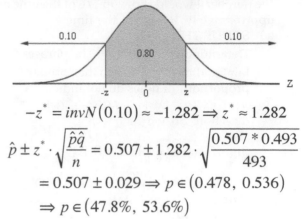

$$-z^* = invN(0.10) \approx -1.282 \Rightarrow z^* \approx 1.282$$

$$\hat{p} \pm z^* \cdot \sqrt{\dfrac{\hat{p}\hat{q}}{n}} = 0.507 \pm 1.282 \cdot \sqrt{\dfrac{0.507 * 0.493}{493}}$$

$$= 0.507 \pm 0.029 \Rightarrow p \in (0.478, 0.536)$$

$$\Rightarrow p \in (47.8\%, 53.6\%)$$

b) We are 80% confident that the percentage of likely voters that will vote for the candidate in question is somewhere between 47.8% and 53.6%. Therefore, it is possible that the candidate will receive less than 50% of the vote. So, we should not reject $H_o : p = 0.5$.

In symbols:

If $p \in (0.478, 0.536) \Rightarrow p$ could be 0.50

$\Rightarrow H_o : p = 0.5$ could be true

$\Rightarrow$ do not reject H_o

73) Givens: $n = 314$, $x = 239$,

$$\hat{p} = \dfrac{x}{n} = \dfrac{239}{314} \approx 0.7611$$

a) We need the z-scores for 98% confidence.

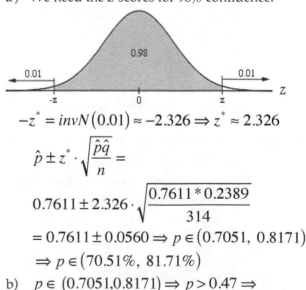

$$-z^* = invN(0.01) \approx -2.326 \Rightarrow z^* \approx 2.326$$

$$\hat{p} \pm z^* \cdot \sqrt{\dfrac{\hat{p}\hat{q}}{n}} =$$

$$0.7611 \pm 2.326 \cdot \sqrt{\dfrac{0.7611 * 0.2389}{314}}$$

$$= 0.7611 \pm 0.0560 \Rightarrow p \in (0.7051, 0.8171)$$

$$\Rightarrow p \in (70.51\%, 81.71\%)$$

b) $p \in (0.7051, 0.8171) \Rightarrow p > 0.47 \Rightarrow$ $H_o : p = 0.47$ is false $\Rightarrow$ We should reject H_o.

Section 9.3

75) We use t rather than z whenever σ is <u>unknown</u> and replaced by <u>s</u>.

76) $\bar{x}$ is the <u>sample</u> mean. μ is the <u>population</u> mean. And μ_o is the <u>claimed</u> mean.

77) In a test of the mean, evidence consists of a large <u>difference</u> between μ and μ_o.

78) In general, evidence in a hypothesis test comes from seeing large differences between what we observed in the <u>sample</u> and what we expected to see if H_o was <u>true</u>.

79) a) Because σ is unknown, we must use s and, therefore, our test statistic is a t-score.

$$t = \frac{42.66 - 41}{4.4524 / \sqrt{22}} \approx 1.749$$

   b) $H_1 : \mu > 41 \Rightarrow$ This is a right-tailed test. Also, $df = n - 1 = 21$.

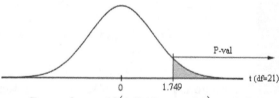

$$P - val = tcdf(1.749, \infty, 21) \approx 0.0474$$

   c) $P - val \approx 0.0474 \le \alpha \Rightarrow$ Reject H_o (Acceptable risk of a type I error.)

81) a) Because σ is unknown, we must use s and, therefore, our test statistic is a t-score.

$$t = \frac{21.074 - 21.8}{2.805 / \sqrt{37}} \approx -1.574$$

   b) $H_1 : \mu \ne 21.8 \Rightarrow$ This is a two-tailed test. Also, $df = n - 1 = 36$.

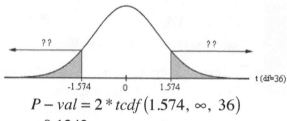

$$P - val = 2 * tcdf(1.574, \infty, 36)$$
$$\approx 0.1242$$

   c) $P - val \approx 0.1242 > \alpha \Rightarrow$ Do not Reject H_o (Too Risky)

83) a) Because σ is unknown, we must use s and, therefore, our test statistic is a t-score.

$$t = \frac{18.90 - 18.3}{0.8557 / \sqrt{42}} \approx 4.544$$

   b) $H_1 : \mu < 18.3 \Rightarrow$ This is a left-tailed test. Also, $df = n - 1 = 41$.

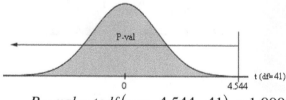

$$P - val = tcdf(-\infty, 4.544, 41) \approx 1.0000$$

   c) $P - val \approx 1.0000 > \alpha \Rightarrow$ Do not Reject H_o (Too Risky)

85) a) SET UP THE TEST:

Determine H_o and H_1: Since we want to know if the true average is different than the author's time, we will use his value as a default for the claimed mean. He wants to see if the true average for all hikers is "**different**".

$H_o : \mu = 5.5$

$H_1 : \mu \neq 5.5$

Significance Level: $\alpha = 0.10$

GATHER AND WEIGH THE EVIDENCE:
Calculate the test statistic: The mean and standard deviation provided are both from the sample. So we have $\bar{x} = 4.91$, $s = 1.682$, and $n = 14$. Since we are using a sample standard deviation, our test statistic is a t-score.

$$t = \frac{4.91 - 5.5}{1.682 / \sqrt{14}} \approx -1.312$$

Calculate the P-value: $H_1 : \mu \neq 5.5 \Rightarrow$ This is a two-tailed test.

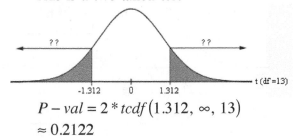

$$P - val = 2 * tcdf(1.312, \infty, 13)$$

$$\approx 0.2122$$

DECISIONS AND CONCLUSIONS:
Decision: $P - val \approx 0.2122 > \alpha \Rightarrow$ Do Not Reject H_o (too risky).

Conclusion: The data did not provide enough evidence, at the 10% significance level, to show that the true average time to the top for hikers is different than 5.5 hours.

b) Since $n = 14 < 15$ and the population is unknown, we must hope that hiking times are normally distributed.

87) a) SET UP THE TEST:

Determine H_o and H_1: The daily average before the toll hike was \$234,018, this will be the claimed value for the mean. They want to see if this average has "**changed**".

$H_o : \mu = 234,018$

$H_1 : \mu \neq 234,018$

Significance Level: $\alpha = 0.05$

GATHER AND WEIGH THE EVIDENCE:
Calculate the test statistic: We are given that $\bar{x} = 249,931$, $s \approx 36,713$, $n = 30$.

$$t = \frac{249,931 - 234,018}{36,713 / \sqrt{30}} \approx 2.374$$

Calculate the P-value:
$H_1 : \mu \neq 234,018 \Rightarrow$ This is a two-tailed test. $df = 30 - 1 = 29$

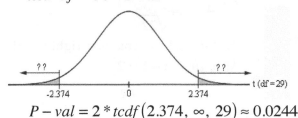

$$P - val = 2 * tcdf(2.374, \infty, 29) \approx 0.0244$$

DECISIONS AND CONCLUSIONS:
Decision: $P - val \approx 0.0244 < \alpha \Rightarrow$ Reject H_o (acceptable risk).

Conclusion: There is enough evidence, at the 5% significance level, to show that the average daily revenue has changed since the toll hike.

b) Since $n = 30 \geq 30$, $\bar{x}$ is normally distributed and the requirements have been met.

89) Givens: Claimed mean is 7 hours per month, $n = 250$, $\bar{x} = 10.77$, $s = 6.793$.

a) SET UP THE TEST:

Determine H_o and H_1: We want to show the mean is "different than" claimed, so we get:

$$H_o : \mu = 7$$
$$H_1 : \mu \neq 7$$

Significance Level: $\alpha = 0.05$

GATHER AND WEIGH THE EVIDENCE:
Calculate the test statistic: Because σ is unknown, we must use s and, therefore, our test statistic is a t-score.

$$t = \frac{10.77 - 7}{6.793 / \sqrt{250}} \approx 8.775$$

Calculate the P-value: $H_1 : \mu \neq 7 \Rightarrow$ This is a two-tailed test. Also, $df = n - 1 = 249$.

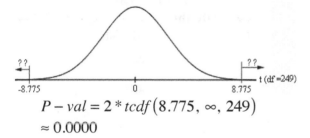

$$P - val = 2 * tcdf(8.775, \infty, 249)$$
$$\approx 0.0000$$

DECISIONS AND CONCLUSIONS:
Decision: $P - val \approx 0.0000 \leq \alpha \Rightarrow$ Reject H_o (Acceptable Risk)

Conclusion: The data does provide enough evidence, at the 5% significance level, to show that the true mean hours per month for students at the teacher's school is different than the average of 7 hours for all users worldwide.

b) $n = 250 \geq 30 \Rightarrow \bar{x}$ is normally distributed. So, the requirements have been met.

c) Maybe, but even if the mean for students at her school is 11 hours per month, that is still less than 0.5 hours per day. Everyone needs a little time away from the books, right?

91) a) SET UP THE TEST:

Determine H_o and H_1: Since the website claims that the mean is 333, we will use this value for the claimed mean. The consumer group wants to see if the true average is "**more than**" claimed.

$$H_o : \mu = 333$$
$$H_1 : \mu > 333$$

Significance Level: $\alpha = 0.01$

GATHER AND WEIGH THE EVIDENCE:
Calculate the test statistic: We calculate the mean and standard deviation from the sample data provided. We get:
$\bar{x} \approx 337.2857$, $s \approx 12.8508$, $n = 14$.
Since we are using a sample standard deviation, our test statistic is a t-score.

$$t = \frac{337.2857 - 333}{12.8508 / \sqrt{14}} \approx 1.248$$

Calculate the P-value:
$H_1 : \mu > 333 \Rightarrow$ This is a right-tailed test.

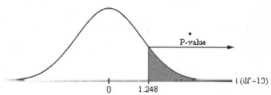

$$P - val = tcdf(1.248, \infty, 13) \approx 0.1170$$

DECISIONS AND CONCLUSIONS:
Decision: $P - val \approx 0.1170 > \alpha \Rightarrow$ Do Not Reject H_o (too risky).

Conclusion: The data did not provide enough evidence, at the 1% significance level, to show that the true mean for these sandwiches is more than claimed on the website.

b) $n = 14 < 15$, but Normtest produced a P-value of 0.646 > 0.05. Therefore, it is reasonable to believe that the population is normal, so it is also reasonable to believe that the requirements have been met.

c) No. The sample average was greater than 333, but the difference is small enough that it could reasonably just be the result of random variation in the sample.

93) a) SET UP THE TEST:

Determine H_o and H_1: Before the new menus were introduced, the mean was known to be $15,470 per day. We will use this value as a default for the claimed mean. They want to see if new menu prices will result in a "**change**" in the average daily revenue.

$H_o : \mu = 15470$

$H_1 : \mu \neq 15470$

Significance Level: $\alpha = 0.05$

GATHER AND WEIGH THE EVIDENCE:
Calculate the test statistic: The mean and standard deviation provided are both from the sample. So we have $\bar{x} = 14312$, $s = 2419$, and $n = 40$. Since we are using a sample standard deviation, our test statistic is a t-score.

$$t = \frac{14312 - 15470}{2419 / \sqrt{40}} \approx -3.028$$

Calculate the P-value: $H_1 : \mu \neq 15470 \Rightarrow$ This is a two-tailed test.

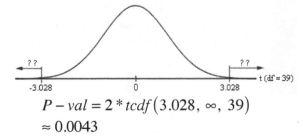

$$P - val = 2 * tcdf(3.028, \infty, 39)$$
$$\approx 0.0043$$

DECISIONS AND CONCLUSIONS:
Decision: $P - val \approx 0.0043 < \alpha \Rightarrow$ Reject H_o (acceptable risk).
Conclusion: The data did provide enough evidence, at the 5% significance level, to show that the true average daily revenue has changed with the introduction of the new menus.

b) Since $n = 40 \geq 30$, $\bar{x}$ will be normally distributed regardless of the distribution of the population. The requirements have been met.

c) No. After the new menus, not only did the average daily revenue change, but it appears to have become lower.

d) Because we rejected H_o, it is not possible that we have made a type II error, but it is possible that we have made a type I error. However, this seems very unlikely with a p-value of approx 0.0043. H_o would have to be true for a type I error to occur.

95) a) SET UP THE TEST:
Determine H_o and H_1: The App claims that the average wait time is 55 minutes. We will use this value for the claimed mean. We want to see if the true mean "differs" from this reported value.

$H_o : \mu = 55$

$H_1 : \mu \neq 55$

Significance Level: $\alpha = 0.10$

GATHER AND WEIGH THE EVIDENCE:
Calculate the test statistic: Using technology to find the mean and standard deviation from the data provided: $\bar{x} \approx 59.636$, $s \approx 9.09145$, $n = 11$. Because we are using a sample standard deviation, our test statistic is a t-score.

$$t = \frac{59.636 - 55}{9.09145 / \sqrt{11}} \approx 1.691$$

Calculate the P-value: $H_1 : \mu \neq 55 \Rightarrow$ This is a two-tailed test.

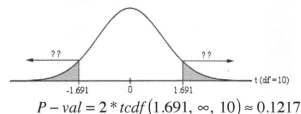

$$P - val = 2 * tcdf(1.691, \infty, 10) \approx 0.1217$$

DECISIONS AND CONCLUSIONS:
Decision: $P - val \approx 0.1217 > \alpha \Rightarrow$ Do Not Reject H_o (too risky).
Conclusion: The data did not provide enough evidence, at the 10% significance level, to show that the true wait time differs from the reported 55 minutes.

b) Because $n = 11 < 15$, we need the population to be normally distributed. The normtest shows a P-val of 0.158. This is greater than 0.05, so there it is reasonable that the population is normal. Therefore, it is reasonable to believe that the requirements are met.

c) Because we did not reject H_o, it is impossible that we have made a type I error. However, if H_o is false, then we have made a type II error.

97) a) SET UP THE TEST:
Determine H_o and H_1: Before the optimization, the average is reported to be 16.67 hits per day. This will be the claimed value for the mean. He wants to see if this average after the optimization has "**increased**".

$H_o : \mu = 16.67$

$H_1 : \mu > 16.67$

Significance Level: $\alpha = 0.01$

GATHER AND WEIGH THE EVIDENCE:
Calculate the test statistic: We are given that $\bar{x} \approx 23.0556$, $s \approx 11.2065$, $n = 18$.

$$t = \dfrac{23.0556 - 16.67}{11.2065 / \sqrt{18}} \approx 2.418$$

Calculate the P-value:
$H_1 : \mu > 16.67 \Rightarrow$ This is a right-tailed test.

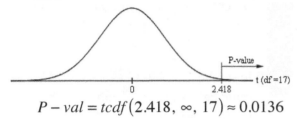

$$P - val = tcdf\left(2.418,\ \infty,\ 17\right) \approx 0.0136$$

DECISIONS AND CONCLUSIONS:
Decision: $P - val \approx 0.0136 > \alpha \Rightarrow$ Do Not Reject H_o (too risky).
Conclusion: There is not enough evidence, at the 1% significance level, to show that the true average number of hits has increased since the optimization.

b) Since $15 \le n = 18 < 30$, we need the population to not be severely skewed to ensure that $\bar{x}$ is normally distributed and the requirements have been met. The boxplot does not have one whisker that is much larger than the other, so it does not look like the population is severely skewed. So, it is reasonable to assume that the requirements have been met.

c) No, not at the 1% significance level. There is over a 1% chance of seeing a sample mean that much higher than 16.67 even if the population mean was still at that value. This difference could just be the result of random variation.

97) d) Since we Did Not Reject H_o, it is not possible that we have made a type I error. However, a type II error is possible if H_o is actually false.

99) a) SET UP THE TEST:
Determine H_o and H_1: Since we want to show that the true average year of mint is after 1993, we will use 1993 as a default value for the claimed mean. We want to see if the true mean year is "**greater than**" 1993.

$H_o : \mu = 1993$

$H_1 : \mu > 1993$

Significance Level: $\alpha = 0.01$

GATHER AND WEIGH THE EVIDENCE:
Calculate the test statistic: We are given: $\bar{x} = 1990.8$, $s \approx 11.601$, $n = 30$. Since we are using a sample standard deviation, our test statistic is a t-score.

$$t = \dfrac{1990.8 - 1993}{11.601 / \sqrt{30}} \approx -1.039$$

Calculate the P-value: $H_1 : \mu > 1993 \Rightarrow$ This is a right-tailed test.

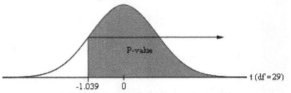

$$P - val = tcdf\left(-1.039,\ \infty,\ 29\right) \approx 0.8463$$

DECISIONS AND CONCLUSIONS:
Decision: $P - val \approx 0.8463 > \alpha \Rightarrow$ Do Not Reject H_o (too risky).
Conclusion: The data did not provide enough evidence, at the 1% significance level, to show that the true mean year of mint for nickels is greater than 1993.

b) Since $n = 30 \ge 30$, $\bar{x}$ will be normally distributed regardless of the distribution of the population. The requirements have been met.

c) $\mu = 1994.2 \Rightarrow H_o : \mu = 1993$ is false. In part (a), we did Not Reject H_o. Not Rejecting a false claim is a type II error.

d) Because the difference was not large enough to lead to the rejection of H_0, it is neither statistically significant nor practically significant.

101) a) SET UP THE TEST:

Determine H_o and H_1: We will use the 2005 average for the claimed mean. We want to see if the true average cost has "increased" from the 2005 level.

$H_o : \mu = 3991$

$H_1 : \mu > 3991$

Significance Level: $\alpha = 0.05$

GATHER AND WEIGH THE EVIDENCE:
Calculate the test statistic: We are given: $\bar{x} = 5311$, $s = 1195$, $n = 60$. Since we are using a sample standard deviation, our test statistic is a t-score.

$t = \dfrac{5311 - 3991}{1195 / \sqrt{60}} \approx 8.556$

Calculate the P-value: $H_1 : \mu > 3991 \Rightarrow$ This is a right-tailed test.

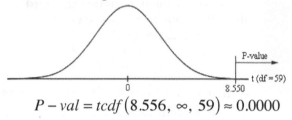

$P - val = tcdf(8.556,\ \infty,\ 59) \approx 0.0000$

DECISIONS AND CONCLUSIONS:
Decision: $P - val \approx 0.0000 \leq \alpha \Rightarrow$ Reject H_o (acceptable risk).
Conclusion: The data did provide enough evidence, at the 5% significance level, to show that the true mean healthcare costs have increased since 2005.

b) Since $n = 60 \geq 30$, $\bar{x}$ will be normally distributed regardless of the distribution of the population. The requirements have been met.

c) $\mu = 4250 \Rightarrow H_o : \mu = 3991$ is false. In part (a), we did Reject H_o. Rejecting a false claim is a correct decision.

d) Because the difference was large enough to lead to the rejection of H_0, it is considered to be statistically significant. The difference between $5311 and $3991 is $1320. This represents 33.07% increase over a two-year time span. I would consider such a large percentage change in the cost to be practically significant as well. That $1320 coast can have a large impact on a person's budget.

103) Givens: $n = 14$, $\bar{x} = 337.3$, $s = 12.851$.
a) We need the t-scores for 98% confidence with $df = n - 1 = 13$.

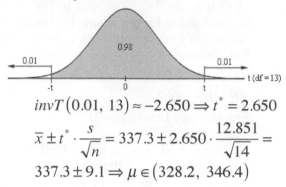

$invT(0.01,\ 13) \approx -2.650 \Rightarrow t^* = 2.650$

$\bar{x} \pm t^* \cdot \dfrac{s}{\sqrt{n}} = 337.3 \pm 2.650 \cdot \dfrac{12.851}{\sqrt{14}} =$

$337.3 \pm 9.1 \Rightarrow \mu \in (328.2,\ 346.4)$

b) We are 98% confident that the true population mean for the sandwiches is somewhere between 328.2 and 346.4 calories. This means that it could be 333 calories. If it is possible that the mean really is 333 calories, then we should not reject Subway's claim that it is 333 calories. This was the decision we reached on Exercise (91).

In symbols: If $\mu \in (328.2,\ 346.4) \Rightarrow \mu$ could be 333 $H_o : \mu = 333$ could be true $\Rightarrow$ Do Not Reject H_o

105)   Givens: $n = 40$, $\bar{x} = 14312$, $s = 2419$.
a) We need the t-scores for 95% confidence with $df = n - 1 = 39$.

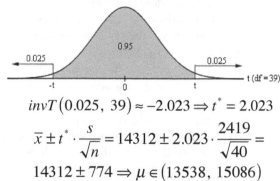

$invT(0.025,\ 39) \approx -2.023 \Rightarrow t^* = 2.023$

$\bar{x} \pm t^* \cdot \dfrac{s}{\sqrt{n}} = 14312 \pm 2.023 \cdot \dfrac{2419}{\sqrt{40}} =$

$14312 \pm 774 \Rightarrow \mu \in (13538,\ 15086)$

b) We are 95% confident that the true population mean for the revenue is somewhere between $13538 and $15086. This implies that it is less than $15470. Because we are confident that the true mean is less than $15470, we should reject the claim that it equals $15470. This was the decision we reached on Exercise (89).

In symbols: If $\mu \in (13538,\ 15086) \Rightarrow$

$\mu < 15470 \Rightarrow H_o : u = 15470$ is false $\Rightarrow$

Reject H_o

107) Givens: $n = 60$, $\bar{x} = 5311$, $s = 1195$.
   a) We need the t-scores for 90% confidence
       with $df = n - 1 = 59$.

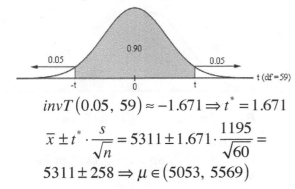

$invT(0.05,\ 59) \approx -1.671 \Rightarrow t^* = 1.671$

$\bar{x} \pm t^* \cdot \dfrac{s}{\sqrt{n}} = 5311 \pm 1.671 \cdot \dfrac{1195}{\sqrt{60}} =$

$5311 \pm 258 \Rightarrow \mu \in (5053,\ 5569)$

   b) We are 90% confident that the true
       population mean for the healthcare costs is
       somewhere between \$5053 and \$5569. This
       implies that it is more than \$3991. Because
       we are confident that the true mean is more
       than \$3991, we should reject the claim that
       it equals \$3991. This was the decision we
       reached on Exercise (97).

       In symbols: If $\mu \in (5053,\ 5569) \Rightarrow$

       $\mu > 3991 \Rightarrow H_o : u = 3991$ is false $\Rightarrow$

       Reject H_o

Chapter Problem:

   a) SET UP THE TEST:
       Determine H_o and H_1: It is stated that
       the pregnant women made up 1% of the
       population at that time. Because we wish
       to show that the proportion of flu deaths is
       "**greater than**" the proportion of pregnant
       women in the overall population, we will
       use 1% as a default for the claimed
       proportion.

       $H_o : p = 0.01$

       $H_1 : p > 0.01$

       Significance Level: $\alpha = 0.05$

   b) $30 = 0.05 * n \Rightarrow \dfrac{30}{0.05} = n \Rightarrow n = 600$

   c) GATHER AND WEIGH THE EVIDENCE:
       Calculate the test statistic: The sample
       proportion was actually given, but we can
       also calculate it from the given data. So we

       have $\hat{p} = \dfrac{x}{n} = \dfrac{30}{600} = 0.05$.

       $z = \dfrac{0.05 - 0.01}{\sqrt{\dfrac{0.01 * 0.99}{600}}} \approx 9.847$

       Calculate the P-value: $H_1 : p > 0.01 \Rightarrow$
       This is a right-tailed test.

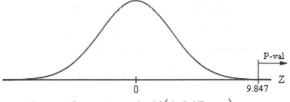

       $P - val = normalcdf(9.847,\ \infty)$

       ≈ 0.0000

   d) DECISIONS AND CONCLUSIONS:
       Decision: $P - val \approx 0.0000 \leq \alpha \Rightarrow$ Reject
       H_o (acceptable risk).
       Conclusion: The data did provide enough
       evidence, at the 5% significance level, to
       show that the proportion of pregnant
       women among the swine flu deaths is
       greater than the proportion of pregnant
       women in the overall population.

e) $np_o = 600(0.01) = 6 < 10$

     $nq_o = 600(0.99) = 594 \geq 10$

Because np_o was smaller than 10, the requirements are not met. This means the P-value may have substantial error in it. However, the z-score of $z \approx 9.847$ does not depend on a normal distribution for $\hat{p}$. So, we can still say that it would be highly unusual to see such a large difference between our sample proportion and the claimed proportion if H_0 were true. We should probably still be confident with our decision to Reject H_o.

Ch 9: Review Exercises

1)   a)   Because σ is unknown, we must use s and, therefore, our test statistic is a t-score.

     $t = \dfrac{11.58 - 14}{5.8762 / \sqrt{38}} \approx -2.539$

   b) $H_1 : \mu < 14 \Rightarrow$ This is a left-tailed test. Also, $df = n - 1 = 37$.

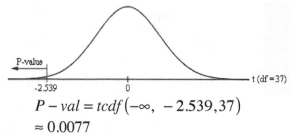

     $P - val = tcdf(-\infty, -2.539, 37)$

     ≈ 0.0077

   c) $P - val \approx 0.0077 \leq \alpha \Rightarrow$ Reject H_o (Acceptable risk of a type I error.)

3)   a) $\hat{p} = \dfrac{x}{n} = \dfrac{235}{612} \approx 0.3840 \Rightarrow$

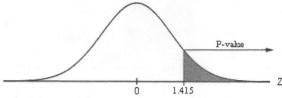

   b) $H_1 : p > 0.3566 \Rightarrow$ This is a right-tailed test.

     $P - val = normalcdf(1.415, \infty)$

     ≈ 0.0785

   c) $P - val \approx 0.0785 > \alpha \Rightarrow$ Do Not Reject H_o (too risky.)

5) Givens: $n = 519$, $x = 291$

   a) SET UP THE TEST:

   Determine H_o and H_1: We want to show that the proportion is "more than half".

   $H_o : p = 0.5$

   $H_1 : p > 0.5$

   Significance Level: $\alpha = 0.10$

   GATHER AND WEIGH THE EVIDENCE:
   Calculate the test statistic:

   $$\hat{p} = \frac{x}{n} = \frac{291}{519} \approx 0.5607 \Rightarrow$$

   $$z = \frac{0.5607 - 0.5}{\sqrt{\dfrac{0.5 * 0.5}{519}}} \approx 2.766$$

   Calculate the P-value: $H_1 : p > 0.5 \Rightarrow$ This is a right-tailed test.

   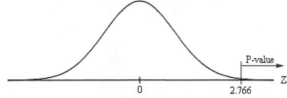

   $$P - val = normalcdf(2.766, \infty) \approx 0.0028$$

   DECISIONS AND CONCLUSIONS:
   Decision: $P - val \approx 0.0028 \leq \alpha \Rightarrow$ Reject H_o (Acceptable risk of making a type I error)

   Conclusion: The data does provide enough evidence, at the 10% significance level, to show that the true proportion of women that do the bills is more than half of all married couples.

   b) $np_0 = 519 * 0.5 = 259.5 \geq 10$ and

   $nq_0 = 519 * 0.5 = 259.5 \geq 10$, so $\hat{p}$ is approximately normal and the requirements are met.

   c) Because we rejected H_o, it is not possible that we have made a type II error. However, if it turns out that H_o is true, then we have made a type I error. The perceived risk of a type I error was about 0.0028 or 0.28%.

6) a) $H_o : \mu = 400$

   $H_1 : \mu > 400$

   $\alpha = 0.05$

   $t \approx 2.230$

   $P - val \approx 0.0238$

   Reject H_o

   In words . . . .

   b) Since $n = 12 < 15$, we must hope that the number of words per day for Giselle are normally distributed. Since the P-value from the normtest is greater than 0.05, a normal population is a reasonable assumption.

   c) If we had enough evidence to show that Giselle's true average number of questions per day is greater than 400, when in fact her true average is not greater than 400.

7) a) SET UP THE TEST:

Determine H_o **and** H_1: The commonly accepted sleep number is 8 hours. We will use this value as a default for the claimed mean. We want to see if Fridays for teens is "greater" than 8 hours.

$H_o : \mu = 8$

$H_1 : \mu > 8$

Significance Level: $\alpha = 0.01$

GATHER AND WEIGH THE EVIDENCE:
Calculate the test statistic: We are given $\bar{x} \approx 9.33$, $s = 1.6985$, and $n = 28$. Since we are using a sample standard deviation, our test statistic is a t-score.

$t = \dfrac{9.33 - 8}{1.6985 / \sqrt{28}} \approx 4.143$

Calculate the P-value: $H_1 : \mu > 8 \Rightarrow$ This is a right-tailed test.

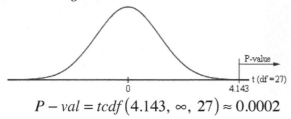

$P - val = tcdf(4.143, \infty, 27) \approx 0.0002$

DECISIONS AND CONCLUSIONS:
Decision: $P - val \approx 0.0002 < \alpha \Rightarrow$ Reject H_o (acceptable risk).

Conclusion: The data did provide enough evidence, at the 1% significance level, to show that the true average Friday night sleep times for teenagers is greater than 8 hours.

b) Because $15 \leq n = 28 < 30$ and the population distribution is unknown, we must hope that the population is not severely skewed so that $\bar{x}$ will be normally distributed.

c) $\mu = 9.1 \Rightarrow H_o : \mu = 8$ is false. Therefore, when we rejected H_o is part (a), that was a correct decision.

9) a) SET UP THE TEST:

Determine H_o **and** H_1: We are comparing to the MLB lifetime of 7 pitches. So, we will use his value as a default for the claimed mean. We want to see if the average for college baseball is "different".

$H_o : \mu = 7$

$H_1 : \mu \neq 7$

Significance Level: $\alpha = 0.10$

GATHER AND WEIGH THE EVIDENCE:
Calculate the test statistic: Using technology with the sample data, we find $\bar{x} = 8.5$, $s \approx 5.2587$, and $n = 14$.

$t = \dfrac{8.5 - 7}{5.2587 / \sqrt{14}} \approx 1.067$

Calculate the P-value: $H_1 : \mu \neq 7 \Rightarrow$ This is a two-tailed test.

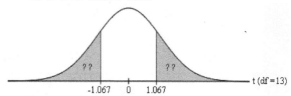

$P - val = 2 * tcdf(1.067, \infty, 13) \approx 0.3054$

DECISIONS AND CONCLUSIONS:
Decision: $P - val \approx 0.3054 > \alpha \Rightarrow$ Do Not Reject H_o (too risky).

Conclusion: The data did not provide enough evidence, at the 10% significance level, to show that the true average lifetime for a college baseball is different than the mean of 7 pitches in MLB.

b) Because $n = 14 < 15$, we need the population to be normally distributed. The P-value from the normtest is $0.829 > 0.05$. Therefore, it is reasonable to believe that the population is normal. So, it is reasonable that the requirements have been met.

c) Because we did not reject H_o, it is not possible that we have made a type I error. However, if it turns out that H_o is false, then we have made a type II error.

11) a) SET UP THE TEST:

Determine H_o and H_1: The average for all Americans is 65 oz. This will be the claimed value for the mean. She wants to show that the average for college students during finals week "exceeds" this amount.

$H_o : \mu = 65$

$H_1 : \mu > 65$

Significance Level: $\alpha = 0.05$

GATHER AND WEIGH THE EVIDENCE:
Calculate the test statistic: We are given that $\bar{x} = 90.54$, $s = 68.422$, $n = 40$.

$$t = \frac{90.54 - 65}{68.422 / \sqrt{40}} \approx 2.361$$

Calculate the P-value: $H_1 : \mu > 65 \Rightarrow$ This is a right-tailed test.

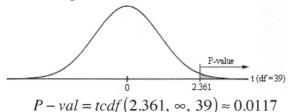

$$P - val = tcdf(2.361, \infty, 39) \approx 0.0117$$

DECISIONS AND CONCLUSIONS:
Decision: $P - val \approx 0.0117 < \alpha \Rightarrow$ Reject H_o (acceptable risk).

Conclusion: There is enough evidence, at the 5% significance level, to show that the true average number of ounces of coffee for college students during finals week does exceed the 65 ounce average for all Americans.

b) A type I error will occur if the data provides enough evidence to show that the true average coffee consumption for college students during finals week exceeds the national average, when in fact the true average for college students is not higher.

12) a)

$H_o : p = 0.5$

$H_1 : p \neq 0.5$

$\alpha = 0.05$

$z \approx 3.382$

$P - val \approx 0.0007$

Reject H_o

In words . . . .

b) $np_0 = 73.5 \geq 10$ and $nq_0 = 73.5 \geq 10$, so $\hat{p}$ is approximately normal and the requirements are met.

c) A type I error will occur if the data provides enough evidence to show that the true percentage of heads for spins of these coins is not 50% when, in fact, the true percentage is 50%.

d) Because we rejected H_0, the difference is considered to be statistically significant. With $\hat{p} \approx 0.6395$, I would say this is also far enough away from 50% to be practically significant as well. I would not feel that it would be a big unfair advantage to know that calling "heads" in this situation would be correct about 63.95% of the time.

13) a) SET UP THE TEST:
Determine H_o and H_1: With properly inflated tires, the true average mileage is 23.9 mpg. We will use this value for the claimed mean. We want to see if the average is has "lowered" with the slightly deflated tires.

$H_o : \mu = 23.8$

$H_1 : \mu < 23.8$

Significance Level: $\alpha = 0.10$

GATHER AND WEIGH THE EVIDENCE:
Calculate the test statistic: The mean and standard deviation from the sample are provided. So we have $\bar{x} \approx 21.381$, $s \approx 4.9859$, and $n = 16$.

$$t = \frac{21.381 - 23.8}{4.9859 / \sqrt{16}} \approx -1.941$$

Calculate the P-value: $H_1 : \mu < 23.8 \Rightarrow$ This is a left-tailed test.

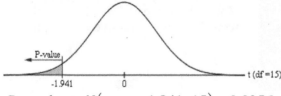

$$P - val = tcdf\left(-\infty, \ -1.941, \ 15\right) \approx 0.0356$$

DECISIONS AND CONCLUSIONS:
Decision: $P - val \approx 0.0356 < \alpha \Rightarrow$ Reject H_o (acceptable risk).

Conclusion: The data did provide enough evidence, at the 10% significance level, to show that the true mileage for cars will be lower if the tires were under inflated by 10 psi.

b) Since $15 \le n = 16 < 30$, we must hope that the population is not severely skewed. The given boxplot seems roughly symmetric rather than skewed. So, since the boxplot does not point towards a severely skewed population, it is reasonable to believe that the requirements have been met.

c) Yes, there is only a 3.56% chance of seeing a difference like we saw between our sample mean and 23.8 mpg just due to random variation. This means that properly inflated tires lead to an improvement in mileage that was statistically significant. The difference between the sample value of 21.381 and 23.8 is 2.419 miles per gallon. This would mean saving over 10% on gas use and on gas costs. I think most people would feel this difference was big enough to be of practical significance in their lives.

d) A type I error would occur on this problem if we had enough evidence to show that the true mileage for cars will be lower if the tires were under inflated by 10 psi, when in fact the true mileage would not actually be lower.

15) a) SET UP THE TEST:

Determine H_o and H_1: We are trying to compare the current percentage to the percentage from 2004. So, we will use the 25.6% from 2004 as the claimed proportion. They want to see percentage has "decreased" in the current population.

$H_o : p = 0.256$

$H_1 : p < 0.256$

Significance Level: $\alpha = 0.05$

GATHER AND WEIGH THE EVIDENCE:
Calculate the test statistic: They give us the percentage from the current sample. If we convert this to a decimal, we have $\hat{p} = 0.2426$.

$$z = \frac{0.2426 - 0.256}{\sqrt{\frac{0.256 * 0.744}{713}}} \approx -0.820$$

Calculate the P-value: $H_1 : p < 0.256 \Rightarrow$ This is a left-tailed test.

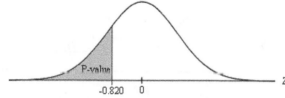

$$P - val = normalcdf(-\infty, -0.820) \approx 0.2061$$

DECISIONS AND CONCLUSIONS:
Decision: $P - val \approx 0.2061 > \alpha \Rightarrow$ Do Not Reject H_o (too risky).

Conclusion: The data did not provide enough evidence, at the 5% significance level, to show that the true percentage of smokers in the adult population has decreased since 2004.

b) No. We did have some evidence from our sample that the percentage had decreased from 2004, just not enough to convince us that this difference not just caused by random variation. When we fail to reject H_o, it means that H_o is a reasonable possibility. We should not be convinced that H_o is true. Also, we should not be trying to decide cause and effect from an observational study.

c) Because the difference was not large enough to lead to the rejection of H_0, it should not be considered to be statistically significant or practically significant.

17) Givens: $n = 713$, $\hat{p} = 0.2426$

a) We need the z-scores for 90% confidence.

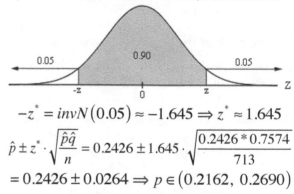

$$-z^* = invN(0.05) \approx -1.645 \Rightarrow z^* \approx 1.645$$

$$\hat{p} \pm z^* \cdot \sqrt{\frac{\hat{p}\hat{q}}{n}} = 0.2426 \pm 1.645 \cdot \sqrt{\frac{0.2426 * 0.7574}{713}}$$

$$= 0.2426 \pm 0.0264 \Rightarrow p \in (0.2162, 0.2690)$$

b) In symbols:

If $p \in (0.2162, 0.2690) \Rightarrow p$ could be $0.256 \Rightarrow H_o : p = 0.256$ could be true $\Rightarrow$ do not reject H_o

19) Givens: $n = 16$, $\bar{x} \approx 21.381$, $s \approx 4.9859$

a) We need the t-scores for 80% confidence.

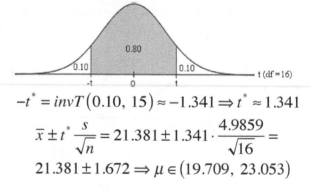

$$-t^* = invT(0.10, 15) \approx -1.341 \Rightarrow t^* \approx 1.341$$

$$\bar{x} \pm t^* \frac{s}{\sqrt{n}} = 21.381 \pm 1.341 \cdot \frac{4.9859}{\sqrt{16}} =$$

$$21.381 \pm 1.672 \Rightarrow \mu \in (19.709, 23.053)$$

b) In symbols:

If $\mu \in (19.709, 23.053) \Rightarrow \mu < 23.8$ $\Rightarrow H_1 : \mu < 23.8$ is true and $H_o : \mu = 23.8$ is false $\Rightarrow$ Reject H_o

Section 10.1

1) χ^2 curves are <u>right</u>-skewed. They are NOT <u>symmetric</u>.

2) χ^2 curves start at <u>zero</u> and extend indefinitely to the <u>right</u> while the height of the curves approach zero.

3) The peak of the curve will occur slightly <u>before</u> the χ^2 value corresponding to the number of degrees of <u>freedom</u> .

4) When using the $\chi^2 cdf$ function, we input left and right <u>boundaries</u> as well as the <u>df</u> and the function gives us <u>area</u> as an output.

5) When using the $inv\chi^2$ function, we input the <u>area</u> to the <u>left</u> and the function give us the <u>chi-square</u> boundary as an output.

6) When finding the boundaries that trap a specified amount of area in the middle, we must compute the left and right hand boundaries <u>separately</u> because of the lack of <u>symmetry</u> in the graph.

7) a) df of 10 is just to the right of the peak.

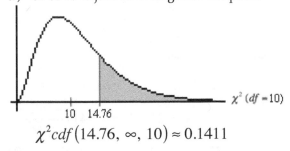

$$\chi^2 cdf\left(14.76,\ \infty,\ 10\right) \approx 0.1411$$

b) df of 5 is just to the right of the peak.

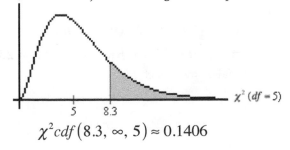

$$\chi^2 cdf\left(8.3,\ \infty,\ 5\right) \approx 0.1406$$

c) df of 6 is just to the right of the peak.

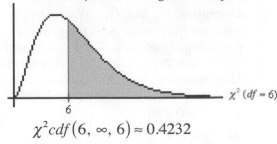

$$\chi^2 cdf\left(6,\ \infty,\ 6\right) \approx 0.4232$$

9) a) df of 6 is just to the right of the peak.

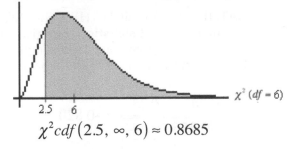

$$\chi^2 cdf\left(2.5,\ \infty,\ 6\right) \approx 0.8685$$

b) df of 4 is just to the right of the peak.

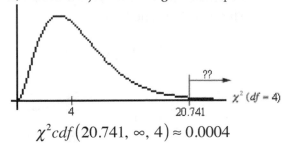

$$\chi^2 cdf\left(20.741,\ \infty,\ 4\right) \approx 0.0004$$

c) df of 21 is just to the right of the peak.

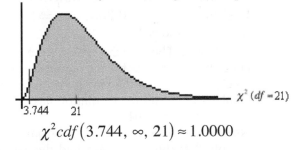

$$\chi^2 cdf\left(3.744,\ \infty,\ 21\right) \approx 1.0000$$

11) a) df of 4 is just to the right of the peak.

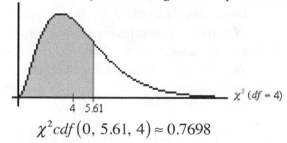

$$\chi^2 cdf\,(0,\ 5.61,\ 4) \approx 0.7698$$

b) df of 9 is just to the right of the peak.

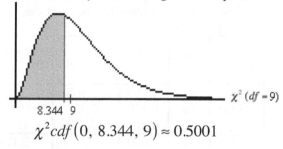

$$\chi^2 cdf\,(0,\ 8.344,\ 9) \approx 0.5001$$

c) df of 11 is just to the right of the peak.

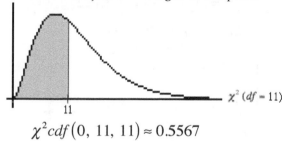

$$\chi^2 cdf\,(0,\ 11,\ 11) \approx 0.5567$$

13) a) df of 12 is just to the right of the peak.

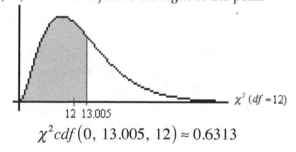

$$\chi^2 cdf\,(0,\ 13.005,\ 12) \approx 0.6313$$

b) df of 3 is just to the right of the peak.

$$\chi^2 cdf\,(0,\ 18.504,\ 3) \approx 0.9997$$

c) df of 19 is just to the right of the peak.

$$\chi^2 cdf\,(0,\ 2.899,\ 19) \approx 0.0000$$

15) a) df of 14 is just to the right of the peak.

$$\chi^2 = inv\chi^2\,(0.90,\ 14) \approx 21.064$$

b) df of 10 is just to the right of the peak.

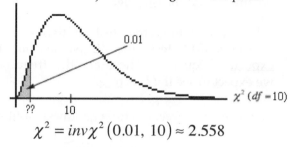

$$\chi^2 = inv\chi^2\,(0.01,\ 10) \approx 2.558$$

17) a) df of 6 is just to the right of the peak.

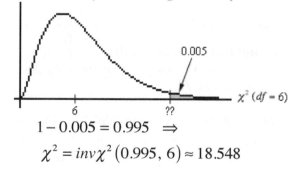

$$1 - 0.005 = 0.995 \ \Rightarrow$$
$$\chi^2 = inv\chi^2\,(0.995,\ 6) \approx 18.548$$

b) df of 17 is just to the right of the peak.

$$1 - 0.95 = 0.05 \ \Rightarrow$$
$$\chi^2 = inv\chi^2\,(0.05,\ 17) \approx 8.672$$

19) a) df of 5 is just to the right of the peak.

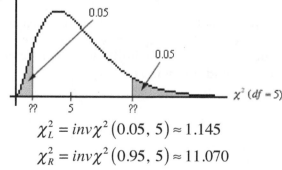

$$\chi_L^2 = inv\chi^2\,(0.05,\ 5) \approx 1.145$$
$$\chi_R^2 = inv\chi^2\,(0.95,\ 5) \approx 11.070$$

b) df of 35 is just to the right of the peak.

$$\chi_L^2 = inv\chi^2\,(0.025,\ 35) \approx 20.569$$
$$\chi_R^2 = inv\chi^2\,(0.975,\ 35) \approx 53.203$$

Section 10.2

21) When calculating the test statistic for a Goodness-of-fit test, the 'O' stands for the observed frequency and the values of 'O' are obtained from the sample.

22) When calculating the test statistics for a goodness-of-fit test, the 'E' stands for the expected frequency. These are the frequencies we expect to see if H_o is true.

23) The degrees of freedom for a goodness-of-fit test is given by the formula $df = k - 1$, where the k stands for the number of categories.

24) The individual values of $\dfrac{(O-E)^2}{E}$ can be thought of as being similar to z-scores. The larger these values get, the more evidence we have against H_o.

25) H_o must always include a phrase like 'is the same as', 'has not changed', etc. This is because H_o must always include the possibility of equality.

26) Because of the squaring step in calculating the test statistic, all Goodness-of-fit tests are right- tailed.

27) The requirement for a Goodness-of-fit test is that all expected frequencies must be at least 5.

28) If no percentages are given to help us calculate the expected frequencies, then we will substitute the probability for each category that would apply if H_o was true.

29) a) SET UP THE TEST:
Determine H_o and H_1:
H_o: the success rates for student athletes are the same as those of all the students
H_1: the success rates for student athletes are different from those of all the students
Significance Level: $\alpha = 0.01$

GATHER AND WEIGH THE EVIDENCE:
Calculate the test statistic: We need to make a table to get the test statistic. The observed frequencies, O, are from the sample. The values of p, are given.

Grade	O	p_i	$E = np_i$	$\dfrac{(O-E)^2}{E}$
Pass	43	0.665	40.565	0.146
Not P	10	0.120	7.32	0.981
W	8	0.215	13.115	1.995
	61	1.000	61	3.122

$$\chi^2 = \sum \frac{(O-E)^2}{E} \approx 3.122$$

Calculate the P-value:
$df = k - 1 = 3 - 1 = 2$

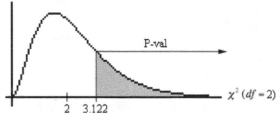

$$P - val \approx \chi^2 cdf(3.122, \infty, 2) \approx 0.2099$$

DECISIONS AND CONCLUSIONS:
Decision: $P - val \approx 0.2099 > \alpha \Rightarrow$ Do Not Reject H_o (Too Risky)
Conclusion: There is not enough evidence, at the 1% significance level, to show that the success rates for student athletes are different from those of all the students.

b) All expected frequencies ≥ 5, so the requirements have been met.

31) a) SET UP THE TEST:

Determine H_o and H_1:

H_o: the true ethnic distribution among heart attack victims is the same as the ethnic distribtution in the U.S.

H_1: the true ethnic distribution among heart attack victims is different from the ethnic distribtution in the U.S.

Significance Level: $\alpha = 0.05$

GATHER AND WEIGH THE EVIDENCE:
Calculate the test statistic: The values of O are from the sample, and we convert the given percentages to decimals to get p.

Ethn	O	p_i	$E = np_i$	$\dfrac{(O-E)^2}{E}$
White	333	0.637	318.5	0.660
Black	62	0.122	61	0.016
Asian	23	0.047	23.5	-0.011
Hispa	71	0.164	82	1.476
Other	11	0.030	15	1.067
	500	1.000	500	3.230

$$\chi^2 = \sum \frac{(O-E)^2}{E} \approx 3.230$$

Calculate the P-value:

$df = k - 1 = 5 - 1 = 4$

$P-val \approx \chi^2 cdf(3.230, \infty, 4) \approx 0.5201$

DECISIONS AND CONCLUSIONS:
Decision: $P-val \approx 0.5201 > \alpha \Rightarrow$ Do Not Reject H_o (too risky)

Conclusion: There is not enough evidence, at the 5% significance level, to show that the true ethnic distribution among heart attack victims is different from the ethnic distribtution in the U.S.

b) All of the E's are at least 5, so the requirements have been met.

c) Because we did not reject H_o, we can't say that heart attacks affect the given ethnicities at different rates. The differences we saw are small enough that they can just be attributed to random variation.

d) We Did NOT Reject H_o so it is impossible that we have made a type I error. Because we did Not Reject H_o, it is possible that we have made a type II error. This will be the case if H_o turns out to be false.

33) a) SET UP THE TEST:

Determine H_o and H_1:

H_o: the true distribution of the use of hands-free devices did not change after the law went into effect.

H_1: the true distribution of the use of hands-free devices changed after the law went into effect.

Significance Level: $\alpha = 0.01$

GATHER AND WEIGH THE EVIDENCE:
Calculate the test statistic: The values of O are from the sample, and we convert the given percentages to decimals to get p.

Answer	O	p_i	$E = np_i$	$\dfrac{(O-E)^2}{E}$
Always	158	0.481	249.158	33.351
Some	170	0.306	158.508	0.833
Never	190	0.213	110.334	57.522
	518	1.000	518	91.706

$$\chi^2 = \sum \frac{(O-E)^2}{E} \approx 91.706$$

Calculate the P-value:

$df = k - 1 = 3 - 1 = 2$

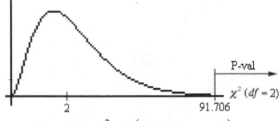

$P-val \approx \chi^2 cdf(91.706, \infty, 2) \approx 0.0000$

DECISIONS AND CONCLUSIONS:
Decision: $P-val \approx 0.0000 \leq \alpha \Rightarrow$ Reject H_o (Acceptable risk of making a type I error)

Conclusion: There is enough evidence, at the 1% significance level, to show that the distribution of the use of hands-free devices changed after the law went into effect.

b) All of the E's are at least 5, so the requirements have been met.

c) 'Never' provided the most evidence against H_o (its $\frac{(O-E)^2}{E}$ provides the biggest contribution to the test stat) 'Sometimes' provided the least evidence against H_o (its $\frac{(O-E)^2}{E}$ provides the smallest contribution to the test stat)

d) We observed a lot less people 'Always' talking on their cell phones without using handsfree than expected and we observed a lot more people saying 'Never' than we expected. Because this is an observational study, we don't know if the cause was the new law.

(35) a) SET UP THE TEST:

Determine H_o and H_1:

H_o: the colors on the wheel are showing up in the proper proportion.

H_1: the colors on the wheel are not showing up in the proper proportion.

Significance Level: $\alpha = 0.01$

GATHER AND WEIGH THE EVIDENCE:
Calculate the test statistic: The values of O are from the sample. The values of p are not given. However, if the wheel is working correctly, then red and black would have a 18/38 chance of occurring and green would have a 2/38 chance.

Color	O	p_i	$E = np_i$	$\frac{(O-E)^2}{E}$
Red	99	18/38	118.42	3.185
Black	140	18/38	118.42	3.933
Green	11	2/38	13.16	0.355
	250	1	250	7.473

$$\chi^2 = \sum \frac{(O-E)^2}{E} = 7.473$$

Calculate the P-value:

$df = k - 1 = 3 - 1 = 2$

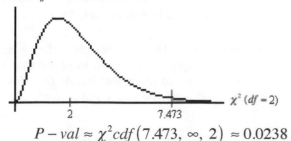

$$P - val \approx \chi^2 cdf\left(7.473, \infty, 2\right) \approx 0.0238$$

DECISIONS AND CONCLUSIONS:
Decision: $P - val \approx 0.0238 > \alpha \Rightarrow$ Do Not Reject H_o (Too risky)

Conclusion: There is not enough evidence, at the 1% significance level, to show that the colors on the wheel are not showing up in the proper proportion.

b) Because we did not reject H_o, it is possible these differences from the expected values could just be the result of random variation on a properly functioning wheel. However, the P-value was close. So, if I were going to play roulette anyway, then I would probably bet on Black, because it occurred more than expected.

c) If n = 90, then for the color green, $E = np = 90 * \frac{2}{38} \approx 4.74 < 5$. So, the requirements would not be met in this case.

37) a) SET UP THE TEST:
Determine H_o and H_1:

H_o: the true distribution of colors of all the candy in the bag is as claimed by the web site.

H_1: the true distribution of colors of all the candy in the bag is not as claimed by the web site.

Significance Level: $\alpha = 0.10$

GATHER AND WEIGH THE EVIDENCE:
Calculate the test statistic: The values of O are from the sample, and we convert the given percentages from the web site to decimals to get p.

Color	O	p_i	$E = np_i$	$\dfrac{(O-E)^2}{E}$
Brown	26	0.13	15.21	7.654
Yellow	13	0.14	16.38	0.697
Red	21	0.13	15.21	2.204
Blue	11	0.24	28.08	10.389
Orange	21	0.20	23.4	0.246
Green	25	0.16	18.72	2.107
	117	1	117	23.297

$$\chi^2 = \sum \frac{(O-E)^2}{E} = 23.297$$

Calculate the P-value:
$$df = k - 1 = 6 - 1 = 5$$

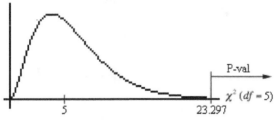

$$P-val \approx \chi^2 cdf(23.297, \infty, 5)$$
$$\approx 0.000296 \approx 0.0003$$

DECISIONS AND CONCLUSIONS:
Decision: $P - val \approx 0.0003 \le \alpha \Rightarrow$ Reject H_o (acceptable risk)

Conclusion: There is enough evidence, at the 10% significance level, to show that the true distribution of colors of all the candy in the bag is not as claimed by the web site.

c) A type I error would occur if we had enough evidence to show that the true distribution of colors of all the candy in the bag is not as claimed by the web site, when in fact it is really the same as claimed. (It is possible that we have made a type I error in our work above, but the risk is low.)

d) A type II error would occur if we did not have enough evidence to show that the true distribution of colors of all the candy in the bag is not as claimed by the web site, when in fact it is really is not the same as claimed.

Section 10.3

41) For a chi-square test of independence, the degrees of freedom is given by the formula $df = (r-1)(c-1)$, where r is the number of <u>row</u> categories and c is the number of <u>column</u> categories.

42) In the test statistic for a chi-square test of independence, the 'E' stands for the frequency we expect if H_o is <u>true</u> . This means that it is calculated under the assumption that the variables in question are <u>independent</u> .

43) H_o must always include a phrase like 'is independent of' or 'is <u>not</u> associated with' because the probability formulas for independence have an <u>equal</u> sign in them and H_o must always include <u>equality</u>.

44) Despite the name, a Test of Independence can only show that the variables are <u>dependent</u>. This test cannot show that the variables are <u>independent</u>.

45) a) SET UP THE TEST:

Determine H_o and H_1:

H_o: American's opinion of the health care law is independent of their political affiliation.

H_1: American's opinion of the health care law is dependent on their political affiliation.

Significance Level: $\alpha = 0.05$

GATHER AND WEIGH THE EVIDENCE:

Calculate the test statistic: Calculate the expected frequencies for each cell using the formula: $E = \dfrac{R \cdot C}{n}$.

	Throw it out	Fix it	Keep it as is	Totals
Democ	83	288	65	436
	200.66	188.10	47.24	
Repub	320	93	32	445
	204.81	191.98	48.22	
Indep	60	53	12	125
	57.53	53.93	13.54	
Totals	463	434	109	1,006

$$\chi^2 = \sum \dfrac{(O-E)^2}{E}$$

$\approx 68.992 + 53.057 + 6.677$

$\quad + 64.786 + 51.032 + 5.456$

$\quad + 0.106 + 0.016 + 0.175$

$\quad = 250.297$

Calculate the P-value:

$df = (r-1)(c-1) = 2*2 = 4$

P-val $\approx \chi^2 cdf(250.297, \infty, 4) \approx 0.0000$

DECISIONS AND CONCLUSIONS:

Decision:: $P-val \approx 0.0000 \le \alpha \Rightarrow$ Reject H_o (Acceptable risk of making a type I error)

Conclusion: There is enough evidence, at the 5% significance level, to show that American's opinion of the health care law is dependent on their political affiliation.

b) All of the E's are at least 5, so the requirements have been met.

c) Highest percentage for "Throw it out" was for Republicans at 71.91%.

$\dfrac{320}{445} \approx 0.7191 = 71.91\%$

47) a) SET UP THE TEST:

Determine H_o and H_1:

H_o: the level of coffee drinking of Chabot students is independent of the season in which they were born.

H_1: the level of coffee drinking of Chabot students is dependent on the season in which they were born.

Significance Level: $\alpha = 0.10$

GATHER AND WEIGH THE EVIDENCE:

Calculate the test statistic: Calculate the expected frequencies for each cell using the formula: $E = \dfrac{R \cdot C}{n}$.

How often do you drink coffee?

	Daily	Sometimes	Never	Totals
Autumn	32	79	47	158
	32.15	76.47	49.37	
Winter	45	95	49	189
	38.46	91.48	59.06	
Spring	39	87	71	197
	40.09	95.35	61.56	
Summer	24	72	48	144
	29.30	69.70	45.00	
Totals	140	333	215	688

$$\chi^2 = \sum \frac{(O-E)^2}{E}$$

$\approx 0.001 + 0.084 + 0.114$

$+ 1.112 + 0.135 + 1.714$

$+ 0.030 + 0.731 + 1.448$

$+ 0.959 + 0.076 + 0.200$

$= 6.604$

Calculate the P-value:

$df = (r-1)(c-1) = 3 * 2 = 6$

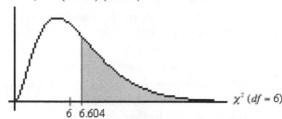

P-val $\approx \chi^2 cdf(6.604, \infty, 6) \approx 0.3590$

DECISIONS AND CONCLUSIONS:

Decision: $P-val \approx 0.3590 > \alpha \Rightarrow$ Do Not Reject H_o (Too risky)

Conclusion: There is not enough evidence, at the 10% significance level, to show that the level of coffee drinking of Chabot students is dependent on the season in which they were born.

b) All of the E's are at least 5, so the requirements have been met.

c) Since we did not reject H_o, it is possible that we have made a type II error. This will be the case if it turns out that H_o is false. It is impossible that we have made a type I error.

49) a) SET UP THE TEST:

Determine H_o and H_1:

H_o: American's priority between creating additional energy sources and protecting the environment is independent of their political affiliation.

H_1: American's priority between creating additional energy sources and protecting the environment is dependent on their political affiliation.

Significance Level: $\alpha = 0.05$

GATHER AND WEIGH THE EVIDENCE:

Calculate the test statistic: Calculate the expected frequencies for each cell using the formula: $E = \dfrac{R \cdot C}{n}$.

Which takes priority?

	Energy	Environ	Don't Know	Totals
Repub	261 208.03	228 277.52	55 58.45	544
Democ	148 189.67	297 253.04	51 53.29	496
Indep	43 54.30	78 72.44	21 15.26	142
Totals	452	603	127	1,182

$$\chi^2 = \sum \frac{(O-E)^2}{E}$$

$\approx 13.488 + 8.836 + 0.204$

$+ 9.155 + 7.637 + 0.098$

$+ 2.352 + 0.427 + 2.159$

$= 44.356$

Calculate the P-value:

$df = (r-1)(c-1) = 2*2 = 4$

P-val $\approx \chi^2 cdf(44.356, \infty, 4) \approx 0.0000$

DECISIONS AND CONCLUSIONS:

Decision:: $P - val \approx 0.0000 \leq \alpha \Rightarrow$ Reject H_o (Acceptable risk of making a type I error)

Conclusion: There is enough evidence, at the 5% significance level, to show that American's priority between creating additional energy sources and protecting the environment is dependent on their political affiliation.

b) Most evidence was from the Repub/Energy cell, because it contributed the largest amount to the test stat. The least was from the Democ/Don't know cell, because it contributed the smallest amount to the test statistic.

c) Highest percentage for the Environment as the top priority was for Democrats at 59.88%.

$$\frac{297}{496} \approx 0.5988 = 59.88\%$$

d) $E = n \cdot p = n \cdot P(\text{Repub \& Energy})$
$= n \cdot P(\text{Repub}) \cdot P(\text{Energy})$

$\approx 1182 \cdot \dfrac{544}{1182} \cdot \dfrac{452}{1182} = \dfrac{544 \cdot 452}{1182}$

≈ 208.03

51) a) SET UP THE TEST:

Determine H_o and H_1:

H_o: A person's smoking status is independent of their education level.

H_1: A person's smoking status is dependent on their education level.

Significance Level: $\alpha = 0.05$

GATHER AND WEIGH THE EVIDENCE:

Calculate the test statistic: Calculate the expected frequencies for each cell using the formula: $E = \dfrac{R \cdot C}{n}$.

	Smoke	Don't Smoke	Totals
No HS Diploma	20 15.02	52 56.98	72
High School Only	53 46.10	168 174.90	221
Some College	25 24.40	92 92.60	117
Bachelor's or Higher	9 21.48	94 81.52	103
Totals	107	406	513

$$\chi^2 = \sum \frac{(O-E)^2}{E}$$

$\approx 1.651 + 0.435$

$+ 1.033 + 0.272$

$+ 0.015 + 0.004$

$+ 7.251 + 1.911$

$= 12.572$

Calculate the P-value:

$df = (r-1)(c-1) = 3*1 = 3$

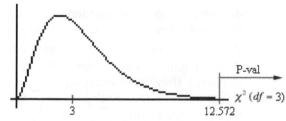

P-val $\approx \chi^2 cdf(12.572, \infty, 3) \approx 0.0057$

DECISIONS AND CONCLUSIONS:

Decision:: $P - val \approx 0.0057 \leq \alpha \Rightarrow$ Reject H_o (Acceptable risk of making a type I error)

Conclusion: There is enough evidence, at the 5% significance level, to show that a person's smoking status is dependent on their education level.

b) Highest percentage for "Smoke" was for "No High School Diploma" at 27.78%.

$\dfrac{20}{72} \approx 0.2778 = 27.78\%$

c) Because we Rejected H_o, it is not possible that we have made a type II error. It is possible that we have made a type I error. A type I error has happened only if H_o turns out to be a true claim.

53) a) SET UP THE TEST:

Determine H_o and H_1:
H_o : The number of injuries a team has during a game is independent of the day of the week they were playing.
H_1 : The number of injuries a team has during a game is dependent on the day of the week they were playing.

Significance Level: $\alpha = 0.05$

GATHER AND WEIGH THE EVIDENCE:

Calculate the test statistic: Calculate the expected frequencies for each cell using the formula: $E = \dfrac{R \cdot C}{n}$.

	Thur	Not Thur	Totals
0	8	55	63
	8.15	54.85	
1	12	81	93
	12.03	80.97	
2+	10	66	76
	9.83	66.17	
Totals	30	202	232

$$\chi^2 = \sum \frac{(O-E)^2}{E}$$
$$\approx 0.003 + 0.000$$
$$+ 0.000 + 0.000$$
$$+ 0.003 + 0.000$$
$$= 0.006$$

Calculate the P-value:
$$df = (r-1)(c-1) = 2*1 = 2$$

$\chi^2\,(df=2)$

0.006   2

P-val $\approx \chi^2 cdf\left(0.006,\ \infty,\ 2\right) \approx 0.9970$

DECISIONS AND CONCLUSIONS:

Decision:: $P-val \approx 0.9970 > \alpha \Rightarrow$ Do Not Reject H_o (way too risky)

Conclusion: There is not enough evidence, at the 5% significance level, to show that the number of injuries a team has during a game is dependent on the day of the week they were playing.

b) All of the E's are at least 5, so the requirements have been met.

c) Not really. Every observed frequency was as close as possible to the expected frequencies which resulted in a test statistic that was nearly 0. The evidence against H_o was as weak as can be.

Section 10.4

57) When computing confidence intervals for σ, or when performing hypothesis tests on the value of σ, we use the Chi-Square distribution with $df = n-1$.

58) In order to use the Chi-Square distribution for inferences involving σ, it is important that our sample be taken from a population that is normally distributed.

59) Because χ^2 curves are right-skewed rather than symmetric, we must find two separate Chi-Square values when computing the endpoints of our confidence interval.

60) For two-tailed tests of , we must find either the area to the left or to the right of our test statistic, whichever is smaller. The P-value is double the smaller area.

61) Givens: $n = 19$, $s = 157.26$, $1-\alpha = 0.99$

We need to find the two χ^2 values that trap an area of 0.99 between them with equal outside areas of 0.005 on each side. We will use the Chi-Square curve with $df = 19 - 1 = 18$.

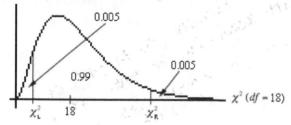

$\chi_L^2 = inv\chi^2(0.005,\ 18) \approx 6.265$ and
$\chi_R^2 = inv\chi^2(0.995,\ 18) \approx 37.156$.

Left Endpoimt $= \sqrt{\dfrac{18*(157.26)^2}{37.156}} \approx 109.46$

Right Endpoint $= \sqrt{\dfrac{18*(157.26)^2}{6.265}} \approx 266.56$

$\Rightarrow\ \sigma \in (109.46,\ 266.56)$

63) Givens: $n = 41$, $s = 5.7709$, $1-\alpha = 0.90$

We need to find the two χ^2 values that trap an area of 0.90 between them with equal outside areas of 0.05 on each side. We will use the Chi-Square curve with $df = 41 - 1 = 40$.

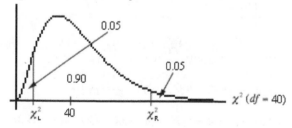

$\chi_L^2 = inv\chi^2(0.05,\ 40) \approx 26.509$ and
$\chi_R^2 = inv\chi^2(0.95,\ 40) \approx 55.758$.

Left Endpoimt $= \sqrt{\dfrac{40*(5.7709)^2}{55.758}} \approx 4.8879$

Right Endpoint $= \sqrt{\dfrac{40*(5.7709)^2}{26.509}} \approx 7.0889$

$\Rightarrow\ \sigma \in (4.8879,\ 7.0889)$

65) Givens: $n = 28$, $s = 9.9448$, $\alpha = 0.05$

a) $\chi^2 = \dfrac{27*(9.9448)^2}{(15)^2} \approx 11.868$

b) Based on $H_1 : \sigma < 15$, this is a left-tailed test. Also, $df = 28 - 1 = 27$.

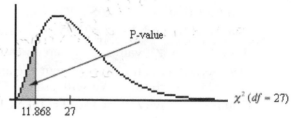

$P - value =$
$\chi^2 cdf(0,\ 11.868,\ 27) \approx 0.0052$

c) Because $P - value = 0.0052 < 0.05$, we will Reject H_0.

67) Givens: $n = 14$, $s = 17.095$, $\alpha = 0.05$

a) $\chi^2 = \dfrac{13*(17.095)^2}{(18)^2} \approx 11.726$

b) Based on $H_1 : \sigma \neq 18$, this is a two-tailed test. Also, $df = 14 - 1 = 13$.

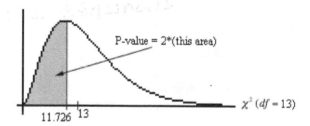

The area on the left side of the test statistic appears to be the smaller one. We will find that and double it.

$P - value = 2 * \chi^2 cdf(0,\ 11.726,\ 13)$
$\approx 2 * 0.44977 \approx 0.8995$

c) Because $P - value = 0.8995 > 0.05$, we Do Not Reject H_0.

69) a) We need our sample to be from a normal population. The P-value $= 0.2946 > 0.05$. So, there is a reasonable possibility that the population is normal and that the requirement is met. We can proceed with our interval.

b) Using technology on the sample data, we can find that $s \approx 434.65$. We were given that $n = 16$ and $1 - \alpha = 0.95$. We need to find the two χ^2 values that trap an area of 0.95 between them with equal outside areas of 0.025 on each side. We will use the Chi-Square curve with $df = 16 - 1 = 15$.

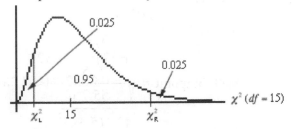

$\chi_L^2 = inv\chi^2\,(0.025,\ 15) \approx 6.262$ and
$\chi_R^2 = inv\chi^2\,(0.975,\ 15) \approx 27.488$.

$$\text{Left Endpt} = \sqrt{\frac{15*(434.65)^2}{27.488}} \approx 321.08$$

$$\text{Right Endpt} = \sqrt{\frac{15*(434.65)^2}{6.262}} \approx 672.71$$

$$\Rightarrow\ \sigma \in (321.08,\ 672.71)$$

c) We are 95% confident that the true standard deviation for the number of calories eaten per day during this 4-month period is somewhere between 321.08 calories and 672.71 calories.

d) Yes, because a more consistent diet would have a smaller standard deviation. And $\sigma \in (321.08,\ 672.71)\ \Rightarrow\ \sigma < 750$.

71) a) We need our sample to be from a normal population. The P-value $= 0.5522 > 0.05$. So, there is a reasonable possibility that the population is normal and that the requirement is met. We can proceed with the hypothesis test.

b) SET UP THE TEST:

Determine H_o and H_1:
Because we are told that the standard deviation in San Francisco is 10.8, we will use that number in H_0. The key word for H_1 is "higher". So we get:

$H_0 : \sigma = 10.8$

$H_1 : \sigma > 10.8$

Significance Level: $\alpha = 0.01$

GATHER AND WEIGH THE EVIDENCE:

Calculate the test statistic: Using technology, we find that $s \approx 18.471$. We also know that $n = 12$.

$$\chi^2 = \frac{11*(18.471)^2}{(10.8)^2} \approx 32.176$$

Calculate the P-value: Because of the '>' in H_1, we know this is a right-tailed test and $df = n - 1 = 12 - 1 = 11$.

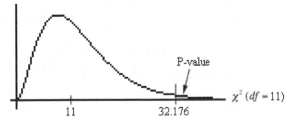

$$\text{P-val} \approx \chi^2 cdf\,(32.176,\ \infty,\ 11) \approx 0.0007$$

DECISIONS AND CONCLUSIONS:

Decision:: $P - val \approx 0.0007 < \alpha \Rightarrow$ Reject H_o (acceptable risk)

Conclusion: There is enough evidence, at the 1% significance level, to show that the true standard deviation of the daily high temperatures in Toronto is higher than it is in San Francisco.

c) Toronto is probably a better fit for her, because we have shown that Toronto has a larger standard deviation in the daily high temperature. This higher standard deviation suggests a larger variation in the weather.

73) a) We need our sample to be from a normal population. Because the population distribution is unknown and we do not have the raw sample data, we can only hope that the population is normal and that the requirements are met.

b) SET UP THE TEST:

Determine H_o and H_1:
Because we are told that the standard deviation for all the servers' tips is $4.75, we will use that number in H_0. The key word for H_1 is "greater". So we get:

$H_0 : \sigma = 4.75$

$H_1 : \sigma > 4.75$

Significance Level: $\alpha = 0.05$

GATHER AND WEIGH THE EVIDENCE:

Calculate the test statistic: We were given $s \approx 5.14$ and $n = 41$.

$$\chi^2 = \frac{40*(5.14)^2}{(4.75)^2} \approx 46.838$$

Calculate the P-value: Because of the '>' in H_1, we know this is a right-tailed test and $df = n - 1 = 41 - 1 = 40$.

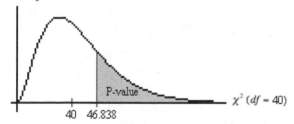

P-val $\approx \chi^2 cdf(46.838, \infty, 40) \approx 0.2123$

DECISIONS AND CONCLUSIONS:

Decision:: $P - val \approx 0.2123 > \alpha \Rightarrow$ Do Not Reject H_0 (too risky)

Conclusion: There is not enough evidence, at the 5% significance level, to show that the true standard deviation of this server's dinner tips is greater than the standard deviation of the combined tips for all the other servers.

c) We are given that $1 - \alpha = 0.90$. We need to find the two χ^2 values that trap an area of 0.90 between them with equal outside areas of 0.05 on each side. We will use the Chi-Square curve with $df = 41 - 1 = 40$.

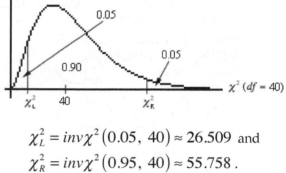

$\chi_L^2 = inv\chi^2(0.05, 40) \approx 26.509$ and
$\chi_R^2 = inv\chi^2(0.95, 40) \approx 55.758$.

Left Endpoint $= \sqrt{\dfrac{40*(5.14)^2}{55.758}} \approx 4.3535$

Right Endpt $= \sqrt{\dfrac{40*(5.14)^2}{26.509}} \approx 6.3139$

$\Rightarrow \sigma \in (4.3535, 6.3139)$

d) If $\sigma \in (4.3535, 6.3139) \Rightarrow \sigma$ could be $4.75 \Rightarrow H_0 : \sigma = 4.75$ could be true $\Rightarrow$ Do Not Reject H_0

e) We can't tell. The sample standard deviation for this server is larger than the standard deviation for the other servers. However, when we look at the confidence interval, we see that this server's true standard deviation could reasonably be lower, higher, or the same as the standard deviation for the other servers.

75) a) We need our sample to be from a normal population. Because the population distribution is unknown and we do not have the raw sample data, we can only hope that the population is normal and that the requirements are met.

b) SET UP THE TEST:

Determine H_o and H_1:
Because we are told that the multiple line standard deviation was 4.477 minutes, we will use that number in H_0. The key word for H_1 is "different". So we get:

$H_0 : \sigma = 4.477$

$H_1 : \sigma \neq 4.477$

Significance Level: $\alpha = 0.10$

GATHER AND WEIGH THE EVIDENCE:

Calculate the test statistic: We were given $s \approx 2.85$ and $n = 61$.

$$\chi^2 = \frac{60 * (2.85)^2}{(4.477)^2} \approx 24.315$$

Calculate the P-value: Because of the '$\neq$' in H_1, we know this is a two-tailed test and $df = n - 1 = 61 - 1 = 60$.

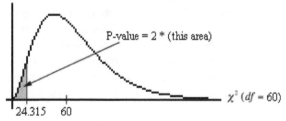

P-val $\approx 2 * \chi^2 cdf(0, 24.315, 60) \approx 0.0000$

DECISIONS AND CONCLUSIONS:

Decision:: $P - val \approx 0.0000 < \alpha \Rightarrow$ Reject H_o (acceptable risk)

Conclusion: There is enough evidence, at the 10% significance level, to show that the true standard deviation of the Friday night wait times is different for the single line system than it was for the multiple line system.

c) We are given that $1 - \alpha = 0.90$. We need to find the two χ^2 values that trap an area of 0.90 between them with equal outside areas of 0.05 on each side. We will use the Chi-Square curve with $df = 61 - 1 = 60$.

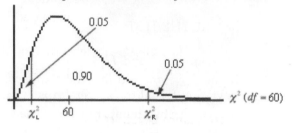

$\chi_L^2 = inv\chi^2(0.05, 60) \approx 43.188$ and
$\chi_R^2 = inv\chi^2(0.95, 60) \approx 79.082$.

$$\text{Left Endpoint} = \sqrt{\frac{60 * (2.85)^2}{79.082}} \approx 2.4825$$

$$\text{Right Endpt} = \sqrt{\frac{60 * (2.85)^2}{43.188}} \approx 3.3592$$

$\Rightarrow \sigma \in (2.4825, 3.3592)$

d) If $\sigma \in (2.4825, 3.3592) \Rightarrow \sigma \neq 4.477$
$\Rightarrow H_0 : \sigma = 4.75$ is False $\Rightarrow$ Reject H_0

e) Yes. Even though the average wait time was about the same as the past, the single line system has a lower standard deviation and, therefore, is more consistent for all the customers.

Chapter Problem:

a) SET UP THE TEST:

Determine H_o and H_1:

H_o: Student GPA's are independent of the amount of financial support provided by the parents.

H_1: Student GPA's are dependent on the amount of financial support provided by the parents.

Significance Level: $\alpha = 0.05$

GATHER AND WEIGH THE EVIDENCE:

Calculate the test statistic: Calculate the expected frequencies for each cell using the

formula: $E = \dfrac{R \cdot C}{n}$.

	0.00- 2.00	2.00- 3.00	3.00 – 4.00	Totals
$0 - $3999	651 709.15	1180 1255.02	3420 3286.83	5251
$4000 - $11,999	517 486.99	913 861.86	2176 2257.15	3606
$12,000 and up	300 271.86	505 481.12	1208 1260.02	2013
Totals	1468	2598	6804	10,870

$$\chi^2 = \sum \frac{(O-E)^2}{E}$$

$$\approx 4.768 + 4.484 + 5.396$$

$$+1.849 + 3.034 + 2.918$$

$$+2.913 + 1.185 + 2.148$$

$$= 28.695$$

Calculate the P-value:

$$df = (r-1)(c-1) = 2 * 2 = 4$$

$$\text{P-val} \approx \chi^2 cdf\left(28.695, \infty, 4\right) \approx 0.0000$$

DECISIONS AND CONCLUSIONS:

Decision:: $P - val \approx 0.0000 \le \alpha \Rightarrow$ Reject H_o (Acceptable risk of making a type I error)

Conclusion: There is enough evidence, at the 5% significance level, to show that Student GPA's are dependent on the amount of financial support provided by the parents.

b) All of the E's are at least 5, so the requirements have been met.

Review Exercises:

1) a) Step 1:

   H_o: the distribution of education levels in his home town is the same as in the city where he plays football.

   H_a: the distribution of education levels in his home town is different than in the city where he plays football.

   Step 2: $\alpha = 0.10$

   Step 3: The values of O are from the sample, and we convert the given percentages to decimals to get p.

Educ	O	p_i	$E = np_i$	$\dfrac{(O-E)^2}{E}$
No HS	32	0.1658	66.32	17.760
HS	219	0.3454	138.16	47.301
Some C	91	0.2787	111.48	3.762
Bach+	58	0.2101	84.04	8.069
	400	1.000	400	76.892

$$\chi^2 = \sum \frac{(O-E)^2}{E} \approx 76.892$$

Step 4: $df = k - 1 = 3$

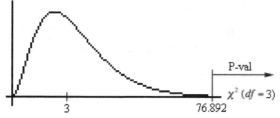

P-val $= \chi^2 cdf(76.892, \infty, 3) \approx 0.0000$

Step 5: $P - val \approx 0.0000 \leq \alpha \Rightarrow$ Reject H_o (Acceptable risk of making a type I error)

Step 6: There is enough evidence, at the 10% significance level, to show that the distribution of education levels in his hometown is different than in the city where he plays football.

b) 100% of the E's are at least 5, so the requirements have been met.

c) Since we rejected H_o, it is possible we have made a type I error. This is the case only if H_o is true. We perceive the risk of this to be nearly zero.

d) The high school only category provided the most evidence against H_o, because it contributed the most to the test statistic.

2) a) Step 1:

   H_o: the dice are producing these sums in the proper proportions

   H_a: the dice are not producing these sums in the proper proportions.

   Step 2: $\alpha = 0.01$

   Step 3: The values of O are from the sample. The values of p are not given, so we must find them using the normal probabilities for these events. To help find these probabilities, we need to make the chart for all possible sums.

	1	2	3	4	5	6
1	2	3	4	5	6	7
2	3	4	5	6	7	8
3	4	5	6	7	8	9
4	5	6	7	8	9	10
5	6	7	8	9	10	11
6	7	8	9	10	11	12

Sum	O	p_i	$E = np_i$	$\dfrac{(O-E)^2}{E}$
2,3,12	24	4/36	20.56	0.576
7,11	51	8/36	41.11	2.379
Other	110	24/36	123.33	1.441
	185	1.000	185	4.396

$$\chi^2 = \sum \frac{(O-E)^2}{E} \approx 4.396$$

Step 4: $df = k - 1 = 2$

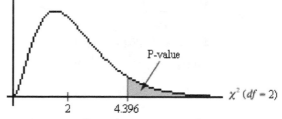

P-val $= \chi^2 cdf(4.396, \infty, 2) \approx 0.1110$

Step 5: $P - val \approx 0.1110 > \alpha \Rightarrow$ Do Not Reject H_o (Too risky)

Step 6: There is not enough evidence, at the 1% significance level, to show that the dice are not producing these sums in the proper proportions.

b) All expected frequencies ≥ 5, so the requirements have been met.

c) A type I error would occur if we had enough evidence to show that the dice are not producing these sums in the proper proportions, when in fact they are producing them in the correct proportions.

d) A type II error would occur if we did not have enough evidence to show that the dice are not producing these sums in the proper proportions, when in fact they are not producing them in the correct proportions.

3) a) Step 1:

H_o: people's opinion on this matter is independent of their political affiliation.
H_a: people's opinion on this matter is dependent on their political affiliation.
Step 2: $\alpha = 0.05$

Step 3: Calculate E's using: $E = \dfrac{R \cdot C}{n}$.

	Dem	Rep	Ind	Totals
Good Idea	62	36	18	116
	51.95	51.14	12.91	
Bad Idea	417	446	103	966
	432.60	425.88	107.52	
Good & Bad	21	10	5	36
	16.12	15.87	4.01	
Not Sure	15	15	2	32
	14.33	14.11	3.56	
Totals	515	507	128	1150

$$\chi^2 = \sum \frac{(O - E)^2}{E}$$

$\approx 1.944 + 4.482 + 2.007$

$+ 0.563 + 0.951 + 0.190$

$+ 1.477 + 2.171 + 0.244$

$+ 0.031 + 0.056 + 0.684$

$= 14.803$

Step 4: $df = (r-1)(c-1) = 3 * 2 = 6$

P-val = $\chi^2 cdf(14.803, \infty, 6) \approx 0.0218$

Step 5: $P - val \approx 0.0218 \le \alpha \Rightarrow$ Reject H_o (Acceptable risk of making a type I error)

Step 6: There is enough evidence, at the 5% significance level, to show that people's opinion on this matter is dependent on their political affiliation.

b) Because two of the E's (4.01 and 3.56) are less than 5, the requirements have NOT been met for this one. This means that we do not have full trust in the accuracy of our P-value.

However, $10/12 \approx 83.33\%$ of the expected frequencies are at least 5, and all of the expected frequencies are at least 1. In such cases, the effect on the P-value is minimal.

c) $E = np = n * P(\text{Good Idea \& Democrat})$
$= n * P(\text{Good Idea}) * P(\text{Democrat})$
$\approx 1150 * \dfrac{116}{1150} * \dfrac{515}{1150} \approx 51.95$

4) a) Step 1:
H_o: The type of phone a person has is independent of whether or not they have ever had sex on the first date.
H_a: The type of phone a person has is dependent of whether or not they have ever had sex on the first date.
Step 2: $\alpha = 0.05$
Step 3: $\chi^2 \approx 3.373$
Step 4: $df = 2$, P-val ≈ 0.1851
Step 5: Do Not Reject H_o
Step 6: There is not enough evidence, at the 5% significance level, to show that the type of phone a person has is dependent on whether or not they have ever had sex on the first date.

b) All of the expected frequencies are at least 5. So, the requirements have been met.

c) No! Even though the sample data did show a higher rate of sex on the first date for Android users than for other phone users, the difference was small enough that there is a reasonable chance that difference is just due to random variation in the sample.

5) a) We need our sample to be from a normal population. The P-value $= 0.3842 > 0.05$. So, there is a reasonable possibility that the population is normal and that the requirement is met. We can proceed with any requested confidence interval or hypothesis test.

b) SET UP THE TEST:

Determine H_o and H_1:
Because we are told that the standard deviation for the U.S. is \$25.91, we will use that number in H_0. The key word for H_1 is "different". So we get:

$H_0 : \sigma = 25.91$

$H_1 : \sigma \neq 25.91$

Significance Level: $\alpha = 0.05$

GATHER AND WEIGH THE EVIDENCE:

Calculate the test statistic: Using technology on the sample data, we find $s \approx 26.579$ and $n = 12$.

$$\chi^2 = \frac{11*(26.579)^2}{(25.91)^2} \approx 11.575$$

Calculate the P-value: Because of the '$\neq$' in H_1, we know this is a two-tailed test and $df = n - 1 = 12 - 1 = 11$.

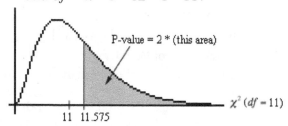

P-val $\approx 2 * \chi^2 cdf(11.575, \infty, 11) \approx 0.7928$

DECISIONS AND CONCLUSIONS:

Decision:: $P - val \approx 0.7928 > \alpha \Rightarrow$ Do Not Reject H_o (too risky)

Conclusion: There is not enough evidence, at the 5% significance level, to show that the true standard deviation of the California lift ticket prices is different than the standard deviation for the prices in the whole U.S.

c) We are given that $1 - \alpha = 0.90$. We need to find the two χ^2 values that trap an area of 0.90 between them with equal outside areas of 0.05 on each side. We will use the Chi-Square curve with $df = 12 - 1 = 11$.

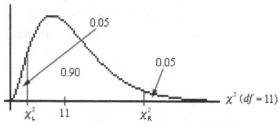

$\chi_L^2 = inv\chi^2(0.05, 11) \approx 4.575$ and
$\chi_R^2 = inv\chi^2(0.95, 11) \approx 19.675$.

Left Endpt $= \sqrt{\dfrac{11*(26.579)^2}{19.675}} \approx 19.874$

Right Endpt $= \sqrt{\dfrac{11*(26.579)^2}{4.575}} \approx 41.213$

$\Rightarrow \sigma \in (19.874, 41.213)$

d) We are 90% confident that the true standard deviation for California lift ticket prices is somewhere between \$19.874 and \$41.213.

e) If $\sigma \in (19.874, 41.213) \Rightarrow \sigma$ could be $25.91 \Rightarrow H_0 : \sigma = 25.91$ could be true $\Rightarrow$ Do Not Reject H_0

f) We can't tell. The sample standard deviation for CA is larger than the standard deviation for the U.S. However, when we look at the confidence interval, we see that CA's true standard deviation could reasonably be lower, higher, or the same as the standard deviation for the U.S. as a whole.

Section 11.1

1) A sample contains paired data if each data value for one variable naturally <u>corresponds</u> to a value for the other variable.

2) $\mu_1 - \mu_2 < 0 \Rightarrow \mu_1$ is <u>smaller</u> than μ_2.
   $\mu_1 - \mu_2 > 0 \Rightarrow \mu_1$ is <u>larger</u> than μ_2.

3) a) $t = \dfrac{\bar{d}}{s_d / \sqrt{n}} = \dfrac{14.25}{31.185 / \sqrt{12}} \approx 1.583$

   b) $H_a : \mu_1 > \mu_2 \Rightarrow$ This is a right-tailed test. $df = n - 1 = 11$

   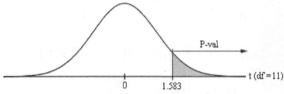

   $P - val = tcdf(1.583, \infty, 11) \approx 0.0709$

   c) $P - val \approx 0.0709 > \alpha \Rightarrow$ Do Not Reject H_o
   (Too Risky)

5) a) $t = \dfrac{\bar{d}}{s_d / \sqrt{n}} = \dfrac{-22.88}{61.007 / \sqrt{40}} \approx -2.372$

   b) $H_a : \mu_1 \neq \mu_2 \Rightarrow$ This is a two-tailed test. $df = n - 1 = 39$

   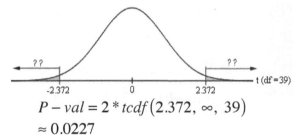

   $P - val = 2 * tcdf(2.372, \infty, 39)$
   ≈ 0.0227

   c) $P - val \approx 0.0227 \leq \alpha \Rightarrow$ Reject H_o
   (Acceptable risk of making a type I error)

7) a) Step 1: We want to show that the average is "lower" after than before the drug.
   $H_o : \mu_1 = \mu_2$
   $H_1 : \mu_1 > \mu_2$
   Step 2: $\alpha = 0.05$

Step 3: Because $\bar{d}$ is not given, we will find it using the calculator. Enter the before values into L1 and the after values into L2. Then let L3 = L1 – L2. Finally choose STAT > CALC > 1-Var Stats L3 and we get:

$\bar{d} = 47.0$, $s_d \approx 25.640$, $n = 14$

$t = \dfrac{\bar{d}}{s_d / \sqrt{n}} = \dfrac{47.0}{25.64 / \sqrt{14}} \approx 6.859$

Step 4: $H_1 : \mu_1 > \mu_2 \Rightarrow$ This is a right-tailed test. $df = n - 1 = 13$

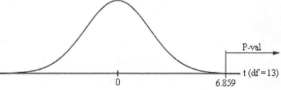

$P - val = tcdf(6.859, \infty, 13) \approx 0.0000$

Step 5: $P - val \approx 0.0000 \leq \alpha \Rightarrow$ Reject H_o
(Acceptable risk of making a type I error)
Step 6: There is enough evidence, at the 5% significance level, to show that the drug will lower, on average, the level of bad cholesterol in patients who take it.

b) We need the t-scores for 90% confidence.

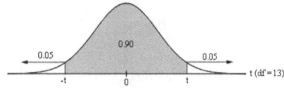

From the t-table with df = 13, we get $t_{0.05} = 1.771$.

$\bar{d} \pm t^* \cdot \dfrac{s_d}{\sqrt{n}} = 47.0 \pm 1.771 \cdot \dfrac{25.64}{\sqrt{14}} =$
$47.0 \pm 12.1 \Rightarrow \mu_1 - \mu_2 \in (34.9, \ 59.1)$

c) We are 90% confident that the average bad cholesterol level after treatment is somewhere between 34.9 and 59.1 points lower than before the treatment.

d) If $\mu_1 - \mu_2 \in (34.9, \ 59.1) \Rightarrow \mu_1 - \mu_2 > 0$
   $\Rightarrow \mu_1 > \mu_2 \Rightarrow H_1 : \mu_1 > \mu_2$ is true and
   $H_o : \mu_1 = \mu_2$ is false $\Rightarrow$ Reject H_o

e) Because $n = 14 < 15$, we must hope that the before and after differences in the population are normally distributed.

9) a) Step 1: We are trying to show a "difference", so we get:
$$H_o : \mu_1 = \mu_2$$
$$H_1 : \mu_1 \neq \mu_2$$

Step 2: $\alpha = 0.10$

Step 3: Because $\bar{d}$ is not given, we will find it using the calculator. Enter the before values into L1 and the after values into L2. Then let L3 = L1 – L2. Finally choose STAT > CALC > 1-Var Stats L3 and we get:

$\bar{d} \approx 0.91667$, $s_d \approx 2.7455$, $n = 12$

$$t = \frac{\bar{d}}{s_d / \sqrt{n}} = \frac{0.91667}{2.7455 / \sqrt{12}} \approx 1.157$$

Note: It is a good idea to use more decimals than normal for $\bar{d}$ when calculating the test statistic. This helps avoid rounding error.

Step 4: $H_1 : \mu_1 \neq \mu_2 \Rightarrow$ This is a two-tailed test. $df = n - 1 = 11$

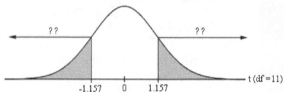

$$P - val = 2 * tcdf(1.157, \infty, 11)$$
$$\approx 0.2718$$

Step 5: $P - val \approx 0.2718 > \alpha \Rightarrow$ Do Not Reject H_o (Too Risky)

Step 6: There is not enough evidence, at the 10% significance level, to show that there is a difference in average score at the two courses for pro players.

b) We need the t-scores for 90% confidence.

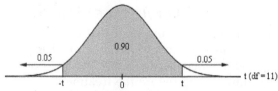

From the t-table with df = 11, we get $t_{0.05} = 1.796$.

$$\bar{d} \pm t^* \cdot \frac{s_d}{\sqrt{n}} = 0.92 \pm 1.796 \cdot \frac{2.7455}{\sqrt{12}} =$$

$$0.92 \pm 1.42 \Rightarrow \mu_1 - \mu_2 \in (-0.50, \ 2.34)$$

Note: It is typically fine to use less decimal places for $\bar{d}$ when computing a confidence interval.

c) We are 90% confident that the average score at Poppy Hills is somewhere between 0.50 strokes lower than the average at Spyglass to 2.34 strokes higher than the average at Spyglass.

d) If $\mu_1 - \mu_2 \in (-0.50, 2.34) \Rightarrow \mu_1 - \mu_2$ could be equal zero $\Rightarrow \mu_1$ could equal μ_2 $\Rightarrow H_o : \mu_1 = \mu_2$ could be true $\Rightarrow$ Do Not Reject H_o.

e) Because $n = 12 < 30$, we must hope that the differences between Poppy Hills and Spyglass Hill in the population are normally distributed.

f) Because we did not reject H_o, it is possible that we have made a type II error. This is the case if H_o turns out to be a false claim.

11) Givens: $n = 31$, $\bar{d} \approx -0.226$, $s_d \approx 1.820$

a) Step 1: The want to see if the sales after are "higher" than before, so we get:
$$H_o : \mu_1 = \mu_2$$
$$H_1 : \mu_1 < \mu_2$$

Step 2: $\alpha = 0.05$

Step 3: $t = \dfrac{\bar{d}}{s_d / \sqrt{n}} = \dfrac{-0.226}{1.82 / \sqrt{31}} \approx -0.691$

Step 4: $H_1 : \mu_1 < \mu_2 \Rightarrow$ This is a left-tailed test. $df = n - 1 = 30$

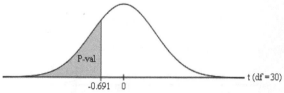

$$P - val = tcdf(-\infty, \ -0.691, 30)$$
$$\approx 0.2474$$

Step 5: $P - val \approx 0.2474 > \alpha \Rightarrow$ Do Not Reject H_o (Too risky)

Step 6: There is not enough evidence, at the 5% significance level, to show that there is, on average, a larger number of units sold by all the sales personnel after the incentive plan.

b) We need the t-score for 90% confidence.

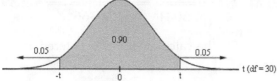

From the t-table with df = 30, we get
$t_{0.05} = 1.697$.

$$\bar{d} \pm t^* \cdot \frac{s_d}{\sqrt{n}} = -0.226 \pm 1.697 \cdot \frac{1.82}{\sqrt{31}} =$$

$$-0.226 \pm 0.555 \Rightarrow \mu_1 - \mu_2 \in (-0.781, 0.329)$$

c) We are 90% confident that the average number of units sold by the sales personnel with the incentive plan is somewhere between 7.81 units higher and 0.329 units lower than the average before the plan.

d) If $\mu_1 - \mu_2 \in (-0.781, 0.329) \Rightarrow \mu_1 - \mu_2$ could be equal to zero $\Rightarrow \mu_1$ could equal μ_2 $\Rightarrow H_o : \mu_1 = \mu_2$ could be true $\Rightarrow$ Do Not Reject H_o.

e) Because $n = 31 \ge 30$, we know that $\bar{d}$ is normally distributed. So the requirements have been met.

f) $\mu_1 - \mu_2 = 0.53 \Rightarrow \mu_1 > \mu_2 \Rightarrow$
$H_1 : \mu_1 < \mu_2$ is false and, thus
$H_o : \mu_1 = \mu_2$ is considered true.
In part (a), we decided not to reject H_o.
Therefore, we have made a correct decision.

13) Givens: $n = 25$, $\bar{d} \approx -18.12$, $s_d \approx 11.322$
a) Step 1: We want to show that the average is "better" after passing the practice quiz than it was before.
$$H_o : \mu_1 = \mu_2$$
$$H_1 : \mu_1 < \mu_2$$
Step 2: $\alpha = 0.01$

Step 3: $t = \dfrac{\bar{d}}{s_d / \sqrt{n}} = \dfrac{-18.12}{11.322 / \sqrt{25}} \approx -8.002$

Step 4: $H_1 : \mu_1 < \mu_2 \Rightarrow$ This is a left-tailed test. $df = n - 1 = 24$

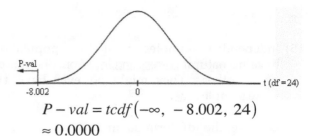

$$P - val = tcdf(-\infty, -8.002, 24)$$
$$\approx 0.0000$$
Step 5: $P - val \approx 0.0000 \le \alpha \Rightarrow$ Reject H_o
(Acceptable risk of making a type I error)
Step 6: There is enough evidence, at the 1% significance level, to show that the students, on average, do better after having passed the practice quiz.

b) We need the t-scores for 98% confidence.

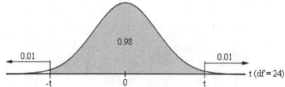

From the t-table with df = 24, we get
$t_{0.01} = 2.492$.

$$\bar{d} \pm t^* \cdot \frac{s_d}{\sqrt{n}} = -18.12 \pm 2.492 \cdot \frac{11.322}{\sqrt{25}} =$$

$$-18.12 \pm 5.64 \Rightarrow \mu_1 - \mu_2 \in (-23.76, -12.48)$$

c) We are 98% confident that the average quiz score after passing the practice quiz is somewhere between 12.48 and 23.76 points higher than before the practice quiz.

d) If $\mu_1 - \mu_2 \in (-23.76, -12.48)$
$\Rightarrow \mu_1 - \mu_2 < 0 \Rightarrow \mu_1 < \mu_2 \Rightarrow$
$H_1 : \mu_1 < \mu_2$ is true and
$H_o : \mu_1 = \mu_2$ is false $\Rightarrow$ Reject H_o

e) Because $15 \le n = 25 < 30$, we must hope that the before and after differences in the population are not severely skewed.

f) A type I error would occur if we had enough evidence to show that the average scores were higher after the practice quiz, when in fact, they actually were not.

g) A type II error would occur if we did not have enough evidence to show that the average scores were higher after the practice quiz, when in fact, they actually were higher.

Section 11.2

15) Independent samples from two populations have no natural <u>correspondence</u> from one sample to the other. They might not even have the same sample <u>size</u>.

16) Because the df formula in this section is so complicated, it is good to have an <u>estimate</u> of the size of your answer. Use the fact that $\min\{n_1, n_2\} - 1 \le df \le n_1 + n_2 - 2$ to help with this.

17) a) $t = \dfrac{15.392 - 13.899}{\sqrt{\dfrac{3.908^2}{19} + \dfrac{2.471^2}{14}}} \approx 1.341$

On the calculator, this is entered as:

```
(15.392-13.899)/
√(3.908²/19+2.47
1²/14)
                1.340783102
```

b) $H_a : \mu_1 > \mu_2 \Rightarrow$ This is a right-tailed test.

$$df = \dfrac{\left(\dfrac{3.908^2}{19} + \dfrac{2.471^2}{14}\right)^2}{\dfrac{\left(\dfrac{3.908^2}{19}\right)^2}{18} + \dfrac{\left(\dfrac{2.471^2}{14}\right)^2}{13}} \approx 30.43$$

```
(3.908²/19+2.471
²/14)²/((3.908²/
19)²/18+(2.471²/
14)²/13)
                30.42859392
```

We round this down and get $df = 30$.

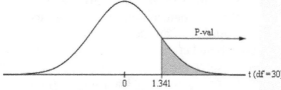

$P - val = tcdf(1.341, \infty, 30) \approx 0.0950$

c) $P - val \approx 0.0950 > \alpha \Rightarrow$ Do Not Reject H_o
(Too risky)

19) a) $t = \dfrac{1.537 - 1.209}{\sqrt{\dfrac{0.5081^2}{35} + \dfrac{0.4366^2}{35}}} \approx 2.897$

On the calculator, this is entered as:

```
(1.537-1.209)/√(
0.5081²/35+0.436
6²/35)
                2.896600606
```

b) $H_a : \mu_1 \ne \mu_2 \Rightarrow$ This is a two-tailed test.

$$df = \dfrac{\left(\dfrac{0.5081^2}{35} + \dfrac{0.4366^2}{35}\right)^2}{\dfrac{\left(\dfrac{0.5081^2}{35}\right)^2}{34} + \dfrac{\left(\dfrac{0.4366^2}{35}\right)^2}{34}} \approx 66.49$$

On the calculator, this is entered as:

```
(0.5081²/35+0.43
66²/35)²/((0.508
1²/35)²/34+(0.43
66²/35)²/34)
                66.49372732
```

We round this down and get $df = 66$.

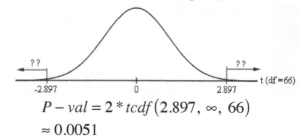

$P - val = 2 * tcdf(2.897, \infty, 66)$
≈ 0.0051

c) $P - val \approx 0.0051 \le \alpha \Rightarrow$ Reject H_o
(Acceptable risk of making a type I error)

21) Givens: Sample 1 (Bay Area), $n_1 = 27$, $\bar{x}_1 = 3.541$, $s_1 = 0.176$. Sample 2 (Statewide), $n_2 = 60$, $\bar{x}_2 = 3.387$, $s_2 = 0.1625$.

a) Step 1: We want to show that the bay area average is "larger", so we get: $H_o : \mu_1 = \mu_2$ $H_1 : \mu_1 > \mu_2$

Step 2: $\alpha = 0.05$

Step 3:

$$t = \frac{3.541 - 3.387}{\sqrt{\frac{0.176^2}{27} + \frac{0.1625^2}{60}}} \approx 3.865$$

On the calculator, this is entered as:

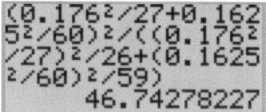

Step 4: $H_1 : \mu_1 > \mu_2 \Rightarrow$ This is a right-tailed test.

$$df = \frac{\left(\frac{0.176^2}{27} + \frac{0.1625^2}{60}\right)^2}{\frac{\left(\frac{0.176^2}{27}\right)^2}{26} + \frac{\left(\frac{0.1625^2}{60}\right)^2}{59}} \approx 46.74$$

On the calculator, this is entered as:

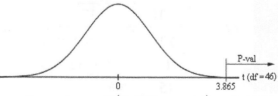

We round this down and get $df = 46$.

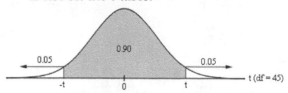

$$P - val = tcdf(3.865, \infty, 46) \approx 0.0002$$

Step 5: $P - val \approx 0.0002 \leq \alpha \Rightarrow$ Reject H_o (Acceptable risk of making a type I error)

Step 6: There is enough evidence, at the 5% significance level, to show that the average gas price in the bay area is higher than the statewide average.

b) We need the t-scores for 90% confidence. We will also round our df down to 45 because 46 is not on the t-table.

From the t-table we get $t_{0.05} = 1.679$.

$$(3.541 - 3.387) \pm 1.679 \cdot \sqrt{\frac{0.176^2}{27} + \frac{0.1625^2}{60}} =$$

$$0.154 \pm 0.067 \Rightarrow \mu_1 - \mu_2 \in (0.087, 0.221)$$

Note: The margin of error is entered in the calculator as:

```
1.679*√(0.176²/2
7+0.1625²/60)
          .0668942642
```

c) We are 90% confident that the average price per gallon in the bay area is somewhere between 8.7 and 22.1 cents more expensive than the statewide average.

d) If $\mu_1 - \mu_2 \in (0.087, 0.221) \Rightarrow \mu_1 - \mu_2 > 0$ $\Rightarrow \mu_1 > \mu_2 \Rightarrow H_1 : \mu_1 < \mu_2$ is true and $H_o : \mu_1 = \mu_2$ is false $\Rightarrow$ Reject H_o

e) Bay Area: $15 \leq n_1 = 27 < 30 \Rightarrow$ We need a population for gas prices in the bay area that is not severely skewed.
Statewide: $n_2 = 60 \geq 30 \Rightarrow \bar{x}_1$ is normally distributed regardless of the distribution of the population.

f) Because we Rejected H_o, we know we did not make a type II error. If H_o is true, then we have made a type I error. If H_o is false, then we have made a correct decision.

23) a) Step 1: We are trying to show that there is

$$H_o : \mu_1 = \mu_2$$

a difference in the means.

$$H_1 : \mu_1 \neq \mu_2$$

Step 2: $\alpha = 0.05$

Step 3:

$$t = \frac{1394.6 - 1524.3}{\sqrt{\dfrac{282.75^2}{126} + \dfrac{226.65^2}{81}}} \approx -3.641$$

Step 4: $H_1 : \mu_1 \neq \mu_2 \Rightarrow$ This is a two-tailed test.

$$df = \frac{\left(\dfrac{282.75^2}{126} + \dfrac{226.65^2}{81}\right)^2}{\dfrac{\left(\dfrac{282.75^2}{126}\right)^2}{125} + \dfrac{\left(\dfrac{226.65^2}{81}\right)^2}{80}} \approx 195.14$$

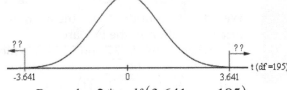

$$P - val = 2 * tcdf(3.641, \infty, 195)$$

$$\approx 0.0003$$

Step 5: $P - val \approx 0.0003 \leq \alpha \Rightarrow$ Reject H_o
(Acceptable risk of making a type I error)

Step 6: There is enough evidence, at the 5% significance level, to show that there is a difference between the average combined SAT scores of public and private schools students.

b) We need the t-scores for 95% confidence. We will round our df down to 100, because 195 is not on the t-table.

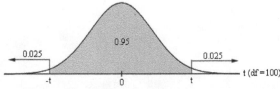

From the t-table we get $t_{0.025} = 1.984$.

$$(1394.6 - 1524.3) \pm 1.984 \cdot \sqrt{\frac{282.75^2}{126} + \frac{226.65^2}{81}} =$$

$$-129.7 \pm 70.7 \Rightarrow \mu_1 - \mu_2 \in (-200.4, -59.0)$$

c) We are 95% confident that average combined SAT score for private schools students is somewhere between 59.0 points and 200.4 points above that of the public school students.

d) If

$$\mu_1 - \mu_2 \in (-200.4, -59.0) \Rightarrow \mu_1 - \mu_2 < 0$$

$$\Rightarrow \mu_1 < \mu_2 \Rightarrow H_o : \mu_1 = \mu_2 \text{ is false}$$

$$\Rightarrow \text{ Reject } H_o$$

e) $\mu_1 - \mu_2 = -9.9 \Rightarrow \mu_1 \neq \mu_2 \Rightarrow H_o : \mu_1 = \mu_2$ is false. In part (a), we decided to reject H_o. Therefore, we have made a correct decision.

25) a) Step 1: We are trying to show that there is

$$H_o : \mu_1 = \mu_2$$

a "difference", so we get:

$$H_1 : \mu_1 \neq \mu_2$$

Step 2: $\alpha = 0.01$

Step 3: Because we have only been given the sample data, we must use it to find the means and standard deviations that we need. Do this one sample at a time. Enter the California prices into L1. Then choose STAT > CALC > 1-Var Stats L1. This yields:

$n_1 = 16$, $\bar{x}_1 = 55.6875$, $s_1 \approx 15.226$

Repeating this process with the Colorado prices produces the following results:

$n_2 = 12$, $\bar{x}_2 \approx 65.8333$, $s_2 \approx 16.275$

$$t = \frac{55.6875 - 65.8333}{\sqrt{\dfrac{15.226^2}{16} + \dfrac{16.275^2}{12}}} \approx -1.678$$

Step 4: $H_1 : \mu_1 \neq \mu_2 \Rightarrow$ This is a two-tailed test.

$$df = \frac{\left(\dfrac{15.226^2}{16} + \dfrac{16.275^2}{12}\right)^2}{\dfrac{\left(\dfrac{15.226^2}{16}\right)^2}{15} + \dfrac{\left(\dfrac{16.275^2}{12}\right)^2}{11}} \approx 22.93$$

$$P - val = 2 * tcdf(1.678, \infty, 22)$$

$$\approx 0.1075$$

Step 5: $P-val \approx 0.1075 > \alpha \Rightarrow$ Do Not Reject H_o (Too risky)

Step 6: There is not enough evidence, at the 1% significance level, to show that there is a difference in average adult lift ticket price between California and Colorado resorts.

b) California: $15 \le n_1 = 16 < 30 \Rightarrow$ We need a population for adult lift ticket prices that is not severely skewed.
Colorado: $n_2 = 12 < 30 \Rightarrow$ We need the prices of adult lift tickets in Colorado to be normally distributed.

c) We need to find the t-scores for 99% confidence with df = 22.

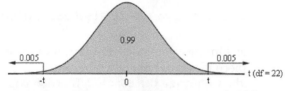

From the t-table we get $t_{0.005} = 2.819$.

$$(55.6875 - 65.8333) \pm 2.819 \cdot \sqrt{\frac{15.226^2}{16} + \frac{16.275^2}{12}} =$$

$$-10.14 \pm 17.05 \Rightarrow \mu_1 - \mu_2 \in (-27.19,\ 6.91)$$

d) We are 99% confident that, on average, adult lift tickets at California resorts are somewhere between \$27.19 less and \$6.91 higher than those in Colorado.

e) If $\mu_1 - \mu_2 \in (-27.19,\ 6.91) \Rightarrow \mu_1 - \mu_2$ could be equal to zero $\Rightarrow \mu_1$ could equal $\mu_2 \Rightarrow H_o : \mu_1 = \mu_2$ could be true $\Rightarrow$ Do Not Reject H_o.

Section 11.3

27) The requirements for two-sample proportion studies are that each <u>sample</u> must contain at least 10 <u>successes</u> and at least 10 <u>failures</u>.

28) $p_1 - p_2 < 0 \Rightarrow p_1$ is <u>smaller</u> than p_2.
$p_1 - p_2 > 0 \Rightarrow p_1$ is <u>larger</u> than p_2.

29) a) $\hat{p}_1 = \dfrac{122}{195} \approx 0.6256$, $\hat{p}_2 = \dfrac{89}{147} \approx 0.6054$,

$$\hat{p}_p = \frac{122 + 89}{195 + 147} \approx 0.6170$$

$$z = \frac{0.6256 - 0.6054}{\sqrt{0.617 * 0.383\left(\dfrac{1}{195} + \dfrac{1}{147}\right)}} \approx 0.380$$

On the calculator, this is entered as:

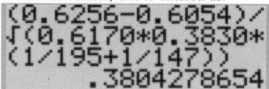

b) $H_a : p_1 > p_2 \Rightarrow$ This is a right-tailed test.

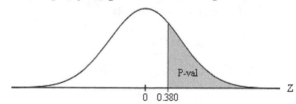

$$P - val = normalcdf(0.380,\ \infty)$$

$$\approx 0.3520$$

c) $P - val \approx 0.3520 > \alpha \Rightarrow$ Do Not Reject H_o (Too risky)

31) a) $\hat{p}_1 = \dfrac{350}{675} \approx 0.5185$, $\hat{p}_2 = \dfrac{309}{692} \approx 0.4465$,

$$\hat{p}_p = \frac{350 + 309}{675 + 692} \approx 0.4821$$

$$z = \frac{0.5185 - 0.4465}{\sqrt{0.4821 * 0.5179\left(\dfrac{1}{675} + \dfrac{1}{692}\right)}} \approx 2.664$$

On the calculator, this is entered as:

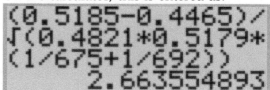

b) $H_a : p_1 \neq p_2 \Rightarrow$ This is a two-tailed test.

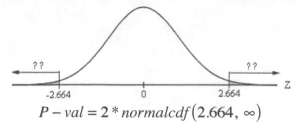

$$P - val = 2 * normalcdf(2.664, \infty)$$
$$\approx 0.0077$$

c) $P - val \approx 0.0077 \leq \alpha \Rightarrow$ Reject H_o
(Acceptable risk of making a type I error)

33) Givens:

Sample 1 (America): $x_1 = 157$, $n_1 = 419$

Sample 2 (Canada): $x_2 = 151$, $n_2 = 387$

a)   Step 1: We are trying to show a

"difference", so we get: $\begin{aligned} H_o &: p_1 = p_2 \\ H_1 &: p_1 \neq p_2 \end{aligned}$

Step 2: $\alpha = 0.05$

Step 3: $\hat{p}_1 = \dfrac{157}{419} \approx 0.3747$,

$\hat{p}_2 = \dfrac{151}{387} \approx 0.3902$,

$\hat{p}_p = \dfrac{157 + 151}{419 + 387} \approx 0.3821$

$$z = \dfrac{0.3747 - 0.3902}{\sqrt{0.3821 * 0.6179 \left(\dfrac{1}{419} + \dfrac{1}{387} \right)}} \approx -0.452$$

On the calculator, this is entered as:

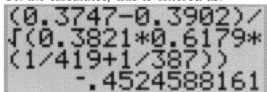

Step 4: $H_1 : p_1 \neq p_2 \Rightarrow$ This is a two-tailed test.

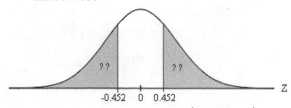

$$P - val = 2 * normalcdf(0.452, \infty)$$
$$\approx 0.6513$$

Step 5: $P - val \approx 0.6513 > \alpha \Rightarrow$ Do Not Reject H_o (Too risky)

Step 6: There is not enough evidence, at the 5% significance level, to show that there is a difference in the proportion of people with type O+ blood between the U.S. and Canada.

b)   We need the z-scores for 95% confidence.

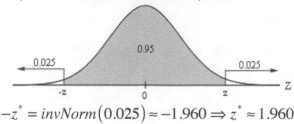

$$-z^* = invNorm(0.025) \approx -1.960 \Rightarrow z^* \approx 1.960$$

$$(0.3747 - 0.3902) \pm 1.96 \cdot \sqrt{\dfrac{0.3747 * 0.6253}{419} + \dfrac{0.3902 * 0.6098}{387}} =$$

$$-0.0155 \pm 0.0672 \Rightarrow p_1 - p_2 \in (-0.0827, 0.0517)$$

Note: On the calculator, the margin of error piece is entered as shown below.

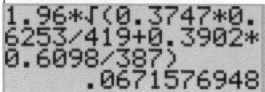

c)   We are 95% confident that the proportion of people in the U.S with type O+ blood is somewhere between 8.27% less and 5.17% more than the proportion in Canada.

d)   If $p_1 - p_2 \in (-0.0827, 0.0517) \Rightarrow p_1 - p_2$ could be equal to zero $\Rightarrow p_1$ could equal $p_2 \Rightarrow H_o : p_1 = p_2$ could be true $\Rightarrow$ Do Not Reject H_o.

e)   There were at least 10 people with type O+ blood and without type O+ blood in each sample, so the requirements have been met.

f)   Because we did not reject $H_o \Rightarrow$ it is possible that we have made a type II error. This has occurred only if H_o is actually false.

35) Givens:

Sample 1 (HF Laws): $x_1 = 259$, $n_1 = 473$

Sample 2 (No HF Laws): $x_2 = 235$, $n_2 = 831$

a) Step 1: We are trying to show that the proportion is "higher" in the states with the hands free laws, so we get:

$H_o : p_1 = p_2$

$H_1 : p_1 > p_2$

Step 2: $\alpha = 0.01$

Step 3: $\hat{p}_1 = \dfrac{259}{473} \approx 0.5476$,

$\hat{p}_2 = \dfrac{235}{831} \approx 0.2828$,

$\hat{p}_p = \dfrac{259 + 235}{473 + 831} \approx 0.3788$

$z = \dfrac{0.5476 - 0.2828}{\sqrt{0.3788 * 0.6212 \left(\dfrac{1}{473} + \dfrac{1}{831} \right)}} \approx 9.477$

Step 4: $H_1 : p_1 > p_2 \Rightarrow$ This is a right-tailed test.

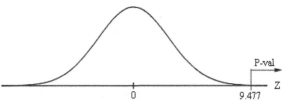

$P - val = normalcdf(9.477, \infty)$

≈ 0.0000

Step 5: $P - val \approx 0.0000 \leq \alpha \Rightarrow$ Reject H_o (Acceptable risk of making a type I error)

Step 6: There is enough evidence, at the 1% significance level, to show that the proportion of use of hands-free devices while driving is higher in states that have laws requiring them.

b) We need the z-scores for 98% confidence.

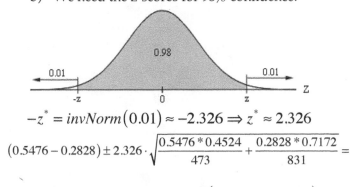

$-z^* = invNorm(0.01) \approx -2.326 \Rightarrow z^* \approx 2.326$

$(0.5476 - 0.2828) \pm 2.326 \cdot \sqrt{\dfrac{0.5476 * 0.4524}{473} + \dfrac{0.2828 * 0.7172}{831}} =$

$0.2648 \pm 0.0645 \Rightarrow p_1 - p_2 \in (0.2003, 0.3293)$

c) We are 98% confident that the proportion of people that use a hands-free device in states that require them is somewhere between 20.03% and 32.93% higher than in states that do not.

d) If $p_1 - p_2 \in (0.2003, 0.3293)$

$\Rightarrow p_1 - p_2 > 0 \Rightarrow p_1 > p_2 \Rightarrow$

$H_1 : p_1 > p_2$ is true and

$H_o : p_1 = p_2$ is false $\Rightarrow$ Reject H_o

e) There were at least 10 people using and not using hands-free devices in each sample, so the requirements have been met.

f) A type I error would occur if we had enough evidence to show that a higher proportion of the people in states with hands-free than people in states with such laws use such a device, when in fact the proportion is not higher.

37) Givens:

Sample 1 (Men): $\hat{p}_1 \approx 0.132$, $n_1 = 258$

Sample 2: (Women): $\hat{p}_2 \approx 0.104$, $n_2 = 241$

a) Step 1: We are trying to show a "difference", so we get: $\begin{aligned} H_o &: p_1 = p_2 \\ H_1 &: p_1 \neq p_2 \end{aligned}$

Step 2: $\alpha = 0.10$

Step 3: This time, we were given the sample proportions rather than the number of successes in each sample. This seems like a head start, but we actually need the number of successes in each sample to calculate the value of $\hat{p}_p$.

$x_1 = n_1 \cdot \hat{p}_1 = 258(0.132) = 34.056 \Rightarrow$

$x_1 = 34$

$x_2 = n_2 \cdot \hat{p}_2 = 241(0.104) = 25.064 \Rightarrow$

$x_2 = 25$

$\hat{p}_p = \dfrac{34 + 25}{258 + 241} \approx 0.1182$

$z = \dfrac{0.132 - 0.104}{\sqrt{0.1182 * 0.8818 \left(\dfrac{1}{258} + \dfrac{1}{241} \right)}} \approx 0.968$

Step 4: $H_1 : p_1 \neq p_2 \Rightarrow$ This is a two-tailed test.

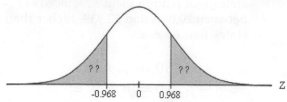

$P - val = 2 * normalcdf(0.968, \infty)$

≈ 0.3330

Step 5: $P - val \approx 0.3330 > \alpha \Rightarrow$ Do Not Reject H_o (Too risky)

Step 6: There is not enough evidence, at the 10% significance level, to show that there is a difference in the proportion of men and women that live in cell phone only households.

b) There were at least 10 people in cell phone only households and at least 10 people with landlines in each sample, so the requirements have been met.

c) We need the z-scores for 90% confidence.

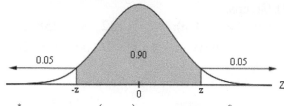

$-z^* = invNorm(0.05) \approx -1.645 \Rightarrow z^* \approx 1.645$

$(0.132 - 0.104) \pm 1.645 \cdot \sqrt{\dfrac{0.132 * 0.868}{258} + \dfrac{0.104 * 0.896}{241}} =$

$0.028 \pm 0.047 \Rightarrow p_1 - p_2 \in (-0.019, \ 0.075)$

d) We are 90% confident that the proportion of men living in cell phone only households is somewhere between 1.9% less and 7.5% more than the proportion of women in such households.

e) If $p_1 - p_2 \in (-0.019, \ 0.075) \Rightarrow p_1 - p_2$ could be equal to zero $\Rightarrow p_1$ could equal $p_2 \Rightarrow H_o : p_1 = p_2$ could be true $\Rightarrow$ Do Not Reject H_o.

Ch 11: Review Exercises

1) a) Step 1: We are trying to show that there is
a "difference", so we get:

$$H_o : \mu_1 = \mu_2$$
$$H_1 : \mu_1 \neq \mu_2$$

Step 2: $\alpha = 0.01$

Step 3:

$$t = \frac{134.9 - 141.4}{\sqrt{\dfrac{6.4904^2}{12} + \dfrac{7.2017^2}{9}}} \approx -2.135$$

Step 4: $H_1 : \mu_1 \neq \mu_2 \Rightarrow$ This is a two-tailed test.

$$df = \frac{\left(\dfrac{6.4904^2}{12} + \dfrac{7.2017^2}{9}\right)^2}{\dfrac{\left(\dfrac{6.4904^2}{12}\right)^2}{11} + \dfrac{\left(\dfrac{7.2017^2}{9}\right)^2}{8}} \approx 16.31$$

??   ??

-2.135   0   2.135   t (df = 16)

$$P - val = 2 * tcdf(2.135, \infty, 16)$$
$$\approx 0.0486$$

Step 5: $P - val \approx 0.0486 > \alpha \Rightarrow$ Do Not Reject H_o (Too risky)

Step 6: There is not enough evidence, at the 1% significance level, to show that there is a difference between the average breaking distance of cars and SUVs.

b) We need the t-scores for 99% confidence.

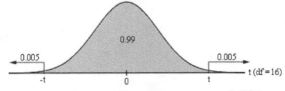

0.005   0.99   0.005

-t   0   t   t (df = 16)

From the t-table, we get $t_{0.005} = 2.921$.

$$(134.9 - 141.4) \pm 2.921 \cdot \sqrt{\frac{6.4902^2}{12} + \frac{7.2017^2}{9}}$$

$$= -6.5 \pm 8.9 \Rightarrow \mu_1 - \mu_2 \in (-15.4, 2.4)$$

c) We are 99% confident that the average breaking distance for SUVs is somewhere between 2.4 feet less than and 15.4 feet more than the average for cars.

d) If $\mu_1 - \mu_2 \in (-15.4, 2.4) \Rightarrow \mu_1 - \mu_2$ could be equal to zero $\Rightarrow \mu_1$ could equal $\mu_2 \Rightarrow H_o : \mu_1 = \mu_2$ could be true $\Rightarrow$ Do Not Reject H_o.

e) Cars: $n_2 = 12 < 30 \Rightarrow$ We need the breaking distances for cars to be normally distributed.
SUVs: $n_2 = 9 < 30 \Rightarrow$ We need the breaking distances for SUVs to be normally distributed.

f) $\mu_1 - \mu_2 = -7.7 \Rightarrow \mu_1 \neq \mu_2 \Rightarrow H_o : \mu_1 = \mu_2$ is false $\Rightarrow$ by not rejecting H_o we have made a type II error.

2) Givens:
   Sample 1 (18-39): $x_1 = 146$, $n_1 = 212$
   Sample 2 (40+): $x_2 = 77$, $n_2 = 219$

a) Step 1: We are trying to show that there is
   a "difference", so we get: $\begin{aligned} H_o &: p_1 = p_2 \\ H_1 &: p_1 \neq p_2 \end{aligned}$

   Step 2: $\alpha = 0.10$

   Step 3: $\hat{p}_1 = \dfrac{x_1}{n_1} = \dfrac{146}{212} \approx 0.6887$,

   $\hat{p}_2 = \dfrac{x_2}{n_2} = \dfrac{77}{219} \approx 0.3516$,

   $\hat{p}_p = \dfrac{x_1 + x_2}{n_1 + n_2} = \dfrac{146 + 77}{212 + 219} \approx 0.5174$

   $z = \dfrac{0.6887 - 0.3516}{\sqrt{0.5174 * 0.4826 \left(\dfrac{1}{212} + \dfrac{1}{219}\right)}} \approx 7.002$

   Step 4: $H_1 : p_1 \neq p_2 \Rightarrow$ This is a two-tailed test.

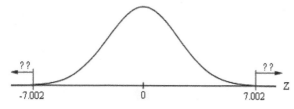

   $P - val = 2 * normalcdf(7.002, \infty)$
   ≈ 0.0000

   Step 5: $P - val \approx 0.0000 \leq \alpha \Rightarrow$ Reject H_o
   (Acceptable risk of making a type I error)
   Step 6: There is enough evidence, at the
   10% significance level, to show that there
   is a difference between the proportion of
   text message users among the younger and
   older age groups.

b) There were at least 10 people using and not
   using text messaging services in each
   sample, so the requirements have been met.

c) We need the z-scores for 90% confidence.

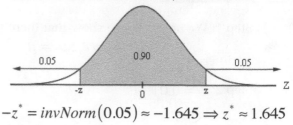

   $-z^* = invNorm(0.05) \approx -1.645 \Rightarrow z^* \approx 1.645$

   $(0.6887 - 0.3516) \pm 1.645 \cdot \sqrt{\dfrac{0.6887 * 0.3113}{212} + \dfrac{0.3516 * 0.6484}{219}}$

   $= 0.3371 \pm 0.0745 \Rightarrow p_1 - p_2 \in (0.2626, 0.4116)$

d) We are 90% confident that the proportion
   of people in the 18 – 39 age group that use
   text messaging is somewhere between
   26.26% and 41.16% higher than for the 40 –
   54 age group.

e) If $p_1 - p_2 \in (0.2626, 0.4116)$
   $\Rightarrow p_1 - p_2 > 0 \Rightarrow p_1 > p_2 \Rightarrow H_o : p_1 = p_2$
   is false $\Rightarrow$ Reject H_o.

f) I would recommend that the focus their
   marketing dollars on the younger group. A
   much higher percentage of this group is
   interested in what they are selling than in
   the older group.

3) a) Step 1: We are trying to show that the second attempt is "better", meaning a higher percentage, than the first attempt,

so we get:
$$H_o : \mu_1 = \mu_2$$
$$H_1 : \mu_1 < \mu_2$$

Step 2: $\alpha = 0.05$

Step 3: Because $\bar{d}$ is not given, we will find it using the calculator. Enter the before values into L1 and the after values into L2. Then let L3 = L1 – L2. Finally choose STAT > CALC > 1-Var Stats L3 and we get:

$$\bar{d} \approx -2.3333, \; s_d \approx 2.2254, \; n = 15$$

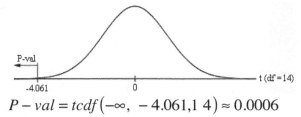

$$t = \frac{\bar{d}}{s_d / \sqrt{n}} = \frac{-2.3333}{2.2254 / \sqrt{15}} \approx -4.061$$

Step 4: $H_1 : \mu_1 < \mu_2 \Rightarrow$ This is a left-tailed test. $df = n - 1 = 14$

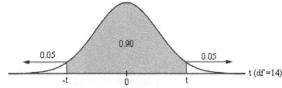

$$P - val = tcdf(-\infty, \; -4.061, 1\,4) \approx 0.0006$$

Step 5: $P - val \approx 0.0006 \leq \alpha \Rightarrow$ Reject H_o (Acceptable risk of making a type I error)

Step 6: There is enough evidence, at the 5% significance level, to show that the second attempt at a song will be, on average, better than the first attempt.

b) We need the t-scores for 90% confidence.

From the t-table, we get $t_{0.05} = 1.761$.

$$-2.33 \pm 1.761 \cdot \frac{2.2254}{\sqrt{15}} = -2.33 \pm 1.01$$

$$\Rightarrow \mu_1 - \mu_2 \in (-3.34, \; -1.32)$$

c) We are 90% confident that the average percentage of notes successfully played is somewhere between 1.32% and 3.34% higher on the second attempt of a song.

d) If $\mu_1 - \mu_2 \in (-3.34, -1.32)$
$$\Rightarrow \mu_1 - \mu_2 < 0 \Rightarrow \mu_1 < \mu_2$$
$$\Rightarrow H_1 : \mu_1 < \mu_2 \text{ is true and}$$
$$H_o : \mu_1 = \mu_2 \text{ is false} \Rightarrow \text{ Reject } H_o$$

e) Because $15 \leq n = 15 < 30$, we must hope that the before and after differences in the population are not severely skewed.

f) Because we rejected H_o, it is not a type II error, it is either a type I error (if H_o is true), or a correct decision (if H_o is false). We perceive the risk of a type I error to only be about 0.06%.

Index

Meaningful Statistics
FORMULA SHEET & *t-table*

Chapter 3:

$$s = \sqrt{\frac{\sum (x - \bar{x})^2}{n-1}} \qquad s = \sqrt{\frac{\sum (x - \bar{x})^2 f}{n-1}} \qquad \sigma = \sqrt{\frac{\sum (x - \mu)^2}{N}} \qquad \sigma = \sqrt{\frac{\sum (x - \mu)^2 f}{N}}$$

$$L_{P_k} = \frac{k}{100}(N+1) \qquad IQR = Q_3 - Q_1 \qquad \text{Boxplot fences: } Q_1 - 1.5 \cdot IQR \ \& \ Q_3 + 1.5 \cdot IQR$$

Chapter 4:

Regression line: $\hat{y} = b_o + b_1 x$ where $b_1 = \dfrac{\sum (x - \bar{x})(y - \bar{y})}{\sum (x - \bar{x})^2}$ & $b_0 = \bar{y} - b_1 \bar{x}$ $\qquad e = y - \hat{y}$

$$r^2 = \frac{\sum (y - \bar{y})^2 - \sum (y - \hat{y})^2}{\sum (y - \bar{y})^2} \qquad r = \frac{\sum (x - \bar{x})(y - \bar{y})}{\sqrt{\sum (x - \bar{x})^2 \sum (y - \bar{y})^2}} \qquad r = \frac{\sum z_x z_y}{n-1}$$

Chapter 5:

$$P(A \text{ or } B) = P(A) + P(B) - P(A \& B) \qquad P(B|A) = \frac{P(A \& B)}{P(A)} \qquad P(A \& B) = P(A)P(B|A)$$

A & B are mutually exclusive IFF $\{P(A \& B) = 0 \qquad P(A \text{ or } B) = P(A) + P(B)\}$

A & B are independent IFF $\{P(A|B) = P(A) \qquad P(A \& B) = P(A)P(B)\}$

$$\mu_x = \sum xP(x) \qquad \sigma_x = \sqrt{\sum (x - \mu_x)^2 P(x)} \qquad \binom{n}{x} = \frac{n!}{x!(n-x)!}$$

For a Binomial Distribution: $P(x) = \dbinom{n}{x} p^x q^{n-x}$ where $q = 1 - p$ $\qquad \mu_x = n \cdot p \qquad \sigma_x = \sqrt{n \cdot p \cdot q}$

Chapter 7: $\qquad \mu_{\hat{p}} = p \qquad \sigma_{\hat{p}} = \sqrt{\dfrac{pq}{n}} \qquad SE = |\hat{p} - p| \qquad \mu_{\bar{x}} = \mu \qquad \sigma_{\bar{x}} \approx \dfrac{\sigma}{\sqrt{n}} \qquad SE = |\bar{x} - \mu|$

Chapter 8: $\qquad \bar{x} \pm t^* \cdot \dfrac{s}{\sqrt{n}} \qquad E = t^* \cdot \dfrac{s}{\sqrt{n}} \qquad (df = n-1) \qquad n = \left[\dfrac{t^* \cdot s}{E} \right]^2 \text{ OR } n = \left[\dfrac{z^* \cdot \sigma_g}{E} \right]^2$

$$\hat{p} = \frac{x}{n} \qquad \hat{p} \pm z^* \cdot \sqrt{\frac{\hat{p}(1 - \hat{p})}{n}} \qquad E = z^* \cdot \sqrt{\frac{\hat{p}(1 - \hat{p})}{n}} \qquad n = p_g (1 - p_g) \left(\frac{z^*}{E} \right)^2$$